D1497849

DAT

Codes of Professional Responsibility

Ethics Standards
in
Business, Health, and Law

Fourth Edition

Codes of Professional Responsibility

Ethics Standards
in
Business, Health, and Law

Fourth Edition

Edited by
RENA A. GORLIN

The Bureau of National Affairs, Inc., Washington, D.C.

Copyright © 1986, 1990, 1994, 1999
The Bureau of National Affairs, Inc.

Library of Congress Cataloging-in-Publication Data

Codes of professional responsibility : ethics standards in business,
   health, and law / edited by Rena A. Gorlin. — 4th ed.
         P. cm.
      Includes bibliographical references and indexes.
      ISBN 1-57018-148-9
      1. Professional ethics—United States.
   BJ125.C57 1999
   174—dc21   98-31152
                                                                               CIP

Published by BNA Books
1250 23rd Street, N.W., Washington, D.C. 20037-1165

International Standard Book Number: 1-57018-148-9
Printed in the United States of America

FOREWORD

More than three and a half decades ago, as an undergraduate, I was introduced to the study of ethics in formal university course work. Little did I understand or appreciate then the extent to which ethics and ethical values had already become an important part of the way I lived my life and viewed the world around me. It was just something that *was*, something one took for granted in those times.

Over the years, the world has become vastly different—immensely more complex, much smaller, and a great deal more vulnerable to acts of violence, both random and planned, on all scales—than the world in which persons of my generation grew up. Yet this same world has developed, as never before in human history, the capacity to build up rather than tear down . . . to save and prolong lives rather than destroy them . . . and to make life better and more noble for even the least of us.

It is in this context that we continue to struggle today with our values and beliefs concerning the morality of our conduct: what constitutes right, wrong, good, bad, acceptable and unacceptable actions and behaviors.

The professions have long carried distinct moral obligations concerning public and private decisionmaking and behavior. The standards we set as professionals—what we do and how we do it, our sense of integrity, our regard and respect for self and others—affect the lives of everyone we deal with. No individual or group is not touched, directly or indirectly, for better or worse, by *how* we deal with increasingly difficult and varied ethical matters. To highly value these matters, and address them, is our task, our privilege, and our greatest responsibility.

We have known along the way, even over the 13 years since the first edition of *Codes of Professional Responsibility* was published, that many questions of ethics would be revisited—those related to our personal, social, and professional responsibility and accountability in our private, public, and corporate lives. And new ethical issues have continued to emerge, which also must be addressed in novel and creative ways.

This *Fourth Edition* of *Codes of Professional Responsibility* gives professionals in the areas of business, health, and law a frame of reference with respect to ethical standards, as we aim to "do the right thing" in difficult and complex situations. Several new organizations and two important categories, computing and the judiciary, have been added. The Resources section has been completely reorganized and greatly expanded. It now includes websites and online publications, resources that did not exist at the time of the book's first release in 1986; even at the time of the *Third Edition,* in 1994, this would have constituted a small list, of interest to relatively few.

Ms. Gorlin has brought us an excellent book on ethics, which any person with an interest in the subject would want to use. Its structure and organization, including its helpful indexes, are user-friendly. A wide range of persons—students and academicians, researchers, practitioners and providers of services as well as clients, patients, and consumers—might legitimately read and benefit from this book, obtaining important information on professional standards and ethics. All of us are stakeholders in the subject, regardless of our individual level of study.

As we stand at the doorway of the 21st century, we continue to face human crises of enormous dimensions; to the extent that these crises are man-made, the result of individual or collective action or inaction in dealing with right and wrong, perhaps there is reason for hope. As the world continues to become smaller, our interdependence on one another increases; perhaps we will be able to see that we are more alike than different, and have the capacity to live together in peace (if not without conflict), in a way that was not possible for generations before us.

One of the values of this book may be in the instruction and guidance it gives us as we attempt to reexamine and fine-tune our ethical beliefs and values, so that they will be sturdy and keep us on course as we journey into the future.

Frances B. Thomas, M.S.W.

Washington, DC
September 1998

INTRODUCTION

This book is intended to be both a catalyst and a reflection of increased public awareness of the ethical conduct of professionals.

Issues of ethics and professional responsibility continue to make headlines, with both positive and negative overtones—as they have since the first edition of this book was published more than 12 years ago. Recent news stories are still reporting on all-too-common political scandals and white-collar crimes, as well as unprecedented moral dilemmas raised by ever more amazing medical and scientific breakthroughs.

All of these events involve the professions. They involve individuals—professionals and clients—whose daily interactions and decisions together make an ethical impact on society as a whole.

Codes of Professional Responsibility: Ethics Standards in Business, Health, and Law presents the statements of major professional organizations all in one place, in an accessible format. While the increased availability of computerized resources has made such material less difficult to find than in previous years, this volume nevertheless makes the information easier to use, understand, and consult readily.

This new *Fourth Edition* revises and updates the previous volumes, which were published in 1986, 1990, and 1994. It expands its coverage to include a greater number and variety of professions, associations, and codes. It also includes more resources on ethics, professionalism, and public policy, notably World Wide Web sites on the Internet and online discussion lists. There are expanded listings in both the individual introductory sections preceding each code, and in the Resources section as a whole.

Most of the codes of ethics appear in full text. In the few instances where excerpts are used, the selected portions address concepts familiar to virtually every profession, such as confidentiality, fees, competence, advertising, and conflicts of interest.

Each text section is preceded by a brief listing of the organization's contacts, membership, and code authority and availability online. Ethics-related organizational resources listed include divisions, programs, and services; informational resources listed include publications, videos, and seminars. There are descriptions of the group's activities and goals, and discussions of its code's implementation, enforcement, history, and development.

This prefatory information was culled from materials supplied by the contributing organizations themselves, such as bylaws, procedural rules, brochures, and annual reports; from conversations and correspondence with association officials responsible for ethics matters, publications, or public affairs; and from the organizations' official Internet websites. These introductions are neither critical nor exhaustive.

Primarily a reference volume, *Codes of Professional Responsibility* is designed for use by researchers in public, academic, business, medical, science, and law libraries; educators and students in professional schools; insurers and lawyers specializing in professional malpractice, negligence, and liability; health care ethics committees and patients' representatives; state bar association disciplinary boards; state peer review bodies and government licensing authorities; trade and professional associations; and public- and private-sector policymakers. It is also meant to assist present and future participants in any kind of professional-client relationship.

The information in this book is current through August 1998. The contact information, the language of each code, and the implementation and enforcement procedures described in the introductory sections are subject to revision. Readers are advised to contact an organization or listed publisher directly. Additional data has been provided, where available, to facilitate a search for the material in the event that an organization or its website moves or is renamed.

Readers should note that the organizations represented here are not necessarily the sole representatives of their respective professions, and that their codes of ethics are not necessarily the only rules governing their members or governing other members of that profession. Federal, state, and local statutes, regulations, and licensure laws may—and usually do—apply.

It is hoped that the publication of the *Fourth Edition* of *Codes of Professional Responsibility* will benefit both professionals and clients, as they continue to learn about each others' rights, responsibilities, expectations, and limitations.

RENA A. GORLIN
Washington, DC
September 1998

ACKNOWLEDGMENTS

The contributions of the following professionals, representing the organizations whose codes of ethics are included in this book, are gratefully acknowledged:

Academy of Family Mediators: Susan M. Costello
Academy of Management: Nancy Urban
American Arbitration Association: Toni L. Griffin and
    Janet C. DeNunzio
American Association of Advertising Agencies: John Wolfe and
    Cathay Brackman
American Association of Law Libraries: Peter Beck and
    Margaret Axtmann
American Bankers Association: Carole McGuinn
American Bar Association: Richard J. Vittenson
American Chiropractic Association: Desiree E. Townes
American College of Healthcare Executives: Karen L. Hackett and
    Monica Reichert
American College of Physicians-American Society of Internal
    Medicine: Joshua Roberts and Lois Snyder
American Counseling Association: Cynthia D. Morrison
American Dental Association: Wendy J. Wils
American Dental Hygienists' Association: Kim Dulany
American Hospital Association: Sharon Alborn
American Institute for Chartered Property Casualty Underwriters:
    Eric A. Wiening
American Institute of Architects: Cassandra Brown
American Institute of Certified Public Accountants: Jessica Cedar and
    Herbert Finkston
American League of Lobbyists: Patti Jo Baber
American Medical Association: Blaire S. Osgood
American Nurses Association: Barbara L. Ross
American Payroll Association: Michael P. O'Toole
American Pharmaceutical Association: Jann B. Hinkle
American Psychiatric Association: Belinda Josey
American Psychological Association: Curtis Nichols and
    Karen Thomas
American Society for Public Administration: John Larkin
American Society of Association Executives: Ann Mahoney
American Society of Journalists and Authors: Alexandra Cantor Owens
American Society of Newspaper Editors: Craig Branson

Association for Computing Machinery: Deborah Cotton
Association for Investment Management and Research:
    Lorna D. Christie
Association of Executive Search Consultants: Nancy DeKoven
Association of Trial Lawyers of America: Michael S. Starr
Certified Financial Planner Board of Standards: Noel Maye
Clinical Social Work Federation: Linda O'Leary and Betty Jean Synar
Direct Marketing Association: Marsha Goldberger
Direct Selling Association: Elizabeth M. Doherty
Federal Bar Association: Liza Blas and Stacy King
Institute of Management Accountants: Jeff Albrechtson
International Association for Financial Planning: Michael Herndon
International Personnel Management Association: Karen D. Smith and
    Diane Brooks
National Association of Exclusive Buyer Agents: Kathleen Chiras
National Association of Legal Assistants: Marge Dover
National Association of REALTORS®: Lorraine Connors Cates,
    Kevin Milligan, and Diane M. Noetzel
National Association of Social Workers: Lori Eatmon
National District Attorneys Association: Jean Holt
National Society of Fund Raising Executives: Maurice R. Levite and
    Michael Nilsen
National Society of Professional Engineers: Arthur E. Schwartz and
    Mary Ann Diggs
Public Relations Society of America: Ray Gaulke
Society of Financial Service Professionals (American Society of CLU
    and ChFC): Anne Rigney
Society of Professional Journalists: Julie Grimes
Society of Professionals in Dispute Resolution: Janice Robertson.

For their advice and contributions, I'd like to thank:
Michael Daigneault, Ethics Resource Center
Mark S. Frankel, American Association for the Advancement of
    Science, Professional Society Ethics Group
Daniel Terris, International Center for Ethics, Justice, and Public Life,
    Brandeis University
Frances B. Thomas, M.S.W.

At The Bureau of National Affairs, Inc., thanks to Jim Fattibene, Mike Kleist, Bob Robbins, Kammie Hedges, Paul Esche, and my friends and colleagues in the Sales & Marketing Division.

Special thanks to my husband, Raymond R. Plante, for his advice and encouragement.

TABLE OF CONTENTS

FOREWORD
Page v

INTRODUCTION
Page vii

ACKNOWLEDGMENTS
Page ix

ETHICS STANDARDS

I. BUSINESS

II.   HEALTH

III. LAW

RESOURCES on ETHICS, PROFESSIONALISM, and PUBLIC POLICY

INDEXES

I. BUSINESS

1. ACCOUNTING

2. ADVERTISING & MARKETING

3. ARCHITECTURE

4. BANKING

5. COMPUTING

6.   ENGINEERING

7.   FINANCIAL PLANNING

8.   HUMAN RESOURCE MANAGEMENT

9.   INSURANCE

10.   JOURNALISM

11.   MANAGEMENT

12.   REAL ESTATE

1. ACCOUNTING

Organization

AMERICAN INSTITUTE OF CERTIFIED PUBLIC ACCOUNTANTS

Headquarters:
1211 Avenue of the Americas
New York, NY 10036-8775
Telephone: (212) 596-6200
Fax: (212) 596-6213

Additional offices:
Harborside Financial Center
201 Plaza Three
Jersey City, NJ 07311-3881
Telephone: (201) 938-3000
Fax: (201) 938-3329

1455 Pennsylvania Avenue, NW
Washington, DC 20004-1081
Telephone: (202) 737-6600
Fax: (202) 638-4512

Website: http://www.aicpa.org
Ethics Hotline: Technical Inquiry Service (800) 862-4272

Date founded: 1887
Former names include the American Association of Public Accountants, Institute of Public Accountants, and American Institute of Accountants; merged with American Society of Certified Public Accountants in 1936

Membership: approximately 330,000 certified public accountants in public practice, industry, government, and education; regular voting members must pass the Uniform CPA Examination and have a valid CPA certificate

Code of Ethics

Official name: *Code of Professional Conduct*
History: Adopted January 1988, amended January 1992, October 1997;
    revised periodically
Authority: Professional Ethics Division; Professional Ethics Executive
    Committee
Code is available on Website

Additional Resources

Organizational (Divisions, Programs, Services, etc.):

Center for Excellence in Financial Management (information clearing-
    house for CPAs in business and industry)
CPA Vision Project
Joint Ethics Enforcement Program (JEEP)
Peer Review Board
Various committees: Accountant's Legal Liability; Professional Liability
    Insurance Programs; Professional Standards and Services; Technical
    Standards Subcommittee on Ethics
Various conferences: Best Practices; Fraud; Peer Review; Tax Contro-
    versies

Informational (Publications, Videos, Seminars, etc.):

Articles in *Journal of Accountancy, The CPA Letter,* and *The Practic-
    ing CPA*
AICPA Professional Standards, Vol. 1 (includes Accounting Standards)
AICPA Professional Standards, Vol. 2 (includes Rules of Conduct, Inter-
    pretations of the Rules, and Ethics Rulings)
AICPA Statements of Position
AICPA Technical Practice Aids
Codification of Statements on Auditing Standards
CPA's Guide to Information Security
JEEP Manual of Procedures
JEEP Semiannual Statistical Reports
Management of an Accounting Practice (MAP) Handbook
The New Finance: A Handbook of Business Management series titles:
    *Codes of Ethics, Practice and Conduct; Implementing Ethics Strate-
    gies Within Organizations; Managing Quality Improvements; Human
    Resources Management—Accountability; Information Systems and
    Service Management—Accountability*
Peer Review Program Manual
Professional Ethics for CPAs (course)
Professional Ethics Quiz in *Journal of Accountancy*
State legislative issues documents and charts: *Tort Reform Issues in the
    Uniform Accountancy Act; States That Have Passed the 150-Hour*

Education Requirement; AICPA/NASBA Guide Implementing the 150-Hour Requirement; State Rules on Commissions and Contingent Fees; CPA Certificate and Permit to Practice Requirements

Goals and Activities of Organization

Among the goals of the American Institute of Certified Public Accountants (AICPA) are to promote uniform certification and licensing standards for accountants; to protect the CPA designation; to encourage public confidence in the integrity, objectivity, competence, and professionalism of members; and to serve as the national representative of CPAs to the government and other organizations.

The AICPA creates and grades the Uniform CPA Examination; provides continuing professional education; issues, monitors, and enforces standards of professional conduct, performance, and expertise; develops auditing standards; and contributes technical advice to rulemaking bodies in such areas as accounting standards, taxation, and banking.

Implementation and Enforcement of Code

All members are required to conform to the Code, which is upheld through the Professional Ethics Division's administration of the Joint Ethics Enforcement Program (JEEP). JEEP was established to integrate the ethics enforcement efforts of state societies and AICPA, and to encourage greater uniformity in standards interpretation and disciplinary action.

The Professional Ethics Executive Committee interprets the Code, proposes amendments, and adopts procedural rules for the investigation of potential disciplinary matters. Cases in which it finds evidence of an infraction are presented to the Joint Trial Board for a possible hearing, on its own behalf or jointly with state societies participating in JEEP. A complaint may be referred to the ethics committee of a state CPA society. A state society may elect to have the Division conduct all investigations.

Where a complaint clearly demonstrates a violation of the Code, the Committee may settle the matter without a full investigation if the member agrees to specified corrective actions or discipline. The Joint Trial Board also may accept, without a hearing, a guilty plea from an accused member.

The Trial Board adjudicates disciplinary charges and adopts procedural rules for cases before hearing panels. A hearing panel may impose discipline on a member who infringes any Rule of the Code, who performs an act discreditable to the profession, who is convicted of fraud, or who fails to cooperate in a disciplinary investigation. Sanctions include suspension or expulsion from AICPA, which is publicized to the membership.

If a Code violation is not serious enough to require Trial Board action, the member may be directed to take certain remedial or corrective measures. If, however, the member has been convicted of certain criminal offenses, the case may be serious enough to warrant suspension and termination without a hearing.

The Division's Technical Inquiry Service (Ethics Hotline) provides education and guidance to members regarding specific issues.

AICPA disciplinary procedures do not affect licenses to practice issued by state regulatory agencies, who may discipline CPAs under state laws and regulations. The U.S. Securities and Exchange Commission and other government agencies may discipline CPAs who practice before them under federal laws and regulations.

History and Development of Code

AICPA's first ethics committee was formed in 1906. The organization issued the Code in its current format in 1973. A major revision of the Code was adopted January 12, 1988.

The Code undergoes constant update and revision. Amendments may be proposed by the Council, Board of Directors, Professional Ethics Division, or the general membership; drafts of proposals are presented for comment by AICPA members and other interested parties. A membership ballot is required for rule changes.

Ethics interpretations and rulings are promulgated by the Professional Ethics Executive Committee to provide guidelines as to the scope and application of the rules.

Among several revisions proposed in April 1998 (upon which action is expected in late 1999) are changes to the definition of "client" and to the interpretation addressing applicability of the Code.

Code of Professional Conduct*

INTRODUCTION

Composition, Applicability, and Compliance

The Code of Professional Conduct of the American Institute of Certified Public Accountants consists of two sections—(1) the Principles and (2) the Rules. The Principles provide the framework for the Rules, which govern the performance of professional services by members. The Council of the American Institute of Certified Public Accountants is authorized to designate bodies to promulgate technical standards under the Rules, and the bylaws require adherence to those Rules and standards.

The Code of Professional Conduct was adopted by the membership to provide guidance and rules to all members—those in public practice, in industry, in government, and in education—in the performance of their professional responsibilities.

Compliance with the Code of Professional Conduct, as with all standards in an open society, depends primarily on members' understanding and voluntary actions, secondarily on reinforcement by peers and public opinion, and ultimately on disciplinary proceedings, when necessary, against members who fail to comply with the Rules.

Other Guidance

Interpretations of Rules of Conduct consist of interpretations which have been adopted, after exposure to state societies, state boards, practice units and other interested parties, by the professional ethics division's executive committee to provide guidelines as to the scope and application of the Rules but are not intended to limit such scope or application. A member who departs from such guidelines shall have the burden of justifying such departure in any disciplinary hearing. *Interpretations* which existed before the adoption of the Code of Professional Conduct on January 12, 1988, will remain in effect until further action is deemed necessary by the appropriate senior technical committee.

Ethics Rulings consist of formal rulings made by the professional ethics division's executive committee after exposure to state societies, state boards, practice units and other interested parties. These rulings summarize the application of Rules of Conduct and Interpretations to a particular set of factual circumstances. Members who depart from such rulings in similar circumstances will be requested to justify such departures. *Ethics Rulings* which existed before the adoption of the Code of Professional Conduct on January 12, 1988, will remain in effect until further action is deemed necessary by the appropriate senior technical committee.

---

*As adopted January 12, 1988, amended January 14, 1992 and October 26, 1997.

This reprint contains the full text of the Introduction, Principles, and Rules of Conduct. All Interpretations of the Rules and Ethics Rulings have been omitted, as well as references in text as to revision dates of individual provisions.

Publication of an Interpretation or Ethics Ruling in *The Journal of Accountancy* constitutes notice to members. Hence, the effective date of the pronouncement is the last day of the month in which the pronouncement is published in *The Journal of Accountancy*. The professional ethics division will take into consideration the time that would have been reasonable for the member to comply with the pronouncement.

A member should also consult, if applicable, the ethical standards of his state CPA society, state board of accountancy, the Securities and Exchange Commission, and any other governmental agency which may regulate his client's business or use his report to evaluate the client's compliance with applicable laws and related regulations.

PRINCIPLES OF PROFESSIONAL CONDUCT

Preamble

Membership in the American Institute of Certified Public Accountants is voluntary. By accepting membership, a certified public accountant assumes an obligation of self-discipline above and beyond the requirements of laws and regulations.

These Principles of the Code of Professional Conduct of the American Institute of Certified Public Accountants express the profession's recognition of its responsibilities to the public, to clients, and to colleagues. They guide members in the performance of their professional responsibilities and express the basic tenets of ethical and professional conduct. The Principles call for an unswerving commitment to honorable behavior, even at the sacrifice of personal advantage.

Article I

Responsibilities

In carrying out their responsibilities as professionals, members should exercise sensitive professional and moral judgments in all their activities.

As professionals, certified public accountants perform an essential role in society. Consistent with that role, members of the American Institute of Certified Public Accountants have responsibilities to all those who use their professional services. Members also have a continuing responsibility to cooperate with each other to improve the art of accounting, maintain the public's confidence, and carry out the profession's special responsibilities for self-governance. The collective efforts of all members are required to maintain and enhance the traditions of the profession.

Article II

The Public Interest

Members should accept the obligation to act in a way that will serve the public interest, honor the public trust, and demonstrate commitment to professionalism.

A distinguishing mark of a profession is acceptance of its responsibility to the public. The accounting profession's public consists of clients, credit grantors, governments, employers, investors, the business and financial community, and others who rely on the objectivity and integrity of certified public accountants to maintain the orderly functioning of commerce. This reliance imposes a public interest responsibility on certified public accountants. The public interest is defined as the collective well-being of the community of people and institutions the profession serves.

In discharging their professional responsibilities, members may encounter conflicting pressures from among each of those groups. In resolving those conflicts, members should act with integrity, guided by the precept that when members fulfill their responsibility to the public, clients' and employers' interests are best served.

Those who rely on certified public accountants expect them to discharge their responsibilities with integrity, objectivity, due professional care, and a genuine interest in serving the public. They are expected to provide quality services, enter into fee arrangements, and offer a range of services—all in a manner that demonstrates a level of professionalism consistent with these Principles of the Code of Professional Conduct.

All who accept membership in the American Institute of Certified Public Accountants commit themselves to honor the public trust. In return for the faith that the public reposes in them, members should seek continually to demonstrate their dedication to professional excellence.

Article III

Integrity

To maintain and broaden public confidence, members should perform all professional responsibilities with the highest sense of integrity.

Integrity is an element of character fundamental to professional recognition. It is the quality from which the public trust derives and the benchmark against which a member must ultimately test all decisions.

Integrity requires a member to be, among other things, honest and candid within the constraints of client confidentiality. Service and the public trust should not be subordinated to personal gain and advantage. Integrity can accommodate the inadvertent error and the honest difference of opinion; it cannot accommodate deceit or subordination of principle.

Integrity is measured in terms of what is right and just. In the absence of specific rules, standards, or guidance, or in the face of conflicting opinions, a member should test decisions and deeds by asking: "Am I doing what a person of integrity would do? Have I retained my integrity?" Integrity requires a member to observe both the form and the spirit of technical and ethical standards; circumvention of those standards constitutes subordination of judgment.

Integrity also requires a member to observe the principles of objectivity and independence and of due care.

Article IV

Objectivity and Independence

A member should maintain objectivity and be free of conflicts of interest in discharging professional responsibilities. A member in public practice should be independent in fact and appearance when providing auditing and other attestation services.

Objectivity is a state of mind, a quality that lends value to a member's services. It is a distinguishing feature of the profession. The principle of objectivity imposes the obligation to be impartial, intellectually honest, and free of conflicts of interest. Independence precludes relationships that may appear to impair a member's objectivity in rendering attestation services.

Members often serve multiple interests in many different capacities and must demonstrate their objectivity in varying circumstances. Members in public practice render attest, tax, and management advisory services. Other members prepare financial statements in the employment of others, perform internal auditing services, and serve in financial and management capacities in industry, education, and government. They also educate and train those who aspire to admission into the profession. Regardless of service or capacity, members should protect the integrity of their work, maintain objectivity, and avoid any subordination of their judgment.

For a member in public practice, the maintenance of objectivity and independence requires a continuing assessment of client relationships and public responsibility. Such a member who provides auditing and other attestation services should be independent in fact and appearance. In providing all other services, a member should maintain objectivity and avoid conflicts of interest.

Although members not in public practice cannot maintain the appearance of independence, they nevertheless have the responsibility to maintain objectivity in rendering professional services. Members employed by others to prepare financial statements or to perform auditing, tax, or consulting services are charged with the same responsibility for objectivity as members in public practice and must be scrupulous in their application of generally accepted accounting principles and candid in all their dealings with members in public practice.

Article V
Due Care

A member should observe the profession's technical and ethical standards, strive continually to improve competence and the quality of services, and discharge professional responsibility to the best of the member's ability.

The quest for excellence is the essence of due care. Due care requires a member to discharge professional responsibilities with competence and diligence. It imposes the obligation to perform professional services to the best of a member's ability with concern for the best interest of those for whom the services are performed and consistent with the profession's responsibility to the public.

Competence is derived from a synthesis of education and experience. It begins with a mastery of the common body of knowledge required for designation as a certified public accountant. The maintenance of competence requires a commitment to learning and professional improvement that must continue throughout a member's professional life. It is a member's individual responsibility. In all engagements and in all responsibilities, each member should undertake to achieve a level of competence that will assure that the quality of the member's services meets the high level of professionalism required by these Principles.

Competence represents the attainment and maintenance of a level of understanding and knowledge that enables a member to render services with facility and acumen. It also establishes the limitations of a member's capabilities by dictating that consultation or referral may be required when a professional engagement exceeds the personal competence of a member or a member's firm. Each member is responsible for assessing his or her own competence—of evaluating whether education, experience, and judgment are adequate for the responsibility to be assumed.

Members should be diligent in discharging responsibilities to clients, employers, and the public. Diligence imposes the responsibility to render services promptly and carefully, to be thorough, and to observe applicable technical and ethical standards.

Due care requires a member to plan and supervise adequately any professional activity for which he or she is responsible.

Article VI

Scope and Nature of Services

A member in public practice should observe the Principles of the Code of Professional Conduct in determining the scope and nature of services to be provided.

The public interest aspect of certified public accountants' services requires that such services be consistent with acceptable professional behavior for certified public accountants. Integrity requires that service and the public trust not be subordinated to personal gain and advantage. Objectivity and independence require that members be free from conflicts of interest in discharging professional responsibilities. Due care requires that services be provided with competence and diligence.

Each of these Principles should be considered by members in determining whether or not to provide specific services in individual circumstances. In some instances, they may represent an overall constraint on the nonaudit services that might be offered to a specific client. No hard-and-fast rules can be developed to help members reach these judgments, but they must be satisfied that they are meeting the spirit of the Principles in this regard.

In order to accomplish this, members should

- Practice in firms that have in place internal quality-control procedures to ensure that services are competently delivered and adequately supervised.
- Determine, in their individual judgments, whether the scope and nature of other services provided to an audit client would create a conflict of interest in the performance of the audit function for that client.
- Assess, in their individual judgments, whether an activity is consistent with their role as professionals (for example, Is such activity a reasonable extension or variation of existing services offered by the member or others in the profession?).

RULES: APPLICABILITY AND DEFINITIONS

Applicability

The bylaws of the American Institute of Certified Public Accountants require that members adhere to the Rules of the Code of Professional Conduct. Members must be prepared to justify departures from these Rules.

Interpretation Addressing the Applicability of the AICPA Code of Professional Conduct. For purposes of the applicability section of the Code, a "member" is a member or international associate of the American Institute of CPAs.

1. The Rules of Conduct that follow apply to all professional services performed except (a) where the wording of the rule indicates otherwise and (b) that a member who is practicing outside the United States will not be subject to discipline for departing from any of the rules stated herein as long as the member's conduct is in accord with the rules of the organized accounting profession in the country in which he or she is practicing. However, where a member's name is associated with financial statements under circumstances that would entitle the reader to assume that United States practices were followed, the member must comply with the requirements of Rules 202 and 203.

2. A member may be held responsible for compliance with the rules by all persons associated with him or her in the practice of public accounting who are either under the member's supervision or are the member's partners or shareholders in the practice.

3. A member shall not permit others to carry out on his or her behalf, either with or without compensation, acts which, if carried out by the member, would place the member in violation of the rules.

Definitions

Client. A client is any person or entity, other than the member's employer, that engages a member or a member's firm to perform professional services or a person or entity with respect to which professional services are performed. The term "employer" for these purposes does not include those entities engaged in the practice of public accounting.

Council. The Council of the American Institute of Certified Public Accountants.

Enterprise. For purposes of the Code, the term "enterprise" is synonymous with the term "client."

Financial statements. A presentation of financial data, including accompanying notes, if any, intended to communicate an entity's economic resources and/or obligations at a point in time or the changes therein for a period of time, in accordance with generally accepted accounting principles or a comprehensive basis of accounting other than generally accepted accounting principles.

Incidental financial data to support recommendations to a client or in documents for which the reporting is governed by Statements on Standards for Attestation Engagements and tax returns and supporting schedules do not, for this purpose, constitute financial statements. The statement, affidavit, or signature of preparers required on tax returns neither constitutes an opinion on financial statements nor requires a disclaimer of such opinion.

Firm. A form of organization permitted by state law or regulation whose characteristics conform to resolutions of Council that is engaged in the practice of public accounting, including the individual owners thereof.

Holding out. In general, any action initiated by a member that informs others of his or her status as a CPA or AICPA-accredited specialist constitutes holding out as a CPA. This would include, for example, any oral or written representation to another regarding CPA status, use of the CPA designation on business cards or letterhead, the display of a certificate evidencing a member's CPA designation, or listing as a CPA in local telephone directories.

Institute. The American Institute of Certified Public Accountants.

Interpretations of rules of conduct. Pronouncements issued by the division of professional ethics to provide guidelines concerning the scope and application of the rules of conduct.

Member. A member, associate member, or international associate of the American Institute of Certified Public Accountants.

Practice of public accounting. The practice of public accounting consists of the performance for a client, by a member or a member's firm, while holding out as CPA(s), of the professional services of accounting, tax, personal financial planning, litigation support services, and those professional services for which standards are promulgated by bodies designated by Council, such as Statements of Financial Accounting Standards, Statements on Auditing Standards, Statements on Standards for Accounting and Review Services, Statement on Standards for Consulting Services, Statements of Governmental Accounting Standards, Statements on Standards for Attestation Engagements, and Statement on Standards for Accountants' Services on Prospective Financial Information.

However, a member or a member's firm, while holding out as CPA(s), is not considered to be in the practice of public accounting if the member or the member's firm does not perform, for any client, any of the professional services described in the preceding paragraph.

Professional services. Professional services include all services performed by a member while holding out as a CPA.

INDEPENDENCE, INTEGRITY, AND OBJECTIVITY

Rule 101   Independence

A member in public practice shall be independent in the performance of professional services as required by standards promulgated by bodies designated by Council.

Rule 102   Integrity and Objectivity

In the performance of any professional service, a member shall maintain objectivity and integrity, shall be free of conflicts of interest, and shall not knowingly misrepresent facts or subordinate his or her judgment to others.

GENERAL STANDARDS, ACCOUNTING PRINCIPLES

Rule 201   General Standards

A member shall comply with the following standards and with any interpretations thereof by bodies designated by Council.

A. *Professional Competence.* Undertake only those professional services that the member or the member's firm can reasonably expect to be completed with professional competence.

B. *Due Professional Care.* Exercise due professional care in the performance of professional services.

C. *Planning and Supervision.* Adequately plan and supervise the performance of professional services.

D. *Sufficient Relevant Data.* Obtain sufficient relevant data to afford a reasonable basis for conclusions or recommendations in relation to any professional services performed.

* * *

Rule 202   Compliance With Standards

A member who performs auditing, review, compilation, management consulting, tax, or other professional services shall comply with standards promulgated by bodies designated by Council.

* * *

Rule 203   Accounting Principles

A member shall not (1) express an opinion or state affirmatively that the financial statements or other financial data of any entity are presented in conformity with generally accepted accounting principles or (2) state that he or she is not aware of any material modifications that should be made to such statements or data in order for them to be in conformity with generally accepted accounting principles, if such statements or data contain any departure from an accounting principle promulgated by bodies designated by Council to establish such principles that has a material effect on the statements or data taken as a whole. If, however, the statements or data contain such a departure and the member can demonstrate that due to unusual circumstances the financial statements or data would otherwise have been misleading, the member can comply with the rule by describing the departure, its approximate effects, if practicable, and the reasons why compliance with the principle would result in a misleading statement.

* * *

RESPONSIBILITIES TO CLIENTS

Rule 301   Confidential Client Information

A member in public practice shall not disclose any confidential client information without the specific consent of the client.

This rule shall not be construed (1) to relieve a member of his or her professional obligations under rules 202 and 203, (2) to affect in any way the member's obligation to comply with a validly issued and enforceable subpoena or summons, or to prohibit a member's compliance with applicable laws and government regulations, (3) to prohibit review of a member's professional practice under AICPA or state CPA society or Board of Accountancy authorization, or (4) to preclude a member from initiating a complaint with, or responding to any inquiry made by, the professional ethics division or trial board of the Institute or a duly constituted investigative or disciplinary body of a state CPA society or Board of Accountancy.

Members of any of the bodies identified in (4) above and members involved with professional practice reviews identified in (3) above shall not use to their own advantage or disclose any member's confidential client information that comes to their attention in carrying out those activities. This prohibition shall not restrict members' exchange of information in connection with the investigative or disciplinary proceedings described in (4) above or the professional practice reviews described in (3) above.

Rule 302   Contingent Fees

A member in public practice shall not
(1) Perform for a contingent fee any professional services for, or receive such a fee from a client for whom the member or the member's firm performs
   (a) an audit or review of a financial statement; or
   (b) a compilation of a financial statement when the member expects, or reasonably might expect, that a third party will use the financial statement and the member's compilation report does not disclose a lack of independence; or
   (c) an examination of prospective financial information;
   or
(2) Prepare an original or amended tax return or claim for a tax refund for a contingent fee for any client.
The prohibition in (1) above applies during the period in which the member or the member's firm is engaged to perform any of the services listed above and the period covered by any historical financial statements involved in any such listed services.

Except as stated in the next sentence, a contingent fee is a fee established for the performance of any service pursuant to an arrangement in which no fee will be charged unless a specified finding or result is attained, or in which the amount of the fee is otherwise dependent upon the finding or result of such service. Solely for purposes of this rule, fees are not regarded as being contingent if fixed by courts or other public authorities, or, in tax matters, if determined based on the results of judicial proceedings or the findings of governmental agencies.

A member's fees may vary depending, for example, on the complexity of services rendered.

RESPONSIBILITIES TO COLLEAGUES

Rule 401   *(Reserved.)*

OTHER RESPONSIBILITIES AND PRACTICES

Rule 501   Acts Discreditable

A member shall not commit an act discreditable to the profession.

Rule 502   Advertising and Other Forms of Solicitation

A member in public practice shall not seek to obtain clients by advertising or other forms of solicitation in a manner that is false, misleading, or deceptive. Solicitation by the use of coercion, over-reaching, or harassing conduct is prohibited.

Rule 503   Commissions and Referral Fees

A. *Prohibited commissions*

A member in public practice shall not for a commission recommend or refer to a client any product or service, or for a commission recommend or refer any

product or service to be supplied by a client, or receive a commission, when the member or the member's firm also performs for that client
  (a) an audit or review of a financial statement; or
  (b) a compilation of a financial statement when the member expects, or reasonably might expect, that a third party will use the financial statement and the member's compilation report does not disclose a lack of independence; or
  (c) an examination of prospective financial information.
This prohibition applies during the period in which the member is engaged to perform any of the services listed above and the period covered by any historical financial statements involved in such listed services.

B. *Disclosure of permitted commissions*

A member in public practice who is not prohibited by this rule from performing services for or receiving a commission and who is paid or expects to be paid a commission shall disclose that fact to any person or entity to whom the member recommends or refers a product or service to which the commission relates.

C. *Referral fees*

Any member who accepts a referral fee for recommending or referring any service of a CPA to any person or entity or who pays a referral fee to obtain a client shall disclose such acceptance or payment to the client.

* * *

Rule 504   *(Deleted.)*

Rule 505   Form of Organization and Name

A member may practice public accounting only in a form of organization permitted by state law or regulation whose characteristics conform to resolutions of Council.

A member shall not practice public accounting under a firm name that is misleading. Names of one or more past owners may be included in the firm name of a successor organization.

A firm may not designate itself as "Members of the American Institute of Certified Public Accountants" unless all of its owners are members of the Institute.

* * *

APPENDIX A

Council Resolution Designating Bodies to Promulgate Technical Standards

[Omitted.]

APPENDIX B

Council Resolution Concerning Rule 505—Form of Organization and Name

RESOLVED: That with respect to a firm or organization which performs (1) any audit or other engagement performed in accordance with the Statements on Auditing Standards, (2) any review of a financial statement or compilation of a financial statement performed in accordance with the Statements on Standards for Accounting and Review Services, or (3) any examination of prospective financial information performed in accordance with the Statements on Standards for Attestation Engagements, or which holds itself out as a firm of certified public accountants or uses the term "certified public accountant(s)" or the designation "CPA" in connection with its name, the characteristics of such a firm or organization under rule 505 are as set forth below. The characteristics of all other firms or organizations are deemed to be whatever is legally permissible under applicable law or regulation.

1. A majority of the ownership of the firm in terms of financial interests and voting rights must belong to CPAs. The non-CPA owner would have to be actively engaged as a firm member in providing services to the firm's clients as his or her principal occupation. Ownership by investors or commercial enterprises not actively engaged as firm members in providing services to the firm's clients as their principal occupation is against the public interest and continues to be prohibited.
2. There must be a CPA who has ultimate responsibility for all the services provided by the firm and by each business unit[1] performing financial statement attest and compilation services and other engagements governed by Statements on Auditing Standards or Statements on Standards for Accounting and Review Services.
3. Non-CPA owners could not assume ultimate responsibility for any financial statement attest or compilation engagement.
4. Non-CPAs becoming owners after adoption of Council's resolution would have to possess a baccalaureate degree and, beginning in the year 2010, have obtained 150 semester hours of education at an accredited college or university.
5. Non-CPA owners would be permitted to use the title "principal," "owner," "officer," "member," or "shareholder," or any other title permitted by state law, but not hold themselves out to be CPAs.
6. Non-CPA owners would have to abide by the AICPA Code of Professional Conduct. AICPA members may be held responsible under the Code for acts of co-owners.
7. Non-CPA owners would have to complete the same work-related CPE requirements as set forth under AICPA bylaw section 2.3 for AICPA members.
8. Owners shall at all times own their equity in their own right and shall be the beneficial owners of the equity capital ascribed to them. Provision would have to be made for the ownership to be transferred to the firm or to other qualified owners if the non-CPA ceases to be actively engaged in the firm.
9. Non-CPA owners would not be eligible for membership in the AICPA.

---

[1]"Business unit" is meant to indicate geographic (such as offices) and functional arrangements (such as tax and management consulting services).

Organization

INSTITUTE OF MANAGEMENT ACCOUNTANTS

Headquarters:
10 Paragon Drive
Montvale, NJ 07645-1760
Telephone: (800) 638-4427
(201) 573-9000
Fax: (201) 573-8601
Website: http://www.imanet.org
Ethics Hotline: 1-800-6ETHICS

Date founded: 1919
> Originally the National Association of Cost Accountants; became the National Association of Accountants in 1957, renamed in 1991

Membership: approximately 80,000 practitioners and students of management accounting and financial management

Code of Ethics

Official name: *Standards of Ethical Conduct for Practitioners of Management Accounting and Financial Management*
History: Adopted April 1997
Authority: Committee on Ethics
Code is available on Website

Additional Resources

Organizational (Divisions, Programs, Services, etc.):

Certified in Financial Management (CFM) Program
Certified Management Accountant (CMA) Program
Ethics Counseling Service
Ethics Enforcement Program
Ethics Retention Policy
Institute of Certified Management Accountants

Performance Management Project
Self-Assessment Project
Various committees: Education; Professional Issues

Informational (Publications, Videos, Seminars, etc.):

Articles in *Management Accounting, Controller's Quarterly, Cost Management Update,* and *IMA Focus*
Corporate Codes of Conduct: An Examination and Implementation Guide
Ethics Enforcement Program Administrative Procedures Manual
Ethics video
Management Accountants: Responding to Change
The Road to Excellence: Becoming a Process-Based Company
The Role of Analytical Procedures in Detecting Management Fraud
Statements on Management Accounting

Goals and Activities of Organization

The Institute of Management Accountants (IMA) is the leading professional organization devoted exclusively to management accounting and financial management. Its provides members with professional development through education, association with other practitioners, certification in skills, and information on changes affecting the management accounting and financial management professions. It offers guidance on ethical practices to members as well as to the broader financial community.

The Institute of Certified Management Accountants (ICMA) implements and administers the CMA and CFM Programs; ethics topics constitute a significant part of the examination.

Implementation and Enforcement of Code

All IMA members are responsible for adherence to the Standards of Ethical Conduct. Members should neither commit acts contrary to the Standards nor condone the commission of such acts by others.

The Standards were developed to help accountants assess their individual ethical situations and make the right decisions. The last section of the Standards contains recommendations for the resolution of ethical conflicts.

The IMA Ethics Committee meets periodically to discuss ethics cases and to determine actions to be taken. Through its subcommittees, it operates the Ethics Consultation Service and other member ethics programs; updates the various ethics procedural manuals and documents; and recommends related modifications to the IMA bylaws.

The confidential Ethics Hotline, exclusively for members, was initiated in 1991. Callers are referred to a counselor who explains how an ethical dilemma relates to provisions of the Standards. The ethics counselor will not provide a specific resolution of the problem, however.

Standards of Ethical Conduct for Practitioners of Management Accounting and Financial Management*

ETHICAL BEHAVIOR FOR PRACTITIONERS OF MANAGEMENT ACCOUNTING AND FINANCIAL MANAGEMENT

In today's modern world of business, individuals in management accounting and financial management constantly face ethical dilemmas. For example, if the accountant's immediate superior instructs the accountant to record the physical inventory at its original costs when it is obvious that the inventory has a reduced value due to obsolescence, what should the accountant do? To help make such a decision, here is a brief general discussion of ethics and the "Standards of Ethical Conduct for Practitioners of Management Accounting and Financial Management."

Ethics, in its broader sense, deals with human conduct in relation to what is morally good and bad, right and wrong. To determine whether a decision is good or bad, the decision maker must compare his/her options with some standard of perfection. This standard of perfection is not a statement of static position but requires the decision maker to assess the situation and the values of the parties affected by the decision. The decision maker must then estimate the outcome of the decision and be responsible for its results. Two good questions to ask when faced with an ethical dilemma are, "Will my actions be fair and just to all parties affected?" and "Would I be pleased to have my closest friends learn of my actions?"

Individuals in management accounting and financial management have a unique set of circumstances relating to their employment. To help them assess their situation, the Institute of Management Accountants has developed the following "Standards of Ethical Conduct for Practitioners of Management Accounting and Financial Management."

STANDARDS OF ETHICAL CONDUCT FOR PRACTITIONERS OF MANAGEMENT ACCOUNTING AND FINANCIAL MANAGEMENT

Practitioners of management accounting and financial management have an obligation to the public, their profession, the organization they serve, and themselves, to maintain the highest standards of ethical conduct. In recognition of this obligation, the Institute of Management Accountants has promulgated the following standards of ethical conduct for practitioners of management accounting and financial management. Adherence to these standards, both domestically and internationally, is integral to achieving the *Objectives of Management Accounting.* Practitioners of management accounting and financial management shall not commit acts contrary to these standards nor shall they condone the commission of such acts by others within their organizations.

---

*Publication SMA 1C, April 1997 (Statements on Management Accounting). Reprinted with permission of the Institute of Management Accountants.

Competence

Practitioners of management accounting and financial management have a responsibility to:

- Maintain an appropriate level of professional competence by ongoing development of their knowledge and skills.
- Perform their professional duties in accordance with relevant laws, regulations, and technical standards.
- Prepare complete and clear reports and recommendations after appropriate analyses of relevant and reliable information.

Confidentiality

Practitioners of management accounting and financial management have a responsibility to:

- Refrain from disclosing confidential information acquired in the course of their work except when authorized, unless legally obligated to do so.
- Inform subordinates as appropriate regarding the confidentiality of information acquired in the course of their work and monitor their activities to assure the maintenance of that confidentiality.
- Refrain from using or appearing to use confidential information acquired in the course of their work for unethical or illegal advantage either personally or through third parties.

Integrity

Practitioners of management accounting and financial management have a responsibility to:

- Avoid actual or apparent conflicts of interest and advise all appropriate parties of any potential conflict.
- Refrain from engaging in any activity that would prejudice their ability to carry out their duties ethically.
- Refuse any gift, favor, or hospitality that would influence or would appear to influence their actions.
- Refrain from either actively or passively subverting the attainment of the organization's legitimate and ethical objectives.
- Recognize and communicate professional limitations or other constraints that would preclude responsible judgment or successful performance of an activity.
- Communicate unfavorable as well as favorable information and professional judgments or opinions.
- Refrain from engaging in or supporting any activity that would discredit the profession.

Objectivity

Practitioners of management accounting and financial management have a responsibility to:

- Communicate information fairly and objectively.
- Disclose fully all relevant information that could reasonably be expected to influence an intended user's understanding of the reports, comments, and recommendations presented.

RESOLUTION OF ETHICAL CONFLICT

In applying the standards of ethical conduct, practitioners of management accounting and financial management may encounter problems in identifying unethical behavior or in resolving an ethical conflict. When faced with significant ethical issues, practitioners of management accounting and financial management should follow the established policies of the organization bearing on the resolution of such conflict. If these policies do not resolve the ethical conflict, such practitioners should consider the following courses of action.

- Discuss such problems with the immediate superior except when it appears that the superior is involved, in which case the problem should be presented initially to the next higher managerial level. If a satisfactory resolution cannot be achieved when the problem is initially presented, submit the issues to the next higher managerial level. If the immediate superior is the chief executive officer, or equivalent, the acceptable reviewing authority may be a group such as the audit committee, executive committee, board of directors, board of trustees, or owners. Contact with levels above the immediate superior should be initiated only with the superior's knowledge, assuming the superior is not involved. Except where legally prescribed, communication of such problems to authorities or individuals not employed or engaged by the organization is not considered appropriate.
- Clarify relevant ethical issues by confidential discussion with an objective advisor (e.g., IMA Ethics Counseling service) to obtain a better understanding of possible courses of action. Consult your own attorney as to legal obligations and rights concerning the ethical conflict.
- If the ethical conflict still exists after exhausting all levels of internal review, there may be no other recourse on significant matters than to resign from the organization and to submit an informative memorandum to an appropriate representative of the organization. After resignation, depending on the nature of the ethical conflict, it may also be appropriate to notify other parties.

2. ADVERTISING & MARKETING

Organization

AMERICAN ASSOCIATION OF ADVERTISING AGENCIES

Headquarters:
405 Lexington Avenue
New York, NY 10174-1801
Telephone: (212) 682-2500
Fax: (212) 682-8391
E-mail: aaaa@aaaa.org
Website: http://www.aaaa.org

Date founded: 1917
Membership: approximately 575 agencies, operating more than 1,215 offices in the U.S.

Codes of Ethics

Official names: *Qualifications for Membership* and *Standards of Practice*
History: First adopted 1920 and 1924, respectively; most recently revised September 1990
Authority: Board of Directors

Additional Resources

Organizational (Divisions, Programs, Services, etc.):

Advertising agency liability insurance
Coalition for Advertising Supported Information and Entertainment (CASIE)
Institutes of Advanced Advertising Studies
Professional Development Division (training programs)

Informational (Publications, Videos, Seminars, etc.):

Another Side of Advertising (video)
A Client's Guide to the Law and Advertising

A Client's Guide to Agency/Client Contracts
CASIE Goals for Privacy for Marketing on Interactive Media
CASIE Guiding Principles of Interactive Media Measurement
CASIE and IAB Voluntary Guidelines for Banner Advertising
Human Resource Policies & Practices in AAAA Agencies
Protection Against Damage Claims
*Questions and Answers Pertaining to the Settlement of the Anti-Trust
    Action with Respect to AAAA*
What Every Account Executive Should Know About Law and Advertising
What Should an Ad Agency Expect from its Attorney? Banker? CPA?
Why We Fight The Tobacco Advertising Battle

Goals and Activities of Organization

The American Association of Advertising Agencies (AAAA) is a management-oriented national trade organization whose members place 75 percent of all agency-produced national U.S. advertising. Its mission is "to improve, strengthen, and interpret the advertising agency business," by counseling its members on operations and management, fostering their professional development, and encouraging the highest creative and business standards.

The organization works with federal, state, and local governments to help achieve desirable social and civic goals, influence public policy, and resist unwise or unfair legislation and regulation. It studies and promotes the ways in which advertising contributes to the economy and society. The AAAA also facilitates members' pro bono efforts on behalf of worthwhile social and community causes.

By exchanging information and advice with advertisers, the media, and the public, and by representing to them the agency point of view, the AAAA aims to solve mutual problems and resolve collective issues in the advertising business.

Implementation and Enforcement of Code

The Qualifications for Membership provide that only an advertising agency that can "give reasonable assurance" of its "readiness and ability to uphold the highest ethical standards" may join the organization to begin with. By accepting membership, an agency agrees to abide by the Standards of Practice, including its Creative Code.

Compliance with the Standards is voluntary, inasmuch as its provisions "serve as a guide" to "wise, foresighted, and constructive" conduct. Nevertheless, "clear and willful violations" are referred to the Board of Directors for appropriate action, which may include annulment of membership.

History and Development of Code

When the Qualifications for Membership were updated in 1990, a separate set of guidelines—the *Agency Service Standards* (adopted in

1918 and revised in 1956)—was incorporated as the section on "Service Standards." The last time the Qualifications had been amended was in June 1983.

As for the Standards of Practice, the 1990 revision focused attention on the Creative Code. The earlier version dated from April 1962.

In August 1998, the Board of Directors appointed a subcommittee to consider modifications to these materials.

Qualifications for Membership*

Membership in the American Association of Advertising Agencies is by application and election after the applicant agency meets the following A.A.A.A. Qualifications for Membership:

OVERVIEW

These qualifications for membership are intended as a definition of the kind of advertising agency most likely to develop advertising that succeeds for advertisers. They are based on the premise that the agency should be *independent, unbiased, and objective; should offer adequate staff and experience; should be ethically operated; and should be soundly financed.*

1. TYPE OF BUSINESS

Applicants shall be primarily in the advertising agency business. A minimum of 50 percent of the agency's gross income must result from payment for services usually performed by advertising agencies (as defined in the Service Standards section herein).

2. SIZE OF AGENCY

The size of any applicant shall not be a factor in determining qualifications for membership, except that an agency inadequately equipped to service its business shall not be considered eligible.

3. AGE OF AGENCY

No agency shall be considered for election unless its principal owners have been doing business as an advertising agency for at least two years. This qualification may be waived by the Board of Directors only in exceptional circumstances.

4. LOCATION OF AGENCY

Only agencies maintaining an office(s) in the United States, its territories, and possessions shall be considered for membership.

5. OWNERSHIP, CONTROL, AND BIAS

a. No agency shall be eligible unless the persons who exercise operating control of it are employees of the agency.
b. No agency shall be eligible if it is controlled or operated by, or on behalf of, one or more advertisers.
c. In the interest of objectivity, where an agency owns an interest in a medium or supplier or where a medium or supplier owns an interest in the agency, it is required that such interest be disclosed to the Association, to the agency's clients, and, in the case of media ownership, to other media as

---

*Reprinted with permission of the American Association of Advertising Agencies.

well. Where there is substantial ownership of such interest by one or more officers or employees of the agency, similar disclosure is required.

d. An applicant must disclose all facts necessary to determine its eligibility with respect to ownership, control, and possible bias and must agree that, if elected to membership, it will notify the Association promptly of any change that might affect its continued eligibility under these provisions.

6. SERVICE STANDARDS

a. Only agencies that are qualified by experience to provide an adequate quantity and quality of advertising agency service shall be eligible for membership. Advertising agency service consists of *interpreting to the public, or to desired segments of the public, information regarding a legally marketed product or service.* An individual agency is, of course, free to determine with its clients what services it will perform. But, this typically includes:

1. A study of the product or service in order to determine the advantages and disadvantages inherent in the product or service itself, and in its relation to competition.
2. An analysis of the present and potential market (and target audiences) for the product or service.
3. A knowledge of the factors of distribution and sales and their methods of operation.
4. A knowledge of all the available media and means that can be used to effectively carry the interpretation of the product or service to target audiences.
5. Formulation of a definite plan.
6. Execution of this plan:
   (a) Developing creative concepts for advertisements or other appropriate forms of the message.
   (b) Writing, designing, and producing advertising.
   (c) Ordering the space, time, or other means of advertising.
   (d) Proper incorporation of the message in mechanical form and forwarding it with proper instructions for the fulfillment of the contract.
   (e) Checking and verifying of insertions, display, affidavits, or other means used.
   (f) Auditing and billing for the service, broadcast time, space, and preparation/production.
7. Cooperation with the advertiser's sales organization to insure the greatest effect from advertising.

7. CHARACTER

Applicants will be evaluated regarding their business record, policies and principles, ethical practices, reputation for honesty, integrity, and sincerity of purpose.

Only agencies who give reasonable assurance of their readiness and ability to uphold the highest ethical standards of the business will be received into membership.

8. ABILITY

a. Advertising ability varies with individual talent and need; it is difficult to standardize. Nevertheless, sound judgment regarding the applicant agency's ability can and should be formed by a proper study of:
   1. Its staff and facilities
   2. Its past service and work produced for clients.
b. The applicant agency is required to furnish a representative list of its present clients, indicating the nature of the advertising handled for them, how long it has held each listed account, and a representative list of media with whom it has done business.

9. FINANCIAL RESPONSIBILITY

a. Financial stability, indicated by a satisfactory balance sheet, is important in determining the applicant's qualification. Such statement should either be verified by a Certified Public Accountant, or, if this is not available, sworn to by the applicant.
b. Each applicant is required not only to fill out the balance sheet accompanying the application blank but also to give other such evidence of its financial condition as may be required.
c. The applicant shall be required to furnish as financial references its banking connections, six media owners, and six suppliers with whom it has done business.
d. No applicant agency shall be admitted to membership until its balance sheet has been approved in accordance with sound banking and accounting standards, except that an applicant whose financial condition does not fully meet the Association's requirement may, in event of unusual merit or desirability in other respects, be admitted by the Board of Directors.

10. METHOD OF APPLICATION/ELECTION

[Omitted.]

Standards of Practice*

We hold that a responsibility of advertising agencies is to be a constructive force in business.

We hold that, to discharge this responsibility, advertising agencies must recognize an obligation, not only to their clients, but to the public, the media they employ and to each other. As a business, the advertising agency must operate within the framework of competition. It is recognized that keen and vigorous competition, honestly conducted, is necessary to the growth and the health of American business. However, unethical competitive practices in the advertising agency business lead to financial waste, dilution of service, diversion of manpower, loss of prestige, and tend to weaken public confidence both in advertisements and in the institution of advertising.

We hold that the advertising agency should compete on merit and not by attempts at discrediting or disparaging a competitor agency, or its work, directly or by inference, or by circulating harmful rumors about another agency, or by making unwarranted claims of particular skill in judging or prejudging advertising copy.

We hold that the responsibility will best be discharged if all agencies observe a common set of standards of practice.

To these ends, the American Association of Advertising Agencies has adopted the following Creative Code as being in the best interests of the public, the advertisers, the media, and the agencies themselves.

The A.A.A.A. believes the Code's provisions serve as a guide to the kind of agency conduct that experience has shown to be wise, foresighted, and constructive. In accepting membership, an agency agrees to follow it.

Creative Code

We, the members of the American Association of Advertising Agencies, in addition to supporting and obeying the laws and legal regulations pertaining to advertising, undertake to extend and broaden the application of high ethical standards. Specifically, we will not knowingly produce advertising that contains:

    a. False or misleading statements or exaggerations, visual or verbal.

    b. Testimonials that do not reflect the real opinions of the individuals involved.

    c. Price claims that are misleading.

    d. Claims insufficiently supported or that distort the true meaning or practicable application of statements made by professional or scientific authority.

    e. Statements, suggestions or pictures offensive to public decency or minority segments of the population.

We recognize that there are areas that are subject to honestly different interpretations and judgment.

Nevertheless, we agree not to recommend to an advertiser, and to discourage the use of, advertising that is in poor or questionable taste or that is deliberately irritating through aural or visual content or presentation.

Comparative advertising shall be governed by the same standards of truthfulness, claim substantiation, tastefulness, etc., as apply to other types of advertising.

These Standards of Practice of the American Association of Advertising Agencies come from the belief that sound and ethical practice is good business. Confidence and respect are indispensable to success in a business embracing the many intangibles of agency service and involving relationships so dependent upon good faith.

Clear and willful violations of these Standards of Practice may be referred to the Board of Directors of the American Association of Advertising Agencies for appropriate action, including possible annulment of membership * * *.

Organization

DIRECT MARKETING ASSOCIATION

Headquarters:
1120 Avenue of the Americas
New York, NY 10036-6700
Telephone: (212) 768-7277
Fax: (212) 302-6714
E-mail: dma@the-dma.org

Additional offices:
1111 19th Street, NW
Suite 1100
Washington, DC 20036-3603
Telephone: (202) 955-5030
Fax: (202) 955-0085
E-mail: consumer@the-dma.org

Website: http://www.the-dma.org

Date founded: 1917
Membership: approximately 3800 companies in the U.S. and 49 other
nations

Code of Ethics

Official name: *Guidelines for Ethical Business Practice*
History: First adopted 1960; current version issued January 1998, amended
June 1998
Authority: Ethics and Consumer Affairs Department: Committee on
Ethical Business Practice and Ethics Policy Committee
Code is available on Website

Additional Resources

Organizational (Divisions, Programs, Services, etc.):

Mail Order Action Line (complaint mediation service for resolving direct
marketing transactional disputes)

Mail Preference Service (to remove names from mailing lists)
Privacy Action Now! (industry initiative to ensure consumer privacy expectations and to develop standard protective practices)
Telephone Preference Service (to remove names from telemarketing lists)

Informational (Publications, Videos, Seminars, etc.):

Articles in *The DMA News*
Best Practices in Interactive Marketing
Compendium of Government Issues Affecting Direct Marketing (annual)
Direct Marketing: Opening the Door to Opportunity: A Simple Guide to Understanding How Direct Marketers Use Information
Excellence in Fulfillment & Customer Service (seminar)
Fair Information Practices Manual (includes *Checklist of Fair Information Practices*)
Guidelines for Acceptance of Direct Response Broadcast Advertising
Guidelines for Acceptance of Print Mail Order Advertising
Guidelines for Mailing List Practices
Guidelines for Marketing by Telephone
Guidelines for Personal Information Protection
Law & Direct Marketing (seminar)
Marketing Online: Privacy Principles and Guidance
Mail Preference Service Subscriber Brochure
Telephone Preference Service Subscriber Brochure
Information for Direct Marketers: Business Check Lists, Recommended Practices for Customer Service, Telephone Consumer Protection Act, Telephone Order Rule

Goals and Activities of Organization

The Direct Marketing Association (the DMA) provides members with educational seminars and conferences; disseminates information on state-of-the-art direct response; represents members' interests to federal and state governments on matters affecting direct marketing; acts as a liaison with consumer affairs and regulatory agencies; and facilitates increased communication between the industry and its customers.

Ethics activities are administered by the Ethics and Consumer Affairs Department, whose long-range goal is to create a positive environment for marketing and to improve the climate for direct marketing in particular. It initiates programs and projects that advance good business practices and educate the public as to the benefits of direct marketing. The Ethics Policy Committee develops and revises the Guidelines, taking into consideration the recommendations of the Committee on Ethical Business Practice.

Implementation and Enforcement of Code

The DMA's guidelines are maintained, updated, and distributed to the industry by the Ethics and Consumer Affairs Department.

The Committee on Ethical Business Practice enforces the Guidelines by monitoring mailings and offerings made to the public, and investigating complaints brought to its attention. This role is designed to help develop good business practices in the industry, provide a device for consumer protection, and counter direct marketing techniques that detract from the industry's image.

Once the Committee determines that there has been a violation of the Guidelines, it notifies the company of its concerns and offers to work with it to resolve the matter. Members who refuse to do so can be censured, suspended, or expelled. Nonmembers who refuse to work with the Committee are denied membership until their solicitations comply with the Guidelines. The fact that a company does not cooperate with the Committee can be made public. If the company has violated the law, the case is referred to the appropriate government agency.

History and Development of Code

The Ethics Policy Committee undertook an extensive revision of the Guidelines in January 1998, approved by the Board of Directors. It strengthened and expanded the previous version, especially in the areas of privacy, sweepstakes, and marketing to children.

The Guidelines are periodically amended to address new issues in the field. This reprint includes amendments through June 1998.

Guidelines for Ethical Business Practice*

The Direct Marketing Association's Guidelines for Ethical Business Practice are intended to provide individuals and organizations involved in direct marketing in all media with generally accepted principles of conduct. These guidelines reflect The DMA's long-standing policy of high levels of ethics and the responsibility of the Association, its members, and all marketers to maintain consumer and community relationships that are based on fair and ethical principles. In addition to providing general guidance to the industry, the Guidelines for Ethical Business Practice are used by The DMA's Committee on Ethical Business Practice, an industry peer review committee, as the standard to which direct marketing promotions, that are the subject of complaint to The DMA, are compared.

These self-regulatory guidelines are intended to be honored in light of their aims and principles. All marketers should support the guidelines in spirit and not treat their provisions as obstacles to be circumvented by legal ingenuity.

These guidelines also represent The DMA's general philosophy that self-regulatory measures are preferable to governmental mandates. Self-regulatory actions are more readily adaptable to changing techniques and economic and social conditions. They encourage widespread use of sound business practices.

Because dishonest, misleading or offensive communications discredit all means of advertising and marketing, including direct marketing, observance of these guidelines by all concerned is expected. All persons involved in direct marketing should take reasonable steps to encourage other industry members to follow these guidelines as well.

THE TERMS OF THE OFFER

Honesty and Clarity of Offer
Article #1

All offers should be clear, honest and complete so that the consumer may know the exact nature of what is being offered, the price, the terms of payment (including all extra charges) and the commitment involved in the placing of an order. Before publication of an offer, marketers should be prepared to substantiate any claims or offers made. Advertisements or specific claims which are untrue, misleading, deceptive or fraudulent should not be used.

Accuracy and Consistency
Article #2

Simple and consistent statements or representations of all the essential points of the offer should appear in the promotional material. The overall impression of an offer should not be contradicted by individual statements, representations or disclaimers.

*Revised January 1998, June 1998. Copyright © Direct Marketing Association 1998. All Rights Reserved. Reprinted with permission of The Direct Marketing Association, Inc.

Clarity of Representations
Article #3
Representations which, by their size, placement, duration or other characteristics, are unlikely to be noticed or are difficult to understand should not be used if they are material to the offer.

Actual Conditions
Article #4
All descriptions, promises and claims of limitation should be in accordance with actual conditions, situations and circumstances existing at the time of the promotion.

Disparagement
Article #5
Disparagement of any person or group on grounds addressed by federal or state laws that prohibit discrimination is unacceptable.

Decency
Article #6
Solicitations should not be sent to consumers who have indicated to the marketer that they consider those solicitations to be vulgar, immoral, profane, pornographic or offensive in any way and who do not want to receive them.

Photographs and Art Work
Article #7
Photographs, illustrations, artwork and the situations they describe should be accurate portrayals and current reproductions of the products, services or other subjects they represent.

Disclosure of Sponsor and Intent
Article #8
All marketing contacts should disclose the name of the sponsor and each purpose of the contact. No one should make offers or solicitations in the guise of one purpose when the intent is a different purpose.

Accessibility
Article #9
Every offer and shipment should clearly identify the marketer's name and postal address or telephone number, or both, at which the consumer may obtain service. If an offer is made online, an e-mail address should also be identified.

Solicitation in the Guise of an Invoice or Governmental Notification
Article #10
Offers that are likely to be mistaken for bills, invoices or notices from public utilities or governmental agencies should not be used.

Postage, Shipping or Handling Charges
Article #11
Postage, shipping or handling charges, if any, should bear a reasonable relationship to actual costs incurred.

MARKETING TO CHILDREN

Marketing to Children
Article #12
Offers and the manner in which they are presented that are suitable for adults only should not be made to children. In determining the suitability of a communication with children online or in any other media, marketers should address the age range, knowledge, sophistication and maturity of their intended audience.

Parental Responsibility and Choice
Article #13
Marketers should provide notice and an opportunity to opt out of the marketing process so that parents have the ability to limit the collection, use and disclosure of their children's names, addresses or other personally identifiable information.

Information From or About Children
Article #14
Marketers should take into account the age range, knowledge, sophistication and maturity of children when collecting information from them. Marketers should limit the collection, use and dissemination of information collected from or about children to information required for the promotion, sale and delivery of goods and services, provision of customer services, conducting market research and engaging in other appropriate marketing activities.

Marketers should effectively explain that the information is being requested for marketing purposes. Information not appropriate for marketing purposes should not be collected.

Upon request from a parent, marketers should promptly provide the source and general nature of information maintained about a child. Marketers should implement strict security measures to ensure against unauthorized access, alteration or dissemination of the data collected from or about children.

SPECIAL OFFERS AND CLAIMS

Use of the Word "Free" and Other Similar Representations
Article #15
A product or service which is offered without cost or obligation to the recipient may be unqualifiedly described as "free."

If a product or service is offered as "free," all qualifications and conditions should be clearly and conspicuously disclosed, in close conjunction with the use of the term "free" or other similar phrase.

When the term "free" or other similar representations are made (for example, 2-for-1, half-price or 1-cent offers), the product or service required to be purchased should not have been increased in price or decreased in quality or quantity.

Price Comparisons
Article #16

Price comparisons including those between a marketer's current price and a former, future or suggested price, or between a marketer's price and the price of a competitor's comparable product should be fair and accurate.

In each case of comparison to a former, manufacturer's suggested or competitor's comparable product price, recent substantial sales should have been made at that price in the same trade area.

For comparisons with a future price, there should be a reasonable expectation that the new price will be charged in the foreseeable future.

Guarantees
Article #17

If a product or service is offered with a guarantee or a warranty, either the terms and conditions should be set forth in full in the promotion, or the promotion should state how the consumer may obtain a copy. The guarantee should clearly state the name and address of the guarantor and the duration of the guarantee.

Any requests for repair, replacement or refund under the terms of a guarantee or warranty should be honored promptly. In an unqualified offer of refund, repair or replacement, the customer's preference shall prevail.

Use of Test or Survey Data
Article #18

All test or survey data referred to in advertising should be valid and reliable as to source and methodology, and should support the specific claim for which it is cited. Advertising claims should not distort test or survey results or take them out of context.

Testimonials and Endorsements
Article #19

Testimonials and endorsements should be used only if they are:
a. Authorized by the person quoted;
b. Genuine and related to the experience of the person giving them both at the time made and at the time of the promotion; and
c. Not taken out of context so as to distort the endorser's opinion or experience with the product.

SWEEPSTAKES

Use of the Term "Sweepstakes"
Article #20

Sweepstakes are promotional devices by which items of value (prizes) are awarded to participants by chance without the promoter's requiring the participants to render something of value (consideration) to be eligible to participate. The co-existence of all three elements—prize, chance and consideration—in the same promotion constitutes a lottery. It is illegal for any private enterprise to run a lottery without specific governmental authorization.

When skill replaces chance, the promotion becomes a skill contest. When gifts (premiums or other items of value) are given to all participants independent of the element of chance, the promotion is not a sweepstakes. Promotions that are not sweepstakes should not be held out as such.

Only those promotional devices which satisfy the definition stated above should be called or held out to be a sweepstakes.

No-Purchase Option
Article #21

Promotions should clearly state that no purchase is required to win sweepstakes prizes. They should not represent that those who make a purchase or otherwise render consideration with their entry will have a better chance of winning or will be eligible to win more or larger prizes than those who do not make a purchase or otherwise render consideration. The method for entering without ordering should be easy to find, read and understand. When response devices used only for entering the sweepstakes are provided, they should be as easy to find as those utilized for ordering the product or service.

Chances of Winning
Article #22

No sweepstakes promotion, or any of its parts, should represent that a recipient or entrant has won a prize or that any entry stands a greater chance of winning a prize than any other entry when this is not the case. Winners should be selected in a manner that ensures fair application of the laws of chance.

Prizes
Article #23

Sweepstakes prizes should be advertised in a manner that is clear, honest and complete so that the consumer may know the exact nature of what is being offered. For prizes paid over time, the annual payment schedule and number of years should be clearly disclosed.

Photographs, illustrations, artwork and the situations they represent should be accurate portrayals of the prizes listed in the promotion.

No award or prize should be held forth directly or by implication as having substantial monetary value if it is of nominal worth. The value of a non-cash prize should be stated at regular retail value, whether actual cost to the sponsor is greater or less.

All prizes should be awarded and delivered without cost to the participant. If there are certain conditions under which a prize or prizes will not be awarded, that fact should be disclosed in a manner that is easy to find, read and understand.

Premiums
Article #24

Premiums should be advertised in a manner that is clear, honest and complete so that the consumer may know the exact nature of what is being offered.

A premium, gift or item should not be called or held out to be a "prize" if it is offered to every recipient of or participant in a promotion. If all participants will receive a premium, gift or item, that fact should be clearly disclosed.

Disclosure of Rules
Article #25

All terms and conditions of the sweepstakes, including entry procedures and rules, should be easy to find, read and understand. Disclosures set out in the rules section concerning no-purchase option, prizes and chances of winning should not contradict the overall impression created by the promotion.

The following should be set forth clearly in the rules:
- No purchase of the advertised product or service is required in order to win a prize.
- Procedures for entry.
- If applicable, disclosure that a facsimile of the entry blank or other alternate means (such as a 3" × 5" card) may be used to enter the sweepstakes.
- The termination date for eligibility in the sweepstakes. The termination date should specify whether it is a date of mailing or receipt of entry deadline.
- The number, retail value (of non-cash prizes) and complete description of all prizes offered, and whether cash may be awarded instead of merchandise. If a cash prize is to be awarded by installment payments, that fact should be clearly disclosed, along with the nature and timing of the payments.
- The approximate odds of winning each prize or a statement that such odds depend on number of entrants.
- The method by which winners will be selected.
- The geographic area covered by the sweepstakes and those areas in which the offer is void.
- All eligibility requirements, if any.
- Approximate dates when winners will be selected and notified.
- Publicity rights regarding the use of winner's name.
- Taxes are the responsibility of the winner.
- Provision of a mailing address to allow consumers to receive a list of winners of prizes over $25.00 in value.

FULFILLMENT

Unordered Merchandise
Article #26

Merchandise should not be shipped without having first received the customer's permission. The exceptions are samples or gifts clearly marked as such, and merchandise mailed by a charitable organization soliciting contributions, as long as all items are sent with a clear and conspicuous statement informing the recipient of an unqualified right to treat the product as a gift and to do with it as the recipient sees fit, at no cost or obligation to the recipient.

Product Availability and Shipment
Article #27

Direct marketers should offer merchandise only when it is on hand or when there is a reasonable expectation of its timely receipt.

Direct marketers should ship all orders according to the terms of the offer or within 30 days where there is no promised shipping date, unless otherwise directed by the consumer, and should promptly notify consumers of any delays.

Dry Testing
Article #28
Direct marketers should engage in dry testing only when the special nature of the offer is made clear in the promotion.

COLLECTION, USE AND MAINTENANCE OF MARKETING DATA

Collection, Use and Transfer of Personally Identifiable Data
Article #29
Consumers who provide data that may be rented, sold or exchanged for marketing purposes should be informed periodically by marketers of their policy concerning the rental, sale or exchange of such data and of the opportunity to opt out of the marketing process. Should that policy substantially change, marketers have an obligation to inform consumers of that change prior to the rental, sale or exchange of such data, and to offer consumers an opportunity to opt out of the marketing process at that time. All individual opt-out requests should be honored. Marketers should maintain and use their own systems, policies and procedures, and, at no cost to consumers, refrain from using or transferring such data, as the case may be, as requested by consumers.

List compilers should maintain and use their own systems, policies and procedures, and at no cost to consumers refrain from using or transferring data, as the case may be, as requested by consumers.

For each list that is rented, sold or exchanged, the applicable DMA Preference Service name removal list (e.g., Mail Preference Service, Telephone Preference Service) should be employed prior to use.

Data about consumers who have opted out of use or transfer should not, per their requests, be used, rented, sold or exchanged.

Upon request by a consumer, marketers should disclose the source from which they obtained personally identifiable data about that consumer.

Personal Data
Article #30
Marketers should be sensitive to the issue of consumer privacy and should only collect, combine, rent, sell, exchange or use marketing data. Marketing data should be used only for marketing purposes.

Data and selection criteria that by reasonable standards may be considered sensitive and/or intimate should not be disclosed, displayed or provide the basis for lists made available for rental, sale or exchange when there is a reasonable expectation by the consumer that the information will be kept confidential.

Promotion of Marketing Lists
Article #31
Any advertising or promotion for marketing lists being offered for rental, sale or exchange should reflect the fact that a marketing list is an aggregate

collection of marketing data. Such promotions should also reflect a sensitivity for the consumers on those lists.

Marketing List Usage
Article #32
   List owners, brokers, managers, compilers and users of marketing lists should ascertain the nature of the list's intended usage for each materially different marketing use prior to rental, sale, exchange, transfer or use of the list. List owners, brokers, managers and compilers should not permit the rental, sale, exchange or transfer of their marketing lists, nor should users use any marketing lists for an offer that is in violation of these guidelines.

TELEPHONE MARKETING

Reasonable Hours
Article #33
   Telephone contacts should be made during reasonable hours as specified by federal and state laws and regulations.

Taping of Conversations
Article #34
   Taping of telephone conversations by telemarketers should only be conducted with notice to or consent of all parties, or the use of a beeping device, as required by applicable federal and state laws and regulations.

Restricted Contacts
Article #35
   A telephone marketer should not knowingly call a consumer who has an unlisted or unpublished telephone number, or a telephone number for which the called party must pay the charges, except in instances where the number was provided by the consumer to that marketer.
   Random dialing techniques, whether manual or automated, in which those parties to be called are left to chance should not be used in sales and marketing solicitations.
   Sequential dialing techniques, whether a manual or automated process, in which selection of those parties to be called is based on the location of their telephone numbers in a sequence of telephone numbers should not be used.

Use of Automated Dialing Equipment
Article #36
   When using automated dialing equipment for any reason, telephone marketers should only use equipment which allows the telephone to immediately release the line when the called party terminates the connection. ADRMPS (Automatic Dialers and Recorded Message Players) and prerecorded messages should be used only in accordance with tariffs, federal, state, and local laws, FCC regulations and these guidelines. Telephone marketers should use a live operator to obtain a consumer's permission before delivering a recorded message.

When using any automated dialing equipment to reach a multi-line location, the equipment should release each line used before connecting to another.

Use of Telephone Facsimile Machines
Article #37
Unless there is a prior business relationship with the recipient, or unless the recipient has given prior permission, unsolicited advertisements should not be transmitted by facsimile. Each permitted transmission to a fax machine must clearly contain on each page or on the first page, the date and time the transmission is sent, the identity of the sender and the telephone number of the sender or the sending machine.

Promotions for Response by Toll-Free and Pay-Per-Call Numbers
Article #38
Promotions for response by 800 or other toll-free numbers should be used only when there is no charge to the consumer for the call itself and when there is no transfer from a toll-free number to a pay call.

Promotions for response by using 900 numbers or any other type of pay-per-call programs should clearly and conspicuously disclose all charges for the call. A preamble at the beginning of the 900 or other pay-per-call should include the nature of the service or program, charge per minute and the total estimated charge for the call, as well as the name, address and telephone number of the sponsor. The caller should be given the option to disconnect the call at any time during the preamble without incurring any charge.

The 900 number or other pay-per-call should only use equipment that ceases accumulating time and charges immediately upon disconnection by the caller.

Disclosure and Tactics
Article #39
Prior to asking consumers for payment authorization, telephone marketers should disclose the cost of the merchandise or service and all terms and conditions, including payment plans, whether or not there is a no-refund or a no-cancellation policy in place, limitations, and the amount or existence of any extra charges such as shipping and handling and insurance. At no time should high pressure tactics be utilized.

FUND-RAISING

Article #40
In addition to compliance with these guidelines, fund-raisers and other charitable solicitors should, whenever requested by donors or potential donors, provide financial information regarding use of funds.

LAWS, CODES, AND REGULATIONS

Article #41
Direct marketers should operate in accordance with laws and regulations of the United States Postal Service, the Federal Trade Commission, the Federal Communications Commission, the Federal Reserve Board, and other applicable

federal, state and local laws governing advertising, marketing practices and the transaction of business.

APPENDIX 1

Other DMA Resources
[see introductory pages]

The DMA can also provide your company with information on the following Federal Trade Commission (FTC) and Federal Communications Commission (FCC) regulations and rules affecting direct marketers:

FTC:

Mail or Telephone Order Merchandise Rule
Telemarketing Sales Rule
Negative Option Rule
Guides Against Deceptive Pricing
Guarantees and Warranties
Equal Credit Opportunity Act
Fair Debt Collection Practices Act
Telephone Disclosure and Dispute Resolution Act

FCC:

Telephone Consumer Protection Act

Other DMA and government titles are available, as well as a variety of consumer education brochures. Contact the Ethics and Consumer Affairs Department in Washington, D.C. for more information.

APPENDIX 2

Introduction
DMA Interpretations Under the Ethical Guidelines

The Direct Marketing Association's Guidelines for Ethical Business Practice are principles that direct marketers should follow to ensure that they are conducting their business in an ethical manner. Guidelines, by their very nature, are meant to be general tenets. However, sometimes more specific guidance is needed to address various marketing practices. When such situations arise, The DMA issues specific guidance which expands on the ethical guidelines.

"Interpretations" are used to respond to consumer and regulatory concerns regarding specific issues and to educate industry members on acceptable industry practice.

As other interpretations of the guidelines are issued, they will be included herein.

#1
Interpretation on Use of Automatic Number Identification and Caller ID Under Ethical Guideline #35

The Direct Marketing Association (The DMA) recognizes that the proper use of technology such as automatic number identification (ANI) and Caller ID benefits consumers. The DMA also acknowledges the privacy concerns that may arise with the use of such technology.

The DMA Guidelines for Marketing by Telephone require that telephone marketers who receive or collect consumer data as a result of a telephone marketing contact, and who intend to rent, sell or exchange those data for direct marketing purposes should notify the consumer of that fact. Consumer requests regarding restrictions on the collection, rental, sale or exchange of data relating to them should be honored. Telephone marketers using Automatic Number Identification (ANI) should not rent, sell, transfer or exchange, without customer consent, telephone numbers gained from ANI except where a prior business relationship exists for the sale of directly related goods or services.

#2
Interpretation on Use of Financial Information by Direct Marketers Under Ethical Guidelines #29 and #30

The DMA considers credit card numbers, checking account numbers and debit account numbers to be personal information and therefore should not be transferred, rented, sold or exchanged when there is a reasonable expectation by the consumer that the information will be kept confidential. Because of the confidential nature of such personally identifying numbers, they should not be publicly displayed on direct marketing promotions or otherwise made public by direct marketers.

#3
Interpretation on Disclosure of Health and Medical Data Under Ethical Guidelines #29 and #30

Direct marketers understand the sensitivity of collecting and using certain types of data, including health-related data. In the management of health-related data, fair information principles outlined in The DMA's Guidelines for Personal Information Protection would apply.

Information derived from the relationship between a patient and a medical care provider should never be disclosed or used for marketing purposes.

Health and medical data not derived from the provider-patient relationship should nonetheless be considered sensitive and personal in nature and should be rented, sold, transferred or exchanged only where appropriate privacy safeguards are in place. Such data may include, but are not limited to, data voluntarily provided by the consumer and compiled by way of questionnaires and/or compiled list methods and marketed with the knowledge of the consumer.

Consumers who provide health and medical information that may be rented, sold, transferred or exchanged for marketing purposes should be informed at the point of providing the information of the potential for the rental, sale, transfer or exchange of such data. Marketers should offer an opportunity to have a consumer's name deleted or suppressed upon request.

Marketers should ensure that safeguards are built into their systems to protect health and medical data from abuse, theft or misappropriation. The text and nature of solicitations directed to consumers on the basis of health-related data should take into account the sensitive nature of such data.

ADDENDA

Interpretation on the Use of Social Security Numbers by Direct Marketers Under Ethical Guidelines #29 and #30

The DMA considers Social Security numbers to be personal information and therefore they should not be transferred, rented, sold or exchanged for use by a third party when there is a reasonable expectation by the consumer that the information will be kept confidential. Because of the confidential nature of Social Security numbers, they should not be publicly displayed on direct marketing promotions or otherwise made public by direct marketers. The DMA acknowledges, however, that Social Security numbers are used by direct marketers as part of the process of extending credit to consumers or for matching or verification purposes.

Position on Marketing to Children Online

The DMA recognizes that online communications present challenges for families and for companies that are different from, and more complex than, those of communicating in traditional media. Families are understandably concerned about their young children's experience online and, in response, The DMA has committed resources to educate families, develop and promote technology tools for parents, and set a firm course for responsible corporate policy development.

While parents understand their responsibility to set and enforce online rules for their families, The DMA also acknowledges the duty of business to be responsible online marketers in addressing the special needs of young children. The DMA proposes the following guidelines for marketers operating online sites targeted to children under 13:

Marketers should not collect personally identifiable information online from a child under 13 without prior parental consent or direct parental notification of the nature and intended use of such information online and an opportunity for the parent to prevent such use and participation in the activity. Online contact information shall only be used to directly respond to an activity initiated by a child and not to recontact a child for other purposes without prior parental consent. However, a marketer may contact and get information from a child for the purpose of obtaining parental consent.

Marketers should not collect, without prior parental permission, personally identifiable information online from children that would permit any off-line contact with the child.

Marketers should not distribute to third parties, without prior parental permission, information collected from a child that would permit any contact with that child.

Marketers should take reasonable steps to prevent the online publication or posting of information that would allow a third party to contact a child off-line unless the marketer has prior parental consent.

Marketers should not entice a child to divulge personally identifiable information by the prospect of a special game, prize or other offer.

Marketers should not make a child's access to a Web site contingent on the collection of personally identifiable information. Only online contact information used to enhance the interactivity of the site is permitted.

The following assumptions underlie these online guidelines:

When a marketer directs a site at a certain age group, it can expect that the visitors to that site are in that age range; and

When a marketer asks the age of the child, the marketer can assume the answer to be truthful.

Organization

DIRECT SELLING ASSOCIATION

Headquarters:
1666 K Street, NW
Suite 1010
Washington, DC 20006-2808
Telephone: (202) 293-5760
Fax: (202) 463-4569
E-mail: info@dsa.org
Website: http://www.dsa.org

Date founded: 1910
> Known as the National Association of Direct Selling Companies until 1969; formerly the Agents Credit Association

Membership: approximately 150 direct selling companies

Code of Ethics

Official name: *Code of Ethics*
History: First adopted June 1970; current version issued March 11, 1997; amended May 30, 1998
Authority: Ethics and Self-Regulation Committee; Board of Directors
Code is available on Website

Additional Resources

Organizational (Divisions, Programs, Services, etc.):

Direct Selling Education Foundation (conferences, seminars, research, and publications)
World Federation of Direct Selling Associations

Informational (Publications, Videos, Seminars, etc.):

DSA Delivers Extra Value

*Moral Suasion: Development of the U.S. Direct Selling Association
    Industry Code of Ethics*
Pyramid Schemes: Not What They Seem!
World Code of Conduct for Direct Selling
World Federation News

Goals and Activities of Organization

The Direct Selling Association (DSA) is the national trade association of companies that manufacture and distribute goods and services sold directly to consumers "in a face-to-face manner away from a fixed retail location." It works to ensure that its member companies conduct their marketing efforts "with the highest level of business ethics and service to consumers"; the DSA considers its Code of Ethics the "cornerstone" of this commitment.

The Board of Directors establishes regulations for the administration of the Code and appoints an independent Code Administrator, "a person of recognized integrity, knowledgeable in the industry," who is not connected with any member company. In addition to the duties of Code enforcement, the Administrator's office maintains relations with Better Business Bureaus and other public and private organizations.

The DSA also serves as the secretariat for the World Federation of Direct Selling Associations, a nongovernmental organization that represents the industry globally. Among its goals is the adoption and promotion of codes of conduct governing direct selling.

Implementation and Enforcement of Code

Applicants for DSA membership undergo a one-year screening process during which their marketing plans and sales literature are reviewed for compliance with state and federal laws and the Code of Ethics. Member companies must abide by the Code and recertify annually that they are in compliance with it. They agree to be bound by the Code Administrator's decisions. Members may not encourage anyone else to violate the Code.

The Code Administrator has the power to hear and determine all complaints against members for alleged Code violations, brought by consumers or initiated by the DSA. The Administrator also suggests to the Board of Directors new regulations or definitions to make the Code more effective.

All parties to a complaint are afforded notice and an opportunity to be heard in confidential formal or informal proceedings. An accused member who refuses to cooperate with the Administrator risks a separate hearing before the Board to show cause why membership should not be terminated.

Alleged violations may be determined to be "of such a nature, scope or frequency so as to require remedial action" in "the best interests of consumers, the association and the direct selling industry." The member may voluntarily consent to accept the suggested remedies without a formal hearing.

If a formal hearing is called for, the Administrator gathers evidence, takes testimony surrounding the complaint, determines whether a Code violation has occurred, and issues a decision. The member may comment on the findings and request an appeal to an independent arbitrator (whose final decision, after a separate arbitration proceeding, is binding on all parties).

Remedies for Code violations include monetary restitution to the consumer, replacement or repair of products, contribution to a special fund used to promote ethical standards, and/or a written commitment to abide by the Code in the future and exercise due diligence to prevent recurrence of the practice that led to the complaint. Compliance with remedies terminates the matter.

If a member refuses to comply with a decision or remedy, the Administrator may consult independent legal counsel to determine whether the Code violation involves any state or federal laws; with notice to the member, the Administrator may inform appropriate government agencies.

Members who have been suspended or terminated may eventually request a reinstatement hearing before the Board of Directors. A company's resignation from DSA membership before complaint proceedings are over neither ends the matter, nor prevents a final decision by the Administrator or arbitrator as to whether the Code has been violated.

History and Development of Code

A voluntary Consumer Relations Code was adopted by the organization in 1940.

The first mandatory DSA Code of Ethics was instituted in 1970, during the burgeoning consumer movement. The DSA was motivated to stop direct selling companies from engaging in disreputable practices harmful to consumers, to head off government regulations aimed at those practices, and to counteract negative images of the industry.

The Code was first amended in 1974 to address pyramid sales schemes. A major revision in 1978–79 specified sanctions for Code violations. Amendments passed in the 1980s enabled complaints to proceed without various formalities; the organization also set out to more actively promote and publicize the Code. An Ethics Task Force set up in 1990 led to amendments regarding such issues as exaggerated earnings claims in the recruitment of salespeople, inventory loading, and multi-level marketing.

The Code was most recently amended in May 1998 to address, among other matters, the purchase of company-produced promotional materials.

Code of Ethics*

PREAMBLE

The Direct Selling Association, recognizing that companies engaged in direct selling assume certain responsibilities toward consumers arising out of the personal-contact method of distribution of their products and services, hereby sets forth the basic fair and ethical principles and practices to which member companies of the association will continue to adhere in the conduct of their business.

A. CODE OF CONDUCT

1. Deceptive or Unlawful Consumer or Recruiting Practices

No member company of the Association shall engage in any deceptive, unlawful, or unethical consumer or recruiting practice. Member companies shall ensure that no statements, promises or testimonials are made which are likely to mislead consumers or prospective salespeople.

2. Products or Services

The offer of products or services for sale by member companies of the Association shall be accurate and truthful as to price, grade, quality, make, value, performance, quantity, currency of model, and availability. A consumer's order for products and services shall be fulfilled in a timely manner.

3. Terms of Sale

A written order or receipt shall be delivered to the customer at the time of sale, which sets forth in language that is clear and free of ambiguity:
A. All the terms and conditions of sale, with specification of the total amount the customer will be required to pay, including all interest, service charges and fees, and other costs and expenses as required by federal and state law;
B. The name and address of the salesperson or the member firm represented.

4. Warranties and Guarantees

The terms of any warranty or guarantee offered by the seller in connection with the sale shall be furnished to the buyer in a manner that fully conforms to federal and state warranty and guarantee laws and regulations. The manufacturer,

*As Adopted June 15, 1970. As Amended by Board of Directors through May 30, 1998. Copyright © 1998 Direct Selling Association. All rights reserved. Reprinted with permission of the Direct Selling Association.

This reprint includes the full text of the Preamble, Code of Conduct, and Responsibilities and Duties. The sections on administration, enforcement, and appeal have been omitted, but are summarized in the preceding introductory pages.

distributor and/or seller shall fully and promptly perform in accordance with the terms of all warranties and guarantees offered to consumers.

5. Identification and Privacy

Sellers shall truthfully identify themselves, their company, their products and the purposes of their solicitation to the prospective customer. Contact with the consumer shall be made in a reasonable manner and during reasonable hours to avoid intrusiveness. A demonstration or sales presentation shall discontinue upon the request of the consumer.

6. Pyramid Schemes

For the purpose of this Code, pyramid or endless chain schemes shall be considered consumer transactions actionable under this Code. The Code Administrator shall determine whether such pyramid or endless chain schemes constitute a violation of this Code in accordance with applicable federal, state and/or local law or regulation.

7. Inventory Purchases

A. Any member company with a marketing plan that involves selling products directly or indirectly to independent salespeople shall clearly state, in its recruiting literature, sales manual, or contract with the independent salespeople, that the company will repurchase on reasonable commercial terms currently marketable inventory, in the possession of that salesperson and purchased by that salesperson for resale prior to the date of termination of the salesperson's business relationship with the company or its independent salespeople. For purposes of this Code, "reasonable commercial terms" shall include the repurchase of marketable inventory within twelve (12) months from the salesperson's date of purchase at not less than 90% of the salesperson's original net cost less appropriate set-offs and legal claims, if any. For purposes of this Code, products shall not be considered "currently marketable" if returned for repurchase after the products' commercially reasonable usable or shelf-life period has passed; nor shall products be considered "currently marketable" if the company clearly discloses to salespeople prior to purchase that the products are seasonal, discontinued, or special promotion products and are not subject to the repurchase obligation.

B. Any member company with a marketing plan which requires independent salespeople to purchase company produced promotional materials, sales aids or kits shall clearly state, in its recruiting literature, sales manual, or contract with the independent salespeople that the company will repurchase these items on reasonable commercial terms.

Any member company with a marketing plan which provides its independent salespeople with any financial benefit related to the sales of company produced promotional materials, sales aids or kits shall clearly state, in its recruiting literature, sales manual, or contract with the independent salespeople that the company will repurchase, on reasonable commercial terms, currently marketable company produced promotional materials, sales aids or kits.

A member company shall clearly state in its recruiting literature, sales manual, or contract with the independent salespeople if any items not otherwise covered by this Section are ineligible for repurchase by the company.

8. Earnings Representations

No member company shall misrepresent the actual or potential sales or earnings of its independent salespeople. Any earnings or sales representations that are made by member companies shall be based on documented facts.

9. Inventory Loading

A member company shall not require or encourage an independent salesperson to purchase inventory in an amount which unreasonably exceeds that which can be expected to be resold and/or consumed within a reasonable period of time.

10. Payment of Fees

Neither member companies nor their representatives shall ask individuals to assume unreasonably high entrance fees, training fees, franchise fees, fees for promotional materials or other fees related solely to the right to participate in the direct selling business.

B. RESPONSIBILITIES AND DUTIES

In the event any consumer shall complain that the salesperson or representative offering for sale the products or services of a member company has engaged in any improper course of conduct pertaining to the sales presentation of its goods or services, the member company shall promptly investigate the complaint and shall take such steps as it may find appropriate and necessary under the circumstances to cause the redress of any wrongs which its investigation discloses to have been committed.

Member companies will be considered responsible for Code violations by their solicitors and representatives where the Administrator finds, after considering all the facts, that a violation of the Code has occurred. For the purposes of this Code, in the interest of fostering consumer protection, companies shall voluntarily not raise the independent contractor status of salespersons distributing their products or services under its trademark or trade name as a defense against Code violation allegations and such action shall not be construed to be a waiver of the companies' right to raise such defense under any other circumstance.

The members subscribing to this Code recognize that its success will require diligence in creating an awareness among their employees and/or the independent wholesalers and retailers marketing the member's products or services of the member's obligations under the Code. No subscribing party shall in any way attempt to persuade, induce or coerce another party to breach this Code, and the subscribers hereto agree that the inducing of the breach of this Code is considered a violation of the Code.

* * *

Organization

PUBLIC RELATIONS SOCIETY OF AMERICA

Headquarters:
33 Irving Place
New York, NY 10003-2376
Telephone: (212) 995-2230
Fax: (212) 995-0757
E-mail: hq@prsa.org
Website: http://www.prsa.org

Date founded: 1947
Membership: approximately 18,000 public relations professionals in business, industry, counseling firms, government, associations, hospitals, schools, firms, and nonprofit organizations

Code of Ethics

Official name: *Code of Professional Standards for the Practice of Public Relations*
History: Adopted 1988; replaces a 1950 Code revised in 1954, 1959, 1963, 1977, and 1983
Authority: Board of Ethics and Professional Standards; PRSA Assembly
Code is available on Website

Additional Resources

Organizational (Divisions, Programs, Services, etc.):

Professional Practice Center (information clearinghouse)
Public Relations Student Society of America
Public Relations Internships to Develop Expertise
Universal Accreditation Program
Various sections: Best Practices in Corporate Communications; Environment; Financial Communications; Public Affairs and Government

Informational (Publications, Videos, Seminars, etc.):

Articles in *Public Relations Strategist* and *Public Relations Tactics*

Accountability: The Watchwords of the 90s
APR Accreditation Sourcebook
Best Practices in Corporate Communications Reports
Changing the Rules for Issues Management
Corporate Response to Ethical Dilemmas
Developing a Corporate Mission Statement
Environmental Public Relations and the PRSA Code of Ethics
Equity Research Today: New Sources, New Challenges
Managing Your Career: Mapping and Mentoring and Other Professional
    Growth Strategies
Practical Public Affairs in an Era of Change
Public Relations Law
Strategies for Dealing With Ethical Dilemmas

Goals and Activities of Organization

The Public Relations Society of America (PRSA) seeks to advance the practice of public relations through continuing education; taking an active role in matters affecting the profession; formulating the objectives of the profession and interpreting its functions to the public; strengthening relationships with employers, clients, government, educators, media, and the public; and promoting high standards of conduct and service.

The organization serves as a forum for members to address professional issues and to exchange information and experiences with peers. It provides resources for promoting ethical standards and for advancing members' skills and knowledge. The Accreditation Program, for instance, covers ethics among a variety of topics.

Implementation and Enforcement of Code

Upon joining PRSA, members agree to adhere to the Code of Professional Standards. The Code itself provides that a member "sever relations with any organization or individual if such relationship requires conduct contrary" to its provisions.

The Assembly adopts and amends the Code. The Board of Directors proposes amendments, adopts procedural rules for enforcement, issues official interpretations of the Code, and expresses opinions as to what constitutes proper professional conduct.

The Board of Ethics and Professional Standards is made up of accredited members appointed by the PRSA president with the approval of the Board of Directors. It has the power to conduct investigations regarding Code violations, bring complaints before a Judicial Panel, and prosecute complaints. Individual members also may bring complaints.

A complaint is heard in a closed, confidential disciplinary proceeding before a Judicial Panel, which, if it determines that the Code was violated, recommends disciplinary action to the Board of Directors. Sanctions for violation include warning, reprimand, censure, suspension, and expulsion;

the Board has the discretion to make this information public. A disciplinary investigation or proceeding will continue to a determination even if the accused member resigns while the matter is pending.

History and Development of Code

The present Code, adopted in 1988, replaced one that had been in force since 1950, which was periodically revised—in 1954, 1959, 1963, 1977, and 1983.

The Board of Ethics and Professional Standards regularly considers issues that may affect Code provisions. Recent discussions have touched on such matters as: the identification of clients; professional practices on the Internet; how confidentiality affects PRSA's role in educating the public about ethics standards; defining a "dubious client"; and whether firms employing PRSA members should be required to comply with the Code as an organization.

Code of Professional Standards for the Practice of Public Relations*

DECLARATION OF PRINCIPLES

Members of the Public Relations Society of America base their professional principles on the fundamental value and dignity of the individual, holding that the free exercise of human rights, especially freedom of speech, freedom of assembly, and freedom of the press, is essential to the practice of public relations.

In serving the interests of clients and employers, we dedicate ourselves to the goals of better communication, understanding, and cooperation among the diverse individuals, groups, and institutions of society, and of equal opportunity of employment in the public relations profession.

We pledge:

To conduct ourselves professionally, with truth, accuracy, fairness, and responsibility to the public;

To improve our individual competence and advance the knowledge and proficiency of the profession through continuing research and education;

And to adhere to the articles of the Code of Professional Standards for the Practice of Public Relations as adopted by the governing Assembly of the Society.

CODE OF PROFESSIONAL STANDARDS FOR THE PRACTICE OF PUBLIC RELATIONS

These articles have been adopted by the Public Relations Society of America to promote and maintain high standards of public service and ethical conduct among its members.

1. A member shall conduct his or her professional life in accord with the **public interest**.
2. A member shall exemplify high standards of **honesty and integrity** while carrying out dual obligations to a client or employer and to the democratic process.
3. A member shall **deal fairly** with the public, with past or present clients or employers, and with fellow practitioners, giving due respect to the ideal of free inquiry and to the opinions of others.
4. A member shall adhere to the highest standards of **accuracy and truth**, avoiding extravagant claims or unfair comparisons and giving credit for ideas and words borrowed from others.
5. A member shall not knowingly disseminate **false or misleading information** and shall act promptly to correct erroneous communications for which he or she is responsible.
6. A member shall not engage in any practice which has the purpose of **corrupting** the integrity of channels of communications or the processes of government.

---

*Reprinted with permission of the Public Relations Society of America.

This Code was adopted by the PRSA Assembly in 1988. It replaces a Code of Ethics in force since 1950 and revised in 1954, 1959, 1963, 1977, and 1983. For information on the Code and enforcement procedures, please call the chair of the Board of Ethics through PRSA Headquarters.

7. A member shall be prepared to **identify publicly** the name of the client or employer on whose behalf any public communication is made.
8. A member shall not use any individual or organization professing to serve or represent an announced cause, or professing to be independent or unbiased, but actually serving another or **undisclosed interest**.
9. A member shall **not guarantee the achievement** of specified results beyond the member's direct control.
10. A member shall **not represent conflicting** or competing interests without the express consent of those concerned, given after a full disclosure of the facts.
11. A member shall not place himself or herself in a position where the member's **personal interest is or may be in conflict** with an obligation to an employer or client, or others, without full disclosure of such interests to all involved.
12. A member shall **not accept fees, commissions, gifts or any other consideration** from anyone except clients or employers for whom services are performed without their express consent, given after full disclosure of the facts.
13. A member shall scrupulously safeguard the **confidences and privacy rights** of present, former, and prospective clients or employers.
14. A member shall not intentionally **damage the professional reputation** or practice of another practitioner.
15. If a member has evidence that another member has been guilty of unethical, illegal, or unfair practices, including those in violation of this Code, the member is obligated to present the information promptly to the proper authorities of the Society for action in accordance with the procedure set forth in Article XII of the Bylaws.
16. A member called as a witness in a proceeding for enforcement of this Code is obligated to appear, unless excused for sufficient reason by the judicial panel.
17. A member shall, as soon as possible, sever relations with any organization or individual if such relationship requires conduct contrary to the articles of this Code.

OFFICIAL INTERPRETATIONS OF THE CODE

Interpretation of Code Paragraph 1, which reads, "A member shall conduct his or her professional life in accord with the public interest."

The public interest is here defined primarily as comprising respect for and enforcement of the rights guaranteed by the Constitution of the United States of America.

Interpretation of Code Paragraph 6, which reads, "A member shall not engage in any practice which has the purpose of corrupting the integrity of channels of communication or the processes of government."
1. Among the practices prohibited by this paragraph are those that tend to place representatives of media or government under any obligation to the member, or the member's employer or client, which is in conflict with their obligations to media or government, such as:
   a. the giving of gifts of more than nominal value;
   b. any form of payment or compensation to a member of the media in order to obtain preferential or guaranteed news or editorial coverage in the medium;
   c. any retainer or fee to a media employee or use of such employee if retained by a client or employer, where the circumstances are not fully disclosed to and accepted by the media employer;

   d. providing trips, for media representatives, that are unrelated to legitimate news interest;

   e. the use by a member of an investment or loan or advertising commitment made by the member, or the member's client or employer, to obtain preferential or guaranteed coverage in the medium.

2. This Code paragraph does not prohibit hosting media or government representatives at meals, cocktails, or news functions and special events that are occasions for the exchange of news information or views, or the furtherance of understanding, which is part of the public relations function. Nor does it prohibit the bona fide press event or tour when media or government representatives are given the opportunity for an on-the-spot viewing of a newsworthy product, process, or event in which the media or government representatives have a legitimate interest. What is customary or reasonable hospitality has to be a matter of particular judgment in specific situations. In all of these cases, however, it is, or should be, understood that no preferential treatment or guarantees are expected or implied and that complete independence always is left to the media or government representative.

3. This paragraph does not prohibit the reasonable giving or lending of sample products or services to media representatives who have a legitimate interest in the products or services.

4. It is permissible, under Article 6 of the Code, to offer complimentary or discount rates to the media (travel writers, for example) if the rate is for business use and is made available to all writers. Considerable question exists as to the propriety of extending such rates for personal use.

Interpretation of Code Paragraph 9, which reads, "A member shall not guarantee the achievement of specified results beyond the member's direct control."

This Code paragraph, in effect, prohibits misleading a client or employer as to what professional public relations can accomplish. It does not prohibit guarantees of quality of service. But it does prohibit guaranteeing specific results which, by their very nature, cannot be guaranteed because they are not subject to the member's control. As an example, a guarantee that a news release will appear specifically in a particular publication would be prohibited. This paragraph should not be interpreted as prohibiting contingent fees.

Interpretation of Code Paragraph 13, which reads, "A member shall scrupulously safeguard the confidences and privacy rights of present, former, and prospective clients or employers."

1. This article does not prohibit a member who has knowledge of client or employer activities that are illegal from making such disclosures to the proper authorities as he or she believes are legally required.

2. Communications between a practitioner and client/employer are deemed to be confidential under Article 13 of the Code of Professional Standards. However, although practitioner/client/employer communications are considered confidential between the parties, such communications are not privileged against disclosure in a court of law.

3. Under the copyright laws of the United States, the copyright in a work is generally owned initially by the author or authors. In the case of a "work made for hire" by an employee acting within the scope of his or her employment, the employer is considered to be the author and owns the copyright in the absence of an express, signed written agreement to the contrary. A freelancer who is the author of the work and is not an employee may be the owner of

the copyright. A member should consult legal counsel for detailed advice concerning the scope and application of the copyright laws.

Interpretation of Code Paragraph 14, which reads, "A member shall not intentionally damage the professional reputation or practice of another practitioner."

1. Blind solicitation, on its face, is not prohibited by the Code. However, if the customer lists were improperly obtained, or if the solicitation contained references reflecting adversely on the quality of current services, a complaint might be justified.

2. This article applies to statements, true or false, or acts, made or undertaken with malice and with the specific purpose of harming the reputation or practice of another member. This article does not prohibit honest employee evaluations or similar reviews, made without malice and as part of ordinary business practice, even though this activity may have a harmful effect.

AN OFFICIAL INTERPRETATION OF THE CODE AS IT APPLIES TO POLITICAL PUBLIC RELATIONS

Preamble

In the practice of political public relations, a PRSA member must have professional capabilities to offer an employer or client quite apart from any political relationships of value, and members may serve their employer or client without necessarily having attributed to them the character, reputation, or beliefs of those they serve. It is understood that members may choose to serve only those interests with whose political philosophy they are personally comfortable.

Definition

"Political Public Relations" is defined as those areas of public relations that relate to:

a. the counseling of political organizations, committees, candidates, or potential candidates for public office; and groups constituted for the purpose of influencing the vote on any ballot issue;

b. the counseling of holders of public office;

c. the management, or direction, of a political campaign for or against a candidate for political office; or for or against a ballot issue to be determined by voter approval or rejection;

d. the practice of public relations on behalf of a client or an employer in connection with that client's or employer's relationships with any candidates or holders of public office, with the purpose of influencing legislation or government regulation or treatment of a client or employer, regardless of whether the PRSA member is a recognized lobbyist;

e. the counseling of government bodies, or segments thereof, either domestic or foreign.

Precepts

1. It is the responsibility of PRSA members practicing political public relations, as defined above, to be conversant with the various statutes, local, state, and federal, governing such activities and to adhere to them strictly. This includes, but is not limited to, the various local, state, and federal laws, court decisions,

and official interpretations governing lobbying, political contributions, disclosure, elections, libel, slander, and the like. In carrying out this responsibility, members shall seek appropriate counseling whenever necessary.

2. It is also the responsibility of the members to abide by PRSA's Code of Professional Standards.

3. Members shall represent clients or employers in good faith, and while partisan advocacy on behalf of a candidate or public issue may be expected, members shall act in accord with the public interest and adhere to truth and accuracy and to generally accepted standards of good taste.

4. Members shall not issue descriptive material or any advertising or publicity information or participate in the preparation or use thereof that is not signed by responsible persons or is false, misleading, or unlabeled as to its source, and are obligated to use care to avoid dissemination of any such material.

5. Members have an obligation to clients to disclose what remuneration beyond their fees they expect to receive as a result of their relationship, such as commissions for media advertising, printing, and the like, and should not accept such extra payment without their client's consent.

6. Members shall not improperly use their positions to encourage additional future employment or compensation. It is understood that successful campaign directors or managers, because of the performance of their duties and the working relationship that develops, may well continue to assist and counsel, for pay, the successful candidate.

7. Members shall voluntarily disclose to employers or clients the identity of other employers or clients with whom they are currently associated, and whose interests might be affected favorably or unfavorably by their political representation.

8. Members shall respect the confidentiality of information pertaining to employers or clients past, present, and potential, even after the relationships cease, avoiding future associations wherein insider information is sought that would give a desired advantage over a member's previous clients.

9. In avoiding practices that might tend to corrupt the processes of government, members shall not make undisclosed gifts of cash or other valuable considerations that are designed to influence specific decisions of voters, legislators, or public officials on public matters. A business lunch or dinner, or other comparable expenditure made in the course of communicating a point of view or public position, would not constitute such a violation. Nor, for example, would a plant visit designed and financed to provide useful background information to an interested legislator or candidate.

10. Nothing herein should be construed as prohibiting members from making legal, properly disclosed contributions to the candidates, party, or referenda issues of their choice.

11. Members shall not, through use of information known to be false or misleading, conveyed directly or through a third party, intentionally injure the public reputation of an opposing interest.

AN OFFICIAL INTERPRETATION OF THE CODE AS IT APPLIES TO FINANCIAL PUBLIC RELATIONS

This interpretation of the Society Code as it applies to financial public relations was originally adopted in 1963 and amended in 1972, 1977, 1983 and 1988 by action of the PRSA Board of Directors. "Financial public relations" is defined as "that area of public relations which relates to the dissemination of information that affects the understanding of stockholders and investors generally concerning the financial position and prospects of a company, and includes among its objectives the improvement of relations between corporations and their stockholders." The interpretation was prepared in 1963 by the Society's Financial Relations Committee, working with the Securities and Exchange Commission and with the advice of the Society's legal counsel. It is rooted directly in the Code with the full force of the Code behind it, and a violation of any of the following paragraphs is subject to the same procedures and penalties as violation of the Code.

1. It is the responsibility of PRSA members who practice financial public relations to be thoroughly familiar with and understand the rules and regulations of the SEC and the laws it administers, as well as other laws, rules, and regulations affecting financial public relations, and to act in accordance with their letter and spirit. In carrying out this responsibility, members shall also seek legal counsel, when appropriate, on matters concerning financial public relations.

2. Members shall adhere to the general policy of making full and timely disclosure of corporate information on behalf of clients or employers. The information disclosed shall be accurate, clear, and understandable. The purpose of such disclosure is to provide the investing public with all material information affecting security values or influencing investment decisions. In complying with the duty of full and timely disclosure, members shall present all material facts, including those adverse to the company. They shall exercise care to ascertain the facts and to disseminate only information they believe to be accurate. They shall not knowingly omit information, the omission of which might make a release false or misleading. Under no circumstances shall members participate in any activity designed to mislead or manipulate the price of a company's securities.

3. Members shall publicly disclose or release information promptly so as to avoid the possibility of any use of the information by any insider or third party. To that end, members shall make every effort to comply with the spirit and intent of the timely-disclosure policies of the stock exchanges, NASD, and the SEC. Material information shall be made available on an equal basis.

4. Members shall not disclose confidential information the disclosure of which might be adverse to a valid corporate purpose or interest and whose disclosure is not required by the timely-disclosure provisions of the law. During any such period of nondisclosure members shall not directly or indirectly (a) communicate the confidential information to any other person or (b) buy or sell or in any other way deal in the company's securities where the confidential information may materially affect the market for the security when disclosed. Material information shall be disclosed publicly as soon as its confidential status has terminated or the requirement of timely disclosure takes effect.

5. During the registration period, members shall not engage in practices designed to precondition the market for such securities. During registration, the issuance of forecasts, projections, predictions about sales and earnings, or opinions concerning security values or other aspects of the future performance of the company, shall be in accordance with current SEC regulations and statements of policy. In the case of companies whose securities are publicly held, the normal flow of factual information to shareholders and the investing public shall continue during the registration period.

6. Where members have any reason to doubt that projections have an adequate basis in fact, they shall satisfy themselves as to the adequacy of the projections prior to disseminating them.

7. Acting in concert with clients or employers, members shall act promptly to correct false or misleading information or rumors concerning clients' or employers' securities or business whenever they have reason to believe such information or rumors are materially affecting investor attitudes.

8. Members shall not issue descriptive materials designed or written in such a fashion as to appear to be, contrary to fact, an independent third-party endorsement or recommendation of a company or a security. Whenever members issue material for clients or employers, either in their own names or in the names of someone other than the clients or employers, they shall disclose in large type and in a prominent position on the face of the material the source of such material and the existence of the issuer's client or employer relationship.

9. Members shall not use inside information for personal gain. However, this is not intended to prohibit members from making bona fide investments in their company's or client's securities insofar as they can make such investments without the benefit of material inside information.

10. Members shall not accept compensation that would place them in a position of conflict with their duty to a client, employer, or the investing public. Members shall not accept stock options from clients or employers nor accept securities as compensation at a price below market price except as part of an overall plan for corporate employees.

11. Members shall act so as to maintain the integrity of channels of public communication. They shall not pay or permit to be paid to any publication or other communications medium any consideration in exchange for publicizing a company, except through clearly recognizable paid advertising.

12. Members shall in general be guided by the PRSA Declaration of Principles and the Code of Professional Standards for the Practice of Public Relations of which this is an official interpretation.

3. ARCHITECTURE

Organization

AMERICAN INSTITUTE OF ARCHITECTS

Headquarters:
1735 New York Avenue, NW
Washington, DC 20006-5292
Telephone: (202) 626-7300
800-AIA-3837
Fax: (202) 626-7420
Website: http://www.e-architect.com

Date founded: 1857
Membership: approximately 59,000 architects, planners, landscape architects, engineers, and others directly involved in the practice of architecture, in 300 state and local chapters

Code of Ethics

Official name: *Code of Ethics and Professional Conduct*
History: Current as of March 1997; revised periodically
Authority: National Ethics Council; General Counsel's Office; Code issued by a Task Force of members and adopted by general membership
Code is available on Website

Additional Resources

Organizational (Divisions, Programs, Services, etc.):

AIA/American Consulting Engineers Council (ACEC) Organizational Peer Review Program
AIA/Architectural Society of China (ASC) Professional Practice Commission
Educators and Practitioners Net
Interfaith Forum on Religion, Art, and Architecture
Practice Management Professional Interest Area
Professional liability insurance program
Various committees: Regional and Urban Design; Risk Management

Informational (Publications, Videos, Seminars, etc.):

Articles in *Architectural Record* and *AIArchitect*
Building a Better Building Industry: Evaluating and Implementing Total Quality Management
Current Issues in the Management of Service Quality (course)
The Architect's Handbook of Professional Practice
Practical and Civic Ethics (course)
Redefining the Architecture Profession
Statement on Urban Design and Quality of Life in Communities

Goals and Activities of Organization

The American Institute of Architects (AIA) is the umbrella organization of the architectural profession, representing the majority of licensed architects in the United States. It provides education, advice, and information to members on architectural practice, methods and materials, professional liability, marketing, and financial management; draws up industry standards; collaborates with other institutions in the design field; and addresses the government on key issues affecting architecture.

The group also works for the preservation of historic buildings; helps influence the direction of change and improvement in architecture; encourages innovation and creativity by recognizing design excellence; and promotes professionalism and accountability.

Members' adherence to the Code "assures the client, the public, and colleagues of an architect's dedication to the highest standards of professional practice."

The AIA and the Architectural Society of China serve as the joint secretariat to a Professional Practice Commission, established by the International Union of Architects. This commission studies international professional standards by conducting research and documentation on architecture practices throughout the world (including education, registration, codes of conduct and ethics, and public protection); by reviewing the professional liability and risk management issues for firms engaged in international practice; and by recommending international standards of professionalism.

Implementation and Enforcement of Code

The Code applies to the professional activities of all AIA members and members emeritus. It consists of three tiers of statements: Canons, broad principles; Ethical Standards, more specific aspirational goals; and Rules of Conduct, mandatory provisions whose violation is grounds for disciplinary action. Commentaries for some of the Rules, while not part of the Code, guide those charged with their enforcement.

Enforcement of the Code is administered through the National Ethics Council, whose members are appointed by the Board of Directors. Formal charges are filed directly with the Council by members, components, or anyone else directly aggrieved by a member's conduct.

Proceedings are confidential. Penalties for violation of the Code include admonition, censure, and suspension or termination of membership. All penalties except an admonishment are to be made public. There is an appellate process.

History and Development of Code

The AIA's first code of ethics, "Circular of Advice Relative to Principles of Professional Practice and the Canon of Ethics," was adopted in 1909. The voluntary statement of Ethical Principles issued in 1980 contained unenforced guidelines. The present Code, with its mandatory, enforceable provisions, was adopted in 1987, and is indicative of the AIA's efforts to increase the status of the architecture profession. It is periodically revised, most recently in March 1997.

The Code may be amended in the same manner as Bylaws, or by the Board of Directors.

Code of Ethics and Professional Conduct[*]

PREAMBLE

Members of The American Institute of Architects are dedicated to the highest standards of professionalism, integrity, and competence. This Code of Ethics and Professional Conduct states guidelines for the conduct of Members in fulfilling those obligations. The Code is arranged in three tiers of statements: Canons, Ethical Standards, and Rules of Conduct.

- **CANONS** are broad principles of conduct.
- *Ethical Standards (E.S.)* are more specific goals toward which Members should aspire in professional performance and behavior.
- **Rules of Conduct (Rule)** are mandatory; violation of a rule is grounds for disciplinary action by the Institute. Rules of Conduct, in some instances, implement more than one Canon or Ethical Standard.

The Code applies to the professional activities of all classes of Members, wherever they occur. It addresses responsibilities to the public, which the profession serves and enriches; to the clients and users of architecture and in the building industries, who help to shape the built environment; and to the art and science of architecture, that continuum of knowledge and creation which is the heritage and legacy of the profession.

Commentary is provided for some of the Rules of Conduct. That commentary is meant to clarify or elaborate the intent of the Rule. The commentary is not part of the Code. Enforcement will be determined by application of the Rules of Conduct alone; the commentary will assist those seeking to conform their conduct to the Code and those charged with its enforcement.

Statement in Compliance With the 1990 Consent Decree

The following practices are not, in themselves, unethical, unprofessional, or contrary to any policy of The American Institute of Architects or any of its components:

1. submitting, at any time, competitive bids or price quotations, including in circumstances where price is the sole or principal consideration in the selection of an architect;
2. providing discounts; or
3. providing free services.

Individual architects or architecture firms, acting alone and not on behalf of the Institute or any of its components, are free to decide for themselves whether or not to engage in any of these practices. The Consent Decree permits the Institute, its components, or Members to advocate legislative or other government policies or actions relating to these practices. Finally, architects should continue to consult with state laws or regulations governing the practice of architecture.

---

[*]1997 edition. This copy of the Code of Ethics is current as of March 22, 1997. Contact the General Counsel's Office for further information at 202-626-7391.

©1997 The American Institute of Architects. Reproduced with the permission of the American Institute of Architects, 1735 New York Avenue, NW, Washington, DC 20006. This reprint contains the full text of the Canons, Ethical Standards, and Rules of Conduct. The Rules of application, enforcement, and amendment have been omitted, but are summarized in the preceding introductory pages.

CANON I
GENERAL OBLIGATIONS

Members should maintain and advance their knowledge of the art and science of architecture, respect the body of architectural accomplishment, contribute to its growth, thoughtfully consider the social and environmental impact of their professional activities, and exercise learned and uncompromised professional judgment.

E.S. 1.1 Knowledge and Skill
Members should strive to improve their professional knowledge and skill.

Rule 1.101
In practicing architecture, Members shall demonstrate a consistent pattern of reasonable care and competence, and shall apply the technical knowledge and skill which is ordinarily applied by architects of good standing practicing in the same locality.

> Commentary:
> By requiring a "consistent pattern" of adherence to the common law standard of competence, this rule allows for discipline of a Member who more than infrequently does not achieve that standard. Isolated instances of minor lapses would not provide the basis for discipline.

E.S. 1.2 Standards of Excellence
Members should continually seek to raise the standards of aesthetic excellence, architectural education, research, training, and practice.

E.S. 1.3 Natural and Cultural Heritage
Members should respect and help conserve their natural and cultural heritage while striving to improve the environment and the quality of life within it.

E.S. 1.4 Human Rights
Members should uphold human rights in all their professional endeavors.

Rule 1.401
Members shall not discriminate in their professional activities on the basis of race, religion, gender, national origin, age, disability, or sexual orientation.

E.S. 1.5 Allied Arts & Industries
Members should promote allied arts and contribute to the knowledge and capability of the building industries as a whole.

CANON II
OBLIGATIONS TO THE PUBLIC

Members should embrace the spirit and letter of the law governing their professional affairs and should promote and serve the public interest in their personal and professional activities.

E.S. 2.1 Conduct
Members should uphold the law in the conduct of their professional activities.

Rule 2.101
Members shall not, in the conduct of their professional practice, knowingly violate the law.

> Commentary:
> The violation of any law, local, state or federal, occurring in the conduct of a Member's professional practice, is made the basis for discipline by this rule. This includes the federal Copyright Act, which prohibits copying architectural works without the permission of the copyright owner. Allegations of violations of this rule must be based on an independent finding of a violation of the law by a court of competent jurisdiction or an administrative or regulatory body.

Rule 2.102
Members shall neither offer nor make any payment or gift to a public official with the intent of influencing the official's judgment in connection with an existing or prospective project in which the Members are interested.

> Commentary:
> This rule does not prohibit campaign contributions made in conformity with applicable campaign financing laws.

Rule 2.103
Members serving in a public capacity shall not accept payments or gifts which are intended to influence their judgment.

Rule 2.104
Members shall not engage in conduct involving fraud or wanton disregard of the rights of others.

> Commentary:
> This rule addresses serious misconduct whether or not related to a Member's professional practice. When an alleged violation of this rule is based on a violation of a law, then its proof must be based on an independent finding of a violation of the law by a court of competent jurisdiction or an administrative or regulatory body.

Rule 2.105
If, in the course of their work on a project, the Members become aware of a decision taken by their employer or client which violates any law or regulation and which will, in the Members' judgment, materially affect adversely the safety to the public of the finished project, the Members shall:
(a) advise their employer or client against the decision,
(b) refuse to consent to the decision, and
(c) report the decision to the local building inspector or other public official charged with the enforcement of the applicable laws and regulations, unless the Members are able to cause the matter to be satisfactorily resolved by other means.

Commentary:
This rule extends only to violations of the building laws that threaten the public safety. The obligation under this rule applies only to the safety of the finished project, an obligation coextensive with the usual undertaking of an architect.

Rule 2.106
Members shall not counsel or assist a client in conduct that the architect knows, or reasonably should know, is fraudulent or illegal.

E.S. 2.2 Public Interest Services
Members should render public interest professional services and encourage their employees to render such services.

E.S. 2.3 Civic Responsibility
Members should be involved in civic activities as citizens and professionals, and should strive to improve public appreciation and understanding of architecture and the functions and responsibilities of architects.

Rule 2.301
Members making public statements on architectural issues shall disclose when they are being compensated for making such statements or when they have an economic interest in the issue.

CANON III
OBLIGATIONS TO THE CLIENT

Members should serve their clients competently and in a professional manner, and should exercise unprejudiced and unbiased judgment when performing all professional services.

E.S. 3.1 Competence
Members should serve their clients in a timely and competent manner.

Rule 3.101
In performing professional services, Members shall take into account applicable laws and regulations. Members may rely on the advice of other qualified persons as to the intent and meaning of such regulations.

Rule 3.102
Members shall undertake to perform professional services only when they, together with those whom they may engage as consultants, are qualified by education, training, or experience in the specific technical areas involved.

Commentary:
This rule is meant to ensure that Members not undertake projects which are beyond their professional capacity. Members venturing into areas which require expertise they do not possess may obtain that expertise by additional

education, training, or through the retention of consultants with the necessary expertise.

Rule 3.103
Members shall not materially alter the scope or objectives of a project without the client's consent.

E.S. 3.2 Conflict of Interest
Members should avoid conflicts of interest in their professional practices and fully disclose all unavoidable conflicts as they arise.

Rule 3.201
A Member shall not render professional services if the Member's professional judgment could be affected by responsibilities to another project or person, or by the Member's own interests, unless all those who rely on the Member's judgment consent after full disclosure.

> Commentary:
> This rule is intended to embrace the full range of situations that may present a Member with a conflict between his interests or responsibilities and the interests of others. Those who are entitled to disclosure may include a client, owner, employee, contractor, or others who rely on or are affected by the Member's professional decisions. A Member who cannot appropriately communicate about a conflict directly with an affected person must take steps to ensure that disclosure is made by other means.

Rule 3.202
When acting by agreement of the parties as the independent interpreter of building contract documents and the judge of contract performance, Members shall render decisions impartially.

> Commentary:
> This rule applies when the Member, though paid by the owner and owing the owner loyalty, is nonetheless required to act with impartiality in fulfilling the architect's professional responsibilities.

E.S. 3.3 Candor and Truthfulness
Members should be candid and truthful in their professional communications and keep their clients reasonably informed about the clients' projects.

Rule 3.301
Members shall not intentionally or recklessly mislead existing or prospective clients about the results that can be achieved through the use of the Members' services, nor shall the Members state that they can achieve results by means that violate applicable law or this Code.

> Commentary:
> This rule is meant to preclude dishonest, reckless, or illegal representations by a Member either in the course of soliciting a client or during performance.

E.S. 3.4 Confidentiality
Members should safeguard the trust placed in them by their clients.

Rule 3.401
Members shall not knowingly disclose information that would adversely affect their client or that they have been asked to maintain in confidence, except as otherwise allowed or required by this Code or applicable law.

Commentary:
To encourage the full and open exchange of information necessary for a successful professional relationship, Members must recognize and respect the sensitive nature of confidential client communications. Because the law does not recognize an architect-client privilege, however, the rule permits a Member to reveal a confidence when a failure to do so would be unlawful or contrary to another ethical duty imposed by this Code.

CANON IV
OBLIGATIONS TO THE PROFESSION

Members should uphold the integrity and dignity of the profession.

E.S. 4.1 Honesty and Fairness
Members should pursue their professional activities with honesty and fairness.

Rule 4.101
Members having substantial information which leads to a reasonable belief that another Member has committed a violation of this Code which raises a serious question as to that Member's honesty, trustworthiness, or fitness as a Member, shall file a complaint with the National Ethics Council.

Commentary:
Often, only an architect can recognize that the behavior of another architect poses a serious question as to that other's professional integrity. In those circumstances, the duty to the professional's calling requires that a complaint be filed. In most jurisdictions, a complaint that invokes professional standards is protected from a libel or slander action if the complaint was made in good faith. If in doubt, a Member should seek counsel before reporting on another under this rule.

Rule 4.102
Members shall not sign or seal drawings, specifications, reports, or other professional work for which they do not have responsible control.

Commentary:
Responsible control means the degree of knowledge and supervision ordinarily required by the professional standard of care. With respect to the work of licensed consultants, Members may sign or seal such work if they have reviewed it, coordinated its preparation, or intend to be responsible for its adequacy.

Rule 4.103
Members speaking in their professional capacity shall not knowingly make false statements of material fact.

> Commentary:
> This rule applies to statements in all professional contexts, including applications for licensure and AIA membership.

E.S. 4.2 Dignity and Integrity
Members should strive, through their actions, to promote the dignity and integrity of the profession, and to ensure that their representatives and employees conform their conduct to this Code.

Rule 4.201
Members shall not make misleading, deceptive, or false statements or claims about their professional qualifications, experience, or performance and shall accurately state the scope and nature of their responsibilities in connection with work for which they are claiming credit.

> Commentary:
> This rule is meant to prevent Members from claiming or implying credit for work which they did not do, misleading others, and denying other participants in a project their proper share of credit.

Rule 4.202
Members shall make reasonable efforts to ensure that those over whom they have supervisory authority conform their conduct to this Code.

> Commentary:
> What constitutes "reasonable efforts" under this rule is a common sense matter. As it makes sense to ensure that those over whom the architect exercises supervision be made generally aware of the Code, it can also make sense to bring a particular provision to the attention of a particular employee when a situation is present which might give rise to violation.

CANON V
OBLIGATIONS TO COLLEAGUES

Members should respect the rights and acknowledge the professional aspirations and contributions of their colleagues.

E.S. 5.1 Professional Environment
Members should provide their associates and employees with a suitable working environment, compensate them fairly, and facilitate their professional development.

E.S. 5.2 Professional Recognition
Members should build their professional reputation on the merits of their own service and performance and should recognize and give credit to others for the professional work they have performed.

Rule 5.201
Members shall recognize and respect the professional contributions of their employees, employers, professional colleagues, and business associates.

Rule 5.202
Members leaving a firm shall not, without the permission of their employer or partner, take designs, drawings, data, reports, notes, or other materials relating to the firm's work, whether or not performed by the Member.

Rule 5.203
A Member shall not unreasonably withhold permission from a departing employee or partner to take copies of designs, drawings, data, reports, notes, or other materials relating to work performed by the employee or partner that are not confidential.

>   Commentary:
>   A Member may impose reasonable conditions, such as the payment of copying costs, on the right of departing persons to take copies of their work.

* * *

4. BANKING

Organization

AMERICAN BANKERS ASSOCIATION

Headquarters:
1120 Connecticut Avenue, NW
Washington, DC 20036
Telephone: (202) 663-5000
(800) 338-0626
Fax: (202) 296-9258
E-mail: custserv@aba.com
Website: http://www.aba.com

Date founded: 1875
Membership: approximately 13,000 commercial banks of all types and
sizes

Code of Ethics

Official name: *Developing or Revising a Bank Code of Ethics*
History: Issued July 1986
Authority: Safety and Soundness Commission

Additional Resources

Organizational (Divisions, Programs, Services, etc.):

ABA Compliance Connection: 1-800-551-2572 or compliance@aba.com
(legal and regulatory questions)
American Financial Skylink (educational TV network)
American Institute of Banking (continuing education and training)
Center for Banking Information (research)
Center for Community Development
Center for Legal and Regulatory Compliance (bank compliance officers)
CEO Peer Group Program
Government Relations Council
Institute of Certified Bankers certification programs
National Compliance School

National Graduate School of Compliance Management
Various conferences: Attorneys' Conference; National Conference for
    Community Bankers; Regulatory Compliance; Security and Fraud Pre-
    vention

Informational (Publications, Videos, Seminars, etc.):

Articles in *ABA Bank Compliance, ABA Bank Security & Fraud Prevention,*
    and *Regulatory and Legislative Advisory*
A Guide to IRS Information Reporting for Financial Institutions
ABA Bank Counsel Directory
*ABA's Compliance Sourcebook: A Manual for Implementing and Manag-
    ing the Compliance Program*
Bank Secrecy
Bank Security Issues and Practices
Banking Industry Privacy Principles for U.S. Financial Institutions
*Bridging the Gap from Affirmative Action to Cultural Diversity: The Legal,
    Societal, and Cultural Issues*
Codes of Conduct and Ethics (course)
Community BankTools Policy and Business Guides: *Writing a Compliance
    Policy; Writing an Insider Activities Policy; Writing a Security Policy;
    Starting Out Right with Advisory Boards; Focus on the Bank Director*
Compliance Audit Manual
Compliance Briefings (telephone seminar)
Ethics: Conflicts of Interest (course)
Federal Advertising and Marketing Law Guide
*Financial Institutions as Good Corporate Citizens: Value to Organiza-
    tions' Marketing Efforts and CRA* [Community Reinvestment Act] *Re-
    quirements*
Law and Banking: Applications
Law and Banking: Principles
Measuring and Improving Customer Service Quality
Money Laundering Enforcement (seminar)
Quick Reference Guide to Banking Regulations
Reference Guide to Regulatory Compliance
Regulation O: Insider Lending Compliance Guide
Setting Up and Using Advisory Boards
The Money Series for Kids (videos)
Year 2000: Fiduciary Liability (telephone seminar)

Goals and Activities of Organization

The American Bankers Association (ABA) represents the full-
spectrum financial-services industry; its member banks' combined assets
represent about 90% of the industry total. It was organized to enhance the
ability of banks and bankers to serve the needs and desires of the public.
Its activities include determining commercial banking's position on federal

regulation and national legislation; establishing and maintaining communications programs; upgrading bankers' skills through seminars, conferences, and educational programs; and promoting the competitiveness, profitability, and effectiveness of banks.

The Institute of Certified Bankers (ICB) is a national association of certified financial professionals, developed to meet industry needs for programs that help bankers improve competency levels, and dedicated to promoting excellence and professionalism.

The ABA Compliance Connection is a telephone and e-mail service staffed by experts who will answer members' legal and regulatory questions, providing interpretations of regulations and information on professional development programs.

Implementation and Enforcement of Code

Developing or Revising a Bank Code of Ethics is a comprehensive set of recommendations aimed at excellence in banking practice, not a definitive code for the entire financial institution industry. Individual banks must formulate their own codes because of differences in bank size, activities, and obligations to customers. These materials are intended to assist banks in adopting or revising their codes of ethics, and may be adopted in whole or in part by any bank.

As for the enforcement of individual codes, this document points out that a code is ineffective without a meaningful enforcement policy. It recommends that a code provide for reprimands, demotions, or dismissals for violations, and that immediate supervisors or managers act as the first line of enforcement. Having senior management responsible for formulating, implementing, revising, and auditing compliance with the code also strengthens its effectiveness more readily than one developed by less influential persons.

History and Development of Code

The creation of this document was an essential part of the review made by the Safety and Soundness Commission in 1985 of all areas of the banking industry that affect the stability of the system. It is based on the Commission's analysis of the economic, regulatory, and legislative environment; determination of industry priorities; examination of codes of ethics from various large and mid-size banks; and assessment of options for action.

Developing or Revising a Bank Code of Ethics supersedes the earlier ABA document, *The Drafting of a Banker's Code*.

Developing or Revising a Bank Code of Ethics*

The Safety and Soundness Commission, recognizing that a key element of any attempt on the part of the financial institution industry to regulate itself is a strong policy on business behavior, recommends that all banks work toward developing or revising a written code of ethics. The Commission understands the difficulty of fashioning a universal code to fit the myriad of financial institutions that differ in size and activity. Therefore, while a model code will not fit all institutions, certain basic components are necessary for any effective code. It is to this end that the Safety and Soundness Commission proposes several options for language to be utilized in any industry code. The Commission makes no attempt to establish a definitive code of ethics for the financial institution industry. Banks must formulate their own codes due in part to the reasons mentioned above, but more important because only each individual bank can understand the obligations it has to its own customers and implement its policies accordingly.

The Commission offers this document as an aid to financial institutions which are initiating or revising their codes of ethics. The following components are provided to aid the banking community in meeting the continuing challenge of ensuring the safety and soundness of the financial industry.

I. Introduction

Bankers need to establish written policies on accepted business practices because a bank's reputation for integrity is its most valuable asset. This reputation is often determined by the conduct of its officers and other employees. Each must manage his personal and business affairs so as to avoid situations that might lead to a conflict or even a suspected conflict between his self-interest and his duty to the bank, its customers, and its shareholders. A code provides guidance for the exercise of personal judgment in the avoidance of conflicts of interest and the appearance of such conflicts.

The reputation of any financial institution depends on the conduct and moral values of its staff. Building and ensuring a superior reputation for an institution involves shaping the judgment of each individual on basic matters of policy, in providing specific direction for each staff member's approach to a variety of situations, and in accepting responsibility for judgment based on those guidelines. Since the role of the bank director has changed dramatically in recent years, it has become necessary to consider either inclusion of director responsibility in a bank's code or the preparation of a separate code of ethics designed exclusively for directors.

A bank is an institution of public trust that is dependent upon public confidence. Inherent in the trust is the responsibility not only to preserve and safeguard public confidence but also to strengthen and renew such confidence. The reputation and soundness of a bank are measured by its basic philosophical principles and practical implementation of those principles. It is to this end that codes of ethics are adopted.

---

*Reprinted with permission of the American Bankers Association.

II. General Rationale for Bank Codes

In general, a strongly-worded document on bank ethics will be ineffective without a concomitant enforcement policy. Codes fail or succeed based on the prevailing perception of enforcement. Banks need to inform employees and directors that any lack of compliance will result in reprimands, denied promotions, demotions or dismissals. A swift response to any infraction is a major factor in ensuring respect for bank policy.

Other factors necessary for an effective code have historically included the use of immediate supervisors or managers as the first line of enforcement. The authority to issue reminders on code provisions or, in some circumstances, fire employees or dismiss directors for violations has greatly enhanced internal respect for a code.

Many companies with internal codes of ethics require that employees acknowledge the existence of a code every year. A 1977 study of corporate ethics codes shows that on the average 71% of all companies required a signature on a form relating to company policy. However, the same study showed that only 57% of all banks required employee attestation. While these statistics are clearly dated, they can be seen as an indication of the need for banks to increase awareness of internal policy.

Finally, the effectiveness of a code of ethics may also be strengthened by having senior management responsible for code formulation and enforcement. Some have suggested that a code prepared by a bank's Chairman, Executive Committee, or Board of Directors will more readily ensure compliance than a code formed by less influential persons.

In connection with the preparation of the code, an effective policy will also be ensured if a higher level of management is responsible for auditing compliance. Having a code monitored by the Board of Directors, Chief Executive Officer or other Executive Officer will emphasize to employees the importance of the code to the institution. In addition, the permanent establishment of an ethics committee or ethics director will guarantee frequent review of institution policy and support effective compliance.

III. Necessary Code Provisions

Current codes utilized by member banks are fairly standard, covering the same core of commercial banking practices. However, the codes differ dramatically in the extent and breadth of the provisions. Some institutions address all general business practices including public communication and contact with the media, as well as preparation of speeches and publications. Others contain general statements of philosophy or focus only on one aspect of business behavior (e.g., receipt and giving of gifts). Additional codes detail the parameters for personal indebtedness, trust relationships and the reporting of irregularities and defalcations. A good code must be an ever-changing document with the flexibility for frequent revisions and interpretations.

The most important topics to be included in any standard of conduct for banks are:

1. Conflicts of interest, since a bank is judged by the conduct of its employees. A definitive statement on procedures for dealing with conflicts will prove to the public that a bank is working hard toward attaining the confidence of the local community.

2. Personal borrowing, investments and outside employment activities, since these activities can easily become potential conflicts.

3. Arm's-length transactions with suppliers, because no employee should take advantage of his position as a banker.

4. Confidentiality of corporate records and a policy on release of customer information.

5. Bribery and other aspects of insider abuse.

6. Political contributions and overall legal compliance.

As stated previously, the increased role of the bank director and the risks involved in serving as a director confirm the need for a code of ethics or at a minimum a set of guidelines for directors. Directors should:

1. Familiarize themselves with their statutory responsibilities at the state and federal levels.

2. Exercise reasonable diligence and common sense. It is certainly reasonable to trust bank officers, but a director's duty does not end once the officers have been selected. There is also a duty of supervision. Furthermore, the books should be checked. If discrepancies or shortages are discovered, the explanations of trusted officers and employees will not save the directors from responsibility. Directors have a duty to inquire. If any irregularities or discrepancies arise, directors are obligated to investigate them fully.

3. Make sure their personal assets are insured. Bank bylaws should be examined for indemnification provisions, and insurance should be arranged for exposures that are not indemnifiable.

4. Exercise ordinary care and prudence. A director may not be legally liable for making an erroneous judgment if it was based on a sincere effort and if the duty to inquire was exercised. Lack of knowledge, however, can be a breach of duty. Care and prudence require the director not to overlook any facts and not to fail to take action on known problems.

5. Pay particular attention to the things courts will consider if a bank gets into trouble. Consider, for example, the nature of the records a court will requisition in deciding a case.

   a. The examination committee function over the last 10 years. The courts will want to know if the examination committee saw to it that the bank was examined at regular intervals, that there were no omissions in the examination, and that action was taken on suspected irregularities or other problems indicated in the examination reports.

   b. The dates and regularity of board meetings. Different state or national charters set requirements for the frequency of board meetings. The courts will look to see that at least the required minimum number of meetings was held.

   c. Each director's attendance pattern. Lack of attendance at board meetings can be considered negligence. Unawareness of an issue that was discussed in the director's absence does not necessarily exempt the director from liability.

   d. The integration of management reports into the minutes. The board's meeting minutes should indicate the nature and scope of management reports and any action initiated.

   e. The loan and discount committee activities. The loan and discount committee is responsible for the approval and/or review of the bank's loans. Any illegal activity, failure to be alerted to potential trouble, or neglect may be detected from a review of these activities.

f. Abnormal fluctuations in savings and checking account totals. A major loss of accounts could signify a loss of confidence in the bank or the loss of a major depositor. Fluctuations in the account totals that have gone uninvestigated may be questioned by the court.

g. The volume and nature of the loan and investment portfolios. An investigation of the loan and investment portfolio may give evidence of unsound lending practices, speculative investments, or other irregularities.

h. Action taken on known or irregular acts of officers and employees. If action has not been taken by the board regarding activities of officers and employees, or if such activities have not been detected, directors could be liable for negligence.

i. Evidence regarding officers who appear to be living beyond their means. In event of bank loss or failure, officers, employees, or directors who appear to be living beyond their means may be suspected of criminal activity. If a director senses this situation, he or she is obligated to investigate, even though there may be no wrongdoing.

j. Evidence of self-dealing (preferential treatment not in the bank's best interest). Directors can be held liable for any action, such as making loans, that is more in the interest of the recipient than the bank or the stockholders.

IV. Is There a Need for More Than One Code?

Separate codes for internal and regulatory oversight and codes appropriate only for external disclosure may be too cumbersome and could cause confusion for bank employees. To retain the public's trust and confidence in bank practices, disclosure of all bank policies should be seriously considered. Some have suggested that a code is a public warranty and that therefore all policies relating to bank practices will be relevant to the public's awareness of sound, ethical banking activity. Some banks allow ready access to any bank information that will enable a potential customer to judge an institution. While these "codes of disclosure" refer to internal and external audits, bank examinations and other outside evaluations whose disclosure is not prohibited by law, external disclosure of the code itself may be appropriate. In addition, it has been pointed out that publishing a bank's code of ethics is a valuable public relations tool. To respond to questions on bank failures, insider abuse or other problems, a bank can improve its image by disclosing its code of ethics and the bank's consistent enforcement of the code.

V. Code Enforcement

Internal enforcement and disclosure of compliance are essential to a code's effectiveness. As stated above, compliance will only be achieved by strong responses to code infractions. This position needs full support of the bank's top management. The penalties must be realistic in application and consistently applied to all employees.

Compliance with the code will be greatly enhanced by disclosure to the board of directors and all employees of penalties for violations. Periodic compliance reports and reports of disciplinary action should be part of any bank's administration. However, general reports (e.g., "There have been no violations . . .") will probably not increase effectiveness, and detailed reporting of infractions may violate employee privacy rights. A policy on disclosure must be carefully prepared and analyzed prior to implementation. Public disclosure of adherence to codes of conduct may present similar problems. In order to have effective disclosure, each institution should consider establishing a code compliance committee to address these concerns.

Codes will fail if the perception exists that they are unenforceable, too general, ambiguous or not publicized. There is a need to continually revise a code, not because of sweeping changes in the banking industry (although this is always possible) but to strengthen the perception that management considers codes of conduct integral to the bank's business.

Some of the codes reviewed by the Commission were extremely out of date, without supplements or revisions reflecting new regulations or laws * * *. Others, however, were current and detailed and prove industry concern for ethical policy. A formal compliance and/or revision report to the CEO or board of directors can help prevent bank code failures. Finally, any compliance requirements must include a mechanism for employees to seek timely guidance regarding the interpretation of any provision of an ethical code, either through the office of an ethics director, committee or the institution's General Counsel.

VI. Commercial Banking Activity Covered by Codes

Primary activities for code development include lending policy, employee participation in outside directorships, fiduciary or other trust account relationships, and protection of customer bank records. Requiring codes is beyond the scope of the Commission's role in developing standards of conduct, but any activities of a bank that customers may use as a barometer of an institution's soundness should be included. Some banks include in their general policy of conduct summaries of general credit policies and lending guidelines as well as standard terms and conditions of selected types of domestic consumer loans. These areas do not have to be a part of any formal code, but the information may be made available in some form to the public.

VII. Market Evaluation of a Banker's Code

Any market evaluation of a bank code of ethics would have to be based on how effectively compliance with bank policy is enforced. A strong code backed by equally strong sanctions for violations will tell a prospective individual or corporate customer that the institution will do everything to assure the safety of their funds.

Public confidence will be generated by any bank code that deals seriously with fraud and abuse by bank employees. There is nothing magical in that formula, but effective communication will further enhance public trust. Communication of a bank's code, as stated above, should include disclosure of penalties, sanctions and other evidence of compliance. A strong document must be seen as the result of a formal policy decision on the part of top administrative officers after careful consideration of problems inherent in bank management.

VIII. Implementation

Any recommendations of the Commission in the area of bank codes are meant as a starting point. Any standards for code development should be put forward only after extensive input from the banking community and should be framed as guideline options to be considered at the discretion of management of each institution. The following is a brief sample code for member banks, as well as a list of topics that should be considered for inclusion in any banker's code:

A. *Political Contributions/Corporate Payments*

Federal and some state laws prohibit the bank or its subsidiaries from contributing corporate funds or property in support of a political party or a candidate for public office. Similarly, the bank may not compensate employees for time so dedicated (i.e., normal working hours). Questions as to the propriety of any action that may involve a political candidate or campaign should be discussed with managing officers before any steps are taken that may involve any employee or the bank in possible violation of the law. It should be clearly understood that no action is to be undertaken for the perceived benefit of the bank if the bank could not legally take such action directly. There should be sensitivity to possible criticism of the bank or staff members on the grounds of self-dealing for personal advantage. For this reason, no employee may purchase any property directly or indirectly from the bank or its subsidiaries. This includes bank premises and equipment, collateral disposed of in settlement of an obligation or property held as a fiduciary. It is contrary to the bank's policy and intent to encourage or permit either directly or indirectly the payment of bank funds or use of bank property to secure favored business treatment for the bank or its subsidiaries. This policy applies domestically and outside the United States to inter-business contacts in the private sector, as well as transactions involving government at all levels. Customary nominal gratuities for services received are permitted if lawful, as are gifts, favors of nominal value or entertainment to the extent they meet the standards of ethical business as explained in section D. Each such payment, gift or expense must be appropriately disclosed on the financial records of the bank. Expenses for travel and entertainment incurred on behalf of the bank or its subsidiaries should be ordinary and necessary to accomplish a business purpose and be documented in conformity with the established requirements for reimbursement. Other than as an approved signature authority, no officer, employee or third party acting for the bank shall control disbursements from a domestic or foreign branch of the bank or its subsidiaries. Further, disbursements from such bank accounts shall be only for legitimate bank purposes, and each shall be clearly disclosed in the financial records.

B. *Investments*

The investment of personal funds as a way to participate in the growth of the economy and to provide for the future is proper and worthwhile. However, employees and directors must be aware that personal financial affairs reflect to the public the character of the organization. The following standards are guides to minimize the risks that may arise from the way investments are selected and financed.

(1) Although the choice of investments is a personal matter, the nature of an employee's position with a commercial bank or bank holding company requires adherence to an appropriate and prudent investment policy.

(2) In-and-out trading and speculative trading involve a degree of risk that may embarrass both the individual and the organization. Such trading is not consistent with the personal conduct expected of bank employees.

(3) The selection of a brokerage firm is a personal decision. Contact with brokers during business hours should be kept to a minimum and must not interfere with one's normal duties.

(4) Employees of the bank may not maintain brokerage margin accounts, directly or indirectly.

(5) Information provided by customers in the normal course of business that is not available to the general public is confidential and must be held inviolate. Such information must never be used as a basis for personal investment decisions.

(6) Commissions paid to brokers to purchase or sell securities for customers must never be used to obtain special concessions from brokerage firms.

C. *Confidentiality of Corporate Records*

All relationships between the bank and its customers are confidential. No information should be disclosed except as authorized by the customer or as required by statute or a court of competent jurisdiction. All employees should use care not to discuss corporate business in any place or manner that risks violation of such confidentiality or that would in any way impair the bank's competitive position. Financial information about the bank or any of its subsidiaries is not to be given to persons outside the bank unless it has been reported to the shareholders or otherwise made available to the public. No one with commercial banking responsibilities who has information not publicly known or available that may bear on a credit or investment decision shall give such information to anyone who has trust responsibilities.

D. *Receipt of Gifts*

Gifts to employees from customers generally are intended as sincere expressions of friendship and appreciation based on the personal relationships that often develop in the normal conduct of business. Nevertheless, substantial gifts of any kind, whether in the form of food, merchandise, unusual discounts, entertainment or the undue use of customer or supplier facilities should be courteously declined as contrary to policy. It is neither practical nor desirable to have an inflexible rule against gifts of any specific kind, or to precisely define a "substantial gift." Any doubt about the proper course of action should be discussed with the employee's managing officer or division head.

E. *Conflict of Interest*

(1) Business Affiliations

Employees should not commence or continue any relationships with outsiders that might, even by implication, cause embarrassment to themselves or impair the bank's best interests or public position. Employees are to avoid conflicts involving business opportunities which come to their attention as a result of their duties with the bank. Periodically, the corporate secretary will distribute a questionnaire dealing with outside business affiliations to be completed and returned as instructed.

(2) Board Directorships

Employees are encouraged to participate in appropriate professional groups and responsible civic organizations if such service does not interfere with their duties in the bank, provided such relationships would not be prohibited or limited because of statutory or administrative requirements regarding conflicts of interest. When participation as a director or officer of a major outside organization serves the best interest of the bank, the office of the chairman will designate the appropriate employee for the assignment. All other participation requires approval of the employee's division head. An employee may be asked by an organization to participate both because of individual talents and because the employee represents the bank. Employees who are approached directly by an outside organization to join the board of directors must first obtain the approval of their managing officer or division head. The types of organizations covered by this policy are both profit and non-profit in nature. This does not apply to participation in religious and political organizations. Employees should seek guidance from their managing officer regarding interpretations or applicability of this policy prior to making any commitments to the outside organization.

Other issues and subjects for possible inclusion in any code are:

A. Outside employment:
   (1) with a competitor
   (2) as an auditor or accountant
   (3) as an investment advisor
   (4) as an insurance broker or agent
   (5) as a real estate broker, contractor or agent
   (6) with any other employer
B. Loans to brokers
C. Making stock recommendations
D. Serving as executor or administrator of estates
E. Bequests from non-relatives
F. Establishment of interest rates, terms of loans, service charges, etc.

5.   COMPUTING

Organization

ASSOCIATION FOR COMPUTING MACHINERY

Headquarters:
One Astor Plaza
1515 Broadway
New York, NY 10036
Telephone: (212) 869-7440
Fax: (212) 944-1318
E-mail: ACMHELP@acm.org

Additional offices:
Public Policy Office
666 Pennsylvania Avenue, SE
Suite 302b
Washington, DC 20003
Telephone: (202) 544-4859
Fax: (202) 547-5482
E-mail: USACM_DC@acm.org

European Service Center
108 Cowley Road
Oxford, OX4 1JF
UK
Telephone: +44-1-865-382-338
Fax: +44-1-865-381-338
E-mail: acm_europe@acm.org

Website: http://www.acm.org

Date founded: 1947
Membership: approximately 80,000 computing professionals in more than
   100 countries, in all areas of industry, academia, and government

Code of Ethics

Official name: *Code of Ethics and Professional Conduct*
History: Adopted October 1992
Authority: ACM Council; Special Interest Group on Computers and Society (SIGCAS); Committee on Professional Ethics
Code is available on Website

Additional Resources

Organizational (Divisions, Programs, Services, etc.):

Computing Sciences Accreditation Board
Computer Science Accreditation Commission
Institute of Electrical and Electronics Engineers-Computer Society (IEEE-CS)/ACM Joint Task Force on Software Engineering Ethics and Professional Practices
Special Interest Groups on: Computer-Human Interaction; Computer Science Education; Security, Audit and Control
Task Force on Licensing and Certification of Computer Professionals (SIGCAS)
Various committees: Computers and Public Policy; Scientific Freedom and Human Rights
Various conferences: Computer and Communications Security; Computer Ethics; Computers and Quality of Life Symposium; Computers, Freedom and Privacy; International Conference on Artificial Intelligence and Law; National Educational Conference; Policy Conference/Ethics and Social Impact Component; Society and the Future of Computing

Informational (Publications, Videos, Seminars, etc.):

Articles in *Journal of the Association for Computing Machinery, Communications of the ACM, Computers and Society Newsletter, Crossroads,* and *Interactions*
Beyond Calculation: The Next 50 Years of Computing
Civilizing Cyberspace: Policy, Power and the Information Superhighway
Computer Related Risks
Computers Under Attack: Intruders, Worms and Viruses
Computing: A Human Activity
Durango Declarations (statement of ethics and action for social and computer scientists)
Ethics in the Computer Age (conference proceedings)
Ethics, Lies and Videotape (conference proceedings)
Forum on Risks to the Public in Computers and Related Systems
Human Factors in Computing Systems (conference proceedings)
Inside Risks column in *Communications of the ACM*
Internet Besieged: Countering Cyber Scofflaws
PRIVACY Forum Digest

RISKS newsgroup and book
Software Engineering Code of Ethics and Professional Practice (draft)
Software Quality: A Framework for Success in Software Development and Support
Using the New ACM Code of Ethics in Decision Making
World-Wide CHI [Computer-Human Interaction]*: Future Ethics*

Goals and Activities of Organization

The Association for Computing Machinery (ACM) is the oldest and largest international scientific and educational organization devoted to the advancement of "the arts, sciences, and applications" of information technology. Several of ACM's many subgroups are involved in activities related to ethics and professionalism.

The Education Board develops and recommends computer curricula, provides self-assessment procedures, and offers professional development seminars. As part of the Computer Sciences Accreditation Board, the ACM evaluates and accredits educational programs in colleges and universities.

The Committee on Computers and Public Policy educates members and the public about computer-related risks. One of its goals is to develop the ACM as a source of responsible advice on public policy matters.

The multidisciplinary Special Interest Group on Computers and Society (SIGCAS) addresses the ethical and societal impact of computers. One of its Task Forces was responsible for the development of the Code of Ethics and Guidelines.

A joint task force of the ACM and the Institute of Electrical and Electronics Engineers (IEEE) is codifying the software engineering profession's practices for resolving ethical conflicts and delivering quality service.

Implementation and Enforcement of Code

The ACM Council adopts, maintains, enforces, and publicizes the Code, which is binding on all members. Together with the Guidelines, these materials are intended to aid members in their individual decisionmaking as to the conduct of their professional activities.

While the Code itself recognizes that "adherence . . . is largely a voluntary matter," it does provide that "if a member does not follow this code by engaging in gross misconduct, membership in ACM may be terminated."

The Code and Guidelines also serve as a basis for judging the merits of formal complaints pertaining to the violation of ethical standards.

History and Development of Code

The Code and the supplemental Guidelines were developed by a Task Force organized by SIGCAS. They were adopted by the ACM Council on October 16, 1992.

Code of Ethics and Professional Conduct*

PREAMBLE

Commitment to ethical professional conduct is expected of every member (voting members, associate members, and student members) of the Association for Computing Machinery (ACM).

This Code, consisting of 24 imperatives formulated as statements of personal responsibility, identifies the elements of such a commitment. It contains many, but not all, issues professionals are likely to face. Section 1 outlines fundamental ethical considerations, while Section 2 addresses additional, more specific considerations of professional conduct. Statements in Section 3 pertain more specifically to individuals who have a leadership role, whether in the workplace or in a volunteer capacity such as with organizations like ACM. Principles involving compliance with this Code are given in Section 4.

The Code shall be supplemented by a set of Guidelines, which provide explanation to assist members in dealing with the various issues contained in the Code. It is expected that the Guidelines will be changed more frequently than the Code.

The Code and its supplemented Guidelines are intended to serve as a basis for ethical decision making in the conduct of professional work. Secondarily, they may serve as a basis for judging the merit of a formal complaint pertaining to violation of professional ethical standards.

It should be noted that although computing is not mentioned in the imperatives of Section 1, the Code is concerned with how these fundamental imperatives apply to one's conduct as a computing professional. These imperatives are expressed in a general form to emphasize that ethical principles which apply to computer ethics are derived from more general ethical principles.

It is understood that some words and phrases in a code of ethics are subject to varying interpretations, and that any ethical principle may conflict with other ethical principles in specific situations. Questions related to ethical conflicts can best be answered by thoughtful consideration of fundamental principles, rather than reliance on detailed regulations.

1. GENERAL MORAL IMPERATIVES

As an ACM member I will . . .

1.1 Contribute to society and human well-being.

This principle concerning the quality of life of all people affirms an obligation to protect fundamental human rights and to respect the diversity of all cultures.

An essential aim of computing professionals is to minimize negative consequences of computing systems, including threats to health and safety. When designing or implementing systems, computing professionals must attempt to ensure that the products of their efforts will be used in socially responsible ways, will meet social needs, and will avoid harmful effects to health and welfare.

In addition to a safe social environment, human well-being includes a safe natural environment. Therefore, computing professionals who design and develop systems must be alert to, and make others aware of, any potential damage to the local or global environment.

1.2 Avoid harm to others.

"Harm" means injury or negative consequences, such as undesirable loss of information, loss of property, property damage, or unwanted environmental impacts. This principle prohibits use of computing technology in ways that result in harm to any of the following: users, the general public, employees, employers. Harmful actions include intentional destruction or modification of files and programs leading to serious loss of resources or unnecessary expenditure of human resources such as the time and effort required to purge systems of "computer viruses."

Well-intended actions, including those that accomplish assigned duties, may lead to harm unexpectedly. In such an event the responsible person or persons are obligated to undo or mitigate the negative consequences as much as possible. One way to avoid unintentional harm is to carefully consider potential impacts on all those affected by decisions made during design and implementation.

To minimize the possibility of indirectly harming others, computing professionals must minimize malfunctions by following generally accepted standards for system design and testing. Furthermore, it is often necessary to assess the social consequences of systems to project the likelihood of any serious harm to others. If system features are misrepresented to users, coworkers, or supervisors, the individual computing professional is responsible for any resulting injury.

In the work environment the computing professional has the additional obligation to report any signs of system dangers that might result in serious personal or social damage. If one's superiors do not act to curtail or mitigate such dangers, it may be necessary to "blow the whistle" to help correct the problem or reduce the risk. However, capricious or misguided reporting of violations can, itself, be harmful. Before reporting violations, all relevant aspects of the incident must be thoroughly assessed. In particular, the assessment of risk and responsibility must be credible. It is suggested that advice be sought from other computing professionals. See principle 2.5 regarding thorough evaluations.

1.3 Be honest and trustworthy.

Honesty is an essential component of trust. Without trust an organization cannot function effectively. The honest computing professional will not make deliberately false or deceptive claims about a system or system design, but will instead provide full disclosure of all pertinent system limitations and problems.

A computer professional has a duty to be honest about his or her own qualifications, and about any circumstances that might lead to conflicts of interest.

Membership in volunteer organizations such as ACM may at times place individuals in situations where their statements or actions could be interpreted as carrying the "weight" of a larger group of professionals. An ACM member will exercise care to not misrepresent ACM or positions and policies of ACM or any ACM units.

1.4 Be fair and take action not to discriminate.

The values of equality, tolerance, respect for others, and the principles of equal justice govern this imperative. Discrimination on the basis of race, sex, religion, age, disability, national origin, or other such factors is an explicit violation of ACM policy and will not be tolerated.

Inequities between different groups of people may result from the use or misuse of information and technology. In a fair society, all individuals would have equal opportunity to participate in, or benefit from, the use of computer resources regardless of race, sex, religion, age, disability, national origin or other such similar factors. However, these ideals do not justify unauthorized use of computer resources nor do they provide an adequate basis for violation of any other ethical imperatives of this code.

1.5 Honor property rights including copyrights and patent.

Violation of copyrights, patents, trade secrets and the terms of license agreements is prohibited by law in most circumstances. Even when software is not so protected, such violations are contrary to professional behavior. Copies of software should be made only with proper authorization. Unauthorized duplication of materials must not be condoned.

1.6 Give proper credit for intellectual property.

Computing professionals are obligated to protect the integrity of intellectual property. Specifically, one must not take credit for others' ideas or work, even in cases where the work has not been explicitly protected by copyright, patent, etc.

1.7 Respect the privacy of others.

Computing and communication technology enables the collection and exchange of personal information on a scale unprecedented in the history of civilization. Thus there is increased potential for violating the privacy of individuals and groups. It is the responsibility of professionals to maintain the privacy and integrity of data describing individuals. This includes taking precautions to ensure the accuracy of data, as well as protecting it from unauthorized access or accidental disclosure to inappropriate individuals. Furthermore, procedures must be established to allow individuals to review their records and correct inaccuracies.

This imperative implies that only the necessary amount of personal information be collected in a system, that retention and disposal periods for that information be clearly defined and enforced, and that personal information gathered for a specific purpose not be used for other purposes without consent of the individual(s). These principles apply to electronic communications, including electronic mail, and prohibit procedures that capture or monitor electronic user data, including messages, without the permission of users or bona fide authorization related to system operation and maintenance. User data observed during the normal duties of system operation and maintenance must be treated with strictest confidentiality, except in cases where it is evidence for the violation of law, organizational regulations, or this Code. In these cases, the nature or contents of that information must be disclosed only to proper authorities.

1.8 Honor confidentiality.

The principle of honesty extends to issues of confidentiality of information whenever one has made an explicit promise to honor confidentiality or, implicitly, when private information not directly related to the performance of one's duties becomes available. The ethical concern is to respect all obligations of confidentiality to employers, clients, and users unless discharged from such obligations by requirements of the law or other principles of this Code.

2. MORE SPECIFIC PROFESSIONAL RESPONSIBILITIES

As an ACM computing professional I will . . .

2.1 Strive to achieve the highest quality, effectiveness and dignity in both the process and products of professional work.

Excellence is perhaps the most important obligation of a professional. The computing professional must strive to achieve quality and to be cognizant of the serious negative consequences that may result from poor quality in a system.

2.2 Acquire and maintain professional competence.

Excellence depends on individuals who take responsibility for acquiring and maintaining professional competence. A professional must participate in setting standards for appropriate levels of competence, and strive to achieve those standards. Upgrading technical knowledge and competence can be achieved in several ways: doing independent study; attending seminars, conferences, or courses; and being involved in professional organizations.

2.3 Know and respect existing laws pertaining to professional work.

ACM members must obey existing local, state, province, national, and international laws unless there is a compelling ethical basis not to do so. Policies and procedures of the organizations in which one participates must also be obeyed. But compliance must be balanced with the recognition that sometimes existing laws and rules may be immoral or inappropriate and, therefore, must be challenged. Violation of a law or regulation may be ethical when that law or rule has inadequate moral basis or when it conflicts with another law judged to be more important. If one decides to violate a law or rule because it is viewed as unethical, or for any other reason, one must fully accept responsibility for one's actions and for the consequences.

2.4 Accept and provide appropriate professional review.

Quality professional work, especially in the computing profession, depends on professional reviewing and critiquing. Whenever appropriate, individual members should seek and utilize peer review as well as provide critical review of the work of others.

2.5 Give comprehensive and thorough evaluations of computer systems and their impacts, including analysis of possible risks.

Computer professionals must strive to be perceptive, thorough, and objective when evaluating, recommending, and presenting system descriptions and alternatives. Computer professionals are in a position of special trust, and therefore have a special responsibility to provide objective, credible evaluations to employers, clients, users, and the public. When providing evaluations the professional must also identify any relevant conflicts of interest, as stated in imperative 1.3.

As noted in the discussion of principle 1.2 on avoiding harm, any signs of danger from systems must be reported to those who have opportunity and/or responsibility to resolve them. See the guidelines for imperative 1.2 for more details concerning harm, including the reporting of professional violations.

2.6 Honor contracts, agreements, and assigned responsibilities.

Honoring one's commitments is a matter of integrity and honesty. For the computer professional this includes ensuring that system elements perform as intended. Also, when one contracts for work with another party, one has an obligation to keep that party properly informed about progress toward completing that work.

A computing professional has a responsibility to request a change in any assignment that he or she feels cannot be completed as defined. Only after serious consideration and with full disclosure of risks and concerns to the employer or client, should one accept the assignment. The major underlying principle here is the obligation to accept personal accountability for professional work. On some occasions other ethical principles may take greater priority.

A judgment that a specific assignment should not be performed may not be accepted. Having clearly identified one's concerns and reasons for that judgment, but failing to procure a change in that assignment, one may yet be obligated, by contract or by law, to proceed as directed. The computing professional's ethical judgment should be the final guide in deciding whether or not to proceed. Regardless of the decision, one must accept the responsibility for the consequences.

However, performing assignments "against one's own judgment" does not relieve the professional of responsibility for any negative consequences.

2.7 Improve public understanding of computing and its consequences.

Computing professionals have a responsibility to share technical knowledge with the public by encouraging understanding of computing, including the impacts of computer systems and their limitations. This imperative implies an obligation to counter any false views related to computing.

2.8 Access computing and communication resources only when authorized to do so.

Theft or destruction of tangible and electronic property is prohibited by imperative 1.2—"Avoid harm to others." Trespassing and unauthorized use of a computer or communication system is addressed by this imperative. Trespassing includes accessing communication networks and computer systems, or accounts and/or files associated with those systems, without explicit authorization to do so. Individuals and organizations have the right to restrict access to their systems so long as they do not violate the discrimination principle (see 1.4). No one should enter or use another's computer system, software, or data files without permission. One must always have appropriate approval before using system resources, including communication ports, file space, other system peripherals, and computer time.

3. ORGANIZATIONAL LEADERSHIP IMPERATIVES

BACKGROUND NOTE: * * * The ethical obligations of organizations tend to be neglected in most codes of professional conduct, perhaps because these codes are written from the perspective of the individual member. This dilemma is addressed by stating these imperatives from the perspective of the organizational leader. In this context "leader" is viewed as any organizational member who has leadership or educational responsibilities. These imperatives generally may apply to organizations as well as their leaders. In this context "organizations" are corporations, government agencies, and other "employers," as well as volunteer professional organizations.

As an ACM member and an organizational leader, I will . . .

3.1 Articulate social responsibilities of members of an organizational unit and encourage full acceptance of those responsibilities.

Because organizations of all kinds have impacts on the public, they must accept responsibilities to society. Organizational procedures and attitudes oriented toward quality and the welfare of society will reduce harm to members of the public, thereby serving public interest and fulfilling social responsibility. Therefore, organizational leaders must encourage full participation in meeting social responsibilities as well as quality performance.

3.2 Manage personnel and resources to design and build information systems that enhance the quality of working life.

Organizational leaders are responsible for ensuring that computer systems enhance, not degrade, the quality of working life. When implementing a computer system, organizations must consider the personal and professional development, physical safety, and human dignity of all workers. Appropriate human-computer ergonomic standards should be considered in system design and in the workplace.

3.3 Acknowledge and support proper and authorized uses of an organization's computing and communication resources.

Because computer systems can become tools to harm as well as to benefit an organization, the leadership has the responsibility to clearly define appropriate and inappropriate uses of organizational computing resources. While the number and scope of such rules should be minimal, they should be fully enforced when established.

3.4 Ensure that users and those who will be affected by a system have their needs clearly articulated during the assessment and design of requirements; later the system must be validated to meet requirements.

Current system users, potential users and other persons whose lives may be affected by a system must have their needs assessed and incorporated in the statement of requirements. System validation should ensure compliance with those requirements.

3.5 Articulate and support policies that protect the dignity of users and others affected by a computing system.

Designing or implementing systems that deliberately or inadvertently demean individuals or groups is ethically unacceptable. Computer professionals who are in decision making positions should verify that systems are designed and implemented to protect personal privacy and enhance personal dignity.

3.6 Create opportunities for members of the organization to learn the principles and limitations of computer systems.

This complements the imperative on public understanding (2.7). Educational opportunities are essential to facilitate optimal participation of all organizational members. Opportunities must be available to all members to help them improve their knowledge and skills in computing, including courses that familiarize them with the consequences and limitations of particular types of systems. In particular, professionals must be made aware of the dangers of building systems around oversimplified models, the improbability of anticipating and designing for every possible operating condition, and other issues related to the complexity of this profession.

4. COMPLIANCE WITH THE CODE

As an ACM member I will . . .

4.1 Uphold and promote the principles of this Code.

The future of the computing profession depends on both technical and ethical excellence. Not only is it important for ACM computing professionals to adhere to the principles expressed in this Code, each member should encourage and support adherence by other members.

4.2 Treat violations of this code as inconsistent with membership in the ACM.

Adherence of professionals to a code of ethics is largely a voluntary matter. However, if a member does not follow this code by engaging in gross misconduct, membership in ACM may be terminated.

6. ENGINEERING

Organization

NATIONAL SOCIETY OF PROFESSIONAL ENGINEERS

Headquarters:
1420 King Street
Alexandria, VA 22314-2794
Telephone: (703) 684-2800
Fax: (703) 836-4875
E-mail: customer.service@nspe.org
Website: http://www.nspe.org

Date founded: 1934
Membership: approximately 65,000 licensed professional engineers in private practice, industry, education, construction, and government, in 52 state societies and more than 500 chapters

Code of Ethics

Official name: *Code of Ethics for Engineers*
History: Originally issued 1946; revised periodically; current version issued July 1996
Authority: Board of Ethical Review; Board of Directors
Code is available on Website

Additional Resources

Organizational (Divisions, Programs, Services, etc.):

Annual Ethics Essay Contest
National Institute for Engineering Ethics (originally established by NSPE in 1988; independent as of 1996)
Professional Edge (continuing education program)

Informational (Publications, Videos, Seminars, etc.):

Articles in *Engineering Times*
A State-by-State Summary of Engineering Liability Laws

*Building for Professional Growth: A History of the National Society of
   Professional Engineers, 1934-1984*
Directory of Professional Liability Insurance Carriers
Engineering Ethics Update (newsletter)
Engineering Licensure Laws: A State-by-State Summary and Analysis
Engineering Licensure Manual
The Engineers' Creed
Ethics Corner in *Engineering Times*
Ethics Reference Guide (breaks down cases by topic and related Code
   section)
Ethics Resources Guide
Gilbane Gold (video and study guide)
Guides to the Practice of Professional Engineering
National Council for Examiners of Engineering and Surveying (NCEES)
   Model Rules of Professional Conduct (guidance for state licensing
   boards)
Opinions of the Board of Ethical Review
Professional Engineers in Private Practice (seminars)
Professional Liability (video)
Proposed National Model for Engineering Licensing and Registration
Quality First—Selected Papers on Quality & Productivity Improvement
*Quality, Risk, & Project Management: Guidelines for Engineers and Archi-
   tects*
State-by-State Summary of Engineering Corporate Practice Laws

Goals and Activities of Organization

The National Society of Professional Engineers (NSPE) represents
the interests of licensed professional engineers from all technical disciplines. Its primary stated goal is to formulate high ethical standards for
the practice of engineering and to lead the profession in adhering to them.
The NSPE promotes engineering licensure and the enforcement of uniform
licensing laws; helps establish educational standards; and provides continuing education opportunities for engineers to maintain practice competency.

The organization seeks to incorporate engineering principles and perspectives in government decisions that protect the public and foster technological development. It also keeps members informed of professional,
political, social, economic, and business developments that affect them.

Implementation and Enforcement of Code

The Code is intended to establish ethical standards of conduct for all
engineers. It is enforceable, however, only to NSPE members, through
affiliated state societies whose primary function is the administration of
disciplinary action. These organizations have adopted the NSPE Code as
their state society's code of ethics, with minor changes in some jurisdictions.

Formal complaint procedures include a hearing with a right of appeal to the state board of directors. Sanctions for code violation include reprimand, censure, and suspension or revocation of membership.

The NSPE Board of Ethical Review (BER) was established in the 1950s to review factual situations involving ethical dilemmas, which may be submitted by engineers, government officials, and the public. It renders opinions on the interpretation and intent of the Code under real or hypothetical situations; the opinions are published for the guidance of members and the public. The BER also conducts an ongoing review of the Code and recommends changes to the NSPE Board of Directors; develops educational materials; and evaluates the degree to which ethical standards are being met.

State engineering licensure examinations now contain ethics questions that follow the National Council for Examiners of Engineering and Surveying *Model Rules of Professional Conduct,* which are based largely on the NSPE Code.

History and Development of Code

The NSPE's ethics standards have been periodically revised every few years since the first "Canons of Ethics for Engineers" were issued in 1946. (For example, the Professional Rules were incorporated into the Code of Ethics in 1961.) The present document includes the most recent changes made, through July 1996.

Sources include earlier codes developed by other engineering and professional groups.

Code of Ethics for Engineers*

Preamble

Engineering is an important and learned profession. As members of this profession, engineers are expected to exhibit the highest standards of honesty and integrity. Engineering has a direct and vital impact on the quality of life for all people. Accordingly, the services provided by engineers require honesty, impartiality, fairness and equity, and must be dedicated to the protection of the public health, safety and welfare. Engineers must perform under a standard of professional behavior which requires adherence to the highest principles of ethical conduct.

I. FUNDAMENTAL CANONS

Engineers, in the fulfillment of their professional duties, shall:
1. Hold paramount the safety, health and welfare of the public.
2. Perform services only in areas of their competence.
3. Issue public statements only in an objective and truthful manner.
4. Act for each employer or client as faithful agents or trustees.
5. Avoid deceptive acts.
6. Conduct themselves honorably, responsibly, ethically and lawfully so as to enhance the honor, reputation and usefulness of the profession.

II. RULES OF PRACTICE

1. **Engineers shall hold paramount the safety, health and welfare of the public.**
   a. If engineers' judgment is overruled under circumstances that endanger life or property, they shall notify their employer or client and such other authority as may be appropriate.
   b. Engineers shall approve only those engineering documents that are in conformity with applicable standards.
   c. Engineers shall not reveal facts, data or information without the prior consent of the client or employer except as authorized or required by law or this Code.
   d. Engineers shall not permit the use of their name or associate in business ventures with any person or firm that they believe is engaged in fraudulent or dishonest enterprise.
   e. Engineers having knowledge of any alleged violation of this Code shall report thereon to appropriate professional bodies and, when relevant, also to public authorities, and cooperate with the proper authorities in furnishing such information or assistance as may be required.

2. **Engineers shall perform services only in the areas of their competence.**
   a. Engineers shall undertake assignments only when qualified by education or experience in the specific technical fields involved.
   b. Engineers shall not affix their signatures to any plans or documents dealing with subject matter in which they lack competence, nor to any plan or document not prepared under their direction and control.
   c. Engineers may accept assignments and assume responsibility for coordina-

---

*Publication date as revised: July 1996. Publication #1102. Copyright © National Society of Professional Engineers. Reprinted with permission.

tion of an entire project and sign and seal the engineering documents for the entire project, provided that each technical segment is signed and sealed only by the qualified engineers who prepared the segment.

3. **Engineers shall issue public statements only in an objective and truthful manner.**
   a. Engineers shall be objective and truthful in professional reports, statements, or testimony. They shall include all relevant and pertinent information in such reports, statements, or testimony, which should bear the date indicating when it was current.
   b. Engineers may express publicly technical opinions that are founded upon knowledge of the facts and competence in the subject matter.
   c. Engineers shall issue no statements, criticisms, or arguments on technical matters that are inspired or paid for by interested parties, unless they have prefaced their comments by explicitly identifying the interested parties on whose behalf they are speaking, and by revealing the existence of any interest the engineers may have in the matters.

4. **Engineers shall act for each employer or client as faithful agents or trustees.**
   a. Engineers shall disclose all known or potential conflicts of interest that could influence or appear to influence their judgment or the quality of their services.
   b. Engineers shall not accept compensation, financial or otherwise, from more than one party for services on the same project, or for services pertaining to the same project, unless the circumstances are fully disclosed and agreed to by all interested parties.
   c. Engineers shall not solicit or accept financial or other valuable consideration, directly or indirectly, from outside agents in connection with the work for which they are responsible.
   d. Engineers in public service as members, advisors, or employees of a governmental or quasi-governmental body or department shall not participate in decisions with respect to services solicited or provided by them or their organizations in private or public engineering practice.
   e. Engineers shall not solicit or accept a contract from a governmental body on which a principal or officer of their organization serves as a member.

5. **Engineers shall avoid deceptive acts.**
   a. Engineers shall not falsify their qualifications or permit misrepresentation of their or their associates' qualifications. They shall not misrepresent or exaggerate their responsibility in or for the subject matter of prior assignments. Brochures or other presentations incident to the solicitation of employment shall not misrepresent pertinent facts concerning employers, employees, associates, joint venturers, or past accomplishments.
   b. Engineers shall not offer, give, solicit, or receive, either directly or indirectly, any contribution to influence the award of a contract by public authority, or which may be reasonably construed by the public as having the effect or intent of influencing the awarding of a contract. They shall not offer any gift or other valuable consideration in order to secure work. They shall not pay a commission, percentage, or brokerage fee in order to secure work, except to a bona fide employee or bona fide established commercial or marketing agencies retained by them.

III. PROFESSIONAL OBLIGATIONS

1. Engineers shall be guided in all their relations by the highest standards of honesty and integrity.

    a. Engineers shall acknowledge their errors and shall not distort or alter the facts.

    b. Engineers shall advise their clients or employers when they believe a project will not be successful.

    c. Engineers shall not accept outside employment to the detriment of their regular work or interest. Before accepting any outside engineering employment, they will notify their employers.

    d. Engineers shall not attempt to attract an engineer from another employer by false or misleading pretenses.

    e. Engineers shall not actively participate in strikes, picket lines, or other collective coercive action.

    f. Engineers shall not promote their own interest at the expense of the dignity and integrity of the profession.

2. Engineers shall at all times strive to serve the public interest.

    a. Engineers shall seek opportunities to participate in civic affairs; career guidance for youths; and work for the advancement of the safety, health and well-being of their community.

    b. Engineers shall not complete, sign, or seal plans and/or specifications that are not in conformity with applicable engineering standards. If the client or employer insists on such unprofessional conduct, they shall notify the proper authorities and withdraw from further service on the project.

    c. Engineers shall endeavor to extend public knowledge and appreciation of engineering and its achievements.

3. Engineers shall avoid all conduct or practice that deceives the public.

    a. Engineers shall avoid the use of statements containing a material misrepresentation of fact or omitting a material fact.

    b. Consistent with the foregoing, Engineers may advertise for recruitment of personnel.

    c. Consistent with the foregoing, Engineers may prepare articles for the lay or technical press, but such articles shall not imply credit to the author for work performed by others.

4. Engineers shall not disclose, without consent, confidential information concerning the business affairs or technical processes of any present or former client or employer, or public body on which they serve.

    a. Engineers shall not, without the consent of all interested parties, promote or arrange for new employment or practice in connection with a specific project for which the Engineer has gained particular and specialized knowledge.

    b. Engineers shall not, without the consent of all interested parties, participate in or represent an adversary interest in connection with a specific project or proceeding in which the Engineer has gained particular specialized knowledge on behalf of a former client or employer.

5. Engineers shall not be influenced in their professional duties by conflicting interests.

    a. Engineers shall not accept financial or other considerations, including free engineering designs, from material or equipment suppliers for specifying their product.

b. Engineers shall not accept commissions or allowances, directly or indirectly, from contractors or other parties dealing with clients or employers of the Engineer in connection with work for which the Engineer is responsible.

6. Engineers shall not attempt to obtain employment or advancement or professional engagements by untruthfully criticizing other engineers, or by other improper or questionable methods.

a. Engineers shall not request, propose, or accept a commission on a contingent basis under circumstances in which their judgment may be compromised.

b. Engineers in salaried positions shall accept part-time engineering work only to the extent consistent with policies of the employer and in accordance with ethical considerations.

c. Engineers shall not, without consent, use equipment, supplies, laboratory, or office facilities of an employer to carry on outside private practice.

7. Engineers shall not attempt to injure, maliciously or falsely, directly or indirectly, the professional reputation, prospects, practice, or employment of other engineers. Engineers who believe others are guilty of unethical or illegal practice shall present such information to the proper authority for action.

a. Engineers in private practice shall not review the work of another engineer for the same client, except with the knowledge of such engineer, or unless the connection of such engineer with the work has been terminated.

b. Engineers in governmental, industrial, or educational employ are entitled to review and evaluate the work of other engineers when so required by their employment duties.

c. Engineers in sales or industrial employ are entitled to make engineering comparisons of represented products with products of other suppliers.

8. Engineers shall accept personal responsibility for their professional activities; provided, however, that Engineers may seek indemnification for services arising out of their practice for other than gross negligence, where the Engineer's interests cannot otherwise be protected.

a. Engineers shall conform with state registration laws in the practice of engineering.

b. Engineers shall not use association with a nonengineer, a corporation, or partnership as a "cloak" for unethical acts.

9. Engineers shall give credit for engineering work to those to whom credit is due, and will recognize the proprietary interests of others.

a. Engineers shall, whenever possible, name the person or persons who may be individually responsible for designs, inventions, writings, or other accomplishments.

b. Engineers using designs supplied by a client recognize that the designs remain the property of the client and may not be duplicated by the Engineer for others without express permission.

c. Engineers, before undertaking work for others in connection with which the Engineer may make improvements, plans, designs, inventions, or other records that may justify copyrights or patents, should enter into a positive agreement regarding ownership.

d. Engineers' designs, data, records, and notes referring exclusively to an employer's work are the employer's property. Employer should indemnify the Engineer for use of the information for any purpose other than the original purpose.

"By order of the United States District Court for the District of Columbia, former Section 11(c) of the NSPE Code of Ethics prohibiting competitive bidding, and all policy statements, opinions, rulings or other guidelines interpreting its scope, have been rescinded as unlawfully interfering with the legal right of engineers, protected under the antitrust laws, to provide price information to prospective clients; accordingly, nothing contained in the NSPE Code of Ethics, policy statements, opinions, rulings or other guidelines prohibits the submission of price quotations or competitive bids for engineering services at any time or in any amount."

Statement by NSPE Executive Committee

In order to correct misunderstandings which have been indicated in some instances since the issuance of the Supreme Court decision and the entry of the Final Judgment, it is noted that in its decision of April 25, 1978, the Supreme Court of the United States declared: "The Sherman Act does not require competitive bidding."

It is further noted that as made clear in the Supreme Court decision:
1. Engineers and firms may individually refuse to bid for engineering services.
2. Clients are not required to seek bids for engineering services.
3. Federal, state, and local laws governing procedures to procure engineering services are not affected, and remain in full force and effect.
4. State societies and local chapters are free to actively and aggressively seek legislation for professional selection and negotiation procedures by public agencies.
5. State registration board rules of professional conduct, including rules prohibiting competitive bidding for engineering services, are not affected and remain in full force and effect. State registration boards with authority to adopt rules of professional conduct may adopt rules governing procedures to obtain engineering services.
6. As noted by the Supreme Court, "nothing in the judgment prevents NSPE and its members from attempting to influence governmental action . . . ."

Note:

In regard to the question of application of the Code to corporations vis-a-vis real persons, business form or type should not negate nor influence conformance of individuals to the Code. The Code deals with professional services, which services must be performed by real persons. Real persons in turn establish and implement policies within business structures. The Code is clearly written to apply to the Engineer, and it is incumbent on members of NSPE to endeavor to live up to its provisions. This applies to all pertinent sections of the Code.

7. FINANCIAL PLANNING

Organization

ASSOCIATION FOR INVESTMENT MANAGEMENT AND RESEARCH

Headquarters:
P.O. Box 3668
5 Boar's Head Lane
Charlottesville, VA 22903-0668
Telephone: (800) 247-8132
(804) 980-3668
Fax: (804) 980-9755
E-mail: info@aimr.org
Website: http://www.aimr.org

Date founded: 1990
Formed through the merger of the Financial Analysts Federation, founded in 1947, and the Institute of Chartered Financial Analysts, founded in 1963
Membership: approximately 33,000 investment professionals in 80 affiliated societies and chapters in over 79 countries, including securities analysts, portfolio managers, strategists, and consultants practicing in such fields as banking, insurance, investment counseling, brokerage firms, corporations, and government, of whom over 24,000 hold the Chartered Financial Analyst (CFA) credential; and over 47,000 candidates for the CFA

Code of Ethics

Official name: *Code of Ethics and Standards of Professional Conduct*
History: First issued January 1990; amended periodically; current version as amended and restated May 1996
Authority: Professional Ethics & Responsibility Committee; Professional Conduct Program
Code is available on Website

Additional Resources

Organizational (Divisions, Programs, Services, etc.):

Advocacy and Professional Conduct Board Oversight Committee
Advocacy Program
Global Investment Performance Standards Committee
International Coordinating Committee
Performance Presentation Standards Program
Professional Conduct Complaint Center: fax (804) 980-9730 or e-mail
    pconduct@aimr.org.

Informational (Publications, Videos, Seminars, etc.):

Articles in *Financial Analysts Journal*
AIMR Performance Presentation Standards
AIMR Soft Dollar Standards (Guidance for Ethical Practices Involving
    Client Brokerage)
AIMR Standards Reporter
Ethics in the Investment Profession: A Survey
Ethics in the Investment Profession: An International Survey
Ethics, Fairness, Efficiency, and Financial Markets
Global Investment Performance Standards
Good Ethics: The Essential Element of a Firm's Success (proceedings)
International Code and Standards (draft)
Performance Reporting for Investment Managers: Applying the AIMR
    Performance Presentation Standards (proceedings)
Standards of Practice Casebook
Standards of Practice Handbook

Goals and Activities of Organization

The Association for Investment Management and Research (AIMR) serves its members as a global leader in educating and examining investment managers and analysts, and in sustaining high standards of professional conduct. Its services fall into three main categories: education, professional conduct and ethics, and professional practice and advocacy.

AIMR representatives work with government regulators and other professional organizations in order to identify and influence legislative, regulatory, or technological decisions that have an impact on capital markets and the investment industry, and to assist in the development of professional practice guidelines.

The Professional Conduct Program coordinates ethics-related matters, including education initiatives and publications.

Among the AIMR's additional activities are promoting strong corporate governance, championing stockholder rights, and expanding its international presence. As a member of the International Coordinating Committee, AIMR develops global ethical standards for investment professionals and encourages their adoption.

Implementation and Enforcement of Code

All members of AIMR, the Financial Analysts Federation, and the Institute of Chartered Financial Analysts, and holders of and candidates for the CFA designation, are obliged to follow the Code and Standards, which the organization considers the most stringent in the investment industry and essential to building public trust and investor confidence.

AIMR's Professional Conduct Program relies on self-regulation and a peer review process for enforcement. AIMR actively monitors compliance with the Code and Standards; members and candidates are required to file an annual statement attesting to their compliance and disclosing any relevant complaints that have been made against them. Each disclosure is independently reviewed.

The Program also answers questions concerning ethical issues and compliance.

Complaints are investigated by Professional Conduct volunteers and staff on a confidential basis; cases are reviewed by members of the Professional Ethics and Responsibility Committee. Violators are subject to disciplinary sanctions ranging from private reprimand, to revocation of the CFA charter (or of the opportunity to participate in the CFA Program), to termination of AIMR membership. All information from and about persons subject to an inquiry, including the status or existence of an inquiry, is also kept strictly confidential.

Where the Code or Standard is more stringent than—but does not conflict with—local law, members are held to the higher standard.

History and Development of Code

The first nationwide Code and Standards were adopted by AIMR's predecessors in May 1962. These documents are continually studied and updated in response to changing conditions in the investment industry. The edition reprinted here, which became effective January 1, 1990, was most recently amended May 5, 1996.

Code of Ethics and Standards of Professional Conduct*

THE CODE OF ETHICS

Members of the Association for Investment Management and Research shall:
- Act with integrity, competence, dignity, and in an ethical manner when dealing with the public, clients, prospects, employers, employees, and fellow members.
- Practice and encourage others to practice in a professional and ethical manner that will reflect credit on members and their profession.
- Strive to maintain and improve their competence and the competence of others in the profession.
- Use reasonable care and exercise independent professional judgment.

THE STANDARDS OF PROFESSIONAL CONDUCT

Standard I:
FUNDAMENTAL RESPONSIBILITIES

Members shall:
A. Maintain knowledge of and comply with all applicable laws, rules, and regulations (including AIMR's Code of Ethics and Standards of Professional Conduct) of any government, regulatory organization, licensing agency, or professional association governing the members' professional activities.
B. Not knowingly participate or assist in any violation of such laws, rules, or regulations.

Standard II:
RELATIONSHIPS WITH AND RESPONSIBILITIES
TO THE PROFESSION

A. **Use of Professional Designation.**
   1. Membership in AIMR, the Financial Analysts Federation (FAF), or the Institute for Chartered Financial Analysts (ICFA) may be referenced by members of these organizations only in a dignified and judicious manner. The use of the reference may be accompanied by an accurate explanation of the requirements that have been met to obtain membership in these organizations.
   2. Holders of the Chartered Financial Analyst (CFA) designation may use the professional designation "Chartered Financial Analyst," or the mark "CFA," and are encouraged to do so, but only in a dignified and judicious manner. The use of the designation may be accompanied by an accurate explanation of the requirements that have been met to obtain the designation.

---

*As amended and restated May 5, 1996. Copyright ©1998 Association for Investment Management and Research. Reprinted with permission.

3. Candidates may reference their participation in the CFA Program, but the reference must clearly state that an individual is a candidate for the CFA designation and may not imply that the candidate has achieved any type of partial designation.

B. Professional Misconduct. Members shall not engage in any professional conduct involving dishonesty, fraud, deceit, or misrepresentation or commit any act that reflects adversely on their honesty, trustworthiness, or professional competence.

C. Prohibition against Plagiarism. Members shall not copy or use, in substantially the same form as the original, material prepared by another without acknowledging and identifying the name of the author, publisher, or source of such material. Members may use, without acknowledgment, factual information published by recognized financial and statistical reporting services or similar sources.

Standard III:
RELATIONSHIPS WITH AND RESPONSIBILITIES TO THE EMPLOYER

A. Obligation to Inform Employer of Code and Standards. Members shall:
1. Inform their employer, through their direct supervisor, that they are obligated to comply with the Code and Standards and are subject to disciplinary sanctions for violations thereof.
2. Deliver a copy of the Code and Standards to their employer if the employer does not have a copy.

B. Duty to Employer. Members shall not undertake any independent practice that could result in compensation or other benefit in competition with their employer unless they obtain written consent from both their employer and the persons or entities for whom they undertake independent practice.

C. Disclosure of Conflicts to Employer. Members shall:
1. Disclose to their employer all matters, including beneficial ownership of securities or other investments, that reasonably could be expected to interfere with their duty to their employer or ability to make unbiased and objective recommendations.
2. Comply with any prohibitions on activities imposed by their employer if a conflict of interest exists.

D. Disclosure of Additional Compensation Arrangements. Members shall disclose to their employer in writing all monetary compensation or other benefits that they receive for their services that are in addition to compensation or benefits conferred by a member's employer.

E. Responsibilities of Supervisors. Members with supervisory responsibility, authority, or the ability to influence the conduct of others shall exercise reasonable supervision over those subject to their supervision or authority to prevent any violation of applicable statutes, regulations, or provisions of the Code and Standards. In so doing, members are entitled to rely on reasonable procedures to detect and prevent such violations.

Standard IV:
RELATIONSHIPS WITH AND RESPONSIBILITIES
TO CLIENTS AND PROSPECTS

A. *Investment Process.*

A.1 Reasonable Basis and Representations.   Members shall:
  a. Exercise diligence and thoroughness in making investment recommendations or in taking investment actions.
  b. Have a reasonable and adequate basis, supported by appropriate research and investigation, for such recommendations or actions.
  c. Make reasonable and diligent efforts to avoid any material misrepresentation in any research report or investment recommendation.
  d. Maintain appropriate records to support the reasonableness of such recommendations or actions.

A.2 Research Reports.   Members shall:
  a. Use reasonable judgment regarding the inclusion or exclusion of relevant factors in research reports.
  b. Distinguish between facts and opinions in research reports.
  c. Indicate the basic characteristics of the investment involved when preparing for public distribution a research report that is not directly related to a specific portfolio or client.

A.3 Independence and Objectivity.   Members shall use reasonable care and judgment to achieve and maintain independence and objectivity in making investment recommendations or taking investment action.

B. *Interactions with Clients and Prospects.*

B.1 Fiduciary Duties.   In relationships with clients, members shall use particular care in determining applicable fiduciary duty and shall comply with such duty as to those persons and interests to whom the duty is owed. Members must act for the benefit of their clients and place their clients' interests before their own.

B.2 Portfolio Investment Recommendations and Actions.   Members shall:
  a. Make a reasonable inquiry into a client's financial situation, investment experience, and investment objectives prior to making any investment recommendations and shall update this information as necessary, but no less frequently than annually, to allow the members to adjust their investment recommendations to reflect changed circumstances.
  b. Consider the appropriateness and suitability of investment recommendations or actions for each portfolio or client. In determining appropriateness and suitability, members shall consider applicable relevant factors, including the needs and circumstances of the portfolio or client, the basic characteristics of the investment involved, and the basic characteristics of the total portfolio. Members shall not make a recommendation unless they reasonably determine that the recommendation is suitable to the client's financial situation, investment experience, and investment objectives.
  c. Distinguish between facts and opinions in the presentation of investment recommendations.

d. Disclose to clients and prospects the basic format and general principles of the investment processes by which securities are selected and portfolios are constructed and shall promptly disclose to clients and prospects any changes that might significantly affect those processes.

B.3 Fair Dealing.   Members shall deal fairly and objectively with all clients and prospects when disseminating investment recommendations, disseminating material changes in prior investment recommendations, and taking investment action.

B.4 Priority of Transactions.   Transactions for clients and employers shall have priority over transactions in securities or other investments of which a member is the beneficial owner so that such personal transactions do not operate adversely to their clients' or employer's interests. If members make a recommendation regarding the purchase or sale of a security or other investment, they shall give their clients and employer adequate opportunity to act on the recommendation before acting on their own behalf. For purposes of the Code and Standards, a member is a "beneficial owner" if the member has:

a. a direct or indirect pecuniary interest in the securities;
b. the power to vote or direct the voting of the shares of the securities or investments;
c. the power to dispose or direct the disposition of the security or investment.

B.5 Preservation of Confidentiality.   Members shall preserve the confidentiality of information communicated by clients, prospects, or employers concerning matters within the scope of the client-member, prospect-member, or employer-member relationship unless the member receives information concerning illegal activities on the part of the client, prospect, or employer.

B.6 Prohibition against Misrepresentation.   Members shall not make any statements, orally or in writing, that misrepresent:

a. the services that they or their firms are capable of performing;
b. their qualifications or the qualifications of their firm;
c. the member's academic or professional credentials.

Members shall not make or imply, orally or in writing, any assurances or guarantees regarding any investment except to communicate accurate information regarding the terms of the investment instrument and the issuer's obligations under the instrument.

B.7 Disclosure of Conflicts to Clients and Prospects.   Members shall disclose to their clients and prospects all matters, including beneficial ownership of securities or other investments, that reasonably could be expected to impair the member's ability to make unbiased and objective recommendations.

B.8 Disclosure of Referral Fees.   Members shall disclose to clients and prospects any consideration or benefit received by the member or delivered to others for the recommendation of any services to the client or prospect.

Standard V:
RELATIONSHIPS WITH AND RESPONSIBILITIES
TO THE PUBLIC

A. Prohibition against Use of Material Nonpublic Information.   Members who possess material nonpublic information related to the value of a security shall not trade or cause others to trade in that security if such trading would breach a duty or if the information was misappropriated or relates to a tender offer. If members receive material nonpublic information in confidence, they shall not breach that confidence by trading or causing others to trade in securities to which such information relates. Members shall make reasonable efforts to achieve public dissemination of material nonpublic information disclosed in breach of a duty.

B. Performance Presentation.

1. Members shall not make any statements, orally or in writing, that misrepresent the investment performance that they or their firms have accomplished or can reasonably be expected to achieve.
2. If members communicate individual or firm performance information directly or indirectly to clients or prospective clients, or in a manner intended to be received by clients or prospective clients, members shall make every reasonable effort to assure that such performance information is a fair, accurate, and complete presentation of such performance.

Organization

CERTIFIED FINANCIAL PLANNER BOARD OF STANDARDS

Headquarters:
1700 Broadway, Suite 2100
Denver, CO 80290-2101
Telephone: (303) 830-7500
Fax: (303) 860-7388
E-mail: mail@CFP-Board.org
Website: http://www.CFP-Board.org
Ethics Hotline: 888-CFP-MARK

Date founded: 1985
　　Formerly the International Board of Standards and Practices for Certified Financial Planners
Membership: The CFP Board is a regulatory, not a membership, organization; approximately 32,500 individuals, who meet initial and continuing requirements for education, examination, experience, and ethics, are licensed to use the trademarks Certified Financial Planner and CFP

Code of Ethics

Official name: *Code of Ethics and Professional Responsibility*
History: Originally adopted 1992; revised periodically; current version issued January 1998
Authority: Board of Ethics and Professional Review; CFP Board
Code is available on Website

Additional Resources

Organizational (Divisions, Programs, Services, etc.):

888-CFP-MARK (toll-free number for consumers to check status of or disciplinary action against CFP licensee, or to lodge complaint)
Board of Practice Standards
Continuing education program
Institute of Certified Financial Planners
Mediation Program for Financial Planning Disputes

Informational (Publications, Videos, Seminars, etc.):

Articles in *CFA Digest* and *Financial Analysts Journal*
A Guide to Mediation for Financial Planning Disputes
CFP Licensee and Disciplinary Statistics (online)
Disciplinary Rules and Procedures
List of Publicly Disciplined CFP Licensees (online)
Practice Standards

Goals and Activities of Organization

The Certified Financial Planner Board of Standards (CFP Board) is an independent professional regulatory organization that owns, confers, and controls the federally registered trademarks CFP and Certified Financial Planner. A private, nonprofit, standard-setting, credentialing, licensing, and disciplinary body, it regulates financial planners by licensing individuals who meet its certification requirements to use the marks.

To fulfill its mission to benefit and protect the public, the CFP Board determines the qualifications for initial professional certification, develops and administers post-certification requirements and disciplinary procedures for licensees, and encourages the attainment and retention of certification in order to enhance the professionalism of personal financial planners.

Licensees must make voluntary periodic disclosures of public, government, or civil disciplinary actions taken against them.

While the CFP Board does not have the authority to prohibit an individual financial planner from practicing, a CFP licensee who fails to meet the standards of the Code is subject to disciplinary action. Discipline is handled by the Board of Professional Review, a seven-member peer review group of CFP licensees.

Implementation and Enforcement of Code

All licensees must subscribe to the Code, whose two-part structure consists of Principles and Rules. The Principles are general statements of ethical and professional ideals; they are aspirational in nature, intended as a source of guidance. Comments following individual Principles further explain their meaning. The Rules are practical standards of ethical and professionally responsible conduct expected of CFP licensees; they are mandatory in nature, to be followed in particular situations.

The CFP Board will investigate any written complaint against a designee or licensee, affording all parties due process and confidentiality. It will also initiate its own investigations based on a continuing review of reports from other regulatory bodies and in the press.

Staff Counsel carefully reviews complaints to determine if further action is warranted; if so, an Inquiry Panel is the next level involved. At all junctures the accused is given notice and an opportunity to respond. If the matter proceeds to a hearing, the Hearing Panel eventually will submit its findings to the full Board of Professional Review, which interprets and applies the Code in rendering a final decision. The judgment may be appealed to the Board of Appeals. The matter also may be resolved through an Offer of Settlement.

Penalties for Code violations include private censure, public letter of admonition, temporary suspension of the license to use the CFP mark, or permanent revocation. Mitigating circumstances and the licensee's level of cooperation with the investigation are taken into consideration.

The Board of Professional Review is also responsible for amending the Disciplinary Rules and Procedures, subject to review and approval of the CFP Board of Governors.

A mediation program is available for resolving certain types of financial planning disputes, as an alternative to their presentation as ethics complaints or litigation.

History and Development of Code

The CFP Board promulgates the Code. It adopted the present *Code of Ethics and Professional Responsibility* in 1993—a major revision of the 1988 *Code of Ethics and Standards of Practice* (whose earlier versions dated from 1983 and 1985). The change reflected the input of CFP licensees, other financial services organizations, and consumers.

Provisions are revised fairly regularly. The following document is current as of January 1998.

Code of Ethics and Professional Responsibility*

Preamble and Applicability

The *Code of Ethics and Professional Responsibility* (Code) has been adopted by the Certified Financial Planner Board of Standards, Inc. (CFP Board) to provide principles and rules to all persons whom it has recognized and certified to use the CFP certification mark and the marks CFP and Certified Financial Planner (collectively "the marks"). The CFP Board determines who is recognized and certified to use the marks. Implicit in the acceptance of this authorization is an obligation not only to comply with the mandates and requirements of all applicable laws and regulations but also to take responsibility to act in an ethical and professionally responsible manner in all professional services and activities.

For purposes of this Code, a person recognized and certified by the CFP Board to use the marks is called a CFP designee or Certified Financial Planner designee. This Code applies to CFP designees actively involved in the practice of personal financial planning, in other areas of financial services, in industry, in related professions, in government, in education or in any other professional activity in which the marks are used in the performance of their professional responsibilities. This Code also applies to candidates for the CFP and Certified Financial Planner designation who are registered as such with the CFP Board. For purposes of this Code, the term CFP designee shall be deemed to include candidates.

Composition and Scope

The Code consists of two parts: **Part I—Principles** and **Part II—Rules.** The Principles are statements expressing in general terms the ethical and professional ideals expected of CFP designees and which they should strive to display in their professional activities. As such the Principles are aspirational in character but are intended to provide a source of guidance for a CFP designee. The comments following each Principle further explain the meaning of the Principle. The Rules provide practical guidelines derived from the tenets embodied in the Principles. As such, the Rules set forth the standards of ethical and professionally responsible conduct expected to be followed in particular situations. This Code does not undertake to define standards of professional conduct of CFP designees for purposes of civil liability.

Due to the nature of a CFP designee's particular field of endeavor, certain Rules may not be applicable to that CFP designee's activities. For example, a CFP designee who is engaged solely in the sale of securities as a registered representative is not subject to the written disclosure requirements of Rule 402 (applicable to CFP designees engaged in personal financial planning) although he or she may have disclosure responsibilities under Rule 401. A CFP designee is obligated to determine what responsibilities the CFP designee has in each professional relationship including, for example, duties that arise in particular circum-

---

*Copyright © 1992, 1993, 1994, 1995, 1996, 1997, 1998 Certified Financial Planner Board of Standards, Inc. Revised 1/98. All rights reserved. Permission to reprint the Code has been granted by its owner and developer, the CFP Board. CFP® and Certified Financial Planner® and the CFP certification mark are federally registered trademarks of the Certified Financial Planner Board of Standards.

stances from a position of trust or confidence that a CFP designee may have. The CFP designee is obligated to meet those responsibilities.

The Code is structured so that the presentation of the Rules parallels the presentation of the Principles. For example, the Rules which relate to Principle 1—Integrity, are numbered in the 100 to 199 series while those Rules relating to Principle 2—Objectivity, are numbered in the 200 to 299 series.

Compliance

The CFP Board of Governors requires adherence to this Code by all those it recognizes and certifies to use the marks. Compliance with the Code, individually and by the profession as a whole, depends on each CFP designee's knowledge of and voluntary compliance with the Principles and applicable Rules, on the influence of fellow professionals and public opinion, and on disciplinary proceedings, when necessary, involving CFP designees who fail to comply with the applicable provisions of the Code.

Terminology In This Code

"Client" denotes a person, persons, or entity for whom professional services are rendered. Where the services of the practitioner are provided to an entity (corporation, trust, partnership, estate, etc.), the client is the entity, acting through its legally authorized representative.

"Commission" denotes the compensation received by an agent or broker when the same is calculated as a percentage on the amount of his or her sales or purchase transactions.

"Conflict(s) of interest(s)" denotes circumstances, relationships or other facts about the CFP designee's own financial, business, property and/or personal interests which will or reasonably may impair the CFP designee's rendering of disinterested advice, recommendations or services.

"Fee-only" denotes a method of compensation in which compensation is received solely from a client with neither the personal financial planning practitioner nor any related party receiving compensation which is contingent upon the purchase or sale of any financial product. A "related party" for this purpose shall mean an individual or entity from whom any direct or indirect economic benefit is derived by the personal financial planning practitioner as a result of implementing a recommendation made by the personal financial planning practitioner.

"Personal financial planning" or **"financial planning"** denotes the process of determining whether and how an individual can meet life goals through the proper management of financial resources.

"Personal financial planning process" or **"financial planning process"** denotes the process which typically includes, but is not limited to, the six elements of establishing and defining the client-planner relationship, gathering client data including goals, analyzing and evaluating the client's financial status, developing and presenting financial planning recommendations and/or alternatives, implementing the financial planning recommendations and monitoring the financial planning recommendations.

"Personal financial planning subject areas" or **"financial planning subject areas"** denotes the basic subject fields covered in the financial planning process which typically include, but are not limited to, financial statement preparation and analysis (including cash flow analysis/planning and budgeting), investment planning (including portfolio design, i.e., asset allocation, and portfolio management), income tax planning, education planning, risk management, retirement planning, and estate planning.

"Personal financial planning professional" or **"financial planning professional"** denotes a person who is capable and qualified to offer objective, integrated, and comprehensive financial advice to or for the benefit of individuals to help them achieve their financial objectives. A financial planning professional must have the ability to provide financial planning services to clients, using the financial planning process covering the basic financial planning subjects.

"Personal financial planning practitioner" or **"financial planning practitioner"** denotes a person who is capable and qualified to offer objective, integrated, and comprehensive financial advice to or for the benefit of clients to help them achieve their financial objectives and who engages in financial planning using the financial planning process in working with clients.

Part I—PRINCIPLES

Introduction

These Principles of the Code express the profession's recognition of its responsibilities to the public, to clients, to colleagues, and to employers. They apply to all CFP designees and provide guidance to them in the performance of their professional services.

Principle 1—**Integrity**

A CFP designee shall offer and provide professional services with integrity.

As discussed in Composition and Scope, CFP designees may be placed by clients in positions of trust and confidence. The ultimate source of such public trust is the CFP designee's personal integrity. In deciding what is right and just, a CFP designee should rely on his or her integrity as the appropriate touchstone. Integrity demands honesty and candor which must not be subordinated to personal gain and advantage. Within the characteristic of integrity, allowance can be made for innocent error and legitimate difference of opinion; but integrity cannot co-exist with deceit or subordination of one's principles. Integrity requires a CFP designee to observe not only the letter but also the spirit of this Code.

Principle 2—**Objectivity**

A CFP designee shall be objective in providing professional services to clients.

Objectivity requires intellectual honesty and impartiality. It is an essential quality for any professional. Regardless of the particular service rendered or the capacity in which a CFP designee functions, a CFP designee should protect the integrity of his or her work, maintain objectivity, and avoid subordination of his or her judgment that would be in violation of this Code.

Principle 3—**Competence**

A CFP designee shall provide services to clients competently and maintain the necessary knowledge and skill to continue to do so in those areas in which the designee is engaged.

One is competent only when he or she has attained and maintained an adequate level of knowledge and skill, and applies that knowledge effectively in providing services to clients. Competence also includes the wisdom to recognize the limitations of that knowledge and when consultation or client referral is appropriate. A CFP designee, by virtue of having earned the CFP designation, is deemed to be qualified to practice financial planning. However, in addition to assimilating the common body of knowledge required and acquiring the necessary experience for designation, a CFP designee shall make a continuing commitment to learning and professional improvement.

Principle 4—**Fairness**

A CFP designee shall perform professional services in a manner that is fair and reasonable to clients, principals, partners, and employers and shall disclose conflict(s) of interest(s) in providing such services.

Fairness requires impartiality, intellectual honesty, and disclosure of conflict(s) of interest(s). It involves a subordination of one's own feelings, prejudices, and desires so as to achieve a proper balance of conflicting interests. Fairness is treating others in the same fashion that you would want to be treated and is an essential trait of any professional.

Principle 5—**Confidentiality**

A CFP designee shall not disclose any confidential client information without the specific consent of the client unless in response to proper legal process, to defend against charges of wrongdoing by the CFP designee or in connection with a civil dispute between the CFP designee and client.

A client, by seeking the services of a CFP designee, may be interested in creating a relationship of personal trust and confidence with the CFP designee. This type of relationship can only be built upon the understanding that information supplied to the CFP designee or other information will be confidential. In order to provide the contemplated services effectively and to protect the client's privacy, the CFP designee shall safeguard the confidentiality of such information.

Principle 6—**Professionalism**

A CFP designee's conduct in all matters shall reflect credit upon the profession.

Because of the importance of the professional services rendered by CFP designees, there are attendant responsibilities to behave with dignity and courtesy to all those who use those services, fellow professionals, and those in related professions. A CFP designee also has an obligation to cooperate with fellow CFP designees to enhance and maintain the profession's public image and to work jointly with other CFP designees to improve the quality of services. It is only through the combined efforts of all CFP designees in cooperation with other professionals, that this vision can be realized.

Principle 7—**Diligence**

A CFP designee shall act diligently in providing professional services.

Diligence is the provision of services in a reasonably prompt and thorough manner. Diligence also includes proper planning for and supervision of the rendering of professional services.

Part II—RULES

Introduction

As stated in **Part I—Principles,** the Principles apply to all CFP designees. However, due to the nature of a CFP designee's particular field of endeavor, certain Rules may not be applicable to that CFP designee's activities. The universe of activities by CFP designees is indeed diverse and a particular CFP designee may be performing all, some or none of the typical services provided by financial planning professionals. As a result, in considering the Rules in Part II, a CFP designee must first recognize what specific services he or she is rendering and then determine whether or not a specific Rule is applicable to those services. To assist the CFP designee in making these determinations, this Code includes a series of definitions of terminology used throughout the Code. Based upon these definitions, a CFP designee should be able to determine which services he or she provides and, therefore, which Rules are applicable to those services.

Rules that Relate to the Principle of Integrity

Rule 101

A CFP designee shall not solicit clients through false or misleading communications or advertisements:

(a) *Misleading Advertising:* A CFP designee shall not make a false or misleading communication about the size, scope or areas of competence of the CFP designee's practice or of any organization with which the CFP designee is associated; and

(b) *Promotional Activities:* In promotional activities, a CFP designee shall not make materially false or misleading communications to the public or create unjustified expectations regarding matters relating to financial planning or the professional activities and competence of the CFP designee. The term "promotional activities" includes, but is not limited to, speeches, interviews, books and/or printed publications, seminars, radio and television shows, and video cassettes; and

(c) *Representation of Authority:* A CFP designee shall not give the impression that a CFP designee is representing the views of the CFP Board or any other group unless the CFP designee has been authorized to do so. Personal opinions shall be clearly identified as such.

Rule 102

In the course of professional activities, a CFP designee shall not engage in conduct involving dishonesty, fraud, deceit or misrepresentation, or knowingly make a false or misleading statement to a client, employer, employee, professional colleague, governmental or other regulatory body or official, or any other person or entity.

Rule 103

A CFP designee has the following responsibilities regarding funds and/or other property of clients:

(a) In exercising custody of or discretionary authority over client funds or other property, a CFP designee shall act only in accordance with the authority set forth in the governing legal instrument (e.g., special power of attorney, trust, letters testamentary, etc.); and

(b) A CFP designee shall identify and keep complete records of all funds or other property of a client in the custody of or under the discretionary authority of the CFP designee; and

(c) Upon receiving funds or other property of a client, a CFP designee shall promptly or as otherwise permitted by law or provided by agreement with the client, deliver to the client or third party any funds or other property which the client or third party is entitled to receive and, upon request by the client, render a full accounting regarding such funds or other property; and

(d) A CFP designee shall not commingle client funds or other property with a CFP designee's personal funds and/or other property or the funds and/or other property of a CFP designee's firm. Commingling one or more clients' funds or other property together is permitted, subject to compliance with applicable legal requirements and provided accurate records are maintained for each client's funds or other property; and

(e) A CFP designee who takes custody of all or any part of a client's assets for investment purposes, shall do so with the care required of a fiduciary.

Rules that Relate to the Principle of Objectivity

Rule 201

A CFP designee shall exercise reasonable and prudent professional judgment in providing professional services.

Rule 202

A financial planning practitioner shall act in the interest of the client.

Rules that Relate to the Principle of Competence

Rule 301

A CFP designee shall keep informed of developments in the field of financial planning and participate in continuing education throughout the CFP designee's professional career in order to improve professional competence in all areas in which the CFP designee is engaged. As a distinct part of this requirement, a CFP designee shall satisfy all minimum continuing education requirements established for CFP designees by the CFP Board.

Rule 302

A CFP designee shall offer advice only in those areas in which the CFP designee has competence. In areas where the CFP designee is not professionally competent, the CFP designee shall seek the counsel of qualified individuals and/ or refer clients to such parties.

Rules that Relate to the Principle of Fairness

Rule 401

In rendering professional services, a CFP designee shall disclose to the client:
(a) Material information relevant to the professional relationship, including but not limited to conflict(s) of interest(s), changes in the CFP designee's business affiliation, address, telephone number, credentials, qualifications, licenses, compensation structure and any agency relationships, and the scope of the CFP designee's authority in that capacity.
(b) The information required by all laws applicable to the relationship in a manner complying with such laws.

Rule 402

A financial planning practitioner shall make timely written disclosure of all material information relative to the professional relationship. In all circumstances such disclosure shall include conflict(s) of interest(s) and sources of compensation. Written disclosures that include the following information are considered to be in compliance with this Rule:
(a) A statement of the basic philosophy of the CFP designee (or firm) in working with clients. The disclosure shall include the philosophy, theory and/or principles of financial planning which will be utilized by the CFP designee; and
(b) Resumes of principals and employees of a firm who are expected to provide financial planning services to the client and a description of those services. Such disclosures shall include educational background, professional/employment history, professional designations and licenses held, and areas of competence and specialization; and
(c) A statement of compensation, which in reasonable detail discloses the source(s) and any contingencies or other aspects material to the fee and/or commission arrangement. Any estimates made shall be clearly

identified as such and shall be based on reasonable assumptions. Referral fees, if any, shall be fully disclosed; and

(d) A statement indicating whether the CFP designee's compensation arrangements involve fee-only, commission-only, or fee and commission. A CFP designee shall not hold out as a fee-only financial planning practitioner if the CFP designee receives commissions or other forms of economic benefit from related parties; and

(e) A statement describing material agency or employment relationships a CFP designee (or firm) has with third parties and the fees or commissions resulting from such relationships; and

(f) A statement identifying conflict(s) of interest(s).

Rule 403

A CFP designee providing financial planning shall disclose in writing, prior to establishing a client relationship, relationships which reasonably may compromise the CFP designee's objectivity or independence.

Rule 404

Should conflict(s) of interest(s) develop after a professional relationship has been commenced, but before the services contemplated by that relationship have been completed, a CFP designee shall promptly disclose the conflict(s) of interest(s) to the client or other necessary persons.

Rule 405

In addition to the disclosure by financial planning practitioners regarding sources of compensation required under Rule 402, such disclosure shall be made annually thereafter for ongoing clients. The annual disclosure requirement may be satisfied by offering to provide clients with the current copy of SEC form ADV, Part II or the disclosure called for by Rule 402.

Rule 406

A CFP designee's compensation shall be fair and reasonable.

Rule 407

Prior to establishing a client relationship, and consistent with the confidentiality requirements of Rule 501, a CFP designee may provide references which may include recommendations from present and/or former clients.

Rule 408

When acting as an agent for a principal, a CFP designee shall assure that the scope of his or her authority is clearly defined and properly documented.

Rule 409

Whether a CFP designee is employed by a financial planning firm, an investment institution, or serves as an agent for such an organization, or is self-employed, all CFP designees shall adhere to the same standards of disclosure and service.

Rule 410

A CFP designee who is an employee shall perform professional services with dedication to the lawful objectives of the employer and in accordance with this Code.

Rule 411

A CFP designee shall:
(a) Advise the CFP designee's employer of outside affiliations which reasonably may compromise service to an employer; and
(b) Provide timely notice to the employer and clients, unless precluded by contractual obligation, in the event of change of employment or CFP Board licensing status.

Rule 412

A CFP designee doing business as a partner or principal of a financial services firm owes to the CFP designee's partners or co-owners a responsibility to act in good faith. This includes, but is not limited to, disclosure of relevant and material financial information while in business together.

Rule 413

A CFP designee shall join a financial planning firm as a partner or principal only on the basis of mutual disclosure of relevant and material information regarding credentials, competence, experience, licensing and/or legal status, and financial stability of the parties involved.

Rule 414

A CFP designee who is a partner or co-owner of a financial services firm who elects to withdraw from the firm shall do so in compliance with any applicable agreement, and shall deal with his or her business interest in a fair and equitable manner.

Rule 415

A CFP designee shall inform his or her employer, partners or co-owners of compensation or other benefit arrangements in connection with his or her services to clients which are in addition to compensation from the employer, partners or co-owners for such services.

Rule 416

If a CFP designee enters into a business transaction with a client, the transaction shall be on terms which are fair and reasonable to the client and the CFP designee shall disclose the risks of the transaction, conflict(s) of interest(s) of the CFP designee, and other relevant information, if any, necessary to make the transaction fair to the client.

Rules that Relate to the Principle of Confidentiality

Rule 501

A CFP designee shall not reveal—or use for his or her own benefit—without the client's consent, any personally identifiable information relating to the client relationship or the affairs of the client, except and to the extent disclosure or use is reasonably necessary:
  (a) To establish an advisory or brokerage account, to effect a transaction for the client, or as otherwise impliedly authorized in order to carry out the client engagement; or
  (b) To comply with legal requirements or legal process; or
  (c) To defend the CFP designee against charges of wrongdoing; or
  (d) In connection with a civil dispute between the CFP designee and the client.
For purposes of this rule, the proscribed use of client information is improper whether or not it actually causes harm to the client.

Rule 502

A CFP designee shall maintain the same standards of confidentiality to employers as to clients.

Rule 503

A CFP designee doing business as a partner or principal of a financial services firm owes to the CFP designee's partners or co-owners a responsibility to act in good faith. This includes, but is not limited to, adherence to reasonable expectations of confidentiality both while in business together and thereafter.

Rules that Relate to the Principle of Professionalism

Rule 601

A CFP designee shall use the marks in compliance with the rules and regulations of the CFP Board, as established and amended from time to time.

Rule 602

A CFP designee shall show respect for other financial planning professionals, and related occupational groups, by engaging in fair and honorable competitive practices. Collegiality among CFP designees shall not, however, impede enforcement of this Code.

Rule 603

A CFP designee who has knowledge, which is not required to be kept confidential under this Code, that another CFP designee has committed a violation of this Code which raises substantial questions as to the designee's honesty, trustworthiness, or fitness as a CFP designee in other respects, shall promptly inform the CFP Board. This rule does not require disclosure of information or reporting based on knowledge gained as a consultant or expert witness in anticipation of or related to litigation or other dispute resolution mechanisms. For purposes of this rule, knowledge means no substantial doubt.

Rule 604

A CFP designee who has knowledge, which is not required under this Code to be kept confidential, and which raises a substantial question of unprofessional, fraudulent, or illegal conduct by a CFP designee or other financial professional, shall promptly inform the appropriate regulatory and/or professional disciplinary body. This rule does not require disclosure or reporting of information gained as a consultant or expert witness in anticipation of or related to litigation or other dispute resolution mechanisms. For purposes of this rule, knowledge means no substantial doubt.

Rule 605

A CFP designee who has reason to suspect illegal conduct within the CFP designee's organization shall make timely disclosure of the available evidence to the CFP designee's immediate supervisor and/or partners or co-owners. If the CFP designee is convinced that illegal conduct exists within the CFP designee's organization, and that appropriate measures are not taken to remedy the situation, the CFP designee shall, where appropriate, alert the appropriate regulatory authorities including the CFP Board in a timely manner.

Rule 606

In all professional activities a CFP designee shall perform services in accordance with:
  (a) Applicable laws, rules, and regulations of governmental agencies and other applicable authorities; and
  (b) Applicable rules, regulations, and other established policies of the CFP Board.

Rule 607

A CFP designee shall not engage in any conduct which reflects adversely on his or her integrity or fitness as a CFP designee, upon the marks, or upon the profession.

Rule 608

The Investment Advisers Act of 1940 requires registration of investment advisers with the U.S. Securities and Exchange Commission and similar state statutes may require registration with state securities agencies. CFP designees shall disclose to clients their firm's status as registered investment advisers. Under present standards of acceptable business conduct, it is proper to use registered investment adviser if the CFP designee is registered individually. If the CFP designee is registered through his or her firm, then the CFP designee is not a registered investment adviser but a person associated with an investment adviser. The firm is the registered investment adviser. Moreover, RIA or R.I.A. following a CFP designee's name in advertising, letterhead stationery, and business cards may be misleading and is not permitted either by this Code or by SEC regulations.

Rule 609

A CFP designee shall not practice any other profession or offer to provide such services unless the CFP designee is qualified to practice in those fields and is licensed as required by state law.

Rule 610

A CFP designee shall return the client's original records in a timely manner after their return has been requested by a client.

Rule 611

A CFP designee shall not bring or threaten to bring a disciplinary proceeding under this Code, or report or threaten to report information to the CFP Board pursuant to Rules 603 and/or 604, or make or threaten to make use of this Code for no substantial purpose other than to harass, maliciously injure, embarrass and/or unfairly burden another CFP designee.

Rule 612

A CFP designee shall comply with all applicable post-certification requirements established by the CFP Board including, but not limited to, payment of the annual CFP designee fee as well as signing and returning the Licensee's Statement annually in connection with the license renewal process.

Rules that Relate to the Principle of Diligence

Rule 701

A CFP designee shall provide services diligently.

Rule 702

A financial planning practitioner shall enter into an engagement only after securing sufficient information to satisfy the CFP designee that:
    (a) The relationship is warranted by the individual's needs and objectives; and
    (b) The CFP designee has the ability to either provide requisite competent services or to involve other professionals who can provide such services.

Rule 703

A financial planning practitioner shall make and/or implement only recommendations which are suitable for the client.

Rule 704

Consistent with the nature and scope of the engagement, a CFP designee shall make a reasonable investigation regarding the financial products recommended to clients. Such an investigation may be made by the CFP designee or by others provided the CFP designee acts reasonably in relying upon such investigation.

Rule 705

A CFP designee shall properly supervise subordinates with regard to their delivery of financial planning services, and shall not accept or condone conduct in violation of this Code.

Organization

INTERNATIONAL ASSOCIATION FOR FINANCIAL PLANNING

Headquarters:
5775 Glenridge Drive
Suite B-300
Atlanta, GA 30328-5364
Telephone: (404) 845-0011
Fax: (404) 845-3660
E-mail: info@iafp.org
Website: http://www.iafp.org

Date founded: 1969
Membership: approximately 17,000 personal and/or corporate financial advisors who work directly with clients, and providers of services and products to those advisors, in 102 chapters representing all 50 states and 24 countries

Code of Ethics

Official name: *Code of Professional Ethics*
History: Originally adopted May 1988; revised periodically; current version issued June 1992
Authority: Ethics Committee
Code is available on Website

Additional Resources

Organizational (Divisions, Programs, Services, etc.):

Various divisions: Broker-Dealer; Corporate; Practitioner
Broker-Dealer Conference
Conference For Advanced Planning
Continuing education programs

Informational (Publications, Videos, Seminars, etc.):

Articles in *Financial Planning* magazine, *Planning Matters* newsletter, and *The Practicing Professional*
CFP Code of Ethics: A Self-Study Continuing Education Program
The Financial Adviser's Guide to Divorce Settlement: Helping Your Clients Make Sound Financial Decisions (co-published with McGraw-Hill Professional Publishing)
Guidelines for Broker-Dealer Communications with the Public
The Guidelines for Investment Adviser Policy and Procedures
Guidelines for Written Supervisory Procedures
How to Protect Yourself Against Fraud
Seeking Professional Advice

Goals and Activities of Organization

The oldest and largest nonprofit organization of its kind, the International Association for Financial Planning (IAFP) provides members with education, training information, and other products and services to advance their professional expertise; builds public and industry awareness of the benefits of professional financial advice; exchanges information and ideas with other financial services professionals and organizations whose activities are directed toward clients; and develops and maintains high ethical standards for members.

The ethics program is administered by the Ethics Committee, whose role is primarily educational and only secondarily correctional.

The IAFP does not certify, license, register, or confer any designations upon financial planners.

Implementation and Enforcement of Code

The basic objective of the Code of Professional Ethics is to specify the minimal conduct expected of all members and to facilitate voluntary compliance with higher standards. All IAFP members must subscribe to the Code. In order to join, applicants may not have any record of severe disciplinary action.

The Code consists of three kinds of provisions: the Canons express general concepts illustrating exemplary behavior; the Rules of Professional Conduct are specific, mandatory, enforceable standards; and the Guidelines for Professional Conduct are explanatory statements designed to assist members in interpreting, understanding, and applying the Canons and Rules. Violations of Canons or Guidelines do not, in the absence of a Rule violation, constitute grounds for disciplinary action.

Local ethics officers in the chapters are responsible for educating members, handling complaints, and referring cases to the Ethics Committee for evaluation and enforcement. Complaints may be initiated by members, the public, allied organizations, chapter ethics officers, or the Ethics Committee. The IAFP staff prepares a report, which is submitted to the Ethics Committee for review. In applying and interpreting the Rules, the Committee refers to the Canons and Guidelines and to applicable published rulings and opinions in previous cases.

Sanctions include reprimand and suspension or removal from membership. Removal or suspension may be appealed to the Disciplinary Appeals Board. Allegations against members already involved in litigation that may relate to Code violations are not reviewed until after adjudication by the courts.

History and Development of Code

The setting of standards of business practice and conduct has been one of the IAFP's main concerns since its founding in 1969. The current Code, issued in April 1998, is a revision of a May 1988 document.

Code of Professional Ethics*

The objective of the Code of Professional Ethics is to specify and set forth the means to enforce the minimum ethical conduct expected of all members as professionals, and to facilitate voluntary compliance with standards considerably higher than the required minimums.

Accordingly, the Code prescribes two kinds of standards: Canons and Rules of Professional Conduct.

The Canons serve as model standards of exemplary professional conduct. They express the general concepts and principles from which more specific Rules are derived.

The Rules are specific standards of a mandatory and enforceable nature. They prescribe the absolute minimum level of conduct required of every member.

In addition to the Canons and Rules, the Ethics Committee has developed a set of Ethics Policies and Procedures to guide members, the committee and staff in the application and enforcement of the Code of Professional Ethics. A copy of the Ethics Policies and Procedures is available upon request.

Although the official Code of Professional Ethics consists of all Canons and Rules, only a violation of the Rules will constitute sufficient grounds for disciplinary action. The Canons and Ethics Policies and Procedures are used by the Ethics Committee to apply and interpret the Rules uniformly, with reference to the general principles and concepts they embody. The Ethics Committee may also refer to applicable rulings in previous cases brought before the Committee, as well as relevant published opinions of the Ethics Committee.

* * *

THE CODE OF PROFESSIONAL ETHICS

The reliance of the public and the business community on sound financial planning and advice imposes on financial planning professionals an obligation to maintain high standards of technical competence, morality and integrity. To this end, the following Code of Professional Ethics serves as the guiding document.

CANON 1

Members should endeavor as professionals to place the public interest above their own.

Rules of Professional Conduct:

R1.1 A member has a duty to understand and abide by all Rules of Profes-

---

*Reprinted with permission of the International Association for Financial Planning.

This information is offered with the understanding that IAFP is not engaged in rendering legal, accounting, or other professional service. If legal advice or other expert assistance is required, the services of a competent professional person should be sought. The information contained in this document is offered in good faith, developed from sources deemed to be reliable, and believed to be accurate when prepared, but is offered without warranty, express or implied, as to its merchantability, fitness for a particular purpose, or any other matter. IAFP and its members disclaim all responsibility for any loss or damage arising from reliance on such information by any party. In all cases, IAFP has attempted to use the most recently available information at the time of publication.

sional Conduct which are prescribed in the Code of Professional Ethics of the Association.

R1.2 A member shall not directly or indirectly condone any act which the member is prohibited from performing by the Rules of this Code.

CANON 2

Members should seek continually to maintain and improve their professional knowledge, skills, and competence.

Rules of Professional Conduct:

R2.1 A member shall keep informed on all matters that are essential to the maintenance of the member's professional competence in the area in which he/she specializes and/or claims expertise.

CANON 3

Members should obey all laws and regulations and avoid any conduct or activity which would cause unjust harm to those who rely upon the professional judgment and skill of the members.

Rules of Professional Conduct:

R3.1 A member shall be subject to disciplinary action for professional misconduct and has the duty to know and abide by the laws and regulations and all legal limitations pertaining to the member's professional activities.

R3.2 A member shall place the needs and best interest of the client above the needs and interests of the member, the member's employees or business associates in all cases; and shall not allow the pursuit of financial gain or other personal benefit to interfere with the exercise of sound professional judgment and skills.

R3.3 In the conduct of business or professional activities, a member shall not engage in any act or omission of a dishonest, deceitful or fraudulent nature.

R3.4 a member shall not knowingly misrepresent or conceal any material limitation on the member's ability to provide the quantity or quality of service that will adequately meet the financial planning needs of the client.

R3.5 In marketing a product, a member shall not knowingly misrepresent or conceal any material limitations on the product's ability to meet the financial needs of the client, and shall scrupulously avoid any statements which are likely to mislead the client regarding the future results of any recommendation.

R3.6 A member has the duty to disclose fully and accurately the material facts representing the true costs, benefits, and limitations of any service or product recommended; and disclose any actual or potential conflict of interest that could impair objectivity.

R3.7 A member shall not disclose to another person any confidential information entrusted to or obtained by the member in the course of the member's business or professional activities, unless a disclosure of such information is required by law or is made to a person who necessarily must have the information in order to discharge legitimate occupational or professional duties.

R3.8 In the rendering of a professional service to a client, a member has the duty to maintain the type and degree of professional independence that (a) is required of practitioners in the member's occupation, or (b) is otherwise in the public interest, given the specific nature of the service being rendered.

CANON 4

Members should be diligent in the performance of their occupational duties.

Rules of Professional Conduct:

R4.1 A member shall competently and consistently discharge the member's occupational duties to every employer, client, purchaser, or user of the member's services, so long as those duties are consistent with what is in the client's best interests.

R4.2 In the making of oral or written recommendations to clients, a member shall (a) distinguish clearly between fact and opinion, (b) base the recommendations on sound professional evaluation of the client's needs, and (c) support the recommendations with appropriate research and adequate documentation of facts.

CANON 5

Members should assist in improving the public understanding of financial planning.

Rules of Professional Conduct:

R5.1 A member shall support efforts to provide lay persons with objective information concerning their financial planning needs, as well as the resources which are available to meet their needs.

R5.2 A member shall not misrepresent the benefits, costs, or limitations of any financial planning service or product, whether the product or service is offered by the member or by another individual or firm.

CANON 6

Members should use the fact of membership in a manner consistent with the Association's Rules of Professional Conduct.

Rules of Professional Conduct:

R6.1 A member shall not misrepresent the criteria for admission to Association membership, which criteria are: (1) active participation in the financial services industry; and (2) a written commitment to abide by the Bylaws and the Code of Professional Ethics of the Association.

R6.2 A member shall not misstate his/her authority to represent the Association. Specifically, a member shall not write, speak, or act in such a way as to lead another to believe that the member is officially representing the Association, unless the member has been duly authorized to do so by the officers, directors or Bylaws of the national Association.

R6.3 A member shall not use the fact of general membership in the Association for commercial purposes. A member may use the fact of general membership for the following non-commercial purposes: in resumes, prospectus, and in introductions if the speaker clearly states that the opinions and ideas presented are his/her own and not necessarily those of the Association. Fact of Division membership may be used by an individual in the Practitioner Division[1], or by a company in the Corporate or Broker-Dealer Divisions[2].

R6.4 A member or prospective member applying for Association membership shall not misrepresent any credentials or affiliations with other organizations.

CANON 7

Members should assist in maintaining the integrity of the Code of Professional Ethics of the Association.

Rules of Professional Conduct:

R7.1 A member shall not sponsor as a candidate for Association membership any person who is known by the member to engage in business or professional practices which violate the Rules of this Code.

R7.2 A member possessing unprivileged information concerning an alleged violation of this Code shall, upon request, reveal such information to the body or other authority empowered by the Association to investigate or act upon the alleged violation.

R7.3 A member shall immediately notify the IAFP Ethics Committee of any accusation or actual violation of the code of ethics of a professional credentialing organization to which they are subject and forward complete details to IAFP.

---

[1]Individual members in the Practitioner Division (those who have met the necessary requirements of the Division and have signed the Practitioner Division Certificate) may use fact of membership in the following manner:

Member, Practitioner Division,
International Association for Financial Planning

Members of the Practitioner Division should contact the compliance department of their broker-dealer to make sure any state or NASD regulatory concerns are addressed before using fact of membership for commercial purposes.

[2]Companies in the Corporate and Broker-Dealer Divisions may use fact of membership as follows:

Member, Corporate Division,
International Association for Financial Planning;
Member, Broker-Dealer Division,
International Association for Financial Planning

R7.4 A member shall immediately notify the IAFP Ethics Committee of any revocation or suspension by a state or federal licensing or regulatory agency of an investment adviser, securities, or insurance license and forward complete details to IAFP.

8. HUMAN RESOURCE MANAGEMENT

Organization

AMERICAN PAYROLL ASSOCIATION

Headquarters:
30 East 33rd Street
5th Floor
New York, NY 10016-5386
Telephone: (212) 686-2030
Fax: (212) 686-4080

Additional offices:
Membership Services
711 Navarro Street
Suite 100
San Antonio, TX 78205-1721
Telephone: (210) 226-4600
Fax: (210) 226-4027

Government Affairs
1225 I Street, NW
Washington, DC 20005-3914
Telephone: (202) 682-4775
Fax: (202) 371-8892

E-mail: apa@apa-ed.com
Website: http://www.americanpayroll.org

Date founded: 1982
Membership: approximately 15,000 professionals engaged in payroll administration and related fields, in the U.S. and other nations

Code of Ethics

Official name: *Code of Ethics*
History: Issued 1984
Authority: Board of Directors

Additional Resources

Organizational (Divisions, Programs, Services, etc.):

Certification Board
Certified Payroll Professional (CPP) program
Continuing education programs
Education and Operations Division
National Telephone Hotline Referral Service (members' questions referred
    to specialists)
National Payroll Week (public awareness campaign)
Pan Asia Payroll Association
Payroll Best Practices Conference

Informational (Publications, Videos, Seminars, etc.):

Articles in *PayTech* magazine and *Payroll Views & News*
APA Guide to Payroll Practice and Management
APA's Survey of Salaries and the Payroll Profession
Payroll Currently (tax compliance newsletter)
The Payroll Source

Goals and Activities of Organization

The American Payroll Association (APA) pursues the following objectives: to increase members' skill levels through education and support; to obtain recognition for payroll work as practiced in business and legislative environments, and as a professional discipline; to represent payroll practitioners' interests before the government; to educate the public about payroll and employment issues.

APA was founded to help payroll professionals maintain the competencies necessary to perform their jobs under rigid deadlines and close regulation. These duties include knowing how federal, state, and local tax laws affect the payroll process; administering regulations of the Internal Revenue Service, Social Security Administration, Department of Labor, Office of Child Support Enforcement, and other federal agencies; and handling withholding requirements on a variety of complex employee benefit plans.

The organization's services are designed to assist members in continual upgrading of skills and staying abreast of legislative and technological changes.

The Certified Payroll Professional (CPP) program was established to identify those who have met the APA's standard of professional competence, as demonstrated by their knowledge of payroll practice and applicable regulations.

Implementation and Enforcement of Code

The Code of Ethics is widely disseminated through publication in the *APA Directory of Members.*

The Board of Directors can censure, suspend, or expel a member for violating the Code's prohibition against "using Association activities for one's personal self-interest or financial gain." If the Board proposes sanctions, the accused member must be notified in writing of the alleged violation. A hearing is held at least 30 days after notice is served.

Payroll professionals passing the test for CPP certification must agree to abide by the Code.

History and Development of Code

The Code of Ethics was written by the APA staff and issued in 1984, two years after the organization was founded.

Code of Ethics*

1. To be mindful of the personal aspect of the payroll relationship between employer and employee and to ensure that harmony is maintained through constant concern for the Payroll Professional's fellow employees.

2. To strive for perfect compliance, accuracy and timeliness of all payroll activities.

3. To keep abreast of the state of the payroll art with regard to developments in payroll technologies.

4. To be current with legislative developments, actions on the part of regulatory bodies and the like insofar as they affect payroll.

5. To maintain the absolute confidentiality of the payroll within the procedures of the employer.

6. To refrain from using Association activities for one's personal self-interest or financial gain.

7. To take as one's commitment the enhancement of one's professional abilities through the resources of the American Payroll Association.

8. To support one's fellow Payroll Professionals both within and outside one's organization.

Organization

AMERICAN SOCIETY FOR PUBLIC ADMINISTRATION

Headquarters:
1120 G Street, NW, Suite 700
Washington, DC 20005-3885
Telephone: (202) 393-7878
Fax: (202) 638-4952
E-mail: info@aspanet.org
Website: http://www.aspanet.org

Date founded: 1939
Membership: approximately 12,000 public service professionals representing all levels of government and in education, research, and consulting, in 124 chapters

Code of Ethics

Official name: *Code of Ethics*
History: First adopted 1981, revised periodically; current version adopted 1994
Authority: Professional Ethics Committee; National Council
Code is available on Website

Additional Resources

Organizational (Divisions, Programs, Services, etc.):

Center for Accountability and Performance (CAP)
Ethics in Government Conference
Various Sections: Conference of Minority Public Administrators; Criminal Justice Administration; Ethics; Humanistic, Artistic and Reflective Expression; Management Science and Policy Analysis; Professional and Organizational Development; Public Administration Education; Public Administration Research; Public Law and Administration; Women in Public Administration

Informational (Publications, Videos, Seminars, etc.):

Articles in *Journal of Public Administration, Research and Theory; PA Times; Public Administration Review; Public Integrity;* and individual Section periodicals
An Ethics Moment column in *PA Times*
Applying Professional Standards and Ethics in the Nineties: A Workbook and Study Guide with Cases for Public Administration
CAP Federal, State, and Local *Case Studies*
Leadership and Ethics
Performance Measurement: Concepts and Techniques
Conference papers:
> *The Citizen is Always Right: Teaching Administrators to Value the People They Serve*
> *Does Trust Matter? Survey of Local Government*
> *Empirical Research on Public Administration Ethics*
> *Ethical Issues Related to Cryptography and Advertising on the Internet: A New Challenge for Government Regulators*
> *The Ethical Triangle: Synthesizing the Bases of Administrative Ethics*
> *Ethics and Entrepreneurialism*
> *The Ethics of Ethics Training*
> *The Future Fit of Policy Evaluation With Public Management: Edging Away from Conflict and Incorporating Value*
> *Global Ethics and Public Administration*
> *Leadership, Ethics and Change*
> *Professional Development Through Ethics Training: Trends, Issues and Strategies*
> *Profiting from Disaster*
> *Service Quality and Satisfaction: An Empirical Model*
> *Teaching Ethics & Values in Graduate PA Schools in the U.S.: Are We Making a Difference?*
> *Testing the Finding of the Voyeur: An Empirical Investigation of the Unethical Behavior of Public Servants*
> *Two Sides of the Same Coin: An Interpretation of Principle and Purpose in Public Administration*

Goals and Activities of Organization

The American Society for Public Administration (ASPA) is a nonprofit organization of professionals in the public sector. It strives to communicate the importance and value of public service; restore confidence in government and in public servants; encourage high ethical standards; and improve the quality of service at all levels of government, in education, and in the nonprofit private sector.

ASPA's activities include: contributing to the analysis, understanding, and resolution of public issues; recognizing excellence in public service;

advancing members' professional growth; conducting programs and conferences; and issuing policy studies and publications.

The Section on Ethics was established in 1998, consistent with ASPA's mission "to advance the science, processes, and art of public administration" by "affirming the spirit of professionalism" among members. It will offer publications, panels, sessions at conferences, a website, and an ethics online discussion list. The Center for Accountability and Performance (formerly the Government Accomplishment and Accountability Task Force) develops case studies on performance management at all levels of government. Many other entities within ASPA address issues of ethics and professionalism.

Implementation and Enforcement of Code

The Professional Ethics Committee seeks to "empower ASPA members to choose the ethical way and generate a public service culture committed to ethical excellence."

Enforcement of the Code of Ethics is conducted in accordance with ASPA's Bylaws, which provide that "it shall be grounds for investigation, notification, and expulsion . . . if a member violates ASPA's standards of professional conduct in public adminsitration. . . ."

The President must receive a signed allegation that a violation has been committed. The Executive Director investigates the matter and determines if further action is warranted, giving notice to the accused member of the investigation, charges, and right to a hearing. If the member does not resign or waive this right, the President conducts a hearing before the Executive Committee. During this "fair and equitable" proceeding, the accused has the opportunity to refute all charges, obtain counsel, and cross-examine witnesses. Expulsion requires a two-thirds vote by the Committee; reinstatement may be considered at any time.

History and Development of Code

In 1981 the National Council adopted a set of moral principles; in 1984, the Council approved a Code of Ethics. Implementation Guidelines were added later, with the expectation that they would be amended in light of changing management problems. Enforcement was not considered feasible.

The current Code, which is enforced as outlined above, was issued in 1994.

Code of Ethics*

The American Society for Public Administration (ASPA) exists to advance the science, processes, and art of public administration. The Society affirms its responsibility to develop the spirit of professionalism within its membership, and to increase public awareness of ethical principles in public service by its example. To this end, we, the members of the Society, commit ourselves to the following principles:

I Serve the Public Interest
Serve the public, beyond serving oneself.

ASPA members are committed to:
1. Exercise discretionary authority to promote the public interest.
2. Oppose all forms of discrimination and harassment, and promote affirmative action.
3. Recognize and support the public's right to know the public's business.
4. Involve citizens in policy decision-making.
5. Exercise compassion, benevolence, fairness and optimism.
6. Respond to the public in ways that are complete, clear, and easy to understand.
7. Assist citizens in their dealings with government.
8. Be prepared to make decisions that may not be popular.

II Respect the Constitution and the Law
Respect, support, and study government constitutions and laws that define responsibilities of public agencies, employees, and all citizens.

ASPA members are committed to:
1. Understand and apply legislation and regulations relevant to their professional role.
2. Work to improve and change laws and policies that are counterproductive or obsolete.
3. Eliminate unlawful discrimination.
4. Prevent all forms of mismanagement of public funds by establishing and maintaining strong fiscal and management controls, and by supporting audits and investigative activities.
5. Respect and protect privileged information.
6. Encourage and facilitate legitimate dissent activities in government and protect the whistleblowing rights of public employees.
7. Promote constitutional principles of equality, fairness, representativeness, responsiveness and due process in protecting citizens' rights.

---

*Enforcement of the Code of Ethics shall be conducted in accordance with Article I, Section 4 of ASPA's Bylaws. In 1981 the American Society for Public Administration's National Council adopted a set of moral principles. Three years later in 1984, the Council approved a Code of Ethics for ASPA members. In 1994 the Code was revised.

Reprinted with permission of the American Society for Public Administration.

III Demonstrate Personal Integrity

Demonstrate the highest standards in all activities to inspire public confidence and trust in public service.

ASPA members are committed to:
1. Maintain truthfulness and honesty and to not compromise them for advancement, honor, or personal gain.
2. Ensure that others receive credit for their work and contributions.
3. Zealously guard against conflict of interest or its appearance: e.g., nepotism, improper outside employment, misuse of public resources or the acceptance of gifts.
4. Respect superiors, subordinates, colleagues and the public.
5. Take responsibility for their own errors.
6. Conduct official acts without partisanship.

IV Promote Ethical Organizations

Strengthen organizational capabilities to apply ethics, efficiency and effectiveness in serving the public.

ASPA members are committed to:
1. Enhance organizational capacity for open communication, creativity, and dedication.
2. Subordinate institutional loyalties to the public good.
3. Establish procedures that promote ethical behavior and hold individuals and organizations accountable for their conduct.
4. Provide organization members with an administrative means for dissent, assurance of due process and safeguards against reprisal.
5. Promote merit principles that protect against arbitrary and capricious actions.
6. Promote organizational accountability through appropriate controls and procedures.
7. Encourage organizations to adopt, distribute, and periodically review a code of ethics as a living document.

V Strive for Professional Excellence

Strengthen individual capabilities and encourage the professional development of others.

ASPA members are committed to:
1. Provide support and encouragement to upgrade competence.
2. Accept as a personal duty the responsibility to keep up to date on emerging issues and potential problems.
3. Encourage others, throughout their careers, to participate in professional activities and associations.
4. Allocate time to meet with students and provide a bridge between classroom studies and the realities of public service.

Organization

ASSOCIATION OF EXECUTIVE SEARCH CONSULTANTS

Headquarters:
500 Fifth Avenue, Suite 930
New York, NY 10110
Telephone: (212) 398-9556
Fax: (212) 398-9560
E-mail: aesc@aesc.org
Website: http://www.aesc.org

Date founded: 1959
   Formerly the Association of Executive Recruiting Consultants; renamed 1982
Membership: approximately 160 executive search firms worldwide, with about 700 offices and 3,000 retained individuals

Code of Ethics

Official name: *Code of Ethics & Professional Practice Guidelines*
History: *Code* adopted 1977, *Guidelines* adopted 1984; both revised and updated 1996
Authority: AESC
Code is available on Website

Additional Resources

Organizational (Divisions, Programs, Services, etc.):

European Council
North American Council
Professional Development Program
Various committees

Informational (Publications, Videos, Seminars, etc.):

Articles in *Journal of Executive Search Consulting*
Case Study: Same Candidate, Two Searches? New AESC Ethics Guidelines in Practice
Case Study II: What Happens When Clients Want to See Your Research?

Goals and Activities of Organization

The Association of Executive Search Consultants, Inc. (AESC) is a worldwide organization of leading firms engaged in executive search consulting, a specialized form of exclusive senior-level management consulting. Executive search consultants also serve as advisors to management on human resources and executive selection issues.

The AESC's mission is to define, establish, promote, and maintain high ethical and professional standards in the field; to broaden public understanding of executive search consulting; to build the professionalism of member firms; to represent members' interests on legislative and public policy issues; and to provide a forum for the exchange of information.

Committees are organized for professional development seminars and publications; developing and communicating ethics standards and practice guidelines; clarifying the consultant's role to the person changing jobs; and addressing client concerns.

Implementation and Enforcement of Code

Individual consultants, staff, and member firms are required to adhere to the standards outlined in the Code of Ethics and Professional Practice Guidelines.

The Code is designed to guide executive search consultants in performing their duties in various professional relationships. The Guidelines represent "contemporary best practices that exemplify the standards of professionalism expected of executive search consultants."

History and Development of Code

The AESC has sought to promote high standards of professionalism among retained executive search consultants since it was founded. It adopted the Code in 1977 and the Guidelines in 1984. In 1996, with the advice of a panel of AESC member firm leaders and outside experts, these documents were revised and updated to reflect important developments in the profession and the business environment.

Code of Ethics & Professional Practice Guidelines*

INTRODUCTION

The Association of Executive Search Consultants (AESC) is an association of leading retained executive search consulting firms worldwide. Dating from its inception in 1959, the AESC has sought to promote high standards of professionalism among retained executive search consultants. In furtherance of this aim, AESC adopted a Code of Ethics in 1977, and a set of Professional Practice Guidelines in 1984. In 1996, with the advice of a panel of AESC member firm leaders and outside experts, the AESC revised and updated both the Code and the Professional Practice Guidelines to reflect important developments in the profession and the business environment.

"Retained executive search consulting" is a specialized form of senior-level management consulting, conducted through an exclusive engagement. Its purpose is to assist executives of a client organization in defining executive positions, identifying well-qualified and motivated candidates, and selecting those best suited through comprehensive, quality assured search processes.

Executive search is widely-recognized as an indispensable service to organizations worldwide and is generally built on relationships rather than discrete transactions. The services provided by executive search consultants are an integral part of the process of building and maintaining corporate, nonprofit and government clients. Like professionals in the fields of law, public accounting and general management consulting, executive search consultants have a profound influence on the organizations they serve.

AESC and its members recognize that outstanding professional service rests on the quality and integrity of relationships with clients, candidates, employees and the public. Executive search consulting firms depend on all of these groups for their continuing success, and to each group they have important responsibilities.

Clients: AESC members are partners with their clients in a consultative process aimed at selecting organizational leaders. As "leadership" can have many meanings, the professional search consultant identifies the client's specific needs and unique culture as essential elements in recruiting appropriate leaders for client organizations.

Candidates: AESC members maintain professional relationships with candidates and treat them with respect at all times. AESC members regard honesty, objectivity, accuracy and confidentiality as fundamental to their relationships with candidates.

Consultants: AESC members strive to attract and develop their own talent, building the knowledge and experience that will guide the profession into the future. Recognizing the importance of training and education to this process, AESC members provide opportunities for consultants, research professionals and other staff to improve their skills and capabilities. AESC and its member firms are partners in professional development.

The Public: AESC members understand the importance of public trust in the executive search profession. Professional search consultants stay abreast of socio-economic developments in the communities they serve and recognize the need to respond to contemporary developments such as changing demographics,

---

*Copyright © 1997 Association of Executive Search Consultants. Reprinted with permission.

new technologies and changes in the employment relationship. AESC's mission includes understanding these changes and taking constructive positions on public policy issues that affect the executive search profession, client organizations and the public.

The AESC's updated **Code of Ethics** clarifies the fundamental principles that guide executive search consultants in performing their duties and conducting their relationships with these constituencies. The **Professional Practice Guidelines** represent the AESC's view of contemporary best practices that exemplify the standards of professionalism expected of executive search consultants into the 21st Century. Underlying these principles and best practices is the expectation that AESC members will articulate and define clearly for clients the terms of their relationship and the members' commitment to perform their work professionally.

CODE OF ETHICS

* * * In order to perform their duties responsibly, AESC member firms are guided by the following ethical principles.

AESC members will:

Professionalism: conduct their activities in a manner that reflects favorably on the profession.

Integrity: conduct their business activities with integrity and avoid conduct that is deceptive or misleading.

Competence: perform all search consulting assignments competently, and with an appropriate degree of knowledge, thoroughness and urgency.

Objectivity: exercise objective and impartial judgment in each search consulting assignment, giving due consideration to all relevant facts.

Accuracy: strive to be accurate in all communications with clients and candidates and encourage them to exchange relevant and accurate information.

Conflicts of Interest: avoid, or resolve through disclosure and waiver, conflicts of interest.

Confidentiality: respect confidential information entrusted to them by clients and candidates.

Loyalty: serve their clients loyally and protect client interests when performing assignments.

Equal Opportunity: support equal opportunity in employment and objectively evaluate all qualified candidates.

Public Interest: conduct their activities with respect for the public interest.

PROFESSIONAL PRACTICE GUIDELINES

Preamble

The [AESC] strives to enhance the professionalism of its members. Accordingly, AESC has developed the following Professional Practice Guidelines to assist AESC member firms in their business relationships with clients, candidates and the public. As the profession evolves and adapts to developments in business practices, technology and law, the AESC may amend these Guidelines.

Relationships Between AESC Members and their Clients

AESC members are partners with their clients in a consultative process aimed at selecting organizational leaders. The success of these partnerships depends on excellence in client service. The following guidelines describe the processes and professional practices that contribute to outstanding client service.

Accepting Client Assignments

Outstanding client service begins with a full understanding of the client organization, its business needs and the position to be filled. An AESC member should:

- Accept only those assignments that a member is qualified to undertake on the basis of the member's knowledge of the client's needs and the member's ability to perform the specific assignment.
- Accept only those assignments that will not adversely affect the member's objectivity, loyalty and integrity.
- Disclose to present and prospective clients information known to the member about relationships, circumstances or interests that might create actual or potential conflicts of interest, and accept potential assignments only if all affected parties have expressly agreed to waive any conflict.
- Disclose to present and prospective clients limitations arising through service to other clients that may affect the member's ability to perform the search assignment.
- Base acceptances on an understanding that, among other things, defines the scope and character of the services to be provided; the identity of the client organization; the period, if any, during which the member will not recruit from the defined client organization; and the fees and expenses to be charged for the services rendered.
- Discuss with the client when advertising is required by law or is a recommended strategy for the particular search assignment.

Performing Client Assignments

Members should serve their clients with integrity and objectivity, making every effort to conduct search consulting activities on the basis of impartial consideration of relevant facts. Specifically, an AESC member should:

- Conduct an appropriate search for qualified candidates.
- Advise the client promptly, and offer alternative courses of action if it becomes apparent that no qualified candidates can be presented, or that the length of the search will differ considerably from that originally specified.
- Present information about the client, the position, and the candidate honestly and factually, and include reservations that are pertinent and important to an assignment.
- Withdraw from the assignment if a member determines that a client has characterized its organization falsely or misled candidates, provided the situation is not rectified.

- Thoroughly evaluate potential candidates, including: in-depth interviews in person or by video conferencing, verification of credentials, and careful assessment of the candidate's strengths and weaknesses, before presenting candidates for client interviews.
- Complete thorough reference checks and transmit these references to the client.
- Advise the client if advertising becomes necessary.
- Avoid the voluntary presentation of resumes in the absence of an existing client relationship.

Preserving the Confidentiality of Client Information

AESC members should use their best efforts to protect confidential information concerning their clients. Specifically, a member should:

- Use such confidential information received from clients only for purposes of conducting the assignment.
- Disclose such confidential client information only to those individuals within the firm or to potential candidates who have a need to know the information.
- Not use such confidential information for personal gain, nor provide inside information to third parties for their personal gain.

Avoiding Conflicts of Interest

AESC members should protect their integrity, objectivity and loyalty by avoiding conflicts of interest with their clients. For example, a member should:

- Refuse or withdraw from an assignment upon learning of conditions that impair the member's ability to perform services properly, including conflicts of interest that may arise during the assignment (unless all affected parties expressly agree to waive the conflict).
- Inform clients of business or personal relationships with candidates that might affect or appear to affect the member's objectivity in conducting the assignment.
- Not accept payment for assisting an individual in securing employment.
- Avoid knowingly presenting simultaneously, without disclosure to clients, the same candidate to more than one client.

Relationships Between AESC Members and Candidates

Although a member's primary relationship is with the client, member firms seek also to establish professional relationships with candidates. These relationships should be characterized by honesty, objectivity, accuracy and respect for confidentiality. In building such relationships, a member should:

- Provide candidates with relevant and accurate information about the client organization and the position.
- Present to clients accurate and relevant information about candidates, and otherwise maintain the confidentiality of information provided by prospective and actual candidates.
- Encourage candidates to provide accurate information about their qualifications. Upon learning that a candidate has misled the client or member regarding his or her qualifications, the member should reject the candidate,

unless the client, candidate and member agree that the candidacy should continue following disclosure of the facts.

- Advise prospects and candidates of the status and disposition of their candidacies in a timely fashion.
- Consider whether an individual's permission is needed before sharing his or her background information with a client and secure permission as necessary (permission should always be obtained if an executive's "resume" is submitted).
- Advise candidates of any limitations on a member firm's ability to advance them as candidates in future searches.

Relationships Between AESC Members and their Contractors

AESC members sometimes rely on contractors and subcontractors to assist in the search process. A member should:

- Avoid contractors and subcontractors whose practices are inconsistent with the standards of professionalism expected of AESC members.
- Encourage its contractors and subcontractors to adhere to the Code of Ethics and Professional Practice Guidelines.

Relationships Between AESC Members and the Public

AESC members should recognize the importance of public trust and confidence in their profession and seek to serve their clients in a manner consistent with the public interest. Therefore, a member should:

- Observe the principles of equal opportunity in employment and avoid unlawful discrimination against qualified candidates.
- Promote and advertise member firm services in a professional and accurate manner.
- Conduct relations with the media so as to reflect favorably upon the AESC, clients and the executive search consulting profession.

Organization

INTERNATIONAL PERSONNEL MANAGEMENT ASSOCIATION

Headquarters:
1617 Duke Street
Alexandria, VA 22314
Telephone: (703) 549-7100
Fax: (703) 684-0948
E-mail: ipma@ipma-hr.org
Website: http://www.ipma-hr.org

Date founded: 1973
> Formed through the consolidation of the Public Personnel Association, founded 1906, and the Society for Personnel Administration, founded 1937

Membership: approximately 5,000 agencies, individuals, and students in public sector human resources

Code of Ethics

Official name: *Statement of Principles and Values*
History: First adopted 1973; revised periodically; current version issued 1991
Authority: Executive Council

Additional Resources

Organizational (Divisions, Programs, Services, etc.):

Center for Personnel Research
Competency Training Model for Human Resource Professionals
Government Affairs Department
Human Rights Committee
IPMA Assessment Council

Informational (Publications, Videos, Seminars, etc.):

Articles in *IPMA News, Public Personnel Management,* and *Assessment Council News*

Center for Personnel Research Series: *Personnel Practices: Ethics; Disciplinary Procedures; Nepotism; Sexual Harassment; Training*; and others

Ethical Dilemmas

IPMA Assessment Council Professional Principles

Personnel Program Inventory: Emerging Trends (survey)

Position Papers on various issues

Goals and Activities of Organization

The members of the International Personnel Management Association (IPMA) are agencies and public personnel professionals, primarily in federal, state, or local government. The organization's mission is to provide leadership, education, information, and representation to these HR managers so as to advance organizational objectives and quality in the public sector.

IPMA's objectives include promoting excellence through the ongoing development of professional and ethical standards; to enhance the image of HR professionals by recognizing their contributions to public service; to foster fairness and equity through the application of merit principles and equal opportunity; and to encourage research and communication.

For members in the field of personnel assessment, the IPMA Assessment Council offers programs for the exchange of information concerning professional standards and methodology.

Implementation and Enforcement of Code

An unenforced declaration of values rather than a traditional ethics code, the IPMA *Statement* is distributed to all members. Related programs include articles and conference workshops.

History and Development of Code

The first code of ethics was adopted by IPMA's governing body in 1973. Proposed revisions are voted on by the Executive Council. The present document was revised October 5, 1991.

Statement of Principles and Values*

As a member of the International Personnel Management Association, I pledge:

- To support the Association's goals and objectives for developing the human resource management professional and the public's understanding of the role of human resource management;

- To maintain the highest standard of professional competence and of professional and personal conduct;

- To respect the dignity of all individuals, and to protect people's rights to fair and equitable treatment in all aspects of employment without regard to race, sex, religion, age, national origin, disability, or any other non-merit or non-job related factor, and to promote affirmative action;

- To support my employer's legitimate efforts for a qualified and productive workforce to accomplish my employer's mission;

- To emphasize the importance of addressing the impact of management plans and decisions on people;

- To support, mentor and counsel individuals pursuing a career in human resource management;

- To treat as privileged and confidential information accepted in trust;

- To uphold all federal, state and local laws, ordinances and regulations, and endeavor to instill in the public a sense of confidence and trust about the conduct and actions of my employer and myself;

- To avoid a conflict of interest; and

- To not compromise, for personal gain or benefit or special privilege, my integrity or that of my employer.

---

*This Code of Professional Principles and Statement of Values for the International Personnel Management Association was adopted as revised by the Executive Council on Saturday, October 5, 1991.

Copyright © International Personnel Management Association, 1617 Duke Street, Alexandria, VA 22314, 703-549-7100, www.ipma-hr.org. Reprinted with permission.

9.　INSURANCE

Organization

AMERICAN INSTITUTE FOR CHARTERED PROPERTY CASUALTY UNDERWRITERS

Headquarters:
720 Providence Road
P.O. Box 3016
Malvern, PA 19355-0716
Telephone: (610) 644-2100
Fax: (610) 640-9576
E-mail: cserv@cpcuiia.org
Website: http://www.aicpcu.org

Date founded: 1942
　　Formerly the American Institute for Property and Liability Underwriters; renamed 1992
Membership: approximately 47,000 individuals holding the Chartered Property Casualty Underwriter (CPCU) designation, and 30,000 CPCU candidates

Code of Ethics

Official name: *Code of Professional Ethics*
History: Adopted 1978; revised periodically; current edition August 1997
Authority: Executive Committee of Board of Trustees; Ethics Policy Committee; Board of Ethical Inquiry

Additional Resources

Organizational (Divisions, Programs, Services, etc.):

The American College
CPCU Society
Center for Advanced Risk Management Education
Continuing Professional Development Program
Insurance Institute of America (IIA)

Informational (Publications, Videos, Seminars, etc.):

Articles in *Solutions* magazine
Advisory Opinions of the Board of Ethical Inquiry
Disciplinary Rules, Procedures, and Penalties
Education, A Path to Professionalism (video)
Ethics, Insurance Perspectives, and Insurance Contract Analysis (course)
Insurance Issues and Professional Ethics (course)
Statement on Continuous Learning

Goals and Activities of Organization

The American Institute for Chartered Property Casualty Underwriters (Institute) is a nonprofit educational institution whose primary purpose is to establish and uphold standards for property-liability insurance professionals. It awards the Chartered Property Casualty Underwriter (CPCU) designation through a 10-part program, of which the Code is an integral feature. The Institute develops curricula, publishes books for students nationwide, and administers the CPCU examination.

The Ethics Policy Committee of the Board of Trustees and the Board of Ethical Inquiry implement established and approved ethics policies, encourage voluntary compliance, and serve as a liaison on ethics activities with other organizations.

The Center for Advanced Risk Management Education provides new courses, products, and educational services to extend and enhance members' expertise in risk management, and establishes alliances with other organizations to develop specialized and applied curricula.

Implementation and Enforcement of Code

The Code consists of two kinds of standards: Canons, which are general and aspirational, and Rules of Professional Conduct, which are specific, mandatory, and enforceable. Guidelines are designed to assist CPCUs and candidates in interpreting and applying these provisions. Violations of Canons or Guidelines, in the absence of a Rule violation, are not grounds for disciplinary action. Guidelines may be incorporated by reference into the Rules.

All applicants agree to abide by the Code and to be screened by the Board of Ethical Inquiry before they become CPCU candidates. Candidates become subject to the binding effect of the Code at the time they matriculate. Once the CPCU is conferred, the privilege to use it is conditioned on continued compliance with the Code.

Enforcement is handled by the Ethics Policy Committee, Ethics Counsel, and the Board of Ethical Inquiry. Complaints are investigated by Counsel and heard by a panel of the Board, which makes a decision and imposes a penalty, if warranted. Certain matters are reviewed or appealed to the Committee. The Board issues informal unpublished advisory opinions, as well as formal opinions published for the guidance of persons subject to the Code.

Sanctions for Code violation include private admonition, reprimand with limited publication, censure with wide publication, or suspension or revocation of the CPCU designation.

History and Development of Code

The original standard was a one-paragraph Professional Charge similar to the Golden Rule or Hippocratic Oath. In 1974 the Institute set out to develop a more comprehensive, substantive, specific code to address the changing needs of the profession. Between 1974 and 1975, a Task Force consisting of the Institute's Ad Hoc Committee on Professional Ethics, the Ethics Policy Committee, outside legal counsel, and the Board of Trustees researched, drafted, and prepared recommendations for a new Code; it was approved in 1976.

The first edition of the Institute's Code of Professional Ethics was published in 1978. It has been amended in 1983, 1984, 1991, 1995, and 1997.

Changes made through June 1997—concerning such matters as continuing education and the violation of laws and regulations—are included in the fifth edition, reproduced here.

Code of Professional Ethics*

PREAMBLE

In accordance with the basic purposes for which it was formed, the American Institute for Chartered Property Casualty Underwriters is charged with the responsibility of directing a unified effort toward professionalism on the part of CPCUs and CPCU candidates. The American Institute alone is authorized to recognize properly qualified persons with the professional designation, Chartered Property Casualty Underwriter (CPCU), which is conferred only upon individuals who have successfully completed a series of national examinations and have met the experience and ethics requirements established by the Board of Trustees. All holders of the CPCU designation (CPCUs), as well as all CPCU candidates, are expected to comply with both the letter and spirit of the ethical standards set forth explicitly in this *Code of Professional Ethics*.

The basic objective of the *Code* is to serve the public interest, not only by specifying and enforcing the minimum ethical conduct rightfully expected of CPCUs and CPCU candidates, as professionals, but also by facilitating voluntary compliance with standards considerably higher than the required minimums. Accordingly, the *Code* consists of two kinds of standards, Canons and Rules of Professional Conduct.

The Canons are general standards of an aspirational and inspirational nature, lofty goals reflecting the fundamental spirit of altruism which all true professionals share. They are maxims which on their merits serve as model standards of exemplary professional conduct. The Canons also express the general concepts and principles from which the more specific Rules are derived.

Unlike the Canons, the Rules are specific standards of a mandatory and enforceable nature. The Rules prescribe the absolute minimum level of ethical conduct required of every CPCU, regardless of occupational position. Any individual subject to the *Code* who violates a Rule will be exposed to the possibility of disciplinary action.

In addition to the *Code* per se, the Institute periodically publishes Guidelines, advisory Opinions, Summaries of Previous Rulings, and similar materials designed to assist CPCUs and CPCU candidates in interpreting the various *Code* provisions, understanding their rationale, and applying them to frequently encountered situations which require ethical judgments.[1] Individuals subject to the *Code* will be exposed to the possibility of disciplinary action for violations of any Guidelines which have been incorporated by reference into the Rules.[2] In the absence of a

---

*Fifth Edition, August 1997. Copyright ©1997 AMERICAN INSTITUTE FOR CHARTERED PROPERTY CASUALTY UNDERWRITERS. All rights reserved. May not be reproduced without the written permission of the publisher. Reprinted with permission.

[1]In all Institute ethics publications, the Rules and Guidelines are grouped and numbered schematically under one Canon with which they are closely associated. This format is largely an expositional convenience and should not be allowed to obscure the important *interrelationships* between and among the various *Code* standards which have been approved by the Board of Trustees.

[2]For example, the Guidelines on uses of the CPCU designation and CPCU key were incorporated by reference in the Rule R8.1 as of the effective date of this *Code*. Additional Guidelines may be incorporated by reference only through approval of additional Rules by the Board of Trustees.

Rule violation, violations of Canons and/or Guidelines will not constitute sufficient grounds for disciplinary action. However, it should be acknowledged that in applying the Rules and interpreting them uniformly, there may be a reference to the general principles and concepts embodied in the Canons and to applicable published rulings in previous cases. It also should be stressed that since the use of the CPCU designation is a privilege granted by the Board of Trustees and conditioned upon full compliance with the Rules of Professional Conduct, the Board of Trustees reserves the power to suspend or revoke the privilege or approve other penalties recommended by the Board of Ethical Inquiry, which is charged with the responsibility of investigating and adjudicating alleged Rule violations. Disciplinary penalties will be imposed as warranted by the severity of the offense and its attendant circumstances. All disciplinary actions will be undertaken in accordance with published procedures and penalties designed to ensure the proper enforcement of the Rules within the framework of due process and equal protection of the laws.

All CPCU candidates become subject to the binding effect of the Rules when they matriculate with the American Institute and thereafter for as long as they remain candidates. Any such candidate who violates a Rule may have conferment of the designation deferred, at the discretion of a duly authorized tribunal, until the tribunal receives convincing proof of the candidate's full and complete rehabilitation.

The Rules are also enforceable and binding upon every CPCU whose designation is conferred after the effective date of this *Code*. Any such CPCU who violates a Rule may be disciplined by any penalty available to, and imposed by, the enforcing tribunal and/or the Board of Trustees. For a CPCU whose designation was conferred prior to the effective date of this *Code,* no disciplinary penalty will be imposed unless the CPCU voluntarily elects in writing to be bound unconditionally by the mandates of the Rules. Nonetheless, all CPCUs who received their designations before the *Code*'s effective date are strongly urged to file such a written election with the American Institute, as an act of good faith and in the public interest, in order that all objectives of the *Code* may be achieved. The ultimate regulator of human behavior, of course, emerges from the depths of each individual's conscience as a personal commitment to the highest ethical standards, quite apart from whether those standards may be legally enforced. But when individuals hold themselves out to the public as professionals with common professional standards, the public has a right to expect the observance and reasonable enforcement of those standards.

Where there is a good reason for a person subject to this *Code* to be uncertain as to the ethical propriety of a specific activity or type of conduct, that person should refrain from engaging in such activity or conduct until the matter has been clarified. Any CPCU or CPCU candidate who needs assistance in interpreting the *Code* may request an advisory opinion from the American Institute's Board of Ethical Inquiry.[3] Unpublished opinions issued by the Board of Ethical Inquiry are informal and intended solely for the guidance of the individuals to whom they are issued, whereas published Opinions are formal and intended for the guidance

---

[3]An advisory opinion may be obtained by writing to the Board of Ethical Inquiry, American Institute * * *. Only the Board of Ethical Inquiry is authorized to issue such opinions on behalf of the American Institute. In no event will the identity of any inquirer be revealed outside this Board; however, the general nature of an inquiry may be published, together with an advisory Opinion, if it warrants a formal, published reponse.

of all persons subject to the *Code*. Every published Opinion except those identified with the prefix "HCS," below, will have a specified effective date, after which it may be used in interpreting and applying the Rules.[4] An advisory opinion which pertains exclusively to the application or interpretation of a Canon or a Guideline will not become binding on any individual unless and until it has been officially approved and has become effective as an addition or amendment to the Rules of Professional Conduct. Nevertheless, inquiries concerning *all* aspects of the *Code* are strongly encouraged since the ultimate goal is to *prevent* unethical conduct before it occurs, apart from whether it may result in the imposition of a penalty on a violator. Such inquiries also will stimulate continuing improvements in the *Code* by testing its inherent clarity, depth, and scope.

CANON 1

CPCUs should endeavor at all times to place the public interest above their own.

Rules of Professional Conduct

R1.1 A CPCU has a duty to understand and abide by all Rules of conduct which are prescribed in the *Code of Professional Ethics* of the American Institute.

R1.2 A CPCU shall not advocate, sanction, participate in, cause to be accomplished, otherwise carry out through another, or condone any act which the CPCU is prohibited from performing by the Rules of this *Code*.

Guidelines for Professional Conduct

G1.1 By stipulating at the outset that "CPCUs Should Endeavor at All Times to Place the Public Interest Above Their Own," Canon 1 serves as the fundamental goal of the entire *Code of Professional Ethics*. The other *Code* Standards are essentially attempts to define the "public interest" (and hence the ethical obligations of CPCUs) in more specific terms. Accordingly, the format of the *Code* is best understood by reading Canon 1, asking the question "how?" and then reading the first two Rules. That is to say, how do CPCUs go about endeavoring at all times to place the public interest above their own? Answer: at a *minimum,* by understanding and obeying all the Rules in the *Code* (as specified in R1.1 and R1.2) and then, beyond the expected minimums, by *striving* to meet the more lofty standards expressed in the Canons and the Guidelines.

The aspirational goal of Canon 1 is more easily expressed than achieved. Indeed, one doubts whether any profession can ultimately make good the claim that all of its practitioners are forever guided by an attitude of altruism and a spirit of unselfish devotion to the needs of others. Nonetheless, a formal

---

[4]Opinions with the prefix "HCS" pertain to hypothetical case studies designed for educational purposes and are intended to indicate to the reader the manner in which the Board of Ethical Inquiry might generally react to a broad inquiry on the topic addressed. Because the cases are purely hypothetical, they shall not serve as precedent for any action by the Board of Ethical Inquiry or Ethics Policy Committee. Furthermore, to further enhance their educational value, these opinions frequently contain additional commentary that might not be essential to reach the conclusion.

commitment to altruism is probably the single most important characteristic which distinguishes professional from unprofessional behavior.

G1.2 In the performance of his or her professional services, a CPCU should avoid even the appearance of impropriety and should generally do or act each day in a manner that will best serve the CPCU's own professional interests in the long run. This Guideline, when taken along with the other provisions of the *Code,* should pose no insurmountable problems of priority in the context of most everyday situations, since the best long-term professional interests of a CPCU ordinarily do not conflict either with the public interest or with other specific interests. However, it should be acknowledged that potential conflicts of interest may arise, or may appear to arise, because many CPCUs simultaneously serve two or more "masters," and they must somehow balance the various interests with their own personal interests and the best interests of the general public. For example, a CPCU who is employed by an insurance company may serve his or her immediate superior, the corporation, the stockholders, the policyholders, agents, and industry associations. An agent may serve his or her clients, two or more insurers, and his or her business partners, stockholders, or associates.

Strict compliance with all the Rules of this *Code,* including R1.2, should enable a CPCU to resolve such potential conflicts of interest which may arise. However, when there is good reason for a person subject to the *Code* to be uncertain as to the ethical propriety of a specific activity or type of conduct, that person should refrain from engaging in such activity or conduct until the matter has been clarified. Any CPCU or CPCU candidate who needs assistance in interpreting the *Code* is encouraged to request an advisory opinion from the American Institute's Board of Ethical Inquiry.

G1.3 The ethical obligation to place the public interest above personal interests or financial gain extends to every CPCU, regardless of whether or not the CPCU's occupational position requires direct contact with actual or prospective insurance consumers.

G1.4 Nothing in these Guidelines should be interpreted to mean that insurance purchasers should be given priority over deserving insurance claimants since the needs and best interests of insurance purchasers are in fact served only when all deserving insurance claimants, including third-party liability claimants, are accorded prompt, equitable, and otherwise fair treatment.

CANON 2

CPCUs should seek continually to maintain and improve their professional knowledge, skills, and competence.

Rules of Professional Conduct

R2.1 A CPCU shall keep informed on those technical matters that are essential to the maintenance of the CPCU's professional competence in insurance, risk management, or related fields.

Guidelines for Professional Conduct

G2.1 Though knowledge and skills alone do not ensure that an individual will adhere to high ethical standards, knowledge and skills are requisites to the high levels of competence and performance rightfully expected of all professionals. Indeed, to the extent that an individual purports to be a professional and yet does not maintain high levels of competence and performance, that individual engages in unethical conduct which is in the nature of a misrepresentation.

In order to earn the CPCU designation, every CPCU candidate demonstrated a mastery of insurance and related subjects by successfully completing a series of rigorous qualifying examinations of the American Institute for Chartered Property Casualty Underwriters. However, for any individual to maintain and improve the knowledge and skills which are requisites to high levels of competence and performance, it is essential for that individual to continue studying throughout his or her working life. This is especially true for practitioners in a business like insurance, which is characterized not only by its existing complexities but also by rapid changes in the business and in the legal, economic, and social environment within which it operates.

In recognition of the foregoing, each and every CPCU has an *ethical* obligation to engage actively and continuously in appropriate educational activities.

G2.2 At a *minimum,* as specified in Rule R2.1, "A CPCU shall keep informed on those technical matters that are essential to the maintenance of the CPCU's professional competence in insurance, risk management, or related fields." Since CPCUs serve as agents, brokers, underwriters, claims representatives, actuaries, risk managers, regulators, company executives and specialists in a wide variety of insurance-related fields, the Rule does not attempt to prescribe the specific technical matters that are essential to the maintenance of professional competence in each of the numerous specialties. Instead, it is left to the judgment of each CPCU to decide, in the light of his or her occupational position, the content and form of continuing education that will satisfy the ethical obligation under R2.1.

G2.3 A number of other professions have established mandatory continuing education requirements, under the terms of which a member usually faces severe penalties unless he or she periodically certifies that at least one of the specified continuing education options has been met. At present and for the foreseeable future, the Trustees of the American Institute have no plans to require CPCUs to certify periodically that they have met the obligations under Rule R2.1. However, because the maintenance of professional competence is considered a minimum obligation of every CPCU, it has been given the status of a Rule under the *Code.* The Board of Ethical Inquiry will investigate alleged violations of Rule 2.1, and it may impose upon violators such penalties as are warranted. Furthermore, if a CPCU is accused of violating any other Rule in the *Code,* the Board may, at its discretion, require the accused to furnish evidence of compliance with Rule 2.1.

G2.4 Beyond the minimum continuing education requirements referred to in Rule 2.1, all CPCUs are urged to engage in such additional pursuits as will meet the aspirational goal, under Canon 2, of *improving* their professional knowledge, skills, and competence.

For example, the Board of Ethical Inquiry suggests that every CPCU should qualify for recognition under the Continuing Professional Development (CPD) Program which is jointly sponsored by the American Institute and the CPCU Society. The CPD program recognizes those who have met specific criteria. The requirements of the CPD program, which are revised from time to time, are automatically distributed to CPCUs who are members of the CPCU Society and are available to others on request. Current criteria, with points assigned to various activities, include the following:

- Passing an exam or course in a nationally known insurance or business-related program.
- Passing a college or university course in insurance, risk management, or a business-related subject.
- Teaching a course in insurance, risk management, or a business-related subject.
- Authoring or co-authoring an article accepted for publication in the *CPCU Journal* or similar business publication, a CPCU Society section newsletter, or a textbook.
- Conducting a research project.
- Serving as an officer, director, committee chair, or committee member of a national insurance organization or local CPCU chapter.
- Serving as a class coordinator for a CPCU chapter or other course-sponsoring organization.
- Serving on a state insurance advisory committee.
- Grading IIA or CPCU exams.
- Serving on exam development committees for IIA, CPCU, state licensing, or other examination programs.
- Attending the CPCU Annual Meeting and Seminars or the annual meetings of other national insurance organizations.
- Attending educational meetings, seminars, videoconferences, or workshops sponsored by the CPCU Society or others.
- Attending meetings of CPCU chapters or other insurance organizations that include a speaker or an educational program.
- Meeting state continuing education requirements for licensing.
- Being an expert witness.
- Serving as a personal sponsor for CPCU and IIA students.

In 1997 the Board of Trustees of the American Institute reaffirmed its earlier position by adopting the following position:

Continuous Learning for CPCUs

1. We reaffirm that the Code of Professional Ethics of the American Institute requires all CPCUs to continue their professional development, as expressed in the *Statement on Continuous Learning* (below).
2. Because CPCUs are a diverse group with diverse learning needs, we reject the idea of a policing program to determine whether CPCUs have met a defined, measurable minimum standard.
3. We continue to support the Continuing Professional Development (CPD) program, jointly administered by the American Institute and the CPCU Society.
4. We intend to expand Institute services to help CPCUs maintain and enhance their knowledge in a rapidly changing, increasingly complex world.

Statement on Continuous Learning

Continuous learning has always been mandatory for CPCUs subject to the *Code*. Rule R2.1 under Canon 2 of the *CPCU Code of Professional Ethics* requires

CPCUs to "keep informed on those technical matters that are essential to the maintenance of the CPCU's professional competence in insurance, risk management, or related fields." As pointed out in Guideline G2.1, "each and every CPCU has an *ethical* obligation to engage actively and continuously in appropriate educational activities.

Although the CPCU Society and the American Institute for CPCU jointly administer a voluntary Continuing Professional Development program, the American Institute has never imposed a mandatory reporting system for determining whether all CPCUs have complied with Rule R2.1. In fact, Guideline G2.2 states that "it is left to the judgment of each CPCU to decide, in light of his or her occupational position, the content and form of continuing education that will satisfy the ethical obligation under Rule R2.1." However, Guideline G2.3 allows the Board of Ethical Inquiry, while conducting investigations of other alleged violations of the *Code,* to "require the accused to furnish evidence of compliance with Rule R2.1."

Virtually any mandatory system that the American Institute could implement for determining whether CPCUs have complied with Rule R2.1 would entail the use of an artificial minimum standard. Such a system, by emphasizing an artificial minimum, would serve to undermine the responsibility of each CPCU to identify and pursue "appropriate educational activities."

CANON 3

CPCUs should obey all laws and regulations, and should avoid any conduct or activity which would cause unjust harm to others.

Rules of Professional Conduct

R3.1 In the conduct of business or professional activities, a CPCU shall not engage in any act or omission of a dishonest, deceitful, or fraudulent nature.

R3.2 A CPCU shall not allow the pursuit of financial gain or other personal benefit to interfere with the exercise of sound professional judgment and skills.

R3.3 A CPCU shall not violate any law or regulation relating to professional activities or commit any felony.

Guidelines for Professional Conduct

G3.1 A CPCU should neither misrepresent nor conceal a fact or information which is material to determining the suitability, efficacy, scope, or limitations of an insurance contract or surety bond. Nor should a CPCU materially misrepresent or conceal the financial condition, or the quality of services, of any insurer or reinsurer. The extent to which a CPCU should volunteer information and facts must necessarily be left to sound professional judgment of what is required under the circumstances. This Guideline is intended to illustrate the kinds of acts and omissions which can be "dishonest, deceitful, or fraudulent," in violation of Rule R3.1, and which normally "would cause unjust harm to others," thus violating the spirit of Canon 3.

G3.2 A CPCU should not, to the detriment of the insuring public, engage in any business practice or activity designed to restrict fair competition. However, this Guideline does not prohibit a CPCU's participation in a legally enforceable covenant not to compete, in a rating bureau, or in a similar activity specifically sanctioned or required by law.

G3.3 In the performance of the CPCU's own occupational function, a CPCU should not deliberately achieve or seek to achieve, at the expense of the uninformed, financial gains for the CPCU, or the CPCU's employer, which are unconscionable relative to the customary gains for the quantity and quality of services actually rendered.

Generally, no CPCU should seek or accept compensation which is neither for nor commensurate with professional services actually rendered or to be rendered. Nor should any CPCU seek or accept compensation under any other terms, conditions, or circumstances which would violate any Canon, Guideline, or Rule in this *Code*. However, nothing in this Guideline is intended to prohibit the seeking or acceptance of gifts from family or personal friends, income from investments, or income from any other activity which would neither (a) prevent or inherently impair the free and complete exercise of the CPCU's sound professional judgment and skills nor (b) otherwise violate this *Code*.

A CPCU should not perform professional services under terms, conditions, or circumstances which would prevent or inherently impair the free and complete exercise of the CPCU's sound professional judgment and skills. This guideline does not prohibit a CPCU from being compensated under the terms of a legally acceptable commission arrangement since such an arrangement, in itself, does not prevent or inherently impair the CPCU's sound professional judgment and skills. But it does serve to remind a CPCU so compensated of his or her ethical obligation to avoid any recommendation to a consumer of the CPCU's services that would increase the CPCU's compensation, unless such recommendation clearly meets the consumer's legitimate needs and best interests. The guideline also serves to remind every CPCU, regardless of his or her basis of compensation, of the ethical obligation to render fully such services as are contemplated and rightfully owed under the terms of the applicable compensation arrangement.

G3.4 While the Institute's standards of ethical conduct are by no means limited to the duties and obligations imposed upon CPCUs by the laws and regulations which govern the conduct of all insurance practitioners, obedience to and respect for law and regulatory authority should be viewed as an absolute minimum standard of professional conduct below which no CPCU should fall. The potential consequences of violating this admonition extend beyond those which may fall upon the violator since one CPCU may indeed bring discredit upon the CPCU designation, and thus all who hold it, by violating laws or regulations which govern the conduct of a CPCU's business activities.

A CPCU is obligated to keep fully informed of each and every law and regulation governing or otherwise pertaining to his business activities. In so doing, a CPCU should not hesitate to seek interpretive assistance from the appropriate regulatory officials and/or retain the services of competent legal counsel. When in doubt as to the legality of a particular kind of business conduct or activity, the CPCU should refrain from such conduct or activity.

A CPCU may not plead lack of knowledge as a defense for improper conduct under Rule 3.3, unless the CPCU can demonstrate that he or she had made a reasonable effort in good faith to obtain such knowledge, and it was not available.

CANON 4

CPCUs should be diligent in the performance of their occupational duties and should continually strive to improve the functioning of the insurance mechanism.

Rules of Professional Conduct

R4.1 A CPCU shall competently and consistently discharge his or her occupational duties.

R4.2 A CPCU shall support efforts to effect such improvements in claims settlement, contract design, investment, marketing, pricing, reinsurance, safety engineering, underwriting, and other insurance operations as will both inure to the benefit of the public and improve the overall efficiency with which the insurance mechanism functions.

Guidelines for Professional Conduct

G4.1 From one who purports to be a true professional, the public has a right to expect both competence, in the sense of abilities, and diligent performance, in the sense of consistently applying those abilities in the service of others. Thus, to complement Rule R2.1, which obligates a CPCU to maintain professional competence by keeping informed, the Institute also promulgated Rule R4.1, which stipulates that "a CPCU shall competently and consistently *discharge* his or her occupational duties."

Although the Board of Ethical Inquiry earnestly believes that diligent performance should be an ethical obligation of all professionals, including CPCUs, the Board will not intervene or arbitrate between the parties in an employment or contractual relationship or civil dispute. Nor does the Board feel that the Institute's disciplinary procedures should become a substitute for legal and other remedies available to such parties. In the event of an alleged violation of Rule R4.1, therefore, the Board will hear the case only after all other remedies have been exhausted, and it generally will take disciplinary action only under circumstances where (1) a proven violation has caused unjust harm to another person, and the violation brings substantial discredit upon the CPCU designation; or, (2) it would otherwise be in the *public* interest to take disciplinary action under the ethics code.

G4.2 In addition to competently and consistently discharging his or her own occupational duties, a CPCU is obligated by Rule R4.2 "to support efforts to effect such improvements (in insurer functions and operations) as will both inure to the benefit of the public and improve the overall efficiency with which the insurance mechanism functions." Note that the obligation is to support the kinds of improvements which will *both* improve the efficiency of the insurance mechanism *and* benefit the public. The drafters of the *Code* worded the rule in this fashion to focus attention on the fact that it is possible to effect improvements in insurer efficiency and profitability at least in the short run, in a manner contrary to the public interest. Granted, it is sometimes very difficult to determine whether a proposed change will both improve overall efficiency and inure to the benefit of the public, but the ethical obligation, consistent with the theme expressed in Canon 1, is to support *efforts* to effect such improvements. The kinds of efforts which satisfy both criteria, and which the Board feels a CPCU should support, are illustrated in the Guidelines immediately following.

G4.3 A CPCU should assist in improving the language, suitability, adaptability, and general efficacy of insurance contracts and surety bonds.

G4.4 A CPCU should assist in ensuring protection and security for the public, and in maintaining and improving the integrity of the insurance institution, by helping to preserve and improve the financial strength of all private insurers.

G4.5 A CPCU should assist in providing an adequate supply of insurance and surety bonds to meet public demands and needs.

G4.6 A CPCU should do the utmost to assist in minimizing the cost to the public of insurance and suretyship, without compromising the quality of benefits or services they provide, not only by helping to improve the operational efficiency of insurers and their representatives but also by contributing to the solution of economic, legal, political and other social problems which demonstrably increase the cost of insurance and suretyship without enhancing their quality or otherwise improving the public well-being. Examples of such problems include, though are not limited to, inflation, unemployment, crime, inequities and inefficiencies in our legal system, inequities and inefficiencies in our health care delivery system, riots, floods and other highly destructive natural catastrophes, and the physical deterioration of property in the nation's cities. The ready availability of insurance alone will not solve such problems. And a CPCU should not neglect his or her personal duty, as a good citizen and a professional, to become actively involved in the search for underlying causes of, and long-run solutions to, such problems.

G4.7 Because of a CPCU's professional capabilities and firsthand knowledge of a tragic magnitude of human and dollar losses suffered annually, a CPCU should assume an especially active role in private and public loss prevention and reduction efforts. A CPCU should do the utmost to preserve each and every human life, maintain and improve the physical and mental health of all human beings, and prevent the damage, destruction, and abstraction of property.

G4.8 A CPCU should make an effort to participate in and support research which promises to assist in improving the functioning of the private insurance mechanism and/or in reducing losses of life, health, or property.

G4.9 The ethical obligation under this *Code* to strive for improvement in the functioning of the private insurance mechanism does not bar a CPCU from serving in the public sector. Nor does it bar a CPCU, as an *individual* citizen, from supporting a governmental role in providing economic security for the citizenry. But a CPCU should be mindful of the restriction imposed by Rule R8.4, and should avoid even the appearance of speaking on behalf of the Institute, especially on political matters.

CANON 5

CPCUs should assist in maintaining and raising professional standards in the insurance business.

Rules of Professional Conduct

R5.1 A CPCU shall support personnel policies and practices which will attract qualified individuals to the insurance business, provide them with ample and equal opportunities for advancement, and encourage them to aspire to the highest levels of professional competence and achievement.

R5.2 A CPCU shall encourage and assist qualified individuals who wish to pursue CPCU or other studies which will enhance their professional competence.

R5.3 A CPCU shall support the development, improvement, and enforcement of such laws, regulations, and codes as will foster competence and ethical conduct on the part of all insurance practitioners and inure to the benefit of the public.

R5.4 A CPCU shall not withhold information or assistance officially requested by appropriate regulatory authorities who are investigating or prosecuting any alleged violation of the laws or regulations governing the qualifications or conduct of insurance practitioners.

Guidelines for Professional Conduct

G5.1 A CPCU should assist in the raising of professional standards in the insurance business. At a minimum, every CPCU should conduct his or her own business activities in a manner which will, by the CPCU's precept and example, inspire other practitioners to do likewise.

G5.2 Both the insuring public and the insurance industry will benefit from continued growth in the number of insurance practitioners who achieve a high level of professional attainment. Thus, Rule R5.2 stipulates that "A CPCU shall encourage and assist qualified individuals who wish to pursue CPCU or other studies which will enhance their professional competence."

A CPCU should share with all other insurance practitioners, as well as fellow CPCUs, the benefits of the CPCU's professional attainments. A CPCU's conduct should be guided by a spirit of altruistic concern for the public interest, and the public interest is best served when all insurance practitioners are well informed.

Moreover, any professional who has acquired a unified body of knowledge is invariably indebted to innumerable predecessors and contemporaries for having made available the benefits of their professional attainments, that is, for having shared freely with others their knowledge, accumulated experiences, skills, and insights into understanding. So also should a CPCU, as a professional who has subscribed to high ethical standards, share freely with contemporaries and, thus, future generations, the benefits of his or her own professional attainments, apart from any hope or expectation of immediate financial gain, because of the CPCU's ethical obligations to repay an indebtedness to forebears, contribute to the efficient advancement of human knowledge, and manifest an altruistic concern for the public interest.

A CPCU should support and participate in educational activities which will assist other practitioners in their professional development. Examples of such activities include seminars, lectures, research projects, teaching, preparation of educational materials for training programs, and preparation of professional articles for professional or lay publications. In writing or speaking publicly as a CPCU, however, the CPCU should maintain the dignity and high professional standards appropriate to the designation.

This Guideline does not obligate a CPCU to divulge trade secrets or other information which would put the CPCU at a competitive disadvantage. Instead, it serves as a reminder that just as the truly professional physician demonstrates a commitment to the advancement of medicine by sharing his or her knowledge and experiences with other physicians and aspiring physicians, so also should a CPCU play a role in the development of the field of insurance, in part by sharing knowledge with other practitioners as well as students.

CANON 6

CPCUs should strive to establish and maintain dignified and honorable relationships with those whom they serve, with fellow insurance practitioners, and with members of other professions.

Rules of Professional Conduct

R6.1 A CPCU shall keep informed on the legal limitations imposed upon the scope of his or her professional activities.

R6.2 A CPCU shall not disclose to another person any confidential information entrusted to, or obtained by, the CPCU in the course of the CPCU's business or professional activities, unless a disclosure of such information is required by law or is made to a person who necessarily must have the information in order to discharge legitimate occupational or professional duties.

R6.3 In rendering or proposing to render professional services for others, a CPCU shall not knowingly misrepresent or conceal any limitations on the CPCU's ability to provide the quantity or quality of professional services required by the circumstances.

Guidelines for Professional Conduct

G6.1 First and foremost by exhibiting high levels of professional competence and ethical conduct, a CPCU should constantly strive to *merit* the confidence and respect of those whom they serve, fellow practitioners, and members of other professions.

G6.2 A CPCU should strive to establish and maintain dignified and honorable relationships with competitors, as well as with other fellow practitioners.

G6.3 A CPCU should strive to establish and maintain dignified and honorable relationships with members of other professions, including but not limited to law, medicine, and accounting. The insurance industry relies heavily on the expertise and cooperation of such professionals in fulfilling its obligation to deliver insurance benefits promptly and otherwise render high quality insurance services to the public.

G6.4 Like other professionals, a CPCU should maintain the knowledge and skills necessary to exercise independent judgment in the performance of his or her professional services. However, a CPCU should always be mindful of his or her personal limitations. A CPCU should not hesitate to seek the counsel of other professionals, therefore, not only at the request of those whom the CPCU may serve but also on the CPCU's own initiative, particularly in doubtful or difficult situations or when the quality of professional service may otherwise be enhanced by such consultation.

G6.5 A CPCU is obligated to keep fully informed on any and all legal limitations imposed upon the scope of his or her professional activities. A CPCU should always exercise caution to avoid engaging in, or giving the appearance of engaging in, the unauthorized practice of law. However, nothing herein should be construed as prohibiting the practice of law by a CPCU who is otherwise qualified by virtue of his or her admission to the bar.

G6.6 Beyond the obligations under Rule R6.2, a CPCU should exercise caution and sound judgment in dealing with any confidential or privileged information.

CANON 7

CPCUs should assist in improving the public understanding of insurance and risk management.

Rules of Professional Conduct

R7.1 A CPCU shall support efforts to provide members of the public with objective information concerning their risk management and insurance needs, and the products, services, and techniques which are available to meet their needs.

R7.2 A CPCU shall not misrepresent the benefits, costs, or limitations of any risk management technique or any product or service of an insurer.

Guidelines for Professional Conduct

G7.1 Fulfillment of all the public's insurance needs would appreciably enhance the economic and social well-being of society. But the public's insurance needs can be fully met only if every citizen recognizes his or her insurance needs and appreciates the importance of seeking competent and ethical assistance in analyzing and meeting these needs. The achievement of this result requires the combined efforts of all knowledgeable insurance professionals. Accordingly, every CPCU should assist in every practical manner to improve the public understanding of insurance and risk management even if the CPCU does not specialize in insurance education, marketing, claims settlement, safety engineering, advertising, or other professional activities which provide frequent opportunities to communicate directly to the public.

G7.2 A CPCU should keep abreast of legislation, changing conditions and/or other developments which may affect the insuring public, and should assist in keeping the public informed of such.

G7.3 In order to contribute to a better public understanding of insurance and risk management, it is essential for every CPCU to maintain and improve his or her own knowledge and communicative skills. However, no CPCU should hesitate to admit freely that he or she does not know the answer to a question. Nor should a CPCU attempt to answer such a question if it lies outside the realm of the CPCU's professional competence, authority, or proper function.

G7.4 A CPCU should neither engage in nor condone deceptive advertising or business practices which significantly mislead the public or otherwise contribute to the widespread misunderstanding or misuse of insurance. The minimum goal of all a CPCU's communications with the public should be to provide objective and factual information.

G7.5 It is highly desirable for the public to recognize its overall risk management needs and the limitations and advantages of insurance in meeting such needs. For instance, a CPCU should seize every opportunity to stress the importance of loss prevention and reduction in any well-conceived risk management program.

G7.6 Rule R7.1 stipulates that "A CPCU shall support efforts to provide members of the public with objective information concerning their risk management and insurance needs, and the products, services, and techniques which are available to meet their needs." Both in the Rules and in the Guidelines above, the needs referred to are those which exist (at a point in time, understood) and the products, services, and techniques referred to are those which are available (at a point in time, understood). Neither the Rules nor the Guidelines require a CPCU to support lobbying efforts or proposed legislation, or the taking of positions on controversial issues. Nor do any of the *Code* standards prohibit a CPCU from engaging in such activities, in his or her own name and as an individual. However, a CPCU who elects to engage in such activities should take great care to avoid violating Rule R8.4.

CANON 8

CPCUs should honor the integrity of the CPCU designation and respect the limitations placed on its use.

Rules of Professional Conduct

R8.1 A CPCU shall use the CPCU designation and the CPCU key only in accordance with the relevant Guidelines promulgated by the American Institute.

R8.2 A CPCU shall not attribute to the mere possession of the designation depth or scope of knowledge, skills, and professional capabilities greater than those demonstrated by successful completion of the CPCU program.

R8.3 A CPCU shall not make unfair comparisons between a person who holds the CPCU designation and one who does not.

R8.4 A CPCU shall not write, speak, or act in such a way as to lead another to reasonably believe the CPCU is officially representing the American Institute, unless the CPCU has been duly authorized to do so by the American Institute.

Guidelines for Professional Conduct

G8.1 Rule 8.1 of the *Code of Professional Ethics* stipulates that "A CPCU shall use the CPCU designation and the CPCU key only in accordance with the relevant Guidelines promulgated by the American Institute." These Guidelines, which define and impose restrictions upon the privilege to use the CPCU designation and key, are set forth below. They are designed to prevent undignified commercialization of the designation, unfair comparisons with able and well-established insurance practitioners who do not hold the designation, and other unethical practices which are inconsistent with the professional concepts which CPCU represents. Specifically, every CPCU has an ethical obligation to comply with the following minimum standards:

a. The designation Chartered Property Casualty Underwriter, the initials CPCU, and the CPCU key may be used only in a dignified and professional manner.

1. The designation or initials may be used after the holder's name on business cards, stationery, office advertising, signed articles, business and professional listings, and telephone listings, except where such use would conflict with the provisions of subparagraph a.3. below.

2. The CPCU key (actual size or reduced, but not enlarged) may be imprinted only on business cards and stationery used exclusively by CPCUs. Copies of the CPCU key suitable for reproduction are available from the American Institute.

3. The CPCU designation being personal in nature, the designation itself, the initials CPCU, and the CPCU key are not to be used as part of a firm, partnership, or corporate name, trademark, or logo, or affixed to any object, product, property, or for any purpose whatsoever, except by the American Institute.

b. The designation Chartered Property Casualty Underwriter, the initials CPCU, and the CPCU key may be used to announce the conferment of the designation.

1. News releases prepared by the American Institute are mailed to all new CPCU designees. Only these approved releases, with the addition of personal biographical information, may be used by individual CPCU designees in preparing material for the business and community press.

2. Announcement cards may be purchased from the American Institute, or printed locally using a reproduction copy supplied by the Institute without charge, to send to friends, relatives, associates, and clients.

3. The American Institute encourages employers of new designees to publish in company publications articles congratulating the new designees. The American Institute's official listing of new designees, published at the time of the conferment ceremony, should be used to verify the names of new designees. Copies of the CPCU key are available from the American Institute for reproduction in such articles.

4. The American Institute encourages the appearance of dignified advertisements congratulating new designees on earning the CPCU designation. Copies of the CPCU key are available from the American Institute for reproduction in such advertisements. These advertisements must be strictly congratulatory in nature, however, and should not include the business conducted by the firm, the lines of insurance carried by the firm, the firm's telephone number, or any copy soliciting business.

c. The designation Chartered Property Casualty Underwriter, the initials CPCU, and the CPCU key may be used by the CPCU Society in a manner which complies with the Rules and Guidelines of the American Institute's *Code of Professional Ethics,* and which has first been authorized in writing by the American Institute's Management Council.

d. The designation Chartered Property Casualty Underwriter, the initials CPCU, and the CPCU key may not be used in any manner which violates a Rule of the *Code of Professional Ethics.* Rules 8.2, 8.3, and 8.4 deserve special mention in this context since they relate directly to, and impose restrictions upon, the privilege to use the CPCU designation.

e. The designation Chartered Property Casualty Underwriter, the initials CPCU, and the CPCU key may be used in any other manner which has received prior approval in writing from the American Institute's Management Council.

Any questions regarding the interpretation of these Guidelines should be directed to the American Institute's Board of Ethical Inquiry. A prompt response will be made to all such requests.

G8.2 Rule R8.2 stipulates that "A CPCU shall not attribute to the *mere possession of the designation* (emphasis supplied) depth or scope of knowledge, skills, and professional capabilities greater than those demonstrated by successful completion of the CPCU program." Unless this Rule is strictly observed by all CPCUs, the public will be misled and the integrity of the designation, as well as the integrity of the violator, will be significantly diminished.

CPCUs can be justifiably proud of having passed the rigorous qualifying exams and of having met the ethical and experience requirements imposed by the American Institute. But the CPCU curriculum, comprehensive though it is, does not in itself make a person an expert in every insurance and insurance-related area. Moreover, the CPCU curriculum has been periodically altered over the years to accommodate revised educational needs and objectives.

Consider, for instance, the case of an agent whose CPCU designation was conferred in a year prior to 1978. Such an agent would clearly violate R8.2 if he or she led a prospective client to believe that the possession of the CPCU designation made him or her a qualified expert in life, health, or group insurance, particularly since the curriculum at that time provided little or no study or testing in these areas. The agent might otherwise have become a qualified expert in life, health, or group insurance, perhaps through experience and/or other formal educational programs, but it would be unethical to attribute this expertise to his or her possession of the CPCU designation per se. In short, the public is protected and the integrity of the designation and its holder are best preserved by avoiding any misrepresentations of the nature and significance of the CPCU designation.

CANON 9

CPCUs should assist in maintaining the integrity of the *Code of Professional Ethics*.

Rules of Professional Conduct

R9.1 A CPCU shall not initiate or support the CPCU candidacy of any individual known by the CPCU to engage in business practices which violate the ethical standards prescribed by this *Code*.

R9.2 A CPCU possessing unprivileged information concerning an alleged violation of this *Code* shall, upon request, reveal such information to the tribunal or other authority empowered by the American Institute to investigate or act upon the alleged violation.

R9.3 A CPCU shall report promptly to the American Institute any information concerning the use of the CPCU designation by an unauthorized person.

Guidelines for Professional Conduct

G9.1 It is *not* an objective of the American Institute to achieve growth in the number of CPCUs at the expense of professional standards, but rather to encourage more qualified individuals to meet the high standards which have always characterized the CPCU designation requirements. A CPCU should assist in upholding the experience, educational, and ethical standards prescribed for prospective CPCU designees by the American Institute for Chartered Property Casualty Underwriters.

G9.2 A CPCU should assist the American Institute in preserving the integrity of the *Code of Professional Ethics,* first and foremost by *voluntarily* complying with both the letter and the spirit of the *Code.* Ultimately, however, the public can be protected and the integrity of the *Code* can be maintained only if the *Code* is strictly but fairly enforced, and this, in turn, can be achieved only if *Code* violations are promptly brought to the attention of the proper officials. Although a CPCU should not become a self-appointed investigator or judge on matters properly left to the Board of Ethical Inquiry, every CPCU should comply with the mandates of Rules R9.1, R9.2, and R9.3. Except for the comparatively rare but troublesome situation covered by R9.3, whether a CPCU should *volunteer* adverse information is left to the judgment of the CPCU.

G9.3 Upon request, a CPCU should serve on such committees, boards, or tribunals as are prescribed by the Institute for the administration or enforcement of the *Code.* A CPCU is obligated to disqualify himself or herself from such service (i) if the CPCU believes, in good conscience, that he or she could not serve in a fair and impartial manner or (ii) upon request.

Organization

SOCIETY OF FINANCIAL SERVICE PROFESSIONALS (AMERICAN SOCIETY OF CLU & ChFC)

Headquarters:
270 South Bryn Mawr Avenue
Bryn Mawr, PA 19010-2195
Telephone: (610) 526-2500
Fax: (610) 527-4010
E-mail: custserv@asclu.org
Website: http://www.agents-online.com/ASCLU/web/index.html

Date founded: 1928
   Name changed in October 1998
Membership: approximately 33,000 insurance and financial services professionals holding the Chartered Life Underwriter (CLU) or Chartered Financial Consultant (ChFC) designations, in 220 chapters nationwide

Code of Ethics

Official name: *Code of Ethics*
History: Issued 1987
Authority: Ethical Guidance & Professional Standards Committee
Code is available on Website

Additional Resources

Organizational (Divisions, Programs, Services, etc.):

American Business Ethics Awards program
The American College
Ethics Awareness Month

Informational (Publications, Videos, Seminars, etc.):

Articles in *CLU Journal*
The Best of Strictly Speaking

Chapter Handbook for Ethical Guidance & Professional Standards Committee
Code of Ethics of The American College
Consumer Disclosure Documents
Ethical Decisions in Life Insurance (course)
Ethical Guidance Procedures
Ethical Guidance Cost Sharing Guidelines
Ethical Selling: An Oxymoron?
Ethics in Life Insurance and Related Financial Services
Ethics Research Studies (co-sponsored with Ethics Officer Association): *Sources and Consequences of Workplace Pressure; Technology & Ethics in the Workplace: The Ethical Impact of New Technologies on Workers*
Insurance Illustration Questionnaires (IQ)
IQ: Understanding the Illustration Puzzle
Life Insurance Company Rating Services and Business Ethics (survey)
Life Insurance Proposals and the Agent's Ethical Dilemma
Professional Achievement in Continuing Education (guidelines)

Goals and Activities of Organization

The American Society of CLU & ChFC (Society) was founded as the alumni association of The American College, which confers the Chartered Life Underwriter (CLU) and Chartered Financial Consultant (ChFC) designations. All members of the Society have completed the required 10-course program to earn the designations, of which ethics is an integral part.

The Society strives to advance the educational and professional qualifications of providers of insurance and financial services; foster ethical and social responsibility; and promote public awareness and recognition of the profession. It also develops professional standards and provides continuing education and other services to members that enhance their ability to serve the public. The Society recommends that all agents adhere to its Code of Ethics as a means of building consumer trust in the insurance industry.

Implementation and Enforcement of Code

Upon conferment of the CLU or ChFC designation, members pledge themselves to a basic "Golden Rule" of ethical conduct: that in all professional relationships and in light of "all conditions surrounding those I serve, which I will make every conscientious effort to ascertain and understand," they will render the kind of service they would apply to themselves.

All members of the Society are subject to the provisions of its Code of Ethics. The Code presents two Ethical Imperatives, which are supported by more specific Guides, and by Interpretive Comments intended to aid in uniform understanding of the document. The Code is violated when a member breaches an Ethical Imperative through failure to adhere to a

Guide. Sanctions for Code violation include reprimand, censure, or suspension or revocation of membership.

Virtually all complaints are handled at the state chapter level in accordance with elaborate due process procedures—including notice, investigation, and a quasi-judicial hearing before a Chapter Tribunal. Matters are supervised by the chapter's Ethical Guidance Chair, who regularly serves as an advisor to members on ethics issues.

Appeals of disciplinary action are heard at the national level by a National Tribunal. A complaint is handled at the national level, by the Ethical Guidance & Professional Standards Committee, only in limited circumstances—such as when a member's license to practice is suspended or revoked or the member is convicted of a felony.

The Committee also makes recommendations to the Society as to ethics-related continuing education materials.

History and Development of Code

The present Code has not been changed since 1987. To assure the continuing professionalism of its members, the Society frequently adds to and updates its consumer and membership information and educational documents.

Code of Ethics*

Men and women who have chosen to enter into membership in the American Society are automatically bound to the Code of Ethics of their professional organization.

The purpose of the Code is to give further force to the pledge taken by all holders of the CLU and ChFC designations and to provide a series of standards by which those involved in providing insurance and financial planning and economic security may conduct themselves. The Code is founded upon the two ethical imperatives of competent advice and service to the client and enhancement of the public regard for the CLU and ChFC designations.

Competent advice and service to the client is at the very essence of any professional calling. Enhancement of the public regard for professional designations gives voice to the concept that in accepting Society membership an obligation is also accepted to all other holders of similar and allied professional designations and degrees.

In its design, the Code presents the two ethical Imperatives, supported by Guides which give specificity to the Imperatives, and interpretive comment which is intended to aid in a uniform understanding of the Guides.

A violation of the Code would expose a member to sanctions which range from reprimand to revocation of membership in the American Society. A member is in violation of the Code when a final judgment is made that the member has breached an ethical imperative through failure to adhere to one or more of the Guides.

For ease of drafting and reading, the masculine gender and singular number have been used. When appropriate, masculine is to be read as feminine and singular as plural. The word "client" is used under the First Imperative since standards concerning advice and service have greatest applicability to the relationship of client to professional insurance and financial services practitioner.

First Imperative
TO COMPETENTLY ADVISE AND SERVE THE CLIENT

Guide 1.1:
A member shall provide advice and service which are in the client's best interest.

Interpretive Comment
  A. A member possessing a specific body of knowledge which is not possessed by the general public has an obligation to use that knowledge for the benefit of the client and to avoid taking advantage of that knowledge to the detriment of the client.
  B. In a conflict of interest situation the interest of the client must be paramount.
  C. The member must make a conscientious effort to ascertain and to understand all relevant circumstances surrounding the client.
  D. A member is to accord due courtesy and consideration to those engaged in related professions who are also serving the client.

E. A member is to give due regard to any agent-principal relationship which may exist between the member and such companies as he may represent.

Guide 1.2:
A member shall respect the confidential relationship existing between client and member.

Interpretive Comment
  A. Competent advice and service may necessitate the client sharing personal and confidential information with the member. Such information is to be held in confidence by the member unless released from the obligation by the client.

Guide 1.3:
A member shall continue his education throughout his professional life.

Interpretive Comment
  A. To advise and serve competently, a member must continue to maintain and to improve his professional abilities.
  B. Continuing education includes both the member adding to his knowledge of the practice of his profession, and the member keeping abreast of changing economic and legislative conditions which may affect the financial plans of the insuring public.
  C. A member may continue his education through formal or informal programs of study or through other professional experiences.

Guide 1.4:
A member shall render continuing advice and service.

Interpretive Comment
  A. Advice and service, to be competent, must be ongoing as the client's circumstances change and as these changes are made known to the member.
  B. A client with whom a member has an active professional relationship is to be informed of economic and legislative changes which relate to the client-member relationship.

Second Imperative

TO ENHANCE THE PUBLIC REGARD FOR PROFESSIONAL DESIGNATIONS AND ALLIED PROFESSIONAL DEGREES HELD BY MEMBERS

Guide 2.1:
A member shall obey all laws governing his business or professional activities.

Interpretive Comment
  A. Business activities are non-personal activities carried on outside the life insurance community; professional activities are non-personal activities carried on within the life insurance community.
  B. A member has a legal obligation to obey all laws applicable to his business and professional activities. The placement of this Guide within the Code raises this obligation to the level of an ethical obligation.

Guide 2.2:
A member shall avoid all activities which detract from the integrity and professionalism of the Chartered Life Underwriter designation, the Chartered Financial
Consultant designation, or any other allied professional degree or designation held
by members.

Interpretive Comment
- A. Personal, business, and professional activities are encompassed within
   the scope of this Guide.
- B. Activities which could present a violation of this Guide might include:
   - (1) A member's failure to obey a law unrelated to the member's business
      or professional activities.
   - (2) A member impairing the reputation of another practitioner.
   - (3) A member unfairly competing with another practitioner.
   - (4) Actions which result in the member discrediting his own reputation.
   - (5) A member discrediting life underwriting as a profession, the institution
      of life insurance or the American Society of CLU & ChFC.
   - (6) A member advertising the Chartered Life Underwriter or Chartered
      Financial Consultant designation or membership in the American
      Society in an undignified manner, or in a manner prohibited by the
      Bylaws of the American Society.

Guide 2.3:
A member shall encourage others to attain the Chartered Life Underwriter and/
or the Chartered Financial Consultant designations.

Interpretive Comment
- A. Enhancement of the public regard for the CLU and ChFC designations
   depends upon a continuing increase in the number of holders of the
   designations who are available to advise and serve the public.
- B. Encouraging others who might be qualified to enter into a practice is one
   hallmark of a professional.

Guide 2.4:
A member shall avoid using the Chartered Life Underwriter or Chartered Financial
Consultant designation in a false or misleading manner.

Interpretive Comment
- A. The CLU and ChFC designations are granted by the American College
   to specified individuals. Acts which directly or indirectly extend the member's personal designation to others would present a violation of this Guide.
- B. Chartered Life Underwriter (CLU) or Chartered Financial Consultant
   (ChFC) may not be used in a name of a business in a manner which
   would reasonably lead others to conclude that someone other than the
   named member held the designation. Example:
   - (1) John Jones, CLU & Associates is permissible.
   - (2) John Jones & Associates, Chartered Financial Consultants is not per-
      missible.

10. JOURNALISM

Organization

AMERICAN SOCIETY OF JOURNALISTS AND AUTHORS

Headquarters:
1501 Broadway, Suite 302
New York, NY 10036
Telephone: (212) 997-0947
Fax: (212) 768-7414
E-mail: asja@compuserve.com
Website: http://www.asja.org

Date founded: 1948
Formerly the Society of Magazine Writers; renamed in 1975
Membership: approximately 1,000 professional freelance writers of non-fiction for general audiences, whose work is regularly published in periodicals, books, or other media

Code of Ethics

Official name: *Code of Ethics and Fair Practices*
History: Revised periodically; current as of September 1997
Authority: Committee on Editor-Writer Relations

Additional Resources

Organizational (Divisions, Programs, Services, etc.):

Anti-Censorship Campaign
The Authors Registry (Licensing Service, Automated Rights Payment System)
Banned Books Week (public awareness campaign)
Conscience-in-Media Medal (award)
Contracts Committee

Informational (Publications, Videos, Seminars, etc.):

Coming to Terms: The Electronic Rights Clause in Magazine and Newspaper Contracts

Contracts Watch (online newsletter)
E-Wrongs About E-Rights: Electronic Publishing: Fiction and Fact
Protecting Your Writing: Give Yourself Credit
Why Writing for Magazines Isn't What It Used to Be, and What Writers Have to Do About It

Goals and Activities of Organization

A nonprofit literary and educational organization of independent nonfiction writers, the American Society of Journalists and Authors (ASJA) is concerned with encouraging and establishing high professional and ethical standards. In pursuit of this goal, it facilitates communication among working writers; sponsors seminars, lectures, workshops, a referral service, and the Annual Writers' Conference; recognizes accomplishments; and monitors events and trends that affect the production and dissemination of information to the public.

ASJA actively opposes practices by government, industry, or individuals that are likely to diminish the quality or quantity of information to the public, or that encroach upon writers' rights and freedoms, including the right to control and profit from uses of their work in new forms of media.

Members are kept informed of the latest contract terms and negotiations in the newspaper and magazine industry. The Authors Registry, Inc. was launched to facilitate licensing of author-controlled rights and the collection and distribution of royalties. ASJA's anti-censorship campaign publicizes and mobilizes resistance to threats to the First Amendment. The organization is a co-sponsor of Banned Books Week and one of several professional, religious, and educational groups in the National Coalition Against Censorship.

Also worth noting is ASJA's Conscience-in-Media Medal, awarded to those who demonstrate "commitment to the highest principles of journalism at notable personal cost or sacrifice."

Implementation and Enforcement of Code

The Code of Ethics and Fair Practices defines the mutual rights and responsibilities of both writers and editors. Either party may bring a disagreement before the Committee on Editor-Writer Relations, which uses the Code to guide its investigation and mediation of the matter. The Committee resolves more than 150 disputes a year.

History and Development of Code

The Code is based on the "unwritten code governing editor-writer relationships"; it is a compilation of principles "generally recognized as fair and equitable."

Revisions have been made in 1977, 1979, 1982, 1986, 1989, and 1991. The present document incorporates changes from September 1997, to the sections concerning payments and agents.

Code of Ethics and Fair Practices*

Preamble

Over the years, an unwritten code governing editor-writer relationships has arisen. The American Society of Journalists and Authors has compiled the major principles and practices of that code that are generally recognized as fair and equitable.

The ASJA has also established a Committee on Editor-Writer Relations to investigate and mediate disagreements brought before it, either by members or by editors. In its activity this committee shall rely on the following guidelines.

1. Truthfulness, Accuracy, Editing

The writer shall at all times perform professionally and to the best of his or her ability, assuming primary responsibility for truth and accuracy. No writer shall deliberately write into an article a dishonest, distorted, or inaccurate statement.

Editors may correct or delete copy for purposes of style, grammar, conciseness or arrangement, but may not change the intent or sense without the writer's permission.

2. Sources

A writer shall be prepared to support all statements made in his or her manuscripts, if requested. It is understood, however, that the publisher shall respect any and all promises of confidentiality made by the writer in obtaining information.

3. Ideas and Proposals

An idea shall be defined not as a subject alone but as a subject combined with an approach.

A proposal of an idea ("query") by a professional writer shall receive a personal response within three weeks. If such a communication is in writing, it is properly viewed and treated as business correspondence, with no return postage or other materials required for reply.

A writer shall be considered to have a proprietary right to an idea suggested to an editor.

4. Acceptance of an Assignment

A request from an editor that the writer proceed with an idea, however worded and whether oral or written, shall be considered an assignment. (The word "assignment" here is understood to mean a definite order for an article.) It shall be the obligation of the writer to proceed as rapidly as possible toward the completion of an assignment, to meet a deadline mutually agreed upon, and not to agree to unreasonable deadlines.

---

*Revised 9/97. Copyright ©1997 by the American Society of Journalists and Authors, Inc. Reprinted with permission.

5. Conflict of Interest

The writer shall reveal to the editor, before acceptance of an assignment, any actual or potential conflict of interest, including but not limited to any financial interest in any product, firm, or commercial venture relating to the subject of the article.

6. Report on Assignment

If in the course of research or during the writing of the article, the writer concludes that the assignment will not result in a satisfactory article, he or she shall be obliged to so inform the editor.

7. Withdrawal

Should a disagreement arise between the editor and writer as to the merit or handling of an assignment, the editor may remove the writer on payment of mutually satisfactory compensation for the effort already expended, or the writer may withdraw without compensation and, if the idea for the assignment originated with the writer, may take the idea elsewhere without penalty.

8. Agreements

The practice of written confirmation of all agreements between editors and writers is strongly recommended, and such confirmation may originate with the editor, the writer, or an agent. Such a memorandum of confirmation should list all aspects of the assignment including subject, approach, length, special instructions, payments, deadline, and guarantee (if any). Failing prompt contradictory response to such a memorandum, both parties are entitled to assume that the terms set forth therein are binding.

All terms and conditions should be agreed upon at the time of assignment, with no changes permitted except by written agreement signed by both parties.

9. Rewriting

No writer's work shall be rewritten without his or her advance consent. If an editor requests a writer to rewrite a manuscript, the writer shall be obliged to do so but shall alternatively be entitled to withdraw the manuscript and offer it elsewhere.

10. Bylines

Lacking any stipulation to the contrary, a byline is the author's unquestioned right. All advertisements of the article should also carry the author's name. If an author's byline is omitted from a published article, no matter what the cause or reason, the publisher shall be liable to compensate the author financially for the omission.

11. Updating

If delay in publication necessitates extensive updating of an article, such updating shall be done by the author, to whom additional compensation shall be paid.

12. Reversion of Rights

Reasonable and good-faith efforts should be made to schedule an article within six months and publish it within twelve months. In the event that circumstances prevent such timely publication, the writer should be informed within twelve months as to the publication's continued interest in the article and plans to publish it. If publication is unlikely, the manuscript and all rights therein should revert to the author without penalty or cost to the author.

13. Payment for Assignments

An assignment presumes an obligation upon the publisher to pay for the writer's work upon satisfactory completion of the assignment, according to the agreed terms. Should a manuscript that has been accepted, orally or in writing, by a publisher or any representative or employee of the publisher, later be deemed unacceptable, the publisher shall nevertheless be obliged to pay the writer in full according to the agreed terms.

If an editor withdraws or terminates an assignment, due to no fault of the writer, after work has begun but prior to completion of a manuscript, the writer is entitled to compensation for work already put in; such compensation shall be negotiated between editor and author and shall be commensurate with the amount of work already completed. If a completed assignment is not accepted due to no fault of the writer, the writer is still entitled to full payment.

14. Time of Payments

The writer is entitled to full payment for an accepted article within 30 days of delivery. No article payment, or any portion thereof, should ever be subject to publication or to scheduling for publication.

15. Expenses

Unless otherwise stipulated by the editor at the time of an assignment, a writer shall assume that normal, out-of-pocket expenses will be reimbursed by the publisher. Any extraordinary expenses anticipated by the writer shall be discussed with the editor prior to incurring them.

16. Insurance

A magazine that gives a writer an assignment involving any extraordinary hazard shall insure the writer against death or disability during the course of travel or the hazard, or, failing that, shall honor the cost of such temporary insurance as an expense account item.

17. Loss of Personal Belongings

If, as a result of circumstances or events directly connected with a perilous assignment and due to no fault of the writer, a writer suffers loss of personal belongings or professional equipment or incurs bodily injury, the publisher shall compensate the writer in full.

18. Copyright, Additional Rights

It shall be understood, unless otherwise stipulated in writing, that sale of an article manuscript entitles the purchaser to first North American publication rights only, and that all other rights are retained by the author. Under no circumstances shall an independent writer be required to sign a so-called "all rights transferred" or "work made for hire" agreement as a condition of assignment, of payment, or of publication.

19. Reprints

All revenues from reprints shall revert to the author exclusively, and it is incumbent upon a publication to refer all requests for reprint to the author. The author has a right to charge for such reprints and must request that the original publication be credited.

20. Agents

In the absence of any agreement to the contrary, a writer shall not be obliged to pay an agent a fee on work negotiated, accomplished and paid for without the assistance of the agent. An agent should not charge a client a separate fee covering "legal" review of a contract for a book or other project.

21. TV and Radio Promotion

The writer is entitled to be paid for personal participation in TV or radio programs promoting periodicals in which the writer's work appears.

22. Indemnity

No writer should be obliged to indemnify any magazine or book publisher against any claim, actions, or proceedings arising from an article or book, except where there are valid claims of plagiarism or copyright violation.

23. Proofs

The editor shall submit edited proofs of the author's work to the author for approval, sufficiently in advance of publication that any errors may be brought to the editor's attention. If for any reason a publication is unable to so deliver or transmit proofs to the author, the author is entitled to review the proofs in the publication's office.

Organization

AMERICAN SOCIETY OF NEWSPAPER EDITORS

Headquarters:
11690B Sunrise Valley Drive
Reston, VA 20191-1409
Telephone: (703) 453-1122
Fax: (703) 453-1133
E-mail: asne@asne.org
Website: http://www.asne.org

Date founded: 1922
Membership: approximately 850 directing editors of daily newspapers, editorial and opinion pages, or wire services having immediate charge of editorial or news policies

Code of Ethics

Official name: *A Statement of Principles*
History: Adopted October 1975; originally issued 1922
Authority: Ethics and Values Committee; Board of Directors
Code is available on Website

Additional Resources

Organizational (Divisions, Programs, Services, etc.):

Institute for Journalism Excellence Certificate Program
Journalism Credibility Project
Journalism Values Institute (educational program)
Various committees: Change; Diversity; Education for Journalism; Freedom of Information; Management and Human Resources; New Media; Readership Issues

Informational (Publications, Videos, Seminars, etc.):

Articles in *The American Editor* magazine and *Editors' Exchange Newsletter*

Drawing the Line
Ethics on Trial: Retaking Our Readers
Free Press and Fair Trial
Journalism Credibility Studies
Journalism Education: Facing Up to the Challenge of Change
Journalism Values Institute Handbook and focus group video
Journalism Values Institute: Insights on the Values
Journalistic Values, What Do They Mean?
Newspaper Credibility: Building Reader Trust
The Newspaper Journalists of the '90s
Newsroom Diversity Resource Guide
Statement on Newsroom Diversity (draft)
Timeless Values: Staying True to Journalistic Principles in the Age of New Media
What Newspapers and Journalists Are Up Against: An Overview of the Landscape
Why and How Newsrooms are Changing

Goals and Activities of Organization

The principal purpose of the American Society of Newspaper Editors (ASNE) is to serve as a medium for the exchange of ideas and the professional growth and development of its members.

The organization acts to strengthen journalism education, increase private support of journalism schools, and enhance the role of newspaper professionals on journalism faculties, and works on the Accrediting Council on Education in Journalism and Mass Communication; examines complex ethical decisions in journalism; protects First Amendment rights, promotes freedom of information, campaigns against government secrecy, and testifies before legislative hearings at the federal, state, and local levels; and monitors international developments affecting world press freedom and issues statements and protests when foreign governments attempt to censor, threaten, or harm journalists.

ASNE also attempts to stimulate understanding and support between the press and the legal, judicial, and military communities; studies how the press is affected by new technologies and other factors; provides education about illiteracy; heightens industry awareness and hiring of minority journalists; explores public and professional perceptions about newspaper ownership; issues publications on journalism; holds conferences on public and newsroom controversies; sponsors major research projects; and issues writing awards.

Implementation and Enforcement of Code

The Statement is not enforced. It is presented as a part of ASNE's mission to help editors "maintain the highest standards of quality" and its commitment to "preserving and promoting core journalistic values"—

including freedom of information, diversity in news coverage, and accurate, fair, and complete reporting.

ASNE's qualifications for membership state that editors of newspapers which, "in the opinion of the directors, * * * have attained adequate journalistic standards," are eligible to join the organization.

The Ethics and Values Committee and other ASNE entities actively address issues of journalism ethics in studies, seminars, and publications. Projects have focused on credibility and public trust, photojournalism, technological developments, tabloid journalism, the use of unnamed sources, and how newspapers report about themselves.

ASNE opposes efforts to establish an international code of ethics for journalists. In June 1998 it said: "While ASNE believes all media should operate with high standards, it has learned from experience that agreements on standards and their enforcement, even voluntary ones, are dangerous for press freedom. * * * Judges and lawyers have used ethical guidelines, council statements and various agreements as evidence and the basis for court decisions against the press. What is intended as voluntary becomes coercive. * * * We have profound reservations about any kind of an agreement at the international level. Not only would it be used against our press in our courts, it could become mandatory under international law. It would be an open invitation to authorities in other countries to inhibit our press. Our society has discussed these issues virtually annually since its founding in 1922, and long ago it resolved that codes of ethics and their enforcement seriously threaten freedom of the press."

History and Development of Code

The Statement was adopted October 23, 1975. It supplants the 1922 "Canons of Journalism."

A Statement of Principles*

PREAMBLE

The First Amendment, protecting freedom of expression from abridgment by any law, guarantees to the people through their press a constitutional right, and thereby places on newspaper people a particular responsibility.

Thus journalism demands of its practitioners not only industry and knowledge but also the pursuit of a standard of integrity proportionate to the journalist's singular obligation.

To this end the American Society of Newspaper Editors sets forth this Statement of Principles as a standard encouraging the highest ethical and professional performance.

ARTICLE I—Responsibility

The primary purpose of gathering and distributing news and opinion is to serve the general welfare by informing the people and enabling them to make judgments on the issues of the time. Newspapermen and women who abuse the power of their professional role for selfish motives or unworthy purposes are faithless to that public trust.

The American press was made free not just to inform or just to serve as a forum for debate but also to bring an independent scrutiny to bear on the forces of power in the society, including the conduct of official power at all levels of government.

ARTICLE II—Freedom of the Press

Freedom of the press belongs to the people. It must be defended against encroachment or assault from any quarter, public or private.

Journalists must be constantly alert to see that the public's business is conducted in public. They must be vigilant against all who would exploit the press for selfish purposes.

ARTICLE III—Independence

Journalists must avoid impropriety and the appearance of impropriety as well as any conflict of interest or the appearance of conflict. They should neither accept anything nor pursue any activity that might compromise or seem to compromise their integrity.

ARTICLE IV—Truth and Accuracy

Good faith with the reader is the foundation of good journalism. Every effort must be made to assure that the news content is accurate, free from bias and in context, and that all sides are presented fairly. Editorials, analytical articles and

---

*Originally adopted in 1922 as the "Canons of Journalism." The document was revised and renamed "Statement of Principles" in 1975. Copyright © 1996, American Society of Newspaper Editors. Reprinted with permission of the American Society of Newspaper Editors.

commentary should be held to the same standards of accuracy with respect to facts as news reports.

Significant errors of fact, as well as errors of omission, should be corrected promptly and prominently.

ARTICLE V—Impartiality

To be impartial does not require the press to be unquestioning or to refrain from editorial expression. Sound practice, however, demands a clear distinction for the reader between news reports and opinion. Articles that contain opinion or personal interpretation should be clearly identified.

ARTICLE VI—Fair Play

Journalists should respect the rights of people involved in the news, observe the common standards of decency and stand accountable to the public for the fairness and accuracy of their news reports.

Persons publicly accused should be given the earliest opportunity to respond.

Pledges of confidentiality to news sources must be honored at all costs, and therefore should not be given lightly. Unless there is clear and pressing need to maintain confidences, sources of information should be identified.

These principles are intended to preserve, protect and strengthen the bond of trust and respect between American journalists and the American people, a bond that is essential to sustain the grant of freedom entrusted to both by the nation's founders.

Organization

SOCIETY OF PROFESSIONAL JOURNALISTS

Headquarters:
16 South Jackson Street
Greencastle, IN 46135-1514
Telephone: (765) 653-3333
Fax: (765) 653-4631
E-mail: spj@link2000.net
Website: http://www.spj.org
Ethics Hotline: (765) 653-2070, Ext. 208

Date founded: 1909
Founded as Sigma Delta Chi; renamed 1988
Membership: approximately 13,500 professional journalists and journalism educators and students, in more than 300 chapters

Code of Ethics

Official name: *Code of Ethics*
History: First adopted 1926, revised periodically; current version September 1996
Authority: National Ethics Committee
Code is available on Website

Additional Resources

Organizational (Divisions, Programs, Services, etc.):

Continuing Professional Education Program
First Amendment and Freedom of Information Internships
The FOIA Resource Center
Freedom of Information Committee
Jane Pauley Task Force on Mass Communication Education
Media Leaders Forum
Project Sunshine (campaign for access to government information)
Sigma Delta Chi Awards
SPJ-Ethics Listserv

Informational (Publications, Videos, Seminars, etc.):

Articles in *Quill* magazine and *The Electronic Journalist* (online)
A Proposed Curriculum for Tomorrow's Broadcast Journalists
Censored Annual
Doing Ethics in Journalism
FOIA Alert
Lifting the Lid: A Guide to Investigative Research
Making the Tough Decisions (case studies)
Tomorrow's Broadcast Journalists: The Pauley Report on Broadcast Journalism Education
Conference sessions:
> *Biting the Hand that Feeds You: Can Journalists Act Independently?*
> *Divided Loyalties: Sports Journalism in the 90s*
> *Just Because We Can, Should We?*
> *Newsroom Values: Have Journalists Changed or Has the Newsroom Changed?*
> *Victims and Remedies: A New Look at Accountability in the News Media*
> *Where Law and Ethics Converge*
> *Why Journalists Hate Public Journalism (and Why Academics Love It)*

Goals and Activities of Organization

The Society of Professional Journalists (SPJ) seeks to become the preeminent, broad-based journalism organization, "dedicated to a free press, free speech and the ethical practice of journalism."

Its activities are designed to promote the free flow of information; maintain vigilance in the protection of First Amendment guarantees for speech and the press; stimulate high standards and ethical behavior; foster excellence and diversity among journalists; inspire talented individuals to become journalists; and encourage a climate in which journalism can be practiced freely.

SPJ represents the interests of journalists in important court cases and congressional hearings on First Amendment and freedom of information issues; conducts national and regional professional development seminars, ethics programs, public education, conferences, and awards contests; produces publications; and provides members with job search assistance.

Implementation and Enforcement of Code

The Code of Ethics is presented as a model; adherence to it is voluntary. SPJ widely disseminates the Code, however, and encourages journalists and news organizations to adopt it or use it as a basis for developing and adhering to their own standards. SPJ also seeks to promote ethical behavior by conducting and promoting the use of educational programs and seminars during which journalists can actively wrestle with vexing ethics issues.

The SPJ Ethics Hotline, staffed by members of the National Ethics Committee and journalists with experience in ethical decisionmaking, was set up to help journalists become adept at applying the Code, and to work through ethical dilemmas.

History and Development of Code

Sigma Delta Chi's first Code of Ethics was borrowed from the American Society of Newspaper Editors in 1926. In 1973, the organization wrote its own code, which was revised in 1984 and 1987. The present version was adopted in September 1996.

Code of Ethics*

Preamble

Members of the Society of Professional Journalists believe that public enlightenment is the forerunner of justice and the foundation of democracy. The duty of the journalist is to further those ends by seeking truth and providing a fair and comprehensive account of events and issues. Conscientious journalists from all media and specialties strive to serve the public with thoroughness and honesty. Professional integrity is the cornerstone of a journalist's credibility.

Members of the Society share a dedication to ethical behavior and adopt this code to declare the Society's principles and standards of practice.

SEEK TRUTH AND REPORT IT

Journalists should be honest, fair and courageous in gathering, reporting and interpreting information.

Journalists should:

- Test the accuracy of information from all sources and exercise care to avoid inadvertent error. Deliberate distortion is never permissible.
- Diligently seek out subjects of news stories to give them the opportunity to respond to allegations of wrongdoing.
- Identify sources whenever feasible. The public is entitled to as much information as possible on sources' reliability.
- Always question sources' motives before promising anonymity. Clarify conditions attached to any promise made in exchange for information. Keep promises.
- Make certain that headlines, news teases and promotional material, photos, video, audio, graphics, sound bites and quotations do not misrepresent. They should not oversimplify or highlight incidents out of context.
- Never distort the content of news photos or video. Image enhancement for technical clarity is always permissible. Label montages and photo illustrations.
- Avoid misleading re-enactments or staged news events. If re-enactment is necessary to tell a story, label it.
- Avoid undercover or other surreptitious methods of gathering information except when traditional open methods will not yield information vital to the public. Use of such methods should be explained as part of the story.
- Never plagiarize.
- Tell the story of the diversity and magnitude of the human experience boldly, even when it is unpopular to do so.
- Examine their own cultural values and avoid imposing those values on others.

---

*Sigma Delta Chi's first Code of Ethics was borrowed from the American Society of Newspaper Editors in 1926. In 1973, Sigma Delta Chi wrote its own code, which was revised in 1984 and 1987. The present version of the Society of Professional Journalists' Code of Ethics was adopted in September 1996.

- Avoid stereotyping by race, gender, age, religion, ethnicity, geography, sexual orientation, disability, physical appearance or social status.
- Support the open exchange of views, even views they find repugnant.
- Give voice to the voiceless; official and unofficial sources of information can be equally valid.
- Distinguish between advocacy and news reporting. Analysis and commentary should be labeled and not misrepresent fact or context.
- Distinguish news from advertising and shun hybrids that blur the lines between the two.
- Recognize a special obligation to ensure that the public's business is conducted in the open and that government records are open to inspection.

MINIMIZE HARM

Ethical journalists treat sources, subjects and colleagues as human beings deserving of respect.

Journalists should:
- Show compassion for those who may be affected adversely by news coverage. Use special sensitivity when dealing with children and inexperienced sources or subjects.
- Be sensitive when seeking or using interviews or photographs of those affected by tragedy or grief.
- Recognize that gathering and reporting information may cause harm or discomfort. Pursuit of the news is not a license for arrogance.
- Recognize that private people have a greater right to control information about themselves than do public officials and others who seek power, influence or attention. Only an overriding public need can justify intrusion into anyone's privacy.
- Show good taste. Avoid pandering to lurid curiosity.
- Be cautious about identifying juvenile suspects or victims of sex crimes.
- Be judicious about naming criminal suspects before the formal filing of charges.
- Balance a criminal suspect's fair trial rights with the public's right to be informed.

ACT INDEPENDENTLY

Journalists should be free of obligation to any interest other than the public's right to know.

Journalists should:
- Avoid conflicts of interest, real or perceived.
- Remain free of associations and activities that may compromise integrity or damage credibility.
- Refuse gifts, favors, fees, free travel and special treatment, and shun secondary employment, political involvement, public office and service in community organizations if they compromise journalistic integrity.
- Disclose unavoidable conflicts.
- Be vigilant and courageous about holding those with power accountable.
- Deny favored treatment to advertisers and special interests and resist their pressure to influence news coverage.

- Be wary of sources offering information for favors or money; avoid bidding for news.

BE ACCOUNTABLE

Journalists are accountable to their readers, listeners, viewers and each other.

Journalists should:
- Clarify and explain news coverage and invite dialogue with the public over journalistic conduct.
- Encourage the public to voice grievances against the news media.
- Admit mistakes and correct them promptly.
- Expose unethical practices of journalists and the news media.
- Abide by the same high standards to which they hold others.

11. MANAGEMENT

Organization

ACADEMY OF MANAGEMENT

Headquarters:
Pace University
P.O. Box 3020
Briarcliff Manor, NY 10510-8020
Telephone: (914) 923-2607
Fax: (914) 923-2615
E-mail: aom@aom.pace.edu
Website: http://www.aom.pace.edu

Date founded: 1936
Membership: approximately 9,800 business educators and researchers, students of management, management consultants, and executives, 83% from the U.S. and the rest from more than 80 countries, in 22 Divisions and Interest Groups

Code of Ethics

Official name: *Code of Ethical Conduct*
History: Approved 1990, amended April 1994
Authority: Ethics Task Force; Board of Governors

Additional Resources

Organizational (Divisions, Programs, Services, etc.):

Professional Development Workshops
Social Issues in Management Division (affiliated with International Association for Business and Society)
Various divisions: Management Education and Development; Management History; Managerial Consultation; Organization Development & Change; Organizational Behavior; Public and Nonprofit Sector; Research Methods

Informational (Publications, Videos, Seminars, etc.):

Articles in *Academy of Management Executive, Journal,* and *Review,* and in individual Division journals
Ethics column in *Academy of Management News*
Conference sessions and addresses:
  Business Ethics and Corporate Social Policy: Reflections on an Intellectual Journey
  Codes of Ethics and Conduct in Consulting Firms
  Illegal and Unethical Behaviors
  Leadership, Trust, and Effective Organizations
  Private Sources of Funding for Organizational Research: Emerging Ethical Issues
  Reshaping the Management Education Paradigm: A New Focus on Ethics, Public Policy and Society
  Teaching-Research-Service Balance Issues
  Theology and Business: An Imperative for Collaboration

Goals and Activities of Organization

The Academy of Management (Academy) was organized to "advance the philosophy of management," primarily through the support of scholarly research and the presentation and exchange of ideas. Its goals are to foster the general development of teaching, learning, and practice in the management field, and to encourage the extension and unification of management knowledge.

The Academy's publication of several management journals and organization of annual and divisional meetings enables members to fulfill these goals.

Implementation and Enforcement of Code

The Code of Ethical Conduct is re-published every year in the *Academy of Management Journal.* As an aspirational and educational guide, it is not enforced; the Academy does not expel members for ethics violations. (The member's university or employer is considered the appropriate venue for lodging a formal complaint.) To join and remain in the Academy, however, is to acknowledge and agree with its principles.

A member of the Board of Governors serves each year as the Academy's Ethics Coordinator. The Coordinator's job is to update the Code as necessary, to inform the Board of ethical issues important to the Academy or its members, and to counsel members who have ethics questions—such as problems with authorship, plagiarism, and inappropriate situations for job interviews. The Coordinator neither provides legal advice nor has any formal authority.

History and Development of Code

The Board of Governors appointed an Ethics Task Force to create the code, which was completed and approved in 1990. Revisions are the responsibility of the Ethics Coordinator.

The present document was amended April 1994 to include the Academy's sexual harassment policy.

Code of Ethical Conduct*

CREDO

We believe in discovering, sharing and applying managerial knowledge.

PREAMBLE

Our professional goals are to enhance the learning of students, colleagues, and others and to improve the effectiveness of organizations through our teaching, research, and practice of management. We have five major responsibilities:

(1) To our students—Relationships with students require respect, fairness, and caring, along with recognition of our commitment to the subject matter and to teaching excellence.

(2) To managerial knowledge—Prudence in research design, human subject use, confidentiality, result reporting, and proper attribution of work is a necessity.

(3) To the Academy of Management and the larger professional environment—Support of the Academy's mission and objectives, service to the Academy and our institutions, and the recognition of the dignity and personal worth of colleagues is required.

(4) To both managers and the practice of management—Exchange of ideas and information between the academic and organizational communities is essential.

(5) To all people with whom we live and work in the world community—Sensitivity to other people, to diverse cultures, to the needs of the poor and disadvantaged, to ethical issues, and to newly emerging ethical dilemmas is required.

STUDENT RELATIONSHIPS

In our roles as educators, the central principles that underlie appropriate student-educator relationships are professionalism, respect, fairness, and concern.

Striving for Teaching Excellence. It is the duty of Academy members who are educators to prepare themselves carefully. Maintenance of current knowledge in the field requires a broad understanding of management theories, research and practice, and use of current classroom materials. Educators should have or develop expertise in the areas in which they teach. Effective teaching requires sufficient time allocated to preparation, clear classroom communication, timely grading, and a willingness to provide an explanation of a student's grade. Educators should act as role models in their relationships. They should also sensitize students to the ethical dimensions of management. In addition, educators have an obligation to present material without conscious bias and to make their own relevant biases

---

*Approved August 1990 and amended in April 1994. Reprinted from *Academy of Management Journal*, December 1995, Vol. 38, No. 6, pp. 1775–80. Copyright © The Academy of Management. All rights reserved. Reprinted with permission.

known to their students. Educators should attempt to evaluate their teaching through some appropriate outcome assessment method which goes beyond concept retention.

Showing Respect for Students. It is the duty of Academy members who are educators to show appropriate respect for students' feelings, interests, needs, contributions, and intellectual freedom. Students' right to privacy requires maintaining the confidentiality of academic records and private communications unless disclosure is mandated by law, institutional policy, or a morally compelling purpose. Educators must avoid manipulation, coercion or exploitation of students (especially acts directed at securing monetary, ego, or sexual gratification) and should demonstrate a sensitivity to cultural and personal diversity by avoiding racial, sexual, religious, and ethnic discrimination.

Maintenance of Objectivity and Fairness. It is the duty of Academy members who are educators to treat students equitably. Fair treatment of students requires explicitly explaining and adhering to academic requirements or standards. Any subsequent change in these requirements or standards, either of the institution or in an individual course, should appropriately recognize the impact on students. Impartiality, objectivity, and fairness are required in all dealings with students. Examinations should be carefully prepared and written work graded in an impartial manner. Educators should scrupulously avoid entering any overly personal relationship or accepting any gift or favor that might influence, or appear to influence, an objective evaluation of a student's work. Appropriate evaluation of student performance requires test design, assignments, and testing conditions that minimize the possibility of academic misconduct. It is the educator's responsibility to pursue appropriate disciplinary action if necessary.

Counseling of Students. It is the duty of Academy members to be helpful and sensitive in counseling students. When serving as academic advisors, members must be knowledgeable about academic requirements and should communicate these clearly and fully to advisees. Educators may play critical roles in a variety of counseling situations. This requires careful analysis of the student and the situation and calls for special expertise and competence. Counseling advice should be identified as an expression of the member's own opinion. Letters of recommendation require candor and fairness. Members should not make insupportable statements nor fail to disclose material facts.

ADVANCEMENT OF MANAGERIAL KNOWLEDGE

Research of Academy members should be done honestly, have a clear purpose, show respect for the rights of all individuals and organizations, efficiently use resources, and advance knowledge in the field.

Conducting and Reporting. It is the duty of Academy members conducting research to design, implement, analyze, report, and present their findings rigorously. Research rigor includes careful design, execution, analysis, interpretation of results, and retention of data. Presentation of research should include a treatment of the data that is honest and that reveals both strengths and weaknesses of findings. When important alternate hypotheses or explanations exist, they should be noted and data that disconfirm hypotheses should be acknowledged. Authorship and credit should be shared in correct proportion to the various parties' contributions. Whether published or not, ideas or concepts derived from others should be acknowledged, as should advice and assistance received. Many management-related journals have policies prohibiting or restricting potential articles from being reviewed concurrently in other outlets. These policies should be closely observed or there should be explicit discussion with the relevant journal editors concerning the intended multiple submissions. More than one report of essentially the same data and results should not be published unless the reports are explicitly directed to different audiences through different types of outlets. When several separate but related reports result from a single study, the existence of the different reports should be made known to the relevant journal editors and the reports should reference each other. Reviewer comments should be considered thoughtfully before a manuscript is submitted to a different journal.

Participants. It is the duty of Academy members to preserve and protect the privacy, dignity, well-being, and freedom of research participants. This duty requires both careful research design and informed consent from all participants. Risks and the possibility of harm to research participants must be carefully considered, and, to the extent possible, these must be minimized. When there is a degree of risk or potential harm inherent in the research, potential participants— organizations as well as individuals—must be informed. Informed consent means explaining to potential participants the purposes and nature of the research so they can freely choose whether or not to become involved. Such explanations include warning of possible harm and providing explicit opportunities to refuse to participate and to terminate participation at any time. Because students and employees are particularly subject to possible coercion, even when unintended, special care must be taken in obtaining their informed consent. Third-party review is one means of protecting the interests of research participants. Research plans involving human participants should be reviewed by an appropriate third party, such as a university human subjects committee or a focus group of potential participants. Questions regarding confidentiality or anonymity must be resolved between researcher and potential research participants, both individuals and organizations; if confidentiality or anonymity is requested, this must be honored. Deception should be minimized and, when necessary, the degree and effects must be mitigated as much as possible. Researchers should carefully weigh the gains achieved against the cost in human dignity. To the extent that concealment of deception is necessary, the researcher must provide a full and accurate explanation to participants at the conclusion of the study, including counseling, if appropriate.

Dissemination. It is the duty of journal editors and reviewers to exercise their position of privilege in a confidential, unbiased, prompt, constructive, and sensitive manner. They have a duty to judge manuscripts only on their scholarly merits. Conflicts of interest may arise when a reviewer is in basic disagreement with the research approach or the line of research represented by a manuscript. In such cases, a reviewer should consult with the journal editor to decide whether to accept or decline to review the manuscript. Protecting intellectual property is a responsibility of the reviewer and the editor. The content of a manuscript is the property of its author(s). It is therefore inappropriate to use ideas or show another person a manuscript one has been asked to review, without the explicit permission of its authors. Advice regarding specific, limited aspects of the manuscript may be sought from qualified colleagues so long as the author's intellectual property remains secure. Sharing of reviewing responsibilities is inappropriate. The review is the sole responsibility of the person to whom it was assigned by the journal editor. In particular, students and colleagues should not be asked to prepare reviews unless the journal's editor has given explicit approval. Anyone contributing to a review should receive formal recognition. Constructive review means providing critiques and comments in a spirit of collegiality with thoroughness, timeliness, compassion, and respect, and in ways intended to improve the quality of the manuscript.

Grants and Contracts. It is the duty of Academy members to accurately represent themselves and their proposed projects and to manage those projects as promised. Representation means accurate disclosure of one's level of expertise and expected actual involvement, the outcomes that can be reasonably expected, the realistic funding level needed, and any potential conflicts of interest. Grant and contract management requires independence and objectivity such that one does not compromise one's responsibilities or create conflicts of interest. One must also manage time and budget responsibly and use the funds as promised unless permission is explicitly granted to do otherwise.

THE ACADEMY OF MANAGEMENT AND THE LARGER PROFESSIONAL ENVIRONMENT

The Mission Statement of the Academy describes member benefits and professional opportunities of members which impose corresponding duties and service responsibilities.

Sharing and Dissemination of Information. To encourage meaningful exchange, Academy members should foster a climate of free interchange and constructive criticism within the Academy and should be willing to share research findings and insights fully with other members.

Academy Participation. The Academy is a voluntary association whose existence and operations are dependent on cooperation, involvement, and leadership from its members. Members should abide by the constitution, bylaws, policies, and codes of the Academy. Members should consider offering their time and talent to carry out activities necessary to maintain the Academy and its functions. Officers and members should fulfill their Academy obligations and responsibilities in a timely, diligent, and sensitive manner, without regard to friendships or personal gain. Members should honor all professional commitments, including presentation of accepted papers and participation in scheduled roles as chair, discussant, or panel member. If absence from a scheduled meeting is unavoidable, members must contact appropriate individuals and pursue suitable alternative arrangements. One should consider the impact one's projects or activities may have on the integrity or reputation of the Academy, and one should not engage in such projects or activities that may have possible negative implications. Members should not imply that their work is sanctioned by the Academy unless an appropriate Academy body has specifically done so.

Commitment to Professional Standards of Conduct. By this code, the Academy provides ongoing ethical guidance for its members. Members should work to raise the consciousness of other members concerning ethical responsibilities, and they should encourage acceptance of these responsibilities. Members should notify appropriate Academy officers or committees regarding the practices or actions of members they believe may violate Academy regulations or general standards of ethical conduct. In this manner, the aspirational and educational goals of this code are served through discussion of the ethical dilemmas and values of our profession.

Strengthening and Renewal of the Academy. The Academy of Management must have continuous infusions of members and new points of view to remain viable and relevant as a professional association. Members may contribute by encouraging all eligible individuals to participate in the Academy and by assisting new and prospective members in developing their skills, knowledge, and understanding of their professional obligations.

The professional environment for many Academy members includes the university community. The central values that underlie appropriate university participation are understanding, involvement, respect, fairness, and the pursuit of knowledge.

Participation in University Leadership. Professors should take an active interest in university governance. Professors should be aware of university policies that affect the dissemination of policies. Professors should endeavor to positively influence policies relating to the quality of education and service to students. Active organizational involvement requires exercise of personal voting rights and respect for such rights of others, without regard to rank or tenure. Professors should evaluate colleagues for purposes of promotion or tenure on the basis of appropriate academic criteria that is fairly weighted in accordance with standards understood by the faculty and the subject of evaluation. It is the duty of Academy members to treat their colleagues with respect and fairness. Members should safeguard confidential personnel matters and avoid disclosing opinions expressed, attribution of statements, voting behavior, and outcomes. Members should address misunderstandings and conflicts with those directly involved and avoid speculative criticism that might damage the reputations of individuals or groups. When speaking or acting outside their university roles, professors should avoid creating the impression that they are speaking or acting for the university or its administration. Professors should dispose of complimentary books requested from publishers by a manner other than sale.

All Academy members, whether affiliated with a university, business, governmental, service, or consulting organization have an obligation to interact with others in a professional manner.

Membership in the Professional Community. It is the duty of Academy members to interact with others in our community in a manner that recognizes individual dignity and merit. The responsible professional promotes and protects the rights of individuals without regard to race, color, religion, national origin, handicap, sex, sexual orientation, age, political beliefs, or academic ideology, and refrains from sexual harassment. In the spirit of intellectual inquiry, the professional should welcome suggestions and complaints openly without reprisal. Members should ensure that outside activities do not significantly diminish their availability and energy to meet their institutional obligations.

MANAGERS AND THE PRACTICE OF MANAGEMENT

Consulting with client organizations ("clients") has the potential for enriching the teaching and practice of management, for translating theory into practice, and for furthering research and community service. To maximize such poten-

tial benefits, it is essential that members who consult be guided by the ideals of competence, integrity, and objectivity.

Credentials and Capabilities. It is the duty of consultants to represent their credentials and capabilities in an accurate and objective manner. Consultants shall accept only those assignments for which they have appropriate expertise. Consultants shall refrain from exaggerating their professional qualifications to secure prospective assignments. Consultants shall examine any factors (e.g., prior experience, capabilities, other commitments) that might limit their judgment or objectivity in carrying out an assignment. University endorsement of the consulting activities of Academy members employed by academic institutions should not be represented or implied to potential clients unless the assignment is formally under university sponsorship or is so approved.

Obligations to Clients. Consultants have a duty to fulfill their obligations to their present and prospective clients in a professionally responsible and timely manner. Consultants shall place the highest possible priority on their clients' interests. Consultants shall avoid or withdraw from situations in which their clients' interests come into serious conflict with their own. Consultants shall not serve two or more competing clients without the consent of all parties. Consultants shall fully inform their clients. This means presenting results or advice in an unbiased manner and discussing fully with the client the values, risks, and limitations of the recommendations.

Client Relations. Consultants must fulfill duties of confidentiality and efficiency as part of the relationship with their clients. Consultants shall maintain confidentiality with respect to their clients' identities and the assignments undertaken, unless granted permission by the client. Consultants should exercise concern for the protection of clients, employees and other stakeholders by maintaining, in particular, appropriate confidentiality. Consultants shall not take personal or financial advantage of confidential information acquired as a result of their professional relationships, nor shall they provide the basis upon which others may take such advantage. Consultants should meet their time commitments, and they should conserve the resources that are utilized.

Remuneration. It is the duty of consultants to negotiate clear and mutually accepted remuneration agreements for their services. Consultants shall provide a realistic estimate of the fees to be charged in advance of assignments. Fees charged shall be commensurate with the services performed.

Societal Responsibilities. Consultants have a duty to uphold the legal and moral obligations of the society in which they function. Consultants should report to the appropriate authorities any unlawful activities that may have been uncovered during the course of their consulting engagements, except where their functional professional code directs otherwise.

Students and Employees. It is the duty of the consultant to safeguard the rights of students and employees when they are involved in consulting assignments. Consultants may involve students in work generated by consulting engagements, especially if such work possesses learning potential, but students must not be coerced into participation. When they are so involved, students, as well as employees, should be fairly compensated, and they should be made aware of the nature of the work they are doing.

THE WORLD COMMUNITY

As citizens of the world community, Academy members may have much to contribute in shaping global consciousness through their teaching, research, and service.

World View. Academy members have a duty to consider their responsibilities to the world community. In their role as educators, members of the Academy can play a vital role in encouraging a broader horizon for decision making by viewing issues from a multiplicity of perspectives, including the perspectives of those who are least advantaged. As researchers, members of the Academy should consider, where appropriate, increasing their exposure to other cultures via travel, study, and research. Where appropriate, research might highlight the responsible steward-ship of the earth's resources. In addition, members should take as a challenge the ongoing task of identifying evolving ethical issues by listening to those whose welfare is affected and by exploring the interaction of people and technology. In fulfilling their service responsibilities, members of the Academy should consider how they might lend their time and talent to enhance the world community through involvement in uncompensated public service.

SEXUAL HARASSMENT

The Academy of Management and its members are committed to providing academic environments that are free of sexual harassment and all forms of sexual intimidation and exploitation.

Sexual harassment consists of unwelcome sexual advances, requests for sexual favors, and other visual, verbal, or physical conduct of a sexual nature when:

1. It is implicitly or explicitly suggested that submission to or rejection of the conduct will be a factor in academic employment, admission, evaluation, or participation in an academic activity.
2. The conduct has the purpose or effect of interfering with an individual's academic or work performance, by creating an intimidating, hostile, offen-sive, or otherwise unacceptable educational or work environment.

The determination of what constitutes sexual harassment depends upon the specific facts and the context in which conduct occurs. Sexual harassment takes many forms: subtle and indirect or blatant and overt; conduct affecting an individual of the opposite or same sex; between peers or between individuals in a hierarchical relationship; between teacher and student. Regardless of the intentions or the actor, the key question is always whether the conduct is unwelcome to the individual at whom it is directed.

There are special risks in any consensual sexual or romantic relationship between individuals in inherently unequal positions (such as student and faculty, or junior and senior faculty). Relationships in which one party is in a position to review the work or influence the career of the other may constitute sexual harass-ment when that relationship gives undue access or advantage, restricts opportuni-ties, or creates a hostile and unacceptable environment for others in the work or classroom environments. Furthermore, such relationships may be less consensual than the individual whose position confers power believes, because of the complex and subtle effects of that power. Moreover, circumstances may change and conduct that was previously welcome may become unwelcome. Even when both parties have consented at the outset to a romantic involvement, subsequent unwelcome conduct may constitute sexual harassment.

Organization

AMERICAN SOCIETY OF ASSOCIATION EXECUTIVES

Headquarters:
1575 I Street, NW
Washington, DC 20005-1168
Telephone: (202) 626-2723
International (402) 271-9293
Fax: (202) 371-8825
(800) 622-ASAE
E-mail: asae@asaenet.org
Website: http://www.asaenet.org

Date founded: 1920
   Called the American Trade Association Executives until 1956
Membership: approximately 23,500 executives of leading trade associations, membership societies, and voluntary organizations, and suppliers of products and services to the association community, in the U.S. and in 44 nations

Codes of Ethics

Official name: *Standards of Conduct*
History: First adopted 1922; current version 1993
Authority: Ethics Committee; ASAE

Official name: *Guidelines for Association Lobbyists*
History: Adopted and approved March 1997
Authority: Government Relations Section; Board of Directors

Codes available on Website

Additional Resources

Organizational (Divisions, Programs, Services, etc.):

Annual Legal Symposium
Annual Legislative Summit

Associations Advance America (public awareness program)
Association Peer Review Program
CEO Center
Certified Association Executive (CAE) Program
Information Central (research clearinghouse)
Legal, Tax, and Accounting Hotlines
Pathways Groups (education program): Advanced; CAE; Executive Development; Managerial Practices; Professional Development; Professional Practices
State Action Legislative Team (SALT) Advocacy Center
Various Sections: Education; Executive Management; Legal; Marketing; Technology

Informational (Publications, Videos, Seminars, etc.):

Articles in *Association Management* magazine; *Association Educator, Association Law & Policy, The Correspondent, Leadership,* and other individual Section journals
A Sharing of Expertise & Experience Series
Adult Learning in Associations: Models for Good Practice
Antitrust Guide for Association Members: An Outline of Procedures to Maintain Compliance with the Law
Association Law Compendium
Association Peer Reviewers Code of Conduct
Board of Directors resolution to encourage ethical behavior
Codes of Ethics and Other Industry Self Regulation Programs
Current Principles and Practices in Association Self-Regulation
Ethics Background Kit
Ethics Survey (co-sponsored with Ethics Resource Center)
Federal Lobbying Law Handbook
Nonprofit Governance Series: *Ten Basic Responsibilities of Nonprofit Boards; The Nonprofit Board's Role in Reducing Risk: More Than Buying Insurance*
Policies and Procedures in Association Management
Position Papers
Principles of Association Management
Professional Practices in Association Management
The Shape of Things to Come? A Guide to the Changing Nature of Associations (video)
The Value of Associations to American Society
Other *Background Kits: Association Liability; Association Personnel Policies; Association Political Involvement; Associations Online; CEOs and Their Boards; Executive Director Performance Evaluation; Lobbying; Managing Continuing Education Programs; Sample Board Governance Policies*

Goals and Activities of Organization

Pursuant to its stated mission, the American Society of Association Executives (ASAE) is dedicated to enhancing the professionalism and competency of association executives, promoting excellence in association management, and increasing the effectiveness of associations to better serve members and society.

ASAE accomplishes this through diverse programs and activities, for its members and on behalf of associations as a whole; these include advocacy, certification, communications, education, government relations, partnerships with other organizations, peer review, public recognition, publications, and research.

Implementation and Enforcement of Codes

Compliance with the Standards of Conduct is voluntary and not enforced, but "adherence is expected."

Ethical standards play an important role in ASAE's overall operations and plans. The discipline of association management, according to ASAE principles, "is based upon a body of knowledge supported by a code of ethics * * *."

ASAE's number-one strategic goal is professionalism, in support of which individual members are to "maintain the highest standard of personal conduct." The corresponding organizational objective is to promote such standards through "communications and role modeling," including dialogue on ethical issues and accountability, and emphasis on standards of conduct in ASAE publications, educational programs, and meetings.

In 1997 the Board of Directors adopted an Ethics Committee-recommended resolution to encourage ethical behavior, which states in part:

> [T]he adoption by membership organizations of codes of ethics or other similar aspirational or self-regulatory guidelines or requirements in the management and governance of associations * * * is most beneficial for society and the economy.
>
> The ASAE Board of Directors believes that association codes of ethics best serve when they contain these sections:
> a) aspirational
> b) instructional
> c) enforcement and
> d) recovery methods.
>
> * * * Although each association may have reasons for determining that one or more elements are inappropriate for their membership or industry and that additional elements may be more appropriate, the ASAE Board recommends that these issues be considered in the development and review of an association code of ethics.
>
> Aspirational elements should contain a clear description of desired behavior and desired results from those individuals who adhere to the code of ethics. * * *

In the public interest some associations adopt a statement of Enforceability which includes procedures for investigating and resolving situations or possible nonadherence and describes penalties for failure to adhere to the principles of the code of ethics. These tenets of enforceability cross a broad range of possibilities within a field and in fact some associations will conclude that Enforceability is not within the scope of their mission, as has ASAE at this time. * * * [T]he association must be careful to observe all laws and regulations that affect the substance of the code's requirements and the procedures for their enforcement.

While the idea of Recoverability is fairly new to the dialogue of ethics among associations, the notion of the ability to recover from an ethical blunder includes the concepts of disclosure/discovery, confidential counseling, restitution, recovery, and surveillance.

* * *

The Guidelines for Association Lobbyists, developed by the Government Relations Section, are intended to promote ethical participation in the political process, and to improve the public's understanding of association lobbyists' role as ethical advocates for their constituents.

The Ethics Committee views the lobbying guidelines in terms of ASAE's overall ethics effort, and encourages other ASAE sections to draw up similar documents for their specific needs.

History and Development of Codes

The Standards of Conduct were first issued in 1922. The current version was adopted in 1993.

The Guidelines for Association Lobbyists, adopted by the Government Relations Section, were approved by the Board of Directors in March 1997. They are based on the American League of Lobbyists' code of ethics. (See Law section, Legal Support Staff.)

Standards of Conduct*

As a member of the American Society of Association Executives, I pledge myself to:

- Maintain the highest standard of personal conduct.
- Actively promote and encourage the highest level of ethics within the industry or profession my association represents.
- Maintain loyalty to the association that employs me, and pursue its objectives in ways that are consistent with the public interest.
- Recognize and discharge my responsibility and that of my association to uphold all laws and regulations relating to my association's policies and activities.
- Strive for excellence in all aspects of management of my association.
- Use only legal and ethical means in all association activities.
- Serve all members of my association impartially, provide no special privilege to any individual member, and accept no personal compensation from a member except with full disclosure and with the knowledge and consent of my association's governing board.
- Maintain the confidentiality of privileged information entrusted or known to me by virtue of my office.
- Refuse to engage in, or countenance, activities for personal gain at the expense of my association or its industry or profession.
- Refuse to engage in, or countenance, discrimination on the basis of race, sex, age, religion, national origin, sexual orientation, or disability.
- Always communicate association internal and external statements in a truthful and accurate manner by assuring that there is integrity in the data and information used by my association.
- Cooperate in every reasonable and proper way with other association executives, and work with them in the advancement of the profession of association management.
- Use every opportunity to improve public understanding of the role of associations.

This Code of Standards of Conduct for members of the American Society of Association Executives has been adopted to promote and maintain the highest standards of association service and personal conduct among its members. Adherence to these standards is expected from members of the society, and serves to assure public confidence in the integrity and service of association executives.

Guidelines for Association Lobbyists*

As an individual member of the American Society of Association Executives (ASAE), I believe that effective government depends on the greatest possible participation of those being governed. At the federal, state and local level, such participation focuses on the legislative and executive branches where association and citizen lobbyists drawn from every major discipline represent literally every segment of society and every sector of the economy.

ASAE further believes that the heavy responsibility of the association lobbyist, functioning in the eye of public opinion, requires standards of ethical behavior beyond those generally accepted by a free and moral society.

ASAE therefore, offers the following guidelines which it urges be observed by its members and all those whose professional objectives are to influence national, state and local public policy decisions:

- The association lobbyist accepts the fact that it is the system of representative government we enjoy that makes possible the practice of lobbying and, while keeping the interest of employer or client in a position of primacy, will temper the advocacy role with proper consideration for the general public interest.

- The association lobbyist will protect confidences, not only those of the employers or client but also those of elected and appointed officials of government and professional colleagues.

- The association lobbyist will always deal in accurate, current and factual information, whether it is being reported to the employer or client, government officials, the media or professional colleagues, and will not engage in misrepresentation of any nature.

- The association lobbyist will acquire enough knowledge of public policy issues to be able to fairly present all points of view.

- The association lobbyist will avoid conflicts of interest, not only conflict with the interests of the employer or client, but also those of colleagues pursuing the same or similar objectives, and where conflict is unavoidable will communicate the facts fully and freely to those affected.

- The association lobbyist will comply with the laws and regulations governing lobbying as well as the standards of conduct applying to officials and staff of the Congress, the Executive Branch, and individual states and will strive to go one step further and function in a manner that goes beyond these official enactments and promulgations.

- The personal conduct of the association lobbyist should not bring discredit to the profession, government or individual colleagues.

- The association lobbyist will refrain from any form of discrimination which is legally proscribed or simply generally recognized as such.

- A priority goal of the association lobbyist should be to increase public understanding of the process and this objective should be pursued in every possible

---

*Approved by the ASAE Board on March 8, 1997. Copyright ©1997 by the American Society of Association Executives. All rights reserved. Reprinted with permission.

way—public appearances, media contacts, articles in company and other publications, and contacts in the normal course of everyday life.

* The association lobbyist should constantly strive to upgrade the necessary skills by every means available, continuing formal education, attendance at meetings and seminars, and participation in ad hoc groups with like-minded colleagues.

Organization

NATIONAL SOCIETY OF FUND RAISING EXECUTIVES

Headquarters:
1101 King Street, Suite 700
Alexandria, VA 22314
Telephone: (800) 666-FUND
(703) 684-0410
Fax: (703) 684-0540
E-mail: nsfre@nsfre.org
Website: http://www.nsfre.org

Date founded: 1960
Established in present form in 1976; previous names include Association of Fund-Raising Directors and National Society of Fund Raisers
Membership: approximately 18,000 members in 149 chapters throughout North America

Code of Ethics

Official name: *Code of Ethical Principles and Standards of Professional Practice*
History: Issued 1991, revised periodically; current version November 1997
Authority: Ethics Committee; Board of Directors; Delegate Assembly
Code is available on Website

Additional Resources

Organizational (Divisions, Programs, Services, etc.):

Advanced Certified Fund Raising Executive (ACFRE) Program
Certified Fund Raising Executive (CFRE) Program
Continuing Education Approval Program
Excellence in Fund Raising Awards
FRIENDS/Fund Raising in Economically Needful Directions
Fund-Raising Resource Center (information clearinghouse)
International Conference on Fund Raising

National Philanthropy Day
Youth in Philanthropy

Informational (Publications, Videos, Seminars, etc.):

Articles in *Advancing Philanthropy* journal and *NSFRE News*
The Accountable Not-for-Profit Organization
Conference workshops on ethical decisionmaking process
Critical Issues in Fund Raising (co-published with John Wiley & Sons)
Donor Bill of Rights
Education Program Guide for the NSFRE Code of Ethical Principles
Executive Leadership Institute *Ethics* (course)
First Course in Fund Raising
Guidelines to the Standards of Professional Practice
NSFRE Position Papers
Principles and Roles in the Ethics Enforcement Process
Survey Course on Fund Raising and *Self-Study Manual*

Goals and Activities of Organization

The National Society of Fund Raising Executives (NSFRE) focuses on the professional development of managers of nonprofit charitable organizations, and the advancement of philanthropy in general.

To achieve these goals, the NSFRE establishes standards of professional ethics and competence, and requires its members to adhere to them; provides educational and training opportunities; gathers and disseminates research and information about philanthropy and fund raising; implements programs that promote diversity in and public understanding of the field; advocates legislation to encourage giving and ethical fund raising practices; and fosters international cooperation among fund raising executives.

The Code and Standards are widely publicized to both NSFRE members and the public, and are vigorously enforced. They are a major part of the organization's broad emphasis on ethical conduct and professionalism in philanthropy. The NSFRE credentialing program, designed to enhance and verify an executive's experience and knowledge of fund raising, is another.

Implementation and Enforcement of Code

All NSFRE members sign an agreement to abide by the Code, with the understanding that it will be enforced. Holders of the CFRE or ACFRE credential, whether or not they are members of the association, also must sign a compliance form; applicants for recertification must renew their written pledge.

The national Ethics Committee's primary responsibilities are educational and advisory. These duties include revising the Code, providing clarifications of its provisions, responding to members' ethics-related questions, and designing programs on ethical issues.

The Committee also handles enforcement, according to Board-approved procedures. Anyone may submit an ethics query to the Committee to find out whether a practice warrants a formal complaint alleging a Code violation. A complaint, to be submitted within one year of the alleged misconduct, may be filed against a member or against a nonmember who holds the CFRE credential. If the Committee finds the allegation supportable, the accused is given an opportunity to respond and work with the Committee to resolve the dispute informally. The Committee may decide to hold a formal hearing.

A finding that the Code was violated can result in such disciplinary actions as reprimand, censure, suspension of or expulsion from membership, or withdrawal of an NSFRE credential.

The entire enforcement process is confidential; the accused is publicly identified only if removed from membership.

Individual chapters' Ethics Education Committees are not to review, adjudicate, or advise in specific situations regarding the Code.

The national Ethics Committee also distinguishes between violations of ethical standards and violations of law, for which legal remedies should be pursued.

History and Development of Code

The Ethics Committee develops and amends the Code of Ethical Principles; changes are approved by the Board of Directors and ratified by the Delegate Assembly.

The present Code is current as of November 1997. The Statements of Ethical Principles section was adopted in 1991; the Standards of Professional Practice section was adopted and incorporated into the Code in 1992. Amendments were made in 1993, 1994, and 1997.

Code of Ethical Principles and Standards of Professional Practice*

Statements of Ethical Principles
Adopted November 1991

The National Society of Fund Raising Executives exists to foster the development and growth of fund-raising professionals and the profession, to preserve and enhance philanthropy and volunteerism, and to promote high ethical standards in the fund-raising profession.

To these ends, this Code declares the ethical values and standards of professional practice that NSFRE members embrace and that they strive to uphold in their responsibilities for generating philanthropic support.

Members of the National Society of Fund Raising Executives are motivated by an inner drive to improve the quality of life through the causes they serve. They seek to inspire others through their own sense of dedication and high purpose. They are committed to the improvement of their professional knowledge and skills in order that their performance will better serve others. They recognize their stewardship responsibility to ensure that needed resources are vigorously and ethically sought and that the intent of the donor is honestly fulfilled. Such individuals practice their profession with integrity, honesty, truthfulness and adherence to the absolute obligation to safeguard the public trust.

Furthermore, NSFRE members:

- serve the ideal of philanthropy, are committed to the preservation and enhancement of volunteerism, and hold stewardship of these concepts as the overriding principle of professional life;
- put charitable mission above personal gain, accepting compensation by salary or set fee only;
- foster cultural diversity and pluralistic values, and treat all people with dignity and respect;
- affirm, through personal giving, a commitment to philanthropy and its role in society;
- adhere to the spirit as well as the letter of all applicable laws and regulations;
- bring credit to the fund-raising profession by their public demeanor;
- recognize their individual boundaries of competence and are forthcoming about their professional qualifications and credentials;
- value the privacy, freedom of choice and interests of all those affected by their actions;
- disclose all relationships that might constitute, or appear to constitute, conflicts of interest;
- actively encourage all their colleagues to embrace and practice these ethical principles;
- adhere to the following standards of professional practice in their responsibilities for generating philanthropic support.

Standards of Professional Practice
Adopted and incorporated into the NSFRE Code of Ethical Principles
November 1992

1. Members shall act according to the highest standards and visions of their institution, profession and conscience.

2. Members shall avoid even the appearance of any criminal offense or professional misconduct.

3. Members shall be responsible for advocating, within their own organizations, adherence to all applicable laws and regulations.

4. Members shall work for a salary or fee, not percentage-based compensation or a commission.

5. Members may accept performance-based compensation, such as bonuses, provided that such bonuses are in accord with prevailing practices within the members' own organizations and are not based on a percentage of philanthropic funds raised.

6. Members shall not pay, seek or accept finder's fees, commissions or percentage-based compensation for obtaining philanthropic funds and shall, to the best of their ability, discourage their organizations from making such payments.

7. Members shall effectively disclose all conflicts of interest; such disclosure does not preclude or imply ethical impropriety.

8. Members shall accurately state their professional experience, qualifications and expertise.

9. Members shall adhere to the principle that all donor and prospect information created by, or on behalf of, an institution is the property of that institution and shall not be transferred or utilized except on behalf of that institution.

10. Members shall, on a scheduled basis, give donors the opportunity to have their names removed from lists that are sold to, rented to, or exchanged with other organizations.

11. Members shall not disclose privileged information to unauthorized parties.

12. Members shall keep constituent information confidential.

13. Members shall take care to ensure that all solicitation materials are accurate and correctly reflect the organization's mission and use of solicited funds.

14. Members shall, to the best of their ability, ensure that contributions are used in accordance with donors' intentions.

15. Members shall ensure, to the best of their ability, proper stewardship of charitable contributions, including timely reporting on the use and management of funds and explicit consent by the donor before altering the conditions of a gift.

16. Members shall ensure, to the best of their ability, that donors receive informed and ethical advice about the value and tax implications of potential gifts.

17. Members' actions shall reflect concern for the interests and well-being of individuals affected by those actions. Members shall not exploit any relation-

ship with a donor, prospect, volunteer or employee to the benefit of the member or the member's organization.

18. In stating fund-raising results, members shall use accurate and consistent accounting methods that conform to the appropriate guidelines adopted by the American Institute of Certified Public Accountants (AICPA)* for the type of institution involved. (* In countries outside of the United States, comparable authority should be utilized.)

19. All of the above notwithstanding, members shall comply with all applicable local, state, provincial and federal civil and criminal laws.

Amended March 1993, October 1994, November 1997

12. REAL ESTATE

Organization

NATIONAL ASSOCIATION OF EXCLUSIVE BUYER AGENTS

Headquarters:
7652 Gartner Road, Suite 500
Evergreen, CO 80439-5204
Telephone: (800) 986-2322
Fax: (303) 640-7187
E-mail: NAEBAHQ@naeba.org
Website: http://www.naeba.org

Date founded: 1995
Membership: approximately 550 licensed real estate brokers, agents, and affiliates throughout North America, who exclusively represent buyers and whose real estate companies do not accept seller-property listings

Codes of Ethics

Official name: *Code of Ethics*
History: First issued 1995; revised October 1996
Authority: Ethics and Professional Standards Committee; Board of Directors

Official name: *Standards of Practice*
History: Issued 1995
Authority: Ethics and Professional Standards Committee; Board of Directors
Standards available on Website

Additional Resources

Organizational (Divisions, Programs, Services, etc.):

Certified Exclusive Buyer Agent (CEBA) Program
Consumer Inquiry Referral Program
Legal Action Program

Various committees: Advertising Practice; Constitution & Bylaws; Consumer Relations; Education; Government/Regulatory; Legal and Legislation; Standards of Practice; Technology

Informational (Publications, Videos, Seminars, etc.):

Articles in *NAEBAhood Newsletter* and in outside real estate journals
Consumer brochures
Guide to Procuring Cause
Judicial and Disciplinary Standards

Goals and Activities of Organization

The National Association of Exclusive Buyer Agents (NAEBA) is a nonprofit organization dedicated to promoting the rights and representing the interests of buyers in real estate transactions. Members may "never serve as a dual agent, facilitator, statutory appointed or designated agent" nor "promote the sale of real estate on behalf of a seller except as approved by the Board of Directors * * *."

NAEBA educates the public about exclusive buyer agency and serves its members through conferences, publications, consumer assistance, and professional training, especially the Certified Exclusive Buyer Agent Designation. It also works with the National Association of REALTORS®, Consumer Federation of America, and related organizations, on legislation and other matters of common interest.

Implementation and Enforcement of Codes

NAEBA believes that a professional association "has a responsibility to encourage ethical conduct." An agreement to abide by the Code and Standards is a condition of membership; they are distributed to members annually.

A member may not be affiliated with an economic entity whose influence "creates a conflict of interest or the public appearance of a conflict of interest" detrimental to the member's clients or to NAEBA's reputation.

Members may be disciplined by the Ethics and Professional Standards Committee for misconduct, misrepresentation, violations of the Code or governing documents, and other behavior injurious to NAEBA. Complaints may be brought by other members or by the public.

If the Committee Chairperson determines that the allegations are reasonable, a subcommittee investigates and attempts to resolve the matter. The accused is entitled to full due process protections, including notice of charges and the right to a fair formal hearing. The subcommittee decides whether a violation occurred and if so, recommends penalties; its report is reviewed by the whole Committee and forwarded to the Board of Directors for final disposition. The member may appeal for a review of the Committee's actions.

Sanctions include reprimand, fines, suspension, or expulsion. The entire disciplinary process is confidential, unless the Board deems it appropriate in a specific situation to inform the general membership.

History and Development of Codes

The Ethics and Professional Standards Committee develops the Code and Standards, with the approval of the Board of Directors and the membership. The specific language of any proposed amendments is issued prior to the annual meeting, at which Broker and Agent members may vote on them.

NAEBA Bylaws provide that Code provisions may not have an anti-competitive effect, nor may they concern advertising—except to prohibit false, deceptive, or misleading advertising.

Both the Code of Ethics and Standards of Practice date from 1995. The Code was revised in 1996. The Code will be reviewed in February 1999, and some changes are expected.

Code of Ethics*

Preamble

N.A.E.B.A. members recognize that exclusive buyer agency must be founded upon strict adherence to the legal principles of agency with ethical standards that may surpass minimum legal standards. An agency relationship therefore requires that we serve our Clients by providing five (5) measurable commitments of our ethical principles as described below. Through our commitment to those principles, our integrity, and our professionalism we serve our clients, our community, and our country. N.A.E.B.A. therefore sets forth the following Code of Ethics:

Article 1:
FIDUCIARY RESPONSIBILITY

A buyer's agent owes his principal a duty to act in a manner that is trustworthy and which inspires confidence that the agency will always act in the principal's best interest.

1.01 An exclusive buyer's agent shall represent the best interest of the client and only the client while serving in the capacity of agent for the client in any matter related to the purchase of any real estate.

1.02 An exclusive buyer's agent shall not represent any client where a conflict of interest exists.

1.03 An exclusive buyer's agent shall not knowingly direct a client to any service which is less than what is in the best interest of the client.

Article 2:
DUTY OF ACCOUNTING

An exclusive buyer's agent shall provide a true account of money and/or any other property entrusted to them, received by them, or paid out on behalf of the principal whenever requested.

2.01 An exclusive buyer's agent shall be employed by a client as evidenced by a written agreement which specifically states the services to be provided, the service fee structure, the method of payment for services, and the beginning and ending date of the agreement.

2.02 An exclusive buyer's agent shall not accept any compensation or gift resulting from expenditures made by or for their client not specified in the representation agreement.

2.03 An exclusive buyer's agent shall account to his principal by disclosing any referral income that might be received through referring that client to a listing agent.

Article 3:
DUTY OF "CARE" OR COMPETENCE

An exclusive buyer's agent shall act on behalf of a client with diligence, professionalism, and reasonable technical knowledge.

3.01 An exclusive buyer's agent shall hold a valid real estate license issued by the appropriate state governing agency.

3.02 An exclusive buyer's agent shall be accountable for his/her actions and should therefore document all substantive events which occur during the agency relationship.

3.03 An exclusive buyer's agent shall assist in negotiating price and terms as directed by the principal.

3.04 An exclusive buyer's agent shall be responsible for researching a targeted property and its surroundings whenever possible to discover all material information.

3.05 An exclusive buyer's agent shall disclose to other agents or unlicensed individuals upon first contact that he/she is acting as the buyer's agent.

3.06 An exclusive buyer's agent shall not undertake specialized services for which they are not qualified.

Article 4:
DUTY OF LOYALTY

An exclusive buyer's agent shall remain loyal to their principal throughout any real estate purchase and will not reduce the level of that loyalty through "informed consent".

4.01 An exclusive buyer's agent shall be loyal, never doing anything which might jeopardize the client's bargaining position or other interest.

4.02 An exclusive buyer's agent shall keep all sensitive information concerning his/her client confidential unless authorized by client or required by law.

4.03 An exclusive buyer's agent must relate everything material he/she knows about the seller to the client.

Article 5:
DUTY OF OBEDIENCE

N.A.E.B.A. members acknowledge and accept the agency responsibility to obey all reasonable, lawful instructions of their principal in regard to the manner of performing the real estate services contracted. While agreeing to follow the principal's instructions, it is also the member's responsibility to counsel and advise their principal where the principal's action may be unwise based upon the member's real estate experience and professional judgement.

5.01 An exclusive buyer's agent shall obey all lawful instructions of the client.

5.02 An exclusive buyer's agent shall obey all State laws and regulations in the jurisdictions in which they do business.

Standards of Practice*

PREAMBLE

The National Association of Exclusive Buyer Agents is an independent alliance of real estate professionals who provide client-level services and whose real estate companies do not accept seller-property listings. We, the members of this Association, set forth the following principles as the minimum professional standards which will guide us in serving our Buyer-Clients.

An Exclusive Buyer Agency relationship requires that we operate according to these fundamental commitments. The essence of Exclusive Buyer Agency practice is undivided loyalty to our Buyer-Clients. We recognize that it is our duty as real estate professionals to serve our clients with fidelity to these Standards of Practice. We also pledge to adhere to the Code of Ethics established by this Association.

A. Services Provided in the Initial Counseling Interview Phase

Standard A(1): A Buyer Agent will disclose that he/she is a Buyer Agent and define his/her agency relationship to a prospective Buyer-Client. A Buyer Agent will explain how different agency relationships may affect the level and type of service a Buyer-Client may receive from a real estate agent.

Standard A(2): Before entering into an agreement with a Buyer-Client, a Buyer Agent will determine if any conflict of interest may exist on his/her own part or that of a Buyer-Client. If a conflict should occur, a Buyer Agent should be precluded from representing a Buyer-Client, who should have the option of seeking representation elsewhere.

Standard A(3): A Buyer Agent will provide a copy of these professional Standards and answer any questions a Buyer-Client may have about them.

Standard A(4): A Buyer Agent will enter into a written Agency Agreement with his/her Buyer-Client. The agreement will include beginning and ending dates, the service fee structure and payment method, and the responsibilities of both parties.

Standard A(5): A Buyer Agent will make him/herself available to his/her Buyer-Client in a timely manner.

Standard A(6): A Buyer Agent will pledge absolute confidentiality to a Buyer-Client when representing him/her, thereby protecting that Buyer-Client's ability to negotiate all aspects of the transaction.

Standard A(7): A Buyer Agent will counsel a Buyer-Client regarding his/her financial qualifications and will assist that Buyer-Client in seeking and working with mortgage lenders. A Buyer Agent will not steer his/her Buyer-Client to any one lender but instead will assist him/her in evaluating interest rates and closing costs.

---

*Copyright © 1995 The National Association of Exclusive Buyer Agents. All rights reserved. Reprinted with permission.

B. Services Provided in the General Property Search Phase

Standard B(1): A Buyer Agent will discuss objectives and preferences in property styles, age, floor plans, and so forth with a Buyer-Client, then develop from this information a target property profile for him/her.

Standard B(2): Based upon the target property profile, a Buyer Agent and his/her Buyer-Client will determine the appropriate level of property preview services to be provided.

Standard B(3): With a Buyer-Client's target property profile in mind, a Buyer Agent will search the real estate market, including properties for sale by owners and builders, to locate properties to show that Buyer-Client.

C. Services Provided in the Property Selection/Contract Offer Phase

Standard C(1): A Buyer Agent will discuss and evaluate the properties viewed with his/her Buyer-Client, comparing each property shown with the target property profile.

Standard C(2): Before preparing an offer to purchase, a Buyer Agent will inform a Buyer-Client about any defects or problems he/she has observed or in any way discovered regarding the target property.

Standard C(3): Before preparing a contract offer on behalf of a Buyer-Client, a Buyer Agent will prepare a comparative market analysis, including explanations and documentation, to determine the target property's market value. A Buyer Agent will not prepare an offer to purchase a property he/she has not seen.

Standard C(4): Before a Buyer-Client signs an offer to purchase, a Buyer Agent will provide that Buyer-Client with an estimate of closing costs and, whenever possible, with the truth-in-lending estimate provided by the mortgage company.

Standard C(5): A Buyer Agent will counsel his/her Buyer-Client and explain the choices available in completing a real estate contract. This real estate counseling is based upon a Buyer Agent's experience in negotiation and real estate business decisions and is not legal advice. Legal matters should be identified and a Buyer-Client advised to seek legal counsel where appropriate.

Standard C(6): Whenever possible, a Buyer Agent will prepare the contract offer on a form which has been designed to protect a Buyer-Client's interest. A Buyer Agent will provide proper disclosures regarding agency representation and other matters as required by law.

Standard C(7): A Buyer Agent will develop contract negotiation strategies with his/her Buyer-Client, establishing pre-set limits on key points of negotiation when that Buyer-Client wishes to do so. A Buyer Agent will actively negotiate only on behalf of his/her Buyer-Client.

Standard C(8): Before submitting a contract offer to a Seller, a Buyer Agent will counsel his/her Buyer-Client regarding the time requirements specified in the contract and will encourage that Buyer-Client to have professional inspectors inspect the property if the contract is accepted.

D. Services Provided in the Escrow-to-Closing Phase

Standard D(1): A Buyer Agent will counsel a Buyer-Client regarding the types of home inspectors, the suggested criteria for selecting home inspectors, and the comparative costs of inspection services. A Buyer-Client will select real estate inspectors. A Buyer Agent will encourage his/her Buyer-Client to be present during inspections.

Standard D(2): A Buyer Agent will notify a Seller or a Seller's Agent in writing of inspectors' findings and of corrections/repairs mandated by a Buyer-Client. A Buyer Agent will specify a Buyer-Client's desire to proceed or cancel the purchase contract whenever such notification is required.

Standard D(3): A Buyer Agent will maintain contact with a Buyer-Client's title company and mortgage company to make sure that his/her Buyer-Client's interests are being protected.

Standard D(4): A Buyer Agent will review a settlement statement with his/her Buyer-Client at or before closing, if possible.

Standard D(5): A Buyer Agent will accompany a Buyer-Client on a property walk-through before closing.

Standard D(6): A Buyer Agent will attend a closing with a Buyer-Client. A Buyer Agent should be prepared to support his/her Buyer-Client's position at closing.

Standard D(7): A Buyer Agent will keep records of transactions for a reasonable period of time and will provide this information to a Buyer-Client on request.

These Standards of Practice establish obligations that include all those consistent with the "Common Law of Agency" and are considered to be client-level, not customer-level, services. These obligations are, in many instances, higher than those mandated by law. If there is any case where the law requires a greater obligation than these Standards of Practice, then the requirements of the law must be followed. It is the duty of each individual Exclusive Buyer Agent to make himself or herself aware of the laws which may affect him or her.

Organization

NATIONAL ASSOCIATION OF REALTORS®

Headquarters:
430 North Michigan Avenue
Chicago, IL 60611-4087
Telephone: (312) 329-8200
Fax: (312) 329-8576
E-mail: infocentral@realtors.org

Additional offices:
Government Affairs Group
700 11th Street, NW
Washington, DC 20001
Telephone: (202) 383-1194
Fax: (202) 383-7580

Website: http://www.REALTOR.com

Date founded: 1908
> Founded as the National Association of Real Estate Exchanges; became National Association of Real Estate Boards in 1916; acquired current name in 1974

Membership: approximately 720,000 residential and commercial brokers, salespeople, property managers, appraisers, counselors, and other real estate professionals, in some 1,700 local boards and 54 state and territorial associations; the term REALTOR® is a registered collective membership mark and may be used only by a member

Code of Ethics

Official name: *Code of Ethics and Standards of Practice*
History: First adopted 1913, revised periodically; current version effective January 1998
Authority: Professional Standards Committee; Board of Directors
Code is available on Website

Additional Resources

Organizational (Divisions, Programs, Services, etc.):

One Realtor Place™ (online information)
Professional Development Program
REALTOR® Guard (errors and omissions insurance program)
Various subgroups: Appraisal Section; Commercial Investment Real Estate Institute; Counselors of Real Estate; Institute of Real Estate Management; International Section; Real Estate Brokerage Managers Council; Real Estate Buyer's Agent Council; REALTORS® Land Institute; REALTORS® National Marketing Institute; Residential Sales Council; Society of Industrial and Office REALTORS®

Informational (Publications, Videos, Seminars, etc.):

Articles in *Today's REALTOR®* magazine, *Real Estate Outlook*, and individual subgroups' journals
Advanced Administrative Concepts of Self-Study Module/Professional Standards
Code of Ethics and Arbitration Manual and *Diskette*
Code of Ethics Awareness Brochure
Fair Housing Declaration
Interpretations of the Code of Ethics
Position Papers: Lead-Based Paint; Property Condition Disclosure and Risk Management; The Real Estate Settlement Procedures Act; Technology and Real Estate
Professionalism in Real Estate Practice

Goals and Activities of Organization

The National Association of REALTORS® (NAR) aims to promote and improve the availability of affordable housing, and to protect and strengthen the right to own, use, and transfer real property. It assists members in all recognized real estate specialties to increase their productivity, proficiency, and profit; supports the creation and maintenance of a legislative, regulatory, and legal environment at the federal, state, and local levels favorable to its members and beneficial to the public; works to achieve high standards of ethics, integrity, and fair business practices; improves the public awareness of and confidence in the association, its members, and the benefits provided by their services; and identifies and addresses trends and issues in the real estate industry.

NAR members' commitment to its Code of Ethics is widely publicized.

Implementation and Enforcement of Code

The title REALTOR® may be used only by real estate professionals who are members of the Association and who subscribe to the Code of Ethics.

The Code consists of Articles and Standards of Practice. Articles establish specific obligations, and failure to observe these requirements subjects a member to disciplinary action. The Standards are not an integral part of the Code, but rather serve to clarify the ethical obligations imposed by the Articles. A complaint alleging a violation of the Code is read as an allegation that one or more Articles have been violated; a Standard may be cited in support of the charge.

The Standards supplement, but do not substitute for, Case Interpretations, which are published in *Interpretations of the Code of Ethics.*

The Code is approved by the Board of Directors, based on changes and amendments recommended by the Professional Standards Committee when it deems necessary or advisable. Enforcement is specifically delegated through the national organization's Constitution and ByLaws, and constituent State Associations and Member Boards.

The Committee interprets the Code, and considers and recommends appropriate action on inquiries of Member Boards and from members concerning enforcement.

History and Development of Code

The first Code was adopted in 1913, and has been amended at Annual Conventions every few years since then. A significant revision occurred in 1995, when several Articles that had been aspirational were made enforceable.

The present document includes 1997 amendments, and became effective in January 1998. Some changes are expected in November 1998, which would become effective in January 1999.

In light of changing Standards, readers should consult the most recent version of the Code, available from the Association.

Code of Ethics and Standards of Practice of the National Association of REALTORS®*

Where the word REALTORS® is used in this Code and Preamble, it shall be deemed to include REALTOR-ASSOCIATE®s.

While the Code of Ethics establishes obligations that may be higher than those mandated by law, in any instance where the Code of Ethics and the law conflict, the obligations of the law must take precedence.

Preamble . . .

Under all is the land. Upon its wise utilization and widely allocated ownership depend the survival and growth of free institutions and of our civilization. REALTORS® should recognize that the interests of the nation and its citizens require the highest and best use of the land and the widest distribution of land ownership. They require the creation of adequate housing, the building of functioning cities, the development of productive industries and farms, and the preservation of a healthful environment.

Such interests impose obligations beyond those of ordinary commerce. They impose grave social responsibility and a patriotic duty to which REALTORS® should dedicate themselves, and for which they should be diligent in preparing themselves. REALTORS®, therefore, are zealous to maintain and improve the standards of their calling and share with their fellow REALTORS® a common responsibility for its integrity and honor.

In recognition and appreciation of their obligations to clients, customers, the public, and each other, REALTORS® continuously strive to become and remain informed on issues affecting real estate and, as knowledgeable professionals, they willingly share the fruit of their experience and study with others. They identify and take steps, through enforcement of this Code of Ethics and by assisting appropriate regulatory bodies, to eliminate practices which may damage the public or which might discredit or bring dishonor to the real estate profession.

Realizing that cooperation with other real estate professionals promotes the best interests of those who utilize their services, REALTORS® urge exclusive representation of clients; do not attempt to gain any unfair advantage over their competitors; and they refrain from making unsolicited comments about other practitioners. In instances where their opinion is sought, or where REALTORS® believe that comment is necessary, their opinion is offered in an objective, professional manner, uninfluenced by any personal motivation or potential advantage or gain.

The term REALTOR® has come to connote competency, fairness, and high integrity resulting from adherence to a lofty ideal of moral conduct in business

---

*Effective January 1, 1998. Form No. 166–288 (12/97). Copyright ©1998, NATIONAL ASSOCIATION OF REALTORS®—All Rights Reserved. The NATIONAL ASSOCIATION OF REALTORS® has authorship of the CODE and ownership of all right, title, and interest in and to valid and subsisting copyrights therein. Published with the consent of the NATIONAL ASSOCIATION OF REALTORS®.

The NATIONAL ASSOCIATION OF REALTORS® reserves exclusively unto itself the right to officially comment on and interpret the CODE and particular provisions thereof. For the NATIONAL ASSOCIATION's official interpretations of the CODE, see INTERPRETATIONS OF THE CODE OF ETHICS; NATIONAL ASSOCIATION OF REALTORS®.

relations. No inducement of profit and no instruction from clients ever can justify departure from this ideal.

In the interpretation of this obligation, REALTORS® can take no safer guide than that which has been handed down through the centuries, embodied in the Golden Rule, "Whatsoever ye would that others should do to you, do ye even so to them."

Accepting this standard as their own, REALTORS® pledge to observe its spirit in all of their activities and to conduct their business in accordance with the tenets set forth below.

DUTIES TO CLIENTS AND CUSTOMERS

ARTICLE 1

When representing a buyer, seller, landlord, tenant, or other client as an agent, REALTORS® pledge themselves to protect and promote the interests of their client. This obligation of absolute fidelity to the client's interests is primary, but it does not relieve REALTORS® of their obligation to treat all parties honestly. When serving a buyer, seller, landlord, tenant or other party in a non-agency capacity REALTORS® remain obligated to treat all parties honestly. *(Amended 1/93)*

- **Standard of Practice 1–1**
  REALTORS®, when acting as principals in a real estate transaction, remain obligated by the duties imposed by the Code of Ethics. *(Amended 1/93)*

- **Standard of Practice 1–2**
  The duties the Code of Ethics imposes are applicable whether REALTORS® are acting as agents or in legally recognized non-agency capacities except that any duty imposed exclusively on agents by law or regulation shall not be imposed by this Code of Ethics on REALTORS® acting in non-agency capacities.

  As used in this Code of Ethics, "client" means the person(s) or entity(ies) with whom a REALTOR® or a REALTOR®'s firm has an agency or legally recognized non-agency relationship; "customer" means a party to a real estate transaction who receives information, services, or benefits but has no contractual relationship with the REALTOR® or the REALTOR®'s firm; and "agent" means a real estate licensee acting in an agency relationship as defined by state law or regulation. *(Adopted 1/95, Amended 1/98)*

- **Standard of Practice 1–3**
  REALTORS®, in attempting to secure a listing, shall not deliberately mislead the owner as to market value.

- **Standard of Practice 1–4**
  REALTORS®, when seeking to become a buyer/tenant representative, shall not mislead buyers or tenants as to savings or other benefits that might be realized through use of the REALTOR®'s services. *(Amended 1/93)*

- **Standard of Practice 1–5**
  REALTORS® may represent the seller/landlord and buyer/tenant in the same transaction only after full disclosure to and with informed consent of both parties. *(Adopted 1/93)*

- **Standard of Practice 1–6**
  REALTORS® shall submit offers and counter-offers objectively and as quickly as possible. *(Adopted 1/93, Amended 1/95)*

- **Standard of Practice 1–7**
  When acting as listing brokers, REALTORS® shall continue to submit to the seller/landlord all offers and counter-offers until closing or execution of a lease unless the seller/landlord has waived this obligation in writing. REALTORS® shall not be obligated to continue to market the property after an offer has been accepted by the seller/landlord. REALTORS® shall recommend that sellers/ landlords obtain the advice of legal counsel prior to acceptance of a subsequent offer except where the acceptance is contingent on the termination of the pre-existing purchase contract or lease. *(Amended 1/93)*

- **Standard of Practice 1–8**
  REALTORS® acting as agents of buyers/tenants shall submit to buyers/tenants all offers and counter-offers until acceptance but have no obligation to continue to show properties to their clients after an offer has been accepted unless otherwise agreed in writing. REALTORS® acting as agents of buyers/tenants shall recommend that buyers/tenants obtain the advice of legal counsel if there is a question as to whether a pre-existing contract has been terminated. *(Adopted 1/93)*

- **Standard of Practice 1–9**
  The obligation of REALTORS® to preserve confidential information provided by their clients continues after the termination of the agency relationship. REALTORS® shall not knowingly, during or following the termination of a professional relationship with their client:
  1) reveal confidential information of the client; or
  2) use confidential information of the client to the disadvantage of the client; or
  3) use confidential information of the client for the REALTOR®'s advantage or the advantage of a third party unless:
     a) the client consents after full disclosure; or
     b) the REALTOR® is required by court order; or
     c) it is the intention of the client to commit a crime and the information is necessary to prevent the crime; or
     d) it is necessary to defend the REALTOR® or the REALTOR®'s employees or associates against an accusation of wrongful conduct. *(Adopted 1/93, Amended 1/97)*

- **Standard of Practice 1–10**
  REALTORS® shall, consistent with the terms and conditions of their property management agreement, competently manage the property of clients with due regard for the rights, responsibilities, benefits, safety and health of tenants and others lawfully on the premises. *(Adopted 1/95)*

- **Standard of Practice 1–11**
  REALTORS® who are employed to maintain or manage a client's property shall exercise due diligence and make reasonable efforts to protect it against reasonably foreseeable contingencies and losses. *(Adopted 1/95)*

- **Standard of Practice 1–12**
  When entering into listing contracts, REALTORS® must advise sellers/land-lords of:
  1) the REALTOR®'s general company policies regarding cooperation with subagents, buyer/tenant agents, or both;
  2) the fact that buyer/tenant agents, even if compensated by the listing broker, or by the seller/landlord will represent the interests of buyers/tenants; and

3) any potential for the listing broker to act as a disclosed dual agent, e.g. buyer/tenant agent. *(Adopted 1/93, Renumbered 1/98)*

- **Standard of Practice 1–13**
When entering into contracts to represent buyers/tenants, REALTORS® must advise potential clients of:
  1) the REALTOR®'s general company policies regarding cooperation with other firms; and
  2) any potential for the buyer/tenant representative to act as a disclosed dual agent, e.g. listing broker, subagent, landlord's agent, etc. *(Adopted 1/93, Renumbered 1/98)*

ARTICLE 2
REALTORS® shall avoid exaggeration, misrepresentation, or concealment of pertinent facts relating to the property or the transaction. REALTORS® shall not, however, be obligated to discover latent defects in the property, to advise on matters outside the scope of their real estate license, or to disclose facts which are confidential under the scope of agency duties owed to their clients. *(Amended 1/93)*

- **Standard of Practice 2–1**
REALTORS® shall only be obligated to discover and disclose adverse factors reasonably apparent to someone with expertise in those areas required by their real estate licensing authority. Article 2 does not impose upon the REALTOR® the obligation of expertise in other professional or technical disciplines. *(Amended 1/96)*

- **Standard of Practice 2–2**
(Renumbered as Standard of Practice 1–12 1/98)

- **Standard of Practice 2–3**
(Renumbered as Standard of Practice 1–13 1/98)

- **Standard of Practice 2–4**
REALTORS® shall not be parties to the naming of a false consideration in any document, unless it be the naming of an obviously nominal consideration.

- **Standard of Practice 2–5**
Factors defined as "non-material" by law or regulation or which are expressly referenced in law or regulation as not being subject to disclosure are considered not "pertinent" for purposes of Article 2. *(Adopted 1/93)*

ARTICLE 3
REALTORS® shall cooperate with other brokers except when cooperation is not in the client's best interest. The obligation to cooperate does not include the obligation to share commissions, fees, or to otherwise compensate another broker. *(Amended 1/95)*

- **Standard of Practice 3–1**
REALTORS®, acting as exclusive agents of sellers/landlords, establish the terms and conditions of offers to cooperate. Unless expressly indicated in offers to cooperate, cooperating brokers may not assume that the offer of cooperation includes an offer of compensation. Terms of compensation, if any, shall be

ascertained by cooperating brokers before beginning efforts to accept the offer of cooperation. *(Amended 1/94)*

- **Standard of Practice 3–2**
  REALTORS® shall, with respect to offers of compensation to another REALTOR®, timely communicate any change of compensation for cooperative services to the other REALTOR® prior to the time such REALTOR® produces an offer to purchase/lease the property. *(Amended 1/94)*

- **Standard of Practice 3–3**
  Standard of Practice 3–2 does not preclude the listing broker and cooperating broker from entering into an agreement to change cooperative compensation. *(Adopted 1/94)*

- **Standard of Practice 3–4**
  REALTORS®, acting as listing brokers, have an affirmative obligation to disclose the existence of dual or variable rate commission arrangements (i.e., listings where one amount of commission is payable if the listing broker's firm is the procuring cause of sale/lease and a different amount of commission is payable if the sale/lease results through the efforts of the seller/landlord or a cooperating broker). The listing broker shall, as soon as practical, disclose the existence of such arrangements to potential cooperating brokers and shall, in response to inquiries from cooperating brokers, disclose the differential that would result in a cooperative transaction or in a sale/lease that results through the efforts of the seller/landlord. If the cooperating broker is a buyer/tenant representative, the buyer/tenant representative must disclose such information to their client. *(Amended 1/94)*

- **Standard of Practice 3–5**
  It is the obligation of subagents to promptly disclose all pertinent facts to the principal's agent prior to as well as after a purchase or lease agreement is executed. *(Amended 1/93)*

- **Standard of Practice 3–6**
  REALTORS® shall disclose the existence of an accepted offer to any broker seeking cooperation. *(Adopted 5/86)*

- **Standard of Practice 3–7**
  When seeking information from another REALTOR® concerning property under a management or listing agreement, REALTORS® shall disclose their REALTOR® status and whether their interest is personal or on behalf of a client and, if on behalf of a client, their representational status. *(Amended 1/95)*

- **Standard of Practice 3–8**
  REALTORS® shall not misrepresent the availability of access to show or inspect a listed property. *(Amended 11/87)*

ARTICLE 4

REALTORS® shall not acquire an interest in or buy or present offers from themselves, any member of their immediate families, their firms or any member thereof, or any entities in which they have any ownership interest, any real property without making their true position known to the owner or the owner's agent. In selling property they own, or in which they have any interest, REALTORS® shall reveal their ownership or interest in writing to the purchaser or the purchaser's representative. *(Amended 1/91)*

- **Standard of Practice 4–1**
  For the protection of all parties, the disclosures required by Article 4 shall be in writing and provided by REALTORS® prior to the signing of any contract. *(Adopted 2/86)*

ARTICLE 5

REALTORS® shall not undertake to provide professional services concerning a property or its value where they have a present or contemplated interest unless such interest is specifically disclosed to all affected parties.

ARTICLE 6

When acting as agents, REALTORS® shall not accept any commission, rebate, or profit on expenditures made for their principal, without the principal's knowledge and consent. *(Amended 1/92)*

- **Standard of Practice 6–1**
  REALTORS® shall not recommend or suggest to a client or a customer the use of services of another organization or business entity in which they have a direct interest without disclosing such interest at the time of the recommendation or suggestion. *(Amended 5/88)*

- **Standard of Practice 6–2**
  When acting as agents or subagents, REALTORS® shall disclose to a client or customer if there is any financial benefit or fee the REALTOR® or the REALTOR®'s firm may receive as a direct result of having recommended real estate products or services (e.g., homeowner's insurance, warranty programs, mortgage financing, title insurance, etc.) other than real estate referral fees. *(Adopted 5/88)*

ARTICLE 7

In a transaction, REALTORS® shall not accept compensation from more than one party, even if permitted by law, without disclosure to all parties and the informed consent of the REALTOR®'s client or clients. *(Amended 1/93)*

ARTICLE 8

REALTORS® shall keep in a special account in an appropriate financial institution, separated from their own funds, monies coming into their possession in trust for other persons, such as escrows, trust funds, clients' monies, and other like items.

ARTICLE 9

REALTORS®, for the protection of all parties, shall assure whenever possible that agreements shall be in writing, and shall be in clear and understandable language expressing the specific terms, conditions, obligations and commitments of the parties. A copy of each agreement shall be furnished to each party upon their signing or initialing. *(Amended 1/95)*

- **Standard of Practice 9–1**
  For the protection of all parties, REALTORS® shall use reasonable care to ensure that documents pertaining to the purchase, sale, or lease of real estate

are kept current through the use of written extensions or amendments. *(Amended 1/93)*

DUTIES TO THE PUBLIC

ARTICLE 10

REALTORS® shall not deny equal professional services to any person for reasons of race, color, religion, sex, handicap, familial status, or national origin. REALTORS® shall not be parties to any plan or agreement to discriminate against a person or persons on the basis of race, color, religion, sex, handicap, familial status, or national origin. *(Amended 1/90)*

- **Standard of Practice 10–1**
  REALTORS® shall not volunteer information regarding the racial, religious or ethnic composition of any neighborhood and shall not engage in any activity which may result in panic selling. REALTORS® shall not print, display or circulate any statement or advertisement with respect to the selling or renting of a property that indicates any preference, limitations or discrimination based on race, color, religion, sex, handicap, familial status or national origin. *(Adopted 1/94)*

ARTICLE 11

The services which REALTORS® provide to their clients and customers shall conform to the standards of practice and competence which are reasonably expected in the specific real estate disciplines in which they engage; specifically, residential real estate brokerage, real property management, commercial and industrial real estate brokerage, real estate appraisal, real estate counseling, real estate syndication, real estate auction, and international real estate.

REALTORS® shall not undertake to provide specialized professional services concerning a type of property or service that is outside their field of competence unless they engage the assistance of one who is competent on such types of property or service, or unless the facts are fully disclosed to the client. Any persons engaged to provide such assistance shall be so identified to the client and their contribution to the assignment should be set forth. *(Amended 1/95)*

- **Standard of Practice 11–1**
  The obligations of the Code of Ethics shall be supplemented by and construed in a manner consistent with the Uniform Standards of Professional Appraisal Practice (USPAP) promulgated by the Appraisal Standards Board of the Appraisal Foundation.

  The obligations of the Code of Ethics shall not be supplemented by the USPAP where an opinion or recommendation of price or pricing is provided in pursuit of a listing, to assist a potential purchaser in formulating a purchase offer, or to provide a broker's price opinion, whether for a fee or not. *(Amended 1/96)*

- **Standard of Practice 11–2**
  The obligations of the Code of Ethics in respect of real estate disciplines other than appraisal shall be interpreted and applied in accordance with the standards of competence and practice which clients and the public reasonably require to protect their rights and interests considering the complexity of the transaction, the availability of expert assistance, and, where the REALTOR® is an agent or subagent, the obligations of a fiduciary. *(Adopted 1/95)*

- **Standard of Practice 11–3**
  When REALTORS® provide consultive services to clients which involve advice or counsel for a fee (not a commission), such advice shall be rendered in an objective manner and the fee shall not be contingent on the substance of the advice or counsel given. If brokerage or transaction services are to be provided in addition to consultive services, a separate compensation may be paid with prior agreement between the client and REALTOR®. *(Adopted 1/96)*

ARTICLE 12
    REALTORS® shall be careful at all times to present a true picture in their advertising and representations to the public. REALTORS® shall also ensure that their professional status (e.g., broker, appraiser, property manager, etc.) or status as REALTORS® is clearly identifiable in any such advertising. *(Amended 1/93)*

- **Standard of Practice 12–1**
  REALTORS® may use the term "free" and similar terms in their advertising and in other representations provided that all terms governing availability of the offered product or service are clearly disclosed at the same time. *(Amended 1/97)*

- **Standard of Practice 12–2**
  REALTORS® may represent their services as "free" or without cost even if they expect to receive compensation from a source other than their client provided that the potential for the REALTOR® to obtain a benefit from a third party is clearly disclosed at the same time. *(Amended 1/97)*

- **Standard of Practice 12–3**
  The offering of premiums, prizes, merchandise discounts or other inducements to list, sell, purchase, or lease is not, in itself, unethical even if receipt of the benefit is contingent on listing, selling, purchasing, or leasing through the REALTOR® making the offer. However, REALTORS® must exercise care and candor in any such advertising or other public or private representations so that any party interested in receiving or otherwise benefiting from the REALTOR®'s offer will have clear, thorough, advance understanding of all the terms and conditions of the offer. The offering of any inducements to do business is subject to the limitations and restrictions of state law and the ethical obligations established by any applicable Standard of Practice. *(Amended 1/95)*

- **Standard of Practice 12–4**
  REALTORS® shall not offer for sale/lease or advertise property without authority. When acting as listing brokers or as subagents, REALTORS® shall not quote a price different from that agreed upon with the seller/landlord. *(Amended 1/93)*

- **Standard of Practice 12–5**
  REALTORS® shall not advertise nor permit any person employed by or affiliated with them to advertise listed property without disclosing the name of the firm. *(Adopted 11/86)*

- **Standard of Practice 12–6**
  REALTORS®, when advertising unlisted real property for sale/lease in which they have an ownership interest, shall disclose their status as both owners/landlords and as REALTORS® or real estate licensees. *(Amended 1/93)*

- **Standard of Practice 12–7**
Only REALTORS® who participated in the transaction as the listing broker or cooperating broker (selling broker) may claim to have "sold" the property. Prior to closing, a cooperating broker may post a "sold" sign only with the consent of the listing broker. *(Amended 1/96)*

ARTICLE 13
REALTORS® shall not engage in activities that constitute the unauthorized practice of law and shall recommend that legal counsel be obtained when the interest of any party to the transaction requires it.

ARTICLE 14
If charged with unethical practice or asked to present evidence or to cooperate in any other way, in any disciplinary proceeding or investigation, REALTORS® shall place all pertinent facts before the proper tribunals of the Member Board or affiliated institute, society, or council in which membership is held and shall take no action to disrupt or obstruct such processes. *(Amended 1/90)*

- **Standard of Practice 14–1**
REALTORS® shall not be subject to disciplinary proceedings in more than one Board of REALTORS® or affiliated institute, society or council in which they hold membership with respect to alleged violations of the Code of Ethics relating to the same transaction or event. *(Amended 1/95)*

- **Standard of Practice 14–2**
REALTORS® shall not make any unauthorized disclosure or dissemination of the allegations, findings, or decision developed in connection with an ethics hearing or appeal or in connection with an arbitration hearing or procedural review. *(Amended 1/92)*

- **Standard of Practice 14–3**
REALTORS® shall not obstruct the Board's investigative or disciplinary proceedings by instituting or threatening to institute actions for libel, slander or defamation against any party to a professional standards proceeding or their witnesses. *(Adopted 11/87)*

- **Standard of Practice 14–4**
REALTORS® shall not intentionally impede the Board's investigative or disciplinary proceedings by filing multiple ethics complaints based on the same event or transaction. *(Adopted 11/88)*

DUTIES TO REALTORS®

ARTICLE 15
REALTORS® shall not knowingly or recklessly make false or misleading statements about competitors, their businesses, or their business practices. *(Amended 1/92)*

ARTICLE 16
REALTORS® shall not engage in any practice or take any action inconsistent with the agency or other exclusive relationship recognized by law that other REALTORS® have with clients. *(Amended 1/98)*

- **Standard of Practice 16–1**

  Article 16 is not intended to prohibit aggressive or innovative business practices which are otherwise ethical and does not prohibit disagreements with other REALTORS® involving commission, fees, compensation or other forms of payment or expenses. *(Adopted 1/93, Amended 1/95)*

- **Standard of Practice 16–2**

  Article 16 does not preclude REALTORS® from making general announcements to prospective clients describing their services and the terms of their availability even though some recipients may have entered into agency agreements or other exclusive relationships with another REALTOR®. A general telephone canvass, general mailing or distribution addressed to all prospective clients in a given geographical area or in a given profession, business, club, or organization, or other classification or group is deemed "general" for purposes of this standard. *(Amended 1/98)*

  Article 16 is intended to recognize as unethical two basic types of solicitations:

  First, telephone or personal solicitations of property owners who have been identified by a real estate sign, multiple listing compilation, or other information service as having exclusively listed their property with another REALTOR®; and

  Second, mail or other forms of written solicitations of prospective clients whose properties are exclusively listed with another REALTOR® when such solicitations are not part of a general mailing but are directed specifically to property owners identified through compilations of current listings, "for sale" or "for rent" signs, or other sources of information required by Article 3 and Multiple Listing Service rules to be made available to other REALTORS® under offers of subagency or cooperation. *(Amended 1/93)*

- **Standard of Practice 16–3**

  Article 16 does not preclude REALTORS® from contacting the client of another broker for the purpose of offering to provide, or entering into a contract to provide, a different type of real estate service unrelated to the type of service currently being provided (e.g., property management as opposed to brokerage). However, information received through a Multiple Listing Service or any other offer of cooperation may not be used to target clients of other REALTORS® to whom such offers to provide services may be made. *(Amended 1/93)*

- **Standard of Practice 16–4**

  REALTORS® shall not solicit a listing which is currently listed exclusively with another broker. However, if the listing broker, when asked by the REALTOR®, refuses to disclose the expiration date and nature of such listing; i.e., an exclusive right to sell, an exclusive agency, open listing, or other form of contractual agreement between the listing broker and the client, the REALTOR® may contact the owner to secure such information and may discuss the terms upon which the REALTOR® might take a future listing or, alternatively, may take a listing to become effective upon expiration of any existing exclusive listing. *(Amended 1/94)*

- **Standard of Practice 16–5**

  REALTORS® shall not solicit buyer/tenant agreements from buyers/tenants who are subject to exclusive buyer/tenant agreements. However, if asked by a REALTOR®, the broker refuses to disclose the expiration date of the exclusive buyer/tenant agreement, the REALTOR® may contact the buyer/tenant to secure such information and may discuss the terms upon which the REALTOR® might enter into a future buyer/tenant agreement or, alternatively, may enter into a buyer/tenant agreement to become effective upon the expiration of any existing exclusive buyer/tenant agreement. *(Adopted 1/94, Amended 1/98)*

- **Standard of Practice 16–6**
  When REALTORS® are contacted by the client of another REALTOR® regarding the creation of an exclusive relationship to provide the same type of service, and REALTORS® have not directly or indirectly initiated such discussions, they may discuss the terms upon which they might enter into a future agreement or, alternatively, may enter into an agreement which becomes effective upon expiration of any existing exclusive agreement. *(Amended 1/98)*

- **Standard of Practice 16–7**
  The fact that a client has retained a REALTOR® as an agent or in another exclusive relationship in one or more past transactions does not preclude other REALTORS® from seeking such former client's future business. *(Amended 1/98)*

- **Standard of Practice 16–8**
  The fact that an exclusive agreement has been entered into with a REALTOR® shall not preclude or inhibit any other REALTOR® from entering into a similar agreement after the expiration of the prior agreement. *(Amended 1/98)*

- **Standard of Practice 16–9**
  REALTORS®, prior to entering into an agency agreement or other exclusive relationship, have an affirmative obligation to make reasonable efforts to determine whether the client is subject to a current, valid exclusive agreement to provide the same type of real estate service. *(Amended 1/98)*

- **Standard of Practice 16–10**
  REALTORS®, acting as agents of, or in another relationship with, buyers or tenants, shall disclose that relationship to the seller/landlord's agent or broker at first contact and shall provide written confirmation of that disclosure to the seller/landlord's agent or broker not later than execution of a purchase agreement or lease. *(Amended 1/98)*

- **Standard of Practice 16–11**
  On unlisted property, REALTORS® acting as buyer/tenant agents or brokers shall disclose that relationship to the seller/landlord at first contact for that client and shall provide written confirmation of such disclosure to the seller/landlord not later than execution of any purchase or lease agreement.

  REALTORS® shall make any request for anticipated compensation from the seller/landlord at first contact. *(Amended 1/98)*

- **Standard of Practice 16–12**
  REALTORS®, acting as agents or brokers of sellers/landlords or as sub-agents of listing brokers, shall disclose that relationship to buyers/tenants

as soon as practicable and shall provide written confirmation of such disclosure to buyers/tenants not later than execution of any purchase or lease agreement. *(Amended 1/98)*

- **Standard of Practice 16–13**
All dealings concerning property exclusively listed, or with buyer/tenants who are subject to an exclusive agreement shall be carried on with the client's agent or broker, and not with the client, except with the consent of the client's agent or broker or except where such dealings are initiated by the client. *(Adopted 1/93, Amended 1/98)*

- **Standard of Practice 16–14**
REALTORS® are free to enter into contractual relationships or to negotiate with sellers/landlords, buyers/tenants or others who are not subject to an exclusive agreement but shall not knowingly obligate them to pay more than one commission except with their informed consent. *(Amended 1/98)*

- **Standard of Practice 16–15**
In cooperative transactions REALTORS® shall compensate cooperating REALTORS® (principal brokers) and shall not compensate nor offer to compensate, directly or indirectly, any of the sales licensees employed by or affiliated with other REALTORS® without the prior express knowledge and consent of the cooperating broker.

- **Standard of Practice 16–16**
REALTORS®, acting as subagents or buyer/tenant agents or brokers, shall not use the terms of an offer to purchase/lease to attempt to modify the listing broker's offer of compensation to subagents or buyer's agents or brokers nor make the submission of an executed offer to purchase/lease contingent on the listing broker's agreement to modify the offer of compensation. *(Amended 1/98)*

- **Standard of Practice 16–17**
REALTORS® acting as subagents or as buyer/tenant agents or brokers, shall not attempt to extend a listing broker's offer of cooperation and/or compensation to other brokers without the consent of the listing broker. *(Amended 1/98)*

- **Standard of Practice 16–18**
REALTORS® shall not use information obtained by them from the listing broker, through offers to cooperate received through Multiple Listing Services or other sources authorized by the listing broker, for the purpose of creating a referral prospect to a third broker, or for creating a buyer/tenant prospect unless such use is authorized by the listing broker. *(Amended 1/93)*

- **Standard of Practice 16–19**
Signs giving notice of property for sale, rent, lease, or exchange shall not be placed on property without consent of the seller/landlord. *(Amended 1/93)*

- **Standard of Practice 16–20**
REALTORS®, prior to or after terminating their relationship with their current firm, shall not induce clients of their current firm to cancel exclusive contractual agreements between the client and that firm. This does not preclude REALTORS® (principals) from establishing agreements with their

associated licensees governing assignability of exclusive agreements. *(Adopted 1/98)*

ARTICLE 17

In the event of contractual disputes or specific non-contractual disputes as defined in Standard of Practice 17–4 between REALTORS® associated with different firms, arising out of their relationship as REALTORS®, the REALTORS® shall submit the dispute to arbitration in accordance with the regulations of their Board or Boards rather than litigate the matter.

In the event clients of REALTORS® wish to arbitrate contractual disputes arising out of real estate transactions, REALTORS® shall arbitrate those disputes in accordance with the regulations of their Board, provided the clients agree to be bound by the decision. *(Amended 1/97)*

- **Standard of Practice 17–1**
The filing of litigation and refusal to withdraw from it by REALTORS® in an arbitrable matter constitutes a refusal to arbitrate. *(Adopted 2/86)*

- **Standard of Practice 17–2**
Article 17 does not require REALTORS® to arbitrate in those circumstances when all parties to the dispute advise the Board in writing that they choose not to arbitrate before the Board. *(Amended 1/93)*

- **Standard of Practice 17–3**
REALTORS®, when acting solely as principals in a real estate transaction, are not obligated to arbitrate disputes with other REALTORS® absent a specific written agreement to the contrary. *(Adopted 1/96)*

- **Standard of Practice 17–4**
Specific non-contractual disputes that are subject to arbitration pursuant to Article 17 are:

1) Where a listing broker has compensated a cooperating broker and another cooperating broker subsequently claims to be the procuring cause of the sale or lease. In such cases the complainant may name the first cooperating broker as respondent and arbitration may proceed without the listing broker being named as a respondent. Alternatively, if the complaint is brought against the listing broker, the listing broker may name the first cooperating broker as a third-party respondent. In either instance the decision of the hearing panel as to procuring cause shall be conclusive with respect to all current or subsequent claims of the parties for compensation arising out of the underlying cooperative transaction. *(Adopted 1/97)*

2) Where a buyer or tenant representative is compensated by the seller or landlord, and not by the listing broker, and the listing broker, as a result, reduces the commission owed by the seller or landlord and, subsequent to such actions, another cooperating broker claims to be the procuring cause of sale or lease. In such cases the complainant may name the first cooperating broker as respondent and arbitration may proceed without the listing broker being named as a respondent. Alternatively, if the complaint is brought against the listing broker, the listing broker may name the first cooperating broker as a third-party respondent. In either instance the decision of the hearing panel as to procuring cause shall be conclusive with respect to all current or subsequent claims of the parties for compensation arising out of the underlying cooperative transaction. *(Adopted 1/97)*

3) Where a buyer or tenant representative is compensated by the buyer or tenant and, as a result, the listing broker reduces the commission owed by the seller or landlord and, subsequent to such actions, another cooperating broker claims to be the procuring cause of sale or lease. In such cases the complainant may name the first cooperating broker as respondent and arbitration may proceed without the listing broker being named as a respondent. Alternatively, if the complaint is brought against the listing broker, the listing broker may name the first cooperating broker as a third-party respondent. In either instance the decision of the hearing panel as to procuring cause shall be conclusive with respect to all current or subsequent claims of the parties for compensation arising out of the underlying cooperative transaction. *(Adopted 1/97)*

4) Where two or more listing brokers claim entitlement to compensation pursuant to open listings with a seller or landlord who agrees to participate in arbitration (or who requests arbitration) and who agrees to be bound by the decision. In cases where one of the listing brokers has been compensated by the seller or landlord, the other listing broker, as complainant, may name the first listing broker as respondent and arbitration may proceed between the brokers. *(Adopted 1/97)*

The Code of Ethics was adopted in 1913. Amended at the Annual Convention in 1924, 1928, 1950, 1951, 1952, 1955, 1956, 1961, 1962, 1974, 1982, 1986, 1987, 1989, 1990, 1991, 1992, 1993, 1994, 1995, 1996 and 1997.

Explanatory Notes

The reader should be aware of the following policies which have been approved by the Board of Directors of the National Association:

In filing a charge of an alleged violation of the Code of Ethics by a REALTOR®, the charge must read as an alleged violation of one or more Articles of the Code. Standards of Practice may be cited in support of the charge.

The Standards of Practice serve to clarify the ethical obligations imposed by the various Articles and supplement, and do not substitute for, the Case Interpretations in *Interpretations of the Code of Ethics*.

Modifications to existing Standards of Practice and additional new Standards of Practice are approved from time to time. Readers are cautioned to ensure that the most recent publications are utilized.

II.   HEALTH

1.   ALLIED HEALTH

2.   CHIROPRACTIC

3.   DENTISTRY

4.   MEDICINE

5.   MENTAL HEALTH

1. ALLIED HEALTH

Organization

AMERICAN COLLEGE OF HEALTHCARE EXECUTIVES

Headquarters:
One North Franklin Street
Suite 1700
Chicago, IL 60606-3491
Telephone: (312) 424-2800
Fax: (312) 424-0023
E-mail: GenInfo@ache.org
Website: http://www.ache.org

Date founded: 1933
Membership: approximately 30,000 managers and administrators in a wide range of health care settings

Code of Ethics

Official name: *Code of Ethics*
History: Adopted 1939, revised periodically; current version as amended August 1995
Authority: Ethics Committee; Council of Regents
Code is available on Website

Additional Resources

Organizational (Divisions, Programs, Services, etc.):

Annual Congress on Healthcare Management
Annual Ethics Special Seminar
Board of Governors Examination in Healthcare Management
Credentialing Programs: Certified Healthcare Executive (CHE); Fellow of the American College of Healthcare Executives (FACHE)
Ethics Self-Assessment Tool
Health Administration Press
Healthcare Executive Public Policy Institute
Leadership Development Institute

255

Informational (Publications, Videos, Seminars, etc.):
Articles in *Healthcare Executive, Hospital & Health Services Administration,* and research journals
Competition, Regulation, and Rationing in Health Care
Contemporary Managed Care: Readings in Structure, Operations, and Public Policy
Cornerstones of Leadership for Health Services Executives
The Ethics of the Ordinary in Healthcare: Concepts and Cases
Evaluating the Healthcare System: Effectiveness, Efficiency, and Equity
Explorations in Quality Assessment and Monitoring
Health Policymaking in the United States
Hospital Leadership & Accountability
Hospital Staff Privileges: What Every Health Care Practitioner and Lawyer Needs to Know
The Law and the Public's Health
The Law of Hospital and Health Care Administration
The Moral Challenges of Health Care Management
The Politics of Health Legislation: An Economic Perspective
Protocols for Health Care Executive Behavior: A Factor for Success
Ethics Policy Statements:
   Creating an Ethical Environment for Employees
   Decisions Near the End Of Life
   Ethical Decision Making for Healthcare Executives
   Ethical Issues Related to Downsizing
   Health Information Confidentiality
   Impaired Healthcare Executives
Professional and Public Policy Statements:
   Access To Healthcare
   Age Discrimination and the Healthcare Executive
   Board Certification in Healthcare Management
   Educational Training in Ethics for Healthcare Executives
   Enhancing Minority Opportunities in Healthcare Management
   Evaluating the Performance of the Hospital CEO
   The Healthcare Executive's Role in Community Health Improvement
   Healthcare Executives' Responsibility to Their Communities
   Lifelong Learning and the Healthcare Executive
   Medical Records Confidentiality
   Organ Donation
   Organizational Ethical Mechanisms
   Preventing and Addressing Sexual Harassment in the Workplace
   Responsibility For Mentoring
   Strengthening Healthcare Employment Opportunities For Persons With Disabilities
   Voluntary Credentialing
Seminars and conference sessions:
   Critical Ethical Issues in Healthcare Management: When Values Collide

Ethical Dilemmas in Managing Care for the Elderly
Legal Compliance Issues in Building Network Alliances
Meeting the Physician Leadership Challenge
Raising the Standards for American Healthcare: Best People, Best
   Practices, Best Results

Goals and Activities of Organization

The American College of Healthcare Executives (ACHE) works to advance the quality of healthcare by helping leaders in hospitals and other healthcare settings create, manage, and monitor change.

Its programs include: developing and supporting professional and ethical standards and credentials; continuing education on specific healthcare issues; initiating and conducting major research in healthcare management; extensive publishing; building communication among members; and encouraging members' participation in the public policy process and offering guidance on important public policy issues.

ACHE places a strong emphasis on ethical standards. The Board of Governors Examination, for instance, examines candidates on their specific knowledge of the Code of Ethics and Ethical Policy Statements. The Ethics Self-Assessment Tool helps members identify issues in which they are—or are not—"on strong ethical ground," and offers an opportunity for personal reflection.

Implementation and Enforcement of Code

Every ACHE member must agree to uphold the Code, which is administered by an Ethics Committee appointed by the Board of Governors. The Committee evaluates the Code annually, recommends any necessary updates, and refines it to specific applications and membership classifications. It is responsible for developing ethical policy statements to guide members' conduct, and for preparing an annual report of its accomplishments and recommendations.

A complaint alleging an infraction of the Code must be filed in writing with the Ethics Committee within three years of the date of discovery of the incident. The Committee must look into all such complaints, provided the information can be documented or supported; or it may be a matter of public record.

The accused member is notified at various stages of the complaint process and is afforded a reasonable opportunity to consider the charges, and to appear and/or respond in his or her defense.

The Ethics Committee refers the matter to a Regent, who investigates it, makes a report, and recommends an action. The Committee reviews the Regent's report and, in turn, recommends an action to the Board of Governors. If the member files an appeal from the Committee's recommendation, the Board of Governors appoints an ad hoc committee to hear the appeal. This hearing committee then makes a report and recommends an action to the Board.

The Board's ultimate decision on the appeal is final. The Board may accept or reject any of the findings or recommendations of the Regent, the Ethics Committee, or the hearing committee, and order whatever level of discipline it decides is justified. Possible sanctions for Code violation include censure, probation, suspension or expulsion of the member.

At each stage, the Board has the discretion to notify the complainant, beyond the fact that the complaint was reviewed or finalized. All information used during the entire process that is not already publicly known is kept strictly confidential, except as provided by the Board or as required by law.

History and Development of Code

The Code was originally developed in 1933 by a committee of representatives of the American Hospital Association and the American College of Hospital Administrators. The Ethics Committee reviews the Code every year to determine if it needs to be updated.

The document reproduced here was amended by the Council of Regents at its annual meeting August 1995.

The Appendices to the Code, not included in this reprint, detail the grievance procedures summarized above.

Code of Ethics*

PREAMBLE

The purpose of the *Code of Ethics* of the American College of Healthcare Executives is to serve as a guide to conduct for members. It contains standards of ethical behavior for healthcare executives in their professional relationships. These relationships include members of the healthcare executive's organization and other organizations. Also included are patients or others served, colleagues, the community and society as a whole. The *Code of Ethics* also incorporates standards of ethical behavior governing personal behavior, particularly when that conduct directly relates to the role and identity of the healthcare executive.

The fundamental objectives of the healthcare management profession are to enhance overall quality of life, dignity and well-being of every individual needing healthcare services; and to create a more equitable, accessible, effective and efficient healthcare system.

Healthcare executives have an obligation to act in ways that will merit the trust, confidence and respect of healthcare professionals and the general public. Therefore, healthcare executives should lead lives that embody an exemplary system of values and ethics.

In fulfilling their commitments and obligations to patients or others served, healthcare executives function as moral advocates. Since every management decision affects the health and well-being of both individuals and communities, healthcare executives must carefully evaluate the possible outcomes of their decisions. In organizations that deliver healthcare services, they must work to safeguard and foster the rights, interests and prerogatives of patients or others served. The role of moral advocate requires that healthcare executives speak out and take actions necessary to promote such rights, interests and prerogatives if they are threatened.

I. THE HEALTHCARE EXECUTIVE'S RESPONSIBILITIES TO THE PROFESSION OF HEALTHCARE MANAGEMENT

The healthcare executive shall:

A. Uphold the values, ethics and mission of the healthcare management profession;
B. Conduct all personal and professional activities with honesty, integrity, respect, fairness and good faith in a manner that will reflect well upon the profession;
C. Comply with all laws pertaining to healthcare management in the jurisdictions in which the healthcare executive is located, or conducts professional activities;
D. Maintain competence and proficiency in healthcare management by implementing a personal program of assessment and continuing professional education;
E. Avoid the exploitation of professional relationships for personal gain;
F. Use this Code to further the interests of the profession and not for selfish reasons;
G. Respect professional confidences;

---

*As amended by the Council of Regents at its annual meeting on August 22, 1995.

Reprinted with permission of the American College of Healthcare Executives. This reprint contains the full text of the Preamble and numbered sections of the Code. The Preface and the Appendices on Grievance Procedure and Ethics Committee Action (which are a material part of the Code of Ethics and incorporated therein by reference), have been omitted, but are summarized in the preceding introductory pages.

H. Enhance the dignity and image of the healthcare management profession through positive public information programs; and

I. Refrain from participating in any activity that demeans the credibility and dignity of the healthcare management profession.

II. THE HEALTHCARE EXECUTIVE'S RESPONSIBILITIES TO PATIENTS OR OTHERS SERVED, TO THE ORGANIZATION AND TO EMPLOYEES

A. RESPONSIBILITIES TO PATIENTS OR OTHERS SERVED

The healthcare executive shall, within the scope of his or her authority:

1. Work to ensure the existence of a process to evaluate the quality of care or service rendered;

2. Avoid practicing or facilitating discrimination and institute safeguards to prevent discriminatory organizational practices;

3. Work to ensure the existence of a process that will advise patients or others served of the rights, opportunities, responsibilities and risks regarding available healthcare services;

4. Work to provide a process that ensures the autonomy and self-determination of patients or others served; and

5. Work to ensure the existence of procedures that will safeguard the confidentiality and privacy of patients or others served.

B. RESPONSIBILITIES TO THE ORGANIZATION

The healthcare executive shall, within the scope of his or her authority:

1. Provide healthcare services consistent with available resources and work to ensure the existence of a resource allocation process that considers ethical ramifications;

2. Conduct both competitive and cooperative activities in ways that improve community healthcare services;

3. Lead the organization in the use and improvement of standards of management and sound business practices;

4. Respect the customs and practices of patients or others served, consistent with the organization's philosophy; and

5. Be truthful in all forms of professional and organizational communication, and avoid disseminating information that is false, misleading, or deceptive.

C. RESPONSIBILITIES TO EMPLOYEES

Healthcare executives have an ethical and professional obligation to employees of the organizations they manage that encompass but are not limited to:

1. Working to create a working environment conducive for underscoring employee ethical conduct and behavior.

2. Working to ensure that individuals may freely express ethical concerns and providing mechanisms for discussing and addressing such concerns.

3. Working to ensure a working environment that is free from harassment, sexual and other; coercion of any kind, especially to perform illegal or unethical acts; and discrimination on the basis of race, creed, color, sex, ethnic origin, age or disability.

4. Working to ensure a working environment that is conducive to proper utilization of employees' skills and abilities.
5. Paying particular attention to the employee's work environment and job safety.
6. Working to establish appropriate grievance and appeals mechanisms.

III. CONFLICTS OF INTEREST

A conflict of interest may be only a matter of degree, but exists when the healthcare executive:
A. Acts to benefit directly or indirectly by using authority or inside information, or allows a friend, relative or associate to benefit from such authority or information.
B. Uses authority or information to make a decision to intentionally affect the organization in an adverse manner.

The healthcare executive shall:
A. Conduct all personal and professional relationships in such a way that all those affected are assured that management decisions are made in the best interests of the organization and the individuals served by it;
B. Disclose to the appropriate authority any direct or indirect financial or personal interests that pose potential or actual conflicts of interest;
C. Accept no gifts or benefits offered with the express or implied expectation of influencing a management decision; and
D. Inform the appropriate authority and other involved parties of potential or actual conflicts of interest related to appointments or elections to boards or committees inside or outside the healthcare executive's organization.

IV. THE HEALTHCARE EXECUTIVE'S RESPONSIBILITIES TO COMMUNITY AND SOCIETY

The healthcare executive shall:
A. Work to identify and meet the healthcare needs of the community;
B. Work to ensure that all people have reasonable access to healthcare services;
C. Participate in public dialogue on healthcare policy issues and advocate solutions that will improve health status and promote quality healthcare;
D. Consider the short-term and long-term impact of management decisions on both the community and on society; and
E. Provide prospective consumers with adequate and accurate information, enabling them to make enlightened judgments and decisions regarding services.

V. THE HEALTHCARE EXECUTIVE'S RESPONSIBILITY TO REPORT VIOLATIONS OF THE CODE

A member of the College who has reasonable grounds to believe that another member has violated this Code has a duty to communicate such facts to the Ethics Committee.

* * *

Organization

AMERICAN HOSPITAL ASSOCIATION

Headquarters:
One North Franklin
Chicago, IL 60606
Telephone: (312) 422-3000
Fax: (312) 422-4796

Additional offices:
325 7th Street, NW
Washington, DC 20004
Telephone: (202) 638-1100
(800) 424-4301
Fax: (202) 626-2345

E-mail: webmaster@aha.org
Website: http://www.aha.org

Date founded: 1898
Formerly the Association of Hospital Superintendents; renamed 1906
Membership: approximately 5,000 institutions, 600 associates, and 40,000 individuals; members include hospitals, nonhospital facilities, hospital-affiliated educational programs, commercial firms, consultants, suppliers, and health care professionals

Code of Ethics

Official name: *Management Advisory: Ethical Conduct for Health Care Institutions*
History: Originally issued 1973; revised periodically; current version approved 1992
Authority: Technical Panel on Biomedical Ethics; Institutional Practices Committee
Code is available on Website

262

Additional Resources

Organizational (Divisions, Programs, Services, etc.):

AHA/Joint Commission Sentinel Event Legal Issues Task Force
American Organization of Nurse Executives
Award to Recognize Excellence in End-of-Life Care
Center for Health Care Leadership
Center for Hospital and Healthcare Administration History
Compliance Information HelpLine (national compliance experts respond
    to subscribers' questions)
Health Care Compliance Service
Health Policy Tracking Service
Health Research and Educational Trust
HealthSTAR (database)
National Information Center for Health Services Administration
Organizational Ethics Task Force
Quality Initiative: Baldrige Self Assessment for Health Care Organizations
Quality Leadership Team
Society for Healthcare Consumer Advocacy

Informational (Publications, Videos, Seminars, etc.):

Articles in *AHA News, Health Facilities Management, Hospitals & Health
    Networks,* and *Trustee*
Accountability: The Buck Stops in the Boardroom (course)
Choices and Conflict: Explorations in Health Care Ethics
*Community Stewardship: Applying the Five Principles of Contemporary
    Governance*
Compliance Manual/Workbook
Compliance Web Site
*Creating a Secure Workplace: Effective Policies and Practices in Health
    Care*
*Ethics for Everyone: A Practical Guide to Interdisciplinary Biomedical
    Ethics Education*
Framework for Compliance Guide and *Video*
Health Care Ethics Committees: The Next Generation
Health Care Manager's Guide to Continuous Quality Improvement
Legal Issues and the Integrated Delivery System: An Executive Guide
Managed Care Ethics: A Clinician's Concise Guide
Management Advisories:
    A Patient's Bill of Rights
    Advertising
    Discharge Planning
    Disclosure of Financial and Operating Information
    Disclosure of Medical Record Information
    Establishment of an Employee Grievance Procedure

Ethics Committees
Imperatives of Hospital Leadership
The Patient's Choice of Treatment Options
Physician Involvement in Governance
Quality Management
Resolution of Conflicts of Interest
Verifying Physician Credentials
Verifying Credentials of Medical Students and Residents
Principles and Guidelines for Changes in Hospital Ownership
Public Policy Advocacy Papers:
Campaign for Coverage
Enhancing Public Confidence
The False Claims Act and Medicare Billing Disputes
Federal Quality and Consumer Protection Legislation
Risk Management Handbook for Health Care Organizations
Service Quality Improvement: The Customer Satisfaction Strategy for Health Care
Statement on Hospital Compliance Programs
The Trustee Guide to Board Accountability in Health Care
Values in Conflict: Resolving Ethical Issues in Health Care

Goals and Activities of Organization

The American Hospital Association's (AHA) stated mission is to advance the health of individuals and communities by leading, representing, and serving health care provider organizations that are accountable to the community and committed to health improvement.

As an organization of organizations, AHA advocates its members' interests before Congress, federal government agencies, courts, standard-setting organizations, and the media, in an effort to influence legislation and regulatory development. It actively participates in the national debate over health care policy issues and health delivery restructuring.

Members are entitled to a broad spectrum of informational, educational, and data and insurance resources designed to enhance their operational effectiveness and professional growth, and implement change at the community level.

Implementation and Enforcement of Code

The Management Advisory on Ethics examines the ethical responsibilities of health care institutions to the community and to patients, and in their roles as employers and businesses. It is intended to provide general advice to members and to assist them in better defining the ethical aspects and implications of their institution's policies and practices. Each member institution's leadership is expected to take into account the individual needs and values of all those who would be affected by its decisions.

The governing board of the institution is responsible for establishing and periodically evaluating the ethical standards that guide institutional policies and practices, and for assuring that its own actions comply with legal and ethical rules. The chief executive officer is responsible for assuring that all staff, employees, and volunteers understand and adhere to standards of ethical conduct.

The AHA notes that ethical responsibilities may be included in legal and accreditation requirements, but often go beyond them.

History and Development of Code

This 1992 document is the most recent version of the AHA's ethical standards. The revisions it incorporated—which focused on advertising, patient care, and conflicts of interest—were made by the Technical Panel on Biomedical Ethics and approved by the Institutional Practices Committee.

The previous standards, Guidelines on Ethical Conduct for Health Care Institutions, were developed in 1987 by the Advisory Committee on Biomedical Ethics and approved by the Board of Trustees. That document broadened and updated the AHA's first code, Guidelines on Ethical Conduct and Relationships for Health Care Institutions, which was formulated in 1973 by the Special Committee on Ethics and revised in 1981.

Management Advisory: Ethical Conduct for Health Care Institutions*

INTRODUCTION

Health care institutions,[1] by virtue of their roles as health care providers, employers, and community health resources, have special responsibilities for ethical conduct and ethical practices that go beyond meeting minimum legal and regulatory standards. Their broad range of patient care, education, public health, social service, and business functions is essential to the health and well being of their communities. These roles and functions demand that health care organizations conduct themselves in an ethical manner that emphasizes a basic community service orientation and justifies the public trust. The health care institution's mission and values should be embodied in all its programs, services, and activities.

Because health care organizations must frequently seek a balance among the interests and values of individuals, the institution, and society, they often face ethical dilemmas in meeting the needs of their patients and their communities. This advisory is intended to assist members of the American Hospital Association to better identify and understand the ethical aspects and implications of institutional policies and practices. It is offered with the understanding that each institution's leadership in making policy and decisions must take into account the needs and values of the institution, its physicians, other caregivers, and employees and those of individual patients, their families, and the community as a whole.

The governing board of the institution is responsible for establishing and periodically evaluating the ethical standards that guide institutional policies and practices. The governing board must also assure that its own policies, practices, and members comply with both legal and ethical standards of behavior. The chief executive officer is responsible for assuring that hospital medical staff, employees, and volunteers and auxilians understand and adhere to these standards and for promoting a hospital environment sensitive to differing values and conducive to ethical behavior.

This advisory examines the hospital's ethical responsibilities to its community and patients as well as those deriving from its organizational roles as employer and business entity. Although explicit responsibilities also are included in legal and accreditation requirements, it should be remembered that legal, accreditation, and ethical obligations often overlap and that ethical obligations often extend beyond legal and accreditation requirements.

COMMUNITY ROLE

Health care institutions should be concerned with the overall health status of their communities while continuing to provide direct patient services. They should

---

*This advisory was revised by the AHA Technical Panel on Biomedical Ethics and approved by the Institutional Practices Committee in 1992.

© 1992 by the American Hospital Association, [840 North Lake Shore Drive], Chicago, Illinois [60611]. All rights reserved. Order #049732. Reprinted with permission of the American Hospital Association, copyright 1992.

[1]The term "health care institution" represents the mission, programs, and services as defined and implemented by the institution's leadership, including the governing board, executive management, and medical staff leadership. See also management advisories on *Imperatives of Hospital*

take a leadership role in enhancing public health and continuity of care in the community by communicating and working with other health care and social agencies to improve the availability and provision of health promotion, education, and patient care services.

Health care institutions are responsible for fair and effective use of available health care delivery resources to promote access to comprehensive and affordable health care services of high quality. This responsibility extends beyond the resources of the given institution to include efforts to coordinate with other health care organizations and professionals and to share in community solutions for providing care for the medically indigent and others in need of specific health services.

All health care institutions are responsible for meeting community service obligations which may include special initiatives for the poor and uninsured, provision of needed medical or social services, education, and various programs designed to meet the specific needs of their communities.

Health care institutions, being dependent upon community confidence and support, are accountable to the public, and therefore their communications and disclosure of information and data related to the institution should be clear, accurate, and sufficiently complete to assure that it is not misleading. Such disclosure should be aimed primarily at better public understanding of health issues, the services available to prevent and treat illness, and patient rights and responsibilities relating to health care decisions.

Advertising may be used to advance the health care organization's goals and objectives and should, in all cases, support the mission of the health care organization. Advertising may be used to educate the public, to report to the community, to increase awareness of available services, to increase support for the organization, and to recruit employees. Health care advertising should be truthful, fair, accurate, complete, and sensitive to the health care needs of the public. False or misleading statements, or statements that might lead the uninformed to draw false conclusions about the health care facility, its competitors, or other health care providers are unacceptable and unethical.[2]

As health care institutions operate in an increasingly challenging environment, they should consider the overall welfare of their communities and their own missions in determining their activities, service mixes, and business. Health care organizations should be particularly sensitive to potential conflicts of interests involving individuals or groups associated with the medical staff, governing board, or executive management. Examples of such conflicts include ownership or other financial interests in competing provider organizations or groups contracting with the health care institution.

PATIENT CARE

Health care institutions are responsible for providing each patient with care that is both appropriate and necessary for the patient's condition. Development and maintenance of organized programs for utilization review and quality improvement and of procedures to verify the credentials of physicians and other health professionals are basic to this obligation.

Leadership, Role and Functions of Hospital Executive Management, Role and Functions of the Hospital Governing Board, and Role and Functions of the Hospital Medical Staff.
    [2]Adapted from the *AHA Management Advisory on Advertising,* 1990.

Health care institutions in conjunction with attending physicians are responsible for assuring reasonable continuity of care and for informing patients of patient care alternatives when acute care is no longer needed.

Health care institutions should ensure that the health care professionals and organizations with which they are formally or informally affiliated have appropriate credentials and/or accreditation and participate in organized programs to assess and assure continuous improvement in quality of care.

Health care institutions should have policies and practices that assure that patient transfers are medically appropriate and legally permissible. Health care institutions should inform patients of the need for and alternatives to such transfers.

Health care institutions should have policies and practices that support informed consent for diagnostic and therapeutic procedures and use of advance directives. Policies and practices must respect and promote the patient's responsibility for decision making.

Health care institutions are responsible for assuring confidentiality of patient-specific information. They are responsible for providing safeguards to prevent unauthorized release of information and establishing procedures for authorizing release of data.

Health care institutions should assure that the psychological, social, spiritual, and physical needs and cultural beliefs and practices of patients and families are respected and should promote employee and medical staff sensitivity to the full range of such needs and practices. The religious and social beliefs and customs of patients should be accommodated whenever possible.

Health care institutions should have specific mechanisms or procedures to resolve conflicting values and ethical dilemmas as well as complaints and disputes among patients/their families, medical staff, employees, the institution, and the community.

ORGANIZATIONAL CONDUCT

The policies and practices of health care institutions should respect and support the professional ethical codes[3] and responsibilities of their employees and medical staff members and be sensitive to institutional decisions that employees might interpret as compromising their ability to provide high-quality health care.

Health care institutions should provide for fair and equitably administered employee compensation, benefits, and other policies and practices.

To the extent possible and consistent with the ethical commitments of the institution, health care institutions should accommodate the desires of employees and medical staff to embody religious and/or moral values in their professional activities.

Health care institutions should have written policies on conflict of interest that apply to officers, governing board members, and medical staff, as well as others who may make or influence decisions for or on behalf of the institution, including contract employees. Particular attention should be given to potential conflicts related to referral sources, vendors, competing health care services, and investments. These policies should recognize that individuals in decision-making or administrative positions often have duality of interests that may not always

---

[3]For example, the American College of Healthcare Executives' *Code of Ethics,* and professional codes of nursing, medicine, etc.

present conflicts. But they should provide mechanisms for identifying and addressing dualities when they do exist.

Health care institutions should communicate their mission, values, and priorities to their employees and volunteers, whose patient care and service activities are the most visible embodiment of the institution's ethical commitments and values.

AHA RESOURCES

The American Hospital Association developed its first "code of ethics" for health care institutions called *Guidelines on Ethical Conduct and Relationships for Health Care Institutions* in 1973 as a complement to the code of ethics for hospital executives (available from the American College of Healthcare Executives). This management advisory is the most current version of this code. The AHA and its members are committed to regular review and updating of this advisory to assure that it is responsive to contemporary ethical issues facing health care institutions.

This advisory identifies the major areas affecting the ethical conduct of health care institutions. It would be impossible for one advisory document to detail all of the factors and issues relating to each area. Additional information and guidance is available in the following AHA management advisories:

A Patient's Bill of Rights
Advertising
Discharge Planning
Disclosure of Financial and Operating Information
Disclosure of Medical Record Information
Establishment of an Employee Grievance Procedure
Ethics Committees
Imperatives of Hospital Leadership
Physician Involvement in Governance
Quality Management
Resolution of Conflicts of Interest
The Patient's Choice of Treatment Options
Verifying Physician Credentials
Verifying Credentials of Medical Students and Residents

The following AHA publications may also be useful:

Values in Conflict: Resolving Ethical Issues in Hospital Care (AHA#025002)
Effective DNR Policies: Development, Revision, and Implementation (out of print)
Hospital Ethics newsletter (no longer published)

2. CHIROPRACTIC

Organization

AMERICAN CHIROPRACTIC ASSOCIATION

Headquarters:
1701 Clarendon Boulevard
Arlington, VA 22209
Telephone: (703) 276-8800
(800) 986-INFO
Fax: (703) 243-2593
E-mail: memberinfo@amerchiro.org
Website: http://www.amerchiro.org

Date founded: 1932
Membership: approximately 19,000 doctors of chiropractic, representing the majority of licensed practitioners, and students at chiropractic colleges

Code of Ethics

Official name: *Code of Ethics*
History: Adopted 1984; as revised July 1993
Authority: Ethics Committee; House of Delegates

Additional Resources

Organizational (Divisions, Programs, Services, etc.):

Clinical Councils
Committee on Public Health
Council on Chiropractic Education and Commission on Accreditation
Department of Government Relations
Public Health Education Program
Quality Verification System (central clearinghouse for credentials information needed by health plans)
Technology Assessment Panel

271

Informational (Publications, Videos, Seminars, etc.):

Articles in *Journal of the American Chiropractic Association* and *ACA Today*
Chiropractic Care Studies
Chiropractic: State of the Art
Guidelines for Chiropractic Quality Assurance and Practice Parameters
Policies on Public Health and Related Matters (partial listing):
   Certification Programs
   Chiropractic Health Care and Cost Containment
   Chiropractic Practice and Procedures
   Chiropractic Principle
   Continuing Education Programs
   Cooperation with Scientific Community
   Dangers of Unqualified Adjusting
   Disassociation with Cultism
   Fees, Professional Services
   Fraudulent Cures
   Freedom of Choice of Health Care
   High Ethical Conduct
   HIV Policy
   Hospital Staff Privilege Guidelines
   Informed Consent
   Insurance Equality
   Intraprofessional Policy
   Living Wills
   Non-Profit Peer Review Panels
   Organization of National Health Services
   Ownership in Clinical/Therapeutic Facilities
   Position on Postgraduate and Continuing Education
   Practice and Procedures: Facilities
   Public Health Care Goals
   Quality Health Care Services
   Religion
   Research/Patient Solicitation
   Scope of Chiropractic Practice
   Standards of Care
   Standards of Practice, Mercy Center Conference Guidelines
   Uniform Licensure Legislation
   X-Ray: Patient Safeguards

Goals and Activities of Organization

The mission of the American Chiropractic Association (ACA) is to advance chiropractic, promote high standards of professional conduct and patient care, and serve the needs of its members, thereby contributing to the health and welfare of society.

Member services and programs include congressional lobbying and legislative activity, insurance, public relations, scientific and statistical resources, publications, and advocacy of standards of education, ethics, and professional competency.

The ACA's public policies (see above) address many issues of ethics and professionalism. The 1982 statement on *High Ethical Conduct* "vigorously condemns suggestions which infer the application of chiropractic treatment primarily for personal monetary gain rather that for the patients' health, safety and welfare. * * * [T]he ACA emphasizes the highest ethical conduct in both research and patient care."

Implementation and Enforcement of Code

The Code of Ethics was designed primarily "for the guidance of the profession with respect to the responsibilities to patients, the public, and fellow practitioners." It is enforceable as authorized under state law.

The Ethics Committee, appointed by the ACA president, is responsible for managing the promulgation, interpretation, and enforcement of the Code and its administrative procedures. It develops and implements an educational program on the Code and periodically assesses the Code for possible amendment. The Committee also investigates submissions brought before it, in order to make an appropriate recommendation to the executive Board of Governors.

A submission may be brought by the general public, doctors of chiropractic, patients, public agencies, and health care professionals, institutions, or reimbursers. It undergoes a preliminary review (to classify it as an inquiry or challenge), preliminary disposition (to determine whether further action is justified), and investigation (to clarify and expand the facts, and/ or to choose a proper venue for decision).

An ACA member who is the subject of a challenge is notified at the beginning of the investigation of his or her opportunity to be heard and represented.

In the case of an inquiry, the Ethics Committee conducts a public administrative hearing; it may recommend that the Board issue an advisory opinion interpreting the Code.

In the case of a challenge, the Committee conducts a private adjudicative hearing; it may recommend that the Board cite the member for failure to observe the Code and impose an appropriate sanction. Sanctions include reprimand, suspension, or termination of ACA membership.

In either case, the Board of Governors may accept, reject, or modify the Ethics Committee's recommendation.

History and Development of Code

The current Code of Ethics was issued in 1984, and has been amended and readopted several times since, including 1988, 1991, and 1992. The version reprinted here was revised July 1993.

The original Code had been withdrawn in early 1981 under pressure from the Federal Trade Commission (FTC) because of certain advertising restrictions. The new standards fit within the legal requirements established by the courts and government agencies.

Code of Ethics*

Preamble

This Code of Ethics is based upon the fundamental principle that the ultimate end and object of the chiropractor's professional services and effort should be: "The greatest good for the patient."

This Code of Ethics is for the guidance of the profession with respect to responsibilities to patients, the public and to fellow practitioners and for such consideration as may be given to them by state legislatures, state administrative agencies and also by state chiropractic associations to the extent that they are authorized under state law to exercise enforcement or disciplinary functions.

A. Responsibility to the Patient

A (1)   Doctors of chiropractic should hold themselves ready at all times to respond to the call of those needing their professional services, although they are free to accept or reject a particular patient except in an emergency.

A (2)   Doctors of chiropractic should attend their patients as often as they consider necessary to ensure the well-being of their patients.

A (3)   Having once undertaken to serve a patient, doctors of chiropractic should not neglect the patient. Doctors of chiropractic should take reasonable steps to protect their patients prior to withdrawing their professional services; such steps shall include: due notice to them allowing a reasonable time for obtaining professional services of others and delivering to their patients all papers and documents in compliance with A (5) of this Code of Ethics.

A (4)   Doctors of chiropractic should be honest and endeavor to practice with the highest degree of professional competency and honesty in the proper care of their patients.

A (5)   Doctors of chiropractic should comply with a patient's authorization to provide records, or copies of such records, to those whom the patient designates as authorized to inspect or receive all or part of such records. A reasonable charge may be made for the cost of duplicating records.

A (6)   Subject to the foregoing Section A (5), doctors of chiropractic should preserve and protect the patient's confidences and records, except as the patient directs or consents or the law requires otherwise. They should not discuss a patient's history, symptoms, diagnosis, or treatment with any third party until they have received the written consent of the patient or the patient's personal representative. They should not exploit the trust and dependency of their patients.

A (7)   Doctors of chiropractic owe loyalty, compassion and respect to their patients. Their clinical judgment and practice should be objective and exercised solely for the patient's benefit.

---

*©1992–1993 American Chiropractic Association. All rights reserved. Reprinted with permission.

The section on Administrative Procedures has been omitted, but is summarized in the preceding introductory pages.

A (8) Doctors of chiropractic should recognize and respect the right of every person to free choice of chiropractors or other health care providers and to the right to change such choice at will.

A (9) Doctors of chiropractic are entitled to receive proper and reasonable compensation for their professional services commensurate with the value of the services they have rendered taking into consideration their experience, time required, reputation and the nature of the condition involved. Doctors of chiropractic should terminate a professional relationship when it becomes reasonably clear that the patient is not benefiting from it. Doctors of chiropractic should support and participate in proper activities designed to enable access to necessary chiropractic care on the part of persons unable to pay such reasonable fees.

A (10) Doctors of chiropractic should maintain the highest standards of professional and personal conduct, and should refrain from all illegal conduct.

A (11) Doctors of chiropractic should be ready to consult and seek the talents of other health care professionals when such consultation would benefit their patients or when their patients express a desire for such consultation.

A (12) Doctors of chiropractic should employ their best good faith efforts that the patient possesses enough information to enable an intelligent choice in regard to proposed chiropractic treatment. The patient should make his or her own determination on such treatment.

A (13) Doctors of chiropractic should utilize only those laboratory and X-ray procedures, and such devices or nutritional products that are in the best interest of the patient and not in conflict with state statute or administrative rulings.

B. Responsibility to the Public

B (1) Doctors of chiropractic should act as members of a learned profession dedicated to the promotion of health, the prevention of illness and the alleviation of suffering.

B (2) Doctors of chiropractic should observe and comply with all laws, decisions and regulations of state governmental agencies and cooperate with the pertinent activities and policies of associations legally authorized to regulate or assist in the regulation of the chiropractic profession.

B (3) Doctors of chiropractic should comport themselves as responsible citizens in the public affairs of their local community, state and nation in order to improve law, administrative procedures and public policies that pertain to chiropractic and the system of health care delivery. Doctors of chiropractic should stand ready to take the initiative in the proposal and development of measures to benefit the general public health and well-being, and should cooperate in the administration and enforcement of such measures and programs to the extent consistent with law.

B (4) Doctors of chiropractic may advertise but should exercise utmost care that such advertising is relevant to health awareness, is accurate, truthful, not misleading or false or deceptive, and scrupulously accurate in representing the chiropractor's professional status and area of special competence. Communications to the public should not appeal primarily to an individual's anxiety or create unjustified expectations of results. Doctors of chiropractic should conform to all applicable state laws, regulations and judicial decisions in connection with professional advertising.

B (5) Doctors of chiropractic should continually strive to improve their skill and competency by keeping abreast of current developments contained in the health and scientific literature, and by participating in continuing chiropractic educational programs and utilizing other appropriate means.

B (6) Doctors of chiropractic may testify either as experts or when their patients are involved in court cases, worker's compensation proceedings or in other similar administrative proceedings in personal injury or related cases.

B (7) The chiropractic profession should address itself to improvements in licensing procedures consistent with the development of the profession and of relevant advances in science.

B (8) Doctors of chiropractic who are public officers should not engage in activities which are, or may be reasonably perceived to be in conflict with their official duties.

B (9) Doctors of chiropractic should protect the public and reputation of the chiropractic profession by bringing to the attention of the appropriate public or private organizations the actions of chiropractors who engage in deception, fraud or dishonesty, or otherwise engage in conduct inconsistent with this Code of Ethics or relevant provisions of applicable law or regulations within their states.

C. Responsibility to the Profession

C (1) Doctors of chiropractic should assist in maintaining the integrity, competency and highest standards of the chiropractic profession.

C (2) Doctors of chiropractic should by their behavior, avoid even the appearance of professional impropriety and should recognize that their public behavior may have an impact on the ability of the profession to serve the public. Doctors of chiropractic should promote public confidence in the chiropractic profession.

C (3) As teachers, doctors of chiropractic should recognize their obligation to help others acquire knowledge and skill in the practice of the profession. They should maintain high standards of scholarship, education, training and objectivity in the accurate and full dissemination of information and ideas.

C (4) Doctors of chiropractic should attempt to promote and maintain cordial relationships with other members of the chiropractic profession and other professions in an effort to promote information advantageous to the public's health and well-being.

D. Administrative Procedures

[Omitted.]

Addendum
ACA Ethics Committee Advisory Opinions
Rental Arrangements and Clinic or Laboratory Referrals

It is unethical for a doctor of chiropractic to receive a fee, rebate, rental payment or any other form of remuneration for the referral of a patient to a clinic, laboratory or other health service entity.

The ACA Code of Ethics mandates, as primary obligation of the doctor of chiropractic, the exercise of clinical judgement and practice "solely for the patient's benefit." In the view of this association, the receipt of any form of remuneration for a patient referral runs directly counter to this primary obligation and tends to adversely impact upon the relationship between chiropractor and patient.

Arrangements in which "rental fees," "rebates," or free gifts are received in return for patient referrals are, in the ACA's view, unethical and unacceptable in the professional practice of chiropractic.

The ACA recognizes that there are some forms of rental agreements for space or equipment which are legitimate arms-length business transactions not conditioned on patient referrals. However, some forms of rental agreements may be designed to conceal the real nature of the payment, that is, to induce referrals. The ACA also recognizes that the federal government has developed guidelines which outline those circumstances in which space or equipment rentals would not constitute an illegal or improper form of remuneration in return for Medicare or Medicaid referrals.

The ACA feels these federal guidelines provide an excellent basis by which a doctor of chiropractic can ethically evaluate and engage in space or equipment rental agreements. These guidelines * * * may be summarized and adapted for the purposes of our ethical standards as follows:

A lease agreement for space or equipment in which a doctor of chiropractic refers a patient to an entity which either leases to or from the doctor space or equipment, will not constitute an unethical practice where:

1. The lease agreement is in writing and signed by the parties.
2. The lease specifies the space or equipment covered by the lease.
3. If the lease is intended to provide the lessee with access to the premises or equipment for periodic intervals of time, rather than on a full-time basis for the term of the lease, the lease specifies exactly the schedule of such intervals, their precise length, their periodicity, and the exact rent for such intervals.
4. The term of the lease is for not less than one year.
5. The rental charge is consistent with fair market value in arms-length transactions and is not determined in a manner that takes into account the volume or value of any referrals of business between the parties.

Doctors of chiropractic are advised to consult with their local examining board or other regulatory agencies for specific requirements which may relate to clinic or laboratory referrals.

Sexual Intimacies with a Patient

The ACA Ethics Committee ("Committee") has received numerous requests for clarification relative to the ethical implications of sexual intimacies between a doctor of chiropractic and a patient he or she is treating. This advisory opinion is intended to resolve any misunderstanding and to state that it is the opinion of the Committee that sexual intimacies with a patient is unprofessional and unethical based on the existing ethical provisions in the ACA Code of Ethics: A(6), A(7), A(10) and C(2).

The physician/patient relationship requires the doctor of chiropractic to exercise utmost care that he or she will do nothing to "exploit the trust and dependency of the patient." Doctors of chiropractic should make every effort to avoid dual relationships that could impair their professional judgement or risk the possibility of exploiting the confidence placed in them by the patient.

3. DENTISTRY

Organization

AMERICAN DENTAL ASSOCIATION

Headquarters:
211 East Chicago Avenue
Chicago, IL 60611-2678
Telephone: (312) 440-2500
Fax: (312) 440-7494
E-mail: online@ada.org
Website: http://www.ada.org

Date founded: 1859
Membership: approximately 140,000 licensed dentists, and dental students, in 54 constituent (state and territorial) and 529 component (local) dental societies

Code of Ethics

Official name: *Principles of Ethics and Code of Professional Conduct,* with *Official Advisory Opinions*
History: First code adopted 1866, periodically revised; current version August 1998
Authority: Council on Ethics, Bylaws and Judicial Affairs; House of Delegates
Code is available on Website

Additional Resources

Organizational (Divisions, Programs, Services, etc.):

ADA Seal of Acceptance Program
Commission on Dental Accreditation
Continuing Education Home Study Program
Council on Access, Prevention and Interprofessional Relations
Council on Dental Education and Licensure
Council on Dental Practice
Dentist Well-Being and Assistance Programs

Golden Apple Awards Program (for promotion of dental ethics awareness)
Professional Liability Insurance Program

Informational (Publications, Videos, Seminars, etc.):

Articles in *Journal of the American Dental Association, ADA News, InSite*,
    and *ADA Legal Adviser: A Guide to the Law for Dentists*
Accreditation Standards for Dental Education Programs
ADA Guide to Dental Therapeutics
ADA Seal of Acceptance: A Symbol of Safety and Effectiveness
Commission on Dental Accreditation Communications Update
Dental Licensure and the New Graduate
*Dental Management of the HIV-Infected Patient: Legal and Ethical Con-
    siderations*
*Resource Manual for Support of Dentists with HBV, HIV, TB and Other
    Infectious Diseases*
Seminar Series
Statement on Ethical Aspects of Dental Practice Arrangements
Statement on Ethical Aspects of Managed Care

Goals and Activities of Organization

The objective of the American Dental Association (ADA) is to encourage the improvement of the public's health through high-quality, accessible
care, and to promote the art and science of dentistry and the dental profession by enhancing integrity and ethics and strengthening the patient/den-
tist relationship.

Through its Councils, the ADA conducts studies, recommends policies, disseminates information, and formulates programs on dental care,
education, materials, instruments, professional practice, research, and therapeutics, as well as on international relations, community health, hospitals
and health care organizations, government affairs, federal dental services,
and insurance.

The Council on Ethics, Bylaws and Judicial Affairs provides guidance
on ethics and professional issues to the general membership, constituent
and component dental societies, and the public. It issues Advisory Opinions
and position statements, and formulates and disseminates materials related
to ethical and professional conduct in journals, interviews, and continuing
education programs. In disciplinary matters, the Council serves as the
ADA's appellate body.

Implementation and Enforcement of Code

The ADA's ethics standards govern the professional conduct of all
members. There are three main components: the Principles, Code, and
Advisory Opinions. The Opinions, issued by the Council on Ethics, Bylaws
and Judicial Affairs, are interpretations of the Code applied to specific
fact situations.

ADA members are also governed by the codes of ethics of the constituent and component societies within whose jurisdiction they practice or participate in other professional activities. These societies may adopt additional code provisions or interpretations that do not conflict with the national standards, and which would enable them to better serve their members' traditions, customs, and desires.

A member disciplined for violating the ADA Bylaws, Code, or Principles, or the code of ethics of a constituent or component society, is subject to penalties including censure, suspension, expulsion, or probation.

Ethical problems are to be solved at the local level. The member is entitled to notice of the specific charges and to a fair hearing. If a satisfactory decision cannot be reached, the question may be referred on appeal to the constituent society, and ultimately to the national Council on Ethics.

History and Development of Code

Early discussions of dental ethics appear in the bylaws of a dentists' society in 1834 and in publications from 1839. The first ADA code of ethics was promulgated in 1866.

The contemporary ADA Principles and Code result from resolutions that are adopted by the House of Delegates; the Opinions are issued periodically by the Council on Ethics, Bylaws and Judicial Affairs. The Council also considers proposals for amending the Code and Principles in response to evolving issues. Amendments are made through the legislative process of the House of Delegates.

The Code is an evolving document that is subject to continuous review, and changes are issued periodically. In 1996, the Code was reorganized under five fundamental principles that form its foundation.

Among the revisions made in August 1998, in the current version of the Code reprinted here, are those concerning specialists' announcements of credentials, and fellowships.

Principles of Ethics and Code of Professional Conduct*

The Code of Professional Conduct is organized into five sections. Each section falls under the Principle of Ethics that predominately applies to it. Advisory Opinions follow the section of the Code that they interpret.

I. INTRODUCTION

The dental profession holds a special position of trust within society. As a consequence, society affords the profession certain privileges that are not available to members of the public-at-large. In return, the profession makes a commitment to society that its members will adhere to high ethical standards of conduct. These standards are embodied in the *ADA Principles of Ethics and Code of Professional Conduct (ADA Code)*. The *ADA Code* is, in effect, a written expression of the obligations arising from the implied contract between the dental profession and society.

Members of the ADA voluntarily agree to abide by the *ADA Code* as a condition of membership in the Association. They recognize that continued public trust in the dental profession is based on the commitment of individual dentists to high ethical standards of conduct.

The *ADA Code* has three main components: The Principles of Ethics, the Code of Professional Conduct and the Advisory Opinions.

The Principles of Ethics are the aspirational goals of the profession. They provide guidance and offer justification for the Code of Professional Conduct and the Advisory Opinions. There are five fundamental principles that form the foundation of the *ADA Code*: patient autonomy, nonmaleficence, beneficence, justice and veracity. Principles can overlap each other as well as compete with each other for priority. More than one principle can justify a given element of the Code of Professional Conduct. Principles may at times need to be balanced against each other, but, otherwise, they are the profession's firm guideposts.

The Code of Professional Conduct is an expression of specific types of conduct that are either required or prohibited. The Code of Professional Conduct is a product of the ADA's legislative system. All elements of the Code of Professional Conduct result from resolutions that are adopted by the ADA's House of Delegates. The Code of Professional Conduct is binding on members of the ADA, and violations may result in disciplinary action.

The Advisory Opinions are interpretations that apply the Code of Professional Conduct to specific fact situations. They are adopted by the ADA's Council on Ethics, Bylaws and Judicial Affairs to provide guidance to the membership on how the Council might interpret the Code of Professional Conduct in a disciplinary proceeding.

The *ADA Code* is an evolving document and by its very nature cannot be a complete articulation of all ethical obligations. The *ADA Code* is the result of an on-going dialogue between the dental profession and society, and as such, is subject to continuous review.

---

*With official advisory opinions revised to August 1998. American Dental Association, Council on Ethics, Bylaws and Judicial Affairs, 211 East Chicago Avenue, Chicago, Illinois 60611. Copyright © 1998 American Dental Association. Reprinted with permission.

Although ethics and the law are closely related, they are not the same. Ethical obligations may—and often do—exceed legal duties. In resolving any ethical problem not explicitly covered by the *ADA Code,* dentists should consider the ethical principles, the patient's needs and interests, and any applicable laws.

II. PREAMBLE

The American Dental Association calls upon dentists to follow high ethical standards which have the benefit of the patient as their primary goal. Recognition of this goal, and of the education and training of a dentist, has resulted in society affording to the profession the privilege and obligation of self-government.

The Association believes that dentists should possess not only knowledge, skill and technical competence but also those traits of character that foster adherence to ethical principles. Qualities of compassion, kindness, integrity, fairness and charity complement the ethical practice of dentistry and help to define the true professional.

The ethical dentist strives to do that which is right and good. The *ADA Code* is an instrument to help the dentist in this quest.

III. PRINCIPLES, CODE OF PROFESSIONAL CONDUCT AND ADVISORY OPINIONS

SECTION 1

PRINCIPLE: **PATIENT AUTONOMY** ("self-governance"). The dentist has a duty to respect the patient's rights to self-determination and confidentiality.

This principle expresses the concept that professionals have a duty to treat the patient according to the patient's desires, within the bounds of accepted treatment, and to protect the patient's confidentiality. Under this principle, the dentist's primary obligations include involving patients in treatment decisions in a meaningful way, with due consideration being given to the patient's needs, desires and abilities, and safeguarding the patient's privacy.

CODE OF PROFESSIONAL CONDUCT

1.A. Patient Involvement.
The dentist should inform the patient of the proposed treatment, and any reasonable alternatives, in a manner that allows the patient to become involved in treatment decisions.

1.B. Patient Records.
Dentists are obliged to safeguard the confidentiality of patient records. Dentists shall maintain patient records in a manner consistent with the protection of the welfare of the patient. Upon request of a patient or another dental practitioner, dentists shall provide any information that will be beneficial for the future treatment of that patient.

ADVISORY OPINIONS
1.B.1. **Furnishing Copies of Records.**
A dentist has the ethical obligation on request of either the patient or the patient's new dentist to furnish, either gratuitously or for nominal cost, such dental records or copies or summaries of them,

including dental X-rays or copies of them, as will be beneficial for the future treatment of that patient. This obligation exists whether or not the patient's account is paid in full.

1.B.2. **Confidentiality of Patient Records.**
The dominant theme in Code Section 1-B is the protection of the confidentiality of a patient's records. The statement in this section that relevant information in the records should be released to another dental practitioner assumes that the dentist requesting the information is the patient's present dentist. The former dentist should be free to provide the present dentist with relevant information from the patient's records. This may often be required for the protection of both the patient and the present dentist. There may be circumstances where the former dentist has an ethical obligation to inform the present dentist of certain facts. Dentists should be aware, however, that the laws of the various jurisdictions in the United States are not uniform, and some confidentiality laws appear to prohibit the transfer of pertinent information, such as HIV seropositivity. Absent certain knowledge that the laws of the dentist's jurisdiction permit the forwarding of this information, a dentist should obtain the patient's written permission before forwarding health records which contain information of a sensitive nature, such as HIV seropositivity, chemical dependency or sexual preference. If it is necessary for a treating dentist to consult with another dentist or physician with respect to the patient, and the circumstances do not permit the patient to remain anonymous, the treating dentist should seek the permission of the patient prior to the release of data from the patient's records to the consulting practitioner. If the patient refuses, the treating dentist should then contemplate obtaining legal advice regarding the termination of the dentist/patient relationship.

SECTION 2

PRINCIPLE: **NONMALEFICENCE** ("do no harm"). The dentist has a duty to refrain from harming the patient.

This principle expresses the concept that professionals have a duty to protect the patient from harm. Under this principle, the dentist's primary obligations include keeping knowledge and skills current, knowing one's own limitations and when to refer to a specialist or other professional, and knowing when and under what circumstances delegation of patient care to auxiliaries is appropriate.

CODE OF PROFESSIONAL CONDUCT

2.A. Education.
The privilege of dentists to be accorded professional status rests primarily in the knowledge, skill and experience with which they serve their patients and society. All dentists, therefore, have the obligation of keeping their knowledge and skill current.

2.B. Consultation and Referral.
Dentists shall be obliged to seek consultation, if possible, whenever the welfare of patients will be safeguarded or advanced by utilizing those who

have special skills, knowledge, and experience. When patients visit or are referred to specialists or consulting dentists for consultation:

1. The specialists or consulting dentists upon completion of their care shall return the patient, unless the patient expressly reveals a different preference, to the referring dentist, or, if none, to the dentist of record for future care.
2. The specialists shall be obliged when there is no referring dentist and upon a completion of their treatment to inform patients when there is a need for further dental care.

ADVISORY OPINION
2.B.1. **Second Opinions.**
A dentist who has a patient referred by a third party for a "second opinion" regarding a diagnosis or treatment plan recommended by the patient's treating dentist should render the requested second opinion in accordance with this Code of Ethics. In the interest of the patient being afforded quality care, the dentist rendering the second opinion should not have a vested interest in the ensuing recommendation.

2.C. Use of Auxiliary Personnel.
Dentists shall be obliged to protect the health of their patients by only assigning to qualified auxiliaries those duties which can be legally delegated. Dentists shall be further obliged to prescribe and supervise the patient care provided by all auxiliary personnel working under their direction.

2.D. Personal Impairment.
It is unethical for a dentist to practice while abusing controlled substances, alcohol or other chemical agents which impair the ability to practice. All dentists have an ethical obligation to urge chemically impaired colleagues to seek treatment. Dentists with first-hand knowledge that a colleague is practicing dentistry when so impaired have an ethical responsibility to report such evidence to the professional assistance committee of a dental society.

ADVISORY OPINION
2.D.1. **Ability to Practice.**
A dentist who becomes ill from any disease or impaired in any way shall, with consultation and advice from a qualified physician or other authority, limit the activities of practice to those areas that do not endanger the patients or members of the dental staff.

2.E. Patient Abandonment
Once a dentist has undertaken a course of treatment, the dentist should not discontinue that treatment without giving the patient adequate notice and the opportunity to obtain the services of another dentist. Care should be taken that the patient's oral health is not jeopardized in the process.

SECTION 3

PRINCIPLE: **BENEFICENCE** ("do good"). The dentist has a duty to promote the patient's welfare.

This principle expresses the concept that professionals have a duty to act for the benefit of others. Under this principle, the dentist's primary obligation is service to the patient and the public-at-large. The most important aspect of this obligation is the competent and timely delivery of dental care within the bounds of clinical circumstances presented by the patient, with due consideration being given to the needs, desires and values of the patient. The same ethical considerations apply whether the dentist engages in fee-for-service, managed care or some other practice arrangement. Dentists may choose to enter into contracts governing the provision of care to a group of patients; however, contract obligations do not excuse dentists from their ethical duty to put the patient's welfare first.

CODE OF PROFESSIONAL CONDUCT

3.A. Community Service.
    Since dentists have an obligation to use their skills, knowledge and experience for the improvement of the dental health of the public and are encouraged to be leaders in their community, dentists in such service shall conduct themselves in such a manner as to maintain or elevate the esteem of the profession.

3.B. Government of a Profession.
    Every profession owes society the responsibility to regulate itself. Such regulation is achieved largely through the influence of the professional societies. All dentists, therefore, have the dual obligation of making themselves a part of a professional society and of observing its rules of ethics.

3.C. Research and Development.
    Dentists have the obligation of making the results and benefits of their investigative efforts available to all when they are useful in safeguarding or promoting the health of the public.

3.D. Patents and Copyrights.
    Patents and copyrights may be secured by dentists provided that such patents and copyrights shall not be used to restrict research or practice.

3.E. Child Abuse.
    Dentists shall be obliged to become familiar with the perioral signs of child abuse and to report suspected cases to the proper authorities consistent with state laws.

SECTION 4

PRINCIPLE: **JUSTICE** ("fairness"). The dentist has a duty to treat people fairly.

This principle expresses the concept that professionals have a duty to be fair in their dealings with patients, colleagues and society. Under this principle, the dentist's primary obligations include dealing with people justly and delivering dental care without prejudice. In its broadest sense, this principle expresses the concept that the dental profession should actively seek allies throughout society on specific activities that will help improve access to care for all.

CODE OF PROFESSIONAL CONDUCT

4.A. Patient Selection.
    While dentists, in serving the public, may exercise reasonable discretion in selecting patients for their practices, dentists shall not refuse to accept patients

into their practice or deny dental service to patients because of the patient's race, creed, color, sex or national origin.

ADVISORY OPINION

4.A.1. **HIV Positive Patients**.

A dentist has the general obligation to provide care to those in need. A decision not to provide treatment to an individual because the individual has AIDS or is HIV seropositive, based solely on that fact, is unethical. Decisions with regard to the type of dental treatment provided or referrals made or suggested, in such instances should be made on the same basis as they are made with other patients, that is, whether the individual dentist believes he or she has need of another's skills, knowledge, equipment or experience and whether the dentist believes, after consultation with the patient's physician if appropriate, the patient's health status would be significantly compromised by the provision of dental treatment.

4.B. **Emergency Service.**

Dentists shall be obliged to make reasonable arrangements for the emergency care of their patients of record. Dentists shall be obliged when consulted in an emergency by patients not of record to make reasonable arrangements for emergency care. If treatment is provided, the dentist, upon completion of treatment, is obliged to return the patient to his or her regular dentist unless the patient expressly reveals a different preference.

4.C. **Justifiable Criticism.**

Dentists shall be obliged to report to the appropriate reviewing agency as determined by the local component or constituent society instances of gross or continual faulty treatment by other dentists. Patients should be informed of their present oral health status without disparaging comment about prior services. Dentists issuing a public statement with respect to the profession shall have a reasonable basis to believe that the comments made are true.

ADVISORY OPINION

4.C.1. **Meaning of "Justifiable."**

A dentist's duty to the public imposes a responsibility to report instances of gross or continual faulty treatment. However, the heading of this section is "Justifiable Criticism." Therefore, when informing a patient of the status of his or her oral health, the dentist should exercise care that the comments made are justifiable. For example, a difference of opinion as to preferred treatment should not be communicated to the patient in a manner which would imply mistreatment. There will necessarily be cases where it will be difficult to determine whether the comments made are justifiable. Therefore, this section is phrased to address the discretion of dentists and advises against disparaging statements against another dentist. However, it should be noted that, where comments are made which are obviously not supportable and therefore unjustified, such comments can be the basis for the institution of a disciplinary proceeding against the dentist making such statements.

4.D. **Expert Testimony.**

Dentists may provide expert testimony when that testimony is essential to a just and fair disposition of a judicial or administrative action.

ADVISORY OPINION
4.D.1. Contingent Fees.
It is unethical for a dentist to agree to a fee contingent upon the favorable outcome of the litigation in exchange for testifying as a dental expert.

4.E. Rebates and Split Fees.
Dentists shall not accept or tender "rebates" or "split fees."

SECTION 5

PRINCIPLE: **VERACITY** ("truthfulness"). The dentist has a duty to communicate truthfully.

This principle expresses the concept that professionals have a duty to be honest and trustworthy in their dealings with people. Under this principle, the dentist's primary obligations include respecting the position of trust inherent in the dentist-patient relationship, communicating truthfully and without deception, and maintaining intellectual integrity.

CODE OF PROFESSIONAL CONDUCT

5.A. Representation of Care.
Dentists shall not represent the care being rendered to their patients in a false or misleading manner.

ADVISORY OPINIONS
5.A.1. Dental Amalgam.
Based on available scientific data the ADA has determined * * * that the removal of amalgam restorations from the non-allergic patient for the alleged purpose of removing toxic substances from the body, when such treatment is performed solely at the recommendation or suggestion of the dentist, is improper and unethical.
5.A.2. Unsubstantiated Representations.
A dentist who represents that dental treatment recommended or performed by the dentist has the capacity to cure or alleviate diseases, infections or other conditions, when such representations are not based upon accepted scientific knowledge or research, is acting unethically.

5.B. Representation of Fees.
Dentists shall not represent the fees being charged for providing care in a false or misleading manner.

ADVISORY OPINIONS
5.B.1. Waiver of Copayment.
A dentist who accepts a third party[1] payment under a copayment plan as payment in full without disclosing to the third party[1] that the patient's payment portion will not be collected, is engaged in overbilling. The essence of this ethical impropriety is deception and

---

[1]A third party is any party to a dental prepayment contract that may collect premiums, assume financial risks, pay claims and/or provide administrative services.

misrepresentation; an overbilling dentist makes it appear to the third party[1] that the charge to the patient for services rendered is higher than it actually is.

5.B.2. **Overbilling.**
It is unethical for a dentist to increase a fee to a patient solely because the patient is covered under a dental benefits plan.

5.B.3. **Fee Differential.**
Payments accepted by a dentist under a governmentally funded program, a component or constituent dental society sponsored access program, or a participating agreement entered into under a program of a third party[1] shall not be considered as evidence of overbilling in determining whether a charge to a patient, or to another third party[1] in behalf of a patient not covered under any of the aforecited programs constitutes overbilling under this section of the Code.

5.B.4. **Treatment Dates.**
A dentist who submits a claim form to a third party[1] reporting incorrect treatment dates for the purpose of assisting a patient in obtaining benefits under a dental plan, which benefits would otherwise be disallowed, is engaged in making an unethical, false or misleading representation to such third party.[1]

5.B.5. **Dental Procedures.**
A dentist who incorrectly describes on a third party[1] claim form a dental procedure in order to receive a greater payment or reimbursement or incorrectly makes a non-covered procedure appear to be a covered procedure on such a claim form is engaged in making an unethical, false or misleading representation to such third party.[1]

5.B.6. **Unnecessary Services.**
A dentist who recommends and performs unnecessary dental services or procedures is engaged in unethical conduct.

5.C. Disclosure of Conflict of Interest.
A dentist who presents educational or scientific information in an article, seminar or other program shall disclose to the readers or participants any monetary or other special interest the dentist may have with a company whose products are promoted or endorsed in the presentation. Disclosure shall be made in any promotional material and in the presentation itself.

5.D. Devices and Therapeutic Methods.
Except for formal investigative studies, dentists shall be obliged to prescribe, dispense, or promote only those devices, drugs and other agents whose complete formulae are available to the dental profession. Dentists shall have the further obligation of not holding out as exclusive any device, agent, method or technique if that representation would be false or misleading in any material respect.

ADVISORY OPINIONS
5.D.1. **Reporting Adverse Reactions.**
A dentist who suspects the occurrence of an adverse reaction to a drug or dental device has an obligation to communicate that information to

---

[1]See above at Advisory Opinion 5.B.1.

the broader medical and dental community, including, in the case of a serious adverse event, the Food and Drug Administration (FDA).

5.D.2. **Marketing or Sale of Products.**

Dentists who, in the regular conduct of their practices, engage in the marketing or sale of products to their patients must take care not to exploit the trust inherent in the dentist-patient relationship for their own financial gain. Dentists should not induce their patients to buy a product by misrepresenting the product's therapeutic value or the dentist's professional expertise in recommending the product.

In the case of a health-related product, it is not enough for the dentist to rely on the manufacturer's or distributor's representations about the product's safety and efficacy. The dentist has an independent obligation to inquire into the truth and accuracy of such claims and verify that they are founded on accepted scientific knowledge or research.

Dentists should disclose to their patients all relevant information the patient needs to make an informed purchase decision, including whether the product is available elsewhere and whether there are any financial incentives for the dentist to recommend the product that would not be evident to the patient.

5.E. Professional Announcement.

In order to properly serve the public, dentists should represent themselves in a manner that contributes to the esteem of the profession. Dentists should not misrepresent their training and competence in any way that would be false or misleading in any material respect.[2]

5.F. Advertising.

Although any dentist may advertise, no dentist shall advertise or solicit patients in any form of communication in a manner that is false or misleading in any material respect.[2]

ADVISORY OPINIONS

5.F.1. **Articles and Newsletters.**

If a dental health article, message or newsletter is published under a dentist's byline to the public without making truthful disclosure of the source and authorship or is designed to give rise to questionable expectations for the purpose of inducing the public to utilize the services of the sponsoring dentist, the dentist is engaged in making a false or misleading representation to the public in a material respect.

---

[2]Advertising, solicitation of patients or business or other promotional activities by dentists or dental care delivery organizations shall not be considered unethical or improper, except for those promotional activities which are false or misleading in any material respect. Notwithstanding any *ADA Principles of Ethics and Code of Professional Conduct* or other standards of dentist conduct which may be differently worded, this shall be the sole standard for determining the ethical propriety of such promotional activities. Any provision of an ADA constituent or component society's code of ethics or other standard of dentist conduct relating to dentists' or dental care delivery organizations' advertising, solicitation, or other promotional activities which is worded differently from the above standard shall be deemed to be in conflict with the *ADA Principles of Ethics and Code of Professional Conduct.*

5.F.2. **Examples of "False or Misleading."**
The following examples are set forth to provide insight into the meaning of the term "false or misleading in a material respect." These examples are not meant to be all-inclusive. Rather, by restating the concept in alternative language and giving general examples, it is hoped that the membership will gain a better understanding of the term. With this in mind, statements shall be avoided which would: **a)** contain a material misrepresentation of fact, **b)** omit a fact necessary to make the statement considered as a whole not materially misleading, **c)** be intended or be likely to create an unjustified expectation about results the dentist can achieve, and **d)** contain a material, objective representation, whether express or implied, that the advertised services are superior in quality to those of other dentists, if that representation is not subject to reasonable substantiation.

Subjective statements about the quality of dental services can also raise ethical concerns. In particular, statements of opinion may be misleading if they are not honestly held, if they misrepresent the qualifications of the holder, or the basis of the opinion, or if the patient reasonably interprets them as implied statements of fact. Such statements will be evaluated on a case by case basis, considering how patients are likely to respond to the impression made by the advertisement as a whole. The fundamental issue is whether the advertisement, taken as a whole, is false or misleading in a material respect.

5.F.3. **Unearned, Nonhealth Degrees.**
The use of an unearned or nonhealth degree in any general announcements to the public by a dentist may be a representation to the public which is false or misleading in a material respect. A dentist may use the title Doctor, Dentist, DDS, or DMD, or any additional earned advanced degrees in health service areas. The use of unearned or nonhealth degrees could be misleading because of the likelihood that it will indicate to the public the attainment of a specialty or diplomate status.

For purposes of this advisory opinion, an unearned academic degree is one which is awarded by an educational institution not accredited by a generally recognized accrediting body or is an honorary degree. Generally, the use of honorary degrees or nonhealth degrees should be limited to scientific papers and curriculum vitae. In all instances state law should be consulted. In any review by the council of the use of nonhealth degrees or honorary degrees the council will apply the standard of whether the use of such is false or misleading in a material respect.

5.F.4. **Referral Services.**
There are two basic types of referral services for dental care: not-for-profit and the commercial. The not-for-profit is commonly organized by dental societies or community services. It is open to all qualified practitioners in the area served. A fee is sometimes charged the practitioner to be listed with the service. A fee for such referral services is for the purpose of covering the expenses of the service and has no relation to the number of patients referred. In contrast,

some commercial referral services restrict access to the referral service to a limited number of dentists in a particular geographic area. Prospective patients calling the service may be referred to a single subscribing dentist in the geographic area and the respective dentist billed for each patient referred. Commercial referral services often advertise to the public stressing that there is no charge for use of the service and the patient may not be informed of the referral fee paid by the dentist. There is a connotation to such advertisements that the referral that is being made is in the nature of a public service. A dentist is allowed to pay for any advertising permitted by the Code, but is generally not permitted to make payments to another person or entity for the referral of a patient for professional services. While the particular facts and circumstances relating to an individual commercial referral service will vary, the council believes that the aspects outlined above for commercial referral services violate the Code in that it constitutes advertising which is false or misleading in a material respect and violates the prohibitions in the Code against fee splitting.

5.F.5. **HIV Test Results.**

An advertisement or other communication intended to solicit patients which omits a material fact or facts necessary to put the information conveyed in the advertisement in a proper context can be misleading in a material respect. An advertisement to the public of HIV negative test results, without conveying additional information that will clarify the scientific significance of this fact, is an example of a misleading omission. A dental practice should not seek to attract patients on the basis of partial truths which create a false impression.

5.G. Name of Practice.

Since the name under which a dentist conducts his or her practice may be a factor in the selection process of the patient, the use of a trade name or an assumed name that is false or misleading in any material respect is unethical. Use of the name of a dentist no longer actively associated with the practice may be continued for a period not to exceed one year.[2]

ADVISORY OPINION

5.G.1. **Dentist Leaving Practice.**

Dentists leaving a practice who authorize continued use of their names should receive competent advice on the legal implications of this action. With permission of a departing dentist, his or her name may be used for more than one year, if, after the one year grace period has expired, prominent notice is provided to the public through such mediums as a sign at the office and a short statement on stationery and business cards that the departing dentist has retired from the practice.

5.H. Announcement of Specialization and Limitation of Practice.

This section and Section 5-I are designed to help the public make an informed selection between the practitioner who has completed an accredited program beyond the dental degree and a practitioner who has not completed such a program. The special areas of dental practice approved by the American

---

[2]See above at Code Section 5.F.

Dental Association and the designation for ethical specialty announcement and limitation of practice are: dental public health, endodontics, oral and maxillofacial pathology, oral and maxillofacial surgery, orthodontics and dentofacial orthopedics, pediatric dentistry, periodontics and prosthodontics. Dentists who choose to announce specialization should use "specialist in" or "practice limited to" and shall limit their practice exclusively to the announced special area(s) of dental practice, provided at the time of the announcement such dentists have met in each approved specialty for which they announce the existing educational requirements and standards set forth by the American Dental Association. Dentists who use their eligibility to announce as specialists to make the public believe that specialty services rendered in the dental office are being rendered by qualified specialists when such is not the case are engaged in unethical conduct. The burden of responsibility is on specialists to avoid any inference that general practitioners who are associated with specialists are qualified to announce themselves as specialists.

General Standards.
The following are included within the standards of the American Dental Association for determining the education, experience and other appropriate requirements for announcing specialization and limitation of practice:
1. The special area(s) of dental practice and an appropriate certifying board must be approved by the American Dental Association.
2. Dentists who announce as specialists must have successfully completed an educational program accredited by the Commission on Dental Accreditation, two or more years in length, as specified by the Council on Dental Education, or be diplomates of an American Dental Association recognized certifying board. The scope of the individual specialist's practice shall be governed by the educational standards for the specialty in which the specialist is announcing.
3. The practice carried on by dentists who announce as specialists shall be limited exclusively to the special area(s) of dental practices announced by the dentist.

Standards for Multiple-Specialty Announcements.
Educational criteria for announcement by dentists in additional recognized specialty areas are the successful completion of an educational program accredited by the Commission on Dental Accreditation in each area for which the dentist wishes to announce. Dentists who completed their advanced education in programs listed by the Council on Dental Education prior to the initiation of the accreditation process in 1967 and who are currently ethically announcing as specialists in a recognized area may announce in additional areas provided they are educationally qualified or are certified diplomates in each area for which they wish to announce. Documentation of successful completion of the educational program(s) must be submitted to the appropriate constituent society. The documentation must assure that the duration of the program(s) is a minimum of two years except for oral and maxillofacial surgery which must have been a minimum of three years in duration.[2]

---

[2]See above at Code Section 5.F.

ADVISORY OPINIONS

5.H.1. Dual Degreed Dentists.
Nothing in Section 5-H shall be interpreted to prohibit a dual degreed dentist who practices medicine or osteopathy under a valid state license from announcing to the public as a dental specialist provided the dentist meets the educational, experience and other standards set forth in the Code for specialty announcement and further providing that the announcement is truthful and not materially misleading.

5.H.2. Specialist Announcement of Credentials in Non-Specialty Interest Areas.
A dentist who is qualified to announce specialization under this section may not announce to the public that he or she is certified or a diplomate or otherwise similarly credentialed in an area of dentistry not recognized as a specialty area by the American Dental Association unless:

1. The organization granting the credential grants certification or diplomate status based on the following: a) the dentist's successful completion of a formal, full-time advanced education program (graduate or postgraduate level) of at least 12 months' duration; and b) the dentist's training and experience; and c) successful completion of an oral and written examination based on psychometric principles; and

2. The announcement includes the following language: [Name of announced area of dental practice] is not recognized as a specialty area by the American Dental Association.

Nothing in this advisory opinion affects the right of a properly qualified dentist to announce specialization in an ADA-recognized specialty area(s) as provided for under Section 5.H of this Code or the responsibility of such dentist to limit his or her practice exclusively to the special area(s) of dental practice announced. Specialists shall not announce their credentials in a manner that implies specialization in a non-specialty interest area.

5.I. General Practitioner Announcement of Services.
General dentists who wish to announce the services available in their practices are permitted to announce the availability of those services so long as they avoid any communications that express or imply specialization. General dentists shall also state that the services are being provided by general dentists. No dentist shall announce available services in any way that would be false or misleading in any material respect.[2]

ADVISORY OPINIONS

5.I.1. General Practitioner Announcement of Credentials.
A general dentist may not announce to the public that he or she is certified or a diplomate or otherwise similarly credentialed in an area of dentistry not recognized as a specialty area by the American Dental Association unless:

1. The organization granting the credential grants certification or diplomate status based on the following: a) the dentist's successful

---

[2]See above at Code Section 5.F.

completion of a formal, full-time advanced education program
(graduate or postgraduate level) of at least 12 months duration;
and b) the dentist's training and experience; and c) successful
completion of an oral and written examination based on psychometric principles;

2. The dentist discloses that he or she is a general dentist; and

3. The announcement includes the following language: [Name of
announced area of dental practice] is not recognized as a specialty
area by the American Dental Association.

5.I.2. **Fellowships.**
General dentists may announce fellowships or other credentials
earned in the area of general dentistry so long as they avoid any
communications that express or imply specialization and the announcement includes the disclaimer that the dentist is a general
dentist. The use of abbreviations to designate credentials shall be
avoided when such use would lead the reasonable person to believe
that the designation represents an academic degree, when such is not
the case.

IV. INTERPRETATION AND APPLICATION OF *PRINCIPLES OF ETHICS AND CODE OF PROFESSIONAL CONDUCT*

The foregoing *ADA Principles of Ethics and Code of Professional Conduct*
set forth the ethical duties that are binding on members of the American Dental
Association. The component and constituent societies may adopt additional requirements or interpretations not in conflict with the *ADA Code.*

Anyone who believes that a member-dentist has acted unethically may bring
the matter to the attention of the appropriate constituent (state) or component
(local) dental society. Whenever possible, problems involving questions of ethics
should be resolved at the state or local level. If a satisfactory resolution cannot
be reached, the dental society may decide, after proper investigation, that the
matter warrants issuing formal charges and conducting a disciplinary hearing
pursuant to the procedures set forth in the ADA Bylaws * * *. The Council on
Ethics, Bylaws and Judicial Affairs reminds constituent and component societies
that before a dentist can be found to have breached any ethical obligation the
dentist is entitled to a fair hearing.

A member who is found guilty of unethical conduct proscribed by the *ADA
Code* or code of ethics of the constituent or component society, may be placed
under a sentence of censure or suspension or may be expelled from membership
in the Association. A member under a sentence of censure, suspension or expulsion
has the right to appeal the decision to his or her constituent society and the
ADA Council on Ethics, Bylaws and Judicial Affairs, as provided in * * * the
ADA Bylaws.

AMERICAN DENTAL HYGIENISTS' ASSOCIATION

Headquarters:
444 North Michigan Avenue
Suite 3400
Chicago, IL 60611
Telephone: (312) 440-8900
(800) 735-5121
Fax: (312) 440-6780
E-mail: mail@adha.net
Website: http://www.adha.org

Date founded: 1923
Membership: approximately 35,00 licensed and registered dental hygienists, and dental students, in 375 local dental hygiene associations

Code of Ethics

Official name: *Code of Ethics for Dental Hygienists*
History: Approved and ratified 1995
Authority: House of Delegates Special Committee on Ethics

Additional Resources

Organizational (Divisions, Programs, Services, etc.):

ADHA Institute Research Grant Review Program
ADHA Institute Scholarship Program
Continuing Education Programs
Ethics Conference
Malpractice insurance
Various Divisions: Governmental Affairs; Member Services; Professional
    Development

Informational (Publications, Videos, Seminars, etc.):

Articles in *Journal of Dental Hygiene and Access* newsletter
Access to Dental Hygiene Care: A Literature Review

ADHA Policy Manual
Conference Session Proceedings
Employee Rights Handbook for Dental Hygienists
Literature Review: Dental Hygiene Education
Longitudinal Studies:
> *Factors Influencing the Work Roles of Dental Hygienists*
> *Dental Hygienists' Perceptions about Issues in Dental Hygiene Care and Dental Hygiene Professionalization*
> *Dental Hygiene Work—Health, Hazards, Safety and Pay*

Practices and Procedures Survey
Quality Assurance and Its Application to the Delivery of Services Provided by Dental Hygienists
Theory Development and Basic Research in Dental Hygiene: A Review of the Literature and Recommendations

Goals and Activities of Organization

The American Dental Hygienists' Association (ADHA) works to improve the public health by increasing the awareness of and access to quality oral health care. Among its goals are to increase the quality of care provided by dental hygienists; to increase the number of people who utilize the services of hygienists; to reduce obstacles to the public's access to alternate practice settings; and to promote high standards of dental hygiene education, licensure, practice, and research. As the largest national organization representing the profession, ADHA also seeks to represent the majority of licensed hygienists and to enhance their lives as practitioners.

The ADHA focuses its activities on professional development, education, research, government affairs, and member services, including representation on state dental boards and on a joint committee with the American Dental Association.

Implementation and Enforcement of Code

Designed to influence dental hygienists in their careers and stimulate the continuing study of ethical issues and responsibilities, members of the ADHA "endorse and incorporate the Code into our daily lives."

The Code establishes concise standards of behavior to guide the public's expectations of the profession. It supports compliance with existing dental hygiene practice, laws, regulations, universal codes, governmental standards, and professional guidelines.

Members hold themselves "accountable to meeting the standards stated in the Code," thereby enhancing public trust.

History and Development of Code

The present Code was developed by a Special Committee on Ethics over a period of six years; the document was approved and ratified by the House of Delegates in 1995.

The previous Principles of Ethics had been issued in 1988.

A consensus-building process served as a framework for the development of the Code. Input was solicited from a broad range of dental hygiene professionals, whose suggestions were received through a series of ethics conferences and national surveys. This information formed the outline for the new document.

The earlier Standards of Applied Dental Hygiene Practice of 1985, drawn up by the Commission for the Assurance of Competence and the Taskforce to Develop Standards of Practice, are no longer in effect.

Code of Ethics for Dental Hygienists*

1. PREAMBLE

As dental hygienists, we are a community of professionals devoted to the prevention of disease and the promotion and improvement of the public's health. We are preventive oral health professionals who provide educational, clinical, and therapeutic services to the public. We strive to live meaningful, productive, satisfying lives that simultaneously serve us, our profession, our society, and the world. Our actions, behaviors, and attitudes are consistent with our commitment to public service. We endorse and incorporate the Code into our daily lives.

2. PURPOSE

The purpose of a professional code of ethics is to achieve high levels of ethical consciousness, decision making, and practice by the members of the profession. Specific objectives of the Dental Hygiene Code of Ethics are

- to increase our professional and ethical consciousness and sense of ethical responsibility.
- to lead us to recognize ethical issues and choices and to guide us in making more informed ethical decisions.
- to establish a standard for professional judgment and conduct.
- to provide a statement of the ethical behavior the public can expect from us.

The Dental Hygiene Code of Ethics is meant to influence us throughout our careers. It stimulates our continuing study of ethical issues and challenges us to explore our ethical responsibilities. The Code establishes concise standards of behavior to guide the public's expectations of our profession and supports existing dental hygiene practice, laws, and regulations. By holding ourselves accountable to meeting the standards stated in the Code, we enhance the public's trust on which our professional privilege and status are founded.

3. KEY CONCEPTS

Our beliefs, principles, values, and ethics are concepts reflected in the Code. They are the essential elements of our comprehensive and definitive code of ethics, and are interrelated and mutually dependent.

4. BASIC BELIEFS

We recognize the importance of the following beliefs that guide our practice and provide context for our ethics:

*Approved and ratified by the 1995 ADHA House of Delegates. "Code of Ethics for Dental Hygienists" by The 1995 ADHA House of Delegates Special Committee on Ethics. Reprinted from the *Journal of Dental Hygiene* Vol. 69, No. 4, pp. 159–162, copyright ©1995 by the American Dental Hygienists' Association, Chicago, IL. Used by permission.

- The services we provide contribute to the health and well being of society.
- Our education and licensure qualify us to serve the public by preventing and treating oral disease and helping individuals achieve and maintain optimal health.
- Individuals have intrinsic worth, are responsible for their own health, and are entitled to make choices regarding their health.
- Dental hygiene care is an essential component of overall healthcare and we function interdependently with other healthcare providers.
- All people should have access to healthcare, including oral healthcare.
- We are individually responsible for our actions and the quality of care we provide.

5. FUNDAMENTAL PRINCIPLES

These fundamental principles, universal concepts, and general laws of conduct provide the foundation for our ethics.

Universality
The principle of universality assumes that, if one individual judges an action to be right or wrong in a given situation, other people considering the same action in the same situation would make the same judgment.

Complementarity
The principle of complementarity assumes the existence of an obligation to justice and basic human rights. It requires us to act toward others in the same way they would act toward us if roles were reversed. In all relationships, it means considering the values and perspective of others before making decisions or taking actions affecting them.

Ethics
Ethics are the general standards of right and wrong that guide behavior within society. As generally accepted actions, they can be judged by determining the extent to which they promote good and minimize harm. Ethics compel us to engage in health promotion/disease prevention activities.

Community
This principle expresses our concern for the bond between individuals, the community, and society in general. It leads us to preserve natural resources and inspires us to show concern for the global environment.

Responsibility
Responsibility is central to our ethics. We recognize that there are guidelines for making ethical choices and accept responsibility for knowing and applying them. We accept the consequences of our actions or the failure to act and are willing to make ethical choices and publicly affirm them.

6. CORE VALUES

We acknowledge these values as general guides for our choices and actions.

Individual Autonomy and Respect for Human Beings

People have the right to be treated with respect. They have the right to informed consent prior to treatment, and they have the right to full disclosure of all relevant information so that they can make informed choices about their care.

Confidentiality

We respect the confidentiality of client information and relationships as a demonstration of the value we place on individual autonomy. We acknowledge our obligation to justify any violation of a confidence.

Societal Trust

We value client trust and understand that public trust in our profession is based on our actions and behavior.

Nonmaleficence

We accept our fundamental obligation to provide services in a manner that protects all clients and minimizes harm to them and others involved in their treatment.

Beneficence

We have a primary role in promoting the well being of individuals and the public by engaging in health promotion/disease prevention activities.

Justice and Fairness

We value justice and support the fair and equitable distribution of healthcare resources. We believe all people should have access to high-quality, affordable oral healthcare.

Veracity

We accept our obligation to tell the truth and assume that others will do the same. We value self-knowledge and seek truth and honesty in all relationships.

7. STANDARDS OF PROFESSIONAL RESPONSIBILITY

We are obligated to practice our profession in a manner that supports our purpose, beliefs, and values in accordance with the fundamental principles that support our ethics. We acknowledge the following responsibilities:

To Ourselves as Individuals. . .

- Avoid self-deception, and continually strive for knowledge and personal growth.
- Establish and maintain a lifestyle that supports optimal health.

- Create a safe work environment.
- Assert our own interests in ways that are fair and equitable.
- Seek the advice and counsel of others when challenged with ethical dilemmas.
- Have realistic expectations of ourselves and recognize our limitations.

To Ourselves as Professionals. . .
- Enhance professional competencies through continuous learning in order to practice according to high standards of care.
- Support dental hygiene peer-review systems and quality-assurance measures.
- Develop collaborative professional relationships and exchange knowledge to enhance our own life-long professional development.

To Family and Friends. . .
- Support the efforts of others to establish and maintain healthy lifestyles and respect the rights of friends and family.

To Clients. . .
- Provide oral healthcare utilizing high levels of professional knowledge, judgment, and skill.
- Maintain a work environment that minimizes the risk of harm.
- Serve all clients without discrimination and avoid action toward any individual or group that may be interpreted as discriminatory.
- Hold professional client relationships confidential.
- Communicate with clients in a respectful manner.
- Promote ethical behavior and high standards of care by all dental hygienists.
- Serve as an advocate for the welfare of clients.
- Provide clients with the information necessary to make informed decisions about their oral health and encourage their full participation in treatment decisions and goals.
- Refer clients to other healthcare providers when their needs are beyond our ability or scope of practice.
- Educate clients about high-quality oral healthcare.

To Colleagues. . .
- Conduct professional activities and programs, and develop relationships in ways that are honest, responsible, and appropriately open and candid.
- Encourage a work environment that promotes individual professional growth and development.
- Collaborate with others to create a work environment that minimizes risk to the personal health and safety of our colleagues.
- Manage conflicts constructively.
- Support the efforts of other dental hygienists to communicate the dental hygiene philosophy of preventive oral care.
- Inform other healthcare professionals about the relationship between general and oral health.
- Promote human relationships that are mutually beneficial, including those with other healthcare professionals.

To Employees and Employers. . .
- Conduct professional activities and programs, and develop relationships in ways that are honest, responsible, open, and candid.
- Manage conflicts constructively.
- Support the right of our employees and employers to work in an environment that promotes wellness.
- Respect the employment rights of our employers and employees.

To the Dental Hygiene Profession. . .
- Participate in the development and advancement of our profession.
- Avoid conflicts of interest and declare them when they occur.
- Seek opportunities to increase public awareness and understanding of oral health practices.
- Act in ways that bring credit to our profession while demonstrating appropriate respect for colleagues in other professions.
- Contribute time, talent, and financial resources to support and promote our profession.
- Promote a positive image for our profession.
- Promote a framework for professional education that develops dental hygiene competencies to meet the oral and overall health needs of the public.

To the Community and Society. . .
- Recognize and uphold the laws and regulations governing our profession.
- Document and report inappropriate, inadequate, or substandard care and/or illegal activities by any healthcare provider, to the responsible authorities.
- Use peer review as a mechanism for identifying inappropriate, inadequate, or substandard care and for modifying and improving the care provided by dental hygienists.
- Comply with local, state, and federal statutes that promote public health and safety.
- Develop support systems and quality-assurance programs in the workplace to assist dental hygienists in providing the appropriate standard of care.
- Promote access to dental hygiene services for all, supporting justice and fairness in the distribution of healthcare resources.
- Act consistently with the ethics of the global scientific community of which our profession is a part.
- Create a healthful workplace ecosystem to support a healthy environment.
- Recognize and uphold our obligation to provide pro bono service.

To Scientific Investigation. . .
We accept responsibility for conducting research according to the fundamental principles underlying our ethical beliefs in compliance with universal codes, governmental standards, and professional guidelines for the care and management of experimental subjects. We acknowledge our ethical obligations to the scientific community:

- Conduct research that contributes knowledge that is valid and useful to our clients and society.
- Use research methods that meet accepted scientific standards.
- Use research resources appropriately.
- Systematically review and justify research in progress to insure the most favorable benefit-to-risk ratio to research subjects.

- Submit all proposals involving human subjects to an appropriate human subject review committee.
- Secure appropriate institutional committee approval for the conduct of research involving animals.
- Obtain informed consent from human subjects participating in research that is based on specifications published in Title 21 Code of Federal Regulations Part 46.
- Respect the confidentiality and privacy of data.
- Seek opportunities to advance dental hygiene knowledge through research by providing financial, human, and technical resources whenever possible.
- Report research results in a timely manner.
- Report research findings completely and honestly, drawing only those conclusions that are supported by the data presented.
- Report the names of investigators fairly and accurately.
- Interpret the research and the research of others accurately and objectively, drawing conclusions that are supported by the data presented and seeking clarity when uncertain.
- Critically evaluate research methods and results before applying new theory and technology in practice.
- Be knowledgeable concerning currently accepted preventive and therapeutic methods, products, and technology and their application to our practice.

4. MEDICINE

Organization

AMERICAN COLLEGE OF PHYSICIANS— AMERICAN SOCIETY OF INTERNAL MEDICINE

Headquarters:
190 North Independence Mall West
Philadelphia, PA 19106-1572
Telephone: (215) 351-2400
(800) 523-1546
Fax: (215) 351-2869
E-mail: interpub@mail.acponline.org
Website: http://www.acponline.org

Date founded: 1998
Merged the American College of Physicians, founded 1915, and the American Society of Internal Medicine, founded 1956
Membership: approximately 100,000 physicians in general internal medicine (the nonsurgical diagnosis and treatment of disease and illness in adults) and related subspecialties, medical researchers, educators, and students, in 76 chapters in the United States, Canada, and Central and South America

Code of Ethics

Official name: *Ethics Manual*
History: First Edition 1984; revised every 4 to 5 years; Fourth Edition approved October 1997, issued April 1998
Authority: Ethics and Human Rights Committee; Board of Regents
Code is available on Website

Additional Resources

Organizational (Divisions, Programs, Services, etc.):

Clinical Efficacy Assessment Project (develops clinical practice guidelines)
Community-Based Teaching Program

305

Continuing Medical Education (CME) Programs
Council of Medical Societies
Credentials Subcommittee (election to Fellowship, Mastership)
Division of Public Policy
Insurance Program
Library for Internists (LiFI)
Managed Care Resource Center (information clearinghouse and referral network)
Medical Knowledge Self-Assessment Program (MKSAP) and Subspecialty MKSAPs
Office Practice Assessment Program

Informational (Publications, Videos, Seminars, etc.):

Articles in *ACP-ASIM Observer, Annals of Internal Medicine, Evidence-Based Medicine,* and *Today's Internist*
A Manual for Assessing Health Practices and Designing Practice Policies: The Explicit Approach
American College of Physicians Pledge
Authors' Professional and Ethical Responsibilities (Annals of Internal Medicine)
Clinical Practice Guidelines
Ethical Choices: Case Studies for Medical Practice
Ethics Case Studies in *ACP-ASIM Observer*
Ethics Program at Annual Session
Guidelines for the Physician Expert Witness
Home Care Guide for HIV and AIDS
Medical Care of the Nursing Home Resident: What Physicians Need to Know
Medical Ethics: An Annotated Bibliography
On Being a Doctor
One Man's Medicine
Public Policy Position Papers:
  Beyond MICRA: New Ideas for Liability Reform
  The Impact of Managed Care on Medical Education and the Physician Workforce
  Insurance Reform in a Voluntary System: Implications for the Sick, the Well, and Universal Health Care
  Medicare Managed Care: How to Ensure Quality
  Physician-Driven Integration: A Response to the Corporatization of Medicine
  Physician-Run Health Plans and Antitrust
  Physicians and the Pharmaceutical Industry
  Reducing Waste, Fraud and Abuse Without Increasing the Hassle Factor for Physicians and Their Patients
  Statement on Arbitrary Classifications that Restrict the Practice of Internal Medicine

Universal Coverage: Renewing the Call to Action
Voluntary Purchasing Pools: A Market Model for Improving Access,
   Quality, and Cost in Health Care
Procedures for Addressing Ethical Complaints Against ACP Members
Professionalism in Medicine (conference session)
Sacred Space: Stories from a Life in Medicine
Selected Medical Curricula: A Guide to Expanding Educational Objectives
   in Internal Medicine Residency
Who Has Seen a Blood Sugar? Reflections on Medical Education

Goals and Activities of Organization

The American College of Physicians–American Society of Internal Medicine (ACP-ASIM) is the nation's largest medical specialty society, whose mission is to enhance the quality and effectiveness of health care by fostering excellence and professionalism in medical practice, education, and research. The organization, incorporated in July 1998, combines the strengths of ACP and ASIM as advocates in congressional, regulatory, scientific and other arenas.

The ACP-ASIM is active in establishing and promoting clinical standards; developing policy on bioethics, professional ethics, and human rights issues; providing informational and professional resources for internists; promoting responsible public policy positions on health for the benefit of individual patients, society, the medical profession, and members; and recognizing excellence in and contributions to medicine.

The Ethics and Human Rights Committee is composed of practicing physicians, medical ethicists, and educators. It promulgates ethical principles and policy, oversees the review of complaints, and sponsors educational programs.

Implementation and Enforcement of Code

The ACP Ethics Manual was designed to facilitate the ethical decision-making process in clinical practice and medical research. It raises issues for debate and presents general guidelines for reference. A physician is expected to make ethical decisions in light of individual circumstances and his or her own best judgment, keeping in mind the distinctions and potential conflicts between legal and ethical obligations.

In 1997, the ACP revised its procedures for handling ethical complaints.

Any physician or layperson may raise concerns regarding unprofessional, unethical, or illegal conduct by a member of the ACP-ASIM. A formal written complaint details the incident and supplies supporting documentation. Information that does not meet these standards may still be deemed worthy of review.

The accused member is notified of the complaint and all related procedures, and asked to respond. The member is also advised that the laws of various jurisdictions may require the ACP-ASIM to report evidence of unethical or professional conduct or the status of membership.

Upon reviewing the complaint or information, the President, Executive Vice President, and relevant Governor decide whether further action is warranted—to hold a hearing, notify other authorities, or dismiss the matter.

At a hearing, a committee appointed by the Governor, none of whose members are in direct economic competition with the accused, ensures that all sides have an opportunity to present evidence. The proceedings are meant to be intracollegial, not judicial, but on occasion the ACP-ASIM and the accused each may be represented by counsel.

The Hearing Committee's subsequent recommendations are forwarded to the Ethics and Human Rights Committee, which reviews the record of the proceedings and makes its own recommendations to the Board of Regents for further review and implementation. The Ethics Committee's decision is adopted unless the Board considers it arbitrary and capricious. Sanctions may not be appealed.

Possible sanctions against a member include reprimand, probation, suspension of membership, and expulsion.

History and Development of Code

The Ethics Manual is developed through a process of committee consensus and extensive peer review. It is revised in its entirety every four or five years. Previous editions of the Manual were issued in 1984, 1989, and 1992.

The current Fourth Edition was developed by the Ethics and Human Rights Committee, and approved by the Board of Regents in 1997 and published in April 1998.

Changes include: new sections on genetic testing, managed care, organ donation, and disability certification; expanded discussions of patient responsibility and discrimination; and substantial revision of the section on decisions near the end of life, including physician-assisted suicide. (A supplement providing a question-and-answer case method for ethics decisionmaking was also added, but is not reprinted here.)

Ethics Manual*

Medicine, law, and social values are not static. Reexamining the ethical tenets of medical practice and their application in new circumstances is a necessary exercise. The fourth edition of the American College of Physicians *Ethics Manual* covers emerging issues in medical ethics and revisits old ones. It reflects on many of the ethical tensions faced by internists and their patients and attempts to shed light on how existing principles extend to emerging concerns. In addition, by reiterating ethical principles that have provided guidance in resolving past ethical problems, it may help physicians to avert future problems. The *Manual* is not a substitute for the experience and integrity of individual physicians, but it may serve as a reminder of the shared obligations and duties of the medical profession.

. . . the secret of the care of the patient is in caring for the patient.
—*Francis Weld Peabody*

Some aspects of medicine are fundamental and timeless. Medical practice, however, does not stand still. Clinicians must be prepared to deal with changes and reaffirm what is fundamental.

The fourth edition of the American College of Physicians *Ethics Manual* examines emerging issues in medical ethics and revisits older issues that are still very pertinent. Changes in the *Manual* since its last revision in 1992 include new sections on genetic testing, the changing practice environment and managed care, organ donation, and disability certification. A case method for ethics decision making has also been added. Such issues as patient responsibility and discrimination are discussed more extensively, and the section on decisions near the end of life (which includes physician-assisted suicide) has been revised substantially. The literature of biomedical ethics expands at a rate that does not allow a bibliography to remain current; therefore, an exhaustive list of references or suggested readings is not included in this edition of the *Manual*.

The *Manual* is intended to facilitate the process of making ethical decisions in clinical practice and medical research and to describe and explain underlying principles of decision making. Because ethics must be understood within a historical and cultural context, the second edition of the *Manual* included a brief overview of the cultural, philosophical, and religious underpinnings of modern medical ethics. In this edition, we refer the reader to that overview and to other sources that more fully explore the rich heritage of medical ethics.

The *Manual* raises ethical issues and presents general guidelines. In applying these guidelines, physicians should consider the circumstances of the individual patient and use their best judgment. Physicians are morally and legally accountable, and the two may not be concordant. Physician participation in torture, for example, is legal in some countries but is never morally defensible. Physicians must keep in mind the distinctions and potential conflicts between legal and ethical obligations

---

*Fourth Edition. Approved by the Board of Regents on 26 October 1997. Copyright © 1998 by the American College of Physicians, *Annals of Internal Medicine*, April 1, 1998, Vol. 128, No. 7, pp. 576–594. Reprinted with permission of the American College of Physicians.

This reprint contains the main text of the *Manual* in its entirety. The following elements have been omitted: names of members of Ethics and Human Rights Committee, Appendix ("A Case Method to Assist Clinical Ethics Decision Making"), Acknowledgments, citations in text to References, and References.

when making clinical decisions and must seek counsel when they are concerned about the potential legal consequences of decisions. We refer to the law in this *Manual* for illustrative purposes only; these references should not be taken as a statement of the law or of the legal consequences of a physician's actions, which can vary from state to state. Physicians must develop and maintain an adequate knowledge of key components of the laws and regulations that affect their patients and practices.

The law does not always establish positive duties (that is, what one should do) to the extent that professional ethics, especially medical ethics, does. Our current understanding of medical ethics is based on the principles from which positive duties emerge.

These principles include beneficence, a duty to promote good and act in the best interest of the patient and the health of society, and nonmaleficence, the duty to do no harm to patients. Also included is respect for patient autonomy—the duty to protect and foster a patient's free, uncoerced choices. From the principle of respect for autonomy are derived the rules for truth-telling, disclosure, and informed consent. The relative weight granted to these principles and the conflicts among them often account for the ethical problems that physicians face. Physicians who will be challenged to resolve dilemmas must have such virtues as compassion, courage, and patience in all aspects of their practice.

In addition, considerations of justice inform the physician's role as citizen and clinical decisions about resource allocation. The principle of distributive justice requires that we seek to equitably distribute the life-enhancing opportunities afforded by health care. How to accomplish this distribution is the focus of intense debate. More than ever, concerns about justice challenge the traditional role of physician as patient advocate.

The environment for the delivery of health care is changing. Sites of care are shifting and managed care continues to grow, yet the U.S. health care system does not serve all of its citizens well and major reform is needed. It is unclear how to reform the system to achieve that goal. Health care financing is a serious concern, and society's values will be tested in decisions about resource allocation.

Ethical issues attract widespread public attention, and debate about them is covered regularly in the press. Through legislation, administrative action, or judicial decision, government is increasingly involved in medical ethics. Today, the convergence of various forces—scientific advances, public education, the civil rights and consumer movements, the effects of law and economics on medicine, and the heterogeneity of our society—demands that physicians clearly articulate the ethical principles that guide their behavior, whether in clinical care, research, or teaching or as citizens. It is crucial that a responsible physician perspective be heard as societal decisions are made.

From genetic testing before conception to dilemmas at the end of life, physicians, patients and their families are called upon to make difficult ethical decisions. The 1970s saw the development of bioethics as a field, followed by a series of reports by the U.S. President's Commission for the Study of Ethical Problems in Medicine and Biomedical and Behavioral Research. Important issues then and now included informed consent, access to health care, genetic screening and engineering, and forgoing life-sustaining treatment. These and other issues—AIDS, physician-assisted suicide, increasing computerization of medical records, and the physician as entrepreneur—challenge us to periodically reconsider such topics as the patient-physician relationship, decisions to limit treatment, and confidentiality.

This *Manual* was written for our colleagues in medicine. The College believes that the *Manual* provides the best approach to the challenges addressed in it. We hope that it will stimulate reasoned debate and serve as a reference for persons who seek the College's positions on ethical issues. Debates about medical ethics may also stimulate critical evaluation and discussion of law and public policy on the difficult ethical issues facing patients, physicians, and society.

PHYSICIAN AND PATIENT

The patient-physician relationship entails special obligations for the physician to serve the patient's interest because of the specialized knowledge that physicians hold and the imbalance of power between physicians and patients.

The physician's primary commitment must always be to the patient's welfare and best interests, whether the physician is preventing or treating illness or helping patients to cope with illness, disability, and death. The physician must support the dignity of all persons and respect their uniqueness. The interests of the patient should always be promoted regardless of financial arrangements; the health care setting; and patient characteristics, such as decision-making capacity or social status.

At the beginning of a patient-physician relationship, the physician must understand the patient's complaints, underlying feelings, goals, and expectations. After patient and physician agree on the problem and the goal of therapy, the physician presents one or more courses of action. If both parties agree, the patient may authorize the physician to initiate a course of action; the physician can then accept that responsibility. The relationship has mutual obligations: The physician must be professionally competent, act responsibly, and treat the patient with compassion and respect, and the patient should understand and consent to the treatment that is rendered and should participate responsibly in the care. Although the physician should be fairly compensated for services rendered, a sense of duty to the patient should take precedence over concern about compensation when a patient's well-being is at stake.

Initiating and Discontinuing the Patient-Physician Relationship

By history, tradition, and professional oath, physicians have a moral obligation to provide care for ill persons. Although this obligation is collective, each individual physician is obliged to do his or her fair share to ensure that all ill persons receive appropriate treatment. A physician may not discriminate against a class or category of patients.

An individual patient-physician relationship is formed on the basis of mutual agreement on medical care for the patient. In the absence of a preexisting relationship, the physician is not ethically obliged to provide care to an individual person unless no other physician is available, as is the case in some isolated communities or when emergency treatment is required. Under these circumstances, the physician is morally bound to provide care and, if necessary, to arrange for proper follow-up. Physicians may also be bound by contract to provide care to beneficiaries of participating health plans.

Physicians and patients may have different concepts of the meaning and resolution of medical problems. The care of the patient and satisfaction of both parties are best served if physician and patient discuss their expectations and concerns. Although the physician must address the patient's concerns, he or she is not required to violate fundamental personal values, standards of scientific or ethical practice, or the law. When the patient's beliefs—religious, cultural, or otherwise—run counter to medical recommendations, the physician is obliged to try to understand clearly the beliefs and the viewpoints of the patient. If the physician is unable to carry out the patient's wishes after seriously attempting to resolve differences, the physician should transfer the care of the patient.

Under exceptional circumstances, the physician may discontinue the professional relationship by notifying the patient and, with the approval of the patient, transfer to another physician the information in the record, provided that adequate care is available elsewhere and the patient's health is not jeopardized in the process. Continuity of care must be assured to the best of the physician's ability. Physician-initiated termination is a serious event, especially if the patient is acutely ill, and should be undertaken only after genuine attempts are made to understand and resolve differences. A patient is free to change physicians and is entitled to the information contained in the medical records.

Confidentiality

Confidentiality is a fundamental tenet of medical care. It is a matter of respecting the privacy of patients, encouraging them to seek medical care and discuss their problems candidly, and preventing discrimination on the basis of their medical conditions. The physician must not release information without the patient's consent (often termed a "privileged communication"). However, confidentiality, like other ethical duties, is not absolute. It may have to be overridden to protect individual persons or the public—for example, to warn sexual partners that a patient has syphilis or is infected with HIV—or to disclose information when the law requires it. Before breaching confidentiality, the physician should make every effort to discuss the issues with the patient. If breaching confidentiality is necessary, it should be done in a way that minimizes harm to the patient and that heeds applicable federal and state law.

Confidentiality is increasingly difficult to maintain in this era of computerized record keeping and electronic data processing, faxing of patient information, third-party payment for medical services, and sharing of patient care among numerous medical professionals and institutions. Physicians should be aware of the increased risk for invasion of patients' privacy and should help ensure confidentiality. Within their own institutions, physicians should advocate policies and procedures to secure the confidentiality of patient records.

Discussion of the problems of an identified patient by professional staff in public places (for example, in elevators or in cafeterias) violates confidentiality and is unethical. Outside of an educational setting, discussions of a potentially identifiable patient in front of persons who are not involved in that patient's care are unwise and impair the public's confidence in the medical profession. Physicians of patients who are well known to the public should remember that they are not free to discuss or disclose information about a patient's health without the explicit consent of the patient.

In the care of the adolescent patient, family support is important. However, this support must be balanced with confidentiality and respect for the adolescent's autonomy in health care decisions and in relationships with health care providers. Physicians should be knowledgeable about state laws governing the right of adolescent patients to confidentiality and the adolescent's legal right to consent to treatment.

Occasionally, the physician receives information from a patient's friends or relatives and is asked to withhold the source of that information from the patient. The physician is not obliged to keep such secrets from the patient. The informant should be urged to address the patient directly and to encourage the patient to discuss the information with the physician. The physician should use sensitivity and judgment in deciding whether to use the information and whether to reveal its source to the patient. The physician should always act in the best interests of the patient.

The Patient and the Medical Record

Ethically and legally, patients have the right to know what is in their medical records. Legally, the actual chart is the property of the physician or institution, although the information in the chart is the property of the patient. Most states have laws that guarantee the patient personal access to the medical record. The physician must release information to the patient or to a third party at the request of the patient. Physicians should retain the original of the chart and radiographic studies and respond to a patient's request with copies unless the original record is required by law. To protect confidentiality, information should only be released with the written permission of the patient or the patient's legally authorized representative.

Disclosure

To make health care decisions and work intelligently in partnership with the physician, the patient must be well informed. Effective patient-physician communication can dispel uncertainty and fear and can enhance healing and patient satisfaction. Information should be disclosed whenever it is considered material to the patient's understanding of his or her situation, possible treatments, and probable outcomes. This information often includes the costs and burdens of treatment, the experience of the proposed clinician, the nature of the illness, and potential treatments.

However uncomfortable to clinician or patient, information that is essential to the patient must be disclosed. How, when, and to whom information is disclosed are important concerns that must be addressed.

Information should be given in terms that the patient can understand. The physician should be sensitive to the patient's responses in setting the pace of disclosure, particularly if the illness is very serious. Disclosure should never be a mechanical or perfunctory process. Upsetting news and information should be presented to the patient in a way that minimizes distress. If the patient is unable to comprehend his or her condition, it should be fully disclosed to an appropriate surrogate.

In addition, physicians should disclose to patients information about procedural or judgment errors made in the course of care if such information is material to the patient's well-being. Errors do not necessarily constitute improper, negligent, or unethical behavior, but failure to disclose them may.

Informed Consent

Any unauthorized touching of a person is battery, even in the medical setting. The patient's consent allows the physician to provide care.

Consent may be either expressed or implied. Expressed consent most often occurs in the hospital setting, where written or oral consent is given for a particular procedure. In many medical encounters, when the patient presents to a physician for evaluation and care, consent can be presumed. The underlying condition and treatment options are explained to the patient, and treatment is rendered or refused. In medical emergencies, consent to treatment that is necessary to maintain life or restore health is usually implied unless it is known that the patient would refuse the intervention.

The doctrine of informed consent goes beyond the question of whether consent was given for a treatment or intervention. Rather, it focuses on the content and process of consent. The physician is required to provide enough information to allow a patient to make an informed judgment about how to proceed. The physician's presentation should be understandable to the patient, should be unbiased, and should include the physician's recommendation. The patient's or surrogate's concurrence must be free and uncoerced.

The principle and practice of informed consent rely on patients to ask questions when they are uncertain about the information they receive; to think carefully about their choices; and to be forthright with their physicians about their values, concerns, and reservations about a particular recommendation. Once patients and physicians decide on a course of action, patients should make every reasonable effort to carry out the aspects of care that are in their control or to inform their physicians promptly if it is not possible to do so.

The physician is obligated to ensure that the patient or the surrogate is adequately informed about the nature of the patient's medical condition and the objectives of, alternatives to, possible outcomes of, and risks involved with a proposed treatment.

All adult patients are considered competent to make decisions about medical care unless a court declares them incompetent. In clinical practice, however, physicians and family members usually make decisions without a formal competency hearing in the courts for patients who lack decision-making capacity. This clinical approach can be ethically justified if the physician has carefully determined that the patient is incapable of understanding the nature of the proposed treatment; the alternatives to it; and the risks, benefits, and consequences of it.

When a patient lacks decision-making capacity (that is, the ability to receive and express information and to make a choice consonant with that information and one's values), an appropriate surrogate should make decisions with the physician. Ideally, surrogate decision makers should know the patient's preferences and act in the best interests of the patient. If the patient has designated a proxy, as through a durable power of attorney for health care, that choice should be respected. When patients have not selected surrogates, standard clinical practice is that family members serve as surrogates. Some states designate the order in which family members will serve as surrogates. Physicians should be aware of legal requirements in their state for surrogate appointment and decision making. In some cases, all parties may agree that a close friend is a more appropriate surrogate than a relative.

Physicians should take reasonable care to ensure that the surrogate's decisions are consistent with the patient's preferences and best interests. When possible, these decisions should be reached in the medical setting by physicians, surrogates, and other caregivers. Physicians should emphasize to surrogates that decisions should be based on what the patient would want, not what surrogates would choose for themselves. If disagreements cannot be resolved, hospital ethics committees may be helpful. Courts should be used when doing so serves the patient, such as to establish guardianship for an unbefriended, incompetent patient; to resolve a problem when other processes fail; or to comply with state law.

Most adult patients can participate in, and thereby share responsibility for, their health care. Physicians cannot properly diagnose and treat conditions without full disclosure of patients' personal and family medical history, habits, ongoing treatments (medical and otherwise), and symptoms. The physician's obligation to confidentiality exists in part to ensure that patients can be candid without fear of loss of privacy. Physicians must try to create an environment in which honesty can thrive and patient concerns and questions are elicited.

Decisions about Reproduction

The ethical duty to disclose relevant information about human reproduction to the patient may conflict with the physician's personal moral standards on abortion, sterilization, or contraception. A physician who objects to these services need not become involved, whether by offering advice to the patient or by involvement in a procedure. As in any other medical situation, the physician has a duty to refer the patient to an appropriate source for the full range of options so that the patient's legal options are not constrained.

If a patient who is a minor requests termination of pregnancy, advice on contraception, or treatment of sexually transmitted diseases without a parent's knowledge, the physician may wish to attempt to persuade the patient of the benefits of having parents involved but should be aware that a conflict may exist between the legal duty to maintain confidentiality and the obligation toward parents or guardians. Information should not be provided to others without the patient's permission. In such cases, the physician should be guided by his or her conscience in light of the law.

Genetic Testing

Presymptomatic and diagnostic testing raises issues of education, counseling, confidentiality, and justice. Such testing may allow clinicians to predict diseases or clarify susceptibility at a time when medicine may not have the ability to prevent or cure the conditions that are identified. Both the public and health care professionals often have a limited grasp of the distinction between prediction and susceptibility or risk. Genetic testing presents unique problems by identifying risk for disease that has special meaning for patients and for family members who may not be under the care of the clinician providing the test.

Clinicians should discuss with patients the degree to which a particular genetic risk factor correlates with the likelihood of developing disease. Testing should not be undertaken until these issues are fully explored with the patient and the potential consequences of the test, from its impact on the patient's well-being to implications for other family members and use by insurers or other societal institutions, are fully understood.

Because the number of trained genetic counselors is small and is unlikely to match the exponential growth in genetic testing, the generalist clinician is increasingly responsible for conveying genetic test results. Only physicians who are familiar with the skills necessary for pretest and post-test education and counseling should engage in genetic testing. All primary care physicians should develop these skills.

As more information becomes available on the genetic risk for certain diseases, physicians must be aware of the need for confidentiality concerning results of genetic tests. Many state governments and the federal government are promulgating rules and regulations that cover access of employers and insurers to such information. Additional complex ethical problems exist, such as which family member should be informed of the results of genetic tests. Physicians should be sensitive to these ethical problems, and testing should not be undertaken until issues are fully discussed and their consequences are well understood.

The potential for stigmatization and insurance and job discrimination require that physicians ensure the confidentiality of data. However, the presence of a genetic risk factor or genetic disease in a family member raises the possibility that other blood relatives are at risk. The physician should seek the affected patient's consent in encouraging potentially affected family members to seek genetic counseling if it may affect treatment or major life decisions.

Medical Risk to Physician and Patient

Traditionally, the ethical imperative for physicians to provide care has overridden the risk to the treating physician, even during epidemics. In recent decades, with better control of such risks, physicians have practiced medicine in the absence of risk as a prominent concern. However, potential occupational exposures such as HIV, multidrug-resistant tuberculosis, and viral hepatitis necessitate reaffirmation of the ethical imperative.

Physicians should evaluate their risk for becoming infected with pathogens, both in their personal lives and in the workplace, and implement appropriate precautions. Physicians who may have been exposed to pathogens have an ethical obligation to be tested and should do so voluntarily. Infected physicians should place themselves under the guidance of their personal physician or the review of local experts to determine in a confidential manner whether practice restrictions are appropriate on the basis of the physician's compliance with infection control precautions and physical and mental fitness to work. Infection does not in itself justify restrictions on the practice of an otherwise competent health care worker. Health care workers are expected to comply with public health and institutional policies.

Because the diseases mentioned above may be transmitted from patient to physician and because they pose significant risks to physicians' health and are difficult to treat or cure, some physicians may be tempted to avoid the care of infected patients. Physicians and health care organizations are obligated to provide competent and humane care to all patients, regardless of their disease state. Physicians can and should expect their workplace to provide appropriate means to limit occupational exposure through rigorous application of infection control methods. The denial of appropriate care to a class of patients for any reason is unethical.

Whether physicians should disclose their condition depends on the likelihood of risk to the patient and relevant law or regulations in their locales. Physicians should remove themselves from care if it becomes clear that the risk associated with contact or with a procedure is significant even if appropriate preventive measures are taken. Physicians are also obligated to disclose their condition after the fact if a clinically significant exposure has taken place.

Physicians have several obligations concerning nosocomial risk of infection. They should help the public to understand the low level of this risk and put it in the perspective of other medical risks while acknowledging public concern. Physicians provide medical care to health care workers, and part of this care is discussing with health care workers their ethical obligation to know their risk for such diseases as HIV or viral hepatitis, to voluntarily seek testing if they are at risk, and to take reasonable steps to protect patients. The physician who provides care for a seropositive health care worker must determine the health care worker's fitness to work. In some cases, seropositive health care workers cannot be persuaded to comply with accepted infection control guidelines, or impaired physicians cannot be persuaded to restrict their practice. In such exceptional cases, the treating physician may need to breach confidentiality and report the incident to the appropriate authorities in order to protect patients and maintain public trust in the profession, even though such actions may have legal consequences.

Alternative Treatments

Alternative or *complementary medicine* is a common term for health practices that generally are not available from U.S. physicians, are not offered in U.S. hospitals, and are not widely taught in U.S. medical schools. The physician should not abandon the patient who elects to try an alternative treatment. Requests by patients for alternative treatment require balancing the medical standard of care with a patient's right to choose care on the basis of his or her values and preferences. Such a request warrants careful attention from the physician. Before advising a patient, the physician should ascertain the reason for the request: for example, whether it stems from dissatisfaction with current care. The physician should be sure that the patient understands his or her condition, standard medical treatment options, and expected outcomes.

The physician should encourage the patient requesting alternative treatment to seek literature and information from reliable sources. The patient should be clearly informed if the option under consideration is likely to delay access to effective treatment or is known to be harmful. The physician need not participate in the monitoring or delivery of alternative care to the patient. However, physicians should recognize that some patients may select alternative forms of treatment; this decision alone should not be cause to sever the patient-physician relationship.

Disability Certification

Some patients have chronic, overwhelming, or catastrophic illnesses. In these cases, society permits physicians to justify exemption from work and to legitimize other forms of financial support.

In keeping with the role of patient advocate, a physician should assist a patient who is medically disabled in obtaining the appropriate disability status. Disability evaluation forms should be completed factually, honestly, and promptly.

Physicians will often find themselves confronted with a patient whose problems may not fit standard definitions of disability but who nevertheless seems deserving of assistance (for example, the patient may have very limited resources or poor housing). Physicians should not distort medical information or misrepresent the patient's functional status in a misguided attempt to help these patients. The trustworthiness of the physician is jeopardized, as is his or her ability to advocate for patients who truly meet disability or exemption criteria.

Care of the Physician's Family, Friends, and Employees

Physicians should avoid treating themselves, close friends, or members of their own families. Physicians should also be very cautious about assuming the care of closely associated employees. Problems may include inadequate history taking or physical examination as a result of role-related discomfort on the part of patient or physician. The physician's emotional proximity can result in a loss of objectivity. If a physician does treat a close friend, family member, or employee out of necessity, the patient should be transferred to another physician as soon as it is practical. Otherwise, requests for care on the part of employees, family members, or friends should be resolved by assisting them in obtaining appropriate care. Fulfilling the role of informed and loving adviser, however, is not precluded.

Sexual Contact between Physician and Patient

Issues of dependency, trust, and transference and inequalities of power lead to increased vulnerability on the part of the patient and require that a physician not engage in a sexual relationship with a patient. It is unethical for a physician to become sexually involved with a current patient even if the patient initiates or consents to the contact.

Even sexual involvement between physicians and former patients raises concern. The impact of the patient-physician relationship may be viewed very differently by physicians and former patients, and either party may underestimate the influence of the past professional relationship. Many former patients continue to feel dependency and transference toward their physicians long after the professional relationship has ended. The intense trust often established between physician and patient may amplify the patient's vulnerability in a subsequent sexual relationship. A sexual relationship with a former patient is unethical if the physician "uses or exploits the trust, knowledge, emotions or influence derived from the previous professional relationship". Because it may be difficult for the physician to judge this influence, we advise consultation with a colleague or other professional before becoming sexually involved with a former patient.

CARE OF PATIENTS NEAR THE END OF LIFE

End-of-life care is an important aspect of medical practice. Individual physicians and the medical community must be committed to the compassionate and competent provision of care to dying patients and their families. Patients rightfully expect their physicians to care for them and provide them medical assistance as they are dying. Good symptom control; ongoing involvement with the patient; and physical, psychological, and spiritual support are the hallmarks of quality end-of-life care. Care of patients near the end of life, however, has a moral, psychological, and interpersonal intensity that distinguishes it from most other clinical encounters.

Patients Near the End of Life

To care properly for patients near the end of life, the physician must understand that palliative care entails addressing physical, psychosocial, and spiritual needs and that patients may at times require palliative treatment in an acute care context. To provide palliative care, the physician must be up to date on the proper use of opioids and the legality and propriety of using high doses of opioids as necessary to relieve suffering. The physician should know how to refer patients to appropriate palliative care, know how to use home-based and institution-based hospice care, and be aware of the palliative care abilities of the nursing homes to which patients are referred.

Making Decisions Near the End of Life

Informed adults with decision-making capacity almost always have the legal and ethical right to refuse any recommended life-sustaining medical treatment. The patient has this right regardless of whether he or she is terminally or irreversibly ill, has dependents, or is pregnant. The patient's right is based on the philosophical concept of respect for autonomy, the common-law right of self-determination, and the patient's liberty interest under the U.S. Constitution.

Many patients, particularly those with terminal or irreversible illness, elect to forgo certain treatments or pursue treatments that their physicians may consider unwise. These situations demand empathy, thoughtful exploration of all possibilities, negotiation, or compromise and may require time-limited trials and additional consultations.

In the unusual circumstance that no evidence shows that a specific treatment desired by the patient will provide any benefit from any perspective, the physician need not provide such treatment. The more common and much more difficult circumstance occurs when the treatment will offer some small prospect of benefit at a great burden of suffering or financial cost, but the patient or family nevertheless desires it. If the physician and patient cannot agree on how to proceed, there is no easy, automatic solution. Timely transfer of care to another care provider who is willing to pursue the patient's preference may resolve the problem. Consultation with an ethics committee may be helpful. Infrequently, resort to the courts may be necessary.

Patients without decision-making capacity (see the section on informed consent) have the same rights concerning life-sustaining treatment decisions as mentally competent patients. Treatment should conform to what the patient would want on the basis of written or oral advance directives. If these instructions are not available, care decisions should be based on the best evidence of what the patient would have chosen (substituted judgments) or, failing that, on the best interests of the patient. Physicians should be aware that hospital protocols and state legal requirements affecting end-of-life care vary.

Advance Care Planning

Advance care planning allows a competent person to indicate preferences for care or choose a surrogate in the event that the patient cannot make health care decisions. It allows the patient's values and circumstances to shape the plan and allows specific arrangements to be made to ensure implementation of the plan.

Physicians should routinely raise the issue of advance planning with competent adult patients during outpatient visits and encourage them to discuss their values and preferences with their surrogates and family members. These discussions let the physician know the patient's views, enable the physician to update the medical record, and allow the physician to reassure patients that he or she is willing to discuss these sensitive issues and will respect their choices. The patient and the physician should negotiate plans to make sure patient wishes are implemented.

Discussions about patient preferences should be documented in the medical record. The Patient Self-Determination Act of 1990 requires hospitals, nursing homes, health maintenance organizations, and hospices that participate in Medicare and Medicaid programs to ask if the patient has an advance directive, to provide information about advance directives, and to incorporate advance directives into the medical record.

Advance planning takes place in conversations with the physician (with documentation in the medical record) or through written advance directives, such as a living will or durable power of attorney for health care. The latter enables a patient to appoint a surrogate who will make decisions if the patient becomes unable to do so. The surrogate is required to act in accordance with the patient's previously expressed preferences or best interests.

Living wills enable persons to describe the kind of treatment they would like to receive in the event that they lose decision-making capacity. Uncertainty about a future clinical course complicates the interpretation of living wills and emphasizes the need for physicians and patients to discuss patient preferences before a crisis arises. Talking about future medical care is an effective method of planning. Some state laws limit the application of advance directives to terminal illness or deem the advance directives not applicable if, for example, the patient is pregnant. Many states have documents that combine the living will and the durable power of attorney for health care into one document. Some specify requirements for witnessing the document. The primary care physician and other key health care personnel should have a written advance directive in the patient's medical record.

When there is no advance directive and the patient's values and preferences are unknown or unclear, decisions should be based on the patient's best interests whenever possible, as interpreted by a guardian or by a person with loving knowledge of the patient. When making the decision to forgo treatment, many people give the most weight to reversibility of disease or dependence on life support, loss of capacity for social interaction, or nearness to death. Family members and health care workers should avoid projecting their own values or views about quality of life onto the incapacitated patient. Quality of life should be assessed according to the patient's perspective.

Problems of Life-Sustaining Treatments

Withdrawing or Withholding Treatment

Withdrawing and withholding treatment are equally justifiable, ethically and legally. Treatments should not be withheld because of the mistaken fear that if they are started, they cannot be withdrawn. This practice would deny patients potentially beneficial therapies. Instead, a time-limited trial of therapy could be used to clarify the patient's prognosis. At the end of the trial, a conference to review and revise the treatment plan should be held. Some health care workers or family members may be reluctant to withdraw treatments even when they believe that the patient would not have wanted them continued. The physician should prevent or resolve these situations by addressing with families feelings of guilt, fears, and concerns that patients may suffer as life support is withdrawn.

Do-Not-Resuscitate Orders

Intervention in the case of a cardiopulmonary arrest is inappropriate for some patients, particularly those with terminal irreversible illness whose death is expected and imminent. Because the onset of cardiopulmonary arrest does not permit deliberative decision making, decisions about resuscitation must be made in advance. Physicians should especially encourage patients who face serious illness or who are in advanced old age, or their surrogates, to discuss resuscitation.

Although a do-not-resuscitate order applies only to cardiopulmonary resuscitation, discussions about this issue often reflect a revision of the larger goals and means of the care plan. The entire health care team must be carefully apprised of the nature of these changes. Do-not-resuscitate orders or requests for no cardiopulmonary resuscitation should specify care strategies and must be written in the medical record along with notes and orders that describe all other changes in the treatment goals or plans. It is essential that patients or surrogates understand that a do-not-resuscitate order does not mean that the patient will be ineligible for other life-prolonging measures, both therapeutic and palliative. However, the appropriateness of a do-not-resuscitate order during and immediately after any procedure needs to be individually negotiated. It is unethical for physicians or nurses to perform half-hearted resuscitation efforts ("slow codes").

Sometimes a patient or surrogate insists on a resuscitation effort, even when they are informed that it will almost certainly fail. A family's religious or other beliefs or need for closure under such circumstances deserve careful attention. Although the physician need not provide an effort at resuscitation that cannot conceivably restore circulation and breathing, the physician should help the family to understand and accept this position. It is more controversial whether physicians may unilaterally write a do-not-resuscitate order when the patient may survive for a very brief time in the hospital. Some institutions, with forewarning to patients and families, allow physicians to write orders against resuscitation over the patient's or family's objections. Empathy and thoughtful exploration of options for care with patients or surrogate decision makers should make such impasses rare. Full discussion about the issue should include the indications for and outcomes of cardiopulmonary resuscitation, the physical impact on the patient, implications for caregivers, the do-not-resuscitate order, the legal aspects of such orders, and the physician's role as patient advocate. Physicians who write a unilateral do-not-resuscitate order must inform the patient or surrogate.

Determination of Death

The irreversible cessation of all functions of the entire brain is an accepted legal standard for determining death when the use of life support precludes the use of traditional cardiopulmonary criteria. After a patient has been declared dead by brain-death criteria, medical support should ordinarily be discontinued. In some circumstances, such as the need to preserve organs for transplantation, to counsel or accommodate family preferences, or to sustain a viable fetus, physicians may temporarily support bodily functions after death has been determined.

Organ Donation

There is an increasingly unmet need for organs and tissues. Physicians should be involved in community efforts to make potential donors aware of their option to make a gift that would enhance life, health, or sight by organ or tissue donation. Physicians should obtain consent from the patient for the disposal and use of tissue, organs, or other body parts removed during diagnostic or operative procedures. All potential donors should communicate their preference to their families and have it listed on such documents as driver's licenses or organ donor cards.

CODES OF PROFESSIONAL RESPONSIBILITY

Physicians caring for dying or brain-dead patients who are potential donors should inquire about whether the patient had expressed preferences about donation. Federal and state law and health care accreditation bodies require that hospitals have procedures to ensure that families of hospitalized potential donors are made aware of the option to consent to organ donation. The issue of organ donation often arises in very difficult circumstances and may carry significant symbolic import for the family. Physicians should approach families with sensitivity and compassion.

Furthermore, organ procurement raises ethical concerns about the determination of death that have been partly addressed by legislation that defines brain death. It can also create conflict or the appearance of conflict between the care of a potential donor and the needs of a potential recipient. The care of the potential donor must be kept separate from the care of a recipient. The potential donor's physician should not be responsible for the care of the recipient nor be involved in retrieving the organs or tissue. However, the potential donor's physician may alert an organ-tissue procurement team of the existence of a potential donor. Once brain death has occurred and organ donation is authorized, the donor's physician should know how to maintain the viability of organs and tissues in coordination with the procurement team. Before declaration of brain death, treatments proposed to maintain the function of transplantable organs may be used only if they are not expected to harm the potential donor, whether by causing symptoms or by compromising the chance of survival.

Irreversible Loss of Consciousness

Persons who are in a persistent vegetative state are unconscious but are not brain dead. Because their condition is not progressive, patients in a persistent vegetative state are not terminally ill. They lack awareness of their surroundings and the ability to respond purposefully to them. The prognosis for these patients varies with cause. Some physicians and medical societies believe that there are no medical indications for life-prolonging treatment or access to intensive care or respirators when patients are confirmed to be in a persistent vegetative state. They conclude that these patients cannot experience any benefits or suffer any discomfort and that all interventions should therefore be withdrawn. However, many patients or families value life in and of itself regardless of neurologic state. For these reasons, goals of care should guide decisions about life-prolonging treatment for patients in a persistent vegetative state in the same manner as for other patients without decision-making capacity.

Intravenous Fluids and Artificial Feedings

Artificial administration of nutrition and fluids is a life-prolonging treatment. As such, it is subject to the same principles for decisions as other treatments. Some states require high levels of proof before previous statements or advance directives can be accepted as firm evidence that a patient would not want these treatments in the setting of terminal illness, permanent unconsciousness, or advanced dementia. For this reason, physicians should counsel patients to establish advance care directives and complete these parts of living wills especially carefully. Clinically, there is unfounded concern that discontinuing use of feeding tubes will cause suffering from hunger or thirst despite research findings to the contrary. Physicians should carefully address this issue with family and caregivers.

Physician-Assisted Suicide and Euthanasia

The debate over physician-assisted suicide is very important to physicians and patients. Both groups favor easing the dying process, providing adequate pain control, and avoiding unwanted overtreatment and protracted suffering. Patients and physicians may find it difficult at times to distinguish between the need for assistance in the dying process and the practice of assisting suicide.

Physician-assisted suicide occurs when a physician provides a medical means for death, usually a prescription for a lethal amount of medication that the patient takes on his or her own. In euthanasia, the physician directly and intentionally administers a substance to cause death. Physicians and patients should distinguish a decision by patients or their authorized surrogate to refuse life-sustaining treatment or an inadvertent death that occurs during an attempt to relieve suffering from physician-assisted suicide and euthanasia. Laws concerning or moral objections to physician-assisted suicide and euthanasia should not deter physicians from honoring a decision to withhold or withdraw medical interventions in appropriate situations. Fears that unwanted life-sustaining treatment will be imposed continue to motivate some patients to request assisted suicide or euthanasia.

In the clinical setting, all of these acts must be framed within the larger context of good end-of-life care. Many patients who request assisted suicide are depressed, have uncontrolled pain, or have potentially reversible suffering or fears. In the setting of providing comfort to a dying person, most physicians and patients should be able to address these issues. For example, with regard to pain control, the physician may appropriately increase medication to relieve pain, even if this action inadvertently shortens life (the "double effect").

Physician-assisted suicide may be legalized in some states, although no consensus currently exists among patients or physicians or within the College. Many fear that physicians are inadequately trained to arrive at such a conclusion with patients. Concerns focus in particular on vulnerable populations—poor persons, persons with costly chronic diseases, demented persons, disabled persons, and very young children. Physicians and patients must continue to search together for answers to these problems without violating the physician's personal and professional values and without abandoning the patient to struggle alone. For now, the policy debate continues to evolve rapidly, and physicians should urgently strive to greatly improve the quality of end-of-life care.

THE ETHICS OF PRACTICE

The Changing Practice Environment

Many individual persons, groups, and institutions play a role in and are affected by medical decision making in the current practice environment. Tension and competition among the interests of clinicians, insurers, patients, and institutions for available social and health care resources unavoidably influence the patient-physician relationship. Although this section of the *Manual* will focus specifically on the obligations of physicians in this changing context, it is essential to note that others, such as insurers and health care institutions, bear responsibility for ensuring that the fundamental ethical commitment between physicians and patients is not undermined. Insured patients and their families should try to understand the possible implications of their insurance. Concern about the changing practice environment for physicians and insured patients should not distract our attention from the problems faced by persons who lack insurance.

Physicians must promote their patients' welfare in an increasingly complex health care system. This entails forthrightly helping patients to understand clinical recommendations and to make informed choices among all appropriate care options. It includes management of the conflicts of interest and multiple commitments that arise in any practice environment, especially in an era of cost concerns. It also includes stewardship of health care resources so that finite resources can meet as many health care needs as possible, whether in the physician's office, the hospital, the nursing home, or home care.

The patient-physician relationship and the principles that govern it should be central to the delivery of care. These principles include beneficence, honesty, confidentiality, privacy, and advocacy when patients' interests may be endangered by arbitrary, unjust, or inadequately individualized institutional procedures. Health care, however, does take place in a broader context beyond the patient-physician relationship. A patient's preferences or interests may conflict with the interests or values of the physician, an institution, a payer, other members of a managed care plan who have equal claim to the same health care resources, or society.

The physician's first and primary duty is to the patient. Physicians must base their counsel to patients on the interests of the individual patient, regardless of the insurance or medical care delivery setting in which physicians find themselves. Whether financial incentives in the fee-for-service system prompt physicians to do more rather than less or managed care arrangements encourage the physician to do less rather than more, physicians must not allow such considerations to affect their clinical judgment or counseling on treatment options, including referrals, for the patient. The physician's professional role is to make recommendations on the basis of their medical merit and to pursue options that comport with the patient's unique background and preferences.

Physicians should also contribute to the responsible stewardship of health care resources. With clinical authority and discretion come responsibility. Parsimonious care that utilizes the most efficient means to diagnose a condition and treat a patient respects the need to use resources wisely and to help ensure that resources are equitably available. The recommendations of physicians to patients, in the design of practice guidelines and formularies, and to medical benefits review boards should reflect the best clinical literature. Recommendations should, as much as possible, consider data on the cost-effectiveness of different clinical approaches. When patients ask, they should be informed of the rationale that underlies the physician's recommendation.

Health plans are not obliged to underwrite approaches that patients may value but that are not justifiable on clinical or theoretical scientific grounds or that are relatively cost-ineffective compared with other therapies for the same condition or other therapies offered by the health plan for other conditions. However, the plan must have in place a fair appeals procedure. In instances of disagreement between patient and physician for any reason, the physician is obligated to explain the basis for the disagreement, to educate the patient, and to meet the patient's needs for comfort and reassurance.

The physician's duty further requires that the physician serve as the patient's agent in the health care arena as a whole. In the managed care context, for example, advocacy can operate at many levels. At the individual level, the physician advocate must pursue the necessary avenues to obtain treatment that is essential to the individual patient's care, regardless of the barriers that may discourage the physician from doing so. When barriers diminish care for a class of patients because the patients themselves are less capable of self-representation, physicians must advocate on their behalf for equitable treatment.

Patients may not understand or may fear conflicts of interests for physicians and the multiple commitments that can arise from cost-containment under managed care. Health care plans have duties to foster an ethical practice environment. They should hold physicians accountable for the quality of care and not simply for economic performance. Managed care plans should not restrict the information or counsel that physicians may give patients.

Although the physician must provide information to the patient about all appropriate care and referral options, the health plan must disclose all relevant information about benefits, including any restrictions, and about financial incentives that might negatively affect patient access to care.

When patients enroll in insurance plans, they receive a great deal of information on rules governing benefits and reimbursement. Patients should familiarize themselves with this information. Physicians cannot and should not be expected to advise patients on the particulars of individual insurance contracts and arrangements. Patients should, however, expect their physicians to honor the rules of the insurer unless doing so would endanger the patient's health. Physicians should not collaborate with a patient or engage in efforts to defraud the insurer.

Financial Arrangements

As professionals dedicated to serving the sick, all physicians should do their fair share to provide services to uninsured and underinsured persons.

Financial relationships between patients and physicians vary from fee-for-service to government contractual arrangements and prepaid insurance. Financial arrangements and expectations should be clearly established in advance. Fees for physician services should accurately reflect the services provided. Physicians should be mindful that forgiving copayment may constitute fraud.

When physicians elect to offer professional courtesy to a colleague, physicians and patients should function without feelings of constraints on time or resources and without shortcut approaches. Colleague-patients who initiate questions in informal settings put the treating physician in a less-than-ideal position to provide optimal care. Both parties should avoid this inappropriate practice.

Financial Conflicts of Interest

The physician must seek to ensure that the medically appropriate level of care takes primacy over financial considerations imposed by the physician's own practice, investments, or financial arrangements. Trust in the profession is undermined when there is even the appearance of impropriety.

Potential influences on clinical judgment cover a wide range and include financial incentives inherent in the practice environment (such as incentives to overutilize in the fee-for-service setting or underutilize in the managed care setting), drug industry gifts, and business arrangements involving referrals. Physicians must be conscious of all potential influences and their actions should be guided by appropriate utilization, not by other factors. A fee paid to one physician by another for the referral of a patient, historically known as fee-splitting, is unethical. It is also unethical for a physician to receive a commission or a kickback from anyone, including a company that manufactures or sells medical instruments or medications that are used in the care of the physician's patients. Physicians should not refer patients to an outside facility in which they have invested and at which they do not directly provide care.

Physicians may, however, invest in or own health care facilities when capital funding and necessary services are provided that would otherwise not be made available. In such situations, in addition to disclosing these interests to patients, safeguards must be established against abuse, impropriety, or the appearance of impropriety.

Physicians may invest in publicly traded securities. However, care must be taken to avoid investment decisions that may create a conflict of interest or the perception of a conflict of interest.

The acceptance of individual gifts, hospitality, trips, and subsidies of all types from the health care industry by an individual physician is strongly discouraged. The acceptance of even small gifts has been documented to affect clinical judgment and heightens the perception (as well as the reality) of a conflict of interest. While following the Royal College of Physicians' guideline, "Would I be willing to have this arrangement generally known?", physicians should also ask, "What would the public or my patients think of this arrangement?"

Physicians must critically evaluate medical information provided by detail persons, advertisements, or industry-sponsored educational programs. Physicians with ties to a particular company should disclose their interests when speaking or writing about a company product. Most journal editors require that authors and peer reviewers disclose any potential conflicts of interest. Editors themselves should be free from conflicts of interest concerning particular papers.

Advertising

Advertising by physicians or health care institutions is unethical when it contains statements that are unsubstantiated, false, deceptive, or misleading, including statements that mislead by omitting necessary information.

THE PHYSICIAN AND SOCIETY

Society has conferred professional prerogatives on physicians with the expectation that they will use their position for the benefit of patients. In turn, physicians are responsible and accountable to society for their professional actions. Society grants each physician the rights, privileges, and duties pertinent to the patient-physician relationship and has the right to require that physicians be competent and knowledgeable and that they practice with consideration for the patient as a person.

Obligations of the Physician to Society

Physicians have obligations to society that in many ways parallel their obligations to individual patients. Physicians' conduct as professionals and as individual citizens should merit the respect of the community.

All physicians must fulfill the profession's collective responsibility to advocate the health and well-being of the public. Physicians should protect public health by reporting diseases, as required by law, to the responsible authority. They should support public health endeavors that provide the general public with accurate information about health care and comment on medical subjects in their areas of expertise to keep the public properly informed. Physicians should regard interaction with the news media to provide accurate information as an obligation to society and an extension of medical practice but must always be mindful of patient confidentiality.

Physicians should help the community recognize and deal with the social and environmental causes of disease. They should work toward ensuring access to health care for all persons and help correct deficiencies in the availability, accessibility, and quality of health services in the community.

Resource Allocation

Medical care is delivered within social and institutional systems that must take overall resources into account. Increasingly, decisions about resource allocations challenge the physician's primary role as patient advocate. There have always been limits to this advocacy role: For example, a physician is not obligated to lie to third-party payers for a patient or to provide all treatments regardless of their effectiveness. Resource allocation pushes these limits further by compelling physicians to consider the best interests of all patients and of each patient. The just allocation of resources and changing reimbursement methods present the physician with ethical problems that cannot be ignored. Two principles are agreed upon:

1. As a physician performs his or her primary role as a patient's trusted advocate, he or she has a responsibility to use all health-related resources in a technically appropriate and efficient manner. He or she should plan workups carefully and avoid unnecessary testing, medications, surgery, and consultations.

2. Resource allocation decisions are most appropriately made at the policy level rather than entirely in the context of an individual patient-physician encounter. Physicians should participate in decisions at the policy level; should emphasize the value of health to society; and should base allocations on medical need, cost-effectiveness of treatments, and proper distribution of benefits and burdens in society.

Relation of the Physician to Government

Physicians must not be a party to and must speak out against torture or other abuses of human rights. Participation by physicians in the execution of prisoners except to certify death is unethical. Under no circumstances is it ethical for a physician to be used as an instrument of government to weaken the physical or mental resistance of a human being, nor should a physician participate in or tolerate cruel or unusual punishment or disciplinary activities beyond those permitted by the United Nations Standard Minimum Rules for the Treatment of Prisoners.

Ethics Committees and Consultants

Ethics committees and consultants contribute to achieving patient care goals by facilitating resolution of conflicts in a respectful atmosphere through a fair and inclusive decision-making process, helping institutions to shape policies and practices that conform with the highest ethical standards, and assisting individual persons with handling current and future ethical problems by providing education in health care ethics. Although it is generally agreed that neither ethics committees nor consultants should have decision-making authority, they can advise clinicians, patients, and family members on ethical matters.

328 CODES OF PROFESSIONAL RESPONSIBILITY

Medicine and the Law

Physicians should remember that the presence of illness does not diminish the right or expectation to be treated equally. Stated another way, illness does not in and of itself change a patient's legal rights or permit a physician to ignore those legal rights.

The law is society's mechanism for establishing boundaries for conduct. Society has a right to expect that those boundaries will not be disregarded. In instances of conflict, the physician must decide whether to violate the law for the sake of what he or she considers to be the dictates of medical ethics. Such a violation may jeopardize the physician's legal position or the legal rights of the patient. It should be remembered that ethical concepts are not always fully reflected in or adopted by the law. Violation of the law for purposes of complying with one's ethical standards may have significant consequences for the physician and should be undertaken only after thorough consideration and, generally, after obtaining legal counsel.

Expert Witnesses

Physicians have specialized knowledge and expertise that may be needed in judicial or administrative processes. Often, expert testimony is necessary for a court or administrative agency to understand the patient's condition, treatment, and prognosis. Physicians may be reluctant to become involved in legal proceedings because the process is unfamiliar and time-consuming. Their absence may mean, however, that legal decisions are made without the benefit of all medical facts or opinions. Without the participation of physicians, the mechanisms used to resolve many disputes may be ineffective and patients may suffer.

Although physicians cannot be compelled to participate as expert witnesses, the profession as a whole has the ethical duty to assist patients and society in resolving disputes. In this role, physicians must give an honest and objective interpretation and representation of the medical facts. Physicians should only accept noncontingent compensation for the time and expenses incurred as expert witnesses.

Strikes by Physicians

Physicians should not participate in a strike that adversely affects access to health care. In general, physicians should individually and collectively find alternatives to strikes to address workplace concerns.

THE PHYSICIAN'S RELATIONSHIP TO OTHER CLINICIANS

Physicians share a commitment to care for ill persons with an increasingly broad team of clinicians. The team's ability to care effectively for the patient depends on the ability of individual persons to treat each other with integrity, honesty, and respect in daily professional interactions regardless of race, religion, ethnicity, nationality, sex, sexual orientation, age, or disability. Particular attention is warranted with regard to certain types of relationships and power imbalances that could be abusive or exploitative or lead to harassment, such as those between attending physician and resident, instructor and medical student, or physician and nurse.

Attending Physicians and Physicians in Training

The very title *doctor*, from the Latin *docere*, "to teach," implies that physicians have a responsibility to share knowledge and information with colleagues and patients. This sharing includes teaching clinical skills and reporting results of scientific research to colleagues, medical students, resident physicians, and other health care providers.

The physician has a responsibility to teach the science, art, and ethics of medicine to medical students, resident physicians, and others and to supervise physicians in training. Attending physicians must treat trainees with the same respect and compassion accorded to other colleagues. In the teaching environment, graduated authority for patient management can be delegated to residents, with adequate supervision. All trainees should inform patients of their training status and role in the medical team. Attending physicians, chiefs of service, or consultants should encourage residents to acknowledge their limitations and ask for help or supervision when concerns arise about patient care or the ability of others to perform their duties.

It is unethical to delegate authority for patient care to anyone, including another physician, who is not appropriately qualified and experienced. On a teaching service, the ultimate responsibility for patient welfare and quality of care remains with the patient's attending physician of record.

Consultation

In almost all circumstances, patients should be encouraged to initially seek care from their principal physician. Physicians should in turn obtain competent consultation whenever they and their patients feel the need for assistance in caring for the patient. The level of consultation needed should be established first: a one-visit opinion, continuing cooperative care, or total transfer of authority to the consultant. Patients have the option to seek an independent consultation from another physician but may be held financially responsible for their decision.

The consultant should respect the relationship between the patient and the principal physician, should promptly and effectively communicate recommendations to the principal physicians and should obtain concurrence of the principal physician for major procedures or additional consultants. The care of the patient and the proper records should be transferred back to the principal physician when the consultation is completed, unless another arrangement is agreed upon.

Consultants who need temporary charge of the patient's care should obtain the principal physician's cooperation and assent. The physician who does not agree with the consultant's recommendations is free to call in another consultant. The interests of the patient should remain paramount in this process.

A complex clinical situation may call for multiple consultations. To assure a coordinated effort that is in the best interest of the patient, the principal physician should remain in charge of overall care, communicating with the patient and coordinating care on the basis of information derived from the consultations. Unless authority has been formally transferred elsewhere, the responsibility for the patient's care lies with the principal physician.

The Impaired Physician

Physicians who are impaired for any reason must refrain from assuming patient responsibilities that they cannot discharge safely and effectively. Whenever there is doubt, they should seek assistance in caring for their patients.

Every physician is responsible for protecting patients from an impaired physician and for assisting an impaired colleague. Fear of being wrong, embarrassment, or possible litigation should not deter or delay identification of an impaired colleague. The identifying physician may find it helpful to discuss the issue with the departmental chair or a senior member of the staff or community.

Impairment may result from use of habit-forming agents (alcohol or other substances) or from psychiatric, physiologic, or behavioral disorders. Impairment may also be caused by diseases that affect the cognitive or motor skills necessary to provide adequate care. The presence of these disorders or the fact that a physician is being treated for them do not necessarily imply impairment.

Although the legal responsibility to do so varies among states, there is a clear ethical responsibility to report a physician who seems to be impaired to an appropriate authority (such as a chief of service, chief of staff, institutional committee, state medical board, or regulatory agency). Physicians should aid their impaired colleagues in identifying appropriate sources of help. While undergoing therapy, the impaired physician is entitled to full confidentiality as in any other patient-physician relationship. To protect patients of the impaired physician, someone other than the physician of the impaired physician must monitor the impaired physician's fitness to work. Serious conflicts may occur if the treating physician tries to fill both roles.

Peer Review

It is unethical for a physician to disparage the professional competence, knowledge, qualifications, or services of another physician to a patient or a third party or to state or imply that a patient has been poorly managed or mistreated by a colleague without substantial evidence, especially when such behavior is used to recruit patients.

Of equal importance, a physician is ethically obligated to report fraud, professional misconduct, incompetence, or abandonment of patients by another physician. Professional peer review is critical in assuring fair assessment of physician performance for the benefit of patients. The trust that patients and the public invest in physicians requires disclosure to the appropriate authorities and to patients at risk for immediate harm.

All physicians have a duty to participate in peer review. Fears of retaliation, ostracism by colleagues, loss of referrals, or inconvenience are not adequate reasons for refusing to participate in peer review. Society looks to physicians to establish professional standards of practice, and this obligation can be met only when all physicians participate in the process. Federal law and most states provide legal protection for physicians who participate in peer review in good faith.

Conversely, in the absence of substantial evidence of professional misconduct, negligence, or incompetence, it is unethical to use the peer review process to exclude another physician from practice, to restrict clinical privileges, or to otherwise harm the physician's practice.

Conflicts Among Members of a Health Care Team

All health professionals share a commitment to work together to serve the patient's interests. The best patient care is often a team effort, and mutual respect, cooperation, and communication should govern this effort. Each member of the patient care team has equal moral status. When a health professional has major ethical objections to an attending physician's order, both should discuss the matter thoroughly. Mechanisms should be available in hospitals to resolve differences of opinion among members of the patient care team.

RESEARCH

Medical progress and improved patient care depend on innovative and vigorous research. The basic principle of research is honesty, which must be assured by institutional protocols. Fraud in research must be condemned and punished. Honesty and integrity must govern all stages of research, from the initial grant application to publication of results. Reviewers of grant applications and journal articles must respect the confidentiality of new ideas and information; they must not use what they learn from the review process for their own purposes, and they should not misrepresent the ideas of others as their own.

Scientists have a responsibility to gather data meticulously; to keep impeccable records of work done; to interpret results objectively, not force them into preconceived molds or models; to submit their work to peer review; and to report new knowledge. Self-aggrandizement, public acclaim, recognition by professional peers, or financial gain should never be primary motivations in scientific research.

Clinical Investigation

The medical profession must assume responsibility for assuring that research is potentially of significant value and ethically conducted. Benefits and risks of research must be distributed fairly, and particular care must be taken to avoid exploitation of vulnerable populations. Research participants must be instructed about the nature of the research; consent from the research participant or an authorized representative must be truly informed and given freely; research must be planned thoughtfully, so that it has a high probability of yielding useful results; risks to patients must be minimized; and the benefit-to-risk ratio must be high enough to justify the research effort.

Each institution that receives federal support for research on humans is required to create an institutional review board. All proposed clinical research, regardless of the source of support, should be approved by the local institutional review board to assure that the research plans are reasonable and that research participants are adequately protected.

Although this formal system of review is designed to protect research participants, the premise on which all ethical research is based is mutual trust and respect between research participants and researchers. This premise requires that physician-investigators involved in designing or carrying out research have primary concern for the potential participants in these investigations.

Although the responsibility for assuring reasonable protection of human research participants resides with the investigators and the local institutional review board, the medical profession as a whole also has responsibilities. Clinical investigation is fraught with opportunities for conflicts to arise.

Physicians should avoid situations in which they are rewarded for particular outcomes. Physician-investigators may find themselves in dual roles with respect to patients who are also research participants. The health and welfare of the patient must always be the physician's primary consideration. Physicians who refer patients for participation in research protocols must be satisfied that the program follows established ethical guidelines, provides for realistic informed consent, gives reasonable assurances of safety, and has an acceptable benefit-to-risk ratio. If the risks of the research become too great or if continued participation cannot be justified, the physician must be willing to advise the patient to withdraw. Physicians-of-record should not abdicate overall responsibility for patients whom they have referred to a research project. Giving finder's fees to individual physicians for referring patients to a research project generates an unethical conflict of interest.

Research on delivery of health services raises issues about the protection of participants that have not yet been well examined. Researchers, physicians, and patients should thoughtfully balance the merits of innovation and the available means to monitor and protect research participants.

Innovative Medical Therapies

The use of innovative medical therapies falls along the continuum between established practice and research. Innovative therapies include the use of unconventional dosages of standard medications, previously untried applications of known procedures, and the use of approved drugs for nonapproved indications. The primary purpose of innovative medical therapies is to benefit the individual patient. Clinicians will confront the ethical issues of innovative practice more frequently than the ethical problems of medical research. Important medical advances have emerged from successful innovations, but innovation should always be approached carefully. Medical therapy should be treated as research whenever data are gathered to develop new medical information and for publication. When an innovative therapy has no precedent, consultation with peers, an institutional review board, or another expert group is necessary to assess the risks of the innovation, the probable outcomes of not using a standard therapy, and whether the innovation is in the patient's best interest. Informed consent is particularly important; patients must understand that the therapy is not standard treatment.

Scientific Publication

Authors of research reports must be sufficiently acquainted with the work being reported that they can take public responsibility for the integrity of the study and the validity of the findings, and they must have substantially contributed to the research itself. Sources of funding for the research project must be disclosed to potential collaborators in the research and must be included in the manuscript for publication (see the section on conflicts of interest).

Scientists build on the published work of other researchers and can proceed with confidence only if they can assume that the previously reported facts on which their work is based have been reported accurately. All scientists have a professional responsibility to be honest in their publications. They must describe methods accurately and in sufficient detail, report only observations that were actually made, make clear in the manuscript which information derives from the author's work and which comes from others (and where it was published), assure readers that research has been carried out in accordance with ethical principles, and assign authorship only to persons who merit and accept authorship.

Plagiarism is unethical. Incorporating the words of others or one's own published words, either verbatim or by paraphrasing without appropriate attribution, is unethical and may have legal consequences.

Public Announcement of Research Discoveries

In this era of rapid communication and intense media and public interest in medical news, it has become common for clinical investigators or their institutions to call press conferences and make public announcements of new research developments. Although it is desirable for the media to obtain accurate information about scientific developments, researchers should approach public pronouncements carefully and use language that does not invite misinterpretation or unjustified extrapolation.

In general, press releases should be issued and press conferences held only after the research has been published in a peer-reviewed journal or presented in a proper and complete abstract so that the details of the study are available to the scientific community. Statements of scientists receive great visibility. An announcement of preliminary results, even couched in the most careful terms, is frequently reported by the media as a "breakthrough." Care must be taken to avoid raising false public expectations and embarrassing the scientists involved, both of which reduce the credibility of the scientific community as a whole.

CONCLUSION

We hope that this *Manual* will help physicians, whether they are clinicians, educators, or research scientists, to address some of the challenging ethical dilemmas that confront them each day. The *Manual* is written for physicians by a physician organization as we attempt to find our way through difficult terrain. Our ultimate intent is to improve the quality of care provided to patients and to give an account of the conduct of the virtuous physician in whom patients and the public may justifiably place their trust.

Organization

AMERICAN MEDICAL ASSOCIATION

Headquarters:
515 North State Street
Chicago, IL 60610-4377
Telephone: (312) 464-5000
Fax: (312) 464-4184
Ethics Standards Division
Telephone: (312) 464-5659

Additional offices:
1101 Vermont Avenue, NW
Washington, DC 20005
Telephone: (202) 789-7400

Website: http://www.ama-assn.org

Date founded: 1847
Membership: approximately 287,000 physicians and medical students in about 2,000 local and regional medical societies

Code of Ethics

Official name: *Code of Medical Ethics and Current Opinions*
History: First adopted 1847, revised periodically; 1998–99 Edition, issued and updated June 1998
Authority: Council on Ethical and Judicial Affairs; Board of Trustees; House of Delegates
Code sections are available on Website

Additional Resources

Organizational (Divisions, Programs, Services, etc.):

Accreditation Council for Continuing Medical Education
Accreditation Council for Graduate Medical Education

AMA/State Medical Society Litigation Center (coordinates legal
  representation)
American Medical Accreditation Program (nationwide credential)
Clinical Practice Guideline Recognition Program
Coalition for Quality End-of-Life Care
Consulting Link/Doctors Advisory Network (health care consultants and
  attorneys referral service)
Continuing Medical Education (CME) Programs
Ethics and American Medicine—History, Change and Challenge
  (conference)
Ethics Awareness Program (internal advisory support)
Institute for Ethics
National Patient Safety Foundation
Physician Masterfile (credentialing information database)
Physician Negotiation Office (legal advice)
Physicians Recognition Award (for CME)
Practice Parameter Partnership Program (develops specialty society guide-
  lines)
Quality Agenda
Various Councils: Medical Service, Medical Education, Scientific Affairs
Various departments: Health Law; Health Policy; Professional Relations;
  Professional Standards (Ethics; Medical Education; Quality and Man-
  aged Care; Science, Technology, and Public Health)

Informational (Publications, Videos, Seminars, etc.):

Articles in *Journal of the American Medical Association, American
  Medical News,* and *Archives* medical specialty journals
AMA Health Care Almanac
Buying, Selling, and Owning the Medical Practice
Code of Medical Ethics and Current Opinions with Annotations
Continuing Medical Education Resource Guide
Directory of Clinical Practice Guidelines
The Ethical Question (video series):
  Advance Care Planning
  Death and Dying
  Economics and Healthcare
  Genetics: Fragile X Syndrome
  Informed Consent
  Physician-Assisted Suicide
Guidelines for the Medical Management of the Home Care Patient
How to Be an Effective Medical Witness (video)
Legal Issues for Physicians (online documents):
  Health Care Fraud and Abuse
  Physicians Representation and Contract Negotiation
  Professional Liability Insurance

Principles of Managed Care
U.S. Medical Licensure Statistics and Current Licensure Requirements
WorkPlays™ Sexual Harassment Video/training program

Goals and Activities of Organization

The largest voluntary organization of physicians in the U.S., the American Medical Association (AMA) was founded to promote the science and art of medicine and the betterment of public health. The establishment of a code of ethics and the creation of minimum requirements for medical education and training were the two principal items of business at the first meeting of the AMA in 1847. Its activities are directed toward improving physician competence, medical care for patients, and the use of medical science and knowledge.

The AMA accredits medical school, residency, and continuing medical education programs; works with allied health professions to set practice standards; monitors the quality of hospital services and facilities; serves as a major source of scientific and medical information through publications, libraries, seminars, and conferences; promotes public awareness of and responsibility for health matters; provides financial support for medical education and research; and maintains computerized records on every doctor licensed to practice in the U.S. The AMA also works with Congress, state governments, business, labor, and consumers to influence and analyze legislation and litigation that affect the medical profession and public health.

The AMA's involvement in the areas of medical ethics and professionalism is extensive. The Council on Ethical and Judicial Affairs (CEJA) sets AMA policy, with the assistance of the Ethics Standards Division. The Institute for Ethics, established in 1997, conducts programs for research, conferences, seminars, publications, and hands-on training, and works closely with CEJA.

A task force of experts was set up in 1998 to develop new standards for AMA business dealings with corporations. The Board of Trustees has established a set of interim principles regarding corporate relationships until the task force issues its guidelines.

The American Medical Accreditation Program, almost fully implemented as of 1998, is a voluntary, comprehensive accreditation program based on a nationally standardized review of credentials, professional qualifications, and office operations, as well as ethics, peer review, clinical performance, and patient satisfaction.

The National Patient Safety Foundation was launched by the AMA in 1997 as an independent nonprofit partnership of consumer advocates, health care providers, health product manufacturers, public and private employers and payers, researchers, regulators, and policymakers. Its goal is to ensure that patients in all settings receive health care services safely, consistent with the Hippocratic Oath to "above all, do no harm."

Implementation and Enforcement of Code

The AMA requires all members to endorse and comply with the Principles of Medical Ethics.

Every year, the Council on Ethical and Judicial Affairs writes detailed reports on various ethical issues; those approved by the Board of Trustees and the House of Delegates become official AMA policy. CEJA's digests of these reports become the Advisory Opinions of the Code of Medical Ethics.

Interpretations of the Principles are initiated by CEJA or upon written request. It may decline a case that is not of national interest and that relates to local customs and ideals; these may be readdressed to the component society or state association with primary responsibility for and familiarity with local conventions.

CEJA is also AMA's judicial and disciplinary body. It may independently investigate ethics breaches by AMA members and affiliates.

Council members are physicians, plus one resident physician and one medical student. The student participates in disciplinary functions only if a medical student is the subject of the disciplinary matter.

The AMA has original jurisdiction in all questions involving membership (especially where an applicant denied membership in a constituent or component society alleges discrimination), controversies under the Principles or Bylaws in which the AMA is a party, or in disputes between constituent or component societies.

Discipline is otherwise handled locally, with CEJA acting as the highest court of appeals. When a complaint of unethical conduct is of greater than local concern, CEJA may refer it to an investigating jury appointed by the AMA President. If the jury decides to submit formal charges, the President appoints a prosecutor to bring the case before CEJA. The accused is afforded notice, time to respond, and the right to a formal hearing, where the member conducts a defense and may be accompanied by legal counsel. CEJA may accept any evidence or information it deems reliable or relevant.

Sanctions against an individual member or against a constituent or component society for violation of the Principles or Bylaws include censure, suspension, or expulsion from the AMA.

History and Development of Code

The first AMA Code of Medical Ethics was adopted in 1847; the first Committee on Ethics was organized in 1858 to implement it. The Code was inspired by the Oath of Hippocrates and based in large part on Percival's Code, a set of principles established in 1803 by English physician and philosopher Thomas Percival.

Major revisions to the AMA Code occurred in 1903, 1912, and 1947. In 1957, the Code was made more succinct, to remove the prolixity and ambiguity that hindered practical application. In 1977, the Principles were revised to clarify and update the language, eliminate references to gender, and to seek a better balance between professional and legal standards in a changing society. The House of Delegates adopted the revised Principles in 1980.

The section on Fundamental Elements of the Patient-Physician Relationship was adopted in 1990; the section on Patient Responsibilities was added in 1994.

The Council on Ethical and Judicial Affairs regularly issues new Reports that eventually become the Code's Advisory Opinions. The June 1998 edition, reproduced here, contains many new and revised opinions, including statements on health care rationing, genetic testing, withdrawal of life-sustaining treatment, and family violence. These opinions are based on reports adopted through June 1997.

Code of Medical Ethics and Current Opinions*

PREFACE

This edition of *Current Opinions* of the Council on Ethical and Judicial Affairs replaces all previous editions * * *. It is one component of the American Medical Association's Code of Ethics; the other components are the Principles of Medical Ethics, Fundamental Elements of the Patient-Physician Relationship, and the Reports of the Council on Ethical and Judicial Affairs. * * *

The Principles of Medical Ethics are the primary component of the Code. They establish the core ethical principles from which the other components of the Code are derived. The Principles were revised most recently in 1980.

* * *

Current Opinions reflects the application of the Principles of Medical Ethics to 140 specific ethical issues in medicine, including health care rationing, genetic testing, withdrawal of life-sustaining treatment, and family violence. Much as courts of law elaborate on constitutional principles in their opinions, the Council develops the meaning of the Principles of Medical Ethics in its opinions. Accordingly, each opinion is followed by one or more roman numerals that identify the Principle(s) from which the opinion is derived.

* * *

All four components of the AMA's Code of Ethics need to be consulted to determine the Association's position on ethical issues. In addition, the AMA's House of Delegates at times issues statements on ethical issues. These statements are contained in the AMA *Policy Compendium*. Because the Council on Ethical and Judicial Affairs is responsible for determining the AMA's position on ethical issues, statements by the House of Delegates should be construed as the view of the House of Delegates but not as the ethics policy of the Association.

Medical ethics involve the professional responsibilities and obligations of physicians. Behavior relating to medical etiquette or custom is not addressed in *Current Opinions*. The opinions that follow are intended as guides to responsible professional behavior.

No one Principle of Medical Ethics can stand alone or be individually applied to a situation. In all instances, it is the overall intent and influence of the Principles of Medical Ethics that shall measure ethical behavior for the physician. Council opinions are issued under its authority to interpret the Principles of Medical Ethics and to investigate general ethical conditions and all matters pertaining to the relationship of physicians to one another and to the public.

The Council on Ethical and Judicial Affairs encourages comments and suggestions for future editions of this publication.

HISTORY

The Oath of Hippocrates, a brief statement of principles, has come down through history as a living statement of ideals to be cherished by the physician. This Oath was conceived some time during the period of Grecian greatness, probably in the fifth century B.C. It protected rights of the patient and appealed to the inner and finer instincts of the physician without imposing sanctions or penalties on him or her. Other civilizations subsequently developed written principles, but the Oath of Hippocrates (Christianized in the tenth or eleventh century A.D. to eliminate reference to pagan gods) has remained in Western Civilization as an expression of ideal conduct for the physician.

The most significant contribution to Western medical ethical history subsequent to Hippocrates was made by Thomas Percival, an English physician, philosopher, and writer. In 1803, he published his Code of Medical Ethics. His personality, his interest in sociological matters, and his close association with the Manchester Infirmary led to the preparation of a scheme of professional conduct relative to hospitals and other charities from which he drafted the code which bears his name.

At the first official meeting of the American Medical Association at Philadelphia in 1847, the two principal items of business were the establishment of a code of ethics and the creation of minimum requirements for medical education and training. Although the Medical Society of the State of New York and the Medico-Chirurgical Society of Baltimore had formal written codes of medical ethics prior to this time, it is clear the AMA's first adopted Code of Ethics was based on Percival's Code.

In general, the language and concepts of the original Code adopted by the Association in 1847 remained the same throughout the years. There were revisions, of course, which reflected the temper of the times and the eternal quest to express basic concepts with clarity. Major revisions did occur in 1903, 1912, and 1947.

In December 1955, an attempt was made to distinguish medical ethics from matters of etiquette. A draft of a two-part code seeking to accomplish this was submitted to the House of Delegates at that time but was not accepted. This proposal was, in effect, a separation of then existing statements found in the Principles into two categories. Little or no change was made in the language of the forty-eight sections of the Principles.

Subsequently, in June 1956, a seemingly radical proposal was submitted to the House of Delegates for consideration. This proposal, a short version of the Principles, was discussed at the December 1956 session of the House after wide publication and broad consideration among members of the medical profession. It was postponed for final consideration until the June 1957 meeting of the House of Delegates, when the short version was adopted.

The format of the Principles adopted in June 1957 is a change from the format of the Principles promulgated by Percival in 1803 and accepted by the Association in 1847. Ten short sections, preceded by a preamble, "succinctly express the fundamental concepts embodied in the present (1955) Principles", according to the report of the Council on Constitution and Bylaws. That Council assured the House of Delegates in its June 1957 report that "every basic principle has been preserved; on the other hand, as much as possible of the prolixity and ambiguity which in the past obstructed ready explanation, practical codification and particular selection of basic concepts has been eliminated."

In 1977, the Judicial Council recommended to the House of Delegates that the AMA Principles of Medical Ethics be revised to clarify and update the language, to eliminate reference to gender, and to seek a proper and reasonable balance between professional standards and contemporary legal standards in our changing society. Given the desire of the Judicial Council for a new version of the Principles to be widely accepted and accurately understood, in 1978 the Judicial Council recommended that a special committee of the House be appointed to consider such a revision. This was done in 1980, and the House of Delegates adopted the revision of the AMA Principles of Medical Ethics at its Annual Meeting in June 1980.

In June 1985, the Judicial Council became the Council on Ethical and Judicial Affairs.

PRINCIPLES OF MEDICAL ETHICS

Preamble

The medical profession has long subscribed to a body of ethical statements developed primarily for the benefit of the patient. As a member of this profession, a physician must recognize responsibility not only to patients, but also to society, to other health professionals, and to self. The following Principles adopted by the American Medical Association are not laws, but standards of conduct which define the essentials of honorable behavior for the physician.

I. A physician shall be dedicated to providing competent medical service with compassion and respect for human dignity.

II. A physician shall deal honestly with patients and colleagues, and strive to expose those physicians deficient in character or competence, or who engage in fraud or deception.

III. A physician shall respect the law and also recognize a responsibility to seek changes in those requirements which are contrary to the best interests of the patient.

IV. A physician shall respect the rights of patients, of colleagues, and of other health professionals, and shall safeguard patient confidences within the constraints of the law.

V. A physician shall continue to study, apply and advance scientific knowledge, make relevant information available to patients, colleagues, and the public, obtain consultation, and use the talents of other health professionals when indicated.

VI. A physician shall, in the provision of appropriate patient care, except in emergencies, be free to choose whom to serve, with whom to associate, and the environment in which to provide medical services.

VII. A physician shall recognize a responsibility to participate in activities contributing to an improved community.

FUNDAMENTAL ELEMENTS OF THE
PATIENT-PHYSICIAN RELATIONSHIP

From ancient times, physicians have recognized that the health and well-being of patients depends upon a collaborative effort between physician and patient. Patients share with physicians the responsibility for their own health care. The patient-physician relationship is of greatest benefit to patients when they bring medical problems to the attention of their physicians in a timely fashion, provide information about their medical condition to the best of their ability, and work with their physicians in a mutually respectful alliance. Physicians can best contribute to this alliance by serving as their patients' advocate and by fostering these rights:

1. The patient has the right to receive information from physicians and to discuss the benefits, risks, and costs of appropriate treatment alternatives. Patients should receive guidance from their physicians as to the optimal course of action. Patients are also entitled to obtain copies or summaries of their medical records, to have their questions answered, to be advised of potential conflicts of interest that their physicians might have, and to receive independent professional opinions.
2. The patient has the right to make decisions regarding the health care that is recommended by his or her physician. Accordingly, patients may accept or refuse any recommended medical treatment.
3. The patient has the right to courtesy, respect, dignity, responsiveness, and timely attention to his or her needs.
4. The patient has the right to confidentiality. The physician should not reveal confidential communications or information without the consent of the patient, unless provided for by law or by the need to protect the welfare of the individual or the public interest.
5. The patient has the right to continuity of health care. The physician has an obligation to cooperate in the coordination of medically indicated care with other health care providers treating the patient. The physician may not discontinue treatment of a patient as long as further treatment is medically indicated, without giving the patient reasonable assistance and sufficient opportunity to make alternative arrangements for care.
6. The patient has a basic right to have available adequate health care. Physicians, along with the rest of society, should continue to work toward this goal. Fulfillment of this right is dependent on society providing resources so that no patient is deprived of necessary care because of an inability to pay for the care. Physicians should continue their traditional assumption of a part of the responsibility for the medical care of those who cannot afford essential health care. Physicians should advocate for patients in dealing with third parties when appropriate.

PATIENT RESPONSIBILITIES

It has long been recognized that successful medical care requires an ongoing collaborative effort between patients and physicians. Physicians and patients are bound in a partnership that requires both individuals to take an active role in the healing process. Such a partnership does not imply that both partners have identical responsibilities or equal power. While physicians have the responsibility to provide health care services to patients to the best of their ability, patients have the responsibility to communicate openly, to participate in decisions about the diagnostic and treatment recommendations, and to comply with the agreed upon treatment program.

Like patients' rights, patients' responsibilities are derived from the principle of autonomy. The principle of patient autonomy holds that an individual's physical, emotional, and psychological integrity should be respected and upheld. This principle also recognizes the human capacity to self-govern and choose a course of action from among different alternative options. Autonomous, competent patients assert some control over the decisions which direct their health care. With that exercise of self-governance and free choice comes a number of responsibilities.

1. Good communication is essential to a successful patient-physician relationship. To the extent possible, patients have a responsibility to be truthful and to express their concerns clearly to their physicians.
2. Patients have a responsibility to provide a complete medical history, to the extent possible, including information about past illnesses, medications, hospitalizations, family history of illness, and other matters relating to present health.
3. Patients have a responsibility to request information or clarification about their health status or treatment when they do not fully understand what has been described.
4. Once patients and physicians agree upon the goals of therapy and a treatment plan, patients have a responsibility to cooperate with that treatment plan. Compliance with physician instructions is often essential to public and individual safety. Patients also have a responsibility to disclose whether previously agreed upon treatments are being followed and to indicate when they would like to reconsider the treatment plan.
5. Patients generally have a responsibility to meet their financial obligations with regard to medical care or to discuss financial hardships with their physicians. Patients should be cognizant of the costs associated with using a limited resource like health care and try to use medical resources judiciously.
6. Patients should discuss end-of-life decisions with their physicians and make their wishes known. Such a discussion might also include writing an advanced directive.
7. Patients should be committed to health maintenance through health-enhancing behavior. Illness can often be prevented by a healthy lifestyle, and patients should take personal responsibility when they are able to avert the development of disease.
8. Patients should also have an active interest in the effects of their conduct on others and refrain from behavior that unreasonably places the health of others at risk. Patients should inquire as to the means and likelihood of infectious disease transmission and act upon that information which can best prevent further transmission.
9. Patients should discuss organ donation with their physicians and, if donation is desired, to make applicable provisions. Patients who are part of an organ allocation system and await a needed transplant should not try to go outside of or manipulate the system. A fair system of allocation should be answered with public trust and an awareness of limited resources.
10. Patients should not initiate or participate in fraudulent health care and should report illegal or unethical behavior by physicians or other providers to the appropriate medical societies, licensing boards, or law enforcement authorities.

CURRENT OPINIONS OF THE COUNCIL ON ETHICAL AND JUDICIAL AFFAIRS

1.00 INTRODUCTION

1.01 Terminology.

The term "ethical" is used in opinions of the Council on Ethical and Judicial Affairs to refer to matters involving (1) moral principles or practices and (2) matters of social policy involving issues of morality in the practice of medicine.

The term "unethical" is used to refer to professional conduct which fails to conform to these moral standards or policies.

Many of the Council's opinions lay out specific duties and obligations for physicians. Violation of these principles and opinions represents unethical conduct and may justify disciplinary action such as censure, suspension, or expulsion from medical society membership.

1.02 The Relation of Law and Ethics.

The following statements are intended to clarify the relationship between law and ethics.

Ethical values and legal principles are usually closely related, but ethical obligations typically exceed legal duties. In some cases, the law mandates unethical conduct. In general, when physicians believe a law is unjust, they should work to change the law. In exceptional circumstances of unjust laws, ethical responsibilities should supersede legal obligations.

The fact that a physician charged with allegedly illegal conduct is acquitted or exonerated in civil or criminal proceedings does not necessarily mean that the physician acted ethically.

2.00 OPINIONS ON SOCIAL POLICY ISSUES

2.01 Abortion.

The Principles of Medical Ethics of the AMA do not prohibit a physician from performing an abortion in accordance with good medical practice and under circumstances that do not violate the law. (III, IV)

2.015 Mandatory Parental Consent to Abortion.

Physicians should ascertain the law in their state on parental involvement to ensure that their procedures are consistent with their legal obligations.

Physicians should strongly encourage minors to discuss their pregnancy with their parents. Physicians should explain how parental involvement can be helpful and that parents are generally very understanding and supportive. If a minor expresses concerns about parental involvement, the physician should ensure that the minor's reluctance is not based on any misperceptions about the likely consequences of parental involvement.

Physicians should not feel or be compelled to require minors to involve their parents before deciding whether to undergo an abortion. The patient—even an adolescent—generally must decide whether, on balance, parental involvement is advisable. Accordingly, minors should ultimately be allowed to decide whether parental involvement is appropriate. Physicians should explain under what circumstances (e.g., life-threatening emergency) the minor's confidentiality will need to be abrogated.

Physicians should try to ensure that minor patients have made an informed decision after giving careful consideration to the issues involved. They should encourage their minor patients to consult alternative sources if parents are not going to be involved in the abortion decision. Minors should be urged to seek the advice and counsel of those adults in whom they have confidence, including professional counselors, relatives, friends, teachers, or the clergy. (III, IV)

2.02* Abuse of Spouses, Children, Elderly Persons, and Others at Risk.

The following are guidelines for detecting and treating family violence:
Due to the prevalence and medical consequences of family violence, physicians should routinely inquire about physical, sexual, and psychological abuse as part of the medical history. Physicians must also consider abuse in the differential diagnosis for a number of medical complaints, particularly when treating women.

Physicians who are likely to have the opportunity to detect abuse in the course of their work have an obligation to familiarize themselves with protocols for diagnosing and treating abuse and with community resources for battered women, children, and elderly persons.

Physicians also have a duty to be aware of societal misconceptions about abuse and prevent these from affecting the diagnosis and management of abuse. Such misconceptions include the belief that abuse is a rare occurrence; that abuse does not occur in "normal" families; that abuse is a private problem best resolved without outside interference; and that victims are responsible for the abuse.

In order to improve physician knowledge of family violence, physicians must be better trained to identify signs of abuse and to work cooperatively with the range of community services currently involved. Hospitals should require additional training for those physicians who are likely to see victims of abuse. Comprehensive training on family violence should be required in medical school curricula and in residency programs for specialties in which family violence is likely to be encountered.

The following are guidelines for the reporting of abuse:
Laws that require the reporting of cases of suspected abuse of children and elderly persons often create a difficult dilemma for the physician. The parties involved, both the suspected offenders and the victims, will often plead with the physician that the matter be kept confidential and not be disclosed or reported for investigation by public authorities.

Children who have been seriously injured, apparently by their parents, may nevertheless try to protect their parents by saying that the injuries were caused by an accident, such as a fall. The reason may stem from the natural parent-child relationship or fear of further punishment. Even institutionalized elderly patients who have been physically maltreated may be concerned that disclosure of what has occurred might lead to further and more drastic maltreatment by those responsible.

The physician who fails to comply with the laws requiring reporting of suspected cases of abuse of children and elderly persons and others at risk can expect that the victims could receive more severe abuse that may result in permanent bodily injury, emotional or psychological injury, or even death.

Public officials concerned with the welfare of children and elderly persons have expressed the opinion that the incidence of physical violence to these persons is rapidly increasing and that a very substantial percentage of such cases is unreported by hospital personnel and physicians. A child or elderly person brought to a physician with a suspicious injury is the patient whose interests require the protection of law in a particular situation, even though the physician may also provide services from time to time to parents or other members of the family.

The obligation to comply with statutory requirements is clearly stated in the Principles of Medical Ethics. In addition, physicians have an ethical obligation

---

*This opinion is currently under reconsideration by the Council, and may be amended in the next edition * * * . Contact the Ethics Standards Division of the AMA for the most up-to-date version.

to report abuse even when the law does not require it. However, for mentally competent adult victims of abuse, physicians must not disclose an abuse diagnosis to spouses or any other third party without the consent of the patient. Physicians must discuss the problem of family violence with adult patients in privacy and safety. (I, III)

2.03   Allocation of Limited Medical Resources.

A physician has a duty to do all that he or she can for the benefit of the individual patient. Policies for allocating limited resources have the potential to limit the ability of physicians to fulfill this obligation to patients. Physicians have a responsibility to participate and to contribute their professional expertise in order to safeguard the interests of patients in decisions made at the societal level regarding the allocation or rationing of health resources.

Decisions regarding the allocation of limited medical resources among patients should consider only ethically appropriate criteria relating to medical need. These criteria include likelihood of benefit, urgency of need, change in quality of life, duration of benefit, and, in some cases, the amount of resources required for successful treatment. In general, only very substantial differences among patients are ethically relevant; the greater the disparities, the more justified the use of these criteria becomes. In making quality-of-life judgments, patients should first be prioritized so that death or extremely poor outcomes are avoided; then, patients should be prioritized according to change in quality of life, but only when there are very substantial differences among patients. Non-medical criteria, such as ability to pay, age, social worth, perceived obstacles to treatment, patient contribution to illness, or past use of resources should not be considered.

Allocation decisions should respect the individuality of patients and the particulars of individual cases as much as possible. When very substantial differences do not exist among potential recipients of treatment on the basis of the appropriate criteria defined above, a 'first-come, first-served' approach or some other equal opportunity mechanism should be employed to make final allocation decisions. Though there are several ethically acceptable strategies for implementing these criteria, no single strategy is ethically mandated. Acceptable approaches include a three-tiered system, a minimal threshold approach, and a weighted formula. Decision-making mechanisms should be objective, flexible, and consistent to ensure that all patients are treated equally.

The treating physician must remain a patient advocate and therefore should not make allocation decisions. Patients denied access to resources have the right to be informed of the reasoning behind the decision. The allocation procedures of institutions controlling scarce resources should be disclosed to the public as well as subject to regular peer review from the medical profession. (I, VII)

2.035   Futile Care.

Physicians are not ethically obligated to deliver care that, in their best professional judgment, will not have a reasonable chance of benefiting their patients. Patients should not be given treatments simply because they demand them. Denial of treatment should be justified by reliance on openly stated ethical principles and acceptable standards of care, as defined in Opinions 2.03 and 2.095, not on the concept of "futility," which cannot be meaningfully defined. (I, IV)

2.037 Medical Futility in End-of-Life Care.

When further intervention to prolong the life of a patient becomes futile, physicians have an obligation to shift the intent of care toward comfort and closure. However, there are necessary value judgments involved in coming to the assessment of futility. These judgments must give consideration to the patient or proxy's assessment of worthwhile outcome. They should also take into account the physician or other provider's perception of intent in treatment, which should not be to prolong the dying process without benefit to the patient or to others with legitimate interests. They may also take into account community and institutional standards, which in turn may have used physiological or functional outcome measures.

Nevertheless, conflicts between the parties may persist in determining what is futility in the particular instance. This may interrupt satisfactory decision-making and adversely affect patient care, family satisfaction, and physician-clinical team functioning. To assist in fair and satisfactory decision-making about what constitutes futile intervention:

(1) All health care institutions, whether large or small, should adopt a policy on medical futility; and

(2) Policies on medical futility should follow a due process approach. The following seven steps should be included in such a due process approach to declaring futility in specific cases.

    a. Earnest attempts should be made in advance to deliberate over and negotiate prior understandings between patient, proxy and physician on what constitutes futile care for the patient, and what falls within acceptable limits for the physician, family, and possibly also the institution.

    b. Joint decision-making should occur between patient or proxy and physician to the maximum extent possible.

    c. Attempts should be made to negotiate disagreements if they arise, and to reach resolution within all parties' acceptable limits, with the assistance of consultants as appropriate.

    d. Involvement of an institutional committee, such as the ethics committee, should be requested if disagreements are irresolvable.

    e. If the institutional review supports the patient's position and the physician remains unpersuaded, transfer of care to another physician within the institution may be arranged.

    f. If the process supports the physician's position and the patient/proxy remains unpersuaded, transfer to another institution may be sought and, if done, should be supported by the transferring and receiving institution.

    g. If transfer is not possible, the intervention need not be offered. (I, V)

2.04 Artificial Insemination by Known Donor.

Any individual or couple contemplating artificial insemination by husband, partner, or other known donor should be counseled about the full range of infectious and genetic diseases for which the donor or recipient can be screened, including HIV infection. Full medical history disclosure and appropriate diagnostic screening should be recommended to the donor and recipient, but are not required.

Informed consent for artificial insemination should include disclosure of risks, benefits, and likely success rate of the method proposed and potential alternative methods. Individuals should receive information about screening, costs, and procedures for confidentiality, when applicable. The prospective parents or parent should be informed of the laws regarding the rights of children conceived by artificial insemination, as well as the laws regarding parental rights and obligations. If the donor is married to the recipient, resultant children will have all the rights of a child conceived naturally.

If the donor and recipient are not married, an appropriate legal rule would treat the situation as if the donor were anonymous: the recipient would be considered the sole parent of the child except in cases where both donor and recipient agree to recognize a paternity right.

Sex selection of sperm for the purposes of avoiding a sex-linked inheritable disease is appropriate. However, physicians should not participate in sex selection for reasons of gender preference. Physicians should encourage a prospective parent or parents to consider the value of both sexes.

If semen is frozen and the donor dies before it is used, the frozen semen should not be used or donated for purposes other than those originally intended by the donor. If the donor left no instructions, it is reasonable to allow the remaining partner to use the semen for artificial insemination but not to donate it to someone else. However, the donor should be advised of such a policy at the time of donation and be given an opportunity to override it. (I, V)

2.05 Artificial Insemination by Anonymous Donor.

Thorough medical histories must be taken of all candidates for anonymous semen donation. All potential donors must also be screened for infectious or inheritable diseases which could adversely affect the recipient or the resultant child. Frozen semen should be used for artificial insemination because it enables the donor to be tested for HIV infection at the time of donation, and again after an interval before the original semen is used, thus increasing the likelihood that the semen is free of HIV infection. Physicians should rely on the guidelines formulated by relevant professional organizations, such as the American Society of Reproductive Medicine, the Centers for Disease Control and Prevention, and the Food and Drug Administration, in determining the interval between the initial and final HIV test, which disorders to screen for, and which procedures to use in screening.

Physicians should maintain a permanent record which includes both identifying and non-identifying health and genetic screening information. Other than exceptional situations where identifying information may be required, physicians should release only non-identifying health-related information in order to preserve the confidentiality of the semen donor. Physicians should maintain permanent records of donors to fulfill the following obligations: (1) to exclude individuals from the donor pool who test positive for infectious or inheritable diseases, (2) to limit the number of pregnancies resulting from a single donor source so as to avoid future consanguineous marriages or reproduction, (3) to notify donors of screening results which indicate the presence of an infectious or inheritable disease, and (4) to notify donors if a child born through artificial insemination has a disorder which may have been transmitted by the donor.

Informed consent for artificial insemination should include disclosure of risks, benefits, and likely success rate of the method proposed and potential alternative methods, and costs. Both recipients and donors should be informed of the reasons for screening and confidentiality. They should also know the extent of access to non-identifying and identifying information about the donor. Participants should be advised to consider the legal ramifications, if any, of artificial insemination by anonymous donor.

The consent of the husband is ethically appropriate if he is to become the legal father of the resultant child from artificial insemination by anonymous donor. Anonymous donors cannot assume the rights or responsibilities of parenthood for children born through therapeutic donor insemination, nor should they be required to assume them.

In the case of single women or women who are part of a homosexual couple, it is not unethical to provide artificial insemination as a reproductive option.

Sex selection of sperm for the purposes of avoiding a sex-linked inheritable disease is appropriate. However, physicians should not participate in sex selection of sperm for reasons of gender preference. Physicians should encourage a prospective parent or parents to consider the value of both sexes.

In general, it is inappropriate to offer compensation to donors to encourage donation over and above reimbursement for time and actual expenses. (I, V)

2.06 Capital Punishment.

An individual's opinion on capital punishment is the personal moral decision of the individual. A physician, as a member of a profession dedicated to preserving life when there is hope of doing so, should not be a participant in a legally authorized execution. Physician participation in execution is defined generally as actions which would fall into one or more of the following categories: (1) an action which would directly cause the death of the condemned; (2) an action which would assist, supervise, or contribute to the ability of another individual to directly cause the death of the condemned; and (3) an action which could automatically cause an execution to be carried out on a condemned prisoner.

Physician participation in an execution includes, but is not limited to, the following actions: prescribing or administering tranquilizers and other psychotropic agents and medications that are part of the execution procedure; monitoring vital signs on site or remotely (including monitoring electrocardiograms); attending or observing an execution as a physician; and rendering technical advice regarding execution.

In the case where the method of execution is lethal injection, the following actions by the physician would also constitute physician participation in execution: selecting injection sites; starting intravenous lines as a port for a lethal injection device; prescribing, preparing, administering, or supervising injection drugs or their doses or types; inspecting, testing, or maintaining lethal injection devices; and consulting with or supervising lethal injection personnel.

The following actions do not constitute physician participation in execution: (1) testifying as to medical diagnoses as they relate to competence to stand trial, testifying as to relevant medical evidence during trial, testifying as to medical aspects of aggravating or mitigating circumstances during the penalty phase of a capital case, or testifying to medical diagnoses as they relate to the legal assessment of competence for execution; (2) certifying death, provided that the condemned has been declared dead by another person; (3) witnessing an execution in a totally nonprofessional capacity; (4) witnessing an execution at the specific voluntary request of the condemned person, provided that the physician observes the execution in a nonprofessional capacity; and (5) relieving the acute suffering of a condemned person while awaiting execution, including providing tranquilizers at the specific voluntary request of the condemned person to help relieve pain or anxiety in anticipation of the execution.

When a condemned prisoner has been declared incompetent to be executed, physicians should not treat the prisoner to restore competence unless a commutation order is issued. However, if the incompetent prisoner is undergoing extreme suffering as a result of psychosis or any other illness, medical intervention intended to mitigate the level of suffering is ethically permissible. Provision of medical testimony in the reevaluation of the prisoner's legal competence to be executed should be provided by an independent physician examiner. A physician cannot be compelled to provide medical testimony as it relates to legal competence for execution if it is contrary to the physician's personal beliefs.

Organ donation by condemned prisoners is permissible only if (1) the decision to donate was made before the prisoner's conviction, (2) the donated tissue is harvested after the prisoner has been pronounced dead and the body removed from the death chamber, and (3) physicians do not provide advice on modifying the method of execution for any individual to facilitate donation. (I)

2.07 Clinical Investigation.

The following guidelines are intended to aid physicians in fulfilling their ethical responsibilities when they engage in the clinical investigation of new drugs and procedures.

(1) A physician may participate in clinical investigation only to the extent that those activities are a part of a systematic program competently designed, under accepted standards of scientific research, to produce data which are scientifically valid and significant.

(2) In conducting clinical investigation, the investigator should demonstrate the same concern and caution for the welfare, safety, and comfort of the person involved as is required of a physician who is furnishing medical care to a patient independent of any clinical investigation.

(3) Minors or mentally incompetent persons may be used as subjects in clinical investigation only if:
    (a) The nature of the investigation is such that mentally competent adults would not be suitable subjects.
    (b) Consent, in writing, is given by a legally authorized representative of the subject under circumstances in which informed and prudent adults would reasonably be expected to volunteer themselves or their children as subjects.

(4) In clinical investigation primarily for treatment:
    (a) The physician must recognize that the patient-physician relationship exists and that professional judgment and skill must be exercised in the best interest of the patient.
    (b) Voluntary written consent must be obtained from the patient, or from the patient's legally authorized representative if the patient lacks the capacity to consent, following: (a) disclosure that the physician intends to use an investigational drug or experimental procedure, (b) a reasonable explanation of the nature of the drug or procedure to be used, risks to be expected, and possible therapeutic benefits, (c) an offer to answer any inquiries concerning the drug or procedure, and (d) a disclosure of alternative drugs or procedures that may be available. Physicians should be completely objective in discussing

the details of the drug or procedure to be employed, the pain and discomfort that may be anticipated, known risks and possible hazards, the quality of life to be expected, and particularly the alternatives. Especially, physicians should not use persuasion to obtain consent which otherwise might not be forthcoming, nor should expectations be encouraged beyond those which the circumstances reasonably and realistically justify.

    i. In exceptional circumstances, where the experimental treatment is the only potential treatment for the patient and full disclosure of information concerning the nature of the drug or experimental procedure or risks would pose such a serious psychological threat of detriment to the patient as to be medically contraindicated, such information may be withheld from the patient. In these circumstances, such information should be disclosed to a responsible relative or friend of the patient where possible.

    ii. Ordinarily, consent should be in writing, except where the physician deems it necessary to rely upon consent in other than written form because of the physical or emotional state of the patient.

(5) In clinical investigation primarily for the accumulation of scientific knowledge:

    (a) Adequate safeguards must be provided for the welfare, safety and comfort of the subject. It is fundamental social policy that the advancement of scientific knowledge must always be secondary to primary concern for the individual.

    (b) Consent, in writing, should be obtained from the subject, or from a legally authorized representative if the subject lacks the capacity to consent, following: (a) disclosure of the fact that an investigational drug or procedure is to be used, (b) a reasonable explanation of the nature of the procedure to be used and risks to be expected, and (c) an offer to answer any inquiries concerning the drug or procedure.

(6) No person may be used as a subject in clinical investigation against his or her will.

(7) The overuse of institutionalized persons in research is an unfair distribution of research risks. Participation is coercive and not voluntary if the participant is subjected to powerful incentives and persuasion.

(8) The ultimate responsibility for the ethical conduct of science resides within the institution (academic, industrial, public, or private) which conducts scientific research and with the individual scientist. Research institutions should assure that rigorous scientific standards are upheld by each of their faculty, staff, and students and should extend these standards to all reports, publications, and databases produced by the institution. All medical schools and biomedical research institutions should implement guidelines for a review process for dealing with allegations of fraud. These guidelines should ensure that (a) the process used to resolve allegations of fraud does not damage science, (b) all parties are treated fairly and justly with a sensitivity to reputations and vulnerabilities, (c) the highest degree of confidentiality is maintained, (d) the integrity of the process is maintained by an avoidance of real or apparent conflicts of interest, (e) resolution of charges is expeditious, (f) accurate and detailed documentation is kept throughout the process, and (g) responsibilities to all involved individuals, the public, research sponsors, the scientific literature, and the scientific community is met after resolution of charges. Academic institutions must be capable of, and committed to,

implementing effective procedures for examining allegations of scientific fraud. No system of external monitoring should replace the efforts of an institution to set its own standards which fulfill its responsibility for the proper conduct of science and the training of scientists.

(9) With the approval of the patient or the patient's lawful representative, physicians should cooperate with the press and media to ensure that medical news concerning the progress of clinical investigation or the patient's condition is available more promptly and more accurately than would be possible without their assistance. On the other hand, the Council does not approve of practices designed to create fanfare, sensationalism to attract media attention, and unwarranted expressions of optimism because of short term progress, even though longer range prognosis is known from the beginning to be precarious. With the approval of the patient or the patient's family, the Council, however, encourages the objective disclosure to the press and media of pertinent information. If at all possible, the identity of the patient should remain confidential if the patient or the patient's family so desires. The situation should not be used for the commercial ends of participating physicians or the institutions involved. (I, III, V)

2.075 The Use of Placebo Controls in Clinical Trials.

Placebo controls are an important part of medicine's commitment to ensuring that the safety and efficacy of new drugs are sufficiently established. Used appropriately, placebo controls can safely provide valuable data and should continue to be considered in the design of clinical trials. The existence of an accepted therapy does not necessarily preclude the use of such controls; however, physician-investigators should adhere to the following guidelines to ensure that the interests of patients who participate in clinical trials are protected.

(1) Investigators must be extremely thorough in obtaining informed consent from patients. To the extent that research is dependent upon the willingness of patients to accept a level of risk, their understanding of the potential harms involved must be a top priority of any clinical investigation. The possibility presented in some studies that patients often do not fully understand the research protocol and therefore cannot truly give informed consent demonstrates a need to heighten the efforts of researchers to impress upon their subjects the nature of clinical research and the risks involved. Patients are capable of making decisions when presented with sufficient information and it is the responsibility of the institutional review board (IRB) and the individual investigators involved to ensure that each subject has been adequately informed and has given voluntary consent. Each patient must also be made aware that they can terminate their participation in a study at any time.

(2) Informed consent cannot be invoked to justify an inappropriate trial design. IRBs as well as investigators have an obligation to evaluate each study protocol to determine whether a placebo control is necessary and whether an alternative study design with another type of control would be sufficient for the purposes of research. Protocols that involve conditions causing death or irreversible damage cannot ethically employ a placebo control if alternative treatment would prevent or slow the illness progression. When studying illnesses characterized by severe or painful symptoms, investigators should thoroughly explore alternatives to the use of placebo controls. In general, the more severe the consequences and symptoms of the illness under study, the more difficult it will be to justify the use of a placebo control when alternative therapy exists. Consequently, there will

almost certainly be conditions for which placebo controls cannot be justified. Similarly, the use of a placebo control will more easily be justified as the severity and number of negative side-effects of standard therapy increases.

(3) Researchers and IRBs should continue to minimize the amount of time patients are given placebo. The rationale provided by investigators for the length of study will give IRBs the opportunity to ensure that patients are given placebo therapy for as short a time as possible to provide verifiable results. Additionally, the interim data analysis and monitoring currently in practice will allow researchers to terminate the study because of either positive or negative results, thus protecting patients from remaining on placebo unnecessarily. (I, V)

2.08 Commercial Use of Human Tissue.

The rapid growth of the biotechnology industry has resulted in the commercial availability of numerous therapeutic and other products developed from human tissue. Physicians contemplating the commercial use of human tissue should abide by the following guidelines:

(1) Informed consent must be obtained from patients for the use of organs or tissues in clinical research.

(2) Potential commercial applications must be disclosed to the patient before a profit is realized on products developed from biological materials.

(3) Human tissue and its products may not be used for commercial purposes without the informed consent of the patient who provided the original cellular material.

(4) Profits from the commercial use of human tissue and its products may be shared with patients, in accordance with lawful contractual agreements.

(5) The diagnostic and therapeutic alternatives offered to patients by their physicians should conform to standards of good medical practice and should not be influenced in any way by the commercial potential of the patient's tissue. (II, V)

2.09 Costs.

While the physician should be conscious of costs and not provide or prescribe unnecessary services, concern for the quality of care the patient receives should be the physician's first consideration. This does not preclude the physician, individually or through medical or other organizations, from participating in policy-making with respect to social issues affecting health care. (I, VII)

2.095 The Provision of Adequate Health Care.

Because society has an obligation to make access to an adequate level of health care available to all of its members regardless of ability to pay, physicians should contribute their expertise at a policy-making level to help achieve this goal. In determining whether particular procedures or treatments should be included in the adequate level of health care, the following ethical principles should be considered: (1) degree of benefit (the difference in outcome between treatment and no treatment), (2) likelihood of benefit, (3) duration of benefit, (4) cost, and (5) number of people who will benefit (referring to the fact that a treatment may benefit the patient and others who come into contact with the patient, as with a vaccination or antimicrobial drug).

Ethical principles require that a just process be used to determine the adequate level of health care. To ensure justice, the process for determining the adequate level of health care should include the following considerations: (1) democratic decision-making with broad public input at both the developmental and final approval stages, (2) monitoring for variations in care that cannot be explained on medical grounds with special attention to evidence of discriminatory impact on historically disadvantaged groups, and (3) adjustment of the adequate level over time to ensure continued and broad public acceptance.

Because of the risk that inappropriate biases will influence the content of the basic benefits package, it may be desirable to avoid rigid or precise formulas to define the specific components of the basic benefits package. After applying the five ethical values listed above, it will be possible to designate some kinds of care as either clearly basic or clearly discretionary. However, for care that is not clearly basic or discretionary, seemingly objective formulas may result in choices that are inappropriately biased. For that care, therefore, it may be desirable to give equal consideration (e.g., through a process of random selection) to the different kinds of care when deciding which will be included in the basic benefits package.

The mechanism for providing an adequate level of health care should ensure that health care benefits for the poor will not be eroded over time. (VII)

2.10 Fetal Research Guidelines.

The following guidelines are offered as aids to physicians when they are engaged in fetal research:

(1) Physicians may participate in fetal research when their activities are part of a competently designed program, under accepted standards of scientific research, to produce data which are scientifically valid and significant.

(2) If appropriate, properly performed clinical studies on animals and non-gravid humans should precede any particular fetal research project.

(3) In fetal research projects, the investigator should demonstrate the same care and concern for the fetus as a physician providing fetal care or treatment in a non-research setting.

(4) All valid federal or state legal requirements should be followed.

(5) There should be no monetary payment to obtain any fetal material for fetal research projects.

(6) Competent peer review committees, review boards, or advisory boards should be available, when appropriate, to protect against the possible abuses that could arise in such research.

(7) Research on the so-called 'dead fetus,' macerated fetal material, fetal cells, fetal tissue, or fetal organs should be in accord with state laws on autopsy and state laws on organ transplantation or anatomical gifts.

(8) In fetal research primarily for treatment of the fetus:
   (a) Voluntary and informed consent, in writing, should be given by the gravid woman, acting in the best interest of the fetus.
   (b) Alternative treatment or methods of care, if any, should be carefully evaluated and fully explained. If simpler and safer treatment is available, it should be pursued.

(9) In research primarily for treatment of the gravid female:
   (a) Voluntary and informed consent, in writing, should be given by the patient.

(b) Alternative treatment or methods of care should be carefully evaluated and fully explained to the patient. If simpler and safer treatment is available, it should be pursued.

(c) If possible, the risk to the fetus should be the least possible, consistent with the gravid female's need for treatment.

(10) In fetal research involving a fetus in utero, primarily for the accumulation of scientific knowledge:

(a) Voluntary and informed consent, in writing, should be given by the gravid woman under circumstances in which a prudent and informed adult would reasonably be expected to give such consent.

(b) The risk to the fetus imposed by the research should be the least possible.

(c) The purpose of research is the production of data and knowledge which are scientifically significant and which cannot otherwise be obtained.

(d) In this area of research, it is especially important to emphasize that care and concern for the fetus should be demonstrated. (I, III, V)

2.11 Gene Therapy.

Gene therapy involves the replacement or modification of a genetic variant to restore or enhance cellular function or to improve the reaction of non-genetic therapies.

Two types of gene therapy have been identified: (1) somatic cell therapy, in which human cells other than germ cells are genetically altered, and (2) germ line therapy, in which a replacement gene is integrated into the genome of human gametes or their precursors, resulting in expression of the new gene in the patient's offspring and subsequent generations. The fundamental difference between germ line therapy and somatic cell therapy is that germ line therapy affects the welfare of subsequent generations and may be associated with increased risk and the potential for unpredictable and irreversible results. Because of the far-reaching implications of germ line therapy, it is appropriate to limit genetic intervention to somatic cells at this time.

The goal of both somatic cell and germ line therapy is to alleviate human suffering and disease by remedying disorders for which available therapies are not satisfactory. This goal should be pursued only within the ethical tradition of medicine, which gives primacy to the welfare of the patient, whose safety and well-being must be vigorously protected. To the extent possible, experience with animal studies must be sufficient to assure the effectiveness and safety of the techniques used, and the predictability of the results.

Moreover, genetic manipulation generally should be utilized only for therapeutic purposes. Efforts to enhance "desirable" characteristics through the insertion of a modified or additional gene, or efforts to "improve" complex human traits—the eugenic development of offspring—are contrary not only to the ethical tradition of medicine, but also to the egalitarian values of our society. Because of the potential for abuse, genetic manipulation to affect non-disease traits may never be acceptable and perhaps should never be pursued. If it is ever allowed, at least three conditions would have to be met before it could be deemed ethically acceptable: (1) there would have to be a clear and meaningful benefit to the person; (2) there would have to be no trade-off with other characteristics or traits; and (3) all citizens would have to have equal access to the genetic technology, irrespective of income or other socioeconomic characteristics. These criteria should be viewed as a minimal, not an exhaustive, test of the ethical propriety of non-disease-related genetic intervention. As genetic technology and knowledge of the human genome develop further, additional guidelines may be required.

As gene therapy becomes feasible for a variety of human disorders, there are several practical factors to consider to ensure safe application of this technology in society. First, any gene therapy research should meet the Council's guidelines on clinical investigation (Opinion 2.07) and investigators must adhere to the standards of medical practice and professional responsibility. The proposed procedure must be fully discussed with the patient and the written informed consent of the patient or the patient's legal representative must be voluntary. Investigators must be thorough in their attempts to eliminate any unwanted viral agents from the viral vector containing the corrective gene. The potential for adverse effects of the viral delivery system must be disclosed to the patient. The effectiveness of gene therapy must be evaluated fully, including the determination of the natural history of the disease and follow-up examination of subsequent generations. Gene therapy should be pursued only after the availability or effectiveness of other possible therapies is found to be insufficient. These considerations should be reviewed, as appropriate, as procedures and scientific information develop.

2.12 Genetic Counseling.

Three primary areas of prenatal genetic testing are (1) screening or evaluating prospective parents for genetic disease before conception to predict the likelihood of conceiving an affected child; (2) analysis of a pre-embryo at the preimplantation stage of artificial reproductive techniques; and (3) in utero testing after conception, such as ultrasonography, amniocentesis, fetoscopy, and chorionic villus sampling, to determine the condition of the fetus. Physicians engaged in genetic counseling are ethically obligated to provide prospective parents with the basis for an informed decision for childbearing. Counseling should include reasons for and against testing as well as discussion of inappropriate uses of genetic testing. Prenatal genetic testing is most appropriate for women or couples whose medical histories or family backgrounds indicate an elevated risk of fetal genetic disorders. Women or couples without an elevated risk of genetic disease may legitimately request prenatal diagnosis, provided they understand and accept the risks involved. When counseling prospective parents, physicians should avoid the imposition of their personal moral values and the substitution of their own moral judgment for that of the prospective parents.

The physician should be aware that where a genetic defect is found in the fetus, prospective parents may request or refuse an abortion. Physicians who consider the legal and ethical requirements applicable to genetic counseling to be in conflict with their moral values and conscience may choose to limit their services to preconception diagnosis and advice or not provide any genetic services. However, the physician who is so disposed is nevertheless obligated to alert prospective parents when a potential genetic problem does exist, so that the patient may decide whether to seek further genetic counseling from another qualified specialist.

Genetic selection refers to the abortion or discard of a fetus or pre-embryo with a genetic abnormality. In general, it is ethically permissible for physicians to participate in genetic selection to prevent, cure, or treat genetic disease. However, selection to avoid a genetic disease may not always be appropriate, depending on factors such as the severity of the disease, the probability of its occurrence, the age at onset, and the time of gestation at which selection would occur. It would not be ethical to engage in selection on the basis of non-disease related characteristics or traits. (II, IV, V, VI)

2.13 Genetic Engineering.

Whatever form of regulation of gene splicing, recombinant DNA research, chemical synthesis of DNA molecules, or other genetic engineering research is eventually developed, there should be independent input from the scientific community, organized medicine, industry, and others, in addition to the federal government, to prevent abuse from any sector of society, private or public.

If and when gene replacement with normal DNA becomes a practical reality for the treatment of human disorders, the following factors should be considered:

(1) If procedures are performed in a research setting, reference should be made to the Council's guidelines on clinical investigation.

(2) If procedures are performed in a non-research setting, adherence to usual and customary standards of medical practice and professional responsibility would be required.

(3) Full discussion of the proposed procedure with the patient would be required. The consent of the patient or the patient's legal representative should be informed, voluntary and written.

(4) There must be no hazardous or other unwanted virus on the viral DNA containing the replacement or corrective gene.

(5) The inserted DNA must function under normal control within the recipient cell to prevent metabolic damage that could damage tissue and the patient.

(6) The effectiveness of the gene therapy should be evaluated as well as possible. This will include determination of the natural history of the disease and follow-up examination of subsequent generations.

(7) Such procedures should be undertaken in the future only after careful evaluation of the availability and effectiveness of other possible therapy. If simpler and safer treatment is available, it should be pursued.

(8) These considerations should be reviewed, as appropriate, as procedures and scientific information are developed in the future. (I, V, VII)

2.132 Genetic Testing by Employers.

As a result of the human genome project, physicians will be able to identify a greater number of genetic risks of disease. Among the potential uses of the tests that detect these risks will be screening of potential workers by employers. Employers may want to exclude workers with certain genetic risks from the workplace because these workers may become disabled prematurely, impose higher health care costs, or pose a risk to public safety. In addition, exposure to certain substances in the workplace may increase the likelihood that a disease will develop in the worker with a genetic risk for the disease.

(1) It would generally be inappropriate to exclude workers with genetic risks of disease from the workplace because of their risk. Genetic tests alone do not have sufficient predictive value to be relied upon as a basis for excluding workers. Consequently, use of the tests would result in unfair discrimination against individ-

uals who have positive test results. In addition, there are other ways for employers to serve their legitimate interests. Tests of a worker's actual capacity to meet the demands of the job can be used to ensure future employability and protect the public's safety. Routine monitoring of a worker's exposure can be used to protect workers who have a genetic susceptibility to injury from a substance in the workplace. In addition, employees should be advised of the risks of injury to which they are being exposed.

(2) There may be a role for genetic testing in the exclusion from the workplace of workers who have a genetic susceptibility to injury. At a minimum, several conditions would have to be met:

   (a) The disease develops so rapidly that serious and irreversible injury would occur before monitoring of either the worker's exposure to the toxic substance or the worker's health status could be effective in preventing the harm.
   (b) The genetic testing is highly accurate, with sufficient sensitivity and specificity to minimize the risk of false negative and false positive test results.
   (c) Empirical data demonstrate that the genetic abnormality results in an unusually elevated susceptibility to occupational injury.
   (d) It would require undue cost to protect susceptible employees by lowering the level of the toxic substance in the workplace. The costs of lowering the level of the substance must be extraordinary relative to the employer's other costs of making the product for which the toxic substance is used. Since genetic testing with exclusion of susceptible employees is the alternative to cleaning up the workplace, the cost of lowering the level of the substance must also be extraordinary relative to the costs of using genetic testing.
   (e) Testing must not be performed without the informed consent of the employee or applicant for employment. (IV)

2.135 Insurance Companies and Genetic Information.

Physicians should not participate in genetic testing by health insurance companies to predict a person's predisposition for disease. As a corollary, it may be necessary for physicians to maintain separate files for genetic testing results to ensure that the results are not sent to health insurance companies when requests for copies of patient medical records are fulfilled. Physicians who withhold testing results should inform insurance companies that, when medical records are sent, genetic testing results are not included. This disclosure should occur with all patients, not just those who have undergone genetic testing. (IV)

2.137 Ethical Issues in Carrier Screening of Genetic Disorders.

All carrier testing must be voluntary, and informed consent from screened individuals is required. Confidentiality of results is to be maintained. Results of testing should not be disclosed to third parties without the explicit informed consent of the screened individual. Patients should be informed as to potential uses for the genetic information by third parties, and whether other ways of obtaining the information are available when appropriate.

Carrier testing should be available uniformly among the at-risk population being screened. One legitimate exception to this principle is the limitation of carrier testing to individuals of childbearing age. In pursuit of uniform access, physicians should not limit testing only to patients specifically requesting testing. If testing is offered to some patients, it should be offered to all patients within the same risk category.

The direction of future genetic screening tests should be determined by well-thought out and well-coordinated social policy. Third parties, including insurance companies or employers, should not be permitted to discriminate against carriers of genetic disorders through policies which have the ultimate effect of influencing decisions about testing and reproduction. (IV, V)

2.138 Genetic Testing of Children.

Genetic testing of children implicates important concerns about individual autonomy and the interest of the patients. Before testing of children can be performed, there must be some potential benefit from the testing that can reasonably be viewed as outweighing the disadvantages of testing, particularly the harm from abrogating the children's future choice in knowing their genetic status. When there is such a potential benefit, parents should decide whether their children will undergo testing. If parents unreasonably request or refuse testing of their child, physician should take steps to change or, if necessary, use legal means to override the parents' choice. Applying these principles to specific circumstances yields the following conclusions:

1. When a child is at risk for a genetic condition for which preventive or other therapeutic measures are available, genetic testing should be offered or, in some cases, required.
2. When a child is at risk for a genetic condition with pediatric onset for which preventive or other therapeutic measures are not available, parents generally should have discretion to decide about genetic testing.
3. When a child is at risk for a genetic condition with adult onset for which preventive or other therapeutic measures are not available, genetic testing of children generally should not be undertaken. Families should still be informed of the existence of tests and given the opportunity to discuss the reasons why the tests are generally not offered for children.
4. Genetic testing for carrier status should be deferred until either the child reaches maturity, the child needs to make reproductive decisions or, in the case of children too immature to make their own reproductive decisions, reproductive decisions need to be made for the child.
5. Genetic testing of children for the benefit of a family member should not be performed unless the testing is necessary to prevent substantial harm to the family member.

When a child's genetic status is determined incidentally, the information should be retained by the physician and entered into the patient record. Discussion of the existence of this finding should then be taken up when the child reaches maturity or needs to make reproductive decisions, so that the individual can decide whether to request disclosure of the information. It is important that physicians be consistent in disclosing both positive and negative results in the same way since if physicians raise the existence of the testing results only when the results are positive, individuals will know what the results must be. This information should not be disclosed to third parties. Genetic information should be maintained in a separate portion of the medical record to prevent mistaken disclosure.

When a child is being considered for adoption, the guidelines for genetic testing should be the same as for other children. (I, IV)

2.14 In Vitro Fertilization.

The technique of in vitro fertilization and embryo transplantation enables certain couples previously incapable of conception to bear a child. It is also useful in the field of research directed toward an understanding of how genetic defects arise and are transmitted and how they might be prevented or treated. Because of serious ethical and moral concerns, however, any fertilized egg that has the potential for human life and that will be implanted in the uterus of a woman should not be subjected to laboratory research.

All fertilized ova not utilized for implantation and that are maintained for research purposes shall be handled with the strictest adherence to the Principles of Medical Ethics, to the guidelines for research and medical practice expressed in the Council's opinion on fetal research, and to the highest standards of medical practice. (I, V, VII)

2.141 Frozen Pre-Embryos.

The practice of freezing extra pre-embryos harvested during the in vitro fertilization (IVF) process has enhanced the ability of infertile couples to preserve embryos for future implantation. This practice has also posed a number of ethical and legal dilemmas, including questions regarding decision-making authority over the pre-embryos and appropriate uses of pre-embryos.

This country's cultural and legal traditions indicate that the logical persons to exercise control over a frozen pre-embryo are the woman and man who provided the gametes (the ovum and sperm). The gamete providers have a fundamental interest at stake, their potential for procreation. In addition, the gamete providers are the parties most concerned with the interests of a frozen pre-embryo and most likely to protect those interests.

Gamete providers should be able to use the pre-embryos themselves or donate them for use by other parties, but not sell them. In addition, research on pre-embryos should be permitted as long as the pre-embryos are not destined for transfer to a woman for implantation and as long as the research is conducted in accordance with the Council's guidelines on fetal research. Frozen pre-embryos may also be allowed to thaw and deteriorate.

The gamete providers should have an equal say in the use of their pre-embryos and, therefore, the pre-embryos should not be available for use by either provider or changed from their frozen state without the consent of both providers. The man and woman each has contributed half of the pre-embryo's genetic code. In addition, whether a person chooses to become a parent and assume all of the accompanying obligations is a particularly personal and fundamental decision. Even if the individual could be absolved of any parental obligations, he or she may have a strong desire not to have offspring. The absence of a legal duty does not eliminate the moral duty many would feel toward any genetic offspring.

Advance agreements are recommended for deciding the disposition of frozen pre-embryos in the event of divorce or other changes in circumstances. Advance agreements can help ensure that the gamete providers undergo IVF and pre-embryo freezing after a full contemplation of the consequences, but should not be mandatory. (I, III, IV, V)

2.145 Pre-Embryo Splitting.

The technique of splitting in vitro fertilized pre-embryos may result in multiple genetically identical siblings.

The procedure of pre-embryo splitting should be available as long as both gamete providers agree. This procedure may greatly increase the chances of conception for an infertile couple or for a couple whose future reproductive capacity will likely be diminished. Pre-embryo splitting also can reduce the number of invasive procedures necessary for egg retrieval and the necessity for hormonal stimulants to generate multiple eggs. The use and disposition of any pre-embryos that are frozen for future use should be consistent with the Council's opinion on frozen pre-embryos. (Opinion 2.141)

The use of frozen pre-embryo identical siblings many years after one child has been born raises new ethical issues. Couples might wait until they can discover the mental and physical characteristics of a child before transferring a genetically identical sibling for implantation, they might sell their frozen pre-embryos based upon the outcome of a genetically identical child, or they might decide to transplant a genetically identical sibling based on the need to harvest the child's tissue.

The Council does not find that these considerations are sufficient to prohibit pre-embryo splitting for the following reasons:

(1) It would take many years to determine the outcome of a child and most families want to complete their childbearing within a shorter time.

(2) The sale of pre-embryos can and should be prohibited.

(3) The small number of couples who might bear identical siblings solely for purposes of harvesting their tissue does not outweigh the benefits which might be derived from pre-embryo splitting. Additionally, it is not evident that a sibling would have negative psychological or emotional consequences from having acted as an organ or tissue donor. Indeed, the child may derive psychological benefits from having saved the life of a sibling.

To the extent possible, discussion of these issues should be had with gamete providers prior to pre-embryo splitting and freezing so as to inform the prospective parents of possible future ethical dilemmas. (I, III, IV, V)

2.15 Financial Incentives for Organ Donation.

The voluntary donation of organs in appropriate circumstances is to be encouraged. However, it is not ethical to participate in a procedure to enable a living donor to receive payment, other than for the reimbursement of expenses necessarily incurred in connection with removal, for any of the donor's non-renewable organs.

Procedures involving financial incentives for cadaveric organ donors should have adequate safeguards to ensure that the health of donors and recipients is in no way jeopardized, and that the quality of the organ supply is not degraded. Incentives should be limited to future contracts offered to prospective donors. By entering into a future contract, an adult would agree while still competent to donate his or her organs after death. In return, the donor's family or estate would receive some financial remuneration after the organs have been retrieved and judged medically suitable for transplantation. Several other conditions would apply:

(1) Only the potential donor, and not the donor's family or other third party, may be given the option of accepting financial incentives for cadaveric organ donation. In addition, the potential donor must be a competent adult when the decision to donate is made, and the donor must not have committed suicide.

(2) Any incentive should be of moderate value and should be the lowest amount that can reasonably be expected to encourage organ donation. By designating a state agency to administer the incentive, full control over the level of incentive can be maintained.

(3) Payment should occur only after the organs have been retrieved and judged medically suitable for transplantation. Suitability should continue to be determined in accordance with the procedures of the Organ Procurement and Transplantation Network.

(4) Incentives should play no part in the allocation of donated organs among potential transplant recipients. The distribution of organs for transplantation should continue to be governed only by ethically appropriate criteria relating to medical need. (I, III, V)

2.155 Mandated Choice and Presumed Consent for Cadaveric Organ Donation.

A system of mandated choice for organ donation, in which individuals are required to express their preferences regarding organ donation when renewing their drivers' licenses or performing some other state-mandated task, is an ethically appropriate strategy for encouraging donation and should be pursued. To be effective, information on the importance of organ donation and the success of organ transplantation should be provided when the donation decision is made.

A system of presumed consent for organ donation, in which individuals are assumed to consent to be organ donors after death unless they indicate their refusal to consent, raises serious ethical concerns. For presumed consent to be ethically acceptable, effective mechanisms for documenting and honoring refusals to donate must be in place. In addition, when there is no documented refusal by the individual decedent, the family of the decedent would have to be contacted to verify that they do not know of any objections to donation by the decedent while living. (I, III, V)

2.157 Organ Procurement Following Cardiac Death.

Given the increasing need for donor organs, protocols for procurement following cardiac death have been developed. In some instances, patients or their surrogate decisionmakers request withdrawal of life support and choose to serve as organ donors. In these cases, the organs can be preserved best by discontinuation of life support in the operating room so that organs can be removed two minutes following cardiac death. In other scenarios, patients who suffer unexpected cardiac death may be cannulated and perfused with cold preserving fluid (in situ preservation) to maintain organs. Both of these methods may be ethically permissible, with attention to certain safeguards.

(1) When securing consent for life support withdrawal and organ retrieval, the health care team must be certain that consent is voluntary. This is particularly true where surrogate decisions about life-sustaining treatment may be influenced

by the prospect of organ donation. If there is any reason to suspect undue influence, a full ethics consultation should be required.

(2) In all instances, it is critical that there be no conflict of interest in the health care team. Those health care professionals providing care at the end of life must be separated from providers participating in the transplant team.

(3) Further pilot programs should assess the success and acceptability of organ removal following withdrawal of life-sustaining treatment.

(4) In cases of in situ preservation of cadaveric organs, the prior consent of the decedent or the consent of the decedent's surrogate decisionmaker makes perfusion ethically permissible. Perfusion without either prior specific consent to perfusion or general consent to organ donation violates requirements for informed consent for medical procedures and should not be permitted.

(5) The recipients of such procured organs should be informed of the source of the organs as well as any potential defects in the quality of the organs, so that they may decide with their physicians whether to accept the organs or wait for more suitable ones.

(6) Clear clinical criteria should be developed to ensure that only appropriate candidates, whose organs are reasonably likely to be suitable for transplantation, are considered eligible to donate organs under these protocols.

2.16 Organ Transplantation Guidelines.

The following statement is offered for guidance of physicians as they seek to maintain the highest level of ethical conduct in the transplanting of human organs.

(1) In all professional relationships between a physician and a patient, the physician's primary concern must be the health of the patient. The physician owes the patient primary allegiance. This concern and allegiance must be preserved in all medical procedures, including those which involve the transplantation of an organ from one person to another where both donor and recipient are patients. Care must, therefore, be taken to protect the rights of both the donor and the recipient, and no physician may assume a responsibility in organ transplantation unless the rights of both donor and recipient are equally protected. A prospective organ transplant offers no justification for a relaxation of the usual standard of medical care for the potential donor.

(2) When a vital, single organ is to be transplanted, the death of the donor shall have been determined by at least one physician other than the recipient's physician. Death shall be determined by the clinical judgment of the physician, who should rely on currently accepted and available scientific tests.

(3) Full discussion of the proposed procedure with the donor and the recipient or their responsible relatives or representatives is mandatory. The physician should ensure that consent to the procedure is fully informed and voluntary, in accordance with the Council's guidelines on informed consent. Once such informed consent to donation has been given by the donor in accordance with applicable state law, it cannot be revoked by surviving family members. The physician's interest in advancing scientific knowledge must always be secondary to his or her concern for the patient.

(4) Transplant procedures of body organs should be undertaken (a) only by physicians who possess special medical knowledge and technical competence developed through special training, study, and laboratory experience and practice, and (b) in medical institutions with facilities adequate to protect the health and well-being of the parties to the procedure.

(5) Recipients of organs for transplantation should be determined in accordance with the Council's guidelines on the allocation of limited medical resources.

(6) Organs should be considered a national, rather than a local or regional, resource. Geographical priorities in the allocation of organs should be prohibited except when transportation of organs would threaten their suitability for transplantation.

(7) Patients should not be placed on the waiting lists of multiple local transplant centers, but rather on a single waiting list for each type of organ. (I, III, V)

2.161 Medical Applications of Fetal Tissue Transplantation.

The principal ethical concern in the use of human fetal tissue for transplantation is the degree to which the decision to have an abortion might be influenced by the decision to donate the fetal tissue. In the application of fetal tissue transplantation the following safeguards should apply: (1) The Council's guidelines on clinical investigation and organ transplantation are followed, as they pertain to the recipient of the fetal tissue transplant (see Opinion 2.07, Clinical Investigation, and Opinion 2.16, Organ Transplantation Guidelines); (2) a final decision regarding abortion is made before initiating a discussion of the transplantation use of fetal tissue; (3) decisions regarding the technique used to induce abortion, as well as the timing of the abortion in relation to the gestational age of the fetus, are based on concern for the safety of the pregnant woman; (4) fetal tissue is not provided in exchange for financial remuneration above that which is necessary to cover reasonable expenses; (5) the recipient of the tissue is not designated by the donor; (6) health care personnel involved in the termination of a particular pregnancy do not participate in or receive any benefit from the transplantation of tissue from the abortus of the same pregnancy; and (7) informed consent on behalf of both the donor and the recipient is obtained in accordance with applicable law. (I, IV, V)

2.162 Anencephalic Neonates as Organ Donors.

Anencephaly is a congenital absence of major portions of the brain, skull, and scalp. Anencephalic neonates are thought to be unique from other brain-damaged beings because of a lack of past consciousness with no potential for future consciousness.

Physicians may provide anencephalic neonates with ventilator assistance and other medical therapies that are necessary to sustain organ perfusion and viability until such time as a determination of death can be made in accordance with accepted medical standards, relevant law, and regional organ procurement organization policy. Retrieval and transplantation of the organs of anencephalic infants are ethically permissible only after such determination of death is made, and only in accordance with the Council's guidelines for transplantation.

2.165 Fetal Umbilical Cord Blood.

Human umbilical cord blood has been identified as a viable source of hematopoietic stem cells that can be used as an alternative to bone marrow for transplantation. It is obtained by clamping the umbilical cord immediately after delivery.

The use of umbilical cord blood raises two main ethical problems. First, the exact timing of the clamping has a significant impact on the neonate. Studies indicate that early clamping may cause an abrupt surge in arterial pressure, resulting in intraventricular hemorrhage (particularly in premature infants). Second, there is a risk that the infant donor will develop a need for his or her own cord blood later in life. If that child was a donor and this later need arises, he or she might be without blood, when he or she could have had his or her own blood stored.

To avoid health risks, normal clamping protocol should be followed and not altered in such a way that might endanger the infant. Additionally, parents of the infant must be fully informed of the risks of the donation and written consent should be obtained from them.

The second concern, that the child may need the blood later in life, is more complex. The possibility that an infant donor would be in need of his or her own umbilical cord blood is highly speculative. There are a number of reasons why the infant may not need the blood later. The diseases that are treated by bone marrow transplantation are not common, and there may be other treatment alternatives available, particularly in the future when the illness would occur. Additionally, the demand for fetal umbilical cord blood will increase as it becomes medically certain that the blood may be used in persons unrelated to the donor. This situation will reduce the need to store a particular infant's blood since umbilical cord blood from other donors would be available. If the blood is sufficient for use in unrelated individuals, then the donor may obtain the cord blood from another donor later in life, making the need to store his or her own blood unnecessary. These original donors, however, should be given priority in receipt of such blood if they need a donation later in life.

For all of these reasons, it would generally not be unethical to use the cord blood. However, if the child-donor is known to be at risk for an illness that is treated by bone marrow donation, the child should not be used as a donor, and his or her blood should be stored for future use. (I, V)

2.167 The Use of Minors as Organ and Tissue Donors.

Minors need not be prohibited from acting as sources of organs, but their participation should be limited. Different procedures pose different degrees of risk and do not all require the same restrictions. In general, minors should not be permitted to serve as a source when there is a very serious risk of complications (e.g., partial liver or lung donation, which involve a substantial risk of serious immediate or long-term morbidity). If the safeguards in the remainder of this opinion are followed, minors may be permitted to serve as a source when the risks are low (e.g., blood or skin donation, in which the donated tissue can regenerate and spinal or general anesthesia is not required), moderate (e.g., bone marrow donation, in which the donated tissue can regenerate but brief general or spinal anesthesia is required) or serious (e.g., kidney donation, which involve more extensive anesthesia and major invasive surgery).

If a child is capable of making his or her own medical treatment decisions, he or she should be considered capable of deciding whether to be an organ or tissue donor. However, physicians should not perform organ retrievals of serious risk without first obtaining court authorization. Courts should confirm that the mature minor is acting voluntarily and without coercion.

If a child is not capable of making his or her own medical decisions, all transplantations should have parental approval, and those which pose a serious risk should receive court authorization. In the court authorization process, the evaluation of a child psychiatrist or psychologist must be sought and a guardian ad litem should be assigned to the potential minor donor in order to fully represent the minor's interests.

When deciding on behalf of immature children, parents and courts should ensure that transplantation presents a "clear benefit" to the minor source, which entails meeting the following requirements:

(1) Ideally the minor should be the only possible source. All other available sources of organs, both donor pools and competent adult family members, must be medically inappropriate or significantly inferior. An unwilling potential donor does not qualify him/her as medically inappropriate.

(2) For transplantations of moderate or serious risk, the transplantation must be necessary with some degree of medical certainty to provide a substantial benefit; that is, it both prevents an extremely poor quality of life and ensures a good quality of life for the recipient. A transplant should not be allowed if it merely increases the comfort of the recipient. If a transplant is not presently considered to provide a substantial benefit but is expected to do so within a period of time, the transplant need not be delayed until it meets this criterion, especially if the delay would significantly decrease the benefits derived from the transplant by the recipient.

(3) The organ or tissue transplant must have a reasonable probability of success in order for transplantation to be allowed. What constitutes a reasonable chance of success should be based on medical judgments about the physical condition of the recipient and the likelihood that the transplant will not be rejected or produce benefits which are very transient. Children should not be used for transplants that are considered experimental or non-standard.

(4) Generally, minors should be allowed to serve as a source only to close family members.

(5) Psychological or emotional benefits to the potential source may be considered, though evidence of future benefit to the minor source should be clear and convincing. Possible benefits to a child include continued emotional bonds between the minor and the recipient, increased self-esteem, and prevention of adverse reaction to death of a sibling. Whether a child will capture these benefits depends upon the child's specific circumstances. A minor's assent or dissent to a procedure is an important piece of evidence that demonstrates whether the transplant will offer psychological benefits to the source. Dissent from incompetent minors should be powerful evidence that the donation will not provide a clear benefit, but may not present an absolute bar. Every effort should be made to identify and address the child's concerns in this case.

(6) It is essential to ensure that the potential source does not have any underlying conditions that create an undue individual risk. (I, V)

2.17 Quality of Life.

In the making of decisions for the treatment of seriously disabled newborns or of other persons who are severely disabled by injury or illness, the primary consideration should be what is best for the individual patient and not the avoidance of a burden to the family or to society. Quality of life, as defined by the patient's interests and values, is a factor to be considered in determining what is best for the individual. It is permissible to consider quality of life when deciding about life-sustaining treatment in accordance with Opinions 2.20, 2.215, and 2.22. (I, III, IV)

2.18 Surrogate Mothers.

"Surrogate" motherhood involves the artificial insemination of a woman who agrees, usually in return for payment, to give the resulting child to the child's father by surrendering her parental rights. Often, the father's infertile wife becomes the child's adoptive mother. The woman bearing the child is in most cases genetically related to the child, though gestational surrogacy (in which the ovum is provided by the father's infertile wife or other donor) is possible as well.

Ethical, social, and legal problems may arise in surrogacy arrangements. Surrogate motherhood may render children and women's reproductive capacities into commodities, exploit poor women whose decision to participate may not be wholly voluntary, and improperly discourage or interfere with the formation of a natural maternal-fetal or maternal-child bond. Psychological impairment may occur in a woman who deliberately conceives with the intention of bearing a child which she will give up. In addition, the woman who has contracted to bear the child may decide to have an abortion or to refuse to relinquish her parental rights. Alternatively, if there is a subsequent birth of a disabled child, prospective parents and the birth mother may not want to or will be unable to assume the responsibilities of parenthood.

On the other hand, surrogate motherhood arrangements are often the last hope of prospective parents to have a child who is genetically related to at least one of them. In addition, most surrogacy arrangements are believed by the parties involved to be mutually beneficial, and most are completed without mishap or dispute. In light of the concerns expressed above, however, some safeguards are necessary to protect the welfare of the child and the birth mother. The Council believes that surrogacy contracts, while permissible, should grant the birth mother the right to void the contract within a reasonable period of time after the birth of the child. If the contract is voided, custody of the child should be determined according to the child's best interests.

In gestational surrogacy, in which the surrogate mother has no genetic tie to the fetus, the justification for allowing the surrogate mother to void the contract becomes less clear. Gestational surrogacy contracts should be strictly enforceable (i.e., not voidable by either party). (I, II, IV)

2.19 Unnecessary Services.

Physicians should not provide, prescribe, or seek compensation for services that they know are unnecessary. (II, VII)

2.20 Withholding or Withdrawing Life-Sustaining Medical Treatment.

The social commitment of the physician is to sustain life and relieve suffering. Where the performance of one duty conflicts with the other, the preferences of the patient should prevail. The principle of patient autonomy requires that physicians respect the decision to forego life-sustaining treatment of a patient who possesses decision-making capacity. Life-sustaining treatment is any treatment that serves to prolong life without reversing the underlying medical condition. Life-sustaining treatment may include, but is not limited to, mechanical ventilation, renal dialysis, chemotherapy, antibiotics, and artificial nutrition and hydration.

There is no ethical distinction between withdrawing and withholding life-sustaining treatment.

A competent, adult patient may, in advance, formulate and provide a valid consent to the withholding or withdrawal of life-support systems in the event that injury or illness renders that individual incompetent to make such a decision. A patient may also appoint a surrogate decisionmaker in accordance with state law.

If the patient receiving life-sustaining treatment is incompetent, a surrogate decisionmaker should be identified. Without an advance directive that designates a proxy, the patient's family should become the surrogate decisionmaker. Family includes persons with whom the patient is closely associated. In the case when there is no person closely associated with the patient, but there are persons who both care about the patient and have sufficient relevant knowledge of the patient, such persons may be appropriate surrogates. Physicians should provide all relevant medical information and explain to surrogate decisionmakers that decisions regarding withholding or withdrawing life-sustaining treatment should be based on substituted judgment (what the patient would have decided) when there is evidence of the patient's preferences and values. In making a substituted judgment, decisionmakers may consider the patient's advance directive (if any); the patient's values about life and the way it should be lived; and the patient's attitudes toward sickness, suffering, medical procedures, and death. If there is not adequate evidence of the incompetent patient's preferences and values, the decision should be based on the best interests of the patient (what outcome would most likely promote the patient's well-being).

Though the surrogate's decision for the incompetent patient should almost always be accepted by the physician, there are four situations that may require either institutional or judicial review and/or intervention in the decision-making process: (a) there is no available family member willing to be the patient's surrogate decisionmaker, (b) there is a dispute among family members and there is no decisionmaker designated in an advance directive, (c) a health care provider believes that the family's decision is clearly not what the patient would have decided if competent, and (d) a health care provider believes that the decision is not a decision that could reasonably be judged to be in the patient's best interests. When there are disputes among family members or between family and health care providers, the use of ethics committees specifically designed to facilitate sound decision-making is recommended before resorting to the courts.

When a permanently unconscious patient was never competent or had not left any evidence of previous preferences or values, since there is no objective way to ascertain the best interests of the patient, the surrogate's decision should not be challenged as long as the decision is based on the decisionmaker's true concern for what would be best for the patient.

Physicians have an obligation to relieve pain and suffering and to promote the dignity and autonomy of dying patients in their care. This includes providing effective palliative treatment even though it may foreseeably hasten death.

Even if the patient is not terminally ill or permanently unconscious, it is not unethical to discontinue all means of life-sustaining medical treatment in accordance with a proper substituted judgment or best interests analysis. (I, III, IV, V)

2.21 Euthanasia.

Euthanasia is the administration of a lethal agent by another person to a patient for the purpose of relieving the patient's intolerable and incurable suffering.

It is understandable, though tragic, that some patients in extreme duress—such as those suffering from a terminal, painful, debilitating illness—may come to decide that death is preferable to life. However, permitting physicians to engage in euthanasia would ultimately cause more harm than good. Euthanasia is fundamentally incompatible with the physician's role as healer, would be difficult or impossible to control, and would pose serious societal risks.

The involvement of physicians in euthanasia heightens the significance of its ethical prohibition. The physician who performs euthanasia assumes unique responsibility for the act of ending the patient's life. Euthanasia could also readily be extended to incompetent patients and other vulnerable populations.

Instead of engaging in euthanasia, physicians must aggressively respond to the needs of patients at the end of life. Patients should not be abandoned once it is determined that a cure is impossible. Patients near the end of life must continue to receive emotional support, comfort care, adequate pain control, respect for patient autonomy, and good communication. (I, IV)

2.211 Physician-Assisted Suicide.

Physician-assisted suicide occurs when a physician facilitates a patient's death by providing the necessary means and/or information to enable the patient to perform the life-ending act (e.g., the physician provides sleeping pills and information about the lethal dose, while aware that the patient may commit suicide).

It is understandable, though tragic, that some patients in extreme duress—such as those suffering from a terminal, painful, debilitating illness—may come to decide that death is preferable to life. However, allowing physicians to participate in assisted suicide would cause more harm than good. Physician-assisted suicide is fundamentally incompatible with the physician's role as healer, would be difficult or impossible to control, and would pose serious societal risks.

Instead of participating in assisted suicide, physicians must aggressively respond to the needs of patients at the end of life. Patients should not be abandoned once it is determined that a cure is impossible. Multidisciplinary interventions should be sought including specialty consultation, hospice care, pastoral support, family counseling, and other modalities. Patients near the end of life must continue to receive emotional support, comfort care, adequate pain control, respect for patient autonomy, and good communication. (I, IV)

2.215 Treatment Decisions for Seriously Ill Newborns.

The primary consideration for decisions regarding life-sustaining treatment for seriously ill newborns should be what is best for the newborn. Factors that should be weighed are: (1) the chance that therapy will succeed, (2) the risks involved with treatment and nontreatment, (3) the degree to which the therapy, if successful, will extend life, (4) the pain and discomfort associated with the therapy, and (5) the anticipated quality of life for the newborn with and without treatment.

Care must be taken to evaluate the newborn's expected quality of life from the child's perspective. Life-sustaining treatment may be withheld or withdrawn from a newborn when the pain and suffering expected to be endured by the child will overwhelm any potential for joy, during his or her life. When an infant suffers extreme neurological damage, and is consequently not capable of experiencing either suffering or joy, a decision may be made to withhold or withdraw life-sustaining treatment. When life-sustaining treatment is withheld or withdrawn, comfort care must not be discontinued.

When an infant's prognosis is largely uncertain, as is often the case with extremely premature newborns, all life-sustaining and life-enhancing treatment should be initiated. Decisions about life-sustaining treatment should be made once the prognosis becomes more certain. It is not necessary to attain absolute or near absolute prognostic certainty before life-sustaining treatment is withdrawn, since this goal is often unattainable and risks unnecessarily prolonging the infant's suffering.

Physicians must provide full information to parents of seriously ill newborns regarding the nature of treatments, therapeutic options, and expected prognosis with and without therapy, so that parents can make informed decisions for their children about life-sustaining treatment. Counseling services and an opportunity to talk with persons who have had to make similar decisions should be available to parents. Ethics committees or infant-review committees should also be utilized to facilitate parental decision-making. These committees should help mediate resolutions of conflicts that may arise among parents, physicians, and others involved in the care of the infant. These committees should also be responsible for referring cases to the appropriate public agencies when it is concluded that the parents' decision is not a decision that could reasonably be judged to be in the best interests of the infant. (I, III, IV, V)

2.22 Do-Not-Resuscitate Orders.

Efforts should be made to resuscitate patients who suffer cardiac or respiratory arrest except when circumstances indicate that cardiopulmonary resuscitation (CPR) would be inappropriate or not in accord with the desires or best interests of the patient.

Patients at risk of cardiac or respiratory failure should be encouraged to express in advance their preferences regarding the use of CPR and this should be documented in the patient's medical record. These discussions should include a description of the procedures encompassed by CPR and, when possible, should occur in an outpatient setting when general treatment preferences are discussed, or as early as possible during hospitalization. The physician has an ethical obligation to honor the resuscitation preferences expressed by the patient. Physicians should not permit their personal value judgments about quality of life to obstruct the implementation of a patient's preferences regarding the use of CPR.

If a patient is incapable of rendering a decision regarding the use of CPR, a decision may be made by a surrogate decisionmaker, based upon the previously expressed preferences of the patient or, if such preferences are unknown, in accordance with the patient's best interests.

If, in the judgment of the attending physician, it would be inappropriate to pursue CPR, the attending physician may enter a do-not-resuscitate (DNR) order into the patient's record. Resuscitative efforts should be considered inappropriate by the attending physician only if they cannot be expected either to restore cardiac or respiratory function to the patient or to meet established ethical criteria, as defined in the Principles of Medical Ethics and Opinions 2.03 and 2.095. When there is adequate time to do so, the physician must first inform the patient, or the incompetent patient's surrogate, of the content of the DNR order, as well as the basis for its implementation. The physician also should be prepared to discuss appropriate alternatives, such as obtaining a second opinion (e.g., consulting a bioethics committee) or arranging for transfer of care to another physician.

DNR orders, as well as the basis for their implementation, should be entered by the attending physician in the patient's medical record.

DNR orders only preclude resuscitative efforts in the event of cardiopulmonary arrest and should not influence other therapeutic interventions that may be appropriate for the patient. (I, IV)

2.225 Optimal Use of Orders-Not-to-Intervene and Advance Directives.

More rigorous efforts in advance care planning are required in order to tailor end-of-life care to the preferences of patients so that they can experience a satisfactory last chapter in their lives. There is need for better availability and tracking of advance directives, and more uniform adoption of form documents that can be honored in all states of the United States. The discouraging evidence of inadequate end-of-life decision-making indicates the necessity of several improvement strategies:

(1) Patients and physicians should make use of advisory as well as statutory documents. Advisory documents aim to accurately represent a patient's wishes and are legally binding under law. Statutory documents give physicians immunity from malpractice for following a patient's wishes. If a form is not available that combines the two, an advisory document should be appended to the state statutory form.

(2) Advisory documents should be based on validated worksheets, thus ensuring reasonable confidence that preferences for end-of-life treatment can be fairly and effectively elicited and recorded, and that they are applicable to medical decisions.

(3) Physicians should directly discuss the patient's preferences with the patient and the patient's proxy. These discussions should be held ahead of time whenever possible. The key steps of structuring a core discussion and of signing and recording the document in the medical record should not be delegated to a junior member of the health care team.

(4) Central repositories should be established so that completed advisory documents, state statutory documents, identification of a proxy, and identification of the primary physician, can be obtained efficiently in emergency and urgent circumstances as well as routinely.

(5) Health care facilities should honor, and physicians use, a range of orders on the Doctor's Order Sheet to indicate patient wishes regarding avoidable treatments that might otherwise be given on an emergency basis or by a covering physician with less knowledge of the patient's wishes. Treatment avoidance orders might include, along with a Do Not Resuscitate (DNR) order, some of the following: Full Comfort Care Only (FCCO); Do Not Intubate (DNI); Do Not Defibrillate (DND); Do Not Leave Home (DNLH); Do Not Transfer (DNTransfer); No Intravenous Lines (NIL); No Blood Draws (NBD); No Feeding Tube (NFT); No Vital Signs (NVS); and so forth. One common new order, Do Not Treat (DNT), is specifically not included in this list, since it may unintentionally convey the message that no care should be given and the patient may lose the intense attention due to a dying person; FCCO serves the same purpose without the likely misinterpretation. As with DNR orders, these treatment avoidance orders should be revisited periodically to ensure their continued applicability. Active comfort care orders might include Allow Visitors Extended Hours (AVEH); and Inquire About Comfort (IAC) b.i.d. (twice daily).(I)

2.23 HIV Testing.

Human Immunodeficiency Virus (HIV) testing is appropriate and should be encouraged for diagnosis and treatment of HIV infection or of medical conditions that may be affected by HIV. Treatment may prolong the lives of those with AIDS and prolong the symptom-free period in those with an asymptomatic HIV infection. Wider testing is imperative to ensure that individuals in need of treatment are identified and treated.

Physicians should ensure that HIV testing is conducted in a way that respects patient autonomy and assures patient confidentiality as much as possible.

The physician should secure the patient's informed consent specific for HIV testing before testing is performed. Because of the need for pretest counseling and the potential consequences of an HIV test on an individual's job, housing, insurability, and social relationships, the consent should be specific for HIV testing. Consent for HIV testing cannot be inferred from a general consent to treatment.

When a health care provider is at risk for HIV infection because of the occurrence of puncture injury or mucosal contact with potentially infected bodily fluids, it is acceptable to test the patient for HIV infection even if the patient refuses consent. When testing without consent is performed in accordance with the law, the patient should be given the customary pretest counseling.

The confidentiality of the results of HIV testing must be maintained as much as possible and the limits of a patient's confidentiality should be known to the patient before consent is given.

Exceptions to confidentiality are appropriate when necessary to protect the public health or when necessary to protect individuals, including health care workers, who are endangered by persons infected with HIV. If a physician knows that a seropositive individual is endangering a third party, the physician should, within the constraints of the law: (1) attempt to persuade the infected patient to cease endangering the third party; (2) if persuasion fails, notify authorities; and (3) if the authorities take no action, notify the endangered third party.

In order to limit the public spread of HIV infection, physicians should encourage voluntary testing of patients at risk for infection.

It is unethical to deny treatment to HIV-infected individuals because they are HIV seropositive or because they are unwilling to undergo HIV testing, except in the instance where knowledge of the patient's HIV status is vital to the appropriate treatment of the patient. When a patient refuses to be tested after being informed of the physician's medical opinion, the physician may transfer the patient to a second physician who is willing to manage the patient's care in accordance with the patient's preferences about testing. (I, IV)

3.00 OPINIONS ON INTERPROFESSIONAL RELATIONS

3.01 Nonscientific Practitioners.

It is unethical to engage in or to aid and abet in treatment which has no scientific basis and is dangerous, is calculated to deceive the patient by giving false hope, or which may cause the patient to delay in seeking proper care.

Physicians should also be mindful of state laws which prohibit a physician from aiding and abetting an unlicensed person in the practice of medicine, aiding or abetting a person with a limited license in providing services beyond the scope of his or her license, or undertaking the joint medical treatment of patients under the foregoing circumstances.

Physicians are otherwise free to accept or decline to serve anyone who seeks their services, regardless of who has recommended that the individual see the physician. (III, VI)

3.02 Nurses.

The primary bond between the practices of medicine and nursing is mutual ethical concern for patients. One of the duties in providing reasonable care is fulfilled by a nurse who carries out the orders of the attending physician. Where orders appear to the nurse to be in error or contrary to customary medical and nursing practice, the physician has an ethical obligation to hear the nurse's concern and explain those orders to the nurse involved. The ethical physician should neither expect nor insist that nurses follow orders contrary to standards of good medical and nursing practice. In emergencies, when prompt action is necessary and the physician is not immediately available, a nurse may be justified in acting contrary to the physician's standing orders for the safety of the patient. Such occurrences should not be considered to be a breakdown in professional relations. (IV, V)

3.03 Allied Health Professionals.

Physicians often practice in concert with allied health professionals such as, but not limited to, optometrists, nurse anesthetists, nurse midwives, and physician assistants in the course of delivering appropriate medical care to their patients. In doing so, physicians should be guided by the following principles:

(1) It is ethical for a physician to work in consultation with or employ allied health professionals, as long as they are appropriately trained and duly licensed to perform the activities being requested.

(2) Physicians have an ethical obligation to the patients for whom they are responsible to insure that medical and surgical conditions are appropriately evaluated and treated.

(3) Physicians may teach in recognized schools for the allied health professionals for the purpose of improving the quality of their education. The scope of teaching may embrace subjects that are within the legitimate scope of the allied health profession and which are designed to prepare students to engage in the practice of the profession within the limits prescribed by law.

(4) It is inappropriate to substitute the services of an allied health professional for those of a physician when the allied health professional is not appropriately trained and duly licensed to provide the medical services being requested. (I, II, VII)

3.04 Referral of Patients.

A physician may refer a patient for diagnostic or therapeutic services to another physician, limited practitioner, or any other provider of health care services permitted by law to furnish such services, whenever he or she believes that this may benefit the patient. As in the case of referrals to physician-specialists, referrals to limited practitioners should be based on their individual competence and ability to perform the services needed by the patient. A physician should not so refer a patient unless the physician is confident that the services provided on referral will be performed competently and in accordance with accepted scientific standards and legal requirements. (V, VI)

3.041 Chiropractic.

It is ethical for a physician to associate professionally with chiropractors provided that the physician believes that such association is in the best interests of his or her patient. A physician may refer a patient for diagnostic or therapeutic services to a chiropractor permitted by law to furnish such services whenever the physician believes that this may benefit his or her patient. Physicians may also ethically teach in recognized schools of chiropractic. (V, VI)

[**3.05** Deleted.]

3.06 Sports Medicine.

Physicians should assist athletes to make informed decisions about their participation in amateur and professional contact sports which entail risks of bodily injury.

The professional responsibility of the physician who serves in a medical capacity at an athletic contest or sporting event is to protect the health and safety of the contestants. The desire of spectators, promoters of the event, or even the injured athlete that he or she not be removed from the contest should not be controlling. The physician's judgment should be governed only by medical considerations. (I, VII)

[**3.07** Deleted.]

3.08 Sexual Harassment and Exploitation Between Medical Supervisors and Trainees.

Sexual harassment may be defined as sexual advances, requests for sexual favors, and other verbal or physical conduct of a sexual nature when (1) such conduct interferes with an individual's work or academic performance or creates an intimidating, hostile, or offensive work or academic environment or (2) accepting or rejecting such conduct affects or may be perceived to affect employment decisions or academic evaluations concerning the individual. Sexual harassment is unethical.

Sexual relationships between medical supervisors and their medical trainees raise concerns because of inherent inequalities in the status and power that medical supervisors wield in relation to medical trainees and may adversely affect patient care. Sexual relationships between a medical trainee and a supervisor even when consensual are not acceptable regardless of the degree of supervision in any given situation. The supervisory role should be eliminated if the parties involved wish to pursue their relationship. (II, IV, VII)

4.00 OPINIONS ON HOSPITAL RELATIONS

4.01 Admission Fee.

Charging a separate and distinct fee for the incidental, administrative, non-medical service the physician performs in securing the admission of a patient to a hospital is unethical. Physicians should derive their income from medical services rendered, in keeping with the traditions of the American Medical Association. (IV)

4.02 Assessments, Compulsory.

It is improper to condition medical staff membership or privileges on compulsory assessments for any purpose. However, self-imposed assessments by vote of the medical staff are acceptable. (IV)

4.03 Billing for House Staff and Student Services.

When a physician assumes responsibility for the services rendered to a patient by a resident or student, the physician may ethically bill the patient for services which were performed under the physician's direct personal observation, direction and supervision. (II)

4.04 Economic Incentives and Levels of Care.

The primary obligation of the hospital medical staff is to safeguard the quality of care provided within the institution. The medical staff has the responsibility to perform essential functions on behalf of the hospital in accordance with licensing laws and accreditation requirements. Treatment or hospitalization that is willfully excessive or inadequate constitutes unethical practice. The organized medical staff has an obligation to avoid wasteful practices and unnecessary treatment that may cause the hospital needless expense. In a situation where the economic interests of the hospital are in conflict with patient welfare, patient welfare takes priority. (I, II, IV, V, VI)

4.05 Organized Medical Staff.

The organized medical staff performs essential hospital functions even though it may often consist primarily of independent practicing physicians who are not hospital employees. As a practical matter, however, the organized medical staff may enjoy a dual status. In addition to functioning as a division of the hospital, members of the organized medical staff may choose to act as a group for the purpose of communicating and dealing with the governing board and others with respect to matters that concern the interest of the organized medical staff and its members. This is ethical as long as there is no adverse interference with patient care or violation of applicable laws. (IV, VI)

4.06 Physician-Hospital Contractual Relations.

There are various financial or contractual arrangements that physicians and hospitals may enter into and find mutually satisfactory. A physician may, for example, be a hospital employee, a hospital-associated medical specialist, or an independent practitioner with staff privileges. The form of the contractual or financial arrangement between physicians and hospitals depends on the facts and circumstances of each situation. A physician may be employed by a hospital for a fixed annual amount, for a certain amount per hour, or pursuant to other similar arrangements that are related to the professional services, skill, education, expertise, or time involved. (VI)

4.07 Staff Privileges.

The mutual objective of both the governing board and the medical staff is to improve the quality and efficiency of patient care in the hospital. Decisions regarding hospital privileges should be based upon the training, experience, and demonstrated competence of candidates, taking into consideration the availability of facilities and the overall medical needs of the community, the hospital, and especially patients. Privileges should not be based on numbers of patients admitted to the facility or the economic or insurance status of the patient. Personal friendships, antagonisms, jurisdictional disputes, or fear of competition should not play a role in making these decisions. Physicians who are involved in the granting, denying, or termination of hospital privileges have an ethical responsibility to be guided primarily by concern for the welfare and best interests of patients in discharging this responsibility. (IV, VI, VII)

5.00 OPINIONS ON CONFIDENTIALITY, ADVERTISING, AND COMMUNICATIONS MEDIA RELATIONS

5.01 Advertising and Managed Care Organizations.

A physician may provide medical services to members of a prepaid medical care plan or to members of a health maintenance organization which seeks members or subscribers through advertising. Physicians practicing in prepaid plans or managed care organizations are subject to the same ethical principles as are other physicians. Advertising which would lead prospective members or subscribers to believe that the services of a named physician who has a reputation for outstanding skill would be routinely available to all members or subscribers, if in fact this is not so, is deceptive. However, the publication by name of the roster of physicians who provide services to members, the type of practice in which each is engaged, biographical and other relevant information is not a deceptive practice. (II, VI)

5.02 Advertising and Publicity.

There are no restrictions on advertising by physicians except those that can be specifically justified to protect the public from deceptive practices. A physician may publicize himself or herself as a physician through any commercial publicity or other form of public communication (including any newspaper, magazine, telephone directory, radio, television, direct mail, or other advertising) provided that the communication shall not be misleading because of the omission of necessary material information, shall not contain any false or misleading statement, or shall not otherwise operate to deceive.

Because the public can sometimes be deceived by the use of medical terms or illustrations that are difficult to understand, physicians should design the form of communication to communicate the information contained therein to the public in a readily comprehensible manner. Aggressive, high pressure advertising and publicity should be avoided if they create unjustified medical expectations or are accompanied by deceptive claims. The key issue, however, is whether advertising or publicity, regardless of format or content, is true and not materially misleading.

The communication may include: (a) the educational background of the physician; (b) the basis on which fees are determined (including charges for specific services); (c) available credit or other methods of payment; and (d) any other nondeceptive information.

Nothing in this opinion is intended to discourage or to limit advertising and representations which are not false or deceptive within the meaning of Section 5 of the Federal Trade Commission Act. At the same time, however, physicians are advised that certain types of communications have a significant potential for deception and should therefore receive special attention. For example, testimonials of patients as to the physician's skill or the quality of the physician's professional services tend to be deceptive when they do not reflect the results that patients with conditions comparable to the testimoniant's condition generally receive.

Objective claims regarding experience, competence and the quality of the physicians and the services they provide may be made only if they are factually supportable. Similarly, generalized statements of satisfaction with a physician's services may be made if they are representative of the experiences of that physician's patients.

Because physicians have an ethical obligation to share medical advances, it is unlikely that a physician will have a truly exclusive or unique skill or remedy. Claims that imply such a skill or remedy therefore can be deceptive. Statements that a physician has an exclusive or unique skill or remedy in a particular geographic area, if true, however, are permissible. Similarly, a statement that a physician has cured or successfully treated a large number of cases involving a particular serious ailment is deceptive if it implies a certainty of result and creates unjustified and misleading expectations in prospective patients.

Consistent with federal regulatory standards which apply to commercial advertising, a physician who is considering the placement of an advertisement or publicity release, whether in print, radio or television, should determine in advance that the communication or message is explicitly and implicitly truthful and not misleading. These standards require the advertiser to have a reasonable basis for claims before they are used in advertising. The reasonable basis must be established by those facts known to the advertiser, and those which a reasonable, prudent advertiser should have discovered. Inclusion of the physician's name in advertising may help to assure that these guidelines are being met. (II)

5.025 Physician Advisory or Referral Services by Telecommunications.

Telecommunication advisory services, by way of phone, fax, or computer, distinct from an existing patient-physician relationship can be a helpful source of medical information for the public. Often, people are not sure where to turn for information of a general medical nature or do not have easy access to other sources of information. Individuals also may be embarrassed about directly bringing up certain questions with their physicians. Although telecommunication advisory services can only provide limited medical services, they can be a useful complement to more comprehensive services, if used properly.

Any telecommunication advisory service should employ certain safeguards to prevent misuse. For example, the physician responding to the call should not make a clinical diagnosis. Diagnosis by telecommunication is done without the benefit of a physician examination or even a face-to-face meeting with the caller. Critical medical data may be unavailable to the physician. Physicians who respond to callers should therefore act within the limitations of telecommunication services and ensure that callers understand the limitations of the services. Under no circumstances should medications be prescribed.

Physicians who respond to the calls should elicit all necessary information from the callers. When callers are charged by the minute, they may try to hurry their calls to limit their costs. As a result, important information may not be disclosed to the physician. Physicians should also ensure that callers do not incur large bills inadvertently or without understanding the billing system.

Physician referral services can also offer important information to the public. Referral services are often provided by medical societies, hospitals and for-profit entities. To ensure that the service bases its recommendation on medically legitimate considerations rather than the likelihood of being paid by the physician, when the service charges physicians a fee to participate, physicians should not pay the service per referral. Also, callers should be told how the list is created. For example, callers should be informed whether the list includes physicians who pay a flat fee to be listed, members of a particular hospital staff or medical society, or physicians who meet some general quality-based criteria.

While these safeguards are described as applying primarily to telephone services, they should be considered equally applicable to any other communication media, such as radio, or television, in which the physician and patient do not meet face-to-face. (I, IV, VI)

[**5.03** Deleted.]

5.04 Communications Media: Standards of Professional Responsibility.

Physicians are ethically and legally required to protect the personal privacy and other legal rights of patients. When information concerning a specific patient is requested by the media, the physician must obtain the consent of the patient or an authorized representative before releasing such information. The physician may release only the authorized information or that which is public knowledge. The physician-patient relationship and its confidential nature must be maintained.

With these considerations in mind, the physician may assist the representatives of the media in every way possible. When the patient or authorized representative consents to the release of information, physicians should cooperate with the press to insure that medical news is available more promptly and more accurately than would be possible without their assistance. Inasmuch as a diagnosis may be made only by a physician and may depend upon X-ray and laboratory studies, no statement regarding diagnosis should be made except by or on behalf of the attending physician. For the same reason, prognosis will be given only by the attending physician or at the attending physician's direction.

Statements regarding the circumstances surrounding shootings, knifings, and poisonings are properly police matters, and questions whether they were accidental should be referred to the appropriate authorities.

Certain news that is part of the public record, such as deaths, may be made available without the consent of the patient or authorized representative. (IV)

5.05 Confidentiality.

The information disclosed to a physician during the course of the relationship between physician and patient is confidential to the greatest possible degree. The patient should feel free to make a full disclosure of information to the physician in order that the physician may most effectively provide needed services. The patient should be able to make this disclosure with the knowledge that the physician will respect the confidential nature of the communication. The physician should not reveal confidential communications or information without the express consent of the patient, unless required to do so by law.

The obligation to safeguard patient confidences is subject to certain exceptions which are ethically and legally justified because of overriding social considerations.

Where a patient threatens to inflict serious bodily harm to another person or to him or herself and there is a reasonable probability that the patient may carry out the threat, the physician should take reasonable precautions for the protection of the intended victim, including notification of law enforcement authorities. Also, communicable diseases, gunshot and knife wounds should be reported as required by applicable statutes or ordinances. (IV)

5.055 Confidential Care for Minors.

Physicians who treat minors have an ethical duty to promote the autonomy of minor patients by involving them in the medical decision-making process to a degree commensurate with their abilities.

When minors request confidential services, physicians should encourage them to involve their parents. This includes making efforts to obtain the minor's reasons for not involving their parents and correcting misconceptions that may be motivating their objections.

Where the law does not require otherwise, physicians should permit a competent minor to consent to medical care and should not notify parents without the patient's consent. Depending on the seriousness of the decision, competence may be evaluated by physicians for most minors. When necessary, experts in adolescent medicine or child psychological development should be consulted. Use of the courts for competence determinations should be made only as a last resort.

When an immature minor requests contraceptive services, pregnancy-related care (including pregnancy testing, prenatal and postnatal care, and delivery services), or treatment for sexually transmitted disease, drug and alcohol abuse, or mental illness, physicians must recognize that requiring parental involvement may be counterproductive to the health of the patient. Physicians should encourage parental involvement in these situations. However, if the minor continues to object, his or her wishes ordinarily should be respected. If the physician is uncomfortable with providing services without parental involvement, and alternative confidential services are available, the minor may be referred to those services. In cases when the physician believes that without parental involvement and guidance, the minor will face a serious health threat, and there is reason to believe that the parents will be helpful and understanding, disclosing the problem to the parents is ethically justified. When the physician does breach confidentiality to the parents, he or she must discuss the reasons for the breach with the minor prior to the disclosure.

For minors who are mature enough to be unaccompanied by their parents for their examination, confidentiality of information disclosed during an exam, interview, or in counseling should be maintained. Such information may be disclosed to parents when the patient consents to disclosure. Confidentiality may be justifiably breached in situations for which confidentiality for adults may be breached, according to Opinion 5.05. In addition, confidentiality for immature minors may be ethically breached when necessary to enable the parent(s) to make an informed decision about treatment for the minor or when such a breach is necessary to avert serious harm to the minor. (IV)

5.057 Confidentiality of HIV Status on Autopsy Reports.

Physicians should maintain the confidentiality of HIV status on autopsy reports to the greatest extent possible.

Physicians who perform autopsies or who have access to autopsy information regarding a patient's HIV status should be familiar with state law governing (1) the reporting of HIV and AIDS to public health authorities; (2) obligations to inform third parties who may be at risk for HIV infection through contact with an HIV-infected decedent; (3) other parties to whom reporting may be required (e.g., funeral directors, health care personnel involved in the care of the patient); and (4) the extent of confidentiality of autopsy records.

HIV status which appears on autopsy records performed under the authority of a hospital are part of the decedent's medical record and should be held confidential. The physician should comply with state laws regarding disclosure to public health authorities and at-risk third parties, and, where such laws are absent, fulfill ethical obligations to notify endangered third parties (e.g., identified sexual or needle-sharing partners). This includes reporting to organ or tissue procurement agencies if any parts of the decedent's body were taken for use in transplantation.

HIV status which appears on autopsy records performed by a medical examiner in the case of suspicious, accidental, on unexplained death should be kept confidential where autopsy records are not accessible to the public. The physician should comply with state laws regarding disclosure to public health authorities and at-risk third parties, and, where such laws are absent, fulfill ethical obligations to notify endangered third parties (e.g., sexual and needle-sharing partners). This includes reporting to organ or tissue procurement agencies if any parts of the decedent's body were taken for use in transplantation.

In cases where autopsies are done under the auspices of the medical examiner's office and state law mandates that the autopsy information be accessible to the public, then physicians should comply with state law. However, in these instances, HIV status should only be recorded when the HIV status of the decedent would be relevant to determining the patient's cause of death. In addition, although a patient's HIV status may be learned from public records in some jurisdictions, it is still unethical for a physician to make a public disclosure of an individual patient's HIV status independent of the legal requirements governing the filing or processing of autopsy records. The physician should comply with state laws regarding disclosure to public health authorities and at-risk third parties, and, where such laws are absent, fulfill ethical obligations to notify endangered third parties (e.g., sexual and needle-sharing partners). This includes reporting to organ or tissue procurement agencies if any parts of the decedent's body were taken for use in transplantation. (IV)

5.06 Confidentiality: Physician-Attorney Relation.

The patient's history, diagnosis, treatment, and prognosis may be discussed with the patient's attorney with the consent of the patient or the patient's lawful representative.

A physician may testify in court or before a worker's compensation board or the like in any personal injury or related case. (IV)

5.07 Confidentiality: Computers.

The utmost effort and care must be taken to protect the confidentiality of all medical records, including computerized medical records.

The guidelines below are offered to assist physicians and computer service organizations in maintaining the confidentiality of information in medical records when that information is stored in computerized data bases:

(1) Confidential medical information should be entered into the computer-based patient record only by authorized personnel. Additions to the record should be time and date stamped, and the person making the additions should be identified in the record.

(2) The patient and physician should be advised about the existence of computerized data bases in which medical information concerning the patient is stored. Such information should be communicated to the physician and patient prior to the physician's release of the medical information to the entity or entities maintaining the computer data bases. All individuals and organizations with some form of access to the computerized data bases, and the level of access permitted, should be specifically identified in advance. Full disclosure of this information to the patient is necessary in obtaining informed consent to treatment. Patient data should be assigned a security level appropriate for the data's degree of sensitivity, which should be used to control who has access to the information.

(3) The physician and patient should be notified of the distribution of all reports reflecting identifiable patient data prior to distribution of the reports by the computer facility. There should be approval by the patient and notification of the physician prior to the release of patient-identifiable clinical and administrative data to individuals or organizations external to the medical care environment. Such information should not be released without the express permission of the patient.

(4) The dissemination of confidential medical data should be limited to only those individuals or agencies with a bona fide use for the data. Only the data necessary for the bona fide use should be released. Patient identifiers should be omitted when appropriate. Release of confidential medical information from the data base should be confined to the specific purpose for which the information is requested and limited to the specific time frame requested. All such organizations or individuals should be advised that authorized release of data to them does not authorize their further release of the data to additional individuals or organizations, or subsequent use of the data for other purposes.

(5) Procedures for adding to or changing data on the computerized data base should indicate individuals authorized to make changes, time periods in which changes take place, and those individuals who will be informed about changes in the data from the medical records.

(6) Procedures for purging the computerized data base of archaic or inaccurate data should be established and the patient and physician should be notified before and after the data has been purged. There should be no mixing of a physician's computerized patient records with those of other computer service bureau clients. In addition, procedures should be developed to protect against inadvertent mixing of individual reports or segments thereof.

(7) The computerized medical data base should be on-line to the computer terminal only when authorized computer programs requiring the medical data are being used. Individuals and organizations external to the clinical facility should not be provided on-line access to a computerized data base containing identifiable data from medical records concerning patients. Access to the computerized data base should be controlled through security measures such as passwords, encryption (encoding) of information, and scannable badges or other user identification.

(8) Back-up systems and other mechanisms should be in place to prevent data loss and downtime as a result of hardware or software failure.

(9) Security:
  (a) Stringent security procedures should be in place to prevent unauthorized access to computer-based patient records. Personnel audit proce-

dures should be developed to establish a record in the event of unauthorized disclosure of medical data. Terminated or former employees in the data processing environment should have no access to data from the medical records concerning patients.

(b) Upon termination of computer services for a physician, those computer files maintained for the physician should be physically turned over to the physician. They may be destroyed (erased) only if it is established that the physician has another copy (in some form). In the event of file erasure, the computer service bureau should verify in writing to the physician that the erasure has taken place. (IV)

5.075 Confidentiality: Disclosure of Records to Data Collection Companies.

Data-collection from computerized or other patient records for marketing purposes raises serious ethical concerns. In some cases, firms have sought to amass information on physicians' prescribing practices on behalf of pharmaceutical houses for marketing purposes. Often, physicians are offered incentives such as computer hardware and software packages in return for agreeing to such an arrangement. They may be told that data-collecting software does not capture patients' names.

These arrangements may violate principles of informed consent and patient confidentiality. Patients divulge information to their physicians only for purposes of diagnosis and treatment. If other uses are to be made of the information, patients must give their permission after being fully informed about the purpose of such disclosures. If permission is not obtained, physicians violate patient confidentiality by sharing specific and intimate information from patients' records with commercial interests.

Arrangements of this kind may also violate Opinion 8.061 on gifts to physicians from industry.

Finally, these arrangements may harm the integrity of the patient-physician relationship. The trust that is fundamental to this relationship is based on the principle that the physicians are the agents first and foremost of their patients. (I, II, IV)

5.08 Confidentiality: Insurance Company Representative.

History, diagnosis, prognosis, and the like acquired during the patient-physician relationship may be disclosed to an insurance company representative only if the patient or a lawful representative has consented to the disclosure. A physician's responsibilities to patients are not limited to the actual practice of medicine. They also include the performance of some services ancillary to the practice of medicine. These services might include certification that the patient was under the physician's care and comment on the diagnosis and therapy in the particular case. See also Opinion 2.135. (IV)

5.09 Confidentiality: Physicians in Industry.

Where a physician's services are limited to pre-employment physical examinations or examinations to determine if an employee who has been ill or injured is able to return to work, no patient-physician relationship should be considered to exist between the physician and those individuals. However, a physician is obligated to divulge important health information to the patient which the physician discovers as a result of the examination. Nevertheless, the information obtained by the physician as a result of such examinations is confidential and should not be communicated to a third party without the individual's prior written consent, unless it is required by law. If the individual authorized the release of medical information to an employer or a potential employer, the physician should release only that information which is reasonably relevant to the employer's decision regarding that individual's ability to perform the work required by the job.

A physician-patient relationship does exist when a physician renders treatment to an employee, even though the physician is paid by the employer. If the employee's illness or injury is work-related, the release of medical information to the employer as to the treatment provided may be subject to the provisions of worker's compensation laws. The physician must comply with the requirements of such laws, if applicable. However, the physician may not otherwise discuss the employee's health condition with the employer without the employee's consent or, in the event of the employee's incapacity, the family's consent.

Whenever statistical information about employees' health is released, all employee identities should be deleted. (IV)

6.00 OPINIONS ON FEES AND CHARGES

6.01 Contingent Physician Fees.

If a physician's fee for medical service is contingent on the successful outcome of a claim, such as a malpractice or worker's compensation claim, there is the ever-present danger that the physician may become less of a healer and more of an advocate or partisan in the proceedings. Accordingly, a physician's fee for medical services should be based on the value of the service provided by the physician to the patient and not on the uncertain outcome of a contingency that does not in any way relate to the value of the medical service.

A physician's fee should not be made contingent on the successful outcome of medical treatment. Such arrangements are unethical because they imply that successful outcomes from treatment are guaranteed, thus creating unrealistic expectations of medicine and false promises to consumers. (VI)

6.02 Fee Splitting.

Payment by or to a physician solely for the referral of a patient is fee splitting and is unethical.

A physician may not accept payment of any kind, in any form, from any source, such as a pharmaceutical company or pharmacist, an optical company or the manufacturer of medical appliances and devices, for prescribing or referring a patient to said source.

In each case, the payment violates the requirement to deal honestly with patients and colleagues. The patient relies upon the advice of the physician on matters of referral. All referrals and prescriptions must be based on the skill and quality of the physician to whom the patient has been referred or the quality and efficacy of the drug or product prescribed. (II)

6.03 Fee Splitting: Referrals to Health Care Facilities.

Clinics, laboratories, hospitals, or other health care facilities that compensate physicians for referral of patients are engaged in fee splitting which is unethical.

Health care facilities should not compensate a physician who refers patients there for the physician's cognitive services in prescribing, monitoring, or revising the patient's course of treatment. Payment for these cognitive services is acceptable when it comes from patients, who are the beneficiaries of the physician's services, or from the patient's designated third-party payer.

Offering or accepting payment for referring patients to research studies (finder's fees) is also unethical. (II)

6.04 Fee Splitting: Drug or Device Prescription Rebates.

A physician may not accept any kind of payment or compensation from a drug company or device manufacturer for prescribing its products. The physician should keep the following considerations in mind:

(1) A physician should only prescribe a drug or device based on reasonable expectations of the effectiveness of the drug or device for the particular patient.

(2) The quantity of the drug prescribed should be no greater than that which is reasonably required for the patient's condition. (II)

6.05 Fees for Medical Services.

A physician should not charge or collect an illegal or excessive fee. For example, an illegal fee occurs when a physician accepts an assignment as full payment for services rendered to a Medicare patient and then bills the patient for an additional amount. A fee is excessive when after a review of the facts a person knowledgeable as to current charges made by physicians would be left with a definite and firm conviction that the fee is in excess of a reasonable fee. Factors to be considered as guides in determining the reasonableness of a fee include the following:

(1) the difficulty and/or uniqueness of the services performed and the time, skill, and experience required;
(2) the fee customarily charged in the locality for similar physician services;
(3) the amount of the charges involved;
(4) the quality of performance;
(5) the experience, reputation, and ability of the physician in performing the kind of services involved. (II)

[**6.06** Deleted.]

6.07 Insurance Form Completion Charges.

The attending physician should complete without charge the appropriate "simplified" insurance claim form as a part of service to the patient to enable the patient to receive his or her benefits. A charge for more complex or multiple forms may be made in conformity with local custom. (II)

6.08 Interest Charges and Finance Charges.

Although harsh or commercial collection practices are discouraged in the practice of medicine, a physician who has experienced problems with delinquent accounts may properly choose to request that payment be made at the time of treatment or add interest or other reasonable charges to delinquent accounts. The patient must be notified in advance of the interest or other reasonable finance or service charges by such means as the posting of a notice in the physician's waiting room, the distribution of leaflets describing the office billing practices and appropriate notations on the billing statement. The physician must comply with state and federal laws and regulations applicable to the imposition of such charges. Physicians are encouraged to review their accounting/collection policies to ensure that no patient's account is sent to collection without the physician's knowledge. Physicians who choose to add an interest or finance charge to accounts not paid within a reasonable time are encouraged to use compassion and discretion in hardship cases. (II)

6.09 Laboratory Bill.

When it is not possible for the laboratory bill to be sent directly to the patient, the referring physician's bill to the patient should indicate the actual charges for laboratory services, including the name of the laboratory, as well as any separate charges for the physician's own professional services. (II)

6.10 Services Provided by Multiple Physicians.

Each physician engaged in the care of the patient is entitled to compensation commensurate with the value of the service he or she has personally rendered. No physician should bill or be paid for a service which is not performed; mere referral does not constitute a professional service for which a professional charge should be made or for which a fee may be ethically paid or received.

When services are provided by more than one physician, each physician should submit his or her own bill to the patient and be compensated separately, if possible. A physician should not charge a markup, commission, or profit on the services rendered by others.

It is ethically permissible in certain circumstances, however, for a surgeon to engage other physicians to assist in the performance of a surgical procedure and to pay a reasonable amount for such assistance, provided the nature of the financial arrangement is made known to the patient. This principle applies whether or not the assisting physician is the referring physician. (II)

6.11 Competition.

Competition between and among physicians and other health care practitioners on the basis of competitive factors such as quality of services, skill, experience, miscellaneous conveniences offered to patients, credit terms, fees charged, etc., is not only ethical but is encouraged. Ethical medical practice thrives best under free market conditions when prospective patients have adequate information and opportunity to choose freely between and among competing physicians and alternate systems of medical care. (VII)

6.12 Forgiveness or Waiver of Insurance Copayments.

Under the terms of many health insurance policies or programs, patients are made more conscious of the cost of their medical care through copayments. By imposing copayments for office visits and other medical services, insurers hope to discourage unnecessary health care. In some cases, financial hardship may deter patients from seeking necessary care if they would be responsible for a copayment for the care. Physicians commonly forgive or waive copayments to facilitate patient access to needed medical care. When a copayment is a barrier to needed care because of financial hardship, physicians should forgive or waive the copayment. A number of clinics have advertised their willingness to provide detailed medical evaluations and accept the insurer's payment but waive the copayment for all patients. Cases have been reported in which some of these clinics have conducted excessive and unnecessary medical testing while certifying to insurers that the testing is medically necessary. Such fraudulent activity exacerbates the high cost of health care, violates Opinion 2.19 and is unethical.

Physicians should be aware that forgiveness or waiver of copayments may violate the policies of some insurers, both public and private; other insurers may permit forgiveness or waiver if they are aware of the reasons for the forgiveness or waiver. Routine forgiveness or waiver of copayments may constitute fraud under state and federal law. Physicians should ensure that their policies on copayments are consistent with applicable law and with the requirements of their agreements with insurers. (II)

6.13 Professional Courtesy.

Professional courtesy refers to the provision of medical care to physician colleagues or their families free of charge or at a reduced rate. While professional courtesy is a long-standing tradition in the medical profession, it is not an ethical requirement. Physicians should use their own judgment in deciding whether to waive or reduce their fees when treating fellow physicians or their families. Physicians should be aware that accepting insurance payments while waiving patient copayments may violate Opinion 6.12. (II, IV)

7.00 OPINIONS ON PHYSICIAN RECORDS

7.01 Records of Physicians: Availability of Information to Other Physicians.

The interest of the patient is paramount in the practice of medicine, and everything that can reasonably and lawfully be done to serve that interest must be done by all physicians who have served or are serving the patient. A physician who formerly treated a patient should not refuse for any reason to make records of that patient promptly available on request to another physician presently treating the patient. Proper authorization for the use of records must be granted by the patient. Medical reports should not be withheld because of an unpaid bill for medical services. (IV)

7.02 Records of Physicians: Information and Patients.

Notes made in treating a patient are primarily for the physician's own use and constitute his or her personal property. However, on request of the patient a physician should provide a copy or a summary of the record to the patient or to another physician, an attorney, or other person designated by the patient.

Most states have enacted statutes that authorize patient access to medical records. These statutes vary in scope and mechanism for permitting patients to review or copy medical records. Access to mental health records, particularly, may be limited by statute or regulation. A physician should become familiar with the applicable laws, rules, or regulations on patient access to medical records.

The record is a confidential document involving the patient-physician relationship and should not be communicated to a third party without the patient's prior written consent, unless required by law or to protect the welfare of the individual or the community. Medical reports should not be withheld because of an unpaid bill for medical services. Physicians may charge a reasonable fee for copying medical records. (IV)

7.03 Records of Physicians upon Retirement or Departure from a Group.

A patient's records may be necessary to the patient in the future not only for medical care but also for employment, insurance, litigation, or other reasons. When a physician retires or dies, patients should be notified and urged to find a new physician and should be informed that upon authorization, records will be sent to the new physician. Records which may be of value to a patient and which are not forwarded to a new physician should be retained, either by the treating physician, another physician, or such other person lawfully permitted to act as a custodian of the records.

The patients of a physician who leaves a group practice must be notified that the physician is leaving the group. Patients of the physician must also be notified of the physician's new address and offered the opportunity to have their medical records forwarded to the departing physician at his or her new practice. It is unethical to withhold such information upon request of a patient. If the responsibility for notifying patients falls to the departing physician rather than to the group, the group should not interfere with the discharge of these duties by withholding patient lists or other necessary information. (IV)

7.04 Sale of a Medical Practice.

A physician or the estate of a deceased physician may sell to another physician the elements which comprise his or her practice, such as furniture, fixtures, equipment, office leasehold, and goodwill. In the sale of a medical practice, the purchaser is buying not only furniture and fixtures, but also goodwill, i.e., the opportunity to take over the patients of the seller.

The transfer of records of patients is subject, however, to the following:

(1) All active patients should be notified that the physician (or the estate) is transferring the practice to another physician who will retain custody of their records and that at their written request, within a reasonable time as specified in the notice, the records or copies will be sent to any other physician of their choice. Rather than destroy the records of a deceased physician, it is better that they be transferred to a practicing physician who will retain them subject to requests from patients that they be sent to another physician.

(2) A reasonable charge may be made for the cost of duplicating records. (IV)

7.05 Retention of Medical Records.

Physicians have an obligation to retain patient records which may reasonably be of value to a patient. The following guidelines are offered to assist physicians in meeting their ethical and legal obligations:

(1) Medical considerations are the primary basis for deciding how long to retain medical records. For example, operative notes and chemotherapy records should always be part of the patient's chart. In deciding whether to keep certain parts of the record, an appropriate criterion is whether a physician would want the information if he or she were seeing the patient for the first time.

(2) If a particular record no longer needs to be kept for medical reasons, the physician should check state laws to see if there is a requirement that records be kept for a minimum length of time. Most states will not have such a provision. If they do, it will be part of the statutory code or state licensing board.

(3) In all cases, medical records should be kept for at least as long as the length of time of the statute of limitations for medical malpractice claims. The statute of limitations may be three or more years, depending on the state law. State medical associations and insurance carriers are the best resources for this information.

(4) Whatever the statute of limitations, a physician should measure time from the last professional contact with the patient.

(5) If a patient is a minor, the statute of limitations for medical malpractice claims may not apply until the patient reaches the age of majority.

(6) Immunization records always must be kept.

(7) The records of any patient covered by Medicare or Medicaid must be kept at least five years.

(8) In order to preserve confidentiality when discarding old records, all documents should be destroyed.

(9) Before discarding old records, patients should be given an opportunity to claim the records or have them sent to another physician, if it is feasible to give them the opportunity.

8.00 OPINIONS ON PRACTICE MATTERS

8.01 Appointment Charges.

A physician may charge a patient for a missed appointment or for one not canceled 24 hours in advance if the patient is fully advised that the physician will make such a charge. (VI)

8.02 Ethical Guidelines for Physicians in Management Positions and Other Non-Clinical Roles.

Physicians in administrative and other nonclinical roles must put the needs of patients first. At least since the time of Hippocrates, physicians have cultivated the trust of their patients by placing patient welfare before all other concerns. The ethical obligations of physicians are not suspended when a physician assumes a position that does not directly involve patient care. (I, VII)

8.03 Conflicts of Interest: Guidelines.

Under no circumstances may physicians place their own financial interests above the welfare of their patients. The primary objective of the medical profession is to render service to humanity; reward or financial gain is a subordinate consideration. For a physician unnecessarily to hospitalize a patient, prescribe a drug, or conduct diagnostic tests for the physician's financial benefit is unethical. If a conflict develops between the physician's financial interest and the physician's responsibilities to the patient, the conflict must be resolved to the patient's benefit. (II)

8.031 Conflicts of Interest: Biomedical Research.

Avoidance of real or perceived conflicts of interest in clinical research is imperative if the medical community is to ensure objectivity and maintain individual and institutional integrity. All medical centers should develop specific guidelines for their clinical staff on conflicts of interest. These guidelines should include the following rules: (1) once a clinical investigator becomes involved in a research project for a company or knows that he or she might become involved, she or he, as an individual cannot ethically buy or sell the company's stock until the involvement ends and the results of the research are published or otherwise disseminated to the public; (2) any remuneration received by the researcher from the company whose product is being studied must be commensurate with the efforts of the researcher on behalf of the company; (3) clinical investigators should disclose any material ties to companies whose products they are investigating. They should disclose their financial ties, participation in educational activities supported by the companies, participation in other research projects funded by the companies, consulting arrangements, and any other ties. The disclosures should be made in writing to the medical center where the research is conducted, organizations that are funding the research, and journals that publish the results of the research.

In addition, medical centers should form review committees to examine disclosures by clinical staff about financial associations with commercial corporations. (II, IV)

8.032 Conflicts of Interest: Health Facility Ownership by a Physician.

Physician ownership interests in commercial ventures can provide important benefits in patient care. Physicians are free to enter lawful contractual relationships, including the acquisition of ownership interests in health facilities, products, or equipment. However, when physicians refer patients to facilities in which they have an ownership interest, a potential conflict of interest exists. In general, physicians should not refer patients to a health care facility which is outside their office practice and at which they do not directly provide care or services when they have an investment interest in that facility. The requirement that the physician *directly* provide the care or services should be interpreted as commonly understood. The physician needs to have personal involvement with the provision of care on site.

There may be situations in which a needed facility would not be built if referring physicians were prohibited from investing in the facility. Physicians may invest in and refer to an outside facility, whether or not they provide direct care or services at the facility, if there is a demonstrated need in the community for the facility and alternative financing is not available. Need might exist when there is no facility of reasonable quality in the community or when use of existing facilities is onerous for patients. Self-referral based on demonstrated need cannot be justified simply if the facility would offer some marginal improvement over the quality of services in the community. The potential benefits of the facility should be substantial. The use of existing facilities may be considered onerous when patients face undue delays in receiving services, delays that compromise the patient's care or affect the curability or reversibility of the patient's condition. The requirement that alternative financing not be available carries a burden of proof. The builder would have to undertake efforts to secure funding from banks, other financial institutions, and venture capitalists before turning to self-referring physicians.

Where there is a true demonstrated need in the community for the facility, the following requirements should also be met: (1) physicians should disclose their investment interest to their patients when making a referral, provide a list of effective alternative facilities if they are available, inform their patients that they have free choice to obtain the medical services elsewhere, and assure their patients that they will not be treated differently if they do not choose the physician-owned facility; (2) individuals not in a position to refer patients to the facility should be given a bona fide opportunity to invest in the facility on the same terms that are offered to referring physicians; (3) the opportunity to invest and the terms of investment should not be related to the past or expected volume of referrals or other business generated by the physician investor or owner; (4) there should be no requirement that a physician investor make referrals to the entity or otherwise generate business as a condition for remaining an investor; (5) the return on the physician's investment should be tied to the physician's equity in the facility rather than to the volume of referrals; (6) the entity should not loan funds or guarantee a loan for physicians in a position to refer to the entity; (7) investment contracts should not include 'noncompetition clauses' that prevent physicians from investing in other facilities; (8) the physician's ownership interest should be disclosed to third party payers upon request; (9) an internal utilization review program should be established to ensure that investing physicians do not exploit their patients in any way, as by inappropriate or unnecessary utilization; (10) when a physician's commercial interest conflicts to the detriment of the patient, the physician should make alternative arrangements for the care of the patient. (II, III, IV)

8.035 Conflicts of Interest in Home Health Care.

Physicians who refer patients to home care providers or any other outside facility should avoid possible conflicts of interest by not accepting payment from those providers or facilities for referrals or as compensation for their cognitive services in prescribing, monitoring, or revising a patient's course of treatment. Payment for these cognitive services is acceptable when it comes from patients, who are the beneficiaries of the physician's services, or from the patients' designated third-party payers.

In accordance with Opinion 8.032, physicians may refer patients to home care facilities in which they have an ownership interest if they actively participate on-site in the care provided to patients. Since the appropriate frequency and duration of home visits is a medical decision that should be made on a case-by-case basis, there is no specific minimum number of home visits that may be identified as a conclusive test of the physician's involvement in the patient's home care regimen. Although different patients will have different needs, physicians who directly provide care in the patient's home on at least every fourth visit may presumptively be considered to have made home care a true extension of practice. (II, III, IV)

8.04 Consultation.

Physicians should obtain consultation whenever they believe that it would be medically indicated in the care of the patient or when requested by the patient or the patient's representative. When a patient is referred to a consultant, the referring physician should provide a history of the case and such other information as the consultant may need, calling to the attention of the consultant any specific questions about which guidance is sought, and the consultant should advise the referring physician of the results of the consultant's examination and recommendations. (V)

8.041 Second Opinions.

Physicians should recommend that a patient obtain a second opinion whenever they believe it would be helpful in the care of the patient. When recommending a second opinion, physicians should explain the reasons for the recommendation and inform their patients that patients are free to choose a second-opinion physician on their own or with the assistance of the first physician. Patients are also free to obtain second opinions on their own initiative, with or without their physician's knowledge.

With the patient's consent, the first physician should provide a history of the case and such other information as the second-opinion physician may need, including the recommendations about management. The second-opinion physician should maintain the confidentiality of the evaluation and should report to the first physician if the consent of the patient has been obtained.

After evaluating the patient, a second-opinion physician should provide the patient with a clear understanding of the opinion, whether or not it agrees with the recommendations of the first physician.

When a patient initiates a second opinion, it is inappropriate for the primary physician to terminate the patient-physician relationship solely because of the patient's decision to obtain a second opinion.

In some cases, patients may ask the second-opinion physician to provide the needed medical care. In general, second-opinion physicians are free to assume responsibility for the care of the patient. It is not unethical to enter into a patient-physician relationship with a patient who has been receiving care from another physician. By accepting second-opinion patients for treatment, physicians affirm the right of patients to have free choice in the selection of their physicians.

There are situations in which physicians may choose not to treat patients for whom they provide second opinions. Physicians may decide not to treat the patient in order to avoid any perceived conflict of interest or loss of objectivity in rendering the requested second opinion. However, the concern about conflicts of interest does not require physicians to decline to treat second-opinion patients. This inherent conflict in the practice of medicine is resolved by the responsible exercise of professional judgment.

Physicians may agree not to treat second-opinion patients as part of their arrangements with insurers or other third-party payers. Physicians who enter into such contractual agreements must honor their commitments.

Physicians must decide independently of their colleagues whether to treat second-opinion patients. Physicians may not establish an agreement or understanding among themselves that they will refuse to treat each others' patients when asked to provide a second opinion. Such agreements compromise the ability of patients to receive care from the physicians of their choice and are therefore not only unethical but also unlawful. (IV, V)

8.05 Contractual Relationships.

The contractual relationships that physicians assume when they join or affiliate with group practices or agree to provide services to the patients of an insurance plan are varied.

Income arrangements may include hourly wages for physicians working part time, annual salaries for those working full time, and share of group income for physicians who are partners in groups that are somewhat autonomous and contract with plans to provide the required medical care. Arrangements also usually include a range of fringe benefits, such as paid vacations, insurance, and pension plans.

Physicians may work directly for plans or may be employed by the medical group or the hospital that has contracted with the plan to provide services. In the operation of such plans, physicians should not be subjected to lay interference in professional medical matters and their primary responsibility should be to the patients they serve. (VI)

8.051 Conflict of Interest Under Capitation.

The application of capitation to physicians' practices can result in the provision of cost-effective, quality medical care. It is important to note, however, that the potential for conflict exists under such systems. Managed care organizations and the physicians who contract with them should attempt to minimize these conflicts and to ensure that capitation is applied in a manner consistent with the interests of patients.

(1) Physicians have an obligation to evaluate a health plan's capitation payments prior to contracting with that plan to ensure that the quality of patient care is not threatened by inadequate rates of capitation. Capitation payments should be calculated primarily on relevant medical factors, available outcomes data, the costs associated with involved providers, and consensus-oriented standards of necessary care. Furthermore, the predictable costs resulting from existing conditions of enrolled patients should be considered when determining the rate of capitation. Different populations of patients have different medical needs and the costs associated with those needs should be reflected in the per member per month payment. Physicians should seek agreements with plans that provide sufficient financial resources for all necessary care and should refuse to sign agreements that fail in this regard.

(2) Physicians must not assume inordinate levels of financial risk and should therefore consider a number of factors when deciding whether or not to sign a provider agreement. The size of the plan and the time period over which the rate is figured should be considered by physicians evaluating a plan as well as in determinations of the per member per month payment. The capitation rate for large plans can be calculated more accurately than for smaller plans because of the mitigating influence of probability and the behavior of large systems. Similarly, length of time will influence the predictability of patient expenditures and should be considered accordingly. Capitation rates calculated for large plans over an extended period of time are able to be more accurate and are therefore preferable to those calculated for small groups over a short time period.

(3) Stop-loss plans should be in effect to prevent the potential of catastrophic expenses from influencing physician behavior. Physicians should attempt to ensure that such arrangements are finalized prior to signing an agreement to provide services in a health plan.

(4) Physicians must be prepared to discuss with patients any financial arrangements which could impact patient care. Physicians should avoid reimbursement systems that cannot be disclosed to patients without negatively affecting the patient-physician relationship. (I, II)

8.052 Negotiating Discounts for Specialty Care.

Patients are entitled to all the benefits outlined in their insurance plan. Therefore, it is unethical for a referring physician to restrict the referral options of patients who have chosen a plan that provides for access to an unlimited or broad selection of specialist physicians. It is also unethical to base the referral of these patients on a discount for the capitated patients in a primary care physician's practice. (I,II)

8.06 Drugs and Devices: Prescribing.

(1) A physician should not be influenced in the prescribing of drugs, devices, or appliances by a direct or indirect financial interest in a pharmaceutical firm or other supplier. Whether the firm is a manufacturer, distributor, wholesaler, or repackager of the products involved is immaterial.

(2) A physician may own or operate a pharmacy but generally may not refer his or her patients to the pharmacy. However, a physician may refer patients to his or her pharmacy if there is a demonstrated need for the pharmacy in the community and alternative financing is unavailable (as defined in Opinion 8.032). Physicians may dispense drugs within their office practices provided there is no resulting exploitation of patients.

(3) A physician should not give patients prescriptions in code or enter into agreements with pharmacies or other suppliers regarding the filling of prescriptions by code.

(4) Patients are entitled to the same freedom of choice in selecting who will fill their prescription needs as they are in the choice of a physician. (See 9.06 and 8.03.) The prescription is a written direction for a therapeutic or corrective agent. A patient is entitled to a copy of the physician's prescription for drugs, eyeglasses, contact lenses, or other devices as required by the Principles of Medical Ethics and as required by law. The patient has the right to have the prescription filled wherever the patient wishes.

(5) Patients have an ethically and legally recognized right to prompt access to the information contained in their individual medical records. The prescription is an essential part of the patient's medical record. Physicians should not discourage patients from requesting a written prescription or urge them to fill prescriptions from an establishment which has a direct telephone line or which has entered into a business or other preferential arrangement with the physician with respect to the filling of the physician's prescriptions. (I, II, III, IV, V)

8.061 Gifts to Physicians from Industry.

Many gifts given to physicians by companies in the pharmaceutical, device, and medical equipment industries serve an important and socially beneficial function. For example, companies have long provided funds for educational seminars and conferences. However, there has been growing concern about certain gifts from industry to physicians. Some gifts that reflect customary practices of industry may not be consistent with the Principles of Medical Ethics. To avoid the acceptance of inappropriate gifts, physicians should observe the following guidelines:

(1) Any gifts accepted by physicians individually should primarily entail a benefit to patients and should not be of substantial value. Accordingly, textbooks, modest meals, and other gifts are appropriate if they serve a genuine educational function. Cash payments should not be accepted. The use of drug samples for personal or family use is permissible as long as these practices do not interfere with patient access to drug samples. It would not be acceptable for non-retired physicians to request free pharmaceuticals for personal use or use by family members.

(2) Individual gifts of minimal value are permissible as long as the gifts are related to the physician's work (e.g., pens and notepads).

(3) The Council on Ethical and Judicial Affairs defines a legitimate "conference" or "meeting" as any activity, held at an appropriate location where (a) the gathering is primarily dedicated, in both time and effort, to promoting objective scientific and educational activities and discourse (one or more educational presentation(s) should be the highlight of the gathering), and (b) the main incentive for bringing attendees together is to further their knowledge on the topic(s) being presented. An appropriate disclosure of financial support or conflict of interest should be made.

(4) Subsidies to underwrite the costs of continuing medical education conferences or professional meetings can contribute to the improvement of patient care and therefore are permissible. Since the giving of a subsidy directly to a physician by a company's representative may create a relationship that could influence the use of the company's products, any subsidy should be accepted by the conference's sponsor who in turn can use the money to reduce the conference's registration fee. Payments to defray the costs of a conference should not be accepted directly from the company by the physicians attending the conference.

(5) Subsidies from industry should not be accepted directly or indirectly to pay for the costs of travel, lodging, or other personal expenses of physicians attending conferences or meetings, nor should subsidies be accepted to compensate for the physicians' time. Subsidies for hospitality should not be accepted outside of modest meals or social events held as a part of a conference or meeting. It is appropriate for faculty at conferences or meetings to accept reasonable honoraria and to accept reimbursement for reasonable travel, lodging, and meal expenses. It is also appropriate for consultants who provide genuine services to receive reasonable compensation and to accept reimbursement for reasonable travel, lodging, and meal expenses. Token consulting or advisory arrangements cannot be used to justify the compensation of physicians for their time or their travel, lodging, and other out-of-pocket expenses.

(6) Scholarship or other special funds to permit medical students, residents, and fellows to attend carefully selected educational conferences may be permissible as long as the selection of students, residents, or fellows who will receive the funds is made by the academic or training institution. Carefully selected educational conferences are generally defined as the major educational, scientific or policymaking meetings of national, regional or specialty medical associations.

(7) No gifts should be accepted if there are strings attached. For example, physicians should not accept gifts if they are given in relation to the physician's

prescribing practices. In addition, when companies underwrite medical conferences or lectures other than their own, responsibility for and control over the selection of content, faculty, educational methods, and materials should belong to the organizers of the conferences or lectures. (II)

8.07 Gifts to Physicians: Offers of Indemnity.

Physicians should prescribe drugs, devices, and other treatments based solely upon medical considerations and patient needs. A third party's offer to indemnify a physician for lawsuits arising from the physician's prescription or use of the third party's drug, device, or other product, introduces inappropriate factors into medical decision-making. Such offers, regardless of their limitations, therefore constitute unacceptable gifts.

This opinion does not address contractual assignments of liability between employers or in research arrangements, nor does it address government indemnification plans. (II)

8.08 Informed Consent.

The patient's right of self-decision can be effectively exercised only if the patient possesses enough information to enable an intelligent choice. The patient should make his or her own determination on treatment. The physician's obligation is to present the medical facts accurately to the patient or to the individual responsible for the patient's care and to make recommendations for management in accordance with good medical practice. The physician has an ethical obligation to help the patient make choices from among the therapeutic alternatives consistent with good medical practice. Informed consent is a basic social policy for which exceptions are permitted: (1) where the patient is unconscious or otherwise incapable of consenting and harm from failure to treat is imminent; or (2) when risk-disclosure poses such a serious psychological threat of detriment to the patient as to be medically contraindicated. Social policy does not accept the paternalistic view that the physician may remain silent because divulgence might prompt the patient to forego needed therapy. Rational, informed patients should not be expected to act uniformly, even under similar circumstances, in agreeing to or refusing treatment. (I, II, III, IV, V)

8.085 Waiver of Informed Consent for Research in Emergency Situations.

The current state of emergency medicine and research has resulted in the application of standard treatments that often have not been scientifically evaluated for safety and effectiveness and may render unsatisfactory outcomes. Given the insufficiency of standard treatment alternatives it is appropriate, in certain situations and with special safeguards, to provide experimental treatments without obtaining the informed consent of the subject. However, in order to protect the rights and welfare of the subjects several conditions must be met:

(1) This type of research is limited to emergency, life-threatening situations, and may involve only experimental treatments that are ready for trials involving human subjects.

(2) The subject must lack the capacity to give informed consent for participation in the research.

(3) The window of opportunity for intervention must be so narrow as to make obtaining surrogate consent unfeasible.

(4) Obtaining prospective informed consent for the protocol must not be feasible (i.e., the life-threatening emergency situation could not have been anticipated).

(5) The experimental treatment must have a realistic probability of benefit equal to or greater than standard care.

(6) The risks associated with the research should be reasonable in light of the critical nature of the conditions and the risks associated with standard treatment.

(7) Where informed consent is waived, subjects or their representatives must be informed as soon as possible about inclusion in the study and asked to consent to further participation. Subjects, or their representatives, may choose to discontinue participation at any time after being fully informed about the possible consequences. Additionally, if the patient dies while participating in the research protocol, the patient's family or representative must be informed that the patient was involved in an experimental protocol.

(8) Community input should be sought prior to approval of the protocol, and public disclosure should be made of study results. Fair randomization of research subjects should be given thorough consideration. Moreover, an independent data monitoring board should be established to oversee the ongoing trial. (I, V).

8.09 Laboratory Services.

(1) A physician should not misrepresent or aid in the misrepresentation of laboratory services performed and supervised by a non-physician as the physician's professional services. Such situations could involve a laboratory owned by a physician who directs and manages its financial and business affairs with no professional medical services being provided; laboratory work being performed by technicians and directly supervised by a medical technologist with no participation by the physician; or the physician's name being used in connection with the laboratory so as to create the appearance that it is owned, operated, and supervised by a physician when this is not so.

(2) If a laboratory is owned, operated, and supervised by a non-physician in accordance with state law and performs tests exclusively for physicians who receive the results and make their own medical interpretations, the following considerations would apply:

The physician's ethical responsibility is to provide patients with high quality services. This includes services that the physician performs personally and those that are delegated to others. A physician should not utilize the services of any laboratory, irrespective of whether it is operated by a physician or non-physician, unless she or he has the utmost confidence in the quality of its services. A physician must always assume personal responsibility for the best interests of his or her patients. Medical judgment based upon inferior laboratory work is likewise inferior. Medical considerations, not cost, must be paramount when the physician chooses a laboratory. The physician who disregards quality as the primary criterion or who chooses a laboratory solely because it provides low cost laboratory services on which the patient is charged a profit, is not acting in the best interests of the patient. However, if reliable, quality laboratory services are available at lower cost, the patient should have the benefit of the savings. As a professional, the physician is entitled to fair compensation for his or her services. A physician should not charge a markup, commission, or profit on the services rendered by others. A markup is an excessive charge that exploits patients if it is nothing more than a tacked on amount for a service already provided and accounted for by the laboratory. A physician may make an acquisition charge or processing charge. The patient should be notified of any such charge in advance. (I, II, III, IV, V)

8.10 Lien Laws.

In states where there are lien laws, a physician may file a lien as a means of assuring payment of his or her fee provided the fee is fixed in amount and not contingent on the amount of settlement of the patient's claim against a third party. (I, VI)

8.11 Neglect of Patient.

Physicians are free to choose whom they will serve. The physician should, however, respond to the best of his or her ability in cases of emergency where first aid treatment is essential. Once having undertaken a case, the physician should not neglect the patient. (I, VI)

8.115 Termination of the Physician-Patient Relationship.

Physicians have an obligation to support continuity of care for their patients. While physicians have the option of withdrawing from a case, they cannot do so without giving notice to the patient, the relatives, or responsible friends sufficiently long in advance of withdrawal to permit another medical attendant to be secured. (I, VI)

8.12 Patient Information.

It is a fundamental ethical requirement that a physician should at all times deal honestly and openly with patients. Patients have a right to know their past and present medical status and to be free of any mistaken beliefs concerning their conditions. Situations occasionally occur in which a patient suffers significant medical complications that may have resulted from the physician's mistake or judgment. In these situations, the physician is ethically required to inform the patient of all the facts necessary to ensure understanding of what has occurred. Only through full disclosure is a patient able to make informed decisions regarding future medical care.

Ethical responsibility includes informing patients of changes in their diagnoses resulting from retrospective review of test results or any other information. This obligation holds even though the patient's medical treatment or therapeutic options may not be altered by the new information.

Concern regarding legal liability which might result following truthful disclosure should not affect the physician's honesty with a patient. (I, II, III, IV)

8.13 Managed Care.

The expansion of managed care has brought a variety of changes to medicine including new and different reimbursement systems for physicians with complex referral restrictions and benefits packages for patients. Some of these changes have raised concerns that a physician's ability to practice ethical medicine will be adversely affected by the modifications in the system. In response to these concerns, the following points were developed to provide physicians with general guidelines that will assist them in fulfilling their ethical responsibilities to patients given the changes heralded by managed care.

(1) The duty of patient advocacy is a fundamental element of the patient-physician relationship that should not be altered by the system of health care delivery in which physicians practice. Physicians must continue to place the interests of their patients first.

(2) When managed care plans place restrictions on the care that physicians in the plan may provide to their patients, the following principles should be followed:

   (a) Any broad allocation guidelines that restrict care and choices—which go beyond the cost/benefit judgments made by physicians as a part of their normal professional responsibilities—should be established at a policy making level so that individual physicians are not asked to engage in bedside rationing.

   (b) Regardless of any allocation guidelines or gatekeeper directives, physicians must advocate for any care they believe will materially benefit their patients.

   (c) Physicians should be given an active role in contributing their expertise to any allocation process and should advocate for guidelines that are sensitive to differences among patients. Managed care plans should create structures similar to hospital medical staffs that allow physicians to have meaningful input into the plan's development of allocation guidelines. Guidelines for allocating health care should be reviewed on a regular basis and updated to reflect advances in medical knowledge and changes in relative costs.

   (d) Adequate appellate mechanisms for both patients and physicians should be in place to address disputes regarding medically necessary care. In some circumstances, physicians have an obligation to initiate appeals on behalf of their patients. Cases may arise in which a health plan has an allocation guideline that is generally fair but in particular circumstances results in unfair denials of care, i.e., denial of care that, in the physician's judgment, would materially benefit the patient. In such cases, the physician's duty as patient advocate requires that the physician challenge the denial and argue for the provision of treatment in the specific case. Cases may also arise when a health plan has an allocation guideline that is generally unfair in its operations. In such cases, the physician's duty as patient advocate requires not only a challenge to any denials of treatment from the guideline but also advocacy at the health plan's policy-making level to seek an elimination or modification of the guideline.

   Physicians should assist patients who wish to seek additional, appropriate care outside the plan when the physician believes the care is in the patient's best interests.

   (e) Managed care plans must adhere to the requirement of informed consent that patients be given full disclosure of material information. Full disclosure requires that managed care plans inform potential subscribers of limitations or restrictions on the benefits package when they are considering entering the plan.

   (f) Physicians also should continue to promote full disclosure to patients enrolled in managed care organizations. The physician's obligation to disclose treatment alternatives to patients is not altered by any limitations in the coverage provided by the patient's managed care plan. Full disclosure includes informing patients of all of their treatment options, even those that may not be covered under the terms of the managed care plan. Patients may then determine whether an appeal is appropriate, or whether they wish to seek care outside the plan for treatment alternatives that are not covered.

   (g) Physicians should not participate in any plan that encourages or requires care below minimum professional standards.

(3) When physicians are employed or reimbursed by managed care plans that offer financial incentives to limit care, serious potential conflicts are created between the physicians' personal financial interests and the needs of their patients. Efforts to contain health care costs should not place patient welfare at risk. Thus, financial incentives are permissible only if they promote the cost-effective delivery of health care and not the withholding of medically necessary care.

   (a) Any incentives to limit care must be disclosed fully to patients by plan administrators upon enrollment and at least annually thereafter.

   (b) Limits should be placed on the magnitude of fee withholds, bonuses and other financial incentives to limit care. Calculating incentive payments according to the performance of a sizable group of physicians rather than on an individual basis should be encouraged.

   (c) Health plans or other groups should develop financial incentives based on quality of care. Such incentives should complement financial incentives based on the quantity of services used.

(4) Patients have an individual responsibility to be aware of the benefits and limitations of their health care coverage. Patients should exercise their autonomy by public participation in the formulation of benefits packages and by prudent selection of health care coverage that best suits their needs.

8.132 Referral of Patients: Disclosure of Limitations.

When a physician agrees to provide treatment, he or she thereby enters into a contractual relationship and assumes an ethical obligation to treat the patient to the best of his or her ability. Preferred provider organization (PPO) and health maintenance organization (HMO) contracts generally restrict the participating physician's scope of referral to medical specialists, diagnostic laboratories, and hospitals that have contractual arrangements with the PPO and HMO. Some plans also restrict the circumstances under which referrals may be made to contracting medical specialists. If the PPO or HMO does not permit referral to a noncontracting medical specialist or to a diagnostic or treatment facility when the physician believes that the patient's condition requires such services, the physician should so inform the patient so that the patient may decide whether to accept the outside referral at his or her own expense or confine herself or himself to services available within the PPO or HMO. In determining whether treatment or diagnosis requires referral to outside specialty services, the physician should be guided by standards of good medical practice.

Physicians must not deny their patients access to appropriate medical services based upon the promise of personal financial reward, or the avoidance of financial penalties. Because patients must have the necessary information to make informed decisions about their care, physicians have an obligation to assure the disclosure of medically appropriate treatment alternatives, regardless of cost.

Physicians must assure disclosure of any financial inducements that may tend to limit the diagnostic and therapeutic alternatives that are offered to patients or that may tend to limit patients' overall access to care. Physicians may satisfy their obligation by assuring that the managed care plan makes adequate disclosure to patients enrolled in the plan. Physicians should also promote an effective program of peer review to monitor and evaluate the quality of the patient care services within their practice setting. (II, IV)

8.135 Managed Care Cost Containment Involving Prescription Drugs.

Managed care organizations establish drug formulary systems so that physicians will supplement medical judgment with cost considerations in drug selection. To ensure optimal patient care, various ethical requirements must be established for formulary application.

(1) Physicians who participate in managed care plans should maintain awareness of plan decisions about drug selection by staying informed about pharmacy and therapeutics (P&T) committee actions and by ongoing personal review of formulary composition. P&T committee members should include independent physician representatives. Mechanisms should be established for ongoing peer review of formulary policy. Physicians who perceive inappropriate influence on formulary development from pharmaceutical industry consolidation should notify the proper regulatory authorities.

(2) Physicians should be particularly vigilant to ensure that formulary decisions adequately reflect the needs of individual patients and that individual needs are not unfairly sacrificed by decisions based on the needs of the average patient. Physicians are ethically required to advocate for additions to the formulary when they think patients would benefit materially and for exceptions to the formulary on a case-by-case basis when justified by the health care needs [of] particular patients. Mechanisms to appeal formulary exclusions should be established. Other cost-containment mechanisms, including prescription caps and prior authorization, should not unduly burden physicians or patients in accessing optimal drug therapy.

(3) Limits should be placed on the extent to which managed care plans use incentives or pressures to lower prescription drug costs. Financial incentives are permissible when they promote cost-effectiveness, not when they require withholding medically necessary care. Physicians should not be made to feel that they jeopardize their compensation or participation in a managed care plan if they prescribe drugs that are necessary for their patients but that may also be costly. There should be limits on the magnitude of financial incentives, incentives should be calculated according to the practices of a sizable group of physicians rather than on an individual basis, and incentives based on quality of care rather than cost of care should be used. Prescriptions should not be changed without physicians having a chance to discuss the change with the patient.

(4) Managed care plans should develop and implement educational programs on cost-effective prescribing practices. Such initiatives are preferable to financial incentives or pressures by HMOs or hospitals, which can be ethically problematic.

(5) Patients must be informed of the methods used by their managed care plans to limit prescription drug costs. During enrollment, the plan should disclose the existence of formularies, the provisions for cases in which the physician prescribes a drug that is not included in the formulary, and the incentives or other mechanisms used to encourage physicians to consider costs when prescribing drugs. In addition, plans should disclose any relationships with pharmaceutical

benefit management companies or pharmaceutical companies that could influence the composition of the formulary. If physicians exhaust all avenues to secure a formulary exception for a significantly advantageous drug, they are still obligated to disclose the option of the more beneficial, more costly drug to the patient, so that the patient can decide whether to pay out-of-pocket.

8.137 Restrictions on Disclosure in Managed Care Contracts.

Managed care organizations have the right to protect proprietary information as long as such protection does not inhibit physicians from disclosing relevant information to patients. Contract clauses which could be applied to prevent physicians from raising or discussing matters relevant to patients' medical care are unethical and should be removed to safeguard the health of plan subscribers. (I, II)

8.14 Sexual Misconduct in the Practice of Medicine.

Sexual contact that occurs concurrent with the patient-physician relationship constitutes sexual misconduct. Sexual or romantic interactions between physicians and patients detract from the goals of the patient-physician relationship, may exploit the vulnerability of the patient, may obscure the physician's objective judgment concerning the patient's health care, and ultimately may be detrimental to the patient's well-being.

If a physician has reason to believe that non-sexual contact with a patient may be perceived as or may lead to sexual contact, then he or she should avoid the non-sexual contact. At a minimum, a physician's ethical duties include terminating the physician-patient relationship before initiating a dating, romantic, or sexual relationship with a patient.

Sexual or romantic relationships between a physician and a former patient may be unduly influenced by the previous physician-patient relationship. Sexual or romantic relationships with former patients are unethical if the physician uses or exploits trust, knowledge, emotions, or influence derived from the previous professional relationship. (I, II, IV)

8.15 Substance Abuse.

It is unethical for a physician to practice medicine while under the influence of a controlled substance, alcohol, or other chemical agents which impair the ability to practice medicine. (I)

8.16 Substitution of Surgeon without Patient's Knowledge or Consent.

A surgeon who allows a substitute to operate on his or her patient without the patient's knowledge and consent is deceitful. The patient is entitled to choose his or her own physician and should be permitted to acquiesce to or refuse the substitution.

The surgeon's obligation to the patient requires the surgeon to perform the surgical operation: (1) within the scope of authority granted by the consent to the operation; (2) in accordance with the terms of the contractual relationship; (3) with complete disclosure of facts relevant to the need and the performance of the operation; and (4) utilizing best skill.

It should be noted that it is the operating surgeon to whom the patient grants consent to perform the operation. The patient is entitled to the services of the particular surgeon with whom he or she contracts. The operating surgeon, in accepting the patient, is obligated to utilize his or her personal talents in the performance of the operation to the extent required by the agreement creating the patient-physician relationship. The surgeon cannot properly delegate to another the duties which he or she is required to perform personally.

Under the normal and customary arrangement with patients, and with reference to the usual form of consent to operation, the operating surgeon is obligated to perform the operation but may be assisted by residents or other surgeons. With the consent of the patient, it is not unethical for the operating surgeon to delegate the performance of certain aspects of the operation to the assistant provided this is done under the surgeon's participatory supervision, i.e., the surgeon must scrub. If a resident or other physician is to perform the operation under non-participatory supervision, it is necessary to make a full disclosure of this fact to the patient, and this should be evidenced by an appropriate statement contained in the consent. Under these circumstances, it is the resident or other physician who becomes the operating surgeon. (I, II, IV, V)

8.17 Use of Restraints.

All individuals have a fundamental right to be free from unreasonable bodily restraint. Physical and chemical restraints should therefore be used only in the best interest of the patient and in accordance with the following guidelines:

(1) The use of restraints, except in emergencies, may be implemented only upon the explicit order of a physician, in conformance with reasonable professional judgment.

(2) Judgment should be exercised in issuing pro re nata (PRN) orders for the use of physical or chemical restraints, and the implementation of such orders should be frequently reviewed and documented by the physician.

(3) The use of restraints should not be punitive, nor should they be used for convenience or as an alternative to reasonable staffing.

(4) Restraints should be used only in accordance with appropriate clinical indications.

(5) As with all therapeutic interventions, informed consent by the patient or surrogate decisionmaker is a key element in the application of physical and chemical restraints, and should be incorporated into institutional policy.

(6) In certain limited situations, it may be appropriate to restrain a patient involuntarily. For example, restraints may be needed for the safety of the patient or others in the area. When restraints are used involuntarily, the restraints should be removed when they are no longer needed. (I, IV)

8.18 Informing Families of a Patient's Death.

Disclosing the death of a patient to the patient's family is a duty which goes to the very heart of the physician-patient relationship and should not be readily delegated to others by the attending physician. The emotional needs of the family and the integrity of the physician-patient relationship must at all times be given foremost consideration.

Physicians in residency training may be asked to participate in the communication of information about a patient's death, if that request is commensurate with the physician's prior training or experience and previous close personal relationship with the family.

It would not be appropriate for the attending physician or resident to request that a medical student notify family members of a patient's death. Medical students should be trained in issues of death and dying, and should be encouraged to accompany attending physicians when news of a patient's death is conveyed to the family members. (I, IV)

8.19 Self-Treatment or Treatment of Immediate Family Members.

Physicians generally should not treat themselves or members of their immediate families. Professional objectivity may be compromised when an immediate family member or the physician is the patient; the physician's personal feelings may unduly influence his or her professional medical judgment, thereby interfering with the care being delivered. Physicians may fail to probe sensitive areas when taking the medical history or may fail to perform intimate parts of the physical examination. Similarly, patients may feel uncomfortable disclosing sensitive information or undergoing an intimate examination when the physician is an immediate family member. This discomfort is particularly the case when the patient is a minor child, and sensitive or intimate care should especially be avoided for such patients. When treating themselves or immediate family members, physicians may be inclined to treat problems that are beyond their expertise or training. If tensions develop in a physician's professional relationship with a family member, perhaps as a result of a negative medical outcome, such difficulties may be carried over into the family member's personal relationship with the physician.

Concerns regarding patient autonomy and informed consent are also relevant when physicians attempt to treat members of their immediate family. Family members may be reluctant to state their preference for another physician or decline a recommendation for fear of offending the physician. In particular, minor children will generally not feel free to refuse care from their parents. Likewise, physicians may feel obligated to provide care to immediate family members even if they feel uncomfortable providing care.

It would not always be inappropriate to undertake self-treatment or treatment of immediate family members. In emergency settings or isolated settings where there is no other qualified physician available, physicians should not hesitate to treat themselves or family members until another physician becomes available. In addition, while physicians should not serve as primary or regular care providers for immediate family members, there are situations in which routine care is acceptable for short-term, minor problems.

Except in emergencies, it is not appropriate for physicians to write prescriptions for controlled substances for themselves or immediate family members. (I, II, IV)

9.00 OPINIONS ON PROFESSIONAL RIGHTS AND RESPONSIBILITIES

9.01 Accreditation.

Physicians who engage in activities that involve the accreditation, approval, or certification of institutions, facilities, and programs that provide patient care or medical education or certify the attainment of specialized professional competence have the ethical responsibility to apply standards that are relevant, fair, reasonable, and nondiscriminatory. The accreditation of institutions and facilities that provide patient care should be based upon standards that focus upon the quality of patient care achieved. Standards used in the accreditation of patient care and medical education, or the certification of specialized professional attainment should not be adopted or used as a means of economic regulation. (II, IV, VII)

9.011 Continuing Medical Education.

Physicians should strive to further their medical education throughout their careers, for only by participating in continuing medical education (CME) can they continue to serve patients to the best of their abilities and live up to professional standards of excellence. Fulfillment of mandatory state CME requirements does not necessarily fulfill the physician's ethical obligation to maintain his or her medical expertise.

Attendees. Guidelines for physicians attending a CME conference or activity are as follows:

(1) The physician choosing among CME activities should assess their educational value and select only those activities which are of high quality and appropriate for the physician's educational needs. When selecting formal CME activities, the physician should, at a minimum, choose only those activities that (a) are offered by sponsors accredited by the Accreditation Council for Continuing Medical Education (ACCME), the American Academy of Family Physicians (AAFP), or a state medical society; (b) contain information on subjects relevant to the physician's needs; (c) are responsibly conducted by qualified faculty; (d) conform to Opinion 8.061: "Gifts to Physicians from Industry."

(2) The educational value of the CME conference or activity must be the primary consideration in the physician's decision to attend or participate. Though amenities unrelated to the educational purpose of the activity may play a role in the physician's decision to participate, this role should be secondary to the educational content of the conference.

(3) Physicians should claim credit commensurate with only the actual time spent attending a CME activity or in studying a CME enduring material.

(4) Attending promotional activities put on by industry or their designees is not unethical as long as the conference conforms to Opinion 8.061: "Gifts to Physicians from Industry" and is clearly identified as promotional to all participants.

Faculty. Guidelines for physicians serving as presenters, moderators, or other faculty at a CME conference are as follows:

(1) Physicians serving as presenters, moderators, or other faculty at a CME conference should ensure that (a) research findings and therapeutic recommendations are based on scientifically accurate, up-to-date information and are presented in a balanced, objective manner and (b) the content of their presentation is not modified or influenced by representatives of industry or other financial contributors, and they do not employ materials whose content is shaped by industry. Faculty may, however, use scientific data generated from industry-sponsored research, and they may also accept technical assistance from industry in preparing slides or other presentation materials, as long as this assistance is of only nominal monetary value and the company has no input in the actual content of the material.

(2) When invited to present at non-CME activities that are primarily promotional, faculty should avoid participation unless the activity is clearly identified as promotional in its program announcements and other advertising.

(3) All conflicts of interest or biases, such as a financial connection to a particular commercial firm or product, should be disclosed by faculty members to the activity's sponsor and to the audience. Faculty may accept reasonable honoraria and reimbursement for expenses in accordance with Opinion 8.061: "Gifts to Physicians from Industry."

Sponsors. Guidelines for physicians involved in the sponsorship of CME activities are as follows:

(1) Physicians involved in the sponsorship of CME activities should ensure that (a) the program is balanced, with faculty members presenting a broad range of scientifically supportable viewpoints related to the topic at hand; (b) representatives of industry or other financial contributors do not exert control over the choice of moderators, presenters, or other faculty, or modify the content of faculty presentations. Funding from industry or others may be accepted in accordance with Opinion 8.061: "Gifts to Physicians from Industry."

(2) Sponsors should not promote CME activities in a way that encourages attendees to violate the guidelines of the Council on Ethical and Judicial Affairs, including Opinion 8.061: "Gifts to Physicians from Industry," or the principles established for the American Medical Association's Physician Recognition Award. CME activities should be developed and promoted consistent with guideline (2) for Attendees.

(3) Any non-CME activity that is primarily promotional must be identified as such to faculty and participants, both in its advertising and at the conference itself.

(4) The entity presenting the program should not profit unfairly or charge a fee which is excessive for the content and length of the program.

(5) The program, content, duration, and ancillary activities should be consistent with the ideals of the AMA CME program. (I, V)

9.02 Restrictive Covenants and the Practice of Medicine.

Covenants-not-to-compete restrict competition, disrupt continuity of care, and potentially deprive the public of medical services. The Council on Ethical and Judicial Affairs discourages any agreement which restricts the right of a physician to practice medicine for a specified period of time or in a specified area upon termination of an employment, partnership or corporate agreement. Restrictive covenants are unethical if they are excessive in geographic scope or duration in the circumstances presented, or if they fail to make reasonable accommodation of patients' choice of physician. (VI, VII)

9.021 Covenants-Not-To-Compete for Physicians-In-Training.

It is unethical for a teaching institution to seek a non-competition guarantee in return for fulfilling its educational obligations. Physicians-in-training (residents in programs approved by the Accreditation Council on Graduate Medical Education, fellows in ACGM-approved fellowship programs, and fellows in programs approved by one of the American Board of Medical Specialty's specialty boards) should not be asked to sign covenants-not-to-compete as a condition of their entry into any residency or fellowship program. (VI, VII)

9.03 Civil Rights and Professional Responsibility.

Opportunities in medical society activities or membership, medical education and training, employment and all other aspects of professional endeavors should not be denied to any duly licensed physician because of race, color, religion, creed, ethnic affiliation, national origin, sex, sexual orientation, age, or handicap. (IV)

9.031 Reporting Impaired, Incompetent, or Unethical Colleagues.

Physicians have an ethical obligation to report impaired, incompetent, and unethical colleagues in accordance with the legal requirements in each state and assisted by the following guidelines:

Impairment. Impairment should be reported to the hospital's in-house impairment program, if available. Otherwise, either the chief of an appropriate clinical service or the chief of the hospital staff should be alerted. Reports may also be made directly to an external impaired physician program. Practicing physicians who do not have hospital privileges should be reported directly to an impaired physician program, such as those run by medical societies, when appropriate. If none of these steps would facilitate the entrance of the impaired physician into an impairment program, then the impaired physician should be reported directly to the state licensing board.

Incompetence. Initial reports of incompetence should be made to the appropriate clinical authority who would be empowered to assess the potential impact on patient welfare and to facilitate remedial action. The hospital peer review body should be notified where appropriate. Incompetence which poses an immediate threat to the health of patients should be reported directly to the state licensing board. Incompetence by physicians without a hospital affiliation should be reported to the local or state medical society and/or the state licensing or disciplinary board.

Unethical conduct. With the exception of incompetence or impairment, unethical behavior should be reported in accordance with the following guidelines:

Unethical conduct that threatens patient care or welfare should be reported to the appropriate authority for a particular clinical service. Unethical behavior which violates state licensing provisions should be reported to the state licensing board or impaired physician programs, when appropriate. Unethical conduct which violates criminal statutes must be reported to the appropriate law enforcement authorities. All other unethical conduct should be reported to the local or state medical society.

Where the inappropriate behavior of a physician continues despite the initial report(s), the reporting physician should report to a higher or additional authority. The person or body receiving the initial report should notify the reporting physician when appropriate action has been taken. Physicians who receive reports of inappropriate behavior have an ethical duty to critically and objectively evaluate the reported information and to assure that identified deficiencies are either remedied or further reported to a higher or additional authority. Anonymous reports should receive appropriate review and confidential investigation. Physicians who are under scrutiny or charge should be protected by the rules of confidentiality until such charges are proven or until the physician is exonerated. (II)

9.032 Reporting Adverse Drug or Device Events.

A physician who suspects the occurrence of an adverse reaction to a drug or medical device has an obligation to communicate that information to the broader medical community (e.g., through submitting a report or letter to a medical journal or informing the manufacturer of the suspect drug or device). In the case of a serious adverse event, the event should be reported to the Food and Drug Administration (FDA). Spontaneous reports of adverse events are irreplaceable as a source of valuable information about drugs and medical devices, particularly their rare or delayed effects, as well as their safety in vulnerable patient populations. Although premarketing and mandated postmarketing studies provide basic safeguards for the public health, they suffer from inherent deficiencies that limit their ability to detect rare or unexpected consequences of drug or medical device use. Physicians who prescribe and monitor the use of drugs and medical devices constitute the group best able to observe and communicate information about resulting adverse events.

Serious adverse events, such as those resulting in death, hospitalization, or medical or surgical intervention, are the most important to report and are the only adverse events for which the FDA desires a report. Certainty, or even reasonable likelihood, of a causal relationship between the drug or medical device and the serious adverse event will rarely exist and is not required before reporting the event to the FDA. Suspicion of such a relationship is sufficient to give rise to an obligation to participate in the reporting system. (I, V, VII)

9.035 Gender Discrimination in the Medical Profession.

Physician leaders in medical schools and other medical institutions should take immediate steps to increase the number of women in leadership positions as such positions become open. There is already a large enough pool of female physicians to provide strong candidates for such positions. Also, adjustments should be made to ensure that all physicians are equitably compensated for their work. Women and men in the same specialty with the same experience and doing the same work should be paid the same compensation.

Physicians in the workplace should actively develop the following: (a) Retraining or other programs which facilitate the reentry of physicians who take time away from their careers to have a family; (b) On-site child care services for dependent children; (c) Policies providing job security for physicians who are temporarily not in practice due to pregnancy or family obligations.

Physicians in the academic medical setting should strive to promote the following: (a) Extension of tenure decisions through "stop the clock" programs, relaxation of the seven-year rule, or part-time appointments that would give faculty members longer to achieve standards for promotion and tenure; (b) More reasonable guidelines regarding the appropriate quantity and timing of published material needed for promotion or tenure that would emphasize quality over quantity and that would encourage the pursuit of careers based on individual talent rather than tenure standards that undervalue teaching ability and overvalue research; (c) Fair distribution of teaching, clinical, research, administrative responsibilities, and access to tenure tracks between men and women. Also, physicians in academic institutions should consider formally structuring the mentoring process, possibly matching students or faculty with advisors through a fair and visible system.

Where such policies do not exist or have not been followed, all medical workplaces and institutions should create strict policies to deal with sexual harassment. Grievance committees should have broad representation of both sexes and other groups. Such committees should have the power to enforce harassment policies and be accessible to those persons they are meant to serve.

Grantors of research funds and editors of scientific or medical journals should consider blind peer review of grant proposals and articles for publication to help prevent bias. However, grantors and editors will be able to consider the author's identity and give it appropriate weight. (II, VII)

9.04 Discipline and Medicine.

Incompetence, corruption, or dishonest or unethical conduct on the part of members of the medical profession is reprehensible. In addition to posing a real or potential threat to patients, such conduct undermines the public's confidence in the profession. A physician should expose, without fear or loss of favor, incompetent or corrupt, dishonest or unethical conduct on the part of members of the profession. Questions of such conduct should be reported and reviewed in accordance with Opinion 9.031: "Reporting Impaired, Incompetent, or Unethical Colleagues."

Violation of governmental laws may subject the physician to civil or criminal liability. Expulsion from membership is the maximum penalty that may be imposed by a medical society upon a physician who violates the ethical standards involving a breach of moral duty or principle. However, medical societies have a civic and professional obligation to report to the appropriate governmental body or state board of medical examiners credible evidence that may come to their attention involving the alleged criminal conduct of any physician relating to the practice of medicine.

Although a physician charged with allegedly illegal conduct may be acquitted or exonerated in civil or criminal proceedings, this does not discharge a medical society from its obligation to initiate a disciplinary proceeding against a member with reference to the same conduct where there is credible evidence tending to establish unethical conduct.

The Council cannot pass judgment in advance on a situation that may later come before it on appeal. The Council cannot be an attorney for a society or a member thereof and later judge in the same factual situation. The local medical society has the initial obligation of determining all the facts and whether or not disciplinary action is indicated. Questions asking for a review of a proposed course of action or an evaluation of an existing factual situation should be presented to the appropriate official of the physician's local society. (II, III, VII)

9.05 Due Process.

The basic principles of a fair and objective hearing should always be accorded to the physician or medical student whose professional conduct is being reviewed. The fundamental aspects of a fair hearing are a listing of specific charges, adequate notice of the right of a hearing, the opportunity to be present and to rebut the evidence, and the opportunity to present a defense. These principles apply when the hearing body is a medical society tribunal, medical staff committee, or other similar body composed of peers. The composition of committees sitting in judgment of medical students, residents, or fellows should include a significant number of persons at a similar level of training.

These principles of fair play apply in all disciplinary hearings and in any other type of hearing in which the reputation, professional status, or livelihood of the physician or medical student may be negatively impacted.

All physicians and medical students are urged to observe diligently these fundamental safeguards of due process whenever they are called upon to serve on a committee which will pass judgment on a peer. All medical societies and institutions are urged to review their constitutions and bylaws and/or policies to make sure that these instruments provide for such procedural safeguards. (II, III, VII)

9.055 Disputes Between Medical Supervisors and Trainees.

Clear policies for handling complaints from medical students, resident physicians, and other staff should be established. These policies should include adequate provisions for protecting the confidentiality of complainants whenever possible. Confidentiality of complainants should be protected when doing so does not hinder the subject's ability to respond to the complaint. Access to employment and evaluation files should be carefully monitored to remove the possibility of tampering. Resident physicians should be permitted access to their employment files and also the right to copy the contents thereof, within the provisions of applicable federal and state laws.

Medical students, resident physicians, and other staff should refuse to participate in patient care ordered by their supervisors in those rare cases in which they believe the orders reflect serious errors in clinical or ethical judgment, or physician impairment, that could result in a threat of imminent harm to the patient or to others. In these rare cases, the complainant may withdraw from the care ordered by the supervisor, provided withdrawal does not itself threaten the patient's immediate welfare. The complainant should communicate his or her concerns to the physician issuing the orders and, if necessary, to the appropriate persons for mediating such disputes. Mechanisms for resolving these disputes, which require immediate resolution, should be in place. Third-party mediators of such disputes may include the chief of staff or the involved service, the chief resident, a designated member of the institutional grievance committee, or, in large institutions, an institutional ombudsperson largely outside of the established hospital staff hierarchy.

Retaliatory or punitive actions against those who raise complaints are unethical and are a legitimate cause for filing a grievance with the appropriate institutional committee. (II, III, VII)

9.06 Free Choice.

Free choice of physicians is the right of every individual. One may select and change at will one's physicians, or one may choose a medical care plan such as that provided by a closed panel or group practice or health maintenance or service organization. The individual's freedom to select a preferred system of health care and free competition among physicians and alternative systems of care are prerequisites of ethical practice and optimal patient care.

In choosing to subscribe to a health maintenance or service organization or in choosing or accepting treatment in a particular hospital, the patient is thereby accepting limitations upon free choice of medical services.

The need of an individual for emergency treatment in cases of accident or sudden illness may, as a practical matter, preclude free choice of a physician, particularly where there is loss of consciousness.

Although the concept of free choice assures that an individual can generally choose a physician, likewise a physician may decline to accept that individual as a patient. In selecting the physician of choice, the patient may sometimes be obliged to pay for medical services which might otherwise be paid by a third party. (IV)

9.065 Caring for the Poor.

Each physician has an obligation to share in providing care to the indigent. The measure of what constitutes an appropriate contribution may vary with circumstances such as community characteristics, geographic location, the nature of the physician's practice and specialty, and other conditions. All physicians should work to ensure that the needs of the poor in their communities are met. Caring for the poor should be a regular part of the physician's practice schedule.

In the poorest communities, it may not be possible to meet the needs of the indigent for physicians' services by relying solely on local physicians. The local physicians should be able to turn for assistance to their colleagues in prosperous communities, particularly those in close proximity.

Physicians are meeting their obligation, and are encouraged to continue to do so, in a number of ways such as seeing indigent patients in their offices at no cost or at reduced cost, serving at freestanding or hospital clinics that treat the poor, and participating in government programs that provide health care to the poor. Physicians can also volunteer their services at weekend clinics for the poor and at shelters for battered women or the homeless.

In addition to meeting their obligation to care for the indigent, physicians can devote their energy, knowledge, and prestige to designing and lobbying at all levels for better programs to provide care for the poor. (I, VII)

9.07 Medical Testimony.

As a citizen and as a professional with special training and experience, the physician has an ethical obligation to assist in the administration of justice. If a patient who has a legal claim requests a physician's assistance, the physician should furnish medical evidence, with the patient's consent, in order to secure the patient's legal rights.

Medical experts should have recent and substantive experience in the area in which they testify and should limit testimony to their sphere of medical expertise. Medical witnesses should be adequately prepared and should testify honestly and truthfully to the best of their medical knowledge.

The medical witness must not become an advocate or a partisan in the legal proceeding. The medical witness should be adequately prepared and should testify honestly and truthfully. The attorney for the party who calls the physician as a witness should be informed of all favorable and unfavorable information developed by the physician's evaluation of the case. It is unethical for a physician to accept compensation that is contingent upon the outcome of litigation. (II, IV, V, VII)

9.08 New Medical Procedures.

In the ethical tradition expressed by Hippocrates and continuously affirmed thereafter, the role of the physician has been that of a healer who serves patients, a teacher who imparts knowledge of skills and techniques to colleagues, and a student who constantly seeks to keep abreast of new medical knowledge.

Physicians have an obligation to share their knowledge and skills and to report the results of clinical and laboratory research. Both positive and negative studies should be included even though they may not support the author's hypothesis. This tradition enhances patient care, leads to the early evaluation of new technologies, and permits the rapid dissemination of improved techniques.

The intentional withholding of new medical knowledge, skills, and techniques from colleagues for reasons of personal gain is detrimental to the medical profession and to society and is to be condemned.

Prompt presentation before scientific organizations and timely publication of clinical and laboratory research in scientific journals are essential elements in the foundation of good medical care. (I, II, V, VII)

9.09 Patent for Surgical or Diagnostic Instrument.

A physician may patent a surgical or diagnostic instrument he or she has discovered or developed. The laws governing patents are based on the sound doctrine that one is entitled to protect one's discovery. (V, VII)

9.095 Patenting of Medical Procedures.

A physician has the ethical responsibility not only to learn from but also to contribute to the total store of scientific knowledge when possible. Physicians should strive to advance medical science and make their advances known to patients, colleagues and the public. This obligation provides not merely incentive but imperative to innovate and share the ensuing advances. The patenting of medical procedures poses substantial risks to the effective practice of medicine by limiting the availability of new procedures to patients and should be condemned on this basis. Accordingly, it is unethical for physicians to seek, secure or enforce patents on medical procedures.

9.10 Peer Review.

Medical society ethics committees, hospital credentials and utilization committees, and other forms of peer review have been long established by organized medicine to scrutinize physicians' professional conduct. At least to some extent, each of these types of peer review can be said to impinge upon the absolute professional freedom of physicians. They are, nonetheless, recognized and accepted. They are necessary and committees performing such work act ethically as long as principles of due process (Opinion 9.05) are observed. They balance the physician's right to exercise medical judgment freely with the obligation to do so wisely and temperately. (II, III, VII)

9.11 Ethics Committees in Health Care Institutions.

The following guidelines have been developed to aid in the establishment and functioning of ethics committees in hospitals and other health care institutions that may choose to form such committees.

(1) Ethics committees in health care institutions should be educational and advisory in purpose. Generally, the function of the ethics committee should be to consider and assist in resolving unusual, complicated ethical problems involving issues that affect the care and treatment of patients within the health care institution.

Recommendations of the ethics committee should impose no obligation for acceptance on the part of the institution, its governing board, medical staff, attending physician, or other persons. However, it should be expected that the recommendations of a dedicated ethics committee will receive serious consideration by decision-makers.

(2) The size of the committee should be consistent with the needs of the institution but not so large as to be unwieldy. Committee members should be selected on the basis of their concern for the welfare of the sick and infirm, their interest in ethical matters, and their reputation in the community and among their peers for integrity and mature judgment. Experience as a member of hospital or medical society committees concerned with ethical conduct or quality assurance should be considered in selecting ethics committee members. Committee members should not have other responsibilities that are likely to prove incompatible with their duties as members of the ethics committee. Preferably, a majority of the committee should consist of physicians, nurses, and other health care providers. In hospitals, medical staff bylaws should delineate the functions of the committee, general qualifications for membership, and manner of selection of members, in accordance with these guidelines.

(3) The functions of the ethics committee should be confined exclusively to ethical matters. The Code of Medical Ethics of the American Medical Association is recommended for the guidance of ethics committees in making their own recommendations. The matters to be considered by the committee should consist of ethical subjects that a majority of its members may choose to discuss on its own initiative, matters referred to it by the executive committee of the organized medical staff or by the governing board of the institution, or appropriate requests from patients, families, or health care providers.

(4) In denominational health care institutions or those operated by religious orders, the recommendations of the ethics committee may be anticipated to be consistent with published religious tenets and principles. Where particular religious beliefs are to be taken into consideration in the committee's recommendations, this fact should be publicized to physicians, patients, and others concerned with the committee's recommendations.

(5) In its deliberations and communication of recommendations, the procedures followed by the ethics committee should comply with institutional and ethical policies for preserving the confidentiality of information regarding patients.

(6) Committee members should be prepared to meet on short notice and to render their recommendations in a timely and prompt fashion in accordance with the demands of the situation and the issues involved. (II, IV, VII)

9.12 Physician-Patient Relationship: Respect for Law and Human Rights.

The creation of the physician-patient relationship is contractual in nature. Generally, both the physician and the patient are free to enter into or decline the relationship. A physician may decline to undertake the care of a patient whose medical condition is not within the physician's current competence. However, physicians who offer their services to the public may not decline to accept patients because of race, color, religion, national origin, sexual orientation, or any other basis that would constitute invidious discrimination. Furthermore, physicians who are obligated under preexisting contractual arrangements may not decline to accept patients as provided by those arrangements. (I, III, V, VI)

9.121 Racial Disparities in Health Care.

Disparities in medical care based on immutable characteristics such as race must be avoided. Whether such disparities in health care are caused by treatment decisions, differences in income and education, social and cultural factors, or failures by the medical profession, they are unjustifiable and must be eliminated. Physicians should examine their own practices to ensure that racial prejudice does not affect clinical judgment in medical care. (I, IV)

9.122 Gender Disparities in Health Care.

A patient's gender plays an appropriate role in medical decision-making when biological differences between the sexes are considered. However, some data suggest that gender bias may be playing a role in medical decision-making. Social attitudes, including stereotypes, prejudices and other evaluations based on gender role expectations may play themselves out in a variety of subtle ways. Physicians must ensure that gender is not used inappropriately as a consideration in clinical decision-making. Physicians should examine their practices and attitudes for influence of social or cultural biases which could be inadvertently affecting the delivery of medical care.

Research on health problems that affect both genders should include male and female subjects, and results of medical research done solely on males should not be generalized to females without evidence that results apply to both sexes. Medicine and society in general should ensure that resources for medical research should be distributed in a manner which promotes the health of both sexes to the greatest extent possible. (I, IV)

9.13 Physicians and Infectious Diseases.

A physician who knows that he or she has an infectious disease, which if contracted by the patient would pose a significant risk to the patient, should not engage in any activity that creates an identified risk of transmission of that disease to the patient. The precautions taken to prevent the transmission of a contagious disease to a patient should be appropriate to the seriousness of the disease and must be particularly stringent in the case of a disease that is potentially fatal. (I, IV)

9.131 HIV-Infected Patients and Physicians.

A physician may not ethically refuse to treat a patient whose condition is within the physician's current realm of competence solely because the patient is seropositive for HIV. Persons who are seropositive should not be subjected to discrimination based on fear or prejudice.

When physicians are unable to provide the services required by an HIV-infected patient, they should make appropriate referrals to those physicians or facilities equipped to provide such services.

A physician who knows that he or she is seropositive should not engage in any activity that creates an identified risk of transmission of the disease to others. A physician who is seropositive should consult colleagues as to which activities the physician can pursue without creating a risk to patients. (I, II, IV)

5. MENTAL HEALTH

Organization

AMERICAN COUNSELING ASSOCIATION

Headquarters:
5999 Stevenson Avenue
Alexandria, VA 22304-3300
Telephone: (703) 823-9800
(800) 347-6647
Fax: (703) 823-0252
Website: http://www.counseling.org
Ethics Hotline: Center for Effective Counseling Practice
(800) 347-6647, Ext. 271
E-mail: cecp@counseling.org

Date founded: 1952
   Former names include the American Personnel and Guidance Association and the American Association of Counseling and Development; renamed 1992
Membership: approximately 51,000 counselors in schools, universities, rehabilitation, mental health, career guidance, hospices, hospitals, business, and industry, in 56 chartered branches in the U.S., Europe, and Latin America

Code of Ethics

Official name: *Code of Ethics and Standards of Practice*
History: First adopted 1959, revised periodically; current version
   July 1997
Authority: Ethics Committee; Governing Council
Code is available on Website

Additional Resources

Organizational (Divisions, Programs, Services, etc.):

ACA Insurance Trust (liability insurance)
Center for Effective Counseling Practice

Continuing Education Program
Council for Accreditation of Counseling and Related Educational Programs
(corporate affiliate)
Counseling and Human Development Foundation
Ethics in Professional Counseling (national videoconference)
Mental Health Bill of Rights Project
Divisions:
Association for Assessment in Counseling
Association for Adult Development and Aging
American College Counseling Association
Association for Counselors and Educators in Government
Association for Counselor Education and Supervision
Association for Gay, Lesbian and Bisexual Issues in Counseling
Association for Humanistic Education and Development
Association for Multicultural Counseling and Development
American Mental Health Counselors Association
American Rehabilitation Counseling Association
American School Counselor Association
Association for Spiritual, Ethical, and Religious Values in Counseling
Association for Specialists in Group Work
International Association of Addiction and Offender Counselors
International Association of Marriage and Family Counselors
National Career Development Association
National Employment Counseling Association
Various committees: Human Rights; Interprofessional International Collaboration; Professional Development; Professionalization; Public Awareness and Support; Public Policy and Legislation; Research and Knowledge

Informational (Publications, Videos, Seminars, etc.):

Articles in *ACAeNews, Counseling Today, CTOnline, Journal of Counseling and Development,* and individual Division journals
A Practitioner's Guide to Ethical Decision Making
ACA Ethical Standards Casebook
ACA Legal Series:
Avoiding Counselor Malpractice
Confidentiality and Privileged Communication
Counseling Minor Clients
The Counselor as Expert Witness
The Danger-to-Self-or-Others Exception to Confidentiality
Legal Issues in Clinical Supervision
Legal Issues in Licensure
Legal Issues in Marriage and Family Counseling
Preparing for Court Appearances
Boundary Issues in Counseling: Multiple Roles and Responsibilities

Child Abuse Reporting: A Strategy for Acting on Ethical Responsibilities (video)
Counseling and Values (journal)
Counseling in a Dynamic Society: Opportunities and Challenges
Counseling: The Spiritual Dimension
The Counselor and the Law
Credentialing in Counseling
Cultural and Diversity Issues in Counseling
Dual Relationships in Counseling
The Emerging Professional Counselor: Student Dreams to Professional Realities
Ethics in Counseling (video)
Ethics in Counseling column in *Counseling Today*
Finding Your Way As a Counselor
Legal Aspects of Counseling (video)
Multicultural Counseling Competencies: Implications For Training and Practice
Office of Public Policy and Information Special Reports: School Counseling Mandate; Sexual Harassment; Third Party Reimbursement
Policies and Procedures for Processing Complaints of Ethical Violations
Principles for the Provision of Mental Health and Substance Abuse Prevention Treatment Services: A Bill of Rights
The Professional Counselor: Competencies, Performance Guidelines, and Assessments
Professional Resource Bibliography: Ethical and Legal Issues
Responsibilities of Users of Standardized Tests (RUST Statement)
School Counselors and Censorship: Facing the Challenge
Social Action: A Mandate for Counselors
State Licensure Chart
The 2001 Standards (Council for Accreditation of Counseling and Related Educational Programs)

Goals and Activities of Organization

The American Counseling Association (ACA) is a partnership of organizations that supports the professional growth of its members; promotes state and national credentialing and licensure; collects and disseminates information on counseling; supports major social programs; acts as an advocate for counselors and clients of counseling; sets professional and ethical standards; and creates counselor accreditation and certification programs. It also represents its members' interests before Congress and federal agencies, and strives to promote public recognition of the profession.

The Center for Effective Counseling Practice, established in 1996, provides workshops and publications, and responds to members' inquiries on issues relating to ethics, licensure, and professional standards.

Implementation and Enforcement of Code

All members are required to adhere to the Code of Ethics and the Standards of Practice. The ACA monitors the professional conduct of its members in order to promote sound ethical practices (but does not warrant an individual's performance).

The Code is developed, revised, and approved by the ACA Governing Council. The Policies and Procedures for Processing Complaints of Ethical Violations were most recently revised in 1997.

The ACA Ethics Committee is responsible for educating members as to the Code, reviewing the standards and recommending changes, administering the complaint process, and handling requests for interpretations of the Code.

In processing complaints against members for alleged misconduct, the Committee compiles an objective factual account of the dispute and makes a recommendation for its resolution. Disciplinary action must be fair, reasonable, based on a proper cause, and, in general, in the interests of the ACA and its membership. Committee members must be unbiased and have no conflict of interest with any party. Individuals are encouraged to try to resolve a dispute personally before filing an ethical complaint.

Only written, signed complaints are permitted. The complaint is reviewed, investigated, and subject to a preliminary determination. The accused member is notified and will be asked to respond regarding each section of the Code of Ethics that he or she allegedly violated. If the Committee does not dismiss the matter, it may impose sanctions or hold a formal hearing.

The hearing, like the entire complaint process, is conducted in a manner guaranteeing confidentiality and due process rights to all concerned. (It is not a court of law, however, and the committee is not required to observe formal legal rules.) The Ethics Committee's subsequent decision may be appealed.

Even if the charging party and the accused both agree to discontinue the complaint, the Committee may decide to complete the adjudication process in light of the evidence.

Sanctions against members for ethical violations include remedial measures, probation, suspension, or expulsion. Licensure, certification, or registry boards and professional associations, as well as ACA divisions and entities, may be notified when a member is suspended or expelled.

Substantial new evidence capable of exonerating an expelled member may lead the Ethics Committee to reopen the case and repeat the entire complaint process.

History and Development of Code

In 1953, the Ethical Practices Committee resolved to study ways in which it and the American Psychological Association might coordinate their work in the ethics field. A draft was issued in 1958 and a code of ethics was published in 1959.

Sources include standards of the American Psychological Association, American Educational Research Association, and National Council of Measurement in Education, and various federal regulations and state privacy acts.

Revisions to the Code were made in 1974, 1981, 1988, and 1995. The Policies and Procedures for Processing Complaints of Ethical Violations, appended to the Code in 1991, are also revised periodically.

The present document became effective July 1997.

Code of Ethics and Standards of Practice*

Preamble

The American Counseling Association is an educational, scientific, and professional organization whose members are dedicated to the enhancement of human development throughout the life-span. Association members recognize diversity in our society and embrace a cross-cultural approach in support of the worth, dignity, potential, and uniqueness of each individual.

The specification of a code of ethics enables the association to clarify to current and future members, and to those served by members, the nature of the ethical responsibilities held in common by its members. As the code of ethics of the association, this document establishes principles that define the ethical behavior of association members. All members of the American Counseling Association are required to adhere to the Code of Ethics and the Standards of Practice. The Code of Ethics will serve as the basis for processing ethical complaints initiated against members of the association.

Section A:
THE COUNSELING RELATIONSHIP

A.1. Client Welfare

a. *Primary Responsibility.*
The primary responsibility of counselors is to respect the dignity and to promote the welfare of clients.

b. *Positive Growth and Development.*
Counselors encourage client growth and development in ways that foster the clients' interest and welfare; counselors avoid fostering dependent counseling relationships.

c. *Counseling Plans.*
Counselors and their clients work jointly in devising integrated, individual counseling plans that offer reasonable promise of success and are consistent with abilities and circumstances of clients. Counselors and clients regularly review counseling plans to ensure their continued viability and effectiveness, respecting clients' freedom of choice.

d. *Family Involvement.*
Counselors recognize that families are usually important in clients' lives and strive to enlist family understanding and involvement as a positive resource when appropriate.

e. *Career and Employment Needs.*
Counselors work with their clients in considering employment in jobs and circumstances that are consistent with the clients' overall abilities, vocational

---

*As approved by Governing Council, April 1997, Effective July 1, 1997. Copyright ©1997 by the American Counseling Association. All rights reserved. Reprinted with permission. No further reproduction authorized without written permission of the American Counseling Association.

All cross-references in the text of the Code have been omitted. (They are retained in the Standards.)

limitations, physical restrictions, general temperament, interest and aptitude patterns, social skills, education, general qualifications, and other relevant characteristics and needs. Counselors neither place nor participate in placing clients in positions that will result in damaging the interest and the welfare of clients, employers, or the public.

A.2. Respecting Diversity

a. *Nondiscrimination.*
Counselors do not condone or engage in discrimination based on age, color, culture, disability, ethnic group, gender, race, religion, sexual orientation, marital status, or socioeconomic status.

b. *Respecting Differences.*
Counselors will actively attempt to understand the diverse cultural backgrounds of the clients with whom they work. This includes, but is not limited to, learning how the counselor's own cultural/ethnic/racial identity impacts her or his values and beliefs about the counseling process.

A.3. Client Rights

a. *Disclosure to Clients.*
When counseling is initiated, and throughout the counseling process as necessary, counselors inform clients of the purposes, goals, techniques, procedures, limitations, potential risks, and benefits of services to be performed, and other pertinent information. Counselors take steps to ensure that clients understand the implications of diagnosis, the intended use of tests and reports, fees, and billing arrangements. Clients have the right to expect confidentiality and to be provided with an explanation of its limitations, including supervision and/or treatment team professionals; to obtain clear information about their case records; to participate in the ongoing counseling plans; and to refuse any recommended services and be advised of the consequences of such refusal.

b. *Freedom of Choice.*
Counselors offer clients the freedom to choose whether to enter into a counseling relationship and to determine which professional(s) will provide counseling. Restrictions that limit choices of clients are fully explained.

c. *Inability to Give Consent.*
When counseling minors or persons unable to give voluntary informed consent, counselors act in these clients' best interests.

A.4. Clients Served by Others

If a client is receiving services from another mental health professional, counselors, with client consent, inform the professional persons already involved and develop clear agreements to avoid confusion and conflict for the client.

A.5. Personal Needs and Values

a. *Personal Needs.*
In the counseling relationship, counselors are aware of the intimacy and responsibilities inherent in the counseling relationship, maintain respect for clients, and avoid actions that seek to meet their personal needs at the expense of clients.

b. *Personal Values.*
Counselors are aware of their own values, attitudes, beliefs, and behaviors and how these apply in a diverse society, and avoid imposing their values on clients.

A.6. Dual Relationships

a. *Avoid When Possible.*
Counselors are aware of their influential positions with respect to clients, and they avoid exploiting the trust and dependency of clients. Counselors make every effort to avoid dual relationships with clients that could impair professional judgment or increase the risk of harm to clients. (Examples of such relationships include, but are not limited to, familial, social, financial, business, or close personal relationships with clients.) When a dual relationship cannot be avoided, counselors take appropriate professional precautions such as informed consent, consultation, supervision, and documentation to ensure that judgment is not impaired and no exploitation occurs.

b. *Superior/Subordinate Relationships.*
Counselors do not accept as clients superiors or subordinates with whom they have administrative, supervisory, or evaluative relationships.

A.7. Sexual Intimacies With Clients

a. *Current Clients.*
Counselors do not have any type of sexual intimacies with clients and do not counsel persons with whom they have had a sexual relationship.

b. *Former Clients.*
Counselors do not engage in sexual intimacies with former clients within a minimum of 2 years after terminating the counseling relationship. Counselors who engage in such relationship after 2 years following termination have the responsibility to thoroughly examine and document that such relations did not have an exploitative nature, based on factors such as duration of counseling, amount of time since counseling, termination circumstances, client's personal history and mental status, adverse impact on the client, and actions by the counselor suggesting a plan to initiate a sexual relationship with the client after termination.

A.8. Multiple Clients

When counselors agree to provide counseling services to two or more persons who have a relationship (such as husband and wife, or parents and children), counselors clarify at the outset which person or persons are clients and the nature of the relationships they will have with each involved person. If it becomes apparent that counselors may be called upon to perform potentially conflicting roles, they clarify, adjust, or withdraw from roles appropriately.

A.9. Group Work

a. *Screening.*
Counselors screen prospective group counseling/therapy participants. To the extent possible, counselors select members whose needs and goals are compatible with goals of the group, who will not impede the group process, and whose well-being will not be jeopardized by the group experience.

b. *Protecting Clients.*
In a group setting, counselors take reasonable precautions to protect clients from physical or psychological trauma.

A.10. Fees and Bartering

a. *Advance Understanding.*
Counselors clearly explain to clients, prior to entering the counseling relationship, all financial arrangements related to professional services including the use of collection agencies or legal measures for nonpayment.

b. *Establishing Fees.*
In establishing fees for professional counseling services, counselors consider the financial status of clients and locality. In the event that the established fee structure is inappropriate for a client, assistance is provided in attempting to find comparable services of acceptable cost.

c. *Bartering Discouraged.*
Counselors ordinarily refrain from accepting goods or services from clients in return for counseling services because such arrangements create inherent potential for conflicts, exploitation, and distortion of the professional relationship. Counselors may participate in bartering only if the relationship is not exploitative, if the client requests it, if a clear written contract is established, and if such arrangements are an accepted practice among professionals in the community.

d. *Pro Bono Service.*
Counselors contribute to society by devoting a portion of their professional activity to services for which there is little or no financial return (pro bono).

A.11. Termination and Referral

a. *Abandonment Prohibited.*
Counselors do not abandon or neglect clients in counseling. Counselors assist in making appropriate arrangements for the continuation of treatment, when necessary, during interruptions such as vacations, and following termination.

b. *Inability to Assist Clients.*
If counselors determine an inability to be of professional assistance to clients, they avoid entering or immediately terminate a counseling relationship. Counselors are knowledgeable about referral resources and suggest appropriate alternatives. If clients decline the suggested referral, counselors should discontinue the relationship.

c. *Appropriate Termination.*
Counselors terminate a counseling relationship, securing client agreement when possible, when it is reasonably clear that the client is no longer benefiting, when services are no longer required, when counseling no longer serves the client's needs or interests, when clients do not pay fees charged, or when agency or institution limits do not allow provision of further counseling services.

A.12. Computer Technology

a. *Use of Computers.*
When computer applications are used in counseling services, counselors ensure that (1) the client is intellectually, emotionally, and physically capable of using the computer application; (2) the computer application is appropriate for the

needs of the client; (3) the client understands the purpose and operation of the computer applications; and (4) a follow-up of client use of a computer application is provided to correct possible misconceptions, discover inappropriate use, and assess subsequent needs.

b. *Explanation of Limitations.*
Counselors ensure that clients are provided information as a part of the counseling relationship that adequately explains the limitations of computer technology.

c. *Access to Computer Applications.*
Counselors provide for equal access to computer applications in counseling services.

Section B:
CONFIDENTIALITY

B.1. Right to Privacy

a. *Respect for Privacy.*
Counselors respect their clients right to privacy and avoid illegal and unwarranted disclosures of confidential information.

b. *Client Waiver.*
The right to privacy may be waived by the client or their legally recognized representative.

c. *Exceptions.*
The general requirement that counselors keep information confidential does not apply when disclosure is required to prevent clear and imminent danger to the client or others or when legal requirements demand that confidential information be revealed. Counselors consult with other professionals when in doubt as to the validity of an exception.

d. *Contagious, Fatal Diseases.*
A counselor who receives information confirming that a client has a disease commonly known to be both communicable and fatal is justified in disclosing information to an identifiable third party, who by his or her relationship with the client is at a high risk of contracting the disease. Prior to making a disclosure the counselor should ascertain that the client has not already informed the third party about his or her disease and that the client is not intending to inform the third party in the immediate future.

e. *Court-Ordered Disclosure.*
When court ordered to release confidential information without a client's permission, counselors request to the court that the disclosure not be required due to potential harm to the client or counseling relationship.

f. *Minimal Disclosure.*
When circumstances require the disclosure of confidential information, only essential information is revealed. To the extent possible, clients are informed before confidential information is disclosed.

g. *Explanation of Limitations.*
When counseling is initiated and throughout the counseling process as necessary, counselors inform clients of the limitations of confidentiality and identify foreseeable situations in which confidentiality must be breached.

h. *Subordinates.*
Counselors make every effort to ensure that privacy and confidentiality of clients are maintained by subordinates including employees, supervisees, clerical assistants, and volunteers.

i. *Treatment Teams.*
If client treatment will involve a continued review by a treatment team, the client will be informed of the team's existence and composition.

B.2. Groups and Families

a. *Group Work.*
In group work, counselors clearly define confidentiality and the parameters for the specific group being entered, explain its importance, and discuss the difficulties related to confidentiality involved in group work. The fact that confidentiality cannot be guaranteed is clearly communicated to group members.

b. *Family Counseling.*
In family counseling, information about one family member cannot be disclosed to another member without permission. Counselors protect the privacy rights of each family member.

B.3. Minor or Incompetent Clients

When counseling clients who are minors or individuals who are unable to give voluntary, informed consent, parents or guardians may be included in the counseling process as appropriate. Counselors act in the best interests of clients and take measures to safeguard confidentiality.

B.4. Records

a. *Requirement of Records.*
Counselors maintain records necessary for rendering professional services to their clients and as required by laws, regulations, or agency or institution procedures.

b. *Confidentiality of Records.*
Counselors are responsible for securing the safety and confidentiality of any counseling records they create, maintain, transfer, or destroy whether the records are written, taped, computerized, or stored in any other medium.

c. *Permission to Record or Observe.*
Counselors obtain permission from clients prior to electronically recording or observing sessions.

d. *Client Access.*
Counselors recognize that counseling records are kept for the benefit of clients and, therefore, provide access to records and copies of records when requested by competent clients, unless the records contain information that may be misleading and detrimental to the client. In situations involving multiple clients, access to records is limited to those parts of records that do not include confidential information related to another client.

e. *Disclosure or Transfer.*
Counselors obtain written permission from clients to disclose or transfer records to legitimate third parties unless exceptions to confidentiality exist as listed in Section B.1. Steps are taken to ensure that receivers of counseling records are sensitive to their confidential nature.

B.5. Research and Training

a. *Data Disguise Required.*
Use of data derived from counseling relationships for purposes of training, research, or publication is confined to content that is disguised to ensure the anonymity of the individuals involved.

b. *Agreement for Identification.*
Identification of a client in a presentation or publication is permissible only when the client has reviewed the material and has agreed to its presentation or publication.

B.6. Consultation

a. *Respect for Privacy.*
Information obtained in a consulting relationship is discussed for professional purposes only with persons clearly concerned with the case. Written and oral reports present data germane to the purposes of the consultation, and every effort is made to protect client identity and avoid undue invasion of privacy.

b. *Cooperating Agencies.*
Before sharing information, counselors make efforts to ensure that there are defined policies in other agencies serving the counselor's clients that effectively protect the confidentiality of information.

Section C:
PROFESSIONAL RESPONSIBILITY

C.1. Standards Knowledge

Counselors have a responsibility to read, understand, and follow the Code of Ethics and the Standards of Practice.

C.2. Professional Competence

a. *Boundaries of Competence.*
Counselors practice only within the boundaries of their competence, based on their education, training, supervised experience, state and national professional credentials, and appropriate professional experience. Counselors will demonstrate a commitment to gain knowledge, personal awareness, sensitivity, and skills pertinent to working with a diverse client population.

b. *New Specialty Areas of Practice.*
Counselors practice in specialty areas new to them only after appropriate education, training, and supervised experience. While developing skills in new specialty areas, counselors take steps to ensure the competence of their work and to protect others from possible harm.

c. *Qualified for Employment.*
Counselors accept employment only for positions for which they are qualified by education, training, supervised experience, state and national professional credentials, and appropriate professional experience. Counselors hire for professional counseling positions only individuals who are qualified and competent.

d. *Monitor Effectiveness.*
Counselors continually monitor their effectiveness as professionals and take steps to improve when necessary. Counselors in private practice take reasonable steps to seek out peer supervision to evaluate their efficacy as counselors.

e. *Ethical Issues Consultation.*
Counselors take reasonable steps to consult with other counselors or related professionals when they have questions regarding their ethical obligations or professional practice.

f. *Continuing Education.*
Counselors recognize the need for continuing education to maintain a reasonable level of awareness of current scientific and professional information in their fields of activity. They take steps to maintain competence in the skills they use, are open to new procedures, and keep current with the diverse and/or special populations with whom they work.

g. *Impairment.*
Counselors refrain from offering or accepting professional services when their physical, mental, or emotional problems are likely to harm a client or others. They are alert to the signs of impairment, seek assistance for problems, and, if necessary, limit, suspend, or terminate their professional responsibilities.

C.3. Advertising and Soliciting Clients

a. *Accurate Advertising.*
There are no restrictions on advertising by counselors except those that can be specifically justified to protect the public from deceptive practices. Counselors advertise or represent their services to the public by identifying their credentials in an accurate manner that is not false, misleading, deceptive, or fraudulent. Counselors may only advertise the highest degree earned which is in counseling or a closely related field from a college or university that was accredited when the degree was awarded by one of the regional accrediting bodies recognized by the Council on Postsecondary Accreditation.

b. *Testimonials.*
Counselors who use testimonials do not solicit them from clients or other persons who, because of their particular circumstances, may be vulnerable to undue influence.

c. *Statements by Others.*
Counselors make reasonable efforts to ensure that statements made by others about them or the profession of counseling are accurate.

d. *Recruiting Through Employment.*
Counselors do not use their places of employment or institutional affiliation to recruit or gain clients, supervisees, or consultees for their private practices.

e. *Products and Training Advertisements.*
Counselors who develop products related to their profession or conduct workshops or training events ensure that the advertisements concerning these products or events are accurate and disclose adequate information for consumers to make informed choices.

f. *Promoting to Those Served.*
Counselors do not use counseling, teaching, training, or supervisory relationships to promote their products or training events in a manner that is deceptive or would exert undue influence on individuals who may be vulnerable. Counselors may adopt textbooks they have authored for instruction purposes.

g. *Professional Association Involvement.*
Counselors actively participate in local, state, and national associations that foster the development and improvement of counseling.

C.4. Credentials

a. *Credentials Claimed.*
Counselors claim or imply only professional credentials possessed and are responsible for correcting any known misrepresentations of their credentials by others. Professional credentials include graduate degrees in counseling or closely related mental health fields, accreditation of graduate programs, national voluntary certifications, government-issued certifications or licenses, ACA professional membership, or any other credential that might indicate to the public specialized knowledge or expertise in counseling.

b. *ACA Professional Membership.*
ACA professional members may announce to the public their membership status. Regular members may not announce their ACA membership in a manner that might imply they are credentialed counselors.

c. *Credential Guidelines.*
Counselors follow the guidelines for use of credentials that have been established by the entities that issue the credentials.

d. *Misrepresentation of Credentials.*
Counselors do not attribute more to their credentials than the credentials represent and do not imply that other counselors are not qualified because they do not possess certain credentials.

e. *Doctoral Degrees From Other Fields.*
Counselors who hold a master's degree in counseling or a closely related mental health field, but hold a doctoral degree from other than counseling or a closely related field, do not use the title "Dr." in their practices and do not announce to the public in relation to their practice or status as a counselor that they hold a doctorate.

C.5. Public Responsibility

a. *Nondiscrimination.*
Counselors do not discriminate against clients, students, or supervisees in a manner that has a negative impact based on their age, color, culture, disability, ethnic group, gender, race, religion, sexual orientation, or socioeconomic status, or for any other reason.

b. *Sexual Harassment.*
Counselors do not engage in sexual harassment. Sexual harassment is defined as sexual solicitation, physical advances, or verbal or nonverbal conduct that is sexual in nature, that occurs in connection with professional activities or roles, and that either (1) is unwelcome, is offensive, or creates a hostile workplace environment, and counselors know or are told this; or (2) is sufficiently severe or intense to be perceived as harassment to a reasonable person in the context. Sexual harassment can consist of a single intense or severe act or multiple persistent or pervasive acts.

c. *Reports to Third Parties.*
Counselors are accurate, honest, and unbiased in reporting their professional activities and judgments to appropriate third parties including courts, health insurance companies, those who are the recipients of evaluation reports, and others.

d. *Media Presentations.*
When counselors provide advice or comment by means of public lectures, demonstrations, radio or television programs, prerecorded tapes, printed articles, mailed material, or other media, they take reasonable precautions to ensure that (1) the statements are based on appropriate professional counseling litera-ture and practice; (2) the statements are otherwise consistent with the Code of Ethics and the Standards of Practice; and (3) the recipients of the information are not encouraged to infer that a professional counseling relationship has been established.

e. *Unjustified Gains.*
Counselors do not use their professional positions to seek or receive unjustified personal gains, sexual favors, unfair advantage, or unearned goods or services.

C.6. Responsibility to Other Professionals

a. *Different Approaches.*
Counselors are respectful of approaches to professional counseling that differ from their own. Counselors know and take into account the traditions and practices of other professional groups with which they work.

b. *Personal Public Statements.*
When making personal statements in a public context, counselors clarify that they are speaking from their personal perspectives and that they are not speaking on behalf of all counselors or the profession.

c. *Clients Served by Others.*
When counselors learn that their clients are in a professional relationship with another mental health professional, they request release from clients to inform the other professionals and strive to establish positive and collaborative profes-sional relationships.

Section D:
RELATIONSHIPS WITH OTHER PROFESSIONALS

D.1. Relationships With Employers and Employees

a. *Role Definition.*
Counselors define and describe for their employers and employees the parame-ters and levels of their professional roles.

b. *Agreements.*
Counselors establish working agreements with supervisors, colleagues, and subordinates regarding counseling or clinical relationships, confidentiality, adherence to professional standards, distinction between public and private material, maintenance and dissemination of recorded information, workload, and accountability. Working agreements in each instance are specified and made known to those concerned.

c. *Negative Conditions.*
Counselors alert their employers to conditions that may be potentially disruptive or damaging to the counselor's professional responsibilities or that may limit their effectiveness.

d. *Evaluation.*
Counselors submit regularly to professional review and evaluation by their supervisor or the appropriate representative of the employer.

e. *In-Service.*
Counselors are responsible for in-service development of self and staff.

f. *Goals.*
Counselors inform their staff of goals and programs.

g. *Practices.*
Counselors provide personnel and agency practices that respect and enhance the rights and welfare of each employee and recipient of agency services. Counselors strive to maintain the highest levels of professional services.

h. *Personnel Selection and Assignment.*
Counselors select competent staff and assign responsibilities compatible with their skills and experiences.

i. *Discrimination.*
Counselors, as either employers or employees, do not engage in or condone practices that are inhumane, illegal, or unjustifiable (such as considerations based on age, color, culture, disability, ethnic group, gender, race, religion, sexual orientation, or socioeconomic status) in hiring, promotion, or training.

j. *Professional Conduct.*
Counselors have a responsibility both to clients and to the agency or institution within which services are performed to maintain high standards of professional conduct.

k. *Exploitive Relationships.*
Counselors do not engage in exploitive relationships with individuals over whom they have supervisory, evaluative, or instructional control or authority.

l. *Employer Policies.*
The acceptance of employment in an agency or institution implies that counselors are in agreement with its general policies and principles. Counselors strive to reach agreement with employers as to acceptable standards of conduct that allow for changes in institutional policy conducive to the growth and development of clients.

D.2. Consultation

a. *Consultation as an Option.*
Counselors may choose to consult with any other professionally competent

persons about their clients. In choosing consultants, counselors avoid placing the consultant in a conflict of interest situation that would preclude the consultant being a proper party to the counselor's efforts to help the client. Should counselors be engaged in a work setting that compromises this consultation standard, they consult with other professionals whenever possible to consider justifiable alternatives.

b. *Consultant Competency.*
Counselors are reasonably certain that they have or the organization represented has the necessary competencies and resources for giving the kind of consulting services needed and that appropriate referral resources are available.

c. *Understanding With Clients.*
When providing consultation, counselors attempt to develop with their clients a clear understanding of problem definition, goals for change, and predicted consequences of interventions selected.

d. *Consultant Goals.*
The consulting relationship is one in which client adaptability and growth toward self-direction are consistently encouraged and cultivated.

D.3. Fees for Referral

a. *Accepting Fees From Agency Clients.*
Counselors refuse a private fee or other remuneration for rendering services to persons who are entitled to such services through the counselor's employing agency or institution. The policies of a particular agency may make explicit provisions for agency clients to receive counseling services from members of its staff in private practice. In such instances, the clients must be informed of other options open to them should they seek private counseling services.

b. *Referral Fees.*
Counselors do not accept a referral fee from other professionals.

D.4. Subcontractor Arrangements

When counselors work as subcontractors for counseling services for a third party, they have a duty to inform clients of the limitations of confidentiality that the organization may place on counselors in providing counseling services to clients. The limits of such confidentiality ordinarily are discussed as part of the intake session.

Section E:
EVALUATION, ASSESSMENT, AND INTERPRETATION

E.1. General

a. *Appraisal Techniques.*
The primary purpose of educational and psychological assessment is to provide measures that are objective and interpretable in either comparative or absolute terms. Counselors recognize the need to interpret the statements in this section as applying to the whole range of appraisal techniques, including test and nontest data.

b. *Client Welfare.*

Counselors promote the welfare and best interests of the client in the development, publication, and utilization of educational and psychological assessment techniques. They do not misuse assessment results and interpretations and take reasonable steps to prevent others from misusing the information these techniques provide. They respect the client's right to know the results, the interpretations made, and the bases for their conclusions and recommendations.

E.2. Competence to Use and Interpret Tests

a. *Limits of Competence.*

Counselors recognize the limits of their competence and perform only those testing and assessment services for which they have been trained. They are familiar with reliability, validity, related standardization, error of measurement, and proper application of any technique utilized. Counselors using computer-based test interpretations are trained in the construct being measured and the specific instrument being used prior to using this type of computer application. Counselors take reasonable measures to ensure the proper use of psychological assessment techniques by persons under their supervision.

b. *Appropriate Use.*

Counselors are responsible for the appropriate application, scoring, interpretation, and use of assessment instruments, whether they score and interpret such tests themselves or use computerized or other services.

c. *Decisions Based on Results.*

Counselors responsible for decisions involving individuals or policies that are based on assessment results have a thorough understanding of educational and psychological measurement, including validation criteria, test research, and guidelines for test development and use.

d. *Accurate Information.*

Counselors provide accurate information and avoid false claims or misconceptions when making statements about assessment instruments or techniques. Special efforts are made to avoid unwarranted connotations of such terms as IQ and grade equivalent scores.

E.3. Informed Consent

a. *Explanation to Clients.*

Prior to assessment, counselors explain the nature and purposes of assessment and the specific use of results in language the client (or other legally authorized person on behalf of the client) can understand unless an explicit exception to this right has been agreed upon in advance. Regardless of whether scoring and interpretation are completed by counselors, by assistants, or by computer or other outside services, counselors take reasonable steps to ensure that appropriate explanations are given to the client.

b. *Recipients of Results.*

The examinee's welfare, explicit understanding, and prior agreement determine the recipients of test results. Counselors include accurate and appropriate interpretations with any release of individual or group test results.

E.4. Release of Information to Competent Professionals

a. *Misuse of Results.*
Counselors do not misuse assessment results, including test results, and interpretations and take reasonable steps to prevent the misuse of such by others.

b. *Release of Raw Data.*
Counselors ordinarily release data (e.g., protocols, counseling or interview notes, or questionnaires) in which the client is identified only with the consent of the client or the client's legal representative. Such data are usually released only to persons recognized by counselors as competent to interpret the data.

E.5. Proper Diagnosis of Mental Disorders

a. *Proper Diagnosis.*
Counselors take special care to provide proper diagnosis of mental disorders. Assessment techniques (including personal interview) used to determine client care (e.g., locus of treatment, type of treatment, or recommended follow-up) are carefully selected and appropriately used.

b. *Cultural Sensitivity.*
Counselors recognize that culture affects the manner in which clients' problems are defined. Clients' socioeconomic and cultural experience is considered when diagnosing mental disorders.

E.6. Test Selection

a. *Appropriateness of Instruments.*
Counselors carefully consider the validity, reliability, psychometric limitations, and appropriateness of instruments when selecting tests for use in a given situation or with a particular client.

b. *Culturally Diverse Populations.*
Counselors are cautious when selecting tests for culturally diverse populations to avoid inappropriateness of testing that may be outside of socialized behavioral or cognitive patterns.

E.7. Conditions of Test Administration

a. *Administration Conditions.*
Counselors administer tests under the same conditions that were established in their standardization. When tests are not administered under standard conditions or when unusual behavior or irregularities occur during the testing session, those conditions are noted in interpretation, and the results may be designated as invalid or of questionable validity.

b. *Computer Administration.*
Counselors are responsible for ensuring that administration programs function properly to provide clients with accurate results when a computer or other electronic methods are used for test administration.

c. *Unsupervised Test Taking.*
Counselors do not permit unsupervised or inadequately supervised use of tests or assessments unless the tests or assessments are designed, intended, and validated for self-administration and/or scoring.

d. *Disclosure of Favorable Conditions.*
Prior to test administration, conditions that produce most favorable test results are made known to the examinee.

E.8. Diversity in Testing

Counselors are cautious in using assessment techniques, making evaluations, and interpreting the performance of populations not represented in the norm group on which an instrument was standardized. They recognize the effects of age, color, culture, disability, ethnic group, gender, race, religion, sexual orientation, and socioeconomic status on test administration and interpretation and place test results in proper perspective with other relevant factors.

E.9. Test Scoring and Interpretation

a. *Reporting Reservations.*
In reporting assessment results, counselors indicate any reservations that exist regarding validity or reliability because of the circumstances of the assessment or the inappropriateness of the norms for the person tested.

b. *Research Instruments.*
Counselors exercise caution when interpreting the results of research instruments possessing insufficient technical data to support respondent results. The specific purposes for the use of such instruments are stated explicitly to the examinee.

c. *Testing Services.*
Counselors who provide test scoring and test interpretation services to support the assessment process confirm the validity of such interpretations. They accurately describe the purpose, norms, validity, reliability, and applications of the procedures and any special qualifications applicable to their use. The public offering of an automated test interpretations service is considered a professional-to-professional consultation. The formal responsibility of the consultant is to the consultee, but the ultimate and overriding responsibility is to the client.

E.10. Test Security

Counselors maintain the integrity and security of tests and other assessment techniques consistent with legal and contractual obligations. Counselors do not appropriate, reproduce, or modify published tests or parts thereof without acknowledgment and permission from the publisher.

E.11. Obsolete Tests and Outdated Test Results

Counselors do not use data or test results that are obsolete or outdated for the current purpose. Counselors make every effort to prevent the misuse of obsolete measures and test data by others.

E.12. Test Construction

Counselors use established scientific procedures, relevant standards, and current professional knowledge for test design in the development, publication, and utilization of educational and psychological assessment techniques.

Section F:
TEACHING, TRAINING, AND SUPERVISION

F.1. Counselor Educators and Trainers

a. *Educators as Teachers and Practitioners.*
   Counselors who are responsible for developing, implementing, and supervising educational programs are skilled as teachers and practitioners. They are knowledgeable regarding the ethical, legal, and regulatory aspects of the profession, are skilled in applying that knowledge, and make students and supervisees aware of their responsibilities. Counselors conduct counselor education and training programs in an ethical manner and serve as role models for professional behavior. Counselor educators should make an effort to infuse material related to human diversity into all courses and/or workshops that are designed to promote the development of professional counselors.

b. *Relationship Boundaries With Students and Supervisees.*
   Counselors clearly define and maintain ethical, professional, and social relationship boundaries with their students and supervisees. They are aware of the differential in power that exists and the student's or supervisee's possible incomprehension of that power differential. Counselors explain to students and supervisees the potential for the relationship to become exploitive.

c. *Sexual Relationships.*
   Counselors do not engage in sexual relationships with students or supervisees and do not subject them to sexual harassment.

d. *Contributions to Research.*
   Counselors give credit to students or supervisees for their contributions to research and scholarly projects. Credit is given through coauthorship, acknowledgment, footnote statement, or other appropriate means, in accordance with such contributions.

e. *Close Relatives.*
   Counselors do not accept close relatives as students or supervisees.

f. *Supervision Preparation.*
   Counselors who offer clinical supervision services are adequately prepared in supervision methods and techniques. Counselors who are doctoral students serving as practicum or internship supervisors to master's level students are adequately prepared and supervised by the training program.

g. *Responsibility for Services to Clients.*
   Counselors who supervise the counseling services of others take reasonable measures to ensure that counseling services provided to clients are professional.

h. *Endorsement.*
   Counselors do not endorse students or supervisees for certification, licensure, employment, or completion of an academic or training program if they believe students or supervisees are not qualified for the endorsement. Counselors take reasonable steps to assist students or supervisees who are not qualified for endorsement to become qualified.

F.2. Counselor Education and Training Programs

a. *Orientation.*
Prior to admission, counselors orient prospective students to the counselor education or training program's expectations, including but not limited to the following: (1) the type and level of skill acquisition required for successful completion of the training, (2) subject matter to be covered, (3) basis for evaluation, (4) training components that encourage self-growth or self-disclosure as part of the training process, (5) the type of supervision settings and requirements of the sites for required clinical field experiences, (6) student and supervisee evaluation and dismissal policies and procedures, and (7) up-to-date employment prospects for graduates.

b. *Integration of Study and Practice.*
Counselors establish counselor education and training programs that integrate academic study and supervised practice.

c. *Evaluation.*
Counselors clearly state to students and supervisees, in advance of training, the levels of competency expected, appraisal methods, and timing of evaluations for both didactic and experiential components. Counselors provide students and supervisees with periodic performance appraisal and evaluation feedback throughout the training program.

d. *Teaching Ethics.*
Counselors make students and supervisees aware of the ethical responsibilities and standards of the profession and the students' and supervisees' ethical responsibilities to the profession.

e. *Peer Relationships.*
When students or supervisees are assigned to lead counseling groups or provide clinical supervision for their peers, counselors take steps to ensure that students and supervisees placed in these roles do not have personal or adverse relationships with peers and that they understand they have the same ethical obligations as counselor educators, trainers, and supervisors. Counselors make every effort to ensure that the rights of peers are not compromised when students or supervisees are assigned to lead counseling groups or provide clinical supervision.

f. *Varied Theoretical Positions.*
Counselors present varied theoretical positions so that students and supervisees may make comparisons and have opportunities to develop their own positions. Counselors provide information concerning the scientific bases of professional practice.

g. *Field Placements.*
Counselors develop clear policies within their training program regarding field placement and other clinical experiences. Counselors provide clearly stated roles and responsibilities for the student or supervisee, the site supervisor, and the program supervisor. They confirm that site supervisors are qualified to provide supervision and are informed of their professional and ethical responsibilities in this role.

h. *Dual Relationships as Supervisors.*
Counselors avoid dual relationships, such as performing the role of site supervi-

sor and training program supervisor in the student's or supervisee's training program. Counselors do not accept any form of professional services, fees, commissions, reimbursement, or remuneration from a site for student or supervisee placement.

i. *Diversity in Programs.*
Counselors are responsive to their institution's and program's recruitment and retention needs for training program administrators, faculty, and students with diverse backgrounds and special needs.

F.3. Students and Supervisees

a. *Limitations.*
Counselors, through ongoing evaluation and appraisal, are aware of the academic and personal limitations of students and supervisees that might impede performance. Counselors assist students and supervisees in securing remedial assistance when needed and dismiss from the training program supervisees who are unable to provide competent service due to academic or personal limitations. Counselors seek professional consultation and document their decision to dismiss or refer students or supervisees for assistance. Counselors ensure that students and supervisees have recourse to address decisions made, to require them to seek assistance, or to dismiss them.

b. *Self-Growth Experiences.*
Counselors use professional judgment when designing training experiences conducted by the counselors themselves that require student and supervisee self-growth or self-disclosure. Safeguards are provided so that students and supervisees are aware of the ramifications their self-disclosure may have on counselors whose primary role as teacher, trainer, or supervisor requires acting on ethical obligations to the profession. Evaluative components of experiential training experiences explicitly delineate predetermined academic standards that are separate and do not depend on the student's level of self-disclosure.

c. *Counseling for Students and Supervisees.*
If students or supervisees request counseling, supervisors or counselor educators provide them with acceptable referrals. Supervisors or counselor educators do not serve as counselor to students or supervisees over whom they hold administrative, teaching, or evaluative roles unless this is a brief role associated with a training experience.

d. *Clients of Students and Supervisees.*
Counselors make every effort to ensure that the clients at field placements are aware of the services rendered and the qualifications of the students and supervisees rendering those services. Clients receive professional disclosure information and are informed of the limits of confidentiality. Client permission is obtained in order for the students and supervisees to use any information concerning the counseling relationship in the training process.

e. *Standards for Students and Supervisees.*
Students and supervisees preparing to become counselors adhere to the Code of Ethics and the Standards of Practice. Students and supervisees have the same obligations to clients as those required of counselors.

Section G:
RESEARCH AND PUBLICATION

G.1. Research Responsibilities

a. *Use of Human Subjects.*
Counselors plan, design, conduct, and report research in a manner consistent with pertinent ethical principles, federal and state laws, host institutional regulations, and scientific standards governing research with human subjects. Counselors design and conduct research that reflects cultural sensitivity appropriateness.

b. *Deviation From Standard Practices.*
Counselors seek consultation and observe stringent safeguards to protect the rights of research participants when a research problem suggests a deviation from standard acceptable practices.

c. *Precautions to Avoid Injury.*
Counselors who conduct research with human subjects are responsible for the subjects' welfare throughout the experiment and take reasonable precautions to avoid causing injurious psychological, physical, or social effects to their subjects.

d. *Principal Researcher Responsibility.*
The ultimate responsibility for ethical research practice lies with the principal researcher. All others involved in the research activities share ethical obligations and full responsibility for their own actions.

e. *Minimal Interference.*
Counselors take reasonable precautions to avoid causing disruptions in subjects' lives due to participation in research.

f. *Diversity.*
Counselors are sensitive to diversity and research issues with special populations. They seek consultation when appropriate.

G.2. Informed Consent

a. *Topics Disclosed.*
In obtaining informed consent for research, counselors use language that is understandable to research participants and that (1) accurately explains the purpose and procedures to be followed; (2) identifies any procedures that are experimental or relatively untried; (3) describes the attendant discomforts and risks; (4) describes the benefits or changes in individuals or organizations that might be reasonably expected; (5) discloses appropriate alternative procedures that would be advantageous for subjects; (6) offers to answer any inquiries concerning the procedures; (7) describes any limitations on confidentiality; and (8) instructs that subjects are free to withdraw their consent and to discontinue participation in the project at any time.

b. *Deception.*
Counselors do not conduct research involving deception unless alternative procedures are not feasible and the prospective value of the research justifies the deception. When the methodological requirements of a study necessitate concealment or deception, the investigator is required to explain clearly the reasons for this action as soon as possible.

c. *Voluntary Participation.*
Participation in research is typically voluntary and without any penalty for refusal to participate. Involuntary participation is appropriate only when it can be demonstrated that participation will have no harmful effects on subjects and is essential to the investigation.

d. *Confidentiality of Information.*
Information obtained about research participants during the course of an investigation is confidential. When the possibility exists that others may obtain access to such information, ethical research practice requires that the possibility, together with the plans for protecting confidentiality, be explained to participants as a part of the procedure for obtaining informed consent.

e. *Persons Incapable of Giving Informed Consent.*
When a person is incapable of giving informed consent, counselors provide an appropriate explanation, obtain agreement for participation, and obtain appropriate consent from a legally authorized person.

f. *Commitments to Participants.*
Counselors take reasonable measures to honor all commitments to research participants.

g. *Explanations After Data Collection.*
After data are collected, counselors provide participants with full clarification of the nature of the study to remove any misconceptions. Where scientific or human values justify delaying or withholding information, counselors take reasonable measures to avoid causing harm.

h. *Agreements to Cooperate.*
Counselors who agree to cooperate with another individual in research or publication incur an obligation to cooperate as promised in terms of punctuality of performance and with regard to the completeness and accuracy of the information required.

i. *Informed Consent for Sponsors.*
In the pursuit of research, counselors give sponsors, institutions, and publication channels the same respect and opportunity for giving informed consent that they accord to individual research participants. Counselors are aware of their obligation to future research workers and ensure that host institutions are given feedback information and proper acknowledgment.

G.3. Reporting Results

a. *Information Affecting Outcome.*
When reporting research results, counselors explicitly mention all variables and conditions known to the investigator that may have affected the outcome of a study or the interpretation of data.

b. *Accurate Results.*
Counselors plan, conduct, and report research accurately and in a manner that minimizes the possibility that results will be misleading. They provide thorough discussions of the limitations of their data and alternative hypotheses. Counselors do not engage in fraudulent research, distort data, misrepresent data, or deliberately bias their results.

c. *Obligation to Report Unfavorable Results.*
Counselors communicate to other counselors the results of any research judged to be of professional value. Results that reflect unfavorably on institutions, programs, services, prevailing opinions, or vested interests are not withheld.

d. *Identity of Subjects.*
Counselors who supply data, aid in the research of another person, report research results, or make original data available take due care to disguise the identity of respective subjects in the absence of specific authorization from the subjects to do otherwise.

e. *Replication Studies.*
Counselors are obligated to make available sufficient original research data to qualified professionals who may wish to replicate the study.

G.4. Publication

a. *Recognition of Others.*
When conducting and reporting research, counselors are familiar with and give recognition to previous work on the topic, observe copyright laws, and give full credit to those to whom credit is due.

b. *Contributors.*
Counselors give credit through joint authorship, acknowledgment, footnote statements, or other appropriate means to those who have contributed significantly to research or concept development in accordance with such contributions. The principal contributor is listed first and minor technical or professional contributions are acknowledged in notes or introductory statements.

c. *Student Research.*
For an article that is substantially based on a student's dissertation or thesis, the student is listed as the principal author.

d. *Duplicate Submission.*
Counselors submit manuscripts for consideration to only one journal at a time. Manuscripts that are published in whole or in substantial part in another journal or published work are not submitted for publication without acknowledgment and permission from the previous publication.

e. *Professional Review.*
Counselors who review material submitted for publication, research, or other scholarly purposes respect the confidentiality and proprietary rights of those who submitted it.

Section H:
RESOLVING ETHICAL ISSUES

H.1. Knowledge of Standards

Counselors are familiar with the Code of Ethics and the Standards of Practice and other applicable ethics codes from other professional organizations of which they are members, or from certification and licensure bodies. Lack of knowledge or misunderstanding of an ethical responsibility is not a defense against a charge of unethical conduct.

H.2. Suspected Violations

a. *Ethical Behavior Expected.*
Counselors expect professional associates to adhere to the Code of Ethics. When counselors possess reasonable cause that raises doubts as to whether a counselor is acting in an ethical manner, they take appropriate action.

b. *Consultation.*
When uncertain as to whether a particular situation or course of action may be in violation of the Code of Ethics, counselors consult with other counselors who are knowledgeable about ethics, with colleagues, or with appropriate authorities.

c. *Organization Conflicts.*
If the demands of an organization with which counselors are affiliated pose a conflict with the Code of Ethics, counselors specify the nature of such conflicts and express to their supervisors or other responsible officials their commitment to the Code of Ethics. When possible, counselors work toward change within the organization to allow full adherence to the Code of Ethics.

d. *Informal Resolution.*
When counselors have reasonable cause to believe that another counselor is violating an ethical standard, they attempt to first resolve the issue informally with the other counselor if feasible, providing that such action does not violate confidentiality rights that may be involved.

e. *Reporting Suspected Violations.*
When an informal resolution is not appropriate or feasible, counselors, upon reasonable cause, take action, such as reporting the suspected ethical violation to state or national ethics committees, unless this action conflicts with confidentiality rights that cannot be resolved.

f. *Unwarranted Complaints.*
Counselors do not initiate, participate in, or encourage the filing of ethics complaints that are unwarranted or intend to harm a counselor rather than to protect clients or the public.

H.3. Cooperation With Ethics Committees

Counselors assist in the process of enforcing the Code of Ethics. Counselors cooperate with investigations, proceedings, and requirements of the ACA Ethics Committee or ethics committees of other duly constituted associations or boards having jurisdiction over those charged with a violation. Counselors are familiar with the ACA Policies and Procedures and use it as a reference in assisting the enforcement of the Code of Ethics.

STANDARDS OF PRACTICE

All members of the American Counseling Association (ACA) are required to adhere to the Standards of Practice and the Code of Ethics. The Standards of Practice represent minimal behavioral statements of the Code of Ethics. Members should refer to the applicable section of the Code of Ethics for further interpretation and amplification of the applicable Standard of Practice.

Section A:
THE COUNSELING RELATIONSHIP

STANDARD OF PRACTICE One (SP-1):
Nondiscrimination.
Counselors respect diversity and must not discriminate against clients because of age, color, culture, disability, ethnic group, gender, race, religion, sexual orientation, marital status, or socioeconomic status. (See A.2.a.)

STANDARD OF PRACTICE Two (SP-2):
Disclosure to Clients.
Counselors must adequately inform clients, preferably in writing, regarding the counseling process and counseling relationship at or before the time it begins and throughout the relationship. (See A.3.a.)

STANDARD OF PRACTICE Three (SP-3):
Dual Relationships.
Counselors must make every effort to avoid dual relationships with clients that could impair their professional judgment or increase the risk of harm to clients. When a dual relationship cannot be avoided, counselors must take appropriate steps to ensure that judgment is not impaired and that no exploitation occurs. (See A.6.a. and A.6.b.)

STANDARD OF PRACTICE Four (SP-4):
Sexual Intimacies With Clients.
Counselors must not engage in any type of sexual intimacies with current clients and must not engage in sexual intimacies with former clients within a minimum of 2 years after terminating the counseling relationship. Counselors who engage in such relationship after 2 years following termination have the responsibility to thoroughly examine and document that such relations did not have an exploitative nature.

STANDARD OF PRACTICE Five (SP-5):
Protecting Clients During Group Work.
Counselors must take steps to protect clients from physical or psychological trauma resulting from interactions during group work. (See A.9.b.)

STANDARD OF PRACTICE Six (SP-6):
Advance Understanding of Fees.
Counselors must explain to clients, prior to their entering the counseling relationship, financial arrangements related to professional services. (See A.10. a.–d. and A.11.c.)

STANDARD OF PRACTICE Seven (SP-7):
Termination.

Counselors must assist in making appropriate arrangements for the continuation of treatment of clients, when necessary, following termination of counseling relationships. (See A.11.a.)

STANDARD OF PRACTICE Eight (SP-8):
Inability to Assist Clients.
Counselors must avoid entering or immediately terminate a counseling relationship if it is determined that they are unable to be of professional assistance to a client. The counselor may assist in making an appropriate referral for the client. (See A.11.b.)

Section B:
CONFIDENTIALITY

STANDARD OF PRACTICE Nine (SP-9):
Confidentiality Requirement.
Counselors must keep information related to counseling services confidential unless disclosure is in the best interest of clients, is required for the welfare of others, or is required by law. When disclosure is required, only information that is essential is revealed and the client is informed of such disclosure. (See B.1. a.–f.)

STANDARD OF PRACTICE Ten (SP-10):
Confidentiality Requirements for Subordinates.
Counselors must take measures to ensure that privacy and confidentiality of clients are maintained by subordinates. (See B.1.h.)

STANDARD OF PRACTICE Eleven (SP-11):
Confidentiality in Group Work.
Counselors must clearly communicate to group members that confidentiality cannot be guaranteed in group work. (See B.2.a.)

STANDARD OF PRACTICE Twelve (SP-12):
Confidentiality in Family Counseling.
Counselors must not disclose information about one family member in counseling to another family member without prior consent. (See B.2.b.)

STANDARD OF PRACTICE Thirteen (SP-13):
Confidentiality of Records.
Counselors must maintain appropriate confidentiality in creating, storing, accessing, transferring, and disposing of counseling records. (See B.4.b.)

STANDARD OF PRACTICE Fourteen (SP-14):
Permission to Record or Observe.
Counselors must obtain prior consent from clients in order to electronically record or observe sessions. (See B.4.c.)

STANDARD OF PRACTICE Fifteen (SP-15):
Disclosure or Transfer of Records.
Counselors must obtain client consent to disclose or transfer records to third parties, unless exceptions listed in SP-9 exist. (See B.4.e.)

STANDARD OF PRACTICE Sixteen (SP-16):
Data Disguise Required.
Counselors must disguise the identity of the client when using data for training, research, or publication. (See B.5.a.)

Section C:
PROFESSIONAL RESPONSIBILITY

STANDARD OF PRACTICE Seventeen (SP-17):
Boundaries of Competence.
Counselors must practice only within the boundaries of their competence. (See C.2.a.)

STANDARD OF PRACTICE Eighteen (SP-18):
Continuing Education.
Counselors must engage in continuing education to maintain their professional competence. (See C.2.f.)

STANDARD OF PRACTICE Nineteen (SP-19):
Impairment of Professionals.
Counselors must refrain from offering professional services when their personal problems or conflicts may cause harm to a client or others. (See C.2.g.)

STANDARD OF PRACTICE Twenty (SP-20):
Accurate Advertising.
Counselors must accurately represent their credentials and services when advertising. (See C.3.a.)

STANDARD OF PRACTICE Twenty-One (SP-21):
Recruiting Through Employment.
Counselors must not use their place of employment or institutional affiliation to recruit clients for their private practices. (See C.3.d.)

STANDARD OF PRACTICE Twenty-Two (SP-22):
Credentials Claimed.
Counselors must claim or imply only professional credentials possessed and must correct any known misrepresentations of their credentials by others. (See C.4.a.)

STANDARD OF PRACTICE Twenty-Three (SP-23):
Sexual Harassment.
Counselors must not engage in sexual harassment. (See C.5.b.)

STANDARD OF PRACTICE Twenty-Four (SP-24):
Unjustified Gains.
Counselors must not use their professional positions to seek or receive unjustified personal gains, sexual favors, unfair advantage, or unearned goods or services. (See C.5.e.)

STANDARD OF PRACTICE Twenty-Five (SP-25):
Clients Served by Others.
With the consent of the client, counselors must inform other mental health professionals serving the same client that a counseling relationship between the counselor and client exists. (See C.6.c.)

STANDARD OF PRACTICE Twenty-Six (SP-26):
Negative Employment Conditions.
Counselors must alert their employers to institutional policy or conditions that may be potentially disruptive or damaging to the counselor's professional responsibilities, or that may limit their effectiveness or deny clients' rights. (See D.1.c.)

STANDARD OF PRACTICE Twenty-Seven (SP-27):
Personnel Selection and Assignment.
Counselors must select competent staff and must assign responsibilities compatible with staff skills and experiences. (See D.1.h.)

STANDARD OF PRACTICE Twenty-Eight (SP-28):
Exploitive Relationships With Subordinates.
Counselors must not engage in exploitive relationships with individuals over whom they have supervisory, evaluative, or instructional control or authority. (See D.1.k.)

Section D:
RELATIONSHIPS WITH OTHER PROFESSIONALS

STANDARD OF PRACTICE Twenty-Nine (SP-29):
Accepting Fees From Agency Clients.
Counselors must not accept fees or other remuneration for consultation with persons entitled to such services through the counselor's employing agency or institution. (See D.3.a.)

STANDARD OF PRACTICE Thirty (SP-30):
Referral Fees.
Counselors must not accept referral fees. (See D.3.b.)

Section E:
EVALUATION, ASSESSMENT, AND INTERPRETATION

STANDARD OF PRACTICE Thirty-One (SP-31):
Limits of Competence.
Counselors must perform only testing and assessment services for which they are competent. Counselors must not allow the use of psychological assessment techniques by unqualified persons under their supervision. (See E.2.a.)

STANDARD OF PRACTICE Thirty-Two (SP-32):
Appropriate Use of Assessment Instruments.
Counselors must use assessment instruments in the manner for which they were intended. (See E.2.b.)

STANDARD OF PRACTICE Thirty-Three (SP-33):
Assessment Explanations to Clients.
Counselors must provide explanations to clients prior to assessment about the nature and purposes of assessment and the specific uses of results. (See E.3.a.)

STANDARD OF PRACTICE Thirty-Four (SP-34):
Recipients of Test Results.
Counselors must ensure that accurate and appropriate interpretations accompany any release of testing and assessment information. (See E.3.b.)

STANDARD OF PRACTICE Thirty-Five (SP-35):
Obsolete Tests and Outdated Test Results.
Counselors must not base their assessment or intervention decisions or recommendations on data or test results that are obsolete or outdated for the current purpose. (See E.11.)

Section F:
TEACHING, TRAINING, AND SUPERVISION

STANDARD OF PRACTICE Thirty-Six (SP-36):
Sexual Relationships With Students or Supervisees.
Counselors must not engage in sexual relationships with their students and supervisees. (See F.1.c.)

STANDARD OF PRACTICE Thirty-Seven (SP-37):
Credit for Contributions to Research.
Counselors must give credit to students or supervisees for their contributions to research and scholarly projects. (See F.1.d.)

STANDARD OF PRACTICE Thirty-Eight (SP-38):
Supervision Preparation.
Counselors who offer clinical supervision services must be trained and prepared in supervision methods and techniques. (See F.1.f.)

STANDARD OF PRACTICE Thirty-Nine (SP-39):
Evaluation Information.
Counselors must clearly state to students and supervisees, in advance of training, the levels of competency expected, appraisal methods, and timing of evaluations. Counselors must provide students and supervisees with periodic performance appraisal and evaluation feedback throughout the training program. (See F.2.c.)

STANDARD OF PRACTICE Forty (SP-40):
Peer Relationships in Training.
Counselors must make every effort to ensure that the rights of peers are not violated when students and supervisees are assigned to lead counseling groups or provide clinical supervision. (See F.2.e.)

STANDARD OF PRACTICE Forty-One (SP-41):
Limitations of Students and Supervisees.
Counselors must assist students and supervisees in securing remedial assistance, when needed, and must dismiss from the training program students and supervisees who are unable to provide competent service due to academic or personal limitations. (See F.3.a.)

STANDARD OF PRACTICE Forty-Two (SP-42):
Self-Growth Experiences.
Counselors who conduct experiences for students or supervisees that include self-growth or self-disclosure must inform participants of counselors' ethical obligations to the profession and must not grade participants based on their nonacademic performance. (See F.3.b.)

STANDARD OF PRACTICE Forty-Three (SP-43):
Standards for Students and Supervisees.
Students and supervisees preparing to become counselors must adhere to the Code of Ethics and the Standards of Practice of counselors. (See F.3.e.)

Section G:
RESEARCH AND PUBLICATION

STANDARD OF PRACTICE Forty-Four (SP-44):
Precautions to Avoid Injury in Research.
Counselors must avoid causing physical, social, or psychological harm or injury to subjects in research. (See G.1.c.)

STANDARD OF PRACTICE Forty-Five (SP-45):
Confidentiality of Research Information.
Counselors must keep confidential information obtained about research participants. (See G.2.d.)

STANDARD OF PRACTICE Forty-Six (SP-46):
Information Affecting Research Outcome.
Counselors must report all variables and conditions known to the investigator that may have affected research data or outcomes. (See G.3.a.)

STANDARD OF PRACTICE Forty-Seven (SP-47):
Accurate Research Results.
Counselors must not distort or misrepresent research data, nor fabricate or intentionally bias research results. (See G.3.b.)

STANDARD OF PRACTICE Forty-Eight (SP-48):
Publication Contributors.
Counselors must give appropriate credit to those who have contributed to research. (See G.4.a. and G.4.b.)

Section H:
RESOLVING ETHICAL ISSUES

STANDARD OF PRACTICE Forty-Nine (SP-49):
Ethical Behavior Expected.
Counselors must take appropriate action when they possess reasonable cause that raises doubts as to whether counselors or other mental health professionals are acting in an ethical manner. (See H.2.a.)

STANDARD OF PRACTICE Fifty (SP-50):
Unwarranted Complaints.
Counselors must not initiate, participate in, or encourage the filing of ethics complaints that are unwarranted or intended to harm a mental health professional rather than to protect clients or the public. (See H.2.f.)

STANDARD OF PRACTICE Fifty-One (SP-51):
Cooperation With Ethics Committees.
Counselors must cooperate with investigations, proceedings, and requirements of the ACA Ethics Committee or ethics committees of other duly constituted associations or boards having jurisdiction over those charged with a violation. (See H.3.)

Organization

AMERICAN PSYCHIATRIC ASSOCIATION

Headquarters:
1400 K Street, NW
Washington, DC 20005
Telephone: (202) 682-6000
Fax: (202) 682-6850
E-mail: apa@psych.org
Website: http://www.psych.org

Date founded: 1844
   Former names include the American Medico-Psychological Association; renamed 1921
Membership: approximately 42,000 U.S. and international physicians with special training in psychiatry

Code of Ethics

Official name: *Principles of Medical Ethics With Annotations Especially Applicable to Psychiatry*
History: First edition 1973, revised periodically; current edition 1998
Authority: Ethics Committee; Board of Trustees; Assembly
Code is available on Website

Additional Resources

Organizational (Divisions, Programs, Services, etc.):

American Psychiatric Press, Inc.
Committee on Interprofessional Affairs
Ethics Appeals Board
Ethics in Managed Care Conference
Legal Consultation Plan
Practice Research Network (psychiatrists who cooperate to collect data and conduct research studies on clinical and health services delivery issues)

Professional Liability Insurance Program
Task Force on Clinician Safety
Task Force to Develop Model Curricular Material on Medical/
    Psychiatric Ethics
Various Commissions: AIDS; Judicial Action; Psychotherapy by
    Psychiatrists
Various Councils: Medical Education and Career Development;
    Psychiatric Services; Psychiatry and Law; Research
Work Group on National Data Bases for Psychiatry

Informational (Publications, Videos, Seminars, etc.):

Articles in *American Journal of Psychiatry, Psychiatric News,* and
    Psychiatric Annals
*A Comprehensive Guide to Malpractice Risk Management in
    Psychiatry*
*Allies and Adversaries: The Impact of Managed Care on Mental Health
    Services*
APA Practice Guidelines
*Assessing Competence to Consent to Treatment: A Guide to Physicians
    and Other Health Professionals*
Basic Model Ethics Curriculum for Psychiatric Residents
Briefings, Position Papers, and *Fact Sheets:*
    Confidentiality
    Graduate Medical Education Policy for Psychiatry
    Insanity Defense
    Insurance Coverage Parity for Mental Illness Treatment
    Legal Sanctions for Mental Health Professional/Patient Sex
    Memories of Sexual Abuse
    Non-Physician Mental Health Practitioners
    Patient Protection and Managed Care
    Patient-Therapist Sexual Contact
    Principles for Medical Record Privacy Legislation
    Towards the Millennium: Universal Access to Psychiatric Care
Certification, Recertification, and Lifetime Learning in Psychiatry
Child Psychiatry and the Law
Clinical Psychiatry and the Law
Concise Guide to Psychiatry and Law for Clinicians
*Confidentiality Versus the Duty to Protect: Foreseeable Harm in the
    Practice of Psychiatry*
Consent and the Incompetent Patient: Ethics, Law, and Medicine
*Continuing Medical Education Mission Statement and Policy on Full
    Disclosure*
Controversies in Managed Mental Health Care
*Demanding Medical Excellence: Doctors and Accountability in the
    Information Age*

Disclosure Statement of Possible Conflict of Interest
Discussion of Implementation of the Revised Procedures for Handling Complaints of Unethical Conduct
End of Life Decisions: A Psychosocial Perspective
Ethical Concerns about Sexual Involvement Between Psychiatrists and Patients: Videotaped Vignettes for Discussion (video)
Ethics and Psychiatry: Toward Professional Definition
Ethics Complaint Flowchart
The First Psychiatric Institute: How Research and Education Changed Practice
Forced Into Treatment: The Role of Coercion in Clinical Practice
Guidelines: Confidentiality; Psychiatrists in Consultative, Supervisory, or Collaborative Relationships with Nonmedical Therapists; Policy on Physician Impairment; Psychiatrists' Signatures
The History and Influence of the American Psychiatric Association
Keeping Boundaries: Maintaining Safety and Integrity in the Psychotherapeutic Process
Law, Psychiatry, and Morality: Essays and Analysis
Legal and Risk Management
Managed Care Ethics: Essays on the Impact of Managed Care on Traditional Medical Ethics
Manual of Psychiatric Quality Assurance
The Mental Health Practitioner and the Law: A Comprehensive Handbook
Opinions of the Ethics Committee
Perinatal Psychiatry: Use and Misuse of the Edinburgh Postnatal Depression Scale
Physicians Living With Depression
Policy and Procedures for Dealing with and Reporting Possible Misconduct in Science
Principles for the Provision of Mental Health and Substance Abuse Treatment Services: A Bill of Rights
Procedures Governing Appeals to the APA Ethics Appeals Board
Proposed Course for District Branches to Offer to Medical Residents on Psychiatric Ethics
Psychiatric Disability: Clinical, Legal, and Administrative Dimensions
Psychiatric Malpractice: Cases and Comments for Clinicians
Psychiatric Practice Under Fire: The Influence of Government, the Media, and Special Interests on Somatic Therapies
Psychological Evaluations for the Courts: A Handbook for Mental Health Professionals and Lawyers
Reflections on Modern Psychiatry
Reporting Ethical Concerns About Sexual Involvement with Patients (video)
The Right to Die
Rights of the Mentally Disabled: Statements and Standards
Sample Ethics Letters for APA District Branch Ethics Committees
Sexual Exploitation in Professional Relationships

Successful Psychiatric Practice: Current Dilemmas, Choices, and Solutions
Women's Health Research: A Medical and Policy Primer

Goals and Activities of Organization

The objectives of the American Psychiatric Association (APA) are to improve the treatment, rehabilitation, and care of the mentally ill, mentally retarded, and emotionally disturbed; to promote research and professional education in psychiatry and allied fields, and the prevention of psychiatric disabilities; to advance the standards of all psychiatric services and facilities; to foster cooperation among those concerned with the medical, psychological, social, and legal aspects of mental health and illness; to make psychiatric knowledge available to other physicians, scientists, and the public; and to further the best interests of present and potential patients or users of mental health services.

Implementation and Enforcement of Code

The Ethics Committee handles complaints charging members with unethical behavior; drafts complaint procedures; develops new Annotations to the Principles; responds to members' inquiries about ethical issues; maintains contact with other ethics committees; and formulates appropriate educational materials.

Ethics complaints against APA members are investigated, processed, and resolved in accordance with procedures approved by the Assembly and Board of Trustees. Unlike malpractice charges, there is no statute of limitations on charges of unethical conduct; complaints may be filed at any time after the alleged event.

Complaints are referred to the member's district branch Ethics Committee. Investigations and hearings must be comprehensive and satisfy generally accepted tenets of fundamental fairness and respect for all parties. The accused member may be represented by counsel. The complainant must be present at the hearing unless excused by the committee.

The district branch decision is forwarded for review to the national Ethics Committee. Appeals are heard by the Ethics Appeals Board. Sanctions for violations of the Principles include admonishment, reprimand, and suspension or expulsion from the APA.

Generally, ethics investigations are confidential. To protect the public, disclosure of the identity of an accused member may be essential, such as when a member is suspended, expelled, or resigns during an ethics investigation. Disclosure may include publication in *Psychiatric News* and report to a medical licensing authority, medical society, hospital, or other institution, and to the National Practitioner Data Bank for Adverse Information on Physicians and Other Health Care Practitioners.

History and Development of Code

The Principles are those of the American Medical Association. In 1973, the APA published the first edition of Annotated Principles. Amendments were published in 1978 and as the Board of Trustees and the Assembly approved additional Annotations.

In 1980, the AMA approved a new version of the Principles; the APA Ethics Committee incorporated many of its Annotations into these new Principles. The result was the 1981 edition and subsequent revisions through 1995.

An addendum of questions and answers about complaint procedures (not reprinted here) addresses issues that have come up since 1973.

The addendum of Guidelines for Ethical Practice in Organized Settings was added in May 1997.

Principles of Medical Ethics With Annotations Especially Applicable to Psychiatry*

* * *

FOREWORD

All physicians should practice in accordance with the medical code of ethics set forth in the Principles of Medical Ethics of the American Medical Association. An up-to-date expression and elaboration of these statements is found in the Opinions and Reports of the Council on Ethical and Judicial Affairs of the American Medical Association.[2] Psychiatrists are strongly advised to be familiar with these documents.[3]

However, these general guidelines have sometimes been difficult to interpret for psychiatry, so further annotations to the basic principles are offered in this document. While psychiatrists have the same goals as all physicians, there are special ethical problems in psychiatric practice that differ in coloring and degree from ethical problems in other branches of medical practice, even though the basic principles are the same. The annotations are not designed as absolutes and will be revised from time to time so as to be applicable to current practices and problems.

* * *

PREAMBLE

The medical profession has long subscribed to a body of ethical statements developed primarily for the benefit of the patient. As a member of this profession, a physician must recognize responsibility not only to patients, but also to society, to other health professionals, and to self. The following Principles, adopted by the American Medical Association, are not laws but standards of conduct, which define the essentials of honorable behavior for the physician.[4]

---

*1998 Edition (Previous editions 1973, 1978, 1981, 1984, 1985, 1986, 1989, 1992, 1993, 1995 Revised) The Addendum was approved by the Board of Trustees in March 1997, and by the Assembly of District Branches in May 1997.

[1][Omitted]

[2]Current Opinions with Annotations of the Council on Ethical and Judicial Affairs, Chicago, American Medical Association, 1996–1997.

[3]Chapter 8, Section 1 of the Bylaws of the American Psychiatric Association states, "All members of the American Psychiatric Association shall be bound by the ethical code of the medical profession, specifically defined in the Principles of Medical Ethics of the American Medical Association." In interpreting the APA Constitution and Bylaws, it is the opinion of the Board of Trustees that inactive status in no way removes a physician member from responsibility to abide by the Principles of Medical Ethics.

[4]Statements in italics are taken directly from the American Medical Association's Principles of Medical Ethics.

SECTION 1

A physician shall be dedicated to providing competent medical service with compassion and respect for human dignity.

1. The patient may place his/her trust in his/her psychiatrist knowing that the psychiatrist's ethics and professional responsibilities preclude him/her gratifying his/her own needs by exploiting the patient. The psychiatrist shall be ever vigilant about the impact that his/her conduct has upon the boundaries of the doctor/patient relationship, and thus upon the well being of the patient. These requirements become particularly important because of the essentially private, highly personal, and sometimes intensely emotional nature of the relationship established with the psychiatrist.

2. A psychiatrist should not be a party to any type of policy that excludes, segregates, or demeans the dignity of any patient because of ethnic origin, race, sex, creed, age, socioeconomic status, or sexual orientation.

3. In accord with the requirements of law and accepted medical practice, it is ethical for a physician to submit his/her work to peer review and to the ultimate authority of the medical staff executive body and the hospital administration and its governing body. In case of dispute, the ethical psychiatrist has the following steps available:

   a. Seek appeal from the medical staff decision to a joint conference committee, including members of the medical staff executive committee and the executive committee of the governing board. At this appeal, the ethical psychiatrist could request that outside opinions be considered.
   b. Appeal to the governing body itself.
   c. Appeal to state agencies regulating licensure of hospitals if, in the particular state, they concern themselves with matters of professional competency and quality of care.
   d. Attempt to educate colleagues through development of research projects and data and presentations at professional meetings and in professional journals.
   e. Seek redress in local courts, perhaps through an enjoining injunction against the governing body.
   f. Public education as carried out by an ethical psychiatrist would not utilize appeals based solely upon emotion, but would be presented in a professional way and without any potential exploitation of patients through testimonials.

4. A psychiatrist should not be a participant in a legally authorized execution.

SECTION 2

A physician shall deal honestly with patients and colleagues, and strive to expose those physicians deficient in character or competence, or who engage in fraud or deception.

1. The requirement that the physician conduct himself/herself with propriety in his/her profession and in all the actions of his/her life is especially important in the case of the psychiatrist because the patient tends to model his/her behavior after that of his/her psychiatrist by identification. Further, the necessary intensity of the treatment relationship may tend to activate sexual and other needs and fantasies on the part of both patient and psychiatrist, while weakening the objectivity necessary for control. Additionally, the inherent inequality in the doctor-patient

relationship may lead to exploitation of the patient. Sexual activity with a current or former patient is unethical.

2. The psychiatrist should diligently guard against exploiting information furnished by the patient and should not use the unique position of power afforded him/her by the psychotherapeutic situation to influence the patient in any way not directly relevant to the treatment goals.

3. A psychiatrist who regularly practices outside his/her area of professional competence should be considered unethical. Determination of professional competence should be made by peer review boards or other appropriate bodies.

4. Special consideration should be given to those psychiatrists who, because of mental illness, jeopardize the welfare of their patients and their own reputations and practices. It is ethical, even encouraged, for another psychiatrist to intercede in such situations.

5. Psychiatric services, like all medical services, are dispensed in the context of a contractual arrangement between the patient and the treating physician. The provisions of the contractual arrangement, which are binding on the physician as well as on the patient, should be explicitly established.

6. It is ethical for the psychiatrist to make a charge for a missed appointment when this falls within the terms of the specific contractual agreement with the patient. Charging for a missed appointment or for one not cancelled 24 hours in advance need not, in itself, be considered unethical if a patient is fully advised that the physician will make such a charge. The practice, however, should be resorted to infrequently and always with the utmost consideration for the patient and his/her circumstances.

7. An arrangement in which a psychiatrist provides supervision or administration to other physicians or nonmedical persons for a percentage of their fees or gross income is not acceptable; this would constitute fee-splitting. In a team of practitioners, or a multidisciplinary team, it is ethical for the psychiatrist to receive income for administration, research, education, or consultation. This should be based upon a mutually agreed upon and set fee or salary, open to renegotiation when a change in the time demand occurs. (See also Section 5, Annotations 2, 3, and 4.)

SECTION 3

A physician shall respect the law and also recognize a responsibility to seek changes in those requirements which are contrary to the best interests of the patient.

1. It would seem self-evident that a psychiatrist who is a law-breaker might be ethically unsuited to practice his/her profession. When such illegal activities bear directly upon his/her practice, this would obviously be the case. However, in other instances, illegal activities such as those concerning the right to protest social injustices might not bear on either the image of the psychiatrist or the ability of the specific psychiatrist to treat his/her patient ethically and well. While no committee or board could offer prior assurance that any illegal activity would not be considered unethical, it is conceivable that an individual could violate a law without being guilty of professionally unethical behavior. Physicians lose no right of citizenship on entry into the profession of medicine.

2. Where not specifically prohibited by local laws governing medical practice, the practice of acupuncture by a psychiatrist is not unethical per se. The psychiatrist should have professional competence in the use of acupuncture. Or, if he/she is supervising the use of acupuncture by nonmedical individuals, he/she should provide proper medical supervision. (See also Section 5, Annotations 3 and 4.)

SECTION 4

A physician shall respect the rights of patients, of colleagues, and of other health professionals, and shall safeguard patient confidences within the constraints of the law.

1. Psychiatric records, including even the identification of a person as a patient, must be protected with extreme care. Confidentiality is essential to psychiatric treatment. This is based in part on the special nature of psychiatric therapy as well as on the traditional ethical relationship between physician and patient. Growing concern regarding the civil rights of patients and the possible adverse effects of computerization, duplication equipment, and data banks makes the dissemination of confidential information an increasing hazard. Because of the sensitive and private nature of the information with which the psychiatrist deals, he/she must be circumspect in the information that he/she chooses to disclose to others about a patient. The welfare of the patient must be a continuing consideration.

2. A psychiatrist may release confidential information only with the authorization of the patient or under proper legal compulsion. The continuing duty of the psychiatrist to protect the patient includes fully apprising him/her of the connotations of waiving the privilege of privacy. This may become an issue when the patient is being investigated by a government agency, is applying for a position, or is involved in legal action. The same principles apply to the release of information concerning treatment to medical departments of government agencies, business organizations, labor unions, and insurance companies. Information gained in confidence about patients seen in student health services should not be released without the students' explicit permission.

3. Clinical and other materials used in teaching and writing must be adequately disguised in order to preserve the anonymity of the individuals involved.

4. The ethical responsibility of maintaining confidentiality holds equally for the consultations in which the patient may not have been present and in which the consultee was not a physician. In such instances, the physician consultant should alert the consultee to his/her duty of confidentiality.

5. Ethically the psychiatrist may disclose only that information which is relevant to a given situation. He/she should avoid offering speculation as fact. Sensitive information such as an individual's sexual orientation or fantasy material is usually unnecessary.

6. Psychiatrists are often asked to examine individuals for security purposes, to determine suitability for various jobs, and to determine legal competence. The psychiatrist must fully describe the nature and purpose and lack of confidentiality of the examination to the examinee at the beginning of the examination.

7. Careful judgment must be exercised by the psychiatrist in order to include, when appropriate, the parents or guardian in the treatment of a minor. At the same time, the psychiatrist must assure the minor proper confidentiality.

8. Psychiatrists at times may find it necessary, in order to protect the patient or the community from imminent danger, to reveal confidential information disclosed by the patient.

9. When the psychiatrist is ordered by the court to reveal the confidences entrusted to him/her by patients, he/she may comply or he/she may ethically hold the right to dissent within the framework of the law. When the psychiatrist is in doubt, the right of the patient to confidentiality and, by extension, to unimpaired treatment should be given priority. The psychiatrist should reserve the right to

raise the question of adequate need for disclosure. In the event that the necessity for legal disclosure is demonstrated by the court, the psychiatrist may request the right to disclosure of only that information which is relevant to the legal question at hand.

10. With regard for the person's dignity and privacy and with truly informed consent, it is ethical to present a patient to a scientific gathering, if the confidentiality of the presentation is understood and accepted by the audience.

11. It is ethical to present a patient or former patient to a public gathering or to the news media only if the patient is fully informed of enduring loss of confidentiality, is competent, and consents in writing without coercion.

12. When involved in funded research, the ethical psychiatrist will advise human subjects of the funding source, retain his/her freedom to reveal data and results, and follow all appropriate and current guidelines relative to human subject protection.

13. Ethical considerations in medical practice preclude the psychiatric evaluation of any person charged with criminal acts prior to access to, or availability of, legal counsel. The only exception is the rendering of care to the person for the sole purpose of medical treatment.

14. Sexual involvement between a faculty member or supervisor and a trainee or student, in those situations in which an abuse of power can occur, often takes advantage of inequalities in the working relationship and may be unethical because: (a) any treatment of a patient being supervised may be deleteriously affected; (b) it may damage the trust relationship between teacher and student; and (c) teachers are important professional role models for their trainees and affect their trainees' future professional behavior.

SECTION 5

A physician shall continue to study, apply, and advance scientific knowledge, make relevant information available to patients, colleagues, and the public, obtain consultation, and use the talents of other health professionals when indicated.

1. Psychiatrists are responsible for their own continuing education and should be mindful of the fact that theirs must be a lifetime of learning.

2. In the practice of his/her specialty, the psychiatrist consults, associates, collaborates, or integrates his/her work with that of many professionals, including psychologists, psychometricians, social workers, alcoholism counselors, marriage counselors, public health nurses, etc. Furthermore, the nature of modern psychiatric practice extends his/her contacts to such people as teachers, juvenile and adult probation officers, attorneys, welfare workers, agency volunteers, and neighborhood aides. In referring patients for treatment, counseling, or rehabilitation to any of these practitioners, the psychiatrist should ensure that the allied professional or paraprofessional with whom he/she is dealing is a recognized member of his/her own discipline and is competent to carry out the therapeutic task required. The psychiatrist should have the same attitude toward members of the medical profession to whom he/she refers patients. Whenever he/she has reason to doubt the training, skill, or ethical qualifications of the allied professional, the psychiatrist should not refer cases to him/her.

3. When the psychiatrist assumes a collaborative or supervisory role with another mental health worker, he/she must expend sufficient time to assure that proper care is given. It is contrary to the interests of the patient and to patient care if he/she allows himself/herself to be used as a figurehead.

4. In relationships between psychiatrists and practicing licensed psychologists, the physician should not delegate to the psychologist or, in fact, to any nonmedical person any matter requiring the exercise of professional medical judgment.

5. The psychiatrist should agree to the request of a patient for consultation or to such a request from the family of an incompetent or minor patient. The psychiatrist may suggest possible consultants, but the patient or family should be given free choice of the consultant. If the psychiatrist disapproves of the professional qualifications of the consultant or if there is a difference of opinion that the primary therapist cannot resolve, he/she may, after suitable notice, withdraw from the case. If this disagreement occurs within an institution or agency framework, the differences should be resolved by the mediation or arbitration of higher professional authority within the institution or agency.

SECTION 6

A physician shall, in the provision of appropriate patient care, except in emergencies, be free to choose whom to serve, with whom to associate, and the environment in which to provide medical services.

1. Physicians generally agree that the doctor-patient relationship is such a vital factor in effective treatment of the patient that preservation of optimal conditions for development of a sound working relationship between a doctor and his/her patient should take precedence over all other considerations. Professional courtesy may lead to poor psychiatric care for physicians and their families because of embarrassment over the lack of a complete give-and-take contract.

2. An ethical psychiatrist may refuse to provide psychiatric treatment to a person who, in the psychiatrist's opinion, cannot be diagnosed as having a mental illness amenable to psychiatric treatment.

SECTION 7

A physician shall recognize a responsibility to participate in activities contributing to an improved community.

1. Psychiatrists should foster the cooperation of those legitimately concerned with the medical, psychological, social, and legal aspects of mental health and illness. Psychiatrists are encouraged to serve society by advising and consulting with the executive, legislative, and judiciary branches of the government. A psychiatrist should clarify whether he/she speaks as an individual or as a representative of an organization. Furthermore, psychiatrists should avoid cloaking their public statements with the authority of the profession (e.g., "Psychiatrists know that . . .").

2. Psychiatrists may interpret and share with the public their expertise in the various psychosocial issues that may affect mental health and illness. Psychiatrists should always be mindful of their separate roles as dedicated citizens and as experts in psychological medicine.

3. On occasion psychiatrists are asked for an opinion about an individual who is in the light of public attention, or who has disclosed information about himself/herself through public media. It is unethical for a psychiatrist to offer a professional opinion unless he/she has conducted an examination and has been granted proper authorization for such a statement.

4. The psychiatrist may permit his/her certification to be used for the involuntary treatment of any person only following his/her personal examination of that person. To do so, he/she must find that the person, because of mental illness, cannot form a judgment as to what is in his/her own best interests and that, without such treatment, substantial impairment is likely to occur to the person or others.

ADDENDUM 1
Guidelines for Ethical Practice in Organized Settings

* * * This addendum contains specific guidelines regarding ethical psychiatric practice in organized settings. The addendum is intended to clarify existing ethical standards contained in Sections 1–7 * * *.

Psychiatrists have a long and valued tradition of being essential participants in organizations that deliver health care. Such organizations can enhance medical effectiveness and protect the standards and values of the psychiatric profession by fostering competent, compassionate medical care in a setting in which informed consent and confidentiality are rigorously preserved, conditions essential for the successful treatment of mental illness. However, some organizations may place the psychiatrist in a position where the clinical needs of the patient, the demands of the community and larger society, and even the professional role of the psychiatrist are in conflict with the interests of the organization.

The psychiatrist must consider the consequences of such role conflicts with respect to patients in his or her care, and strive to resolve these conflicts in a manner that is likely to be of greatest benefit to the patient. Whether during treatment or a review process, a psychiatrist shall respect the autonomy, privacy and dignity of the patient and his or her family.

These guidelines are intended to clarify existing standards. They are intended to promote the interests of the patient, and should not be construed to interfere with the ability of a psychiatrist to practice in an organized setting. The principles and annotations noted * * * conform to the statement in the preamble to the Principles of Medical Ethics. These are not laws but standards of conduct, which define the essentials of honorable behavior for the physician.

1. Appropriateness of Treatment and Treatment Options
(a) A psychiatrist shall not withhold information that the patient needs or reasonably could use to make informed treatment decisions, including options for treatment not provided by the psychiatrist. (*Section 2, Annotation 5; Section 5, Annotations 2 and 3*)
(b) A psychiatrist's treatment plan shall be based upon clinical, scientific or generally accepted standards of treatment. This applies to the treating and reviewing psychiatrist. (*Section 5, Annotation 1*)
(c) A psychiatrist shall strive to provide beneficial treatment which shall not be limited to minimum criteria of medical necessity. (*Section 1, Annotation 1; Section 5, Annotations 2 and 3*)

2. Financial Arrangements
When a psychiatrist is aware of financial incentives or penalties which limit the provision of appropriate treatment for that patient, the psychiatrist shall inform the patient and/or designated guardian. (*Section 1, Annotation 1; Section 5, Annotations 2 and 3*)

3. Review Process

A psychiatrist shall not conduct reviews or participate in reviews in a manner likely to demean the dignity of the patient by asking for highly personal material not necessary for the conduct of the review. A reviewing psychiatrist shall strive as hard for a patient he or she reviews as for one he or she treats to prevent the disclosure of sensitive patient material to anyone other than for clear, clinical necessity. (*Section 1, Annotations 1 and 2; Section 4, Annotations 1, 2, 4 and 5*)

Organization

AMERICAN PSYCHOLOGICAL ASSOCIATION

Headquarters:
750 First Street, NE
Washington, DC 20002-4242
Telephone: (202) 336-5500
Website: http://www.apa.org

Date founded: 1892
Membership: approximately 155,000 researchers, educators, clinicians, consultants, and students in 50 subfields of psychology and 59 state and territorial associations in the U.S. and Canada

Code of Ethics

Official name: *Ethical Principles of Psychologists and Code of Conduct*
History: First adopted 1953, revised periodically; current version 1992
Authority: Office of Ethics; Council of Representatives
Code is available on Website

Additional Resources

Organizational (Divisions, Programs, Services, etc.):

American Psychology-Law Society
Board for the Advancement of Psychology in the Public Interest
Commission for the Recognition of Specialties and Proficiencies in Professional Psychology
Research Ethics Office
Society for the Psychological Study of Social Issues
Society for the Teaching of Psychology
Various committees: Accreditation; Advancement of Professional Practice; Animal Research and Ethics; Approval of Continuing Education Sponsors; Continuing Education; Professional Practice and Standards; Psychological Tests and Assessments
Various Divisions: History of Psychology; Humanistic Psychology; Peace Psychology; State Psychological Association Affairs; Theoretical and Philosophical Psychology

461

Informational (Publications, Videos, Seminars, etc.):

Articles in *APA Monitor* and various Division journals:
Contemporary Psychology
History of Psychology
Humanistic Psychologist
Journal of Social Issues
Journal of Theoretical and Philosophical Psychology
Law and Human Behavior
Peace and Conflict: Journal of Peace Psychology
Professional Psychology: Research and Practice
Psychology, Public Policy, and Law
State Psychological Association Affairs
The American Psychological Association: A Historical Perspective
Code of Fair Testing Practices in Education
Ethical Conflicts in Psychology
The Ethical Practice of Psychology in Organizations
Ethics Committee Rules and Procedures
Ethics for Psychologists: A Commentary on the APA Ethics Code
The Ethics of Research With Human Participants (draft)
If Sex Enters Into the Psychotherapy Relationship
Information on Licensure
Law & Mental Health Professionals Series
Mandated Reporting of Suspected Child Abuse: Ethics, Law, and Policy
Practicing in the New Mental Health Marketplace: Ethical, Legal, and Moral Issues
Principles for the Provision of Mental Health and Substance Abuse Treatment Services: A Bill of Rights
Professional Conduct and Discipline in Psychology
Professional Liability and Risk Management
Professional, Ethical, and Legal Issues Concerning Interpersonal Violence, Maltreatment and Related Trauma
Professionals in Distress: Issues, Syndromes, and Solutions in Psychology
Psychology and Public Policy: Balancing Public Service and Professional Need
Psychology in Litigation and Legislation
Quality in Professional Psychology and Training: A National Conference and Self-Study
Responsible Test Use: Case Studies for Assessing Human Behavior
The Right to Refuse Mental Health Treatment
Sexual Feelings in Psychotherapy: Explorations for Therapists and Therapists-in-Training
Sexual Involvement with Therapists: Patient Assessment, Subsequent Therapy, Forensics
Standards for Educational and Psychological Testing
The Suggestibility of Children's Recollections: Implications for Eyewitness Testimony

The Suicidal Patient: Clinical and Legal Standards of Care
Various *Briefing Sheets, Position Papers* and *Policy Statements*
Various conference sessions:
  Ethical and Legal Issues in Geriatric Practice
  Ethical Issues and HIV/AIDS Mental Health Services
  Therapists at Risk: Perils of the Psychotherapeutic Relationship
  Working with Clients Who Want to Hasten Their Deaths
Various *Guidelines*:
  Accreditation of Programs in Professional Psychology
  Avoiding Sexism in Psychological Research
  Ethical Conduct in the Care and Use of Animals
  Involvement in International Human Rights Affairs
  Social Responsibility in Investments

Goals and Activities of Organization

The American Psychological Association (APA) seeks to advance psychology as a science, profession, and means of promoting human welfare. The growth of psychology is reflected in the APA's development of diverse programs and services for: promoting research and improving research methods and conditions; maintaining the qualifications and competence of psychologists through high standards of education, ethical conduct, and professional practice; and disseminating psychological knowledge through meetings and publications.

The Office of Ethics educates the public and the profession on appropriate standards of conduct.

Implementation and Enforcement of Code

Membership in the APA commits a member to adhere to the Code and the rules and procedures that implement it. The Code applies to psychologists, psychology students, and others who do work of a psychological nature under the supervision of a psychologist. The Code also may be applied to members or nonmembers by state psychology boards, courts, and other public bodies.

The APA Code consists of general Principles and specific Ethical Standards. The Principles are aspirational goals; while not enforceable, they guide a professional's decisions and behavior. They also help ethics committees interpret enforceable rules of conduct.

Complaints are evaluated initially by the Ethics Office Director, to determine whether there are grounds for further action. After an investigation, the case is referred to the APA Ethics Committee for review and resolution. If there is neither a dismissal nor stipulated resignation, the accused member has a right to a formal hearing or an independent adjudication.

The Board of Directors adopts the recommendation of the Ethics Committee (if no hearing), or the decision of the hearing committee or independent adjudication panel, unless defects require the matter to be sent back.

Penalties for violations include reprimand, censure, termination, and referral of the matter to other regulatory or professional bodies.

In the absence of a complaint, members convicted of a felony or expelled from an affiliated state psychological association, or whose license has been suspended or revoked, may be asked to show cause why they should not be expelled from the APA.

The Ethics Committee is also responsible for proposing necessary changes or additions to the Code. In 1997, for instance, the Committee issued the *Statement on Services by Telephone, Teleconferencing, and Internet*, recognizing that the Code does not currently address the issue of therapies provided by electronic means. The subject will be considered in a future revision of the Code.

History and Development of Code

The APA issued its first code, Ethical Standards of Psychologists, in 1953. Subsequent versions date from 1958, 1963, 1968, 1977, 1979, 1981, and 1990.

This version of the APA's ethics standards was adopted by the Council of Representatives and became effective in December 1992.

Ethical Principles of Psychologists and Code of Conduct*

INTRODUCTION

The American Psychological Association's (APA's) Ethical Principles of Psychologists and Code of Conduct (hereinafter referred to as the Ethics Code) consists of an Introduction, a Preamble, six General Principles (A-F), and specific Ethical Standards. The Introduction discusses the intent, organization, procedural considerations, and scope of application of the Ethics Code. The Preamble and General Principles are aspirational goals to guide psychologists toward the highest ideals of psychology. Although the Preamble and General Principles are not themselves enforceable rules, they should be considered by psychologists in arriving at an ethical course of action and may be considered by ethics bodies in interpreting the Ethical Standards. The Ethical Standards set forth enforceable rules for conduct as psychologists. Most of the Ethical Standards are written broadly, in order to apply to psychologists in varied roles, although the application of an Ethical Standard may vary depending on the context. The Ethical Standards are not exhaustive. The fact that a given conduct is not specifically addressed by the Ethics Code does not mean that it is necessarily either ethical or unethical.

Membership in the APA commits members to adhere to the APA Ethics Code and to the rules and procedures used to implement it. Psychologists and students, whether or not they are APA members, should be aware that the Ethics Code may be applied to them by state psychology boards, courts, or other public bodies.

This Ethics Code applies only to psychologists' work-related activities, that is, activities that are part of the psychologists' scientific and professional functions or that are psychological in nature. It includes the clinical or counseling practice of psychology, research, teaching, supervision of trainees, development of assessment instruments, conducting assessments, educational counseling, organizational consulting, social intervention, administration, and other activities as well. These work-related activities can be distinguished from the purely private conduct of a psychologist, which ordinarily is not within the purview of the Ethics Code.

The Ethics Code is intended to provide standards of professional conduct that can be applied by the APA and by other bodies that choose to adopt them. Whether or not a psychologist has violated the Ethics Code does not by itself

---

*American Psychological Association. Reprinted from *American Psychologist*, Vol. 47, No. 12, pp. 1597–1611, December 1992. Copyright © 1992 by the American Psychological Association, Inc. Reprinted with permission.

This version of the APA Ethics Code was adopted by the American Psychological Association's Council of Representatives during its meeting, August 13 and 16, 1992, and is effective beginning December 1, 1992. Inquiries concerning the substance or interpretation of the APA Ethics Code should be addressed to the Director, Office of Ethics, American Psychological Association, 750 First Street, NE, Washington, DC 20002-4242.

This Code will be used to adjudicate complaints brought concerning alleged conduct occurring after the effective date. Complaints regarding conduct occurring prior to the effective date will be adjudicated on the basis of the version of the Code that was in effect at the time the conduct occurred, except that no provisions repealed in June 1989, will be enforced even if an earlier version contains the provision. The Ethics Code will undergo continuing review and study for future revisions; comments on the Code may be sent to the above address. * * *

determine whether he or she is legally liable in a court action, whether a contract is enforceable, or whether other legal consequences occur. These results are based on legal rather than ethical rules. However, compliance with or violation of the Ethics Code may be admissible as evidence in some legal proceedings, depending on the circumstances.

In the process of making decisions regarding their professional behavior, psychologists must consider this Ethics Code, in addition to applicable laws and psychology board regulations. If the Ethics Code establishes a higher standard of conduct than is required by law, psychologists must meet the higher ethical standard. If the Ethics Code standard appears to conflict with the requirements of law, then psychologists make known their commitment to the Ethics Code and take steps to resolve the conflict in a responsible manner. If neither law nor the Ethics Code resolves an issue, psychologists should consider other professional materials[1] and the dictates of their own conscience, as well as seek consultation with others within the field when this is practical.

The procedures for filing, investigating, and resolving complaints of unethical conduct are described in the current Rules and Procedures of the APA Ethics Committee. * * *

PREAMBLE

Psychologists work to develop a valid and reliable body of scientific knowledge based on research. They may apply that knowledge to human behavior in a variety of contexts. In doing so, they perform many roles, such as researcher, educator, diagnostician, therapist, supervisor, consultant, administrator, social interventionist, and expert witness. Their goal is to broaden knowledge of behavior and, where appropriate, to apply it pragmatically to improve the condition of both the individual and society. Psychologists respect the central importance of freedom of inquiry and expression in research, teaching, and publication. They also strive to help the public in developing informed judgments and choices concerning human behavior. This Ethics Code provides a common set of values upon which psychologists build their professional and scientific work.

This Code is intended to provide both the general principles and the decision rules to cover most situations encountered by psychologists. It has as its primary goal the welfare and protection of the individuals and groups with whom psychologists work. It is the individual responsibility of each psychologist to aspire to the highest possible standards of conduct. Psychologists respect and protect human and civil rights, and do not knowingly participate in or condone unfair discriminatory practices.

The development of a dynamic set of ethical standards for a psychologist's work-related conduct requires a personal commitment to a lifelong effort to act ethically; to encourage ethical behavior by students, supervisees, employees, and colleagues, as appropriate; and to consult with others, as needed, concerning ethical problems. Each psychologist supplements, but does not violate, the Ethics

---

[1]Professional materials that are most helpful in this regard are guidelines and standards that have been adopted or endorsed by professional psychological organizations. Such guidelines and standards, whether adopted by the American Psychological Association (APA) or its Divisions, are not enforceable as such by this Ethics Code, but are of educative value to psychologists, courts, and professional bodies. * * *

Code's values and rules on the basis of guidance drawn from personal values, culture, and experience.

GENERAL PRINCIPLES

Principle A: **Competence**

Psychologists strive to maintain high standards of competence in their work. They recognize the boundaries of their particular competencies and the limitations of their expertise. They provide only those services and use only those techniques for which they are qualified by education, training, or experience. Psychologists are cognizant of the fact that the competencies required in serving, teaching, and/ or studying groups of people vary with the distinctive characteristics of those groups. In those areas in which recognized professional standards do not yet exist, psychologists exercise careful judgment and take appropriate precautions to protect the welfare of those with whom they work. They maintain knowledge of relevant scientific and professional information related to the services they render, and they recognize the need for ongoing education. Psychologists make appropriate use of scientific, professional, technical, and administrative resources.

Principle B: **Integrity**

Psychologists seek to promote integrity in the science, teaching, and practice of psychology. In these activities psychologists are honest, fair, and respectful of others. In describing or reporting their qualifications, services, products, fees, research, or teaching, they do not make statements that are false, misleading, or deceptive. Psychologists strive to be aware of their own belief systems, values, needs, and limitations and the effect of these on their work. To the extent feasible, they attempt to clarify for relevant parties the roles they are performing and to function appropriately in accordance with those roles. Psychologists avoid improper and potentially harmful dual relationships.

Principle C: **Professional and Scientific Responsibility**

Psychologists uphold professional standards of conduct, clarify their professional roles and obligations, accept appropriate responsibility for their behavior, and adapt their methods to the needs of different populations. Psychologists consult with, refer to, or cooperate with other professionals and institutions to the extent needed to serve the best interests of their patients, clients, or other recipients of their services. Psychologists' moral standards and conduct are personal matters to the same degree as is true for any other person, except as psychologists' conduct may compromise their professional responsibilities or reduce the public's trust in psychology and psychologists. Psychologists are concerned about the ethical compliance of their colleagues' scientific and professional conduct. When appropriate, they consult with colleagues in order to prevent or avoid unethical conduct.

Principle D: **Respect for People's Rights and Dignity**

Psychologists accord appropriate respect to the fundamental rights, dignity, and worth of all people. They respect the rights of individuals to privacy, confidentiality, self-determination, and autonomy, mindful that legal and other obligations may lead to inconsistency and conflict with the exercise of these rights. Psychologists are aware of cultural, individual, and role differences, including those due to age, gender, race, ethnicity, national origin, religion, sexual orientation, disability, language, and socioeconomic status. Psychologists try to eliminate the effect on their work of biases based on those factors, and they do not knowingly participate in or condone unfair discriminatory practices.

Principle E: **Concern for Others' Welfare**

Psychologists seek to contribute to the welfare of those with whom they interact professionally. In their professional actions, psychologists weigh the welfare and rights of their patients or clients, students, supervisees, human research participants, and other affected persons, and the welfare of animal subjects of research. When conflicts occur among psychologists' obligations or concerns, they attempt to resolve these conflicts and to perform their roles in a responsible fashion that avoids or minimizes harm. Psychologists are sensitive to real and ascribed differences in power between themselves and others, and they do not exploit or mislead other people during or after professional relationships.

Principle F: **Social Responsibility**

Psychologists are aware of their professional and scientific responsibilities to the community and the society in which they work and live. They apply and make public their knowledge of psychology in order to contribute to human welfare. Psychologists are concerned about and work to mitigate the causes of human suffering. When undertaking research, they strive to advance human welfare and the science of psychology. Psychologists try to avoid misuse of their work. Psychologists comply with the law and encourage the development of law and social policy that serve the interests of their patients and clients and the public. They are encouraged to contribute a portion of their professional time for little or no personal advantage.

ETHICAL STANDARDS

1. GENERAL STANDARDS

These General Standards are potentially applicable to the professional and scientific activities of all psychologists.

1.01 Applicability of the Ethics Code

The activity of a psychologist subject to the Ethics Code may be reviewed under these Ethical Standards only if the activity is part of his or her work-related functions or the activity is psychological in nature. Personal activities having no connection to or effect on psychological roles are not subject to the Ethics Code.

1.02 Relationship of Ethics and Law

If psychologists' ethical responsibilities conflict with law, psychologists make known their commitment to the Ethics Code and take steps to resolve the conflict in a responsible manner.

1.03 Professional and Scientific Relationship

Psychologists provide diagnostic, therapeutic, teaching, research, supervisory, consultative, or other psychological services only in the context of a defined professional or scientific relationship or role. (See also Standards 2.01 Evaluation, Diagnosis, and Interventions in Professional Context, and 7.02, Forensic Assessments.)

1.04 Boundaries of Competence

(a) Psychologists provide services, teach, and conduct research only within the boundaries of their competence, based on their education, training, supervised experience, or appropriate professional experience.

(b) Psychologists provide services, teach, or conduct research in new areas or involving new techniques only after first undertaking appropriate study, training, supervision, and/or consultation from persons who are competent in those areas or techniques.

(c) In those emerging areas in which generally recognized standards for preparatory training do not yet exist, psychologists nevertheless take reasonable steps to ensure the competence of their work and to protect patients, clients, students, research participants, and others from harm.

1.05 Maintaining Expertise

Psychologists who engage in assessment, therapy, teaching, research, organizational consulting, or other professional activities maintain a reasonable level of awareness of current scientific and professional information in their fields of activity, and undertake ongoing efforts to maintain competence in the skills they use.

1.06 Basis for Scientific and Professional Judgments

Psychologists rely on scientifically and professionally derived knowledge when making scientific or professional judgments or when engaging in scholarly or professional endeavors.

1.07 Describing the Nature and Results of Psychological Services

(a) When psychologists provide assessment, evaluation, treatment, counseling, supervision, teaching, consultation, research, or other psychological services to an individual, a group, or an organization, they provide, using language that is reasonably understandable to the recipient of those services, appropriate information beforehand about the nature of such services and appropriate information later about results and conclusions. (See also Standard 2.09, Explaining Assessment Results.)

(b) If psychologists will be precluded by law or by organizational roles from providing such information to particular individuals or groups, they so inform those individuals or groups at the outset of the service.

1.08 Human Differences

Where differences of age, gender, race, ethnicity, national origin, religion, sexual orientation, disability, language, or socioeconomic status significantly affect psychologists' work concerning particular individuals or groups, psychologists obtain the training, experience, consultation, or supervision necessary to ensure the competence of their services, or they make appropriate referrals.

1.09 Respecting Others

In their work-related activities, psychologists respect the rights of others to hold values, attitudes, and opinions that differ from their own.

1.10 Nondiscrimination

In their work-related activities, psychologists do not engage in unfair discrimination based on age, gender, race, ethnicity, national origin, religion, sexual orientation, disability, socioeconomic status, or any basis proscribed by law.

1.11 Sexual Harassment

(a) Psychologists do not engage in sexual harassment. Sexual harassment is sexual solicitation, physical advances, or verbal or nonverbal conduct that is sexual in nature, that occurs in connection with the psychologist's activities or roles as a psychologist, and that either: (1) is unwelcome, is offensive, or creates a hostile workplace environment, and the psychologist knows or is told this; or (2) is sufficiently severe or intense to be abusive to a reasonable person in the context. Sexual harassment can consist of a single intense or severe act or of multiple persistent or pervasive acts.

(b) Psychologists accord sexual-harassment complainants and respondents dignity and respect. Psychologists do not participate in denying a person academic admittance or advancement, employment, tenure, or promotion, based solely upon their having made, or their being the subject of, sexual-harassment charges. This does not preclude taking action based upon the outcome of such proceedings or consideration of other appropriate information.

1.12 Other Harassment

Psychologists do not knowingly engage in behavior that is harassing or demeaning to persons with whom they interact in their work based on factors such as those persons' age, gender, race, ethnicity, national origin, religion, sexual orientation, disability, language, or socioeconomic status.

1.13 Personal Problems and Conflicts

(a) Psychologists recognize that their personal problems and conflicts may interfere with their effectiveness. Accordingly, they refrain from undertaking an activity when they know or should know that their personal problems are likely to lead to harm to a patient, client, colleague, student, research participant, or other person to whom they may owe a professional or scientific obligation.

(b) In addition, psychologists have an obligation to be alert to signs of, and to obtain assistance for, their personal problems at an early stage, in order to prevent significantly impaired performance.

(c) When psychologists become aware of personal problems that may interfere with their performing work-related duties adequately, they take appropriate measures, such as obtaining professional consultation or assistance, and determine whether they should limit, suspend, or terminate their work-related duties.

1.14 Avoiding Harm

Psychologists take reasonable steps to avoid harming their patients or clients, research participants, students, and others with whom they work, and to minimize harm where it is foreseeable and unavoidable.

1.15 Misuse of Psychologists' Influence

Because psychologists' scientific and professional judgments and actions may affect the lives of others, they are alert to and guard against personal, financial, social, organizational, or political factors that might lead to misuse of their influence.

1.16 Misuse of Psychologists' Work

(a) Psychologists do not participate in activities in which it appears likely that their skills or data will be misused by others, unless corrective mechanisms are available. (See also Standard 7.04, Truthfulness and Candor.)
(b) If psychologists learn of misuse or misrepresentation of their work, they take reasonable steps to correct or minimize the misuse or misrepresentation.

1.17 Multiple Relationships

(a) In many communities and situations, it may not be feasible or reasonable for psychologists to avoid social or other nonprofessional contacts with persons such as patients, clients, students, supervisees, or research participants. Psychologists must always be sensitive to the potential harmful effects of other contacts on their work and on those persons with whom they deal. A psychologist refrains from entering into or promising another personal, scientific, professional, financial, or other relationship with such persons if it appears likely that such a relationship reasonably might impair the psychologist's objectivity or otherwise interfere with the psychologist's effectively performing his or her functions as a psychologist, or might harm or exploit the other party.
(b) Likewise, whenever feasible, a psychologist refrains from taking on professional or scientific obligations when preexisting relationships would create a risk of such harm.
(c) If a psychologist finds that, due to unforeseen factors, a potentially harmful multiple relationship has arisen, the psychologist attempts to resolve it with due regard for the best interests of the affected person and maximal compliance with the Ethics Code.

1.18 Barter (With Patients or Clients)

Psychologists ordinarily refrain from accepting goods, services, or other nonmonetary remuneration from patients or clients in return for psychological services because such arrangements create inherent potential for conflicts, exploitation, and distortion of the professional relationship. A psychologist may participate in bartering *only* if (1) it is not clinically contraindicated, *and* (2) the relationship is not exploitative. (See also Standards 1.17, Multiple Relationships, and 1.25, Fees and Financial Arrangements.)

1.19 Exploitative Relationships

(a) Psychologists do not exploit persons over whom they have supervisory, evaluative, or other authority such as students, supervisees, employees, research participants, and clients or patients. (See also Standards 4.05–4.07 regarding sexual involvement with clients or patients.)

(b) Psychologists do not engage in sexual relationships with students or supervisees in training over whom the psychologist has evaluative or direct authority, because such relationships are so likely to impair judgment or be exploitative.

1.20 Consultations and Referrals

(a) Psychologists arrange for appropriate consultations and referrals based principally on the best interests of their patients or clients, with appropriate consent, and subject to other relevant considerations, including applicable law and contractual obligations. (See also Standards 5.01, Discussing the Limits of Confidentiality, and 5.06, Consultations.)

(b) When indicated and professionally appropriate, psychologists cooperate with other professionals in order to serve their patients or clients effectively and appropriately.

(c) Psychologists' referral practices are consistent with law.

1.21 Third-Party Requests for Services

(a) When a psychologist agrees to provide services to a person or entity at the request of a third party, the psychologist clarifies to the extent feasible, at the outset of the service, the nature of the relationship with each party. This clarification includes the role of the psychologist (such as therapist, organizational consultant, diagnostician, or expert witness), the probable uses of the services provided or the information obtained, and the fact that there may be limits to confidentiality.

(b) If there is a foreseeable risk of the psychologist's being called upon to perform conflicting roles because of the involvement of a third party, the psychologist clarifies the nature and direction of his or her responsibilities, keeps all parties appropriately informed as matters develop, and resolves the situation in accordance with this Ethics Code.

1.22 Delegation to and Supervision of Subordinates

(a) Psychologists delegate to their employees, supervisees, and research assistants only those responsibilities that such persons can reasonably be expected to perform competently, on the basis of their education, training, or experience, either independently or with the level of supervision being provided.

(b) Psychologists provide proper training and supervision to their employees or supervisees and take reasonable steps to see that such persons perform services responsibly, competently, and ethically.

(c) If institutional policies, procedures, or practices prevent fulfillment of this obligation, psychologists attempt to modify their role or to correct the situation to the extent feasible.

1.23 Documentation of Professional and Scientific Work

(a) Psychologists appropriately document their professional and scientific work in order to facilitate provision of services later by them or by other professionals, to ensure accountability, and to meet other requirements of institutions or the law.

(b) When psychologists have reason to believe that records of their professional services will be used in legal proceedings involving recipients of or participants in their work, they have a responsibility to create and maintain documentation in the kind of detail and quality that would be consistent with reasonable scrutiny in an adjudicative forum. (See also Standard 7.01, Professionalism, under Forensic Activities.)

1.24 Records and Data

Psychologists create, maintain, disseminate, store, retain, and dispose of records and data relating to their research, practice, and other work in accordance with law and in a manner that permits compliance with the requirements of this Ethics Code. (See also Standard 5.04, Maintenance of Records.)

1.25 Fees and Financial Arrangements

(a) As early as is feasible in a professional or scientific relationship, the psychologist and the patient, client, or other appropriate recipient of psychological services reach an agreement specifying the compensation and the billing arrangements.

(b) Psychologists do not exploit recipients of services or payors with respect to fees.

(c) Psychologists' fee practices are consistent with law.

(d) Psychologists do not misrepresent their fees.

(e) If limitations to services can be anticipated because of limitations in financing, this is discussed with the patient, client, or other appropriate recipient of services as early as is feasible. (See also Standard 4.08, Interruption of Services.)

(f) If the patient, client, or other recipient of services does not pay for services as agreed, and if the psychologist wishes to use collection agencies or legal measures to collect the fees, the psychologist first informs the person that such measures will be taken and provides that person an opportunity to make prompt payment. (See also Standard 5.11, Withholding Records for Nonpayment.)

1.26 Accuracy in Reports to Payors and Funding Sources

In their reports to payors for services or sources of research funding, psychologists accurately state the nature of the research or service provided, the fees or charges, and where applicable, the identity of the provider, the findings, and the diagnosis. (See also Standard 5.05, Disclosures.)

1.27 Referrals and Fees

When a psychologist pays, receives payment from, or divides fees with another professional other than in an employer-employee relationship, the payment to each is based on the services (clinical, consultative, administrative, or other) provided and is not based on the referral itself.

2. EVALUATION, ASSESSMENT, OR INTERVENTION

2.01 Evaluation, Diagnosis, and Interventions in Professional Context

(a) Psychologists perform evaluations, diagnostic services, or interventions only within the context of a defined professional relationship. (See also Standard 1.03, Professional and Scientific Relationship.)

(b) Psychologists' assessments, recommendations, reports, and psychological diagnostic or evaluative statements are based on information and techniques (including personal interviews of the individual when appropriate) sufficient to provide appropriate substantiation for their findings. (See also Standard 7.02, Forensic Assessments.)

2.02 Competence and Appropriate Use of Assessments and Interventions

(a) Psychologists who develop, administer, score, interpret, or use psychological assessment techniques, interviews, tests, or instruments do so in a manner and for purposes that are appropriate in light of the research on or evidence of the usefulness and proper application of the techniques.

(b) Psychologists refrain from misuse of assessment techniques, interventions, results, and interpretations and take reasonable steps to prevent others from misusing the information these techniques provide. This includes refraining from releasing raw test results or raw data to persons, other than to patients or clients as appropriate, who are not qualified to use such information. (See also Standards 1.02, Relationship of Ethics and Law, and 1.04, Boundaries of Competence.)

2.03 Test Construction

Psychologists who develop and conduct research with tests and other assessment techniques use scientific procedures and current professional knowledge for test design, standardization, validation, reduction or elimination of bias, and recommendations for use.

2.04 Use of Assessment in General and With Special Populations

(a) Psychologists who perform interventions or administer, score, interpret, or use assessment techniques are familiar with the reliability, validation, and related standardization or outcome studies of, and proper applications and uses of, the techniques they use.

(b) Psychologists recognize limits to the certainty with which diagnoses, judgments, or predictions can be made about individuals.

(c) Psychologists attempt to identify situations in which particular interventions or assessment techniques or norms may not be applicable or may require adjustment in administration or interpretation because of factors such as individuals' gender, age, race, ethnicity, national origin, religion, sexual orientation, disability, language, or socioeconomic status.

2.05 Interpreting Assessment Results

When interpreting assessment results, including automated interpretations, psychologists take into account the various test factors and characteristics of the person being assessed that might affect psychologists' judgments or reduce the accuracy of their interpretations. They indicate any significant reservations they have about the accuracy or limitations of their interpretations.

2.06 Unqualified Persons

Psychologists do not promote the use of psychological assessment techniques by unqualified persons. (See also Standard 1.22, Delegation to and Supervision of Subordinates.)

2.07 Obsolete Tests and Outdated Test Results

(a) Psychologists do not base their assessment or intervention decisions or recommendations on data or test results that are outdated for the current purpose.
(b) Similarly, psychologists do not base such decisions or recommendations on tests and measures that are obsolete and not useful for the current purpose.

2.08 Test Scoring and Interpretation Services

(a) Psychologists who offer assessment or scoring procedures to other professionals accurately describe the purpose, norms, validity, reliability, and applications of the procedures and any special qualifications applicable to their use.
(b) Psychologists select scoring and interpretation services (including automated services) on the basis of evidence of the validity of the program and procedures as well as on other appropriate considerations.
(c) Psychologists retain appropriate responsibility for the appropriate application, interpretation, and use of assessment instruments, whether they score and interpret such tests themselves or use automated or other services.

2.09 Explaining Assessment Results

Unless the nature of the relationship is clearly explained to the person being assessed in advance and precludes provision of an explanation of results (such as in some organizational consulting, preemployment or security screenings, and forensic evaluations), psychologists ensure that an explanation of the results is provided using language that is reasonably understandable to the person assessed or to another legally authorized person on behalf of the client. Regardless of whether the scoring and interpretation are done by the psychologist, by assistants, or by automated or other outside services, psychologists take reasonable steps to ensure that appropriate explanations of results are given.

2.10 Maintaining Test Security

Psychologists make reasonable efforts to maintain the integrity and security of tests and other assessment techniques consistent with law, contractual obligations, and in a manner that permits compliance with the requirements of this Ethics Code. (See also Standard 1.02, Relationship of Ethics and Law.)

3. ADVERTISING AND OTHER PUBLIC STATEMENTS

3.01 Definition of Public Statements

Psychologists comply with this Ethics Code in public statements relating to their professional services, products, or publications or to the field of psychology.

Public statements include but are not limited to paid or unpaid advertising, brochures, printed matter, directory listings, personal resumes or curricula vitae, interviews or comments for use in media, statements in legal proceedings, lectures and public oral presentations, and published materials.

3.02 Statements by Others

(a) Psychologists who engage others to create or place public statements that promote their professional practice, products, or activities retain professional responsibility for such statements.
(b) In addition, psychologists make reasonable efforts to prevent others whom they do not control (such as employers, publishers, sponsors, organizational clients, and representatives of the print or broadcast media) from making deceptive statements concerning psychologists' practice or professional or scientific activities.
(c) If psychologists learn of deceptive statements about their work made by others, psychologists make reasonable efforts to correct such statements.
(d) Psychologists do not compensate employees of press, radio, television, or other communication media in return for publicity in a news item.
(e) A paid advertisement relating to the psychologist's activities must be identified as such, unless it is already apparent from the context.

3.03 Avoidance of False or Deceptive Statements

(a) Psychologists do not make public statements that are false, deceptive, misleading, or fraudulent, either because of what they state, convey, or suggest or because of what they omit, concerning their research, practice, or other work activities or those of persons or organizations with which they are affiliated. As examples (and not in limitation) of this standard, psychologists do not make false or deceptive statements concerning (1) their training, experience, or competence; (2) their academic degrees; (3) their credentials; (4) their institutional or association affiliations; (5) their services; (6) the scientific or clinical basis for, or results or degree of success of, their services; (7) their fees; or (8) their publications or research findings. (See also Standards 6.15, Deception in Research, and 6.18, Providing Participants With Information About the Study.)
(b) Psychologists claim as credentials for their psychological work, only degrees that (1) were earned from a regionally accredited educational institution or (2) were the basis for psychology licensure by the state in which they practice.

3.04 Media Presentations

When psychologists provide advice or comment by means of public lectures, demonstrations, radio or television programs, prerecorded tapes, printed articles, mailed material, or other media, they take reasonable precautions to ensure that (1) the statements are based on appropriate psychological literature and practice, (2) the statements are otherwise consistent with this Ethics Code, and (3) the recipients of the information are not encouraged to infer that a relationship has been established with them personally.

3.05 Testimonials

Psychologists do not solicit testimonials from current psychotherapy clients or patients or other persons who because of their particular circumstances are vulnerable to undue influence.

3.06 In-Person Solicitation

Psychologists do not engage, directly or through agents, in uninvited in-person solicitation of business from actual or potential psychotherapy patients or clients or other persons who because of their particular circumstances are vulnerable to undue influence. However, this does not preclude attempting to implement appropriate collateral contacts with significant others for the purpose of benefiting an already engaged therapy patient.

4. THERAPY

4.01 Structuring the Relationship

(a) Psychologists discuss with clients or patients as early as is feasible in the therapeutic relationship appropriate issues, such as the nature and anticipated course of therapy, fees, and confidentiality. (See also Standards 1.25, Fees and Financial Arrangements, and 5.01, Discussing the Limits of Confidentiality.)

(b) When the psychologist's work with clients or patients will be supervised, the above discussion includes that fact, and the name of the supervisor, when the supervisor has legal responsibility for the case.

(c) When the therapist is a student intern, the client or patient is informed of that fact.

(d) Psychologists make reasonable efforts to answer patients' questions and to avoid apparent misunderstandings about therapy. Whenever possible, psychologists provide oral and/or written information, using language that is reasonably understandable to the patient or client.

4.02 Informed Consent to Therapy

(a) Psychologists obtain appropriate informed consent to therapy or related procedures, using language that is reasonably understandable to participants. The content of informed consent will vary depending on many circumstances; however, informed consent generally implies that the person (1) has the capacity to consent, (2) has been informed of significant information concerning the procedure, (3) has freely and without undue influence expressed consent, and (4) consent has been appropriately documented.

(b) When persons are legally incapable of giving informed consent, psychologists obtain informed permission from a legally authorized person, if such substitute consent is permitted by law.

(c) In addition, psychologists (1) inform those persons who are legally incapable of giving informed consent about the proposed interventions in a manner commensurate with the persons' psychological capacities, (2) seek their assent to those interventions, and (3) consider such persons' preferences and best interests.

4.03 Couple and Family Relationships

(a) When a psychologist agrees to provide services to several persons who have a relationship (such as husband and wife or parents and children), the psychologist attempts to clarify at the outset (1) which of the individuals are patients or clients and (2) the relationship the psychologist will have with each person. This clarification includes the role of the psychologist and the probable uses of the services provided or the information obtained. (See also Standard 5.01, Discussing the Limits of Confidentiality.)

(b) As soon as it becomes apparent that the psychologist may be called on to perform potentially conflicting roles (such as marital counselor to husband and wife, and then witness for one party in a divorce proceeding), the psychologist attempts to clarify and adjust, or withdraw from, roles appropriately. (See also Standard 7.03, Clarification of Role, under Forensic Activities.)

4.04 Providing Mental Health Services to Those Served by Others

In deciding whether to offer or provide services to those already receiving mental health services elsewhere, psychologists carefully consider the treatment issues and the potential patient's or client's welfare. The psychologist discusses these issues with the patient or client, or another legally authorized person on behalf of the client, in order to minimize the risk of confusion and conflict, consults with the other service providers when appropriate, and proceeds with caution and sensitivity to the therapeutic issues.

4.05 Sexual Intimacies With Current Patients or Clients

Psychologists do not engage in sexual intimacies with current patients or clients.

4.06 Therapy With Former Sexual Partners

Psychologists do not accept as therapy patients or clients persons with whom they have engaged in sexual intimacies.

4.07 Sexual Intimacies With Former Therapy Patients

(a) Psychologists do not engage in sexual intimacies with a former therapy patient or client for at least two years after cessation or termination of professional services.

(b) Because sexual intimacies with a former therapy patient or client are so frequently harmful to the patient or client, and because such intimacies undermine public confidence in the psychology profession and thereby deter the public's use of needed services, psychologists do not engage in sexual intimacies with former therapy patients and clients even after a two-year interval except in the most unusual circumstances. The psychologist who engages in such activity after the two years following cessation or termination of treatment bears the burden of demonstrating that there has been no exploitation, in light of all relevant factors, including (1) the amount of time that has passed since therapy terminated, (2) the nature and duration of the therapy, (3) the circumstances of termination, (4) the patient's or client's personal history, (5) the patient's or client's current mental status, (6) the likelihood of adverse impact on the patient or client and others, and (7) any statements or actions made by the therapist during the course of therapy suggesting or inviting the possibility of a posttermination sexual or romantic relationship with the patient or client. (See also Standard 1.17, Multiple Relationships.)

4.08 Interruption of Services

(a) Psychologists make reasonable efforts to plan for facilitating care in the event that psychological services are interrupted by factors such as the psychologist's illness, death, unavailability, or relocation or by the client's relocation or financial limitations. (See also Standard 5.09, Preserving Records and Data.)

(b) When entering into employment or contractual relationships, psychologists provide for orderly and appropriate resolution of responsibility for patient or client care in the event that the employment or contractual relationship ends, with paramount consideration given to the welfare of the patient or client.

4.09 Terminating the Professional Relationship

(a) Psychologists do not abandon patients or clients. (See also Standard 1.25e, under Fees and Financial Arrangements.)

(b) Psychologists terminate a professional relationship when it becomes reasonably clear that the patient or client no longer needs the service, is not benefiting, or is being harmed by continued service.

(c) Prior to termination for whatever reason, except where precluded by the patient's or client's conduct, the psychologist discusses the patient's or client's views and needs, provides appropriate pretermination counseling, suggests alternative service providers as appropriate, and takes other reasonable steps to facilitate transfer of responsibility to another provider if the patient or client needs one immediately.

5. PRIVACY AND CONFIDENTIALITY

These Standards are potentially applicable to the professional and scientific activities of all psychologists.

5.01 Discussing the Limits of Confidentiality

(a) Psychologists discuss with persons and organizations with whom they establish a scientific or professional relationship (including, to the extent feasible, minors and their legal representatives) (1) the relevant limitations on confidentiality, including limitations where applicable in group, marital, and family therapy or in organizational consulting, and (2) the foreseeable uses of the information generated through their services.

(b) Unless it is not feasible or is contraindicated, the discussion of confidentiality occurs at the outset of the relationship and thereafter as new circumstances may warrant.

(c) Permission for electronic recording of interviews is secured from clients and patients.

5.02 Maintaining Confidentiality

Psychologists have a primary obligation and take reasonable precautions to respect the confidentiality rights of those with whom they work or consult, recognizing that confidentiality may be established by law, institutional rules, or professional or scientific relationships. (See also Standard 6.26, Professional Reviewers.)

5.03 Minimizing Intrusions on Privacy

(a) In order to minimize intrusions on privacy, psychologists include in written and oral reports, consultations, and the like, only information germane to the purpose for which the communication is made.
(b) Psychologists discuss confidential information obtained in clinical or consulting relationships, or evaluative data concerning patients, individual or organizational clients, students, research participants, supervisees, and employees, only for appropriate scientific or professional purposes and only with persons clearly concerned with such matters.

5.04 Maintenance of Records

Psychologists maintain appropriate confidentiality in creating, storing, accessing, transferring, and disposing of records under their control, whether these are written, automated, or in any other medium. Psychologists maintain and dispose of records in accordance with law and in a manner that permits compliance with the requirements of this Ethics Code.

5.05 Disclosures

(a) Psychologists disclose confidential information without the consent of the individual only as mandated by law, or where permitted by law for a valid purpose, such as (1) to provide needed professional services to the patient or the individual or organizational client, (2) to obtain appropriate professional consultations, (3) to protect the patient or client or others from harm, or (4) to obtain payment for services, in which instance disclosure is limited to the minimum that is necessary to achieve the purpose.
(b) Psychologists also may disclose confidential information with the appropriate consent of the patient or the individual or organizational client (or of another legally authorized person on behalf of the patient or client), unless prohibited by law.

5.06 Consultations

When consulting with colleagues, (1) psychologists do not share confidential information that reasonably could lead to the identification of a patient, client, research participant, or other person or organization with whom they have a confidential relationship unless they have obtained the prior consent of the person or organization or the disclosure cannot be avoided, and (2) they share information only to the extent necessary to achieve the purposes of the consultation. (See also Standard 5.02, Maintaining Confidentiality.)

5.07 Confidential Information in Databases

(a) If confidential information concerning recipients of psychological services is to be entered into databases or systems of records available to persons whose access has not been consented to by the recipient, then psychologists use coding or other techniques to avoid the inclusion of personal identifiers.

(b) If a research protocol approved by an institutional review board or similar body requires the inclusion of personal identifiers, such identifiers are deleted before the information is made accessible to persons other than those of whom the subject was advised.

(c) If such deletion is not feasible, then before psychologists transfer such data to others or review such data collected by others, they take reasonable steps to determine that appropriate consent of personally identifiable individuals has been obtained.

5.08 Use of Confidential Information for Didactic or Other Purposes

(a) Psychologists do not disclose in their writings, lectures, or other public media, confidential, personally identifiable information concerning their patients, individual or organizational clients, students, research participants, or other recipients of their services that they obtained during the course of their work, unless the person or organization has consented in writing or unless there is other ethical or legal authorization for doing so.

(b) Ordinarily, in such scientific and professional presentations, psychologists disguise confidential information concerning such persons or organizations so that they are not individually identifiable to others and so that discussions do not cause harm to subjects who might identify themselves.

5.09 Preserving Records and Data

A psychologist makes plans in advance so that confidentiality of records and data is protected in the event of the psychologist's death, incapacity, or withdrawal from the position or practice.

5.10 Ownership of Records and Data

Recognizing that ownership of records and data is governed by legal principles, psychologists take reasonable and lawful steps so that records and data remain available to the extent needed to serve the best interests of patients, individual or organizational clients, research participants, or appropriate others.

5.11 Withholding Records for Nonpayment

Psychologists may not withhold records under their control that are requested and imminently needed for a patient's or client's treatment solely because payment has not been received, except as otherwise provided by law.

6. TEACHING, TRAINING SUPERVISION, RESEARCH, AND PUBLISHING

6.01 Design of Education and Training Programs

Psychologists who are responsible for education and training programs seek to ensure that the programs are competently designed, provide the proper experiences, and meet the requirements for licensure, certification, or other goals for which claims are made by the program.

6.02 Descriptions of Education and Training Programs

(a) Psychologists responsible for education and training programs seek to ensure that there is a current and accurate description of the program content, training goals and objectives, and requirements that must be met for satisfactory completion of the program. This information must be made readily available to all interested parties.

(b) Psychologists seek to ensure that statements concerning their course outlines are accurate and not misleading, particularly regarding the subject matter to be covered, bases for evaluating progress, and the nature of course experiences. (See also Standard 3.03, Avoidance of False or Deceptive Statements.)

(c) To the degree to which they exercise control, psychologists responsible for announcements, catalogs, brochures, or advertisements describing workshops, seminars, or other non-degree-granting educational programs ensure that they accurately describe the audience for which the program is intended, the educational objectives, the presenters, and the fees involved.

6.03 Accuracy and Objectivity in Teaching

(a) When engaged in teaching or training, psychologists present psychological information accurately and with a reasonable degree of objectivity.

(b) When engaged in teaching or training, psychologists recognize the power they hold over students or supervisees and therefore make reasonable efforts to avoid engaging in conduct that is personally demeaning to students or supervisees. (See also Standards 1.09, Respecting Others, and 1.12, Other Harassment.)

6.04 Limitation on Teaching

Psychologists do not teach the use of techniques or procedures that require specialized training, licensure, or expertise, including but not limited to hypnosis, biofeedback, and projective techniques, to individuals who lack the prerequisite training, legal scope of practice, or expertise.

6.05 Assessing Student and Supervisee Performance

(a) In academic and supervisory relationships, psychologists establish an appropriate process for providing feedback to students and supervisees.

(b) Psychologists evaluate students and supervisees on the basis of their actual performance on relevant and established program requirements.

6.06 Planning Research

(a) Psychologists design, conduct, and report research in accordance with recognized standards of scientific competence and ethical research.

(b) Psychologists plan their research so as to minimize the possibility that results will be misleading.

(c) In planning research, psychologists consider its ethical acceptability under the Ethics Code. If an ethical issue is unclear, psychologists seek to resolve the issue through consultation with institutional review boards, animal care and use committees, peer consultations, or other proper mechanisms.

(d) Psychologists take reasonable steps to implement appropriate protections for the rights and welfare of human participants, other persons affected by the research, and the welfare of animal subjects.

6.07 Responsibility

(a) Psychologists conduct research competently and with due concern for the dignity and welfare of the participants.

(b) Psychologists are responsible for the ethical conduct of research conducted by them or by others under their supervision or control.

(c) Researchers and assistants are permitted to perform only those tasks for which they are appropriately trained and prepared.

(d) As part of the process of development and implementation of research projects, psychologists consult those with expertise concerning any special population under investigation or most likely to be affected.

6.08 Compliance With Law and Standards

Psychologists plan and conduct research in a manner consistent with federal and state law and regulations, as well as professional standards governing the conduct of research, and particularly those standards governing research with human participants and animal subjects.

6.09 Institutional Approval

Psychologists obtain from host institutions or organizations appropriate approval prior to conducting research, and they provide accurate information about their research proposals. They conduct the research in accordance with the approved research protocol.

6.10 Research Responsibilities

Prior to conducting research (except research involving only anonymous surveys, naturalistic observations, or similar research), psychologists enter into an agreement with participants that clarifies the nature of the research and the responsibilities of each party.

6.11 Informed Consent to Research

(a) Psychologists use language that is reasonably understandable to research participants in obtaining their appropriate informed consent (except as provided in Standard 6.12, Dispensing With Informed Consent). Such informed consent is appropriately documented.

(b) Using language that is reasonably understandable to participants, psychologists inform participants of the nature of the research; they inform participants that they are free to participate or to decline to participate or to withdraw from the research; they explain the foreseeable consequences of declining or withdrawing; they inform participants of significant factors that may be expected to influence their willingness to participate (such as risks, discomfort, adverse effects, or limitations on confidentiality, except as provided in Standard 6.15, Deception in Research); and they explain other aspects about which the prospective participants inquire.

(c) When psychologists conduct research with individuals such as students or subordinates, psychologists take special care to protect the prospective participants from adverse consequences of declining or withdrawing from participation.

(d) When research participation is a course requirement or opportunity for extra credit, the prospective participant is given the choice of equitable alternative activities.
(e) For persons who are legally incapable of giving informed consent, psychologists nevertheless (1) provide an appropriate explanation, (2) obtain the participant's assent, and (3) obtain appropriate permission from a legally authorized person, if such substitute consent is permitted by law.

6.12 Dispensing With Informed Consent

Before determining that planned research (such as research involving only anonymous questionnaires, naturalistic observations, or certain kinds of archival research) does not require the informed consent of research participants, psychologists consider applicable regulations and institutional review board requirements, and they consult with colleagues as appropriate.

6.13 Informed Consent in Research Filming or Recording

Psychologists obtain informed consent from research participants prior to filming or recording them in any form, unless the research involves simply naturalistic observations in public places and it is not anticipated that the recording will be used in a manner that could cause personal identification or harm.

6.14 Offering Inducements for Research Participants

(a) In offering professional services as an inducement to obtain research participants, psychologists make clear the nature of the services, as well as the risks, obligations, and limitations. (See also Standard 1.18, Barter [With Patients or Clients].)
(b) Psychologists do not offer excessive or inappropriate financial or other inducements to obtain research participants, particularly when it might tend to coerce participation.

6.15 Deception in Research

(a) Psychologists do not conduct a study involving deception unless they have determined that the use of deceptive techniques is justified by the study's prospective scientific, educational, or applied value and that equally effective alternative procedures that do not use deception are not feasible.
(b) Psychologists never deceive research participants about significant aspects that would affect their willingness to participate, such as physical risks, discomfort, or unpleasant emotional experiences.
(c) Any other deception that is an integral feature of the design and conduct of an experiment must be explained to participants as early as is feasible, preferably at the conclusion of their participation, but no later than at the conclusion of the research. (See also Standard 6.18, Providing Participants With Information About the Study.)

6.16 Sharing and Utilizing Data

Psychologists inform research participants of their anticipated sharing or further use of personally identifiable research data and of the possibility of unanticipated future uses.

6.17 Minimizing Invasiveness

In conducting research, psychologists interfere with the participants or milieu from which data are collected only in a manner that is warranted by an appropriate research design and that is consistent with psychologists' roles as scientific investigators.

6.18 Providing Participants With Information About the Study

(a) Psychologists provide a prompt opportunity for participants to obtain appropriate information about the nature, results, and conclusions of the research, and psychologists attempt to correct any misconceptions that participants may have.
(b) If scientific or humane values justify delaying or withholding this information, psychologists take reasonable measures to reduce the risk of harm.

6.19 Honoring Commitments

Psychologists take reasonable measures to honor all commitments they have made to research participants.

6.20 Care and Use of Animals in Research

(a) Psychologists who conduct research involving animals treat them humanely.
(b) Psychologists acquire, care for, use, and dispose of animals in compliance with current federal, state, and local laws and regulations, and with professional standards.
(c) Psychologists trained in research methods and experienced in the care of laboratory animals supervise all procedures involving animals and are responsible for ensuring appropriate consideration of their comfort, health, and humane treatment.
(d) Psychologists ensure that all individuals using animals under their supervision have received instruction in research methods and in the care, maintenance, and handling of the species being used, to the extent appropriate to their role.
(e) Responsibilities and activities of individuals assisting in a research project are consistent with their respective competencies.
(f) Psychologists make reasonable efforts to minimize the discomfort, infection, illness, and pain of animal subjects.
(g) A procedure subjecting animals to pain, stress, or privation is used only when an alternative procedure is unavailable and the goal is justified by its prospective scientific, educational, or applied value.
(h) Surgical procedures are performed under appropriate anesthesia; techniques to avoid infection and minimize pain are followed during and after surgery.
(i) When it is appropriate that the animal's life be terminated, it is done rapidly, with an effort to minimize pain, and in accordance with accepted procedures.

6.21 Reporting of Results

(a) Psychologists do not fabricate data or falsify results in their publications.
(b) If psychologists discover significant errors in their published data, they take reasonable steps to correct such errors in a correction, retraction, erratum, or other appropriate publication means.

6.22 Plagiarism

Psychologists do not present substantial portions or elements of another's work or data as their own, even if the other work or data source is cited occasionally.

6.23 Publication Credit

(a) Psychologists take responsibility and credit, including authorship credit, only for work they have actually performed or to which they have contributed.
(b) Principal authorship and other publication credits accurately reflect the relative scientific or professional contributions of the individuals involved, regardless of their relative status. Mere possession of an institutional position, such as Department Chair, does not justify authorship credit. Minor contributions to the research or to the writing for publications are appropriately acknowledged, such as in footnotes or in an introductory statement.
(c) A student is usually listed as principal author on any multiple-authored article that is substantially based on the student's dissertation or thesis.

6.24 Duplicate Publication of Data

Psychologists do not publish, as original data, data that have been previously published. This does not preclude republishing data when they are accompanied by proper acknowledgment.

6.25 Sharing Data

After research results are published, psychologists do not withhold the data on which their conclusions are based from other competent professionals who seek to verify the substantive claims through reanalysis and who intend to use such data only for that purpose, provided that the confidentiality of the participants can be protected and unless legal rights concerning proprietary data preclude their release.

6.26 Professional Reviewers

Psychologists who review material submitted for publication, grant, or other research proposal review respect the confidentiality of and the proprietary rights in such information of those who submitted it.

7. FORENSIC ACTIVITIES

7.01 Professionalism

Psychologists who perform forensic functions, such as assessments, interviews, consultations, reports, or expert testimony, must comply with all other provisions of this Ethics Code to the extent that they apply to such activities. In addition, psychologists base their forensic work on appropriate knowledge of and competence in the areas underlying such work, including specialized knowledge concerning special populations. (See also Standards 1.06, Basis for Scientific and Professional Judgments; 1.08, Human Differences; 1.15, Misuse of Psychologists' Influence; and 1.23, Documentation of Professional and Scientific Work.)

7.02 Forensic Assessments

(a) Psychologists' forensic assessments, recommendations, and reports are based on information and techniques (including personal interviews of the individual, when appropriate) sufficient to provide appropriate substantiation for their findings. (See also Standards 1.03, Professional and Scientific Relationship; 1.23, Documentation of Professional and Scientific Work; 2.01, Evaluation, Diagnosis, and Interventions in Professional Context; and 2.05, Interpreting Assessment Results.)

(b) Except as noted in (c), below, psychologists provide written or oral forensic reports or testimony of the psychological characteristics of an individual only after they have conducted an examination of the individual adequate to support their statements or conclusions.

(c) When, despite reasonable efforts, such an examination is not feasible, psychologists clarify the impact of their limited information on the reliability and validity of their reports and testimony, and they appropriately limit the nature and extent of their conclusions or recommendations.

7.03 Clarification of Role

In most circumstances, psychologists avoid performing multiple and potentially conflicting roles in forensic matters. When psychologists may be called on to serve in more than one role in a legal proceeding—for example, as consultant or expert for one party or for the court and as a fact witness—they clarify role expectations and the extent of confidentiality in advance to the extent feasible, and thereafter as changes occur, in order to avoid compromising their professional judgment and objectivity and in order to avoid misleading others regarding their role.

7.04 Truthfulness and Candor

(a) In forensic testimony and reports, psychologists testify truthfully, honestly, and candidly and, consistent with applicable legal procedures, describe fairly the bases for their testimony and conclusions.

(b) Whenever necessary to avoid misleading, psychologists acknowledge the limits of their data or conclusions.

7.05 Prior Relationships

A prior professional relationship with a party does not preclude psychologists from testifying as fact witnesses or from testifying to their services to the extent permitted by applicable law. Psychologists appropriately take into account ways in which the prior relationship might affect their professional objectivity or opinions and disclose the potential conflict to the relevant parties.

7.06 Compliance With Law and Rules

In performing forensic roles, psychologists are reasonably familiar with the rules governing their roles. Psychologists are aware of the occasionally competing demands placed upon them by these principles and the requirements of the court system, and attempt to resolve these conflicts by making known their commitment to this Ethics Code and taking steps to resolve the conflict in a responsible manner. (See also Standard 1.02, Relationship of Ethics and Law.)

8. RESOLVING ETHICAL ISSUES

8.01 Familiarity With Ethics Code

Psychologists have an obligation to be familiar with this Ethics Code, other applicable ethics codes, and their application to psychologists' work. Lack of awareness or misunderstanding of an ethical standard is not itself a defense to a charge of unethical conduct.

8.02 Confronting Ethical Issues

When a psychologist is uncertain whether a particular situation or course of action would violate this Ethics Code, the psychologist ordinarily consults with other psychologists knowledgeable about ethical issues, with state or national psychology ethics committees, or with other appropriate authorities in order to choose a proper response.

8.03 Conflicts Between Ethics and Organizational Demands

If the demands of an organization with which psychologists are affiliated conflict with this Ethics Code, psychologists clarify the nature of the conflict, make known their commitment to the Ethics Code, and to the extent feasible, seek to resolve the conflict in a way that permits the fullest adherence to the Ethics Code.

8.04 Informal Resolution of Ethical Violations

When psychologists believe that there may have been an ethical violation by another psychologist, they attempt to resolve the issue by bringing it to the attention of that individual if an informal resolution appears appropriate and the intervention does not violate any confidentiality rights that may be involved.

8.05 Reporting Ethical Violations

If an apparent ethical violation is not appropriate for informal resolution under Standard 8.04 or is not resolved properly in that fashion, psychologists take further action appropriate to the situation, unless such action conflicts with confidentiality rights in ways that cannot be resolved. Such action might include referral to state or national committees on professional ethics or to state licensing boards.

8.06 Cooperating With Ethics Committees

Psychologists cooperate in ethics investigations, proceedings, and resulting requirements of the APA or any affiliated state psychological association to which they belong. In doing so, they make reasonable efforts to resolve any issues as to confidentiality. Failure to cooperate is itself an ethics violation.

8.07 Improper Complaints

Psychologists do not file or encourage the filing of ethics complaints that are frivolous and are intended to harm the respondent rather than to protect the public.

6. NURSING

Organization

AMERICAN NURSES ASSOCIATION

Headquarters:
600 Maryland Avenue, SW
Suite 100W
Washington, DC 20024-2571
Telephone: (202) 651-7000
(800) 274-4ANA
Fax: (202) 651-7001
Website: http://www.nursingworld.org

Date founded: 1897
   Known as the Nurses Associated Alumnae until 1911
Membership: approximately 180,000 registered nurses in 53 constituent
   state and territorial associations, and students

Code of Ethics

Official name: *Code for Nurses With Interpretive Statements*
History: First adopted 1950; revised 1976; current version 1985
Authority: Committee on Ethics; Congress of Nursing Practice; House
   of Delegates

Additional Resources

Organizational (Divisions, Programs, Services, etc.):

American Academy of Nursing
American Nurses Credentialing Center
American Nurses Foundation
Best Practice Network (information-sharing system created with American
   Association of Critical Care Nurses)
Center for Ethics and Human Rights
Certification Program
Congress of Nursing Practice
Congress on Nursing Economics

Continuing Education Program
Council for Advance Practice Nursing
Council for Nursing Research
Council for Professional Nursing Education and Development
HIV/AIDS Nursing Care Summit
Liability Insurance Program
National Coalition for Health Professional Education in Genetics

Informational (Publications, Videos, Seminars, etc.):

Articles in *American Nurse, Credentialing News, Online Journal of Issues in Nursing,* and *Nursing Trends & Issues*
ANA Model Practice Act
ANA Standards of Practice
Annotated Bibliography for Ethical Guidelines
Bloodborne Diseases: Nurses' Risks, Rights, and Responsibilities
Center for Ethics and Human Rights Communiqué
Consumer Bill of Rights and Responsibilities
Directory of Accredited Organizations
Directory of Certification Examination Review Courses
Diversity, Marginalization and Culturally Competent Health Care: Issues in Knowledge Development
Ethical Dilemmas in Contemporary Nursing Practice
Ethical Guidelines for Nursing Research (International Council of Nurses)
Ethical Guidelines in the Conduct, Dissemination, and Implementation of Nursing Research
The Genetics Revolution: Implications for Nursing
Guidelines on Reporting Incompetent, Unethical, or Illegal Practices
Implementation of Nursing Practice Standards and Guidelines
Knowledge About Care and Caring: State of the Art and Future Developments
Managed Care: Challenges and Opportunities for Nursing
Managing Genetic Information: Implications for Nursing Practice
Manual to Develop Guidelines
Nightingale Pledge
Nurses and Consumers: Partners in Assuring Quality Care in the Home
Nursing and HIV/AIDS
Nursing Quality Indicators: Definitions and Implications and Guide for Implementation
Nursing's Quality Indicators for Acute Care Settings & ANA's Safety and Quality Initiative
Nursing's Social Policy Statement
Practice and Inquiry for Nursing Administration: Intradisciplinary and Interdisciplinary Perspectives
Principles for the Provision of Mental Health and Substance Abuse Treatment Services: A Bill of Rights
Promoting Cultural Competence In and Through Education

Protect Your Patients—Protect Your License
Registered Professional Nurses & Unlicensed Assistive Personnel
Various conference sessions:
    Ensuring Continued Competency for Nursing Licensees
    Ethics of Managed Care
    Licensure and Regulation of Nurses
    Sexual Misconduct
Various *Position Statements*:
    Active Euthanasia
    Assisted Suicide
    Ethics and Human Rights
    Foregoing Nutrition and Hydration
    Guideline for Commercial Support for Continuing Nurse Education
    Guidelines for Disclosure to a Known Third Party About Possible
        HIV Infection
    HIV Infected Nurse, Ethical Obligations and Disclosure
    Joint Statement on Maintaining Professional and Legal Standards
        During a Shortage of Nursing Personnel
    Measuring the Quality of Care at the End of Life
    Mechanisms Through Which State Nurses Associations Consider
        Ethical/Human Rights Issues
    The Non-Negotiable Nature of the Code for Nurses
    Nurses' Participation in Capital Punishment
    Nursing and the Patient Self-Determination Acts
    Nursing Care and Do-Not-Resuscitate Decisions
    Promotion of Comfort and Relief of Pain in Dying Patients
    Registered Nurse Utilization of Unlicensed Assistive Personnel
    The Right to Accept or Reject an Assignment
    Risk Versus Responsibility in Providing Nursing Care
    Sexual Harassment
    Support for Confidential Notification Services and a Limited Privilege
        to Disclose
    Telehealth—Issues for Nursing

Goals and Activities of Organization

The American Nurses Association (ANA) is a professional organization and labor union representing the interests of the nation's 2.2 million registered nurses. A federation of constituent state nurses associations and individual members, its goals are to improve health standards and the availability of health care services; foster high standards of nursing; stimulate and promote the professional development of nurses; project a positive and realistic view of nursing; and advance nurses' economic and general welfare.

The ANA establishes standards of nursing practice, education, services, and ethics; ensures a system of credentialing; initiates and influences legislation, governmental programs, and national and international health policy and reform; supports evaluation and research; serves as a central agency for the collection, analysis, and dissemination of information; ensures a collective bargaining program; acts as a consumer advocate; and represents the profession to health groups, governmental bodies, and the public.

American Nurses Publishing produces many materials dealing with issues of ethics and professionalism. The Committee on Ethics distributes and promotes the Code for Nurses, and issues relevant Position Statements. The Center for Ethics and Human Rights provides educational programs and clearinghouse activities. The American Nurses Credentialing Center provides certification and accreditation in defined functional or clinical areas, based on standards set by the ANA Congress of Nursing Practice.

Implementation and Enforcement of Code

Enforcement is the combined responsibility of the ANA, state associations, and individual nurses. The ANA Bylaws direct constituent state nurses associations to require their members to abide by the Code. Enforcement mechanisms and penalties vary depending upon the state and the member's infraction.

The Board of Directors establishes policies and procedures for disciplinary action, including a fair hearing. Cause for action includes the failure to maintain one's professional qualifications or fulfill one's responsibilities (including the responsibility to abide by the Code).

The Committee on Ethics applies the broad principles in the Code to specific practice issues and develops guidelines for implementing the Code. It offers consultation to state associations upon request. The Congress of Nursing Practice interprets the Code, and also formulates revisions to the Code for approval by the House of Delegates.

History and Development of Code

One of the first goals of the ANA upon its founding in 1897 was to "establish and maintain a code of ethics." The organization adopted a suggested code in 1926; the first official Code of Ethics was adopted in 1950.

The Code for Nurses was issued in 1976. It was revised in 1985 to more fully delineate the nature and scope of nursing practice.

Code for Nurses With Interpretive Statements*

PREAMBLE

A code of ethics makes explicit the primary goals and values of the profession. When individuals become nurses, they make a moral commitment to uphold the values and special moral obligations expressed in their code. The *Code for Nurses* is based on a belief about the nature of individuals, nursing, health, and society. Nursing encompasses the protection, promotion, and restoration of health; the prevention of illness; and the alleviation of suffering in the care of clients, including individuals, families, groups, and communities. In the context of these functions, nursing is defined as the diagnosis and treatment of human responses to actual or potential health problems.

Since clients themselves are the primary decision makers in matters concerning their own health, treatment, and well-being, the goal of nursing actions is to support and enhance the client's responsibility and self-determination to the greatest extent possible. In this context, health is not necessarily an end in itself, but rather a means to a life that is meaningful from the client's perspective.

When making clinical judgments, nurses base their decisions on consideration of consequences and of universal moral principles, both of which prescribe and justify nursing actions. The most fundamental of these principles is respect for persons. Other principles stemming from this basic principle are autonomy (self-determination), beneficence (doing good), nonmaleficence (avoiding harm), veracity (truth-telling), confidentiality (respecting privileged information), fidelity (keeping promises), and justice (treating people fairly).

In brief, then, the statements of the code and their interpretation provide guidance for conduct and relationships in carrying out nursing responsibilities consistent with the ethical obligations of the profession and with high quality in nursing care.

INTRODUCTION

A code of ethics indicates a profession's acceptance of the responsibility and trust with which it has been invested by society. Under the terms of the implicit contract between society and the nursing profession, society grants the profession considerable autonomy and authority to function in the conduct of its affairs. The development of a code of ethics is an essential activity of a profession and provides one means for the exercise of professional self-regulation.

Upon entering the profession, each nurse inherits a measure of both the responsibility and the trust that have accrued to nursing over the years, as well as the corresponding obligation to adhere to the profession's code of conduct and relationships for ethical practice. The *Code for Nurses with Interpretive Statements* is thus more a collective expression of nursing conscience and philosophy than a set of external rules imposed upon an individual practitioner of nursing. Personal

---

*Reprinted from American Nurses Association, *Code for Nurses With Interpretive Statements,* © 1976, 1985 by the American Nurses Association. All rights reserved. Reprinted with permission from American Nurses Publishing, American Nurses Foundation/American Nurses Association, 600 Maryland Avenue, SW, Suite 100W, Washington, DC 20024-2571. To order the current *Code for Nurses With Interpretive Statements* (© 1998) call 800/637-0323, publication code #G-56.

and professional integrity can be assured only if an individual is committed to the profession's code of conduct.

A code of ethical conduct offers general principles to guide and evaluate nursing actions. It does not assure the virtues required for professional practice within the character of each nurse. In particular situations, the justification of behavior as ethical must satisfy not only the individual nurse acting as a moral agent but also the standards for professional peer review.

The *Code for Nurses* was adopted by the American Nurses Association in 1950 and has been revised periodically. It serves to inform both the nurse and society of the profession's expectations and requirements in ethical matters. The code and the interpretive statements together provide a framework within which nurses can make ethical decisions and discharge their responsibilities to the public, to other members of the health team, and to the profession.

Although a particular situation by its nature may determine the use of specific moral principles, the basic philosophical values, directives, and suggestions provided here are widely applicable to situations encountered in clinical practice. The *Code for Nurses* is not open to negotiation in employment settings, nor is it permissible for individuals or groups of nurses to adapt or change the language of this code.

The requirements of the code may often exceed those of the law. Violations of the law may subject the nurse to civil or criminal liability. The state nurses' associations, in fulfilling the profession's duty to society, may discipline their members for violations of the code. Loss of the respect and confidence of society and of one's colleagues is a serious sanction resulting from violation of the code. In addition, every nurse has a personal obligation to uphold and adhere to the code and to ensure that nursing colleagues do likewise.

Guidance and assistance in applying the code to local situations may be obtained from the American Nurses Association and the constituent state nurses' associations.

* * *

1. *The nurse provides services with respect for human dignity and the uniqueness of the client, unrestricted by considerations of social or economic status, personal attributes, or the nature of health problems.*

1.1 Respect for Human Dignity

The fundamental principle of nursing practice is respect for the inherent dignity and worth of every client. Nurses are morally obligated to respect human existence and the individuality of all persons who are the recipients of nursing actions. Nurses therefore must take all reasonable means to protect and preserve human life when there is hope of recovery or reasonable hope of benefit from life-prolonging treatment.

Truth telling and the process of reaching informed choice underlie the exercise of self-determination, which is basic to respect for persons. Clients should be as fully involved as possible in the planning and implementation of their own health care. Clients have the moral right to determine what will be done with their own person; to be given accurate information, and all the information necessary for making informed judgments; to be assisted with weighing the benefits and burdens of options in their treatment; to accept, refuse, or terminate treatment without coercion; and to be given necessary emotional support. Each nurse has an obligation to be knowledgeable about the moral and legal rights of all clients and to protect and support those rights. In situations in which the client lacks the capacity to make a decision, a surrogate decision maker should be designated.

Individuals are interdependent members of the community. Taking into account both individual rights and the interdependence of persons in decision making, the nurse recognizes those situations in which individual rights to autonomy in health care may temporarily be overridden to preserve the life of the human community; for example, when a disaster demands triage or when an individual presents a direct danger to others. The many variables involved make it imperative that each case be considered with full awareness of the need to preserve the rights and responsibilities of clients and the demands of justice. The suspension of individual rights must always be considered a deviation to be tolerated as briefly as possible.

1.2 Status and Attributes of Clients

The need for health care is universal, transcending all national, ethnic, racial, religious, cultural, political, educational, economic, developmental, personality, role, and sexual differences. Nursing care is delivered without prejudicial behavior. Individual value systems and life-styles should be considered in the planning of health care with and for each client. Attributes of clients influence nursing practice to the extent that they represent factors the nurse must understand, consider, and respect in tailoring care to personal needs and in maintaining the individual's self-respect and dignity.

1.3 The Nature of Health Problems

The nurse's respect for the worth and dignity of the individual human being applies, irrespective of the nature of the health problem. It is reflected in care given the person who is disabled as well as one without disability, the person with long-term illness as well as one with acute illness, the recovering patient as well as one in the last phase of life. This respect extends to all who require the services of the nurse for the promotion of health, the prevention of illness, the restoration of health, the alleviation of suffering, and the provision of supportive care of the dying. The nurse does not act deliberately to terminate the life of any person.

The nurse's concern for human dignity and for the provision of high quality nursing care is not limited by personal attitudes or beliefs. If ethically opposed to interventions in a particular case because of the procedures to be used, the nurse is justified in refusing to participate. Such refusal should be made known in advance and in time for other appropriate arrangements to be made for the client's nursing care. If the nurse becomes involved in such a case and the client's life is in jeopardy, the nurse is obliged to provide for the client's safety, to avoid abandonment, and to withdraw only when assured that alternative sources of nursing care are available to the client.

The measures nurses take to care for the dying client and the client's family emphasize human contact. They enable the client to live with as much physical, emotional, and spiritual comfort as possible, and they maximize the values the client has treasured in life. Nursing care is directed toward the prevention and relief of the suffering commonly associated with the dying process. The nurse may provide interventions to relieve symptoms in the dying client even when the interventions entail substantial risks of hastening death.

1.4 The Setting for Health Care

The nurse adheres to the principle of non-discriminatory, nonprejudicial care in every situation and endeavors to promote its acceptance by others. The setting shall not determine the nurse's readiness to respect clients and to render or obtain needed services.

2. *The nurse safeguards the client's right to privacy by judiciously protecting information of a confidential nature.*

2.1 The Client's Right to Privacy

The right to privacy is an inalienable human right. The client trusts the nurse to hold all information in confidence. This trust could be destroyed and the client's welfare jeopardized by injudicious disclosure of information provided in confidence. The duty of confidentiality, however, is not absolute when innocent parties are in direct jeopardy.

2.2 Protection of Information

The rights, well-being, and safety of the individual client should be the determining factors in arriving at any professional judgment concerning the disposition of confidential information received from the client relevant to his or her treatment. The standards of nursing practice and the nursing responsibility to provide high quality health services require that relevant data be shared with members of the health team. Only information pertinent to a client's treatment and welfare is disclosed, and it is disclosed only to those directly concerned with the client's care.

Information documenting the appropriateness, necessity, and quality of care required for the purposes of peer review, third-party payment, and other quality assurance mechanisms must be disclosed only under defined policies, mandates, or protocols. These written guidelines must assure that the rights, well-being, and safety of the client are maintained.

2.3 Access to Records

If in the course of providing care there is a need for the nurse to have access to the records of persons not under the nurse's care, the persons affected should be notified and, whenever possible, permission should be obtained first. Although records belong to the agency where the data are collected, the individual maintains the right of control over the information in the record. Similarly, professionals may exercise the right of control over information they have generated in the course of health care.

If the nurse wishes to use a client's treatment record for research or nonclinical purposes in which anonymity cannot be guaranteed, the client's consent must be obtained first. Ethically, this ensures the client's right to privacy; legally, it protects the client against unlawful invasion of privacy.

3. The nurse acts to safeguard the client and the public when health care and safety are affected by incompetent, unethical, or illegal practice by any person.

3.1 Safeguarding the Health and Safety of the Client

The nurse's primary commitment is to the health, welfare, and safety of the client. As an advocate for the client, the nurse must be alert to and take appropriate action regarding any instances of incompetent, unethical, or illegal practice by any member of the health care team or the health care system, or any action on the part of others that places the rights or best interests of the client in jeopardy. To function effectively in this role, nurses must be aware of the employing institution's policies and procedures, nursing standards of practice, the *Code for Nurses,* and laws governing nursing and health care practice with regard to incompetent, unethical, or illegal practice.

3.2 Acting on Questionable Practice

When the nurse is aware of inappropriate or questionable practice in the provision of health care, concern should be expressed to the person carrying out the questionable practice and attention called to the possible detrimental effect upon the client's welfare. When factors in the health care delivery system threaten the welfare of the client, similar action should be directed to the responsible administrative person. If indicated, the practice should then be reported to the appropriate authority within the institution, agency, or larger system.

There should be an established process for the reporting and handling of incompetent, unethical, or illegal practice within the employment setting so that such reporting can go through official channels without causing fear of reprisal. The nurse should be knowledgeable about the process and be prepared to use it if necessary. When questions are raised about the practices of individual practitioners or of health care systems, written documentation of the observed practices or behaviors must be available to the appropriate authorities. State nurses associations should be prepared to provide assistance and support in the development and evaluation of such processes and in reporting procedures.

When incompetent, unethical, or illegal practice on the part of anyone concerned with the client's care is not corrected within the employment setting and continues to jeopardize the client's welfare and safety, the problem should be reported to other appropriate authorities such as practice committees of the pertinent professional organizations or the legally constituted bodies concerned with licensing of specific categories of health workers or professional practitioners. Some situations may warrant the concern and involvement of all such groups. Accurate reporting and documentation undergird all actions.

3.3 Review Mechanisms

The nurse should participate in the planning, establishment, implementation, and evaluation of review mechanisms that serve to safeguard clients, such as duly constituted peer review processes or committees and ethics committees. Such ongoing review mechanisms are based on established criteria, have stated purposes, include a process for making recommendations, and facilitate improved delivery of nursing and other health services to clients wherever nursing services are provided.

4. *The nurse assumes responsibility and accountability for individual nursing judgments and actions.*

4.1 Acceptance of Responsibility and Accountability

The recipients of professional nursing services are entitled to high quality nursing care. Individual professional licensure is the protective mechanism legislated by the public to ensure the basic and minimum competencies of the professional nurse. Beyond that, society has accorded to the nursing profession the right to regulate its own practice. The regulation and control of nursing practice by nurses demand that individual practitioners of professional nursing must bear primary responsibility for the nursing care clients receive and must be individually accountable for their own practice.

4.2 Responsibility for Nursing Judgment and Action

Responsibility refers to the carrying out of duties associated with a particular role assumed by the nurse. Nursing obligations are reflected in the ANA publications *Nursing: A Social Policy Statement* and *Standards of Clinical Nursing Practice*. In recognizing the rights of clients, the standards describe a collaborative relationship between the nurse and the client through use of the nursing process. Nursing responsibilities include data collection and assessment of the health status of the client; formation of nursing diagnoses derived from client assessment; development of a nursing care plan that is directed toward designated goals, assists the client in maximizing his or her health capabilities, and provides for the client's participation in promoting, maintaining, and restoring his or her health; evaluation of the effectiveness of nursing care in achieving goals as determined by the client and the nurse; and subsequent reassessment and revision of the nursing care plan as warranted. In the process of assuming these responsibilities, the nurse is held accountable for them.

4.3 Accountability for Nursing Judgment and Action

Accountability refers to being answerable to someone for something one has done. It means providing an explanation or rationale to oneself, to clients, to peers, to the nursing profession, and to society. In order to be accountable, nurses act under a code of ethical conduct that is grounded in the moral principles of fidelity and respect for the dignity, worth, and self-determination of clients.

The nursing profession continues to develop ways to clarify nursing's accountability to society. The contract between the profession and society is made explicit through such mechanisms as (a) the *Code for Nurses*, (b) the standards of nursing practice, (c) the development of nursing theory derived from nursing research in order to guide nursing actions, (d) educational requirements for practice, (e) certification, and (f) mechanisms for evaluating the effectiveness of the nurse's performance of nursing responsibilities.

Nurses are accountable for judgments made and actions taken in the course of nursing practice. Neither physicians' orders nor the employing agency's policies relieve the nurse of accountability for actions taken and judgments made.

5. *The nurse maintains competence in nursing.*

5.1 Personal Responsibility for Competence

The profession of nursing is obligated to provide adequate and competent nursing care. Therefore it is the personal responsibility of each nurse to maintain competency in practice. For the client's optimum well-being and for the nurse's own professional development, the care of the client reflects and incorporates new techniques and knowledge in health care as these develop, especially as they relate to the nurse's particular field of practice. The nurse must be aware of the need for continued professional learning and must assume personal responsibility for currency of knowledge and skills.

5.2 Measurement of Competence in Nursing Practice

Evaluation of one's performance by peers is a hallmark of professionalism and a method by which the profession is held accountable to society. Nurses must be willing to have their practice reviewed and evaluated by their peers. Guidelines for evaluating the scope of practice and the appropriateness, effectiveness, and efficiency of nursing practice are found in nursing practice acts, ANA standards of practice, and other quality assurance mechanisms. Each nurse is responsible for participating in the development of objective criteria for evaluation. In addition, the nurse engages in ongoing self-evaluation of clinical competency, decision-making abilities, and professional judgments.

5.3 Intraprofessional Responsibility for Competence in Nursing Care

Nurses share responsibility for high quality nursing care. Nurses are required to have knowledge relevant to the current scope of nursing practice, changing issues and concerns, and ethical concepts and principles. Since individual competencies vary, nurses refer clients to and consult with other nurses with expertise and recognized competencies in various fields of practice.

6. *The nurse exercises informed judgment and uses individual competency and qualifications as criteria in seeking consultation, accepting responsibilities, and delegating nursing activities.*

6.1 Changing Functions

Nurses are faced with decisions in the context of the increased complexity of health care, changing patterns in the delivery of health services, and the development of evolving nursing practice in response to the health needs of clients. As the scope of nursing practice changes, the nurse must exercise judgment in accepting responsibilities, seeking consultation, and assigning responsibilities to others who carry out nursing care.

6.2 Accepting Responsibilities

The nurse must not engage in practices prohibited by law or delegate to others activities prohibited by practice acts of other health care personnel or by other laws. Nurses determine the scope of their practice in light of their education, knowledge, competency, and extent of experience. If the nurse concludes that he or she lacks competence or is inadequately prepared to carry out a specific function, the nurse has the responsibility to refuse that work and to seek alternative sources of care based on concern for the client's welfare. In that refusal, both the client and the nurse are protected. Inasmuch as the nurse is responsible for the continuous care of patients in health care settings, the nurse is frequently called upon to carry out components of care delegated by other health professionals as part of the client's treatment regimen. The nurse should not accept these interdependent functions if they are so extensive as to prevent the nurse from fulfilling the responsibility to provide appropriate nursing care to clients.

6.3 Consultation and Collaboration

The provision of health and illness care to clients is a complex process that requires a wide range of knowledge, skills, and collaborative efforts. Nurses must be aware of their own individual competencies. When the needs of the client are beyond the qualifications and competencies of the nurse, consultation and collaboration must be sought from qualified nurses, other health professionals, or other appropriate sources. Participation on intradisciplinary or interdisciplinary teams is often an effective approach to the provision of high quality total health services.

6.4 Delegation of Nursing Activities

Inasmuch as the nurse is accountable for the quality of nursing care rendered to clients, nurses are accountable for the delegation of nursing care activities to other health workers. Therefore, the nurse must assess individual competency in assigning selected components of nursing care to other nursing service personnel. The nurse should not delegate to any member of the nursing team a function for which that person is not prepared or qualified. Employer policies or directives do not relieve the nurse of accountability for making judgments about the delegation of nursing care activities.

7. *The nurse participates in activities that contribute to the ongoing development of the profession's body of knowledge.*

7.1 The Nurse and Development of Knowledge

Every profession must engage in scholarly inquiry to identify, verify, and continually enlarge the body of knowledge that forms the foundation for its practice. A unique body of verified knowledge provides both framework and direction for the profession in all of its activities and for the practitioner in the provision of nursing care. The accrual of scientific and humanistic knowledge promotes the advancement of practice and the well-being of the profession's clients. Ongoing scholarly activity such as research and the development of theory is indispensable to the full discharge of a profession's obligations to society. Each nurse has a role in this area of professional activity, whether as an investigator in furthering knowledge, as a participant in research, or as a user of theoretical and empirical knowledge.

7.2 Protection of Rights of Human Participants in Research

Individual rights valued by society and by the nursing profession that have particular application in research include the right of adequately informed consent, the right to freedom from risk of injury, and the right of privacy and preservation of dignity. Inherent in these rights is respect for each individual's rights to exercise self-determination, to choose to participate or not, to have full information, and to terminate participation in research without penalty.

It is the duty of the nurse functioning in any research role to maintain vigilance in protecting the life, health, and privacy of human subjects from both anticipated and unanticipated risks and in assuring informed consent. Subjects' integrity, privacy, and rights must be especially safeguarded if the subjects are unable to protect themselves because of incapacity or because they are in a dependent relationship to the investigator. The investigation should be discontinued if its continuance might be harmful to the subject.

7.3 General Guidelines for Participating in Research

Before participating in research conducted by others, the nurse has an obligation to (a) obtain information about the intent and the nature of the research and (b) ascertain that the study proposal is approved by the appropriate bodies, such as institutional review boards.

Research should be conducted and directed by qualified persons. The nurse who participates in research in any capacity should be fully informed about both the nurse's and the client's rights and obligations.

8. *The nurse participates in the profession's efforts to implement and improve standards of nursing.*

8.1 Responsibility to the Public for Standards

Nursing is responsible and accountable for admitting to the profession only those individuals who have demonstrated the knowledge, skills, and commitment considered essential to professional practice. Nurse educators have a major responsibility for ensuring that these competencies and a demonstrated commitment to professional practice have been achieved before the entry of an individual into the practice of professional nursing.

Established standards and guidelines for nursing practice provide guidance for the delivery of professional nursing care and are a means for evaluating care received by the public. The nurse has a personal responsibility and commitment to clients for implementation and maintenance of optimal standards of nursing practice.

8.3 Responsibility to the Profession for Standards

Established standards reflect the practice of nursing grounded in ethical commitments and a body of knowledge. Professional standards or guidelines exist in nursing practice, nursing service, nursing education, and nursing research. The nurse has the responsibility to monitor these standards in daily practice and to participate actively in the profession's ongoing efforts to foster optimal standards of practice at the local, regional, state, and national levels of the health care system.

Nurse educators have the additional responsibility to maintain optimal standards of nursing practice and education in nursing education programs and in any other settings where planned learning activities for nursing students take place.

9. *The nurse participates in the profession's efforts to establish and maintain conditions of employment conducive to high quality nursing care.*

9.1 Responsibility for Conditions of Employment

The nurse must be concerned with conditions of employment that (a) enable the nurse to practice in accordance with the standards of nursing practice and (b) provide a care environment that meets the standards of nursing service. The provision of high quality nursing care is the responsibility of both the individual nurse and the nursing profession. Professional autonomy and self-regulation in the control of conditions of practice are necessary for implementing nursing standards.

9.2 Maintaining Conditions for High Quality Nursing Care

Articulation and control of nursing practice can be accomplished through individual agreement and collective action. A nurse may enter into an agreement with individuals or organizations to provide health care. Nurses may participate in collective action such as collective bargaining through their state nurses' association to determine the terms and conditions of employment conducive to high quality nursing care. Such agreements should be consistent with the profession's standards of practice, the state law regulating nursing practice, and the *Code for Nurses.*

10. *The nurse participates in the profession's effort to protect the public from misinformation and misrepresentation and to maintain the integrity of nursing.*

10.1 Protection from Misinformation and Misrepresentation

Nurses are responsible for advising clients against the use of products that endanger the clients' safety and welfare. The nurse shall not use any form of public or professional communication to make claims that are false, fraudulent, misleading, deceptive, or unfair.

The nurse does not give or imply endorsement to advertising, promotion, or sale of commercial products or services in a manner that may be interpreted as reflecting the opinion or judgment of the profession as a whole. The nurse may use knowledge of specific services or products in advising an individual client, since this may contribute to the client's health and well-being. In the course of providing information or education to clients or other practitioners about commercial products or services, however, a variety of similar products or services should be offered or described so the client or practitioner can make an informed choice.

10.2 Maintaining the Integrity of Nursing

The use of the title *registered nurse* is granted by state governments for the protection of the public. Use of that title carries with it the responsibility to act in the public interest. The nurse may use the title *R.N.* and symbols of academic degrees or other earned or honorary professional symbols of recognition in all ways that are legal and appropriate. The title and other symbols of the profession should not be used, however, for benefits unrelated to nursing practice or the profession, or used by those who may seek to exploit them for other purposes.

Nurses should refrain from casting a vote in any deliberations involving health care services or facilities where the nurse has business or other interests that could be construed as a conflict of interest.

11. *The nurse collaborates with members of the health professions and other citizens in promoting community and national efforts to meet the health needs of the public.*

11.1 Collaboration with Others to Meet Health Needs

The availability and accessibility of high quality health services to all people require collaborative planning at the local, state, national, and international levels that respects the interdependence of health professionals and clients in health care systems. Nursing care is an integral part of high quality health care, and nurses have an obligation to promote equitable access to nursing and health care for all people.

11.2 Responsibility to the Public

The nursing profession is committed to promoting the welfare and safety of all people. The goals and values of nursing are essential to effective delivery of health services. For the benefit of the individual client and the public at large, nursing's goals and commitments need adequate representation. Nurses should ensure this representation by active participation in decision making in institutional and political arenas to assure a just distribution of health care and nursing resources.

11.3 Relationships with Other Disciplines

The complexity of health care delivery systems requires a multidisciplinary approach to delivery of services that has the strong support and active participation of all the health professions. Nurses should actively promote the collaborative planning required to ensure the availability and accessibility of high quality health services to all persons whose health needs are unmet.

7. PHARMACY

Organization

AMERICAN PHARMACEUTICAL ASSOCIATION

Headquarters:
2215 Constitution Avenue, NW
Washington, DC 20037-2985
Telephone: (202) 628-4410
(800) 237-APHA
Fax: (202) 783-2351
E-mail: membership@mail.aphanet.org
Website: http://www.aphanet.org

Date founded: 1852
Membership: approximately 50,000 pharmacists and scientists practicing in the community, hospitals, research, and industry, and students of pharmacy

Code of Ethics

Official name: *Code of Ethics for Pharmacists*
History: First issued 1969, revised periodically; current version adopted October 1994
Authority: Code of Ethics Review Committee; Board of Trustees; Judicial Board
Code is available on Website

Additional Resources

Organizational (Divisions, Programs, Services, etc.):

Academy of Pharmaceutical Research and Science
Academy of Pharmacy Practice and Management
Board of Pharmaceutical Specialties (certification)
Continuing Education Program
National Pharmacy Week (public awareness campaign)
Pharmacy Recovery Program (for impaired professionals)
Pharmacy Service Quality Research Initiative

Policy and Advocacy Department
Policy Committees: Educational Affairs; Professional Affairs; Public
    Affairs; and Scientific Affairs
Professional Liability Plan
Quality Center
Strategic and Tactical Analysis Team on Practice Environment/Quality of
    Worklife Issues

Informational (Publications, Videos, Seminars, etc.):

Articles in *Journal of the American Pharmaceutical Association* and
    Pharmacy Today
Continuing Education Special Reports
Essential Elements: The Dynamics of Pharmaceutical Care
Guidelines for Medication Incentive Programs
Guidelines for Pharmacy-Based Immunization Advocacy
Innovation and Regulation: Challenges of a Changing Environment
Pharmacist Conscience Clause
*The Pharmacy Technician Companion: Your Road Map to Technician
    Training and Careers*
Policy Committee Reports
Policy Manual
Principles of Practice
Statement of Values and Guiding Principles

Goals and Activities of Organization

The American Pharmaceutical Association (APhA) represents the third largest health profession in the U.S. It was founded to advance pharmacy as a profession and a science, and to safeguard the well-being of individual patients.

The APhA keeps members informed of the latest developments in pharmacy practice; promotes high professional and ethical standards; provides the profession with a forum for the discussion and development of progressive policies and positions; represents members' interests before federal and state legislatures, regulatory agencies, and allied health care organizations; communicates with the public, the media, and other professional groups about the pharmacist's vital role in the community; fosters science and research in support of the practice of pharmacy; and offers career, financial, insurance, and continuing education services.

One of the organization's major strategic goals is the creation and implementation of pharmacy guidelines, quality standards, and programs for self-evaluation, improvement, and recognition. The APhA Quality Center was established in 1997 as a research and information clearinghouse on quality assessment in pharmacy practice.

The Policy and Advocacy Department examines current ethical and professional issues, which include: the impact of managed care; expansion of state practice acts to allow pharmacists to collaborate with physicians;

workplace issues; antitrust exemptions for pharmacy providers; confidentiality of patient data in electronic communication systems; and the right to exercise conscientious refusal.

Implementation and Enforcement of Code

The Code of Ethics for Pharmacists is a public statement of the principles underlying pharmacists' professional roles and responsibilities, and a guide for pharmacists in their relationships with patients and colleagues.

Proposed amendments to the Code are approved by the Board of Trustees and submitted to the voting membership for approval.

Complaints against members for unprofessional conduct are handled by a Judicial Board, appointed by the APhA President on an ad hoc basis.

Unprofessional conduct is defined in the Bylaws as a violation of "the principles embodied in the Code." It also covers conduct that a federal or state judicial or disciplinary body has found to be a violation of a law or regulation.

The Board of Trustees establishes rules for disciplinary proceedings. A complaint must be filed within three years of the alleged misconduct. The accused has the right to notice and a hearing before the Judicial Board, which may impose such sanctions as reprimand, suspension, or expulsion from APhA. The decision may be appealed to the Board of Trustees, which may affirm, reverse, or modify it.

The Judicial Board also renders advisory opinions interpreting the Code upon request or on its own motion.

History and Development of Code

Previous Codes have been issued or revised in 1969, 1975, and 1981.

The present document was developed in 1993 by the Code of Ethics Review Committee, and was approved by the membership in 1994.

Code of Ethics for Pharmacists*

PREAMBLE

Pharmacists are health professionals who assist individuals in making the best use of medications. This Code, prepared and supported by pharmacists, is intended to state publicly the principles that form the fundamental basis of the roles and responsibilities of pharmacists. These principles, based on moral obligations and virtues, are established to guide pharmacists in relationships with patients, health professionals, and society.

I. **A pharmacist respects the covenantal relationship between the patient and pharmacist.**
Considering the patient-pharmacist relationship as a covenant means that a pharmacist has moral obligations in response to the gift of trust received from society. In return for this gift, a pharmacist promises to help individuals achieve optimum benefit from their medications, to be committed to their welfare, and to maintain their trust.

II. **A pharmacist promotes the good of every patient in a caring, compassionate, and confidential manner.**
A pharmacist places concern for the well-being of the patient at the center of professional practice. In doing so, a pharmacist considers needs stated by the patient as well as those defined by health science. A pharmacist is dedicated to protecting the dignity of the patient. With a caring attitude and a compassionate spirit, a pharmacist focuses on serving the patient in a private and confidential manner.

III. **A pharmacist respects the autonomy and dignity of each patient.**
A pharmacist promotes the right of self-determination and recognizes individual self-worth by encouraging patients to participate in decisions about their health. A pharmacist communicates with patients in terms that are understandable. In all cases, a pharmacist respects personal and cultural differences among patients.

IV. **A pharmacist acts with honesty and integrity in professional relationships.**
A pharmacist has a duty to tell the truth and to act with conviction of conscience. A pharmacist avoids discriminatory practices, behavior or work conditions that impair professional judgment, and actions that compromise dedication to the best interests of patients.

V. **A pharmacist maintains professional competence.**
A pharmacist has a duty to maintain knowledge and abilities as new medications, devices, and technologies become available and as health information advances.

VI. **A pharmacist respects the values and abilities of colleagues and other health professionals.**
When appropriate, a pharmacist asks for the consultation of colleagues or

---

*Adopted by the membership of the American Pharmaceutical Association October 27, 1994. Reprinted with permission. Copyright ©1998 American Pharmaceutical Association. All rights reserved.

other health professionals or refers the patient. A pharmacist acknowledges that colleagues and other health professionals may differ in the beliefs and values they apply to the care of the patient.

VII. A pharmacist serves individual, community, and societal needs.

The primary obligation of a pharmacist is to individual patients. However, the obligations of a pharmacist may at times extend beyond the individual to the community and society. In these situations, the pharmacist recognizes the responsibilities that accompany these obligations and acts accordingly.

VIII. A pharmacist seeks justice in the distribution of health resources.

When health resources are allocated, a pharmacist is fair and equitable, balancing the needs of patients and society.

8. SOCIAL WORK

Organization

CLINICAL SOCIAL WORK FEDERATION

Headquarters:
P.O. Box 3740
Arlington, VA 22203
Street Address:
239 North Highland Street
Arlington, VA 22201
Telephone: (703) 522-3866
(800) 270-9739
Fax: (703) 522-9441
E-mail: nfscswlo@aol.com
Website: http://www.cswf.org

Date founded: 1971
    Formerly the National Federation of Societies for Clinical Social Work
Membership: approximately 11,000 clinical social workers in 34 state
    societies

Code of Ethics

Official name: *Code of Ethics*
History: First published 1976, revised periodically; current edition
    revised 1997
Authority: Professional Standards Committee; CSWF Board
Code is available on Website

Additional Resources

Organizational (Divisions, Programs, Services, etc.):

Clinical Conference
Clinical Social Work & the Law/Forensic Practice Committee
Family Therapy Practice Academy (FTPA)
Government Relations Committee
Healthcare Systems Committee

Office and Professional Employees International Union, AFL-CIO
(affiliation)
Professional Liability Protection Insurance Plan

Informational (Publications, Videos, Seminars, etc.):

Articles in *Clinical Social Work Journal, CSWF Progress Notes, Managed
Care News,* and *FTPA News Notes*
Adjudication Guidelines
Government Relations Committee Reports, Position Papers, and Surveys
National Advocates' Reports
Position Paper on Managed Care
*Principles for the Provision of Mental Health and Substance Abuse Treat-
ment Services: A Bill of Rights*
Standards of Practice for Clinical Social Work
Statement of Principles of the Family Therapy Practice Academy (draft)

Goals and Activities of Organization

The Clinical Social Work Federation (CSWF) represents the interests
of social workers engaged in direct clinical practice, the only national
organization with this specific focus. It assists its member societies by
providing state- and national-level advocacy on behalf of clinical social
work; developing and promulgating standards for education, practice, ethics, and achievement; working towards the universal legal regulation of
clinical social workers; and advocating more adequate and appropriate
public and private support for mental health services and coverage.

The state societies are voluntary associations formed for the purpose
of promoting the highest standards of professional education and clinical
practice. The Board of the CSWF supports the state societies in education,
marketing, reimbursement, research, image building, promoting standards
and competence, legislation and regulation, and related areas at the state
and national level.

The Committee on Professional Standards creates and maintains model
standards and offers consultation to member societies on ethical issues.

Implementation and Enforcement of Code

Clinical social workers are expected to take into consideration all the
principles of the Code that have a bearing upon any situation that requires
the exercise of ethical judgment. They are to act consistently with the
spirit as well as the letter of the Code.

State societies adopt the Code, adherence to which is required of all
members. Disciplinary actions are handled at the state level by state ethics
committees. Members agree to abide by the recommendations of state
society disciplinary panels.

State licensure laws also regulate an individual's ethical conduct.

The national Committee on Professional Standards monitors both the
standards for professional practice and the Code of Ethics. It has developed

and distributed Adjudication Guidelines for use by state societies, which may modify them to conform with local needs. These Guidelines are designed to assure fairness to both complainant and respondent, spelling out procedures and conditions for complaints, hearings, sanctions, appeals, and recordkeeping.

History and Development of Code

The CSWF's first model set of standards was published in 1976. By 1984, a revision was approved, and further refinements were made in 1985 and 1988.

Many years of work by the Professional Standards Committee resulted in a major revision of the Code, issued in late 1997, reprinted here.

Sources include the ethics standards of several state clinical social work societies, the National Association of Social Workers, American Psychological Association, American Bar Association, and American Psychiatric Association.

Code of Ethics*

PREAMBLE

The principal objective of the profession of clinical social work is the enhancement of the mental health and the well-being of the individuals and families who seek services from its practitioners. The professional practice of clinical social workers is shaped by ethical principles which are rooted in the basic values of the social work profession. These core values include a commitment to the dignity, well-being, and self-determination of the individual; a commitment to professional practice characterized by competence and integrity, and a commitment to a society which offers opportunities to all its members in a just and non-discriminatory manner.

Clinical social workers examine practice situations in terms of the ethical dilemmas that they present, with a critical analysis of how the formulation of a solution fulfills the core requirements of ethical practice; non-malfeasance, (doing no harm to clients); beneficence, (helping clients), and autonomy (enhancing the self-determination of clients).

The following represents a specific codification of those ethical principles. It is intended to serve as a standard for clinical social workers in all of their professional functions, and to inspire their will to act in a manner consistent with those tenets. The clinical social worker is expected to take into consideration all principles in this code that have a bearing upon any situation in which ethical judgment is to be exercised, and to select a course of action consistent with the spirit, as well as the letter of the code.

Individual members of the Clinical Social Work Federation and of the various State Societies for Clinical Social Work agree to adhere to the precepts expressed in this Code, and to practice in a manner which is consistent with them. When the practice of a member is alleged to deviate from the Code of Ethics, the Code is to be used as a standard for the evaluation of the nature and seriousness of the deviation.

Principle I
GENERAL RESPONSIBILITIES OF
CLINICAL SOCIAL WORKERS

Clinical social workers maintain high standards in all of their professional roles, and value professional competence, objectivity, and integrity. They accept responsibility for the consequences of their work, and ensure that their services are used in an appropriate manner.

a) Clinical social workers bear a heavy professional responsibility because their actions and recommendations may significantly affect the lives of others. They practice only within their sphere of competence, and maintain and enhance that competence through participation in continuing professional development throughout their careers. They refrain from undertaking or continuing any professional activity in which their personal difficulties, or any other limitations, might lead to the inadequate provision of service.

---

*Revised 1997. Copyright © Clinical Social Work Federation. Reprinted with permission.

b) Clinical social workers do not exploit professional relationships sexually, financially, or for any other professional and/or personal advantage. They maintain this standard of conduct toward all those who may be professionally associated with them.

c) Clinical social workers often function as employees in clinics, hospitals, and agencies, or, as providers on managed care panels. In these positions, they are responsible for identifying and actively working to modify policies or procedures which may come into conflict with the standards of their profession. If such a conflict arises, the primary responsibility of the clinical social worker is to uphold the ethical standards of the profession. These standards require that commitment to the welfare of the client(s) is the primary obligation.

d) Clinical social workers have an additional responsibility, both to the profession which provides the basis of their practice, and to those who are entering that profession. As teachers, supervisors, and mentors, they are responsible for maintaining high standards of objectivity and scholarship. In all of their professional activities they consistently examine, and attempt to expand, the knowledge base on which practice in the profession is centered.

Principle II
RESPONSIBILITY TO CLIENTS

The primary responsibility of the clinical social worker is to the individual client, the family or the group with whom he or she has a professional relationship. Clinical social workers respect the dignity, protect the welfare, and maximize the self-determination of the clients with whom they work.

1. INFORMED CONSENT TO TREATMENT

a) Clinical social work treatment takes place within a context of informed consent. This requires that the client(s) be informed of the extent and nature of the services being offered as well as the mutual limits, rights, opportunities, and obligations associated with the provision of and payment for those services. In order for the consent to be valid, the client(s) must be informed in a manner which is clear to them, must choose freely and without undue influence, and must have the capacity to make an informed choice. In instances where clients are not of legal age or competent to give a meaningful consent, they will be informed in a manner which is consistent with their level of understanding. In such situations, authorization for treatment will be obtained from an appropriate third party, such as a parent or other legal guardian.

b) Clinical social workers have a duty to understand the potential impact on all aspects of treatment resulting from participation in various third party payment mechanisms, and to disclose fully their knowledge of these features to the client. Such features might include, but are not limited to; limitations of confidentiality; payment limitations related to provider choice; a summary of the treatment review process required by the plan; the comparative treatment orientations of the plan and of the clinical social worker; the possibility that benefits may be limited under the plan; the clinical social worker's relationship to the plan and any incentives to limit or deny care; and, the availability of alternative treatment options.

2. PRACTICE MANAGEMENT AND TERMINATION

a) Clinical social workers enter into and/or continue professional relationships based on their ability to meet the needs of clients appropriately. The clinical social worker terminates services and relationships with clients when such services and relationships are no longer in the client's best interest. Clinical social workers do not abandon clients by withdrawing services precipitously, except under extraordinary circumstances.

   Clinical social workers give careful consideration to all factors involved in termination and take care to minimize the possible adverse effects it might have on the client(s). When interruption or termination of service is anticipated, the clinical social worker gives reasonable notification and provides for transfer, referral, or continuation of service in a manner as consistent as possible with the client's needs and preferences.

b) Clinical social workers providing services which are reimbursed by third party payers continue to have primary responsibility for the welfare of the client(s). The failure of the third party to authorize continued benefits does not remove the obligation of the clinical social worker to assure necessary treatment, if this is in the client's best interests. When benefits are ended, the clinical social worker has a number of options including: acceptance of private payment for continued services, at either regular or reduced rates; provision of services on an unpaid basis; and, referral to appropriate alternative treatment sources.

c) A clinical social worker who disagrees with the denial of continued benefits by a third party payer is responsible for discussing this action with the client(s), and for devising a clinically appropriate plan, which may or may not include appeal of the decision. Further pursuit of the appeals process will be based on such factors as; the degree to which the clinical social worker believes that further treatment is necessary for the client's well-being; the degree to which the client(s) wishes to pursue the appeals process, and; the degree to which there are alternative means available for the client(s) to continue treatment.

d) Clinical social workers keep records for each individual and family they treat which reflect relevant administrative rules, contractual obligations, and local and federal statutes. They are required to be knowledgeable about statutes relating to client access to records, and to fulfill their responsibility as required by law. When access to records is permitted, the clinical social worker will take appropriate, legally permitted steps to protect the privacy of all third parties who may be named in the records.

e) All requirements regarding the establishment, maintenance, and disposal of records relate equally to written and to electronic records.

   Clinical social workers establish a policy on record retention and disposal, or are aware of agency policies regarding these issues, and communicate it to the client. In the event of the death or incapacity of a client, they safeguard the record, within existing statues, and the information contained therein. Clinical social workers have a plan or procedure for the proper handling of client records in the event of their own death or disability which both protects privacy, and ensures that legitimate access functions can be properly carried out.

3. RELATIONSHIPS WITH CLIENTS

a) Clinical social workers are responsible for setting clear and appropriate professional boundaries, especially in those instances in which dual or multiple relationships are unavoidable. They do not engage in dual or multiple relationships in which there is any risk of their professional judgment being compromised, or of the client being harmed or exploited. When clinical social workers provide services to two or more persons who have a relationship with each other, they clarify with all parties the nature of the professional responsibilities to each of them, and the ways in which appropriate boundaries will be maintained.

b) Clinical social workers do not, under any circumstances, engage in romantic or sexual contact with either current or former clients. Clinical social workers are also mindful of how their relationship with the family and/or friends of their clients might affect their work with the client. Consequently, they also avoid romantic or sexual involvements with members of the client's family, or with others with whom the client has a close, personal relationship.

c) Clinical social workers are aware of the authority which is inherent in their professional role. They do not engage in any activity that will abuse their professional relationships or exploit others for personal, political, or business interests. As practitioners, supervisors, teachers, administrators, and researchers their primary professional responsibility is always the welfare of the client(s) with whom they work.

d) When the clinical social worker must act on behalf of a client, that action should always safeguard the interests and concerns of that client. When another person has been authorized to act on behalf of a client, the clinical social worker should deal with that person in a manner which will safeguard the interests and concerns of the client.

e) Clinical social workers recognize and support the right to self-determination of clients who may choose not to relinquish their privacy by pursuing third party reimbursement for treatment, even when they are eligible for such reimbursement. In such instances, the clinical social worker makes every effort to assist the client in making alternative financial arrangements so that treatment can proceed.

f) When a clinical social worker determines that a conflict potentially detrimental to the treatment process has arisen, he or she should inform the individual(s) to whom he or she has a professional responsibility of the nature of the conflict and the way in which it might affect the provision of service.

4. COMPETENCE

a) Clinical social workers are aware of the scope in which they are entitled to practice. This scope is defined by their areas of personal competence; by their license or other legal recognition; and by their training and/or experience. They are responsible for confining their practice to those areas in which they are legally authorized and in which they are qualified to practice. When necessary, they utilize the knowledge and experience of members of other professions. In using such consultants or supervisors, the clinical social worker is responsible for ensuring that they are recognized members of their own profession, and are qualified and competent to carry out the service required.

b) Clinical social workers recognize that the privacy and intimacy of the therapeutic relationship may unrealistically intensify the client's feelings for them. The maintenance of professional boundaries and objectivity is crucial to effective and responsible treatment. Clinical social workers maintain self awareness and take care to prevent the possible harmful intrusion of their own unresolved personal issues into the therapeutic relationship. They take appropriate steps to resolve the situation when there is a danger of this occurring. Such steps could include, but are not limited to: seeking additional supervision or consultation; seeking additional personal treatment; and, if necessary, making alternative arrangements for the treatment of the client(s).

c) Clinical social workers recognize the responsibility to remain abreast of knowledge and developments in the field which may benefit their client(s). Ongoing involvement in supervision, consultation, and continuing education are some of the ways in which this responsibility can be fulfilled. It is particularly important for the clinical social worker to secure appropriate training, supervision, or consultation when attempting to use a treatment technique with which he or she is unfamiliar.

Principle III
CONFIDENTIALITY

Clinical social workers have a primary obligation to maintain the privacy of both current and former clients, whether living or deceased, and to maintain the confidentiality of material that has been transmitted to them in any of their professional roles. Exceptions to this responsibility will occur only when there are overriding legal or professional reasons and, whenever possible, with the written informed consent of the client(s).

a) Clinical social workers discuss fully with clients both the nature of confidentiality, and potential limits to confidentiality which may arise during the course of their work. Confidential information should only be released, whenever possible, with the written permission of the client(s). As part of the process of obtaining such a release, the clinical social worker should inform the client(s) about the nature of the information being sought, the purpose(s) for which it is being sought, to whom the information will be released, how the client(s) may withdraw permission for its release, and, the length of time that the release will be in effect.

b) Clinical social workers know and observe both legal and professional standards for maintaining the privacy of records, and mandatory reporting obligations. Mandatory reporting obligations may include, but are not limited to: the reporting of the abuse or neglect of children or of vulnerable adults; the duty to take steps to protect or warn a third party who may be endangered by the client(s); and, any duty to report the misconduct or impairment of another professional. Additional limits to confidentiality may occur because of parental access to the records of a minor, the access of legal guardians to the records of some adults, access by the courts to mandated reports, and access by third party payers to information for the purpose of treatment authorization or audit. When confidential information is released to a third party, the clinical social worker will ensure that the information divulged is limited to the minimum amount required to accomplish the purpose for which the release is being made.

c) Clinical social workers treating couples, families, and groups seek agreement among the parties involved regarding each individual's right to confidentiality, and the mutual obligation to protect the confidentiality of information shared by other parties to the treatment. Clients involved in this type of treatment should, however, be informed that the clinical social worker cannot guarantee that all participants will honor their agreement to maintain confidentiality.

d) When confidential information is used for purposes of professional education, research, or publication, the primary responsibility of the clinical social worker is the protection of the client(s) from possible harm, embarrassment, or exploitation. When extensive material is used for any of these purposes the clinical social worker makes every effort to obtain the informed consent of the client(s) for such use, and will not proceed if the client(s) denies this consent. Whether or not a consent is obtained, every effort will be made to protect the true identity of the client. Any such presentation will be limited to the amount necessary for the professional purpose, and will be shared only with other responsible individuals.

e) The development of new technologies for the storage and transmission of data poses a great danger to the privacy of individuals. Clinical social workers take special precautions to protect the confidentiality of material stored or transmitted through computers, electronic mail, facsimile machines, telephones, telephone answering machines, and all other electronic or computer technology. When using these technologies, disclosure of identifying information regarding the client(s) should be avoided whenever possible.

Principle IV
RELATIONSHIPS WITH COLLEAGUES

Clinical social workers act with integrity in their relationships with colleagues and members of other professions. They know and take into account the traditions, practices, and areas of competence of other professionals and cooperate with them fully for the welfare of clients.

a) Clinical social workers represent accurately the views, qualifications, and findings of colleagues. When expressing judgment on these matters they do so in a manner that is sensitive to the best interests of both colleagues and clients.

b) If a clinical social worker's services are sought by an individual who is already receiving similar services from another professional, consideration for the client's welfare is the primary concern. This concern requires that the clinical social worker proceed with great caution, carefully considering the existing professional relationship, the therapeutic issues involved, and whether it is therapeutically and ethically appropriate to be involved in the situation.

c) As supervisors, consultants, or employers, clinical social workers are responsible for providing competent professional guidance and a role model to colleagues, employees, and students. They foster working conditions that assure consistency, respect, privacy, and protection from physical or mental harm. Clinical social workers do not abuse the authority of their position by harassing or pressuring colleagues, employees, or students for sexual reasons, financial gain, or any other purpose. They refrain from actions that are unwanted by the recipient, and can reasonably be interpreted as pressuring or intimidating the recipient.

d) Clinical social workers carry out their responsibility to both clients and the profession by maintaining high standards of practice within the professional community. They take appropriate measures to discourage, prevent, expose, and correct unethical or incompetent behavior by colleagues, and also assist and defend colleagues believed to be unjustly charged with such conduct. They discourage the practice of clinical social work by those who fail to meet accepted standards of training and experience, or who are practicing outside of their area of competence.

e) Clinical social workers who have knowledge of a colleague's impairment, misconduct, or incompetence attempt to bring about remediation through whatever means is appropriate. Such actions may include, but are not limited to: direct discussion with the colleague, with permission from the client(s) if this is needed; a report, if mandatory, to a regulatory body, professional organization, or employer; a report to a supervisor, or other agency administrator.

Principle V
FEE ARRANGEMENTS

When setting fees, clinical social workers should give consideration to the client's ability to pay and make every effort to establish fees that are fair, reasonable, and commensurate with the value of the service performed.

a) In the initial contact with the client(s) fees for services and policies regarding fee collection should be clarified. This clarification should also take into account any financial constraint which may affect the treatment process.

b) It is unethical for a clinical social worker to offer, give, solicit, or receive any fee or other consideration to or from a third party for the referral of a client. They accept reimbursement from clients and from third party payers only for services directly rendered to the client(s). Clinical social workers may, however, participate in contractual arrangements in which they agree to discount their fees.

c) A clinical social worker who contracts with a third party payer agrees to abide by the conditions of the contract. If, however, the clinical social worker believes the contract contains elements which violate the ethics of the profession, the clinical social worker seeks to redress this situation through appropriate courses of action which may include: obtaining the other party's agreement to delete the clause; or, refusing to sign the contract.

d) Barter arrangements, in which goods or services are accepted from clients as payment for professional services, should be avoided as much as possible.

Such plans, especially when they involve provision of services by the client(s), have the potential to constitute dual relationships which will damage the treatment. Barter arrangements may be entered into only in rare situations, and may only involve provision of goods, as opposed to services, in exchange for treatment. Such arrangements can only be entered into upon the specific request of the client, and when the following additional criteria are met: traditional payment methods are not possible; the client(s) is not coerced or exploited in any way, and; the arrangement is not detrimental to the client(s) or to the professional relationship.

e) Clinical social workers employed by an agency or clinic, and also engaged in private practice, conform to contractual agreements with the employing facility. They do not solicit or accept a private fee or consideration of any kind for providing a service to which the client is entitled through the employing facility.

Principle VI
CLINICAL SOCIAL WORKERS' RESPONSIBILITIES TO THE COMMUNITY

Clinical social workers are aware of the social codes and ethical expectations in their communities, and recognize that violation of accepted societal, ethical, legal, and moral standards on their part may compromise the fulfillment of their professional responsibilities and/or reduce public trust in the profession.

a) Clinical social workers do not, in any of their capacities, practice, condone, facilitate, or collaborate with any form of discrimination on the basis of race, religion, color, national origin, gender, sexual orientation, age, socioeconomic status, or physical or emotional disability.

b) Clinical social workers practice their profession in compliance with legal standards, and do not participate in arrangements or activities which undermine or violate the law. When they believe, however, that laws or community standards are in conflict with the principles and ethics of the profession, they make known the conflict and work responsibly toward change that is in the public interest.

c) Clinical social workers recognize a responsibility to participate in activities leading toward improved social conditions. They should advocate and work for conditions and resources that give all persons equal access to the services and opportunities required to meet basic needs and to develop to the fullest potential.

Principle VII
RESEARCH AND SCHOLARLY ACTIVITIES

In planning, conducting, and reporting a study, the investigator has the responsibility to make a careful evaluation of its ethical acceptability, taking into account the following additional principles for research with human subjects. To the extent that this appraisal, weighing scientific and humane values, suggests a compromise of any principle, the investigator incurs an increasingly serious obligation to observe stringent safeguards to protect the rights and well-being of research participants.

a) In conducting research in institutions or organizations, clinical social workers obtain appropriate authority to carry out their work. Host organizations are given proper credit for their contributions to the project.

b) Ethically acceptable research begins with the establishment of a clear and fair agreement between the investigator and the research participant that clarifies the responsibilities of each. The investigator has the obligation to honor all commitments included in that agreement.

c) Responsibility for the establishment and maintenance of acceptable ethical practice in research always remains with the investigator. The investigator is also responsible for the ethical treatment of research participants by collaborators, assistants, students, and employees, all of whom incur parallel obligations.

d) Ethical practice requires the investigator to inform the participant of all features of the research that might reasonably be expected to influence willingness to participate, and to explain all other aspects of the research about which the participant inquires. After the data are collected, the investigator provides the participant with information about the nature of the study in order to remove any misconceptions that may have arisen.

e) The ethical investigator protects participants from physical and mental discomfort, harm, and danger. If a risk of such consequences exists, the investigator is required to inform the participant of that fact, secure consent before proceeding, and take all possible measures to minimize distress. A research procedure must not be used if it is likely to cause serious or lasting harm to a participant.

f) The methodological requirements of the study may necessitate concealment, deception, or minimal risk to participants. In such cases, the investigator must be able to justify the use of these techniques and to ensure, as soon as possible, the participant's understanding of the reasons and sufficient justification for the procedure in question.

g) Ethical practice requires the investigator to respect the individual's freedom to decline to participate in, or withdraw from, research and to so inform prospective participants. The obligation to protect this freedom requires special vigilance when the investigator is, in any manner, in a position of authority over the participant. It is unethical to penalize a participant in any way for withdrawing from or refusing to participate in a research project.

h) Information obtained about the individual research participants during the course of an investigation is confidential unless otherwise agreed to in advance.

i) Investigation of human subjects in studies which use drugs, are conducted only in conjunction with licensed physicians.

j) Clinical social workers take credit only for work actually done in scholarly and research projects, and give appropriate credit to the contributions of others in a manner which is proportional to the degree to which those contributions are represented in the final product.

k) Research findings must be presented accurately and completely, with full discussion of both their usefulness and their limitations. Clinical social workers are responsible for attempting to prevent any distortion or misuse of their findings.

Principle VIII
PUBLIC STATEMENTS

Public statements, announcements of services, and promotional activities of clinical social workers serve the purpose of providing sufficient information to aid consumers in making informed judgments and choices. Clinical social workers state accurately, objectively, and without misrepresentation their professional qualifications, affiliations, and functions as well as those of the institutions or organizations with which they or their statements may be associated. In addition, they should correct the misrepresentations of others with respect to these matters.

a) In announcing availability for professional services, protection of the public is the primary concern. A clinical social worker may use any information so long as it describes his or her credentials and the services provided accurately and without misrepresentation. Information usually found helpful by the public includes the name of the professional; highest relevant academic degree from an accredited institution; specialized post-graduate training; type and level of state certification or license; any advanced certifications held; address and telephone number; office hours; type of service provided; languages spoken; and, policy with regard to third party payments.

b) In announcements of available professional services, information regarding fees and fee policies may also be found helpful by prospective clients. Appropriate announcements of this type could include such general terms as "moderate fees." It is unethical to make statements regarding fees or fee policies which are deceptive, or misrepresent the actual fee arrangements.

c) The clinical social worker is responsible for assuring that all advertising is in conformity with the ethical standards of the profession. Publications announcing any type of clinic social work service describe those services accurately. They do not falsely or deceptively claim or imply superior personal or professional competence.

d) Clinical social workers are free to make public appearances and engage in public discussion regarding issues such as, for example, the relative value of alternative treatment approaches. Diagnostic and therapeutic services for clients, however, are rendered only in the context of a professional relationship. Such services are not given by means of public lectures, newspaper or magazine articles, radio or television programs, or anything of a similar nature. Professional use of the media or of other public forums is appropriate when the purpose is to educate the public about professional matters regarding which the clinical social worker has special knowledge or expertise.

e) Clinical social workers respect the rights and reputation of any professional organization with which they are affiliated, and do not falsely imply sponsorship or certification by any organization. When making public statements, the clinical social worker will make clear which are personal opinions, and which are authorized statements on behalf of the organization.

Organization

NATIONAL ASSOCIATION OF SOCIAL WORKERS

Headquarters:
750 First Street, NE
Suite 700
Washington, DC 20002-4241
Telephone: (202) 408-8600
Fax: (202) 336-8311
E-mail: info@naswdc.org
Website: http://www.socialworkers.org

Date founded: 1955
Merged the American Association of Social Workers, Social Work Research Group, and five other predecessor social work organizations
Membership: approximately 155,000 social workers in 55 chapters throughout the U.S., Puerto Rico, Virgin Islands, and other nations

Code of Ethics

Official name: *Code of Ethics*
History: First issued 1960, revised periodically; current version adopted August 1996, effective January 1997
Authority: Code of Ethics Review Task Force; Delegate Assembly
Code is available on Website

Additional Resources

Organizational (Divisions, Programs, Services, etc.):

Academy of Certified Social Workers (ACSW) Program
Diplomate in Clinical Social Work (DCSW) Program
Ethics and Adjudication Manager
NASW Press
NASW Register of Clinical Social Workers (roster of clinical practitioners)
Office of Quality Assurance
Professional Liability Insurance Program

Qualified Clinical Social Worker (QCSW) Program
School Social Work Specialist (SSWS) Program
Social Work Month (public awareness campaign)

Informational (Publications, Videos, Seminars, etc.):

Articles in *Health & Social Work* journal, *Social Work, Social Work in Education, Social Work Research,* and *NASW News*
Community Building: Renewal, Well-Being, and Shared Responsibility
Continuing Education Standards
The Diverse Society: Implications for Social Policy
Ethical Standards in Social Work: Commentary on the NASW Code of Ethics
Gender Dilemmas in Social Work: Issues Affecting Women in the Profession
Guidelines and Documentation Requirements for Social Workers in Home Health Care
Issues in International Social Work
The Legal Environment of Social Work
Managed Care Principles (with Campaign for Health Security)
Multicultural Issues in Social Work
NASW Guidelines on the Private Practice of Clinical Social Work
Perspectives on the Small Community: Humanistic Views for Practitioners
Practical Politics: Social Work and Political Responsibility
Principles for the Provision of Mental Health and Substance Abuse Treatment Services: A Bill of Rights
Procedures for the Adjudication of Grievances
Professional Choices: Ethics at Work (video)
Prudent Practice: A Guide for Managing Malpractice Risk
Social Policy: Reform, Research, and Practice
Social Work Speaks: NASW Policy Statements
The Vulnerable Social Worker: Liability for Serving Children with Families
Women & Social Change: Nonprofits and Social Policy
Workplace Diversity: Issues and Perspectives

Goals and Activities of Organization

Among the major goals of the National Association of Social Workers (NASW) are to promote the social work profession, advance social work practice, and shape public policy.

The world's largest organization of professional social workers, the NASW has established major priorities in several areas: lobbying for legislation to improve health, welfare, and other human services programs; advocating for civil rights and for appropriate recognition of the social work profession; and supporting political candidates who back sound social policies. To meet its consumer protection goals, NASW sets practice standards, enforces a code of ethics, and works to improve state regulation of social work. It offers voluntary professional social work credentials and publishes a national roster of clinical practitioners.

Implementation and Enforcement of Code

All members pledge to abide by the Code, which is intended to serve as a guide to the everyday professional conduct of social workers. It does not specify which values, principles, and standards are most important, or which prevail when they conflict. In a specific situation, the individual social worker is to use informed judgment, and to consider how the matter would be dealt with in a peer review process where the ethical standards of the profession would apply.

Members' behavior is to conform with both the spirit and the letter of the Code, in light of all the values, principles, and standards therein. Additional sources of helpful information include general ethical theory, social work theory and research, laws, regulations, agency policies, and other codes of ethics; but the NASW Code should be regarded as the primary source.

Where ethical obligations conflict with agency policies or relevant laws or regulations, members must make a responsible effort to resolve the conflict in a manner consistent with the Code, or seek proper consultation before making a decision.

Individuals, agencies, organizations, licensing boards, insurance providers, courts, and other professional groups may adopt the NASW Code or use it as a frame of reference.

A violation of the Code does not automatically imply a violation of law, which is determined in legal and judicial proceedings; the profession counsels and disciplines its own members. Complaints alleging ethical violations are handled at the state chapter level in a disciplinary process that includes evaluations, hearings, findings, decisions, sanctions, and appeals.

History and Development of Code

The Code was originally adopted in 1960, five years after the formation of the NASW. Revisions have been made in 1980, 1990, 1994, and 1996.

These most recent amendments became effective in January 1997, and reflect changes in service delivery and insurance coverage, privacy concerns precipitated by technology, and a better informed public.

Code of Ethics*

Overview

The *NASW Code of Ethics* is intended to serve as a guide to the everyday professional conduct of social workers. This *Code* includes four sections. The first Section, "Preamble," summarizes the social work profession's mission and core values. The second section, "Purpose of the *NASW Code of Ethics*," provides an overview of the *Code*'s main functions and a brief guide for dealing with ethical issues or dilemmas in social work practice. The third section, "Ethical Principles," presents broad ethical principles, based on social work's core values, that inform social work practice. The final section, "Ethical Standards," includes specific ethical standards to guide social workers' conduct and to provide a basis for adjudication.

Preamble

The primary mission of the social work profession is to enhance human well-being and help meet the basic human needs of all people, with particular attention to the needs and empowerment of people who are vulnerable, oppressed, and living in poverty. A historic and defining feature of social work is the profession's focus on individual well-being in a social context and the well-being of society. Fundamental to social work is attention to the environmental forces that create, contribute to, and address problems in living.

Social workers promote social justice and social change with and on behalf of clients. "Clients" is used inclusively to refer to individuals, families, groups, organizations, and communities. Social workers are sensitive to cultural and ethnic diversity and strive to end discrimination, oppression, poverty, and other forms of social injustice. These activities may be in the form of direct practice, community organizing, supervision, consultation, administration, advocacy, social and political action, policy development and implementation, education, and research and evaluation. Social workers seek to enhance the capacity of people to address their own needs. Social workers also seek to promote the responsiveness of organizations, communities, and other social institutions to individuals' needs and social problems.

The mission of the social work profession is rooted in a set of core values. These core values, embraced by social workers throughout the profession's history, are the foundation of social work's unique purpose and perspective:

- service
- social justice
- dignity and worth of the person
- importance of human relationships
- integrity
- competence.

This constellation of core values reflects what is unique to the social work profession. Core values, and the principles that flow from them, must be balanced within the context and complexity of the human experience.

---

*Approved by the 1996 NASW Delegate Assembly. Adopted August, 1996—Effective January, 1997. Copyright © 1996, National Association of Social Workers, Inc. Reprinted with permission.

Purpose of the *NASW Code of Ethics*

Professional ethics are at the core of social work. The profession has an obligation to articulate its basic values, ethical principles, and ethical standards. The *NASW Code of Ethics* sets forth these values, principles, and standards to guide social workers' conduct. The *Code* is relevant to all social workers and social work students, regardless of their professional functions, the settings in which they work, or the populations they serve.

The *NASW Code of Ethics* serves six purposes:

1. The *Code* identifies core values on which social work's mission is based.
2. The *Code* summarizes broad ethical principles that reflect the profession's core values and establishes a set of specific ethical standards that should be used to guide social work practice.
3. The *Code* is designed to help social workers identify relevant considerations when professional obligations conflict or ethical uncertainties arise.
4. The *Code* provides ethical standards to which the general public can hold the social work profession accountable.
5. The *Code* socializes practitioners new to the field to social work's mission, values, ethical principles, and ethical standards.
6. The *Code* articulates standards that the social work profession itself can use to assess whether social workers have engaged in unethical conduct. NASW has formal procedures to adjudicate ethics complaints filed against its members.[1] In subscribing to this *Code,* social workers are required to cooperate in its implementation, participate in NASW adjudication proceedings, and abide by any NASW disciplinary rulings or sanctions based on it.

The *Code* offers a set of values, principles, and standards to guide decision making and conduct when ethical issues arise. It does not provide a set of rules that prescribe how social workers should act in all situations. Specific applications of the *Code* must take into account the context in which it is being considered and the possibility of conflicts among the *Code*'s values, principles, and standards. Ethical responsibilities flow from all human relationships, from the personal and familial to the social and professional.

Further, the *NASW Code of Ethics* does not specify which values, principles, and standards are most important and ought to outweigh others in instances when they conflict. Reasonable differences of opinion can and do exist among social workers with respect to the ways in which values, ethical principles, and ethical standards should be rank ordered when they conflict. Ethical decision making in a given situation must apply the informed judgment of the individual social worker and should also consider how the issues would be judged in a peer review process where the ethical standards of the profession would be applied.

Ethical decision making is a process. There are many instances in social work where simple answers are not available to resolve complex ethical issues. Social workers should take into consideration all the values, principles, and standards in this *Code* that are relevant to any situation in which ethical judgment is warranted. Social workers' decisions and actions should be consistent with the spirit as well as the letter of this *Code.*

---

[1] For information on NASW adjudication procedures, see *NASW Procedures for the Adjudication of Grievances.*

In addition to this *Code*, there are many other sources of information about ethical thinking that may be useful. Social workers should consider ethical theory and principles generally, social work theory and research, laws, regulations, agency policies, and other relevant codes of ethics, recognizing that among codes of ethics social workers should consider the *NASW Code of Ethics* as their primary source. Social workers also should be aware of the impact on ethical decision making of their clients' and their own personal values and cultural and religious beliefs and practices. They should be aware of any conflicts between personal and professional values and deal with them responsibly. For additional guidance social workers should consult the relevant literature on professional ethics and ethical decision making and seek appropriate consultation when faced with ethical dilemmas. This may involve consultation with an agency-based or social work organization's ethics committee, a regulatory body, knowledgeable colleagues, supervisors, or legal counsel.

Instances may arise when social workers' ethical obligations conflict with agency policies or relevant laws or regulations. When such conflicts occur, social workers must make a responsible effort to resolve the conflict in a manner that is consistent with the values, principles, and standards expressed in this *Code*. If a reasonable resolution of the conflict does not appear possible, social workers should seek proper consultation before making a decision.

The *NASW Code of Ethics* is to be used by NASW and by individuals, agencies, organizations, and bodies (such as licensing and regulatory boards, professional liability insurance providers, courts of law, agency boards of directors, government agencies, and other professional groups) that choose to adopt it or use it as a frame of reference. Violation of standards in this *Code* does not automatically imply legal liability or violation of the law. Such determination can only be made in the context of legal and judicial proceedings. Alleged violations of the *Code* would be subject to a peer review process. Such processes are generally separate from legal or administrative procedures and insulated from legal review or proceedings to allow the profession to counsel and discipline its own members.

A code of ethics cannot guarantee ethical behavior. Moreover, a code of ethics cannot resolve all ethical issues or disputes or capture the richness and complexity involved in striving to make responsible choices within a moral community. Rather, a code of ethics sets forth values, ethical principles, and ethical standards to which professionals aspire and by which their actions can be judged. Social workers' ethical behavior should result from their personal commitment to engage in ethical practice. The *NASW Code of Ethics* reflects the commitment of all social workers to uphold the profession's values and to act ethically. Principles and standards must be applied by individuals of good character who discern moral questions and, in good faith, seek to make reliable ethical judgments.

ETHICAL PRINCIPLES

The following broad ethical principles are based on social work's core values of service, social justice, dignity and worth of the person, importance of human relationships, integrity, and competence. These principles set forth ideals to which all social workers should aspire.

Value: *Service*
Ethical Principle: *Social workers' primary goal is to help people in need and to address social problems.*

Social workers elevate service to others above self-interest. Social workers draw on their knowledge, values, and skills to help people in need and to address social problems. Social workers are encouraged to volunteer some portion of their professional skills with no expectation of significant financial return (pro bono service).

Value: *Social Justice*
Ethical Principle: *Social workers challenge social injustice.*
Social workers pursue social change, particularly with and on behalf of vulnerable and oppressed individuals and groups of people. Social workers' social change efforts are focused primarily on issues of poverty, unemployment, discrimination, and other forms of social injustice. These activities seek to promote sensitivity to and knowledge about oppression and cultural and ethnic diversity. Social workers strive to ensure access to needed information, services, and resources; equality of opportunity; and meaningful participation in decision making for all people.

Value: *Dignity and Worth of the Person*
Ethical Principle: *Social workers respect the inherent dignity and worth of the person.*
Social workers treat each person in a caring and respectful fashion, mindful of individual differences and cultural and ethnic diversity. Social workers promote clients' socially responsible self-determination. Social workers seek to enhance clients' capacity and opportunity to change and to address their own needs. Social workers are cognizant of their dual responsibility to clients and to the broader society. They seek to resolve conflicts between clients' interests and the broader society's interests in a socially responsible manner consistent with the values, ethical principles, and ethical standards of the profession.

Value: *Importance of Human Relationships*
Ethical Principle: *Social workers recognize the central importance of human relationships.*
Social workers understand that relationships between and among people are an important vehicle for change. Social workers engage people as partners in the helping process. Social workers seek to strengthen relationships among people in a purposeful effort to promote, restore, maintain, and enhance the well-being of individuals, families, social groups, organizations, and communities.

Value: *Integrity*
Ethical Principle: *Social workers behave in a trustworthy manner.*
Social workers are continually aware of the profession's mission, values, ethical principles, and ethical standards and practice in a manner consistent with them. Social workers act honestly and responsibly and promote ethical practices on the part of the organizations with which they are affiliated.

Value: *Competence*
Ethical Principle: *Social workers practice within their areas of competence and develop and enhance their professional expertise.*
Social workers continually strive to increase their professional knowledge and skills and to apply them in practice. Social workers should aspire to contribute to the knowledge base of the profession.

ETHICAL STANDARDS

The following standards are relevant to the professional activities of all social workers. * * *

Some of the standards that follow are enforceable guidelines for professional conduct, and some are aspirational. The extent to which each standard is enforceable is a matter of professional judgment to be exercised by those responsible for reviewing alleged violations of ethical standards.

1. SOCIAL WORKERS' ETHICAL RESPONSIBILITIES TO CLIENTS

1.01 Commitment to Clients

Social workers' primary responsibility is to promote the well-being of clients. In general, clients' interests are primary. However, social workers' responsibility to the larger society or specific legal obligations may on limited occasions supersede the loyalty owed clients, and clients should be so advised. (Examples include when a social worker is required by law to report that a client has abused a child or has threatened to harm self or others.)

1.02 Self-Determination

Social workers respect and promote the right of clients to self-determination and assist clients in their efforts to identify and clarify their goals. Social workers may limit clients' right to self-determination when, in the social workers' professional judgment, clients' actions or potential actions pose a serious, foreseeable, and imminent risk to themselves or others.

1.03 Informed Consent

(a) Social workers should provide services to clients only in the context of a professional relationship based, when appropriate, on valid informed consent. Social workers should use clear and understandable language to inform clients of the purpose of the services, risks related to the services, limits to services because of the requirements of a third-party payer, relevant costs, reasonable alternatives, clients' right to refuse or withdraw consent, and the time frame covered by the consent. Social workers should provide clients with an opportunity to ask questions.

(b) In instances when clients are not literate or have difficulty understanding the primary language used in the practice setting, social workers should take steps to ensure clients' comprehension. This may include providing clients with a detailed verbal explanation or arranging for a qualified interpreter or translator whenever possible.

(c) In instances when clients lack the capacity to provide informed consent, social workers should protect clients' interests by seeking permission from an appropriate third party, informing clients consistent with the clients' level of understanding. In such instances social workers should seek to ensure that the third party acts in a manner consistent with clients' wishes and interests. Social workers should take reasonable steps to enhance such clients' ability to give informed consent.

(d) In instances when clients are receiving services involuntarily, social workers should provide information about the nature and extent of services and about the extent of clients' right to refuse service.
(e) Social workers who provide services via electronic media (such as computer, telephone, radio, and television) should inform recipients of the limitations and risks associated with such services.
(f) Social workers should obtain clients' informed consent before audiotaping or videotaping clients or permitting observation of services to clients by a third party.

1.04 Competence

(a) Social workers should provide services and represent themselves as competent only within the boundaries of their education, training, license, certification, consultation received, supervised experience, or other relevant professional experience.
(b) Social workers should provide services in substantive areas or use intervention techniques or approaches that are new to them only after engaging in appropriate study, training, consultation, and supervision from people who are competent in those interventions or techniques.
(c) When generally recognized standards do not exist with respect to an emerging area of practice, social workers should exercise careful judgment and take responsible steps (including appropriate education, research, training, consultation, and supervision) to ensure the competence of their work and to protect clients from harm.

1.05 Cultural Competence and Social Diversity

(a) Social workers should understand culture and its function in human behavior and society, recognizing the strengths that exist in all cultures.
(b) Social workers should have a knowledge base of their clients' cultures and be able to demonstrate competence in the provision of services that are sensitive to clients' cultures and to differences among people and cultural groups.
(c) Social workers should obtain education about and seek to understand the nature of social diversity and oppression with respect to race, ethnicity, national origin, color, sex, sexual orientation, age, marital status, political belief, religion, and mental or physical disability.

1.06 Conflicts of Interest

(a) Social workers should be alert to and avoid conflicts of interest that interfere with the exercise of professional discretion and impartial judgment. Social workers should inform clients when a real or potential conflict of interest arises and take reasonable steps to resolve the issue in a manner that makes the clients' interests primary and protects clients' interests to the greatest extent possible. In some cases, protecting clients' interests may require termination of the professional relationship with proper referral of the client.
(b) Social workers should not take unfair advantage of any professional relationship or exploit others to further their personal, religious, political, or business interests.
(c) Social workers should not engage in dual or multiple relationships with clients or former clients in which there is a risk of exploitation or potential harm to

the client. In instances when dual or multiple relationships are unavoidable, social workers should take steps to protect clients and are responsible for setting clear, appropriate, and culturally sensitive boundaries. (Dual or multiple relationships occur when social workers relate to clients in more than one relationship, whether professional, social, or business. Dual or multiple relationships can occur simultaneously or consecutively.)

(d) When social workers provide services to two or more people who have a relationship with each other (for example, couples, family members), social workers should clarify with all parties which individuals will be considered clients and the nature of social workers' professional obligations to the various individuals who are receiving services. Social workers who anticipate a conflict of interest among the individuals receiving services or who anticipate having to perform in potentially conflicting roles (for example, when a social worker is asked to testify in a child custody dispute or divorce proceedings involving clients) should clarify their role with the parties involved and take appropriate action to minimize any conflict of interest.

1.07 Privacy and Confidentiality

(a) Social workers should respect clients' right to privacy. Social workers should not solicit private information from clients unless it is essential to providing services or conducting social work evaluation or research. Once private information is shared, standards of confidentiality apply.

(b) Social workers may disclose confidential information when appropriate with valid consent from a client or a person legally authorized to consent on behalf of a client.

(c) Social workers should protect the confidentiality of all information obtained in the course of professional service, except for compelling professional reasons. The general expectation that social workers will keep information confidential does not apply when disclosure is necessary to prevent serious, foreseeable, and imminent harm to a client or other identifiable person or when laws or regulations require disclosure without a client's consent. In all instances, social workers should disclose the least amount of confidential information necessary to achieve the desired purpose; only information that is directly relevant to the purpose for which the disclosure is made should be revealed.

(d) Social workers should inform clients, to the extent possible, about the disclosure of confidential information and the potential consequences, when feasible before the disclosure is made. This applies whether social workers disclose confidential information on the basis of a legal requirement or client consent.

(e) Social workers should discuss with clients and other interested parties the nature of confidentiality and limitations of clients' right to confidentiality. Social workers should review with clients circumstances where confidential information may be requested and where disclosure of confidential information may be legally required. This discussion should occur as soon as possible in the social worker–client relationship and as needed throughout the course of the relationship.

(f) When social workers provide counseling services to families, couples, or groups, social workers should seek agreement among the parties involved concerning each individual's right to confidentiality and obligation to preserve the confidentiality of information shared by others. Social workers should inform participants in family, couples, or group counseling that social workers cannot guarantee that all participants will honor such agreements.

(g) Social workers should inform clients involved in family, couples, marital, or group counseling of the social worker's, employer's, and agency's policy concerning the social worker's disclosure of confidential information among the parties involved in the counseling.

(h) Social workers should not disclose confidential information to third-party payers unless clients have authorized such disclosure.

(i) Social workers should not discuss confidential information in any setting unless privacy can be ensured. Social workers should not discuss confidential information in public or semipublic areas such as hallways, waiting rooms, elevators, and restaurants.

(j) Social workers should protect the confidentiality of clients during legal proceedings to the extent permitted by law. When a court of law or other legally authorized body orders social workers to disclose confidential or privileged information without a client's consent and such disclosure could cause harm to the client, social workers should request that the court withdraw the order or limit the order as narrowly as possible or maintain the records under seal, unavailable for public inspection.

(k) Social workers should protect the confidentiality of clients when responding to requests from members of the media.

(l) Social workers should protect the confidentiality of clients' written and electronic records and other sensitive information. Social workers should take reasonable steps to ensure that clients' records are stored in a secure location and that clients' records are not available to others who are not authorized to have access.

(m) Social workers should take precautions to ensure and maintain the confidentiality of information transmitted to other parties through the use of computers, electronic mail, facsimile machines, telephones and telephone answering machines, and other electronic or computer technology. Disclosure of identifying information should be avoided whenever possible.

(n) Social workers should transfer or dispose of clients' records in a manner that protects clients' confidentiality and is consistent with state statutes governing records and social work licensure.

(o) Social workers should take reasonable precautions to protect client confidentiality in the event of the social worker's termination of practice, incapacitation, or death.

(p) Social workers should not disclose identifying information when discussing clients for teaching or training purposes unless the client has consented to disclosure of confidential information.

(q) Social workers should not disclose identifying information when discussing clients with consultants unless the client has consented to disclosure of confidential information or there is a compelling need for such disclosure.

(r) Social workers should protect the confidentiality of deceased clients consistent with the preceding standards.

1.08 Access to Records

(a) Social workers should provide clients with reasonable access to records concerning the clients. Social workers who are concerned that clients' access to their records could cause serious misunderstanding or harm to the client should provide assistance in interpreting the records and consultation with the client regarding the records. Social workers should limit clients' access to their records, or portions of their records, only in exceptional circumstances when there is compelling evidence that such access would cause serious harm to the client. Both clients' requests and the rationale for withholding some or all of the record should be documented in clients' files.

(b) When providing clients with access to their records, social workers should take steps to protect the confidentiality of other individuals identified or discussed in such records.

1.09 Sexual Relationships

(a) Social workers should under no circumstances engage in sexual activities or sexual contact with current clients, whether such contact is consensual or forced.

(b) Social workers should not engage in sexual activities or sexual contact with clients' relatives or other individuals with whom clients maintain a close personal relationship when there is a risk of exploitation or potential harm to the client. Sexual activity or sexual contact with clients' relatives or other individuals with whom clients maintain a personal relationship has the potential to be harmful to the client and may make it difficult for the social worker and client to maintain appropriate professional boundaries. Social workers— not their clients, their clients' relatives, or other individuals with whom the client maintains a personal relationship—assume the full burden for setting clear, appropriate, and culturally sensitive boundaries.

(c) Social workers should not engage in sexual activities or sexual contact with former clients because of the potential for harm to the client. If social workers engage in conduct contrary to this prohibition or claim that an exception to this prohibition is warranted because of extraordinary circumstances, it is social workers—not their clients—who assume the full burden of demonstrating that the former client has not been exploited, coerced, or manipulated, intentionally or unintentionally.

(d) Social workers should not provide clinical services to individuals with whom they have had a prior sexual relationship. Providing clinical services to a former sexual partner has the potential to be harmful to the individual and is likely to make it difficult for the social worker and individual to maintain appropriate professional boundaries.

1.10 Physical Contact

Social workers should not engage in physical contact with clients when there is a possibility of psychological harm to the client as a result of the contact (such as cradling or caressing clients). Social workers who engage in appropriate physical contact with clients are responsible for setting clear, appropriate, and culturally sensitive boundaries that govern such physical contact.

1.11 Sexual Harassment

Social workers should not sexually harass clients. Sexual harassment includes sexual advances, sexual solicitation, requests for sexual favors, and other verbal or physical conduct of a sexual nature.

1.12 Derogatory Language

Social workers should not use derogatory language in their written or verbal communications to or about clients. Social workers should use accurate and respectful language in all communications to and about clients.

1.13 Payment for Services

(a) When setting fees, social workers should ensure that the fees are fair, reasonable, and commensurate with the services performed. Consideration should be given to clients' ability to pay.
(b) Social workers should avoid accepting goods or services from clients as payment for professional services. Bartering arrangements, particularly involving services, create the potential for conflicts of interest, exploitation, and inappropriate boundaries in social workers' relationships with clients. Social workers should explore and may participate in bartering only in very limited circumstances when it can be demonstrated that such arrangements are an accepted practice among professionals in the local community, considered to be essential for the provision of services, negotiated without coercion, and entered into at the client's initiative and with the client's informed consent. Social workers who accept goods or services from clients as payment for professional services assume the full burden of demonstrating that this arrangement will not be detrimental to the client or the professional relationship.
(c) Social workers should not solicit a private fee or other remuneration for providing services to clients who are entitled to such available services through the social workers' employer or agency.

1.14 Clients Who Lack Decision-Making Capacity

When social workers act on behalf of clients who lack the capacity to make informed decisions, social workers should take reasonable steps to safeguard the interests and rights of those clients.

1.15 Interruption of Services

Social workers should make reasonable efforts to ensure continuity of services in the event that services are interrupted by factors such as unavailability, relocation, illness, disability, or death.

1.16 Termination of Services

(a) Social workers should terminate services to clients and professional relationships with them when such services and relationships are no longer required or no longer serve the clients' needs or interests.
(b) Social workers should take reasonable steps to avoid abandoning clients who are still in need of services. Social workers should withdraw services precipitously only under unusual circumstances, giving careful consideration to all factors in the situation and taking care to minimize possible adverse effects. Social workers should assist in making appropriate arrangements for continuation of services when necessary.
(c) Social workers in fee-for-service settings may terminate services to clients who are not paying an overdue balance if the financial contractual arrangements

have been made clear to the client, if the client does not pose an imminent danger to self or others, and if the clinical and other consequences of the current nonpayment have been addressed and discussed with the client.
(d) Social workers should not terminate services to pursue a social, financial, or sexual relationship with a client.
(e) Social workers who anticipate the termination or interruption of services to clients should notify clients promptly and seek the transfer, referral, or continuation of services in relation to the clients' needs and preferences.
(f) Social workers who are leaving an employment setting should inform clients of appropriate options for the continuation of services and of the benefits and risks of the options.

2. SOCIAL WORKERS' ETHICAL RESPONSIBILITIES TO COLLEAGUES

2.01 Respect

(a) Social workers should treat colleagues with respect and should represent accurately and fairly the qualifications, views, and obligations of colleagues.
(b) Social workers should avoid unwarranted negative criticism of colleagues in communications with clients or with other professionals. Unwarranted negative criticism may include demeaning comments that refer to colleagues' level of competence or to individuals' attributes such as race, ethnicity, national origin, color, sex, sexual orientation, age, marital status, political belief, religion, and mental or physical disability.
(c) Social workers should cooperate with social work colleagues and with colleagues of other professions when such cooperation serves the well-being of clients.

2.02 Confidentiality

Social workers should respect confidential information shared by colleagues in the course of their professional relationships and transactions. Social workers should ensure that such colleagues understand social workers' obligation to respect confidentiality and any exceptions related to it.

2.03 Interdisciplinary Collaboration

(a) Social workers who are members of an interdisciplinary team should participate in and contribute to decisions that affect the well-being of clients by drawing on the perspectives, values, and experiences of the social work profession. Professional and ethical obligations of the interdisciplinary team as a whole and of its individual members should be clearly established.
(b) Social workers for whom a team decision raises ethical concerns should attempt to resolve the disagreement through appropriate channels. If the disagreement cannot be resolved, social workers should pursue other avenues to address their concerns consistent with client well-being.

2.04 Disputes Involving Colleagues

(a) Social workers should not take advantage of a dispute between a colleague and an employer to obtain a position or otherwise advance the social workers' own interests.

(b) Social workers should not exploit clients in disputes with colleagues or engage clients in any inappropriate discussion of conflicts between social workers and their colleagues.

2.05 Consultation

(a) Social workers should seek the advice and counsel of colleagues whenever such consultation is in the best interests of clients.
(b) Social workers should keep themselves informed about colleagues' areas of expertise and competencies. Social workers should seek consultation only from colleagues who have demonstrated knowledge, expertise, and competence related to the subject of the consultation.
(c) When consulting with colleagues about clients, social workers should disclose the least amount of information necessary to achieve the purposes of the consultation.

2.06 Referral for Services

(a) Social workers should refer clients to other professionals when the other professionals' specialized knowledge or expertise is needed to serve clients fully or when social workers believe that they are not being effective or making reasonable progress with clients and that additional service is required.
(b) Social workers who refer clients to other professionals should take appropriate steps to facilitate an orderly transfer of responsibility. Social workers who refer clients to other professionals should disclose, with clients' consent, all pertinent information to the new service providers.
(c) Social workers are prohibited from giving or receiving payment for a referral when no professional service is provided by the referring social worker.

2.07 Sexual Relationships

(a) Social workers who function as supervisors or educators should not engage in sexual activities or contact with supervisees, students, trainees, or other colleagues over whom they exercise professional authority.
(b) Social workers should avoid engaging in sexual relationships with colleagues when there is potential for a conflict of interest. Social workers who become involved in, or anticipate becoming involved in, a sexual relationship with a colleague have a duty to transfer professional responsibilities, when necessary, to avoid a conflict of interest.

2.08 Sexual Harassment

Social workers should not sexually harass supervisees, students, trainees, or colleagues. Sexual harassment includes sexual advances, sexual solicitation, requests for sexual favors, and other verbal or physical conduct of a sexual nature.

2.09 Impairment of Colleagues

(a) Social workers who have direct knowledge of a social work colleague's impairment that is due to personal problems, psychosocial distress, substance abuse, or mental health difficulties and that interferes with practice effectiveness should consult with that colleague when feasible and assist the colleague in taking remedial action.

(b) Social workers who believe that a social work colleague's impairment interferes with practice effectiveness and that the colleague has not taken adequate steps to address the impairment should take action through appropriate channels established by employers, agencies, NASW, licensing and regulatory bodies, and other professional organizations.

2.10 Incompetence of Colleagues

(a) Social workers who have direct knowledge of a social work colleague's incompetence should consult with that colleague when feasible and assist the colleague in taking remedial action.

(b) Social workers who believe that a social work colleague is incompetent and has not taken adequate steps to address the incompetence should take action through appropriate channels established by employers, agencies, NASW, licensing and regulatory bodies, and other professional organizations.

2.11 Unethical Conduct of Colleagues

(a) Social workers should take adequate measures to discourage, prevent, expose, and correct the unethical conduct of colleagues.

(b) Social workers should be knowledgeable about established policies and procedures for handling concerns about colleagues' unethical behavior. Social workers should be familiar with national, state, and local procedures for handling ethics complaints. These include policies and procedures created by NASW, licensing and regulatory bodies, employers, agencies, and other professional organizations.

(c) Social workers who believe that a colleague has acted unethically should seek resolution by discussing their concerns with the colleague when feasible and when such discussion is likely to be productive.

(d) When necessary, social workers who believe that a colleague has acted unethically should take action through appropriate formal channels (such as contacting a state licensing board or regulatory body, an NASW committee on inquiry, or other professional ethics committees).

(e) Social workers should defend and assist colleagues who are unjustly charged with unethical conduct.

3. SOCIAL WORKERS' ETHICAL RESPONSIBILITIES IN PRACTICE SETTINGS

3.01 Supervision and Consultation

(a) Social workers who provide supervision or consultation should have the necessary knowledge and skill to supervise or consult appropriately and should do so only within their areas of knowledge and competence.

(b) Social workers who provide supervision or consultation are responsible for setting clear, appropriate, and culturally sensitive boundaries.

(c) Social workers should not engage in any dual or multiple relationships with supervisees in which there is a risk of exploitation of or potential harm to the supervisee.

(d) Social workers who provide supervision should evaluate supervisees' performance in a manner that is fair and respectful.

3.02 Education and Training

(a) Social workers who function as educators, field instructors for students, or trainers should provide instruction only within their areas of knowledge and competence and should provide instruction based on the most current information and knowledge available in the profession.
(b) Social workers who function as educators or field instructors for students should evaluate students' performance in a manner that is fair and respectful.
(c) Social workers who function as educators or field instructors for students should take reasonable steps to ensure that clients are routinely informed when services are being provided by students.
(d) Social workers who function as educators or field instructors for students should not engage in any dual or multiple relationships with students in which there is a risk of exploitation or potential harm to the student. Social work educators and field instructors are responsible for setting clear, appropriate, and culturally sensitive boundaries.

3.03 Performance Evaluation

Social workers who have responsibility for evaluating the performance of others should fulfill such responsibility in a fair and considerate manner and on the basis of clearly stated criteria.

3.04 Client Records

(a) Social workers should take reasonable steps to ensure that documentation in records is accurate and reflects the services provided.
(b) Social workers should include sufficient and timely documentation in records to facilitate the delivery of services and to ensure continuity of services provided to clients in the future.
(c) Social workers' documentation should protect clients' privacy to the extent that is possible and appropriate and should include only information that is directly relevant to the delivery of services.
(d) Social workers should store records following the termination of services to ensure reasonable future access. Records should be maintained for the number of years required by state statutes or relevant contracts.

3.05 Billing

Social workers should establish and maintain billing practices that accurately reflect the nature and extent of services provided and that identify who provided the service in the practice setting.

3.06 Client Transfer

(a) When an individual who is receiving services from another agency or colleague contacts a social worker for services, the social worker should carefully consider the client's needs before agreeing to provide services. To minimize possible confusion and conflict, social workers should discuss with potential clients the nature of the clients' current relationship with other service providers and the implications, including possible benefits or risks, of entering into a relationship with a new service provider.

(b) If a new client has been served by another agency or colleague, social workers should discuss with the client whether consultation with the previous service provider is in the client's best interest.

3.07 Administration

(a) Social work administrators should advocate within and outside their agencies for adequate resources to meet clients' needs.
(b) Social workers should advocate for resource allocation procedures that are open and fair. When not all clients' needs can be met, an allocation procedure should be developed that is nondiscriminatory and based on appropriate and consistently applied principles.
(c) Social workers who are administrators should take reasonable steps to ensure that adequate agency or organizational resources are available to provide appropriate staff supervision.
(d) Social work administrators should take reasonable steps to ensure that the working environment for which they are responsible is consistent with and encourages compliance with the *NASW Code of Ethics*. Social work administrators should take reasonable steps to eliminate any conditions in their organizations that violate, interfere with, or discourage compliance with the Code.

3.08 Continuing Education and Staff Development

Social work administrators and supervisors should take reasonable steps to provide or arrange for continuing education and staff development for all staff for whom they are responsible. Continuing education and staff development should address current knowledge and emerging developments related to social work practice and ethics.

3.09 Commitments to Employers

(a) Social workers generally should adhere to commitments made to employers and employing organizations.
(b) Social workers should work to improve employing agencies' policies and procedures and the efficiency and effectiveness of their services.
(c) Social workers should take reasonable steps to ensure that employers are aware of social workers' ethical obligations as set forth in the *NASW Code of Ethics* and of the implications of those obligations for social work practice.
(d) Social workers should not allow an employing organization's policies, procedures, regulations, or administrative orders to interfere with their ethical practice of social work. Social workers should take reasonable steps to ensure that their employing organizations' practices are consistent with the *NASW Code of Ethics*.
(e) Social workers should act to prevent and eliminate discrimination in the employing organization's work assignments and in its employment policies and practices.
(f) Social workers should accept employment or arrange student field placements only in organizations that exercise fair personnel practices.
(g) Social workers should be diligent stewards of the resources of their employing organizations, wisely conserving funds where appropriate and never misappropriating funds or using them for unintended purposes.

544 CODES OF PROFESSIONAL RESPONSIBILITY

3.10 Labor–Management Disputes

(a) Social workers may engage in organized action, including the formation of and participation in labor unions, to improve services to clients and working conditions.
(b) The actions of social workers who are involved in labor–management disputes, job actions, or labor strikes should be guided by the profession's values, ethical principles, and ethical standards. Reasonable differences of opinion exist among social workers concerning their primary obligation as professionals during an actual or threatened labor strike or job action. Social workers should carefully examine relevant issues and their possible impact on clients before deciding on a course of action.

4. SOCIAL WORKERS' ETHICAL RESPONSIBILITIES AS PROFESSIONALS

4.01 Competence

(a) Social workers should accept responsibility or employment only on the basis of existing competence or the intention to acquire the necessary competence.
(b) Social workers should strive to become and remain proficient in professional practice and the performance of professional functions. Social workers should critically examine and keep current with emerging knowledge relevant to social work. Social workers should routinely review the professional literature and participate in continuing education relevant to social work practice and social work ethics.
(c) Social workers should base practice on recognized knowledge, including empirically based knowledge, relevant to social work and social work ethics.

4.02 Discrimination

Social workers should not practice, condone, facilitate, or collaborate with any form of discrimination on the basis of race, ethnicity, national origin, color, sex, sexual orientation, age, marital status, political belief, religion, or mental or physical disability.

4.03 Private Conduct

Social workers should not permit their private conduct to interfere with their ability to fulfill their professional responsibilities.

4.04 Dishonesty, Fraud, and Deception

Social workers should not participate in, condone, or be associated with dishonesty, fraud, or deception.

4.05 Impairment

(a) Social workers should not allow their own personal problems, psychosocial distress, legal problems, substance abuse, or mental health difficulties to interfere with their professional judgment and performance or to jeopardize the best interests of people for whom they have a professional responsibility.

(b) Social workers whose personal problems, psychosocial distress, legal problems, substance abuse, or mental health difficulties interfere with their professional judgment and performance should immediately seek consultation and take appropriate remedial action by seeking professional help, making adjustments in workload, terminating practice, or taking any other steps necessary to protect clients and others.

4.06 Misrepresentation

(a) Social workers should make clear distinctions between statements made and actions engaged in as a private individual and as a representative of the social work profession, a professional social work organization, or the social worker's employing agency.
(b) Social workers who speak on behalf of professional social work organizations should accurately represent the official and authorized positions of the organizations.
(c) Social workers should ensure that their representations to clients, agencies, and the public of professional qualifications, credentials, education, competence, affiliations, services provided, or results to be achieved are accurate. Social workers should claim only those relevant professional credentials they actually possess and take steps to correct any inaccuracies or misrepresentations of their credentials by others.

4.07 Solicitations

(a) Social workers should not engage in uninvited solicitation of potential clients who, because of their circumstances, are vulnerable to undue influence, manipulation, or coercion.
(b) Social workers should not engage in solicitation of testimonial endorsements (including solicitation of consent to use a client's prior statement as a testimonial endorsement) from current clients or from other people who, because of their particular circumstances, are vulnerable to undue influence.

4.08 Acknowledging Credit

(a) Social workers should take responsibility and credit, including authorship credit, only for work they have actually performed and to which they have contributed.
(b) Social workers should honestly acknowledge the work of and the contributions made by others.

5. SOCIAL WORKERS' ETHICAL RESPONSIBILITIES TO THE SOCIAL WORK PROFESSION

5.01 Integrity of the Profession

(a) Social workers should work toward the maintenance and promotion of high standards of practice.
(b) Social workers should uphold and advance the values, ethics, knowledge, and mission of the profession. Social workers should protect, enhance, and improve the integrity of the profession through appropriate study and research, active discussion, and responsible criticism of the profession.

(c) Social workers should contribute time and professional expertise to activities that promote respect for the value, integrity, and competence of the social work profession. These activities may include teaching, research, consultation, service, legislative testimony, presentations in the community, and participation in their professional organizations.

(d) Social workers should contribute to the knowledge base of social work and share with colleagues their knowledge related to practice, research, and ethics. Social workers should seek to contribute to the profession's literature and to share their knowledge at professional meetings and conferences.

(e) Social workers should act to prevent the unauthorized and unqualified practice of social work.

5.02 Evaluation and Research

(a) Social workers should monitor and evaluate policies, the implementation of programs, and practice interventions.

(b) Social workers should promote and facilitate evaluation and research to contribute to the development of knowledge.

(c) Social workers should critically examine and keep current with emerging knowledge relevant to social work and fully use evaluation and research evidence in their professional practice.

(d) Social workers engaged in evaluation or research should carefully consider possible consequences and should follow guidelines developed for the protection of evaluation and research participants. Appropriate institutional review boards should be consulted.

(e) Social workers engaged in evaluation or research should obtain voluntary and written informed consent from participants, when appropriate, without any implied or actual deprivation or penalty for refusal to participate; without undue inducement to participate; and with due regard for participants' well-being, privacy, and dignity. Informed consent should include information about the nature, extent, and duration of the participation requested and disclosure of the risks and benefits of participation in the research.

(f) When evaluation or research participants are incapable of giving informed consent, social workers should provide an appropriate explanation to the participants, obtain the participants' assent to the extent they are able, and obtain written consent from an appropriate proxy.

(g) Social workers should never design or conduct evaluation or research that does not use consent procedures, such as certain forms of naturalistic observation and archival research, unless rigorous and responsible review of the research has found it to be justified because of its prospective scientific, educational, or applied value and unless equally effective alternative procedures that do not involve waiver of consent are not feasible.

(h) Social workers should inform participants of their right to withdraw from evaluation and research at any time without penalty.

(i) Social workers should take appropriate steps to ensure that participants in evaluation and research have access to appropriate supportive services.

(j) Social workers engaged in evaluation or research should protect participants from unwarranted physical or mental distress, harm, danger, or deprivation.

(k) Social workers engaged in the evaluation of services should discuss collected information only for professional purposes and only with people professionally concerned with this information.

(l) Social workers engaged in evaluation or research should ensure the anonymity or confidentiality of participants and of the data obtained from them. Social workers should inform participants of any limits of confidentiality, the measures that will be taken to ensure confidentiality, and when any records containing research data will be destroyed.

(m) Social workers who report evaluation and research results should protect participants' confidentiality by omitting identifying information unless proper consent has been obtained authorizing disclosure.

(n) Social workers should report evaluation and research findings accurately. They should not fabricate or falsify results and should take steps to correct any errors later found in published data using standard publication methods.

(o) Social workers engaged in evaluation or research should be alert to and avoid conflicts of interest and dual relationships with participants, should inform participants when a real or potential conflict of interest arises, and should take steps to resolve the issue in a manner that makes participants' interests primary.

(p) Social workers should educate themselves, their students, and their colleagues about responsible research practices.

6. SOCIAL WORKERS' ETHICAL RESPONSIBILITIES TO THE BROADER SOCIETY

6.01 Social Welfare

Social workers should promote the general welfare of society, from local to global levels, and the development of people, their communities, and their environments. Social workers should advocate for living conditions conducive to the fulfillment of basic human needs and should promote social, economic, political, and cultural values and institutions that are compatible with the realization of social justice.

6.02 Public Participation

Social workers should facilitate informed participation by the public in shaping social policies and institutions.

6.03 Public Emergencies

Social workers should provide appropriate professional services in public emergencies to the greatest extent possible.

6.04 Social and Political Action

(a) Social workers should engage in social and political action that seeks to ensure that all people have equal access to the resources, employment, services, and opportunities they require to meet their basic human needs and to develop fully. Social workers should be aware of the impact of the political arena on practice and should advocate for changes in policy and legislation to improve social conditions in order to meet basic human needs and promote social justice.

(b) Social workers should act to expand choice and opportunity for all people, with special regard for vulnerable, disadvantaged, oppressed, and exploited people and groups.
(c) Social workers should promote conditions that encourage respect for cultural and social diversity within the United States and globally. Social workers should promote policies and practices that demonstrate respect for difference, support the expansion of cultural knowledge and resources, advocate for programs and institutions that demonstrate cultural competence, and promote policies that safeguard the rights of and confirm equity and social justice for all people.
(d) Social workers should act to prevent and eliminate domination of, exploitation of, and discrimination against any person, group, or class on the basis of race, ethnicity, national origin, color, sex, sexual orientation, age, marital status, political belief, religion, or mental or physical disability.

III. LAW

1. DISPUTE RESOLUTION

2. JUDICIARY

3. LAW PRACTICE

4. LEGAL SUPPORT STAFF

5.   LITIGATION

1. DISPUTE RESOLUTION

Organization

ACADEMY OF FAMILY MEDIATORS

Headquarters:
4 Militia Drive
Lexington, MA 02421
Telephone: (781) 674-2663
Fax: (781) 674-2690
E-mail: afmoffice@mediators.org
Website: http://www.mediators.org

Date founded: 1981
Membership: approximately 3,700 individuals with backgrounds in behavioral science, conflict resolution, or law, who specialize in mediating family disputes and divorce, in private practice, courts, schools, and government, in the U.S. and other nations

Code of Ethics

Official name: *Standards of Practice for Family and Divorce Mediation*
History: Adopted 1983; updated 1988
Authority: Ethics & Grievance Committee
Code is available on Website

Additional Resources

Organizational (Divisions, Programs, Services, etc.):

Family Mediators Professional Liability Insurance
Legislative & Public Policy Committee
Membership Committee/Certification & Qualifications Workgroup
Presidential Training Program
Task Force on Spousal and Child Abuse

Informational (Publications, Videos, Seminars, etc.):

Articles in *Mediation News* and *Mediation Quarterly*
The Attorney-Mediator Relationship: Competition vs. Collaboration
    (audio)

Ethical Decision-Making and Values Skills and Knowledge (audio)
Ethics Forum in *Mediation News*
Guidelines for Mediation of Family Disputes Involving Domestic Violence
The Hopeless Case, the Helpless Mediator (audio)
*Managing Legal Issues and Information in Mediation: A Practice Guide
    for Non-Attorney Mediators* (conference session)
Professional Skills and Knowledge (audio)
Protocol on Use of the Academy Name or Membership Designation

Goals and Activities of Organization

The Academy of Family Mediators (AFM) was founded to support the professional and social development of mediation, which it recognizes as a rapidly expanding and maturing profession. Through professional and public education, the AFM serves the needs of mediators and enhances the public's awareness of mediation as a form of alternative dispute resolution.

The AFM develops and refines criteria for appropriate mediator education, training, experience, and ethical practice in cooperation with other state, regional, and national organizations. It also provides a National Referral Service to the public.

The Ethics & Grievance Committee advises members on ethical problems encountered in practice, either informally through individual consultation or by issuing an advisory opinion upon request.

Implementation and Enforcement of Code

All members agree to subscribe to the Standards of Practice as they currently exist and as they are amended. The Board of Directors adopts procedures for reviewing violations of the Standards.

A complaint is initially reviewed by the Executive Director to determine, among other things, whether it arises out of mediation services, as distinct from psychotherapeutic, legal, or other professional services offered by the member. Disputes involving fees are not reviewed unless the conduct alleged also constitutes a violation of a Standard.

If the parties have attempted to mediate a resolution of their disagreement, the Executive Director will accept such a resolution and stop further proceedings, unless the situation involves repeated code violations, gross professional misconduct, or serious harm to a client.

Complaints not resolved by the parties are forwarded to the Ethics & Grievance Committee, which may appoint a Reviewing Panel to conduct a full evaluation of the complaint and of the member's response. Decisions generally may be appealed to an Appeal Board appointed by the AFM President.

Sanctions for violation of the Standards include reprimand, suspension or expulsion from the AFM, or, if the violation relates to fees, restitution. All proceedings are confidential. The names of suspended or expelled members are published to the membership after completion of any appeal.

History and Development of Code

The following version of the Standards was issued in 1983, and updated in 1988 to add sections on training and education, advertising, and interprofessional relations.

Standards of Practice for Family and Divorce Mediation*

I. PREAMBLE

Mediation is a family-centered conflict resolution process in which an impartial third party assists the participants to negotiate a consensual and informed settlement. In mediation, whether private or public, decision-making authority rests with the parties. The role of the mediator includes reducing the obstacles to communication, maximizing the exploration of alternatives, and addressing the needs of those it is agreed are involved or affected.

Mediation is based on principles of problem solving that focus on the needs and interests of the participants; fairness; privacy; self determination; and the best interest of all family members.

These standards are intended to assist and guide public, private, voluntary, and mandatory mediation. It is understood that the manner of implementation and mediator adherence to these standards may be influenced by local law or court rule.

II. INITIATING THE PROCESS

A. **Definition and Description of Mediation.** The mediator shall define mediation and describe the differences and similarities between mediation and other procedures for dispute resolution. In defining the process, the mediator shall delineate it from therapy, counseling, custody evaluation, arbitration, and advocacy.

B. **Identification of Issues.** The mediation shall elicit sufficient information from the participants so that they can mutually define and agree on the issues to be resolved in mediation.

C. **Appropriateness of Mediation.** The mediator shall help the participants evaluate the benefits, risks, and costs of mediation and the alternatives available to them.

D. **Mediator's Duty of Disclosure**
   1. *Biases.* The mediator shall disclose to the participants any biases or strong views relating to the issues to be mediated.
   2. *Training and Experience.* The mediator's education, training, and experience to mediate the issues should be accurately described to the participants.

III. PROCEDURES

The mediator shall reach an understanding with the participants regarding the procedures to be followed in mediation. This includes but is not limited to the practice as to separate meetings between a participant and the mediator, confidentiality, use of legal services, the involvement of additional parties, and conditions under which mediation may be terminated.

A. Mutual Duties and Responsibilities. The mediator and the participants shall agree upon the duties and responsibilities that each is accepting in the mediation process. This may be a written or verbal agreement.

IV. IMPARTIALITY AND NEUTRALITY

A. Impartiality. The mediator is obligated to maintain impartiality toward all participants. Impartiality means freedom from favoritism or bias, either in word or action. Impartiality implies a commitment to aid all participants, as opposed to a single individual, in reaching a mutually satisfactory agreement. Impartiality means that a mediator will not play an adversarial role. The mediator has a responsibility to maintain impartiality while raising questions for the parties to consider as to the fairness, equity, and feasibility of proposed options for settlement.

B. Neutrality. Neutrality refers to the relationship that the mediator has with the disputing parties. If the mediator feels, or any one of the participants states, that the mediator's background or personal experiences would prejudice the mediator's performance, the mediator should withdraw from mediation unless all agree to proceed.

C. Prior Relationships. A mediator's actual or perceived impartiality may be compromised by social or professional relationships with one of the participants at any point in time. The mediator shall not proceed if previous legal or counseling services have been provided to one of the participants. If such services have been provided to both participants, mediation shall not proceed unless the prior relationship has been discussed, the role of the mediator made distinct from the earlier relationship, and the participants given the opportunity to freely choose to proceed.

D. Relationship to Participants. The mediator should be aware that post-mediation professional or social relationships may compromise the mediator's continued availability as a neutral third party.

E. Conflict of Interest. A mediator should disclose any circumstance to the participants that might cause a conflict of interest.

V. COSTS AND FEES

A. Explanation of Fees. The mediator shall explain the fees to be charged for mediation and any related costs and shall agree with the participants on how the fees will be shared and the manner of payment.

B. Reasonable Fees. When setting fees, the mediator shall ensure that they are explicit, fair, reasonable, and commensurate with the service to be performed. Unearned fees should be promptly returned to the clients.

C. Contingent Fees. It is inappropriate for a mediator to charge contingent fees or to base fees on the outcome of mediation.

D. Referrals and Commissions. No commissions, rebates, or similar forms of remuneration shall be given or received for referral of clients for mediation services.

VI. CONFIDENTIALITY AND EXCHANGE OF INFORMATION

A. Confidentiality. Confidentiality relates to the full and open disclosure necessary for the mediation process. A mediator shall foster the confidentiality of the process.

B. Limits of Confidentiality. The mediator shall inform the parties at the initial meeting of limitations on confidentiality, such as statutorily or judicially mandated reporting.

C. Appearing in Court. The mediator shall inform the parties of circumstances under which mediators may be compelled to testify in court.

D. Consequences of Disclosure of Facts Between Parties. The mediator shall discuss with the participants the potential consequences of their disclosure of facts to each other during the mediation process.

E. Release of Information. The mediator shall obtain the consent of the participants prior to releasing information to others. The mediator shall maintain confidentiality and render anonymous all identifying information when materials are used for research or training purposes.

F. Caucus. The mediator shall discuss policy regarding confidentiality for individual caucuses. In the event that a mediator, on consent of the participants, speaks privately with any person not represented in mediation, including children, the mediator shall define how information received will be used.

G. Storage and Disposal of Records. The mediator shall maintain confidentiality in the storage and disposal of records.

H. Full Disclosure. The mediator shall require disclosure of all relevant information in the mediation process, as would reasonably occur in the judicial discovery process.

VII. SELF-DETERMINATION

A. Responsibilities of the Participants and the Mediator. The primary responsibility for the resolution of a dispute rests with the participants. The mediator's obligation is to assist the disputants in reaching an informed and voluntary settlement. At no time shall a mediator coerce a participant into agreement or make a substantive decision for any participant.

B. Responsibility to Third Parties. The mediator has a responsibility to promote the participants' consideration of the interests of children and other persons affected by the agreement. The mediator also has a duty to assist parents to examine, apart from their own desires, the separate and individual needs of such people. The participants shall be encouraged to seek outside professional consultation when appropriate or when they are otherwise unable to agree on the needs of any individual affected by the agreement.

VIII. PROFESSIONAL ADVICE

A. Independent Advice and Information. The mediator shall encourage and assist the participants to obtain independent expert information and advice when such information is needed to reach an informed agreement or to protect the rights of a participant.

B. Providing Information. A mediator shall give information only in those areas where qualified by training or experience.

C. Independent Legal Counsel. When the mediation may affect legal rights or obligations, the mediator shall advise the participants to seek independent legal counsel prior to resolving the issues and in conjunction with formalizing an agreement.

IX. PARTIES' ABILITY TO NEGOTIATE

The mediator shall ensure that each participant has had an opportunity to understand the implications and ramifications of available options. In the event a participant needs either additional information or assistance in order for the negotiations to proceed in a fair and orderly manner or for an agreement to be reached, the mediator shall refer the individual to appropriate resources.

A. **Procedural Factors.** The mediator has a duty to ensure balanced negotiations and should not permit manipulative or intimidating negotiation techniques.

B. **Psychological Factors.** The mediator shall explore whether the participants are capable of participating in informed negotiations. The mediator may postpone mediation and refer the parties to appropriate resources if necessary.

X. CONCLUDING MEDIATION

A. **Full Agreement.** The mediator shall discuss with the participants the process for formalization and implementation of the agreement.

B. **Partial Agreement.** When the participants reach a partial agreement, the mediator shall discuss with them procedures available to resolve the remaining issues. The mediator shall inform the participants of their right to withdraw from mediation at any time and for any reason.

C. **Termination by Participants.** The mediator shall inform the participants of their right to withdraw from mediation at any time and for any reason.

D. **Termination by Mediator.** If the mediator believes that participants are unable or unwilling to participate meaningfully in the process or that a reasonable agreement is unlikely, the mediator may suspend or terminate mediation and should encourage the parties to seek appropriate professional help.

E. **Impasse.** If the participants reach a final impasse, the mediator should not prolong unproductive discussions that would result in emotional and monetary costs to the participants.

XI. TRAINING AND EDUCATION

A. **Training.** A mediator shall acquire substantive knowledge and procedural skill in the specialized area of practice. This may include but is not limited to family and human development, family law, divorce procedures, family finances, community resources, the mediation process, and professional ethics.

B. **Continuing Education.** A mediator shall participate in continuing education and be personally responsible for ongoing professional growth. A mediator is encouraged to join with other mediators and members of related professions to promote mutual professional development.

XII. ADVERTISING

A mediator shall make only accurate statements about the mediation process, its costs and benefits, and the mediator's qualifications.

XIII. RELATIONSHIP WITH OTHER PROFESSIONALS

A. **The Responsibility of the Mediator Toward Other Mediators/Relationship with Other Mediators.** A mediator should not mediate any dispute that is being mediated by another mediator without first endeavoring to consult with the person or persons conducting the mediation.

B. Co-mediation. In those situations where more than one mediator is participating in a particular case, each mediator has a responsibility to keep the others informed of developments essential to a cooperative effort.

C. Relationships with Other Professionals. A mediator should respect the complementary relationship between mediation and legal, mental health, and other social services and should promote cooperation with other professionals.

XIV. ADVANCEMENT OF MEDIATION

A. Mediation Service. A mediator is encouraged to provide some mediation service in the community for nominal or no fee.

B. Promotion of Mediation. A mediator shall promote the advancement of mediation by encouraging and participating in research, publishing, or other forms of professional and public education.

Organization

AMERICAN ARBITRATION ASSOCIATION

Headquarters:
335 Madison Avenue
New York, NY 10017
Telephone: (212) 716-5800
E-mail: usadrsrv@arb.com
Website: http://www.adr.org

Date founded: 1926
  Formed by a merger of the Arbitration Society of America and the
  Arbitration Foundation
Membership: approximately 9,000 businesses, unions, trade and educational associations, law firms, arbitrators, and individuals who support
  voluntary dispute settlement, in 38 regional offices; approximately
  18,000 neutrals listed on National Roster of Arbitrators and Mediators;
  53 cooperative agreements with arbitral institutions in 38 other nations

Codes of Ethics

Official name: *Code of Ethics for Arbitrators in Commercial Disputes*
History: Adopted 1977; updated 1993, 1997
Authority: Joint Committee consisting of Special Committees of AAA
  and American Bar Association (ABA)

Official name: *Code of Professional Responsibility for Arbitrators of
  Labor-Management Disputes*
History: Adopted 1975; amended 1985
Authority: Committee of AAA, National Academy of Arbitrators, and
  Federal Mediation and Conciliation Service; Joint Steering Committee

559

Official name: *Model Standards of Conduct for Mediators*
History: Prepared 1992-94
Authority: Joint Committee of AAA, American Bar Association, and
 Society of Professionals in Dispute Resolution; ABA Litigation Sec-
 tion; ABA Dispute Resolution Section

Codes are available on Website

Additional Resources

Organizational (Divisions, Programs, Services, etc.):

ADR Systems Assessment Program (advice on program design, clause
 construction, training)
Center for Educational Outreach (external education and training
 programs)
Commission on Health Care Dispute Resolution (with American Bar
 Association and American Medical Association)
Dispute Avoidance and Resolution Task Force
Focus Areas: Commercial; Construction; Developing a Corporate ADR
 Policy; Federal and State Statutes; Insurance; International; Labor
 & Employment
National Consumer Disputes Advisory Committee
National Roster of Arbitrators and Mediators (individuals available to hear
 and decide cases)
Neutrals' Retreat (annual conference)
President's Panel of Mediators

Informational (Publications, Videos, Seminars, etc.):

Articles in *ADR Currents, Dispute Resolution Journal, Dispute Resolution
 Times,* and *Punch List*
*A Due Process Protocol for Mediation and Arbitration of Statutory
 Disputes Arising Out of the Employment Relationship*
A Guide for Construction Industry Arbitrators
A Guide to Mediation and Arbitration for Business People
A Handbook for Grievance Arbitration: Procedural and Ethical Issues
ADR & the Law
Beginner's Guide to ADR
Bibliographies and Reading Lists
*Building Success into the 21st Century: A Guide to Partnering in the
 Construction Industry*
Commercial/Business Rules and Procedures
*Consumer Due Process Protocol: Statement of Principles of the National
 Consumer Disputes Advisory Committee*
Dispute Resolution Program for Insurance Claims: A Procedural Guide
Drafting Dispute Resolution Clauses: A Practical Guide

Due Process Protocol for Mediation and Arbitration of Consumer Disputes
Ethics and Disclosure (conference session)
Guide for Commercial Arbitrators
Guide for Employment Arbitrators
Labor and Employment Rules and Procedures
Labor Arbitration: Procedures and Techniques
Labor Arbitration: What You Need to Know
Labor Arbitration in America: The Profession and Practice
NAA Formal Advisory Opinions
*Qualification Criteria for Admittance to the AAA National Roster of
    Arbitrators and Mediators*
Resolving Employment Disputes: A Practical Guide

Goals and Activities of Organization

The American Arbitration Association (AAA) is a public service organization dedicated to the resolution of disputes through voluntary methods. As a leading advocate of alternative dispute resolution (ADR), it offers a broad range of services, including the administration of arbitration, mediation, mini-trials, elections, and other settlement procedures, as alternatives to litigation. It serves as a center for education and training, issues specialized publications, conducts research, maintains a library, and offers consultation on special problems. The AAA also assists in the design and implementation of specialized ADR systems for corporations, government agencies, law firms, courts, and other institutions.

In addition, the AAA develops standard clauses that many businesses and unions insert in their contractual agreements, and formulates specialized rules and procedures for settling disputes involving labor-management relations, business, construction, insurance, international trade, real estate valuation, and family relationships.

The National Roster of Arbitrators and Mediators is a group of 18,000 impartial experts available to hear and resolve cases, who demonstrate high levels of knowledge, ability, and integrity. Their performance is monitored and evaluated on an ongoing basis in several areas, including reputation and dedication to upholding AAA ethical standards.

The AAA has had a Code of Ethics for Arbitrators since 1946.

Code of Ethics for Arbitrators in Commercial Disputes

Implementation and Enforcement of Code

The Code of Ethics for Arbitrators in Commercial Disputes is intended to provide guidelines to arbitrators but does not form any part of the arbitration rules of the AAA or any other organization. It is presented as a public service, to provide guidance in all types of commercial arbitration. Its use is not limited to arbitrations administered by the AAA or to cases in which the arbitrators are lawyers.

The ethical principles embodied in the Code are implemented through training seminars, guides, and videos.

History and Development of Code

The Code was prepared in 1977 by a Joint Committee consisting of a Special Committee of the AAA and a Special Committee of the American Bar Association (ABA). It has been approved and recommended by both organizations.

An updated version with minor changes was issued in August 1993.

In August 1998, the Arbitration Committee of the ABA Section of Dispute Resolution proposed revisions to update the Code.

Code of Professional Responsibility for Arbitrators of Labor-Management Disputes

Implementation and Enforcement of Code

The Code of Professional Responsibility for Arbitrators of Labor-Management Disputes leaves the gravity of alleged misconduct, and the extent to which ethical standards have been violated, to be assessed in the light of the facts and circumstances of each particular case.

The AAA, National Academy of Arbitrators (NAA), and the Federal Mediation and Conciliation Service (FMCS) apply the Code to the arbitrators on their rosters in cases handled under their individual appointment or referral procedures. The three organizations stopped short of developing an enforcement mechanism in the Code itself.

The AAA deals with violations on an ad hoc basis, without formal procedures. An unethical arbitrator is usually removed from the roster.

The NAA Committee on Professional Responsibility and Grievances has specific procedures, restricted to its members, for handling complaints, interpreting and revising the Code, and providing training on ethical issues. The NAA Committee also issues Advisory Opinions on the Code.

The FMCS considers knowledge and observance of the Code a qualification of its arbitrators and considers it as protection for the parties. It maintains a log of actionable complaints against each arbitrator.

History and Development of Code

The first Code of Ethics and Procedural Standards for Labor-Management Arbitration was approved in 1951 by a Committee of the AAA, by the NAA, and by representatives of the FMCS.

Revision of the 1951 document was initiated in 1972; the resulting Code was adopted in 1975, and last amended in May 1985.

The NAA is an organization of about approximately 700 arbitrators, lawyers, and educators interested in the resolution of labor-management disputes. The FMCS is an independent agency of the federal government that provides mediators to parties in labor-management disputes.

Model Standards of Conduct for Mediators

Implementation and Enforcement of Code

The Model Standards of Conduct for Mediators are presented as a general framework for the practice of all types of mediation, offered as a step in the development of the field and a tool to assist practitioners. They serve an educational and assistive function for individuals, organizations, and institutions involved in mediation.

The Standards are to perform three major functions: as a guide for the conduct of mediators; to inform the mediating parties; and to promote public confidence in mediation as a process for resolving disputes.

In some cases the application of the Standards may be affected by laws or contractual agreements.

History and Development of Code

The Standards draw on existing codes of conduct for mediators, while taking into account issues and problems that have surfaced in mediation practice.

The document was prepared from 1992 through 1994 by a joint committee of delegates from the AAA, ABA, and the Society of Professionals in Dispute Resolution (SPIDR). It was approved by AAA, SPIDR, and the ABA's Litigation and Dispute Resolution Sections.

Code of Ethics for Arbitrators in Commercial Disputes[*]

PREAMBLE

The use of commercial arbitration to resolve a wide variety of disputes has grown extensively and forms a significant part of the system of justice on which our society relies for fair determination of legal rights. Persons who act as commercial arbitrators therefore undertake serious responsibilities to the public as well as to the parties. Those responsibilities include important ethical obligations.

Few cases of unethical behavior by commercial arbitrators have arisen. Nevertheless, the American Bar Association and the American Arbitration Association believe that it is in the public interest to set forth generally accepted standards of ethical conduct for guidance of arbitrators and parties in commercial disputes. By establishing this Code, the sponsors hope to contribute to the maintenance of high standards and continued confidence in the process of arbitration.

There are many different types of commercial arbitration. Some cases are conducted under arbitration rules established by various organizations and trade associations, while others are conducted without such rules. Although most cases are arbitrated pursuant to voluntary agreement of the parties, certain types of dispute are submitted to arbitration by reason of particular laws. This Code is intended to apply to all such proceedings in which disputes or claims are submitted for decision to one or more arbitrators appointed in a manner provided by an agreement of the parties, by applicable arbitration rules, or by law. In all such cases, the persons who have the power to decide should observe fundamental standards of ethical conduct. In this Code all such persons are called "arbitrators" although, in some types of case, they might be called "umpires" or have some other title.

Various aspects of the conduct of arbitrators, including some matters covered by this Code, may be governed by agreements of the parties, by arbitration rules to which the parties have agreed, or by applicable law. This Code does not take the place of or supersede such agreements, rules, or laws and does not establish new or additional grounds for judicial review of arbitration awards.

While this Code is intended to provide ethical guidelines in many types of arbitration, it does not form a part of the arbitration rules of the American Arbitration Association or of any other organization, nor is it intended to apply to mediation or conciliation. Labor arbitration is governed by the Code of Professional Responsibility for Arbitrators of Labor-Management Disputes, not by this Code.

Arbitrators, like judges, have the power to decide cases. However, unlike full-time judges, arbitrators are usually engaged in other occupations before, during, and after the time that they serve as arbitrators. Often, arbitrators are purposely chosen from the same trade or industry as the parties in order to bring special knowledge to the task of deciding. This Code recognizes these fundamental differences between arbitrators and judges.

---

[*]Prepared in 1977 by a joint committee consisting of a special committee of the American Arbitration Association and a special committee of the American Bar Association. It has been approved and recommended by both organizations. Rules, forms, procedures and guides are subject to periodic change and updating. To ensure that you have the most current information, see the AAA World Wide Web home page at **http://www.adr.org**
Reprinted with permission of the American Arbitration Association.

In some types of arbitration, there are three or more arbitrators. In these cases, it is sometimes the practice for each party, acting alone, to appoint one arbitrator and for the other arbitrators to be designated by those two, by the parties, or by an independent institution or individual. The sponsors of this Code believe that it is preferable for parties to agree that all arbitrators should comply with the same ethical standards. However, it is recognized that there is a long-established practice in some types of arbitration for the arbitrators who are appointed by one party, acting alone, to be governed by special ethical considerations. Those special considerations are set forth in the last section of the Code, headed "Ethical Considerations Relating to Arbitrators Appointed By One Party."

Although this Code is sponsored by the American Arbitration Association and the American Bar Association, its use is not limited to arbitrations administered by the AAA or to cases in which the arbitrators are lawyers. Rather, it is presented as a public service to provide guidance in all types of commercial arbitration.

Canon I

AN ARBITRATOR SHOULD UPHOLD THE INTEGRITY AND FAIRNESS OF THE ARBITRATION PROCESS

A. Fair and just processes for resolving disputes are indispensable in our society. Commercial arbitration is an important method for deciding many types of disputes. In order for commercial arbitration to be effective, there must be broad public confidence in the integrity and fairness of the process. Therefore, an arbitrator has a responsibility not only to the parties but also the process of arbitration itself, and must observe high standards of conduct so that the integrity and fairness of the process will be preserved. Accordingly, an arbitrator should recognize a responsibility to the public, to the parties whose rights will be decided, and to all other participants in the proceeding. The provisions of this Code should be construed and applied to further these objectives.

B. It is inconsistent with the integrity of the arbitration process for persons to solicit appointment for themselves. However, a person may indicate a general willingness to serve as an arbitrator.

C. Persons should accept appointment as arbitrators only if they believe that they can be available to conduct the arbitration promptly.

D. After accepting appointment and while serving as an arbitrator, a person should avoid entering into any financial, business, professional, family or social relationship, or acquiring any financial or personal interest, which is likely to affect impartiality or which might reasonably create the appearance of partiality or bias. For a reasonable period of time after the decision of a case, persons who have served as arbitrators should avoid entering into any such relationship, or acquiring any such interest, in circumstances which might reasonably create the appearance that they had been influenced in the arbitration by the anticipation or expectation of the relationship or interest.

E. Arbitrators should conduct themselves in a way that is fair to all parties and should not be swayed by outside pressure, by public clamor, by fear of criticism or by self-interest.

F. When an arbitrator's authority is derived from an agreement of the parties, the arbitrator should neither exceed that authority nor do less than is required to exercise that authority completely. Where the agreement of the parties sets forth procedures to be followed in conducting the arbitration or refers to rules to be followed, it is the obligation of the arbitrator to comply with such procedures or rules.

G. An arbitrator should make all reasonable efforts to prevent delaying tactics, harassment of parties or other participants, or other abuse or disruption of the arbitration process.

H. The ethical obligations of an arbitrator begin upon acceptance of the appointment and continue throughout all stages of the proceeding. In addition, wherever specifically set forth in this Code, certain ethical obligations begin as soon as a person is requested to serve as an arbitrator and certain ethical obligations continue even after the decision in the case has been given to the parties.

Canon II

AN ARBITRATOR SHOULD DISCLOSE ANY INTEREST OR RELATIONSHIP LIKELY TO AFFECT IMPARTIALITY OR WHICH MIGHT CREATE AN APPEARANCE OF PARTIALITY OR BIAS

Introductory Note

This Code reflects the prevailing principle that arbitrators should disclose the existence of any interests or relationships that are likely to affect their impartiality or that might reasonably create an appearance that they are biased against one party or favorable to another. These provisions of the Code are intended to be applied realistically so that the burden of detailed disclosure does not become so great that it is impractical for persons in the business world to be arbitrators, thereby depriving parties of the services of those who might be best informed and qualified to decide particular types of cases.*

This Code does not limit the freedom of parties to agree on whomever they choose as an arbitrator. When parties, with knowledge of a person's interests and relationships, nevertheless desire that individual to serve as an arbitrator, that person may properly serve.

Disclosure

A. Persons who are requested to serve as arbitrators should, before accepting, disclose

---

*In applying the provisions of this code relating to disclosure, it might be helpful to recall the words of the concurring opinion, in a case decided by the US Supreme Court, that arbitrators "should err on the side of disclosure" because "it is better that the relationship be disclosed at the outset when the parties are free to reject the arbitrator or accept him with knowledge of the relationship." At the same time, it must be recognized that "an arbitrator's business relationships may be diverse indeed, involving more or less remote commercial connections with great numbers of people." Accordingly, an arbitrator "cannot be expected to provide the parties with his complete and unexpurgated business biography," nor is an arbitrator called on to disclose interests or relationships that are merely "trivial" (a concurring opinion in *Commonwealth Coatings Corp. v. Continental Casualty Co.*, 393 US 145, 151–152, 1968).

(1) any direct or indirect financial or personal interest in the outcome of the arbitration;

(2) any existing or past financial, business, professional, family or social relationships which are likely to affect impartiality or which might reasonably create an appearance of partiality or bias. Persons requested to serve as arbitrators should disclose any such relationships which they personally have with any party or its lawyer, or with any individual whom they have been told will be a witness. They should also disclose any such relationships involving members of their families or their current employers, partners or business associates.

B. Persons who are requested to accept appointment as arbitrators should make a reasonable effort to inform themselves of any interests or relationships described in the preceding paragraph A.

C. The obligation to disclose interests or relationships described in the preceding paragraph A is a continuing duty which requires a person who accepts appointment as an arbitrator to disclose, at any stage of the arbitration, any such interests or relationships which may arise, or which are recalled or discovered.

D. Disclosure should be made to all parties unless other procedures for disclosure are provided in the rules or practices of an institution which is administering the arbitration. Where more than one arbitrator has been appointed, each should inform the others of the interests and relationships which have been disclosed.

E. In the event that an arbitrator is requested by all parties to withdraw, the arbitrator should do so. In the event that an arbitrator is requested to withdraw by less than all of the parties because of alleged partiality or bias, the arbitrator should withdraw unless either of the following circumstances exists.

(1) If an agreement of the parties, or arbitration rules agreed to by the parties, establishes procedures for determining challenges to arbitrators, then those procedures should be followed; or,

(2) if the arbitrator, after carefully considering the matter, determines that the reason for the challenge is not substantial, and that he or she can nevertheless act and decide the case impartially and fairly, and that withdrawal would cause unfair delay or expense to another party or would be contrary to the ends of justice.

Canon III

AN ARBITRATOR IN COMMUNICATING WITH THE PARTIES SHOULD AVOID IMPROPRIETY OR THE APPEARANCE OF IMPROPRIETY

A. If an agreement of the parties or applicable arbitration rules referred to in that agreement, establishes the manner or content of communications between the arbitrator and the parties, the arbitrator should follow those procedures notwithstanding any contrary provisions of the following paragraphs B and C.

B. Unless otherwise provided in applicable arbitration rules or in an agreement of the parties, arbitrators should not discuss a case with any party in the absence of each other party, except in any of the following circumstances.

(1) Discussions may be had with a party concerning such matters as setting the time and place of hearings or making other arrangements for the conduct of the proceedings. However, the arbitrator should promptly inform each other party of the discussion and should not make any final determination concerning the matter discussed before giving each absent party an opportunity to express its views.

(2) If a party fails to be present at a hearing after having been given due notice, the arbitrator may discuss the case with any party who is present.

(3) If all parties request or consent to it, such discussion may take place.

C. Unless otherwise provided in applicable arbitration rules or in an agreement of the parties, whenever an arbitrator communicates in writing with one party, the arbitrator should at the same time send a copy of the communication to each other party. Whenever the arbitrator receives any written communication concerning the case from one party which has not already been sent to each other party, the arbitrator should do so.

Canon IV

AN ARBITRATOR SHOULD CONDUCT THE PROCEEDINGS FAIRLY AND DILIGENTLY

A. An arbitrator should conduct the proceedings in an evenhanded manner and treat all parties with equality and fairness at all stages of the proceedings.

B. An arbitrator should perform duties diligently and conclude the case as promptly as the circumstances reasonably permit.

C. An arbitrator should be patient and courteous to the parties, to their lawyers and to the witnesses and should encourage similar conduct by all participants in the proceedings.

D. Unless otherwise agreed by the parties or provided in arbitration rules agreed to by the parties, an arbitrator should accord to all parties the right to appear in person and to be heard after due notice of the time and place of hearing.

E. An arbitrator should not deny any party the opportunity to be represented by counsel.

F. If a party fails to appear after due notice, an arbitrator should proceed with the arbitration when authorized to do so by the agreement of the parties, the rules agreed to by the parties or by law. However, an arbitrator should do so only after receiving assurance that notice has been given to the absent party.

G. When an arbitrator determines that more information than has been presented by the parties is required to decide the case, it is not improper for the arbitrator to ask questions, call witnesses, and request documents or other evidence.

H. It is not improper for an arbitrator to suggest to the parties that they discuss the possibility of settlement of the case. However, an arbitrator should not be present or otherwise participate in the settlement discussions unless requested to do so by all parties. An arbitrator should not exert pressure on any party to settle.

I. Nothing in this Code is intended to prevent a person from acting as a mediator or conciliator of a dispute in which he or she has been appointed as arbitrator, if requested to do so by all parties or where authorized or required to do so by applicable laws or rules.

J. When there is more than one arbitrator, the arbitrators should afford each other the full opportunity to participate in all aspects of the proceedings.

Canon V

AN ARBITRATOR SHOULD MAKE DECISIONS IN A JUST, INDEPENDENT AND DELIBERATE MANNER

A. An arbitrator should, after careful deliberation, decide all issues submitted for determination. An arbitrator should decide no other issues.

B. An arbitrator should decide all matters justly, exercising independent judgment, and should not permit outside pressure to affect the decision.

C. An arbitrator should not delegate the duty to decide to any other person.

D. In the event that all parties agree upon a settlement of issues in dispute and request an arbitrator to embody that agreement in an award, an arbitrator may do so, but is not required to do so unless satisfied with the propriety or the terms of settlement. Whenever an arbitrator embodies a settlement by the parties in an award, the arbitrator should state in the award that it is based on an agreement of the parties.

Canon VI

AN ARBITRATOR SHOULD BE FAITHFUL TO THE RELATIONSHIP OF TRUST AND CONFIDENTIALITY INHERENT IN THAT OFFICE

A. An arbitrator is in a relationship of trust to the parties and should not, at any time, use confidential information acquired during the arbitration proceeding to gain personal advantage or advantage for others, or to affect adversely the interest of another.

B. Unless otherwise agreed by the parties, or required by applicable rules or law, an arbitrator should keep confidential all matters relating to the arbitration proceedings and decision.

C. It is not proper at any time for an arbitrator to inform anyone of the decision in advance of the time it is given to all parties. In a case in which there is more than one arbitrator, it is not proper at any time for an arbitrator to inform anyone concerning the deliberations of the arbitrators. After an arbitration award has been made, it is not proper for an arbitrator to assist in postarbitral proceedings, except as is required by law.

D. In many types of arbitration it is customary practice for the arbitrators to serve without pay. However, in some types of cases it is customary for arbitrators to receive compensation for their services and reimbursement for their expenses. In cases in which any such payments are to be made, all persons who are requested to serve, or who are serving as arbitrators, should be governed by the same high standards of integrity and fairness as apply to their other activities in the case.

Accordingly, such persons should scrupulously avoid bargaining with parties over the amount of payments or engaging in any communications concerning payments which would create an appearance of coercion or other impropriety. In the absence of governing provisions in the agreement of the parties or in rules agreed to by the parties or in applicable law, certain parties, relating to payments are generally recognized as being preferable in order to preserve the integrity and fairness of the arbitration process. These practices include the following.

(1) It is preferable that before the arbitrator finally accepts appointment the basis of payment be established and that all parties be informed thereof in writing.

(2) In cases conducted under the rules or administration of an institution that is available to assist in making arrangements for payments, the payments should be arranged by the institution to avoid the necessity for communication by the arbitrators directly with the parties concerning the subject.

(3) In cases where no institution is available to assist in making arrangement for payments, it is preferable that any discussions with arbitrators concerning payments should take place in the presence of all parties.

Canon VII

ETHICAL CONSIDERATIONS RELATING TO ARBITRATORS APPOINTED BY ONE PARTY

Introductory Note

In some types of arbitration in which there are three arbitrators, it is customary for each party, acting alone, to appoint one arbitrator. The third arbitrator is then appointed by agreement either of the parties or of the two arbitrators, or, failing such agreement, by an independent institution or individual. In some of these types of arbitration, all three arbitrators are customarily considered to be neutral and are expected to observe the same standards of ethical conduct. However, there are also many types of tripartite arbitration in which it has been the practice that the two arbitrators appointed by the parties are not considered to be neutral and are expected to observe many—but not all—of the same ethical standards as the neutral third arbitrator. For the purposes of this Code, an arbitrator appointed by one party who is not expected to observe all of the same standards as the third arbitrator is called a "nonneutral arbitrator." This Canon VII describes the ethical obligations that nonneutral party-appointed arbitrators should observe and those that are not applicable to them.

In all arbitrations in which there are two or more party-appointed arbitrators, it is important for everyone concerned to know from the start whether the party-appointed arbitrators are expected to be neutrals or nonneutrals. In such arbitrations, the two party-appointed arbitrators should be considered nonneutrals unless both parties inform the arbitrators that all three arbitrators are to be neutral or unless the contract, the applicable arbitration rules, or any governing law requires that all three arbitrators be neutral.

It should be noted that, in cases conducted outside the United States, the applicable law might require that all arbitrators be neutral. Accordingly, in such cases the governing law should be considered before applying any of the following provisions relating to nonneutral party-appointed arbitrators.

A. Obligations under Canon I

Nonneutral party-appointed arbitrators should observe all of the obligations of Canon I to uphold the integrity and fairness of the arbitration process, subject only to the following provisions.

(1) Nonneutral arbitrators may be predisposed toward the party who appointed them but in all other respects are obligated to act in good faith and with integrity and fairness. For example, nonneutral arbitrators should not engage in delaying tactics or harassment of any party or witness and should not knowingly make untrue or misleading statements to the other arbitrators.

(2) The provisions of Canon I.D relating to relationships and interests are not applicable to nonneutral arbitrators.

B. Obligations under Canon II

Nonneutral party-appointed arbitrators should disclose to all parties, and to the other arbitrators, all interests and relationships which Canon II requires be disclosed. Disclosure as required by Canon II is for the benefit not only of the party who appointed the nonneutral arbitrator, but also for the benefit of the other parties and arbitrators so that they may know of any bias which may exist or appear to exist. However, this obligation is subject to the following provisions.

(1) Disclosure by nonneutral arbitrators should be sufficient to describe the general nature and scope of any interest or relationship, but need not include as detailed information as is expected from persons appointed as neutral arbitrators.

(2) Nonneutral arbitrators are not obliged to withdraw if requested to do so by the party who did not appoint them, notwithstanding the provisions of Canon II.E.

C. Obligations under Canon III

Nonneutral party-appointed arbitrators should observe all of the obligations of Canon III concerning communications with the parties, subject only to the following provisions.

(1) In an arbitration in which the two party-appointed arbitrators are expected to appoint the third arbitrator, nonneutral arbitrators may consult with the party who appointed them concerning the acceptability of persons under consideration for appointment as the third arbitrator.

(2) Nonneutral arbitrators may communicate with the party who appointed them concerning any other aspect of the case, provided they first inform the other arbitrators and the parties that they intend to do so. If such communication occurred prior to the time the person was appointed as arbitrator, or prior to the first hearing or other meeting of the parties with the arbitrators, the nonneutral arbitrator should, at the first hearing or meeting, disclose the fact that such communication has taken place. In complying with the provisions of this paragraph, it is sufficient that there be disclosure of the fact that such communication has occurred without disclosing the content of the communication. It is also sufficient to disclose

at any time the intention to follow the procedure of having such communications in the future and there is no requirement thereafter that there be disclosure before each separate occasion on which such a communication occurs.

(3) When nonneutral arbitrators communicate in writing with the party who appointed them concerning any matter as to which communication is permitted under this Code, they are not required to send copies of any such written communication to any other party or arbitrator.

D. Obligations under Canon IV

Nonneutral party-appointed arbitrators should observe all of the obligations of Canon IV to conduct the proceedings fairly and diligently.

E. Obligations under Canon V

Nonneutral party-appointed arbitrators should observe all of the obligations of Canon V concerning making decisions, subject only to the following provision.

(1) Nonneutral arbitrators are permitted to be predisposed toward deciding in favor of the party who appointed them.

F. Obligations under Canon VI

Nonneutral party-appointed arbitrators should observe all of the obligations of Canon VI to be faithful to the relationship of trust inherent in the office of arbitrator, subject only to the following provision.

(1) Nonneutral arbitrators are not subject to the provisions of Canon VI.D with respect to any payments by the party who appointed them.

Code of Professional Responsibility for Arbitrators of Labor-Management Disputes*

* * *

PREAMBLE

Background

Voluntary arbitration rests upon the mutual desire of management and labor in each collective bargaining relationship to develop procedures for dispute settlement which meet their own particular needs and obligations. No two voluntary systems, therefore, are likely to be identical in practice. Words used to describe arbitrators (Arbitrator, Umpire, Impartial Chairman, Chairman of Arbitration Board, etc.) may suggest typical approaches but actual differences within any general type of arrangement may be as great as distinctions often made among the several types.

Some arbitration and related procedures, however, are not the product of voluntary agreement. These procedures, primarily but not exclusively applicable in the public sector, sometimes utilize other third party titles (Fact Finder, Impasse Panel, Board of Inquiry, etc.). These procedures range all the way from arbitration prescribed by statute to arrangements substantially indistinguishable from voluntary procedures.

The standards of professional responsibility set forth in this Code are designed to guide the impartial third party serving in these diverse labor-management relationships.

Scope of Code

This Code is a privately developed set of standards of professional behavior. It applies to voluntary arbitration of labor-management grievance disputes and of disputes concerning new or revised contract terms. Both "ad hoc" and "permanent" varieties of voluntary arbitration, private and public sector, are included. To the extent relevant in any specific case, it also applies to advisory arbitration, impasse resolution panels, arbitration prescribed by statutes, fact-finding, and other special procedures.

The word "arbitrator," as used hereinafter in the Code, is intended to apply to any impartial person, irrespective of specific title, who serves in a labor-management dispute procedure in which there is conferred authority to decide issues or to make formal recommendations.

The Code is not designed to apply to mediation or conciliation, as distinguished from arbitration, nor to other procedures in which the third party is not authorized in advance to make decisions or recommendations. It does not apply to partisan representatives on tripartite boards. It does not apply to commercial arbitration or to other uses of arbitration outside the labor-management dispute area.

---

*National Academy of Arbitrators, American Arbitration Association, and Federal Mediation and Conciliation Service. As amended and in effect May 29, 1985. Reprinted with permission of the American Arbitration Association. The Foreword has been omitted.

Format of Code

Bold Face type, sometimes including explanatory material, is used to set forth general principles. *Italics* are used for amplification of general principles. Ordinary type is used primarily for illustrative or explanatory comment.

Application of Code

Faithful adherence by an arbitrator to this Code is basic to professional responsibility.

The National Academy of Arbitrators will expect its members to be governed in their professional conduct by this Code and stands ready, through its Committee on Ethics and Grievances, to advise its members as to the Code's interpretation. The American Arbitration Association and the Federal Mediation and Conciliation Service will apply the Code to the arbitrators on their rosters in cases handled under their respective appointment or referral procedures. Other arbitrators and administrative agencies may, of course, voluntarily adopt the Code and be governed by it.

In interpreting the Code and applying it to charges of professional misconduct, under existing or revised procedures of the National Academy of Arbitrators and of the administrative agencies, it should be recognized that while some of its standards express ethical principles basic to the arbitration profession, others rest less on ethics than on considerations of good practice. Experience has shown the difficulty of drawing rigid lines of distinction between ethics and good practice and this Code does not attempt to do so. Rather, it leaves the gravity of alleged misconduct and the extent to which ethical standards have been violated to be assessed in the light of the facts and circumstances of each particular case.

1
ARBITRATOR'S QUALIFICATIONS AND RESPONSIBILITIES TO THE PROFESSION

A. General Qualifications

1. Essential personal qualifications of an arbitrator include honesty, integrity, impartiality and general competence in labor relations matters.

An arbitrator must demonstrate ability to exercise these personal qualities faithfully and with good judgment, both in procedural matters and in substantive decisions.

a. Selection by mutual agreement of the parties or direct designation by an administrative agency are the effective methods of appraisal of this combination of an individual's potential and performance, rather than the fact of placement on a roster of an administrative agency or membership in a professional association of arbitrators.

2. An arbitrator must be as ready to rule for one party as for the other on each issue, either in a single case or in a group of cases. Compromise by an arbitrator for the sake of attempting to achieve personal acceptability is unprofessional.

B. Qualifications for Special Cases

1. An arbitrator must decline appointment, withdraw, or request technical assistance when he or she decides that a case is beyond his or her competence.

a. An arbitrator may be qualified generally but not for specialized assignments. Some types of incentive, work standard, job evaluation, welfare program, pension, or insurance cases may require specialized knowledge, experience or competence. Arbitration of contract terms also may require distinctive background and experience.

b. Effective appraisal by an administrative agency or by an arbitrator of the need for special qualifications requires that both parties make known the special nature of the case prior to appointment of the arbitrator.

C. Responsibilities to the Profession

1. An arbitrator must uphold the dignity and integrity of the office and endeavor to provide effective service to the parties.

a. To this end, an arbitrator should keep current with principles, practices and developments that are relevant to his or her own field of arbitration practice.

2. An experienced arbitrator should cooperate in the training of new arbitrators.

3. An arbitrator must not advertise or solicit arbitration assignments.

a. It is a matter of personal preference whether an arbitrator includes "Labor Arbitrator" or similar notation on letterheads, cards, or announcements. *It is inappropriate, however, to include memberships or offices held in professional societies or listings on rosters of administrative agencies.*

b. *Information provided for published biographical sketches, as well as that supplied to administrative agencies, must be accurate.* Such information may include membership in professional organizations (including reference to significant offices held), and listings on rosters of administrative agencies.

2
RESPONSIBILITIES TO THE PARTIES

A. Recognition of Diversity in Arbitration Arrangements

1. An arbitrator should conscientiously endeavor to understand and observe, to the extent consistent with professional responsibility, the significant principles governing each arbitration system in which he or she serves.

a. Recognition of special features of a particular arbitration arrangement can be essential with respect to procedural matters and may influence other aspects of the arbitration process.

2. Such understanding does not relieve an arbitrator from a corollary responsibility to seek to discern and refuse to lend approval or consent to any collusive attempt by the parties to use arbitration for an improper purpose.

B. Required Disclosures

1. Before accepting an appointment, an arbitrator must disclose directly or through the administrative agency involved, any current or past managerial, representational, or consultative relationship with any company or union involved in a proceeding in which he or she is being considered for appointment or has been tentatively designated to serve. Disclosure must also be made of any pertinent pecuniary interest.

a. The duty to disclose includes membership on a Board of Directors, full-time or part-time service as a representative or advocate, consultation work for a fee, current stock or bond ownership (other than mutual fund shares or appropriate trust arrangements) or any other pertinent form of managerial, financial or immediate family interest in the company or union involved.

2. When an arbitrator is serving concurrently as an advocate for or representative of other companies or unions in labor relations matters, or has done so in recent years, he or she must disclose such activities before accepting appointment as an arbitrator.

An arbitrator must disclose such activities to an administrative agency if he or she is on that agency's active roster or seeks placement on a roster. Such disclosure then satisfies this requirement for cases handled under that agency's referral.

a. It is not necessary to disclose names of clients or other specific details. It is necessary to indicate the general nature of the labor relations advocacy or representational work involved, whether for companies or unions or both, and a reasonable approximation of the extent of such activity.

b. *An arbitrator on an administrative agency's roster has a continuing obligation to notify the agency of any significant changes pertinent to this requirement.*

c. When an administrative agency is not involved, an arbitrator must make such disclosure directly unless he or she is certain that both parties to the case are fully aware of such activities.

3. An arbitrator must not permit personal relationships to affect decision-making.

Prior to acceptance of an appointment, an arbitrator must disclose to the parties or to the administrative agency involved any close personal relationship or other circumstance, in addition to those specifically mentioned earlier in this section, which might reasonably raise a question as to the arbitrator's impartiality.

a. Arbitrators establish personal relationships with many company and union representatives, with fellow arbitrators, and with fellow members of various professional associations. There should be no attempt to be secretive about such friendships or acquaintances but disclosure is not necessary unless some feature of a particular relationship might reasonably appear to impair impartiality.

4. If the circumstances requiring disclosure are not known to the arbitrator prior to acceptance of appointment, disclosure must be made when such circumstances become known to the arbitrator.

5. The burden of disclosure rests on the arbitrator. After appropriate disclosure, the arbitrator may serve if both parties so desire. If the arbitrator believes or perceives that there is a clear conflict of interest, he or she should withdraw, irrespective of the expressed desires of the parties.

C. Privacy of Arbitration

1. All significant aspects of an arbitration proceeding must be treated by the arbitrator as confidential unless this requirement is waived by both parties or disclosure is required or permitted by law.

a. Attendance at hearings by persons not representing the parties or invited by either or both of them should be permitted only when the parties agree or when an applicable law requires or permits. Occasionally, special circumstances may require that an arbitrator rule on such matters as attendance and degree of participation of counsel selected by a grievant.

b. *Discussion of a case at any time by an arbitrator with persons not involved directly should be limited to situations where advance approval or consent of both parties is obtained or where the identity of the parties and details of the case are sufficiently obscured to eliminate any realistic probability of identification.*

A commonly recognized exception is discussion of a problem in a case with a fellow arbitrator. *Any such discussion does not relieve the arbitrator who is acting in the case from sole responsibility for the decision and the discussion must be considered as confidential.*

Discussion of aspects of a case in a classroom without prior specific approval of the parties is not a violation provided the arbitrator is satisfied that there is no breach of essential confidentiality.

c. *It is a violation of professional responsibility for an arbitrator to make public an award without the consent of the parties.*

An arbitrator may ask the parties whether they consent to the publication of the award either at the hearing or at the time the award is issued.

(1) *If such question is asked at the hearing it should be asked in writing as follows:*

"*Do you consent to the submission of the award in this matter for publication?*   (   )   (   )
                                                                YES   NO

If you consent you have the right to notify the arbitrator within 30 days after the date of the award that you revoke your consent."

It is desirable but not required that the arbitrator remind the parties at the time of the issuance of the award of their right to withdraw their consent to publication.

(2) If the question of consent to the publication of the award is raised at the time the award is issued, the arbitrator may state in writing to each party that failure to answer the inquiry within 30 days will be considered an implied consent to publish.

d. It is not improper for an arbitrator to donate arbitration files to a library of a college, university or similar institution without prior consent of all the parties involved. When the circumstances permit, there should be deleted from such donations any cases concerning which one or both of the parties have expressed a desire for privacy. As an additional safeguard, an arbitrator may also decide to withhold recent cases or indicate to the donee a time interval before such cases can be made generally available.

e. *Applicable laws, regulations, or practices of the parties may permit or even require exceptions to the above noted principles of privacy.*

D. Personal Relationships with the Parties

1. An arbitrator must make every reasonable effort to conform to arrangements required by an administrative agency or mutually desired by the parties regarding communications and personal relationships with the parties.

a. *Only an "arms-length" relationship may be acceptable to the parties in some arbitration arrangements or may be required by the rules of an administrative agency. The arbitrator should then have no contact of consequence with representatives of either party while handling a case without the other party's presence or consent.*

b. *In other situations, both parties may want communications and personal relationships to be less formal. It is then appropriate for the other party to respond accordingly.*

E. Jurisdiction

1. An arbitrator must observe faithfully both the limitations and inclusions of the jurisdiction conferred by an agreement or other submission under which he or she serves.

2. A direct settlement by the parties of some or all issues in a case, at any stage of the proceedings, must be accepted by the arbitrator as relieving him or her of further jurisdiction over such issues.

F. Mediation by an Arbitrator

1. When the parties wish at the outset to give an arbitrator authority both to mediate and to decide or submit recommendations regarding residual issues, if any, they should so advise the arbitrator prior to appointment. If the appointment is accepted, the arbitrator must perform a mediation role consistent with the circumstances of the case.

a. Direct appointments, also, may require a dual role as mediator and arbitrator of residual issues. This is most likely to occur in some public sector cases.

2. When a request to mediate is first made after appointment, the arbitrator may either accept or decline a mediation role.

a. *Once arbitration has been invoked, either party normally has a right to insist that the process be continued to decision.*

b. *If one party requests that the arbitrator mediate and the other party objects, the arbitrator should decline the request.*

c. *An arbitrator is not precluded from making a suggestion that he or she mediate. To avoid the possibility of improper pressure, the arbitrator should not so suggest unless it can be discerned that both parties are likely to be receptive. In any event, the arbitrator's suggestion should not be pursued unless both parties readily agree.*

G. Reliance by an Arbitrator on Other Arbitration Awards or on Independent Research

1. An arbitrator must assume full personal responsibility for the decision in each case decided.

a. *The extent, if any, to which an arbitrator properly may rely on precedent, on guidance of other awards, or on independent research is dependent primarily on the policies of the parties on these matters, as expressed in the contract, or other agreement, or at the hearing.*

b. When the mutual desires of the parties are not known or when the parties express differing opinions or policies, the arbitrator may exercise discretion as to these matters, consistent with acceptance of full personal responsibility for the award.

H. Use of Assistants

1. An arbitrator must not delegate any decision-making function to another person without consent of the parties.

a. *Without prior consent of the parties, an arbitrator may use the services of an assistant for research, clerical duties, or preliminary drafting under the direction of the arbitrator, which does not involve the delegation of any decision-making function.*

b. *If an arbitrator is unable, because of time limitations or other reasons, to handle all decision-making aspects of a case, it is not a violation of professional responsibility to suggest to the parties an allocation of responsibility between the arbitrator and an assistant or associate. The arbitrator must not exert pressure on the parties to accept such a suggestion.*

I. Consent Awards

1. Prior to issuance of an award, the parties may jointly request the arbitrator to include in the award certain agreements between them, concerning some or all of the issues. If the arbitrator believes that a suggested award is proper, fair, sound, and lawful, it is consistent with professional responsibility to adopt it.

a. *Before complying with such a request, an arbitrator must be certain that he or she understands the suggested settlement adequately in order to be able to appraise its terms. If it appears that pertinent facts or circumstances may not have been disclosed, the arbitrator should take the initiative to assure that all significant aspects of the case are fully understood. To this end, the arbitrator may request additional specific information and may question witnesses at a hearing.*

J. Avoidance of Delay

1. It is a basic professional responsibility of an arbitrator to plan his or her work schedule so that present and future commitments will be fulfilled in a timely manner.

a. *When planning is upset for reasons beyond the control of the arbitrator, he or she, nevertheless, should exert every reasonable effort to fulfill all commitments. If this is not possible, prompt notice at the arbitrator's initiative should be given to all parties affected. Such notices should include reasonably accurate estimates of any additional time required. To the extent possible, priority should be given to cases in process so that other parties may make alternative arbitration arrangements.*

2. An arbitrator must cooperate with the parties and with any administrative agency involved in avoiding delays.

a. *An arbitrator on the active roster of an administrative agency must take the initiative in advising the agency of any scheduling difficulties that he or she can foresee.*

b. *Requests for services, whether received directly or through an administrative agency, should be declined if the arbitrator is unable to schedule a hearing as soon as the parties wish. If the parties, nevertheless, jointly desire to obtain the services of the arbitrator and the arbitrator agrees, arrangements should be made by agreement that the arbitrator confidently expects to fulfill.*

c. *An arbitrator may properly seek to persuade the parties to alter or eliminate arbitration procedures or tactics that cause unnecessary delay.*

3. Once the case record has been closed, an arbitrator must adhere to the time limits for an award, as stipulated in the labor agreement or as provided by regulation of an administrative agency or as otherwise agreed.

a. *If an appropriate award cannot be rendered within the required time, it is incumbent on the arbitrator to seek an extension of time from the parties.*

b. If the parties have agreed upon abnormally short time limits for an award after a case is closed, the arbitrator should be so advised by the parties or by the administrative agency involved, prior to acceptance of appointment.

K. Fees and Expenses

1. An arbitrator occupies a position of trust in respect to the parties and the administrative agencies. In charging for services and expenses, the arbitrator must be governed by the same high standards of honor and integrity that apply to all other phases of his or her work.

An arbitrator must endeavor to keep total charges for services and expenses reasonable and consistent with the nature of the case or cases decided.

Prior to appointment, the parties should be aware of or be able readily to determine all significant aspects of an arbitrator's bases for charges for fees and expenses.

a. *Services Not Primarily Chargeable on a Per Diem Basis*

By agreement with the parties, the financial aspects of many "permanent" arbitration assignments, of some interest disputes, and of some "ad hoc" grievance assignments do not include a per diem fee for services as a primary part of the total understanding. *In such situations, the arbitrator must adhere faithfully to all agreed-upon arrangements governing fees and expenses.*

b. *Per Diem Basis for Charges for Services*

(1) *When an arbitrator's charges for services are determined primarily by a stipulated per diem fee, the arbitrator should establish in advance his or her bases for application of such per diem fee and for determination of reimbursable expenses.*

Practices established by an arbitrator should include the basis for charges, if any, for:

(a) hearing time, including the application of the stipulated basis per diem hearing fee to hearing days of varying lengths;

(b) study time;

(c) necessary travel time when not included in charges for hearing time;

(d) postponement or cancellation of hearings by the parties and the circumstances in which such charges will normally be assessed or waived;

(e) office overhead expenses (secretarial, telephone, postage, etc.);

(f) the work of paid assistants or associates.

(2) *Each arbitrator should be guided by the following general principles:*
   (a) *Per diem charges for a hearing should not be in excess of actual time spent or allocated for the hearing.*
   (b) *Per diem charges for study time should not be in excess of actual time spent.*
   (c) *Any fixed ratio of study days to hearing days, not agreed to specifically by the parties, is inconsistent with the per diem method of charges for services.*
   (d) *Charges for expenses must not be in excess of actual expenses normally reimbursable and incurred in connection with the case or cases involved.*
   (e) *When time or expense charges are involved for two or more sets of parties on the same day or trip, such time or expense charges should be appropriately prorated.*
   (f) *An arbitrator may stipulate in advance a minimum charge for a hearing without violation of (a) or (e) above.*

(3) *An arbitrator on the active roster of an administrative agency must file with the agency his or her individual bases for determination of fees and expenses if the agency so requires. Thereafter, it is the responsibility of each such arbitrator to advise the agency promptly of any change in any basis for charges.*

   Such filing may be in the form of answers to a questionnaire devised by an agency or by any other method adopted by or approved by an agency.

   Having supplied an administrative agency with the information noted above, an arbitrator's professional responsibility of disclosure under this Code with respect to fees and expenses has been satisfied for cases referred by that agency.

(4) *If an administrative agency promulgates specific standards with respect to any of these matters which are in addition to or more restrictive than an individual arbitrator's standards, an arbitrator on its active roster must observe the agency standards for cases handled under the auspices of that agency, or decline to serve.*

(5) *When an arbitrator is contacted directly by the parties for a case or cases, the arbitrator has a professional responsibility to respond to questions by submitting his or her bases for fees and charges.*

(6) *When it is known to the arbitrator that one or both of the parties cannot afford normal charges, it is consistent with professional responsibility to charge lesser amounts to both parties or to one of the parties if the other party is made aware of the difference and agrees.*

(7) *If an arbitrator concludes that the total of charges derived from his or her normal basis of calculation is not compatible with the case decided, it is consistent with professional responsibility to charge lesser amounts to both parties.*

2. An arbitrator must maintain adequate records to support charges for services and expenses and must make an accounting to the parties or to an involved administrative agency on request.

3
RESPONSIBILITIES TO ADMINISTRATIVE AGENCIES
A. General Responsibilities

1. An arbitrator must be candid, accurate, and fully responsive to an administrative agency concerning his or her qualifications, availability, and all other pertinent matters.

2. An arbitrator must observe policies and rules of an administrative agency in cases referred by that agency.

3. An arbitrator must not seek to influence an administrative agency by any improper means, including gifts or other inducements to agency personnel.

a. It is not improper for a person seeking placement on a roster to request references from individuals having knowledge of the applicant's experience and qualifications.

b. Arbitrators should recognize that the primary responsibility of an administrative agency is to serve the parties.

4
PREHEARING CONDUCT

1. All prehearing matters must be handled in a manner that fosters complete impartiality by the arbitrator.

a. The primary purpose of prehearing discussions involving the arbitrator is to obtain agreement on procedural matters so that the hearing can proceed without unnecessary obstacles. If differences of opinion should arise during such discussions and, particularly, if such differences appear to impinge on substantive matters, the circumstances will suggest whether the matter can be resolved informally or may require a prehearing conference or, more rarely, a formal preliminary hearing. When an administrative agency handles some or all aspects of the arrangements prior to a hearing, the arbitrator will become involved only if differences of some substance arise.

b. *Copies of any prehearing correspondence between the arbitrator and either party must be made available to both parties.*

5
HEARING CONDUCT
A. General Principles

1. An arbitrator must provide a fair and adequate hearing which assures that both parties have sufficient opportunity to present their respective evidence and argument.

a. *Within the limits of this responsibility, an arbitrator should conform to the various types of hearing procedures desired by the parties.*

b. An arbitrator may: encourage stipulations of fact; restate the substance of issues or arguments to promote or verify understanding; question the parties' representatives or witnesses, when necessary or advisable, to obtain additional pertinent information; and request that the parties submit additional evidence, either at the hearing or by subsequent filing.

c. An arbitrator should not intrude into a party's presentation so as to prevent that party from putting forward its case fairly and adequately.

B. Transcripts or Recordings

1. Mutual agreement of the parties as to use or non-use of a transcript must be respected by the arbitrator.

a. *A transcript is the official record of a hearing only when both parties agree to a transcript or an applicable law or regulation so provides.*

b. An arbitrator may seek to persuade the parties to avoid use of a transcript, or to use a transcript if the nature of the case appears to require one. *However, if an arbitrator intends to make his or her appointment to a case contingent on mutual agreement to a transcript, that requirement must be made known to both parties prior to appointment.*

c. If the parties do not agree to a transcript, an arbitrator may permit one party to take a transcript at its own cost. The arbitrator may also make appropriate arrangements under which the other party may have access to a copy, if a copy is provided to the arbitrator.

d. Without prior approval, an arbitrator may seek to use his or her own tape recorder to supplement note taking. The arbitrator should not insist on such a tape recording if either or both parties object.

C. Ex Parte Hearings

1. In determining whether to conduct an ex parte hearing, an arbitrator must consider relevant legal, contractual, and other pertinent circumstances.

2. An arbitrator must be certain, before proceeding ex parte, that the party refusing or failing to attend the hearing has been given adequate notice of the time, place, and purposes of the hearing.

D. Plant Visits

1. An arbitrator should comply with a request of any party that he or she visit a work area pertinent to the dispute prior to, during, or after a hearing. An arbitrator may also initiate such a request.

a. *Procedures for such visits should be agreed to by the parties in consultation with the arbitrator.*

E. Bench Decisions or Expedited Awards

1. When an arbitrator understands, prior to acceptance of appointment, that a bench decision is expected at the conclusion of the hearing, the arbitrator must comply with the understanding unless both parties agree otherwise.

a. *If notice of the parties' desire for a bench decision is not given prior to the arbitrator's acceptance of the case, issuance of such a bench decision is discretionary.*

b. *When only one party makes the request and the other objects, the arbitrator should not render a bench decision except under most unusual circumstances.*

2. When an arbitrator understands, prior to acceptance of appointment, that a concise written award is expected within a stated time period after the

hearing, the arbitrator must comply with the understanding unless both parties agree otherwise.

6
POST HEARING CONDUCT

A. Post Hearing Briefs and Submissions

1. An arbitrator must comply with mutual agreements in respect to the filing or nonfiling of post hearing briefs or submissions.

a. An arbitrator, in his or her discretion, may either suggest the filing of post hearing briefs or other submissions or suggest that none be filed.

b. When the parties disagree as to the need for briefs, an arbitrator may permit filing but may determine a reasonable time limitation.

2. An arbitrator must not consider a post hearing brief or submission that has not been provided to the other party.

B. Disclosure of Terms of Award

1. An arbitrator must not disclose a prospective award to either party prior to its simultaneous issuance to both parties or explore possible alternative awards unilaterally with one party, unless both parties so agree.

a. Partisan members of tripartite boards may know prospective terms of an award in advance of its issuance. Similar situations may exist in other less formal arrangements mutually agreed to by the parties. In any such situation, the arbitrator should determine and observe the mutually desired degree of confidentiality.

C. Awards and Opinions

1. The award should be definite, certain, and as concise as possible.

a. When an opinion is required, factors to be considered by an arbitrator include: desirability of brevity, consistent with the nature of the case and any expressed desires of the parties; need to use a style and form that is understandable to responsible representatives of the parties, to the grievant and supervisors, and to others in the collective bargaining relationship; necessity of meeting the significant issues; forthrightness to an extent not harmful to the relationship of the parties; and avoidance of gratuitous advice or discourse not essential to disposition of the issues.

D. Clarification or Interpretation of Awards

1. No clarification or interpretation of an award is permissible without the consent of both parties.

2. Under agreements which permit or require clarification or interpretation of an award, an arbitrator must afford both parties an opportunity to be heard.

E. Enforcement of Award

1. The arbitrator's responsibility does not extend to the enforcement of an award.

   2. **In view of the professional and confidential nature of the arbitration relationship, an arbitrator should not voluntarily participate in legal enforcement proceedings.**

Model Standards of Conduct for Mediators*

Introductory Note

The initiative for these standards came from three professional groups: The American Arbitration Association, the American Bar Association, and the Society of Professionals in Dispute Resolution.

The purpose of this initiative was to develop a set of standards to serve as a general framework for the practice of mediation. The effort is a step in the development of the field and a tool to assist practitioners in it—a beginning, not an end. The model standards are intended to apply to all types of mediation. It is recognized, however, that in some cases the application of these standards may be affected by laws or contractual agreements.

Preface

The model standards of conduct for mediators are intended to perform three major functions: to serve as a guide for the conduct of mediators; to inform the mediating parties; and to promote public confidence in mediation as a process for resolving disputes. The standards draw on existing codes of conduct for mediators and take into account issues and problems that have surfaced in mediation practice. They are offered in the hope that they will serve an educational function and provide assistance to individuals, organizations, and institutions involved in mediation.

Mediation is a process in which an impartial third party—a mediator—facilitates the resolution of a dispute by promoting voluntary agreement (or "self-determination") by the parties to the dispute. A mediator facilitates communications, promotes understanding, focuses the parties on their interests, and seeks creative problem solving to enable the parties to reach their own agreement. These standards give meaning to this definition of mediation.

I. SELF-DETERMINATION:

A mediator shall recognize that mediation is based on the principle of self-determination by the parties.

Self-determination is the fundamental principle of mediation. It requires that the mediation process rely upon the ability of the parties to reach a voluntary, uncoerced agreement. Any party may withdraw from mediation at any time.

COMMENTS:
- The mediator may provide information about the process, raise issues, and help parties explore options. The primary role of the mediator is to facilitate a voluntary resolution of a dispute. Parties shall be given the opportunity to consider all proposed options.

---

*Prepared from 1992 through 1994 by a joint committee of delegates from the American Arbitration Association, American Bar Association, and Society of Professionals in Dispute Resolution. Approved by the American Arbitration Association, the Litigation Section and Dispute Resolution Section of the American Bar Association, and the Society of Professionals in Dispute Resolution. The views set out in this publication have not been considered by the American Bar Association House of Delegates and do not constitute the policy of the American Bar Association. Reprinted with permission of the American Arbitration Association.

- A mediator cannot personally ensure that each party has made a fully informed choice to reach a particular agreement, but it is a good practice for the mediator to make the parties aware of the importance of consulting other professionals, where appropriate, to help them make informed decisions.

II. IMPARTIALITY:
A mediator shall conduct the mediation in an impartial manner.

The concept of mediator impartiality is central to the mediation process. A mediator shall mediate only those matters in which she or he can remain impartial and evenhanded. If at any time the mediator is unable to conduct the process in an impartial manner, the mediator is obligated to withdraw.

COMMENTS:
- A mediator shall avoid conduct that gives the appearance of partiality toward one of the parties. The quality of the mediation process is enhanced when the parties have confidence in the impartiality of the mediator.
- When mediators are appointed by a court or institution, the appointing agency shall make reasonable efforts to ensure that mediators serve impartially.
- A mediator should guard against partiality or prejudice based on the parties' personal characteristics, background or performance at the mediation.

III. CONFLICTS OF INTEREST:
A mediator shall disclose all actual and potential conflicts of interest reasonably known to the mediator. After disclosure, the mediator shall decline to mediate unless all parties choose to retain the mediator. The need to protect against conflicts of interest also governs conduct that occurs during and after the mediation.

A conflict of interest is a dealing or relationship that might create an impression of possible bias. The basic approach to questions of conflict of interest is consistent with the concept of self-determination. The mediator has a responsibility to disclose all actual and potential conflicts that are reasonably known to the mediator and could reasonably be seen as raising a question about impartiality. If all parties agree to mediate after being informed of conflicts, the mediator may proceed with the mediation. If, however, the conflict of interest casts serious doubt on the integrity of the process, the mediator shall decline to proceed.

A mediator must avoid the appearance of conflict of interest both during and after the mediation. Without the consent of all parties, a mediator shall not subsequently establish a professional relationship with one of the parties in a related matter, or in an unrelated matter under circumstances which would raise legitimate questions about the integrity of the mediation process.

COMMENTS:
- A mediator shall avoid conflicts of interest in recommending the services of other professionals. A mediator may make reference to professional referral services or associations which maintain rosters of qualified professionals.
- Potential conflicts of interest may arise between administrators of mediation programs and mediators and there may be strong pressures on the mediator to settle a particular case or cases. The mediator's commitment must be

to the parties and the process. Pressure from outside of the mediation process should never influence the mediator to coerce parties to settle.

IV. COMPETENCE:

A mediator shall mediate only when the mediator has the necessary qualifications to satisfy the reasonable expectations of the parties.

Any person may be selected as a mediator, provided that the parties are satisfied with the mediator's qualifications. Training and experience in mediation, however, are often necessary for effective mediation. A person who offers herself or himself as available to serve as a mediator gives parties and the public the expectation that she or he has the competency to mediate effectively. In court-connected or other forms of mandated mediation, it is essential that mediators assigned to the parties have the requisite training and experience.

COMMENTS:
- Mediators should have information available for the parties regarding their relevant training, education and experience.
- The requirements for appearing on a list of mediators must be made public and available to interested persons.
- When mediators are appointed by a court or institution, the appointing agency shall make reasonable efforts to ensure that each mediator is qualified for the particular mediation.

V. CONFIDENTIALITY:

A mediator shall maintain the reasonable expectations of the parties with regard to confidentiality.

The reasonable expectations of the parties with regard to confidentiality shall be met by the mediator. The parties' expectations of confidentiality depend on the circumstances of the mediation and any agreements they may make. The mediator shall not disclose any matter that a party expects to be confidential unless given permission by all parties or unless required by law or other public policy.

COMMENTS:
- The parties may make their own rules with respect to confidentiality, or other accepted practice of an individual mediator or institution may dictate a particular set of expectations. Since the parties' expectations regarding confidentiality are important, the mediator should discuss these expectations with the parties.
- If the mediator holds private sessions with a party, the nature of these sessions with regard to confidentiality should be discussed prior to undertaking such sessions.
- In order to protect the integrity of the mediation, a mediator should avoid communicating information about how the parties acted in the mediation process, the merits of the case, or settlement offers. The mediator may report, if required, whether parties appeared at a scheduled mediation.
- Where the parties have agreed that all or a portion of the information disclosed during a mediation is confidential, the parties' agreement should be respected by the mediator.
- Confidentiality should not be construed to limit or prohibit the effective monitoring, research, or evaluation of mediation programs by responsible persons. Under appropriate circumstances, researchers may be permitted

to obtain access to the statistical data and, with the permission of the parties, to individual case files, observations of live mediations, and interviews with participants.

VI. QUALITY OF THE PROCESS:
A mediator shall conduct the mediation fairly, diligently, and in a manner consistent with the principle of self-determination by the parties.

A mediator shall work to ensure a quality process and to encourage mutual respect among the parties. A quality process requires a commitment by the mediator to diligence and procedural fairness. There should be adequate opportunity for each party in the mediation to participate in the discussions. The parties decide when and under what conditions they will reach an agreement or terminate a mediation.

COMMENTS:
- A mediator may agree to mediate only when he or she is prepared to commit the attention essential to an effective mediation.
- Mediators should only accept cases when they can satisfy the reasonable expectations of the parties concerning the timing of the process. A mediator should not allow a mediation to be unduly delayed by the parties or their representatives.
- The presence or absence of persons at a mediation depends on the agreement of the parties and the mediator. The parties and mediator may agree that others may be excluded from particular sessions or from the entire mediation process.
- The primary purpose of a mediator is to facilitate the parties' voluntary agreement. This role differs substantially from other professional-client relationships. Mixing the role of a mediator and the role of a professional advising a client is problematic, and mediators must strive to distinguish between the roles. A mediator should, therefore, refrain from providing professional advice. Where appropriate, a mediator should recommend that parties seek outside professional advice, or consider resolving their dispute through arbitration, counseling, neutral evaluation, or other processes. A mediator who undertakes, at the request of the parties, an additional dispute resolution role in the same matter assumes increased responsibilities and obligations that may be governed by the standards of other processes.
- A mediator shall withdraw from a mediation when incapable of serving or when unable to remain impartial.
- A mediator shall withdraw from a mediation or postpone a session if the mediation is being used to further illegal conduct, or if a party is unable to participate due to drug, alcohol, or other physical or mental incapacity.
- Mediators should not permit their behavior in the mediation process to be guided by a desire for a high settlement rate.

VII. ADVERTISING AND SOLICITATION:
A mediator shall be truthful in advertising and solicitation for mediation.

Advertising or any other communication with the public concerning services offered or regarding the education, training, and expertise of the mediator shall be truthful. Mediators shall refrain from promises and guarantees of results.

COMMENTS:
- It is imperative that communication with the public educate and instill confidence in the process.
- In an advertisement or other communication to the public, a mediator may make reference to meeting state, national, or private organization qualifications only if the entity referred to has a procedure for qualifying mediators and the mediator has been duly granted the requisite status.

VIII. FEES:
A mediator shall fully disclose and explain the basis of compensation, fees, and charges to the parties.

The parties should be provided sufficient information about fees at the outset of a mediation to determine if they wish to retain the services of a mediator. If a mediator charges fees, the fees shall be reasonable, considering, among other things, the mediation service, the type and complexity of the matter, the expertise of the mediator, the time required, and the rates customary in the community. The better practice in reaching an understanding about fees is to set down the arrangements in a written agreement.

COMMENTS:
- A mediator who withdraws from a mediation should return any unearned fee to the parties.
- A mediator should not enter into a fee agreement which is contingent upon the result of the mediation or amount of the settlement.
- Co-mediators who share a fee should hold to standards of reasonableness in determining the allocation of fees.
- A mediator should not accept a fee for referral of a matter to another mediator or to any other person.

IX. OBLIGATIONS TO THE MEDIATION PROCESS:
Mediators have a duty to improve the practice of mediation.

COMMENT:
- Mediators are regarded as knowledgeable in the process of mediation. They have an obligation to use their knowledge to help educate the public about mediation; to make mediation accessible to those who would like to use it; to correct abuses; and to improve their professional skills and abilities.

Organization

SOCIETY OF PROFESSIONALS IN DISPUTE RESOLUTION

Headquarters:
1621 Connecticut Avenue, NW
Suite 400
Washington, DC 20009
Telephone: (202) 265-1927
Fax: (202) 265-1968
E-mail: spidr@spidr.org
Website: http://www.spidr.org

Date founded: 1972
Membership: approximately 3,500 neutrals and educators in dispute resolution processes, including arbitrators, mediators, ombudsmen, fact-
finders, conciliators, trial examiners, and hearing officers

Code of Ethics

Official name: *Ethical Standards of Professional Responsibility*
History: Adopted 1986;, revised March 1992
Authority: Ethics Committee; Board of Directors
Code is available on Website

Additional Resources

Organizational (Divisions, Programs, Services, etc.):

Commission on Qualifications
Law and Public Policy Committee
Participatory Dialogues on Diversity
Professional Liability Insurance

Informational (Publications, Videos, Seminars, etc.):

Articles in *SPIDR News*
Competencies for Mediators of Complex Public Disputes

Democracy and Dispute Resolution: Power, Principle and Practice (conference proceedings)
Diversity Policy
Duty to Keep Secrets: A Re-Evaluation
Elements of Good Practice in Dispute Resolution
Ensuring Competence and Quality in Dispute Resolution Practice
Guidelines for Voluntary Mediation Programs Instituted by Agencies Charged with Enforcing Workplace Rights
Making the Tough Calls—Ethical Exercises for Neutral Dispute Resolvers
Mandated Participation and Settlement Coercion: Dispute Resolution As It Relates to the Courts
Mediator Practice Styles and Ethics: Exploratory Survey (conference session)
Open Forum on Competencies, Credentials, Best Practices (e-mail forum)
Principles and Policies to Guide State Courts in the Selection, Training, Qualification and Evaluation of Neutrals (with National Center for State Courts)
Public Encouragement of Private Dispute Resolution: Implications, Issues, and Recommendations
Qualifying Dispute Resolution Practitioners: Guidelines for Court-Connected Programs
Qualifying Neutrals: The Basic Principles
SPIDR Ethics (e-mail forum)

Goals and Activities of Organization

The Society of Professionals in Dispute Resolution (SPIDR) is an international membership association committed to the advancement of the highest standards of ethics and practice for dispute resolvers. Established to promote the peaceful resolution of disputes, SPIDR works to enhance the professional skills and interests of all neutrals; aid the structure and institutions through which dispute resolution services are provided; and promote professionalism at local, regional, and national levels. SPIDR also strives to increase public understanding of dispute resolution processes; further potential parties' acceptability and understanding of the role of neutrals; and promote the recruitment and educational development of dispute resolution personnel.

In addition, SPIDR serves as a clearinghouse for information and research, and sponsors research leading to the development of innovative impasse resolution techniques and procedures.

Implementation and Enforcement of Code

The Standards are broad in scope and general in nature. They were written with the expectation that as they are applied to specific cases and ethical problems, they will be refined and clarified.

The Ethics Committee welcomes members' and other practitioners' comments as to how the Standards should be further implemented and whether and how they should be enforced.

History and Development of Code

The Ethics Committee, supported by a grant from the National Institute for Dispute Resolution, began developing a code of professional ethics in 1983 at the request of the SPIDR Board of Directors.

The Committee members represented all the various sectors and disciplines within SPIDR. They reviewed and analyzed a variety of existing codes, including those of the Academy of Family Mediators, Association of Family and Conciliation Courts, and organizations in law and medicine.

A first draft was produced in 1985 and submitted for comment by the entire membership. The new draft incorporated much of this input, the result of discussion and consensus among practitioners in all areas of dispute resolution. The Board adopted the present Standards in 1986. The version reproduced here contains minor revisions made in March 1992.

Ethical Standards of Professional Responsibility*

INTRODUCTION

The Society of Professionals in Dispute Resolution (SPIDR) was established in 1973 to promote the peaceful resolution of disputes. Members of the Society believe that resolving disputes through negotiation, mediation, arbitration and other neutral interventions can be of great benefit to disputing parties and to society. In 1983, the SPIDR Board of Directors charged the Ethics Committee with the task of developing ethical standards of professional responsibility. The Committee membership represented all the various sectors and disciplines within SPIDR. This document, adopted by the Board on June 2, 1986, is the result of that charge.

The purpose of this document is to promote among SPIDR members and associates ethical conduct and a high level of competency among SPIDR members, including honesty, integrity, impartiality, and the exercise of good judgment in their dispute resolution efforts. It is hoped that this document also will help to (1) define the profession of dispute resolution, (2) educate the public, and (3) inform users of dispute resolution services.

APPLICATION OF STANDARDS

Adherence to these ethical standards by SPIDR members and associates is basic to professional responsibility. SPIDR members and associates commit themselves to be guided in their professional conduct by these standards. The SPIDR Board of Directors or its designee is available to advise members and associates about the interpretation of these standards. Other neutral practitioners and organizations are welcome to follow these standards.

SCOPE

It is recognized that SPIDR members and associates resolve disputes in various sectors within the disciplines of dispute resolution and have their own codes of professional conduct. These standards have been developed as general guidelines of practice for neutral disciplines represented in the SPIDR membership. Ethical considerations relevant to some, but not to all, of these disciplines are not covered by these standards.

GENERAL RESPONSIBILITIES

Neutrals have a duty to the parties, to the profession, and to themselves. They should be honest and unbiased, act in good faith, be diligent, and not seek to advance their own interests at the expense of their parties'.

Neutrals must act fairly in dealing with the parties, have no personal interest in the terms of the settlement, show no bias toward individuals and institutions involved in the dispute, be reasonably available as requested by the parties, and be certain that the parties are informed of the process in which they are involved.

---

*Adopted June 1986. Reprinted with permission from the Society of Professionals in Dispute Resolution, Inc.

RESPONSIBILITIES TO THE PARTIES

1. Impartiality

The neutral must maintain impartiality toward all parties. Impartiality means freedom from favoritism or bias either by word or by action, and a commitment to serve all parties as opposed to a single party.

2. Informed Consent

The neutral has an obligation to assure that all parties understand the nature of the process, the procedures, the particular role of the neutral, and the parties' relationship to the neutral.

3. Confidentiality

Maintaining confidentiality is critical to the dispute resolution process. Confidentiality encourages candor, a full exploration of the issues, and a neutral's acceptability. There may be some types of cases, however, in which confidentiality is not protected. In such cases, the neutral must advise the parties, when appropriate in the dispute resolution process, that the confidentiality of the proceedings cannot necessarily be maintained. Except in such instances, the neutral must resist all attempts to cause him or her to reveal any information outside the process. A commitment by the neutral to hold information in confidence within the process also must be honored.

4. Conflict of Interest

The neutral must refrain from entering or continuing in any dispute if he or she believes or perceives that participation as a neutral would be a clear conflict of interest and any circumstances that may reasonably raise a question as to the neutral's impartiality.

The duty to disclose is a continuing obligation throughout the process.

5. Promptness

The neutral shall exert every reasonable effort to expedite the process.

6. The Settlement and Its Consequences

The dispute resolution process belongs to the parties. The neutral has no vested interest in the terms of a settlement, but must be satisfied that agreements in which he or she has participated will not impugn the integrity of the process. The neutral has a responsibility to see that the parties consider the terms of a settlement. If the neutral is concerned about the possible consequences of a proposed agreement, and the needs of the parties dictate, the neutral must inform the parties of that concern. In adhering to this standard, the neutral may find it advisable to educate the parties, to refer one or more parties for specialized advice, or to withdraw from the case. In no case, however, shall the neutral violate Section 3, Confidentiality, of these standards.

UNREPRESENTED INTERESTS

The neutral must consider circumstances where interests are not represented in the process. The neutral has an obligation, where in his or her judgment the needs of the parties dictate, to assure that such interests have been considered by the principal parties.

USE OF MULTIPLE PROCEDURES

The use of more than one dispute resolution procedure by the same neutral involves additional responsibilities. Where the use of more than one procedure is initially contemplated, the neutral must take care at the outset to advise the parties of the nature of the procedures and the consequences of revealing information during any one procedure which the neutral may later use for decision making or may share with another decision maker. Where the use of more than one procedure is contemplated after the initiation of the dispute resolution process, the neutral must explain the consequences and afford the parties an opportunity to select another neutral for the subsequent procedures. It is also incumbent upon the neutral to advise the parties of the transition from one dispute resolution process to another.

BACKGROUND AND QUALIFICATIONS

A neutral should accept responsibility only in cases where the neutral has sufficient knowledge regarding the appropriate process and subject matter to be effective. A neutral has a responsibility to maintain and improve his or her professional skills.

DISCLOSURE OF FEES

It is the duty of the neutral to explain to the parties at the outset of the process the bases of compensation, fees, and charges, if any.

SUPPORT OF THE PROFESSION

The experienced neutral should participate in the development of new practitioners in the field and engage in efforts to educate the public about the value and use of neutral dispute resolution procedures. The neutral should provide *pro bono* services, where appropriate.

RESPONSIBILITIES OF NEUTRALS
WORKING ON THE SAME CASE

In the event that more than one neutral is involved in the resolution of a dispute, each has an obligation to inform the others regarding his or her entry in the case. Neutrals working with the same parties should maintain an open and professional relationship with each other.

ADVERTISING AND SOLICITATION

A neutral must be aware that some form of advertising and solitations are inappropriate and in some conflict resolution disciplines, such as labor arbitration, are impermissible. All advertising must honestly represent the services to be rendered. No claims of specific results or promises which imply favor of one side over another for the purpose of obtaining business should be made. No commissions, rebates, or other similar forms of remuneration should be given or received by a neutral for the referral of clients.

2. JUDICIARY

Organization

AMERICAN BAR ASSOCIATION

Headquarters:
750 North Lake Shore Drive
Chicago, IL 60611-6281
Telephone: (312) 988-5000
Fax: (312) 988-6281
E-mail: info@abanet.org
Website: http://www.abanet.org

Additional offices:
Judicial Division
Telephone: (800) 238-2667, Ext. 5705
E-mail: abajd@abanet.org
Website: www.abanet.org/jd/home.html

Center for Professional Responsibility
541 North Fairbanks Court
Chicago, IL 60611-3314
Telephone: (312) 988-5304
E-mail: ctrprofresp@abanet.org
Website: http://www.abanet.org/cpr

Date founded: 1878 (Judicial Division: 1913)
Membership: approximately 350,000 lawyers, judges, court administrators, educators, law students, legal assistants, criminal justice professionals, government officials, and business executives, plus state and
local bar associations and law-related organizations
(Judicial Division: approximately 5,000 federal, state and local trial,
appellate and administrative judges, court administrators, practicing
lawyers, and staff counsel)

Code of Ethics

Official name: *Model Code of Judicial Conduct*
History: First adopted 1924; revised 1972; current version adopted 1990, revised periodically; as amended August 1997
Authority: Standing Committee on Ethics and Professional Responsibility; House of Delegates; Judicial Division

Additional Resources

Organizational (Divisions, Programs, Services, etc.):

Center for Professional Responsibility
ETHICSearch (legal research service)
Judges' Professional Liability Policy
Judicial Division Conferences (sections):
    Administrative Law Judges
    Appellate Judges
    Federal Trial Judges
    Lawyers Conference
    Special Court Judges
    State Trial Judges
Judicial Education Project (concerning judges' response to lawyer misconduct)
Various Committees and Subcommittees (ABA):
    Ethics and Professional Responsibility
    Federal Judicial Improvements
    Federal Judiciary
    Judicial Discipline
    Professionalism
    Professionalism and Ethics
Various Committees and Subcommittees (Judicial Division):
    Court Technology
    Courts and Community
    Judicial Ethics
    Judicial Independence
    Minorities in the Judiciary
    Programs & Education
    Publications
    Standards

Informational (Publications, Videos, Seminars, etc.):

Articles in *The Judges' Journal* and individual Conference journals
ABA/BNA Lawyers' Manual on Professional Conduct
Compendium of Professional Responsibility Rules and Standards
Crisis Points for Justice

Dealing Ethically with Unfair Media Criticism (video)
The Development of the ABA Judicial Code
Ethics Opinions
Guidelines for Evaluation of Judicial Performance
Guidelines for Reviewing Qualifications Of Candidates for State Judicial Office
In the Spirit of Public Service: A Blueprint for the Rekindling of Professionalism
The Judge's Book
Judicial Implementation of Permanency Planning Reforms: One Court That Works
Judicial Independence: Real Threat or Feeling Threatened? (video)
Judicial Performance Evaluation Handbook
The Judicial Response to Lawyer Misconduct
Merit Selection Commissions: What Do They Do? How Effective Are They?
Model Code of Judicial Conduct for Federal Administrative Law Judges
Model Code of Judicial Conduct for State Administrative Law Judges
Model Judicial Article
Model Program for State, Local and Territorial Bar Associations: Suggested Program for the Appropriate Response to Criticism of Judges and Courts
Model Rules for Judicial Disciplinary Enforcement
Professional Discipline for Lawyers and Judges
Reporter's Notes to Code of Judicial Conduct
Standards Benchbooks
The Standing Committee on Federal Judiciary: What It Is and How It Works
Survey of State Judicial Fringe Benefits
Surviving the Pressure Cooker: A Workshop to Help Judges Maintain the Balance Between Agency Objectives and Judicial Independence (video)
Various Annual Meeting sessions:
Civility Among Judges: Living in Glass Houses
Courtroom Civility: Three Part Harmony
Judicial Independence: Politics, Paradox or Pandering
Judicial Role: Step Up to the Mike
Prime Time Trials: Fair Trial/Fair Press
Special Committee on Judicial Independence: Speaking Out for Justice
Technology in Litigation and the Courtroom: Access to Justice for All or Just the Elite?
Various *Standards: Appellate Courts; Court Organization; Judicial Compensation; Judicial Education; Juror Use and Management; Traffic Justice; Trial Courts; Trial Management*

Goals and Activities of Organization

The American Bar Association (ABA) is the national organization of the legal profession in the U.S. Among its goals are to advance the science of jurisprudence; promote improvements in the justice system, the uniformity of legislation and judicial decisions, and the delivery of legal services; increase the public's understanding of the law and the role of lawyers; assure high standards of professional competence and ethical conduct; enhance members' professional growth; encourage cordial relations among lawyers; urge full and equal participation in the profession by minorities and women; and advance the rule of law in the world.

The ABA analyzes issues that affect the legal profession and develops effective remedial responses, ranging from policy positions to demonstration projects to conferences. These activities are conducted through the ABA's many sections, divisions, commissions, and committees, which are semi-autonomous and focus on the different areas of legal practice. They coordinate their efforts with those of the national organization, in order to publish books and journals, offer continuing legal education programs, influence legislation and litigation, create model rules and laws, work with affiliated professions, evaluate judicial performance, and provide information on the law and lawyers to the public.

The ABA Center for Professional Responsibility coordinates, collects, analyzes, and publishes research, statistical, and educational materials on all aspects of legal and judicial ethics. It maintains close liaison with federal and state courts, disciplinary agencies, and advisory committees.

The ABA Judicial Division monitors and recommends improvements in the administration of justice, and supports the highest quality of professionalism for its members. Its goals are to educate the public about the judicial system, and to evaluate and assist in the adoption of improved procedures and technologies by the courts.

Implementation and Enforcement of Code

The Code of Judicial Conduct is intended to establish standards for ethical conduct of judges, and to assist judges in maintaining them.

It consists of broadly stated Canons, specific rules (in Sections under each Canon), Terminology, Application, and Commentary. The Canons, Sections, Terminology, and Application are authoritative. The Commentaries provide guidance as to the purpose and meaning of the Canons and Sections they accompany; they are not additional rules.

The use in the text of "shall" imposes binding obligations, the violation of which can result in disciplinary action. The use of "should" applies to appropriate conduct but is not a binding rule under which a judge may be disciplined. The use of "may" denotes permissible discretion or conduct that is not covered by specific provisions.

The Canons and Sections are to be applied consistent with constitutional requirements, statutes, court rules, and decisional law, and in the context of all relevant circumstances. They are not to be construed in a manner that impinges on judges' independence in making judicial decisions.

The Code is designed to provide guidance to judges and a structure for regulating conduct through disciplinary agencies. It is not to be used as a basis for civil liability or criminal prosecution, or to be invoked by lawyers for tactical advantage in a proceeding.

While the Canons and Sections are binding on judges' conduct, not every transgression will result in disciplinary action. Whether and to what degree discipline is appropriate should be determined through a reasonable application of the Code, considering such factors as the seriousness of the misconduct, a pattern of improper activity, and its effect on others or on the judicial system.

The Standing Committee on Ethics and Professional Responsibility is responsible for providing interpretations of the Code. It will issue ethics opinions in response to formal or informal requests from judges, judicial conduct organizations, state and local ethics committees, and lawyers. The Judges' Advisory Committee reviews these opinions at the draft stage, to insure that they adequately meet specific administrative and substantive concerns of the judiciary.

The Code applies to all judges, which includes "[a]nyone, whether or not a lawyer, who is an officer of a judicial system and who performs judicial functions, including an officer such as a magistrate, court commissioner, special master or referee * * *." Some exceptions apply to these categories of judicial service: retired judge subject to recall; continuing part-time judge; periodic part-time judge; and pro tempore part-time judge. Whether the Code applies to administrative law judges—who are usually affiliated with the executive, not the judicial branch of government—is to be determined by each adopting jurisdiction.

The topics covered in the complete Model Code of Judicial Conduct are:

> **Canon 1:** integrity and independence
> **Canon 2:** impropriety and the appearance of impropriety
> **Canon 3:** impartiality and diligence
> **Canon 4:** conflicts between extra-judicial activities and judicial obligations
> **Canon 5:** inappropriate political activity
> **Application of the Code**

The ABA Model Code of Professional Responsibility and Model Rules of Professional Conduct also impose ethical obligations on judges. The ABA Model Rules for Judicial Disciplinary Enforcement are designed to assist in upholding these and other standards.

History and Development of Code

The first ABA standards specifically for judges were the 1924 Canons of Judicial Ethics. In 1972, the Code of Judicial Conduct was issued; it was revised periodically, and last amended in 1984.

Between 1987 and 1990 the Standing Committee on Ethics and Professional Responsibility developed a revised document, the result of drafters' deliberations and public hearings. It was adopted by the House of Delegates in 1990 and replaced the 1972 Code.

This 1998 edition of the Model Code, excerpted here, contains amendments through August 1997.

Model Code of Judicial Conduct*

PREAMBLE

Our legal system is based on the principle that an independent, fair and competent judiciary will interpret and apply the laws that govern us. The role of the judiciary is central to American concepts of justice and the rule of law. Intrinsic to all sections of this Code are the precepts that judges, individually and collectively, must respect and honor the judicial office as a public trust and strive to enhance and maintain confidence in our legal system. The judge is an arbiter of facts and law for the resolution of disputes and a highly visible symbol of government under the rule of law.

The Code of Judicial Conduct is intended to establish standards for ethical conduct of judges. It consists of broad statements called Canons, specific rules set forth in Sections under each Canon, a Terminology Section, an Application Section and Commentary. The text of the Canons and the Sections, including the Terminology and Application Sections, is authoritative. The Commentary, by explanation and example, provides guidance with respect to the purpose and meaning of the Canons and Sections. The Commentary is not intended as a statement of additional rules. When the text uses "shall" or "shall not," it is intended to impose binding obligations the violation of which can result in disciplinary action. When "should" or "should not" is used, the text is intended as hortatory and as a statement of what is or is not appropriate conduct but not as a binding rule under which a judge may be disciplined. When "may" is used, it denotes permissible discretion or, depending on the context, it refers to action that is not covered by specific proscriptions.

The Canons and Sections are rules of reason. They should be applied consistent with constitutional requirements, statutes, other court rules and decisional law and in the context of all relevant circumstances. The Code is to be construed so as not to impinge on the essential independence of judges in making judicial decisions.

The Code is designed to provide guidance to judges and candidates for judicial office and to provide a structure for regulating conduct through disciplinary agencies. It is not designed or intended as a basis for civil liability or criminal prosecution. Furthermore, the purpose of the Code would be subverted if the Code were invoked by lawyers for mere tactical advantage in a proceeding.

The text of the Canons and Sections is intended to govern conduct of judges and to be binding upon them. It is not intended, however, that every transgression will result in disciplinary action. Whether disciplinary action is appropriate, and the degree of discipline to be imposed, should be determined through a reasonable and reasoned application of the text and should depend on such factors as the

---

*ABA *Model Code of Judicial Conduct*, copyright ©1998 by the American Bar Association. All rights reserved. Reprinted by permission of the American Bar Association. Copies of the *Model Code of Judicial Conduct* (1998) are available from Service Center, American Bar Association, 750 North Lake Shore Drive, Chicago, IL 60611, 1-800-285-2221.

ABA policy prohibits the reprinting of more than a limited percentage of the text of its publications. The policy of the ABA Center for Professional Responsibility prohibits the reprinting of only the black-letter (boldface) sections without all accompanying Commentary. This reprint of the *Model Code of Judicial Conduct* contains the full text of the Preamble, Terminology, and Canons 1 through 3 with Commentary. (For Canons 4 and 5, Application, and additional materials, see ***ABA/BNA Lawyers' Manual on Professional Conduct***, tab 01, pages 01:3001*ff.*)

seriousness of the transgression, whether there is a pattern of improper activity and the effect of the improper activity on others or on the judicial system. See ABA Standards Relating to Judicial Discipline and Disability Retirement.[1]

The Code of Judicial Conduct is not intended as an exhaustive guide for the conduct of judges. They should also be governed in their judicial and personal conduct by general ethical standards. The Code is intended, however, to state basic standards which should govern the conduct of all judges and to provide guidance to assist judges in establishing and maintaining high standards of judicial and personal conduct.

TERMINOLOGY

Terms explained below are noted with an asterisk (*) in the Sections where they appear. In addition, the Sections where terms appear are referred to after the explanation of each term below.

"Appropriate authority" denotes the authority with responsibility for initiation of disciplinary process with respect to the violation to be reported. See Sections 3D(1) and 3D(2).

"Candidate." A candidate is a person seeking selection for or retention in judicial office by election or appointment. A person becomes a candidate for judicial office as soon as he or she makes a public announcement of candidacy, declares or files as a candidate with the election or appointment authority, or authorizes solicitation or acceptance of contributions or support. The term "candidate" has the same meaning when applied to a judge seeking election or appointment to non-judicial office. See Preamble and Sections 5A, 5B, 5C and 5E.

"Continuing part-time judge." A continuing part-time judge is a judge who serves repeatedly on a part-time basis by election or under a continuing appointment, including a retired judge subject to recall who is permitted to practice law. See Application Section C.

"Court personnel" does not include the lawyers in a proceeding before a judge. See Sections 3B(7)(c) and 3B(9).

"De minimis" denotes an insignificant interest that could not raise reasonable question as to a judge's impartiality. See Sections 3E(1)(c) and 3E(1)(d).

"Economic interest" denotes ownership of a more than de minimis legal or equitable interest, or a relationship as officer, director, advisor or other active participant in the affairs of a party, except that:

(i) ownership of an interest in a mutual or common investment fund that holds securities is not an economic interest in such securities unless the judge participates in the management of the fund or a proceeding pending or impending before the judge could substantially affect the value of the interest;

(ii) service by a judge as an officer, director, advisor or other active participant in an educational, religious, charitable, fraternal or civic organization, or service by a judge's spouse, parent or child as an officer, director, advisor or other active participant in any organization does not create an economic interest in securities held by that organization;

---

[1]Judicial disciplinary procedures adopted in the jurisdictions should comport with the requirements of due process. The ABA Standards Relating to Judicial Discipline and Disability Retirement are cited as an example of how these due process requirements may be satisfied.

(iii) a deposit in a financial institution, the proprietary interest of a policy holder in a mutual insurance company, of a depositor in a mutual savings association or of a member in a credit union, or a similar proprietary interest, is not an economic interest in the organization unless a proceeding pending or impending before the judge could substantially affect the value of the interest;

(iv) ownership of government securities is not an economic interest in the issuer unless a proceeding pending or impending before the judge could substantially affect the value of the securities. See Sections 3E(1)(c) and 3E(2).

"Fiduciary" includes such relationships as executor, administrator, trustee, and guardian. See Sections 3E(2) and 4E.

"Knowingly," "knowledge," "known" or "knows" denotes actual knowledge of the fact in question. A person's knowledge may be inferred from circumstances. See Sections 3D, 3E(1), and 5A(3).

"Law" denotes court rules as well as statutes, constitutional provisions and decisional law. See Sections 2A, 3A, 3B(2), 3B(6), 4B, 4C, 4D(5), 4F, 4I, 5A(2), 5A(3), 5B(2), 5C(1), 5C(3) and 5D.

"Member of the candidate's family" denotes a spouse, child, grandchild, parent, grandparent or other relative or person with whom the candidate maintains a close familial relationship. See Section 5A(3)(a).

"Member of the judge's family" denotes a spouse, child, grandchild, parent, grandparent, or other relative or person with whom the judge maintains a close familial relationship. See Sections 4D(3), 4E and 4G.

"Member of the judge's family residing in the judge's household" denotes any relative of a judge by blood or marriage, or a person treated by a judge as a member of the judge's family, who resides in the judge's household. See Sections 3E(1) and 4D(5).

"Nonpublic information" denotes information that, by law, is not available to the public. Nonpublic information may include but is not limited to: information that is sealed by statute or court order, impounded or communicated in camera; and information offered in grand jury proceedings, presentencing reports, dependency cases or psychiatric reports. See Section 3B(11).

"Periodic part-time judge." A periodic part-time judge is a judge who serves or expects to serve repeatedly on a part-time basis but under a separate appointment for each limited period of service or for each matter. See Application Section D.

"Political organization" denotes a political party or other group, the principal purpose of which is to further the election or appointment of candidates to political office. See Sections 5A(1), 5B(2) and 5C(1).

"Pro tempore part-time judge." A pro tempore part-time judge is a judge who serves or expects to serve once or only sporadically on a part-time basis under a separate appointment for each period of service or for each case heard. See Application Section E.

"Public election." This term includes primary and general elections; it includes partisan elections, nonpartisan elections and retention elections. See Section 5C.

"Require." The rules prescribing that a judge "require" certain conduct of others are, like all of the rules in this Code, rules of reason. The use of the term "require" in that context means a judge is to exercise reasonable direction and control over the conduct of those persons subject to the judge's direction and control. See Sections 3B(3), 3B(4), 3B(5), 3B(6), 3B(9) and 3C(2).

"Third degree of relationship." The following persons are relatives within the third degree of relationship: great-grandparent, grandparent, parent, uncle, aunt, brother, sister, child, grandchild, great-grandchild, nephew or niece. See Section 3E(1)(d).

Canon 1

A JUDGE SHALL UPHOLD THE INTEGRITY AND INDEPENDENCE OF THE JUDICIARY

A. An independent and honorable judiciary is indispensable to justice in our society. A judge should participate in establishing, maintaining and enforcing high standards of conduct, and shall personally observe those standards so that the integrity and independence of the judiciary will be preserved. The provisions of this Code are to be construed and applied to further that objective.

Commentary:

Deference to the judgments and rulings of courts depends upon public confidence in the integrity and independence of judges. The integrity and independence of judges depends in turn upon their acting without fear or favor. Although judges should be independent, they must comply with the law, including the provisions of this Code. Public confidence in the impartiality of the judiciary is maintained by the adherence of each judge to this responsibility. Conversely, violation of this Code diminishes public confidence in the judiciary and thereby does injury to the system of government under law.

Canon 2

A JUDGE SHALL AVOID IMPROPRIETY AND THE APPEARANCE OF IMPROPRIETY IN ALL OF THE JUDGE'S ACTIVITIES

A. A judge shall respect and comply with the law* and shall act at all times in a manner that promotes public confidence in the integrity and impartiality of the judiciary.

Commentary:

Public confidence in the judiciary is eroded by irresponsible or improper conduct by judges. A judge must avoid all impropriety and appearance of impropriety. A judge must expect to be the subject of constant public scrutiny. A judge must therefore accept restrictions on the judge's conduct that might be viewed as burdensome by the ordinary citizen and should do so freely and willingly.

The prohibition against behaving with impropriety or the appearance of impropriety applies to both the professional and personal conduct of a judge. Because it is not practicable to list all prohibited acts, the proscription is necessarily cast in general terms that extend to conduct by judges that is harmful although not specifically mentioned in the Code. Actual improprieties under this standard include violations of law, court rules or other specific provisions of this Code. The test for appearance of impropriety is whether the conduct would create in reasonable minds a perception that the judge's ability to carry out judicial responsibilities with integrity, impartiality and competence is impaired.

See also Commentary under Section 2C.

B. A judge shall not allow family, social, political or other relationships to influence the judge's judicial conduct or judgment. A judge shall not lend

the prestige of judicial office to advance the private interests of the judge or others; nor shall a judge convey or permit others to convey the impression that they are in a special position to influence the judge. A judge shall not testify voluntarily as a character witness.

Commentary:

Maintaining the prestige of judicial office is essential to a system of government in which the judiciary functions independently of the executive and legislative branches. Respect for the judicial office facilitates the orderly conduct of legitimate judicial functions. Judges should distinguish between proper and improper use of the prestige of office in all of their activities. For example, it would be improper for a judge to allude to his or her judgeship to gain a personal advantage such as deferential treatment when stopped by a police officer for a traffic offense. Similarly, judicial letterhead must not be used for conducting a judge's personal business.

A judge must avoid lending the prestige of judicial office for the advancement of the private interests of others. For example, a judge must not use the judge's judicial position to gain advantage in a civil suit involving a member of the judge's family. In contracts for publication of a judge's writings, a judge should retain control over the advertising to avoid exploitation of the judge's office. As to the acceptance of awards, see Section 4D(5)(a) and Commentary.

Although a judge should be sensitive to possible abuse of the prestige of office, a judge may, based on the judge's personal knowledge, serve as a reference or provide a letter of recommendation. However, a judge must not initiate the communication of information to a sentencing judge or a probation or corrections officer but may provide to such persons information for the record in response to a formal request.

Judges may participate in the process of judicial selection by cooperating with appointing authorities and screening committees seeking names for consideration, and by responding to official inquiries concerning a person being considered for a judgeship. See also Canon 5 regarding use of a judge's name in political activities.

A judge must not testify voluntarily as a character witness because to do so may lend the prestige of the judicial office in support of the party for whom the judge testifies. Moreover, when a judge testifies as a witness, a lawyer who regularly appears before the judge may be placed in the awkward position of cross-examining the judge. A judge may, however, testify when properly summoned. Except in unusual circumstances where the demands of justice require, a judge should discourage a party from requiring the judge to testify as a character witness.

C. A judge shall not hold membership in any organization that practices invidious discrimination on the basis of race, sex, religion or national origin.

Commentary:

Membership of a judge in an organization that practices invidious discrimination gives rise to perceptions that the judge's impartiality is impaired. Section 2C refers to the current practices of the organization. Whether an organization practices invidious discrimination is often a complex question to which judges should be sensitive. The answer cannot be determined from a mere examination of an organization's current membership rolls but rather depends on how the organization selects members and other relevant factors, such as that the organization is dedicated to the preservation of religious, ethnic or cultural values of legitimate common interest to its members, or that it is in fact and effect an intimate, purely private organization whose membership limitations could not be constitutionally prohibited. Absent such factors, an organization is generally said to discriminate invidiously if it arbitrarily excludes from membership on the basis of race, religion, sex or national origin persons who would otherwise be admitted to membership. * * *

Although Section 2C relates only to membership in organizations that invidiously discriminate on the basis of race, sex, religion or national origin, a judge's membership in an organization that engages in any discriminatory membership practices prohibited by the law of the jurisdiction also violates Canon 2 and Section 2A and gives the appearance of impropriety. In addition, it would be a violation of Canon 2 and Section 2A for a judge to arrange a meeting at a club that the judge knows practices invidious discrimination on the basis of race, sex, religion or national origin in its membership or other policies, or for the judge to regularly use such a club. Moreover, public manifestation by a judge of the judge's knowing approval of invidious discrimination on any basis gives the appearance of impropriety under Canon 2 and diminishes public confidence in the integrity and impartiality of the judiciary, in violation of Section 2A.

When a person who is a judge on the date this Code becomes effective [in the jurisdiction in which the person is a judge][2] learns that an organization to which the judge belongs engages in invidious discrimination that would preclude membership under Section 2C or under Canon 2 and Section 2A, the judge is permitted, in lieu of resigning, to make immediate efforts to have the organization discontinue its invidiously discriminatory practices, but is required to suspend participation in any other activities of the organization. If the organization fails to discontinue its invidiously discriminatory practices as promptly as possible (and in all events within a year of the judge's first learning of the practices), the judge is required to resign immediately from the organization.

Canon 3

A JUDGE SHALL PERFORM THE DUTIES OF JUDICIAL OFFICE IMPARTIALLY AND DILIGENTLY

A. *Judicial Duties in General.* **The judicial duties of a judge take precedence over all the judge's other activities. The judge's judicial duties include all the duties of the judge's office prescribed by law*. In the performance of these duties, the following standards apply.**

B. *Adjudicative Responsibilities.*

(1) A judge shall hear and decide matters assigned to the judge except those in which disqualification is required.

(2) A judge shall be faithful to the law* and maintain professional competence in it. A judge shall not be swayed by partisan interests, public clamor or fear of criticism.

(3) A judge shall require* order and decorum in proceedings before the judge.

---

[2]The language within the brackets should be deleted when the jurisdiction adopts this provision.

(4) A judge shall be patient, dignified and courteous to litigants, jurors, witnesses, lawyers and others with whom the judge deals in an official capacity, and shall require* similar conduct of lawyers, and of staff, court officials and others subject to the judge's direction and control.

Commentary:

The duty to hear all proceedings fairly and with patience is not inconsistent with the duty to dispose promptly of the business of the court. Judges can be efficient and businesslike while being patient and deliberate.

A judge must refrain from speech, gestures or other conduct that could reasonably be perceived as sexual harassment and must require the same standard of conduct of others subject to the judge's direction and control.

(5) A judge shall perform judicial duties without bias or prejudice. A judge shall not, in the performance of judicial duties, by words or conduct manifest bias or prejudice, including but not limited to bias or prejudice based upon race, sex, religion, national origin, disability, age, sexual orientation or socioeconomic status, and shall not permit staff, court officials and others subject to the judge's direction and control to do so.

Commentary:

A judge must perform judicial duties impartially and fairly. A judge who manifests bias on any basis in a proceeding impairs the fairness of the proceeding and brings the judiciary into disrepute. Facial expression and body language, in addition to oral communication, can give to parties or lawyers in the proceeding, jurors, the media and others an appearance of judicial bias. A judge must be alert to avoid behavior that may be perceived as prejudicial.

(6) A judge shall require* lawyers in proceedings before the judge to refrain from manifesting, by words or conduct, bias or prejudice based upon race, sex, religion, national origin, disability, age, sexual orientation or socioeconomic status, against parties, witnesses, counsel or others. This Section 3B(6) does not preclude legitimate advocacy when race, sex, religion, national origin, disability, age, sexual orientation or socioeconomic status, or other similar factors, are issues in the proceeding.

(7) A judge shall accord to every person who has a legal interest in a proceeding, or that person's lawyer, the right to be heard according to law*. A judge shall not initiate, permit, or consider ex parte communications, or consider other communications made to the judge outside the presence of the parties concerning a pending or impending proceeding except that:

(a) Where circumstances require, ex parte communications for scheduling, administrative purposes or emergencies that do not deal with substantive matters or issues on the merits are authorized; provided:

(i) the judge reasonably believes that no party will gain a procedural or tactical advantage as a result of the ex parte communication, and

(ii) the judge makes provision promptly to notify all other parties of the substance of the ex parte communication and allows an opportunity to respond.

(b) A judge may obtain the advice of a disinterested expert on the law* applicable to a proceeding before the judge if the judge gives notice to the parties of the person consulted and the substance of the advice, and affords the parties reasonable opportunity to respond.

(c) A judge may consult with court personnel* whose function is to aid the judge in carrying out the judge's adjudicative responsibilities or with other judges.

(d) A judge may, with the consent of the parties, confer separately with the parties and their lawyers in an effort to mediate or settle matters pending before the judge.

(e) A judge may initiate or consider any ex parte communications when expressly authorized by law* to do so.

Commentary:

The proscription against communications concerning a proceeding includes communications from lawyers, law teachers, and other persons who are not participants in the proceeding, except to the limited extent permitted.

To the extent reasonably possible, all parties or their lawyers shall be included in communications with a judge.

Whenever presence of a party or notice to a party is required by Section 3B(7), it is the party's lawyer, or if the party is unrepresented the party, who is to be present or to whom notice is to be given.

An appropriate and often desirable procedure for a court to obtain the advice of a disinterested expert on legal issues is to invite the expert to file a brief *amicus curiae.*

Certain ex parte communication is approved by Section 3B(7) to facilitate scheduling and other administrative purposes and to accommodate emergencies. In general, however, a judge must discourage ex parte communication and allow it only if all the criteria stated in Section 3B(7) are clearly met. A judge must disclose to all parties all ex parte communications described in Sections 3B(7)(a) and 3B(7)(b) regarding a proceeding pending or impending before the judge.

A judge must not independently investigate facts in a case and must consider only the evidence presented.

A judge may request a party to submit proposed findings of fact and conclusions of law, so long as the other parties are apprised of the request and are given an opportunity to respond to the proposed findings and conclusions.

A judge must make reasonable efforts, including the provision of appropriate supervision, to ensure that Section 3B(7) is not violated through law clerks or other personnel on the judge's staff.

If communication between the trial judge and the appellate court with respect to a proceeding is permitted, a copy of any written communication or the substance of any oral communication should be provided to all parties.

(8) A judge shall dispose of all judicial matters promptly, efficiently and fairly.

Commentary:

In disposing of matters promptly, efficiently and fairly, a judge must demonstrate due regard for the rights of the parties to be heard and to have issues resolved without unnecessary cost or delay. Containing costs while preserving fundamental rights of parties also protects the interests of witnesses and the general public. A judge should monitor and supervise cases so as to reduce or eliminate dilatory practices, avoidable delays and unnecessary costs. A judge should encourage and seek to facilitate settlement, but parties should not feel coerced into surrendering the right to have their controversy resolved by the courts.

Prompt disposition of the court's business requires a judge to devote adequate time to judicial duties, to be punctual in attending court and expeditious in determining matters under submission, and to insist that court officials, litigants and their lawyers cooperate with the judge to that end.

(9) A judge shall not, while a proceeding is pending or impending in any court, make any public comment that might reasonably be expected to affect its outcome or impair its fairness or make any nonpublic comment that might substantially interfere with a fair trial or hearing. The judge shall require* similar abstention on the part of court personnel* subject to the judge's direction and control. This Section does not prohibit judges from making public statements in the course of their official duties or from explaining for public information the procedures of the court. This Section does not apply to proceedings in which the judge is a litigant in a personal capacity.

Commentary:

The requirement that judges abstain from public comment regarding a pending or impending proceeding continues during any appellate process and until final disposition. This Section does not prohibit a judge from commenting on proceedings in which the judge is a litigant in a personal capacity, but in cases such as a writ of mandamus where the judge is a litigant in an official capacity, the judge must not comment publicly. The conduct of lawyers relating to trial publicity is governed by [Rule 3.6 of the ABA Model Rules of Professional Conduct]. (Each jurisdiction should substitute an appropriate reference to its rule.)

(10) A judge shall not commend or criticize jurors for their verdict other than in a court order or opinion in a proceeding, but may express appreciation to jurors for their service to the judicial system and the community.

Commentary:

Commending or criticizing jurors for their verdict may imply a judicial expectation in future cases and may impair a juror's ability to be fair and impartial in a subsequent case.

(11) A judge shall not disclose or use, for any purpose unrelated to judicial duties, nonpublic information* acquired in a judicial capacity.

C. *Administrative Responsibilities.*

(1) A judge shall diligently discharge the judge's administrative responsibilities without bias or prejudice and maintain professional competence in judicial administration, and should cooperate with other judges and court officials in the administration of court business.

(2) A judge shall require* staff, court officials and others subject to the judge's direction and control to observe the standards of fidelity and diligence that apply to the judge and to refrain from manifesting bias or prejudice in the performance of their official duties.

(3) A judge with supervisory authority for the judicial performance of other judges shall take reasonable measures to assure the prompt disposition of matters before them and the proper performance of their other judicial responsibilities.

(4) A judge shall not make unnecessary appointments. A judge shall exercise the power of appointment impartially and on the basis of merit. A judge shall avoid nepotism and favoritism. A judge shall not approve compensation of appointees beyond the fair value of services rendered.

Commentary:

Appointees of a judge include assigned counsel, officials such as referees, commissioners, special masters, receivers and guardians and personnel such as clerks, secretaries and bailiffs. Consent by the parties to an appointment or an award of compensation does not relieve the judge of the obligation prescribed by Section 3C(4).

D. *Disciplinary Responsibilities.*

(1) A judge who receives information indicating a substantial likelihood that another judge has committed a violation of this Code should take appropriate action. A judge having knowledge* that another judge has committed a violation of this Code that raises a substantial question as to the other judge's fitness for office shall inform the appropriate authority*.

(2) A judge who receives information indicating a substantial likelihood that a lawyer has committed a violation of the Rules of Professional Conduct [substitute correct title if the applicable rules of lawyer conduct have a different title] should take appropriate action. A judge having knowledge* that a lawyer has committed a violation of the Rules of Professional Conduct [substitute correct title if the applicable rules of lawyer conduct have a different title] that raises a substantial question as to the lawyer's honesty, trustworthiness or fitness as a lawyer in other respects shall inform the appropriate authority*.

(3) Acts of a judge, in the discharge of disciplinary responsibilities, required or permitted by Sections 3D(1) and 3D(2) are part of a judge's judicial duties and shall be absolutely privileged, and no civil action predicated thereon may be instituted against the judge.

Commentary:

Appropriate action may include direct communication with the judge or lawyer who has committed the violation, other direct action if available, and reporting the violation to the appropriate authority or other agency or body.

E. *Disqualification.*

(1) A judge shall disqualify himself or herself in a proceeding in which the judge's impartiality might reasonably be questioned, including but not limited to instances where:

Commentary:

Under this rule, a judge is disqualified whenever the judge's impartiality might reasonably be questioned, regardless whether any of the specific rules in Section 3E(1) apply. For example, if a judge were in the process of negotiating for employment with a law firm, the judge would be disqualified from any matters in which that law firm appeared, unless the disqualification was waived by the parties after disclosure by the judge.

A judge should disclose on the record information that the judge believes the parties or their lawyers might consider relevant to the question of disqualification, even if the judge believes there is no real basis for disqualification.

By decisional law, the rule of necessity may override the rule of disqualification. For example, a judge might be required to participate in judicial review of a judicial salary statute, or might be the only judge available in a matter requiring immediate judicial action, such as a hearing on probable cause or a temporary restraining order. In the latter case, the judge must disclose on the record the basis for possible disqualification and use reasonable efforts to transfer the matter to another judge as soon as practicable.

(a) **the judge has a personal bias or prejudice concerning a party or a party's lawyer, or personal knowledge* of disputed evidentiary facts concerning the proceeding;**

(b) **the judge served as a lawyer in the matter in controversy, or a lawyer with whom the judge previously practiced law served during such association as a lawyer concerning the matter, or the judge has been a material witness concerning it;**

Commentary:

A lawyer in a government agency does not ordinarily have an association with other lawyers employed by that agency within the meaning of Section 3E(1)(b); a judge formerly employed by a government agency, however, should disqualify himself or herself in a proceeding if the judge's impartiality might reasonably be questioned because of such association.

(c) **the judge knows* that he or she, individually or as a fiduciary, or the judge's spouse, parent or child wherever residing, or any other member of the judge's family residing in the judge's household*, has an economic interest* in the subject matter in controversy or in a party to the proceeding or has any other more than de minimis* interest that could be substantially affected by the proceeding;**

(d) **the judge or the judge's spouse, or a person within the third degree of relationship* to either of them, or the spouse of such a person:**

(i) **is a party to the proceeding, or an officer, director or trustee of a party;**

(ii) **is acting as a lawyer in the proceeding;**

(iii) **is known* by the judge to have a more than de minimis* interest that could be substantially affected by the proceeding;**

(iv) **is to the judge's knowledge* likely to be a material witness in the proceeding.**

Commentary:

The fact that a lawyer in a proceeding is affiliated with a law firm with which a relative of the judge is affiliated does not of itself disqualify the judge. Under appropriate circumstances, the fact that "the judge's impartiality might reasonably be questioned" under Section 3E(1), or that the relative is known by the judge to have an interest in the law firm that could be "substantially affected by the outcome of the proceeding" under Section 3E(1)(d)(iii) may require the judge's disqualification.

(2) A judge shall keep informed about the judge's personal and fiduciary* economic interests*, and make a reasonable effort to keep informed about the personal economic interests of the judge's spouse and minor children residing in the judge's household.

F. *Remittal of Disqualification.* A judge disqualified by the terms of Section 3E may disclose on the record the basis of the judge's disqualification and may ask the parties and their lawyers to consider, out of the presence of the judge, whether to waive disqualification. If following disclosure of any basis for disqualification other than personal bias or prejudice concerning a party, the parties and lawyers, without participation by the judge, all agree that the judge should not be disqualified, and the judge is then willing to participate, the judge may participate in the proceeding. The agreement shall be incorporated in the record of the proceeding.

Commentary:

A remittal procedure provides the parties an opportunity to proceed without delay if they wish to waive the disqualification. To assure that consideration of the question of remittal is made independently of the judge, a judge must not solicit, seek or hear comment on possible remittal or waiver of the disqualification unless the lawyers jointly propose remittal after consultation as provided in the rule. A party may act through counsel if counsel represents on the record that the party has been consulted and consents. As a practical matter, a judge may wish to have all parties and their lawyers sign the remittal agreement.

* * *

3. LAW PRACTICE

Organization

AMERICAN BAR ASSOCIATION

Headquarters:
750 North Lake Shore Drive
Chicago, IL 60611-6281
Telephone: (312) 988-5000
Fax: (312) 988-6281
E-mail: info@abanet.org
Website: http://www.abanet.org
Ethics Hotline: Lawyers' Professional Liability
    Hotline: (312) 988-5754

Additional offices:
Center for Professional Responsibility
541 North Fairbanks Court
Chicago, IL 60611-3314
Telephone: (312) 988-5304
E-mail: ctrprofresp@abanet.org
Website: http://www.abanet.org/cpr

Date founded: 1878
Membership: approximately 350,000 lawyers, judges, court administra-
    tors, educators, law students, legal assistants, criminal justice profes-
    sionals, government officials, and business executives, plus state and
    local bar associations and law-related organizations

Official name: *Model Rules of Professional Conduct*
History: Adopted 1983; revised periodically; as amended August 1997
Authority: Standing Committee on Ethics and Professional Responsibility;
    House of Delegates

Additional Resources

Organizational (Divisions, Programs, Services, etc.):

Center for Professional Responsibility
Character and Fitness Project

Continuing Legal Education (CLE) Programs
Coordinating Group on Bioethics and the Law
CoverageQuest (computer software to analyze state legal malpractice
    insurance policies)
E. Smythe Gambrell Professionalism Awards
ETHICSearch (legal research service)
Forum on Health Law
Judicial Education Project
Lawyer Assistance Clearinghouse
Lawyer Regulation Outreach Project
National Conference on Professional Responsibility
National Forum on Client Protection
National Lawyer Regulatory Data Bank
National Legal Malpractice Data Center
National Organization of Bar Counsel
National Professionalism Research Service
National Workshop for Lawyer Assistance Programs
Professionalism Outreach Project
State Disciplinary System Consultations
Various Commissions: Advertising; Evaluation of Disciplinary
    Enforcement (McKay Commission); Evaluation of the Rules of
    Professional Conduct (Ethics 2000); Impaired Attorneys; Lawyers'
    Assistance Programs; Lawyers' Funds for Client Protection; Legal
    Education; Nonlawyer Practice
Various Committees and Subcommittees: Client Protection; Continuing
    Education of the Bar; Lawyer Competence; Lawyer Regulation;
    Lawyers' Professional Liability; Lawyers' Public Service
    Responsibility; Professional Discipline; Professionalism;
    Professionalism and Ethics; Specialization
Various Sections: Legal Education and Admissions to the Bar;
    Individual Rights and Responsibilities; Young Lawyers
West Professional Responsibility Law Library

Informational (Publications, Videos, Seminars, etc.):

Articles in *ABA Journal* and individual Section journals
Various periodicals:
    ABA Bioethics Bulletin
    ABA/BNA Lawyers' Manual on Professional Conduct
    Law Practice Management
    Lawyers' Professional Liability Update
    The Professional Lawyer
Various publications:
    A Survey on the Teaching of Professional Responsibility
    *Advertising in the Legal Profession: A Descriptive Bibliography and
        Reference Guide*

AIDS and Government Liability: State and Local Government Guide to Legislation, Legal Issues, and Liability

AIDS/HIV and Confidentiality

Annotated Model Rules of Professional Conduct

Antitrust and Trade Associations: How Trade Regulation Laws Apply to Trade and Professional Associations

Attorney-Client Privilege and the Work-Product Doctrine

Attorney-Client Privilege in Civil Litigation

Attorney-Client Privilege Under Siege: Preserving and Protecting It in Civil Cases

Avoiding Client Grievances

Bar Response to a Mass Disaster: Protecting the Victims from Unethical Lawyer Conduct

Compendium of Professional Responsibility Rules and Standards

Competence in the Law Firm

Connecting with Your Client

Directories: Lawyer Disciplinary Agencies; Lawyers' Funds for Client Protection; State and Local Lawyer Assistance Programs

Disclosure Roles of Counsel in State and Local Government Securities Offerings

The Ethical Family Lawyer: A Practical Guide to Avoiding Professional Dilemmas

Ethical Problems Facing the Criminal Defense Lawyer: Practical Answers to Tough Questions

Ethics Opinions

The Impact of Advertising on the Image of Lawyers

In the Spirit of Public Service: A Blueprint for the Rekindling of Professionalism

Invited Papers on Privacy: Law, Ethics and Technology

Issues in Forming a Bar-Related Professional Liability Insurance Company

Law Partnership: Its Rights and Responsibilities

Lawyer Advertising at the Crossroads: Professional Policy Considerations

Lawyer Specialization Bibliography

The Lawyer's Desk Guide to Legal Malpractice

Lawyers and Certified Public Accountants: A Study of Interprofessional Relations

Lawyers On Line: Ethical Perspectives in the Use of Telecomputer Communication

The Legal Assistant's Practical Guide to Professional Responsibility

Legal Education and Professional Development: An Educational Continuum

Legal Tender: A Lawyer's Guide to Handling Professional Dilemmas

The Lobbying Manual: A Compliance Guide for Lawyers and Lobbyists

Making the Competent Lawyer: A Model for Law School Action
Non-Lawyer Practice in the United States
Organizational Conflicts of Interest in Government Contracting
Personal Conflicts of Interest in Government Contracting
Practicing Law Without Clients
Problems and Recommendations in Disciplinary Enforcement ("The Clark Report")
Professional Discipline for Lawyers and Judges
Profile of Legal Malpractice: A Statistical Study of Determinative Characteristics of Claims Asserted Against Attorneys
Provisions of State Codes of Professional Responsibility Governing Lawyer Advertising and Solicitation
The Quality Pursuit: Assuring Standards in the Practice of Law
Serving Two Masters: The Law of Lawyer Disqualification
Statement of Fundamental Lawyering Skills and Professional Values
Statement of Standards & Practices for a Lawyer Referral & Information Service
Survey and Related Materials on the Unauthorized Practice of Law/Nonlawyer Practice
Survey on Lawyer Discipline
Teaching and Learning Professionalism
Various *Model Codes, Rules,* and *Standards*
Various videos and audiotapes:
Client Confidentiality
Conflicts of Interest
Corporate Counsel: Confidences and Conflicts
Emerging Issues in Professional Responsibility and Malpractice
Ethical and Aggressive Use of the Federal Rules to Gain an Advantage in Litigation
Ethical Dilemmas and Professionalism
Ethics Decisions Regarding the Representation of a Client Under a Disability
The Ethics of Race in Criminal Defense Practice
Government Lawyers and the Rules of Legal Ethics
Imposing Discipline on Criminal Lawyers: Different Rules, Different Procedures?
Independence of Counsel
The Judicial Response to Lawyer Misconduct
Lawyer Advertising: How Far Can Regulation Go?
Lawyers Impaired by Alcohol/Drugs: The Interaction Between Disciplinary and Assistance Programs
The Model Rules of Professional Conduct: Have We Lost Our Professional Values?
Preventing Legal Malpractice: A Guide series
Professional Responsibility and the Solo or Small Firm Practitioner
The S.O.B. Litigator Vignettes

Video Depositions: What You Don't Know Can Hurt You
White Collar Crime
Winning. . . Without Losing Your Professionalism

Goals and Activities of Organization

The American Bar Association (ABA) is the national organization of the legal profession in the U.S. Among its goals are to advance the science of jurisprudence; promote improvements in the justice system, the uniformity of legislation and judicial decisions, and the delivery of legal services; increase the public's understanding of the law and the role of lawyers; assure high standards of professional competence and ethical conduct; enhance members' professional growth; encourage cordial relations among lawyers; urge full and equal participation in the profession by minorities and women; and advance the rule of law in the world.

The ABA analyzes issues that affect the legal profession and develops effective remedial responses, ranging from policy positions to demonstration projects to conferences. These activities are conducted through the ABA's many sections, divisions, commissions, and committees, which are semi-autonomous and focus on the different areas of legal practice. They coordinate their efforts with those of the national organization, in order to publish books and journals, offer continuing legal education programs, influence legislation and litigation, create model rules and laws, work with affiliated professions, evaluate judicial performance, and provide information on the law and lawyers to the public.

The ABA Center for Professional Responsibility coordinates, collects, analyzes, and publishes research, statistical, and educational materials on all aspects of legal and judicial ethics. It maintains close liaison with federal and state courts, disciplinary agencies, and advisory committees.

Implementation and Enforcement of Code

The ABA does not have the power to discipline attorneys or enforce the Rules it develops. The Rules are designed to serve as model legislation for the state and federal bars in creating their own rules of professional responsibility, applicable to the attorneys who practice within their jurisdictions.

The majority of states have fashioned their standards after the Model Rules of Professional Conduct. The remaining states' standards are based on the older ABA Model Code of Professional Responsibility.

Only the "black-letter" (boldface) Rules are intended to be enforceable and controlling; the accompanying Comments are intended to explain and interpret them. The Model Code Comparisons are included to assist the reader in comparing the Model Rules with the Model Code; they are not official ABA policy.

The Standing Committee on Ethics and Professional Responsibility assists state bar organizations and courts in their study of the Model Rules and their modification and/or implementation in their own jurisdictions. The Committee also issues formal and informal Ethics Opinions interpreting the Rules, either at the request of a lawyer or judge (whether or not a member of the ABA) or on its own initiative.

The topics covered in the complete Model Rules are:

Client-Lawyer Relationship
Rule 1.1 Competence
     1.2 Scope of Representation
     1.3 Diligence
     1.4 Communication
     1.5 Fees
     1.6 Confidentiality of Information
     1.7 Conflict of Interest: General Rule
     1.8 Conflict of Interest: Prohibited Transactions
     1.9 Conflict of Interest: Former Client
     1.10 Imputed Disqualification: General Rule
     1.11 Successive Government and Private Employment
     1.12 Former Judge or Arbitrator
     1.13 Organization as Client
     1.14 Client Under a Disability
     1.15 Safekeeping Property
     1.16 Declining or Terminating Representation
     1.17 Sale of Law Practice

Counselor
Rule 2.1 Advisor
     2.2 Intermediary
     2.3 Evaluation for Use by Third Persons

Advocate
Rule 3.1 Meritorious Claims and Contentions
     3.2 Expediting Litigation
     3.3 Candor Toward the Tribunal
     3.4 Fairness to Opposing Party and Counsel
     3.5 Impartiality and Decorum of the Tribunal
     3.6 Trial Publicity
     3.7 Lawyer as Witness
     3.8 Special Responsibilities of a Prosecutor
     3.9 Advocate in Nonadjudicative Proceedings

Transactions with Persons Other Than Clients
Rule 4.1 Truthfulness in Statements to Others
     4.2 Communication with Person Represented by Counsel
     4.3 Dealing with Unrepresented Person
     4.4 Respect for Rights of Third Persons

Law Firms and Associations
Rule 5.1 Responsibilities of a Partner or Supervisory Lawyer
     5.2 Responsibilities of a Subordinate Lawyer
     5.3 Responsibilities Regarding Nonlawyer Assistants

History and Development of Code

The Model Rules of Professional Conduct, including Preamble, Scope, Terminology, and Comment, were adopted by the House of Delegates in August 1983, and have been periodically amended.

The drafting process began in 1977 with the appointment of a Commission on Evaluation of Professional Standards, which examined the effectiveness of the existing set of disciplinary rules, the Model Code of Professional Responsibility adopted in 1969. It determined that the patchwork amendment of the Code would not adequately address lawyers' growing need for consistent, comprehensive ethical guidance in a more complex society; creation of a new set of standards was necessary.

One of the major changes was in format. The previous Model Code of 1969 consisted of general Canons, aspirational Ethical Considerations, and enforceable Disciplinary Rules. The current standards consist of enforceable black-letter Rules and explanatory Comments—a more convenient, understandable, and readily applicable structure.

The 1969 Code had replaced the original ABA Standards—the 1908 Canons of Professional Ethics. The Canons were adapted from the Alabama Bar Association's 1887 Code of Ethics, which was in turn based on two earlier legal works published in 1854 and 1836.

The Model Rules are amended upon recommendation of the Standing Committee on Ethics and Professional Responsibility and adoption by the House of Delegates.

As of August 1998, a new Special Commission on Evaluation of the Rules of Professional Conduct, or Ethics 2000, is reviewing and evaluating the ABA Model Rules, state and federal rules of professional conduct, and other ethics standards governing the legal profession, and will make further recommendations.

Model Rules of Professional Conduct*

PREAMBLE: A LAWYER'S RESPONSIBILITIES

A lawyer is a representative of clients, an officer of the legal system and a public citizen having special responsibility for the quality of justice.

As a representative of clients, a lawyer performs various functions. As advisor, a lawyer provides a client with an informed understanding of the client's legal rights and obligations and explains their practical implications. As advocate, a lawyer zealously asserts the client's position under the rules of the adversary system. As negotiator, a lawyer seeks a result advantageous to the client but consistent with requirements of honest dealing with others. As intermediary between clients, a lawyer seeks to reconcile their divergent interests as an advisor and, to a limited extent, as a spokesperson for each client. A lawyer acts as evaluator by examining a client's legal affairs and reporting about them to the client or to others.

In all professional functions a lawyer should be competent, prompt and diligent. A lawyer should maintain communication with a client concerning the representation. A lawyer should keep in confidence information relating to representation of a client except so far as disclosure is required or permitted by the Rules of Professional Conduct or other law.

A lawyer's conduct should conform to the requirements of the law, both in professional service to clients and in the lawyer's business and personal affairs. A lawyer should use the law's procedures only for legitimate purposes and not to harass or intimidate others. A lawyer should demonstrate respect for the legal system and for those who serve it, including judges, other lawyers and public officials. While it is a lawyer's duty, when necessary, to challenge the rectitude of official action, it is also a lawyer's duty to uphold legal process.

As a public citizen, a lawyer should seek improvement of the law, the administration of justice and the quality of service rendered by the legal profession. As a member of a learned profession, a lawyer should cultivate knowledge of the law beyond its use for clients, employ that knowledge in reform of the law and work to strengthen legal education. A lawyer should be mindful of deficiencies in the administration of justice and of the fact that the poor, and sometimes persons who are not poor, cannot afford adequate legal assistance, and should therefore devote professional time and civic influence in their behalf. A lawyer should aid the legal profession in pursuing these objectives and should help the bar regulate itself in the public interest.

Many of a lawyer's professional responsibilities are prescribed in the Rules of Professional Conduct, as well as substantive and procedural law. However, a

---

lawyer is also guided by personal conscience and the approbation of professional peers. A lawyer should strive to attain the highest level of skill, to improve the law and the legal profession and to exemplify the legal profession's ideals of public service.

A lawyer's responsibilities as a representative of clients, an officer of the legal system and a public citizen are usually harmonious. Thus, when an opposing party is well represented, a lawyer can be a zealous advocate on behalf of a client and at the same time assume that justice is being done. So also, a lawyer can be sure that preserving client confidences ordinarily serves the public interest because people are more likely to seek legal advice, and thereby heed their legal obligations, when they know their communications will be private.

In the nature of law practice, however, conflicting responsibilities are encountered. Virtually all difficult ethical problems arise from conflict between a lawyer's responsibilities to clients, to the legal system and to the lawyer's own interest in remaining an upright person while earning a satisfactory living. The Rules of Professional Conduct prescribe terms for resolving such conflicts. Within the framework of these Rules many difficult issues of professional discretion can arise. Such issues must be resolved through the exercise of sensitive professional and moral judgment guided by the basic principles underlying the Rules.

The legal profession is largely self-governing. Although other professions also have been granted powers of self-government, the legal profession is unique in this respect because of the close relationship between the profession and the processes of government and law enforcement. This connection is manifested in the fact that ultimate authority over the legal profession is vested largely in the courts.

To the extent that lawyers meet the obligations of their professional calling, the occasion for government regulation is obviated. Self-regulation also helps maintain the legal profession's independence from government domination. An independent legal profession is an important force in preserving government under law, for abuse of legal authority is more readily challenged by a profession whose members are not dependent on government for the right to practice.

The legal profession's relative autonomy carries with it special responsibilities of self-government. The profession has a responsibility to assure that its regulations are conceived in the public interest and not in furtherance of parochial or self-interested concerns of the bar. Every lawyer is responsible for observance of the Rules of Professional Conduct. A lawyer should also aid in securing their observance by other lawyers. Neglect of these responsibilities compromises the independence of the profession and the public interest which it serves.

Lawyers play a vital role in the preservation of society. The fulfillment of this role requires an understanding by lawyers of their relationship to our legal system. The Rules of Professional Conduct, when properly applied, serve to define that relationship.

SCOPE

The Rules of Professional Conduct are rules of reason. They should be interpreted with reference to the purposes of legal representation and of the law itself. Some of the Rules are imperatives, cast in the terms "shall" or "shall not." These define proper conduct for purposes of professional discipline. Others, generally cast in the term "may," are permissive and define areas under the Rules in which the lawyer has professional discretion. No disciplinary action should be taken when the lawyer chooses not to act or acts within the bounds of such discretion. Other Rules define the nature of relationships between the lawyer and others. The Rules are thus partly obligatory and disciplinary and partly constitutive and descriptive in that they define a lawyer's professional role. Many of the Comments use the term "should." Comments do not add obligations to the Rules but provide guidance for practicing in compliance with the Rules.

The Rules presuppose a larger legal context shaping the lawyer's role. That context includes court rules and statutes relating to matters of licensure, laws defining specific obligations of lawyers and substantive and procedural law in general. Compliance with the Rules, as with all law in an open society, depends primarily upon understanding and voluntary compliance, secondarily upon reinforcement by peer and public opinion and finally, when necessary, upon enforcement through disciplinary proceedings. The Rules do not, however, exhaust the moral and ethical considerations that should inform a lawyer, for no worthwhile human activity can be completely defined by legal rules. The Rules simply provide a framework for the ethical practice of law.

Furthermore, for purposes of determining the lawyer's authority and responsibility, principles of substantive law external to these Rules determine whether a client-lawyer relationship exists. Most of the duties flowing from the client-lawyer relationship attach only after the client has requested the lawyer to render legal services and the lawyer has agreed to do so. But there are some duties, such as that of confidentiality under Rule 1.6, that may attach when the lawyer agrees to consider whether a client-lawyer relationship shall be established. Whether a client-lawyer relationship exists for any specific purpose can depend on the circumstances and may be a question of fact.

Under various legal provisions, including constitutional, statutory and common law, the responsibilities of government lawyers may include authority concerning legal matters that ordinarily reposes in the client in private client-lawyer relationships. For example, a lawyer for a government agency may have authority on behalf of the government to decide upon settlement or whether to appeal from an adverse judgment. Such authority in various respects is generally vested in the attorney general and the state's attorney in state government, and their federal counterparts, and the same may be true of other government law officers. Also, lawyers under the supervision of these officers may be authorized to represent several government agencies in intragovernmental legal controversies in circumstances where a private lawyer could not represent multiple private clients. They also may have authority to represent the "public interest" in circumstances where a private lawyer would not be authorized to do so. These Rules do not abrogate any such authority.

Failure to comply with an obligation or prohibition imposed by a Rule is a basis for invoking the disciplinary process. The Rules presuppose that disciplinary assessment of a lawyer's conduct will be made on the basis of the facts and circumstances as they existed at the time of the conduct in question and in recognition of the fact that a lawyer often has to act upon uncertain or incomplete evidence of the situation. Moreover, the Rules presuppose that whether or not discipline should be imposed for a violation, and the severity of a sanction, depend on all the circumstances, such as the willfulness and seriousness of the violation, extenuating factors and whether there have been previous violations.

Violation of a Rule should not give rise to a cause of action nor should it create any presumption that a legal duty has been breached. The Rules are designed to provide guidance to lawyers and to provide a structure for regulating conduct through disciplinary agencies. They are not designed to be a basis for civil liability. Furthermore, the purpose of the Rules can be subverted when they are invoked by opposing parties as procedural weapons. The fact that a Rule is a just basis for a lawyer's self-assessment, or for sanctioning a lawyer under the administration of a disciplinary authority, does not imply that an antagonist in a collateral proceeding or transaction has standing to seek enforcement of the Rule. Accordingly, nothing in the Rules should be deemed to augment any substantive legal duty of lawyers or the extra-disciplinary consequences of violating such duty.

Moreover, these Rules are not intended to govern or affect judicial application of either the attorney-client or work product privilege. Those privileges were developed to promote compliance with law and fairness in litigation. In reliance on the attorney-client privilege, clients are entitled to expect that communications within the scope of the privilege will be protected against compelled disclosure. The attorney-client privilege is that of the client and not of the lawyer. The fact that in exceptional situations the lawyer under the Rules has a limited discretion to disclose a client confidence does not vitiate the proposition that, as a general matter, the client has a reasonable expectation that information relating to the client will not be voluntarily disclosed and that disclosure of such information may be judicially compelled only in accordance with recognized exceptions to the attorney-client and work product privileges.

The lawyer's exercise of discretion not to disclose information under Rule 1.6 should not be subject to reexamination. Permitting such reexamination would be incompatible with the general policy of promoting compliance with law through assurances that communications will be protected against disclosure.

The Comment accompanying each Rule explains and illustrates the meaning and purpose of the Rule. The Preamble and this note on Scope provide general orientation. The Comments are intended as guides to interpretation, but the text of each Rule is authoritative. Research notes were prepared to compare counterparts in the ABA Model Code of Professional Responsibility (adopted 1969, as amended) and to provide selected references to other authorities. The notes have not been adopted, do not constitute part of the Model Rules, and are not intended to affect the application or interpretation of the Rules and Comments.

TERMINOLOGY

"Belief" or "Believes" denotes that the person involved actually supposed the fact in question to be true. A person's belief may be inferred from circumstances.

"Consult" or "Consultation" denotes communication of information reasonably sufficient to permit the client to appreciate the significance of the matter in question.

"Firm" or "Law firm" denotes a lawyer or lawyers in a private firm, lawyers employed in the legal department of a corporation or other organization and lawyers employed in a legal services organization. See Comment, Rule 1.10.

"Fraud" or "Fraudulent" denotes conduct having a purpose to deceive and not merely negligent misrepresentation or failure to apprise another of relevant information.

"Knowingly," "Known," or "Knows" denotes actual knowledge of the fact in question. A person's knowledge may be inferred from circumstances.

"Partner" denotes a member of a partnership and a shareholder in a law firm organized as a professional corporation.

"Reasonable" or "Reasonably" when used in relation to conduct by a lawyer denotes the conduct of a reasonably prudent and competent lawyer.

"Reasonable belief" or "Reasonably believes" when used in reference to a lawyer denotes that the lawyer believes the matter in question and that the circumstances are such that the belief is reasonable.

"Reasonably should know" when used in reference to a lawyer denotes that a lawyer of reasonable prudence and competence would ascertain the matter in question.

"Substantial" when used in reference to degree or extent denotes a material matter of clear and weighty importance.

CLIENT-LAWYER RELATIONSHIP

Rule 1.1 COMPETENCE

A lawyer shall provide competent representation to a client. Competent representation requires the legal knowledge, skill, thoroughness and preparation reasonably necessary for the representation.

COMMENT:

Legal Knowledge and Skill

In determining whether a lawyer employs the requisite knowledge and skill in a particular matter, relevant factors include the relative complexity and specialized nature of the matter, the lawyer's general experience, the lawyer's training and experience in the field in question, the preparation and study the lawyer is able to give the matter and whether it is feasible to refer the matter to, or associate or consult with, a lawyer of established competence in the field in question. In many instances, the required proficiency is that of a general practitioner. Expertise in a particular field of law may be required in some circumstances.

A lawyer need not necessarily have special training or prior experience to handle legal problems of a type with which the lawyer is unfamiliar. A newly admitted lawyer can be as competent as a practitioner with long experience. Some important legal skills, such as the analysis of precedent, the evaluation of evidence and legal drafting, are required in all legal problems. Perhaps the most fundamental legal skill consists of determining what kind of legal problems a situation may involve, a skill that necessarily transcends any particular specialized knowledge. A lawyer can provide adequate representation in a wholly novel field through necessary study. Competent representation can also be provided through the association of a lawyer of established competence in the field in question.

In an emergency a lawyer may give advice or assistance in a matter in which the lawyer does not have the skill ordinarily required where referral to or consultation or association with another lawyer would be impractical. Even in an emergency, however, assistance should be limited to that reasonably necessary in the circumstances, for ill-considered action under emergency conditions can jeopardize the client's interest.

A lawyer may accept representation where the requisite level of competence can be achieved by reasonable preparation. This applies as well to a lawyer who is appointed as counsel for an unrepresented person. See also Rule 6.2.

Thoroughness and Preparation

Competent handling of a particular matter includes inquiry into and analysis of the factual and legal elements of the problem, and use of methods and procedures meeting the standards of competent practitioners. It also includes adequate preparation. The required attention and preparation are determined in part by what is at stake; major litigation and complex transactions ordinarily require more elaborate treatment than matters of lesser consequence.

Maintaining Competence

To maintain the requisite knowledge and skill, a lawyer should engage in continuing study and education. If a system of peer review has been established, the lawyer should consider making use of it in appropriate circumstances.

MODEL CODE COMPARISON

DR 6-101(A)(1) provided that a lawyer shall not handle a matter "which he knows or should know that he is not competent to handle, without associating himself with a lawyer who is competent to handle it;" DR 6-101(A)(2) required "preparation adequate in the circumstances." Rule 1.1 more fully particularizes the elements of competence. Whereas DR 6-101(A)(3) prohibited the "[n]eglect of a legal matter," Rule 1.1 does not contain such a prohibition. Instead, Rule 1.1 affirmatively requires the lawyer to be competent.

Rule 1.2 SCOPE OF REPRESENTATION

(a) A lawyer shall abide by a client's decisions concerning the objectives of representation, subject to paragraphs (c), (d) and (e), and shall consult with the client as to the means by which they are to be pursued. A lawyer shall abide by a client's decision whether to accept an offer of settlement of a matter. In a criminal case, the lawyer shall abide by the client's decision, after consultation with the lawyer, as to a plea to be entered, whether to waive jury trial and whether the client will testify.

(b) A lawyer's representation of a client, including representation by appointment, does not constitute an endorsement of the client's political, economic, social or moral views or activities.

(c) A lawyer may limit the objectives of the representation if the client consents after consultation.

(d) A lawyer shall not counsel a client to engage, or assist a client, in conduct that the lawyer knows is criminal or fraudulent, but a lawyer may discuss the legal consequences of any proposed course of conduct with a client and may counsel or assist a client to make a good faith effort to determine the validity, scope, meaning or application of the law.

(e) When a lawyer knows that a client expects assistance not permitted by the Rules of Professional Conduct or other law, the lawyer shall consult with the client regarding the relevant limitations on the lawyer's conduct.

COMMENT:

Scope of Representation

Both lawyer and client have authority and responsibility in the objectives and means of representation. The client has ultimate authority to determine the purposes to be served by legal representation, within the limits imposed by law and the lawyer's professional obligations. Within those limits, a client also has a right to consult with the lawyer about the means to be used in pursuing those objectives. At the same time, a lawyer is not required to pursue objectives or employ means simply because a client may wish that the lawyer do so. A clear distinction between objectives and means sometimes cannot be drawn, and in many cases the client-lawyer relationship partakes of a joint undertaking. In questions of means, the lawyer should assume responsibility for technical and legal tactical issues, but should defer to the client regarding such questions as the expense to be incurred and concern for third persons who might be adversely affected. Law defining the lawyer's scope of authority in litigation varies among jurisdictions.

In a case in which the client appears to be suffering mental disability, the lawyer's duty to abide by the client's decisions is to be guided by reference to Rule 1.14.

Independence From Client's Views or Activities

Legal representation should not be denied to people who are unable to afford legal services, or whose cause is controversial or the subject of popular disapproval. By the same token, representing a client does not constitute approval of the client's views or activities.

Services Limited in Objectives or Means

The objectives or scope of services provided by a lawyer may be limited by agreement with the client or by the terms under which the lawyer's services are made available to the client. For example, a retainer may be for a specifically defined purpose. Representation provided through a legal aid agency may be subject to limitations on the types of cases the agency handles. When a lawyer has been retained by an insurer to represent an insured, the representation may be limited to matters related to the insurance coverage. The terms upon which representation is undertaken may exclude specific objectives or means. Such limitations may exclude objectives or means that the lawyer regards as repugnant or imprudent.

An agreement concerning the scope of representation must accord with the Rules of Professional Conduct and other law. Thus, the client may not be asked to agree to representation so limited in scope as to violate Rule 1.1, or to surrender the right to terminate the lawyer's services or the right to settle litigation that the lawyer might wish to continue.

Criminal, Fraudulent and Prohibited Transactions

A lawyer is required to give an honest opinion about the actual consequences that appear likely to result from a client's conduct. The fact that a client uses advice in a course of action that is criminal or fraudulent does not, of itself, make a lawyer a party to the course of action. However, a lawyer may not knowingly assist a client in criminal or fraudulent conduct. There is a critical distinction between presenting an analysis of legal aspects of questionable conduct and recommending the means by which a crime or fraud might be committed with impunity.

When the client's course of action has already begun and is continuing, the lawyer's responsibility is especially delicate. The lawyer is not permitted to reveal the client's wrongdoing, except where permitted by Rule 1.6. However, the lawyer is required to avoid furthering the purpose, for example, by suggesting how it might be concealed. A lawyer may not continue assisting a client in conduct that the lawyer originally supposes is legally proper but then discovers is criminal or fraudulent. Withdrawal from the representation, therefore, may be required.

Where the client is a fiduciary, the lawyer may be charged with special obligations in dealings with a beneficiary.

Paragraph (d) applies whether or not the defrauded party is a party to the transaction. Hence, a lawyer should not participate in a sham transaction; for example, a transaction to effectuate criminal or fraudulent escape of tax liability. Paragraph (d) does not preclude undertaking a criminal defense incident to a general retainer for legal services to a lawful enterprise. The last clause of paragraph (d) recognizes that determining the validity or interpretation of a statute or regulation may require a course of action involving disobedience of the statute or regulation or of the interpretation placed upon it by governmental authorities.

MODEL CODE COMPARISON

Paragraph (a) has no counterpart in the Disciplinary Rules of the Model Code. EC 7-7 stated: "In certain areas of legal representation not affecting the merits of the cause or substantially prejudicing the rights of a client, a lawyer is entitled to make decisions on his own. But otherwise the authority to make decisions is exclusively that of the client. . . ." EC 7-8 stated that "[i]n the final analysis, however, the . . . decision whether to forego legally available objectives or methods because of nonlegal factors is ultimately for the client. . . . In the event that the client in a nonadjudicatory matter insists upon a course of conduct that is contrary to the judgment and advice of the lawyer but not prohibited by Disciplinary Rules, the lawyer may withdraw from the employment." DR 7-101(A)(1) provided that a lawyer "shall not intentionally . . . fail to seek the lawful objectives of his client through reasonably available means permitted by law. . . . A lawyer does not violate this Disciplinary Rule, however, by . . . avoiding offensive tactics. . . ."

Paragraph (b) has no counterpart in the Model Code.

With regard to paragraph (c), DR 7-101(B)(1) provided that a lawyer may, "where permissible, exercise his professional judgment to waive or fail to assert a right or position of his client."

With regard to paragraph (d), DR 7-102(A)(7) provided that a lawyer shall not "counsel or assist his client in conduct that the lawyer knows to be illegal or fraudulent." DR 7-102(A)(6) provided that a lawyer shall not "participate in the creation or preservation of evidence when he knows or it is obvious that the evidence is false." DR 7-106 provided that a lawyer shall not "advise his client to disregard a standing rule of a tribunal or a ruling of a tribunal . . . but he may take appropriate steps in good faith to test the validity of such rule or ruling." EC 7-5 stated that a lawyer "should never encourage or aid his client to commit criminal acts or counsel his client on how to violate the law and avoid punishment therefor."

With regard to paragraph (e), DR 2-110(C)(1)(c) provided that a lawyer may withdraw from representation if a client "insists" that the lawyer engage in "conduct that is illegal or that is prohibited under the Disciplinary Rules." DR 9-101(C) provided that "a lawyer shall not state or imply that he is able to influence improperly . . . any tribunal, legislative body or public official."

Rule 1.3 DILIGENCE

A lawyer shall act with reasonable diligence and promptness in representing a client.

COMMENT:

A lawyer should pursue a matter on behalf of a client despite opposition, obstruction or personal inconvenience to the lawyer, and may take whatever lawful and ethical measures are required to vindicate a client's cause or endeavor. A lawyer should act with commitment and dedication to the interests of the client and with zeal in advocacy upon the client's behalf. However, a lawyer is not bound to press for every advantage that might be realized for a client. A lawyer has professional discretion in determining the means by which a matter should be pursued. See Rule 1.2. A lawyer's workload should be controlled so that each matter can be handled adequately.

Perhaps no professional shortcoming is more widely resented than procrastination. A client's interests often can be adversely affected by the passage of time or the change of conditions; in extreme instances, as when a lawyer overlooks a statute of limitations, the client's legal position may be destroyed. Even when the client's interests are not affected in substance, however, unreasonable delay can cause a client needless anxiety and undermine confidence in the lawyer's trustworthiness.

Unless the relationship is terminated as provided in Rule 1.16, a lawyer should carry through to conclusion all matters undertaken for a client. If a lawyer's employment is limited to a specific matter, the relationship terminates when the matter has been resolved. If a lawyer has served a client over a substantial period in a variety of matters, the client sometimes may assume that the lawyer will continue to serve on a continuing basis unless the lawyer gives notice of withdrawal. Doubt about whether a client-lawyer relationship still exists should be clarified by the lawyer, preferably in writing, so that the client will not mistakenly suppose the lawyer is looking after the client's affairs when the lawyer has ceased to do so. For example, if a lawyer has handled a judicial or administrative proceeding that produced a result adverse to the client but has not been specifically instructed concerning pursuit of an appeal, the lawyer should advise the client of the possibility of appeal before relinquishing responsibility for the matter.

MODEL CODE COMPARISON

DR 6-101(A)(3) required that a lawyer not "[n]eglect a legal matter entrusted to him." EC 6-4 stated that a lawyer should "give appropriate attention to his legal work." Canon 7 stated that "a lawyer should represent a client zealously within the bounds of the law." DR 7-101(A)(1) provided that a lawyer "shall not intentionally . . . fail to seek the lawful objectives of his client through reasonably available means permitted by law and the Disciplinary Rules. . . ." DR 7-101(A)(3) provided that a lawyer "shall not intentionally . . . [p]rejudice or damage his client during the course of the relationship. . . ."

Rule 1.4 COMMUNICATION

(a) A lawyer shall keep a client reasonably informed about the status of a matter and promptly comply with reasonable requests for information.

(b) A lawyer shall explain a matter to the extent reasonably necessary to permit the client to make informed decisions regarding the representation.

COMMENT:

The client should have sufficient information to participate intelligently in decisions concerning the objectives of the representation and the means by which they are to be pursued, to the extent the client is willing and able to do so. For example, a lawyer negotiating on behalf of a client should provide the client with facts relevant to the matter, inform the client of communications from another party and take other reasonable steps that permit the client to make a decision regarding a serious offer from another party. A lawyer who receives from opposing counsel an offer of settlement in a civil controversy or a proffered plea bargain in a criminal case should promptly inform the client of its substance unless prior discussions with the client have left it clear that the proposal will be unacceptable. See Rule 1.2(a). Even when a client delegates authority to the lawyer, the client should be kept advised of the status of the matter.

Adequacy of communication depends in part on the kind of advice or assistance involved. For example, in negotiations where there is time to explain a proposal, the lawyer should review all important provisions with the client before proceeding to an agreement. In litigation a lawyer should explain the general strategy and prospects of success and ordinarily should consult the client on tactics that might injure or coerce others. On the other hand, a lawyer ordinarily cannot be expected to describe trial or negotiation strategy in detail. The guiding principle is that the lawyer should fulfill reasonable client expectations for information consistent with the duty to act in the client's best interests, and the client's overall requirements as to the character of representation.

Ordinarily, the information to be provided is that appropriate for a client who is a comprehending and responsible adult. However, fully informing the client according to this standard may be impracticable, for example, where the client is a child or suffers from mental disability. See Rule 1.14. When the client is an organization or group, it is often impossible or inappropriate to inform every one of its members about its legal affairs; ordinarily, the lawyer should address communications to the appropriate officials of the organization. See Rule 1.13. Where many routine matters are involved, a system of limited or occasional reporting may be arranged with the client. Practical exigency may also require a lawyer to act for a client without prior consultation.

Withholding Information

In some circumstances, a lawyer may be justified in delaying transmission of information when the client would be likely to react imprudently to an immediate communication. Thus, a lawyer might withhold a psychiatric diagnosis of a client when the examining psychiatrist indicates that disclosure would harm the client. A lawyer may not withhold information to serve the lawyer's own interest or convenience. Rules or court orders governing litigation may provide that information supplied to a lawyer may not be disclosed to the client. Rule 3.4(c) directs compliance with such rules or orders.

MODEL CODE COMPARISON

Rule 1.4 has no direct counterpart in the Disciplinary Rules of the Model Code. DR 6-101(A)(3) provided that a lawyer shall not "[n]eglect a legal matter entrusted to him." DR 9-102(B)(1) provided that a lawyer shall "[p]romptly notify a client of the receipt of his funds, securities, or other properties." EC 7-8 stated that a lawyer "should exert his best efforts to insure that decisions of his client are made only after the client has been informed of relevant considerations." EC 9-2 stated that "a lawyer should fully and promptly inform his client of material developments in the matters being handled for the client."

Rule 1.5 FEES

(a) A lawyer's fee shall be reasonable. The factors to be considered in determining the reasonableness of a fee include the following:

(1) the time and labor required, the novelty and difficulty of the questions involved, and the skill requisite to perform the legal service properly;

(2) the likelihood, if apparent to the client, that the acceptance of the particular employment will preclude other employment by the lawyer;

(3) the fee customarily charged in the locality for similar legal services;

(4) the amount involved and the results obtained;

(5) the time limitations imposed by the client or by the circumstances;

(6) the nature and length of the professional relationship with the client;

(7) the experience, reputation, and ability of the lawyer or lawyers performing the services; and;

(8) whether the fee is fixed or contingent.

(b) When the lawyer has not regularly represented the client, the basis or rate of the fee shall be communicated to the client, preferably in writing, before or within a reasonable time after commencing the representation.

(c) A fee may be contingent on the outcome of the matter for which the service is rendered, except in a matter in which a contingent fee is prohibited by paragraph (d) or other law. A contingent fee agreement shall be in writing and shall state the method by which the fee is to be determined, including the percentage or percentages that shall accrue to the lawyer in the event of settlement, trial or appeal, litigation and other expenses to be deducted from the recovery, and whether such expenses are to be deducted before or after the contingent fee is calculated. Upon conclusion of a contingent fee matter, the lawyer shall provide the client with a written statement stating the outcome of the matter and, if there is a recovery, showing the remittance to the client and the method of its determination.

(d) A lawyer shall not enter into an arrangement for, charge, or collect:

(1) any fee in a domestic relations matter, the payment or amount of which is contingent upon the securing of a divorce or

upon the amount of alimony or support, or property settlement in lieu thereof; or

(2) a contingent fee for representing a defendant in a criminal case.

(e) A division of fee between lawyers who are not in the same firm may be made only if:

(1) the division is in proportion to the services performed by each lawyer or, by written agreement with the client, each lawyer assumes joint responsibility for the representation;

(2) the client is advised of and does not object to the participation of all the lawyers involved; and

(3) the total fee is reasonable.

COMMENT:

Basis or Rate of Fee

When the lawyer has regularly represented a client, they ordinarily will have evolved an understanding concerning the basis or rate of the fee. In a new client-lawyer relationship, however, an understanding as to the fee should be promptly established. It is not necessary to recite all the factors that underlie the basis of the fee, but only those that are directly involved in its computation. It is sufficient, for example, to state that the basic rate is an hourly charge or a fixed amount or an estimated amount, or to identify the factors that may be taken into account in finally fixing the fee. When developments occur during the representation that render an earlier estimate substantially inaccurate, a revised estimate should be provided to the client. A written statement concerning the fee reduces the possibility of misunderstanding. Furnishing the client with a simple memorandum or a copy of the lawyer's customary fee schedule is sufficient if the basis or rate of the fee is set forth.

Terms of Payment

A lawyer may require advance payment of a fee, but is obliged to return any unearned portion. See Rule 1.16(d). A lawyer may accept property in payment for services, such as an ownership interest in an enterprise, providing this does not involve acquisition of a proprietary interest in the cause of action or subject matter of the litigation contrary to Rule 1.8(j). However, a fee paid in property instead of money may be subject to special scrutiny because it involves questions concerning both the value of the services and the lawyer's special knowledge of the value of the property.

An agreement may not be made whose terms might induce the lawyer improperly to curtail services for the client or perform them in a way contrary to the client's interest. For example, a lawyer should not enter into an agreement whereby services are to be provided only up to a stated amount when it is foreseeable that more extensive services probably will be required, unless the situation is adequately explained to the client. Otherwise, the client might have to bargain for further assistance in the midst of a proceeding or transaction. However, it is proper to define the extent of services in light of the client's ability to pay. A lawyer should not exploit a fee arrangement based primarily on hourly charges by using wasteful procedures. When there is doubt whether a contingent fee is consistent with the client's best interest, the lawyer should offer the client alternative bases for the fee and explain their implications. Applicable law may impose limitations on contingent fees, such as a ceiling on the percentage.

Division of Fee

A division of fee is a single billing to a client covering the fee of two or more lawyers who are not in the same firm. A division of fee facilitates association of more than one lawyer in a matter in which neither alone could serve the client as well, and most often is used when the fee is contingent and the division is between a referring lawyer and a trial specialist. Paragraph (e) permits the lawyers to divide a fee on either the basis of the proportion of services they render or by agreement between the participating lawyers if all assume responsibility for the representation as a whole and the client is advised and does not object. It does not require disclosure to the client of the share that each lawyer is to receive. Joint responsibility for the representation entails the obligations stated in Rule 5.1 for purposes of the matter involved.

Disputes over Fees

If a procedure has been established for resolution of fee disputes, such as an arbitration or mediation procedure established by the bar, the lawyer should conscientiously consider submitting to it. Law may prescribe a procedure for determining a lawyer's fee, for example, in representation of an executor or administrator, a class or a person entitled to a reasonable fee as part of the measure of damages. The lawyer entitled to such a fee and a lawyer representing another party concerned with the fee should comply with the prescribed procedure.

MODEL CODE COMPARISON

DR 2-106(A) provided that a lawyer "shall not enter into an agreement for, charge, or collect an illegal or clearly excessive fee." DR 2-106(B) provided that a fee is "clearly excessive when, after a review of the facts, a lawyer of ordinary prudence would be left with a definite and firm conviction that the fee is in excess of a reasonable fee." The factors of a reasonable fee in Rule 1.5(a) are substantially identical to those listed in DR 2-106(B). EC 2-17 states that a lawyer "should not charge more than a reasonable fee. . . ."

There was no counterpart to paragraph (b) in the Disciplinary Rules of the Model Code. EC 2-19 stated that it is "usually beneficial to reduce to writing the understanding of the parties regarding the fee, particularly when it is contingent."

There was also no counterpart to paragraph (c) in the Disciplinary Rules of the Model Code. EC 2-20 provided that "[c]ontingent fee arrangements in civil cases have long been commonly accepted in the United States," but that "a lawyer generally should decline to accept employment on a contingent fee basis by one who is able to pay a reasonable fixed fee. . . ."

With regard to paragraph (d), DR 2-106(C) prohibited "a contingent fee in a criminal case." EC 2-20 provided that "contingent fee arrangements in domestic relation cases are rarely justified."

With regard to paragraph (e), DR 2-107(A) permitted division of fees only if: "(1) The client consents to employment of the other lawyer after a full disclosure that a division of fees will be made. (2) The division is in proportion to the services performed and responsibility assumed by each. (3) The total fee does not exceed clearly reasonable compensation. . . ." Paragraph (e) permits division without regard to the services rendered by each lawyer if they assume joint responsibility for the representation.

Rule 1.6 CONFIDENTIALITY OF INFORMATION

(a) **A lawyer shall not reveal information relating to representation of a client unless the client consents after consultation, except for disclosures that are impliedly authorized in order to carry out the representation, and except as stated in paragraph (b).**

(b) **A lawyer may reveal such information to the extent the lawyer reasonably believes necessary:**

(1) **to prevent the client from committing a criminal act that the lawyer believes is likely to result in imminent death or substantial bodily harm; or**

(2) **to establish a claim or defense on behalf of the lawyer in a controversy between the lawyer and the client, to establish a defense to a criminal charge or civil claim against the lawyer based upon conduct in which the client was involved, or to respond to allegations in any proceeding concerning the lawyer's representation of the client.**

COMMENT:

The lawyer is part of a judicial system charged with upholding the law. One of the lawyer's functions is to advise clients so that they avoid any violation of the law in the proper exercise of their rights.

The observance of the ethical obligation of a lawyer to hold inviolate confidential information of the client not only facilitates the full development of facts essential to proper representation of the client but also encourages people to seek early legal assistance.

Almost without exception, clients come to lawyers in order to determine what their rights are and what is, in the maze of laws and regulations, deemed to be legal and correct. The common law recognizes that the client's confidences must be protected from disclosure. Based upon experience, lawyers know that almost all clients follow the advice given, and the law is upheld.

A fundamental principle in the client-lawyer relationship is that the lawyer maintain confidentiality of information relating to the representation. The client is thereby encouraged to communicate fully and frankly with the lawyer even as to embarrassing or legally damaging subject matter.

The principle of confidentiality is given effect in two related bodies of law, the attorney-client privilege (which includes the work product doctrine) in the law of evidence and the rule of confidentiality established in professional ethics. The attorney-client privilege applies in judicial and other proceedings in which a lawyer may be called as a witness or otherwise required to produce evidence concerning a client. The rule of client-lawyer confidentiality applies in situations other than those where evidence is sought from the lawyer through compulsion of law. The confidentiality rule applies not merely to matters communicated in confidence by the client but also to all information relating to the representation, whatever its source. A lawyer may not disclose such information except as authorized or required by the Rules of Professional Conduct or other law. See also Scope.

The requirement of maintaining confidentiality of information relating to representation applies to government lawyers who may disagree with the policy goals that their representation is designed to advance.

Authorized Disclosure

A lawyer is impliedly authorized to make disclosures about a client when appropriate in carrying out the representation, except to the extent that the client's instructions or special circumstances limit that authority. In litigation, for example, a lawyer may disclose information by admitting a fact that cannot properly be disputed, or in negotiation by making a disclosure that facilities a satisfactory conclusion.

Lawyers in a firm may, in the course of the firm's practice, disclose to each other information relating to a client of the firm, unless the client has instructed that particular information be confined to specified lawyers.

Disclosure Adverse to Client

The confidentiality rule is subject to limited exceptions. In becoming privy to information about a client, a lawyer may foresee that the client intends serious harm to another person. However, to the extent a lawyer is required or permitted to disclose a client's purposes, the client will be inhibited from revealing facts which would enable the lawyer to counsel against a wrongful course of action. The public is better protected if full and open communication by the client is encouraged than if it is inhibited.

Several situations must be distinguished. First, the lawyer may not counsel or assist a client in conduct that is criminal or fraudulent. See Rule 1.2(d). Similarly, a lawyer has a duty under Rule 3.3 (a)(4) not to use false evidence. This duty is essentially a special instance of the duty prescribed in Rule 1.2(d) to avoid assisting a client in criminal or fraudulent conduct.

Second, the lawyer may have been innocently involved in past conduct by the client that was criminal or fraudulent. In such a situation the lawyer has not violated Rule 1.2 (d), because to "counsel or assist" criminal or fraudulent conduct requires knowing that the conduct is of that character.

Third, the lawyer may learn that a client intends prospective conduct that is criminal and likely to result in imminent death or substantial bodily harm. As stated in paragraph (b)(1), the lawyer has professional discretion to reveal information in order to prevent such consequences. The lawyer may make a disclosure in order to prevent homicide or serious bodily injury which the lawyer reasonably believes is intended by a client. It is very difficult for a lawyer to "know" when such a heinous purpose will actually be carried out, for the client may have a change of mind.

The lawyer's exercise of discretion requires consideration of such factors as the nature of the lawyer's relationship with the client and with those who might be injured by the client, the lawyer's own involvement in the transaction and factors that may extenuate the conduct in question. Where practical, the lawyer should seek to persuade the client to take suitable action. In any case, a disclosure adverse to the client's interest should be no greater than the lawyer reasonably believes necessary to the purpose. A lawyer's decision not to take preventive action permitted by paragraph (b)(1) does not violate this Rule.

Withdrawal

If the lawyer's services will be used by the client in materially furthering a course of criminal or fraudulent conduct, the lawyer must withdraw, as stated in Rule 1.16(a)(1).

After withdrawal the lawyer is required to refrain from making disclosure of the client's confidences, except as otherwise provided in Rule 1.6. Neither this rule nor Rule 1.8(b) nor Rule 1.16(d) prevents the lawyer from giving notice of the fact of withdrawal, and the lawyer may also withdraw or disaffirm any opinion, document, affirmation, or the like.

Where the client is an organization, the lawyer may be in doubt whether contemplated conduct will actually be carried out by the organization. Where necessary to guide conduct in connection with this Rule, the lawyer may make inquiry within the organization as indicated in Rule 1.13(b).

Dispute Concerning Lawyer's Conduct

Where a legal claim or disciplinary charge alleges complicity of the lawyer in a client's conduct or other misconduct of the lawyer involving representation of the client, the lawyer may respond to the extent the lawyer reasonably believes necessary to establish a defense. The same is true with respect to a claim involving the conduct or representation of a former client. The lawyer's right to respond arises when an assertion of such complicity has been made. Paragraph (b)(2) does not require the lawyer to await the commencement of an action or proceeding that charges such complicity, so that the defense may be established by responding directly to a third party who has made such an assertion. The right to defend, of course, applies where a proceeding has been commenced. Where practicable and not prejudicial to the lawyer's ability to establish the defense, the lawyer should advise the client of the third party's assertion and request that the client respond appropriately. In any event, disclosure should be no greater than the lawyer reasonably believes is necessary to vindicate innocence, the disclosure should be made in a manner which limits access to the information to the tribunal or other persons having a need to know it, and appropriate protective orders or other arrangements should be sought by the lawyer to the fullest extent practicable.

If the lawyer is charged with wrongdoing in which the client's conduct is implicated, the rule of confidentiality should not prevent the lawyer from defending against the charge. Such a charge can arise in a civil, criminal or professional disciplinary proceeding, and can be based on a wrong allegedly committed by the lawyer against the client, or on a wrong alleged by a third person; for example, a person claiming to have been defrauded by the lawyer and client acting together. A lawyer entitled to a fee is permitted by paragraph (b)(2) to prove the services rendered in an action to collect it. This aspect of the rule expresses the principle that the beneficiary of a fiduciary relationship may not exploit it to the detriment of the fiduciary. As stated above, the lawyer must make every effort practicable to avoid unnecessary disclosure of information relating to a representation, to limit disclosure to those having the need to know it, and to obtain protective orders or make other arrangements minimizing the risk of disclosure.

Disclosures Otherwise Required or Authorized

The attorney-client privilege is differently defined in various jurisdictions. If a lawyer is called as a witness to give testimony concerning a client, absent waiver by the client, Rule 1.6(a) requires the lawyer to invoke the privilege when it is applicable. The lawyer must comply with the final orders of a court or other tribunal of competent jurisdiction requiring the lawyer to give information about the client.

The Rules of Professional Conduct in various circumstances permit or require a lawyer to disclose information relating to the representation. See Rules 2.2, 2.3, 3.3 and 4.1. In addition to these provisions, a lawyer may be obligated or permitted by other provisions of law to give information about a client. Whether another provision of law supersedes Rule 1.6 is a matter of interpretation beyond the scope of these Rules, but a presumption should exist against such a supersession.

Former Client

The duty of confidentiality continues after the client-lawyer relationship has terminated.

MODEL CODE COMPARISON

Rule 1.6 eliminates the two-pronged duty under the Model Code in favor of a single standard protecting all information about a client "relating to representation." Under DR 4-101, the requirement applied to information protected by the attorney-client privilege and to information "gained in" the professional relationship that "the client has requested be held inviolate or the disclosure of which would be embarrassing or would be likely to be detrimental to the client." EC 4-4 added that the duty differed from the evidentiary privilege in that it existed "without regard to the nature or source of information or the fact that others share the knowledge." Rule 1.6 imposes confidentiality on information relating to the representation even if it is acquired before or after the relationship existed. It does not require the client to indicate information that is to be confidential, or permit the lawyer to speculate whether particular information might be embarrassing or detrimental.

Paragraph (a) permits a lawyer to disclose information where impliedly authorized to do so in order to carry out the representation. Under DR 4-101(B) and (C), a lawyer was not permitted to reveal "confidences" unless the client first consented after disclosure.

Paragraph (b) redefines the exceptions to the requirement of confidentiality. Regarding paragraph (b)(1), DR 4-101(C)(3) provided that a lawyer "may reveal . . . [t]he intention of his client to commit a crime and the information necessary to prevent the crime." This option existed regardless of the seriousness of the proposed crime.

With regard to paragraph (b)(2), DR 4-101(C)(4) provided that a lawyer may reveal "[c]onfidences or secrets necessary to establish or collect his fee or to defend himself or his employers or associates against an accusation of wrongful conduct." Paragraph (b)(2) enlarges the exception to include disclosure of information relating to claims by the lawyer other than for the lawyer's fee; for example, recovery of property from the client.

Rule 1.7 CONFLICT OF INTEREST: GENERAL RULE

(a) A lawyer shall not represent a client if the representation of that client will be directly adverse to another client, unless:

(1) the lawyer reasonably believes the representation will not adversely affect the relationship with the other client; and

(2) each client consents after consultation.

(b) A lawyer shall not represent a client if the representation of that client may be materially limited by the lawyer's responsibilities to another client or to a third person, or by the lawyer's own interests, unless:

(1) the lawyer reasonably believes the representation will not be adversely affected; and

(2) the client consents after consultation. When representation of multiple clients in a single matter is undertaken, the consultation shall include explanation of the implications of the common representation and the advantages and risks involved.

COMMENT:

Loyalty to a Client

Loyalty is an essential element in the lawyer's relationship to a client. An impermissible conflict of interest may exist before representation is undertaken, in which event the representation should be declined. The lawyer should adopt reasonable procedures, appropriate for the size and type of firm and practice, to determine in both litigation and non-litigation matters the parties and issues involved and to determine whether there are actual or potential conflicts of interest.

If such a conflict arises after representation has been undertaken, the lawyer should withdraw from the representation. See Rule 1.16. Where more than one client is involved and the lawyer withdraws because a conflict arises after representation, whether the lawyer may continue to represent any of the clients is determined by Rule 1.9. See also Rule 2.2(c). As to whether a client-lawyer relationship exists or, having once been established, is continuing, see Comment to Rule 1.3 and Scope.

As a general proposition, loyalty to a client prohibits undertaking representation directly adverse to that client without that client's consent. Paragraph (a) expresses that general rule. Thus, a lawyer ordinarily may not act as advocate against a person the lawyer represents in some other matter, even if it is wholly unrelated. On the other hand, simultaneous representation in unrelated matters of clients whose interests are only generally adverse, such as competing economic enterprises, does not require consent of the respective clients. Paragraph (a) applies only when the representation of one client would be directly adverse to the other.

Loyalty to a client is also impaired when a lawyer cannot consider, recommend or carry out an appropriate course of action for the client because of the lawyer's other responsibilities or interests. The conflict in effect forecloses alternatives that would otherwise be available to the client. Paragraph (b) addresses such situations. A possible conflict does not itself preclude the representation. The critical questions are the likelihood that a conflict will eventuate and, if it does, whether it will materially interfere with the lawyer's independent professional judgment in considering alternatives or foreclose courses of action that reasonably should be pursued on behalf of the client. Consideration should be given to whether the client wishes to accommodate the other interest involved.

Consultation and Consent

A client may consent to representation notwithstanding a conflict. However, as indicated in paragraph (a)(1) with respect to representation directly adverse to a client, and paragraph (b)(1) with respect to material limitations on representation of a client, when a disinterested lawyer would conclude that the client should not agree to the representation under the circumstances, the lawyer involved cannot properly ask for such agreement or provide representation on the basis of the client's consent. When more than one client is involved, the question of conflict must be resolved as to each client. Moreover, there may be circumstances where it is impossible to make the disclosure necessary to obtain consent. For example, when the lawyer represents different clients in related matters and one of the clients refuses to consent to the disclosure necessary to permit the other client to make an informed decision, the lawyer cannot properly ask the latter to consent.

Lawyer's Interests

The lawyer's own interests should not be permitted to have adverse effect on representation of a client. For example, a lawyer's need for income should not lead the lawyer to undertake matters that cannot be handled competently and at a reasonable fee. See Rules 1.1 and 1.5. If the probity of a lawyer's own conduct in a transaction is in serious question, it may be difficult or impossible for the lawyer to give a client detached advice. A lawyer may not allow related business interests to affect representation, for example, by referring clients to an enterprise in which the lawyer has an undisclosed interest.

Conflicts in Litigation

Paragraph (a) prohibits representation of opposing parties in litigation. Simultaneous representation of parties whose interests in litigation may conflict, such as co-plaintiffs or co-defendants, is governed by paragraph (b). An impermissible conflict may exist by reason of substantial discrepancy in the parties' testimony, incompatibility in positions in relation to an opposing party or the fact that there are substantially different possibilities of settlement of the claims or liabilities in question. Such conflicts can arise in criminal cases as well as civil. The potential for conflict of interest in representing multiple defendants in a criminal case is so grave that ordinarily a lawyer should decline to represent more than one codefendant. On the other hand, common representation of persons having similar interests is proper if the risk of adverse effect is minimal and the requirements of paragraph (b) are met. Compare Rule 2.2 involving intermediation between clients.

Ordinarily, a lawyer may not act as advocate against a client the lawyer represents in some other matter, even if the other matter is wholly unrelated. However, there are circumstances in which a lawyer may act as advocate against a client. For example, a lawyer representing an enterprise with diverse operations may accept employment as an advocate against the enterprise in an unrelated matter if doing so will not adversely affect the lawyer's relationship with the enterprise or conduct of the suit and if both clients consent upon consultation. By the same token, government lawyers in some circumstances may represent government employees in proceedings in which a government agency is the opposing party. The propriety of concurrent representation can depend on the nature of the litigation. For example, a suit charging fraud entails conflict to a degree not involved in a suit for a declaratory judgment concerning statutory interpretation.

A lawyer may represent parties having antagonistic positions on a legal question that has arisen in different cases, unless representation of either client would be adversely affected. Thus, it is ordinarily not improper to assert such positions in cases pending in differential trial courts, but it may be improper to do so in cases pending at the same time in an appellate court.

Interest of Person Paying for a Lawyer's Service

A lawyer may be paid from a source other than the client, if the client is informed of that fact and consents and the arrangement does not compromise the lawyer's duty of loyalty to the client. See Rule 1.8(f). For example, when an insurer and its insured have conflicting interests in a matter arising from a liability insurance agreement, and the insurer is required to provide special counsel for the insured, the arrangement should assure the special counsel's professional independence. So also, when a corporation and its directors or employees are involved in a controversy in which they have conflicting interests, the corporation may provide funds for separate legal representation of the directors or employees, if the clients consent after consultation and the arrangement ensures the lawyer's professional independence.

Other Conflict Situations

Conflicts of interest in contexts other than litigation sometimes may be difficult to assess. Relevant factors in determining whether there is potential for adverse effect include the duration and intimacy of the lawyer's relationship with the client or clients involved, the functions being performed by the lawyer, the likelihood that actual conflict will arise and the likely prejudice to the client from the conflict if it does arise. The question is often one of proximity and degree.

For example, a lawyer may not represent multiple parties to a negotiation whose interests are fundamentally antagonistic to each other, but common representation is permissible where the clients are generally aligned in interest even though there is some difference of interest among them.

Conflict questions may also arise in estate planning and estate administration. A lawyer may be called upon to prepare wills for several family members, such as husband and wife, and, depending upon the circumstances, a conflict of interest may arise. In estate administration the identity of the client may be unclear under the law of a particular jurisdiction. Under one view, the client is the fiduciary; under another view the client is the estate or trust, including its beneficiaries. The lawyer should make clear the relationship to the parties involved.

A lawyer for a corporation or other organization who is also a member of its board of directors should determine whether the responsibilities of the two roles may conflict. The lawyer may be called on to advise the corporation in matters involving actions of the directors. Consideration should be given to the frequency with which such situations may arise, the potential intensity of the conflict, the effect of the lawyer's resignation from the board and the possibility of the corporation's obtaining legal advice from another lawyer in such situations. If there is material risk that the dual role will compromise the lawyer's independence of professional judgment, the lawyer should not serve as a director.

Conflict Charged by an Opposing Party

Resolving questions of conflict of interest is primarily the responsibility of the lawyer undertaking the representation. In litigation, a court may raise the question when there is reason to infer that the lawyer has neglected the responsibility. In a criminal case, inquiry by the court is generally required when a lawyer represents multiple defendants. Where the conflict is such as clearly to call in question the fair or efficient administration of justice, opposing counsel may properly raise the question. Such an objection should be viewed with caution, however, for it can be misused as a technique of harassment. See Scope.

MODEL CODE COMPARISON

DR 5-101(A) provided that "[e]xcept with the consent of his client after full disclosure, a lawyer shall not accept employment if the exercise of his professional judgment on behalf of the client will be or reasonably may be affected by his own financial, business, property, or personal interests." DR 5-105(A) provided that a lawyer "shall decline proffered employment if the exercise of his independent professional judgment in behalf of a client will be or is likely to be adversely affected by the acceptance of the proffered employment, or if it would be likely to involve him in representing differing interests, except to the extent permitted under DR 5-105(C)." DR 5-105(C) provided that "a lawyer may represent multiple clients if it is obvious that he can adequately represent the interest of each and if each consents to the representation after full disclosure of the possible effect of such representation on the exercise of his independent professional judgment on behalf of each." DR 5-107(B) provided that a lawyer "shall not permit a person who recommends, employs, or pays him to render legal services for another to direct or regulate his professional judgment in rendering such services."

Rule 1.7 clarifies DR 5-105(A) by requiring that, when the lawyer's other interests are involved, not only must the client consent after consultation but also that, independent of such consent, the representation reasonably appears not to be adversely affected by the lawyer's other interests. This requirement appears to be the intended meaning of the provision in DR 5-105(C) that "it is obvious that he can adequately represent" the client, and was implicit in EC 5-2, which stated that a lawyer "should not accept proffered employment if his personal interests or desires will, or there is a reasonable probability that they will, affect adversely the advice to be given or services to be rendered the prospective client."

Rule 1.8 CONFLICT OF INTEREST: PROHIBITED TRANSACTIONS

(a) A lawyer shall not enter into a business transaction with a client or knowingly acquire an ownership, possessory, security or other pecuniary interest adverse to a client unless:

(1) the transaction and terms on which the lawyer acquires the interest are fair and reasonable to the client and are fully disclosed and transmitted in writing to the client in a manner which can be reasonably understood by the client;

(2) the client is given a reasonable opportunity to seek the advice of independent counsel in the transaction; and

(3) the client consents in writing thereto.

(b) A lawyer shall not use information relating to representation of a client to the disadvantage of the client unless the client consents after consultation, except as permitted or required by Rule 1.6 or Rule 3.3.

(c) A lawyer shall not prepare an instrument giving the lawyer or a person related to the lawyer as parent, child, sibling, or spouse any substantial gift from a client, including a testamentary gift, except where the client is related to the donee.

(d) Prior to the conclusion of representation of a client, a lawyer shall not make or negotiate an agreement giving the lawyer literary or media rights to a portrayal or account based in substantial part on information relating to the representation.

(e) A lawyer shall not provide financial assistance to a client in connection with pending or contemplated litigation, except that:

(1) a lawyer may advance court costs and expenses of litigation, the repayment of which may be contingent on the outcome of the matter; and

(2) a lawyer representing an indigent client may pay court costs and expenses of litigation on behalf of the client.

(f) A lawyer shall not accept compensation for representing a client from one other than the client unless:

(1) the client consents after consultation;

(2) there is no interference with the lawyer's independence of professional judgment or with the client-lawyer relationship; and

(3) information relating to representation of a client is protected as required by Rule 1.6.

(g) A lawyer who represents two or more clients shall not participate in making an aggregate settlement of the claims of or against the clients, or in a criminal case an aggregated agreement as to guilty or nolo contendere pleas, unless each client consents after consultation, including disclosure of the existence and nature of all the claims or pleas involved and of the participation of each person in the settlement.

(h) A lawyer shall not make an agreement prospectively limiting the lawyer's liability to a client for malpractice unless permitted by law and the client is independently represented in making the agreement, or settle a claim for such liability with an unrepresented client or former client without first advising that person in writing that independent representation is appropriate in connection therewith.

(i) A lawyer related to another lawyer as parent, child, sibling or spouse shall not represent a client in a representation directly adverse to a person who the lawyer knows is represented by the other lawyer except upon consent by the client after consultation regarding the relationship.

(j) A lawyer shall not acquire a proprietary interest in the cause of action or subject matter of litigation the lawyer is conducting for a client, except that the lawyer may:

(1) acquire a lien granted by law to secure the lawyer's fee or expenses; and

(2) contract with a client for a reasonable contingent fee in a civil case.

COMMENT:

Transactions Between Client and Lawyer

As a general principle, all transactions between client and lawyer should be fair and reasonable to the client. In such transactions a review by independent counsel on behalf of the client is often advisable. Furthermore, a lawyer may not exploit information relating to the representation to the client's disadvantage. For example, a lawyer who has learned that the client is investing in specific real estate may not, without the client's consent, seek to acquire nearby property where doing so would adversely affect the client's plan for investment. Paragraph (a) does not, however, apply to standard commercial transactions between the lawyer and the client for products or services that the client generally markets to others, for example, banking or brokerage services, medical services, products manufactured or distributed by the client, and utilities services. In such transactions, the lawyer has no advantage in dealing with the client, and the restrictions in paragraph (a) are unnecessary and impracticable.

A lawyer may accept a gift from a client, if the transaction meets general standards of fairness. For example, a simple gift such as a present given at a holiday or as a token of appreciation is permitted. If effectuation of a substantial gift requires preparing a legal instrument such as a will or conveyance, however, the client should have the detached advice that another lawyer can provide. Paragraph (c) recognizes an exception where the client is a relative of the donee or the gift is not substantial.

Literary Rights

An agreement by which a lawyer acquires literary or media rights concerning the conduct of the representation creates a conflict between the interests of the client and the personal interests of the lawyer. Measures suitable in the representation of the client may detract from the publication value of an account of the representation. Paragraph (d) does not prohibit a lawyer representing a client in a transaction concerning literary property from agreeing that the lawyer's fee shall consist of a share in ownership in the property, if the arrangement conforms to Rule 1.5 and paragraph (j).

Person Paying for Lawyer's Services

Rule 1.8(f) requires disclosure of the fact that the lawyer's services are being paid for by a third party. Such an arrangement must also conform to the requirements of Rule 1.6 concerning confidentiality and Rule 1.7 concerning conflict of interest. Where the client is a class, consent may be obtained on behalf of the class by court-supervised procedure.

Family Relationships Between Lawyers

Rule 1.8(i) applies to related lawyers who are in different firms. Related lawyers in the same firm are governed by Rules 1.7, 1.9, and 1.10. The disqualification stated in Rule 1.8(i) is personal and is not imputed to members of firms with whom the lawyers are associated.

Acquisition of Interest in Litigation

Paragraph (j) states the traditional general rule that lawyers are prohibited from acquiring a proprietary interest in litigation. This general rule, which has its basis in common law champerty and maintenance, is subject to specific exceptions developed in decisional law and continued in these Rules, such as the exception for reasonable contingent fees set forth in Rule 1.5 and the exception for certain advances of the costs of litigation set forth in paragraph (e).

This Rule is not intended to apply to customary qualification and limitations in legal opinions and memoranda.

MODEL CODE COMPARISON

With regard to paragraph (a), DR 5-104(A) provided that a lawyer "shall not enter into a business transaction with a client if they have differing interests therein and if the client expects the lawyer to exercise his professional judgment therein for the protection of the client, unless the client has consented after full disclosure." EC 5-3 stated that a lawyer "should not seek to persuade his client to permit him to invest in an undertaking of his client nor make improper use of his professional relationship to influence his client to invest in an enterprise in which the lawyer is interested."

With regard to paragraph (b), DR 4-101(B)(3) provided that a lawyer should not use "a confidence or secret of his client for the advantage of himself, or of a third person, unless the client consents after full disclosure."

There was no counterpart to paragraph (c) in the Disciplinary Rules of the Model Code. EC 5-5 stated that a lawyer "should not suggest to his client that a gift be made to himself or for his benefit. If a lawyer accepts a gift from his client, he is peculiarly susceptible to the charge that he unduly influenced or overreached the client. If a client voluntarily offers to make a gift to his lawyer, the lawyer may accept the gift, but before doing so, he should urge that the client secure disinterested advice from an independent, competent person who is cognizant of all the circumstances. Other than in exceptional circumstances, a lawyer should insist that an instrument in which his client desires to name him beneficially be prepared by another lawyer selected by the client."

Paragraph (d) is substantially similar to DR 5-104(B), but refers to "literary or media" rights, a more generally inclusive term than "publication" rights.

Paragraph (e)(1) is similar to DR 5-103(B), but eliminates the requirement that "the client remains ultimately liable for such expenses."

Paragraph (e)(2) has no counterpart in the Model Code.

Paragraph (f) is substantially identical to DR 5-107(A)(1).

Paragraph (g) is substantially identical to DR 5-106.

The first clause of paragraph (h) is similar to DR 6-102(A). There was no counterpart in the Model Code to the second clause of paragraph (h).

Paragraph (i) has no counterpart in the Model Code.

Paragraph (j) is substantially identical to DR 5-103(A).

Rule 1.9 CONFLICT OF INTEREST: FORMER CLIENT

(a) A lawyer who has formerly represented a client in a matter shall not thereafter represent another person in the same or a substantially related matter in which that person's interests are materially adverse to the interests of the former client unless the former client consents after consultation.

(b) A lawyer shall not knowingly represent a person in the same or a substantially related matter in which a firm with which the lawyer formerly was associated had previously represented a client
    (1) whose interests are materially adverse to that person; and
    (2) about whom the lawyer had acquired information protected by Rules 1.6 and 1.9(c) that is material to the matter;
unless the former client consents after consultation.

(c) A lawyer who has formerly represented a client in a matter or whose present or former firm has formerly represented a client in a matter shall not thereafter:
    (1) use information relating to the representation to the disadvantage of the former client except as Rule 1.6 or Rule 3.3 would permit or require with respect to a client, or when the information has become generally known; or
    (2) reveal information relating to the representation except as Rule 1.6 or Rule 3.3 would permit or require with respect to a client.

COMMENT:

After termination of a client-lawyer relationship, a lawyer may not represent another client except in conformity with this Rule. The principles in Rule 1.7 determine whether the interests of the present and former client are adverse. Thus, a lawyer could not properly seek to rescind on behalf of a new client a contract drafted on behalf of the former client. So also a lawyer who has prosecuted an accused person could not properly represent the accused in a subsequent civil action against the government concerning the same transaction.

The scope of a "matter" for purposes of this Rule may depend on the facts of a particular situation or transaction. The lawyer's involvement in a matter can also be a question of degree. When a lawyer has been directly involved in a specific transaction, subsequent representation of other clients with materially adverse interests clearly is prohibited. On the other hand, a lawyer who recurrently handled a type of problem for a former client is not precluded from later representing another client in a wholly distinct problem of that type even though the subsequent representation involves a position adverse to the prior client. Similar considerations can apply to the reassignment of military lawyers between defense and prosecution functions within the same military jurisdiction. The underlying question is whether the lawyer was so involved in the matter that the subsequent representation can be justly regarded as a changing of sides in the matter in question.

Lawyers Moving Between Firms

When lawyers have been associated within a firm but then end their association, the question of whether a lawyer should undertake representation is more complicated. There are several competing considerations. First, the client previously represented by the former firm must be reasonably assured that the principle of loyalty to the client is not compromised. Second, the rule should not be so broadly cast as to preclude other persons from having reasonable choice of legal counsel. Third, the rule should not unreasonably hamper lawyers from forming new associations and taking on new clients after having left a previous association. In this connection, it should be recognized that today many lawyers practice in firms, that many lawyers to some degree limit their practice to one field or another, and that many move from one association to another several times in their careers. If the concept of imputation were applied with unqualified rigor, the result would be radical curtailment of the opportunity of lawyers to move from one practice setting to another and of the opportunity of clients to change counsel.

Reconciliation of these competing principles in the past has been attempted under two rubrics. One approach has been to seek per se rules of disqualification. For example, it has been held that a partner in a law firm is conclusively presumed to have access to all confidences concerning all clients of the firm. Under this analysis, if a lawyer has been a partner in one law firm and then becomes a partner in another law firm, there maybe a presumption that all confidences known by the partner in the first firm are known to all partners in the second firm. This presumption might properly be applied in some circumstances, especially where the client has been extensively represented, but may be unrealistic where the client was represented only for limited purposes. Furthermore, such a rigid rule exaggerates the difference between a partner and an associate in modern law firms.

The other rubric formerly used for dealing with disqualification is the appearance of impropriety proscribed in Canon 9 of the ABA Model Code of Professional Responsibility. This rubric has a two fold problem. First, the appearance of impropriety can be taken to include any new client-lawyer relationship that might make a former client feel anxious. If that meaning were adopted, disqualification would become little more than a question of subjective judgment by the former client. Second, since "impropriety" is undefined, the term "appearance of impropriety" is question-begging. It therefore has to be recognized that the problem of disqualification cannot be properly resolved either by simple analogy to a lawyer practicing alone or by the very general concept of appearance of impropriety.

Confidentiality

Preserving confidentiality is a question of access to information. Access to information, in turn, is essentially a question of fact in particular circumstances, aided by inferences, deductions or working presumptions that reasonably may be made about the way in which lawyers work together. A lawyer may have general access to files of all clients of a law firm and may regularly participate in discussions of their affairs; it should be inferred that such a lawyer in fact is privy to all information about all the firm's clients. In contrast, another lawyer may have access to the files of only a limited number of clients and participate in discussions of the affairs of no other clients; in the absence of information to the contrary, it should be inferred that such a lawyer in fact is privy to information about the clients actually served but not those of other clients.

Application of paragraph (b) depends on a situation's particular facts. In such an inquiry, the burden of proof should rest upon the firm whose disqualification is sought.

Paragraph (b) operates to disqualify the lawyer only when the lawyer involved has actual knowledge of information protected by Rules 1.6 and 1.9(b). Thus, if a lawyer while with one firm acquired no knowledge or information relating to a particular client of the firm, and that lawyer later joined another firm, neither the lawyer individually nor the second firm is disqualified from representing another client in the same or a related matter even though the interests of the two clients conflict. See Rule 1.10(b) for the restrictions on a firm once a lawyer has terminated association with the firm.

Independent of the question of disqualification of a firm, a lawyer changing professional association has a continuing duty to preserve confidentiality of information about a client formerly represented. See Rules 1.6 and 1.9.

Adverse Positions

The second aspect of loyalty to a client is the lawyer's obligation to decline subsequent representations involving positions adverse to a former client arising in substantially related matters. This obligation requires abstention from adverse representation by the individual lawyer involved, but does not properly entail abstention of other lawyers through imputed disqualification. Hence, this aspect of the problem is governed by Rule 1.9(a). Thus, if a lawyer left one firm for another, the new affiliation would not preclude the firms involved from continuing to represent clients with adverse interests in the same or related matters, so long as the conditions of paragraphs (b) and (c) concerning confidentiality have been met.

Information acquired by the lawyer in the course of representing a client may not subsequently be used or revealed by the lawyer to the disadvantage of the client. However, the fact that a lawyer has once served a client does not preclude the lawyer from using generally known information about that client when later representing another client.

Disqualification from subsequent representation is for the protection of former clients and can be waived by them. A waiver is effective only if there is disclosure of the circumstances, including the lawyer's intended role in behalf of the new client.

With regard to an opposing party's raising a question of conflict of interest, see Comment to Rule 1.7. With regard to disqualification of a firm with which a lawyer is or was formerly associated, see Rule 1.10.

MODEL CODE COMPARISON

There was no counterpart to this Rule in the Disciplinary Rules of the Model Code. Representation adverse to a former client was sometimes dealt with under the rubric of Canon 9 of the Model Code, which provided: "A lawyer should avoid even the appearance of impropriety." Also applicable were EC 4-6 which stated that the "obligation of a lawyer to preserve the confidences and secrets of his client continues after the termination of his employment" and Canon 5 which stated that "[a] lawyer should exercise independent professional judgment on behalf of a client."

The provision for waiver by the former client in paragraphs (a) and (b) is similar to DR 5-105(C).

The exception in the last clause of paragraph (c)(1) permits a lawyer to use information relating to a former client that is in the "public domain," a use that was also not prohibited by the Model Code, which protected only "confidences and secrets." Since the scope of paragraphs (a) and (b) is much broader than "confidences and secrets," it is necessary to define when a lawyer may make use of information about a client after the client-lawyer relationship has terminated.

Rule 1.10 IMPUTED DISQUALIFICATION: GENERAL RULE

(a) While lawyers are associated in a firm, none of them shall knowingly represent a client when any one of them practicing alone would be prohibited from doing so by Rules 1.7, 1.8(c), 1.9 or 2.2.

(b) When a lawyer has terminated an association with a firm, the firm is not prohibited from thereafter representing a person with interests materially adverse to those of a client represented by the formerly associated lawyer and not currently represented by the firm, unless:

(1) the matter is the same or substantially related to that in which the formerly associated lawyer represented the client; and

(2) any lawyer remaining in the firm has information protected by Rules 1.6 and 1.9(c) that is material to the matter.

(c) A disqualification prescribed by this rule may be waived by the affected client under the conditions stated in Rule 1.7.

COMMENT:

Definition of "Firm"

For purposes of the Rules of Professional Conduct, the term "firm" includes lawyers in a private firm, and lawyers in the legal department of a corporation or other organization, or in a legal services organization. Whether two or more lawyers constitute a firm within this definition can depend on the specific facts. For example, two practitioners who share office space and occasionally consult or assist each other ordinarily would not be regarded as constituting a firm. However, if they present themselves to the public in a way suggesting that they are a firm or conduct themselves as a firm, they should be regarded as a firm for the purposes of the Rules. The terms of any formal agreement between associated lawyers are relevant in determining whether they are a firm, as is the fact that they have mutual access to information concerning the clients they serve. Furthermore, it is relevant in doubtful cases to consider the underlying purpose of the Rule that is involved. A group of lawyers could be regarded as a firm for purposes of the rule that the same lawyer should not represent opposing parties in litigation, while it might not be so regarded for purposes of the rule that information acquired by one lawyer is attributed to the other.

With respect to the law department of an organization, there is ordinarily no question that the members of the department constitute a firm within the meaning of the Rules of Professional Conduct. However, there can be uncertainty as to the identity of the client. For example, it may not be clear whether the law department of a corporation represents a subsidiary or an affiliated corporation, as well as the corporation by which the members of the department are directly employed. A similar question can arise concerning an unincorporated association and its local affiliates.

Similar questions can also arise with respect to lawyers in legal aid. Lawyers employed in the same unit of a legal service organization constitute a firm, but not necessarily those employed in separate units. As in the case of independent practitioners, whether the lawyers should be treated as associated with each other can depend on the particular rule that is involved, and on the specific facts of the situation.

Where a lawyer has joined a private firm after having represented the government, the situation is governed by Rule 1.11(a) and (b); where a lawyer represents the government after having served private clients, the situation is governed by Rule 1.11(c)(1). The individual lawyer involved is bound by the Rules generally, including Rules 1.6, 1.7 and 1.9.

Different provisions are thus made for movement of a lawyer from one private firm to another and for movement of a lawyer between a private firm and the government. The government is entitled to protection of its client confidences and, therefore, to the protections provided in Rules 1.6, 1.9 and 1.11. However, if the more extensive disqualification in Rule 1.10 were applied to former government lawyers, the potential effect on the government would be unduly burdensome. The government deals with all private citizens and organizations and, thus, has a much wider circle of adverse legal interests than does any private law firm. In these circumstances, the government's recruitment of lawyers would be seriously impaired if Rule 1.10 were applied to the government. On balance, therefore, the government is better served in the long run by the protections stated in Rule 1.11.

Principles of Imputed Disqualification

The rule of imputed disqualification stated in paragraph (a) gives effect to the principle of loyalty to the client as it applies to lawyers who practice in a law firm. Such situations can be considered from the premise that a firm of lawyers is essentially one lawyer for purposes of the rules governing loyalty to the client, or from the premise that each lawyer is vicariously bound by the obligation of loyalty owed by each lawyer with whom the lawyer is associated. Paragraph (a) operates only among the lawyers currently associated in a firm. When a lawyer moves from one firm to another, the situation is governed by Rules 1.9(b) and 1.10(b).

Rule 1.10(b) operates to permit a law firm, under certain circumstances, to represent a person with interests directly adverse to those of a client represented by a lawyer who formerly was associated with the firm. The Rule applies regardless of when the formerly associated lawyer represented the client. However, the law firm may not represent a person with interests adverse to those of a present client of the firm, which would violate Rule 1.7. Moreover, the firm may not represent the person where the matter is the same or substantially related to that in which the formerly associated lawyer represented the client and any other lawyer currently in the firm has material information protected by Rules 1.6 and 1.9(c).

MODEL CODE COMPARISON

DR 5-105(D) provided that "[i]f a lawyer is required to decline or to withdraw from employment under a Disciplinary Rule, no partner, or associate, or any other lawyer affiliated with him or his firm, may accept or continue such employment."

Rule 1.11 SUCCESSIVE GOVERNMENT AND PRIVATE EMPLOYMENT

(a) Except as law may otherwise expressly permit, a lawyer shall not represent a private client in connection with a matter in which the lawyer participated personally and substantially as a public officer or employee, unless the appropriate government agency consents after consultation. No lawyer in a firm with which that lawyer is associated may knowingly undertake or continue representation in such a matter unless:

(1) the disqualified lawyer is screened from any participation in the matter and is apportioned no part of the fee therefrom; and

(2) written notice is promptly given to the appropriate government agency to enable it to ascertain compliance with the provisions of this Rule.

(b) Except as law may otherwise expressly permit, a lawyer having information that the lawyer knows is confidential government information about a person acquired when the lawyer was a public officer or employee, may not represent a private client whose interests are adverse to that person in a matter in which the information could be used to the material disadvantage of that person. A firm with which that lawyer is associated may undertake or continue representation in the matter only if the disqualified lawyer is screened from any participation in the matter and is apportioned no part of the fee therefrom.

(c) Except as law may otherwise expressly permit, a lawyer serving as a public officer or employee shall not:

(1) participate in a matter in which the lawyer participated personally and substantially while in private practice or nongovernmental employment, unless under applicable law no one is, or by lawful delegation may be, authorized to act in the lawyer's stead in the matter; or

(2) negotiate for private employment with any person who is involved as a party or as attorney for a party in a matter in which the lawyer is participating personally and substantially, except that a lawyer serving as a law clerk to a judge, other adjudicative officer or arbitrator may negotiate for private employment as permitted by Rule 1.12(b) and subject to the conditions stated in Rule 1.12(b).

(d) As used in this Rule, the term "matter" includes:

(1) any judicial or other proceeding, application, request for a ruling or other determination, contract, claim, controversy, investigation, charge, accusation, arrest or other particular matter involving a specific party or parties; and

(2) any other matter covered by the conflict of interest rules of the appropriate government agency.

(e) As used in this Rule, the term "confidential government information" means information which has been obtained under governmental authority and which, at the time this Rule is applied, the government is prohibited by law from disclosing to the public or has a legal privilege not to disclose, and which is not otherwise available to the public.

COMMENT:

This Rule prevents a lawyer from exploiting public office for the advantage of a private client. It is a counterpart of Rule 1.10(b), which applies to lawyers moving from one firm to another.

A lawyer representing a government agency, whether employed or specially retained by the government, is subject to the Rules of Professional Conduct, including the prohibition against representing adverse interests stated in Rule 1.7 and the protections afforded former clients in Rule 1.9. In addition, such a lawyer is subject to Rule 1.11 and to statutes and government regulations regarding conflict of interest. Such statutes and regulations may circumscribe the extent to which the government agency may give consent under this Rule.

Where the successive clients are a public agency and a private client, the risk exists that power or discretion vested in public authority might be used for the special benefit of a private client. A lawyer should not be in a position where benefit to a private client might affect performance of the lawyer's professional functions on behalf of public authority. Also, unfair advantage could accrue to the private client by reason of access to confidential government information about the client's adversary obtainable only through the lawyer's government service. However, the rules governing lawyers presently or formerly employed by a government agency should not be so restrictive as to inhibit transfer of employment to and from the government. The government has a legitimate need to attract qualified lawyers as well as to maintain high ethical standards. The provisions for screening and waiver are necessary to prevent the disqualification rule from imposing too severe a deterrent against entering public service.

When the client is an agency of one government, that agency should be treated as a private client for purposes of this Rule if the lawyer thereafter represents an agency of another government, as when a lawyer represents a city and subsequently is employed by a federal agency.

Paragraphs (a)(1) and (b) do not prohibit a lawyer from receiving a salary or partnership share established by prior independent agreement. They prohibit directly relating the attorney's compensation to the fee in the matter in which the lawyer is disqualified.

Paragraph (a)(2) does not require that a lawyer give notice to the government agency at a time when premature disclosure would injure the client; a requirement for premature disclosure might preclude engagement of the lawyer. Such notice is, however, required to be given as soon as practicable in order that the government agency will have a reasonable opportunity to ascertain that the lawyer is complying with Rule 1.11 and to take appropriate action if it believes the lawyer is not complying.

Paragraph (b) operates only when the lawyer in question has knowledge of the information, which means actual knowledge; it does not operate with respect to information that merely could be imputed to the lawyer.

Paragraphs (a) and (c) do not prohibit a lawyer from jointly representing a private party and a government agency when doing so is permitted by Rule 1.7 and is not otherwise prohibited by law.

Paragraph (c) does not disqualify other lawyers in the agency with which the lawyer in question has become associated.

MODEL CODE COMPARISON

Paragraph (a) is similar to DR 9-101(B), except that the latter used the terms "in which he had substantial responsibility while he was a public employee." Paragraphs (b), (c), (d) and (e) have no counterparts in the Model Code.

Rule 1.12 FORMER JUDGE OR ARBITRATOR

(a) Except as stated in paragraph (d), a lawyer shall not represent anyone in connection with a matter in which the lawyer participated personally and substantially as a judge or other adjudicative officer, arbitrator or law clerk to such a person, unless all parties to the proceeding consent after consultation.

(b) A lawyer shall not negotiate for employment with any person who is involved as a party or as attorney for a party in a matter in which the lawyer is participating personally and substantially as a judge or other adjudicative officer, or arbitrator. A lawyer serving as a law clerk to a judge, other adjudicative officer or arbitrator may negotiate for employment with a party or attorney involved in a matter in which the clerk is participating personally and substantially, but only after the lawyer has notified the judge, other adjudicative officer or arbitrator.

(c) If a lawyer is disqualified by paragraph (a), no lawyer in a firm with which that lawyer is associated may knowingly undertake or continue representation in the matter unless:

(1) the disqualified lawyer is screened from any participation in the matter and is apportioned no part of the fee therefrom; and

(2) written notice is promptly given to the appropriate tribunal to enable it to ascertain compliance with the provisions of this Rule.

(d) An arbitrator selected as a partisan of a party in a multi-member arbitration panel is not prohibited from subsequently representing that party.

COMMENT:

This Rule generally parallels Rule 1.11. The term "personally and substantially" signifies that a judge who was a member of a multimember court, and thereafter left judicial office to practice law, is not prohibited from representing a client in a matter pending in the court, but in which the former judge did not participate. So also the fact that a former judge exercised administrative responsibility in a court does not prevent the former judge from acting as a lawyer in a matter where the judge had previously exercised remote or incidental administrative responsibility that did not affect the merits. Compare the Comment to Rule 1.11. The term "adjudicative officer" includes such officials as judges pro tempore, referees, special masters, hearing officers and other parajudicial officers, and also lawyers who serve as part-time judges. Compliance Canons A(2), B(2) and C of the Model Code of Judicial Conduct provide that a part-time judge, judge pro tempore or retired judge recalled to active service, may not "act as a lawyer in any proceeding in which he served as a judge or in any other proceeding related thereto." Although phrased differently from this Rule, those rules correspond in meaning.

MODEL CODE COMPARISON

Paragraph (a) is substantially similar to DR 9-101(A), which provided that a lawyer "shall not accept private employment in a matter upon the merits of which he has acted in a judicial capacity." Paragraph (a) differs, however, in that it is broader in scope and states more specifically the persons to whom it applies. There was no counterpart in the Model Code to paragraphs (b), (c) or (d).

With regard to arbitrators, EC 5-20 stated that "a lawyer [who] has undertaken to act as an impartial arbitrator or mediator, . . . should not thereafter represent in the dispute any of the parties involved." DR 9-101(A) did not permit a waiver of the disqualification applied to former judges by consent of the parties. However, DR 5-105(C) was similar in effect and could be construed to permit waiver.

Rule 1.13 ORGANIZATION AS CLIENT

(a) A lawyer employed or retained by an organization represents the organization acting through its duly authorized constituents.

(b) If a lawyer for an organization knows that an officer, employee or other person associated with the organization is engaged in action, intends to act or refuses to act in a matter related to the representation that is a violation of a legal obligation to the organization, or a violation of law which reasonably might be imputed to the organization, and is likely to result in substantial injury to the organization, the lawyer shall proceed as is reasonably necessary in the best interest of the organization. In determining how to proceed, the lawyer shall give due consideration to the seriousness of the violation and its consequences, the scope and nature of the lawyer's representation, the responsibility in the organization and the apparent motivation of the person involved, the policies of the organization concerning such matters and any other relevant considerations. Any measures taken shall be designed to minimize disruption of the organization and the risk of revealing information relating to the representation to persons outside the organization. Such measures may include among others:

(1) asking reconsideration of the matter;

(2) advising that a separate legal opinion on the matter be sought for presentation to appropriate authority in the organization; and

(3) referring the matter to higher authority in the organization, including, if warranted by the seriousness of the matter, referral to the highest authority that can act in behalf of the organization as determined by applicable law.

(c) If, despite the lawyer's efforts in accordance with paragraph (b), the highest authority that can act on behalf of the organization insists upon action, or a refusal to act, that is clearly a violation of law and is likely to result in substantial injury to the organization, the lawyer may resign in accordance with Rule 1.16.

(d) In dealing with an organization's directors, officers, employees, members, shareholders or other constituents, a lawyer shall explain the identity of the client when it is apparent that the organization's interests are adverse to those of the constituents with whom the lawyer is dealing.

(e) A lawyer representing an organization may also represent any of its directors, officers, employees, members, shareholders or other constituents, subject to the provisions of Rule 1.7. If the organization's consent to the dual representation is required by Rule 1.7, the consent shall be given by an appropriate official of the organization other than the individual who is to be represented, or by the shareholders.

COMMENT:

The Entity as the Client

An organizational client is a legal entity, but it cannot act except through its officers, directors, employees, shareholders and other constituents. Officers, directors, employees and shareholders are the constituents of the corporate organizational client. The duties defined in this Comment apply equally to unincorporated associations. "Other constituents" as used in this Comment means the positions equivalent to officers, directors, employees and shareholders held by persons acting for organizational clients that are not corporations.

When one of the constituents of an organizational client communicates with the organization's lawyer in that person's organizational capacity, the communication is protected by Rule 1.6. Thus, by way of example, if an organizational client requests its lawyer to investigate allegations of wrongdoing, interviews made in the course of that investigation between the lawyer and the client's employees or other constituents are covered by Rule 1.6. This does not mean, however, that constituents of an organizational client are the clients of the lawyer. The lawyer may not disclose to such constituents information relating to the representation except for disclosures explicitly or impliedly authorized by the organizational client in order to carry out the representation or as otherwise permitted by Rule 1.6.

When constituents of the organization make decisions for it, the decisions ordinarily must be accepted by the lawyer even if their utility or prudence is doubtful. Decisions concerning policy and operations, including ones entailing serious risk, are not as such in the lawyer's province. However, different considerations arise when the lawyer knows that the organization may be substantially injured by action of constituent that is in violation of law. In such a circumstance, it may be reasonably necessary for the lawyer to ask the constituent to reconsider the matter. If that fails, or if the matter is of sufficient seriousness and importance to the organization, it may be reasonably necessary for the lawyer to take steps to have the matter reviewed by a higher authority in the organization. Clear justification should exist for seeking review over the head of the constituent normally responsible for it. The stated policy of the organization may define circumstances and prescribe channels for such review, and a lawyer should encourage the formulation of such a policy. Even in the absence of organization policy, however, the lawyer may have an obligation to refer a matter to higher authority, depending on the seriousness of the matter and whether the constituent in question has apparent motives to act at variance with the organization's interest. Review by the chief executive officer or by the board of directors may be required when the matter is of importance commensurate with their authority. At some point it may be useful or essential to obtain an independent legal opinion.

In an extreme case, it may be reasonably necessary for the lawyer to refer the matter to the organization's highest authority. Ordinarily, that is the board of directors or similar governing body. However, applicable law may prescribe that under certain conditions highest authority reposes elsewhere; for example, in the independent directors of a corporation.

Relation to Other Rules

The authority and responsibility provided in paragraph (b) are concurrent with the authority and responsibility provided in other Rules. In particular, this Rule does not limit or expand the lawyer's responsibility under Rule 1.6, 1.8, 1.16, 3.3 or 4.1. If the lawyer's services are being used by an organization to further a crime or fraud by the organization, Rule 1.2(d) can be applicable.

Government Agency

The duty defined in this Rule applies to governmental organizations. However, when the client is a governmental organization, a different balance may be appropriate between maintaining confidentiality and assuring that the wrongful official act is prevented or rectified, for public business is involved. In addition, duties of lawyers employed by the government or lawyers in military service may be defined by statutes and regulation. Therefore, defining precisely the identity of the client and prescribing the resulting obligations of such lawyers may be more difficult in the government context. Although in some circumstances the client may be a specific agency, it is generally the government as a whole. For example, if the action or failure to act involves the head of a bureau, either the department of which the bureau is a part or the government as a whole may be the client for purpose of this Rule. Moreover, in a matter involving the conduct of government officials, a government lawyer may have authority to question such conduct more extensively than that of a lawyer for a private organization in similar circumstances. This Rule does not limit that authority. See note on Scope.

Clarifying the Lawyer's Role

There are times when the organization's interest may be or become adverse to those of one or more of its constituents. In such circumstances the lawyer should advise any constituent, whose interest the lawyer finds adverse to that of the organization of the conflict or potential conflict of interest, that the lawyer cannot represent such constituent, and that such person may wish to obtain independent representation. Care must be taken to assure that the individual understands that, when there is such adversity of interest, the lawyer for the organization cannot provide legal representation for that constituent individual, and that discussions between the lawyer for the organization and the individual may not be privileged.

Whether such a warning should be given by the lawyer for the organization to any constituent individual may turn on the facts of each case.

Dual Representation

Paragraph (e) recognizes that a lawyer for an organization may also represent a principal officer or major shareholder.

Derivative Actions

Under generally prevailing law, the shareholders or members of a corporation may bring suit to compel the directors to perform their legal obligations in the supervision of the organization. Members of unincorporated associations have essentially the same right. Such an action may be brought nominally by the organization, but usually is, in fact, a legal controversy over management of the organization.

The question can arise whether counsel for the organization may defend such an action. The proposition that the organization is the lawyer's client does not alone resolve the issue. Most derivative actions are a normal incident of an organization's affairs, to be defended by the organization's lawyer like any other suit. However, if the claim involves serious charges of wrongdoing by those in control of the organization, a conflict may arise between the lawyer's duty to the organization and the lawyer's relationship with the board. In those circumstances, Rule 1.7 governs who should represent the directors and the organization.

MODEL CODE COMPARISON

There was no counterpart to this Rule in the Disciplinary Rules of the Model Code. EC 5-18 stated that a "lawyer employed or retained by a corporation or similar entity owes his allegiance to the entity and not to a stockholder, director, officer, employee, representative, or other person connected with the entity. In advising the entity, a lawyer should keep paramount its interests and his professional judgment should not be influenced by the personal desires of any person or organization. Occasionally, a lawyer for an entity is requested by a stockholder, director, officer, employee, representative, or other person connected with the entity to represent him in an individual capacity; in such case the lawyer may serve the individual only if the lawyer is convinced that differing interests are not present." EC 5-24 stated that although a lawyer "may be employed by a business corporation with non-lawyers serving as directors or officers, and they necessarily have the right to make decisions of business policy, a lawyer must decline to accept direction of his professional judgment from any layman." DR 5-107(B) provided that a lawyer "shall not permit a person who . . . employs . . . him to render legal services for another to direct or regulate his professional judgment in rendering such legal services."

* * *

Organization

FEDERAL BAR ASSOCIATION

Headquarters:
1815 H Street, NW
Suite 408
Washington, DC 20006-3697
Telephone: (202) 638-0252
Fax: (202) 775-0295
E-mail: fba@fedbar.org
Website: http://www.fedbar.org

Date founded: 1920
Membership: approximately 15,000 public and government lawyers and
judges involved in federal legal practice, including members of Congress, military attorneys, and corporate counsel

Codes of Ethics

Official name: *Model Rules of Professional Conduct for Federal
Lawyers*
History: Adopted December 1990
Authority: Professional Ethics Committee; National Council

Official name: *Standards for Civility in Professional Conduct*
History: Adopted November 1997, issued January 1998
Authority: Professional Ethics Committee; Executive Committee
Standards available on Website

Additional Resources

Organizational (Divisions, Programs, Services, etc.):

Continuing Legal Education (CLE) Program
Divisions: Administration of Justice; Administrative Law; Antitrust and
Trade Regulation; Bankruptcy Law; Corporate and Association Coun-

sels; Environment, Energy, and Natural Resources; Federal Career
Service; Federal Litigation; Financial Institutions and the Economy;
General Counsels; Government Contracts; Health and Human Ser-
vices; Immigration Law; Indian Law; Intellectual Property and Com-
munications Law; International Law; Judiciary; Labor & Employment
Law; Senior Lawyers; State & Local Government Relations; Taxation;
Transportation Law; Veterans Law; Younger Lawyers
Various committees: Administrative Law; Career Service; Federal Litiga-
tion; Government Contracts; Taxation
Various conferences

Informational (Publications, Videos, Seminars, etc.):

Articles in *The Federal Lawyer* and *Newsbriefs—Administration of Justice
Section Newsletter*
The Ballad of Halibut Klutz, An Interactive Legal Ethics Epic
Bankruptcy Law Isn't Just for Bankruptcy Lawyers
Ethics
Ethics: Attorney vs. Tribe, Who's In Control? (conference materials)
Gender-Based Issues in Asylum Claims (seminar)
*Government Ethics for Federal Attorneys: An Overview of Ethics Law
and Regulations*
Guidelines Manual
Hypothetically Speaking: Legal Ethics for Federal Bar Practitioners
Professional Responsibility for Government Attorneys
*Professional Responsibility for Government Attorneys: Ethics for
Litigators and Non-Litigators*
*Professional Responsibility for Government Attorneys: Who Is the Client
and What Are Your Responsibilities to Your Client?*
*Robert Poling Symposium on Professional Responsibility for
Government Attorneys*
Rule 11 Sanctions in Civil Litigation
*Standards of Conduct for the Evolving Natural Gas & Electric
Industries* (seminar)

Goals and Activities of Organization

The Federal Bar Association (FBA) was organized to serve as the
national representative of the federal judiciary and bar and to promote the
sound administration of justice. It supports its members' professional
growth and development, sponsoring substantive law programs, seminars,
and conferences, including continuing legal education programs designed
to meet mandatory state requirements. It promotes the welfare of attorneys
and judges employed by the government, advocating their interests before
courts, departments, and agencies of the U.S.

The FBA develops high standards of professional competence and ethical conduct; keeps members informed of developments in their respective fields of interest; and facilitates interaction among federal legal professionals.

The Professional Ethics Committee is responsible for formulating and recommending standards of ethics and conduct for the federal legal profession.

Implementation and Enforcement of Codes

Model Rules of Professional Conduct for Federal Lawyers

The FBA is not empowered to discipline members or enforce the Model Rules. Federal lawyers are urged, however, to "carefully consider" them "as guidance in specific situations." Partly obligatory and partly descriptive, the Rules provide a structure for directing and regulating minimum standards of ethical conduct.

Federal agencies are encouraged to use the Rules as a model for developing and adopting their own standards of conduct for the lawyers they employ or who practice before them. Federal lawyers are bound by their agencies' rules of professional responsibility.

Therefore, the FBA Rules are enforceable only to the extent that they have been adopted by a federal agency. A federal lawyer who violates the agency's rules—or any applicable statutes or regulations governing lawyers—may be subject to disciplinary proceedings and sanctions.

The Comments accompanying the Rules are to be used as interpretive tools, explaining or amplifying the Rules, placing them in context, and providing additional guidance for understanding and using them.

Standards for Civility in Professional Conduct

These Standards are voluntary. While they cannot be used as a basis for litigation or sanctions, the FBA expects lawyers and judges in the federal system to make a commitment to adhere to them in all aspects of their dealings with one another and with other participants in the legal process.

The FBA considers the Standards an integral component of professionalism instruction for both law students and practicing lawyers. It recommends that they be incorporated in law school curricula, and in continuing legal education programs for lawyers in the federal sector, law firms, government agencies, and other legal institutions.

Apart from any ethical standards, the FBA National Council may expel a member for good cause—knowingly engaging in conduct designed to overthrow the U.S. government by force or violence; disbarment by any state or federal court; or violating the FBA Constitution or Bylaws. A member so charged is entitled to notice, hearing, and appeal before expulsion takes effect.

History and Development of Codes

Model Rules of Professional Conduct for Federal Lawyers

The Rules were developed by the FBA Professional Ethics Committee and an Advisory Committee in 1989-90, and adopted by the National Council in December 1990.

The American Bar Association's Model Rules of Professional Responsibility are the primary basis for the FBA Rules. Additional sources include the standards of conduct for lawyers in the Army, Navy, Air Force, Coast Guard, and District of Columbia Bar.

Portions of earlier FBA standards, the 1972 Canons of Professional Ethics and Federal Ethical Considerations, were incorporated into the new document where appropriate.

Standards for Civility in Professional Conduct

These Standards were adapted from those of the District of Columbia Bar, published in 1996, by the FBA Professional Ethics Committee. In November 1997, the FBA Executive Committee adopted the Standards as official policy. They were issued to the membership in January 1998. In his accompanying message, the FBA president characterized the Standards' adoption as an example of the organization's leadership efforts in the area of professionalism.

Model Rules of Professional Conduct for Federal Lawyers*

PREFACE

The Federal Bar Association (FBA) has adopted the Federal Bar Association's Model Rules of Professional Conduct for Federal Lawyers (Rules) to serve as a guide for all lawyers involved in Federal practice, both Government lawyers and Non-Government lawyers. These Rules recognize many of the special aspects of the practice of law with the Federal Government.

The FBA is not empowered to discipline members or enforce these Rules. However, the FBA encourages Federal Agencies to adopt rules of professional responsibility based on these Rules to govern the conduct of lawyers employed by the Federal Agency and lawyers who practice before the Federal Agency and its tribunals.

* * *

While the [American Bar Association Model Rules of Professional Conduct] were the basis of these Rules, changes were required to ensure that these Rules met the needs of the Federal lawyer. Reasons for the changes include but are not limited to—an ABA Rule's inapplicability to practice within or before a Federal Agency; the need for guidance tailored to Federal government practice; differences in approach to the resolution of specific ethical issues for Federal lawyers; and editorial and stylist changes. Some ABA Rules that do not pertain to the practice of law within the Federal Government were omitted. In these cases the Non-Government lawyer should consult the applicable rules of the various states in which the Non-Government lawyer practicing before Federal agencies and courts is licensed. In particular, deference has been given to state rules involving the setting of fees, advertising, and the organization of private law firms.

The Rules contain Comment sections, designed to explain or amplify the Rules place them in context, or provide additional guidance. The Comments are interpretive tools, not binding upon Federal lawyers, but helpful in understanding and using the Rules. In doing so, Federal lawyers must be aware that these Rules were specifically adapted to the unique needs and demands of the Federal lawyer. Federal lawyers should carefully consider these Rules as guidance in specific situations.

Federal lawyers shall be thoroughly acquainted with and shall adhere at all times to the rules of professional responsibility adopted by the Federal Agency that employs them or before which they practice. In the absence of Federal Agency rules, they should comply with the rules of the state bars in which they are licensed to practice.

* * *

The Rules seek to balance the Federal Agency's needs with the needs of the Federal lawyers, who are members, and often leaders, in the mainstream of the legal profession. It is an appropriate balance, but one that carries heavy obligations to the service and the profession.

STATUTES, REGULATIONS, AND GUIDANCE

The Federal lawyer, particularly Government and former Government lawyers, may be bound by statutory provisions; * * * the Ethics in Government Act; relevant Executive Orders; Federal Agency rules and directives including, but not limited to, Federal Agency Standards of Conduct regulations; * * *; Office of Government Ethics Regulations and Formal Advisory Opinions; Memoranda of Attorney General; and state Rules of Professional Conduct. Federal lawyers admitted to practice in more than one jurisdiction should exercise caution in ascertaining the content of ethical requirements in each state and the application of such requirements to their practice.

One of the most difficult issues Government lawyers may confront is the identity of the client and where counsel's loyalties belong. Rule 1.13 addresses this question at length and cautions that under some circumstances, a Government lawyer may encounter a conflict between his or her obligation to the Federal Agency as the client, and the needs and interests of individual officials, employees, and agents of the Federal Agency. Another difficult area, addressed in Rule 1.6, is the question of client confidentiality. The Comments to both of these Rules are extensive and intended to offer additional guidance.

Another area in which a Government lawyer's actions may be regulated by law involves the release of information, which is also regulated by the Freedom of Information Act, * * * the Privacy Act, * * * and the laws governing the protection of national security and defense information.

* * *

PREAMBLE: A FEDERAL LAWYER'S RESPONSIBILITIES

A Federal lawyer is a representative of clients, an officer of the legal system, and a public citizen having special responsibility for the quality of justice. The Federal lawyer should demonstrate the highest standards of ethical conduct, personal dignity, truthfulness, honesty, fortitude, and professional integrity. The Federal lawyer should also promote public service.

As a representative of clients, a Federal lawyer performs various functions. As an advisor, a Federal lawyer provides a client with informed understanding of the client's rights and obligations and explains their practical implications. As an advocate, a Federal lawyer zealously asserts the client's position under the law and the ethical rules of the adversary system. As negotiator, a Federal lawyer seeks results advantageous to the client, but consistent with the requirement of honest dealing with others. As a mediator between clients, a Federal lawyer seeks to reconcile their divergent interests as an advisor and, to a limited extent, as a spokesperson for each client. A Federal lawyer acts as evaluator by examining client's legal affairs and reporting about them to the client or to others.

In all professional functions a Federal lawyer should be competent, prompt, diligent, and honest. A Federal lawyer should maintain communication with a client concerning the representation. A Federal lawyer should keep in confidence information relating to representation of a client, except insofar as disclosure is required or permitted by these Rules or other law.

A Federal lawyer's conduct should conform to the requirements of the law, both in professional service to clients and in the Federal lawyer's personal affairs. A Federal lawyer should use legal procedures only for their lawfully intended purposes and not to harass or intimidate others. A Federal lawyer should demonstrate respect for the legal system and for those who serve it, including judges, other Federal lawyers, and public officials. To the Federal Agency, the Federal lawyer owes the duties of professional dignity and integrity. While it is a Federal lawyer's duty, when necessary, to challenge the rectitude of official action, it is also a Federal lawyer's duty to uphold legal process.

As a public citizen, a Federal lawyer should seek improvement of the law, the administration of justice, and the quality of service rendered by the legal profession. Federal lawyers should strive at all times to uphold the honor and dignity of the Federal legal profession and to improve the administration of justice. As a member of a learned profession, a Federal lawyer should cultivate knowledge of the law beyond its use for clients, employ that knowledge in reform of the law where needed, and work to strengthen legal education.

Many of a Federal lawyer's professional responsibilities are prescribed in these Rules, as well as in substantive and procedural law. However, a Federal lawyer is also guided by personal conscience and the approbation of professional peers. A Federal lawyer should strive to attain the highest level of skill, to improve the law and the legal profession, to exemplify the legal profession's ideals of public service, and to respect the truth finding role of the courts.

A Federal lawyer's responsibilities as a representative of clients, an officer of the legal system, and a public citizen are usually harmonious. Thus, when an opposing party is well represented, a Federal lawyer can be zealous in advocating the interests of a client and justice will be served. A Federal lawyer also can be sure that preserving client confidence ordinarily serves the public interest because people are more likely to ask legal advice, and thereby heed their legal obligations, when they know their communications will be private.

A Federal lawyer should always uphold and promote the highest standards for the practice of law within the Federal sector. A Federal lawyer should seek to advance the development of sound Federal laws and the establishment and maintenance of an efficient Federal legal and judicial system. A Federal lawyer should promote the public's confidence in the Federal legal system. A Federal lawyer also should promote the highest professional standards for and the professional well being of all Federal lawyers. A Federal lawyer should seek to encourage outstanding lawyers to enter the Federal service.

In addition to the high standards of conduct expected of all Federal lawyers, the Government lawyer has a specific responsibility to strive to promote the public interest. The Government lawyer should not realize personal gain from the performance of official duties and should avoid any interest or activity that is in conflict with the Government lawyer's official duties. The Government lawyer should strive for personal professional excellence and encourage the professional development of other staff members and those seeking to enter the field of Government law practice.

Due to the nature of legal practice, however, Federal lawyers encounter conflicting responsibilities. Virtually all difficult ethical problems arise from conflicts between a Federal lawyer's responsibilities to clients, to the legal system, and to the Federal lawyer's own interest in remaining an upright person. These Rules prescribe terms for resolving such conflicts. Within the framework of these Rules many difficult issues of professional discretion can arise. Such issues must be resolved through the exercise of sensitive professional and moral judgment guided by the basic principles underlying these Rules.

SCOPE

These Rules, in conjunction with laws and regulations that control the practice of Federal lawyers, are intended to govern the ethical conduct of Federal lawyers.

They have been adopted by the National Council of the Federal Bar Association. The Federal Bar Association is not empowered to discipline members or enforce these Rules. As such, these Rules regulate professional conduct of Federal lawyers and impose certain duties only to the extent to which they are adopted by a Federal Agency. The Federal Bar Association encourages Federal agencies to adopt rules of professional responsibility based, in whole or in part, on these Rules. If so adopted, failure to comply with an obligation or prohibition imposed by a Rule may be the basis for invoking administrative or disciplinary action. The Rules presuppose that disciplinary assessment of a Federal lawyer's conduct will be made on the basis of the facts and circumstances as they existed at the time of the conduct in question and in recognition of the fact that a Federal lawyer often has to act upon uncertain or incomplete evidence of the situation. Moreover, these Rules presuppose that whether or not discipline should be imposed for a violation, and severity of a sanction, depend on all of the circumstances, such as the willfulness and seriousness of the violation, extenuating factors, and whether there have been previous violations. Violations of a Rule should not give rise to a cause of action nor should they create a presumption that a legal duty has been breached. These Rules are designed to provide guidance to Federal lawyers and to provide a structure for regulating conduct. They are not designed to be a basis for civil liability.

Furthermore, the purpose of these Rules can be subverted when they are invoked by opposing parties as procedural weapons. The fact that a Rule is a just basis for a Federal lawyer's self-assessment, or for sanctioning a Federal lawyer under the administration of a disciplinary authority, does not imply that an antagonist in a collateral proceeding or transaction has standing to seek enforcement of the Rule. Accordingly, nothing in these Rules should be deemed to augment any substantive legal duty of Federal lawyers or the extra-disciplinary consequences of violating such duty.

They are to be used in conjunction with laws and regulation that control the practice of Federal lawyers. Although not punitive in nature, the Rules establish the minimum standards of ethical conduct demanded of Federal lawyers.

The ethical conduct of lawyers specially retained by the Government is also intended to be governed by these Rules of Professional Conduct.

These Rules presuppose a larger legal context shaping the Federal lawyer's role. That context includes statutes and court rules relating to matters of licensing, laws defining specific obligations of Federal lawyers, and substantive and procedural law in general. Compliance with these Rules, as with all laws in an open society, depends primarily upon understanding and voluntary compliance, secondarily upon reinforcement by peer and public opinion, and finally, when applicable and necessary, upon enforcement through disciplinary proceedings. These Rules do not, however, exhaust the moral and ethical considerations that should inform a Federal lawyer, for no worthwhile human activity can be completely defined by legal rules. These Rules simply provide a framework for the ethical practice of law.

Furthermore, for purposes of determining the Federal lawyer's authority and responsibility, principles of substantive law external to these Rules determine whether a client-lawyer relationship exists. Whether a client-lawyer relationship exists for any specific purpose can depend on the circumstances and may be a question of fact.

Moreover, these Rules are not intended to govern or affect judicial application of either the attorney-client or work product privilege. Those privileges were developed to promote compliance with law and fairness in litigation. In reliance on the attorney-client privilege, clients are entitled to expect that communications within the scope of the privilege will be protected against compelled disclosure. The attorney-client privilege is that of the client and not of the Federal lawyer. The fact that in exceptional situations the Federal lawyer under these Rules is required or permitted to disclose client confidence does not vitiate the proposition that, as a general matter, the client has a reasonable expectation that information relating to the client will not be voluntarily disclosed and that disclosure of such information may be compelled only in accordance with recognized exceptions to the attorney-client and work product privileges.

The Federal lawyer's exercise of discretion not to disclose information under Rule 1.6(c) should not be subject to reexamination. Permitting such reexamination would be incompatible with the general policy of promoting compliance with law through assurances that communications will be protected against disclosure.

These Rules of Professional Conduct are rules of reason. They should be interpreted with reference to the purposes of legal representation and of the law itself. Some of these Rules are imperative, cast in the terms "shall" or "shall not." These define proper conduct for purposes of professional discipline. Others, generally cast in the term "may" are permissive and define areas under these Rules in which the Federal lawyer has professional discretion. No disciplinary action should be taken when the Federal lawyer chooses not to act or acts within the bounds of such discretion. Other Rules define the nature of relationships between the Federal lawyer and others. These Rules are thus partly obligatory and partly descriptive in that they define a Federal lawyer's professional role. Many of the comments use the term "should." Comments do not add obligations to these Rules, but provide guidance for practicing in compliance with these Rules. The comments are interpretative, while the text of each Rule is authoritative.

The Preamble and this note on Scope provide general orientation.

DEFINITIONS

Within the scope of these Rules:

"Attorney-client" is the term used to describe the evidentiary privilege against disclosure of communications between a Federal lawyer's client and the Federal lawyer. It is not used to describe the relationship between a Federal lawyer and the lawyer's client.

"Belief" or "believes" means that the individual involved actually concludes the fact in question to be true. An individual's belief may be inferred from circumstances.

"Client-lawyer" is used to express the professional relationship between a Federal lawyer and the lawyer's client. The term is not used to reference any evidentiary privileges, such as the "attorney-client" privilege.

"Consult" or "consultation" means communication of information reasonably sufficient to permit the client to appreciate the significance of the matter in question.

"Federal Agency" means: (1) An Executive agency, including an Executive department, military department, Government corporation, Government controlled corporation, and an independent establishment; (2) The Congress, committees of Congress, members of Congress who employ lawyers, and Congressional agencies; (3) The courts of the United States and agencies of the Judiciary; (4) The Governments of the territories and possessions of the United States; or (5) The Government of the District of Columbia.

"Federal lawyer" means a Government lawyer or a Non-Government lawyer, as hereinafter defined.

"Firm" means the organizational entity through which Non-Government lawyers transact business. The term includes private law firms, the legal departments of corporations and other business entities that hire lawyers as employees, and legal service organizations. The term does not include a Federal Agency.

"Fraud" or "fraudulent" means conduct having deceit as its purpose and does not encompass merely negligent misrepresentation or failure to apprise another of relevant information.

"Government employee" means an officer or employee of a Federal Agency. The term includes members of the Armed Forces.

"Government lawyer" means a Government employee who holds a position as an attorney with a Federal Agency or serves as a judge advocate in one of the Armed Forces, but only while performing official duties. The term includes a lawyer in private practice who has contracted with or been specially retained by a Federal Agency to represent the Agency or another person while engaged in the performance of the contractual obligation.

"Individual" is used to describe a single human being.

"Knowingly," "known," or "knows" means actual knowledge of the fact in question. A person's knowledge may be inferred from circumstances.

"Law" as used in these Rules includes statutes, treaties and international agreements, legal precedents, Federal Agency regulations, directives, and orders.

"Non-Government lawyer" means an individual who is a member of the bar of a Federal court or the highest court of a State or Territory, who represents persons before a Federal Agency. When a Government lawyer is engaged in the private practice of law or pro bono representation not related to the Government lawyer's official duties, the lawyer is considered a Non-Government lawyer.

"Person" means an individual, a corporation, a company, an association, a firm, a partnership, a society, a joint stock company, or any other legal entity.

"Reasonable" or "reasonably" when used in relation to conduct by a Federal lawyer means the conduct of a reasonably prudent and competent lawyer.

"Reasonable belief" or "reasonably believes" when used in reference to a Federal lawyer means that the lawyer believes the matter in question and that the circumstances are such that the belief is reasonable.

"Reasonably should know" when used in reference to a Federal lawyer means that a lawyer of reasonable prudence and competence would ascertain the matter in question.

"Substantial" when used in reference to degree or extent means a material matter of clear and weighty importance.

"Supervisory lawyer" means a Federal lawyer within an office or organization with authority over or responsibility for the direction, coordination, evaluation, or assignment of responsibilities and work of subordinate lawyers, contract legal representation, nonlawyer assistants (e.g., paralegals), and clerical personnel.

"Tribunal" means a court, board, hearing officer, investigating officer, judge, jury, panel, or other body or official that receives evidence and makes a ruling or determination.

CLIENT-LAWYER RELATIONSHIP

Rule 1.1 COMPETENCE

A federal lawyer shall provide competent representation to a client. Competent representation requires the legal knowledge, skill, thoroughness, and preparation reasonably necessary for the representation.

COMMENT:

Legal Knowledge and Skill

In determining whether a Federal lawyer employs the requisite knowledge and skill in a particular matter, relevant factors include the relative complexity and specialized nature of the matter, the lawyer's general experience, the lawyer's training and experience in the field in question, the preparation and study the lawyer is able to give the matter, and whether it is feasible to refer the matter to, or consult with, a lawyer of established competence in the field in question. In most instances, the required proficiency is that generally afforded to clients by other lawyers in similar matters. Expertise in a particular field of law may be required in some circumstances.

Initial determinations as to the competence of a Government lawyer for a particular assignment will be made by a supervisory lawyer prior to case or issue assignments. However, once assigned, a Government lawyer may consult with the supervisory lawyer concerning competence to continue handling a particular case or issue. See Rules 5.1 and 5.2.

A Federal lawyer need not necessarily have special training or prior experience to handle legal problems of a type with which the Federal lawyer is unfamiliar. A newly admitted Federal lawyer can be as competent as a practitioner with long experience. Some important legal skills, such as the analysis of precedent, the evaluation of evidence, and legal drafting, are required in all legal problems. Perhaps the most fundamental legal skill consists of determining what kind of legal problems a situation may involve, a skill that necessarily transcends any particular specialized knowledge. A Federal lawyer can provide adequate representation in a wholly novel field through necessary study or consultation with a Federal lawyer of established competence in the field in question.

A Federal lawyer may become involved in representing a client whose needs exceed either the lawyer's competence or authority to act in the client's behalf. In such a situation, the Federal lawyer should refer the matter to another Federal lawyer who has the requisite competence or authority to meet the client's needs. For Non-Government lawyers practicing before Federal agencies, competent representation may also be provided through the association of a Non-Government lawyer of established competence in the field in question.

A Federal lawyer may give advice or assistance in a matter in which the Federal lawyer does not have the skill ordinarily required where referral to or consultation with another Federal lawyer would be impractical. However, assistance should be limited to that reasonably necessary in the circumstances, for ill-considered action can jeopardize the client's interest.

Thoroughness and Preparation

Competent handling of a particular matter includes inquiry into and analysis of the factual and legal elements of the problem, and use of methods and procedures meeting the standards of competent practitioners. It also includes adequate preparation. The attention and preparation required are determined in part by what is at stake; major litigation and complex transactions ordinarily require more elaborate treatment than matters of lesser consequence.

Maintaining Competence

To maintain the requisite knowledge and skill, a Federal lawyer should engage in continuing study and education.

Rule 1.2 SCOPE OF REPRESENTATION

(a) A Federal lawyer shall abide by a client's decisions concerning the objectives of representation, subject to paragraphs (c), (d), (e), and (f), and shall consult with the client as to the means by which these decisions are to be pursued. A Federal lawyer shall abide by a client's decision whether to accept an offer of settlement of a matter. In a criminal case, and to the extent applicable in civil cases and administrative hearings, the Federal lawyer shall abide by the client's decision, after consultation with the Federal lawyer, as to choice of counsel (as provided by law), a plea to be entered, selection of trial forum, whether to enter into a pretrial agreement, and whether the client will testify.

(b) A Federal lawyer's representation of a client, including representation by appointment, does not constitute an endorsement of the client's political, economic, social, or moral views or activities.

(c) A Federal lawyer may limit the objectives of the representation if the client consents after consultation or as required by law and communicated to the client.

(d) A Federal lawyer shall not counsel a client to engage, or assist a client, in conduct that the lawyer knows is criminal or fraudulent, but a Federal lawyer may discuss the legal and moral consequences of any proposed course of conduct with a client and may counsel or assist a client to make a good faith effort to determine the validity, scope, meaning, or application of the law.

(e) When a Federal lawyer knows that a client expects assistance not permitted by these Rules of Professional Conduct or other law, the lawyer shall advise the client of the relevant limitations on the lawyer's conduct.

(f) A Government lawyer's authority and control over decisions concerning the representation may, by law, be expanded beyond the limits imposed by paragraphs (a) and (c).

COMMENT:

General

In many cases, straightforward application of Rule 1.2 is possible. However, in other cases, primarily in the litigation context, the scope of representation is necessarily altered and set out by law. For example, a Government lawyer representing an individual may have significant control over the litigation decisions. Similarly, except as otherwise provided by law, the Department of Justice, under 28 U.S.C. § 516, is given the authority to represent certain Federal agencies in litigation. Procedures for resolving inter-agency disputes should be followed in cases of conflict between a position recommended by the litigating attorney and the Federal Agency being represented.

Scope of Representation

Both Federal lawyer and client have authority and responsibility in the objectives and means of representation. The client has ultimate authority to determine the purposes to be served by legal representation, within the limits imposed by law and the Federal lawyer's professional obligations. Within those limits, a client also has a right to consult with the Federal lawyer about the means to be used in pursuing those objectives. At the same time, a Federal lawyer is not required to pursue objectives or employ means simply because a client may wish that the Federal lawyer do so. A clear distinction between objectives and means sometimes cannot be drawn, and in many cases the client-lawyer relationship becomes a joint undertaking. In question of means, the Federal lawyer should assume responsibility for technical and legal tactical issues, such as what witnesses to call, whether and how to conduct cross-examination, what court members to challenge, and what options to make. Except where precluded by Rule 4.4, the Federal lawyer should defer to the client regarding such questions as expenses to be incurred and concern for third persons who might be affected adversely.

When the client appears to be suffering mental disability, the Federal lawyer's duty to abide by the client's decisions is to be guided by Rule 1.14.

Service Limited in Objectives or Means

The objectives or scope of services provided by a Federal lawyer may be limited by agreement with the client or by the law governing the conditions under which the Federal lawyer's services are made available to the client. Formation of client-lawyer relationships and representation of clients by a Government lawyer is permissible only when authorized by competent authority. When the objectives or scope of services provided by a Federal lawyer are limited by law, the Federal lawyer should inform the client of such limitations at the earliest opportunity.

If a Government lawyer is uncertain of the scope of services permitted by the law governing the conditions under which the Federal lawyer's services are made available to a client, the Government lawyer should consult with the Government lawyer's supervisory lawyer concerning the matter. See Rule 5.2.

An agreement concerning the scope of representation must accord with these Rules of Professional Conduct and other law. Thus, the client shall not be asked to agree to representation so limited in scope as to violate Rule 1.1, to surrender the right to terminate the Federal lawyer's services, or to conclude a matter that the Federal lawyer might wish to continue.

Criminal, Fraudulent, and Prohibited Transactions

A Federal lawyer is required to give an honest opinion about the consequences likely to result from a client's conduct. Simply because a client uses advice in a course of action that is criminal or fraudulent does not, of itself, make a Federal lawyer a party to the course of action. However, a Federal lawyer shall not knowingly assist a client in criminal or fraudulent conduct. A critical distinction exists between presenting an analysis of legal aspects of questionable conduct and recommending the means by which a crime or fraud might be committed with impunity.

When the client's course of action has already begun and is continuing, the Federal lawyer's responsibility is especially delicate. The Federal lawyer is not permitted to reveal the client's wrongdoing, except where required or permitted by Rule 1.6 or Rule 3.3. However, the Federal lawyer is required to avoid furthering an illegal purpose, for example, by suggesting how it might be concealed. A Federal lawyer shall not continue assisting a client in conduct that the Federal lawyer originally supposes is legally proper but then discovers is criminal or fraudulent. Seeking to withdraw from the representation, therefore, may be appropriate.

Paragraph (d) applies whether or not the defrauded party is a party to the transaction. Hence, a Federal lawyer should not participate in a sham transaction; for example, a transaction to effectuate criminal or fraudulent escape of tax liability. The last clause of paragraph (d) recognizes that determining the validity or interpretation of a statute or regulation may include a course of action contrary to the terms of the statute or regulation or of the interpretation placed upon it by governmental authorities.

Rule 1.3. DILIGENCE

A Federal lawyer shall act with reasonable diligence and promptness in representing a client.

COMMENT:

A Federal lawyer should pursue a matter on behalf of a client despite opposition, obstruction, or personal inconvenience to the Federal lawyer, and may take whatever lawful and ethical measures are required to vindicate a client's cause or endeavor. A Federal lawyer should act with commitment and dedication to the interests of the client and with morality in advocating the client's position. However, a Federal lawyer is not bound to press for every advantage that might be realized for a client. Although a Federal lawyer may be bound by court precedent to pursue certain matters on behalf of a client, a Federal lawyer has professional discretion in determining the means by which a matter should be pursued. See Rules 1.2 and 1.4(b). A Federal lawyer's work load should be managed by both the Federal lawyer and a supervisory lawyer so that each matter can be handled adequately. See Rule 5.1.

Perhaps no professional shortcoming is more widely resented than procrastination. A client's interest often can be adversely affected by the passage of time or the chance of condition; in extreme instances, as when a Federal lawyer overlooks a statute of limitation, the client's legal position may be destroyed. Even when the client's interests are not affected in substance, however, unreasonable delay can cause a client needless anxiety and undermine confidence in the Federal lawyer's trustworthiness.

Unless the relationship is terminated as provided in Rule 1.16, and to the extent permitted by law, a Federal lawyer should carry through to conclusion all matters undertaken for a client. If a Federal lawyer's representation is limited to a specific matter, the relationship terminates when the matter has been resolved. Doubt about whether a client-lawyer relationship exists should be clarified by the Federal lawyer, preferably in writing, so that the client will not mistakenly suppose the Federal lawyer is looking after the client's affairs when the Federal lawyer has ceased to do so. For example, a Federal lawyer who has handled a judicial or administrative proceeding that produced a result adverse to the client should advise the client of the possibility of appeal before relinquishing responsibility for the matter.

Rule 1.4 COMMUNICATION

(a) A Federal lawyer shall keep a client reasonably informed about the status of a matter and promptly comply with reasonable requests for information.

(b) A Federal lawyer shall explain a matter to the extent reasonably necessary to permit the client to make informed decisions regarding the representation.

COMMENT:

A client should have sufficient information to participate intelligently in decisions concerning the objectives of the representation and the means by which they are to be pursued, to the extent a client is willing and able to do so. For example, a Federal lawyer negotiating a pretrial agreement on behalf of a client should provide the client with facts relevant to the matter, inform the client of communications from the Government, and take other reasonable steps that permit the client to make a decision regarding the feasibility of further negotiation with the Government. A Federal lawyer representing the Government who receives from the defendant an offer for a pretrial agreement must communicate that offer, and should provide advice as to that offer, to the appropriate authority.

Adequacy of communications depends in part on the kind of advice or assistance involved. For example, in negotiations where there is time to explain a proposal, a Federal lawyer should review all important provisions with the client before proceeding to an agreement. In litigation, a Federal lawyer should explain the general strategy and prospects of success and ordinarily should consult the client on tactics that might injure or coerce another. On the other hand, a Federal lawyer ordinarily cannot be expected to describe trial or negotiation strategy in detail. The guiding principle is that a Federal lawyer should fulfill reasonable client expectations for information consistent with the duty to act in the client's best interests, taking into account client's overall requirements as to the character of representation.

When the client is the Federal Agency, it is often impossible or inappropriate to inform all of its members about its legal affairs. Ordinarily, a Government lawyer should address communications to the appropriate officials of the Federal Agency. See Rule 1.13.

When the representation involves many routine matters, a system of limited or occasional reporting may be arranged with the client. Practical exigencies may limit the opportunity for consultation and also require a Federal lawyer to act for a client without prior consultation.

In some circumstances, a Federal lawyer may be required to withhold information from a client. For example, classified information shall not be disclosed without proper authority. In other circumstances, a Federal lawyer may be justified in delaying transmission of information when the client would be likely to react imprudently to an immediate communication. Thus, a Federal lawyer might withhold a psychiatric diagnosis of a client when the examining psychiatrist indicates that disclosure would harm the client. A Federal lawyer shall not withhold information to serve the Federal lawyer's own interest or convenience, or where disclosure would be favorable to the defense of a criminal defendant. Rules or court orders governing litigation may provide that information supplied to a Federal lawyer shall not be disclosed to the client. Rule 3.4(c) directs compliance with such rules or orders.

Rule 1.5 FEES

(a) A Federal lawyer shall be regulated by the Rules of Professional Conduct or other applicable rules of the jurisdictions in which the Federal lawyer is licensed or is practicing law, and otherwise by law in regard to matters concerning fees.

(b) A Government lawyer, in connection with the Government lawyer's official duties, may not request or accept any compensation from a client other than that provided by the United States for the performance of duties.

COMMENT:

Non-Government Lawyers

Rather than adopting a rule based on Rule 1.5 of the ABA Model Rule of Professional Conduct that would apply only to Non-Government lawyers practicing before Federal agencies, the Federal Agency defers on this matter to the rules of the jurisdictions in which these Non-Government lawyers are licensed, and otherwise by law.

Government Lawyers

Government lawyers are prohibited by statute from accepting, as compensation for services as a Government employee any salary or contribution to or supplementation of salary from any source other than the Government of the United States. See, for example, 18 U.S.C. § 203 and § 209.

A Government lawyer shall not request or accept any gratuity, salary, or other compensation from a client, other than the Federal Agency that employs the Government lawyer, incident to the performance of duties as a Government employee.

However, to the extent permitted by applicable laws, a Government lawyer who is active in a non-Government organization or who delivers a speech to an organization may accept reimbursement from the organization for the Government lawyer's costs incurred as a result of the Government lawyer's participation, on the Government lawyer's own time, in that organization's activities.

While a Government lawyer may be able to represent clients in a private or pro bono capacity, the Rule prohibits the Government lawyer from using the Government lawyer's official position to solicit or obtain clients for the Government lawyer's private practice.

Rule 1.6 CONFIDENTIALITY OF INFORMATION

(a) A Federal lawyer shall not reveal information relating to the representation of a client unless the client consents after consultation, except for disclosures that are impliedly authorized in order to carry out the representation, and except as stated in paragraphs (b), (c), and (d).

(b) A Federal lawyer shall reveal such information to the extent the Federal lawyer reasonably believes necessary to prevent the client from committing a criminal act that the Federal lawyer believes is likely to result in imminent death or substantial bodily harm, or imminent and significant impairment of national security or defense.

(c) A Federal lawyer may reveal such information to the extent the Federal lawyer reasonably believes necessary to establish a claim or defense on behalf of the Federal lawyer in a controversy between the Federal lawyer and the client, to establish a defense to a criminal charge or civil claim against the Federal lawyer based upon conduct in which the client was involved, or to respond to allegations in any proceeding concerning the Federal lawyer's representation of the client.

(d) A Government lawyer may reveal such information when required or authorized by law.

COMMENT:

The Federal lawyer is part of a judicial system charged with upholding the law. One of the Federal lawyer's functions is to advise clients so that they avoid any violation of the law in the proper exercise of their rights.

The observance of the ethical obligation of a Federal lawyer to hold inviolate confidential information of the client not only facilitates the full development of facts essential to proper representation of the client but also encourages people to seek early legal assistance.

Almost without exception, clients come to Federal lawyers in order to determine what their rights are and what, in the maze of laws and regulations, is deemed to be legal and correct. The common law recognizes that the client's confidences must be protected from disclosure. Based upon experience, Federal lawyers know that most clients follow the advice given, and the law is upheld.

A fundamental principle in the client-lawyer relationship is that the Federal lawyer maintains confidentiality of information relating to the representation. The client is thereby encouraged to communicate fully and frankly with the Federal lawyer even as to embarrassing or legally damaging matters.

The principle of confidentiality is given effect in two related bodies of law— the attorney-client privilege (which includes the work product doctrine) in the law of evidence and the rule of confidentiality established in professional ethics. The attorney-client privilege applies in judicial and other proceedings in which a Federal lawyer may be called as a witness or otherwise required to produce evidence concerning a client. The rule of client-lawyer confidentiality applies in situations other than those where evidence is sought from the Federal lawyer through compulsion of law. The confidentiality rule applies not merely to matters communicated in confidence by the client but also to all information relating to the representation, whatever its source. A Federal lawyer shall not disclose such information except as authorized or required by these Rules of Professional Conduct or other lawful order, directive, regulation, or statute. See also Scope.

The requirement of maintaining confidentiality of information relating to representation applies to Government lawyers, even those who may disagree with the policy goals that their representation is designed to advance.

Authorized Disclosure

A Federal lawyer is impliedly authorized to make disclosures about a client when appropriate in carrying out the representation, except to the extent that the client's instructions or special circumstances limit that authority. For example, a Federal lawyer may disclose information in litigation by admitting a fact that cannot properly be disputed, or in negotiation by making a disclosure that facilitates a satisfactory conclusion.

Federal lawyers may disclose to supervisory lawyers within the office and to nonlawyer assistants subject to the direction and control of the lawyer or the lawyer's supervisory lawyer information relating to a client, unless the client has instructed that particular information be confined to specified lawyers, or unless otherwise prohibited by these Rules of Professional Conduct or by law.

Disclosure Adverse to Client

The confidentiality rule is subject to limited exceptions. In becoming privy to information about a client, a Federal lawyer may foresee that the client intends serious harm to another person. However, to the extent a Federal lawyer is required or permitted to disclose a client's purposes, the client will be inhibited from revealing facts which would enable the Federal lawyer to counsel against a wrongful course of action. The public is better protected if full and open communication by the client is encouraged than if it is inhibited.

Several situations must be distinguished.

First, the Federal lawyer shall not counsel or assist a client in conduct that is criminal or fraudulent. See Rule 1.2(d). Similarly, a Federal lawyer owes a duty of candor to the court and has a duty under Rule 3.3(a)(3) not to use false evidence. These duties are essentially special instances of the duty prescribed in Rule 1.2(d) to avoid assisting a client in criminal or fraudulent conduct.

Second, the Federal lawyer may have been innocently involved in past conduct by the client that was criminal or fraudulent. In such a situation the Federal lawyer has not violated Rule 1.2(d), because to "counsel or assist" criminal or fraudulent conduct requires knowing that the conduct is of that character.

Third, the Federal lawyer may learn that a client intends prospective conduct that is criminal and likely to result in imminent death or substantial bodily harm, or imminent and significant impairment of national security or defense. As stated in paragraph (b), the Federal lawyer has a professional obligation to reveal the information to the extent that Federal lawyer reasonably believes necessary to prevent such consequences.

In any case, a disclosure adverse to the client's interest should be no greater than the Federal lawyer reasonably believes necessary to the purpose giving rise to the disclosure.

Withdrawal

If a Federal lawyer's services will be used by a client in materially furthering a course of criminal or fraudulent conduct, the Federal lawyer must seek to withdraw, as stated in Rule 1.16(a)(1).

After withdrawal the Federal lawyer is required to refrain from making disclosure of the client's confidence, except as otherwise provided in this Rule. Nothing in this Rule, Rule 1.8(b), or Rule 1.16(d) prevents the Federal lawyer from giving notice of the fact of withdrawal, and the Federal lawyer may also withdraw or disaffirm any opinion, document, affirmation, or the like.

When the client is a Federal Agency, the Federal lawyer may doubt whether contemplated conduct will actually be carried out. When necessary to guide conduct in connection with the Rule, the Federal lawyer may make inquiry within the Federal Agency as indicated in Rule 1.13(b).

Dispute Concerning a Federal Lawyer's Conduct

When a legal claim or disciplinary charge alleges complicity of the Federal lawyer in a client's conduct, or other misconduct of the Federal lawyer involving representation of the client, the Federal lawyer may respond to the extent the Federal lawyer reasonably believes necessary to establish a defense. The same is true with respect to a claim involving the conduct or representation of a former client. The Federal lawyer's right to respond arises when an assertion of such complicity has been made. Paragraph (c) does not require the Federal lawyer to await the commencement of an action or proceeding that charges such complicity. The defense may be established by responding directly to a third party who has made such an assertion. The right to defend, of course, applies where a proceeding has been commenced. Where practicable and not prejudicial to the Federal lawyer's ability to establish the defense, the Federal lawyer should advise the client of the third party's assertion and request that the client respond appropriately. In any event, disclosure should be no greater than the Federal lawyer reasonably believes is necessary to vindicate innocence; the disclosure should be made in a manner which limits access to the information to the tribunal or other persons having a need to know it; and appropriate protective orders or other arrangements should be sought by the Federal lawyer to the fullest extent practicable.

If a Federal lawyer is charged with wrongdoing in which the client's conduct is implicated, the rule of confidentiality should not prevent the Federal lawyer from defending against the charge. Such a charge can arise in a civil, criminal, or professional disciplinary proceeding, and can be based on a wrong allegedly committed by the Federal lawyer against the client, or a wrong alleged by a third person; for example, a person claiming to have been defrauded by the Federal lawyer and client acting together. A Non-Government lawyer entitled to a fee is permitted by paragraph (c) to prove the services rendered in an action to collect it. This aspect of the Rule expresses the principle that the beneficiary of a fiduciary relationship shall not exploit it to the detriment of the fiduciary. As stated above, the Federal lawyer must make every effort practicable to avoid unnecessary disclosure of information relating to a representation, to limit disclosure to those having the need to know it, and to obtain protective orders or make other arrangements to minimize the risk of disclosure.

Disclosure Otherwise Required or Authorized

If a Federal lawyer is called as a witness to give testimony concerning a client, absent waiver by the client, paragraph (a) requires the Federal lawyer to invoke the attorney-client privilege when it is applicable. The Federal lawyer must comply with the final orders of a court or other tribunal of competent jurisdiction requiring the Federal lawyer to give information about the client.

These Rules of Professional Conduct in various circumstances permit or require a Federal lawyer to disclose information relating to the representation.

See Rules 2.2, 2.3, 3.3, and 4.1. In addition to these provisions, a Federal lawyer may be obligated or permitted by other provision of law to give information about a client. Whether another provision of law supersedes Rule 1.6 is a matter of interpretation beyond the scope of these Rules, but a presumption should exist against such a supersession.

Former Client

The duty of confidentiality continues after the client-lawyer relationship has terminated.

Government Lawyers

The identification of the client, for purposes of the Government lawyer, is critical to the application of this Rule. Generally, a Federal Agency is the Government lawyer's client for the purposes of this Rule. Communications by the Government lawyer, both outside and within the Federal Agency, may or may not be considered breaches of this Rule. There are numerous statutes, regulations, and directives that may affect the Government lawyer's obligations under this Rule. A secondary issue concerns statutory protections against reprisal for Government employees who disclose violations or abuses—the "whistleblower statutes." However, in such situations there may be a conflict with attorney-client privileges.

Government lawyers are often formally employed by a Federal Agency but assigned to an organizational element within the Federal Agency. Unless otherwise specifically provided, the Federal Agency, not the organizational element, is ordinarily considered the client.

Paragraph (d) permits disclosures that the Government authorizes its lawyers to make in connection with their professional services to the Government. Such disclosures may be authorized or required by statute, Executive Order, regulation, or directive, depending on the constitutional or statutory powers of the authorizing entity. This paragraph also clarifies that, under 28 U.S.C. § 516, Government lawyers may disclose all information relevant to representation by the Department of Justice to the Department's assigned attorney, and authorizes such information to be further disclosed by the assigned attorney to other Department of Justice lawyers concerned with the representation.

There are circumstances in which a Government lawyer may be assigned to provide an individual with counsel or representation in which it is clear that an obligation of confidentiality runs directly to that individual and not to the Federal Agency. Examples of such representation include a Government lawyer representing a defendant sued for damages arising out of the performance of the defendant's Government employment, a judge advocate representing an accused in a court-martial, or representation by a public defender.

The relevant circumstances may indicate the extent to which the individual client will be deemed to have granted or denied consent to disclosures by the Government lawyer to the Government lawyer's employing Agency under paragraph (d).

While the general thrust of this Rule may serve as guidance for the Government attorney, the Government lawyer's actions are defined and circumscribed by various Federal laws and these Rules. As a practical matter, in addition to determining the extent to which Rule 1.6 applies to a given situation, it is always advisable for Government lawyers to review the applicable Federal law that may govern their conduct under the circumstances, and to consult with their supervisors.

For example, Government employees are prohibited from using, for financial gain or other improper purposes, non-public information obtained by reason of their status as an employee. See 5 CFR 735.206. See also 28 CFR Part 17, which sets out regulations protecting confidential information relating to national security; 28 CFR 50.2, which establishes policy regarding the release of information relating to criminal and civil proceedings; 28 CFR 50.15(a)(3), which regulates the treatment of confidential attorney-client information in the context of Department of Justice representation of individual Government employees. The Privacy Act and other laws also prohibit the disclosure of certain types of confidential Government information. * * * Unique Government privileges also play a role in shaping a Government lawyer's duties and responsibilities regarding confidential Government information. Thus, for example, the law recognizes a deliberative process privilege, which protects from public disclosure predecisional communications that are part of the decision making process of government agencies. * * *

Rule 1.7 CONFLICT OF INTEREST: GENERAL RULE

(a) A Federal lawyer shall not represent a client if the representation of that client will be directly adverse to another client, unless:
    (1) The Federal lawyer reasonably believes the representation will not adversely affect the relationship with the other client; and
    (2) Each client consents after consultation.
(b) A Federal lawyer shall not represent a client if the representation of that client may be materially limited by the lawyer's responsibilities to another client or to a third person, or by the Federal lawyer's own interests, unless:
    (1) The Federal lawyer reasonably believes the representation will not be adversely affected; and
    (2) The client consents after consultation. When representation of multiple clients in a single matter is undertaken, the consultation shall include explanation of the implications of the common representation and the advantages and risks involved.

COMMENT:

Loyalty is an essential element in the Federal lawyer's relationship to a client. If an impermissible conflict of interest exists before representation, the Federal lawyer should decline to represent the client. If such a conflict arises after representation has been undertaken, the Federal lawyer should seek to withdraw from representation of the subsequent client. See Rule 1.16. When more than one client is involved and the Federal lawyer is permitted to withdraw because a conflict arises after the representation has begun, the Federal lawyer's ethical ability to continue to represent any of the clients is determined by Rule 1.9. See also Rule 2.2(c). As to whether a client-lawyer relationship exists or, having once been established, is continuing, see Comment to Rule 1.3.

As a general proposition, loyalty to a client prohibits undertaking representation directly adverse to that client without that client's consent. Paragraph (a) expresses that general rule. Thus, a Federal lawyer ordinarily shall not act as advocate against a person the Federal lawyer represents in some other matter even if it is wholly unrelated. On the other hand, simultaneous representation in unrelated matters of clients whose interests are only generally adverse, does not require consent of either client. Paragraph (a) applies only when the representation of one client would be directly adverse to the other.

Loyalty to a client is also impaired when a Federal lawyer cannot consider, recommend, or carry out an appropriate course of action for the client because of the Federal lawyer's other responsibilities or interests. This type of conflict effectively forecloses alternatives that would otherwise be available to the client. Paragraph (b) addresses such situations. A possible conflict does not itself preclude the representation. The critical questions are—the likelihood that a conflict will eventuate and, if it does, whether it will materially interfere with the Federal lawyer's independent professional judgment in considering alternatives or foreclose courses of action that reasonably should be pursued on behalf of the client. Consideration should be given to whether the client wishes to accommodate the other interest involved.

Consultation and Consent

A client, including an organization (see Rule 1.13(b)), may consent to representation notwithstanding a conflict. However, as indicated in paragraph (a)(1) with respect to representation directly adverse to a client, and paragraph (b)(1) with respect to material limitations on representation of a client, when a disinterested Federal lawyer would conclude that the client should not agree to the representation under the circumstances, the Federal lawyer involved cannot properly ask for such agreement to provide representation on the basis of the client's consent. When more than one client is involved, the question of conflict must be resolved as to each client. Moreover, there may be circumstances where it is impossible to make the disclosure necessary to obtain consent.

Federal Lawyer's Interests

The Federal lawyer's own interests should not be permitted to have an adverse effect on representation of a client. * * * If the probity of a Federal lawyer's own conduct in a transaction is in serious question, it may be difficult or impossible for the Federal lawyer to give a client detached advice. A Federal lawyer shall not allow related business interests to affect representation, for example, by referring clients to an enterprise in which the Federal lawyer has an undisclosed interest.

Conflict of Litigation

Paragraph (a) prohibits representation of opposing parties in litigation. Simultaneous representation of parties whose interest in litigation may conflict, such as co-plaintiffs or co-defendants, is governed by paragraph (b). An impermissible conflict may exist by reason of substantial discrepancy in the parties' testimony, incompatibility in position in relation to an opposing party, or the fact that there are substantially different possibilities of settlement of the claims or liabilities in question. Such conflicts can arise in criminal cases, as well as, civil matters. The potential for a conflict of interest in representing multiple defendants in a criminal case is so grave that ordinarily a Federal lawyer should not represent more than one co-defendant. On the other hand, common representation of persons having similar interests is proper if the risk of adverse effect is minimal and the requirements of paragraph (b) are met. Compare Rule 2.2 involving intermediation between clients.

Ordinarily, a Federal lawyer shall not act as advocate against a client the Federal lawyer represents in some other matter, even if the other matter is wholly unrelated. However, there are circumstances in which a Government lawyer may act as advocate against the Government lawyer's Federal Agency. For example, Government lawyers in some circumstances may represent another Government employee in proceedings (e.g., courts-martial or adverse personnel action proceedings) in which a Federal Agency is the opposing party. The propriety of concurrent representation can depend on the nature of the litigation. For example, a suit charging fraud entails conflict to a degree not involved in a suit for declaratory judgment concerning statutory interpretation.

A Federal lawyer may represent parties having antagonistic positions on a legal question that has arisen in different cases, unless representation of either client would be adversely affected. Thus, it is ordinarily proper to assert such positions in cases pending in different trial courts, but it may be improper to do so in cases pending in an appellate court.

Interest of a Person Paying for a Federal Lawyer's Service

A Non-Government lawyer may be paid from a source other than the client, if the client is informed of that fact, consents, and the arrangement does not compromise the Federal lawyer's duty of loyalty to the client. See Rule 1.8(f). For example, a defendant's family may pay a Non-Government lawyer to represent a defendant at trial.

Other Conflict Situations

Conflicts of interest in contexts other than litigation sometimes may be difficult to assess. Relevant factors in determining whether there is potential for adverse effect include the duration and intimacy of the Federal lawyer's relationship with the client or clients involved, the functions being performed by the Federal lawyer, the likelihood that actual conflict will arise and the likely prejudice to the client from the conflict if it does arise. The question is often one of proximity and degree.

Although the Federal lawyer must be careful to avoid conflict of interest situations, resolving questions of conflict of interest is primarily the responsibility of the supervisory lawyer or the judge. See also Rule 5.1.

Conflict Charged by an Opposing Party

In litigation, courts raise conflict of interest issues when reason exists to believe that a Federal lawyer may have neglected his or her responsibilities. In a criminal case, inquiry by the court is generally required when a Federal lawyer represents multiple defendants. When an apparent conflict calls into question the fair or efficient administration of justice, opposing counsel may properly raise the issue. Such objections should be viewed with caution, however, for they can be misused as a technique of harassment. See Scope.

Government Lawyers

This Rule is not intended to apply to conflicts between Federal agencies or components of government (Federal, State or local), where the resolution of such conflicts has been entrusted by law to a specific individual or entity. Thus, for example, 28 U.S.C. § 516, authorizes the Attorney General and the Government lawyers of the Justice Department to resolve conflicts between certain Government agencies for purposes of litigation and even to assert positions in litigation that might be adverse to positions urged upon the Department of Justice by a client Agency. (See also Executive Order 12146, sections 1–4, which directs Executive agencies that are unable to resolve a legal dispute to submit the dispute to the Attorney General). Moreover, this rule is not intended to supersede Government regulations * * * governing the resolution of conflicts in the context of representation of Government employees sued in their individual or personal capacities.

Rule 1.8 CONFLICT OF INTEREST: PROHIBITED TRANSACTIONS

(a) A Federal lawyer shall not enter into a business transaction with a client or knowingly acquire an ownership, possessory, security, or other pecuniary interest adverse to a client unless:
  (1) The transaction and terms on which the Federal lawyer requires the interest are fair and reasonable to the client and are fully disclosed and transmitted in writing to the client in a manner which can be reasonably understood by the client;
  (2) The client is given a reasonable opportunity to seek the advice of independent counsel in the transaction; and
  (3) The client consents in writing thereto.
(b) A Federal lawyer shall not use information relating to representation of a client to the disadvantage of the client unless the client consents after consultation.
(c) A Federal lawyer shall not prepare an instrument giving the lawyer or an individual related to the lawyer as parent, child, sibling, or spouse any substantial gift from a client, including a testamentary gift, except where the client is related to the donee.
(d) While representing a client, a Federal lawyer shall not make or negotiate an agreement giving the lawyer literary or edit rights to a portrayal or account based in substantial part on information relating to the representation.
(e) A Federal lawyer shall not provide financial assistance to a client in connection with pending or contemplated litigation, except that:
  (1) A Non-Government lawyer practicing before a Federal Agency may advance court costs and expenses of litigation, the repayment of which may be contingent on the outcome of the matter; and
  (2) A Non-Government lawyer practicing before a Federal Agency representing an indigent client may pay court costs and expenses of litigation on behalf of the client.
(f) A Federal lawyer shall not accept compensation for representing a client from one other than the client unless:
  (1) The client consents after consultation;
  (2) There is no interference with the Federal lawyer's independence of professional judgment or with the Federal lawyer-client relationship; and
  (3) Information relative to representation of a client is protected as required by Rule 1.6.

(g) A Federal lawyer who represents two or more clients shall not participate in making an aggregate settlement of the claims of or against the clients, or in a criminal case an aggregate agreement as to guilty pleas or nolo contendere pleas, unless each client consents after consultation, including disclosure of the existence and nature of all the claims or pleas involved and of the participation of each person in the settlement.

(h) A Federal lawyer shall not:

    (1) Make an agreement prospectively limiting the lawyer's liability to a client for malpractice unless permitted by law and the client is independently represented in making the agreement.

    (2) Settle a claim for liability due to allegations of malpractice with an unrepresented client or former client without first advising that person in writing that independent representation is appropriate in connection therewith.

(i) A Federal lawyer related to another lawyer as parent, child, sibling, or spouse shall not represent a client if the client's interest is directly adverse to a person who the Federal lawyer knows is represented by the other lawyer, except with the consent of the client after consultation regarding the relationship.

(j) A Non-Government lawyer shall not acquire a proprietary interest in the cause of action or subject matter of litigation the lawyer is conducting for a client, except that the lawyer may:

    (1) Acquire a lien granted by law to secure the Non-Government lawyer's fee or expenses; and

    (2) Contract with a client for a reasonable contingent fee in a civil case.

COMMENT:

Government Lawyers

Government lawyers shall strictly adhere to Federal Agency standards of conduct regulations and applicable laws in all dealings with individual clients. (See generally 18 U.S.C. §§ 202–211.) Such laws generally prohibit entering into business transactions with clients, deriving financial benefit from representations of clients, and accepting gifts from clients or other entities for the performance of official duties. This Rule does not authorize otherwise prohibited by such regulations. A Government lawyer shall not refer legal or other business to any private Non-Government lawyer or enterprise with whom the Government lawyer has any present or expected direct or indirect personal interest. Special care will be taken to avoid giving preferential treatment to other Government lawyers in their private capacities.

A Government lawyer shall not request or accept any gratuity, salary, or other compensation from a client incident to the performance of duties as a Government employee.

Transactions Between Client and Federal Lawyer

As a general principle, all business transactions between client and Federal lawyer should be fair and reasonable to the client. In such transactions, a review by independent counsel on behalf of the client is often advisable. Furthermore, a Federal lawyer shall not exploit information relating to the representation to the client's disadvantage. For example, a Federal lawyer who has learned that the client is investing in specific real estate shall not, without the client's consent, seek to acquire nearby property where doing so would adversely affect the client's plan for investment. Paragraph (a) does not apply to standard commercial transactions between the Federal lawyer and the client for products or services that the client generally markets to others, for example, banking or brokerage services, medical services, products manufactured or distributed by the client, and utility services. In such transactions, the lawyer has no advantage in dealing with the client, and the restrictions in paragraph (a) are unnecessary and impracticable. All transactions must comply with promulgated standards of conduct and other laws. See also Rule 1.5.

Literary Rights

An agreement by which a Federal lawyer acquires literary or media rights concerning the conduct of the representation creates a conflict between the interests of the client and the personal interests of the Federal lawyer. Measures suitable in the representation of the client may detract from the publication value of an account of that representation.

Person Paying for a Federal Lawyer's Services

Paragraph (f) requires the Federal lawyer to disclose the fact that the Federal lawyer's services are being paid for by a third party. Such an arrangement must also conform to the requirements of Rule 1.6 concerning confidentiality and Rule 1.7 concerning conflict of interest.

Family Relationships Between Federal Lawyers

Paragraph (i) applies to related Federal lawyers who are in the same or different Federal Agency. Related Federal lawyers in the same office also are governed by Rules 1.7, 1.9, and 1.10. The disqualification stated in paragraph (i) is personal and is not imputed to other Federal lawyers in the offices with whom the Federal lawyer performs duty.

Acquisition of Interest in Litigation

Paragraph (j) states the traditional general rule that Federal lawyers are prohibited from acquiring a proprietary interest in litigation. This general rule, which has its basis in common law champerty and maintenance, is subject to specific exceptions developed in decisional law and continued in these Rules, such as the exception for reasonable contingent fees set forth in Rule 1.5 of the ABA Model Rules of Professional Conduct and the exception for certain advances of the costs of litigation set forth in paragraph (e).

The Rule is not intended to apply to customary qualifications and limitations in legal opinions and memoranda.

Rule 1.9 CONFLICT OF INTEREST: FORMER CLIENT

(a) A Federal lawyer who has formerly represented a client in a matter shall not thereafter represent another person in the same or a substantially related matter in which the person's interests are materially adverse to the interests of the client unless the former client consents after consultation.

(b) A Federal lawyer shall not knowingly represent a person in the same or a substantially related matter in which a firm with which the lawyer formerly was associated had previously represented a client:

(1) Whose interests are materially adverse to that person; and

(2) About whom the lawyer had acquired information protected by Rules 1.6 and 1.9(c) that is material to the matter; unless the former client consents after consultation.

(c) A Federal lawyer who has formerly represented a client in a matter or whose present or former firm has formerly represented a client in a matter shall not thereafter:

(1) Use information relating to the representation to the disadvantage of the former client except as Rule 1.6 would permit with respect to a client or when the information has become generally known.

(2) Reveal information relating to the representation except as Rule 1.6 or Rule 3.3 would permit or require with respect to a client.

COMMENT:

After termination of a client-lawyer relationship, a Federal lawyer shall not represent another client except in conformity with this Rule. The principles in Rule 1.7 determine whether the interests of the present and former client are adverse. The principles in Rule 1.11 govern successive Government and private employment.

The scope of a "matter" for purposes of paragraph (a) may depend on the facts of a particular situation or transaction. The Federal lawyer's involvement in a matter can also be a question of degree. When a Federal lawyer has been directly involved in a specific transaction, subsequent representation of other clients with materially adverse interest clearly is prohibited. On the other hand, a Federal lawyer who recurrently handled a type of problem for a former client is not precluded from later representing another client in a wholly distinct problem of that type, even though the subsequent representation involves a position adverse to the prior client. Thus, the reassignment of judge advocates between defense, prosecution, review, claim, and legal assistance functions within the same legal office is not precluded by this Rule.

Lawyers Moving Between Firms

When Non-Government lawyers have been associated within a firm, but then end their association, the question of whether the Non-Government lawyer should undertake representation is more complicated. There are several competing considerations. First, the client previously represented by the former firm must be reasonably assured that the principle of loyalty to the client is not compromised. Second, the rule should not be so broadly cast as to preclude other persons from having reasonable choice of legal counsel. Third, the rule should not unreasonably hamper lawyers from forming new associations and taking on new clients after having left a previous association. In this connection, it should be recognized that today many lawyers practice in firms, that many lawyers to some degree limit their practice to one field or another, and that many move from one association to another several times in their careers. If the concept of imputation were applied with unqualified rigor, the result would be radical curtailment of the opportunity of lawyers to move from one practice setting to another and of the opportunity of clients to change counsel.

Reconciliation of these competing principles in the past has been attempted under two rubrics. One approach has been to seek per se rules of disqualification. For example, it has been held that a partner in a law firm is conclusively presumed to have access to all confidences concerning all clients of the firm. Under this analysis, if a lawyer has been a partner in one law firm and then becomes a partner in another law firm, there may be a presumption that all confidences known by the partner in the first firm are known to all partners in the second firm. This presumption might properly be applied in some circumstances, especially where the client has been extensively represented, but may be unrealistic where the client was represented only for limited purposes. Furthermore, such a rigid rule exaggerates the difference between a partner and an associate in modern law firms.

The other rubric formerly used for dealing with disqualification is the appearance of impropriety prescribed in Canon 9 of the ABA Model Code of Professional Responsibility. This rubric has a twofold problem. First, the appearance of impropriety can be taken to include any new client-lawyer relationship that might make a former client feel anxious. If that meaning were adopted, disqualification would become little more than a question of subjective judgment by the former client. Second, since "impropriety" is undefined, the term "appearance of impropriety" is question-begging. It therefore has to be recognized that the problem of disqualification cannot be properly resolved either by simple analogy to a lawyer practicing alone or by the very general concept of appearance of impropriety.

Confidentiality

Preserving confidentiality is a question of access to information. Access to information, in turn, is essentially a question of fact in particular circumstances, aided by inferences, deductions, or working presumptions that reasonably may be made about the way in which lawyers work together. A lawyer may have general access to files of all clients of a law firm and may regularly participate in discussions of their affairs; it should be inferred that such a lawyer in fact is privy to all information about all of the firm's clients. In contrast, another lawyer may have access to the files of only a limited number of clients and participate in discussions of the affairs of no other clients; in the absence of information to the contrary, it should be inferred that such a lawyer in fact is privy to information about the clients actually served but not those of other clients.

Application of paragraph (b) depends on a situation's particular facts. In such an inquiry, the burden of proof should rest upon the lawyer whose disqualification is sought.

Paragraph (b) operates to disqualify the lawyer only when the lawyer involved has actual knowledge of information protected by Rules 1.6 and 1.9(c). Thus, if a lawyer while with one firm acquired no knowledge or information relating to a particular client of the firm, and that lawyer later joins another firm, neither the lawyer individually nor the second firm is disqualified from representing another client in the same or a related matter even though the interests of the two clients conflict. See Rule 1.10(b) for the restrictions on a firm once a lawyer has terminated association [with] the firm.

Independent of the question of disqualification of a firm, a lawyer changing professional association has a continuing duty to preserve confidentiality of information about a client formerly represented. See Rules 1.6 and 1.9.

Adverse Positions

The underlying question is whether the Federal lawyer was so involved in a particular matter that the subsequent representation can be justly regarded as a changing of sides in the matter in question.

Information acquired by the Federal lawyer in the course of representing a client shall not later be used by the Federal lawyer to the disadvantage of the client. However, just because a Federal lawyer once represented a client does not preclude the Federal lawyer from using generally known information about that client when later representing another client.

Disqualification from subsequent representation is for the protection of clients and can be waived by them. A waiver is effective only if it is preceded by full disclosure of the circumstances, including the Federal lawyer's role in behalf of the new client.

With regard to an opposing party's raising a question of conflict of interest, see Comment to Rule 1.7.

Rule 1.10 IMPUTED DISQUALIFICATION: GENERAL RULE

(a) Government lawyers working in the same Federal Agency are not automatically disqualified from representing a client because any of them practicing alone would be prohibited from doing so by Rules 1.7, 1.8(c), 1.9, or 2.2.

(b) When a Federal lawyer has terminated an association with a firm, the firm is not prohibited from thereafter representing a person with interests materially adverse to those of a client represented by the formerly associated lawyer and not currently represented by the firm, unless:

(1) The matter is the same or substantially related to that in which the formerly associated lawyer represented the client; and

(2) Any Federal lawyer remaining in the firm has information protected by Rules 1.6 and 1.9(c) that is material to the matter.

(c) A disqualification under this Rule may be waived by the affected client under the conditions stated in Rule 1.7.

COMMENT:

Government Federal Agency Practice

The circumstances of Government service may require representation of opposing sides by Government lawyers working in the same Federal Agency. Such representation is permissible so long as conflicts of interest are avoided and independent judgment, zealous representation, and protection of confidences are not compromised. Thus, the principle of imputed disqualification is not automatically controlling for Government lawyers. The knowledge, action, and conflicts of interest of one Government lawyer are not to be imputed to another simply because they operate from the same office. For example, a number of military defense counsels or public defenders operating from one office under a common supervisory lawyer and sharing clerical assistance are not prohibited from representing co-defendants at trial.

While it is permissible under this rule for a Government lawyer to represent an individual client in a military justice or an administrative proceeding that is under the control of a superior of the Government lawyer, particular care and attention is required when potential conflicts of interest exist between the organizational client of a supervisory lawyer and the individual clients of the Government lawyer being supervised.

Preserving confidentiality is a question of access to information. Access to information, in turn, is essentially a question of fact in particular circumstance, aided by inferences, deductions, or working presumptions that reasonably may be made about the way in which Government lawyers work together. A Government lawyer may have general access to files of all clients of a Federal Agency legal staff and may regularly participate in discussions of their affairs. It may be inferred that such a Government lawyer in fact is privy to all information about all the office's clients. In contrast, another Government lawyer may have access only to the files of his or her clients and does not participate in discussion of the affairs of other clients. In the absence of information to the contrary, it should be inferred that such a Government lawyer in fact is privy to information about the clients actually served, but not to information of other clients.

General

Whether a Federal lawyer is disqualified requires a functional analysis of the facts in a specific situation. The analysis should include consideration of whether the following will be compromised: preserving attorney-client confidentiality; maintaining independence of judgment; and avoiding positions adverse to a client.

Additionally, a Federal lawyer changing jobs has a continuing duty to preserve confidentiality of information about a client formerly represented. See Rules 1.6 and 1.9.

Maintaining independent judgment allows a Federal lawyer to consider, recommend, and carry out any appropriate course of action for a client without regard to the Federal lawyer's personal interests or the interests of another. When such independence is lacking or unlikely, representation cannot be zealous.

Another aspect of loyalty to a client is the Federal lawyer's obligation to decline subsequent representation involving positions adverse to a former client in substantially related matters. This obligation requires abstention from adverse representation by the individual Federal lawyer involved, but does not properly entail abstention of other Federal lawyers through imputed disqualification. Hence this aspect of the problem is governed by Rule 1.9(a).

Rule 1.11 SUCCESSIVE GOVERNMENT AND PRIVATE EMPLOYMENT

(a) Except as law may otherwise expressly permit, a Federal lawyer shall not represent a private client in connection with a matter in which the Federal lawyer participated personally and substantially as a Government employee unless the appropriate Government Agency consents after consultation. No lawyer in a firm with which that lawyer is associated may knowingly undertake or continue representation in such matter unless:

(1) The disqualified Federal lawyer is screened from any participation in the matter and is apportioned no part of the fee therefrom; and

(2) Written notice is promptly given to the appropriate government Agency to enable it to ascertain compliance with the provisions of this Rule.

(b) Except as law may otherwise expressly permit, a Federal lawyer having information that the lawyer knows is confidential Government information about a person acquired when the lawyer was a Government employee shall not represent a private client whose interests are adverse to that person in a matter in which the information could be used to the material disadvantage of that person. A firm with which that lawyer is associated may undertake or continue representation in the matter only if the disqualified lawyer is screened from any participation in the matter and is apportioned no part of the fee therefrom.

(c) Except as law may otherwise expressly permit, a Federal lawyer serving as a Government employee shall not:

    (1) Participate in a matter in which the Federal lawyer participated personally and substantially while in private practice or nongovernmental employment, unless under applicable law no one is, or by lawful delegation may be, authorized to act in the lawyer's stead in the matter.

    (2) Negotiate for private employment with any person who is involved as a party or as attorney for a party in a matter in which the Federal lawyer is participating personally and substantially.

(d) As used in this Rule, the term "matter" includes:

    (1) Any judicial or other proceeding, application, request for a ruling or other determination, contract, claim, controversy, investigation, charge, accusation, arrest, or other particular matter involving a specific party or parties.

    (2) Any other matter covered by the conflict of interest rules of the appropriate Federal Agency.

(e) As used in this Rule, the term "confidential Governmental information" means information which has been obtained under Governmental authority and that, at the time this Rule is applied, the Government is prohibited by law from disclosing to the public or has a legal privilege not to disclose, and which is not otherwise available to the public.

COMMENT:

This Rule prevents a Federal lawyer from exploiting public office for the advantage of a private client.

A Government lawyer representing a Federal Agency is subject to these Rules of Professional Conduct, including the prohibition against representing adverse interests stated in Rule 1.7 and the protections afforded former clients in Rule 1.9. In addition, such a Government lawyer is subject to Rule 1.11 and to laws regarding conflicts of interest, including 18 U.S.C. § 205 (prohibits Government employees from representing parties in actions against the United States), § 207 (restrictions on successive Government and private employment), § 208 (financial conflict of interest restrictions), and § 281 (restrictions on retired military officers); 5 CFR Part 2637 (regulations concerning post Government employment); and any Federal Agency regulations or directives. Such statutes and regulations may circumscribe the extent to which the Federal Agency may give consent under this Rule. If a Federal Agency has adopted rules governing practice before the agency by former federal lawyers, such issues (e.g., notice requirements) are governed by the Federal Agency rules and this Rule is not intended to displace such Agency requirements.

Where the successive clients are a Federal Agency and a private client, the risk exists that power or discretion vested in public authority might be used for the special benefit of a private client. A Federal lawyer should not be in a position in which benefit to a private client might affect performance of the Federal lawyer's professional functions on behalf of public authority. Also, unfair advantage could accrue to the private client by reason of access to confidential Government information about the client or by reason of access to confidential Government information about the client's adversary obtainable only through the Federal lawyer's government service. The rules governing Federal lawyers presently or formerly employed by a Federal Agency, however, should not be so restrictive as to inhibit transfer of employment to and from the Government. The Government has a legitimate need to attract qualified Federal lawyers as well as to maintain high ethical standards. The provisions for screening and waiver are necessary to prevent the disqualification rule from imposing too severe a deterrent against entering public service.

When the client is an agency of one government, that agency should be treated as a private client for purposes of this Rule if the Federal lawyer thereafter represents an agency of another government; as when a Federal lawyer represents a city and subsequently is employed by a Federal Agency.

Paragraphs (a)(1) and (b) do not prohibit a Federal lawyer from receiving salary or partnership income where established by prior independent agreement. They prohibit directly relating the Federal lawyer's compensation to the fee in the matter in which the Federal lawyer is disqualified.

Paragraph (a)(2) does not require that a Federal lawyer give notice to the Federal Agency at a time when premature disclosure would injure the client; a requirement for premature disclosure might preclude engagement of the Federal lawyer. Such notice is, however, required to be given as soon as practicable to give the Federal Agency a reasonable opportunity to determine if the Federal lawyer is complying with Rule 1.11 and to take appropriate action if it believes the Federal lawyer is not complying.

Paragraph (b) operates only when the Federal lawyer in question has knowledge of the information. This means actual knowledge. Paragraph (b) does not operate with respect to information that merely could be imputed to the Federal lawyer.

Rule 1.12 FORMER JUDGE OR ARBITRATOR

(a) Except as stated in paragraph (d), a Federal lawyer shall not represent anyone in connection with a matter in which the lawyer participated personally and substantially as a judge or other adjudicative officer, arbitrator, or law clerk to such a person, unless all parties to the proceeding consent after disclosure.

(b) A Federal lawyer shall not negotiate for employment with any person who is involved as a party or as attorney for a party in a matter in which the lawyer is participating personally and substantially as a judge or other adjudicative officer, or arbitrator.

(c) If a Federal lawyer is disqualified by paragraph (a), no Federal lawyer in a firm with which the lawyer is associated may knowingly undertake or continue representation in the matter unless:

(1) The disqualified Federal lawyer is screened from any participation in the matter and is apportioned no part of the fee therefrom.

(2) Written notice is promptly given to the appropriate tribunal to enable it to ascertain compliance with the provisions of this Rule.

(d) An arbitrator selected as a partisan of a party in a multi-member arbitration panel is not prohibited from subsequently representing that party.

COMMENT:

This Rule generally parallels Rule 1.11. The term "personally and substantially" means that a judge who was a member of a multi-member court, and thereafter left judicial office, is not prohibited from representing a client in a matter pending in the court, so long as it is a matter in which the former judge did not participate. Likewise, a former judge's exercise of administrative responsibility in a court or judiciary office does not prevent the former judge from acting as a Federal lawyer in a matter in which the judge had previously exercised remote or incidental administrative responsibility that did not affect the merits. Compare the Comment to Rule 1.11. The term "adjudicative officer" includes such officials as hearing officers, legal advisors to administrative boards, and investigating officers.

Rule 1.13 THE FEDERAL AGENCY AS THE CLIENT

(a) Except when representing another client pursuant to paragraphs (e), (f) and (g), a Government lawyer represents the Federal Agency that employs the Government lawyer. Government lawyers are often formally employed by a Federal Agency but assigned to an organizational element within the Federal Agency. Unless otherwise specifically provided, the Federal Agency, not the organizational element, is ordinarily considered the client. The Federal Agency acts through its authorized officials. These officials include the heads of organizational elements within the Federal Agency. When a Government lawyer is assigned to an organizational element and designated to provide legal services and advice to the head of that organization, the client-lawyer relationship exists between the Government lawyer and the Federal agency, as represented by the head of the organization, as to matters within the scope of the official business of the organization. The head of the organization may only invoke the attorney-client privilege or the rule of confidentiality for the benefit of the Federal Agency. In so invoking, either the attorney-client privilege or attorney-client confidentiality on behalf of the Federal Agency, the head of the organization is subject to being overruled by higher agency authority.

(b) If a Government lawyer knows that a Government employee is acting, intending to act, or refusing to act in a matter related to the representation in a manner such that either a violation of a legal obligation to the Federal Agency or a violation of law reasonably might be imputed to the Federal Agency, the Government lawyer shall proceed as is reasonably necessary in the best interest of the Federal Agency. In determining how to proceed, the Government lawyer shall give due consideration to the seriousness of the violation and its consequences, the scope and nature of the Government lawyer's representation, the responsibility in the Federal Agency, the apparent motivation of the person involved, the policies of the Federal Agency concerning such matters, and any other relevant considerations.

Any measures taken shall be designed to minimize disruption of the Federal Agency and the risk of revealing information relating to the representation to persons outside the Federal Agency. Such measures may include, among others:

(1) Advising the person that, in the Government lawyer's opinion, the action, planned action, or refusal to act is contrary to law; advising the person of the Federal Agency's policy on the matter concerned; advising the person that his or her personal legal interests are at risk and that he or she should consult independent counsel, because there may be a conflict of interest with the Government lawyer's responsibility to the organization; and asking the person to reconsider the matter.

(2) Advising the person that a separate legal opinion on the matter be sought for presentation to appropriate authority in Federal Agency.

(3) Advising the person that the lawyer is ethically obligated to preserve the interests of the Federal Agency and, as a result, must consider discussing the matter with supervisory lawyers within the Government lawyer's office or at a higher level within the Federal Agency.

(4) Referring the matter to or seeking guidance from higher authority in the Federal Agency, including, if warranted by the seriousness of the matter, referral to the highest authority that can act on behalf of the Federal Agency.

(c) If, despite the Government lawyer's efforts in accordance with paragraph (b), the highest authority that can act concerning the matter insists upon action, or refusal to act, that is clearly a violation of law, the Government lawyer shall terminate representation with respect to the matter in question. In no event may the Government lawyer participate or assist in the illegal activity.

(d) In dealing with the Government employee, a Government lawyer shall explain the identity of the client when it is apparent that the Federal Agency's interests are adverse to those of the Government employee.

(e) A Government lawyer shall not form a client-lawyer relationship or represent a client other than the Federal Agency unless specifically assigned or authorized by competent authority.

(f) A Government lawyer representing the Federal Agency may also represent any of its Government employees subject to the provisions of paragraph (f), Rule 1.7, and other applicable authority. If the Federal Agency's consent to dual representation is required by Rule 1.7, the consent shall be given by an appropriate official of the Federal Agency, other than the individual to be represented.

(g) A Government lawyer who has been duly assigned or authorized to represent an individual who is subject to disciplinary action or administrative proceedings, or to provide civil legal assistance to an individual, has, for those purposes, a lawyer-client relationship with that individual.

COMMENT:

The Comment to the ABA Model Rule acknowledges the applicability of this Rule to governmental organizations; the balance between maintaining confidentiality and assuring that wrongful official acts are prevented or rectified; and the difficulty in defining precisely the identity of the client (and prescribing the resulting obligations of such lawyers) in the government context.

Except when a Government lawyer is assigned to represent the interest of another client, the Federal Agency that employs the Government lawyer is the client. This principle is critical to the application of these Rules, since the identity of the client affects significant confidentiality and conflict issues.

Because the Federal Agency is the Government lawyer's client, the Government lawyer represents the Federal Agency acting through its duly authorized constituents. Any application of Rule 1.13 to Government lawyers must, however, take into account the differences between Federal agencies and other organizations. These exceptions include, but are not limited to, Government lawyers assigned to represent individuals under subsection (g); prosecutors who represent the Government of the United States; Government lawyers authorized to represent several Federal agencies in intragovernmental legal controversies; and counsel assigned to perform special duties, such as assignment to other Federal agencies or sub-agencies.

In most cases, the Federal Agency will be a discrete entity with identifiable lines of authority. Federal Agency regulations and directives provide clear benchmarks for assessing conduct. In some situations, the Government lawyer may represent a branch of Government rather than a Federal Agency. Although arguments have been made that the Government lawyer's ultimate obligation is to serve the public interest or the "government as a whole," for practical purposes, these may be unworkable ethical guidelines, particularly with regard to client control and confidentiality.

A Federal Agency may, of course, establish different client-lawyer obligations by Executive or court order, regulation, or statute. * * *

Nevertheless, the conclusion that the government lawyer's client is the lawyer's employing agency does not answer every ethical question. There are special considerations that affect the ethical responsibilities of the Government lawyer. For example, the Government lawyer has a responsibility to question the conduct of agency officials more extensively than a lawyer for a private organization would in similar circumstances. Government lawyers, in many situations, are asked to represent diverse client interests. For example, Government lawyers in the Executive branch also represent other branches of Government in a number of different situations. Here it becomes especially clear that the Government attorney's responsibilities are affected by the attorney's more general obligations to the United States, as for example, when it is necessary to refuse to defend an unconstitutional statute or regulation or to resist the encroachment by one branch on another's sphere of power. The client-lawyer obligations of Government lawyers in other branches of Government raise still different considerations. For example, lawyers engaged by the Senate or the House of Representatives, by Congressional committees, or on the staffs of individual members of Congress may develop client-lawyer relationships with those bodies, committees or individuals. Yet these relationships must themselves be viewed in the context of the Government lawyer's broader obligations to the Congress as a whole and ultimately to the United States.

Relation to Other Rules

The authority and responsibility provided in paragraph (b) are concurrent with the authority and responsibility provided in other Rules. In particular, this

Rule does not limit or expand the Government lawyer's responsibility under Rules 1.6, 1.8, 1.16, 3.3, or 4.1. If the Government lawyer's services are being used by an organization to further a crime or fraud by the organization, Rule 1.2(d) may be applicable.

Termination of Representation

Paragraph (c) recognizes that the Government lawyer is not always free to withdraw from representation. Specific facts will govern each case.

Clarifying the Government Lawyer's Role

When the Federal Agency's interests are adverse to those of one or more of its Government employees, the Government lawyer should advise the Government employee that the Government lawyer cannot continue to advise that person and that person may wish to obtain independent representation. Care must be taken to ensure that the individual understands that, when there is such adversity of interest, the Government lawyer can no longer provide legal advice to that person on those matters in which the person's interests are adverse, and that discussions between the Government lawyer and the individual are not confidential or privileged.

Whether such a warning should be given by the Government lawyer to any Government employee may turn on the facts of each case.

Dual Representation

Paragraph (e) recognizes that a Government lawyer may only enter into a client-lawyer relationship and represent persons when specifically authorized by a Federal Agency directive or an authorized superior. Unless authorized and assigned to represent a specific person or class of persons, the Government lawyer shall not establish a client-lawyer relationship. If a Government lawyer is uncertain as to the scope of representation authorized, the Government lawyer shall consult the supervisory lawyer. Recognition is given to the Government lawyer representing a Government employee of the Federal Agency.

Paragraph (f) recognizes that a Government lawyer may also represent a Government employee of the Federal Agency.

Paragraph (g) recognizes that the Government lawyer who is designated to represent another individual in Federal Government service against whom disciplinary or administrative proceedings have been brought, establishes a client-lawyer relationship with its privilege and professional responsibility to protect and defend the interest of the individual represented. This is also true for Federal lawyers providing legal assistance. But See Rule 1.2. Representation of members of the Federal Agency, other Government employees, and other individuals in accordance with paragraph (g) and the assumption of the traditional client-lawyer relationship with such individuals is not inconsistent with the Government lawyer's duties to the Federal Agency.

Rule 1.14 CLIENT UNDER A DISABILITY

(a) When a client's ability to make adequately considered decisions in connection with the representation is impaired, whether because of minority, mental disability, or for some other reason, the Federal lawyer shall, as far as reasonably possible, maintain a normal client-lawyer relationship with the client.

(b) A Federal lawyer may seek the appointment of a guardian or take other protective action with respect to a client, only when the Federal lawyer reasonably believes the client cannot adequately act in the client's own interest.

COMMENT:

The normal client-lawyer relationship is based on the assumption that the client, when properly advised and assisted, is capable of making decisions about important matters. When the client is a minor or suffers from a mental disorder or disability, however, maintaining the ordinary client-lawyer relationship shall not be possible in all respects. In particular, an incapacitated person may have no power to make legally binding decisions. Nevertheless, a client lacking legal competence often has the ability to understand, deliberate upon, and reach conclusions about the matters affecting the client's own well-being. Furthermore, to an increasing extent, the law recognizes intermediate degrees of competence. For example, children as young as five or six years of age, and certainly those of ten or twelve, are regarded as having opinions that are entitled to weight in legal proceedings concerning their custody. Also, some persons of advanced age can be quite capable of handling routine financial matters while needing special legal protection concerning major transactions.

Simply because a client is under a disability does not diminish the Federal lawyer's obligation to treat the client with attention and respect. If the person has no guardian or legal representative, the Federal lawyer should take action so that procedures are initiated for the appointment of a guardian by the person's relatives, civil authorities, or the Veterans Administration. Even if the person does have a legal representative, the Federal lawyer should as far as possible accord the represented person the status of client, particularly in maintaining communication.

If a legal representative already has been appointed for the client, the Federal lawyer ordinarily should look to the representative for decisions on behalf of the client. If a legal representative has not been appointed, the Federal lawyer should consider recommending such an appointment when it would serve the client's best interests.

Disclosure of the Client's Conditions

Rules of procedure in civil litigation generally provide that minors or persons suffering mental disability shall be represented by a guardian or next friend if they do not have a general guardian. Disclosure of the client's disability, however, can adversely affect the client's interests. For example, raising the question of disability could, in some circumstances, lead to proceedings for involuntary commitment or to disclosure of information that would be detrimental to a client. The Federal lawyer's position in such cases is an unavoidably difficult one. The Federal lawyer may seek guidance from an appropriate diagnostician but military law does not recognize a physician-patient privilege.

Rule 1.15 SAFEKEEPING PROPERTY

(a) A Federal lawyer shall hold property of clients or third persons that is in the lawyer's possession in connection with a representation separate from the lawyer's own property. Funds shall be kept in a separate account maintained in the state in which the Federal lawyer's office is situated, or elsewhere with the consent of the client or third person. Other property shall be identified as belonging to the client and safeguarded appropriately. Complete records of such account funds and other property shall be kept by the lawyer and shall be preserved for a period of five years after termination of the representation.

(b) Upon receiving funds or other property in which a client or third person has an interest, a Federal lawyer shall promptly notify the client or the third person. Except as stated in this Rule or as otherwise permitted by law or by agreement with the client, the lawyer shall promptly deliver to the client or third person any funds or other property that the client or third person is entitled to receive and, upon request by the client or third person, shall promptly render full accounting regarding such property.

(c) When in the course of representation a Federal lawyer is in possession of property in which both the lawyer and another person claim interests, the property shall be kept separate by the lawyer until an accounting is made and their respective interests are severed. If a dispute arises concerning their respective interests, the portion in dispute shall be kept separate by the lawyer until the dispute is resolved.

(d) When property of a client or third party is admitted into evidence or otherwise included in the record of a proceeding, the Federal lawyer should take reasonable action to ensure its prompt return.

COMMENT:

Government lawyers normally will not hold property of clients or third persons. Should a Government lawyer find it necessary to hold such property, care must be taken to ensure the United States Government does not become responsible for any claims for the property. This rule does not authorize a Government lawyer to hold property of clients or third persons when otherwise prohibited from doing so.

A Federal lawyer should hold property of others with the care required of a professional fiduciary. Securities should be kept in safe deposit boxes, except when some other form of safekeeping is warranted by special circumstances. All property that belongs to clients or third persons should be kept separate from the Federal lawyer's business and personal property and, if money, in one or more trust accounts. Separate trust accounts may be warranted when administering estate monies or acting in a similar fiduciary capacity.

When it is necessary to use a client's property as evidence, a Federal lawyer should seek to obtain court permission to withdraw the property as an exhibit and to substitute a description or photograph after trial. If a Federal lawyer is offered contraband property, the Federal lawyer should refer to Rule 3.4 and its accompanying Comment for guidance.

Federal lawyers often receive funds from third parties from which the Federal lawyer's fee will be paid. If a risk exists that the client may divert the funds without paying the fee, the Federal lawyer is not required to remit the portion from which the fee is to be paid. A Federal lawyer shall not hold funds to coerce a client into accepting the Federal lawyer's contention, however. The disputed portion of the funds should be kept in trust and the Federal lawyer should suggest means such as arbitration for prompt resolution of the dispute. The undisputed portion of the funds shall be distributed promptly.

Third parties, such as a client's creditors, may have just claims against funds or other property in a Federal lawyer's custody. A Federal lawyer may have a duty under applicable law to protect such third-party claims against wrongful interference by the client, and accordingly may refuse to surrender the property to the client. A Federal lawyer should not unilaterally assume to arbitrate a dispute between the client and the third party, however.

The obligations of a Federal lawyer under this Rule are independent of those arising from activity other than rendering legal services. For example, a Federal lawyer who serves as an escrow agent is governed by the applicable law relating to fiduciaries even though the Federal lawyer does not render legal services in the transaction.

A Federal attorney who holds the property of others that was admitted into evidence or otherwise included in the record of a proceeding should take reasonable steps to secure the return of the property to its rightful owner or proper custodian. Where possible copies, descriptions, or photographs should be substituted for the original item in the record.

Rule 1.16 DECLINING OR TERMINATING REPRESENTATION

(a) Except as stated in paragraph (c), a Federal lawyer shall not represent a client, or, once representation has commenced, shall seek to withdraw from the representation of a client, if:
   (1) The representation will result in violation of these Rules of Professional Conduct or law.
   (2) The Federal lawyer's physical or mental condition materially impairs the lawyer's ability to represent the client.
   (3) The Federal lawyer is dismissed by the client.

(b) Except as stated in paragraph (c), a Federal lawyer may seek to withdraw from representing a client if withdrawal can be accomplished without material adverse effect on the interests of the client, or if:
   (1) The client persists in a course of action involving the Federal lawyer's services that the lawyer reasonably believes is criminal or fraudulent.
   (2) The client has used the Federal lawyer's services to perpetrate a crime or fraud.
   (3) A client insists upon pursuing an objective that the Federal lawyer considers repugnant or imprudent.
   (4) The client fails substantially to fulfill an obligation to the Federal lawyer regarding the lawyer's services and has been given reasonable warning that the Federal lawyer will seek to withdraw unless the obligation is fulfilled.
   (5) The representation will result in an unreasonable financial burden on the Federal lawyer or has been rendered unreasonable by the client.
   (6) Other good cause for withdrawal exists.

(c) When properly ordered to do so by a tribunal or other competent authority, a Federal lawyer shall continue representation notwithstanding good cause for terminating the representation.

(d) Upon termination of representation, a Federal lawyer shall take steps to the extent reasonably practicable to protect a client's interests, such as giving reasonable notice to the client, allowing time for employment of other counsel, surrendering papers and property to which the client is entitled, and refunding any advance payment of fees that has not been earned. The Federal lawyer may retain papers relating to the client to the extent permitted by law.

COMMENT:

A Federal lawyer should not represent a client in a matter unless it can be performed competently, promptly, without improper conflict of interest, and to completion.

Mandatory Withdrawal

A Federal lawyer ordinarily must seek to withdraw from representation if the client demands that the Federal lawyer engage in conduct that is illegal or violates these Rules of Professional Conduct or other law. The Federal lawyer is not obliged to seek to withdraw simply because the client suggests such a course of conduct; a client may make such a suggestion in the hope that a Federal lawyer will not be constrained by a professional obligation.

Continued Representation Notwithstanding Good Cause

Notwithstanding the existence of good cause for terminating representation, a Federal lawyer appointed to represent a client shall continue such representation until relieved by competent authority. Who is competent authority will differ with the circumstances. A Government lawyer representing the Federal Agency may be authorized to withdraw from the representation by the Federal Agency's chief legal official or the Federal lawyer's supervisory lawyer. Difficulty may be encountered where competent authority requires an explanation for the termination and such explanation would necessitate the revelation of confidential facts. When necessary and practicable, a Federal lawyer should seek the advice of a supervisory lawyer. The decision by one authority to continue representation does not prevent the Federal lawyer from seeking withdrawal from other competent authority.

Discharge by the Client

A client has a right to discharge a Federal lawyer with or without cause. Where future disputes about the withdrawal are anticipated, it may be advisable to prepare a written statement reciting the circumstances leading to withdrawal.

Whether a client can release appointed counsel may depend on applicable law. A client seeking to release appointed counsel must be given a full explanation of the consequences. Those consequences may include a decision by the appointing authority that appointment of successor counsel is unjustified, thus requiring the client to represent him or herself.

If the client is mentally incompetent, the client may lack the legal capacity to discharge the Federal lawyer, and in any event, the discharge may be seriously adverse to the client's interests. See Rule 1.14.

Optional Withdrawal

A Federal lawyer may seek to withdraw from representation in some circumstances. The Federal lawyer has the option of seeking to withdraw if it can be accomplished without material adverse effect to the client's interests. Seeking to withdraw is also justified if the client persists in a course of action that the Federal lawyer reasonably believes is criminal or fraudulent, for a Federal lawyer is not required to be associated with such conduct even if the Federal lawyer does not further it. Seeking to withdraw also is permitted if the Federal lawyer's services were misused in the past, even if that would materially prejudice the client. The Federal lawyer also may seek to withdraw when the client insists on a repugnant or imprudent objective.

As the scope of a Federal lawyer's representation may be limited by the law under which the Federal lawyer's services are made available to the client, see Comment to Rule 1.2, good cause to seek withdrawal may exist when a Federal lawyer changes duty stations or duties within an office. For example, a legal assistance Federal lawyer has good cause to seek withdrawal when the Federal lawyer is reassigned within the office to duties as prosecutor. In such a circumstance, the legal assistance Federal lawyer has been granted permission to withdraw from representation of legal assistance clients by virtue of the reassignment to prosecutor duties. If a question arises as to whether a Federal lawyer has permission to withdraw from a particular representation, the Federal lawyer should consult with the supervisory lawyer who has the authority to grant permission to withdraw from the representation.

Assisting the Client upon Withdrawal

A Federal lawyer who has withdrawn from representation must take all reasonable steps to mitigate adverse consequences to the client. Such steps may include referring of the client to another Federal lawyer who is able to represent the client further. A Federal lawyer making such a referral should ensure that these Rules and any agency policy governing referral of clients is followed. If a Federal lawyer must refer a client to another Federal lawyer due to a conflict of interest, the referring Federal lawyer should be careful not to disclose confidential information relating to representation of another client.

Government Lawyers

Paragraph (c) recognizes that the Government lawyer is not always free to withdraw from representation. Competent authority may be the Government lawyer's supervisory lawyers or, in some cases, other Federal Agency officials in the Government lawyer's chain of command. Specific facts will govern each case.

Whether a Government lawyer may, under certain unusual circumstances, have a legal obligation to the Federal Agency after withdrawing or being released by the Federal Agency's highest authority is beyond the scope of these Rules.

COUNSELOR

Rule 2.1 ADVISOR

In representing a client, a Federal lawyer shall exercise independent professional judgment and render candid advice. In rendering advice, a Federal lawyer may refer not only to law but to other considerations, such as moral, social, and political factors, that may be relevant to the client's situation, but not in conflict with the law.

COMMENT:

Scope of Advice

A client is entitled to straightforward advice expressing the Federal lawyer's honest assessment. Legal advice often involves unpleasant facts and alternatives that a client may be reluctant to confront. In presenting advice, a Federal lawyer endeavors to sustain the client's morale and may put advice in as acceptable a form as honesty permits. Nevertheless, a Federal lawyer should not be deterred from giving candid advice by the prospect that the advice will be unpalatable to the client.

Advice couched in narrowly legal terms may be of little value to a client, especially where practical considerations, such as cost or effects on other people, are predominant. Purely technical legal advice, therefore, can sometimes be inadequate. It is proper for a Federal lawyer to refer to other relevant considerations in giving advice. Such considerations impinge upon most legal questions and may decisively influence how the law will be applied.

A client may expressly or impliedly ask the Federal lawyer for purely technical advice. When such a request is made by a client experienced in legal matters, the Federal lawyer may accept it at face value. When such a request is made by client inexperienced in legal matters, however, the Federal lawyer's responsibility as advisor may include indicating more may be involved than strictly legal considerations.

Matters that go beyond strictly legal questions may also be in the domain of another profession. Family matters can involve problems within the professional competence of psychiatry, clinical psychology, or social work; business matters can involve problems within the competence of the accounting profession or of financial specialists. When consultation with a professional in another field is itself something a competent Federal lawyer would recommend, the Federal lawyer should make such a recommendation. At the same time, a Federal lawyer's best advice often consists of recommending a course of action in the face of conflicting recommendations of experts.

Offering Advice

When a Non-Government lawyer knows that a client proposes a course of action that is likely to result in substantial adverse legal consequences to the client, however, duty to the client under Rule 1.4 may require that the Non-Government lawyer act if the client's course of action is related to the representation. A Non-Government lawyer ordinarily has no duty to initiate investigation of a client's affairs or to give advice the client has indicated is unwanted, but a Non-Government lawyer should initiate advice to a client when doing so appears to be in the client's interest.

A Government lawyer has an affirmative duty to offer advice to a Government employee of the Federal Agency that employs the Government lawyer, if the Government lawyer knows that the Government employee is engaging in or about to engage in a course of conduct that would be a violation of law or that may result in substantial adverse legal consequences to the Federal Agency. A Government lawyer has the duty to provide the advice, even if the advice is unwanted.

RULE 2.2 INTERMEDIARY

(a) A Federal lawyer may act as an intermediary between individuals if:

(b) While acting as an intermediary, the Federal lawyer shall consult with each client concerning the decisions to be made and the considerations relevant in making them, so each client can make adequately informed decisions.

    (1) The Federal lawyer consults with each client concerning the implications of common representation, including the advantages and risks involved and the effect on the attorney-client confidentiality, and obtains each client's consent to the common representation;

    (2) The Federal lawyer reasonably believes that the matter can be resolved on terms compatible with each client's best interest, that each client will be able to make adequately informed decisions in the matter, and that there is little risk of material prejudice to the interests of any of the clients if the contemplated resolution is unsuccessful; and

    (3) The Federal lawyer reasonably believes that the common representation can be undertaken impartially and without improper effect on other responsibilities the lawyer has to any of the clients.

(c) A Federal lawyer shall withdraw as an intermediary if any of the clients so requests or if any of the conditions stated in paragraph (a) is no longer satisfied. Upon withdrawal, the lawyer shall not represent any of the clients in the matter that was the subject of the common representation unless each client consents.

COMMENT:

A Federal lawyer acts as an intermediary under this Rule when the Federal lawyer represents two or more clients with potentially conflicting interests. Because confusion can arise as to the Federal lawyer's role when each client is not separately represented, it is important that the Federal lawyer make clear the relationship.

A Federal lawyer acts as an intermediary in seeking to establish or adjust a relationship between clients on an amicable and mutually advantageous basis. The Federal lawyer seeks to resolve potentially conflicting interests by developing the clients' mutual interests. The alternative can be that each client may have to obtain separate representation, with the possibility in some situations of incurring additional cost, complications, or even litigation. Given these and other relevant factors, all the clients may prefer the Federal lawyer to act as intermediary.

In considering whether to act as an intermediary, a Federal lawyer should remember that if the common representation fails the result can be additional cost, embarrassment, and recrimination. In some situations the risk of failure is so great that common representation is plainly impossible. For example, a Federal lawyer cannot undertake mediation among clients when contentious litigation is imminent or when contentious negotiations are contemplated. More generally, if the relationship between the clients has already assumed definite antagonism, the possibility that the clients' interests can be adjusted by common representation ordinarily is not very good.

The appropriateness of intermediation can depend on its form. One form may be appropriate in circumstances in which another would not. Other relevant factors include whether the Federal lawyer subsequently will represent either client on a continuing basis and whether the situation involves creating or terminating a relationship between the clients.

Confidentiality and Privilege

A particularly important factor in determining the appropriateness of common representation is the effect on attorney-client confidentiality of information relating to the common representation. See Rules 1.4 and 1.6. As the Federal lawyer represents neither individual in the intermediation there is neither attorney-client privilege nor attorney-client confidentiality.

Since the Federal lawyer is required to be impartial between commonly represented clients, intermediation is improper when that impartiality cannot be maintained. For example, a Federal lawyer who has represented one of the clients for a long period and in a variety of matters might have difficulty being impartial between that client and one to whom the Federal lawyer has only recently been introduced.

Consultation

In acting as a intermediary between clients, the Federal lawyer is required to consult with the clients on the implications of doing so, and proceed only upon consent based on such a consultation. The consultation should make clear that the Federal lawyer's role is not that of partisanship normally expected in other circumstances.

Where the Federal lawyer is an intermediary, the clients ordinarily must assume greater responsibility for decisions than when each client is represented by a Federal lawyer.

Withdrawal

Common representation does not diminish the rights of each client in the client-lawyer relationship. Each client has the right to loyal and diligent representation. Any of the clients may discharge the Federal lawyer as stated in Rule 1.16 and gain the protection of Rule 1.9 concerning obligations to former clients.

Rule 2.3 EVALUATION FOR USE BY THIRD PERSONS

(a) A Federal lawyer may undertake an evaluation of a matter affecting a client for the use of someone other than the client if:
    (1) The Federal lawyer reasonably believes that making the evaluation is compatible with other aspects of the lawyer's relationship with the client, and
    (2) The client consents after sufficient consultation.
(b) Except [when] a disclosure is required in connection with a report of an evaluation, information relating to the evaluation is otherwise protected by Rule 1.6.

COMMENT:

Definition

An evaluation may be performed at the client's direction but for the primary purpose of establishing information for the benefit of third parties; for example, a Government lawyer is asked to prepare a brief setting forth the Federal Agency's position on a situation for use by another Federal Agency or the Congress.

A Government lawyer may be called upon to give a formal opinion on the legality of action contemplated by the Federal Agency. In making such an evaluation, the Government lawyer acts at the behest of the Federal Agency as the client, but for the purpose of establishing the limits of the Federal Agency's authorized activity. Such an opinion may be confidential legal advice, depending on whether the Federal Agency intended it to be confidential.

If a Federal lawyer believes that making an evaluation is incompatible with other aspects of the Federal lawyer's relationship with the client, the Federal lawyer should consult with a supervisory lawyer for advice and guidance.

A legal evaluation should be distinguished from an investigation of a person with whom the Federal lawyer does not have a Federal lawyer-client relationship. For example, a Government lawyer assigned to conduct an investigation of a traffic accident between a private citizen and a Government employee in accordance with applicable Federal Agency regulations and directives does not have a client-lawyer relationship with the Government employee. So also, an investigation into a person's affairs by a Government lawyer is not an evaluation as that term is used in this rule.

The question is whether the Government lawyer represents the person whose affairs are being examined. When the Government lawyer does represent the person, the general rules concerning loyalty to client and preservation of confidences apply. For this reason, the client must be identified. The identity of the client should be made clear not only to the person under examination, but also to others to whom the results are to be made available.

Duty to Third Person

When the evaluation is intended for the information or use of a third person a legal duty to that person may or shall not arise. That legal question is beyond the scope of this rule. However, since such an evaluation involves a departure from the normal client-lawyer relationship, careful analysis of the situation is required. The Federal lawyer must be satisfied as a matter of professional judgment that making the evaluation is compatible with other functions undertaken on behalf of the client. For example, if the Federal lawyer is acting as advocate in defending the client against charges of fraud, it would normally be incompatible with that responsibility for the Federal lawyer to perform an evaluation for others concerning the same or a related transaction. Assuming no such impediment is apparent, however, the Federal lawyer should advise the client of the implications of the evaluation, particularly the Federal lawyer's responsibilities to third persons and the duty to disseminate the findings.

ADVOCATE

Rule 3.1 MERITORIOUS CLAIMS AND CONTENTIONS

A Federal lawyer shall not bring or defend a proceeding, or assert or controvert an issue therein, unless there is a basis for doing so that is not frivolous. This basis may include a good faith argument for an extending, modifying, or reversing existing law. A Federal lawyer for the defendant in a criminal proceeding, or the respondent in a proceeding that could result in incarceration or other adverse action, may nevertheless so defend the proceeding as to require that every element of the case be established.

COMMENT:

The advocate has a duty to use legal procedure for the fullest benefit of the client's cause, but also a duty not to abuse legal procedure. The law, both procedural and substantive, establishes the limits within which an advocate may proceed. Nevertheless, the law is not always clear and is never static. Accordingly, in determining the proper scope of advocacy, account must be taken of the law's ambiguities and potential for change.

The filing of a cause of action, defense, or similar act taken on behalf of a client is not frivolous merely because the facts have not first been fully substantiated or because the Federal lawyer expects vital evidence to develop only through discovery. Such action is not frivolous even though the Federal lawyer believes the client's position ultimately will not prevail. Merely because an issue has never been raised before, or because it may have been raised and resolved under different circumstances, does not make revisiting the issue frivolous. The action is frivolous, however, if the client desires to have the action taken solely for the purpose of harassing or maliciously injuring a person, or if the Federal lawyer is unable either to make a good faith argument on the merits of the action taken or to support the action taken by a good faith argument for an extending, modifying, or reversing of existing law.

A Federal lawyer does not violate this Rule by raising issues in good faith compliance with court precedent.

Rule 3.2 EXPEDITING LITIGATION

A Federal lawyer shall make reasonable efforts to expedite litigation and other proceedings consistent with the interests of the client and the lawyer's responsibilities to the tribunal to avoid unwarranted delay.

COMMENT:

Dilatory practices bring the administration of justice into disrepute. The legitimate interests of the client are rarely well-served by such tactics. Delay exacts a toll upon a litigant in uncertainty, frustration, and apprehension. Expediting litigation, in contrast, often can directly benefit the client's interest in obtaining bargaining concessions and in obtaining an early resolution of the matter. Delay should not be indulged merely for the convenience of the advocates, or for the purpose of frustrating an opposing party's attempt to obtain rightful redress or repose. It is not a justification that similar conduct is often tolerated by the bench and bar. The question is whether a competent Federal lawyer acting in good faith would regard the course of action as having some substantial purpose other than delay. Realizing financial or other benefit from otherwise improper delay in litigation is not a legitimate interest of the client.

Rule 3.3 CANDOR TOWARD THE TRIBUNAL

(a) A Federal lawyer shall not knowingly:
   (1) Make a false statement of material fact or law to a tribunal.
   (2) Fail to disclose a material fact to a tribunal when disclosure is necessary to avoid assisting a criminal or fraudulent act by the client.

(3) Fail to disclose to the tribunal legal authority in the controlling jurisdiction known to the Federal lawyer to be directly adverse to the position of the client and not disclosed by opposing counsel.
(4) Offer evidence that the lawyer knows to be false. If a Federal lawyer has offered material evidence and comes to know of its falsity, the lawyer shall take reasonable remedial measures.
(5) Disobey an obligation or order imposed by a tribunal, unless done openly before the tribunal in a good faith assertion that no valid obligation or order should exist.
(b) The duties stated in paragraph (a) continue to the conclusion of the proceeding, and apply even if compliance requires disclosure of information otherwise protected by Rule 1.6.
(c) A Federal lawyer may refuse to offer evidence that the lawyer reasonably believes to be false.
(d) In an ex parte proceeding, a Federal lawyer shall disclose to the tribunal all material facts known to the lawyer that are reasonably necessary to enable the tribunal to make an informed decision, whether or not the facts are adverse.

COMMENT:

The advocate's task is to present the client's case with persuasive force. Performance of that duty while maintaining confidences of the client is qualified by the advocate's duty of candor to the tribunal. An advocate does not vouch for the evidence submitted in a cause, however. The tribunal is responsible for assessing its probative value.

Relationship with Rule 1.6

The conflicting duties to reveal fraud and to preserve confidences have existed side-by-side for some time. A Federal lawyer should not be confronted with the necessity of either breaching the client's privilege or breaching a disciplinary Rule. This Rule recognizes that the policies underlying Rule 1.6 take precedence over Rule 3.3 in all but the most serious cases. When Rule 1.6 either permits or mandates disclosure of otherwise confidential information, Rule 3.3 requires that the Federal lawyer reveal criminal or fraudulent acts by the client. When Rule 1.6 requires confidentiality of information, Rule 3.3 does not permit the Federal lawyer to disclose such information to a tribunal, even if the disclosure would be necessary to avoid assisting a criminal or fraudulent act by the client. A Federal lawyer who follows the guidance in the Perjury by a Criminal Client section of this comment is not assisting a criminal or fraudulent act by a client for purposes of these Rules. See Rule 1.2(d) and Comment.

Representations by a Federal Lawyer

An advocate is responsible for pleadings and other documents prepared for litigation, but is usually not required to have personal knowledge of matters asserted therein, for litigation documents ordinarily present assertions by the client, or by someone on the client's behalf, not assertions by the Federal lawyer. Compare Rule 3.1. An assertion purporting to be on the Federal lawyer's own knowledge (as in an affidavit by the Federal lawyer or in a statement in open court), however, may properly be made only when the Federal lawyer knows the assertion is true or believes it to be true on the basis of a reasonably diligent inquiry. Circumstances can arise in which failure to make a disclosure is the equivalent of an affirmative misrepresentation. The obligation prescribed in Rule 1.2(d) not to counsel a client to commit or to assist the client in committing a fraud applies in litigation. Regarding compliance with this Rule, see Rule 11 of the Federal Rules of Civil Procedure. * * *

Misleading Legal Argument

Legal argument based on a knowingly false representation of law constitutes dishonesty toward the tribunal. A Federal lawyer is not required to make a disinterested exposition of the law, but must recognize the existence of pertinent legal authorities. Furthermore, as stated in paragraph (a)(3), an advocate has a duty to disclose directly adverse authority in the controlling jurisdiction that has not been disclosed by the opposing party. The underlying concept is that legal argument is a discussion seeking to determine the legal premises properly applicable to the case. A Federal lawyer also should disclose to the tribunal legal authority from a non-controlling jurisdiction, directly adverse to the position of the client and not disclosed by opposing counsel, if the issue being litigated has not been decided by a controlling jurisdiction and the judge would reasonably consider it important to resolving the issue.

False Evidence

When evidence a Federal lawyer knows to be false is provided by a person who is not the client, the Federal lawyer must refuse to offer it regardless of the client's wishes.

When false evidence is offered by the client, however, a conflict may arise between the Federal lawyer's duty to keep revelations of the client confidential and the duty of candor to the tribunal. Upon discovering that material evidence is false, the Federal lawyer should try to persuade the client not to offer it. If the client has already offered the false evidence, the Federal lawyer should try to persuade the client to withdraw it.

If the client cannot be persuaded to withdraw the already offered false evidence, the Federal lawyer generally must disclose the client's deception to the tribunal or to the other party. This disclosure may result in grave consequences to the client, including not only a sense of betrayal, but also loss of the case and perhaps prosecution for perjury. The alternative, however, would be the Federal lawyer's participation in deceiving the tribunal, which would subvert the truth-finding process the adversary system is designed to implement. See Rule 1.2(d). Consequently, in seeking to persuade the client to withdraw false evidence, the Federal lawyer's intention to disclose the falsity if the client does not withdraw it must be made clear. Otherwise the client could simply reject the advice and insist upon the Federal lawyer's silence, thus effectively coercing the Federal lawyer into becoming a party to a fraud on the tribunal.

Perjury by a Criminal Defendant

A criminal case where the defendant insists on offering testimony the Federal lawyer knows is perjurious is the most difficult situation a Federal lawyer faces.

The Federal lawyer's effort to rectify the situation can increase the likelihood of the client's being convicted, as well as, opening the possibility of a prosecution for perjury. On the other hand, if the Federal lawyer does not exercise control over the proof, the Federal lawyer participates, although passively, in deception of the tribunal.

If the defendant has admitted to the Federal lawyer facts that establish guilt and the Federal lawyer's independent investigation establishes the truth of the admissions, but the defendant insists on exercising the right to testify, the Federal lawyer must advise the client against taking the witness stand to testify falsely. If before trial the defendant insists on testifying falsely, the Federal lawyer shall seek to withdraw from representation. See Rule 1.16. If that is not permitted or if the situation arises during the trial or other proceedings and the defendant insists upon testifying falsely, it is unprofessional conduct for the Federal lawyer to lend aid to the client in presenting perjured testimony.

A criminal defendant has a right to the assistance of an advocate, a right to testify, and a right [to] communicate confidentially with counsel. A defendant does not have a right to the assistance of counsel in committing perjury, and an advocate has an obligation, not only in professional ethics but under the law, to avoid implication in the commission of perjury or other falsification of evidence. See Rule 1.2(d).

Remedial Measures

If perjured testimony or false evidence has been offered, the advocate's proper course ordinarily is to remonstrate with the client confidentially. If that effort fails, the advocate should seek to withdraw if that will remedy the situation. If withdrawal will not remedy the situation or is impossible, the advocate should make disclosure to the tribunal, subject to Rule 1.6.

Duration of Obligation

A practical time limit on the obligation to rectify the presentation of false evidence has to be established. The conclusion of the proceeding is a reasonably definite point for the termination of this obligation.

Refusing to Offer Proof Believed to be False

Generally speaking, a Federal lawyer has authority to refuse to offer testimony or other proof the Federal lawyer believes is untrustworthy. Offering such proof may reflect adversely on the Federal lawyer's ability to discriminate in the quality of evidence and thus impair the Federal lawyer's effectiveness as an advocate.

Ex Parte Proceedings

Ordinarily, an advocate has the limited responsibility of presenting one side of the matters that a tribunal should consider in reaching a decision; the conflicting position is expected to be presented by the opposing party. In an ex parte proceeding, however, such as in application for a temporary restraining order, there is no balance of presentation by opposing advocates. The object of an ex parte proceeding is, nevertheless, to yield a substantially just result. The judge, magistrate, or other official has an affirmative responsibility to accord the absent party just consideration. The Federal lawyer for the represented party has the correlative duty to disclose material facts known to the Federal lawyer and reasonably believed to be necessary to an informed decision.

Rule 3.4   FAIRNESS TO OPPOSING PARTY AND COUNSEL

A Federal lawyer shall not:

(a) Unlawfully obstruct another party's access to evidence or unlawfully alter, destroy, or conceal a document or other material having potential evidentiary value. A Federal lawyer shall not counsel or assist another person to do any such act.

(b) Falsify evidence, counsel, or assist a witness to testify falsely, or offer an inducement to a witness that is prohibited by law.

(c) Knowingly disobey an obligation to an opposing party and counsel under the rules of a tribunal, except for an open refusal based on an assertion that no valid obligation exists.

(d) In pretrial procedure, make a frivolous discovery request or fail to make reasonably diligent efforts to comply with a legally proper discovery request by an opposing party.

(e) In trial, allude to any matter that the lawyer does not reasonably believe is relevant or that will not be supported by admissible evidence, assert personal knowledge of facts in issue except when testifying as a witness, or state a personal opinion as to the justness of a cause, the credibility of a witness, the culpability of a civil litigant, or the guilt or innocence of a defendant.

(f) Request a person other than a client to refrain from voluntarily giving relevant information to another party unless:

(1) The person is a relative or an employee or other agent of a client; and

(2) The Federal lawyer reasonably believes the person's interests will not be adversely affected by refraining from giving such information.

COMMENT:

The procedure of the adversary system contemplates that the evidence in a case is to be marshalled competitively by the contending parties. Fair competition in the adversary system is secured by prohibitions against destruction or conceal-ment of evidence, improperly influencing witnesses, obstructive tactics in discovery procedure, and the like.

Documents and other items of evidence are often essential to establish a claim or defense. Subject to evidentiary privileges, the right of an opposing party, including the Government, to obtain evidence through discovery or subpoena is an important procedural right. The exercise of that right can be frustrated if relevant material is altered, concealed, or destroyed. Most criminal codes, including the Uniform Code of Military Justice, proscribe the destruction of material in an attempt to preclude its availability in a pending proceeding or reasonably foresee-able proceeding. Falsifying evidence is also a criminal offense. Paragraph (a) applies to evidentiary material generally, including computerized information.

A Federal lawyer who receives (i.e., has in the Federal lawyer's possession) an item of physical evidence implicating the client in criminal conduct shall disclose the location of or shall deliver that item to proper authorities when required by law or court order. Thus, if a Federal lawyer receives contraband, the

Federal lawyer has no legal right to possess it and must always surrender it to lawful authorities. If a Federal lawyer receives stolen property, the Federal lawyer must surrender it to the owner or lawful authority to avoid violating the law. The appropriate disposition of such physical evidence is a proper subject to discuss confidentially with a supervisory lawyer. When a client informs the Federal lawyer about the existence of material having potential evidentiary value adverse to the client or when the client presents, but does not relinquish possession of such material to the Federal lawyer, the Federal lawyer should inform the client of the Federal lawyer's legal and ethical obligations regarding evidence. Frequently, the best course for the Federal lawyer is to refrain from either taking possession of such material or advising the client as to what course of action should be taken regarding it. See Rules 1.6 and 1.7. If a Federal lawyer discloses the location of or delivers an item of physical evidence to proper authorities, it should be done in the way best designed to protect the client's interest. The Federal lawyer should consider methods of return or disclosure that best protect (a) the client's identity; (b) the client's words concerning the item; (c) other confidential information; and (d) the client's privilege against self-incrimination.

Neither a Federal lawyer when interviewing victims or witnesses not represented by counsel nor another person appointed by a Federal lawyer to act in such capacity unlawfully obstructs another party's access to evidence or to material having potential evidentiary value by performing those duties in accordance with Federal Agency regulations or directives. For example, a Federal lawyer, upon the request of a victim or witness, may require prosecutor and defense counsel to coordinate with another person for interviews of a victim of or witness to the crime that forms the basis of a court-martial.

With regard to paragraph (b), it is not improper to pay a witness expenses or to compensate an expert witness on terms permitted by law. The common law rule in most jurisdictions is that it is improper to pay an occurrence witness any fee for testifying and that it is improper to pay an expert witness a contingent fee.

With regard to paragraph (c), a "rule of a tribunal" includes Rule 6(e) of the Federal Rules of Criminal Procedure governing discussion of grand jury testimony.

Paragraph (f) permits a Federal lawyer to advise relatives, employees, or other agents of a client to refrain from giving information to another party because such persons may identify their interests with those of the client. See also Rule 4.2.

Rule 3.5 IMPARTIALITY AND DECORUM OF THE TRIBUNAL

A Federal lawyer shall not:
(a) Seek to influence a tribunal, a member of a tribunal, a prospective member of a tribunal, or other official by means prohibited by law.
(b) Communicate ex parte with such a person about the matter except as permitted by law.
(c) Engage in conduct intended to disrupt a tribunal.

COMMENT:

Many forms of improper influence upon a tribunal are proscribed by law. The ABA Model Code of Judicial Conduct sets standards for the conduct of judges and other members of a tribunal. An advocate should be familiar with that Code, in order to avoid contributing to a violation by a tribunal.

The advocate's function is to present evidence and argument so that the cause may be decided according to law. Refraining from abusive or obstreperous conduct is a corollary of the advocate's right to speak on behalf of litigants. A Federal lawyer may stand firm against abuse by a judge but should avoid reciprocation; the judge's default is no justification for similar dereliction by an advocate. An advocate can present the cause, protect the record for subsequent review, and preserve professional integrity no less effectively by patient firmness than by belligerence or theatrics.

Because many tribunals are permanent or semi-permanent bodies, it may be impossible for Federal lawyers in the same community to avoid all communications with the members of a tribunal in the course of normal business, social, and professional activities. What is forbidden is any discussion with the individuals regarding a particular case or issue that has been or is likely to be referred to that tribunal for ultimate decision. Any Federal attorney who inadvertently engages in any conversations concerning a prohibitive subject should immediately report the incident to his supervisory lawyer, opposing counsel, and to the tribunal.

However, a Federal lawyer should always strive to avoid contact with a member of a tribunal when such contact could be perceived by an opposing party or member of the public to be an attempt to improperly influence the tribunal.

Rule 3.6 TRIBUNAL PUBLICITY

(a) A Federal lawyer shall not make an extrajudicial statement that a reasonable person would expect to be disseminated by means of public communication if the lawyer knows or reasonably should know that it will have a substantial likelihood of materially prejudicing an adjudicative proceeding or an official review process thereof.

(b) A statement referred to in paragraph (a) ordinarily is likely to have such an effect when it refers to a civil matter triable to a jury, a criminal matter, any other proceeding that could result in incarceration, or other adverse action and that statement relates to:

(1) The character, credibility, reputation, or criminal record of a party, suspect in a criminal investigation, or witness, the identity of a witness, or the expected testimony of a party or witness.

(2) The possibility of a plea of guilty to the offense or the existence or contents of any confession, admission, or statement given by a defendant or suspect, or that person's refusal or failure to make a statement.

(3) The performance or results of any examination or test, the refusal or failure of a person to submit to an examination or test, or the identity or nature of physical evidence expected to be presented.

(4) Any opinion as to the guilt or innocence of a defendant or suspect in an original case or proceeding that could result in incarceration or other adverse action.

(5) Information the Federal lawyer knows or reasonably should know is likely to be inadmissible as evidence in a trial and that would, if disclosed, create a substantial risk of prejudicing an impartial trial.

(6) A defendant's having been charged with a crime, unless included therein is a statement explaining that the charge is merely an accusation and the defendant is presumed innocent until and unless proven guilty.

(c) Notwithstanding paragraphs (a) and (b)(1–5), a Federal lawyer involved in the investigation or litigation of a matter may state without elaboration:

(1) The general nature of the claim or defense.
(2) Information contained in a public record.
(3) That an investigation of the matter is in progress, including the general scope of the investigation, the offense or claim or defense involved and, except when prohibited by law, the identity of the persons involved.
(4) The scheduling or result of any step in litigation.
(5) A request for assistance in obtaining evidence and information necessary in litigation.
(6) A warning of danger concerning the behavior of the person involved, when there is reason to believe the likelihood of substantial harm to an individual or to the public interest exists.
(7) In a criminal case:
    (i) The identity, place of business, occupation, and family status of the defendant.
    (ii) If the defendant has not been apprehended, information necessary to aid in apprehension of that person.
    (iii) The fact, time, and place of apprehension.
    (iv) The identity of investigating and apprehending officers or agencies and the length of the investigation.
(d) The protection and release of information in matters pertaining to the Government shall be consistent with law.

COMMENT:

It is difficult to strike a balance between protecting the right to a fair trial and safeguarding the right of free expression. Preserving the right to a fair trial necessarily entails some curtailment of the information that may be disseminated about a party prior to trial, particularly when trial by jury or members is involved. If there were no such limits, the result would be the practical nullification of the protective effect of the rules of forensic decorum and the exclusionary rules of evidence. On the other hand, there are vital social interests served by the free dissemination of information about events having legal consequences and about legal proceedings themselves. The public has a right to know about threats to its safety and measures aimed at assuring its security. It also has a legitimate interest in the conduct of judicial proceedings, particularly in matters of general public concern. Furthermore, the subject matter of legal proceedings is often of direct significance in debate and deliberation over questions of public policy.

No body of rules can simultaneously satisfy all interests of fair trial and all those of free expression. Special rules of confidentiality may validly govern proceedings involving classified material, juveniles, domestic relations, and mental disability proceedings, and perhaps other types of proceedings. Rule 3.4(c) requires compliance with such Rules.

Special rules of confidentiality may validly govern proceedings involving classified material, juveniles, domestic relations and mental disability proceedings, and perhaps other types of proceedings. Rule 3.4(c) require compliance with such Rules.

Rule 3.6(d) acknowledges that a Government lawyer's release of information is governed not only by Rule 3.6 but also by law. Prior to releasing any information, a Government lawyer should consult the appropriate statute, directive, regulation, or policy guideline.

Rule 3.7 FEDERAL LAWYER AS WITNESS

(a) A Federal lawyer shall not act as advocate at a trial in which the lawyer is likely to be a necessary witness except when:

    (1) The testimony relates to an uncontested issue.

    (2) The testimony relates to the nature, value, and quality of legal services rendered in the case.

    (3) Disqualification of the Federal lawyer would work substantial hardship on the client.

(b) A Federal lawyer may act as advocate in a matter in which another lawyer in the Federal lawyer's agency or firm is likely to be called as a witness unless precluded from doing so by Rule 1.7 or Rule 1.9.

COMMENT:

Combining the roles of advocate and witness can prejudice the opposing party and involve a conflict of interest between the Federal lawyer and client.

The opposing party has a proper objection when the combination of roles may prejudice that party's rights in the litigation. A witness is required to testify on the basis of personal knowledge, while an advocate is expected to explain and comment on evidence given by others. It shall not be clear whether a statement by an advocate-witness should be taken as proof or as an analysis of the proof.

Rule 3.7(a)(1) recognizes that if the testimony will be uncontested, the ambiguities in the dual role are purely theoretical. Rule 3.7(a)(2) recognizes that, if the testimony concerns the value and quality of legal services rendered in the action in which the testimony is offered, permitting the Federal lawyer to testify avoids the need for a second trial with new counsel to resolve this issue. Moreover, in such a situation the judge has firsthand knowledge of the matter in issue; hence, there is less dependence on the adversary process to test the credibility of the testimony.

Apart from these two exceptions, Rule 3.7(a)(3) recognizes that a balancing is required between the interests of the client and those of the opposing party. Whether the opposing party is likely to suffer prejudice depends on the nature of the case, the importance and probable tenor of the Federal lawyer's testimony, and the probability that the Federal lawyer's testimony will conflict with that of other witnesses. Even if there is risk of such prejudice, in determining whether the Federal lawyer should be disqualified, due regard must be given to the effect of disqualification on the Federal lawyer's client. That one or both parties could reasonably have foreseen the probability that the Federal lawyer would be a witness is relevant to this determination.

Whether the combination of roles involves an improper conflict of interest with respect to the client is determined by Rule 1.7 or 1.9. For example, if substantial conflict is likely between the testimony of the client and that of the Federal lawyer the representation is improper. The problem can arise whether the Federal lawyer is called as a witness on behalf of the client or is called by the opposing party. Determining whether such a conflict exists is primarily the responsibility of the Federal lawyer involved. See Comment to Rule 1.7.

Rule 3.8 SPECIAL RESPONSIBILITIES OF A PROSECUTOR

A prosecutor shall:

(a) Refrain from prosecuting a charge that the prosecutor knows is not supported by probable cause, or if not authorized to decline the prosecution of a charge to recommend to the appropriate authority that any charge not warranted by the evidence be withdrawn;

(b) Make reasonable efforts to ensure that the defendant has been advised of the right to and the procedure for obtaining counsel and has been given reasonable opportunity to obtain counsel;

(c) Not seek to obtain from an unrepresented defendant a waiver of important pretrial rights;

(d) Make timely disclosure to the defense of all evidence or information known to the Federal lawyer that tends to negate the guilt of the defendant or mitigates the offense, and, in connection with sentencing, disclose to the defense all unprivileged mitigating information known to the Federal lawyer, except when the Federal lawyer is relieved of this responsibility by a protective order or regulation; and

(e) Exercise reasonable care to prevent investigators, law enforcement personnel, employees, or other persons assisting or associated with the Federal lawyer in a criminal case from making extrajudicial statements that the prosecutor would be prohibited from making under Rule 3.6.

(f) Respect the attorney-client privilege of defendants and not diminish the privilege through investigative or judicial processes.

COMMENT:

A prosecutor is not simply an advocate but is responsible for seeing that the defendant is accorded procedural justice and that guilt is decided upon the basis of sufficient evidence. See also Rule 3.3(d), governing ex parte proceedings. Applicable law may require other measures by the prosecutor and knowing disregard of those obligations or a systematic abuse of prosecutorial discretion could constitute a violation of Rule 8.4.

The exception in Rule 3.8 (d) recognizes that a prosecutor may seek an appropriate protective order from the tribunal if disclosures of information to the defense could result in substantial harm to an individual or organization or to the public interest. This exception also recognizes that applicable regulations may proscribe the disclosure of certain information without proper authorization.

A prosecutor may comply with Rule 3.8(e) in a number of ways. These include personally informing others of the Federal lawyer's obligations under Rule 3.6, promulgating guidelines, conducting training of law enforcement personnel, and appropriately supervising the activities of personnel assisting the prosecutor.

Rule 3.9 ADVOCATE IN NONADJUDICATIVE PROCEEDINGS

A Federal lawyer representing a client before a legislative or administrative tribunal in a nonadjudicative proceeding shall disclose that the appearance is in a representative capacity and shall conform to the provisions of rules 3.3(a)–(c), 3.4(a)–(c), and 3.5.

COMMENT:

In representation before bodies such as legislatures, municipal councils, and executive and administrative agencies acting in a rulemaking or policy-making capacity, Federal lawyers present facts, formulate issues, and advance argument in the matters under consideration. The decision-making body, like a court, should be able to rely on the integrity of the submissions made it. A Federal lawyer appearing before such a body should deal with the tribunal honestly and in conformity with applicable rules of procedure.

Federal lawyers have no exclusive right to appear before nonadjudicative bodies. The requirements of this Rule, therefore, may subject Federal lawyers to regulations inapplicable to advocates who are not lawyers. Legislatures and administrative agencies, however, have a right to expect Federal lawyers to deal with them in the same manner as Federal lawyers deal with courts.

TRANSACTIONS WITH PERSONS OTHER THAN CLIENTS

Rule 4.1 TRUTHFULNESS IN STATEMENTS TO OTHERS

In the course of representing a client a Federal lawyer shall not knowingly:
(a) Make a false statement of material fact or law to a third person.
(b) Fail to disclose a material fact to a third person when disclosure is necessary to avoid assisting a criminal or fraudulent act by a client, unless disclosure is prohibited by Rule 1.6.

COMMENT:

Misrepresentation

A Federal lawyer is required to be truthful when dealing with others on a client's behalf, but generally has no affirmative duty to inform an opposing party of relevant facts. A misrepresentation can occur if the Federal lawyer incorporates or affirms statement of another person the Federal lawyer knows to be false. Misrepresentations also can occur by failing to act.

Statements of Fact

This Rule refers to statements of fact. Whether a particular statement should be regarded as one of fact depends on the circumstances. Under generally accepted conventions in negotiation, certain types of statements ordinarily are not taken as statements of material fact. Estimates of price or value are placed in this category.

Fraud by a Client

Paragraph (b) recognizes that substantive law may require a Federal lawyer to disclose certain information to avoid being deemed to have assisted the client's crime or fraud. The requirement of disclosure created by this paragraph, however, is subject to the obligations created by Rule 1.6.

Rule 4.2 COMMUNICATION WITH PERSONS REPRESENTED BY COUNSEL

(a) In representing a client, a Federal lawyer shall not communicate about the subject of the representation with a party the lawyer knows to be represented by another lawyer in the matter, unless the Federal lawyer has the consent of the other lawyer; in a criminal matter, the individual initiates the communication with the Government lawyer and voluntarily and knowingly waives the right to counsel for the purposes of the communication; or the Federal lawyer otherwise is authorized by law to do so.

(b) This Rule does not prohibit communications by a Non-Government lawyer with Federal Agency officials who have the authority to resolve a matter affecting the lawyer's client, whether or not the lawyer's communications relate to matters that are the subject of the representation, provided that the lawyer discloses the lawyer's identity; the fact that the lawyer represents a client in a matter involving the official's Federal Agency; and that the matter is being handled for the Federal Agency by a Government lawyer.

COMMENT:

This Rule does not prohibit communication with a party, or an employee or agent of a party, concerning matters outside the representation. For example, the existence of a controversy between a Federal Agency and private party does not prohibit a Federal lawyer from either from communicating with nonlawyer representatives of the other regarding a separate matter. Also, parties to a matter may communicate directly with each other and a Federal lawyer having independent justification for communicating with the other party is permitted to do so. Communications authorized by law include, for example, the right of a party to a controversy with a Federal Agency to speak with Federal Agency officials about the matter.

In the case of an organization, other than a Federal Agency, this Rule prohibits communications by a lawyer for one party concerning the matter in representation with individuals that having a managerial responsibility on behalf of the organization, and with any other person whose act or omission in connection with that matter may be imputed to the organization for purposes of civil or criminal liability or whose statement may constitute an admission on the part of the organization. If an agent or employee of the organization is represented in the matter by his or her own counsel, the consent by that counsel to a communication will be sufficient for purposes of this Rule. Compare Rule 3.4(f).

Paragraph (b) permits communications with those in government having the authority to resolve matters without the prior consent of the lawyer representing the government in such cases. A non-government lawyer making such a communication without the prior consent of the lawyer representing the government must make certain disclosures. If known, the lawyer should advise the Federal Agency official of the name of the Government lawyer handling the matter. This paragraph does not permit a lawyer to bypass counsel representing the Federal Agency on every issue which may arise in the course of disputes with the Federal Agency. It is intended to provide lawyers access to decisionmakers in government with respect to genuine grievances and not intended to provide direct access on routine disputes or routine aspects of the resolution of disputes.

This Rule also covers any person, even if not a party to a formal proceeding, who is represented by counsel concerning the matter in question.

In a criminal case there may be times when communications between a defendant and a Federal Agency without notice to defense counsel is in the interest of the defendant. Some communications will serve to protect the defendant and to identify sham representations. For example, in certain criminal enterprises, such as organized crime or drug rings, a defendant may wish to cooperate with a Federal Agency, but the counsel may also be the counsel of others involved in the enterprise.

To ensure that in such instances there is no abuse, this rule would permit communications by the defendant with the Government lawyer, as long as the defendant voluntarily and knowingly waives the right to counsel.

Rule 4.3 DEALING WITH UNREPRESENTED PERSONS

In dealing on behalf of a client with a person who is not represented by counsel, a Federal lawyer shall not state or imply that the lawyer is disinterested. When the Federal lawyer knows or reasonably should know that the unrepresented person misunderstands the lawyer's role in the matter, the lawyer shall make reasonable efforts to correct the misunderstanding.

COMMENT:

An unrepresented person, particularly one not experienced in dealing with legal matters, might assume a Federal lawyer is disinterested in loyalties or is a disinterested authority on the law even when the lawyer represents a client. During the course of a Federal lawyer's representation of a client, the lawyer should not give advice to an unrepresented person other than the advice to obtain counsel.

Rule 4.4 RESPECT FOR RIGHTS OF THIRD PERSONS

In representing a client, a Federal lawyer shall not use means that have no substantial purpose other than to embarrass, delay, or burden a third person, or use methods of obtaining evidence that violate the legal rights of such a person.

COMMENT:

Responsibility to a client requires a Federal lawyer to subordinate the interests of others to those of the client. That responsibility does not imply that a Federal lawyer may disregard the rights of third persons. The duty of a Federal lawyer to represent the client with zeal does not mitigate against his concurrent obligation to treat with consideration all persons involved in the legal process and to avoid the infliction of needless harm. It is impractical to catalogue all such rights, but they include legal restrictions on methods of obtaining evidence from third persons.

LEGAL OFFICES

Rule 5.1 RESPONSIBILITIES OF A SUPERVISORY LAWYER

(a) A supervisory lawyer shall make reasonable efforts to ensure that all Federal lawyers conform to these Rules of Professional Conduct.
(b) A Federal lawyer shall be responsible for another Federal lawyer's violation of these Rules of Professional Conduct if:
   (1) The Federal lawyer orders or, with knowledge of the specific conduct, ratifies the conduct involved; or
   (2) The Federal lawyer has direct supervisory authority over the other Federal lawyer and knows of the conduct at a time when its consequences can be avoided or mitigated, but fails to take reasonable remedial action.

(c) A Federal lawyer, who is a supervisory lawyer, is responsible for ensuring that the subordinate lawyer is properly trained and is competent to perform the duties to which the subordinate lawyer is assigned.

(d) A Government lawyer, who is a supervisory lawyer, should encourage subordinate lawyers to participate in pro bono publico service activities and the activities of bar associations and law reform organizations.

COMMENT:

Paragraph 5.1(a) recognizes the responsibilities of the supervisory lawyers to effect and ultimately to enforce these Rules. The measures required to fulfill the responsibility prescribed in Rule 5.1(a) can depend on the office's structure and the nature of its practice. In a small office, informal supervision and occasional admonition ordinarily might be sufficient. In a large office, or in practice situations in which intensely difficult ethical problems frequently arise, more elaborate procedures may be necessary. In some offices, for example, junior lawyers can make confidential referral of ethical problems directly to a senior lawyer. See Rules 1.13 and 5.2. Offices may also rely on continuing legal education in professional ethics. In any event, the ethical atmosphere of an office can influence the conduct of all its members and a Federal lawyer having authority over the work of another shall not assume the subordinate lawyer will inevitably conform to these Rules.

Supervisory lawyers must be careful to avoid conflicts of interest in providing advice to subordinate lawyers. Depending on the circumstances, the supervisory lawyer may advise one subordinate Federal lawyer and refer the other subordinate Federal lawyer to another supervisory lawyer in a different office. Alternatively, the supervisory lawyer may refer both subordinate Federal lawyers to separate supervisory lawyers in the same or another office.

Paragraph 5.1(b)(1) expresses a general principle of supervisory responsibility for acts of another. See also Rule 8.4(a). Ratification as used in paragraph 5.1(b)(1) means approval of or consent to another Federal lawyer's conduct.

Paragraph 5.1(b)(2) defines the duty of a Federal lawyer having direct supervisory authority over the performance of specific legal work by another Federal lawyer. Whether a Federal lawyer has such supervisory authority in particular circumstances is a question of fact. Appropriate remedial action would depend on the immediacy of the supervisor's involvement and the seriousness of the misconduct. Apart from the responsibility that may be incurred for ordering or ratifying another Federal lawyer's conduct under paragraph 5.1(b)(1), the supervisor is required to intervene to prevent avoidable consequences of misconduct if the supervisor knows the misconduct occurred. Thus, if a supervisory lawyer knows that a subordinate misrepresented a matter to an opposing party in negotiation, the supervisor, as well as the subordinate, has a duty to correct the resulting misapprehension.

Professional misconduct by a Federal lawyer under supervision could reveal a violation [of] paragraph 5.1(a) on the part of the supervisory lawyer even though it does not entail a violation of paragraph 5.1(b) because there was no direction, ratification, or knowledge of the violation.

Apart from this Rule and Rule 8.4(a), a Federal lawyer does not have disciplinary liability for the conduct of subordinate Federal lawyers. Whether a Federal lawyer may be liable civilly or criminally for another Federal lawyer's conduct is a question of law beyond the scope of these Rules.

Rule 5.2 RESPONSIBILITIES OF A SUBORDINATE FEDERAL LAWYER

(a) A Federal lawyer is bound by these Rules of Professional Conduct notwithstanding the Federal lawyer's acting at the direction of another person.
(b) A subordinate Federal lawyer does not violate these Rules of Professional Conduct if that lawyer acts in accordance with a supervisory lawyer's reasonable resolution of an arguable question of professional duty.

COMMENT:

   Although a Federal lawyer is not relieved of responsibility for a violation by the fact that the Federal lawyer acted at the direction of a supervisor, that fact may be relevant in determining whether a Federal lawyer had the knowledge required to render conduct a violation of these Rules. For example, if a subordinate filed a frivolous motion at the direction of a supervisor, the subordinate would not be guilty of a professional violation, unless the subordinate knew of the document's frivolous character.

   When Federal lawyers in a supervisor-subordinate relationship encounter a matter involving professional judgment as to ethical duty, the supervisor may assume responsibility for making the judgment. Otherwise a consistent course of action or position could not be taken. If the question can reasonably be answered only one way, the duty of both Federal lawyers is clear and they are equally responsible for fulfilling it. If the question is reasonably arguable, however, someone has to decide upon the course of action. That authority and responsibility ordinarily reposes in the supervisor, and a subordinate may be guided accordingly. For example, if a question arises whether the interests of two clients conflict under Rule 1.7, the supervisor's reasonable resolution of the question should protect the subordinate professionally if the resolution is subsequently challenged.

Rule 5.3 RESPONSIBILITIES REGARDING NONLAWYER ASSISTANTS

   With respect to a nonlawyer under the authority, supervision, or direction of a Federal lawyer:
(a) A supervisory lawyer shall make reasonable efforts to ensure that the office has in effect measures giving reasonable assurance that the person's conduct is compatible with the professional obligations of the Federal lawyer.
(b) A Federal lawyer having direct supervisory authority over the nonlawyer shall make reasonable efforts to ensure that the nonlawyer's conduct is compatible with the professional obligations of the Federal lawyer.
(c) A Federal lawyer shall be responsible for conduct of the nonlawyer that would be a violation these Rules if engaged in by the Federal lawyer if:
   (1) The Federal lawyer orders or, with the knowledge of the specific conduct, ratifies the conduct involved; or
   (2) The Federal lawyer has direct supervisory authority over the nonlawyer, and knows of the conduct at a time when its consequences can be avoided or mitigated but fails to take reasonable remedial action.

COMMENT:

Various nonlawyer assistants are employed by federal lawyers in their practices, including paralegals, legal technicians, secretaries, clerks, investigators, law student interns, and others. Such assistants act for the Federal lawyer in rendition of the Federal lawyer's professional services. A Federal lawyer should give such assistants appropriate instruction and supervision concerning the ethical aspects of their performance, particularly regarding the obligation not to disclose information relating to representation of the client, and should be responsible for their work product. The measures employed in supervising nonlawyers should take account of their lack of legal training and their not being subject to professional discipline.

Rule 5.4 PROFESSIONAL INDEPENDENCE OF A FEDERAL LAWYER

(a) A Federal lawyer is expected to exercise professional independence of judgment during the representation of a client, consistent with these Rules.

(b) Notwithstanding a Government lawyer's status as a Government employee, a Government lawyer detailed or assigned to represent an individual Government employee or another person as the client is expected to exercise loyalty and professional independence during the representation, consistent with these Rules and to the same extent as required by a Non-Government lawyer in private practice.

(c) A Supervisory Government lawyer may not base an adverse evaluation or other prejudicial action against a Subordinate Government lawyer on the Subordinate Government lawyer's exercise of professional independence under (b) above.

(d) A Government lawyer shall obey the lawful orders of superiors when representing the United States and individual clients, but a Government lawyer shall not permit a nonlawyer to direct or regulate the Government lawyer's professional judgment in rendering legal services.

(e) A Non-Government lawyer shall not permit a nonlawyer who recommends, employs, or pays the Non-Government lawyer to render legal services for another to direct or regulate the Non-Government lawyer's professional judgment in rendering legal services.

(f) A Non-Government lawyer shall comply with the Rules of Professional Conduct or other applicable laws of the jurisdiction in which the Non-Government lawyer is licensed or is practicing law concerning the limitations on sharing fees and the organizational form of their practice.

COMMENT:

Federal Lawyers

A Federal lawyer subjected to outside pressures that might impair or give the appearance of impairing the effectiveness of the representation should make full disclosure of the pressures to the client. If the Federal lawyer or the client believes the effectiveness of the representation has been or will be impaired thereby, the lawyer should take proper steps to withdraw from representation of the client.

Government Lawyers

This Rule recognizes that a Government lawyer is a Government employee required by law to obey the lawful orders of superiors. Nevertheless, the practice of law requires the exercise of judgment solely for the benefit of the client and free of compromising influences and loyalties. Thus, when a Government lawyer is assigned to represent an individual client, neither the lawyer's personal interests, the interests of other clients, nor the interests of third persons should affect loyalty to the individual client.

Non-Government Lawyers

Rather that adopting specific rules on the sharing of fees or the organizational makeup of law practices that would apply only to Non-government lawyers practicing before the Federal Agency, the Federal Agency defers on this matter to the rules and applicable laws of the jurisdictions in which these Non-Government lawyers are licensed.

Rule 5.5 UNAUTHORIZED PRACTICE OF LAW

A Federal lawyer shall not:
(a) Except as authorized by law, practice law in a jurisdiction where doing so violates the regulation of the legal profession in that jurisdiction; or
(b) Assist a person who is not a member of the bar in the performance of activity that constitutes the unauthorized practice of law.

COMMENT:

Limiting the practice of law to members of the bar protects the public against rendition of legal services by unqualified persons. A Government lawyer's performance of legal duties for a Federal Agency, however, is considered a Federal function and not subject to regulation by the states. Paragraph (b) does not prohibit a Federal lawyer from employing the services of nonlawyers and delegating functions to them, so long as the Federal lawyer supervises the delegated work and retains responsibility for their work. See Rule 5.3. Likewise, it does not prohibit Federal lawyers from providing professional advice and instruction to nonlawyers whose employment requires knowledge of law; for example, claims adjusters, social workers, accountants, and persons employed in Government agencies. In addition, a Federal lawyer may counsel nonlawyers who wish to proceed pro se, or nonlawyers authorized by law to practice in military proceedings.

The sole admission to practice requirement is applicable to Government lawyers. As such, admission in any of the several states should preclude the imposition of additional requirements on behalf of the U.S. Government.

PUBLIC SERVICE

Rule 6.1 PRO BONO PUBLICO SERVICE

(a) A Federal lawyer should render public interest legal service. A Federal lawyer may discharge this responsibility by providing professional services at no fee or at a reduced fee to persons of limited means or to public service or charitable groups or organizations, by service in activities for improving the law, the legal system or the legal profession, and by financial support for organizations that provide legal service to persons of limited means.

(b) A Government lawyer should provide pro bono legal services consistent with applicable law.

COMMENT:

Each Federal lawyer has a basic responsibility to provide public interest legal services without fee, or at a substantially reduced fee, in one or more of the following areas: poverty law, civil rights law, public rights law, charitable organization representation, and the administration of justice. This Rule expresses that policy but is not intended to be enforced through disciplinary process.

The rights and responsibilities of individuals and organizations in the United States are increasingly defined in legal terms. As a consequence, legal assistance in coping with the web of laws is imperative for persons of modest and limited means, as well as for the relatively well-to-do.

The basic responsibility for providing legal services for those unable to pay ultimately rests upon the individual lawyer, and personal involvement in the problems of the disadvantaged can be one of the most rewarding experiences in the life of a Federal lawyer. Every Federal lawyer, regardless of professional prominence or professional work load, should find time to participate in or otherwise support the provision of legal services to the disadvantaged. The provision of free legal services to those unable to pay reasonable fees continues to be an obligation of each Federal lawyer as well as the profession generally, but the efforts of individual Federal lawyers are often not enough to meet the need. Thus, it has been necessary for the profession and government to institute additional programs to provide legal services. Accordingly, legal aid offices, lawyer referral services, and other related programs have been developed, and others will be developed by the profession and government. Every Federal lawyer should support all proper efforts to meet this need for legal services.

18 U.S.C. § 205 and § 209 and other laws, including those governing off-duty employment by members of the Armed Forces, may regulate a Government lawyer's ability to provide legal services on a pro bono basis outside the scope of the Government lawyer's official duties.

Rule 6.2 ACCEPTING APPOINTMENTS

A Federal lawyer shall not seek to avoid appointment by a tribunal to represent a person except for good cause, such as:

(a) Representing the client is contrary to law or in violation of these Rules.

(b) Representing the client is likely to result in an unreasonable financial burden on the Federal lawyer.

(c) The client or the cause is so repugnant to the lawyer as to be likely to impair the client-lawyer relationship or the lawyer's ability to represent the client.

COMMENT:

A Federal lawyer ordinarily is not obliged to accept a client whose character or cause the Federal lawyer regards as repugnant. The Federal lawyer's freedom to select clients is, however, qualified. All lawyers have a responsibility to assist in providing pro bono publico service. See Rule 6.1. An individual Federal lawyer fulfills this responsibility by accepting a fair share of unpopular matters or indigent or unpopular clients. A Federal lawyer may also be subject to appointment by a court to serve unpopular clients or persons unable to afford legal services.

Appointed Counsel

For good cause a Federal lawyer may seek to decline an appointment to represent a person who cannot afford to retain counsel or whose cause is unpopular. Good cause exists if the Federal lawyer could not handle the matter competently, see Rule 1.1, or if undertaking the representation would result in an improper conflict of interest, for example, when the client or the cause is so repugnant to the Federal lawyer as to be likely to impair the client-lawyer relationship or the Federal lawyer's ability to represent the client. A Federal lawyer may also seek to decline an appointment if acceptance would be unreasonably burdensome, for example, when it would impose a financial sacrifice so great as to be unjust.

An appointed Federal lawyer has the same obligations to the client as retained counsel, including the obligations of loyalty and confidentiality, and is subject to the same limitations on the client-lawyer relationship, such as the obligation to refrain from assisting the client in violation of the Rules.

18 U.S.C. § 205 and other laws, including those governing off-duty employment, may prevent or restrict the types of cases that a Government lawyer may accept appointment to by a tribunal outside the scope of the Government lawyer's official duties.

Rule 6.3 MEMBERSHIP IN LEGAL SERVICES ORGANIZATION

A Federal lawyer may serve as a director, officer, or member of a legal services organization, apart from the law firm or Federal Agency in which the lawyer practices, notwithstanding that the organization serves persons having interests adverse to a client of the Federal lawyer. The Federal lawyer shall not knowingly participate in a decision or action of the organization:

    (a) If participating in the decision or action would be incompatible with the Federal lawyer's obligations to a client under Rule 1.7; or

    (b) Where the decision or action could have a material adverse effect on the representation of a client of the organization whose interests are adverse to a client of the Federal lawyer.

COMMENT:

Federal lawyers should be encouraged to support and participate in legal service organizations. A Federal lawyer who is an officer or a member of such an organization does not thereby have a client-lawyer relationship with persons served by the organization. However, there is potential conflict between the interests of such persons and the interests of the Federal lawyer's clients. If the possibility of such conflict disqualified a Federal lawyer from serving on the board of a legal services organization, the profession's involvement in such organizations would be severely curtailed.

It may be necessary in appropriate cases to reassure a client of the organization that the representation will not be affected by conflicting loyalties of a member of the board. Established written policies in this respect can enhance the credibility of such assurances.

18 U.S.C. § 205 and § 208 and other laws may prevent or restrict a Government lawyer's participation in a legal services organization.

Rule 6.4 MEMBERSHIP IN BAR ASSOCIATIONS AND LAW REFORM ACTIVITIES AFFECTING CLIENT INTERESTS

A Federal lawyer may serve as a member, director, or officer of a bar association or an organization involved in reform of the law or its administration, notwithstanding that the reform may affect the interests of a client. The Federal lawyer shall not knowingly participate in a decision or action of the organization if participating in the decision would be incompatible with the Federal lawyer's obligations to the client under Rule 1.7. When the Federal lawyer knows the interests of the client may be materially benefited by a decision in which the Federal lawyer participates, the Federal lawyer shall disclose that fact, but need not identify the client.

COMMENT

Federal lawyers involved in organizations seeking law reform generally do not have a client-lawyer relationship with the organization. Otherwise, it might follow that a Government lawyer could not be involved in a bar association law reform program that might indirectly affect the United States. See also Rule 1.2(b). For example, a Government lawyer might be disqualified from participating in drafting proposed regulations. In determining the nature and scope of participation in such activities, a Federal lawyer should be mindful of obligations to clients under other Rules, particularly Rule 1.7. A Federal lawyer is professionally obligated to protect the integrity of the program by making an appropriate disclosure within the organization when the Federal lawyer knows that a client might be materially benefited.

A Government lawyer who is active in bar association activities or who makes a presentation to a bar association in the lawyer's personal capacity, and not as a representative of the Government lawyer's Federal Agency, may accept reimbursement, subject to the provisions of applicable laws, for the Government lawyer's expenses in attending a meeting of the bar association on the Government lawyer's own time.

INFORMATION ABOUT LEGAL SERVICES

Rule 7.1 COMMUNICATIONS CONCERNING A FEDERAL AGENCY'S LEGAL SERVICES

A Government lawyer may advertise the Federal Agency's legal services through the public media, such as a telephone directory, newspaper, or other periodicals, outdoor sign, radio, television, or through written communications.

COMMENT:

To assist members of the public, Government employees, and dependents of Government employees, a Government lawyer may advertise or otherwise conduct information campaigns regarding the legal services that a Federal Agency makes available to the public, Government employees, and dependents of Government employees.

MAINTAINING THE INTEGRITY OF THE PROFESSION

Rule 8.1 BAR ADMISSION AND DISCIPLINARY MATTERS

An applicant for admission to a bar or employment as a lawyer with a Federal Agency, a Federal lawyer seeking the right to practice before a Federal Agency, or a Federal lawyer in connection with a disciplinary matter, shall not:
(a) Knowingly make a false statement of material fact.
(b) Fail to disclose a fact necessary to correct a misapprehension known by the person to have arisen in the matter, or knowingly fail to respond to a lawful demand for information from an admission or disciplinary authority, except that the Rule does not require disclosure of information otherwise protected by Rule 1.6.

COMMENT:

The duty imposed by this Rule extends to applicants seeking admission to the bar or employment with a Federal Agency as well as to Federal lawyers. Hence, if a person makes a material false statement in connection with an application for admission, employment, or certification, it may form the basis for subsequent disciplinary action if the person is admitted or employed, and in any event may be relevant in a subsequent admission application. The duty imposed by this Rule applies to a Federal lawyer's own admission or discipline, as well as to that of others. Thus, it is a separate professional offense for a Federal lawyer to knowingly make a misrepresentation or omission in connection with a disciplinary investigation of the Federal lawyer's own conduct. This Rule also requires affirmative clarification of any misunderstanding on the part of the admission or disciplinary authority of which the person involved becomes aware.

A Federal lawyer representing an applicant for admission to the bar, or representing a Federal lawyer who is the subject of a disciplinary inquiry or proceeding, is governed by the Rules applicable to the client-lawyer relationship.

Rule 8.2 JUDICIAL AND LEGAL OFFICIALS

A Federal lawyer shall not make a statement the lawyer knows to be false or with reckless disregard as to its truth or falsity concerning the qualifications or integrity of a tribunal or of a candidate for election or appointment to judicial or legal office.

COMMENT:

Assessments by Federal lawyers are relied on in evaluating the professional or personal fitness of persons performing legal duties. Expressing honest and candid opinions on such matters contributes to improving the administration of justice. Conversely, false statements by a Federal lawyer can unfairly undermine confidence in the administration of justice.

To maintain the fair and independent administration of justice, Federal lawyers are encouraged to continue traditional efforts to defend judges and courts criticized unjustly.

Rule 8.3 REPORTING PROFESSIONAL MISCONDUCT

(a) A Federal lawyer having knowledge that another Federal lawyer has committed a violation of these Rules of Professional Conduct that raises a substantial question as to that lawyer's honesty, trustworthiness, or fitness as a Federal lawyer in other respects, shall report such a violation to the appropriate official as provided by law.

(b) A Federal lawyer having knowledge that a judge has committed a violation of applicable rules of judicial conduct that raises a substantial question as to the judge's fitness for office shall report such a violation to the appropriate official as provided by law.

(c) This Rule does not require disclosure of information otherwise protected by Rule 1.6.

COMMENT:

Self-regulation of the legal profession requires members of the profession to initiate disciplinary investigations when they know of violations of these Rules of Professional Conduct or other such rules. Federal lawyers have a similar obligation with respect to judicial misconduct. An apparently isolated violation may indicate a pattern of misconduct that only a disciplinary investigation can uncover. Reporting a violation is especially important if the victim is unlikely to discover the offense.

A report about misconduct is not required if it would involve violation of Rule 1.6. A Federal lawyer should, however, encourage a client to consent to disclosure when prosecution would not substantially prejudice the client's interests.

This Rule limits the reporting obligation to those offenses that a self-regulating profession must vigorously endeavor to prevent. A measure of judgment, therefore, is required in complying with this Rule. The term "substantial" refers to the seriousness of the possible offense and not the quantum of evidence of which the Federal lawyer is aware. Any report should be made to the appropriate official under the applicable law.

Rule 8.4 MISCONDUCT

It is professional misconduct for a Federal lawyer to:

(a) Violate or attempt to violate these Rules of Professional Conduct, knowingly assist or induce another to do so, or do so through the acts of another.

(b) Commit a criminal act that reflects adversely on the Federal lawyer's honesty, trustworthiness, or fitness as a Federal lawyer in other respects.

(c) Engage in conduct involving dishonesty, fraud, deceit, or misrepresentation.

(d) Engage in conduct prejudicial to the administration of justice.

(e) State or imply an ability to influence improperly a government Federal Agency or official.

(f) Knowingly assist a judge or judicial officer in conduct that violates applicable rules of judicial conduct or other law.

COMMENT:

Many kinds of illegal conduct reflect adversely on fitness to practice law, such as offenses involving fraud and the offense of willful failure to file an income tax return. However, some kinds of offenses carry no such implication. Traditionally, the distinction was drawn in terms of offenses involving "moral turpitude." That concept can be construed to include offense concerning some matters of personal morality, such as adultery and comparable offenses, which have no specific connection to fitness for the practice of law. Although a Federal lawyer is personally answerable under law, a Federal lawyer should be professionally answerable only for offenses that indicate lack of those characteristics relevant to law practice. Offenses involving violence, dishonesty, breach of truth, or serious interference with the administration of justice are in that category. One example of such conduct is the unlawful, unauthorized, or nonconsentual obtaining of confidential files, including confidential working paper files, of Federal lawyers who are known or reasonably should be known to be representing a client. Such conduct includes the solicitation or prompting of another person, not bound by these Rules, to engage in such activities. A pattern of repeated offenses, even ones of minor significance when considered separately, can indicate indifference to ethical obligations.

A Federal lawyer may refuse to comply with an obligation imposed by law upon a good faith belief that no valid obligation exists. The provision of Rule 1.2(d) concerning a good faith challenge to the validity, scope, meaning or application of the law applies to challenges of legal regulation of the practice of law.

A Government lawyer assumes legal responsibilities beyond those of other citizens. A Government lawyer's abuse of such status can suggest an inability to fulfill the professional role of Government lawyer and Federal lawyer.

Rule 8.5 JURISDICTION

(a) A Federal lawyer shall comply with the rules of professional conduct applicable to the Federal Agency that employs the Government lawyer or the Federal Agency before which the Federal lawyer practices.

(b) If the Federal Agency has not adopted or promulgated rules of professional conduct, the Federal lawyer shall comply with the rules of professional conduct of the state bars in which the Federal lawyer is admitted to practice.

COMMENT:

Many Federal lawyers practicing before Federal Agency tribunals practice outside the territorial limits of the jurisdiction in which they are licensed.

While the Federal lawyer may remain subject to the governing authority of their licensing jurisdiction, the Federal lawyer is also subject to these Rules. However, when a Government lawyer is engaged in the conduct of Federal Agency legal functions, whether servicing the Federal Agency as a client or serving an individual client in the course of official duties, these Rules are regarded as superseding any conflicting rules applicable in the jurisdictions in which the Government lawyer may be licensed.

When a Government lawyer is practicing before a Federal Agency whose rules conflict with these Rules, the Government lawyer shall comply with the rules of that Federal Agency.

A Non-Government lawyer practicing before a Federal Agency tribunal who violates these Rules may be suspended from practice before such tribunals.

Standards for Civility in Professional Conduct*

PREAMBLE

Civility in professional conduct is the responsibility of every lawyer practicing in the federal system. While lawyers have an obligation to represent clients zealously, we must also be mindful of our obligations to the administration of justice. Incivility to opposing counsel, adverse parties, judges inclusive of Article I, III and the administrative judiciary, court[1] and agency personnel, and other participants in the legal process demeans the legal profession, undermines the administration of justice, and diminishes respect for both the legal process and the results of our system of justice.

Our judicial system is a truth-seeking process designed to resolve human and societal problems in a rational, peaceful, and efficient manner and designed to be perceived as producing fair and just results. We must be careful to avoid actions or statements which undermine the system or the public's confidence in it.

The organized bar and the judiciary, in partnership with each other, have a responsibility to promote civility in the practice of law and the administration of justice. Uncivil conduct of lawyers or judges impedes the fundamental goal of resolving disputes rationally, peacefully, and efficiently. Such conduct may delay or deny justice and diminish the respect for law, which is a cornerstone of our society and our profession.

Civility and professionalism are hallmarks of a learned profession dedicated to public service. These standards are designed to encourage us, as lawyers and judges, to meet our obligations of civility and professionalism, to each other, to litigants, and to the system of justice. The goal is to ensure that lawyers and judges will conduct themselves at all times, in both litigated and nonlitigated matters, with personal courtesy and professionalism in the fullest sense of those terms.

While these standards are voluntary and shall not be used as a basis for litigation or sanctions, we expect that lawyers and judges in the federal system will make a commitment to adhere to these standards in all aspects of their dealings with one another and with other participants in the legal process.

Finally, we believe these standards should be incorporated as an integral component of the teaching of professionalism to law students and practicing lawyers alike. We therefore believe that it is important for law schools to incorporate these standards in their curricula and for lawyers in the federal system, law firms, government agencies, and other legal institutions in our country to teach and promote these standards as part of their continuing legal education programs.

PRINCIPLES OF GENERAL APPLICABILITY: LAWYERS' DUTIES TO OTHER COUNSEL, PARTIES AND THE JUDICIARY

General Principles:

1. In carrying out our professional responsibilities, we will treat all participants in the legal process, including counsel and their staff, parties, witnesses, judges,

---

*Federal Bar Association Professional Ethics Committee. Adapted with the consent of the D.C. Bar from their standards published in 1996. Copyright © 1998. Reprinted with permission of the Federal Bar Association, 1815 H Street, NW, Suite 408, Washington, D.C. 20006-3697.

[1]References herein to "court" include agency tribunals.

court personnel, and administrative agency staff, in a civil, professional, and courteous manner, at all times and in all communications, whether oral or written. We will refrain from acting upon or manifesting racial, gender, or other bias or prejudice toward any participant in the legal process. We will treat all participants in the legal process with respect.

2. Except within the bounds of fair argument in pleadings or in formal proceedings, we will not reflect in our conduct, attitude, or demeanor our clients' ill feelings, if any, toward other participants in the legal process.

3. We will not, even if called upon by a client to do so, engage in offensive conduct directed toward other participants in the legal process, nor will we abuse other such participants in the legal process. Except within the bounds of fair argument in pleadings or in formal proceedings, we will abstain from directing disparaging personal remarks or acrimony toward such participants and treat adverse witnesses and parties with fair consideration. We will encourage our clients to act civilly and respectfully to all participants in the legal process.

4. We will not encourage or authorize any person under our control to engage in conduct that would be inappropriate under these standards if we were to engage in such conduct.

5. We will not bring the profession into disrepute by making unfounded accusations of impropriety or making ad hominem attacks on counsel, and, absent good cause, we will not attribute bad motives or improper conduct to other counsel.

6. While we owe our highest loyalty to our clients, we will discharge that obligation in the framework of the federal judicial system in which we apply our learning, skill, and industry in accordance with professional norms. In this context, we will strive for orderly, efficient, ethical, fair, and just disposition of litigation as well as disputed matters that are not, or are not yet, the subject of litigation, and for the efficient, ethical, and fair negotiation and consummation of business transactions.

7. The foregoing General Principles apply to all aspects of the federal legal proceedings, both in the presence and outside the presence of a court or tribunal.

Scheduling Matters:

8. We will endeavor to schedule dates for trials, hearings, depositions, meetings, negotiations, conferences, vacations, seminars, and other functions to avoid creating calendar conflicts for other participants in the legal process, provided our clients' interests will not be adversely affected.

9. We will notify other counsel and, if appropriate, the court or other persons, at the earliest possible time when hearings, depositions, meetings, or conferences need to be canceled or postponed. Early notice avoids unnecessary travel and expense and may enable the court and the other participants in the legal process to use the previously reserved time for other matters.

10. We will agree to reasonable requests for extensions of time and for waiver of procedural formalities provided our clients' interests will not be adversely affected.

11. We will not request an extension of time for the purpose of unjustified delay.

PRINCIPLES PARTICULARLY APPLICABLE TO LITIGATION

Procedural Agreements:

12. We will confer with opposing counsel about procedural issues that arise during the course of litigation, such as requests for extensions of time, discovery

matters, pre-trial matters, and the scheduling of meetings, depositions, hearings, and trial. We will seek to resolve by agreement such procedural issues that do not require court order. For those that do, we will seek to reach agreement with opposing counsel before presenting the matter to the court.

13. We accept primary responsibility, after consultation with the client, for making decisions about procedural agreements. We will explain to our clients that cooperation between counsel in such matters is the professional norm and may be in the client's interest. We will explain the nature of the matter at issue in any such proposed agreements and explain how such agreements do not compromise the client's interests.

Discovery:

14. We will not use any form of discovery or discovery scheduling for harassment, unjustified delay, to increase litigation expenses, or any other improper purpose.
15. We will make good faith efforts to resolve by agreement any disputes with respect to matters contained in pleadings and discovery requests and objections.
16. We will not engage in any conduct during a deposition that would not be appropriate if a judge were present. Accordingly, we will not obstruct questioning during a deposition or object to deposition questions, unless permitted by the applicable rules to preserve an objection or privilege, and we will ask only those questions we reasonably believe are appropriate in discovery under the applicable rules.
17. We will carefully craft document production requests so they are limited to those documents we reasonably believe are appropriate under the applicable rules. We will not design production requests for the purpose of placing an undue burden or expense on a party.
18. We will respond to document requests reasonably and in accordance with what the applicable rules require. We will not interpret the request in an artificially restrictive manner to avoid disclosure of relevant and non-privileged documents. We will not produce documents in a manner designed to hide or obscure the existence of particular documents.
19. We will carefully craft interrogatories so they are limited to those matters we reasonably believe are appropriate under the applicable rules, and we will not design them for the purpose of placing an undue burden or expense on a party.
20. We will respond to interrogatories reasonably and in accordance with what the applicable rules require. We will not interpret interrogatories in an artificially restrictive manner to avoid disclosure of relevant and non-privileged information.
21. We will base our discovery objections on a good faith belief in their merit. We will not object solely for the purpose of withholding or delaying the disclosure of properly discoverable information.
22. During discovery, we will not engage in acrimonious conversations or exchanges with opposing counsel, parties, or witnesses. We will advise our clients to conduct themselves in accordance with these provisions. We will not engage in undignified or discourteous conduct which degrades the legal proceeding.

Sanctions:

23. We will not seek court sanctions or disqualification of counsel unless reasonably justified by the circumstances after conducting a reasonable investigation, which includes attempting to confer with opposing counsel.

Lawyers' Duties to the Court:

24. We recognize that the public's perception of our system of justice is influenced by the relationship between lawyers and judges, and that judges perform a symbolic role. At the same time, lawyers have the right and, at times, the duty to be critical of judges and their rulings. Thus, in all communications with the court, we will speak and write civilly. In expressing criticism of the court to an administrative tribunal, we shall use language that is respectful of courts or tribunals, the system of justice, and the symbolism that these represent.
25. We will not engage in conduct that offends the dignity and decorum of judicial or administrative proceedings, brings disorder or disruption to the courtroom or tribunal, or undermines the image of the legal profession.
26. We will advise clients and witnesses to act civilly and respectfully toward the court, educate them about proper courtroom decorum, and, to the best of our ability, prevent them from creating disorder or disruption in the courtroom.
27. We will not knowingly misrepresent, mischaracterize, misquote, or miscite facts or authorities and will immediately make any clarifications and corrections as these become known to us.
28. We will not degrade the intelligence, ethics, morals, integrity, or personal behavior of others, unless such matters are legitimately at issue in the proceeding.
29. We will act and speak civilly and respectfully to the judge's staff, the courtroom and tribunal staff, and other court or tribunal personnel with an awareness that they, too, are an integral part of the judicial system. We will also advise clients and witnesses to act civilly and respectfully toward these participants in the legal process.
30. We recognize that judicial resources are scarce, that court dockets are crowded, and that justice is undermined when cases are delayed and/or disputes remain unresolved. Therefore, we will be considerate of the time constraints and pressures on the court and court staff inherent in their efforts to administer justice.
31. We recognize that tardiness and neglect show disrespect to the court and the judicial system. Therefore, we will be punctual and prepared for all court appearances so that all hearings, conferences, and trials may commence on time and proceed efficiently. We will also educate clients and witnesses concerning the need to be punctual and prepared. If delayed, we will promptly notify the court and counsel, if at all possible.
32. Before dates for hearings or trials are set, or, if that is not feasible, immediately after such a date has been set, we will attempt to verify the availability of necessary participants and witnesses so we can promptly notify the court of any likely problems.
33. We will avoid ex parte communications with the court or tribunal, including the judge's staff, on pending matters, in person (whether in social, professional, or other contexts), by telephone, and in letters and other forms of written communication, unless such communications relate solely to scheduling or other non-substantive administrative matters, or are made with the consent of all parties, or are otherwise expressly authorized by law or court rule.

Judges' Duties to Lawyers:

34. We will be courteous, respectful, and civil to lawyers, parties, agency personnel, and witnesses. We will maintain control of the proceedings, recognizing

that judges have both the obligation and the authority to ensure that judicial proceedings are conducted with dignity, decorum, and courtesy.

35. We will not employ hostile, demeaning, or humiliating words in opinions or in written or oral communications with lawyers, parties, or witnesses.
36. We will be punctual in convening hearings, meetings, and conferences; if delayed, we will notify counsel as promptly as possible.
37. In scheduling hearings, meetings, and conferences, we will be considerate of time schedules of lawyers, parties, and witnesses and of other courts and tribunals. We will inform counsel promptly of any rescheduling, postponement, or cancellation of hearings, meetings, or conferences.
38. While endeavoring to resolve disputes efficiently, we will be considerate of the time constraints and pressures imposed on lawyers by the exigencies of litigation practice. We will make all reasonable efforts promptly to decide matters presented to us for decision.
39. We recognize that a lawyer has a right and duty to present a cause fully and properly, and that a litigant has a right to a fair and impartial hearing. Within the practical limits of time, we will allow lawyers to present proper arguments, to make a complete and accurate record, and to present a case free from unreasonable or unnecessary judicial interruption.
40. We will not impugn the integrity or professionalism of any lawyer on the basis of the clients whom or the causes which a lawyer represents.
41. We will do our best to ensure that court personnel act civilly toward lawyers, parties, and witnesses.
42. At an appropriate time and in an appropriate manner, we will bring to a lawyer's attention conduct which we observe that is inconsistent with these standards.

Judges' Duties to Each Other:

43. We will treat other judges with courtesy and respect.
44. In written opinions and oral remarks, we will refrain from personally attacking, disparaging, or demeaning other judges.
45. We will endeavor to work cooperatively with other judges with respect to the availability of lawyers, witnesses, parties, and court resources.

PRINCIPLES PARTICULARLY APPLICABLE TO REPRESENTATIONS INVOLVING BUSINESS TRANSACTIONS AND OTHER NEGOTIATIONS

46. We will not knowingly misrepresent or mischaracterize facts or authorities or affirmatively mislead another party or its counsel in negotiations and will immediately make any clarifications and corrections as these become known to us.
47. We will not engage in personal vilification or other abusive or discourteous conduct in negotiations. We will not engage in acrimonious exchanges with opposing counsel or parties at the negotiating table. We will encourage our clients to conduct themselves in accordance with these principles.
48. We will honor all understandings with, and commitments we have made to, other attorneys. We will stand by proposals we have made in negotiations unless newly received information or unforeseen circumstances provide a good faith basis for rescinding them, and we will encourage our clients to conduct themselves in accordance with this principle.

49. We will not make changes to written documents under negotiation in a manner calculated to cause the opposing party or counsel to overlook or fail to appreciate the changes. We will clearly and accurately identify for other counsel and parties all changes that we have made in documents submitted to us for review.

50. In memorializing oral agreements the parties have reached, we will do so without making changes in substance and will strive in good faith to state the oral understandings accurately and completely. In drafting proposed agreements based on letters of intent, we will strive to draft documents that fairly reflect the agreements of the parties.

4. LEGAL SUPPORT STAFF

Organization

AMERICAN ASSOCIATION OF LAW LIBRARIES

Headquarters:
53 West Jackson Boulevard
Suite 940
Chicago, IL 60604
Telephone: (312) 939-4764
Fax: (312) 431-1097
E-mail: aallhq@aall.org
Website: http://www.aallnet.org

Date founded: 1906
Membership: approximately 4,400 librarians and institutions, including academic, law firm, corporate, bar association, state, county, court, and legislative law libraries

Code of Ethics

Official name: *Code of Ethics*
History: Adopted September 1978; currently under revision (January 1999)
Authority: Special Committee on Ethics
Code is available on Website

Additional Resources

Organizational (Divisions, Programs, Services, etc.):

Continuing Education Program
Grants Program
Task Force to Enhance Law Librarianship Education
Task Force on the Value of Law Libraries
Various Special Interest Sections:
    Academic Law Libraries
    Computing Services
    Legal Information Services to the Public

Private Law Libraries
Social Responsibilities
State, Court & County Law Libraries
Various Committees:
Mentoring and Retention
Professional Development
Relations with Information Vendors
Research

Informational (Publications, Videos, Seminars, etc.):

Articles in *AALL Spectrum* and *Law Library Journal*
Biennial Salary Survey
Directory & Handbook
Government Relations Policy
Guidelines for Graduate Programs in Law Librarianship
Guidelines on the Fair Use of Copyrighted Works by Law Libraries
Investment Policies
Law Librarianship: A Handbook
Law Libraries: Making Information Work Resource Guides
Law Library Staff Organization and Administration
Library Bill of Rights (American Library Association)
Manual of Procedures for Private Law Libraries
Model Law Firm Copyright Policy
Occasional Papers Series
Policy on Collaborative Activities and Joint Agreements
Policy Regarding "Speaking for AALL"
Preservation Policy
Principles for Licensing Electronic Resources
Professional Development Policy
Resolution on the Protection of Databases
Setting the Legal Information Agenda for the Year 2000
Telecommunications Policy
Toolkit for Law Firm Managers
*Transfer Guidelines for Records of Educational and Professional
    Associations*

Goals and Activities of Organization

The American Association of Law Libraries (AALL) recognizes that "the availability of legal information to all people is a necessary requirement for a just and democratic society." It is active in the study of matters relating to the successful management of law libraries, the exchange of ideas and information, continuing professional education for law librarians, publishing, and the promotion of the profession.

Through its committees and sections, the AALL also issues awards for distinguished legal bibliographies and publications; monitors federal copyright legislation; provides legal information services to the public; influences legislation affecting the law and law libraries; facilitates relations with publishers and dealers; studies ethical standards in publishing; drafts general guidelines to promote uniformity in the development of standards useful to law libraries; and collects and disseminates library statistics.

Implementation and Enforcement of Code

The Code states goals and guidelines for conduct, and is not enforced. The function of the Special Committee on Ethics is to redraft the Code.

Several groups within AALL frequently deal with ethical matters. The Social Responsibilities Special Interest Section studies aspects of social change and responsibility of concern to members both personally and professionally. The Committee on Relations with Information Vendors works to facilitate communication between law librarians and legal publishers and dealers, monitoring business practices and promoting high ethical standards in the field.

In addition, AALL recognizes the importance of ethics education in the professional curriculum. The Guidelines for Graduate Programs in Law Librarianship specify that accredited library schools offering such programs must provide "basic competencies" in four areas, one of which is Law and Ethics:

Law librarians must understand the legal complexities that affect access to and use of information, including copyright, freedom of information, privacy, and issues related to unauthorized practice of law and/or malpractice. Law librarians must be familiar with and understand any legal requirements and ethical considerations of both the legal profession and librarianship.

History and Development of Code

The Code was adopted in 1978. It incorporates the Statement on Professional Ethics promulgated by the American Library Association.

Planning for a revised Code began in the 1990s. In 1997 a Special Committee on Ethics was appointed by the AALL President to draft a revision to the Code. A discussion draft of ethical principles was distributed to the AALL membership for comment in mid-1998. A final proposed revision will be submitted to the membership for adoption in 1999.

Code of Ethics*

The American Association of Law Libraries espouses the statement of professional ethics promulgated by the American Library Association, which states that: "A librarian

- has a special responsibility to maintain the principles of the Library Bill of Rights.

- should learn and faithfully execute the policies of the institution of which one is a part and should endeavor to change those which conflict with the spirit of the Library Bill of Rights.

- must protect the essential confidential relationship which exists between a library user and the library.

- must avoid any possibility of personal financial gain at the expense of the employing institution.

- has an obligation to insure equality of opportunity and fair judgment of competence in actions dealing with staff appointments, retentions and promotions.

- has an obligation when making appraisal of the qualifications of any individual to report the facts clearly, accurately, and without prejudice, according to generally accepted guidelines concerning the disclosure of personal information."

In addition, the Association, in light of the special character and mission of its membership, espouses the principles that law librarians, while engaged in their professional work,

- have a duty *neither to* engage in the unauthorized practice of law *nor to solicit* an attorney-client relationship.

- have a duty to avoid any situations posing a possible *undisclosed* conflict of interest.

- have a special duty, given the nature of their patron base, to treat confidentially any private information obtained through contact with library patrons and not to divulge any confidential information to persons representing adverse interests.

- have a duty to exercise scrupulous care in avoiding any acts or even the appearance, of misappropriating the work product of library patrons or professional colleagues to their own credit or profit.

- have a duty actively to *promote* free and effective access to legal information.

- have a duty to society and the legal profession to work both individually and through their professional organizations toward *improving* the quality and *minimizing* the cost of the library component of the delivery of legal services.

---

*Adopted, September 1978. © 1996, American Association of Law Libraries. Reprinted with permission of the American Association of Law Libraries.

Organization

AMERICAN LEAGUE OF LOBBYISTS

Headquarters:
P.O. Box 30005
Alexandria VA 22310
Telephone: (703) 960-3011
Fax: (703) 960-4070
E-mail: info@alldc.org
Website: http://www.alldc.org

Date founded: 1979
Membership: approximately 500 government relations and public affairs professionals, including representatives of corporations, trade associations, labor unions, and interest groups; law and lobbying firms; and students and vendor organizations

Code of Ethics

Official name: *Code of Ethics/Guidelines for Professional Conduct*
History: Adopted September 1987
Authority: Professional Ethics & Standards Committee; Board of Directors
Code is available on Website

Additional Resources

Organizational (Divisions, Programs, Services, etc.):

Issue Sections: Defense; Environment & Energy; Health; Infrastructure; Taxation; Trade
Referral Service
Speakers Bureau

Informational (Publications, Videos, Seminars, etc.):

Articles in *ALL News*
Website information:
  How to Retain a Lobbyist
  Lobbying as a Career
  Lobbying Registration
  What is Lobbying?

Goals and Activities of Organization

The American League of Lobbyists (ALL) is a voluntary organization of public affairs professionals engaged in the First Amendment-protected activity of "advocacy of a point of view, either by groups or individuals," through education and persuasion, research and analysis of legislation, communications, and attendance at hearings.

ALL provides its members with exposure to elected officials through a variety of programs with members of Congress and staff; promotes the development of professional skills through conferences and seminars; works to inform the public about the substantive role played by lobbyists in the governmental process; encourages the implementation and advancement of ethical lobbying practices; represents the interests of its own members in legislative, executive, and judicial proceedings; and provides a referral service for pro bono representation of organizations and individuals who lack financial resources.

Implementation and Enforcement of Code

Adherence to the Guidelines is a condition for membership, but there is currently no enforcement mechanism. Rather, the document outlines the basic tenets for responsible representation in Washington, DC. Sanctions may be developed in the future.

The ALL notes that the Lobbying Disclosure Act of 1995, which requires qualified federal lobbyists to register with Congress, is not a credential system to permit lobbying, but rather a reporting system on lobbying activity.

History and Development of Code

The Guidelines were adopted in September 1987.

The American Society of Association Executives cited the ALL Guidelines as a source for the creation of its own lobbying standards, issued in 1997. [See the Business section, Management chapter, above.]

Code of Ethics/Guidelines for Professional Conduct*

The American League of Lobbyists believes that effective government depends on the greatest possible participation of those being governed. At the federal level, such participation focuses on the legislative and executive branches where professional and citizen lobbyists drawn from every major discipline represent literally every segment of society and every sector of the economy.

The League further believes that the heavy responsibility of the professional lobbyist, functioning in the eye of public opinion, requires standards of ethical behavior beyond those generally accepted by a free and moral society.

The League, therefore, offers the following guidelines which it urges be observed by its members and all those whose professional objectives are to influence national public policy decisions—

- The professional lobbyist accepts the fact that it is the system of representative government we enjoy that makes possible the practice of lobbying and, while keeping the interest of employer or client in a position of primacy, will temper the advocacy role with proper consideration for the general public interest.

- The professional lobbyist will protect confidences, not only those of the employer or client, but also those of elected and appointed officials of government and professional colleagues.

- The professional lobbyist will always deal in accurate, current and factual information, whether it is being reported to the employer or client, government officials, the media or professional colleagues, and will not engage in misrepresentation of any nature.

- The professional lobbyist will acquire enough knowledge of public policy issues to be able to fairly present all points of view.

- The professional lobbyist will avoid conflicts of interest, not only conflict with the interests of the employer or client, but also those of colleagues pursuing the same or similar objectives, and where conflict is unavoidable, will communicate the facts fully and freely to those affected.

- The professional lobbyist will comply with the laws and regulations governing lobbying as well as the standards of conduct applying to officials and staff of the Congress and the Executive Branch and will strive to go one step further and function in a manner that goes beyond these official enactments and promulgations.

- The personal conduct of the professional lobbyist should not bring discredit to the profession, government or individual colleagues.

- The professional lobbyist will refrain from any form of discrimination which is legally proscribed or simply generally recognized as such.

---

*Approved by the membership September 28, 1987. Reprinted with permission of the American League of Lobbyists.

- A priority goal of the professional lobbyist should be to increase public understanding of the process and this objective should be pursued in every possible way—public appearances, media contacts, articles in company and other publications, and contacts in the normal course of everyday life.

- The professional lobbyist should constantly strive to upgrade the necessary skills by every means available, continuing formal education, attendance at meetings and seminars, and participation in ad hoc groups with like-minded colleagues.

Organization

NATIONAL ASSOCIATION OF LEGAL ASSISTANTS

Headquarters:
1516 South Boston Avenue
Suite 200
Tulsa, OK 74119
Telephone: (918) 587-6828
Fax: (918) 582-6772
E-mail: nalanet@nala.org
Website: http://www.nala.org

Date founded: 1975
Membership: approximately 6,500 individual legal assistants plus 91 state and local affiliates, with a combined membership in excess of 17,000

Codes of Ethics

Official name: *Code of Ethics and Professional Responsibility*
History: Adopted 1975; revised 1979, 1988, and 1995

Official name: *Model Standards and Guidelines for Utilization of Legal Assistants*
History: Adopted 1984; revised 1991, 1997
Authority: NALA membership

Codes are available on Website

Additional Resources

Organizational (Divisions, Programs, Services, etc.):

Certified Legal Assistant and CLA Specialist Credentials Programs
Continuing Legal Education
Conventions and Workshops
Member Exchange Program (leading special educational seminars)
NALA NET (online information service)

Informational (Publications, Videos, Seminars, etc.):

Articles in *FACTS & FINDINGS* and *NALA News & Information* (online)
Career Chronicle
Ethical Challenges in Today's Environment (conference session)
Licensure and Certification: Myths and Facts
NALA Manual for Legal Assistants
National Utilization and Compensation Survey Report

Goals and Activities of Organization

The promulgation of ethical standards for legal assistants or para-legals—persons who assist lawyers in the delivery of legal services—is the first goal of the National Association of Legal Assistants (NALA). Its activities include the establishment and administration of the Certified Legal Assistant (CLA) program for national voluntary certification; cooperation with local, state, and national bar associations in setting standards for legal assistants; becoming involved in cases affecting the legal assistant career field; promotion of the profession, including educating the public to broaden understanding of the functions of legal assistants; and providing continuing legal education to members.

NALA monitors activities among the states and keeps members informed as to issues of ethics and professionalism as they affect legal assistants. NALA Net, its online information service, tracks pertinent legislation, state ethics opinions, court decisions, bar association guidelines and membership requirements, and journal articles concerning the profession and its role in the delivery of legal services.

The NALA credentialing program is a form of self-regulation designed to strengthen and expand the development of the profession. Ethics is one of the major subject areas of the examination. The CLA designation may be revoked for a violation of the Code of Ethics.

Implementation and Enforcement of Codes

Ethical considerations are stressed throughout all NALA materials. A legal assistant is governed by rules of conduct of the American Bar Association and of state and local courts and bar associations.

All members of NALA and its affiliated organizations agree to be bound by the NALA Code of Ethics by signing a statement on the membership application. The Bylaws provide that violation of the Code is cause for removal.

The following documents describe how legal assistants are expected to conduct themselves, and outline minimum qualifications and standards necessary to assure the public and the legal profession. They are not intended to be exhaustive or comprehensive, but to serve as guides to proper conduct.

While the Code and Standards may not have universal application, they are intended to be definitive models for bar associations and other organizations that are interested in setting up voluntary standards for legal assistants. If regulation is to be imposed, they serve as comprehensive resources and educational tools.

Supervising attorneys must be aware of the specific rules, decisions, and statutes applicable to legal assistants in their particular jurisidictions.

History and Development of Codes

The Code of Ethics was adopted in 1975; revisions were made in 1979, 1988, and July 1995. The Model Standards and Guidelines were adopted in 1984 and revised in 1991 and 1997, primarily to update the annotated discussions. Both documents are current as of April 1998.

Sources for their development and annotation include the codes of ethics of the American Bar Association and various state courts and bar associations, and the reasoning and rules of law in many reported decisions involving professional discipline and the unauthorized practice of law.

Code of Ethics and Professional Responsibility*

Preamble.

A legal assistant must adhere strictly to the accepted standards of legal ethics and to the general principles of proper conduct. The performance of the duties of the legal assistant shall be governed by specific canons as defined herein so that justice will be served and goals of the profession attained.

The canons of ethics set forth hereafter are adopted by the National Association of Legal Assistants, Inc., as a general guide intended to aid legal assistants and attorneys. The enumeration of these rules does not mean there are not others of equal importance although not specifically mentioned. Court rules, agency rules and statutes must be taken into consideration when interpreting the canons.

Definition.

Legal assistants, also known as paralegals, are a distinguishable group of persons who assist attorneys in the delivery of legal services. Through formal education, training and experience, legal assistants have knowledge and expertise regarding the legal system and substantive and procedural law which qualify them to do work of a legal nature under the supervision of an attorney.

Canon 1.

A legal assistant must not perform any of the duties that attorneys only may perform nor take any actions that attorneys may not take.

Canon 2.

A legal assistant may perform any task which is properly delegated and supervised by an attorney, as long as the attorney is ultimately responsible to the client, maintains a direct relationship with the client, and assumes professional responsibility for the work product.

Canon 3.

A legal assistant must not:
(a) engage in, encourage, or contribute to any act which could constitute the unauthorized practice of law; and
(b) establish attorney-client relationships, set fees, give legal opinions or advice, or represent a client before a court or agency unless so authorized by that court or agency; and
(c) engage in conduct or take any action which would assist or involve the attorney in a violation of professional ethics or give the appearance of professional impropriety.

---

*Adopted May 1, 1975. Revised 1979, 1988, and 1995. Copyright © National Association of Legal Assistants, Inc. All rights reserved. Reprinted with permission.

References in the text to the *Model Standards and Guidelines for Utilization of Legal Assistants* have been omitted.

Canon 4.

A legal assistant must use discretion and professional judgment commensurate with knowledge and experience but must not render independent legal judgment in place of an attorney. The services of an attorney are essential in the public interest whenever such legal judgment is required.

Canon 5.

A legal assistant must disclose his or her status as a legal assistant at the outset of any professional relationship with a client, attorney, a court or administrative agency or personnel thereof, or a member of the general public. A legal assistant must act prudently in determining the extent to which a client may be assisted without the presence of an attorney.

Canon 6.

A legal assistant must strive to maintain integrity and a high degree of competency through education and training with respect to professional responsibility, local rules and practice, and through continuing education in substantive areas of law to better assist the legal profession in fulfilling its duty to provide legal service.

Canon 7.

A legal assistant must protect the confidences of a client and must not violate any rule or statute now in effect or hereafter enacted controlling the doctrine of privileged communications between a client and an attorney.

Canon 8.

A legal assistant must do all other things incidental, necessary, or expedient for the attainment of the ethics and responsibilities as defined by statute or rule of court.

Canon 9.

A legal assistant's conduct is guided by bar associations' codes of professional responsibility and rules of professional conduct.

Model Standards and Guidelines for Utilization of Legal Assistants*

INTRODUCTION

* * *

The Guidelines represent a statement of how the legal assistant may function. The Guidelines are not intended to be a comprehensive or exhaustive list of the proper duties of a legal assistant. Rather, they are designed as guides to what may or may not be proper conduct for the legal assistant. In formulating the Guidelines, the reasoning and rules of law in many reported decisions of disciplinary cases and unauthorized practice of law cases have been analyzed and considered. In addition, the provisions of the American Bar Association's Model Rules of Professional Conduct, as well as the ethical promulgations of various state courts and bar associations have been considered in the development of the Guidelines.

These Guidelines form a sound basis for the legal assistant and the supervising attorney to follow. This Model will serve as * * * a definitive, well-reasoned guide to those considering voluntary standards and guidelines for legal assistants.

I. PREAMBLE

Proper utilization of the services of legal assistants contributes to the delivery of cost-effective, high-quality legal services. Legal assistants and the legal profession should be assured that measures exist for identifying legal assistants and their role in assisting attorneys in the delivery of legal services. Therefore, the National Association of Legal Assistants, Inc., hereby adopts these Standards and Guidelines as an educational document for the benefit of legal assistants and the legal profession.

COMMENT

The three most frequently raised questions concerning legal assistants are (1) How do you define a legal assistant; (2) Who is qualified to be identified as a legal assistant; and (3) What duties may a legal assistant perform? The definition adopted in 1984 by the National Association of Legal Assistants answers the first question. The Model sets forth minimum education, training and experience through standards which will assure that an individual utilizing the title "legal assistant" has the qualifications to be held out to the legal community and the public in that capacity. The Guidelines identify those acts which the reported cases hold to be proscribed and give examples of services which the legal assistant may perform under the supervision of a licensed attorney.

These Guidelines constitute a statement relating to services performed by legal assistants, as defined herein, as approved by court decisions and other sources of authority. The purpose of the Guidelines is not to place limitations or restrictions on the legal assistant profession. Rather, the Guidelines are intended to outline

---

*Adopted 1984; Revised 1991, 1997. Copyright © 1997 National Association of Legal Assistants, Inc. All rights reserved. Reprinted with permission.

All legal citations and the entire Addendum (case references) have been omitted.

for the legal profession an acceptable course of conduct. Voluntary recognition and utilization of the Standards and Guidelines will benefit the entire legal profession and the public it serves.

II. DEFINITION

The National Association of Legal Assistants adopted the following definition in 1984:

Legal assistants, also known as paralegals, are a distinguishable group of persons who assist attorneys in the delivery of legal services. Through formal education, training, and experience, legal assistants have knowledge and expertise regarding the legal system and substantive and procedural law which qualify them to do work of a legal nature under the supervision of an attorney.

COMMENT

This definition emphasizes the knowledge and expertise of legal assistants in substantive and procedural law obtained through education and work experience. It further defines the legal assistant or paralegal as a professional working under the supervision of an attorney as distinguished from a non-lawyer who delivers services directly to the public without any intervention or review of work product by an attorney. Statutes, court rules, case law and bar associations are additional sources for legal assistant or paralegal definitions. In applying the Standards and Guidelines, it is important to remember that they were developed to apply to the legal assistant as defined herein.

Lawyers should refrain from labeling those who do not meet the criteria set forth in this definition, such as secretaries and other administrative staff, as legal assistants.

For billing purposes, the services of a legal secretary are considered part of overhead costs and are not recoverable in fee awards. However, the courts have held that fees for paralegal services are recoverable as long as they are not clerical functions, such as organizing files, copying documents, checking docket, updating files, checking court dates and delivering papers. * * * [T]asks performed by legal assistants must be substantive in nature which, absent the legal assistant, the attorney would perform.

There are also case law and Supreme Court Rules addressing the issue of a disbarred attorney serving in the capacity of a legal assistant.

III. STANDARDS

A legal assistant should meet certain minimum qualifications. The following standards may be used to determine an individual's qualifications as a legal assistant:

1. Successful completion of the Certified Legal Assistant ("CLA") certifying examination of the National Association of Legal Assistants, Inc.;
2. Graduation from an ABA approved program of study for legal assistants;
3. Graduation from a course of study for legal assistants which is institutionally accredited but not ABA approved, and which requires not less than the equivalent of 60 semester hours of classroom study;

4. Graduation from a course of study for legal assistants, other than those set forth in (2) and (3) above, plus not less than six months of in-house training as a legal assistant;
5. A baccalaureate degree in any field, plus not less than six months in-house training as a legal assistant;
6. A minimum of three years of law-related experience under the supervision of an attorney, including at least six months of in-house training as a legal assistant; or
7. Two years of in-house training as a legal assistant.

For purposes of these Standards, "in-house training as a legal assistant" means attorney education of the employee concerning legal assistant duties and these Guidelines. In addition to review and analysis of assignments, the legal assistant should receive a reasonable amount of instruction directly related to the duties and obligations of the legal assistant.

COMMENT

The Standards set forth suggest minimum qualifications for a legal assistant. These minimum qualifications, as adopted, recognize legal related work backgrounds and formal education backgrounds, both of which provide the legal assistant with a broad base in exposure to and knowledge of the legal profession. This background is necessary to assure the public and the legal profession that the employee identified as a legal assistant is qualified.

The Certified Legal Assistant ("CLA") examination established by NALA in 1976 is a voluntary nationwide certification program for legal assistants. The CLA designation is a statement to the legal profession and the public that the legal assistant has met the high levels of knowledge and professionalism required by NALA's certification program. Continuing education requirements, which all certified legal assistants must meet, assure that high standards are maintained. The CLA designation has been recognized as a means of establishing the qualifications of a legal assistant in supreme court rules, state court and bar association standards and utilization guidelines.

Certification through NALA is available to all legal assistants meeting the educational and experience requirements. Certified Legal Assistants may also pursue advanced specialty certification ("CLAS") in the areas of bankruptcy, civil litigation, probate and estate planning, corporate and business law, criminal law and procedure, real estate, intellectual property, and may also pursue state certification based on state laws and procedures [* * *].

IV. GUIDELINES

These Guidelines relating to standards of performance and professional responsibility are intended to aid legal assistants and attorneys. The ultimate responsibility rests with an attorney who employs legal assistants to educate them with respect to the duties they are assigned and to supervise the manner in which such duties are accomplished.

COMMENT

In general, a legal assistant is allowed to perform any task which is properly delegated and supervised by an attorney, as long as the attorney is ultimately responsible to the client and assumes complete professional responsibility for the work product.

ABA Model Rules of Professional Conduct, Rule 5.3 provides:

With respect to a non-lawyer employed or retained by or associated with a lawyer:

>   (a) a partner in a law firm shall make reasonable efforts to ensure that the firm has in effect measures giving reasonable assurance that the person's conduct is compatible with the professional obligations of the lawyer;

>   (b) a lawyer having direct supervisory authority over the non-lawyer shall make reasonable efforts to ensure that the person's conduct is compatible with the professional obligations of the lawyer; and

>   (c) a lawyer shall be responsible for conduct of such a person that would be a violation of the rules of professional conduct if engaged in by a lawyer if:

>>   (1) the lawyer orders or, with the knowledge of the specific conduct ratifies the conduct involved; or

>>   (2) the lawyer is a partner in the law firm in which the person is employed, or has direct supervisory authority over the person, and knows of the conduct at a time when its consequences can be avoided or mitigated but fails to take remedial action.

There are many interesting and complex issues involving the use of legal assistants. In any discussion of the proper role of a legal assistant, attention must be directed to what constitutes the practice of law. Proper delegation to legal assistants is further complicated and confused by the lack of an adequate definition of the practice of law.

Kentucky became the first state to adopt a Paralegal Code by Supreme Court Rule. This Code sets forth certain exclusions to the unauthorized practice of law:

For purposes of this rule, the unauthorized practice of law shall not include any service rendered involving legal knowledge or advice, whether representation, counsel or advocacy, in or out of court, rendered in respect to the acts, duties, obligations, liabilities or business relations of the one requiring services where:

A. The client understands that the paralegal is not a lawyer;

B. The lawyer supervises the paralegal in the performance of his or her duties; and

C. The lawyer remains fully responsible for such representation including all actions taken or not taken in connection therewith by the paralegal to the same extent as if such representation had been furnished entirely by the lawyer and all such actions had been taken or not taken directly by the attorney. * * * [Footnote omitted.]

South Dakota['s] Supreme Court Rule * * * states:

The attorney remains responsible for the services performed by the legal assistant to the same extent as though such services had been furnished entirely by the attorney and such actions were those of the attorney.

Guideline 1

Legal assistants should:

1. Disclose their status as legal assistants at the outset of any professional relationship with a client, other attorneys, a court or administrative agency or personnel thereof, or members of the general public;
2. Preserve the confidences and secrets of all clients; and
3. Understand the attorney's Rules of Professional Responsibility and these Guidelines in order to avoid any action which would involve the attorney in a violation of the Rules, or give the appearance of professional impropriety.

COMMENT

Routine early disclosure of the legal assistant's status when dealing with persons outside the attorney's office is necessary to assure that there will be no misunderstanding as to the responsibilities and role of the legal assistant. Disclosure may be made in any way that avoids confusion. If the person dealing with the legal assistant already knows of his/her status, further disclosure is unnecessary. If at any time in written or oral communication the legal assistant becomes aware that the other person may believe the legal assistant is an attorney, immediate disclosure should be made as to the legal assistant's status.

The attorney should exercise care that the legal assistant preserves and refrains from using any confidence or secrets of a client, and should instruct the legal assistant not to disclose or use any such confidences or secrets.

The legal assistant must take any and all steps necessary to prevent conflicts of interest and fully disclose such conflicts to the supervising attorney. Failure to do so may jeopardize both the attorney's representation of the client and the case itself.

* * *

The ultimate responsibility for compliance with approved standards of professional conduct rests with the supervising attorney. The burden rests upon the attorney who employs a legal assistant to educate the latter with respect to the duties which may be assigned and then to supervise the manner in which the legal assistant carries out such duties. However, this does not relieve the legal assistant from an independent obligation to refrain from illegal conduct. Additionally, and notwithstanding that the Rules are not binding upon non-lawyers, the very nature of a legal assistant's employment imposes an obligation not to engage in conduct which would involve the supervising attorney in a violation of the Rules.

The attorney must make sufficient background investigation of the prior activities and character and integrity of his or her legal assistants.

Further, the attorney must take all measures necessary to avoid and fully disclose conflicts of interest due to other employment or interests. Failure to do so may jeopardize both the attorney's representation of the client and the case itself.

Legal assistant associations strive to maintain the high level of integrity and competence expected of the legal profession and, further, strive to uphold the high standards of ethics.

NALA's Code of Ethics and Professional Responsibility states:

A legal assistant's conduct is guided by bar associations' codes of professional responsibility and rules of professional conduct.

Guideline 2

Legal assistants should not:

1. Establish attorney-client relationships; set legal fees; give legal opinions or advice; or represent a client before a court, unless authorized to do so by said court; nor
2. Engage in, encourage, or contribute to any act which could constitute the unauthorized practice law.

COMMENT

Case law, court rules, codes of ethics and professional responsibilities, as well as bar ethics opinions now hold which acts can and cannot be performed by a legal assistant. Generally, the determination of what acts constitute the unauthorized practice of law is made by State Supreme Courts.

Numerous cases exist relating to the unauthorized practice of law. Courts have gone so far as to prohibit the legal assistant from preparation of divorce kits and assisting in preparation of bankruptcy forms and, more specifically, from providing basic information about procedures and requirements, deciding where information should be placed on forms, and responding to questions from debtors regarding the interpretation or definition of terms.

Cases have identified certain areas in which an attorney has a duty to act, but it is interesting to note that none of these cases state that it is improper for an attorney to have the initial work performed by the legal assistant. This again points out the importance of adequate supervision by the employing attorney.

An attorney can be found to have aided in the unauthorized practice of law when delegating acts which cannot be performed by a legal assistant.

Guideline 3

Legal assistants may perform services for an attorney in the representation of a client, provided:

1. The services performed by the legal assistant do not require the exercise of independent professional legal judgment;
2. The attorney maintains a direct relationship with the client and maintains control of all client matters;
3. The attorney supervises the legal assistant;
4. The attorney remains professionally responsible for all work on behalf of the client, including any actions taken or not taken by the legal assistant in connection therewith; and
5. The services performed supplement, merge with and become the attorney's work product.

COMMENT:

Legal assistants, whether employees or independent contractors, perform services for the attorney in the representation of a client. Attorneys should delegate work to legal assistants commensurate with their knowledge and experience and provide appropriate instruction and supervision concerning the delegated work, as well as ethical acts of their employment. Ultimate responsibility for the work product of a legal assistant rests with the attorney. However, a legal assistant must use discretion and professional judgment and must not render independent legal judgment in place of an attorney.

The work product of a legal assistant is subject to civil rules governing discovery of materials prepared in anticipation of litigation, whether the legal assistant is viewed as an extension of the attorney or as another representative of the party itself. * * *

Guideline 4

In the supervision of a legal assistant, consideration should be given to:

1. Designating work assignments that correspond to the legal assistant's abilities, knowledge, training and experience;
2. Educating and training the legal assistant with respect to professional responsibility, local rules and practices, and firm policies;
3. Monitoring the work and professional conduct of the legal assistant to ensure that the work is substantively correct and timely performed;
4. Providing continuing education for the legal assistant in substantive matters through courses, institutes, workshops, seminars and in-house training; and
5. Encouraging and supporting membership and active participation in professional organizations.

COMMENT

Attorneys are responsible for the actions of their employees in both malpractice and disciplinary proceedings. In the vast majority of cases, the courts have not censured attorneys for a particular act delegated to the legal assistant, but rather, have been critical of and imposed sanctions against attorneys for failure to adequately supervise the legal assistant. The attorney's responsibility for supervision of his or her legal assistant must be more than a willingness to accept responsibility and liability for the legal assistant's work. Supervision of a legal assistant must be offered in both the procedural and substantive legal areas. The attorney must delegate work based upon the education, knowledge and abilities of the legal assistant and must monitor the work product and conduct of the legal assistant to insure that the work performed is substantively correct and competently performed in a professional manner.

Michigan * * * guidelines, in part, encourage employers to support legal assistant participation in continuing education programs to ensure that the legal assistant remains competent in the fields of practice in which the legal assistant is assigned.

The working relationship between the lawyer and the legal assistant should extend to cooperative efforts on public service activities wherever possible. Participation in pro bono activities is encouraged in ABA Guideline 10.

Guideline 5

Except as otherwise provided by statute, court rule or decision, administrative rule or regulation, or the attorney's rules of professional responsibility, and within the preceding parameters and proscriptions, a legal assistant may perform any function delegated by an attorney, including, but not limited to the following:

1. Conduct client interviews and maintain general contact with the client after the establishment of the attorney-client relationship, so long as the client is aware of the status and function of the legal assistant, and the client contact is under the supervision of the attorney.
2. Locate and interview witnesses, so long as the witnesses are aware of the status and function of the legal assistant.
3. Conduct investigations and statistical and documentary research for review by the attorney.
4. Conduct legal research for review by the attorney.
5. Draft legal documents for review by the attorney.
6. Draft correspondence and pleadings for review by and signature of the attorney.
7. Summarize depositions, interrogatories and testimony for review by the attorney.
8. Attend executions of wills, real estate closings, depositions, court or administrative hearings and trials with the attorney.
9. Author and sign letters providing the legal assistant's status is clearly indicated and the correspondence does not contain independent legal opinions or legal advice.

COMMENT:

The United States Supreme Court has recognized the variety of tasks being performed by legal assistants and has noted that use of legal assistants encourages cost-effective delivery of legal services * * * . In [*Missouri v. Jenkins*, (1989)], the court further held that legal assistant time should be included in compensation for attorney fee awards at the rate in the relevant community to bill legal assistant time.

Courts have held that legal assistant fees are not a part of the overall overhead of a law firm. Legal assistant services are billed separately by attorneys, and decrease litigation expenses. Tasks performed by legal assistants must contain substantive legal work under the direction or supervision of an attorney, such that if the legal assistant were not present, the work would be performed by the attorney.

[The Oklahoma] Court ruled that attorney fees awarded should include fees for services performed by legal assistants and, further, defined tasks which may be performed by the legal assistant under the supervision of an attorney * * * .

Except for the specific proscription contained in Guideline 1, the reported cases do not limit the duties which may be performed by a legal assistant under the supervision of the attorney.

An attorney may not split legal fees with a legal assistant, nor pay a legal assistant for the referral of legal business. An attorney may compensate a legal assistant based on the quantity and quality of the legal assistant's work and value of that work to a law practice.

CONCLUSION

These Standards and Guidelines were developed from generally accepted practices. Each supervising attorney must be aware of the specific rules, decisions and statutes applicable to legal assistants within his/her jurisdiction.

5. LITIGATION

Organization

ASSOCIATION OF TRIAL LAWYERS OF AMERICA

Headquarters:
1050 31st Street, NW
Washington, DC 20007-4499
Telephone: (202) 965-3500
(800) 424-2725
Fax: (202) 965-0920
E-mail: help@atlahq.org
Website: http://www.atlanet.org

Date founded: 1946
Founded as the National Association of Claimant's Compensation Attorneys; renamed 1964 and 1971
Membership: approximately 60,000 plaintiffs' attorneys, judges, law professors, paralegals, and law students

Code of Ethics

Official name: *Code of Conduct*
History: First issued early 1980s; revised and adopted 1988; implemented 1991
Authority: Committee on Ethical Conduct; ATLA membership; Board of Governors
Code is available on Website (ATLA members only)

Additional Resources

Organizational (Divisions, Programs, Services, etc.):

ATLA Exchange (referral service)
ATLA NET (online information service)
Attorney's Information Exchange Group, Inc. (product defect litigation)
Civil Justice Foundation (coalition with consumer advocacy organizations)
National College of Advocacy (training programs)
Professional Liability Insurance

Roscoe Pound Foundation (programs, publications, and research)
Various Litigation Groups (by subject area)
Various Sections: Admiralty Law; Aviation Law; Civil Rights; Commercial Litigation; Criminal Law; Employment Rights Law; Family Law; Federal Tort Liability and Military Advocacy; Insurance; International Practice; Motor Vehicle Collision, Highway, and Premises Liability; Products Liability; Professional Negligence; Railroad Law; Toxic Environmental, and Pharmaceutical Tort Litigation; Social Security Disability; Workers' Compensation and Workplace Injury

Informational (Publications, Videos, Seminars, etc.):

Articles in *Trial* magazine, *Law Reporter, ATLA Advocate, Civil Justice Digest,* and individual Section publications
Anatomy of a Personal Injury Lawsuit: How to Be a Trial Lawyer
Civil Justice Fact Sheets
Essays on Advocacy
Excellence in Advocacy: Trial Expertise
Full Disclosure: Combatting Stonewalling & Other Discovery Abuses
Procedures for Resolution of Complaints Against Members of the Association
Professional Negligence Law Reporter (newsletter)
Reports of the Chief Justice Earl Warren Conferences on Advocacy: Ethics and Government
Resolution on Professional Ethics Regarding the Use of Contingent Fees
Taking the Rules to Court
What is a Lawyer (video)

Goals and Activities of Organization

The Association of Trial Lawyers of America (ATLA) is the world's largest trial bar association. Among its goals are to seek justice and fairness for injured persons; to safeguard victims' rights, particularly the right to trial by jury; to strengthen the civil justice system through public education; and "uphold the honor and dignity of the legal profession and the highest standards of ethical conduct and integrity."

ATLA takes a stand on public policy issues that affect the trial bar and individual litigants. It opposes legislation that would erode victims' rights, and any form of secrecy in the courts that limits the disclosure of information critical to public health and safety.

ATLA encourages lawyers to report dangerous products and other hazards to appropriate regulatory authorities, since lawyers are often the first to uncover design defects, and have the responsibility to act in the public interest.

The Professional Negligence Section promotes research and study in cases concerning liability in a wide range of professions, such as medicine, engineering, architecture, clergy, and the law.

Implementation and Enforcement of Code

The Code is intended to make paramount the interests of clients and potential clients—victims of injuries and their families. The Code's ban on lawyer solicitation is designed to protect a victim's privacy, emotional well-being, and right to make an unpressured decision about legal representation.

Recent federal proposals to restrict the time within which lawyers may contact accident victims do not go as far as ATLA policy, which prohibits members or their representatives from initiating contact intended to solicit a potential client, regardless of when the accident occurred.

Regarding the use of contingent fees, the Board of Governors adopted in 1986 a professional ethics resolution that states in part:

> [T]here is absolutely no proof, nor data, that the contingent fee bears any relationship to the cost of insurance or the size of awards or settlements, or the encouragement of frivolous lawsuits.
> We support the freedom of contract between attorneys and the public.
> We oppose any legislative regulation of attorneys' fees.
> We recognize the right of the judiciary to supervise attorneys' fees * * *.

The resolution recommends that lawyers "exercise sound judgment" in setting contingent fees, and opposes "excessive and unnecessary" plaintiff or defense fees.

ATLA's Committee on Ethical Conduct administers disciplinary procedures involving members. It may review allegations of misconduct based on information that comes to its attention from any source.

After a preliminary investigation, the Committee may dismiss the matter or issue a public or private reprimand against the member; or it may institute formal charges and arrange to hold a procedural (as opposed to a formal, legal) due process hearing. The accused has rights to notice and an opportunity to respond, and to conduct a defense represented by counsel. The member's resignation from ATLA while charges are pending may be interpreted as an admission of the allegations, and may not necessarily terminate the proceedings.

Sanctions for a finding of misconduct are censure, suspension, or expulsion from ATLA. The decision and penalties may be reviewed by an Appellate Board appointed by the President. The Committee may report to the general membership the status of any action arising from non-confidential investigations.

History and Development of Code

The present Code was adopted by the membership in July 1988. ATLA requested an advisory opinion from the Federal Trade Commission as to whether one of the Code sanctions, expulsion from membership, constituted an unlawful restraint of trade. The FTC found that the Code would not have an "anticompetitive effect"; ATLA gave members notice of the Code's implementation in March 1991.

ATLA's previous set of standards was "The American Lawyer's Code of Conduct," developed in the early 1980s by the Commission on Professional Responsibility. Its creation, largely in response to the American Bar Association's rules, followed a 1978 ATLA Conference on Ethics and Advocacy.

Procedures for resolving complaints against members were established by the Board of Governors in November 1994.

Code of Conduct*

1. No ATLA member shall personally, or through a representative, contact any party, or an aggrieved survivor in an attempt to solicit a potential client when there has been no request for such contact from the injured party, an aggrieved survivor, or a relative of either, or the injured parties' union representative.

2. No ATLA member shall go to the scene of an event which caused injury unless requested to do so by an interested party, an aggrieved survivor, a relative of either, or by an attorney representing an injured party or survivor.

3. No ATLA member shall initiate a television appearance or initiate any comment to any news media concerning an event causing injury within 10 days of the event unless the member forgoes any financial return from the compensation of those injured or killed, provided, however, that an individual designated by a bar association to state the official position of such bar association may initiate such media contact to communicate such position.

4. No ATLA member shall personally, or through an associate attorney, file a complaint with a specific *ad damnum* amount unless required by local rules of court. If such amount is stated, it shall be based upon good faith evaluation of facts which the member can demonstrate.

5. No ATLA member shall personally, or through a representative, make representations of trial experience or past results of litigation either of which is in any way false or misleading.

6. No ATLA member shall personally, or through a representative, initiate personal contact with a potential client (who is not a client, former client, relative or close personal friend of the attorney) for the purpose of advising that individual of the possibility of an unrecognized legal claim for damages unless the member forgoes any financial interest in the compensation of the injured party.

7. No ATLA member shall file or maintain a frivolous suit, issue, or position. However, no ATLA member should refrain from urging or arguing any suit, issue or position that he believes in good faith to have merit.

8. The ATLA Board of Governors has condemned attorneys or legal clinics who advertise for clients in personal injury cases and who have no intention of handling the cases themselves, but do so for the sole purpose of brokering the case to other attorneys. Any ATLA member who enters a contract of representation on behalf of a claimant shall, at the time of retention, fully advise the client, in writing, of all relationships with other attorneys who will be involved in the presentation, the role each attorney shall play, and the proposed division of fees among them. The client shall also be promptly advised of all changes affecting the representation.

9. No ATLA member shall knowingly accept a referral from a person, whether an ATLA member or not, who obtained the representation by conduct which this code prohibits.

---

*Adopted by the membership of the Association of Trial Lawyers of America, July 31, 1988. Reprinted with permission.

Organization

NATIONAL DISTRICT ATTORNEYS ASSOCIATION

Headquarters:
99 Canal Center Plaza
Suite 510
Alexandria, VA 22314
Telephone: (703) 549-9222
Fax: (703) 836-3195
Website: http://www.ndaa.org/ndaa.htm

Date founded: 1950
 Was the National Association of County and Prosecuting Attorneys until 1959
Membership: approximately 7,000 state and local prosecuting attorneys, assistant prosecutors, investigators, victim witness advocates, and paralegals

Code of Ethics

Official name: *National Prosecution Standards*
History: First Edition 1977; Second Edition 1991, amended January/ February 1997
Authority: Prosecution Standards and Ethics Committee; National Prosecution Standards Advisory Committee; Board of Directors

Additional Resources

Organizational (Divisions, Programs, Services, etc.):
America's Prosecutors Annual Conference
American Prosecutors Research Institute (APRI) (research, programs, publications, and training)
Emerging Technologies Ad Hoc Subcommittee
National Advocacy Center (training facility operated with U.S. Department of Justice Executive Office of U.S. Attorneys)
National College of District Attorneys (trial advocacy programs)

Policy and Legislation Committee
Professional Liability Insurance Protection

Informational (Publications, Videos, Seminars, etc.):

Articles in *The Prosecutor* magazine
Case Commentaries & Briefs (newsletter)
Community Prosecution Implementation Manual (APRI)
Domestic Violence: Prosecutors Take the Lead (APRI)
Environmental Crime Prosecution: A Comprehensive Analysis of District Attorneys' Efforts in this Emerging Area of Criminal Enforcement (APRI)
Investigation and Prosecution of Child Abuse (APRI)
Investigation and Prosecution of Parental Abduction (APRI)
National Prosecution Standards, First Edition
When You're in the News . . . You are the News (video)

Goals and Activities of Organization

The National District Attorneys Association (NDAA) is a nonprofit institution originally founded in response to the growth of organized crime and the increasing difficulty in monitoring interstate crime, and represents the interests of district attorneys from the largest to the smallest jurisdictions.

The NDAA sponsors seminars, undertakes special projects, serves as an educational resource, acts as a legislative advocate, and provides professional liability insurance. The governmental relations office assists members in their work with Congress, courts, regulatory agencies, and the executive branch, with legislative research and by locating key personnel.

The training arm of NDAA, the National College of District Attorneys, conducts trial advocacy programs at the National Advocacy Center, a facility to be operated jointly with the U.S. Department of Justice Executive Office of U.S. Attorneys.

The American Prosecutors Research Institute (APRI) is a nonprofit research and program development resource and national clearinghouse of information on the prosecutorial function. It supports high professional standards and specialized training for prosecutors.

Implementation and Enforcement of Code

The NDAA Standards are "a necessary part of an optimal system of justice," to be considered directional and flexible. They are the reactions and reflections of the nation's prosecutors, as represented by the NDAA and the Task Forces and Committees that developed and revised the Standards.

Prosecutors are not to be sanctioned for not following the Standards. The Standards are not intended to ignore or usurp the authority of current case law or ethics opinions. Prosecutors must be thoroughly aware of and comply with the controlling legal authority of their jurisdictions, including codes of professional responsibility as adopted by the state and local bar associations.

The Standards should be applied where possible, with prosecutors expanding or modifying them to suit local needs. Prosecutors are to urge their widespread adoption and cooperatively seek the support of a wide spectrum of agencies and organizations, including state legislatures, courts, and police.

Any amendments to the Standards must be approved by the Prosecution Management and Standards Committee. The Committee's work focuses on issues of management of the prosecutor's office. It also discusses modifications to the American Bar Association's standards regarding prosecution.

History and Development of Code

The First Edition of the Standards was developed between 1974 and 1977 by several Task Forces of prosecutors. Their work was reviewed by other Task Forces, the NDAA Board of Directors, and individuals outside of prosecution. The whole project was subject to a multi-faceted evaluation process. A post-project analysis was used to determine the impact of the material.

The NDAA initiated the revision of the Standards in 1989. Through a series of meetings held over 13 months, the Prosecution Management and Standards Committee reviewed, revised, and adopted the new rules as they progressed through a series of drafts. The Committee frequently turned to the original Standards for direction, ideas, and language. The drafts were later scrutinized by the National Prosecution Standards Advisory Committee, before their adoption by the Board of Directors.

The most dramatic differences between the First and Second Editions are: the new Standards are not limited to ethical provisions, nor to matters under the direct control of local prosecutors; they have been restructured and reorganized to focus attention in the opening section on prosecutorial functions, administration, and relationships, and in the remaining sections, to focus on prosecutorial procedures; many topics have been deleted or added, to reduce repetition and maintain relevance to the times; and finally, the Commentaries are less detailed.

Among the sources for the Standards are the American Bar Association's Standards for Criminal Justice, the National Advisory Commission on Criminal Justice's Standards and Goals, the American Law Institute's Code of Criminal Procedure and Model Penal Code, and the codes of ethics of "virtually every analogous standard-setting body in America."

In 1997, the NDAA issued amendments to the Standards addressing prosecutors' relationships with the public and the media. The new and revised Sections are:

Protections of Rights of Accused and Public
Prosecutors and the Media
Media Comments—Judicial Decisions, Jury Verdicts and Conduct

National Prosecution Standards*

INTRODUCTION

Background

* * *

While the *National Prosecution Standards* (1977) "NPS" continue to serve as a reference source on the prosecution function, the passage of time has diminished its original intent and impact. The applicability of standards established within a system at a particular point in time is often reduced quickly when that system is as dynamic as that of criminal justice. Even though the original standards had a visionary perspective, the passage of * * * years has resulted in a natural consequence of limited direction for subsequent future changes in the criminal justice system and the prosecution function.

* * *

Changes in fundamental approaches to the practice of law have been profound as well. In 1983, the rules of ethics took a substantial change of direction when the American Bar Association promulgated the Model Rules of Professional Conduct, replacing the Model Code of Professional Responsibility. Additionally, the profession elevated its focus on ethics and professionalism. Many jurisdictions have developed codes of professionalism as a method of enhancing civility in the courtroom. The quality of life of lawyers working long, hard hours in contentious, adversarial environments has emerged as an issue at the same time that the beginning salaries of new associates in major law firms have approached that of the chief prosecutor.

New social problems have emerged * * *, creating a need for new prosecution standards. * * *

As case law and statutes sometimes are reflective of social change, they, too, have influenced the need to revise the standards, as well as rendered direction for that revision. * * * [O]nly contemporary standards can be used by prosecutors to demonstrate issues and serve as persuasion before courts, legislatures, and other governing bodies.

All of these circumstances combine to create the need to revise prosecution standards. While the original work is far from obsolete, its utility could only be made contemporary by thorough review, revision, and the development of new standards.

---

*Second Edition. © 1991, 1997 by the National District Attorneys Association. Amendments reprinted from *The Prosecutor*, Vol. 31, No. 1, January/February 1997. All rights reserved. Reprinted with permission. First edition published 1977. This publication was developed under a grant from the State Justice Institute. Points of view expressed herein are those of the author [National District Attorneys Association] and do not necessarily represent the official position or policies of the State Justice Institute.

This reprint contains selected excerpts from the Introduction and Application sections, the full text of most of the Standards in the Functions/Relations section, and selected excerpts from the Commentaries accompanying those Standards. The Pre-Trial, Trial, Post-Trial, and Juvenile Justice sections, and the Appendix, have been omitted.

Methodology

* * *

The Prosecution Management and Standards Committee * * * first decided that the standards should not be limited to ethical provisions. Nor were the standards to be limited in scope or subject matter to those things under the direct control of local prosecutors. In both respects, the revision was to be consistent with the original standards, which had set out to balance a pragmatic approach with a visionary design. The revised standards were to address the problems of the prosecution function, and would necessarily include reform and revision of statutes and action of related segments of the criminal justice system.

With this perspective, the Committee undertook a thorough review of the original standards, focusing on the numerous subjects needing attention and improvement. In many areas, the standards and commentaries were too detailed, serving better as a resource for scholarly research rather than the more necessary blueprint for improvement of the prosecution function.

The organization of the standards needed improvement as well. Originally separated into three parts, the standards are now divided into five; the first focusing on the function and administration of prosecution and its relations with other entities, while the three parts entitled "pre-trial," "trial," and "post-trial" provide a procedural sequence of activities from charging to appeal. The last part, "juvenile justice," stands alone because that standard was considered separately by NDAA's Juvenile Justice Committee.

The Prosecution Management and Standards Committee also reorganized the topics to reduce any repetition by deleting topics which it found to be no longer relevant and adding new subjects.

Results

* * *

Many * * * additions emphasize the prosecutor's responsibility to upgrade the functions of the office and his role in the criminal justice system.

* * *

While some elements of deleted standards are incorporated into revised standards, the orientation of the deletions has resulted in more of a concentration in those areas within the prosecutor's domain.

* * *

Many other standards in the first part, "functions/relations," have seen less dramatic, yet not insignificant, revisions consistent with the objectives detailed above.

* * *

Due to the self-governing nature of the legal profession, the role of these standards should be noted. While each standard is viewed by NDAA as a necessary part of an optimal system of justice, it is not the intent of NDAA that these standards serve in any way as a basis to sanction a prosecutor who has deemed it more appropriate to vary his practice from the standards. The word "should" is used in the standards to indicate the suggestive nature of the standards.

Whenever the personal pronouns "he," "him," or "they" are used in the standards and commentaries, they refer to both masculine and feminine genders.

Finally, the distinctions in the commentaries should be mentioned. In the original standards, the commentaries were frequently so long and detailed that they overshadowed the standards themselves. As a reference source, they undoubtedly were the premier comprehensive work on prosecution at the time and still serve as a valuable resource. However, in the revision, the commentaries have been rendered more readable. They serve to explain and justify the standards in a manner designed to enhance the utilization of the entire work. They also conform to the contemporary format for commentaries now used in the NDAA Juvenile Justice Standards and by other standard-setting bodies, such as the American Bar Association in the Model Rules of Professional Conduct * * *.

APPLICATION

A unique feature of the original standards was the incorporation of viewpoints of prosecutors from a complete range of jurisdictional size and variation. In some of the original standards, a minority view from the task forces was presented as an alternative for offices of comparable demographics.

In the revision of the standards, the Prosecution Management and Standards Committee considered the perspective of different sizes and types of offices and was able to promulgate unified standards on the various topics. The Committee did this with the view that the standards would be considered directional and flexible. Clearly, not every standard is applicable in every jurisdiction. Many standards can be modified to fit local needs. Prosecutors are encouraged to consider the extent to which they are applicable and to expand, modify, or alter them to reflect jurisdictional needs and realities.

In terms of application and implementation, there are two types of standards: those that can be implemented through the authority of the prosecutor and those that require more than that authority. Prosecutors are encouraged to review the standards to make this distinction and structure plans for short-term and long-term implementation. The greatest responsibility for the prosecutor is in the effort to implement those standards beyond the authority of the prosecutor. As agents for institutional and system changes, those standards which require change by legislation, case law, or through other entities, are capable of effecting dramatic improvement in the effectiveness of prosecution. It is, therefore, the responsibility of prosecutors to urge the adoption of the concepts found in the standards by all reasonable methods.

While prosecutors are seeking change within a visionary design, caution must also be exercised in relying on standards which lack immediate authority. Indeed, some standards may be ahead of current case law, ethics opinions, or other authority. It is not the intent or purpose of NDAA to ignore or usurp such authority. Prosecutors are specifically cautioned to be aware of and comply with controlling legal authority. At the same time, prosecutors have a responsibility to work toward modifications to enhance their function. The standards themselves give direction for such modification. Beyond that, prosecutors should not hesitate to cite these standards in any persuasive manner to bar associations, legislatures, courts, budget authorities and any other entities with the ability to effectuate implementation. These standards are quite literally the voice of prosecution present and future.

THE PROSECUTION FUNCTION

1.1 Primary Responsibility

The primary responsibility of prosecution is to see that justice is accomplished.

1.2 Civil/Criminal Jurisdiction

The prosecutor should represent the case of the people as to both civil and criminal jurisdiction. The criminal representation should be the primary responsibility. In jurisdictions where civil and criminal responsibilities are vested in the prosecutor, provisions for alternative representation in conflicts of interest must be made.

1.3 Societal Rights

The prosecutor should at all times be zealous in the need to protect the rights of individuals, but must place the rights of society in a paramount position in exercising prosecutorial discretion in individual cases and in the approach to the larger issues of improving the law and making the law conform to the needs of society.

1.4 Full-Time/Part-Time

The office of the prosecutor should be a full-time profession. The prosecutor should neither maintain nor profit from a private legal practice. In those jurisdictions unable to justify the employment of a full-time prosecutor, the prosecutor may serve part-time until the state determines that the merger of jurisdictions or growth of caseload necessitates a full-time prosecutor.

The prosecutor should devote primary effort to his office and should have no outside financial interests which could conflict with that duty.

1.5 Rules of Conduct

At a minimum, the prosecutor should abide by all applicable provisions of the Rules of Professional Conduct or Code of Professional Responsibility as adopted by the state of his jurisdiction.

1.6 Inconsistency in Rules of Conduct

To the extent that prosecutors are bound by Rules of Professional Conduct inconsistent with these National Prosecution Standards, prosecutors should endeavor to modify the Rules of Professional Conduct to make them consistent with these Standards.

COMMENTARY

The standard recognizes that the prosecutor is primarily responsible for criminal prosecution in his jurisdiction. It is to be read in conjunction with Standards 2.1 thru 2.5, Civil Representation, which set forth the civil representation responsibilities of the prosecutor's office.

The standard recognizes that there are many part-time prosecutors in the United States, both elected prosecutors and staff attorneys. This is an economic fact of life created by the overriding benefit of local accountability and control. Where the position is part-time, it is usually because the sparse population, geographic size of the jurisdiction, budget, and caseload do not warrant that the position be approached as a full-time position. The position of the standard is that the office be approached on a full-time basis, *insofar as that is possible in any given jurisdiction.* While the standard favors the concept of a full-time position (resulting in reduced potential for conflicts of interest, greater availability, and increased accountability), the existence of the position as part-time due to the considerations enumerated, is not forbidden by the standard. The standard merely means that the concept of full-time can be considered a goal where such is not presently feasible.

Whether full-time or part-time, the position should be approached as a career and not as a stepping-stone or sideline. This means that the prosecutor is prepared to bring to his public duties an orientation of *primacy.* No matter what other activities the prosecutor is involved in, his public duties come first. The fostering of such an attitude will not only serve the immediate public interest but also the prosecutor's professional responsibility in resolving problems that may occur where a potential conflict of interest exists.

The standard does not endorse any particular code of professional responsibility. Indeed, some prosecutors have had considerable differences of opinion over the years with the various codes and standards promulgated by the American Bar Association. These materials have often not fully addressed the special concerns of prosecutors in carrying out their public duties and responsibilities. The standard merely means that the prosecutor—as a member of the bar—is expected to abide by existing rules and codes.

This does not mean, however, that a prosecutor cannot challenge in appropriate *fora* and procedures such code provisions as are believed in good faith to be unjust or inapplicable. The existence of a code or rule does not eliminate the duty of the prosecutor to seek justice and serve the public interest. In this sense, the role of the prosecutor is not always the same as other members of the bar.

Furthermore, the prosecutor should work to modify code provisions which are not in the best interest of the prosecution function. The standards promulgated by the National District Attorneys Association may serve as a guide to assist in the identification of such inconsistent provisions.

While the standard recognizes that the prosecutor is to discharge his duties with fairness to all constituents, the standard—indeed all of the standards— recognizes that the prosecutor has a client not shared with other members of the bar, *i.e.,* society as a whole. No other member of the bar has this broad responsibility. The prosecutor must seek justice. In doing so there is a need to balance the interests of *all* members of society, but when the balance cannot be struck in an individual case, the interest of society is *paramount* for the prosecutor.

This is a principle that runs through all of the standards. Some of the individual standards that follow are couched in terms of "rules" (although not in the sense of being mandatory and sanctionable). Every such "rule" must be read and applied with reference to the underlying principle. In an individual case, application of the principle may dictate a departure from the rule; where there is a conflict, the principle controls. The prosecutor who applies the principle in good faith—meaning in the context of objective reasonableness—should not be faulted if a "rule" must be varied.

CIVIL REPRESENTATION

2.1 Scope

In jurisdictions where the prosecutor has civil representation responsibilities, he should provide civil representation to agencies and persons designated within the local governmental framework.

2.2 Specific Assignment

In carrying out such responsibilities, the prosecutor should, where practicable, designate a specific staff person or persons responsible for interacting with the appropriate local agencies.

2.3 Concentration

The prosecutor, in designating the person referred to in standard 2.2, should emphasize that civil representation is considered to be an area of concentration within his office.

2.4. Training

The prosecutor should, where practicable, institute an in-house training program for his staff on civil responsibilities, with emphasis on civil liability issues.

2.5 Risk Management

The prosecutor should, where practicable, initiate appropriate preventive programs among governmental agencies within his jurisdiction on civil liability risk avoidance. These programs should include training lectures and publications on civil liability topics.

COMMENTARY

The standards in general concentrate on criminal prosecution, but that focus should not imply that civil representation is not an important function in jurisdictions where civil representation is a designated function. It is essential that the staff assigned to the civil arena be competent and, therefore, the standards recommend that specific staff be assigned and concentrate in these responsibilities.

Virtually all actions taken in the prosecutor's office have civil liability risks. It is essential for local government officials to be alert to the actions that could expose them to liability risks as well. It should be the prosecutor's function to initiate and maintain a civil liability risk avoidance program for his office and those agencies which the prosecutor is responsible to defend in civil litigation.

SELECTION

3.1 Local Control

The prosecutor should be a locally elected official with a term of office of no less than four years.

3.2 Qualifications

At the time of filing for election, where applicable, and for the duration of the term of office, the prosecutor should be a member of the state's bar in good standing, a resident of the jurisdiction, and otherwise qualified to seek and hold the office under state law.

COMMENTARY

The standards favor the election of the prosecutor at the local level. The reason for this has not diminished since it was recognized by the President's Commission on Law Enforcement and the Administration of Justice, * * * when it noted * * * that the election of prosecutors at the local level:

> ... increases the likelihood that the prosecutor will be responsive to the dominant law enforcement views and demands of the community. Since he is not dependent on another official for reappointment, the prosecutor possesses a degree of political independence that is desirable in an officer charged with the investigation and the prosecution of charges of bribery and corruption.
> ... The election of local prosecutors is ingrained in our political traditions. Moreover, experience in several large cities has shown that the elective process can produce dedicated career prosecutors who are highly professional and competent.

The key to election at the local level is public accountability and the need for autonomy within the local jurisdiction. Prosecutors must never be placed in positions where their accountability lies elsewhere. The prosecutor's ability, competence, and performance can and should be judged by the citizens of the jurisdiction he serves. This system also works well to control individual prosecutors in the exercise of sound discretion which is vital to the successful management of crime control.

The standard is recommended notwithstanding the negative aspects of the election process, including the costs of campaigns and of the election itself. Good lawyers who seek prosecution as a career are sometimes unseated. Nevertheless, the benefits of accountability to the local electorate prevails over such drawbacks. The standard takes note of the fact that some jurisdictions have experimented over the years with systems of appointed prosecutors, rather than locally elected. In no case has it been demonstrated that a non-elective office is superior to that of the elective office or can effectively maintain the degree of accountability that the elective office provides. There is no reason to depart from the model that predominates in the overwhelming number of jurisdictions in the United States.

The provision that the prosecutor—both elected and staff—be a member of the bar in good standing at the commencement of his duties and throughout such duties, may seem a truism. Yet, there have been cases where individuals who were not members of the bar sought to serve on the prosecutor's staff.

It is in the public interest that any action resulting in the disbarment of a prosecutor renders him unqualified to continue in office.

REMOVAL

4.1 Procedure

Each state should provide and maintain a system for removal of the prosecutor which clearly defines the conduct subject to removal and provides notice, hearing, and due process to the prosecutor.

4.2 Replacement

Each state should provide and maintain a system of interim or permanent replacement of the prosecutor upon removal which is consistent with that state's traditional prosecutorial selection process.

4.3 Inappropriate Factors

Factors which should never be considered in the removal of the prosecutor include, but are not limited to:

    a. Characteristics of the prosecutor which are legally recognized to be deemed the basis of invidious discrimination, such as race, national origin, religion, age, and gender;

    b. Arrest or indictment alone;

    c. Actions and statements within the purview of prosecutorial discretion; and

    d. Partisan activities which are legal and ethical.

COMMENTARY

This standard addresses the removal of prosecutors. It does not address the grounds or basis for removal proceedings, but leaves that up to the individual states. Procedural due process, however, must be accorded the prosecutor subjected to removal proceedings.

The standard *does* address a number of factors which NDAA believes should *not* be the basis of removal proceedings. Two such factors warrant comment here.

Because the office of the prosecutor may sometimes involve unpopular decisions, the prosecutor stands to be a target of allegations which could lead to arrest or indictment. While not ignoring possible legitimacy of such allegations, the prosecutor in such a situation, like anyone else, is innocent until proven guilty. The removal of an unpopular prosecutor would be too easily subject to manipulation if it could be based on mere arrest or indictment. Therefore, these factors should not be a criteria for removal. Conversely, this is an area where the prosecutor must exercise personal judgment. In some instances, the prosecutor may find the circumstances such as to make it impossible to carry out the duties of the office. A prolonged trial might create a situation in which it is not in the best interest of society for him to continue and resignation should be considered.

The standard otherwise makes it clear that the exercise of a prosecutor's discretion that is not influenced by what could be considered a corrupt motive is not to be a basis for removal, even though the prosecutor's action might be subject to criticism. The standard seeks to protect a key element of the prosecutor's office, *i.e.,* prosecutorial discretion. This element is the cornerstone of the prosecutor's office; perceived abuses of prosecutorial discretion are addressed in our society through the mechanism of the ballot box, not removal * * *.

COMPENSATION

5.1 Responsibilities

The compensation of the prosecutor should be commensurate with the responsibilities of the office.

5.2 Factors to Consider

Factors in determining the compensation of the prosecutor should include, but are not limited to:

    a. The benefits to the jurisdiction of encouraging highly competent persons to seek the position with a career orientation;

b. The level of compensation of persons with analogous responsibilities in the private practice of law and private industry;
c. The level of compensation of persons with analogous responsibilities in public service.

5.3 Salary Ranges

The salary of the full-time prosecutor should be at least that of the salary of the chief judge of general trial jurisdiction of the district of the prosecutor. The compensation of the elected prosecutor should not serve as a basis for the highest compensation of assistant prosecutors.

5.4 Factors Not Considered

Factors which should never be considered in determining compensation of the prosecutor include, but are not limited to:
a. Characteristics of the prosecutor which are legally recognized to be deemed the basis of invidious discrimination, such as race, national origin, religion, age, and gender;
b. Partisan political affiliation;
c. Revenues generated by the prosecution function.

5.5 Benefits

A program of benefits, including health and pension provisions, should be established to complement the salary of the prosecutor and be at least equal to that provided to members of the state judiciary. The prosecutor's benefits should include indemnification or insurance to pay all costs of defense against, and judgments rendered, in civil lawsuits arising from the prosecutor's performance of his official duties.

COMMENTARY

Provision of an adequate salary is an absolute necessity if the office of prosecutor is to function at maximum efficiency. An adequate salary is essential for attracting capable candidates to the position of prosecutor. Without such compensation, capable persons who might otherwise be attracted to the prosecutor's office are diverted to private practice of law or other endeavors.

Provision for an adequate salary level is also essential to reduce the rapid turnover of local prosecutors. Turnover in prosecutors' offices across the country has been traditionally high. The primary reason for this high turnover is inadequate financial compensation. In both initial hiring and retention, the prosecutor's office competes for talented, skilled staff with law firms with rapidly escalating financial opportunities.

Provision of adequate salaries will also act to reduce the likelihood of prosecutorial misconduct, since adequately paid, full-time prosecutors and their staffs will be less susceptible to temptations of offers of money or favors in return for accommodating individuals whose cases come before them.

The salary provided the prosecutor should be at least that of the salary of the judge of general trial jurisdiction in the district of the prosecutor. As noted by the National Advisory Commission on Criminal Justice Standards and Goals * * *:

For purposes of salary, the prosecutor should be considered to be on the same level as the chief judge of the highest trial court of the local criminal justice system. Both positions require the exercise of broad professional discretion in the discharge of the duties of the offices. It is therefore reasonable that the compensation for the holders of these offices have the same base.

Those jurisdictions which have part-time prosecutors should have salaries set by a professional compensation board at the state level, in order to assure uniformity within each state.

A review mechanism should be established to periodically examine and evaluate the salary of the prosecutor in light of changing economic conditions. Current practice in many jurisdictions is to provide review and alteration of the prosecutor's salary only at the beginning of each term. This frequently results in an erosion of the prosecutor's salary, which is a disincentive for qualified seekers of the office. Unless statutory provision is made for periodic in-term increases in salary, a board or other mechanism should be established with authority to review and revise prosecutors' salaries in light of changing economic conditions. This periodic review of salaries is very important.

* * *

PROFESSIONALISM

6.1 Standard of Professionalism

The prosecutor should conduct himself with a high level of dignity and professionalism.

6.2 Code Compliance

In those jurisdictions where a code of professionalism has been promulgated, all participants in the system of justice should abide by its provisions, where applicable.

6.3 Code Promulgation

In those jurisdictions where no code of professionalism has been promulgated or where such a code is inapplicable or insufficient, the prosecutor should provide leadership in its promulgation and should design and implement a code to be followed by the prosecutor and staff.

6.4 Scope and Code

A code of professionalism developed or expanded by the prosecutor should address appropriate conduct in and out of court and include all professional relationships.

6.5 Code Provisions

The prosecutor's code of professionalism should include, among other provisions, the following:

  a. Counsel should proceed with candor, good faith, and courtesy in all relations with opposing counsel and should act with integrity in all communications, interactions, and agreements with opposing counsel.
  b. Counsel should avoid the expression of personal animosity toward opposing counsel, regardless of personal opinion.
  c. Counsel should at all times display proper respect and consideration for the judiciary, without foregoing the right to justifiably criticize individual members of the judiciary.
  d. Counsel should be punctual in all court appearances. When absence or tardiness is unavoidable, prompt notice should be given to the court and opposing counsel.
  e. Counsel should conduct himself with proper restraint and dignity throughout the course of proceedings. Disruptive conduct or argument is always improper.
  f. Counsel should treat witnesses fairly and with due consideration. Counsel should take no action in taking testimony of a witness to abuse, insult, or degrade the witness. Examination of a witness's credibility should be limited to accepted impeachment procedures.
  g. Counsel should avoid obstructive tactics including, but not limited to, the following:
     (1) Bringing frivolous objections, including unfounded objections intended only to disrupt opposing counsel;
     (2) Attempting to proceed in a manner previously barred by the court;
     (3) Attempting to ask improper questions or to introduce inadmissible evidence;
     (4) Using dilatory actions or tactics;
     (5) Creating prejudicial or inflammatory argument or publicity.

COMMENTARY

The prosecutor's obligation to comply with the ethical code and rules of his jurisdiction is a fundamental and minimal requirement. When the prosecutor falls below that standard, he may expect sanctions impacting on a particular case or on the individual prosecutor.

However, the dignity and honor of the profession call for compliance with a higher standard of conduct, one of professionalism. This standard requires the prosecutor to bring integrity, fairness, and courtesy into all interactions, be they with opposing counsel, the court, jurors, or defendants.

Many state and local bar associations have created codes of professionalism. Such codes are generally non-binding but strongly encouraged and used to inspire and invigorate both recently admitted and long-standing lawyers. Codes are usually aimed at the litigation bar where emotions run highest and the adversary setting generates a competitive orientation. Combining these factors with the axiomatic concept that the prosecutor's function is to seek justice and not merely convict, the need for a code of professionalism is perhaps greater in criminal trial work than any other area of law practice.

Incorporating the elements of professionalism for both the prosecutor and staff is unquestionably beneficial. As an elected official, the prosecutor is always under public scrutiny and, at the same time, has responsibility for the conduct of his staff. A code of professionalism directs staff to expectations regarding conduct, a breach of which can be embarrassing and politically detrimental to the prosecutor.

A professional orientation in the courtroom takes the judge out of the position of referee and allows him to be more attentive to the proceedings. This, too frequently, is contrary to the goal of a disruptive lawyer who may have too weak a case to be favorably decided on the merits. Defense counsel may sometimes engage in a flamboyant, theatrical, and disruptive style. If a prosecutor allows himself to be provoked into similar tactics, he detracts from the merits of the case and serves no useful purpose.

The standards suggest that the prosecutor determine the existence of a state or local code of professionalism and adapt or adopt one if it exists or create one if it does not.

While professionalism is a word of elusive definition, the standard lists a number of types of conduct which must be considered. It is strongly recommended that wherever prosecution adopts and abides by a code of professionalism, the defense bar should reciprocate.

CONFLICTS OF INTEREST

7.1 Conflict Avoidance

The prosecutor should avoid interests and activities which are likely to appear to, or in fact do, conflict with the duties and responsibilities of the prosecutor's office.

7.2 Conflicts with Private Practice

In those jurisdictions which do not prohibit private practice by a prosecutor:
a. The prosecutor should avoid representation in all criminal and quasi-criminal defense regardless of the jurisdiction.
b. The prosecutor should avoid any representation in which there is a reasonable belief that the subject matter will be that of a criminal investigation.
c. The prosecutor should avoid any representation of a person who is under criminal investigation, charged or indicted, and any agent or close relative of such a person.
d. The prosecutor should avoid any representation to private clients or prospective clients that the status as prosecutor is or could be an advantage in the private representation.
e. The prosecutor may not designate the status as prosecutor on any letterhead, announcements, advertising, or other communications involved in the private practice and may not in any manner use the resources of the prosecutor's office for the purpose of such non-prosecutorial activities.
f. The prosecutor should excuse himself from the investigation and prosecution of any client of the prosecutor and should withdraw from the representation of that client.

7.3 Specific Conflicts

In all jurisdictions, including those prohibiting private practice by prosecutors:
a. The prosecutor should excuse himself from the investigation and prosecution of any former client involving or substantially related to the subject matter of the former representation, unless, after full disclosure, the former client makes a counseled waiver permitting the prosecutor's involvement in the investigation or prosecution.

    b. The prosecutor should excuse himself from the investigation and prosecution of any matter where information known to the prosecutor by virtue of prior representation and subject to the attorney-client privilege would be pertinent to the investigation or prosecution, unless, after full disclosure, the individual makes a counseled waiver permitting the prosecutor's involvement in the investigation or prosecution.

    c. The prosecutor should excuse himself from the investigation and prosecution of any person who is represented by a lawyer related to the prosecutor as a parent, child, sibling, or spouse or who has a significant financial relationship with the prosecutor.

    d. The prosecutor should avoid any private interests, financial or otherwise, which may affect his professional judgment in the exercise of the duties and responsibilities of the prosecutor's office.

7.4 The Special Prosecutor

    a. The prosecutor should have the discretion to appoint or to petition the court for an appointment of a special prosecutor in cases where actual or potential conflicts of interest exist.

    b. The special prosecutor should have authority only over the case or cases for which he is appointed.

    c. The special prosecutor should be a member of the state bar in good standing with appropriate experience in the subject matter of the appointment.

    d. In those jurisdictions where the prosecutor does not have authority to appoint a special prosecutor, he may petition the court to assign a special prosecutor who should be selected by the presiding judge of the court of general jurisdiction with consideration given to the reciprocal appointment of local prosecutors from among those of the state.

    e. The special prosecutor should be compensated from general funds at a reasonable and necessary rate as determined and ordered by the court. Jurisdictions within a state should develop a system of reciprocal appointments from other prosecution offices.

COMMENTARY

There are few topics of ethical orientation more pervasive than conflicts of interest. Major law firms contend with conflicts searches when accepting new clients and face the withdrawal of existing clients when making collateral hires of partners.

Conflicts of interest problems are founded on the premise of the inability to serve clients which foreseeably have interests which compete or contend and the representation of one interest would therefore be to the detriment of the other.

Conflicts present themselves differently to the prosecutor, compared to the private practitioner, because the prosecutor does not initially select those subject to prosecution. Nor is there a choice of which prosecution office should proceed.

The standards dichotomize prosecution jurisdictions into those which prohibit private practice, generally considered full-time prosecutors, and those which permit private practice, those considered part-time. In recognition of geographic, demographic, and economic constraints, the standards address the problem posed by the part-time circumstance.

Notwithstanding a part-time prosecutor's right to represent criminal defendants in neighboring jurisdictions, the standard finds this inappropriate as a conflict of interest. Furthermore, the standards indicate that it is inappropriate for a part-time prosecutor to use his status as prosecutor to represent that he can somehow provide more effective legal representation.

The standards recognize potential conflicts in all jurisdictions involving former clients or information obtained by virtue of former representation and allow the prosecutor to proceed on the case only if the individual makes a counseled waiver permitting the prosecutor's involvement.

When the prosecutor has an actual or potential conflict, it is his responsibility to seek a special prosecutor. The standards further address this circumstance.

Jurisdictions within a state should employ a system of reciprocity in which prosecutors from other jurisdictions would be available for exchange as special prosecutors. Such a system would be cost-efficient, provide independence, and assure prosecutorial competence.

STAFFING

* * *

8.8 Affirmative Action

The prosecutor's staff should be hired on the basis of merit: however, as much as possible, it should represent a cross-section of the local community and statewide legal community including racial, ethnic, and religious minority groups. In order to achieve this representation, the prosecutor should actively recruit persons for employment.

COMMENTARY

The prosecutor's office should be considered a law firm whose client is the general public. As such, the client deserves the best possible legal representation. In addition to qualified staff, the prosecuting attorney should be funded to hire sufficient staff to adequately handle the office workload. The standard stresses the need for adequate funding, since the prosecutor cannot be faulted for having a less than adequate staff if necessary funds are not provided by the funding agency.

While the size of the jurisdiction will necessarily contribute to determining staffing resources, it should not act as a rigid constriction; the caseload, plus the workload which the existing staff bears, and the availability of outside resources should also be considered in determining the additional need. In general, referring to assistant prosecutors, the criminal trial division of each prosecutor's office should have at least two full-time attorneys for each trial judge conducting felony trials on a full-time basis, or the equivalent part-time situations. In jurisdictions with heavy caseloads, more than two assistant prosecutors per trial judge will be required.

It is desirable for the prosecuting attorney to require a minimum commitment of at least two years service from all deputy prosecutors. This period may be lengthened within the discretion of the prosecutor if a longer requirement is feasible and in the best interests of the community. Experience shows that most deputies do not receive adequate training until at least one year has been completed. A time requirement itself, however, will not be sufficient to retain qualified and competent staff. Proper salary, benefits, and working condition incentives must be arranged so that the prosecutor's office can compete effectively with the private sector.

The office of the prosecutor must be made competitive with private firms and offer pay scales that are comparable to those offered attorneys in private law firms within the same jurisdiction. Suggestions have been made that salary scales for the prosecuting attorneys' staff lawyers be determined by the formulation of an equation based on local economic indicators. Such an equation could be based on estimating the general income levels of numerous sectors of the work force in the local area and calculating the effects of the cost of local housing, food, etc.

Similar competitive situations should be taken into consideration when establishing salary and benefit levels for other members of the prosecutor's staff. Legal secretaries who are highly skilled and trained should be compensated at the same level as legal secretaries working in local private firms.

Many managerial and clerical positions within the prosecuting attorney's office can be filled with permanent employees utilizing either the local or state civil service or state merit systems as an aid in recruiting and also as a guide to qualified individuals. The advantage of such a process is to be able to maintain trained support staff from administration to administration, and be able to offer wages and benefits that are on the same level as those offered at other public service agencies within the state.

In large offices, the office manager should possess a high degree of skill in administration. A good office manager can analyze office systems and anticipate problem areas, make changes and forecast future needs of the office. This individual will take into consideration crime reports of the area, caseload of the courts, police arrest statistics, etc., and present them to the prosecutor so that together they can plan and allocate the necessary expenditures of both manpower and budget.

Office managers are responsible for non-lawyer personnel, file maintenance, and case flow. A complete and accessible library is also under the supervision of the office manager. The skills of a management specialist are utilized in close association with the prosecutor to initiate useful policies for an efficient organization.

Some positions, such as chief assistant prosecutors, special investigators, and personal secretaries, should serve at the pleasure of the prosecuting attorney. These positions must remain responsive to enforcing the policy decisions of the elected prosecuting attorney. In order to attract and keep the most highly qualified personnel, benefits should be comparable to those available to the judiciary and state employees.

In keeping with the affirmative duty to investigate found in these standards, it is expedient for the prosecutor to maintain a staff of professional investigators, independent of the police and responsible solely to the prosecutor's office. The actual number of full-time or part-time investigators for the particular office should be determined by the size of the office and the needs of the office. The prosecutor must estimate the continuous and seasonal fluctuation needs of the office and determine the number of full-time and part-time investigators which will best meet those needs.

It can no longer remain a distant goal but must become a necessary standard that the prosecutor who serves rural or medium-sized, as well as large metropolitan communities, have sufficient investigative resources for thorough case preparation. Of equal importance, the prosecutor, as the chief law enforcement official, has both the discretion and the responsibility to initiate and control investigations of certain areas, which, by virtue of their complexity or sensitivity, are frequently not handled by law enforcement agencies. The prosecutor may find it necessary to initiate investigations of alleged child abuse, environmental law suits, economic crime, bias/hate crime, or public assistance fraud, for example. In those jurisdictions where state agencies or a particular department are responsible for these technical, skilled investigations, the prosecutorial investigator may assist the investigation by interpreting the scientific or empirical data in terms of the existing and applicable law. Or the particular agency may have the power to require an investigation by the prosecutor's office.

Since the investigator is to be a regular and essential feature of the prosecutor's office, the training for this role must necessarily be comprehensive and of the highest quality. The prosecutorial investigator, because of the association with an elected public official, must reflect the same standards of professional behavior.

Investigators should not be viewed as merely a supplemental police force and their training should compare to the variety of their expertise.

It is the responsibility of the prosecutor to hire staff which reflects the composition of the community, where possible. The recruitment of qualified minorities is an essential aspect of this goal and should be incorporated into the hiring practices and procedures of all prosecution offices. While it is not the responsibility of the prosecutor to meet predetermined quotas, the office benefits by strong representation that reflects the community that is served.

TRAINING

9.1 Orientation

After election or appointment, but prior to assuming office, or as soon thereafter as possible, the prosecutor should participate in a formal orientation program sponsored by a state or national association or organization.

9.2 Prosecution Standards

Pursuant to orientation, incoming prosecutors should become familiar with the standards promulgated herein.

9.3 Transitional Cooperation

Where an individual has been elected or appointed prosecutor, the incumbent prosecutor should cooperate in an in-house orientation of the incoming prosecutor to allow for an effective transition consistent with principles of professional courtesy.

9.4 Funding

The prosecutor should establish and maintain a program of orientation for all new staff personnel which should include in-house and outside training components.

The prosecutor's budget should include a line item for training, adequate to allow both internal activities and for prosecutor attendance at programs conducted outside the office.

Funding must be provided for development and implementation of in-house training for staff and for local, state, and national level training of the prosecutor and staff.

9.5 Continuing Legal Education

The prosecutor and legal staff should participate in formal continuing legal education. The prosecutor and supervisory staff should include the study of management issues, such as staff relations, budget preparation, and planning principles, in continuing legal education participation.

9.6 CLE Exclusive to Prosecutors

States should provide continuing legal education that is available exclusively to prosecutors.

9.7 Mandatory CLE Compliance

The prosecutor and legal staff should be diligent in meeting or exceeding requirements of continuing legal education in those states where requirements are mandatory.

9.8 Support Staff Training

The prosecutor should provide for continuing training of non-legal staff to allow for their professional development and enhancement.

9.9 Code of Professionalism

Where the prosecutor has adopted a code of professionalism, he is responsible for the incorporation of the code into the training and orientation programs of all staff.

9.10 National Resources

The prosecutor should be knowledgeable of and utilize appropriate national training programs for both initial orientation and continuing legal education, for both himself and his staff.

COMMENTARY

In addition to assuring that each prosecutor attains a level of proficiency in criminal law/trial advocacy, there is a need to provide professional personnel with specific knowledge of the policies and procedures of the individual office to which they are assigned. Furthermore, it is increasingly necessary to assure that the level of competence achieved through training programs is maintained through awareness of changes in the law. The standard addresses the need for training programs for both legal and non-legal staff.

Conceptually, staff training can be divided into two broad categories. The first, which might be termed "orientation," would seek to provide new assistants or deputies, as well as chief prosecutors, with an understanding of their responsibilities in the criminal justice system, and with the technical skills they will be required to utilize. Orientation for the chief prosecutor should center on office management skills, especially for larger jurisdictions. A basic orientation package for assistants could include familiarization with office structure, procedures, and policies; the local court system; the operation of local police agencies; and training in ethics, professional conduct, courtroom decorum, and relations with the court and the defense bar. A second aspect of training which should be included in each prosecutor's training program is continuing education. Much continuing education is traditionally provided within prosecutors' offices, particularly larger offices which can justify employment of training officers and development of a formal array of lectures. Most common of these would be labeled "refresher" training—providing maintenance of existing proficiency by seminars and discussions on basic topics such as the impact of recent court decisions or statutory change on substantive law, search and seizure, rules of evidence, etc. Similar programs on trial practice might be held. Another target of continuing education could be the broadening of the scope of the prosecutor's knowledge of the entire criminal justice system; both review of functions traditionally exercised by prosecution, as well as a consideration of new areas of endeavor.

The standard calls for the allocation of funds specifically through a line item in the budget. This may help to emphasize the essential role of training in assuring efficient and effective performance of duties—and disabuse those who have the notion that training is a frill, an extra to be cut at the first sign of any pressure on the budget. Justification of the budget, of course, imposes certain duties on the prosecutor. He must continually re-evaluate the cost-effectiveness of training activities. Training *per se* is neither good nor bad—its value comes from the extent to which it responds to the needs of the prosecution function.

Continuing legal education is usually provided within the prosecutor's office, especially in large offices where special training, personnel, and additional budget allocations are easier to justify. Such programs can play a useful role whenever they are possible. While in most states a range of continuing education courses is currently available, NDAA does not believe that mere availability of programs will suffice. Therefore, it is suggested that each jurisdiction establish a minimum level of training which each prosecutor and assistant would be required to participate in annually. Programs of continuing education that are designed for prosecutors and their staffs need not be open to non-prosecutors, *i.e.,* defense attorneys. To do so may well defeat the purpose of such training programs.

The concern for training in the standard has focused primarily on programs for legal personnel—the prosecutor and assistants. In general, legal positions require the greatest amount of specialized expertise. However, there is no intention to slight programs which would prepare paralegal personnel to fulfill roles in intake review, division, mediation of citizen complaints, consumer fraud enforcement, non-support, spouse and child abuse investigation, etc., or for continued upgrading of investigative, secretarial, and clerical personnel in relevant skills.

It is important not to overlook the benefits of training at the national level. Both litigation and management skills have many features in common regardless of local practice rules. Prosecutors from all demographics stand to gain substantial insight and skill through the use of such resources.

OFFICE MANUALS

10.1 Policies and Procedures

To the extent merited by the size of the office, each prosecutor's office should develop statements of general policies and procedures of the office. The objectives of these policies and procedures are to establish the office as a place for the fair,

efficient, and effective enforcement of the criminal law. The policies and procedures should give guidance in the exercise of prosecutorial discretion and should
provide information necessary for the performance of the duties of the staff.

10.2 Manual Development and Maintenance

In the interest of continuity and clarity, such statements of policies and
procedures should be maintained in a manual of internal policies of the office. In
addition, the office manual should be periodically updated to assure accuracy
and completeness.

10.3 Manual Availability

Each office manual should contain policies which define the acceptability of
public access, or access of other criminal justice agencies, to particular portions
of the document. Certain portions may be established as confidential, while others
should be subject to access by the general public and/or law enforcement agencies
or the defense bar. In the alternative, the prosecutor may develop separate manuals
for internal use and for external availability.

COMMENTARY

A primary benefit of drafting written policies and placing them in an office
manual is uniformity. The prosecutorial discretion that has been recognized in
many of the standards most correctly belongs to the chief prosecutor only, being
the elected official ultimately responsible to the community for the performance
of the prosecution function. In promoting uniformity, the emphasis is on assuring
that assistant prosecutors and other personnel perform in a manner consistent with
the policy of the chief prosecutor. Given that the individual assistants must be
delegated the authority to apply their best judgment to the facts of particular cases,
there is yet little justification for victim or accused to receive substantially different
treatment because the case was assigned to one individual in the office and not
to another.

NDAA recognizes a distinction between the operation of small and large
offices. In a small office, the long personal association of a prosecutor's staff will
have created a completely shared understanding of the tenets of each prosecutor's
individual policies. In those cases, the written policy may serve as no more than
a cross-reference and as a guard against any misunderstanding. Thus, it may not
always be necessary for the office manual of a small office to be as detailed as
that of a large office. However, in a larger office, where there is frequent staff
turnover and a variety of staff positions or where assistants serve part-time and
operate in widely separated locales within the jurisdiction, the office manual should
represent an enormous stride toward uniformity and continuity in the execution
of prosecutorial discretion.

Another benefit in the adoption of office policies and procedures will be a
more effective orientation and training of new staff. A new attorney, paralegal,
clerical employee, or intern may bring to the job little or no experience in the
operations of a prosecutor's office. No matter what the size of the office, existing
staff may be already overburdened, with little or no time to devote to thorough
training of new employees. Even when time is taken to explain to an individual his
duties, the amount of information conveyed can generally not be fully assimilated.

Written explanation of policy and office procedure can serve as an extremely valuable reinforcement to oral instruction and as a constant guide and reference to an individual during employment in the office.

An additional benefit to be derived from the adoption of an office manual will be improvement of the knowledge and technical proficiency of staff members in performing the various tasks required in the prosecutor's office. * * *

Lastly, the standard recognizes the confidential aspect of the prosecutor's office manual. This may quite properly lead the prosecutor to conclude that not all portions of the manual should be accessible to the public, or that separate works be available—one for internal management and another for public information. This approach is fully justified by the nature of the prosecution function, which in large part deals with confidential matters.

* * * Prosecutors without manuals should consult with their association and other prosecution offices to lessen the burden of the initial manual development.

FUNCTIONAL OFFICE DIVISIONS

11.1 Features of Divisions

Prosecuting attorneys may find that a particular function or program conducted by their office is of sufficient importance and generates enough volume to constitute a distinct unit or division within the office. * * *

COMMENTARY

The larger the size of the prosecution office, in terms of caseload and staff, the greater the need for areas to which the creation of a separate functional office division is appropriate. The smallest prosecution offices are not likely to possess either a sufficient volume of complaints or a sufficient number of assistant prosecutors to warrant distinct office divisions.

Where functional office divisions or units are created, they should be established as miniature prosecution offices within the parent prosecution facilities. The division should possess a separate managerial person. Where possible, separate facilities in the office should be provided for the division. To facilitate planning and operation, the division should develop and manage its internal budget arrangements.

Since a primary justification for the establishment of a separate office unit is the need for special expertise in a given area, each office division should be assigned permanent legal and support staff, on a full-time basis where appropriate. These staff members should receive special training upon assignment to the division and should be required to continue acquiring and updating competence in that area. Such training is particularly essential where the office division or unit is concerned with a particular subject orientation. To make full use of this expertise, policies should be implemented which mandate the referral of all developing cases to the office division having responsibility for that area.

PLANNING, MONITORING, AND EVALUATION

12.1 In-House Capacity

Prosecutors should have the in-house capability to plan, monitor, and evaluate the operation of their offices and overall function.

* * *

COMMENTARY

Prosecutors are, in effect, administrators of a business. Prosecutor's offices operate on a budget, utilize manpower, and have to report to other levels of authority for economic and manpower allocations. Because of their public accountability, prosecutors also have to be concerned with intake levels, case backlogs, file systems, statistical tabulation and collection systems, etc. When reviewed closely, prosecutors are in need of planning, monitoring, and evaluation techniques to a greater extent than most private concerns.

Planning, monitoring, and evaluation are interrelated concepts. Though they can be defined separately, they must be considered together if they are to be properly applied.

Planning involves three activities. First, goals have to be established. A clear idea of the objectives must be formed and a definite purpose must be established before work can proceed. Second, an estimate of the available resources must be made and plans to secure any other needed resources must be formulated. "Resources" include both manpower and physical facilities. Third, these resources must be efficiently organized and directed in such a way as to expedite the completion of the plan.

Monitoring is an ongoing activity performed concurrently with the work itself, which assures that any given project or operating system pursues its identified objectives and adheres to its agenda of tasks and activities.

Evaluation is a technique which attempts to assess the extent to which an organization has accomplished the goals it has set for itself. Further, evaluation is intended to analyze the varying contributions of planned accomplishments, rather than unanticipated occurrences. Also, it seeks to interpret and categorize phenomena which may be detrimental to success so as to remove possible causes of failure and thus avoid future low benefit/high cost activities.

When an organization is faced with limited resources and multiple objectives, the proper use of planning, monitoring, and evaluation can be an effective tool. Those prosecutors with limited resources at their disposal and whose operations encompass a wide range of legal and administrative tasks will find these techniques helpful.

At the same time, NDAA recognizes that this important office function is frequently neglected for the simple reason that performance of the function has not been budgeted into anyone's responsibilities within the prosecutor's office. To the extent office size makes it necessary and feasible, this should be addressed by a separate and distinct budget line item.

STATISTICAL SYSTEMS

13.1 Prosecution Data Base

The prosecutor's office should maintain sufficient data to evaluate and monitor the performance of the office. * * *

COMMENTARY

The development and use of a good office statistical system has benefits for both the prosecutor and for the criminal justice system as a whole. One of the problems of the criminal justice system has been its traditional inability to generate and maintain records on its processes. This inability is especially evident in those processes between arrest and incarceration. Good statistical recordkeeping can supply the information needed for a better understanding of the system as a whole and for needed innovation in attempting to fight crime more efficiently.

The prosecutor can utilize a statistical system for the improvement of his own operation. Receiving regular reports on the functioning of the prosecutor's office gives the prosecutor a more accurate picture of what is happening in the community in the area of crime and an idea of how well the prosecutor's office is responding. It allows for the best allocation of present available resources, as well as providing a basis for requesting additional resources and making plans to meet future needs.

Statistical analysis can also provide a look at the comparative functions of different aspects of the operation. Statistical methods that have been developed for both public and private sectors allow the prosecuting attorney to pinpoint bottlenecks in the prosecutorial system accurately, identifying areas for corrective action within a generally viable system.

Good recordkeeping is essential to an effective public relations program. The prosecutor should utilize office statistics to keep the community informed of the trends in local crime and with the efforts of the prosecutor's office to combat crime.

Effective statistics are essential for the prosecutor when dealing with funding boards or agencies. They are crucial in any attempt to rally public support to the maintenance of an effective criminal justice program.

There is a key relationship between good filing practices and a useful statistical system. A statistical system can be generated more easily in an office which has an orderly and methodical approach to maintaining its case files. The use of innovative management tools such as the model case jacket, or efficient case numbering systems, makes it possible for the prosecutor to collect statistics about the flow of cases through the prosecutor's office.

The only efficient way to manage and effectively use a sound statistical system is through computerization. It is the hallmark of a professional office, no matter what size, to have and use the best technical resources available. The range of computer hardware and software available today provides reasonably priced systems which can be highly effective in impacting criminal activity. Funding agencies should make automation of the prosecutor's office a high priority where it does not exist or is outmoded or inadequate.

NDAA recognizes that the prosecutor does not always have the expertise or the manpower available to develop these systems. National programs are available through such organizations as the American Prosecutors Research Institute in assisting the local prosecutor to generate these capabilities. Local government should make necessary funds available so that the prosecuting attorney can improve the management efficiency and capability of the office in these two key areas.

* * * Statistics are not an end in themselves. Their use is the critical issue. Therefore, prosecutors should make individual determinations of those specific statistics to maintain and put to use.

FACILITIES

[Standards omitted.]

COMMENTARY

To provide the necessary services, proper facilities must be provided. It does little good to employ a full staff complement if the needed space is not available. Likewise, the needed tools to complete any given task must be available.

Rural and small offices have different needs from large and urban offices. But there are universal needs in all types and sizes of offices. These standards take this into account and differentiate where necessary, but are also specific enough to give guidelines for facility and space optimum utilization.

* * *

The office complex must be conducive to both the function of prosecution and to the judicial hallmark that the image of prosecution deserves. The facility must be designed so that future expansion is possible. Often new equipment and refurbishing will suffice, but sometimes a totally new complex may be the sole solution. Also, as new modes of equipment become commonly available, * * * such items should be considered necessary adjuncts to the prosecutor's facilities.

Large urban offices are best located near or in criminal justice complexes. Practicality may preclude this in small office situations. However, even one-person offices should have facilities designed for the demands of prosecution. All offices should be publicly financed and devoted exclusively to prosecution. Many rural prosecutors are still expected to use their personal, private law offices for prosecution facilities; this practice is unwarranted and demeaning to the profession. * * *

These standards address those items and issues that affect the prosecutor's working environment. They range in scope from office configuration and location through basic equipment for internal operations.

The proper plan and design is not the only answer to maximizing the efficiency within a prosecutor's office. However, it will definitely enhance the capabilities of the prosecutor and all related activities. * * *

* * *

RELATIONS WITH LOCAL CRIMINAL JUSTICE ORGANIZATIONS

15.1 Prosecutor's Involvement

The prosecutor should be involved in local entities established and maintained for the enhancement of the effectiveness, efficiency, and fairness of the administration of justice in that jurisdiction.

15.2 Information Input

The prosecutor should provide such entities with information, advice, and data pertinent to the solution of problems identified in the jurisdiction and should consider the implementation of proposals designed to address and resolve such problems.

15.3 Organization Establishment

In those jurisdictions where there are no local inter-agency entities established for the enhancement of the effective, efficient, and fair administration of justice, the prosecutor should determine the potential benefits of such an organization and provide leadership in its establishment, if deemed beneficial.

15.4 Enhancing Prosecution

The prosecutor should participate in local bar associations for the purpose of enhancing and advancing the goals of the prosecution function.

RELATIONS WITH STATE CRIMINAL JUSTICE ORGANIZATIONS

16.1 Need for State Association

Each state should have a professional association of prosecuting attorneys for the purpose of serving and responding to the needs of its membership and enhancing the prosecution function.

The prosecutor should be an active member of his state association.

Each state association should provide services that are most conducive to development at the state-wide level. * * *

16.2 Enhancing Prosecution

The prosecutor should participate in other state-wide entities, such as state bar associations, for the purpose of enhancing and advancing the goals of the prosecution function.

16.3 Fulfillment of Obligation

The obligations a prosecutor undertakes on behalf of state organizations should extend only to those which he can fulfill in a diligent and competent manner.

16.4 Prosecutorial Input

State organizations should take all reasonable measures to include the involvement and view of incumbent local prosecutors in the research of studies and promulgation of standards, rules, and the like (disciplinary, aspirational, or otherwise) which impact on the prosecutor and the prosecution function.

RELATIONS WITH NATIONAL CRIMINAL JUSTICE ORGANIZATIONS

17.1 Enhancing Prosecution

The prosecutor should take an active role in national level organizations for the purpose of enhancing and advancing the goals of the prosecution function. The obligations a prosecutor undertakes on behalf of national organizations should extend only to those which he can fulfill in a diligent and competent manner.

17.2 Prosecutorial Input

National organizations should undertake all reasonable measures to include the involvement and views of the incumbent local prosecutors in the research of studies and promulgation of standards, rules, and the like (disciplinary, aspirational, or otherwise), which impact on the prosecutor and the prosecution function.

COMMENTARY

The prosecutor should participate in local, state, and national affairs for the improvement of the criminal justice sytem. Activities which the prosecutor might undertake include provisions of information and advice to governmental bodies and citizens' groups, review and consideration of pending state and national legislation, and participation in criminal justice-related programs or projects. A good prosecutor is a good attorney and would be expected to be active in his local and state bar associations.

The standards recognize the rapid growth in community organizations in the last 20 years devoted to specific interests, such as DUI enforcement, rape prevention/counseling programs, spousal and child abuse prevention, drug education programs, neighborhood watch programs, to name just a few. An interested and informed citizenry can be a valuable partner in law enforcement. The standards encourage prosecutors in communities lacking such grass-roots organizations to consider appropriate ways and means whereby citizen interest in their formation can be stimulated.

Because the office of the prosecutor is a local one, the responsibilities placed on this office are probably more diverse than those at any other level of government, which may have the capacities for specialization. For example, citizen complaints may range from how to cope with a neighbor's children to how to collect on a bad check. Expectations from law enforcement agencies and the courts are equally diverse and more demanding. In many jurisdictions, the prosecutor is also the attorney for his county. This responsibility may demand an expertise in taxation, school law, zoning, property law, employee disciplinary law, health law, environmental law, and labor relations.

If every prosecutor's office were designed on a level of specialization necessary to address each area it is responsible for, it would not only be a tremendous (and no doubt prohibitive) financial burden, but also an enormous duplication of effort on a county-by-county or district-by-district basis. On the other hand, local initiative, flexibility, and accountability are essential factors which must be maintained in prosecution. Thus, one method of alleviating this problem is through a state-wide association of prosecuting attorneys, a concept that NDAA has long fostered.

Such an association should be made up of all local prosecutors in a state and should have a full-time staff. This organization must be responsive to the needs of its members. As a result, the various functions will differ. However, those areas of concentration may include: training, information dissemination, technical assistance, resource provisions, legislative development, review and liaison, support of innovative programs, and informal professional conduct review.

Because the purpose of such an association is to serve prosecutors, it is imperative that they be involved and support the operation of the association. Membership should be the responsibility of all prosecuting attorneys, and dues should be paid through the prosecutor's budget. Membership should not be limited to elected prosecutors but rather be open to other interested parties such as assistants, former prosecutors, state attorney general staff members, investigation staff, and law students.

* * *

RELATIONS WITH OTHER PROSECUTORIAL ENTITIES

18.1 Prosecutorial Cooperation

In recognition of the common goal of serving the interest of justice, the prosecutor should cooperate with all applicable federal, state, and local prosecutorial entities in the investigation, charging, dismissal, or prosecution of cases which may be of concern to such entities.

18.2 Coordination Mechanisms

The prosecutor should establish and maintain mechanisms for determining the possibility of other prosecution which would avoid double jeopardy defense claims and avoid detriment to prosecution resulting from a grant of immunity.

18.3 Resource Sharing

The prosecutor should share resources and investigative information with other prosecutorial entities commensurate with the fullest attainment of the interests of justice.

18.4 Non-Partisan Relations

All relations with other prosecutorial entities should be maintained on a non-partisan basis.

18.5 Duty to Report Misconduct

When the prosecutor has knowledge of misconduct or incompetency in another entity of prosecution, he should report that information to the supervisory authority and take such other actions necessary to sanction the misconduct and remedy the incompetence.

18.6 Furtherance of Justice

The office of the prosecutor and the office of the state attorney general, where separate and distinct entities, should cooperate in the furtherance of justice.

18.7 Intervention on Request

The state attorney general should intervene in or assist in local prosecutions at the request, and only at the request, of the local prosecutor.

18.8 Availability of Resources

The state attorney general should make the resources of his office available to assist the local prosecutor.

COMMENTARY

Relations between the local prosecutor, attorney general, special prosecutors, and other prosecutorial agencies have overlapping jurisdictions, vary considerably from state to state and have not always been smooth.

While the standard counsels that cooperation among agencies is the key to effective law enforcement, it does not diminish the position that the individual with primary responsibility and authority to make decisions and take action on local crime problems is the locally elected prosecutor. The prosecutor is in the best position to make correct decisions regarding local crime problems, reform of local court procedures, and the allocation of local resources to effectively fight crime.

State and federal authorities should recognize the primacy of the locally elected prosecutor. Intervention which is not requested is not likely to foster necessary, positive working relations. * * *

POLICE LIAISON

POLICE LEGAL ADVICE AND TRAINING

POLICE LIAISON OFFICER

POLICE LEGAL ADVISOR

[Standards omitted.]

COMMENTARY

The maintenance of good relations between the prosecuting attorney and the law enforcement agencies within the community is essential for the smooth functioning of the criminal justice system. Both parties have the burden of fostering, maintaining, and improving their working relationship, and developing an atmosphere conducive to a positive exchange of ideas and information.

The criminal justice system, of which the police are only one element, is a structure of law. Many times this structure suffers from seemingly contradictory court decisions, public pressure, and the problems that arise in trying to balance effective law enforcement and the protection of the rights of individuals. The police face many of these problems. To alleviate these problems, the prosecutor should educate the police in the area of pre-trial criminal procedure * * *. [T]he prosecutor has a responsibility to educate the police on the effect of court decisions in general and their application in specific cases * * *.

The prosecutor has a large stake in the training and professionalization of local law enforcement. Their handling of a case is often crucial to the prosecutor's success. Therefore, the prosecutor should encourage the local police to participate to the fullest extent possible in training programs operated on state, regional, and national levels. If such a program does not exist or is not available to police in the jurisdiction, it is in the prosecutor's best interest to promote the development of such a program. Such training should result in more successful prosecutions. Besides the face value effectiveness of police training, it is an excellent opportunity to establish personal rapport and communications with individual police officers.

The prosecutor should advise the police on the legal aspects of criminal investigations. This advisory function pertains only to criminal matters and should not be confused with the function of police in-house counsel. Assuming the role of an advisor to any member of the police department on civil or personal matters is beyond the scope of the duties of the office of prosecuting attorney. In many cases, such a role would place the prosecutor in a position of possible conflict of interest with other duties prosecution is obliged to perform.

Furthermore, the prosecuting attorney may be restricted from any active participation in the police function by the threatened loss of immunity to civil damages in instances where participation is beyond the scope of advisor and, therefore, not an integral part of the judicial process. The prosecutor must always be cognizant that his quasi-judicial immunity afforded by the courts in civil liability suits is limited to actions taken in advancement of the traditional prosecution function.

The responsibility for sound communications between the prosecutor and law enforcement agencies is mutual. It is a goal of the prosecutor to keep police informed of developments in investigations, trials, and related matters. Both entities must seek to develop and implement systems and procedures which facilitate and enhance communications.

* * *

RELATIONS WITH THE COURT

23.1 Judicial Respect

Proper respect for the judicial system and appropriate respect for the court should be maintained at all times.

23.2 Respect in the Courtroom

While counsel is entitled to vigorously pursue all proper avenues of argument, such action must be undertaken in a fashion that does not undermine respect for the judicial function.

23.3 Improper Influence

Counsel should not seek to unfairly influence the proper course of justice by any relationship, communication, or pressure upon the court.

23.4 Respect From the Court

The court should display appropriate respect for the prosecution and defense. The court should not express or demonstrate any personal preferences or opinions.

23.5 Limitations of Resources/Abolition of Trial *De Novo*

The prosecutor should recognize the limitations of the resources of the courts and avoid all dilatory action inconsistent with such limitations. It is recommended that all trial *de novo*, whereby appellate review of a lower court verdict is systematically conducted in the form of a new trial before a higher court, be abolished.

23.6 Suspicion of Misconduct

When a prosecutor has reasonable suspicion of misconduct by a member of the judiciary, the prosecutor has a responsibility to take such action necessary to substantiate or dispel such suspicions.

23.7 Responsibility to Report Misconduct

When a prosecutor has knowledge of misconduct or unfitness to serve by a member of the judiciary, the prosecutor has the responsibility to report that knowledge to the appropriate authority and take such other action as is necessary to remedy the misconduct.

23.8 Application for Recusal

When a prosecutor has a sound basis to believe that a judge is unfit or unqualified to sit on a particular case, the prosecutor may properly seek that judge's recusal.

COMMENTARY

The prosecutor is an officer of the court, a public official accountable to those of his jurisdiction as a hub of the criminal justice system. All of these dimensions influence the prosecutor's relations with the court.

The standard recognizes that judges, like all figures in the criminal justice system, are individuals of diverse talents, skills, and temperaments. While some are of superior character, others suffer from human frailties not uncommon in our society. Thus, while the prosecutor needs to have proper respect for the institution of the judiciary, he, at the same time, has a responsibility to guard against the infrequent abuses from those who fail to honor their responsibilities while serving on the bench.

While this approach may require a delicate balance, it is necessary both inside and out of the courtroom. As is true of all National Prosecution Standards, effective justice is the paramount issue. Therefore, the prosecutor should neither undermine respect for the judicial function nor in any manner attempt to unfairly influence the court. In these respects, the prosecutor has the right to expect nothing less from the court.

Nevertheless, the prosecutor must assume the role of guardian against injustice and corruption. It is unacceptable to turn a deaf ear to suspicions of misconduct. The standard places a duty on the prosecutor to follow through when there is reasonable suspicion of misconduct by a member of the judiciary. When judicial scandals are uncovered, they become an indictment of the entire criminal justice system, creating a public perception that all those involved in the system are corrupt. Because of the prosecutor's close contact with the judiciary, he has the best opportunity to observe suspicious patterns of behavior. Because of the prosecutor's role in the criminal justice system, he has the obligation to investigate and address the misconduct with at least the vigor and the resources of any other allegations of corruption within the jurisdiction.

The standards make it clear that the prosecutor has responsibilities not only when misconduct is at the level of criminal activity, but also when a judge demonstrates the inability to carry out his duties with a minimal level of competence.

RELATIONS WITH THE DEFENDANT

24.1 Communications with Defendants

In most instances involving felonies or serious misdemeanors, it is desirable that a prosecutor communicate with a defendant through counsel; however, even in felonies or serious misdemeanors, there are occasions when it is in the best interest of justice that a prosecutor communicate with a defendant not represented by counsel or whose counsel is not present.

24.2 Disclosure

When a prosecutor communicates with a defendant not represented by counsel or whose counsel is not present, the prosecutor should make certain that the defendant is treated with honesty, fairness, and full disclosure of his liabilities in the matter under discussion. If legally required, under the circumstances, the prosecutor should advise the defendant of his rights. If the prosecutor contemplates using statements made by the defendant against him, the prosecutor should advise the defendant to that effect.

24.3 Unsolicited Communications

When a defendant is represented by counsel, but requests to communicate with a prosecutor out of the presence of his counsel, the prosecutor should ascertain if there is a valid reason to allow such communication and allow the communication only if a valid reason exists. The prosecutor has a right to receive unsolicited communications from defendants, of which he has no advance notice, without the duty of ascertaining whether or not there is a valid reason for the communication.

24.4 Safeguards

If a prosecutor enters into a plea negotiation with a defendant not represented by counsel or whose counsel is not present, he should make certain that the defendant understands his rights, duties, and liabilities under the agreement. When possible, the agreement should be reduced to writing and a copy provided to the defendant. The prosecutor should never take unfair advantage of an unrepresented defendant.

24.5 Right to Counsel

If a prosecutor is engaged in communications with a defendant not represented by counsel or whose counsel is not present, and the defendant changes his mind and expresses a desire to obtain counsel or to have counsel present (when represented by counsel), the prosecutor should allow him to obtain counsel or secure the presence of counsel and, when necessary, give him advice on obtaining appointed counsel.

24.6 Communications with Represented Defendants During Investigations

A prosecutor performing his duty to investigate should neither be intimidated nor discouraged from communicating with a defendant in the absence of counsel when the communication is "authorized by law." Such communication is allowed. A prosecutor who communicates with a witness who is also charged as a defendant in an unrelated matter, is not communicating about the subject of the representation, so long as the prosecutor keeps that matter entirely separate from the investigation or prosecution which the prosecutor is conducting. Similarly, nothing prohibits a prosecutor from advising or authorizing a police officer to engage in communications with an uncharged, represented suspect in the absence of the suspect's counsel provided such a communication is "authorized by law."

COMMENTARY

Relations with defendants is a sensitive area of a prosecutor's function. There must be a balancing of the general desirability to have defendants represented by counsel in their dealings with prosecutors and the right of defendants to represent themselves in traffic cases and minor misdemeanors, and even in felonies or serious misdemeanors under certain circumstances. It must be recognized that even defendants represented by counsel may have the right under certain circumstances to communicate with a prosecutor without the prior knowledge or presence of his attorney.

The standard provides that prosecutors communicating with unrepresented defendants should be certain that they are treated fairly and the defendants be made aware of what could happen to them as a result of whatever actions are taken. * * * The standard assumes that a prosecutor will tell a defendant if he intends to use the communications against him. There are circumstances in which a prosecutor will agree to receive information from a defendant but not use it against him. However, to ensure fairness to an unrepresented defendant, it is felt that he should not be subjected to the liability of incriminating statements without a prior warning and waiver of rights.

The standard recognized that prosecutors are sometimes contacted by defendants without the knowledge of their counsel and given good reasons for their direct communications with the prosecutor. * * * [P]rosecutors and defendants should have a right to communicate as long as legal and fairness requirements are met. Prosecutors also often receive unsolicited telephone calls and letters from defendants. They should have the right to receive them and use them in any legal manner.

The standard recognizes that many defendants wish to negotiate a plea with the prosecutor without representation. Many such defendants are experienced with the system or do not wish the expense of representation. In these circumstances, the prosecutor is held to full disclosure of the defendant's liabilities and a standard of fairness. The prosecutor should make certain that a defendant receives as favorable a disposition as he would have had had he been represented in the circumstances. The desirability of written plea agreements is also noted.

The standard recognizes the general legal requirement of fulfilling a defendant's desire for counsel, even if he originally expressed a desire not to be represented or to have counsel present and assisting him, or to obtain counsel if he cannot afford to pay for representation. The defendant's wishes in this regard are recognized as paramount. The prosecutor should make a record of any communications with represented defendants which take place in the absence of counsel.

Prosecutors have a duty to investigate criminal activity. This may involve communicating with witnesses who are also defendants or suspects in unrelated cases. * * *

In some jurisdictions, these standards may be inconsistent with case precedent and/or rules of professional conduct. The prosecutor must proceed with caution and seek to avoid any action that would jeopardize the case or result in misconduct under applicable rules.

RELATIONS WITH DEFENSE COUNSEL

25.1 Standards of Professionalism

The prosecutor should comply with the provisions of professionalism as identified in Standard 6.5, in his relations with defense counsel, regardless of prior relations or animosity and should maintain uniformity of fairness among different defense counsel.

25.2 Propriety of Relations

In all contacts with members of the defense bar, the prosecutor should strive to preserve the appearance and reality of proper relations.

25.3 Cooperation to Assure Justice

The prosecutor should cooperate with defense counsel at all stages of the criminal process to assure the attainment of justice and the most appropriate disposition of each case.

25.4 Disclosure of Exculpatory Evidence

The prosecutor should disclose the existence or nature of exculpatory evidence pertinent to the defense.

25.5 Pursuit of Misconduct

When a prosecutor has reasonable suspicion of misconduct by defense counsel, the prosecutor has a responsibility to take such action necessary to substantiate or dispel such suspicion.

25.6 Responsibility to Report Misconduct

When a prosecutor has knowledge of misconduct by defense counsel, the prosecutor has the responsibility to report that knowledge to the appropriate authority and take such other actions necessary to sanction the misconduct.

COMMENTARY

As with the judiciary, appropriate prosecutorial consideration is due opposing counsel, and all actions directed at opposing counsel and all deliberations with opposing counsel should be conducted with candor and fairness and should be presented without any express or implied animosity or disrespect.

Underlying the whole area of trial decorum is the question of trial ethics and the philosophical role of the prosecution and defense. It has long been recognized that the responsibility of the prosecutor goes beyond simply seeking indictment and conviction. The duty of the prosecutor is to seek justice, not merely to obtain a conviction. This same type of standard also applies to defense counsel * * *.

A defense attorney does not promote the attainment of justice when he secures his client's freedom through illegal or improper means. Rather, by the use of such methods, he breaches the public trust reposed in him by virtue of his oath of office . . . Neither the presumption of the defendant's innocence nor the government's burden of proof demands that the defense attorney act with anything other than honor and fairness.

The maintenance of this obligation by both sides mandates the fair, impartial, and decorous conduct of all trial proceedings and all relations with opposing counsel, opposing parties, and all officers of the court.

Of course, this admonition would be hollow if the prosecutor did not assume a responsibility to report misconduct of defense counsel to the appropriate professional and judicial authorities. If the prosecutor has a substantial basis for believing that misconduct exists, he should in all cases report that information to the appropriate authorities, at the same time being careful not to take action that would prejudice a defendant's right to a fair trial or precipitate a mistrial of the case. The timing of such report, therefore, may be an important element in a balanced approach to carrying out this responsibility.

One continuing myth that pervades the judicial process is the misconception that the defense attorney should be allowed greater leeway in the presentation of his case than the prosecutor. This leeway is often sought to be justified on the grounds that it is necessary to counter-balance the more prolific resources of the state brought to bear upon a single individual. Such reasoning is fallacious, however, when viewed in relation to the purpose of the adversary proceeding and the safeguards already provided therein. The courtroom is not a stage but a forum, and uniformity of trial decorum by defense and prosecuting attorneys should be maintained by the court to prevent undue influence on judge and jury which might result from theatrical behavior. The prosecutor should be able to bring to the court's attention the failure to maintain such uniformity and should himself maintain the high standards of conduct befitting a professional advocate in public service.

RELATIONS WITH VICTIMS

26.1 Information Conveyed to Victims

Victims of violent crimes, serious felonies, or any actions where it is likely the victim may be the object of physical retaliation, should be informed of all initial stages in the criminal justice proceedings to the extent feasible, including, but not limited to, the following:

a. Acceptance or rejection of a case by the prosecution's screening unit, the return of an indictment, or the filing of criminal charges;

* * *

f. Any proceeding within the knowledge of the prosecutor which does or may result in the defendant no longer being incarcerated, including appellate reversal, parole, release, and escape; and

g. Any other event within the knowledge of the prosecutor which may put the victim at risk of harm or harassment.

26.2 Victim Orientation

To the extent feasible and when it is deemed appropriate by the prosecutor, the prosecution should provide an orientation to the criminal justice process for victims of crime and should explain prosecutorial decisions, including the rationale used to reach their decisions. Special orientation should be given to child and spousal abuse victims and their families.

26.3 Victim Assistance Provisions

To the extent feasible, the prosecution should develop policies and procedures for providing * * * services to victims of crimes * * *.

26.4 Cooperative Assistance

The prosecution should work with other law enforcement agencies to:
a. Cooperate with victim advocates for the benefit of providing direct and referral services to victims of crime; and
b. Assist in the protection of a victim's right to privacy regarding a victim's address and telephone number, place of employment, name when the victim is a minor, or any other personal information unless a court finds it necessary to that proceeding.

* * *

26.6 Victim Compensation Program

Each state should establish and maintain a victim compensation program. The prosecution should be knowledgeable of the criteria for compensation and should inform victims with potential compensable claims of the existence of such programs.

26.7 Victim Assistance Program

To the extent feasible, the prosecutor should develop and maintain a victim/witness assistance program within the staffing structure of the office to provide services and give assistance to victims of, and witnesses to, crimes.

26.8 Victim Protection

Law enforcement agencies should provide protection from intimidation and harm arising from victims' cooperation with such agencies and the prosecution.

RELATIONS WITH WITNESSES

27.1 Information Conveyed to Witnesses

The prosecution should keep witnesses informed of:
a. Notification of all pre-trial hearings which the witnesses may be required to attend; and
b. Notification of trial dates and the scheduling of that witness's appearance.

27.2 Witness Assistance Provisions

To the extent feasible, the prosecution should develop policies and procedures for providing * * * services to witnesses of crimes * * * .

27.3 Witness Protection

Law enforcement agencies should provide protection from intimidation and harm arising from the witness's cooperation with such agencies and prosecution.

* * *

27.5 Protection Enforcement

The prosecutor should assign a high priority to the investigation and prosecution of any type of witness intimidation, harassment, coercion, or retaliation, including any such conduct or threatened conduct against family members or friends.

COMMENTARY

Effective prosecution includes a sound understanding of the value of victims and witnesses within the criminal justice system. The necessity of individuals reporting crimes and following through with identifications, statements, and testimony is self-evident. The standard, however, identifies obligations of the prosecutor and others to facilitate the relationship with victims and witnesses.

* * *

Prosecution should not assume that victims or witnesses are familiar with the terminology, procedures, or even location of the courts. At a minimum, prosecutors should be sensitive to this. Ideally, there should be a formal orientation program available to all victims and witnesses.

Such an orientation program should be part of a number of services provided. Prosecutors should have a leading role in the development and maintenance of victim/witness assistance programs. * * *

* * *

As central a figure as the prosecutor is to relations with victims and witnesses, he is certainly not the sole source to accommodate the needs of victims and witnesses. These needs should be a cooperative effort. For example, one of the greatest needs of victims and witnesses is the assurance of their safety. They are most vulnerable to threats, harassment, and intimidation. Their protection is primarily a law enforcement function. While prosecution should work with the police to minimize this, it is essentially a cooperative effort.

PROBATION

28.1 Role in Pre-Sentence

The prosecutor should take an active role in the process of development and submission of the pre-sentence report, including the following:
  a. The office of the prosecutor should develop a rapport with the probation department to encourage consultation on pre-sentence reports;
     * * *
  d. Upon denoting any information within a pre-sentence report which conflicts with information known to the prosecutor, it is the duty of the prosecutor to notify the appropriate parties of such conflicting information;
     * * *
  f. The office of the prosecutor should assist the probation department in assuring the confidentiality of individuals providing information for pre-sentence reports.

28.2 Prosecutorial Resource

The office of the prosecutor should be available as a source of information to the probation department for ex-offenders under supervision.

28.3 Notice

The office of the prosecutor should be notified of, and has the right to appear at, probation revocation and termination hearings and should be notified of the outcome of such proceedings within the jurisdiction.

COMMUNITY-BASED PROGRAMS

29.1 Knowledge of Programs

The prosecutor should be cognizant of and familiar with all community-based programs to which offenders may be sentenced, referred as a condition of probation, or referred as a diversionary disposition.

29.2 Need for Programs

In jurisdictions where community agencies providing services—such as employment, education, family counseling, and substance abuse counseling—are needed but not provided, the prosecutor should encourage their development. The prosecutor should be available as a source of information for community-based agencies.

29.3 Notice

The prosecutor and the police should be notified of individuals participating in work-release programs in their jurisdiction.

PRISONS

30.1 Knowledge of Facilities

The prosecutor should be cognizant of, and familiar with, all prison facilities and services to which offenders prosecuted in the jurisdiction may be sentenced.

30.2 Improvement of Institutions

The prosecutor should make efforts to upgrade correctional institutions within the state, including the avoidance of prison over-crowding. Adequate and additional facilities, new construction of prison facilities, and the enlargement of existing facilities, services, and trained staff should be primary goals of such upgrading.

30.3 Prosecutor as Resource

The prosecutor should be available as a source of information for prisons and their intake divisions.

30.4 Career Offender Identification

The prosecutor should assist in the identification of multiple and career offenders.

30.5 Appropriate Sentencing

The prosecutor should cooperate with the prison system to assure that realistic sentences are carried out.

30.6 Innovative Improvements

The prosecutor should encourage innovative experimentation which would improve the penal system.

30.7 Notice

Any institution holding an offender should notify both the prosecutor and law enforcement agencies at the time of an escape, prior to any temporary or final release, and prior to parole consideration.

30.8 Corrections Advisory Committee

The prosecutor should encourage the establishment of a state-wide correctional advisory committee involving representatives from all components of the criminal justice system and responsible members of the public.

PAROLE/EARLY RELEASE

31.1 Prosecution as Resource

The prosecutor should be available as a source of information for the parole board and supervisory agency.

31.2 Information System

Where the prosecutor deems it appropriate, he should assist in the development and maintence of an information system to keep the prosecutor's office informed of parole decisions concerning individuals from, or planning to reside in, the jurisdiction.

31.3 Parole Board Discretion

The prosecutor should be cognizant of the parole board's discretion and address abuses of the discretion.

31.4 Right to Appear

The prosecutor should have the opportunity to appear at hearings for parole, pardon, commutation, and grant of executive clemency, and should be notified sufficiently in advance of all such hearings.

31.5 Early Release

The prosecutor should oppose the early release of offenders where the release decision is made by correctional authorities solely or primarily on the basis of overcrowding of the correctional facility. The prosecutor should encourage the adoption of legislation preventing early release programs based on overcrowding of such facilities.

31.6 Notice

The prosecutor and appropriate law enforcement agencies should be notified of all parole, pardon, commutation, or grant of executive clemency concerning individuals from, or planning to reside in, the jurisdiction.

COMMENTARY

In most jurisdictions, probation has two basic functions: pre-sentence investigations and supervision. Pre-sentence investigations lead to reports which are social histories of the convicted offender awaiting sentencing. While the qualifications of probation officers who develop these reports have increased in recent years, the investigations may be inadequate in various jurisdictions because of manpower shortages and time limits. Such inadequacies could include erroneous and/or irrelevant information. In addition, such reports could omit valuable information.

Cooperation between probation and prosecution will not alone resolve the inadequacies of pre-sentence reports; but if prosecution makes itself available and is viewed as a resource by probation, such investigations may be more accurate and may be developed more efficiently. Because the prosecutor and his staff have worked closely on individual cases, they have an insight into the background of the offender prior to the initiation of pre-sentence investigation. Thus, it would be to the advantage of the probation department and ultimately to the community to consult the prosecutor during the development of this report.

* * *

A major function of probation is supervision of offenders sentenced to probation. Here the insight of the prosecutor may merit an active role, particularly in the initial stages of such supervision. As the probation officer strives to develop a relationship with clients, it is important for the officer to have a thorough knowledge of the individual's background and behavior. Therefore, it is to the advantage of the probation department to consult with the prosecutor in this area.

On the other hand, it is to the advantage of the prosecutor to be aware of revocation hearings of those individuals under probation supervision. In many jurisdictions the prosecutor will be present at such hearings. If not present, the prosecutor should be notified of the outcome of these proceedings. Thus, communication is needed at this level.

Another facet of the correctional component where lines of communication and coordination must be developed and enhanced with the prosecutor's office is that of community-based agencies. Such programs represent a wide spectrum of services, including both residential and non-residential facilities. These agencies specialize in meeting such needs as employment, education, family relations, and substance abuse problems.

It is recognized that community-based programs represent viable alternatives to traditional institutions for less-serious offenders. In addition, the concept of supplementing incarceration with community-based services has been advanced in recent years. The responsibilities placed upon community-based agencies mandates an increasing need for coordination and communication with the prosecutor. The degree of the prosecutor's input into such agencies may have as wide a spectrum as those programs do themselves. At the most basic level, the prosecutor must be cognizant of all community services which offenders in the jurisdiction may be sentenced to, referred to as a condition of probation, or referred to as part of a diversionary program. In addition, it is important for the prosecutor to be available as a resource to these services. Prosecution should be in a position to supply these agencies with information concerning clients whom the prosecutor has had contact with.

Some prosecutors have chosen to play an active role in community-based operations. Developing and implementing programs under the auspices of the office has been initiated on a wide scale in recent years. Diversionary and citizen volunteer programs are examples of the input the prosecutor's office may have. In addition, prosecutors are active in local, regional, and state-wide planning boards with an emphasis on developing such programs. Where basic community services such as employment, adult education, family counseling, and substance abuse counseling are not provided or are inadequate, the prosecutor should consider having input in their development or upgrading. The prosecutor's involvement in such planning and advisory boards is important because of his position as the chief local law enforcement official.

It must be recognized that there is a need for the prosecutor's involvement in the prisons and their programs. At its most basic level, the prosecutor must be cognizant of detention facilities and the services they offer to which offenders in the jurisdiction may be sentenced. Also, just as for probation and community agencies, the prosecutor's insight into the background and behavior of individuals should be viewed as a resource by officials in this area. * * *

There are other areas where prosecutors could profitably have input into the prison system, if not because of their positions as prosecutors, then because of their positions as concerned leaders in the criminal justice system. In general, correctional institutions in America need upgrading. The prosecutor should strive for better facilities and services within the prison setting, as well as better trained staff. Since prison overcrowding is a problem that affects the entire criminal justice system, it is natural to expect that the prosecutor will be involved in legislative efforts to build new facilities and enlarge existing ones. * * *

At a basic level, the prosecutor can also assist in the identification of multiple offenders. The prosecutor should also cooperate with prison systems to assure that realistic prison sentences are carried out. The prosecutor should encourage and support experimental efforts in regard to sentencing practices. Concepts such as mandatory prison sentences for multiple offenders of certain crimes should be closely examined.

As with all other components discussed here, the prosecutor must urge cooperation. The prosecutor must be considered a resource to both parole boards and supervisory personnel. In addition, the prosecutor should receive information concerning individuals from, or planning to reside in, the jurisdiction who have been approved for release from institutions. And fundamental to the protective function of the prosecutor, he must have an opportunity to oppose parole release decisions that are not in the best interest of the community.

A phenomenon that has arisen since the original promulgation of the NPS standards in the 1970s is that of early release programs that have as their primary motivation the alleviation of overcrowding in detention facilities. * * * Conditions of incarceration, however, are an improper basis for release of offenders and the standards takes an unequivocal position against it. The solution for prison overcrowding and related problems lies with the appropriate legislative bodies but is not to be found in simply releasing offenders. The prosecutor should support legislative proposals that solve this problem * * *. Inappropriate release of offenders undermines every advance achieved in improving the criminal justice system.

RELATIONS WITH LAW SCHOOLS AND LAW STUDENTS

32.1 Law School Resources

The prosecutor should make regular and efficient use of law students and law schools primarily to foster and encourage interest in the prosecutorial field as a career choice and, secondarily, as a supplement to the resources of his own office.

32.2 Law School Clinics

The prosecutor should actively cooperate with law school clinical programs for prosecution where they exist and actively promote their creation where they do not.

32.3 Internships

The prosecutor should structure and coordinate, through liaison with law schools, an internship program to employ law students in his office. * * * Such a program should permit student participation in a variety of practical functions and real life situations. Appearances in court by legal interns should be only under the supervision of the prosecutor.

32.4 Facilities

The prosecutor should make arrangements for the use of law school facilities, especially law libraries, in order to maximize the research tools available to his office.

32.5 Faculty

Where appropriate, the prosecutor should consult those members of the law school faculty who may have expertise in a field of particular relevance to criminal prosecution.

32.6 Ethics

Legal ethics as taught in law schools should address the practical problems and realistic considerations confronting the prosecutor.

32.7 Recruitment

The prosecutor should maintain close and regular contact with law school placement divisions to encourage an informed consideration of prosecutorial work as a career service.

32.8 Prosecutors as Lecturers

Prosecutors and staff should be available as special lecturers and instructors for relevant law school classes.

32.9 Faculty as Interns

Law professors should be encouraged to intern in prosecutors' offices to develop practical expertise and expand their knowledge.

COMMENTARY

Among other things, the standards recommend that the use of law students be optimized by a program geared to the handling of practical problems grounded in the circumstances of an actual prosecution. The appropriate student practice rule of the jurisdiction should include prosecutorial programs. A properly conducted student intern program can provide not only a stimulus for recruitment of law school graduates but also a method of evaluating aspiring applicants.

* * *

Courses in legal ethics are having a resurgence, driven in large part by the ethical improprieties of members of the profession that have become major public scandals in government and related fields. Unfortunately such courses seldom include the special ethical problems of prosecutors. Prosecutors should seek to remedy it by offering assistance in providing curriculum materials and adjunct faculty services to law schools within their jurisdiction and encouraging the pervasive incorporation of ethics in the law school curriculum.

PROTECTION OF RIGHTS OF ACCUSED AND PUBLIC

33.1 Balancing Interests

The prosecutor should strive to protect both the rights of the individual accused of a crime and the right of the public to know in criminal cases. The prosecutor should provide sufficient information so the public is aware that the alleged perpetrator of a crime has been arrested and that there exists sufficient competent evidence with which to proceed with prosecution. Additional information may be released by the prosecution if such release will aid the law enforcement process, promote public safety, dispel widespread rumor or unrest, or promote confidence in the criminal justice system.

33.2 Media Relations

The prosecutor should seek to maintain a relationship with the media that will facilitate the appropriate flow of information necessary to educate the public.

PROSECUTORS AND THE MEDIA

34.1 Information Appropriate for Media Dissemination by Prosecutors

Prior to and during a criminal trial the prosecutor may comment on the following matters.

   a. The accused's name, age, residence, occupation, family status, and citizenship;

   b. The substance or text of the charge such as complaint, indictment, information, and where appropriate, the identity of the complainant;

   c. The existence of probable cause to believe that the accused committed the offense charged;

   d. The identity of the investigating and arresting agency, the length and scope of the investigation, the thoroughness of the investigative procedures, and the diligence and professionalism of the law enforcement personnel in identifying and apprehending the accused;

   e. The circumstances immediately surrounding the arrest, including the time and place of arrest, the identity of the arresting officer or agency, resistance, pursuit, possession and use of weapons, and a description of items seized at the time of arrest or pursuant to a search warrant; and

   f. Matters which are of public record, the disclosure of which could serve the public interest, including correction and/or clarification of any misstatements, or misrepresentations of any record by other persons.

34.2 Restraints on Information

Prior to and during a criminal trial the prosecutor should only release the following information when the prosecutor believes that dissemination of such information is necessary to fulfill his obligations under 33.1 or under 34.3:

   a. statements as to the character or reputation of an accused person or a prospective witness;

   b. admissions, confessions, or the contents of a statement or alibi attributable to an accused person;

   c. the performance or results of tests or the refusal of the accused to take a test;

   d. statements concerning the credibility or anticipated testimony of prospective witnesses;

   e. the possibility of a plea of guilty to the offense charged or to a lesser offense or other disposition;

   f. information about tactics, strategies or arguments that will be used at trial.

34.3 Public Responses

Nothing in these standards should be deemed to preclude the prosecutor from making reasonable and fair response to comments of defense counsel or others.

34.4 Law Enforcement Policy on Information

Upon requests from local law enforcement agencies, the prosecutor should inform said agencies of the state, court, constitutional and case law provisions, as well as professional codes and standards, concerning fair trial/free press issues, and the prosecutor should encourage local law enforcement agencies to adopt policies which will protect both the rights of the individual and the ability of the prosecution to proceed.

MEDIA COMMENTS—
JUDICIAL DECISIONS, JURY VERDICTS AND CONDUCT

35.1 Judicial Decisions

The prosecutor has the authority to inform the public of judicial decisions that are contrary to law, fact or public interest. The prosecutor should not criticize judicial decisions through malice, politics or any other reason extraneous to the proper role of prosecutor.

35.2 Jury Verdicts and Juror Conduct

The prosecutor has the authority to inform the public of jury verdicts that are clearly contrary to the law and the evidence. The prosecutor also has the authority to inform the public of juror conduct that is plainly contrary to the sworn duties of jurors, such as verdicts that were clearly rendered on the basis of bias, prejudice or sympathy, rather than the law and evidence of a case. The prosecutor should not criticize jury verdicts or jury conduct through malice, politics or any other reason extraneous to the proper role of prosecutor.

COMMENTARY

Fairness in the pursuit of justice governs the conduct of the prosecuting attorney who is charged with representing the people in the community. Professional conduct is expected not only before trial and during the course of the trial but at all times that the prosecution function is being executed. In performing each prosecutorial duty, the prosecuting attorney must conform to the highest standards of justice. These standards were written to guide the prosecutor in public and media relations.

The standards deal with pre-trial and trial statements, post-trial positions, comments on judicial decisions, jury verdicts and juror conduct. The prosecutor has an affirmative duty to maintain and improve the criminal justice system. As an adjunct to this duty, the prosecutor should be allowed to criticize those aspects of a criminal proceeding that warrant improvement. There should be no prohibition on public statements that detract from the prosecutor's representative role. The appropriate public comments following a criminal proceeding where the highest standards of justice have not been satisfied should be determined according to the prosecutor's own conscience. If such statement is not permitted, the public is denied the most knowledgeable voice regarding the facts and circumstances of the proceeding. Unless the prosecutor has the rights under Standard [35.1], Judicial Decisions, the judiciary becomes immune from public censure and evaluation through insulation provided by arbitrary rules that are contrary to rights of free speech preferred in a democracy. Unless the prosecutor has the rights under Standard [35.2], Jury Verdicts and Juror Conduct, juries and jurors become immune from public censure and evaluation necessary for reform. The prosecuting attorney is responsible to his constituency, the general public. When the public should be made cognizant of a particular criminal proceeding, which may involve criticism of a verdict and/or a sentence, the prosecutor should respond only in the capacity as representative of the people. In addition, a response to charges of misconduct during trial which have been leveled against the prosecutor is appropriate.

The standards address the proper role of the prosecutor with respect to statements made by the police. As the chief law enforcement officer in his jurisdiction, the prosecutor has the authority to advise the police to adopt and implement policies on the subject of media comments that are fair to victims, witnesses, defendants and the public. The prosecutor, however, has neither the responsibility nor authority to monitor and discipline the police for improper statements, nor can the prosecutor be culpable for such unauthorized statements. To the extent that such responsibility is imposed on the prosecutor in the ABA Model Rules of Professional Conduct, it is rejected here.

Notwithstanding the specific direction of the standards, and limitations they impose to protect a fair trial, the prosecutor must recognize the value of an informed public. Therefore, the prosecutor has the responsibility of exercising sound judgment after balancing the interests involved and including what information is appropriate for release under all the circumstances.

RELATIONS WITH FUNDING ENTITY

36.1 Necessary Resources

It is the responsibility of the prosecutor's funding authority to provide all resources necessary for fulfillment of the prosecution function and the protection and safety of the public.

36.2 Funds for Standards Compliance

Funding of the prosecutor and other segments of the law enforcement and criminal justice systems must be sufficient for the implementation of compliance with the standards presented herein.

36.3 Assessment of Need

The prosecutor should cooperate with the funding entity in providing an assessment of need to effectively administer the duties of the office.

36.4 Independent Revenue

The budget for prosecution should be independent of and unrelated to revenues resulting from law enforcement and criminal justice activities, such as fines and forfeitures.

COMMENTARY

The basic premise of this standard is adequate funding. Little can happen in the way of system improvements in general, and the prosecutor's office in particular, without adequate funding. In a very real sense, virtually every provision in the National Prosecution Standards is addressed, at least in part, to the prosecutor's funding source. Without sufficient funding, few of these standards are attainable; and this standard in particular draws attention to this crucial fact.

* * *

An expectation persists among funding bodies that funds for law enforcement can be generated from fines and forfeitures. * * * Such remedies were never intended to be primary sources of revenue, and the notion that they can be "budgeted" into criminal justice agencies is totally misguided. To the extent that such remedies provide *some* funds for law enforcement agencies, this benefit is at best collateral to their primary purpose. Such revenues are not predictable; and, therefore, it is doubly wrong for funding sources to rely upon them when considering budget requests from prosecutors.

RELATIONS WITH THE PUBLIC

37.1 Community Organizations

The prosecutor should encourage the formation and growth of community-based organizations interested in aspects of the criminal justice system and crime prevention.

37.2 Staff Liaison

With respect to such organizations and to the extent that the prosecutor has the resources to do so, the prosecutor should assign an appropriate staff member to act as liaison to such organizations and should, in any case, provide qualified speakers from the prosecutor's office to address and appear before such groups on matters of common interest.

37.3 Public Education

The prosecutor should use all available resources to encourage citizen involvement in the support of law enforcement and prosecution programs and issues. The prosecutor should educate the public about the programs, policies, and goals of his office and alert the public to the ways in which the public may be involved and benefit from those programs, policies, and goals.

37.4 Advisory Role

Because the prosecutor has the responsibility of exercising discretion and making ultimate decisions, the role of public interest and citizen groups must be understood to be advisory only.

COMMENTARY

Responses to the problem of increasing crime have, to date, been relatively ineffective. * * * Community leaders, although recognizing the seriousness of the crime problem, often delegate responsibility for crime prevention to the police force and to government agencies which too frequently seem unable to keep up with crime prevention needs. As a result of this delegation, policies with respect to crime prevention are controlled by political and administrative bodies that are far removed from the local communities where crime originates.

Only when local citizens assume responsibility for crime prevention within their own communities will some progress be made in reducing crime rates across the country. * * * Since the prosecutor's work is intimately involved with crime in the community, the prosecutor can contribute significantly to crime prevention by lending personal support, and that of the prosecutor's office, to existing community crime prevention programs. Further, the prosecutor can lend expertise to criminologists, city planners and others as they make plans for the growth and development of the community in a way best suited to deter criminal activity. The standard has been developed to serve as a guide to prosecutors in implementing their role in community crime prevention. It recognizes the need for the prosecutor to not only interact with community crime prevention and social service organizations that are community-based, but also to take a hand in the formation of such citizen groups where they presently do not exist.

In order to assure that available government services do, in fact, reach the people for whom they are designed, positive public information programs should include continuous dissemination of information on available benefits so that individuals can learn how and if they qualify to receive the benefits. * * *

At the same time that governments are bringing services to more citizens, their decision-making processes should become more open. The prosecutor, as a citizen of the community, should contribute to the success of public information programs by lending his personal support to the programs. Further, since the prosecutor is perhaps more familiar than most individuals with government and its function in the community, he should take the lead in publicizing the prosecutor's programs and related community crime prevention programs.

* * *

Notwithstanding the benefits of public interest groups, the prosecutor has the ultimate responsibility for decision-making and the exercise of discretion. Citizen groups must understand these respective roles and operate within these limitations.

PROSECUTORIAL IMMUNITY

38.1 Scope of Immunity

When acting as a quasi-judicial officer, the prosecutor should have the same immunity from civil liability as that of the judiciary.

38.2 Good Faith Defense

In any civil litigation arising from administrative or investigative activities, the prosecutor should have an absolute defense in good faith and probable cause.

38.3 Coverage of Defense Costs

All costs, including attorney's fees and judgments, associated with suits claiming civil liability against the prosecutor and staff arising from the performance of their duties, should be provided by the prosecutor's funding entity.

38.4 Coverage of Judgment

The cost of insuring the prosecutor and staff against judgments from civil liability arising from the performance of their duties should be borne by the funding entity.

38.5 Personal Indemnity

Self-insured funding entities should indemnify the prosecutor and staff from direct losses due to civil liability.

COMMENTARY

In *Imbler v. Pachtman*, 424 U.S. 408 (1976), the U.S. Supreme Court ruled that prosecutors enjoy absolute immunity from Civil Rights Actions brought under Section 1983, 42 U.S.C., when acting within the scope of their duties in initiating and pursuing a criminal prosecution and in presenting the state's case. The Court noted that although such immunity leaves the genuinely wronged criminal defendant without civil redress against a prosecutor whose malicious or dishonest action deprives him of liberty, the alternative of qualifying a prosecutor's immunity would outweigh the broader public interest in that it would prevent the vigorous and fearless performance of the prosecutor's duty that is essential to the proper functioning of the criminal justice system.

The Court did not extend such absolute immunity to actions taken by a prosecutor outside of the scope of his duties as aforesaid. Thus, *Imbler* did not change pre-existing law with respect to the performance of duties that traditionally are viewed as investigative duties falling primarily within the police function.

* * *

The * * * prosecutor's funding source should provide the "costs" of defending civil suits against the prosecutor and his staff. * * * No prosecutor should be expected to function without full insurance coverage or a risk management plan covering intentional and non-intentional torts and all civil rights actions. The standard also implicitly recognizes that insurance costs in general for municipal agencies have greatly increased * * *; this, however, is not a reason for the funding source to provide anything less than full coverage to the prosecutor and staff or a fully adequate risk management plan.

RESOURCES on ETHICS, PROFESSIONALISM, and PUBLIC POLICY

A. ORGANIZATIONAL RESOURCES

B. INFORMATIONAL RESOURCES

A. ORGANIZATIONAL RESOURCES

1. Organizations and Programs Based in the U.S.

This section lists organizations, associations, research centers, educational and training programs, advocacy and watchdog groups, standard-setting bodies, and consultants, that deal with issues of ethics, professionalism, and public policy. It includes entities in academic, professional, nonprofit, and commercial settings, based in the U.S.

Each organization's mail address, telephone, fax number, e-mail address, and World Wide Web site URL are provided, where available. Notable reference works and periodicals (except newsletters of the same name as the organization) are also listed. These and other publications appear in the **Informational Resources** section, following.

Classifications (business, health, law, various professions, etc.) are noted only if an organization's name or affiliation is not self-explanatory.

**Academy of Legal Studies in
  Business**
Miami University
Dept. of Finance
120 Upham Hall
Oxford, OH 45056
Telephone: 800-831-2903
Fax: 513-523-8180
Website: http://miavx1.muohio.edu/
  ~herrondj
Periodical: *American Business Law
  Journal*

**Acadia Institute for the Study of
  Medicine, Science and Society**
118 West Street
Bar Harbor, ME 04604
Telephone: 207-288-4082
Fax: 207-288-3295

Accuracy in Media
4455 Connecticut Avenue, NW,
  Suite 330
Washington, DC 20008

(Accuracy in Media *cont'd*)
Telephone: 202-364-4401
Fax: 202-364-4098
E-mail: info@aim.org
Website: http://www.aim.org

**American Academy of Psychiatry &
  the Law**
1 Regency Drive
P.O. Box 30
Bloomfield, CT 06002
Telephone: 860-242-5450
  800-331-1389
Fax: 860-286-0787

**American Association for the
  Advancement of Science**
Directorate for Science and Policy
  Programs
1200 New York Avenue, NW
Washington, DC 20005
Telephone: 202-326-6600
Fax: 202-289-4950
Website: http://www.aaas.org/spp/
  dspp/dspp.htm

815

(American Association for the
Advancement of Science *cont'd*)
Scientific Freedom, Responsibility
and Law Program
Professional Society Ethics Group
Program of Dialogue Between
Science and Religion
Science and Human Rights Program
Science, Technology and Government
Periodicals: *Professional Ethics
Report*
*Science and Technology Policy
Yearbook*

American Association of Bioethics
(see American Society for Bioethics
and Humanities)

**American Board of Quality
Assurance and Utilization
Review Physicians**
4890 West Kennedy Blvd., Suite 260
Tampa, FL 33609
Telephone: 813-286-4411
Fax: 813-286-4387
Periodical: *Quality Assurance and
Utilization Review: Current
Readings in Concept and Practice*

American Civil Liberties Union
125 Broad Street
New York, NY 10004-2400
Telephone: 212-549-2500
E-mail: aclu@aclu.org
Website: http://www.aclu.org

**American College of Medical
Quality**
P.O. Box 34493
Bethesda, MD 20827
Telephone: 301-365-3570
Fax: 301-365-3202
E-mail: ACMg@aol.com
Periodical: *Journal of the American
College of Medical Quality*

**American Engineers for Social
Responsibility**
P.O. Box 2785
Washington, DC 20013-2785

**American Enterprise Institute for
Public Policy Research**
1150 17th Street, NW
Washington, DC 20036
Telephone: 202-862-5914
Fax: 202-862-7178
Periodical: *American Enterprise*

American Ethical Union
Federation of Ethical Societies in the
United States
2 West 64th Street
New York, NY 10023
Telephone: 212-873-6500
Website: http://www.aeu.org
(humanism)

**American Health Lawyers
Association**
1120 Connecticut Avenue, NW,
Suite 950
Washington, DC 20036-3902
Telephone: 202-833-1100
Fax: 202-833-1105
E-mail: info@healthlawyers.org
Website: http://www.healthlawyers.org
Periodicals: *Health Law Digest*
Health Lawyers News
Journal of Health and Hospital Law
References: *Peer Review Guidebook*
*State Illegal-Remuneration and Self-
Referral Laws*

**American Health Quality
Association**
1140 Connecticut Avenue, NW,
Suite 1050
Washington, DC 20036
Telephone: 202-331-5790
Fax: 202-331-9334

**American Institute of Medical
Ethics**
409 Encina Avenue
Davis, CA 95616
Telephone/Fax: 916-758-0739

**American Medical Peer Review
Association**
(see American Health Quality
Association)

American Psychology-Law Society
American Psychological Association
(see Ethics Standards section)

American Society for Bioethics and Humanities
4700 West Lake Avenue
Glenview, IL 60025-1485
Telephone: 847-375-4745
Fax: 847-375-4777
Website: http://www.asbh.org

American Society for Pharmacy Law
P.O. Box 7163
Auburn, CA 95604-7163
Telephone: 916-823-0667
Fax: 916-823-0669
Periodical: *RX IPSA Loquitur*

American Society for Political and Legal Philosophy
c/o K. Winston
Wheaton College
Dept. of Philosophy
Knapton 120
Norton, MA 02776
Telephone: 508-286-3677
Fax: 508-285-8270

American Society of Law, Medicine and Ethics
765 Commonwealth Avenue,
16th Floor
Boston, MA 02215
Telephone: 617-262-4990
Fax: 617-437-7596
E-mail: aslme@bu.edu
Website: http://www.aslme.org
Periodicals: *American Journal of Law & Medicine*
Journal of Law, Medicine and Ethics

Americans for Effective Law Enforcement
5519 North Cumberland Avenue,
Suite 1008
Chicago, IL 60656-1498

(Americans for Effective Law Enforcement *cont'd*)
Telephone: 773-763-2800
Fax: 773-763-3225
E-mail: AELE@aol.com.
Website: http://www.aele.org
Periodical: *Law Enforcement Liability Reporter*

Americans for the Enforcement of Attorney Ethics
P.O. Box 417-120
Chicago, IL 60641-7120
Telephone: 708-453-0080
Fax: 708-453-0083
Periodical: *Ethics Report*

Americans for the Enforcement of Judicial Ethics
P.O. Box 35189
Chicago, IL 60707-0189
Telephone: 708-453-0080
Fax: 708-453-0083
Periodical: *Judicial Code of Conduct Report*

Amnesty International
322 8th Avenue
New York, NY 10001
Telephone: 212-807-8400
Fax: 212-463-9193
212-627-1451
Additional Office: 304 Pennsylvania Avenue, SE
Washington, DC 20003
Telephone: 202-544-0200
Fax: 202-546-7142
E-mail: admin-us@aiusa.org
Website: http://www.amnesty.org
(human rights)

Applied and Professional Ethics Resource Center
Appalachian State University
Dept. of Philosophy and Religion
Greer Hall
Boone, NC 28608
Telephone: 704-262-3089
(various professions)

Applied Research Ethics National Association
132 Boylston Street, 4th Floor
Boston, MA 02116
Telephone: 617-423-4112
Fax: 617-423-1185
E-mail: PRMR@aol.com
Website: http://www.aamc.org/
  research/primr/arena

Architects, Designers, and Planners for Social Responsibility
P.O. Box 9126
Berkeley, CA 94709-0126
Telephone: 510-273-2428

Association for Moral Education
Wittenberg University
P.O. Box 720
Springfield, OH 45501-0720
Telephone: 800-677-7558
937-327-6231
Fax: 937-327-6340
Website: http://www.wittenberg.
  edu/ame

Association for Politics and the Life Sciences
Lake Superior State University
650 West Easterday Avenue
Sault Ste. Marie, MI 49783-1699
Telephone: 906-635-2757
Fax: 906-635-2111
E-mail: apls@lakers.lssu.edu
Website: http://198.110.216.3/apls
Periodical: *Politics and the Life Sciences*

Association for Practical and Professional Ethics
618 East Third Street
Bloomington, IN 47405
Telephone: 812-855-6450
Fax: 812-855-3315
E-mail: appe@indiana.edu
Website: http://php.indiana.edu/~appe/
  home.html
Intercollegiate Ethics Bowl™
Periodical: *Ethically Speaking*

Association for Spiritual, Ethical, and Religious Values in Counseling
American Counseling Association
(see Ethics Standards section)
Periodical: *Counseling and Values*

Association of Certified Fraud Examiners
Gregor Bldg.
716 West Avenue
Austin, TX 78701
Telephone: 800-245-3321
512-478-9070
Fax: 512-478-9297
E-mail: acfe@cfenet.com
Website: http://www.acfe.org
(business)

Association of Professional Responsibility Lawyers
American Bar Association
(see Ethics Standards section)

Association to Advance Ethical Hypnosis
2675 Oakwood Drive
Cuyahoga Falls, OH 44221
Telephone: 330-923-8880

Augustine Institute
Center for the Advancement of Paleo
  Orthodoxy
190 Manhattan Avenue
Oak Ridge, TN 37830
Telephone: 423-482-7549
Fax: 423-483-5581
Website: http://capo.org/augustine/
  caugust.html

Bacon Center for Ethics in Business
Iowa State University
332 Carver Hall
Ames, IA 50011-2063
Telephone: 515-294-2717
Website: http://www.public.
  iastate.edu/~BACON_CENTER/
  ?homepage.html

Baldy Center for Law and Social Policy
University at Buffalo Law School
State University of New York
511 O'Brian Hall
Buffalo, NY 14260
Telephone: 716-645-2060
Fax: 716-645-2064
Periodical: *Law & Social Policy*

Battelle Endowment for Technology and Human Affairs
Ohio State University
Office of Academic Affairs
203 Bricker Hall
190 North Oval Mall
Columbus, OH 43210
Telephone: 614-292-5881
Fax: 614-292-3658
Website: http://www.admin.ohio-state.edu/provost/betha/index.htm

Beard Center for Leadership in Ethics
Duquesne University
Palumbo School of Business Administration
Rockwell Hall
600 Forbes Avenue
Pittsburgh, PA 15282
Telephone: 412-396-5475
E-mail: weberj@duq2.cc.duq.edu
Website: http://fs2.bus.duq.edu/Beard/info.html

Bioethical Services of Virginia, Inc.
Medical Ethics Program Development and Support
P.O. Box 3468
Lynchburg, VA 24503
Telephone: 804-384-5322
E-mail: bsvinc@aol.com
Website: http://members.aol.com/bsvinc/index.html
Periodical: *Practical Ethics*

Bioethics and Medical Humanities
University of Medicine and Dentistry of New Jersey-Robert Wood Johnson Medical School
675 Hoes Lane
Piscataway, NJ 08855-5635

(Bioethics and Medical Humanities *cont'd*)
Telephone: 732-235-4549
Fax: 732-235-4569
E-mail: rmcintyr@umdnj.edu
Website: http://www2.umdnj.edu/ethicweb/bioethic.htm
Reference: *International Calendar of Bioethics Events* (online)
Periodical: *Trends in Health Care, Law and Ethics*

Bioethics Center
University Health Systems of Eastern Carolina
East Carolina University School of Medicine
Dept. of Medical Humanities
2S-17 Brody Medical Science Bldg.
Greenville, NC 27858-4354
Telephone: 252-816-2361
Fax: 252-816-2319
Website: http://www.ecu.edu/htdocs/med_hum/index.htm
Periodical: *Ethics & Health Care*

Bioethics Consultation Group
2322 Sixth Street, Suite 193
Berkeley, CA 94710
Telephone: 510-486-0626
510-540-7643
E-mail: info@bioethics-inc.com
Website: http://www.bioethics-inc.com
Reference: *Forming a Moral Community: A Resource for Healthcare Ethics Committees*
Periodicals: *Clinical Ethics Report*
Ethical Issues in Managed Care Quarterly

Bioethics Education Project
University of Washington School of Medicine
Dept. of Medical History and Ethics
Box 357120
Seattle, WA 98195
Fax: 206-685-7515
E-mail: bioethx@u.washington.edu
Website: http://eduserv.hscer.washington.edu/bioethics

Bioethics Forum
Princeton University
Dod Hall
Princeton, NJ 08544
E-mail: bioethic@princeton.edu
http://www.princeton.edu/~bioethic
Periodical: *Princeton Journal of
Bioethics*

Bioethics Institute
Program in Law, Ethics, and Health
Johns Hopkins University
School of Public Health
624 North Broadway, Room 511
Baltimore, MD 21205
Telephone: 410-955-3018
410-614-4188
Fax: 410-614-9567
E-mail: rfaden@jhsph.edu
rgaare@jhsph.edu
Website: http://www.sph.jhu.edu/
Departments/HPM/centers.htm

Bioethics Program
Iowa State University
402 Catt Hall
Ames, IA 50011
Telephone: 515-294-0054
Website: http://grad.admin.iastate.edu/
bioethics
Periodical: *Ag Bioethics Forum*

Brookings Institution
1775 Massachusetts Avenue, NW
Washington, DC 20036
Telephone: 202-797-6000
Fax: 202-797-6004
E-mail: brookinfo@brook.edu
Website: http://www.brook.edu
Center for Public Policy Education
Brookings Government Affairs
Institute
(public policy)

**Bureau of Essential Ethics
Education**
P.O. Box 80208
R.S.M., CA 92688-0208

(Bureau of Essential Ethics Education
cont'd)
Telephone: 800-229-3455
E-mail: ethicsusa@earthlink.net
Website: http://www.ethicsusa.com/
viahome.htm
Periodical: *Values in Action!*

**Carol Burnett Fund for
Responsible Journalism**
Dept. of Journalism
University of Hawaii
2550 Campus Road
Honolulu, HI 96822
Telephone: 808-956-6131
Fax: 808-956-5396
E-mail: tbrislin@hawaii.edu
Website: http://www2.hawaii.edu/
~tbrislin/jethics.html

Business Enterprise Trust
706 Cowper Street
Palo Alto, CA 94301
Telephone: 650-321-5100
Fax: 650-321-5774
E-mail: bet@betrust.org
Website: http://www.betrust.org

**Business Ethics Bureau of
Investigation**
P.O. Box 970488
4233 West Hillsboro Blvd.
Coconut Creek, FL 33097
Telephone: 954-341-6567
E-mail: info@bebi.com
Website: http://www.bebi.com

Business Ethics Foundation
28 Marshal Street, Suite 3
Brookline, MA 02146
Telephone: 617-232-1820
Fax: 617-232-2775
Periodical: *Business Ethics Resource:
A Resource on Ethics Management
for the CEO*
Reference: *Henderson's Ethictionary:
A Practical Dictionary of Business
Ethics Terms*

Business for Social Responsibility
609 Mission Street, 2nd Floor
San Francisco, CA 94105
Telephone: 415-537-0888
Fax: 415-537-0889
Website: http://www.bsr.org

**Carnegie Council on Ethics and
International Affairs**
Merrill House
170 East 64th Street
New York, NY 10021-7478
Telephone: 212-838-4120
Fax: 212-752-2432
E-mail: info@cceia.org
Website: http://www.cceia.org
Periodicals: *Ethics & International
Affairs*
Human Rights Dialogue

Cato Institute
1000 Massachusetts Avenue, NW
Washington, DC 20001-5403
Telephone: 202-842-0200
Fax: 202-842-3490
Website: http://www.cato.org
Periodicals: *Cato Journal:
An Interdisciplinary Journal of
Public Policy Analysis*
Cato Policy Report
*Regulation: The Cato Review of
Business & Government*
(public policy)

Caux Round Table
c/o M.A. Olson
4626 France Avenue South
Minneapolis, MN 55410
Telephone: 612-924-9234
Fax: 612-924-0068
Website: http://www.cauxroundtable
.org
Principles for Business
(business)

Center for Academic Ethics
Wayne State University
311 Education Bldg.
Detroit, MI 48202

(Center for Academic Ethics *cont'd*)
Telephone: 313-577-8290
Fax: 313-577-5235
Website: http://www.wayne.edu

Center for Academic Integrity
Duke University
102 West Duke Bldg.
Box 90434
Durham, NC 27708
Telephone: 919-660-3045
Fax: 919-660-3049
E-mail: srcole@acpub.duke.edu
Website: http://www.nwu.edu/uacc/cai

**Center for Accountability and
Performance**
American Society for Public
Administration
(see Ethics Standards section)

**Center for Advanced Study of
Ethics**
Georgetown University
Box 571248
Washington, DC 20057-1248

**Center for Advocacy and
Governmental Ethics**
American Advocacy Project
National Conference of State
Legislatures
1560 Broadway, Suite 700
Denver, CO 80202
Telephone: 303-830-2200
Fax: 303-863-8003
Website: http://www.ncsl.org

**Center for Applied and
Professional Ethics**
Central Missouri State University
Warrensburg, MO 64093
Telephone: 660-543-4268
Fax: 660-543-8445
Website: http://cape.cmsu.edu

**Center for Applied and
Professional Ethics**
University of Tennessee-Knoxville
Dept. of Philosophy
801 McClung Tower
Knoxville, TN 37996

(Center for Applied and Professional
Ethics *cont'd*)
Telephone: 423-974-3255
Fax: 423-974-3509
Website: http://web.utk.edu/~philosop/
department.html#CAPE
(various professions)

Center for Applied Christian Ethics
Wheaton College
Wheaton, IL 60187-5593
Telephone: 630-752-5886
Website: http://www.wheaton.edu:80/
cace

Center for Bioethics
University of Minnesota
Suite N504 Boynton
410 Church Street SE
Minneapolis, MN 55455-0346
Telephone: 612-624-9440
Fax: 612-624-9108
E-mail: bioethx@tc.umn.edu
Website: http://www.med.umn.edu/
bioethics
Periodical: *Bioethics Examiner*

Center for Bioethics
University of Pennsylvania
School of Medicine
3401 Market Street, Suite 320
Philadelphia, PA 19104-3308
Telephone: 215-898-7136
Fax: 215-573-3036
Website: http://www.med.upenn.edu/
~bioethic
*Ethics & Genetics: A Global
Conversation*
Periodical: *American Journal of
Ethics in Medicine: A National
Publication by Medical Students*

Center for Bioethics
University of South Carolina
Institute of Public Affairs
School of Medicine
Columbia, SC 29808
Telephone: 803-777-8157
Fax: 803-777-4575
Website: http://www.iopa.sc.edu/
centers/bioethic.htm

**Center for Bioethics and Human
Dignity**
2065 Half Day Road
Bannockburn, IL 60015
Telephone: 847-317-8180
Fax: 847-317-8153
Website: http://www.bioethix.org
Reference: *Bioethics Bibliographies*
Periodical: *Dignity Newsletter*

Center for Biomedical Ethics
Case Western Reserve University
School of Medicine
10900 Euclid Avenue
Cleveland, OH 44106-4976
Telephone: 216-368-6196
Fax: 216-368-8713
E-mail: xx245@po.cwru.edu
Website: http://www.cwru.edu/med/
bioethics/bioethics.html

Center for Biomedical Ethics
Stanford University
701 Welch Road
Palo Alto, CA 94304
Telephone: 650-723-5760
Fax: 650-725-6131
Website: http://www.stanford
.edu/dept/scbe
Program in Genomics, Ethics and
Society

Center for Biomedical Ethics
University of Virginia Health
Sciences Center
Box 348 HSC
Charlottesville, VA 22908
Telephone: 804-924-5974
Fax: 804-982-3971
E-mail: hsc-webmaster@virginia.edu
Website: http://www.med.Virginia
.EDU/medicine/inter-dis/bio-ethics
Periodical: *Bioethics Matters*

Center for Business Ethics
Bentley College
Adamian Graduate Center, Room 108
Waltham, MA 02452

(Center for Business Ethics *cont'd*)
Telephone: 781-891-2981
Fax: 781-891-2988
E-mail: cbeinfo@bentley.edu
Website: http://www.bentley.edu/
resource/cbe

Center for Business Ethics
Grand Valley State University
1 Campus Drive
Allendale, MI 49401-9403
Telephone: 616-895-6611
Fax: 616-895-3503
Website: http://www.gvsu.edu

Center for Business Ethics
Loyola Marymount University
7900 Loyola Blvd.
Los Angeles, CA 90045-8385
Telephone: 310-338-4523
Fax: 310-338-3000
E-mail: twhite@lmumail.lmu.edu
Website: http://www.lmu.edu/acad/
cenbuseth/cbe_home.htm
Periodical: *Business Ethics Fortnight*

Center for Business Ethics Studies
Cameron School of Business
University of St. Thomas
3800 Montrose Blvd.
Houston, TX 77006-4696
Telephone: 713-942-5917
Fax: 713-525-2110
E-mail: cameron@stthom.edu
Website: http://www.stthom.edu/cbes/
index.html

**Center for Business-Religion-
Professions**
Pittsburgh Theological Seminary
616 North Highland Avenue
Pittsburgh, PA 15206-2596
Telephone: 412-362-5610
Fax: 412-363-3260

Center for Christian Bioethics
Coleman Pavilion, 11121S
Loma Linda University
Loma Linda, CA 92350

(Center for Christian Bioethics
cont'd)
Telephone: 909-558-4956
Website: http://www.llu.edu/llu/
bioethics

Center for Civil and Human Rights
Notre Dame Law School
Notre Dame, IN 46556
Telephone: 219-631-7953
Website: http://www.nd.edu/~cchr

Center for Clinical Bioethics
Georgetown University Medical
Center
4000 Reservoir Road, NW
#D-238
Washington, DC 20007
Telephone: 202-687-2000

Center for Clinical Ethics
Lutheran General Hospital
1775 Dempster Street
9 South Pavilion
Park Ridge, IL 60068
Telephone: 847-723-7847

**Center for Corporate Community
Relations**
Boston College
Carroll School of Management
36 College Road
Chestnut Hill, MA 02467-3835
Telephone: 617-552-4545
Fax: 617-552-8499
E-mail: cccr@bc.edu
Website: http://www.bc.edu/cccr
Periodicals: *Community, Work &
Family*
*Corporate Community Relations
Letter*

**Center for Corporate Public
Involvement**
1001 Pennsylvania Avenue, NW
Washington, DC 20004
Telephone: 202-624-2425

Center for Creative Leadership
P.O. Box 26300
Greensboro, NC 27438-6300

(Center for Creative Leadership
cont'd)
Telephone: 336-545-2810
Fax: 336-282-3284
E-mail: info@leaders.ccl.org
Website: http://www.ccl.org
Periodical: *Leadership in Action*
(business)

Center for Democracy and Technology
1634 I Street NW, Suite 1100
Washington, DC 20006
Telephone: 202-637-9800
Fax: 202-637-0968
Website: http://www.cdt.org
Periodical: *Policy Posts*

Center for Environmental Philosophy
University of North Texas
P.O. Box 310980
Denton, TX 76203-0980
Telephone: 940-565-2727
Fax: 940-565-4439
E-mail: cep@unt.edu
Website: http://www.cep.unt.edu/
centerfo.html
Periodical: *Environmental Ethics:
An Interdisciplinary Journal
Dedicated to the Philosophical
Aspects of Environmental Problems*

Center for Ethics
Loyola University
6525 North Sheridan Road
Chicago, IL 60626-5385
Telephone: 773-508-8349
Fax: 773-508-8879
Website: http://www.luc.edu/depts/
ethics
Periodical: *Ethics Across the
University*

Center for Ethics
University of Tampa
College of Business
401 West Kennedy Blvd.
Tampa, FL 33606-1490

(Center for Ethics *cont'd*)
Telephone: 813-253-3333
E-mail: ethics@alpha.utampa.edu
Website: http://www.utampa.edu/acad/
cob/cfe/cfehome.htm

Center for Ethics and Human Rights
American Nurses Association
(see Ethics Standards section)
Periodical: *Communiqué*

Center for Ethics and Humanities in the Life Sciences
Michigan State University
C-201 East Fee Hall
East Lansing, MI 48824-3316
Telephone: 517-355-7550
E-mail: center@pilot.msu.edu
Website: http://www.chm.msu.edu/
CHM_HTML/CHM_Ethics.html
Medical Ethics Resource Network of
Michigan
Ethics-In-Formation

Center for Ethics and Social Policy
Graduate Theological Union
2400 Ridge Road
Berkeley, CA 94709
Telephone: 510-649-2560
Fax: 510-649-2565
Periodical: *Ethics & Policy Newsletter*

Center for Ethics in Health Care
Oregon Health Sciences University
3181 S.W. Sam Jackson Park Road,
L101
Portland, OR 97201-3098
Telephone: 503-494-8311
Website: http://www.ohsu.edu

Center for Ethics in Managed Care
Harvard Medical School
Division of Medical Ethics
641 Huntington Avenue, 4th Floor
Boston, MA 02115
Telephone: 617-432-3041

Center for Ethics in Public Policy & the Professions
Emory University, Suite 302
1462 Clifton Road, NE
Atlanta, GA 30322
Telephone: 404-727-1208
E-mail: EthicsCenter@learnlink
.emory.edu
Website: http://www.emory.edu/
ETHICS/index.html

Center for Ethics Studies
Marquette University
Academic Support Facility
735 North 17th Street
Milwaukee, WI 53233
Telephone: 414-288-5824

Center for Genetics, Ethics and Women
24 Berkshire Terrace
Amherst, MA 01002-1302
Telephone: 413-549-1925
Fax: 413-549-1226
E-mail: fholmes@pltpath.umass.edu
Website: http://www-unix.oit.umass
.edu/~fholmes

Center for Government Accountability
P.O. Box 50291
Knoxville, TN 37950-0291
Telephone: 423-691-7835
E-mail: whistleblower1@
geocities.com
Website: http://www.geocities.com/
CapitolHill/Lobby/3486
Periodical: *Whistleblower's Gazette*

Center for Health Care Ethics
St. Louis University Health Sciences
Center
1402 South Grand Blvd.
St. Louis, MO 63104
Telephone: 314-577-8195
Fax: 314-268-5150
Periodical: *Health Care Ethics in the
USA*

Center for Health Ethics and Law
Robert C. Byrd Health Sciences Center
West Virginia University
1354 Health Sciences North
P.O. Box 9022
Morgantown, WV 26506-9022
Telephone: 304-293-7618
Fax: 304-293-7442
Website: http://www.hsc.wvu.edu/chel
West Virginia Network of Ethics
Committees

Center for Health Law and Ethics
Institute of Public Law
University of New Mexico School of
Law
1117 Stanford Street NE
Albuquerque, NM 87131
Telephone: 505-277-5006
Fax: 505-277-7064
Website: http://wwwipl.unm.edu/chle/
chle.html

Center for Health Law Studies
St. Louis University School of Law
3700 Lindell Blvd.
St. Louis, MO 63108
Telephone: 314-977-3067
Fax: 314-977-3966
Periodical: *Health Law News
Bibliography of Selected Internet
Resources in Health Law and
Policy*

Center for Health Policy and Ethics
Creighton University
2500 California Plaza
Criss II, #232
Omaha, NE 68178
Telephone: 402-280-2017
Fax: 402-280-5735
Website: http://CHPE.creighton.edu
Periodical: *Focus*

Center for Health Policy and Ethics
George Mason University
College of Nursing and Health Science
Fairfax, VA 22030-4444
Telephone: 703-993-1931
Fax: 703-993-1953
Website: http://www.gmu.edu/
departments/chp

Center for Healthcare Ethics
St. Joseph Health System
P.O. Box 14132
Orange, CA 92863-1532
Telephone: 714-997-7690
Fax: 714-997-7907
E-mail: ethics@corp.stjoe.org
Periodicals: *Bioethics News &
  Reviews
Ethical Currents
Ethical Dimensions
Healthcare Reform & Ethics Review*

**Center for Improving Government
  Performance**
National Academy of Public
  Administration
1120 G Street, NW, Suite 850
Washington, DC 20005
Telephone: 202-347-3190
Fax: 202-393-0993
Website: http://www.NAPAWash.org/
  NAPA/ImprovingGovernment
  .nsf?OpenDatabase

Center for Judicial Accountability
Box 69, Gedney Station
White Plains, NY 10605-0069
Telephone: 914-421-1200
Fax: 914-684-6554
E-mail: probono69@aol.com

**Center for Judicial Conduct
  Organizations**
American Judicature Society
180 North Michigan Avenue,
  Suite 600
Chicago, IL 60601
Telephone: 312-558-6900
Fax: 312-558-9175
Website: http://www.ajs.org
References: *Digest of Judicial Ethics
  Advisory Opinions
Electing Justice: A Handbook of
  Judicial Election Reforms
Judicial Disqualification: An
  Empirical Study of Judicial
  Practices and Attitudes*

(Center for Judicial Conduct
  Organizations *cont'd*)
*Judicial Ethics and the
  Administration of Justice:
  A Videotaped Instructional
  Program on Judicial Ethics
Justice at First Hand: A Videotape
  Curriculum on Ethics &
  Professionalism for Nonjudicial
  Court Personnel
Key Issues in Judicial Ethics Series
Practices and Procedures of State
  Judicial Conduct Organizations*
Periodicals: *Judicature
Judicial Conduct Reporter
Judicial Discipline and Disability
  Digest*

Center for Law and Social Policy
1616 P Street, NW, Suite 150
Washington, DC 20036
Telephone: 202-328-5140
Fax: 202-328-5195
E-mail: info@clasp.org
Website: http://www.clasp.org

Center for Law Enforcement Ethics
Southwestern Law Enforcement
  Institute
Southwestern Legal Foundation
P.O. Box 830707
Richardson, TX 75083-0707
Telephone: 972-699-9501
Fax: 972-699-3870
Website: http://web2.airmail.net/slf/
  clee.html
Periodical: *Ethics Roll Call*

**Center for Literature, Medicine,
  and the Health Care Professions**
Hiram College and Northeastern Ohio
  University College of Medicine
Mahan House
Hiram, OH 44234
Telephone: 330-569-5380
Fax: 330-569-5449
Website: http://www.hiram.edu/
  admin/literature.shtml

Center for Media and Public Affairs
2100 L Street, NW, Suite 300
Washington, DC 20037
Telephone: 202-223-2942
Website: http://www.cmpa.com
Periodical: *Media Monitor*

Center for Medical Ethics
University of Pittsburgh
Medical Arts Bldg., Suite 300
3708 Fifth Avenue
Pittsburgh, PA 15213-3405
Telephone: 412-647-5700
Fax: 412-647-5877
E-mail: bio-ethics@med.pitt.edu
Website: http://www.law.pitt.edu/
    mdethics

Center for Medical Ethics and Health Policy
Baylor College of Medicine
IREL Room 401
One Baylor Plaza
Houston, TX 77030-3498
Telephone: 713-798-6290
Fax: 713-798-5678
Website: http://www.bcm.tmc
    .edu/ethics
Periodical: *Journal of Medicine and Philosophy: A Forum for Bioethics and Philosophy of Medicine*

Center for Medical Ethics and Mediation
1081 Camino Del Rio South, Suite 106
San Diego, CA 92108
Telephone: 619-296-7268
Fax: 619-296-7011
E-mail: cmem@flash.net
Website: http://www.wh.com/cmem

Center for Philosophy, Law, Citizenship
State University of New York-Farmingdale
Knapp Hall 15
Farmingdale, NY 11735
Telephone: 516-420-2047

Center for Philosophy of Science
University of Pittsburgh
817 Cathedral of Learning
Pittsburgh, PA 15260
Telephone: 412-624-1050
Fax: 412-624-3895
Website: http://www.pitt.edu/~pittcntr
Archives of Scientific Philosophy in the 20th Century
University of Pittsburgh Series in the Philosophy of Science
Pittsburgh Series in Philosophy and History of Science

Center for Professional and Applied Ethics
University of North Carolina at Charlotte
9201 University City Blvd.
Charlotte, NC 28223-0001
Telephone: 704-547-3542
Fax: 704-547-2172
E-mail: jmlincou@email.uncc.edu
Website: http://www.uncc.edu/
    colleges/arts_and_sciences/
    philosophy/center.html

Center for Professional and Applied Ethics
Valdosta State University
Dept. of Philosophy
1500 North Patterson Street
Valdosta, GA 31698
Telephone: 912-333-5800
Website: http://www.valdosta
    .edu/cpae

Center for Professional Development in the Law
955 Massachusetts Avenue
Cambridge, MA 02139
Telephone: 617-868-6669
Fax: 617-876-0203
E-mail: cpdl@shore.net
Website: http://www1.shore.net/~cpdl

Center for Professional Ethics
Manhattan College
Manhattan College Parkway
Riverdale, NY 10471

(Center for Professional Ethics
cont'd)
Telephone: 718-862-8000
Fax: 718-862-8016
E-mail: jwilcox@manhattan.edu
Website: http://www.manhattan.edu/
special/prethics/corporat.html
(business)

**Center for Professional
Responsibility**
American Bar Association
(see Ethics Standards section)
Periodicals: *ABA/BNA Lawyers'
Manual on Professional Conduct
Lawyers' Professional Liability Update
The Professional Lawyer*

Center for Professional Well-Being
21 West Colony Place, Suite 150
Durham, NC 27705
Telephone: 919-489-9167
919-419-0011
800-473-5880
Fax: 919-403-8605
Periodical: *Being Well: Bulletin of
the Society for Professional
Well-Being*
(health)

Center for Public Integrity
1634 I Street, NW, Suite 902
Washington, DC 20006
Telephone: 202-783-3900
Fax: 202-783-3906
E-mail: ctrforpi@essential.org

**Center for Religion, Ethics, and
Social Policy**
Cornell University
Annabel Taylor Hall
Ithaca, NY 14853
Telephone: 607-255-5027
Fax: 607-255-9985

**Center for Research in Faith and
Moral Development**
Emory University
Candler School of Theology
Atlanta, GA 30322
Telephone: 404-727-4155
Fax: 404-727-2915

**Center for Reproductive Law &
Policy**
120 Wall Street, 18th Floor
New York, NY 10005
Telephone: 212-514-5534
Fax: 212-514-5538
E-mail: info@crlp.org
Website: http://www.crlp.org
Periodical: *Reproductive Freedom
News*

**Center for Science and Technology
Policy and Ethics**
Texas A&M University
329 Dulie Bell
College Station, TX 77843-4355
Telephone: 409-845-5434
Fax: 409-847-9372
E-mail: susanna@tamu.edu
Website: http://www.tamu.edu/cstpe
Periodical: *Currents*

**Center for Social & Legal
Research**
2 University Plaza, Suite 414
Hackensack, NJ 07601
Telephone: 201-996-1154
Fax: 201-996-1883
E-mail: pab@mail.idt.net
Periodical: *Privacy & American
Business*

**Center for the Advancement of
Applied Ethics**
Carnegie-Mellon University
Philosophy Dept.
135 Baker Hall
Pittsburgh, PA 15213
Telephone: 412-268-8568
Fax: 412-268-1440
Website: http://www.lcl.cmu.edu/
CAAE/Home/CAAE.html

**Center for the Advancement of
Ethics**
University of Wyoming
Laramie, WY 82071-3963
Telephone: 307-766-3368
Website: http://www.uwyo.edu/A&S/
phil/cae

Center for the Advancement of Ethics and Character
Boston University
School of Education
605 Commonwealth Avenue
Boston, MA 02214
Telephone: 617-353-3262
Fax: 617-353-3924

Center for the Health Professions
University of California at San Francisco
1388 Sutter Street, Suite 805
San Francisco, CA 94109
Telephone: 415-476-8181
Fax: 415-476-4113

Center for the Study of Bioethics
Medical College of Wisconsin
8701 Watertown Plank Road
P.O. Box 26509
Milwaukee, WI 53226-050
Telephone: 414-456-4299
Fax: 414-456-6511
Website: http://www.mcw.edu/bioethics
Reference: *Bioethics Online Service*

Center for the Study of Ethics and Contemporary Moral Problems
Hebrew Union College and University of Cincinnati
3101 Clifton Avenue
Cincinnati, OH 45220-2488
Telephone: 513-221-1875
Fax: 513-221-1842

Center for the Study of Ethics in Society
Western Michigan University
1201 Oliver Street
Kalamazoo, MI 49008
Telephone: 616-387-3130
Fax: 616-387-3990

Center for the Study of Ethics in the Professions
Illinois Institute of Technology
10 West 31st Street
Room 102, Stuart Building
Chicago, IL 60616-3793

(Center for the Study of Ethics in the Professions *cont'd*)
Telephone: 312-567-3017
Fax: 312-567-3016
E-mail: csep@charlie.cns.iit.edu
Website: http://csep.iit.edu
Codes of Ethics Online
Professional Ethics and Engineering: A Resource Guide
Periodical: *Perspectives on the Professions: Ethical & Policy Issues*

Center for the Study of Religion and American Culture
Indiana University - Purdue University at Indianapolis
425 University Blvd., Room 344
Indianapolis, IN 46202-5140
Telephone: 317-274-8409
Fax: 317-278-3354
Website: http://www.iupui.edu/it/raac
Periodical: *Religion and American Culture: A Journal of Interpretation*

Center for the Study of Science in Society
Virginia Polytechnic Institute and State University
Center for Interdisciplinary Studies
Science and Technology Studies
131 Lane Hall
Blacksburg, VA 24061-0227
Telephone: 540-231-7615
Fax: 540-231-7013
E-mail: sts@vt.edu
Website: http://www.cis.vt.edu/stshome/frameindex.htm

Center for the Study of Society and Medicine
College of Physicians & Surgeons of Columbia University
630 West 168th Street
P&S Box 11
New York, NY 10032
Telephone: 212-305-4184
Fax: 212-305-6416
E-mail: cssm@columbia.edu
Website: http://cpmcnet.columbia.edu/dept/cssm/cssm.html

Center for the Study of Values in Public Life
Harvard Divinity School
56 Francis Avenue
Cambridge, MA 02138
Telephone: 617-496-3586
E-mail: csvpl@div.harvard.edu
Website: http://divweb.harvard.edu/csvpl
Periodical: *Religion & Values in Public Life*

Center for Theology & the Natural Sciences
Graduate Theological Union
2400 Ridge Road
Berkeley, CA 94709
Telephone: 510-848-8152
Fax: 510-649-1417
E-mail: ctnsinfo@ctns.org
Website: http://www.ctns.org

Center for Values and Social Policy
University of Colorado
Campus Box 232
Boulder, CO 80309
Telephone: 303-492-6364
Fax: 303-492-8386
E-mail: vspctr@spot.Colorado.edu
Website: http://www.colorado.edu/philosophy/Center

Center on Professionalism
University of Pennsylvania Law School
3400 Chestnut Street
Philadelphia, PA 19104-6204
Telephone: 215-898-9812
Fax: 215-573-2056
Website: http://www.law.upenn.edu

Center to Improve Care of the Dying
George Washington University
2175 K Street, NW
Washington, DC 20037
Telephone: 202-467-2222

Character Counts! Coalition
Josephson Institute of Ethics
4640 Admiralty Way, Suite 1001
Marina del Rey, CA 90292-6610
Telephone: 310-306-1868
Fax: 310-827-1864
E-mail: cc@JIethics.org
Website: http://www.charactercounts.org
(youth ethics training)

Character Training Institute
Character and Ethics Training for Schools or Businesses
3018 200th Place SE
Bothell, WA 98012
Telephone: 425-889-7816
E-mail: Mark_Putnam@asd.wednet.edu
Website: http://members.tripod.com/~mput/index.htm

Chicago Center for Religion and Science
Center for Advanced Study in Religion and Science
Lutheran School of Theology at Chicago
1100 East 55th Street
Chicago, IL 60615-5199
Telephone: 773-256-0670
Fax: 773-256-0682/0782
Website: http://192.146.206.5/www/faculty/shaferi/ccrs.html

Choice in Dying
1035 30th Street, NW
Washington, DC 20007
Telephone: 202-338-9790
800-989-WILL
Fax: 202-338-0242
Website: http://www.choices.org

Citizens Against Government Waste
1301 Connecticut Avenue, NW, Suite 400
Washington, DC 20036
Telephone: 202-467-5300
800-BE-ANGRY
Fax: 202-467-4523
Website: http://www.govt-waste.org

Citizens for Leaders with Ethics and Accountability Now!
4301 South Pine Street, Suite 148
Tacoma, WA 98409-7204
Telephone: 253-473-1212
800-219-7332
Fax: 253-473-0704
E-mail: sherry@clean.org
Website: http://www.clean.org
CLEAN Watch
(government)

Citizens United Resisting Euthanasia
812 Stephen Street
Berkeley Springs, WV 25411
Telephone: 304-258-LIFE
Fax: 304-258-5420
E-mail: CUREltd@ix.netcom.com
Website: http://pw2.netcom.com/
~cureltd/index.html

Civic Practices Network
Center for Human Resources
Heller School for Advanced Studies
in Social Welfare
Brandeis University
60 Turner Street
Waltham, MA 02154
Telephone: 617-736-4890
Fax: 617-736-4891
E-mail: cpn@tiac.net
Website: http://www.cpn.org
(citizenship, government)

Cleveland Clinic Foundation
Dept. of Bioethics
9500 Euclid Avenue, P-31
Cleveland, OH 44195
Telephone: 216-444-8720
Fax: 216-444-9275
Website: http://www.ccf.org/ed/
bioethic/biohome.htm
Bioethics Network of Ohio

Clinical Ethics Center
Memorial Medical Center
800 North Rutledge Street
Springfield, IL 62781-0001
Telephone: 217-757-2353
Fax: 217-757-2359

Coalition for Environmentally Responsible Economies
711 Atlantic Avenue
Boston, MA 02111
Telephone: 617-451-0927
Fax: 617-482-2028
Website: http://www.ceres.org

Colloquium on Rational Choice, Legal Institutions, and Political Organization
Law, Philosophy, and Social Theory
Colloquium
New York University School of Law
40 Washington Square South
Vanderbilt Hall
New York, NY 10012
Telephone: 212-998-6100
Fax: 212-995-3156
E-mail: law.jdprograms@nyu.edu
Website: http://www.law.nyu.edu/
featuredarticles/interdisciplinary
studies.html

Commission for Accountability to the Public
3330 Windsong
Rockford, IL 61114-8143
Telephone: 815-282-0205

Committee on Professional Ethics, Rights and Freedoms
American Political Science
Assocation
527 New Hampshire Avenue, NW
Washington, DC 20036-1206
Telephone: 202-483-2512
Fax: 202-483-2657
E-mail: apsa@apsanet.org
Website: http://www.apsanet.org
Reference: *A Guide to Professional
Ethics in Political Science*

Committee to Expose Dishonest and Incompetent Attorneys and Judges
c/o D. Palmer
6140 Henthorne Drive
Maumee, OH 43537

(Committee to Expose Dishonest and
Incompetent Attorneys and Judges
cont'd)
Telephone: 419-866-4606
Fax: 419-866-8774
E-mail: NoEthics1@aol.com
Website: http://www.amoralethics.com

Common Cause
1250 Connecticut Avenue, NW
Washington, DC 20036
Telephone: 202-833-1200
Fax: 202-659-3716
Periodical: *Common Cause Magazine*
(government)

Communitarian Network
2130 H Street, NW, Suite 714
Washington, DC 20052
Telephone: 202-994-7997
E-mail: comnet@gwis2.circ.gwu.edu
Website: http://www.gwu.edu/~ccps
Reference: *Communitarian
Bibliography* (online)
Periodicals: *Communitarian Update
Responsive Community*

**Community-State Partnerships to
Improve End-of-Life Care**
Midwest Bioethics Center
1021-1025 Jefferson Street
Kansas City, MO 64105-1329
Telephone: 816-842-7110
Fax: 816-842-3440
E-mail: partners@midbio.org
Website: http://www.midbio.com
Periodical: *State Initiatives in
End-of-Life Care*

Compassion in Dying
6312 S.W. Capitol Highway,
Suite 415
Portland, OR 97201
Telephone: 503-221-9556
Fax: 503-228-9160
E-mail: info@compassionindying.org
Website: http://www.Compassion
InDying.org

Computer Ethics Institute
11 Dupont Circle, NW, Suite 900
Washington, DC 20036
Telephone: 202-939-3707
Fax: 202-797-7806
Additional Address: P.O. Box 42672
Washington, DC 20015
Telephone/Fax: 301-469-0615
Website: http://www.brook.edu/its/cei/
cei_hp.htm
Reference: *Ten Commandments of
Computer Ethics*

**Computer Professionals for Social
Responsibility**
P.O. Box 717
Palo Alto, CA 94302
Telephone: 650-322-3778
Fax: 650-322-4748
E-mail: cpsr@cpsr.org
Website: http://www.cpsr.org/
home.html
Reference: *Bibliography of
Computing, Ethics, and
Social Responsibility* (online)

Consortium Ethics Program
Center for Medical Ethics
University of Pittsburgh
Medical Arts Bldg., Suite 300
3708 Fifth Avenue
Pittsburgh, PA 15213-3405
Telephone: 412-647-5700
Fax: 412-647-5877
E-mail: cep+@pitt.edu
Website: http://www.pitt.edu/~cep
Periodical: *Community Ethics*

Council for Ethics in Economics
125 East Broad Street
Columbus, OH 43215
Telephone: 614-221-8661
Fax: 614-221-8707
Website: http://www.
businessethics.org
Reference: *i-CASE Series* (interactive
business ethics case studies)
Website: http://www.i-case.com
Periodical: *Ethics in Economics*

Council for Ethics in Legislative Advocacy
c/o NLD
P.O. Box 18416
Capitol Hill Station
Denver, CO 80218-0416
E-mail: nlddirect@aol.com
Website: http://www.lobbyist
  directory.com/indxcela.htm
Periodical: *Ethics in the News*
  (online)

Council for Research in Values & Policy
Catholic University of America
P.O. Box 261 Cardinal Station
003 St. Bonaventure
Washington, DC 20064
Telephone: 202-319-5636
Fax: 202-319-6089

Council for Responsible Genetics
5 Upland Road, Suite 3
Cambridge, MA 02140
Telephone: 617-868-0870
Fax: 617-491-5344
E-mail: crg@essential.org
Website: http://www.essential.org/crg/
  crg.html
Periodical: *GeneWATCH*

Council of Better Business Bureaus
4200 Wilson Blvd., Suite 800
Arlington, VA 22203-1838
Telephone: 703-276-0100
Fax: 703-525-8277
Additional Office: National
  Advertising Division
845 Third Avenue
New York, NY 10022
National Torch Award for
  Marketplace Ethics
Website: http://www.bbb.org

Council on Economic Priorities
30 Irving Place, 9th Floor
New York, NY 10003-2386

(Council on Economic Priorities
  cont'd)
Telephone: 212-420-1133
800-729-4237
Fax: 212-420-0988
E-mail: CEP@echonyc.com
Website: http://www-2.realaudio.com/
  CEP/home.html

Council on Governmental Ethics Laws
10951 West Pico Blvd., Suite 120
Los Angeles, CA 90064-2126
Telephone: 310-470-6590
Fax: 310-475-3752
Website: http://www.cogel
  .org/home.asp
Periodical: *Guardian*

Council on Licensure, Enforcement, and Regulation
P.O. Box 11910
3560 Iron Works Pike
Lexington, KY 40578-1910
Telephone: 606-231-1890
Reference: *Directory of Professional
  and Occupational Regulation in the
  United States and Canada*

Dale Ethics Center
Youngstown State University
Dept. of Philosophy and Religious
  Studies
401 Debartolo Hall
Youngstown, OH 44555-3448
Telephone: 330-742-1463
Fax: 330-742-2304
Website: http://www.as.ysu.edu/
  ~philrel/ethics/mission.htm

Decisions and Ethics Center
Stanford University
Dept. of Engineering-Economic
  Systems and Operations Research
Terman Engineering Center
Stanford, CA 94305-4023
Telephone: 415-326-9613
Fax: 650-723-1614
650-723-4107
E-mail: gkf@leland.stanford.edu
Website: http://www-leland.stanford
  .edu/group/decisions

Defense Industry Initiative on Business Ethics and Conduct
c/o W.E. Prachar
1299 Pennsylvania Avenue, NW,
4th Floor
Washington, DC 20004
Telephone: 202-383-6745
Website: http://www.dii.org
Reference: *DII Information Clearinghouse Index of Corporate Ethics Program Materials* (online)

Dept. of Medical History & Ethics
University of Washington School of Medicine
Health Sciences Bldg., Room A204
Box 357120
Seattle, WA 98195-7120
Telephone: 206-543-5145
Fax: 206-685-7515
Website: http://weber.u.washington.edu/~mhedept

Discussion of Values and Ethics
St. Louis College of Pharmacy
4588 Parkview Place
St. Louis, MO 63110
Telephone: 314-367-8700
E-mail: greynold@rx.stlcop.edu
Website: http://rx.stlcop.edu/dove/index.html

Effective Government Committee
530 7th Street, SE, 2nd Floor
Washington, DC 20003
Telephone: 202-347-6112
Fax: 202-544-8612

Einstein Institute for Science, Health and the Courts
3 Bethesda Metro Center, Suite 750
Bethesda, MD 20814
Telephone: 301-961-1949
E-mail: einshac@aol.com
Website: http://www.ornl.gov/courts/journal1/describe.htm
Periodical: *CASOLM: The Courts & Science On-Line Magazine*

Electronic Frontier Foundation
1550 Bryant Street, Suite 725
San Francisco, CA 94103-4832
Telephone: 415-436-9333
Fax: 415-436-9993
E-mail: ask@eff.org
Website: http://www.eff.org
(computing)

Electronic Privacy Information Center
666 Pennsylvania Avenue, SE, Suite 301
Washington, DC 20003
Telephone: 202-544-9240
Fax: 202-547-5482
E-mail: info@epic.org
Website: http://www.epic.org

Emerson Electric Center for Business Ethics
St. Louis University
School of Business and Administration
3674 Lindell Blvd.
St. Louis, MO 63108-3397
Telephone: 314-977-3836
E-mail: fisherje@sluvca.slu.edu
Website: http://www.slu.edu/centers/eecbe/eecbehome.html

Enjoin for Responsible Government
10450 Lottsford Road, #3103
Mitchellville, MD 20721
Telephone: 301-925-7686
Fax: 301-925-7318

Environmental Ethics and Public Policy Research Program
Center for the Study of Values in Public Life
Harvard Divinity School
56 Francis Avenue
Cambridge, MA 02138
Telephone: 617-496-3586
E-mail: csvpl@div.harvard.edu
Website: http://divweb.harvard.edu/csvpl/ee
Reference: *Subject Bibliographies in Environmental Ethics* (online)

Environmental Ethics Certificate Program
University of Georgia
Dept. of Marine Sciences/Dept. of Philosophy
Peabody Hall, Room 107
Athens, GA 30602
Telephone: 706-542-2823
Fax: 706-542-2839
Website: http://www.phil.uga.edu/eecp
EECPerspectives
Periodicals: *Ethics and the Environment*

Ethics and Public Policy Center
1015 15th Street, NW
Washington, DC 20005
Telephone: 202-682-1200
Fax: 202-408-0632
E-mail: ethics@eppc.org
Website: http://www.eppc.org
Periodicals: *American Character: A Commentary on Domestic Issues* (online)
American Purpose (online)
Unum Conversations (online)

Ethics Center
University of South Florida
100 Fifth Avenue South
St. Petersburg, FL 33701-5016
Telephone: 813-553-3172
Fax: 813-553-3169
Website: http://www.stpt.usf.edu/coas/ethics/main.html
Periodical: *Medical Ethics Newsletter*
(various professions)

Ethics College
Medical-Legal Education Center
2139 North University Drive, Suite 182
Coral Springs, FL 33071
Telephone: 800-984-9853
E-mail: info@cle-ethicsseminar.com
Website: http://www.cle-ethicsseminar.com/ethcoll.html

Ethics Dept.
Northridge Hospital Medical Center
18300 Roscoe Blvd.
Northridge, CA 91328

(Ethics Dept. *cont'd*)
Telephone: 818-885-5479

Ethics Institute
Cedar Crest College
100 College Drive
Allentown, PA 18104-6196
Telephone: 610-740-3792
Fax: 610-606-4613
(health)

Ethics Officer Association
30 Church Street, Suite 331
Belmont, MA 02478
Telephone: 617- 484-9400
Fax: 617-484-8330
E-mail: amujica@eoa.org
Website: http://www.eoa.org
business)

Ethics Resource Center
1747 Pennsylvania Avenue, NW, Suite 400
Washington, DC 20006
Telephone: 202-737-2258
Fax: 202-737-2227
E-mail: ethics@ethics.org
Website: http://www.ethics.org
National Institute for Character Education
Periodical: *Ethics Today*

Ethics Teaching Center
Indiana University at Kokomo
2300 South Washington Street
Kokomo, IN 46902
Telephone: 317-455-9258

Euthanasia Research & Guidance Organization
24829 Norris Lane
Junction City, OR 97448-9559
Telephone/Fax: 541-998-1873
E-mail: ergo@efn.org
Websites: http://www.efn.org/~ergo
http://www.FinalExit.org
Euthanasia World Directory

Fairness and Accuracy in Reporting
30 West 25th Street
New York, NY 10001

(Fairness and Accuracy in Reporting
  cont'd)
Telephone: 212-633-6700
Fax: 212-727-7668
E-mail: FAIR@fair.org
Website: http://www.fair.org
Periodical: *Extra! Magazine*

Federation of American Scientists
307 Massachusetts Avenue, NE
Washington, DC 20002
Telephone: 202-546-3300
Fax: 202-675-1010
E-mail: fas@fas.org
Website: http://www.fas.org
Periodicals: *@ction @lert* (online)
*Public Interest Report: Journal of the
  Federation of American Scientists*
Secrecy and Government Bulletin
(public policy)

First Amendment Center
The Freedom Forum
1207 18th Avenue South
Nashville, TN 37212
Telephone: 615-321-9588
Fax: 615-321-9599
E-mail: info@fac.org
Website: http://www.
  freedomforum.org/first/welcome.asp

**Forest Service Employees for
  Environmental Ethics**
P.O. Box 11615
Eugene, OR 97440
Telephone: 541-484-2692
E-mail: afseee@afseee.org
Website: http://www.afseee.org
Periodical: *Inner Voice*

Forum for Bioethics and Philosophy
University of Miami School of
  Medicine
P.O. Box 016960
M-825
Miami, FL 33101
Telephone: 305-243-5723
E-mail: kwg@paris.cs.miami.edu
Website: http://www.med.miami.edu

**Foundation for Individual
  Responsibility and Social Trust**
2500 One Liberty Place
Philadelphia, PA 19103
Telephone: 888-FIRST96
215-241-7980
Fax: 215-851-1420
E-mail: first@libertynet.org
Website: http://www.libertynet.org/first
(youth ethics training)

Freedom Forum
World Center
1101 Wilson Blvd.
Arlington, VA 22209
Telephone: 703-528-0800
Fax: 703-522-4831
E-mail: news@freedomforum.org
Website: http://www.freedomforum.org
Periodical: *FREE! Freedom Forum
  ONLINE*

Full Disclosure
P.O. Box 1533
Oil City, PA 16301
Telephone: 814-676-2345
E-mail: glr@glr.com
Website: http://www.fulldisclosure.org
(privacy, technology, government)

Funeral Ethics Association
215 South Grand Avenue West
Springfield, IL 62704
Telephone: 217-525-1520
Website: http://www.fea.org

Giraffe Project
P.O. Box 759
Langley, WA 98260
Telephone: 360-221-7989
Fax: 360-221-7817
E-mail: office@giraffe.org
Website: http://www.giraffe.org/giraffe
(youth ethics training)

Global Lawyers and Physicians
Boston University School of Public
  Health
Health Law Dept.
715 Albany Street
Boston, MA 02118

(Global Lawyers and Physicians
  cont'd)
Telephone: 617-638-4626
Fax: 617-414-1464
E-mail: glp@bu.edu
Website: http://www.bumc.bu.edu/
  www/sph/lw/glphr.htm
(human rights)

**Gould Center for Humanistic
  Studies**
Claremont McKenna College
Claremont, CA 91711
Telephone: 909-621-8417
Fax: 909-621-8249
Website: http://www.mckenna.edu/
  academics/index.htm

Government Accountability Project
1402 Third Avenue, Suite 1215
Seattle, WA 98101
Telephone: 206-292-2850
Fax: 206-292-0610
E-mail: gap@whistleblower.org
Additional Office: 1612 K Street, NW
Washington, DC 20036
Telephone: 202-408-0034
Fax: 202-408-9855
E-mail: gap1@erols.com
Website: http://www.whistleblower.org
Periodical: *Bridging the GAP*

**Alan Guttmacher Institute:
  Research, Policy Analysis &
  Public Education**
120 Wall Street
New York, NY 10005
Telephone: 212-248-1111
Fax: 212-248-1951
E-mail: info@agi-usa.org
Additional Office: 1120 Connecticut
  Avenue, NW
Suite 460
Washington, DC 20036
Telephone: 202-296-4012
Fax: 202-223-5756
E-mail: policyinfo@agi-usa.org
Website: http://www.agi-usa.org
Periodical: *Guttmacher Report on
  Public Policy*
(health)

**Hartman Institute for Formal and
  Applied Axiology**
Foley House Inn
14 West Hall
Savannah, GA 31401
Telephone: 912-232-6622
800-647-3708
Fax: 912-231-1218

Hastings Center
255 Elm Road
Briarcliff Manor, NY 10510
Telephone: 914-762-8500
Fax: 914-762-2124
Website: http://www.cpn.org/sections/
  affiliates/hastings_center.html
Hastings Center Report
Periodicals: *IRB: A Review of Human
  Subjects Research*
(health)

Health Care Ethics Center
Duquesne University
Pittsburgh, PA 15282-0504
Telephone: 412-396-5902
Fax: 412-396-5904
Website: http://www.duq.edu/
  liberalarts/gradhealth/
  healthcare.html

Health Law and Policy Institute
University of Houston Law Center
4800 Calhoun Road
Houston, TX 77204
Telephone: 713-743-2101
Website: http://www.law.uh.edu/
  LawCenter/Programs/Health/
  health-law.html
Periodicals: *Health Law News*
*Health Law Perspectives: Analyses of
  Recent Developments in Health
  Law*

Heartland Institute
19 South LaSalle Street #903
Chicago, IL 60603
Telephone: 312-377-4000
Fax: 312-377-5000
E-mail: think@heartland.org
Website: http://www.heartland.org
(public policy)

Hemlock Society USA
P.O. Box 101810
Denver, CO 80250
Telephone: 303-639-1202
800-247-7421
Fax: 303-639-1224
E-mail: hemlock@privatei.com
Website: http://www.hemlock.org/
  hemlock
(euthanasia)

Hispanic Association for Corporate Responsibility
1730 Rhode Island Avenue, NW,
  Suite 505
Washington, DC 20036
Telephone: 202-835-9672
Periodical: *Corporate Observer*

Hoffberger Center for Professional Ethics
University of Baltimore
1420 North Charles Street, AC #204
Baltimore, MD 21201-5779
Telephone: 410-837-5324
Fax: 410-837-4783
E-mail: hoffberger@ubmail.ubalt.edu
Website: http://ubmail.ubalt.edu/
  ~rbento/hoffberger
(various professions)

Hoover Institution on War, Revolution and Peace
Stanford University
Stanford, CA 94305-6010
Telephone: 415-723-0603
Fax: 415-723-1687
Periodical: *Essays in Public Policy*

Human Genetics and Bioethics Education Laboratory
Ball State University
Dept. of Biology
Muncie, IN 47306
Telephone: 317-285-8840
Website: http://www.bsu.edu/bio/sp/
  hgabel.html

Human Rights Center
University of Minnesota
229 19th Avenue South
Minneapolis, MN 55455
Telephone: 612-625-5027
Fax: 612-625-2011
E-mail: humanrts@gold.tc.umn.edu
Websites: http://www.umn.edu/
  humanrts/hrcenter.htm
Human Rights Library

Human Rights Watch
350 Fifth Avenue, 34th Floor
New York, NY 10118-3299
Telephone: 212-290-4700
Fax: 212-736-1300
E-mail: hrwnyc@hrw.org
Website: http://www.hrw.org

Institute for American Values
1841 Broadway, Room 211
New York, NY 10023
Telephone: 212-246-3942
Fax: 212-541-6665

Institute for Business & Professional Ethics
DePaul University
One East Jackson
Chicago, IL 60604
Telephone: 312-362-6569
Fax: 312-362-6973
E-mail: lpincus@wppost.depaul.edu
Website: http://www.depaul.edu/ethics
Periodical: *Online Journal of Ethics*

Institute for Christian Ethics
Stetson University
Dept. of Religious Studies
DeLand, FL 32720-3771
Telephone: 904-822-8931
Website: http://www.stetson.edu/
  departments/religion

Institute for Criminal Justice Ethics
John Jay College of Criminal Justice
City University of New York
899 10th Avenue
New York, NY 10019-1029
Telephone: 212-237-8225
Fax: 212-237-8221
E-mail: cjejj@cunyvm.cuny.edu

(Institute for Criminal Justice Ethics
cont'd)
Website: http://www.lib.jjay.cuny.edu
*Professional Law Enforcement Codes:
A Documentary Collection*
Periodical: *Criminal Justice Ethics*

**Institute for Economic and
Restorative Justice**
P.O. Box 262
Voorheesville, NY 12186
Telephone: 518-765-2468
Fax: 518-765-2468
Periodical: *Contemporary Justice
Review: Issues in Criminal, Social,
and Restorative Justice*

Institute for Ethics
American Medical Association
(see Ethics Standards section)

**Institute for Ethics and Policy
Studies**
University of Nevada, Las Vegas
4505 Maryland Parkway
Las Vegas, NV 89154-5049
Telephone: 702-895-3463
Fax: 702-895-4673
Website: http://www.nscee.edu/unlv/
Colleges/Liberal_Arts/Ethics_
and_Policy/
Periodical: *Studies in Ethics and Policy*

Institute for Global Ethics
11 Main Street
P.O. Box 563
Camden, ME 04843
Telephone: 207-236-6658
Fax: 207-236-4014
E-mail: webethics@globalethics.org
Website: www.globalethics.org

Institute for Health Law
Loyola University Chicago School of
Law
1 East Pearson Street
Chicago, IL 60611
Telephone: 312-915-6304
Fax: 312-915-7201
Website: http://www.luc.edu/schools/
law/hlthlaw/index.htm
Periodical: *Annals of Health Law*

Institute for Jewish Medical Ethics
Hebrew Academy of San Francisco
645 14th Avenue
San Francisco, CA 94118
Telephone: 415-752-7333
800-258-4427
E-mail: director@ijme.org
Website: http://www.ijme.org

**Institute for Medicine in
Contemporary Society**
SUNY Health Sciences Center
State University of New York-Stony
Brook
Division of Medicine in Society
Dept. of Preventive Medicine
Stony Brook, NY 11794-8036
Telephone: 516-444-2765
Website: http://www.uhmc.sunysb
.edu/prevmed/mns/imcs
Periodical: *Contexts*

**Institute for Philosophy and Public
Policy**
University of Maryland
School of Public Affairs
3111 Van Munching Hall
College Park, MD 20742
Telephone: 301-405-4753
Fax: 301-314-9346
Website: http://www.puaf.umd.edu/
ippp
Report from the Institute
Periodical: *Philosophy and Public
Policy*

Institute for Policy Studies
733 15th Street, NW
Washington, DC 20005
Telephone: 202-234-9382
Fax: 202-387-7915

Institute for Social Responsibility
San Jose State University
One Washington Square FO 201
San Jose, CA 95192-0096
Telephone: 408-924-4523
Fax: 408-924-4527
Website: http://www.sjsu.edu/depts/
hum_arts/social_faculty.html

Institute for the Medical Humanities
University of Texas Medical Branch
301 University Blvd.
Galveston, TX 77555-0202
Telephone: 409-747-1230
Fax: 409-747-2255
Website: http://snapper.utmb.edu/ethics
Periodicals: *Literature and Medicine*
Medical Humanities Review

Institute for the Study of Applied and Professional Ethics
Dartmouth College
6031 Parker House
Hanover, NH 03755
Telephone: 603-646-1263
Fax: 603-646-2652
E-mail: ethics.institute@dartmouth.edu
Website: http://www.dartmouth.edu:80/artsci/ethics-inst
Periodical: *Ethics Newsletter*

Institute for the Study of Civic Values
1218 Chestnut Street, Room 702
Philadelphia, PA 19107
Telephone: 215-238-1434
Fax: 215-238-10530

Institute for Theological Encounter with Science & Technology: ITEST Faith/Science
3601 Lindell Blvd.
St. Louis, MO 63108
Telephone: 314-977-2703
Fax: 314-977-7264
Website: http://ITEST.slu.edu

Institute of Ethics
Finkelstein Institute for Religious and Social Studies at the Stein Center
3080 Broadway
New York, NY 10027
Telephone: 212-678-8020
Fax: 212-678-8947

Institute of Human Values in Medicine
Westchester County Medical Center
Division of Cardiology
Valhalla, NY 10595
Telephone: 914-493-8816

Institute on Religion in an Age of Science
c/o Prof. U. Goodenough
Washington University
Dept. of Biology
St. Louis, MO 63130
Telephone: 314-935-6836
Website: http://www.iras.org
Periodicals: *Science & Spirit*
Zygon: Journal of Religion and Science

Interfaith Center on Corporate Responsibility
475 Riverside Drive
New York, NY 10115-0050
Telephone: 212-870-2295
Fax: 212-870-2023
Periodical: *Corporate Examiner*

International Association for Business and Society
c/o Prof. P. Lewellyn
University of South Carolina at Aiken
School of Business Administration
171 University Parkway
Aiken, SC 29801
Website: http://cac.psu.edu/~plc/iabs.html
Periodical: *Business & Society*

International Association of Ethicists
117 West Harrison Bldg.
Suite I-104, 6th Floor
Chicago, IL 60605
Telephone: 817-699-0676
800-423-3844
Periodical: *Journal of Ethical Studies*

International Business Ethics Institute
1000 Connecticut Avenue, NW, Suite 503
Washington, DC 20036

(International Business Ethics
Institute *cont'd*)
Telephone: 202-296-6938
Fax: 202-296-5897
E-mail: info@business-ethics.org
Website: http://www.business-
ethics.org

**International Center for Ethics,
Justice and Public Life**
Brandeis University
P.O. Box 9110
Mailstop 084
Waltham, MA 02254-9110
Telephone: 781-736-8577
Fax: 781-736-2122
E-mail: ethics@brandeis.edu
Website: www.brandeis.edu/sumsch/
ethics

**International Center for Healthcare
Ethics**
St. Francis Medical Center
2230 Liliha Street
Honolulu, HI 96817
Telephone: 808-547-6011
Fax: 808-547-6714

**International Center for the Study
of Education Policy & Human
Values**
University of Maryland
College Park, MD 20742
Telephone: 301-405-3588
Fax: 301-405-3573

**International Foundation for
Ethical Research**
53 West Jackson Blvd., Suite 1552
Chicago, IL 60602-3703
Telephone: 312-427-6025
Fax: 312-427-6524

**International Network on Feminist
Approaches to Bioethics**
Kennedy Institute of Ethics
Box 571212
Georgetown University
Washington, DC 20057

(International Network on Feminist
Approaches to Bioethics *cont'd*)
Telephone: 202-687-2312
Fax: 202-687-8089
E-mail: fabstaff@gunet.georgetown
.edu
Website: http://guweb.georgetown
.edu/kennedy/fab/index.htm

**International Society for
Environmental Ethics**
c/o J. Weir
Morehead State University
Dept. of Philosophy
103 Combs Bldg.
UPO 662
Morehead, KY 40351-1689
Telephone: 606-783-2785
Fax: 606-783-2678
E-mail: iseenewsletter@msuacad
.morehead-st.edu
Website: http://www.cep.unt.edu/
ISEE.html
Reference: *ISEE Master Bibliography*
(online)

**International Society of Business,
Economics and Ethics**
c/o University of Notre Dame
College of Business Administration
Notre Dame, IN 46556
E-mail: georges.enderle.1@nd.edu
Website: http://www.nd.edu/~isbee

**Investor Responsibility Research
Center**
1350 Connecticut Avenue, NW,
Suite 700
Washington, DC 20036
Telephone: 202-833-0700
Fax: 202-833-3555
E-mail: mkt@irrc.org
Website: http://www.irrc.org
Periodicals: *Corporate Governance
Bulletin*
Corporate Social Issues Reporter

**Joint Commission on Accreditation
of Healthcare Organizations**
One Renaissance Blvd.
Oakbrook Terrace, IL 60181

(Joint Commission on Accreditation of Healthcare Organizations *cont'd*)
Telephone: 630-792-5889
Fax: 630-792-5005
Website: http://www.jcaho.org
Periodical: *Health Care Quality Monitor*

Josephson Institute of Ethics
4640 Admiralty Way, Suite 1001
Marina del Rey, CA 90292-6610
Telephone: 310-306-1868
Fax: 310-827-1864
E-mail: JI@JIethics.org
Website: http://www.jiethics.org
Character Counts! Coalition
Periodical: *Ethics: Easier Said Than Done*
(various professions)

Journalism Values Institute
American Society of Newspaper Editors
(see Ethics Standards section)

Kegley Institute of Applied Ethics
California State University, Bakersfield
9001 Stockdale Highway
Bakersfield, CA 93311-1099
Telephone: 805-664-3149
Website: http://www.co.calstate.edu/ CSUI/CSU/baker/kie.html
(various professions)

Kenan Ethics Program
Duke University
102 West Duke Bldg.
Box 90432
Durham, NC 27708
Telephone: 919-660-3033
Fax: 919-660-3049
Website: http://kenan.ethics.duke.edu/ index.html
(various professions)

Kennedy Institute of Ethics
Georgetown University
Box 571212
Washington, DC 20057-1212

(Kennedy Institute of Ethics *cont'd*)
Telephone: 202-687-8099
E-mail: kidirofc@gunet.georgetown.edu
Website: http://guweb.georgetown .edu/kennedy
Kampelman Collection of Jewish Ethics
National Information Resource on Ethics & Human Genetics
National Reference Center for Bioethics Literature
Shriver Collection in Christian Ethics
References: *Bibliography of Bioethics*
Bioethics Thesaurus
Encyclopedia of Bioethics
International Directory of Bioethics Organizations
BIOETHICSLINE (National Library of Medicine) (online)
Scope Note Series
Syllabus Exchange Catalog
Periodicals: *Kennedy Institute of Ethics Journal*
New Titles in Bioethics
Newsletter of the Network on Ethics and Intellectual Disabilities
(health)

Koch Endowed Chair in Business Ethics
University of St. Thomas
Graduate School of Business
2115 Summit Avenue
St. Paul, MN 55105-1096
Website: http://www.gsb.stthomas .edu/ethics

KPMG Business Ethics Institute
2001 M Street, NW
Washington, DC 20036
Telephone: 202-739-8947
Website: http://www.us.kpmg.com/ ethics
Periodical: *Integrity* (online)

Last Acts Campaign: Care and Caring at the End of Life
Robert Wood Johnson Foundation
Route 1 and College Road East
P.O. Box 2316
Princeton, NJ 08543-2316

(Last Acts Campaign: Care and
Caring at the End of Life *cont'd*)
Telephone: 609-243-5926
Fax: 609-452-1865
E-mail: lastacts@aol.com
Websites: http://www.lastacts.org
http://lastacts.rwjf.org
Periodical: *State Initiatives in
End-of-Life Care*

Law and Society Association
University of Massachusetts
Hampshire House
Box 33615
Amherst, MA 01003-3615
Telephone: 413-545-4617
Fax: 413-545-1640
E-mail: lsa@legal.umas.edu
Periodical: *Law & Society Review*

Law, Medicine, and Ethics Program
Patient Rights Program
Boston University School of Public
Health
Health Law Dept.
715 Albany Street
Boston, MA 02118
Telephone: 617-638-4626
Fax: 617-414-1464
Website: http://www.bumc.bu.edu/
Departments/HomeMain.asp?
DepartmentID=95

**Lawyers' Committee for Civil
Rights Under Law**
1450 G Street, NW, Suite 400
Washington, DC 20005
Telephone: 202-662-8600
Fax: 202-783-0857

Lincoln Center for Applied Ethics
Arizona State University
College of Business
P.O. Box 874806
Tempe, AZ 85287-4806
Telephone: 602-965-2710
Fax: 602-965-3995
E-mail: lincoln@asu.edu
Website: http://www.cob.asu.edu/ba/
faculty/lin.html
Periodical: *Managing Ethics*

Loka Institute
P.O. Box 355
Amherst, MA 01004
Telephone: 413-559-5860
Fax: 413-559-5811
E-mail: loka@amherst.edu
Website: http://www.amherst.edu/~loka
(science, technology)

**MacLean Center for Clinical
Medical Ethics**
University of Chicago
MC 6098
5841 South Maryland Avenue
Chicago, IL 60637-1470
Telephone: 773-702-1453
Fax: 773-702-0090
Website: http://ccme-mac4.bsd
.uchicago.edu/CCME.html
Reference: *Beginnings of a Partially
Annotated Bibliography on Advance
Directives* (online)

**Maguire Center for Ethics and
Public Responsibility**
Southern Methodist University
100 McFarlin Auditorium
6405 Boaz
P.O. Box 750316
Dallas, TX 75275-0316
Telephone: 214-768-4255
Fax: 214-768-3391
E-mail: maguire_ethics@mail.smu
.edu
Website: http://www.smu.edu/
~ethics_center

**Markkula Center for Applied
Ethics**
Santa Clara University
500 El Camino Real
Santa Clara, CA 95053-0633
Telephone: 408-554-5319
E-mail: ethics@scu.edu
Website: http://www.scu.edu/ethics
Ethics Camp
Periodical: *Issues in Ethics*

Medical-Legal Consulting Institute, Inc.
National Alliance of Certified Legal
Nurse Consultants
2476 Bolsover Street, Suite 632W
Houston, TX 77005
Telephone: 800-880-0944
713-942-2200
Fax: 713-942-8075
E-mail: mail@legalnurse.com
Website: http://www.legalnurse.com
Periodical: *National Medical-Legal
Journal*

Meiklejohn Civil Liberties Institute
Box 673
Berkeley, CA 94701-0673
Telephone: 510-848-0599
Fax: 510-848-6008
E-mail: mcli@igc.org
Reference: *Human Rights
Organizations and Periodicals
Directory*

Midwest Bioethics Center
1021-1025 Jefferson Street
Kansas City, MO 64105-1329
Telephone: 800-344-3829
816-221-1100
Fax: 816-221-2002
E-mail: bioethic@midbio.org
Website: http://www.midbio.com
Periodical: *Bioethics Forum*

Minnesota Center for Corporate Responsibility
1000 LaSalle Avenue, Suite 153
Minneapolis, MN 55403-2005
Telephone: 651-962-4120
Fax: 651-962-4125
E-mail: MCCR_UST@stthomas.edu
Website: http://www.stthomas.edu/mccr

Morality in Media
475 Riverside Drive, Suite 239
New York, NY 10115
Telephone: 212-870-3222
Fax: 212-870-2765
E-mail: mimnyc@ix.netcom.com
Website: http://pw2.netcom.com/
~mimnyc/index.html

Murata Colloquium for Ethics in Business
Business Ethics Program
Babson College
Babson Park, MA 02457
Telephone: 781-235-1200
E-mail: babsonethics@babson.edu
Website: http://roger.babson.edu/ethics

Murdough Center for Engineering Professionalism
Texas Tech University
Lubbock, TX 79409
Telephone: 806-742-3525
Fax: 806-742-0444
Website: http://www.murdough
.ttu.edu
Periodical: *TexethicS Newsletter:
Engineering Professionalism and
Ethics in Texas*

National Association for Healthcare Quality
4700 West Lake Avenue
Glenview, IL 60025
Telephone: 800-966-9392
Fax: 847-375-4777
Website: http://www.nahq.org
Periodical: *Journal for Healthcare
Quality*

National Catholic Bioethics Center
159 Washington Street
Boston, MA 02135
Telephone: 617-787-1900
Fax: 617-787-4900
E-mail: postmaster@pjcenter.org
Websites: http://www.ncbcenter.org
http://www.pjcenter.org
Periodical: *Ethics & Medics*

National Center for Bioethics
2960 Vecino Drive
Sacramento, CA 95833
Telephone/Fax: 916-921-2205
E-mail: Ethctee@aol.com

National Committee for Quality Assurance
2000 L Street, NW, Suite 500
Washington, DC 20036

(National Committee for Quality
Assurance *cont'd*)
Telephone: 202-955-3500
Fax: 202-955-3599
Website: http://www.ncqa.org
Periodical: *Quality Matters*
(health)

**National Committee for Quality
Health Care**
1800 Massachusetts Avenue, NW,
Suite 401
Washington, DC 20036
Telephone: 202-347-5731
Fax: 202-347-5836
Periodicals: *Quality Bulletin*
Quality Outlook

National Consumers League
1701 K Street, NW, Suite 1201
Washington, DC 20006
Telephone: 202-835-3323
Fax: 202-835-0747
Website: http://www.nclnet.org

**National Council Against Health
Fraud**
National Council for Reliable Health
Information
P.O. Box 1276
Loma Linda, CA 92354
Telephone: 909-824-4690
Fax: 909-824-4838
Website: http://www.ncahf.org

National Fraud Information Center
Alliance Against Fraud in
Telemarketing
Internet Fraud Watch
P.O. Box 65868
Washington, DC 20035
Telephone: 800-876-7060
Website: http://www.fraud.org
Periodical: *Focus on Fraud*

**National Health Care Anti-Fraud
Association**
1255 23rd Street, NW
Washington, DC 20037
Telephone: 202-659-5955
E-mail: fraud@nhcaa.org
Website: http://www2.nhcaa.org/nhcaa

**National Institute for Engineering
Ethics**
One South Main, Suite 102
Webb City, MO 64870
P.O. Box 96163
Washington, DC 20090-6163
E-mail: rgranfeldt@windmill.net
Website: http://www.niee.org
*Engineering Ethics References
Bibliography*
Periodical: *Engineering Ethics Update*

**National Organization for
Competency Assurance**
1200 19th Street, NW, Suite 300
Washington, DC 20036-2401
Telephone: 202-857-1165
Fax: 202-223-4579
Periodical: *Professional Regulation
News*
(various professions)

National Patient Safety Foundation
American Medical Association
(see Ethics Standards section)
Web Bibliography
Periodical: *Focus on Patient Safety*

**National Resource Center for
Consumers of Legal Services**
6596 Main Street
P.O. Box 340
Gloucester, VA 23061
Telephone: 804-693-9330
Fax: 804-693-7363
E-mail: info@nrccls.org
Website: http://www.nrccls.org
Periodical: *Preventive Law Lawyer*

National Right to Life Committee
419 7th Street, NW, Suite 500
Washington, DC 20004
Telephone: 202-626-8800
E-mail: nrlc@nrlc.org
Website: http://www.nrlc.org

National Security Archive
George Washington University
Gelman Library
2130 H Street, NW, Suite 701
Washington, DC 20037

(National Security Archive *cont'd*)
Telephone: 202-994-7000
Fax: 202-994-7005
E-mail: nsarchiv@gwu.edu
Website: http://www.seas.gwu.edu/
   nsarchive
(government)

National Whistleblower Center
P.O. Box 3768
Washington, DC 20007
Telephone: 202-667-7515
Fax: 202-342-6984
E-mail: whistle@whistleblowers.org
Website: http://www.whistleblowers.org

**Navran Associates: Focused on
   Leadership**
3037 Wembley Ridge
Atlanta, GA 30340-4716
Telephone: 770-493-8886
800-635-9540
Fax: 770-493-4162
E-mail: fj@navran.com
Website: http://www.navran.com
*Desktop Guide to Total Ethics
   Management*
(business)

**Network on Ethics and Intellectual
   Disabilities**
Kennedy Institute of Ethics
Georgetown University
Box 571212
Washington, DC 20057-1212
Telephone: 202-687-8099
Fax: 202-687-8089
E-mail: veatchr@guvax.georgetown.edu
Website: http://www.quasar.ualberta
   .ca/ddc/ethics/intro.html

**North American Society for Social
   Philosophy**
Ethics Center
University of South Florida
100 Fifth Avenue South
St. Petersburg, FL 33701-5016

(North American Society for Social
   Philosophy *cont'd*)
Telephone: 813-553-3172
Fax: 813-553-3169
Website: http://www.stpt.usf.edu/coas/
   ethics/main.html
Periodical: *Journal of Social
   Philosophy*

**Northeastern University Center for
   the Advancement of Science
   Education: Addressing Ethical
   Responsibility in Science
   Education**
125 Nightingale Hall
Boston, MA 02115
Telephone: 617-373-3049
Fax: 617-373-8714
E-mail: NUCASE@lynx.neu.edu
Website: http://www.psych.neu.edu/
   Programs/NUCASE

Nursing Ethics Network
Boston College School of Nursing
Cushing Hall
140 Commonwealth Avenue
Chestnut Hill, MA 02467
Telephone: 617-552-4250
Fax: 617-552-0913
E-mail: frys@bc.edu
Website: http://www.bc.edu/bc_org/
   avp/son/ethics/nen.html
Periodical: *Ethics Research Report*

Olsson Center for Applied Ethics
Darden Graduate School of Business
University of Virginia
P.O. Box 6550
Charlottesville, VA 22906-6550
Telephone: 804-924-7281
800-UVA-MBA-1
Website: http://www.darden.virginia
   .edu/research/olsson/olsson.htm

OMB Watch
1742 Connecticut Avenue, NW
Washington, DC 20009

(OMB Watch *cont'd*)
Telephone: 202-234-8494
Fax: 202-234-8584
E-mail: ombwatch@rtk.net
Website: http://www.RTK.NET:80/
  ombwatch
Periodical: *Government Information
  Insider*
(government)

Ombudsmen Association
5521 Greenville Avenue
  Suite 104-265
Dallas, TX 74206
Telephone: 214-553-0043
Fax: 214-348-6621
(business)

Open Society Institute
400 West 59th Street
New York, NY 10019
Telephone: 212-548-0600
212-757-2323
Fax: 212-548-4679
212-548-4600
Website: http://www.soros.org
Center on Crime, Communities &
  Culture
Legal Profession Program
Project on Death in America
(law, medicine, journalism)

Organization of News Ombudsmen
c/o A. Nauman
6307 Surfside Way
Sacramento, CA 95831
Telephone: 916-391-1314
E-mail: artnauman@aol.com
Website: http://www5.infi.net/ono
(journalism)

**Pacific Center for Health Policy
  and Ethics**
University of Southern California
  Law School
Los Angeles, CA 90089-0071
Telephone: 213-740-2541
Fax: 213-740-5502
Website: http://www.usc.edu/dept/
  law-lib

**Pacific Center for the Study of
  Ethics and Values**
Pacific University
2043 College Way
Forest Grove, OR 97116
Telephone: 503-359-2847
Fax: 503-359-2242
(various professions)

**Park Ridge Center for the Study of
  Health, Faith and Ethics**
211 East Ontario, Suite 800
Chicago, IL 60611-3215
Telephone: 312-266-2222
Fax: 312-266-6086
Website: http://www.prchfe.org
Periodical: *Making the Rounds in
  Health, Faith and Ethics*

**People for the Ethical Treatment of
  Animals**
501 Front Street
Norfolk, VA 23510
Telephone: 757-622-PETA
Website: http://www.peta-online.org

**Physicians Committee for
  Responsible Medicine**
5100 Wisconsin Avenue, NW,
  Suite 404
Washington, DC 20016
Telephone: 202-686-2210
Fax: 202-686-2216
Website: http://www.sai.com/pcrm

Physicians for Human Rights
100 Boylston Street, Suite 702
Boston, MA 02116
Telephone: 617-695-0041
Fax: 617-695-0307
Website: http://www.phrusa.org
Periodical: *The Record*

**Physicians for Responsible
  Medicine**
P.O. Box 6322
Washington, DC 20015
Telephone: 202-686-2210
Fax: 202-686-2216
Periodical: *Good Medicine*

Physicians for Social Responsibility
1101 14th Street, NW, Suite 700
Washington, DC 20005
Telephone: 202-898-0150
Fax: 202-898-0172
E-mail: psrnatl@psr.org
Website: http://www.psr.org

Pope John Center
(see National Catholic Bioethics
Center)

**Poynter Center for the Study of
Ethics and American Institutions**
410 North Park Avenue
Bloomington, IN 47405
Telephone: 812-855-0261
Fax: 812-855-3315
Website: http://www.indiana.edu/
~poynter/index.html
Reference: *Annotated Bibliography on
Teaching Research Ethics* (online)
Periodical: *TREnds: Teaching
Research Ethics*

Poynter Institute for Media Studies
801 Third Street South
St. Petersburg, FL 33701
Telephone: 813-821-9494
Fax: 813-821-0583
Website: http://www.poynter.org
Doing Ethics in Journalism
References: *Media Ethics
Bibliography* (online)

Practical Ethics Center
University of Montana-Missoula
Missoula, MT 59812
Telephone: 406-243-5744
Fax: 406-243-6632
E-mail: ethics@selway.umt.edu
Website: http://www.umt.edu/ethics/
program.htm
(various professions)

Privacy & American Business
Center for Social & Legal Research
2 University Plaza
Hackensack, NJ 07601

(Privacy & American Business
cont'd)
Telephone: 201-996-1154
Fax: 201-996-1883
E-mail: pab@mail.idt.net
Website: http://idt.net/~pab

Privacy International
666 Pennsylvania Avenue, SE,
Suite 301
Washington, DC 20003
Telephone: 202-544-9240
Fax: 202-547-5482
E-mail: pi@mail.privacy.org
Website: http://www.privacy.org/pi

Privacy Rights Clearinghouse
Utility Consumers' Action Network
1717 Kettner Avenue, Suite 105
San Diego, CA 92101
Telephone: 619-298-3396
Fax: 619-298-5681
E-mail: prc@privacyrights.org
Website: http://www.privacyrights.org

**Professional Standards Review
Council of America**
200 Madison Avenue, Suite 1910
New York, NY 10016
Telephone: 212-686-9147
Fax: 212-779-9307
Periodical: *Informational Health Care
Bulletin*
(health)

**Program for Ethics, Science and
the Environment**
Oregon State University
Dept. of Philosophy
Corvallis, OR 97331
Telephone: 541-737-5648
Website: http://osu.orst.edu/dept/
philosophy/pese/pese.html
Periodical: *Reflections*

Program in Applied Ethics
Fairfield University
Philosophy Dept.
315 Donnarumma Hall
Fairfield, CT 06430

(Program in Applied Ethics *cont'd*)
Telephone: 203-254-4000, ext. 2851
Website: http://www.fairfield.edu/
academic/artssci/majors/applied/
ugapdept.htm

**Program in Ethics and the
Professions**
Kennedy School of Government
79 John F. Kennedy Street
Cambridge, MA 02138
Telephone: 617-495-1100
Website: http://ksgwww.harvard.edu

**Program in Genomics, Ethics and
Society**
(see Center for Biomedical Ethics,
Stanford University)

**Program in Health Care Ethics,
Humanities and Law**
University of Colorado Health
Sciences Center
4200 East Ninth Avenue
Denver, CO 80262
Telephone: 303-315-5096

Program in Society & Medicine
University of Michigan Medical
School
6312 Medical Science Bldg. I
Box 0604
Ann Arbor, MI 48109
Telephone: 734-647-0571
Fax: 734-647-3301
E-mail: jhowell@umich.edu
Website: http://www.med.umich.edu/
psm/psm.html

**Program on Science, Technology &
Society**
North Carolina State University
College of Humanities and Social
Sciences
Box 7107
Raleigh, NC 27695-7107
Telephone: 919-515-7999
Fax: 919-515-1828
Website: http://www2.ncsu.edu/ncsu/
chass/mds/psts.html

Project on Government Oversight
1900 L Street, NW, Suite 314
Washington, DC 20036
Telephone: 202-466-5539
Fax: 202-466-5596
E-mail: pogo@pogo.org
Website: http://www.pogo.org

**Project on Technology, Work and
Character**
1700 K Street, NW, Suite 306
Washington, DC 20006
Telephone: 202-296-4300

**Psychologists for the Ethical
Treatment of Animals**
P.O. Box 1297
Washington Grove, MD 20880-1297
Telephone/Fax: 301-963-4751
E-mail: kshapiro@capaccess.org
Website: http://www.psyeta.org
Periodicals: *Journal of Applied
Animal Welfare Science*
*Society and Animals: Social Scientific
Studies of the Human Experience*

Public Citizen
1600 20th Street, NW
Washington, DC 20009
Telephone: 202-588-1000
Periodical: *Public Citizen*
(consumers)

**Public Employees for
Environmental Responsibility**
2001 S Street, NW, Suite 570
Washington, DC 20009
Telephone: 202-265-7337
Periodical: *Peer Review*

Public Health Law Project
University of Missouri at Kansas City
School of Law
5100 Rockhill Road
Kansas City, MO 64110-2499

(Public Health Law Project *cont'd*)
Telephone: 816-235-1644
Fax: 816-235-5276
Website: http://www.law.umkc.edu
Medical and Public Health Law Site
Law and the Physician: A Practical
  Guide
Medical Risk Management:
  Preventive Legal Strategies for
  Health Care Providers

Public Responsibility in Medicine
and Research
132 Boylston Street, 4th Floor
Boston, MA 02116
Telephone: 617-423-4112
Fax: 617-423-1185
E-mail: prmr@aol.com
Website: http://www.aamc.org/
  research/primr

Reilly Center for Science,
Technology and Values
University of Notre Dame
346 O'Shaughnessy Hall
Notre Dame, IN 46556
Telephone: 800-813-2304
Fax: 219-631-4268
Website: http://www.nd.edu/~reilly
Periodical: *Studies in Science and the*
  Humanities

Religion and Ethics Institute, Inc.
P.O. Box 5510
Evanston, IL 60204
Telephone: 847-328-4049

Risk Assessment & Policy
Association
Franklin Pierce Law Center
2 White Street
Concord, NH 03301
Telephone: 603-228-1541
Fax: 603-224-3342
E-mail: cruh@fplc.edu
Website: http://www.fplc.edu/tfield/
  rapa.htm
Periodical: *RISK: Health, Safety &*
  Environment

Rockford Institute
934 North Main Street
Rockford, IL 61103-7061
Telephone: 815-964-5053
Fax: 815-965-1826
Periodical: *Religion & Society Report*

Rocky Mountain Center for
Healthcare Ethics
225 East 16th Avenue, Suite 1050
Denver, CO 80203-1614
Telephone: 303-831-4880
Fax: 303-832-7496
E-mail: rmche@ix.netcom.com
Website: http://www.healthcareethics
  .com
Voices

Salvatori Center for the Study of
Individual Freedom in the
Modern World
Claremont McKenna College
Claremont, CA 91711
Telephone: 909-607-3984
Fax: 909-621-8416
Website: http://www.mckenna.edu/
  academics/index.htm

Schweitzer Institute for the
Humanities
P.O. Box 550
700 Christian Street
Wallingford, CT 06492-0550
Telephone: 203-697-ASIH
Fax: 203-697-2748
E-mail: Info@SchweitzerInstitute
Website: http://www.schweitzer
  institute.org
(environment, public policy)

Security Awareness and Ethics
Committee
Loyola University
Division of Information Technologies
Administration Bldg., Room 2332
Medical Center Campus
2160 South 1st Avenue
Maywood, IL 60153
E-mail: sae-committee@luc.edu

Shorenstein Center on the Press, Politics, and Public Policy
Kennedy School of Government
79 John F. Kennedy Street
Cambridge, MA 02138
Telephone: 617-495-8269
Fax: 617-495-8696
Website: http://ksgwww.harvard.edu/
~presspol/home.htm

Silha Center for the Study of Media Ethics and Law
University of Minnesota
School of Journalism and Mass Communication
111 Murphy Hall
206 Church Street SE
Minneapolis, MN 55455
Telephone: 612-625-3421
Fax: 612-626-8012
Website: http://www.sjmc.umn.edu/
silhacenter/silhahome.html

Social Investment Forum
1612 K Street NW, Suite 650
Washington, DC 20006
Telephone: 202-872-5319
Fax: 202-822-8471
E-mail: info@socialinvest.org
Website: http://www.socialinvest.org
Periodical: *Online Guide to Socially Responsible Investing*

Social Philosophy & Policy Center
Bowling Green State University
Dept. of Philosophy
305 Shatzel Hall
Bowling Green, OH 43403-0222
Telephone: 419-372-2117
Fax: 419-372-8191
E-mail: sppc@mailserver.bgsu.edu
Website: http://www.bgsu.edu/offices/
sppc
Periodical: *Social Philosophy & Policy*

Society for Bioethics Consultation
(see American Society for Bioethics and Humanities)

Society for Business Ethics
The American College
270 South Bryn Mawr Avenue
Bryn Mawr, PA 19010
Telephone: 610-526-1387
Fax: 610-526-1359
E-mail: rduska@aol.com
Website: http://www.luc.edu/depts/
business/sbe/index.htm
Periodical: *Business Ethics Quarterly*

Society for Ethics
San Diego State University
Dept. of Philosophy
5500 Campanile Drive
San Diego, CA 92182-8142
E-mail: corlett@rohan.sdsu.edu
Website: http://www-rohan.sdsu.edu/
faculty/corlett/se.html
Periodical: *Journal of Ethics: An International Philosophical Review*

Society for Health and Human Values
(see American Society for Bioethics and Humanities)

Society for Philosophy and Public Affairs
c/o C. Gould
Stevens Institute of Technology
Dept. of Humanities
Hoboken, NJ 07030
Telephone: 201-216-5405
Fax: 201-216-8245

Society for Social Studies of Science
Louisiana State University
Sociology Dept.
Baton Rouge, LA 70803
Telephone: 504-388-5311
Fax: 504-388-5102
E-mail: sowesl@unix1.sncc.lsu.edu
Website: http://its2.ocs.lsu.edu/guests/
ssss/public_html
Periodicals: *Science, Technology, and Human Values*
Technoscience (online)

Society for the Psychological Study of Social Issues
American Psychological Association
(see Ethics Standards section)

Society for the Study of Social Problems
906 McClung Tower
University of Tennessee
Knoxville, TN 37996-0490
Telephone: 423-974-3620
Fax: 423-974-7013
Website: http://web.utk.edu/~sssp
Periodical: *Social Problems*

Society for Values in Higher Education
Georgetown University
Box 571205
Washington, DC 20057-1205

Society of Christian Ethics
Boston University
School of Theology
745 Commonwealth Avenue
Boston, MA 02215
Telephone: 617-353-7322

Society on Social Implications of Technology
Institute of Electrical and Electronics Engineers
445 Hoes Lane
Piscataway, NJ 08855-1331
Telephone: 732-981-0060
Website: http://www4.ncsu.edu/unity/users/j/jherkert/index.html
Periodical: *Technology and Society Magazine*

Software Engineering Ethics Research Institute
East Tennessee State University
Dept. of Computer and Information Sciences
Box 70711
Johnson City, TN 37614-0711
E-mail: gotterba@etsu.edu
Website: http://www-cs.etsu.edu/seeri

Special Interest Group on Professional Licensure and Regulation
American Educational Research Association
1230 17th Street, NW
Washington, DC 20036
Telephone: 202-223-9485
Fax: 202-775-1824

Stein Center on Ethics and Public Interest Law
Fordham University School of Law
140 West 62nd Street
New York, NY 10023
Website: http://www.fordham.edu/law/centers/index.htm
Periodical: *Common Good*

Student Pugwash USA
815 15th Street, NW, Suite 814
Washington, DC 20005
E-mail: spusa@spusa.org
Website: http://www.spusa.org/pugwash/mainpages/programs_activities.html
(science, technology)

Students for Responsible Business
609 Mission Street
San Francisco, CA 94105
Telephone: 415-778-8366
Fax: 415-778-8367
E-mail: Mail@SRB.Org
Website: http://www.srb.org

Taxpayers Against Fraud
False Claims Act Legal Center
1220 19th Street, NW, Suite 501
Washington, DC 20036
Telephone: 202-296-4826
800-USFALSE
Fax: 202-296-4838
E-mail: ams@taf.org
Website: http://www.taf.org/taf
Periodical: *FCA and Qui Tam Quarterly Review*

Texas Center for Legal Ethics and Professionalism
P.O. Box 12487
Austin, TX 78711-2487
Additional Office: 1414 Colorado, Suite 600A
Austin, TX 78701
Telephone: 800-204-2222, ext. 2161
Fax: 512-463-1459
E-mail: info@txethics.org
Website: http://www.txethics.org
Reference: *Bibliography of Professionalism & Ethics Topics* (online)

Union of Concerned Scientists
2 Brattle Square
Cambridge, MA 02238
Telephone: 617-547-5552
Fax: 617-864-9405
E-mail: ucs@ucsusa.org
Website: http://www.ucsusa.org
Periodicals: *The Gene Exchange Nucleus*

University at Buffalo Center for Clinical Ethics and Humanities in Health Care
State University of New York at Buffalo
Veterans Affairs Medical Center
3495 Bailey Avenue
Buffalo, NY 14215
Telephone: 716-862-3412
Fax: 716-862-4748
Website: http://wings.buffalo.edu/faculty/research/bioethics/index.html
Periodical: *Bioethics Bulletin*

University Center for Human Values
Princeton University
Marx Hall
Princeton, NJ 08544
Telephone: 609-258-1460
Website: http://www.princeton.edu/~uchv

U.S. Public Interest Research Group
218 D Street, SE
Washington, DC 20003-1900

(U.S. Public Interest Research Group *cont'd*)
Telephone: 202-546-9707
Fax: 202-546-2461
E-mail: uspirg@pirg.org
Website: http://www.pirg.org/uspirg

Values, Ethics, and Justice Specialty Group
Association of American Geographers
c/o University of California, Santa Barbara
Dept. of Geography
3611 Ellison Hall
Santa Barbara, CA 93106-4060
Telephone: 805-893-3663
Website: http://www.geog.ucsb.edu/vejsg

Values in Bioethics Research Program
University of Michigan Medical School
1018 Fuller Street
Ann Arbor, MI 48109-0708
Telephone: 734-998-7120, ext. 313
E-mail: ddoukas@umich.edu
Website: http://www.med.umich.edu/psm/VBRP.html

Vera Institute of Justice
377 Broadway
New York, NY 10013
Telephone: 212-334-1300
Fax: 212-941-9407
Website: http://www.vera.org
Federal Sentencing Reporter

Wharton Ethics Program
(see Zicklin Center for Business Ethics Research)

Wiener Center for Social Policy
Kennedy School of Government
79 John F. Kennedy Street
Cambridge, MA 02138
Telephone: 617-495-1461
Fax: 617-496-9053
E-mail: mwcenter@harvard.edu
Website: http://ksgwww.harvard.edu/socpol

Woodstock Theological Center
Georgetown University
Box 571137
Washington, DC 20057-1137
Telephone: 202-687-3532
Fax: 202-687-5835
Website: http://guweb.georgetown
  .edu/woodstock
Woodstock Seminars in Business
  Ethics

Zicklin Center for Business Ethics
  Research
University of Pennsylvania
Wharton School
Philadelphia, PA 19104-6369
Telephone: 215-898-7691
E-mail: dunfeet@rider.wharton
  .upenn.edu
Website: http://rider.wharton.upenn
  .edu/~ethics/zicklin
Wharton Ethics Program

2. Organizations and Programs Based Worldwide

This section lists organizations, associations, research centers, educational and training programs, advocacy and watchdog groups, standard-setting bodies, and consultants that deal with issues of ethics, professionalism, and public policy. It includes entities in academic, professional, nonprofit, government, and commercial settings, based worldwide.

Each organization's mail address, telephone, fax number, e-mail address, and World Wide Web site URL are provided, where available. Notable reference works and periodicals (except newsletters of the same name as the organization) are also listed. These and other publications appear in the **Informational Resources** section, following.

Classifications (business, health, law, various professions, etc.) are noted only if an organization's name or affiliation is not self-explanatory.

Aberdeen Centre for Philosophy, Technology and Society
The Old Brewery
King's College
University of Aberdeen
Old Aberdeen AB24 3UB
Scotland
Telephone/Fax: 44 1224 272366
E-mail: cpts@abdn.ac.uk
Website: http://www.abdn.ac.uk/
~phl002/cpts.htm
Periodical: *ENDS and MEANS:
A Journal of Philosophy and
Technology*

**Academy for Ethics
in Medicine**
University Goettingen
Humboldtallee 36
D37073 Goettingen
Germany
Telephone: 49-551-393966
Fax: 49-551-393996
E-mail: UTE@ethik.med.uni-
goettingen.de
Website: http://www.gwdg.de/
~uelsner/euroeth.htm
Information and Documentation
Center for Ethics in Medicine
Periodical: *Ethik in der
Medizin*

**Argentinian Association of Ethical
Investigators**
Tte. Gral J.D. Peron 2395
3o piso
Oficina G
1040 Buenos Aires
Argentina
Telephone/Fax: 54 1 9520183

Asian Bioethics Association
c/o University Research Center
Nihon University
4-8-24 Kudan-Minami
Chiyoda-ku, Tokyo 102
Japan
Telephone: 81-3-5275-8137
Fax: 81-3-5275-8326
E-mail: sakamoto@chs.nihon-u.ac.jp

**Australian Association for
Professional and Applied Ethics**
University of New South Wales
School of Philosophy
Sydney, New South Wales 2052
Australia
Telephone: 61 2 9385 2320
E-mail: s.cohen@unsw.edu.au
Website: http://www.arts.unsw.edu.au/
aapae

Australian Institute of Computer Ethics
c/o Swinburne University of Technology
School of Information Technology
P.O. Box 218
Hawthorn, Victoria 3122
Australia
Telephone: 61 3 9214 8315
Fax: 61 3 9819 0823
E-mail: csimpson@swin.edu.au
Website: http://www.aice.swin.edu.au/AICEhome.htm

Australian Society of CPAs Ethics Centre of Excellence
CPA House
170 Queen Street
Melbourne, Victoria 3000
Australia
Telephone: 61 3 9606 9606
Fax: 61 3 9670 8901
Website: http://www.cpaonline.com.au

Bioethics Research Centre
University of Otago
P.O. Box 913
Dunedin
New Zealand
Telephone: 64-3-474-7977
Fax: 64-3-474-7601
E-mail: bioethics@otago.ac.nz
Website:http://telperion.otago.ac.nz:800/Bioethics
Periodical: *Otago Bioethics Report*
Reference: *Euthanasia: Resourses for Community Discussion*

Bochum Center for Medical Ethics
Ruhr-Universität Bochum
Gebäude GA 3/53
D-44780 Bochum
Germany
Telephone: 49 234 700-2749
Fax: 49 234 7094-288
E-mail: Med.Ethics@ruhr-uni-bochum.de
Website: http://www.ruhr-uni-bochum.de/zme/zme.html#zme-e

Dietrich Bonhoeffer International Institute for Bioethical Studies
G.P.O. Box 588
Adelaide, South Australia 5001
Australia
Telephone: 61 8 83460190
Periodical: *VITA*

British Society for Ethical Theory
University of Keele
Dept. of Philosophy
Keele Hall
Keele, Staffs ST5 5BG
England
Website: http://www.gla.ac.uk/Acad/Philosophy/Lenman/bset.html

Business Ethics and Stakeholder Relations Program
Human Rights Research and Education Centre
University of Ottawa
57 Louis Pasteur
Ottawa, Ontario KIN 6N5
Canada
Telephone: 613-562-5775
Fax: 613-562-5125
E-mail: errol@human-rights.cdp.uottawa.ca
Website: http://www.uottawa.ca/~hrrec/busethics/busmain.html

Business Ethics Network
Small Business Research Centre
Kingston University
Kingston Hill
Kingston-upon-Thames
Surrey KT2 7LB
England
Telephone: 44 181 547 724
E-mail: l.spence@kingston.ac.uk
Website: http://www.bath.ac.uk/Centres/Ethical/EBEN/home.html

Canadian Bioethics Society
Office of Medical Bioethics
University of Calgary
3330 Hospital Drive NW
Calgary, Alberta T2N 4N1
Canada

(Canadian Bioethics Society *cont'd*)
Telephone: 403-220-7990
Fax: 403-220-4740
E-mail: riddell@acs.ucalgary.ca
Website: http://www.bioethics.ca

Canadian Centre for Ethics & Corporate Policy
50 Baldwin Street
Toronto, Ontario M5T 1L4
Canada
Telephone: 416-348-8691
Fax: 416-348-8689
E-mail: ethicctr@interlog.com
Website: http://www.ethicscentre.com
Periodical: *Management Ethics*

Canadian Centre for Ethics in Sport
1600 James Naismith Drive
Gloucester, Ontario K1B 5N4
Canada
Telephone: 613-748-5755
800-672-7775
Fax: 613-748-5746
E-mail: info@cces.ca
Website: http://www.cces.ca

Canadian Institute for Law, Theology, and Public Policy
7203 - 90 Avenue
Edmonton, Alberta T6B 0P5
Canada
Telephone/Fax: 403-465-4581
E-mail: 73421.25@compuserve.com
Website: http://www.lights.com/
    caninst

Canadian Medical Malpractice Prevention Association
1711 McCowan Road, Suite 41653
Scarborough, Ontario M1S 5G8
Canada
Telephone: 416-969-1587

Center for Business Ethics and Social Responsibility
Jerusalem College of Technology-
    Machon Lev
21 HaVaad HaLeumi Street
P.O. Box 16031
91160 Jerusalem
Israel
Telephone: 972-2-675-1117
Fax: 972-2-675-1190
Website: http://www.jct.ac.il

Center for Ethics in Law and Medicine
University Clinic
Elsässer Strasse 2m
Haus 1a
D-79110 Freiburg
Germany

Center for Jewish Medical Ethics
Ben Gurion University of the Negev
Faculty of Health Sciences
P.O. Box 653
84105 Beer-Sheva
Israel
Telephone: 972 7 6400821
Fax: 972 7 6279360
E-mail: yeruham@bgumail.bgu.ac.il
Website: http://www.bgu.ac.il

Center of Environmental Philosophy and Bioethics
University of Ghent
Dept. of Philosophy
Blandijnberg 2
B-9000 Ghent
Belgium
Telephone: 32 9 2644135
Fax: 32 9 2644187

Center of Medical Ethics
North Iranshahr Avenue
Taleghni Crossroad
15836 Tehran
Iran
E-mail: bagheri@farabi.hbi.dmr.or.ir

Center of Studies for Ethics in the Organizations
CENE/EAESP-FGV
Avenida 9 de Julho, 2029
01313-902 São Paulo, SP
Brazil
Telephone: 55-11-281-7749
Fax: 55-11-284-1789
55-11-281-7749
E-mail: cene@eaesp.fgvsp.br

Centre de documentation en éthique des sciences de la vie et de la santé
INSERM
71, rue Saint-Dominique
F-75007 Paris
France
Telephone: 33 1 44 42 48 35
33 1 44 42 48 32
Fax: 33 1 44 42 48 41
E-mail:
  ethique.inserm@dial.oleane.com
Website: http://www.spri.se/spriline/
  inserm.htm

Centre de Recherches Interdisciplinaires en Bioethique
Universite Libre de Bruxelles
Avenue F.D. Roosevelt 50
CP 175/01
B-1050 Brussels
Belgium
Telephone: 32 2 6502628
32 2 6502343
Fax: 32 2 6503647
E-mail: CRIB@resulb.ULB.ac.be
References: *Encyclopedia of Bioethics*
Les Mots de Bioethique

Centre for Accounting Ethics
School of Accountancy
University of Waterloo
Waterloo, Ontario N2L 3G1
Canada
Website: http://www.arts.uwaterloo
  .ca/ACCT/ethics
Reference: *Annotated Bibliography*

Centre for Alleviating Social Problems Through Values Education
85 Argyll Place
Aberdeen AB25 2HU
Scotland
Periodical: *Journal of Values Education*

Centre for Applied Ethics
Hong Kong Baptist University
Kowloon Tong, Kowloon
Hong Kong
China
Telephone: 852-2339-7274
Fax: 852-2339-5151
E-mail: cae@hkbu.edu.hk
Website: http://arts.hkbu.edu.hk/cae
Periodical: *Ethics and Society Newsletter*

Centre for Applied Ethics
University of British Columbia
Computer Science Bldg.
227-6356 Agricultural Road
Vancouver, British Columbia
  V6T 1Z2
Canada
Telephone: 604-822-5139
Fax: 604-822-8627
E-mail: centre@ethics.ubc.ca
Website: http://www.ethics.ubc.ca
Periodical: *ETHICS FAX*
Reference: *Applied Ethics Resources on the WWW* (online)
(various professions)

Centre for Applied Ethics
University of Stellenbosch
Philosophy Dept.
Private Bag X1
Matieland 7602
South Africa
Telephone: 27 21 808-2058
E-mail: jph2@maties.sun.ac.za
Website: http://www.sun.ac.za/local/
  academic/arts/philosophy/
  ethics.html
(health, environment, business)

Centre for Bioethics
Clinical Research Institute of
  Montreal
110 Pine Avenue West
Montreal, Quebec H2W 1R7
Canada
Telephone: 514-842-1481
Fax: 514-987-5695
Website: http://www.ircm
  .umontreal.ca/bioethique
Periodicals: *Au Chevet, Newsletter of
  the FRSQ Network for Research in
  Clinical Ethics*
Cahiers de Bioéthique
*Collection Panétius - Les Archives de
  l'éthique clinique*
Journal of Palliative Care

**Centre for Business and
  Professional Ethics**
University of Leeds
Dept. of Philosophy
Leeds LS2 9JT
England
Telephone: 44 113 233 3280
Fax: 44 113 233 3265
E-mail: j.c.jackson@leeds.ac.uk
Website: http://condor.depaul.edu/
  ethics/mabpe.html

**Centre for Business and Public
  Sector Ethics**
6 Croftgate
Fulbrooke Road
Cambridge CB3 9EG
England

**Centre for Computing and Social
  Responsibility**
De Montfort University
School of Computing Sciences
The Gateway
Leicester LE1 9BH
England
Telephone: 44 116 257 7471
Fax: 44 116 254 1891
Websites: http://www.ccsr.org
http://www.ccsr.cms.dmu.ac.uk
ETHICOMP Annual International
  Conference

**Centre for Corporate Social
  Performance & Ethics**
Rotman School for Management
105 St. George Street
Toronto, Ontario M5S 1A1
Canada
Telephone: 416-978-4930
Fax: 416-978-5433
E-mail: mbaprog@fmgmt.mgmt
  .utoronto.ca

**Centre for Ethics, Law &
  Economics**
Libero Istituto Carlo Cattaneo
Corso Matteotti, 22
I-21053 Castellanza, Varese
Italy
Telephone: 39-331-572-275
Fax: 39-331-572-229
E-mail: sdecolle@liuc.it

**Centre for Health Law, Ethics
  and Policy**
University of Newcastle
University Drive
Callaghan, New South Wales 2308
Australia
Telephone: 61 2 49 215052
Fax: 61 2 49 216931
Website: http://www.law.newcastle
  .edu.au/centre/home.html

Centre for Human Bioethics
Monash University
Clayton, Victoria 3168
Australia
Telephone: 61 3 9905 4279
Fax: 61 3 9905 3279
E-mail: heather.mahamooth@arts
  .monash.edu.au
Website: http://www.arts.monash.edu
  .au/bioethics
Periodical: *Monash Bioethics Review*

**Centre for Medicine, Ethics,
  and Law**
McGill University
3690 Peel Street
Montreal, Quebec H3A 1W9
Canada

(Centre for Medicine, Ethics,
and Law *cont'd*)
Telephone: 514-398-7400
514-398-6980
Fax: 514-398-8349
E-mail: elliot c.@falaw.lan.mcgill.ca
Website: http://mystic.biomed.mcgill
.ca/MedinfHome/DEANBOOK/
public_html/FACULTY/
medicine_law_ethics.html

Centre for Peace and Environmental Ethics

Katholieke Universiteit Leuven
Department of Moral Theology
Sint Michielsstraat 6
B-3000 Leuven
Belgium
Telephone: 32 16 32 38 85
Fax: 32 16 32 38 58
E-mail: Johan.DeTavernier@theo
.kuleuven.ac.be
Website: http://www.kuleuven.ac.be/
facdep/theology/en/peace.htm

Centre for Practical Ethics

Canadian Society for the Study of
Practical Ethics
York University
102 McLaughlin College
4700 Keele Street
North York, Ontario M3J 1PE
Canada
Telephone: 416-736-5128, ext. 30446
Fax: 416-736-5436
E-mail: praceth@nexus.yorku.ca
Website: www.yorku.ca/mclaughlin/
ethics/Ethics.htm

Centre for Professional and Applied Ethics

University of Manitoba
University College
500 Dysart Road
Winnipeg, Manitoba R3T 2M8
Canada
Telephone: 204-474-9107
Fax: 204-261-0021

Centre for Professional Ethics

University of Central Lancashire
Preston PR1 2HE
England
Telephone: 44 1772 892541
Fax: 44 1772 892942
Website: http://www.uclan.ac.uk/facs/
ethics/brochure.htm

Centre for Research Ethics

Göteborg University
Box 700
SE-405 30 Göteborg
Sweden
Telephone: 46-31-7734922
Fax: 46-31-7734863
E-mail: ehagberg@cre.gu.se
swelin@cre.gu.se
Website: http://www.cre.gu.se
(science, social science)

Centre for Research Ethics

Uppsala University and Swedish
University of Agricultural Sciences
c/o Dept. of Theology
P.O. Box 1604
SE-751 46 Uppsala
Sweden
Telephone: 46-18-4712175
Fax: 46-18-710170
Website: http://www.fef.uu.se
Reference: *Studies in Bioethics and
Research Ethics*

Centre for Social and Environmental Accounting Research

University of Dundee
Dept. of Accountancy and Business
Finance
Dundee DD1 4HN
Scotland
Telephone: 44 1382 344789
Fax: 44 1382 224419
E-mail: CSEAR@acc.dundee.ac.uk
Website: http://www.dundee.ac.uk/
accountancy/csear
Periodical: *Social and Environmental
Accounting*

**Centre for Society, Technology
and Values**
University of Waterloo
Systems Design Engineering Dept.
Davis Centre, Room 2722
Waterloo, Ontario N2L 3G1
Canada
Telephone: 519-888-4567, ext. 6215
Fax: 519-884-3644
E-mail: cstv@engmail.uwaterloo.ca
Website: http://sail.uwaterloo.ca/
~cstvwww

Centre for Techno-Ethics
Saint Paul University
233 Main Street
Ottawa, Ontario K1S 1C4
Canada
Telephone: 613-236-1393
Fax: 613-782-3001

**Centre of Medical Law and
Ethics**
King's College London
School of Law
Strand, London WC2R 2LS
England
Telephone: 44-171-873 2382
44-171-836 5454
Fax: 44-171-873 2575
E-mail: cmle.enq@kcl.ac.uk
Website: http://www.kcl.ac.uk/kis/
schools/law/research/cmle/
index.html
Periodical: *Dispatches*

**Centro de Etica Medica de
Ascofame**
Calle 39A, No. 28-63
Santafe de Bogota
Colombia
Telephone: 57 1 3680332
57 1 3685603
Fax: 57 1 2699584
E-mail:
sascome@col1.telecom.com.co

Centro e dell'Istituto di Bioetica
Universita Cattolica del Sacro Cuore
Largo F. Vito
I-00168 Roma
Italy

(Centro e dell'Istituto di Bioetica
cont'd)
E-mail: gmiranda@uni.net
Website: http://www.uni.net/cdb/
med_mor.htm
Periodical: *Medicina e Morale:
Rivista Internazionale bimestrale di
Bioetica, Deontologia e Morale
Medica*

**Centrum voor Bio-Ethiek en
Gezondheidsrecht**
Utrecht University
Heidelberglaan 2
Postbus 80105
Utrecht
Netherlands
Telephone: 31 30 2534399
Fax: 31 30 2539410
E-mail: bergh@cc.run.nl

**Chisholm Centre for Health
Ethics**
166 Gipps Street, 7th Floor
East Melbourne, Victoria 3002
Australia

Clinical Ethics Service
St. Joseph's Health Centre
St. Michael's Hospital
Providence Centre
30 The Queensway
Toronto, Ontario M6R 1B5
Canada
Telephone: 416-530-6750
Fax: 416-530-6621

**Comite de Bioethique de
l'Academie de Medicine**
Institut d'Endocrinologie
Bd. Aviatorilor 34
Bucharest
Romania
Telephone: 40 1 2122010
40 1 2121751
Fax: 40 1 3129927

Comite d'Ethique pour les Sciences
Centre National de la Recherche
  Scientifique
3, rue Michel-Ange
F-75794 Paris Cedex 16
France
Telephone: 33 1 44 96 43 55
Fax: 33 1 44 96 48 42
Website: http://www.cnrs.fr/ethique

Consumers for Ethics in Research
P.O. Box 1365
London N16 0BW
England
Periodical: *Medical Research and You*

Cyber-Rights & Cyber-Liberties
Centre for Criminal Justice Studies
University of Leeds
Leeds LS2 9JT
England
Telephone: 44-113-2335033
Fax: 44-113-2335056
E-mail: lawya@leeds.ac.uk
Website: http://www.leeds.ac.uk/law/
  pgs/yaman/yaman.htm

Danish Council of Ethics
Ravnsborggade 2-4
2200 København N
Denmark
Telephone: 45 3537 5833
Fax: 45 3537 5755
Website: http://www.etiskraad.dk/
  english/english.htm

Dossetor Health Ethics Centre
University of Alberta
Aberhart Centre Two, Room 222
8220 - 114 Street
Edmonton, Alberta T6G 2J3
Canada
Telephone: 403-492 6676
Fax: 403-492 0673
Website: http://www.ualberta.ca/
  ~ethics/bethics.htm
Periodicals: *Bioethics Bulletin*
Health Ethics Today

**Dutch Voluntary Euthanasia
  Society**
Postbus 75331
Leidsegracht 103
1070 AH Amsterdam
Netherlands
Telephone: 31 20-620-0690
Fax: 31 20-420-7216
E-mail: euthanasie@nvve.nl
Website: http://www.nvve.nl/
  ukframe.htm

**Economic and Social Research
  Council**
Polaris House
North Star Avenue
Swindon, Wilts SN2 1UJ
England
Website: http://www.esrc.ac.uk

Engineers for Social Responsibility
P.O. Box 6208
Wellesley Street
Auckland 1
New Zealand

**ETHICA - Ethics and Health:
  An International and
  Comparative Arena**
University of Bergen
Dept. of Philosophy
Centre for International Health
Sydnesplassen 7
N-5007 Bergen
Norway
Telephone: 47 55 58 24 37
Fax: 47 55 58 96 51
Website: http://www.hf.uib.no/i/
  Filosofisk/ethica
South East Asian Health Ethics
  Network
Reference: *Annotated Bibliography on
  Equity and Health Policy* (online)

**Ethical Investment Research
  Service**
504 Bondway Business Centre
71 Bondway
London SW8 1SQ
England

(Ethical Investment Research Service
cont'd)
Telephone: 44 171 735 1351
Fax: 44 171 735 5323
Website: http://www.personal.u-
net.com/~gaeia/gaeiaers.htm

Ethics Centre
Ryerson Polytechnic University
613 Jorgenson Hall
350 Victoria Street
Toronto, Ontario M5B 2K3
Canada
Telephone: 416-979-5000, ext. 6164
E-mail: ethics@acs.ryerson.ca
Website: http://www.ryerson.ca

**Ethics for USS: University
Lecturers' Campaign for Ethical
and Environmental Investment of
Their Pension Fund**
4A East Avenue
Oxford OX4 1XW
England
Website: http://www.dundee.ac.uk/
accountancy/csear/ethics4uss

EthicScan Canada Ltd.
Canadian Clearing-house for
Consumer and Corporate Ethics
P.O. Box 54034
Toronto, Ontario M6A 3B7
Canada
Telephone: 416-783-6776
Fax: 416-783-7386
Website: http://www.ethicscan.on.ca
Periodical: *Corporate Ethics Monitor*

**ETHOS Groupe de Recherche en
Ethique**
Université du Québec à Rimouski
300, avenue des Ursulines
Rimouski, Quebec G5L 3A1
Canada
Telephone: 418-724-1784
Fax: 418-724-1525
Website: http://www.uqar.uquebec.ca/
uqar/ress.htm#Groupes et
laboratoire de recherche
Periodical: *Ethica*

Eubios Ethics Institute
Institute of Biological Sciences
University of Tsukuba
Tsukuba Science City 305
Japan
Telephone: 81-298-53-4662
Fax: 81-298-53-6614
E-mail:
Macer@sakura.cc.tsukuba.ac.jp
Website: http://www.biol.tsukuba
.ac.jp/~macer.index.html
Periodicals: *Eubios Journal of Asian
and International Bioethics*
*Eubios Bioethics and Biotechnology
News*

European Bioethical Research
191 Leith Walk
Edinburgh EH6 8NX
Scotland

**European Business Ethics
Network**
(see European Institute for Business
Ethics)

European Centre for Ethics
European Ethics Network
Katholieke Universiteit Leuven
Deberiotstraat 26
B-3000 Leuven
Belgium
Telephone: 32 16 323787
Fax: 32 16 323788
Website: http://www.kuleuven.ac.be/
oce/ece.html
Periodical: *Ethical Perspectives*

**European Group for Ethics in
Science and New Technologies**
Commission of the European
Community
SG/C/02
Rue de la Loi 200
Brey 07/328
B-1049 Brussels
Belgium
Fax: 32 2 299 45 65
References: *Ethical Aspects of
Cloning Techniques*
Ethical Implications of Biotechnology

European Institute for Business Ethics
European Business Ethics Network
Nijenrode University
Straatweg 25
3621 BG Breukelen
Netherlands
Telephone: 31-3462-91290
Fax: 31-3462-91296
E-mail: eibe@nijenrode.nl
Website: http://www.nijenrode.nl/
    research/eibe.html

European Network on Law and Society
Domaine Saint Louis
F-11160 Rieux-Minervois
France
Telephone: 33 4.68.78.13.15
Fax: 33 4.68.78.23.04
Website: http://www.msh-paris.fr/
    red&s/indexgb.htm

European Society for Philosophy of Medicine and Health Care
Catholic University of Nijmegen
Faculty of Medical Sciences
Dept. of Ethics, Philosophy and
    History of Medicine
Geert Grooteplein 21
P.O. Box 9101
6500 HB Nijmegen
Netherlands
Telephone: 31 24 361 53 20
Fax: 31 24 354 02 54
E-mail: b.gordijn@efg.kun.nl
Website: http://www.azn.nl/fmw/
    maatschp/bioeth1.htm

European Society for the Study of Science and Theology
c/o W.B. Drees
Bezinningscentrum Vrije Universiteit
De Boelelaan 1115
1081 HV Amsterdam
Netherlands
Fax: 31 20 444 5680
Website: http://www.vu.nl/
    Bezinningscentrum/ESSSAT.htm
Periodical: *Studies in Science and
    Theology*

GAEIA: Global And Ethical Investment Advice
Ethical Investment House
425 Wilmslow Road
Manchester M20 4A
England
Telephone: 44 161 434 4681
Fax: 44 161 445 8421
Website: http://www.gaeia.u-net.com

L.J. Goody Bioethics Centre
39 Jugan Street
Glendalough, Western Australia 6016
Australia
Telephone: 61 8 92424066
Fax: 61 92424068 7
E-mail: ljgbc@iinet.net.au
Periodical: *St. Luke's News*

Group of Advisers on the Ethical Aspects of Biotechnology
(see European Group for Ethics
    in Science and New
    Technologies)

Groupe d'Ethique Appliquee
College de Chicoutimi
534, Jacques-Cartier est
Chicoutimi, Quebec G7H 1Z6
Canada
Telephone: 418-549-9520
Fax: 418-549-1315
E-mail: melancon@cegep-
    chicoutimi.qc.ca

Groupe de Recherche en Bioethique et Sante
Universite Laval
Pavillon Paul-Comtois
Laval, Quebec G1K 7P4
Canada
Telephone: 418-656-2131
Fax: 418-656-7747
E-mail:
    Danielle.Blondeau@esi.ulaval.ca
Website: http://www.ulaval.ca/vrr/
    rech/Regr/00087.html

Health Care Ethics Service
St. Boniface General Hospital
409 Tache Avenue
Winnipeg, Manitoba R2H 2A6
Canada
Telephone: 204-237-2990
Fax: 204-235-3527

Health, Ethics and Liberties
95, boulevard Pirel
F-69677 Bron Cedex
France

**Hong Kong Ethics Development
Centre**
1/F, Tung Wah Mansion
199-203 Hennessy Road
Wanchai, Hong Kong
China
Telephone: 852 2587 9812
Fax: 852 2824 9766
E-mail: icac@cuhk.edu.hk
Website: http://www.icac.org.hk/icac/
edc.htm
Periodical: *Ethics in Practice*
(business)

**Hoover Chair in Economic and
Social Ethics**
Catholic University of Louvain
3 Place Montesquieu
B-1348 Louvain-la-Neuve
Belgium
Telephone: 32-10-47.39.51
Fax: 32-10-47.39.52
E-mail: dabeye@etes.ucl.ac.be
Website: http://www.econ.ucl.ac.be/
ETES/chaireEn.html

Hungarian Bioethical Commission
Hungarian Academy of Sciences
Institute of Experimental Medicine
1083 Szigony u. 43
P.O. Box 67
H-1450 Budapest
Hungary
Telephone: 36 1 2100819
Fax: 36 1 2100813

Institut Borja de Bioetica
Centre Borja - Llaseres, 30
Sant Cugat del Valles
Barcelona 08190
Spain
Telephone: 34-3-6741150
Fax: 34-3-6747980

**Institut Medical Ethics and
Bioethics**
Limbova 12
833 03 Bratislava
Slovak Republic
Fax: 42-7-373739
E-mail: @vpkm.sanet.sk

Institute for Bioethics
University of Maastricht
P.O. Box 616
6200 MD Maastricht
Netherlands
Telephone: 31-43-388 21 45
Fax: 31-43-367 10 58
E-mail: secretariaat@ige.unimaas.nl

Institute for Ethics
Free University
Faculty of Theology
13a-10, De Boelelaan 1105
1081 HV Amsterdam
Netherlands
Telephone: 31-20-44 46605
E-mail: j.s.reinders@esau.th.vu.nl

Institute for Global Ethics
16 Northwick Close
London NW8 8JG
England
Telephone: 44-171-266-5404
Fax: 44-171-266-0404
E-mail: northwick@easynet.co.uk
Website: http://www.globalethics.org

Institute of Business Ethics
12 Palace Street
London SW1E 5JA
England
Telephone: 44-171-931.0495
Fax: 44-171-821.5819

**Institute of Law and Ethics in
Medicine**
University of Glasgow
School of Law
Glasgow G12 8QQ
Scotland
Telephone: 44 141 330 3528
Fax: 44 141 330 4698

**Institute of Medicine, Law and
Bioethics**
University of Liverpool
Liverpool L69 3BX
England
Telephone: 44 151 794 2302
Fax: 44 151 794 2311
University of Manchester
Oxford Road
Manchester M13 9PL
England
Telephone: 161 275 7703
Fax: 161 275 7704
E-mail: imlab@liv.ac.uk
Website: http://www.liv.ac.uk/
  ~scooper/imlab.html

**Institute of Practical
Philosophy**
Malaspina University-College
900 Fifth Street
Nanaimo, British Columbia V9R 5S5
Canada
Website: http://www.mala.bc.ca/www/
  ipp/ipp.htm
(various professions)

**Institute of Social and Ethical
AccountAbility**
1st Floor, Vine Court
112-116 Whitechapel Road
London E1 1JE
England
Telephone: 44 171 377 5866
Fax: 44 171 377 5720
Website:
http://www.accountability.org.uk/
Periodical: *AccountAbility Quarterly*
(accounting, business)

Instituto de Filosofia Practica
Viamonte 1596
1055 Buenos Aires
Argentina
Telephone: 54-1-3713315
Periodical: *Ethos: Revista de
  Filosofia Practica*

Instituto Siciliano di Bioetica
Piazza S. Domenico
I-95024 Acireale
Sicily
Italy
Telephone: 39 95 2631324
Fax: 39 95 2632498
Periodical: *Bioetica a Cultura*

**Interfaculty Center for Ethics
in the Sciences and
Humanities**
University of Tübingen
Keplerstrasse 17
D-72074 Tübingen
Germany
Telephone: 49 7071 29-77981
Fax: 49 7071 29-5255
E-mail: zew@uni-tuebingen.de
Website: http://www.uni-tuebingen.de/
  zew
Periodical: *Biomedical Ethics:
  Newsletter of the European
  Network for Biomedical
  Ethics*

**International Association of
Bioethics**
c/o Centre for Professional Ethics
University of Central Lancashire
Preston PR1 2HE
England
Telephone: 44 1772 892541
Fax: 44 1772 892942
E-mail: IAB'ggl.ruu.nl
Website: http://www.uclan.ac.uk/facs/
  ethics/iab.htm
Periodical: *Bioethics: Journal of the
  International Association of
  Bioethics*

International Bioethics Research Center
Institute of Religion and Culture
Kyoto Women's University
35 Kita-Hiyoshi-Cho
Imakumano, Higashiyama-ku
Kyoto 605
Japan
Telephone: 81 75 531-7221
Fax: 81 75 531-7215

International Ethical Business Registry
Box 53529
984 West Broadway
Vancouver, British Columbia
V5Z 4M6
Canada
Telephone/Fax: 604-732-3688
E-mail: ethics@reelwest.bc.ca
Website: http://www.orca.bc.ca/ethics
Periodical: *Connecting Rod: The Networking Newsletter of the International Ethical Business Registry*

International Institute for Sustainable Development
161 Portage Avenue East, 6th Floor
Winnipeg, Manitoba R3B 0Y4
Canada
Telephone: 204-958-7700
Fax: 204-958-7710
Website: http://iisd1.iisd.ca

International Institute for the Sociology of Law
Antigua Universidad
Apartado 28
20560 Oñati, Gipuzkoa
Spain
Telephone: 34 943 78 30 64
Fax: 34 943 78 31 47
Website: http://www.sc.ehu.es/onati
Periodical: *Current Legal Sociology: A Periodical Publication of Abstracts and Bibliography in Law and Society*

(International Institute for the Sociology of Law *cont'd*)
References: *List of Key Words in the Sociology of Law*
Onati International Series in Law and Society

International Network for the Definition of Death
Instituto de Neurologia y Neurocirugia
29 y D, Vedado, Habana 4
Ciudad de La Habana 10400
Apartado Postal 4268
Cuba
Fax: 53-7-336321
E-mail: braind@infomed.hin.gn.apc.org
Website: http://www.changesurfer.com/BD/Network.html

International Network of Engineers and Scientists for Global Responsibility
Post Box 101707
D-44017 Dortmund
Germany
Fax: 49-231-103869
E-mail: uphc01@uxp1.hrz.uni-dortmund.de
Website: http://cac.psu.edu/~duf/social/ines.html

International Society for Quality in Health Care
Lincoln House
625 Swanston Street
Carlton, Victoria 3053
Australia
Telephone: 61.3 9285 5368
Fax: 61.3 9285 5329
61.3 9347 4851
E-mail: isqua@latrobe.edu.au
Website: http://hsfo.health.latrobe.edu.au/isqua/home.html
Periodical: *International Journal for Quality in Health Care*

Joint Centre for Bioethics
University of Toronto
88 College Street
Toronto, Ontario M5G 1L4
Canada
Telephone: 416-978-2709
Fax: 416-978-1911
Website: http://www.utoronto.ca/jcb
*ETHICS OSCE: Standardized Patient
Scenarios for Teaching and
Evaluating Bioethics*

**KPMG Ethics & Integrity
Services**
Commerce Court West, Suite 3300
P.O. Box 31
Station Commerce Court
Toronto, Ontario M5L 1B2
Canada
Telephone: 416-777-8500
Fax: 416-777-3519
Additional Office: 2000, avenue
McGill College
Bureau 1900
Montreal, Quebec H3A 3H8
Canada
Telephone: 514-840-2100
Fax: 514-840-2187
Additional Office: World Exchange
Plaza
45 O'Connor Street, Suite 1000
Ottawa, Ontario K1P 1A4
Canada
Telephone: 613-560-0011
Fax: 613-560-2896
E-mail: ethicsweb@kpmg.com
Website: http://www.kpmg.ca/ethics

Linacre Centre
60 Grove End Road
St. John's Wood
London NW8 9NH
England
Telephone: 44 171 289 3625
E-mail: admin@linacre.org
Website: http://www.linacre.org
Periodical: *Linacre Quarterly*
(health)

**Management Centre for Human
Values**
Indian Institute of Management
Joka, Diamond Harbour Road
Post Box No. 16757
Alipore Post Office
Calcutta 700 027
India
Periodical: *Journal of Human
Values*

**Medical Malpractice Information
Center in Japan**
1-1-35 Haiesto-Hisaya Bldg. 6F
Izumi, Higashi-ku
Nagoya-shi
Aichi-ken 461
Japan
Telephone: 81-52-951-1731
Fax: 81-52-951-1732

**National Committee for Medical
Research Ethics**
Gaustadalleen 21
N-0371 Oslo 3
Norway
Telephone: 47 22958780
Fax: 47 22958492

**National Council on Bioethics in
Human Research**
774 Echo Drive
Ottawa, Ontario K1S 5N8
Canada
Telephone: 613-730-6225
Fax: 613-730-8251

**National Council on Ethics in
Human Research**
774 Echo Drive
Ottawa, Ontario K1S 5N8
Canada
Telephone: 613-730–6225
Fax: 613-730–8251
E-mail: ncehr@rcpsc.edu
Website: http://ncehr.medical.org
Periodical: *Communiqué*

**National Institute for Law, Ethics
and Public Affairs**
Griffith University
Faculty of Arts
Kessels Road
Nathan, Queensland 4111
Australia
Telephone: 61 7 3875 5490
Fax: 61 7 3875 6634
E-mail: C.Sampford@hum.gu.edu.au
Website: http://www.gu.edu.au/gwis/
   hum/nilepa/homepage.htm
Reference: *Law, Ethics and Public
   Affairs Series*

Nuffield Council of Bioethics
28 Bedford Square
London WC1B 3EG
England
Telephone: 44 171 631 0566
Fax: 44 171 323 4877

**Office of Bioethics Education
and Research**
Dalhousie University
Division of Medical Education
5849 University Avenue,
   Room C5CRC
Halifax, Nova Scotia B3H 4H7
Canada
Telephone: 902-494-3801
Fax: 902-494-3865
Website: http://www.mcms.dal.ca/
   dme/dme_bio.html

**Open University Students for
Ethical Science**
Orchard Avenue
Solihull
West Midlands B91 2LS
England
Telephone: 44 121 705 3050
E-mail: ses@masg.demon.co.uk
Website: http://host.envirolink.org/ses/
   index.html
(animal rights)

**Organisation for Economic
Co-operation and Development**
Public Management Service
2, rue André-Pascal
F-75775 Paris Cedex 16
France
Telephone: 33 1.45.24.82.00
Fax: 33 1.45.24.85.00
E-mail: webmaster@oecd.org
Website: http://www.oecd.org/puma/
   gvrnance/ethics/index.htm
(government)

**Oxford Centre for the
Environment, Ethics
& Society**
Mansfield College
Oxford OX1 3TF
England
Telephone/Fax: 44 1865 270886
E-mail: ocees@mansfield.oxford.ac.uk
Website: http://users.ox.ac.uk/~ocees

**Peace, Ethics, Animals and
Connected Human Rights**
88 Cobden Street
Luton, Beds. LU2 0NG
England
Telephone: 44 1582 459943
E-mail: peach@frienchs-for-
   life.demon.co.uk

Plunkett Centre for Ethics
St. Vincents Hospital
Darlinghurst, New South Wales 2010
Australia
Telephone/Fax: 61-2-3612869
E-mail: plunkett@plunkett.edu.au
Periodical: *Bioethics Outlook*

**Research Centre for the Study
of Ethics in the Market,
Government and Professions**
Queensland University of Technology
School of Humanities
Beams Road, Carseldine
Brisbane, Queensland 4034
Australia

(Research Centre for the Study
of Ethics in the Market,
Government and Professions
cont'd)
Telephone: 61 7 3864 4747
Fax: 61 7 3864 4719
E-mail: n.preston@qut.edu.au
Website: http://www.qut.edu.au/arts/
human/ethics/centrehm.htm
Brisbane Ethics Colloquium

**Russian National Committee on
Bioethics**
Russian Academy of Sciences
Volkhonka 14
Moscow
Russia
Telephone/Fax: 7 95 2039169

Salvation Army Ethics Centre
447 Webb Place
Winnipeg, Manitoba R3B 2P2
Canada
Telephone: 204-957-2412
Fax: 204-957-2418
E-mail: saethics@mbnet.mb.ca

**Sheffield Institute of
Biotechnological Law and
Ethics**
University of Sheffield
Western Bank
Sheffield S10 2TN
England
Telephone: 44 114 222 2000
Fax: 44 114 273 9826
Website: http://www.shef.ac.uk/uni/
projects/sible/sible.html

Social Investment Organization
366 Adelaide Street East
Suite 443
Toronto, Ontario M5A 3X9
Canada
Telephone: 416-360-6047
Fax: 416-861-0183
E-mail: sio@web.net
Website: http://www.web.net/~sio

Social Values Research Centre
University of Hull
Hull HU6 7RX
England
Telephone: 44-1482-465.406
Website: http://www.hull.ac.uk/Hull/
centres/svrc.html

**Societe Francaise de Reflexion
Bioethique**
30, rue d'Auteuil
F-75016 Paris
France
Telephone: 33 1 42150462
Periodical: *Ethique: La Vie en
Question*

**Societe Suisse d'Ethique
Biomedicale**
21 Rue de Bugnon
CH-1005 Lausanne
Switzerland
Telephone/Fax: 41 21 3141750
E-mail: sseb@inst.hospvd.ch
Periodicals: *Bioethica Forum
Folia Bioethica*

**Society, Religion and Technology
Project**
Church of Scotland
John Knox House
45 High Street
Edinburgh EH1 1SR
Scotland
Telephone: 44 131-556 2953
Fax: 44 131-556 7478
E-mail: srtscot@dial.pipex.com
Website: http://webzone.ccacyber
.com/www/srtproject/srtpage3.htm

**South East Asian Center for
Bioethics**
St. Martin de Porres Bldg., Rm. 226
Espana, UST
Manila
Philippines
Telephone: 63 2 7313101

South East Asian Health Ethics Network
(see ETHICA - Ethics and Health:
An International and Comparative
Arena, Norway)
Website: http://www.hf.uib.no/i/
Filosofisk/seahen

South Place Ethical Society
25 Red Lion Square
London WC1R 4RL
England
Telephone: 44-171-831-7723
Fax: 44-171-430-1271
Periodical: *Ethical Record*

Southern Cross Bioethics Institute
336 Marion Road
P.O. Box 206
North Plympton
Adelaide, South Australia 5038
Australia
Fax:.61 8 8371 1391
E-mail: scbi@bioethics.org.au
Website: http://www.bio-ethics.com
Periodical: *Bioethics Research Notes*

St. Joseph's College Ethics Centre
University of Alberta
Physicians and Surgeons Bldg.,
Suite 520
8409-112 Street
Edmonton, Alberta T6G 1K6
Canada
Telephone: 403-439-2422
Fax: 403-432-0245
E-mail: ethics@connect.ab.ca
Website: http://www.connect.ab.ca/
~ethics
Periodical: *FOCUS On Ethics*
(various professions)

Strategic Research Centre for Environmental Accountability
University of Tasmania
Faculty of Commerce and Law
GPO Box 252-86
Hobart, Tasmania 7001
Australia

(Strategic Research Centre for
Environmental Accountability
cont'd)
Telephone: 61 3 6226 2758
Fax: 61 3 6226 7845
E-mail: SRCEA@utas.edu.au
Website: http://www.comlaw.utas
.edu.au/srcea

Tompkins Institute for Human Values and Technology
University College of Cape Breton
P.O. Box 5300
Sydney, Nova Scotia B1P 6L2
Canada
Telephone: 888-959-9995
902-539-5300
Fax: 902-562-0119
Website: http://www.uccb.ns.ca

Transparency International: Coalition Against Corruption in International Business Transactions
Otto-Suhr-Allee 97-99
D-10585 Berlin
Germany
Telephone: 49 30-343 820-0
Fax: 49 30-343 820-44
E-mail: ti@transparency.de
Website: http://www.transparency.de

UK Social Investment Forum
1st Floor, Vine Court
112-116 Whitechapel Road
London E1 1JE
England
Telephone: 44 171 377 5907
E-mail: uksif@gn.apc.org
Website: http://www.arq.co.uk/
ethicalbusiness/uksif

UNESCO International Bioethics Committee
1, rue Miollis
F-75732 Paris Cedex 15
France

(UNESCO International Bioethics
Committee *cont'd*)
Telephone: 33 1 45 68 38 58
33 1 45 68 39 39
Fax: 33 1 45 68 55 15
Website: http://www.unesco.org/
ethics/uk

**Walker Tate & Associates
Ethics and Law Reform
Consultants**
129 Foxlow Street
Captain's Flat
New South Wales 2623
Australia
Telephone/Fax: 61 6 2366352
Website: wta@ozemail.com.au

Workplace Ethics Consultancy
131 Sunnyside Avenue
Ottawa, Ontario K1S OR2
Canada
Telephone: 613-730-5184
Fax: 613-730-4246
E-mail: evb@magi.com
Website: http://ethics.hypermart.net

**World Federation of Right to
Die Societies**
61 Minterne Avenue
Norwood Green
Southall, Middlesex UB2 4HP
England
Telephone: 44-181-574-3775
Fax: 44-181-893-5986
Website: http://www.efn.org/~ergo/
world.fed.html

3. Government-Related Organizations and Programs

This section lists organizations and programs within and relating to the U.S. federal government, and some state and local governments, that deal with issues concerning ethics, professionalism, and public policy.

Each entity is listed separately; there may be several within the same Executive Department.

Each organization's mail address, telephone, fax number, e-mail address, and World Wide Web site URL are provided, where available. Notable reference works and periodicals (except newsletters of the same name as the organization) are also listed. These and other publications appear in the **Informational Resources** section, following.

Classifications (business, health, law, various professions, etc.) are noted only if an organization's name or affiliation is not self-explanatory.

Agency for Health Care Policy and Research
Executive Office Center, Suite 600
2101 East Jefferson Street
Rockville, MD 20852
Telephone: 301-594-6662
Website: http://www.ahcpr.gov

Antitrust Division
U.S. Department of Justice
601 D Street, NW
Washington, D.C. 20530
Telephone: 202-514-3543
E-mail: antitrust@usdoj.gov
Website: http://www.usdoj.gov/atr/index.html

Association of Inspectors General
c/o John Jay College of Criminal Justice
City University of New York
899 10th Avenue
New York, NY 10019
Telephone: 212-237-8225
Fax: 212-237-8221
Website:
http://www.lib.jjay.cuny.edu/ig
(state and local Inspectors General)

Bureau of Competition
U.S. Federal Trade Commission
6th Street and Pennsylvania Avenue, NW
Washington, DC 20580
Telephone: 202-326-2180
E-mail: antitrust@ftc.gov
Website: http://www.ftc.gov/ftc/antitrust.htm
(enforcement of antitrust laws)

Bureau of Consumer Protection
U.S. Federal Trade Commission
6th Street and Pennsylvania Avenue, NW
Washington, DC 20580
Telephone: 202-326-3284
202-FTC-HELP
E-mail: crc@ftc.gov
Website: http://www.ftc.gov/bcp/bcp.htm
(enforcement of Telemarketing Sales Rule, Telemarketing Consumer Fraud and Abuse Prevention Act)

Civil Rights Division
U.S. Department of Justice
Office of the Assistant Attorney General
P.O. Box 65808
Washington, DC 20035-5808

(Civil Rights Division *cont'd*)
Telephone: 202-514-2151
Fax: 202-514-0293
(enforcement of civil rights laws)

**Computer Crime and Intellectual
Property Section**
Criminal Division
U.S. Department of Justice
P.O. Box 887
Ben Franklin Station
Washington, DC 20044-0887
Telephone: 202-514-1026
Fax: 202-514-6113
Website: http://www.usdoj.gov/
criminal/cybercrime/index.html

**Department of Clinical
Bioethics**
Clinical Center Bioethics Program
Warren G. Magnuson Clinical
Center
National Institutes of Health
Bldg. 10, Room 1C-116
Bethesda, MD 20892-1154
Telephone: 301-496-2496

Division of Quality Assurance
U.S. Department of Health and
Human Services
Bureau of Health Professions
Health Resources and Services
Administration
5600 Fishers Lane
Rockville, MD 20857
Telephone: 301-443-5794
Websites:
http://www.hrsa.dhhs.gov/bhpr
http://www.hrsa.dhhs.gov/bhpr/dqa/
dqahompg.htm
References: *Healthcare Integrity and
Protection Data Bank* (online)
*Malpractice and Medical Discipline
Research Information* (online)
*National Practitioner Data
Bank* (online)

**Ethical, Legal and Social
Implications Branch**
National Human Genome Research
Institute
Division of Extramural Research
National Institutes of Health
Bldg. 38A, Room 617
38 Library Drive, MSC 6050
Bethesda, MD 20892-6050
Telephone: 301-402-4997
Fax: 301-402-1950
E-mail: elsi@nhgri.nih.gov
Website: http://www.nhgri.nih.gov/
About_NHGRI/Der/Elsi

**Ethical, Legal, and Social Issues
(ELSI) in Science Program**
Lawrence Berkeley National
Laboratory
1 Cyclotron Road
Mail Stop 1-459
Berkeley, CA 94720
Telephone: 510-486-4879
E-mail: SJSpengler@lbl.gov
Website: http://www.lbl.gov/
Education/ELSI/ELSI.html

**Ethics & Lobbyist Registration
Department**
Los Angeles County Metropolitan
Transportation Authority
One Gateway Plaza
M.S.#99-7-5
Los Angeles, CA 90012-2932
Telephone: 213-922-2979
Fax: 213-922-2986
E-mail: ethics@mta.net
Website: http://www.mta.net/
corporate/depts/ethics/
ethics_start.htm

**Federal Mediation and
Conciliation Service**
2100 K Street, NW
Washington, DC 20427
Telephone: 202-606-8100
Fax: 202-606-4216
E-mail: publicinformation@fmcs.gov
Website: http://www.fmcs.gov

**Financial Crimes Enforcement
Network (FinCEN)**
U.S. Department of the Treasury
2070 Chain Bridge Road, Suite 200
Vienna, VA 22182
Telephone: 703-905-3695
Fax: 703-905-3885
E-mail: webmaster@fincen.treas.gov
Website: http://www.treas.gov/fincen/
index.html

Fraud Section
Criminal Division
U.S. Department of Justice
Bond Bldg., Room 2424
1400 New York Avenue, NW
Washington, DC 20530
Telephone: 202-514-0651
Website: http://www.usdoj.gov/
criminal/fraud

**Human Genome Project Ethical,
Legal, and Social Issues (ELSI)
Program**
U.S. Department of Energy
Health Effects and Life Sciences
Division
Office of Biological and
Environmental Research
19901 Germantown Road
ER-72
Germantown, MD 20874-1290
Telephone: 301-903-6488
Fax: 301-903-8521
E-mail: genome@oer.doe.gov
Website: http://www.ornl.gov/
TechResources/Human_Genome/
resource/elsi.html
Periodical: *Human Genome News*

**Jet Propulsion Laboratory Ethics
Office**
National Aeronautics & Space
Administration
P.O. Box 751
La Canada Flintridge, CA 91012
Ethics Hotline

(Jet Propulsion Laboratory Ethics
Office *cont'd*)
Telephone: 818-354-9999
Website: http://www.jpl.nasa.gov/JPL/
ethics
Periodical: *Ethics Briefs*

**Joint Services Conference On
Professional Ethics**
c/o Col. A.E. Hartle
U.S. Military Academy
Dept. of English
West Point, NY 10996-1791
Telephone: 914-938-2501
Fax: 914-938-2562
Website: http://www.usafa.af.mil/
jscope
Reference: *JSCOPE Bibliography*
(online)
(study of military ethics)

**National Bioethics Advisory
Commission**
6100 Executive Blvd., Suite 5B01
Rockville, MD 20892-7508
Telephone: 301-402-4242
Fax: 301-480-6900
Website: http://bioethics.gov/cgi-bin/
bioeth_counter.pl

National Center for Clinical Ethics
U.S. Department of Veterans Affairs
Office of the Under Secretary for
Health
VAM & ROC (10AE)
215 North Main Street
White River Junction, VT
05009-3517
Telephone: 802-296-5145
Fax: 802-296-6316
Website: http://wrjva1.hitchcock.org/
ncce.html
National Headquarters Bioethics
Committee
Ethics Advisory Committees
Reference: *Annotated Bibliographies*
(online)

National Center for Genome Resources
1800-A Old Pecos Trail
Santa Fe, NM 87505
Telephone: 505-982-7840
Fax: 505-995-4432
E-mail: ncgr@ncgr.org
Website: http://www.ncgr.org
(information clearinghouse)

National Endowment for the Humanities
1100 Pennsylvania Ave, NW
Washington, DC 20506
Telephone: 800-NEH-1121
202-606-8400
E-mail: info@neh.gov
Website: http://www.neh.fed.us
Periodical: *Humanities*
(supports programs and research in the humanities)

National Partnership for Reinventing Government
750 17th Street, NW, Suite 200
Washington, DC 20006
Telephone: 202-632-0150
Fax: 202-632-0390
Website: http://www.npr.gov
Formerly National Performance Review
Periodical: *Reinvention Express*
(federal government reform)

National Reference Center for Bioethics Literature
Kennedy Institute of Ethics
Georgetown University
Box 571212
Washington, DC 20057-1212
Telephone: 202-687-3885
800-MED-ETHX
Fax: 202-687-6770
E-mail:
 medethx@gunet.georgetown.edu
Website: http://guweb.georgetown
 .edu/nrcbl/index.htm
Periodical: *New Titles in Bioethics*
Reference: *BIOETHICSLINE*
(National Library of Medicine, online database)

New York State Task Force on Life and the Law
33 West 34th Street, 3rd Floor
New York, NY 10001-3071
Telephone: 212-613-4286
Website: http://www.buffalo.edu/
 faculty/research/bioethics/
 members.html

Office for Protection from Research Risks
Office of Extramural Research
National Institutes of Health
6100 Executive Blvd., Suite 3B01
MSC 7507
Rockville, MD 20892-7507
Telephone: 301-496-7005
E-mail: oprr@od.nih.gov
Website: http://www.nih.gov/grants/
 oprr/oprr.htm
Reference: *Protecting Human Research Subjects: Institutional Review Board Guidebook*

Office of Genome Ethics
National Human Genome Research Institute
Division of Intramural Research
Office of the Clinical Director
National Institutes of Health
Bldg. 9, Room B1E10
9 Memorial Drive, MSC 0965
Bethesda, MD 20892-0965
Telephone: 301-594-2481
Fax: 301-435-2440
E-mail: kberg@nhgri.nih.gov
Website: http://www.nhgri.nih.gov/
 About_NHGRI/Dir/Ethics

Office of Human Subjects Research
Office of the Deputy Director for Intramural Research
National Institutes of Health
Warren G. Magnuson Clinical Center
Bldg. 10, Room 1C-116,
Bethesda, MD 20892-1154
Telephone: 301-402-3444
Fax: 301-402-3443
Website: http://helix.nih.gov:8001/
 ohsr

Office of Information and Privacy
U.S. Department of Justice
Flag Bldg., Suite 570
Washington, DC 20530-0001
Telephone: 202-514-FOIA
Website: http://www.usdoj.gov/oip/
oip.html
(administration of Freedom of
Information Act and Privacy Act)

Office of Professional Responsibility
U.S. Department of Justice
950 Pennsylvania Avenue, NW,
Room 4304
Washington, DC 20530
Website:
http://www.usdoj.gov/opr/index.html
(conduct of federal attorneys)

Office of Research Integrity
Public Health Service
U.S. Department of Health and
Human Services
5515 Security Lane, Suite 700
Rockville, MD 20852
Telephone: 301-443-3400
Fax: 301-443-5351
Website: http://ori.dhhs.gov

**President's Council on Integrity
and Efficiency**
Deputy Director for Management
Office of Management and Budget
Executive Office of the President
New Executive Office Bldg., Room
9026
725 17th Street, NW
Washington, DC 20503
Website: http://www.ignet.gov/ignet/
internal/pcie/pcie.html
Periodical: *Journal of Public Inquiry*
(federal Inspectors General)

Public Integrity Section
Criminal Division
U.S. Department of Justice
10th and Constitution Avenue, NW
Washington, DC 20530
Telephone: 202-514-1412
(conduct of federal and state
government officials)

**Social, Behavioral, and Economic
Research Division**
National Science Foundation
4201 Wilson Blvd., Room 995
Arlington, VA 22230
Fax: 703-306-0485
Website: http://www.nsf.gov:80/sbe/
sber
Law and Social Science Program
Telephone: 703-306-1762
Societal Dimensions of Engineering,
Science, and Technology Program
(formerly Ethics and Values Studies
Program/Research on Science and
Technology Program)
Telephone: 703-306-1743

Standards of Conduct Office
U.S. Department of Defense
Office of General Counsel
1600 Defense Pentagon
Washington, DC 20301-1600
Telephone: 703-695-3272
Fax: 703-697-1640
E-mail: SOCO@OSDGC.OSD.MIL
Website: http://www.defenselink.mil/
dodgc/defense_ethics/index.html
Reference: *Compilation of Federal
Ethics Laws* (online)
(conduct of military personnel)

State Justice Institute
1650 King Street, Suite 600
Alexandria, VA 22314
Telephone: 703-684-6100
Fax: 703-684-7618
E-mail: SJI@clark.net
Website: http://www.clark.net/pub/sji/
home.htm
(awards grants to improve quality of
justice in the state courts)

U.S. Commission on Civil Rights
624 9th Street, NW
Washington, DC 20425
Telephone: 202-376-8312
Complaints Referral

(U.S. Commission on Civil Rights
cont'd)
Telephone: 800-552-6843
202-376-8513
E-mail:
ocre.complaints@usccr.sprint.com
Website: http://www.usccr.gov/
index.html
Periodicals: *Civil Rights Journal*
Civil Rights Update

U.S. Congress
House of Representatives Committee
on Standards of Official Conduct
HT2 O'Neill House Office Bldg.
Washington, DC 20515
Telephone: 202-225-7103
Website: http://www.house.gov/Ethics
(conduct of House Members, staff,
and employees)

U.S. Congress
Senate Select Committee on Ethics
220 Hart Senate Office Bldg.
Washington, DC 20510-6425
Telephone: 202-224-2981
Website: http://www.senate.gov/
committee/ethics.html
(conduct of Senators, staff, and
employees)

**U.S. Consumer Product Safety
Commission**
4330 East-West Highway
Bethesda, MD 20814
Telephone: 301-504-0990
800-638-2772
Fax: 301-504-0124
301-504-0025
Washington, DC 20207
E-mail: info@cpsc.gov
Website: http://www.cpsc.gov

U.S. Food & Drug Administration
5600 Fishers Lane
Rockville, MD 20857
Telephone: 800-532-4440
301-827-4420
Fax: 301-443-9767
E-mail: execsec@oc.fda.gov
Website: http://www.fda.gov

**U.S. Merit Systems Protection
Board**
1120 Vermont Avenue, NW
Washington, DC 20419
Telephone: 202-653-7200
800-209-8960
Fax: 202-653-7130
E-mail: mspb@mspb.gov
Website: http://www.mspb.gov
(adjudication of federal employee
personnel actions)

U.S. Office of Compliance
110 2nd Street, SE
Washington, DC 20540
Telephone: 202-724-9250
Fax: 202-426-1913
Website: http://www.compliance.gov/
index.html
(enforcement of Congressional
Accountability Act)

**U.S. Office of Government
Ethics**
1201 New York Avenue, NW,
Suite 500
Washington, DC 20005-3917
Telephone: 202-208-8000
Fax: 202-208-8039
Website: http://www.usoge.gov
Reference: *Ethics CD-ROM*
Periodicals: *Government Ethics
Newsgram*
*Public Financial Disclosure:
A Reviewer's Reference*
(conduct of federal employees)

U.S. Office of Special Counsel
1730 M Street, NW, Suite 300
Washington, DC 20036-4505
Website: http://www.osc.gov
Complaints Examining
Unit/Prohibited Personal
Practices
Telephone: 800-872-9855
202-653-7188
Hatch Act Unit/Political Activity

(U.S. Office of Special Counsel
   cont'd)
Telephone: 800-85-HATCH
202-653-7143
E-mail: hatchact@osc.gov
Disclosure Unit/Whistleblower
   Disclosure Hotline
Telephone: 800-572-2249
202-653-9125
(conduct of federal employees)

U.S. Sentencing Commission
One Columbus Circle, NE
Washington, DC 20002-8002
Website: http://www.ussc.gov
Periodical: *Guide Lines*
(sentencing guidelines for use by
   federal judiciary)

B. INFORMATIONAL RESOURCES

1. Periodicals

This section lists journals, newsletters, looseleaf services, and annuals, published in print and online, that address issues of ethics, professionalism, and public policy.

For each periodical, the publisher's mail address, telephone, fax number, e-mail address, and World Wide Web site URL are provided, where available. When this information does not appear, reference is made to the organization that publishes the material; these organizations are listed in the **Ethics Standards** or **Organizational Resources** sections.

(Generally, newsletters of the same name as their sponsoring organizations are not included.)

ABA Bank Security & Fraud Prevention
American Bankers Association
(see Ethics Standards section)

ABA Bioethics Bulletin
American Bar Association
(see Ethics Standards section)

ABA/BNA Lawyers' Manual on Professional Conduct
The Bureau of National Affairs, Inc.
1231 25th Street, NW
Washington, DC 20037
Telephone: 800-372-1033
Fax: 800-253-0332
Website: http://www.bna.com

Accountability & Performance: A Journal for Practitioners and Academics
Griffith University
School of Accounting, Banking and Finance
Queensland 4111
Australia

(*Accountability & Performance: A Journal for Practitioners and Academics* cont'd)
Telephone: 61 7 3875 7668
Fax: 61 7 3875 7760
E-mail: AllanHodgson@cad.gu.edu.au
Website: http://www.cad.gu.edu.au/accountability/account.htm

Accountability in Research: Policies and Quality Assurance
Gordon and Breach Publishing Group
Knightsbridge House
8th Floor, North Wing
197 Knightsbridge
London SW7 1RB
England
Telephone: 44 171 584 7676
Fax: 44 171 823 7969
E-mail: info@gbhap.com
Website: http://www.gbhap.com

AccountAbility Quarterly
Institute of Social and Ethical AccountAbility, England
(see Organizations: World)

Accountants' Liability Quarterly
VersusLaw, Inc.
2613 151st Place NE
Redmond, WA 98052
Telephone: 425-250-0142
Fax: 425-250-0157
E-mail: service@versuslaw.com
Website: http://www.versuslaw.com

Accounting, Auditing &
  Accountability Journal
MCB University Press
60/62 Toller Lane
Bradford
West Yorkshire BD8 9BY
England
Telephone: 44 1274 777700
Fax: 44 1274 785200
Website: http://www.mcb.co.uk

Accounting Liability Alert
Harcourt Brace Professional
  Publishing
525 B Street, Suite 1900
San Diego, CA 92101-4495
Telephone: 619-699-6716
Fax: 619-699-6542
E-mail: propub@harcourtbrace.com
Website: http://www.hbpp.com

Accounting, Organizations and
  Society: An International Journal
  Devoted to the Behavioural,
  Organizational & Social Aspects of
  Accounting
Elsevier
P.O. Box 945
New York, NY 10159-0945
Telephone: 212-633-3730
888-4ES-INFO
Fax: 212-633-3680
E-mail: usinfo-f@elsevier.com
Website: http://www.elsevier.nl

@ction @lert (online)
Federation of American Scientists,
  DC
(see Organizations: U.S.)
Website: http://www.fas.org/
  action.htm

Action Kit for Hospital Law
Action Kit for Hospital Trustees
Action Kit Publications
Horty, Springer & Mattern
The Fairfax
4614 Fifth Avenue
Pittsburgh, PA 15213
Telephone: 800-548-9346
Website:
http://www.hortyspringer.com

ADA Legal Advisor: A Guide to the
  Law for Dentists
American Dental Association
(see Ethics Standards section)

Advanced Medical Directives
Clark Boardman Callaghan
West Group
610 Opperman Drive
Eagan, MN 55123
Telephone: 612-687-7000
800-328-4880
Fax: 800-340-9378
Website: http://www.westgroup.com

Ag Bioethics Forum
Bioethics Program, Iowa State
  University
(see Organizations: U.S.)

AI & Society: The Journal of Human-
  Centred Systems and Machine
  Intelligence
Springer-Verlag
Tiergartenstrasse 17
D-69121 Heidelberg
Germany
Telephone: 49 6221 487 0
E-mail: Webmaster@springer.de
Website: http://www.springer.de
U.S. Office: 175 Fifth Avenue
New York, NY 10010
Telephone: 800-SPRINGER
212-460-1500
Fax: 212-473-6272
E-mail: custserv@springer-ny.com
Website: http://www.springer-ny.com

AIDS & Public Policy Journal
AIDS Law & Litigation Reporter
University Publishing Group
12 South Market Street, Suite 300
Frederick, MD 21701-5225
Telephone: 800-654-8188

AIDS Litigation Reporter
Andrews Publications
175 Strafford Avenue
Bldg. 4, Suite 140
Wayne, PA 19087
Telephone: 800-345-1101
610-225-0510
Fax: 610-225-0501
E-mail: customer@andrewspub.com
Website: http://www.andrewspub.com

AIDS Policy & Law
LRP Publications
747 Dresher Road, Suite 500
P.O. Box 980
Horsham, PA 19044-0980
Telephone: 800-341-7874
Fax: 215-784-9639
E-mail: custserve@LRP.com
Website: http://www.lrp.com

American Business Law Journal
Academy of Legal Studies in
   Business, OH
(see Organizations: U.S.)

American Character: A Commentary
   on Domestic Issues (online)
American Purpose (online)
Ethics and Public Policy Center, DC
(see Organizations: U.S.)
Website: http://www.eppc.org/library

American Enterprise
American Enterprise Institute for
   Public Policy Research, DC
(see Organizations: U.S.)

American Journal of Ethics in
   Medicine: A National Publication
   by Medical Students
Center for Bioethics, University of
   Pennsylvania
(see Organizations: U.S.)

American Journal of Jurisprudence
Natural Law Institute
Notre Dame Law School
Notre Dame, IN 46556
Telephone: 219-631-5913
Website: http://www.nd.edu/~ndlaw/
   academic/journals.html

American Journal of Law & Medicine
American Society of Law, Medicine
   and Ethics, MA
(see Organizations: U.S.)

American Journal of Medical Quality
Williams & Wilkins
351 West Camden Street
Baltimore, MD 21201-2436
Telephone: 800-638-6423
410-528-8555
E-mail: custserv@wwilkins.com
Website: http://www.wwilkins.com

Andrews' Professional Liability
   Litigation Reporter
Andrews Publications
(see *AIDS Litigation Reporter*)

Anesthesia Malpractice Prevention
Williams & Wilkins
(see *American Journal of Medical*
   Quality)

Angelaki: Journal of the Theoretical
   Humanities
Carfax Publishing Ltd.
P.O. Box 25
Abingdon
Oxfordshire OX14 3UE
England
Telephone: 44 1235 401000
Fax: 44 1235 401550
U.S. Office: 875-81 Massachusetts
   Avenue
Cambridge, MA 02139
Telephone: 617-354-1425
Fax: 617-354-6875
E-mail: enquiries@carfax.co.uk
Website: http://www.carfax.co.uk/
   index.htm

Annals of Health Law
Institute for Health Law, Loyola
University Chicago School of Law,
IL
(see Organizations: U.S.)

Annual Review of Law and Ethics
Duncker & Humblot GmbH
Carl-Heinrich-Becker-Weg 9
D-12165 Berlin
P.O. Box 41 03 29
D-12113 Berlin
Germany
Telephone: 49 30 79 00 06-0
Fax: 49 30 79 00 06 31
E-mail: duh-werbung@t-online.de
Website: http://www.duncker-
humblot.de/cgi-bin/start.pl/
index.html?onum=2056

Anthropology & Medicine
Carfax Publishing Ltd.
(see *Angelaki*)

Art, Artifact & Architecture Law
Clark Boardman Callaghan
(see *Advanced Medical Directives*)

Association Law & Policy
American Society of Association
Executives
(see Ethics Standards section)

*Astrolabe Online Journal: Ethical
Navigations through Virtual
Technologies*
Advanced Computing Center for the
Arts and Design, Ohio State
University
Website: http://www.cgrg.ohio-state
.edu/Astrolabe/journal

*Au Chevet, Newsletter of the FRSQ
Network for Research in Clinical
Ethics*
Centre for Bioethics, Clinical
Research Institute of Montreal,
Canada
(see Organizations: World)

*Bank Directors', Officers' and
Lawyers' Civil Liabilities*
Aspen Publishers, Inc.
200 Orchard Ridge Drive
Gaithersburg, MD 20878
Telephone: 301-417-7500
800-638-8437
Fax: 301-417-7550
Website: http://www.aspenpub.com

*Bank Policies, Bank Procedures, and
Bank Internal Audit: A Working
Guide to Regulatory Compliance
Bank Secrecy Act and Anti-Money
Laundering Service*
Sheshunoff Information Services Inc.
505 Barton Springs Road, Suite 1200
Austin, TX 78704
Telephone: 512-472-2244
800-456-2340
Fax: 512-305-6575
Website: http://www.sheshunoff.com

Basic and Applied Social Psychology
Lawrence Erlbaum Associates, Inc.
10 Industrial Avenue
Mahwah, NJ 07430-2262
Telephone: 201-236-9500
800-9-BOOKS-9
Fax: 201-236-0072
Website: http://www.erlbaum.com

*BEARS: Brown Electronic Article
Review Service on Moral and
Political Philosophy* (online)
Brown University, Dept. of
Philosophy, RI
Website: http://www.brown.edu/
Departments/Philosophy/bears/
menu.html

*Being Well: Bulletin of the Society for
Professional Well-Being*
Center for Professional Well-Being,
NC
(see Organizations: U.S.)

Berkeley Technology Law Journal
University of California Press
Journals
2120 Berkeley Way
Berkeley, CA 94720

(*Berkeley Technology Law Journal*
   cont'd)
Telephone: 510-643-7154
Fax: 510-642-9917
E-mail: journals@ucop.edu
Website: http://www.ucpress.edu/
   journals

*Between the Species: A Journal of
   Ethics*
Schweitzer Center of the San
   Francisco Bay Institute/
   Congress of Cultures
P.O. Box 8496
Landscape Station
Berkeley, CA 94707
Telephone: 510-526-5346

Bioethica Forum
Societe Suisse d'Ethique Biomedicale,
   Switzerland
(see Organizations: World)

*Bioethics: Journal of the International
   Association of Bioethics (IAB)*
Blackwell Publishers
108 Cowley Road
Oxford OX4 1JF
England
Telephone: 44 1865 791100
Fax: 44 1865 791347
U.S. Office: 350 Main Street
Malden, MA 02148
Telephone: 781-388-8200
Fax: 781-388-8210
Website:
http://www.blackwellpublishers.co.uk

Bioethics Bulletin
Dossetor Health Ethics Centre,
   Canada
(see Organizations: World)

Bioethics Bulletin
University at Buffalo Center for
   Clinical Ethics and Humanities in
   Health Care, State University of
   New York
(see Organizations: U.S.)

Bioethics Examiner
Center for Bioethics, University of
   Minnesota
(see Organizations: U.S.)

Bioethics Forum
Midwest Bioethics Center, MO
(see Organizations: U.S.)

Bioethics Literature Review
University Publishing Group
(see *AIDS & Public Policy Journal*)

Bioethics Matters
Center for Biomedical Ethics,
   University of Virginia Health
   Sciences Center
(see Organizations: U.S.)

Bioethics News & Reviews
Center for Healthcare Ethics,
   St. Joseph Health System, CA
(see Organizations: U.S.)

Bioethics Outlook
Plunkett Centre for Ethics, Australia
(see Organizations: World)

Bioethics Research Notes
Southern Cross Bioethics Institute,
   Australia
(see Organizations: World)

Bioetica
Franco Angeli Editore
Viale Monza 106
I-20127 Milan
Italy
Telephone: 39-28-27-651

Bioetica a Cultura
Instituto Siciliano di Bioetica, Italy
(see Organizations: World)

*Biolaw: A Legal and Ethical Reporter
   on Medicine, Health Care, and
   Bioengineering*
University Publications of America
4520 East-West Highway
Bethesda, MD 20814-3389

(*Biolaw: A Legal and Ethical Reporter on Medicine, Health Care, and Bioengineering* cont'd)
Telephone: 301-657-3200
800-692-6300
Fax: 301-657-3203
E-mail: upainfo@lexis-nexis.com
Website: http://www.upapubs.com

Biology and Philosophy
Kluwer Academic Publishers
P.O. Box 322
3300 AH Dordrecht
Netherlands
Telephone: 31 78 639 23 92
Fax: 31 78 654 64 74
E-mail: services@wkap.nl
Website: http://www.wkap.nl

Biomedical Ethics: Newsletter of the European Network for Biomedical Ethics
Interfaculty Center for Ethics in the Sciences and Humanities, Germany
(see Organizations: World)
E-mail: biomedical.ethics@uni-tuebingen.de

Biotechnology Law Report
Mary Ann Liebert, Inc., Publishers
2 Madison Avenue
Larchmont, NY 10538
Telephone: 914-834-3100
Fax: 914-834-3688
E-mail: info@liebertpub.com
Website: http://www.liebertpub.com

BLAST: Bulletin of Law, Science and Technology
American Bar Association
(see Ethics Standards section)

BNA/ACCA Compliance Manual: Prevention of Corporate Liability
The Bureau of National Affairs, Inc.
(see *ABA/BNA Lawyers' Manual. . .*)

Bowman's Ethics & Malpractice Alert
Forest J. Bowman
P.O. Box 4253
Star City, WV 26504-4253

(*Bowman's Ethics & Malpractice Alert* cont'd)
Telephone: 304-293-7081
Fax: 304-293-6891

Bridging the GAP
Government Accountability Project, WA
(see Organizations: U.S.)

British Journal for the Philosophy of Science
Oxford University Press
Great Clarendon Street
Oxford OX2 6DP
England
U.S. Office: 198 Madison Avenue
New York, NY 10016
Telephone: 212-726-6000
800-451-7556
Fax: 919-677-1303
Website: http://www.oup-usa.org

Bulletin of Medical Ethics (online)
Website:
   http://ourworld.compuserve.com/homepages/Bulletin_of_Medical_Ethics/

Bulletin of Science, Technology & Society
Sage Publications
6 Bonhill Street
London EC2A 4PU
England
Telephone: 44 171 374 0645
Fax: 44 171 374 8741
E-mail: market@sagepub.co.uk
Website: http://www.sagepub.co.uk/ltd_home.html
U.S. Office: 2455 Teller Road
Thousand Oaks, CA 91320
Telephone: 805-499-0721
Fax: 805-499-0871
E-mail: info@sagepub.com

Business & Professional Ethics Journal
Box 15017
Gainesville, FL 32604

(*Business & Professional Ethics
Journal* cont'd)
Telephone: 904-392-2084
Fax: 904-392-5577

Business & Society
Sage Publications
(see *Bulletin of Science, Technology
& Society*)

*Business and Society Review: Journal
of the Center for Business Ethics at
Bentley College*
Blackwell Publishers
(see *Bioethics: Journal of the IAB*)

*Business & the Contemporary World:
An International Journal of
Business, Economics and Social
Policy*
John Wiley & Sons, Inc.
605 Third Avenue
New York, NY 10158-0012
Telephone: 212-850-6645
Fax: 212-850-6021
E-mail: subinfo@wiley.com
Website: http://www.wiley.com

*Business Conduct and Ethics: How to
Set Up a Self-Governance Program*
Business Laws, Inc.
11630 Chillicothe Road
P.O. Box 185
Chesterland, OH 44026-9982
Telephone: 440-729-7996
800-759-0929
Fax: 440-729-0645
E-mail: inquiry@businesslaws.com
Website:
http://www.businesslaws.com

*Business Crimes Bulletin: Compliance
& Litigation Newsletter*
American Lawyer Media, Inc.
Law Journal Seminars-Press
Leader Publications
345 Park Avenue South
New York, NY 10010

(*Business Crimes Bulletin* cont'd)
Telephone: 800-888-8300, ext. 6000
212-545-6000
Fax: 212-481-8110
Website: http://www.lawcatalog.com

Business Ethics: A European Review
Blackwell Publishers
(see *Bioethics: Journal of the IAB*)

*Business Ethics: The Magazine of
Socially Responsible Business*
52 South 10th Street, Suite 110
Minneapolis, MN 55403-2001
Telephone: 612-962-4700
800-601-9010
Fax: 612-962-4706
E-mail: Bizethics@aol.com
Website: http://www.depaul.edu/
ethics/bizethics.html

Business Ethics Fortnight
Center for Business Ethics, Loyola
Marymount University, CA
(see Organizations: U.S.)

Business Ethics Quarterly
Philosophy Documentation Center
Bowling Green State University
Bowling Green, OH 43403-0189
Telephone: 419-372-9902
800-444-2419
Fax: 419-372-6987
E-mail: pdc@mailserver.bgsu.edu
Website: http://www.bgsu.edu/offices/
phildoc/index.html

*Business Ethics Resource: A Resource
on Ethics Management for the CEO*
Business Ethics Foundation, MA
(see Organizations: U.S.)

*Butterworths Human Rights Cases
Butterworths Medico-Legal Reports
Butterworths Professional Negligence
Service*
Butterworths Ltd.
Halsbury House
35 Chancery Lane
London WC2A 1EL
England

(*Butterworths* cont'd)
Telephone: 44 171 400 2500
Fax: 44 171 400 2842
Website:
http://www.butterworths.co.uk
Canadian Office: 75 Clegg Road
Markham, Ontario L6G 1A1
Canada
Telephone: 800-668-6481
905-479-2665
Fax: 905-479-2826
E-mail: info@butterworths.ca
Website: http://www.butterworths.ca

Cahiers de Bioethique
Presses de l'Université Laval
Pavillon Jean-Durand
2336 chemin Sainte-Foy, 2e étage
Sainte-Foy, Quebec G1K 7P4
Canada
Telephone: 418-656-2803
Fax: 418-656-3305
E-mail: Presses@PUL.ULaval.ca

Calyx: Ethical Issues in Pediatrics
Hospital for Sick Children
Dept. of Bioethics
555 University Avenue
Toronto, Ontario M5G 1X8
Canada
Telephone: 416-813-5000
Fax: 416-813-4967

*Cambridge Quarterly of Healthcare
    Ethics: The International Journal
    for Healthcare Ethics and Ethics
    Committees*
Cambridge University Press
Edinburgh Bldg.
Cambridge CB2 2RU
England
Fax: 44 1223 325959
E-mail: customer_service@cup.org
U.S. Office: 110 Midland Avenue
Port Chester, NY 10573
Telephone: 800-872-7423
Fax: 914-937-4712
Website: http://www.cup.org

Canadian Bioethics Report
Canadian Medical Association
1867 Alta Vista Drive
Ottawa, Ontario K1G 3Y6
Canada
Telephone: 800 663-7336
613 731-8610
Fax: 613 731-1779
E-mail: willij@cma.ca
Website: http://www.cma.ca

*CASOLM: The Courts & Science
    On-Line Magazine*
Einstein Institute for Science, Health
    and the Courts, MD
(see Organizations: U.S.)
Website: http://www.ornl.gov/courts

*Cato Journal: An Interdisciplinary
    Journal of Public Policy Analysis*
Cato Policy Report
Cato Institute, DC
(see Organizations: U.S.)

*Christian Bioethics: Non-Ecumenical
    Studies in Medical Morality*
Swets & Zeitlinger Publishers
P.O. Box 825
2160 SZ Lisse
Netherlands
Telephone: 31 252-435111
Fax: 31 252-415888
E-mail: orders@swets.nl
Website: http://www.swets.nl/sps/
    home.html
U.S. Office: P.O. Box 613
Royersford, PA 19468
Telephone: 610-524-5355
Fax: 610-524-5366

Citation
Citation Publishing Corp.
Box 3538 RFD
Long Grove, IL 60047
Telephone: 847-438-2020
800-626-5210
Fax: 847-438-2299
(health law)

Civil Justice Digest
Roscoe Pound Foundation
Association of Trial Lawyers of
America
(see Ethics Standards section)

Civil Rights Journal
Civil Rights Update
U.S. Commission on Civil Rights, DC
(see Organizations: Government)

Civil Rights Update
National Association of Attorneys
General
750 1st Street, NE, Suite 1100
Washington, DC 20002
Telephone: 202-236-6000
Fax: 202-408-7014

Clinical Ethics Report
Bioethics Consultation Group, CA
(see Organizations: U.S.)

*Collection Panétius - Les Archives de
l'éthique clinique*
Centre for Bioethics, Clinical
Research Institute of Montreal,
Canada
(see Organizations: World)

Common Cause Magazine
Common Cause, DC
(see Organizations: U.S.)

Common Good
Stein Center on Ethics and Public
Interest Law, NY
(see Organizations: U.S.)
E-mail: CommonGood@mail.lawnet
.fordham.edu

Communication Law and Policy
Lawrence Erlbaum Associates, Inc.
(see *Basic and Applied Social
Psychology*)

Communiqué
Center for Ethics and Human Rights,
American Nurses Association
(see Ethics Standards section)

Communiqué
National Council on Ethics in Human
Research, Canada
(see Organizations: World)

Communitarian Update
Communitarian Network, DC
(see Organizations: U.S.)

Community Ethics
Consortium Ethics Program, Center
for Medical Ethics, University of
Pittsburgh, PA
(see Organizations: U.S.)

Community, Work & Family
Carfax Publishing Ltd.
(see *Angelaki*)

*Compendium of Government Issues
Affecting Direct Marketing*
Direct Marketing Association
(see Ethics Standards section)

Computer Law & Security Report
Elsevier
(see *Accounting, Organizations and
Society*)

Computer Law Monitor
Research Publications, Inc.
P.O. Box 9267
Asheville, NC 28815
Telephone: 704-298-8291

Computer Security Digest
Computer Protection Systems, Inc.
12275 Appletree Drive
Plymouth, MI 48170
Telephone: 313-459-8787
Fax: 313-459-2720

Computers and the Humanities
Kluwer Academic Publishers
(see *Biology and Philosophy*)

Computers in Human Behavior
Elsevier
(see *Accounting, Organizations and
Society*)

*Configurations: A Journal of
  Literature, Science, and Technology*
Johns Hopkins University Press
2715 North Charles Street
Baltimore, MD 21218-4363
Telephone: 410-516-6900
800-548-1784
Fax: 410-516-6968
Website: http://www.press.jhu.edu/
  press/journals

*Connecting Rod: The Networking
  Newsletter of the International
  Ethical Business Registry*
International Ethical Business
  Registry, Canada
(see *Organizations: World*)

*Consent to Treatment: A Practical
  Guide*
Aspen Publishers, Inc.
(see *Bank Directors'. . .*)

*Contemporary Justice Review: Issues
  in Criminal, Social, and Restorative
  Justice*
Gordon and Breach Publishing Group
(see *Accountability in Research*)

Contexts
Institute for Medicine in
  Contemporary Society, SUNY
  Health Sciences Center, State
  University of New York-Stony
  Brook
(see *Organizations: U.S.*)

*Continuum: Journal of Media and
  Cultural Studies*
Carfax Publishing Ltd.
(see *Angelaki*)

*Convergence: The Journal of
  Research into New Media
  Technologies*
John Libbey Media
University of Luton
Faculty of Humanities
Dept. of Media Arts
75 Castle Street
Luton LU1 3AJ
England

(*Convergence* cont'd)
Telephone: 44 1582 743297
Fax: 44 1582 743298
E-mail: ulp@luton.ac.uk
Website: http://colossus.luton.ac.uk/
  Convergence

Corporate & Computer Fraud
(see *Computer Security Digest*)

*Corporate Community Relations
  Letter*
Center for Corporate Community
  Relations, MA
(see *Organizations: U.S.*)

Corporate Conduct Quarterly
(see *Ethikos and Corporate Conduct
  Quarterly*)

Corporate Crime Reporter
American Communications &
  Publishing Co., Inc.
P.O. Box 18384
Washington, DC 20036
Telephone: 202-737-1680

*Corporate Counsel's Guide to
  Business Ethics Policies*
*Corporate Counsel's Guide to
  Lawyering Laws*
*Corporate Counsel's Guide to the
  Attorney-Client, Work-Product and
  Self-Evaluative Privileges*
*Corporate Counsel's Guide to the
  Organizational Sentencing
  Guidelines*
*Corporate Counsel's Guide to White-
  Collar Crime*
Corporate Crime and Sentencing
Business Laws, Inc.
(see *Business Conduct and Ethics*)

Corporate Ethics Monitor
EthicScan Canada Ltd.
(see *Organizations: World*)

Corporate Examiner
Interfaith Center on Corporate
  Responsibility, NY
(see *Organizations: U.S.*)

*Corporate Governance: An
    International Review*
Blackwell Publishers
(see *Bioethics: Journal of the IAB*)

Corporate Governance Advisor
Aspen Publishers, Inc.
(see *Bank Directors'. . .*)

Corporate Governance Bulletin
Investor Responsibility Research
    Center, Washington, DC
(see Organizations: U.S.)

*Corporate Governance Manual &
    Report*
The Bureau of National Affairs, Inc.
(see *ABA/BNA Lawyers' Manual. . .*)

Corporate Observer
Hispanic Association for Corporate
    Responsibility, DC
(see Organizations: U.S.)

*Corporate Officers & Directors
    Liability Litigation Reporter*
Andrews Publications
(see *AIDS Litigation Reporter*)

Corporate Public Issues
Issue Action Publications
207 Loudoun Street, SE
Leesburg, VA 22075
Telephone: 703-777-8450
Fax: 703-777-8484

Corporate Responsibility
658 Counselors Way
Williamsburg, VA 23185-4059

*Corporate Sentencing Guidelines:
    Compliance and Mitigation*
American Lawyer Media, Inc.
(see *Business Crimes Bulletin*)

Corporate Social Issues Reporter
Investor Responsibility Research
    Center, DC
(see Organizations: U.S.)

Corporate Watch (online)
Transnational Resource and Action
    Center
Institute for Global Communications
Website: http://www.corpwatch.org/
    home.html

Counseling and Values
Association for Spiritual, Ethical, and
    Religious Values in Counseling
P.O. Box 631396
Baltimore, MD 21263-1396
Telephone: 800-422-2648
410-594-7570

Crime, Law and Social Change
Kluwer Academic Publishers
(see *Biology and Philosophy*)

*Criminal Defense Ethics Law and
    Liability*
Clark Boardman Callaghan
(see *Advanced Medical Directives*)

Criminal Justice Ethics
Institute for Criminal Justice Ethics,
    NY
(see Organizations: U.S.)

Cultural Values
Blackwell Publishers
(see *Bioethics: Journal of the IAB*)

Culture, Medicine and Psychiatry
Kluwer Academic Publishers
(see *Biology and Philosophy*)

*Current Legal Sociology:
    A Periodical Publication of
    Abstracts and Bibliography in Law
    and Society*
International Institute for the
    Sociology of Law, Spain
(see Organizations: World)

Currents
Center for Science and Technology
    Policy and Ethics, Texas A&M
    University
(see Organizations: U.S.)

*D&O Book: A Comparison Guide to
  Directors & Officers Liability
  Policies*
Warren, McVeigh & Griffin, Inc.
Griffin Communications, Inc.
1420 Bristol Street North, Suite 220
Newport Beach, CA 92660
Telephone: 949-752-1058
800-205-6218
Fax: 949-955-1929
E-mail: griffcom@ix.netcom.com
Website: http://www.griffincom.com

*DAEOgrams: Designated Agency
  Ethics Officials*
CCH Washington Service Bureau
655 15th Street, NW, Suite 275
Washington, DC 20005
Telephone: 800-955-5219
202-508-0600
Fax: 202-508-0694
E-mail: custserv@wsb.com.
Website: http://www.wsb.com

Dignity Newsletter
Center for Bioethics and Human
  Dignity, IL
(see Organizations: U.S.)

Director & Officer Liability Insurance
Business Laws, Inc.
(see *Business Conduct and Ethics*)

Disability & Society
Carfax Publishing Ltd.
(see *Angelaki*)

Dispatches
Centre of Medical Law and Ethics,
  King's College London
(see Organizations: World)

*Durable Powers of Attorney and
  Health Care Directives*
Clark Boardman Callaghan
(see *Advanced Medical Directives*)

Earth Ethics
Center for Respect of Life and
  Environment
2100 L Street, NW
Washington, DC 20037
Telephone: 202-778-6133
Fax: 202-778-6138
E-mail: crle@aol.com
Website: http://www.center1.com/
  eeidx.html

ED Legal Letter
American Health Consultants, Inc.
3525 Piedmont Road
Bldg. 6, Suite 400
Atlanta, GA 30305
Telephone: 404-262-7436
800-688-2421
Fax: 800-284-3291
Website: http://www.ahcpub.com
(emergency medicine liability)

*Emergences: Journal for the Study of
  Media and Composite Cultures*
Carfax Publishing Ltd.
(see *Angelaki*)

*Employee Responsibilities and Rights
  Journal*
Plenum Publishing Corp.
233 Spring Street
New York, NY 10013-1578
Telephone: 212-620-8000
800-221-9369
Fax: 212-463-0742
E-mail: info@plenum.com
Website: http://www.plenum.com

*Endeavour: A Review of the Progress
  of Science and Technology in the
  Service of Mankind*
Elsevier
(see *Accounting, Organizations and
  Society*)

*ENDS and MEANS: A Journal of
  Philosophy and Technology*
Aberdeen Centre for Philosophy,
  Technology and Society, England
(see Organizations: World)

Engineering Ethics Update
National Institute for Engineering
Ethics, MO
(see Organizations: U.S.)

Environmental Ethics:
An Interdisciplinary Journal
Dedicated to the Philosophical
Aspects of Environmental Problems
Center for Environmental Philosophy,
University of North Texas
(see Organizations: U.S.)

Environmental Values
White Horse Press
10 High Street
Knapwell, Cambridge CB3 8NR
England
Telephone/Fax: 44 1954 267527
Additional Office: 1 Strand
Isle of Harris HS5 3UD
England
Telephone/Fax: 44 1859 520204
E-mail: aj@erica.demon.co.uk

Essays in Public Policy
Hoover Institution on War,
Revolution and Peace, CA
(see Organizations: U.S.)

Ethica
ETHOS Groupe de Recherche en
Ethique, Université du Québec à
Rimouski, Canada
(see Organizations: World)

Ethical Currents
Ethical Dimensions
Center for Healthcare Ethics, St.
Joseph Health System, CA
(see Organizations: U.S.)

Ethical Issues in Managed Care
Quarterly
Bioethics Consultation Group, CA
(see Organizations: U.S.)

Ethical Perspectives: Journal of the
European Ethics Network
Peeters Publishers
Bondgenotenlaan 153
B-3000 Leuven
Belgium
Telephone: 32-16-235170
Fax: 32-16-228500
E-mail: peeters@www.peeters-
leuven.be
Website: http://www.peeters-leuven.be

Ethical Record
South Place Ethical Society, England
(see Organizations: World)

Ethical Spectacle (online)
Website: http://www.spectacle.org

Ethical Theory and Moral Practice
Kluwer Academic Publishers
(see *Biology and Philosophy*)

Ethically Speaking
Association for Practical and
Professional Ethics, IN
(see Organizations: U.S.)

Ethics (Lunlixue)
China People's University
Book & Newspaper Inormation
Center
3 Zhang Zizhung Road
P.O. Box 1122
Beijing 100007
China
Telephone: 86-10-4015080
U.S. Office: China Publications
Services
Box 49614
Chicago, IL 60649
Telephone: 312-288-3291
Fax: 312-288-8570

Ethics: An International Journal of
Social, Political, and Legal
Philosophy
University of Chicago Press
Journals Division
P.O. Box 37005
Chicago, IL 60637

(*Ethics: An International Journal of Social, Political, and Legal Philosophy* cont'd)
Telephone: 773-753-3347
Fax: 773-753-0811
E-mail: orders@journals.uchicago.edu
Website: http://www.journals
.uchicago.edu/home.html

Ethics: Easier Said Than Done
Josephson Institute of Ethics, CA
(see Organizations: U.S.)

Ethics Across the University
Center for Ethics, Loyola University, IL
(see Organizations: U.S.)

Ethics & Behavior
Lawrence Erlbaum Associates, Inc.
(see *Basic and Applied Social Psychology*)

Ethics & Health Care
Bioethics Center, University Health Systems of Eastern Carolina, NC
(see Organizations: U.S.)

Ethics and Information Technology
Kluwer Academic Publishers
(see *Biology and Philosophy*)

Ethics & International Affairs
Carnegie Council on Ethics and International Affairs, NY
(see Organizations: U.S.)

Ethics and Medicine
Paternoster Press
P.O. Box 300
Kingstown Broadway
Carlisle, Cumbria CA3 0QS
England
Telephone: 44-1228-512512
Fax: 44-1228-514949
U.S. Office: P.O. Box 11127
Birmingham, AL 35201-1127

Ethics & Medics
National Catholic Bioethics Center, MA
(see Organizations: U.S.)

Ethics & Policy Newsletter
Center for Ethics and Social Policy, Graduate Theological Union, CA
(see Organizations: U.S.)

Ethics and Society Newsletter
Centre for Applied Ethics, Hong Kong Baptist University, China
(see Organizations: World)

Ethics and the Environment
JAI Press
100 Prospect Street
P.O. Box 811
Stamford, CT 06904
Telephone: 203-323-9606
Fax: 203-357-8446
Website: http://www.jaipress.com

Ethics Briefs
Jet Propulsion Laboratory Ethics Office, CA
(see Organizations: Government)

ETHICS FAX
Centre for Applied Ethics, University of British Columbia, Canada
(see Organizations: World)

Ethics in Economics
Council for Ethics in Economics, OH
(see Organizations: U.S.)

Ethics in Government Reporter
CCH Washington Service Bureau
(see *DAEOgrams*)

Ethics in Practice
Hong Kong Ethics Development Centre, China
(see Organizations: World)

Ethics in the News (online)
Council for Ethics in Legislative
   Advocacy, CO
(see Organizations: U.S.)
Website: http://www
   .lobbyistdirectory.com/indxcela.htm

Ethics Newsletter
Institute for the Study of Applied and
   Professional Ethics, NH
(see Organizations: U.S.)

Ethics, Place and Environment
Carfax Publishing Ltd.
(see *Angelaki*)

Ethics Report
Americans for the Enforcement of
   Attorney Ethics, IL
(see Organizations: U.S.)

Ethics Research Report
Nursing Ethics Network, MA
(see Organizations: U.S.)

Ethics Roll Call
Center for Law Enforcement Ethics,
   TX
(see Organizations: U.S.)

Ethics Today
Ethics Resource Center, DC
(see Organizations: U.S.)

Ethik in der Medizin
Springer-Verlag
(see *AI & Society*)

*Ethikos and Corporate Conduct
   Quarterly*
P.O. Box 31
154 East Boston Post Road
Mamaroneck, NY 10543
Telephone: 800-373-7723
Fax: 914-381-6947
E-mail: ethikos@earthlink.com
Website: http://www.singerpubs.com/
   ethikos

Ethique: La Vie en Question
Societe Francaise de Reflexion
   Bioethique, France
(see Organizations: World)

Ethos: Revista de Filosofia Practica
Instituto de Filosofia Practica,
   Argentina
(see Organizations: World)

*Eubios Bioethics and Biotechnology
   News*
*Eubios Journal of Asian and
   International Bioethics*
Eubios Ethics Institute, Japan
(see Organizations: World)

European Journal of Health Law
Kluwer Academic Publishers
(see *Biology and Philosophy*)

Extra! Magazine
Fairness and Accuracy in Reporting,
   NY
(see Organizations: U.S.)

*False Arrest, Malicious Prosecution,
   and Police Misconduct*
Juris Publishing, Inc.
Executive Park
1 Odell Plaza
Yonkers, NY 10701
Telephone: 800-887-4064
914-375-3400
Fax: 914-375-6047
E-mail: jurispub@aol.com
Website: http://www.jurispub.com

FCA and Qui Tam Quarterly Review
Taxpayers Against Fraud, DC
(see Organizations: U.S.)

Federal Ethics Report
CCH Washington Service Bureau
(see *DAEOgrams*)

*Financial Accountability &
   Management: In Governments,
   Public Services and Charities*
Blackwell Publishers
(see *Bioethics: Journal of the IAB*)

Financial Crimes Report
National Association of Attorneys
  General
(see *Civil Rights Update*)

Focus
Center for Health Policy and Ethics,
  NE
(see Organizations: U.S.)

Focus on Ethics
St. Joseph's College Ethics Centre,
  Canada
(see Organizations: World)

Focus on Fraud
National Fraud Information Center,
  DC
(see Organizations: U.S.)

Focus on Patient Safety
National Patient Safety Foundation,
  American Medical Association
(see Ethics Standards section)

Folia Bioethica
Societe Suisse d'Ethique Biomedicale,
  Switzerland
(see Organizations: World)

*Foreign Corrupt Practices Act
  Reporter*
Business Laws, Inc.
(see *Business Conduct and Ethics*)

Fraud and Abuse Compliance Manual
Aspen Publishers, Inc.
(see *Bank Directors'. . .*)

FREE! Freedom Forum ONLINE
Freedom Forum, VA
(see Organizations: U.S.)
Website:
http://www.freedomforum.org

Free Inquiry
P.O. Box 664
Amherst, NY 14226-9968
Telephone: 800-458-1366
Fax: 716-636-1733

The Gene Exchange
Union of Concerned Scientists, MA
(see Organizations: U.S.)

*Gene Letter: A Newsletter on
  Scientific and Societal Issues in
  Genetics* (online)
Shriver Center
200 Trapelo Road
Waltham, MA 02254
Telephone: 781-642-0001
Website: http://www.geneletter.org

GeneWATCH
Council for Responsible Genetics,
  MA
(see Organizations: U.S.)

Georgetown Journal of Legal Ethics
Georgetown University Law Center
Office of Journal Administration
600 New Jersey Avenue, NW
Washington, DC 20001
Telephone: 202-662-9468
E-mail:
  legal.ethics@law.georgetown.edu
Website: http://www.law.georgetown
  .edu/journals

*Global Society: Journal of
  Interdisciplinary International
  Relations*
Carfax Publishing Ltd.
(see *Angelaki*)

Good Medicine
Physicians for Responsible Medicine,
  DC
(see Organizations: U.S.)

*Governance: An International Journal
  of Policy and Administration*
Blackwell Publishers
(see *Bioethics: Journal of the IAB*)

Government Ethics Newsgram
U.S. Office of Government Ethics,
  DC
(see Organizations: Government)

Government Information Insider
OMB Watch, Washington, DC
(see Organizations: U.S.)

Guardian
Council on Governmental Ethics
    Laws, CA
(see Organizations: U.S.)

Guide Lines
U.S. Sentencing Commission, DC
(see Organizations: Government)

Guide to Fraud Investigations
Practitioners Publishing Co.
3200 Collinsworth
Fort Worth, TX 76107
Telephone: 817-332-3709
800-323-8724
Fax: 817-336-2433

*Guidebook to Freedom of Information
    and Privacy Acts*
Clark Boardman Callaghan
(see *Advanced Medical Directives*)

Guttmacher Report on Public Policy
Alan Guttmacher Institute: Research,
    Policy Analysis & Public
    Education, DC
(see Organizations: U.S.)

*Handling Confidential Information
Handling Government Investigations*
Business Laws, Inc.
(see *Business Conduct and Ethics*)

*Harvard Civil Rights-Civil Liberties
    Law Review*
Harvard Law School
Hastings Hall
Cambridge, MA 02138
Telephone: 617-495-4500
E-mail: hlscrc@law.harvard.edu
Website: http://www.law.harvard.edu/
    Studorgs/crcl_lawreview

*Harvard International Journal of
    Press/Politics*
MIT Press
5 Cambridge Center
Cambridge, MA 02142-1493
Telephone: 617-253-5646
800-356-0343
Fax: 617-258-6779
E-mail: mitpress-orders@mit.edu
Website: http://mitpress.mit.edu

*Health Care Analysis: Journal of
    Health Philosophy and Policy*
John Wiley & Sons, Inc.
(see *Business & the Contemporary
    World*)

Health Care Ethics in the USA
Center for Health Care Ethics, St.
    Louis University Health Sciences
    Center, MO
(see Organizations: U.S.)

Health Care Fraud
American Lawyer Media, Inc.
(see *Business Crimes Bulletin*)

Health Care Fraud & Abuse
Clark Boardman Callaghan
(see *Advanced Medical Directives*)

*Health Care Fraud Litigation
    Reporter*
Andrews Publications
(see *AIDS Litigation Reporter*)

Health Care Fraud Report
The Bureau of National Affairs, Inc.
(see *ABA/BNA Lawyers' Manual. . .*)

Health Care Law Monthly
Matthew Bender & Co., Inc.
11 Penn Plaza
New York, NY 10001
Telephone: 212-967-7707
800-833-9844
Fax: 212-244-3188
Website: http://www.bender.com

Health Care Policy Report
The Bureau of National Affairs, Inc.
(see *ABA/BNA Lawyers' Manual. . .*)

Health Care Quality Monitor
Joint Commission on Accreditation of
    Healthcare Organizations, IL
(see Organizations: U.S.)

Health Ethics Today
Dossetor Health Ethics Centre,
    Canada
(see Organizations: World)

Health Law & Business Series
The Bureau of National Affairs, Inc.
(see *ABA/BNA Lawyers' Manual. . .*)

Health Law Digest
American Health Lawyers
    Association, DC
(see Organizations: U.S.)

Health Law Focus Newsletter
CCH
2700 Lake Cook Road
Riverwoods, IL 60015
Telephone: 847-267-7000
800-835-5224
Fax: 847-224-8299
Website: http://www.cch.com

Health Law Litigation Reporter
Andrews Publications
(see *AIDS Litigation Reporter*)

Health Law News
Center for Health Law Studies,
    St. Louis University School of
    Law, MO
(see Organizations: U.S.)

Health Law News
*Health Law Perspectives: Analyses of
    Recent Developments in Health
    Law*
Health Law and Policy Institute,
    University of Houston Law Center,
    TX
(see Organizations: U.S.)

Health Law Reporter
The Bureau of National Affairs, Inc.
(see *ABA/BNA Lawyers' Manual. . .*)

Health Lawyer
American Bar Association
(see Ethics Standards section)

Health Lawyers News
American Health Lawyers
    Association, DC
(see Organizations: U.S.)

Health, Risk & Society
Carfax Publishing Ltd.
(see *Angelaki*)

Healthcare Ethics Committee Forum
Permanente Medical Group
3400 Delta Fair Blvd.
Antioch, CA 94509

Healthcare Reform & Ethics Review
Center for Healthcare Ethics, St.
    Joseph Health System, CA
(see Organizations: U.S.)

*HEC (HealthCare Ethics Committee)
    Forum: An Interprofessional
    Journal on Healthcare Institutions'
    Ethical and Legal Issues*
Kluwer Academic Publishers
(see *Biology and Philosophy*)

Hospital Consents Manual
Hospital Law Manual
Aspen Publishers, Inc.
(see *Bank Directors'. . .*)

Hospital Peer Review
American Health Consultants, Inc.
(see *ED Legal Letter*)

Human Genome News
Human Genome Management
    Information System
Oak Ridge National Laboratory
1060 Commerce Park, MS 6480
Oak Ridge, TN 37830

(*Human Genome News* cont'd)
Telephone: 423-576-6669
Fax: 423-574-9888
E-mail: bkq@ornl.gov
Website: http://www.ornl.gov/hgmis/
    publicat/publications.html#hgn

Human Rights
American Bar Association
(see Ethics Standards section)

Human Rights Dialogue
Carnegie Council on Ethics and
    International Affairs, NY
(see Organizations: U.S.)

Human Rights Quarterly
Johns Hopkins University Press
(see *Configurations*)

*Human-Computer Interaction:
A Journal of Theoretical,
Empirical, and Methodological
Issues of User Science and of
System Design*
Lawrence Erlbaum Associates, Inc.
(see *Basic and Applied Social
Psychology*)

Humanities
National Endowment for the
    Humanities, DC
(see Organizations: Government)

*IDEA: The Journal of Law and
Technology*
Franklin Pierce Law Center
2 White Street
Concord, NH 03301
Telephone: 603-228-1541
Fax: 603-224-3342
Website: http://www.fplc.edu/IDEA

Ineffective Assistance of Counsel
Clark Boardman Callaghan
(see *Advanced Medical Directives*)

*Information Economics and Policy:
An International and
InterDisciplinary Journal in
Information Economics,
(Tele)Communications and Media*
Elsevier
(see *Accounting, Organizations and
Society*)

Information Technology and People
MCB University Press
(see *Accounting, Auditing &
Accountability Journal*)

Information Technology and the Law
Kluwer Academic Publishers
(see *Biology and Philosophy*)

Informational Health Care Bulletin
Professional Standards Review
    Council of America, NY
(see Organizations: U.S.)

Inner Voice
Forest Service Employees for
    Environmental Ethics, OR
(see Organizations: U.S.)

*Inside Medical Technology: The
Monthly Report on Clinical, Social,
and Policy Trends*
Health Trends, Inc.
4405 East-West Highway, Suite 406
Bethesda, MD 20814
Telephone: 800-945-8816
Fax: 301-907-6790
E-mail: healthtrends@htrinc.com

Integrity (online)
KMPG Business Ethics Institute, DC
(see Organizations: U.S.)
Website:
http://www.us.kpmg.com/ethics

*International Calendar of Bioethics
Events* (online)
Bioethics and Medical Humanities,
    University of Medicine and
    Dentistry of New Jersey-Robert
    Wood Johnson Medical School
(see Organizations: U.S.)
Website: http://www2.umdnj.edu/
    ethicweb/upcome.htm

*International Journal for Quality in
    Health Care*
Oxford University Press
(see *British Journal for the
    Philosophy of Science*)

*International Journal of Applied
    Philosophy*
Philosophy Documentation Center
(see *Business Ethics Quarterly*)

*International Journal of Health Care
    Quality Assurance*
MCB University Press
(see *Accounting, Auditing &
    Accountability Journal*)

*International Journal of Human-
    Computer Studies*
Academic Press
525 B Street, Suite 1900
San Diego, CA 92101-4495
Telephone: 619-231-6616
E-mail: ap@acad.com
app@acad.com
Website: http://www.apnet.com

*International Journal of Law and
    Information Technology*
Oxford University Press
(see *British Journal for the
    Philosophy of Science*)

*International Journal of Law, Policy
    and the Family*
Oxford University Press
(see *British Journal for the
    Philosophy of Science*)

*International Journal of Legal
    Medicine*
Springer-Verlag
(see *AI & Society*)

*International Journal of Politics,
    Culture, and Society*
Plenum Publishing Corp.
(see *Employee Responsibilities and
    Rights Journal*)

*International Journal of the Sociology
    of Law*
Academic Press
(see *International Journal of Human-
    Computer Studies*)

*International Journal of Value-Based
    Management*
Kluwer Academic Publishers
(see *Biology and Philosophy*)

*International Review of Law,
    Computers and Technology*
Carfax Publishing Ltd.
(see *Angelaki*)

*IRB (Institutional Review Board):
    A Review of Human Subjects
    Research*
Hastings Center, NY
(see *Organizations: U.S.*)

*IR&R (Individual Rights and
    Responsibilities) News Report*
American Bar Association
(see Ethics Standards section)

Issues in Ethics
Markkula Center for Applied Ethics,
    Santa Clara University, CA
(see *Organizations: U.S.*)

Issues in Law and Medicine
National Legal Center for the
    Medically Disabled and Dependent
P.O. Box 1586
Terre Haute, IN 47808-1586
Telephone: 812-232-2434

*Journal for General Philosophy of
    Science*
Kluwer Academic Publishers
(see *Biology and Philosophy*)

Journal for Healthcare Quality
National Association for Healthcare
    Quality, IL
(see *Organizations: U.S.*)

*Journal of Accounting and Public
  Policy*
Elsevier
(see *Accounting, Organizations and
  Society*)

*Journal of Accounting, Ethics &
  Public Policy*
c/o R.W. McGee, Editor
236 Johnson Avenue
Dumont, NJ 07628
Telephone: 201-501-8574
Fax: 201-387-0744
E-mail: Dumontinst@aol.com

*Journal of Agricultural and
  Environmental Ethics*
Kluwer Academic Publishers
(see *Biology and Philosophy*)

*Journal of Applied Animal Welfare
  Science*
Lawrence Erlbaum Associates, Inc.
(see *Basic and Applied Social
  Psychology*)

*Journal of Applied Philosophy:
  Journal of the Society for Applied
  Philosophy*
Blackwell Publishers
(see *Bioethics: Journal of the IAB*)

*Journal of Beliefs & Values: Studies
  in Religion & Education*
Carfax Publishing Ltd.
(see *Angelaki*)

*Journal of Biblical Ethics in
  Medicine*
P.O. Box 13231
Florence, SC 29504-3231
Website: http://capo.org/jbem/
  intro_pa.htm

Journal of BioLaw and Business
Aspen Publishers, Inc.
(see *Bank Directors'. . .*)

Journal of Buddhist Ethics (online)
Pennsylvania State University;
  London University, England
Websites: http://jbe.la.psu.edu/jbe.html
http://www.gold.ac.uk/jbe/jbe.html

Journal of Business Ethics
Kluwer Academic Publishers
(see *Biology and Philosophy*)

Journal of Chinese Medical Ethics
Xi'an Medical University
Xi'an, Shaanxi 710061
China
Website: http://www.biol.tsukuba.ac
  .jp/~macer/JCME.html

Journal of Clinical Ethics
University Publishing Group
(see *AIDS & Public Policy Journal*)

*Journal of Computer-Mediated
  Communication: A Journal for New
  Media* (online)
University of Southern California,
  Annenberg School for
  Communication; Hebrew University
  of Jerusalem, School of Business
  Administration, Israel
Websites: http://www.ascusc.org/jcmc
http://jcmc.huji.ac.il

Journal of Ethical Studies
International Association of Ethicists,
  IL
(see *Organizations: U.S.*)

*Journal of Ethics: An International
  Philosophical Review*
Kluwer Academic Publishers
(see *Biology and Philosophy*)

Journal of Ethics, Law and Aging
Springer-Verlag
(see *AI & Society*)

*Journal of Government Information:
An International Review of Policy,
Issues and Resources*
Elsevier
(see *Accounting, Organizations and
Society*)

Journal of Health and Hospital Law
American Health Lawyers
Association, DC
(see Organizations: U.S.)

*Journal of Health Politics, Policy and
Law*
Duke University Press Journals
Box 90660
Durham, NC 27708-0660
Telephone: 919-687-3613
Fax: 919-688-3524
Website: http://www.duke.edu/web/
dupress

Journal of Human Values
Sage Publications
(see *Bulletin of Science, Technology
& Society*)

Journal of Information Ethics
McFarland & Co., Inc.
Box 611
Jefferson, NC 28640
Telephone: 336-246-4460
800-253-2187
Fax: 336-246-5018

*Journal of Interdisciplinary Studies:
An International Journal of
Interdisciplinary and Interfaith
Dialogue*
Institute for Interdisciplinary Research
1065 Pine Bluff Drive
Pasadena, CA 91107-1751
Website: http://www.aaas.org/spp/
dspp/dbsr/RESOURCE/TOC/JIS-
GEN.htm

Journal of Law & Medicine
BC Information Services
50 Waterloo Road
North Ryde, New South Wales 2113
Australia

(*Journal of Law & Medicine* cont'd)
Telephone: 61-2-99366444
Fax: 61-2-98889706

Journal of Law & Society
Blackwell Publishers
(see *Bioethics: Journal of the IAB*)

Journal of Law, Medicine and Ethics
American Society of Law, Medicine
and Ethics, MA
(see Organizations: U.S.)

*Journal of Legislation and Public
Policy*
New York University School of Law
110 West 3rd Street
New York, NY 10012-1074
Telephone: 212-998-6480
E-mail: law.jlpp@nyu.edu
Website: http://www.law.nyu.edu/
journalspublications

Journal of Management Inquiry
Sage Publications
(see *Bulletin of Science, Technology
& Society*)

*Journal of Mass Media Ethics:
Exploring Questions of Media
Morality*
Lawrence Erlbaum Associates, Inc.
(see *Basic and Applied Social
Psychology*)

Journal of Medical Ethics
BMJ Publishing Group
P.O. Box 299
London WC1H 9TD
England
Telephone: 44 171 383 6185/6245
Fax: 44 171 383 6662
E-mail: bmjsubs@dial.pipex.com
Website: http://www.bmjpg.com/data/
jmesub.htm

Journal of Medical Humanities
Plenum Publishing Corp.
(see *Employee Responsibilities and
Rights Journal*)

*Journal of Medicine and Philosophy:
A Forum for Bioethics and
Philosophy of Medicine*
Swets & Zeitlinger Publishers
(see *Christian Bioethics*)

Journal of Moral Education
Carfax Publishing Ltd.
(see *Angelaki*)

Journal of Palliative Care
Centre for Bioethics, Clinical
Research Institute of Montreal,
Canada
(see Organizations: World)

Journal of Palliative Medicine
Mary Ann Liebert, Inc., Publishers
(see *Biotechnology Law Report*)

*Journal of Policy Modeling: A Social
Science Forum of World Issues*
Elsevier
(see *Accounting, Organizations and
Society*)

*Journal of Professional Issues in
Engineering Education & Practice*
American Society of Civil Engineers
1801 Alexander Bell Drive
Reston, VA 20191-4400
Telephone: 800 548-2723
E-mail: marketing@asce.org
Website: http://www.pubs.asce.org/
journals/ei.html

Journal of Psychiatry and Law
Federal Legal Publications, Inc.
157 Chambers Street
New York, NY 10007
Telephone: 212-619-4949
Fax: 212-608-3141

Journal of Public Inquiry
President's Council on Integrity and
Efficiency, DC
(see Organizations: Government)

*Journal of Public Policy &
Marketing*
American Marketing Association
Publications
250 South Wacker Drive, Suite 200
Chicago, IL 60606-5819
Telephone: 800-AMA-1150
Fax: 312-993-7542
Website: http://www.ama.org/pubs/
index.html

Journal of Religious Ethics
Scholars Press
P.O. Box 15399
Atlanta, GA 30333-0399
Telephone: 404-727-2320
Fax: 404-727-2348
E-mail: scholars@unix.cc.emory.edu
Website: http://scholar.cc.emory.edu

*Journal of Social Issues: Journal of
the Society for the Psychological
Study of Social Issues*
Blackwell Publishers
(see *Bioethics: Journal of the IAB*)

Journal of Social Philosophy
North American Society for Social
Philosophy, Ethics Center, FL
(see Organizations: U.S.)

Journal of Social Policy
Cambridge University Press
(see *Cambridge Quarterly of
Healthcare Ethics*)

*Journal of the American College of
Medical Quality*
American College of Medical Quality,
MD
(see Organizations: U.S.)

Journal of Value Inquiry
Kluwer Academic Publishers
(see *Biology and Philosophy*)

Journal of Values Education
Centre for Alleviating Social
Problems Through Values
Education, Scotland
(see Organizations: World)

Judicial Code of Conduct Report
Americans for the Enforcement of
   Judicial Ethics, IL
(see Organizations: U.S.)

Judicial Conduct Reporter
Judicial Discipline and Disability
   Digest
Center for Judicial Conduct
   Organizations, IL
(see Organizations: U.S.)

Jurimetrics: Journal of Law, Science,
   and Technology
American Bar Association
(see Ethics Standards section)

Kennedy Institute of Ethics Journal
Johns Hopkins University Press
(see *Configurations*)

Lahey Hitchcock Medical Ethics
   Newsletter
Lahey Hitchcock Medical Center
41 Mall Road
Burlington, MA 01805

Law &: Southern California
   Interdisciplinary Law Journal
University of Southern California
   Law School
University Park
Los Angeles, CA 90089-0071
Telephone: 213-740-5710
Website:
http://www-bcf.usc.edu/~idjlaw

Law and Ethics Series
Academy of State and Local
   Government
444 North Capitol Street, NE
Suite 345
Washington, DC 20001
Telephone: 202-434-4851
Fax: 202-434-4850

Law and Human Behavior
Plenum Publishing Corp.
(see *Employee Responsibilities and*
   Rights Journal)

Law and Philosophy
Kluwer Academic Publishers
(see *Biology and Philosophy*)

Law & Policy
Blackwell Publishers
(see *Bioethics: Journal of the IAB*)

Law and Policy in International
   Business
Georgetown University Law Center
(see *Georgetown Journal of Legal*
   Ethics)

Law & Social Inquiry
University of Chicago Press
(see *Ethics: An International*
   Journal. . .)

Law & Social Policy
Baldy Center for Law and Social
   Policy, NY
(see Organizations: U.S.)

Law & Society Review
Law and Society Association, MA
(see Organizations: U.S.)

Law Enforcement Liability Reporter
P.O. Box 75401
Chicago, IL 60675-5401
Telephone: 800-763-2802
Fax: 800-763-3221

Law in Society
Ahmadu Bello University
Samaru-Zaria
Kaduna State
Nigeria

Law of Associations: An Operating
   Legal Manual for Executives and
   Counsel
Matthew Bender & Co., Inc.
(see *Health Care Law Monthly*)

Law of Fraud and Related Offences
Carswell Thomson Professional
  Publishing
1 Corporate Plaza, 11th Floor
2075 Kennedy Road
Scarborough, Ontario M1T 3V4
Canada
Telephone: 800-387-5164
416-609-3800
Fax: 416-298-5082
E-mail: orders@carswell.com
Website: http://www.carswell.com

*Law of Lawyering: A Handbook on
  the Model Rules of Professional
  Conduct*
Aspen Publishers, Inc.
(see *Bank Directors'...*)

Lawyer Advertising News
American Bar Association
(see Ethics Standards section)

*Lawyers and Ethics: Professional
  Responsibility and Discipline*
Carswell Thomson Professional
  Publishing
(see *Law of Fraud and Related
  Offences*)

*Lawyers' Liability Review: Reporting
  and Analyzing the Issues and
  Topics of Professional
  Responsibility*
VersusLaw, Inc.
(see *Accountants' Liability Quarterly*)

*Lawyers' Professional Liability
  Update*
American Bar Association
(see Ethics Standards section)

Leadership in Action
Jossey-Bass, Inc., Publisher
350 Sansome Street, 5th Floor
San Francisco, CA 94104
Telephone: 800-956-7739
Fax: 800-605-2665
415-433-0499
Website: http://www.josseybass.com

Legal Aspects of AIDS
Clark Boardman Callaghan
(see *Advanced Medical Directives*)

*Legal Ethics for Management and
  Their Counsel*
LEXIS Law Publishing
P.O. Box 7587
Charlottesville, VA 22906
Telephone: 800-562-1197
Fax: 800-643-1280
Website: http://
  www.lexislawpublishing.com

Legal Malpractice Report
Long & Levit LLP
101 California Street, Suite 2300
San Francisco, CA 94111
Telephone: 415-397-2222
Fax: 415-397-6392
Website: http://www.longlevit.com

*Liability and Risk Management in
  Home Health Care
Liability and Risk Management in
  Managed Care*
Aspen Publishers, Inc.
(see *Bank Directors'...*)

*Liability, Risk & Insurance
  (incorporating Product Liability
  International, Professional Liability
  Today, and Risk Update)*
LLP Limited
Sheepen Place
Colchester
Essex CO3 3LP
England
Telephone: 44 1206 772113
Fax: 44 1206 772771
E-mail: publications@llplimited.com
Website: http://www.llplimited.com

Linacre Quarterly
Linacre Centre, England
(see Organizations: World)

Literature and Medicine
Johns Hopkins University Press
(see *Configurations*)

Making the Rounds in Health, Faith and Ethics
Park Ridge Center for the Study of Health, Faith and Ethics, IL
(see Organizations: U.S.)

Management Ethics
Canadian Centre for Ethics & Corporate Policy
(see Organizations: World)

Managing Corporate Electronic Information: A Risk Manager's Guide
LRP Publications
(see *AIDS Policy & Law*)

Managing Ethics
Lincoln Center for Applied Ethics, AZ
(see Organizations: U.S.)

Mealey's Attorneys Fees
Mealey's Litigation Report: Insurance Fraud
P.O. Box 62090
King of Prussia, PA 19406-0230
Telephone: 610-768-7800
800-MEALEYS
Fax: 610-768-0880
E-mail: news@mealeys.com
Website: http://www.mealeys.com

Media, Culture & Society
Sage Publications
(see *Bulletin of Science, Technology & Society*)

Media Monitor
Center for Media and Public Affairs, DC
(see Organizations: U.S.)

Medicaid Fraud Alert
National Association of Attorneys General
(see *Civil Rights Update*)

Medical Ethics: Policies, Protocols, Guidelines & Programs
Aspen Publishers, Inc.
(see *Bank Directors'. . .*)

Medical Ethics Advisor
American Health Consultants, Inc.
(see *ED Legal Letter*)

Medical Ethics Newsletter
Ethics Center, St. Petersburg, FL
(see Organizations: U.S.)

Medical Humanities Review
Institute for the Medical Humanities, University of Texas Medical Branch
(see Organizations: U.S.)

Medical Law Review
Oxford University Press
(see *British Journal for the Philosophy of Science*)

Medical Liability Monitor
Malpractice Lifeline Inc.
P.O. Box 316
Glenview, IL 60025
Telephone: 312-944-7900
Fax: 312-944-8845

Medical Malpractice Law & Strategy Newsletter
American Lawyer Media, Inc.
(see *Business Crimes Bulletin*)

Medical Malpractice Reports
Matthew Bender & Co., Inc.
(see *Health Care Law Monthly*)

Medical Malpractice Verdicts, Settlements and Experts
Lewis L. Laska Legal Newsletters
901 Church Street
Nashville, TN 37203
Telephone: 615-255-6288
800-298-6288
Fax: 615-255-6289
E-mail: mail@verdictslaska.com
Website: http://www.verdictslaska.com

Medical Research and You
Consumers for Ethics in Research,
England
(see Organizations: World)

Medicina e Morale: Rivista
Internazionale bimestrale di
Bioetica, Deontologia e Morale
Medica
Centro e dell'Istituto di Bioetica, Italy
(see Organizations: World)

Medicine and Philosophy Journal
c/o Prof. Du Zhi Zheng, Editor
No. 4 Chang Bai Street
Dailin
China

Medicine, Health Care and
Philosophy
Kluwer Academic Publishers
(see *Biology and Philosophy*)

Medico-Legal Watch
Andrews Publications
(see *AIDS Litigation Reporter*)

Mental Capacity: Legal and Medical
Aspects of Assessment and
Treatment
Clark Boardman Callaghan
(see *Advanced Medical Directives*)

Mental Health Law Reporter
Business Publishers, Inc.
951 Pershing Drive
Silver Spring, MD 20910-4464
Telephone: 800-274-6737
301-589-5103
Fax: 301-587-4530
E-mail: bpinews@bpinews.com
Website: http://www.bpinews.com

Mental Health, Religion & Culture
Carfax Publishing Ltd.
(see *Angelaki*)

Milbank Quarterly: A Journal of
Public Health and Health Care
Policy
Blackwell Publishers
(see *Bioethics: Journal of the IAB*)

Monash Bioethics Review
Centre for Human Bioethics,
Australia
(see Organizations: World)

Money Laundering Alert
Money Laundering Alert On-Line/
Suspicious Activity Alert
Alert Global Media, Inc.
1101 Brickell Avenue
Suite 601, South Tower
Miami, FL 33131
Telephone: 305-530-0500
Fax: 305-530-9434
E-mail: alert@moneylaundering.com
Website:
http://www.moneylaundering.com

Money Laundering Law Report
Newsletter
American Lawyer Media, Inc.
(see *Business Crimes Bulletin*)

Monitors: A Journal of Human Rights
and Technology (online)
University of Texas at Austin
Dept. of English
Austin, TX 78712
E-mail: monitors@babbage.cwrl
.utexas.edu
Website: http://www.cwrl.utexas.edu/
~monitors

Moral Musings: A Journal of Social
and Political Thought (online)
604-185 Berkshire Drive
London, Ontario N6J 3R6
Canada
Telephone: 519-474-0296
E-mail: musing@plato.ml.org
Website: http://www.plato.ml.org/
integral/musings

Multinational Monitor
Essential Information, Inc.
P.O. Box 19405
Washington, DC 20036
Telephone: 202-387-8030
E-mail: monitor@essential.org
Website: http://www.essential.org:80/
   monitor
(business)

National Medical-Legal Journal
Medical-Legal Consulting Institute,
   Inc., TX
(see Organizations: U.S.)

*National Reporter on Legal Ethics
   and Professional Responsibility*
University Publications of America
(see *Biolaw: A Legal and Ethical
   Reporter*)

New Genetics and Society
Carfax Publishing Ltd.
(see *Angelaki*)

New Media & Society
Sage Publications
(see *Bulletin of Science, Technology
   & Society*)

*New Perspectives Quarterly:
   A Journal of Social and Political
   Thought*
Blackwell Publishers
(see *Bioethics: Journal of the IAB*)

New Titles in Bioethics
National Reference Center for
   Bioethics Literature, DC
(see Organizations: Government)

*Notre Dame Journal of Law, Ethics
   and Public Policy*
White Center on Law and
   Government, IN
(see Organizations: U.S.)
(see *American Journal of
   Jurisprudence*)

Nucleus
Union of Concerned Scientists, MA
(see Organizations: U.S.)

OB-GYN Malpractice Prevention
Williams & Wilkins
(see *American Journal of Medical
   Quality*)

Online Journal of Ethics
Institute for Business & Professional
   Ethics, IL
(see Organizations: U.S.)
Website: http://condor.depaul.edu/
   ethics/ethg1.html

*Organization Studies:
   An International Multidisciplinary
   Journal Devoted to the Study of
   Organizations, Organizing and the
   Organized In and Between Societies*
Walter de Gruyter GmbH & Co.
Genthiner Strasse 13
D-10785 Berlin
Germany
Telephone: 49 30 260 05-0
Fax: 49 30 260 05-222
U.S. Office: 200 Saw Mill River
   Road
Hawthorne, NY 10532
Telephone: 914-747-0110
Fax: 914-747-1326
E-mail: wdg-info@deGruyter.de
Website: http://www.deGruyter.de

Otago Bioethics Report
Bioethics Research Centre, University
   of Otago, New Zealand
(see Organizations: World)

*Pacifica Review: Peace, Strategy and
   Global Change*
Carfax Publishing Ltd.
(see *Angelaki*)

*Patient Care Decision Making: A
   Legal Guide for Providers*
Clark Boardman Callaghan
(see *Advanced Medical Directives*)

Peer Review
Public Employees for Environmental
   Responsibility, DC
(see Organizations: U.S.)

*Perspectives on Science and Christian
   Faith*
American Scientific Affiliation
55 Market Street
Ipswich, MA 01938-0668
Telephone: 508-356-5656
Fax: 508-356-4375
Website: http://asa.calvin.edu/ASA/
   PSCF.html

*Perspectives on Science: Historical,
   Philosophical, Social*
MIT Press
(see *Harvard International Journal of
   Press/Politics*)

*Perspectives on the Professions:
   Ethical & Policy Issues*
Center for the Study of Ethics in the
   Professions, IL
(see Organizations: U.S.)

Pharmacy Law Digest
Facts and Comparisons
111 West Port Plaza, Suite 300
St. Louis, MO 63146-3098
Telephone: 800-223-0554
Website: http://www.fandc.com

Philosophical Psychology
Carfax Publishing Ltd.
(see *Angelaki*)

Philosophy & Public Affairs
Johns Hopkins University Press
(see *Configurations*)

Philosophy and Public Policy
Institute for Philosophy and Public
   Policy, MD
(see Organizations: U.S.)

Philosophy & Social Criticism
Sage Publications
(see *Bulletin of Science, Technology
   & Society*)

Philosophy of Science
University of Chicago Press
(see *Ethics: An International
   Journal. . .*)

Philosophy of the Social Sciences
Sage Publications
(see *Bulletin of Science, Technology
   & Society*)

*Philosophy, Psychiatry, and
   Psychology*
Johns Hopkins University Press
(see *Configurations*)

Police Civil Liability
Matthew Bender & Co., Inc.
(see *Health Care Law Monthly*)

*Police Misconduct and Civil Rights
   Law Report*
Police Misconduct Law and Litigation
Clark Boardman Callaghan
(see *Advanced Medical Directives*)

*Policing and Society:
   An International Journal of
   Research and Policy*
Gordon and Breach Publishing Group
(see *Accountability in Research*)

Policy Posts
Center for Democracy and
   Technology, DC
(see Organizations: U.S.)

Policy Studies
Carfax Publishing Ltd.
(see *Angelaki*)

Politics & Society
Sage Publications
(see *Bulletin of Science, Technology
   & Society*)

Politics and the Life Sciences
Beech Tree Publishing
10 Watford Close
Guildford, Surrey GU1 2EP
England
Telephone/Fax: 44-1483-567497

Practical Ethics
Bioethical Services of Virginia, Inc.
(see Organizations: U.S.)

Preventive Law Journal
University of Denver College of Law
7039 East 18th Avenue
Denver, CO 80220
Telephone: 303-871-6000
Website: http://www.law.du.edu

Preventive Law Lawyer
National Resource Center for
    Consumers of Legal Services, VA
(see Organizations: U.S.)

Princeton Journal of Bioethics
Bioethics Forum, Princeton
    University, NJ
(see Organizations: U.S.)

Privacy & American Business
Center for Social & Legal Research,
    NJ
(see Organizations: U.S.)
E-mail: pab@mail.idt.net

Privacy in the Workplace: Rights,
    Procedures and Policies
LRP Publications
(see *AIDS Policy & Law*)

Privacy Journal
P.O. Box 28577
Providence, RI 02908
Telephone: 401-274-7861
E-mail: 5101719@mcimail.com
Website: http://www.epic.org

Privacy Times
P.O. Box 21501
Washington, DC 20009
Telephone: 202-829-3660
fax 202-829-3653
E-mail: pritimes@nicom.com
Website: http://www.privacytimes
    .com

Procurement Ethics Report
Holbrook & Kellogg Inc.
1964 Gallows Road, Suite 200
Vienna, VA 22182-3814
Telephone: 703-506-0600
800-506-4450
Fax: 703-506-1948

Professional Ethics:
    A Multidisciplinary Journal
(see *Business & Professional Ethics*
    Journal)

Professional Ethics Report
American Association for the
    Advancement of Science, DC
(see Organizations: U.S.)

Professional Lawyer
American Bar Association
(see Ethics Standards section)

Professional Liability
Knowles Publishing
5535 Airport Freeway
P.O. Box 911004
Fort Worth, TX 76111
Telephone: 817-838-0202
Fax: 817-831-4725

Professional Liability in Canada
Carswell Thomson Professional
    Publishing
(see *Law of Fraud and Related*
    Offences)

Professional Liability Insurance
International Risk Management
    Institute, Inc.
12222 Merit Drive #1450
Dallas, TX 75251-2276
Telephone: 800-827-4242
972-960-7693
Fax: 972-960-6037
E-mail: info@irmi.com
Website: http://www.irmi.com/
    pubs.htm

Professional Liability Newsletter
Box 834
Berkeley, CA 94701

(Professional Liability Newsletter
cont'd)
Telephone: 510-741-8723
(health)

Professional Liability Reporter
Clark Boardman Callaghan
(see *Advanced Medical Directives*)

Professional Liability Updates
(online)
Website: http://www.longlevit.com/
updates/update_index_pl.htm
Long & Levit LLP
(see *Legal Malpractice Report*)

Professional Licensing Report
Paxton Associates
4919 Hampden Lane, Suite 201
Bethesda, MD 20814
Telephone: 301-652-8009
Fax: 301-652-8050

*Professional Negligence Law
Reporter*
Association of Trial Lawyers of
America
(see *Ethics Standards section*)

Professional Regulation News
National Organization for
Competency Assurance, DC
(see *Organizations: U.S.*)

*Professional Responsibility of the
Criminal Lawyer*
Clark Boardman Callaghan
(see *Advanced Medical Directives*)

Prosecutorial Misconduct
Clark Boardman Callaghan
(see *Advanced Medical Directives*)

*Protecting Human Research Subjects:
Institutional Review Board
Guidebook*
Office for Protection from Research
Risks, National Institutes of Health,
MD
(see *Organizations: Government*)

*Psychological Inquiry:
An International Journal of Peer
Commentary and Review*
Lawrence Erlbaum Associates, Inc.
(see *Basic and Applied Social
Psychology*)

Psychology, Crime & Law
Gordon and Breach Publishing Group
(see *Accountability in Research*)

Psychology, Health and Medicine
Carfax Publishing Ltd.
(see *Angelaki*)

Psychology, Public Policy, and Law
American Psychological Association
(see *Ethics Standards section*)

Public Affairs Quarterly
Philosophy Documentation Center
(see *Business Ethics Quarterly*)

Public Citizen
Public Citizen, DC
(see *Organizations: U.S.*)

*Public Financial Disclosure:
A Reviewer's Reference*
U.S. Office of Government Ethics,
DC
(see *Organizations: Government*)

Public Integrity
Westview Press
5500 Central Avenue
Boulder, CO 80301-2877
Telephone: 303-444-3541
Fax: 303-449-3356
Website: http://www.hcacademic.com

Public Integrity Annual
Council of State Governments
2760 Research Park Drive
P.O. Box 11910
Lexington, KY 40578-1910
Telephone: 606-244-8000
Fax: 606-244-8001
E-mail: info@csg.org
Website: http://www.statesnews.org/
index.html

Public Interest Law Review
Carolina Academic Press
700 Kent Street
Durham, NC 27701
Telephone: 919-489-7486
Fax: 919-493-5668
E-mail: cap@cap-press.com
Website: http://www.cap-press.com

Public Interest Report: Journal of the Federation of American Scientists
Federation of American Scientists, DC
(see Organizations: U.S.)

Public Opinion Quarterly
University of Chicago Press
(see *Ethics: An International Journal. . .*)

Quality Assurance and Utilization Review: Current Readings in Concept and Practice
American Board of Quality Assurance and Utilization Review Physicians, FL
(see Organizations: U.S.)

Quality Bulletin
National Committee for Quality Health Care, DC
(see Organizations: U.S.)

Quality in Higher Education
Carfax Publishing Ltd.
(see *Angelaki*)

Quality of Life Research
Kluwer Academic Publishers
(see *Biology and Philosophy*)

Quality Matters
National Committee for Quality Assurance, DC
(see Organizations: U.S.)

Quality Outlook
National Committee for Quality Health Care, DC
(see Organizations: U.S.)

Ratio: An International Journal of Analytic Philosophy
Ratio Juris: An International Journal of Jurisprudence and Philosophy of Law
Blackwell Publishers
(see *Bioethics: Journal of the IAB*)

The Record
Physicians for Human Rights, MA
(see Organizations: U.S.)

Reflections
Program for Ethics, Science and the Environment, Oregon State University
(see Organizations: U.S.)

Regan Report on Hospital Law
Regan Report on Medical Law
Regan Report on Nursing Law
Medica Press Inc.
10 Dorrance Street, Suite 500
Providence, RI 02903
Telephone: 401-421-4747
Fax: 401-521-9226

Regulation: The Cato Review of Business & Government
Cato Institute, DC
(see Organizations: U.S.)

Regulation of Professions in Canada
Carswell Thomson Professional Publishing
(see *Law of Fraud and Related Offences*)

Reinvention Express
National Partnership for Reinventing Government, DC
(see Organizations: Government)

Religion and American Culture: A Journal of Interpretation
University of California Press Journals
(see *Berkeley Technology Law Journal*)

Religion & Society Report
Rockford Institute, IL
(see Organizations: U.S.)

Religion & Values in Public Life
Center for the Study of Values in
Public Life, MA
(see Organizations: U.S.)

Religion, State and Society
Carfax Publishing Ltd.
(see *Angelaki*)

*Reporter on Human Reproduction and
the Law*
Legal-Medical Studies Inc.
P.O. Box 8219
JFK Station
Boston, MA 02114
Telephone: 617-742-7959

Reporter on the Legal Profession
Legal-Medical Studies Inc.
(see *Reporter on Human
Reproduction and the Law*)

Reproductive Freedom News
Center for Reproductive Law &
Policy, NY
(see Organizations: U.S.)

*Responsibilities of Insurance Agents
and Brokers*
Matthew Bender & Co., Inc.
(see *Health Care Law Monthly*)

Responsive Community
Communitarian Network, DC
(see Organizations: U.S.)

Review of Law & Social Change
New York University School of Law
E-mail: law.rlsc@nyu.edu
(see *Journal of Legislation and
Public Policy*)

RISK: Health, Safety & Environment
Risk Assessment & Policy
Association, NH
(see Organizations: U.S.)
Website: http://www.fplc.edu/tfield/
PROFRISK.htm

*Rule 11 Sanctions: Case Law
Perspectives and Preventive
Measures*
Aspen Publishers, Inc.
(see *Bank Directors'. . .*)

RX IPSA Loquitur
American Society for Pharmacy Law,
CA
(see Organizations: U.S.)

Science and Engineering Ethics
Opragen Publications
P.O. Box 54
Guildford
Surrey GU1 2YF
England
Telephone/Fax: 44 1483 560074
E-mail: opragen@cableol.co.uk
Website: http://www.cableol.net/
opragen

Science and Public Policy
Beech Tree Publishing
(see *Politics and the Life Sciences*)

Science & Spirit
Science & Spirit Resources
71-B Rumford Street
Concord, NH 03301
Fax: 603-229-0953
Website: http://science-spirit.com

*Science and Technology Policy
Yearbook*
American Association for the
Advancement of Science, DC
(see Organizations: U.S.)

Science As Culture
Carfax Publishing Ltd.
(see *Angelaki*)

Science, Technology, and Human Values
Science Technology & Society
Sage Publications
(see *Bulletin of Science, Technology & Society*)

Secrecy and Government Bulletin
Federation of American Scientists, DC
(see Organizations: U.S.)

Sentencing Guidelines Case Law Guide
American Bar Association
(see Ethics Standards section)

Social Action and the Law
Center for Responsive Psychology
Brooklyn College
511 James Hall
Brooklyn, NY 11210
Telephone: 718-951-5041

Social and Environmental Accounting
Centre for Social and Environmental Accounting Research, Scotland
(see Organizations: World)

Social & Legal Studies
Sage Publications
(see *Bulletin of Science, Technology & Society*)

Social Philosophy & Policy
Cambridge University Press
(see *Cambridge Quarterly of Healthcare Ethics*)

Social Policy & Administration
Blackwell Publishers
(see *Bioethics: Journal of the IAB*)

Social Problems
University of California Press Journals
(see *Berkeley Technology Law Journal*)

Social Responsibilities SIS Newsletter
American Association of Law Libraries
(see Ethics Standards section)

Social Responsibility: Business, Journalism, Law, Medicine
Washington and Lee University
Lexington, VA 24450-0303
Telephone: 540-463-8786
Fax: 540-463-8045
Website: http://www.wlu.edu

Social Science & Medicine
Elsevier
(see *Accounting, Organizations and Society*)

Social Studies of Science
Sage Publications
(see *Bulletin of Science, Technology & Society*)

Social Text
Duke University Press Journals
(see *Journal of Health Politics. . .*)

Society and Animals: Social Scientific Studies of the Human Experience
White Horse Press
(see *Environmental Values*)

Society for Philosophy & Technology
(online)
University of Delaware, Philosophy Dept.
Website: http://scholar.lib.vt.edu/ejournals/SPT/spt.html

Specialty Law Digest: Health Care
Specialty Digest Publications, Inc.
P.O. Box 24439
Minneapolis, MN 55424
Telephone: 612-823-4220
E-mail: sdpubs@earthlink.net

Sports Medicine Standards and Malpractice Reporter
PRC Publishing, Inc.
4418 Delden Village Street, NW
Canton, OH 44718-2516

(*Sports Medicine Standards and Malpractice Reporter* cont'd)
Telephone: 330-492-6063
Fax: 330-492-6176

St. Luke's News
L.J. Goody Bioethics Centre,
    Australia
(see Organizations: World)

State & Local Government Civil Rights Liabilities
Clark Boardman Callaghan
(see *Advanced Medical Directives*)

State Initiatives in End-of-Life Care
Community-State Partnerships to
    Improve End-of-Life Care, MO
Last Acts Campaign, NJ
(see Organizations: U.S.)

Strategies: Journal of Theory, Culture and Politics
Carfax Publishing Ltd.
(see *Angelaki*)

Studia Moralia
Alphonsian Academy of Moral
    Theology, Italy

Studies in Christian Ethics
T & T Clark
59 George Street
Edinburgh EH2 2LQ
Scotland

Studies in Cultures, Organizations and Societies
Gordon and Breach Publishing Group
(see *Accountability in Research*)

Studies in Ethics and Policy
Institute for Ethics and Policy
    Studies, NV
(see Organizations: U.S.)

Studies in History and Philosophy of Science
Elsevier
(see *Accounting, Organizations and Society*)

Studies in Law, Politics, and Society
JAI Press
(see *Ethics and the Environment*)

Studies in Science and the Humanities
Reilly Center for Science,
    Technology, and Values, IN
(see Organizations: U.S.)

Studies in Science and Theology
Labor et Fides
1, rue de Beauregard
CH-1205 Geneva
Switzerland
Fax: 41 22 781 3051
Website: http://www.vu.nl/
    Bezinningscentrum/esssth.htm

Synapse, A Canadian News Service for Biomedical Ethics
(see *Canadian Bioethics Report*)

Teaching Business Ethics - An Interdisciplinary Quarterly Journal
Kluwer Academic Publishers
(see *Biology and Philosophy*)

Technology and Culture: The International Quarterly of the Society for the History of Technology
Johns Hopkins University Press
(see *Configurations*)

Technology and Society Magazine
Society on Social Implications of
    Technology, NJ
(see Organizations: U.S.)
Website: http://www.pontz.com/ts/
    newtsmag.shtml

Technology in Society: An International Journal
Elsevier
(see *Accounting, Organizations and Society*)

Technology, Law and Insurance
Routledge
11 New Fetter Lane
London EC4P 4EE
England
Telephone: 44 171 583 9855
Fax: 44 171 842 2298
E-mail: info@routledge.com
Website: http://www.routledge.com
U.S. Office: 29 West 35th Street
New York, NY 10001
Telephone: 212-216-7800
Fax: 212-564-7854

Technology Studies
Walter de Gruyter GmbH & Co.
(see *Organization Studies*)

Technoscience (online)
Society for Social Studies of Science,
    LA
(see Organizations: U.S.)
Website: http://www.cis.vt.edu/
    technoscience/technohome.html

Terra Nova: Nature & Culture
MIT Press
(see *Harvard International Journal of
    Press/Politics*)

Texas Ethics Reporter (online)
University of Houston Law Center
4800 Calhoun Road
Houston, TX 77204
Telephone: 713-743-2300
Website: http://www.law.uh.edu/ethics

*TexethicS Newsletter: Engineering
    Professionalism and Ethics in
    Texas*
Murdough Center for Engineering
    Professionalism, TX
(see Organizations: U.S.)

Theoretical Medicine and Bioethics
Kluwer Academic Publishers
(see *Biology and Philosophy*)

Theory and Society
Kluwer Academic Publishers
(see *Biology and Philosophy*)

Theory, Culture & Society
Sage Publications
(see *Bulletin of Science, Technology
    & Society*)

*Tikkun: A Jewish Critique of Politics,
    Culture, and Society*
26 Fell Street
San Francisco, CA 94102
Telephone: 415-575-1200
Fax: 415-575-1434
Website: http://www.tikkun.org

*Tolley's Professional Negligence:
    A Journal of Liability, Ethics and
    Discipline*
Tolley Publishing Co.
Butterworths Ltd.
(see *Butterworths Human Rights
    Cases*)

*Trends in Health Care, Law and
    Ethics*
Bioethics and Medical Humanities,
    University of Medicine and
    Dentistry of New Jersey-Robert
    Wood Johnson Medical School
(see Organizations: U.S.)

TREnds: Teaching Research Ethics
Poynter Center for the Study of
    Ethics and American Institutions,
    IN
(see Organizations: U.S.)

Trial Diplomacy Journal
John Wiley & Sons, Inc.
(see *Business & the Contemporary
    World*)

*21C Scanning the Future:
    The Magazine of Culture,
    Technology and Science* (online)
Website: http://www.21c.worldideas
    .com
Gordon and Breach Publishing Group
(see *Accountability in Research*)

Unum Conversations (online)
Ethics and Public Policy Center, DC
(see Organizations: U.S.)
Website: http://www.eppc.org/library/
    unum/index.html

Values in Action!
Bureau of Essential Ethics Education,
    CA
(see Organizations: U.S.)

VITA
Dietrich Bonhoeffer International
    Institute for Bioethical Studies,
    Australia
(see Organizations: World)

Whistleblower's Gazette
Center for Government
    Accountability, TN
(see Organizations: U.S.)

*White Collar Crime: Business and
    Regulatory Offenses*
American Lawyer Media, Inc.
(see *Business Crimes Bulletin*)

White-Collar Crime Reporter
Andrews Publications
(see *AIDS Litigation Reporter*)

Zygon: Journal of Religion & Science
Blackwell Publishers
(see *Bioethics: Journal of the IAB*)

2. Reference Works

This section lists bibliographies, dictionaries, encyclopedias, handbooks, directories, anthologies, CD-ROMs, and similar reference materials, plus notable series of books, on topics in ethics, professionalism, and public policy.

Works are listed by publisher.

Each publisher's mail address, telephone, fax number, e-mail address, and World Wide Web site URL are provided, where available. When this information does not appear, reference is made to the organization that publishes the material; these organizations are listed in the **Ethics Standards** or **Organizational Resources** sections, above.

Bibliographies available online are listed separately, in the **Electronic Media** section, following.

ABBE Publishers Association of Washington, DC
4111 Gallows Road
Annandale, VA 22003-1862
Fax: 703-864-5850
> *Bio-Ethics: Index of New Information and Current Research* (A.G. Skinner)
> *Insurance Liability and Legal Implications: Index of New Information for Consumers and Professional Personnel* (Science, Life Consultants)

ABC-CLIO
130 Cremona Drive
Santa Barbara, CA 93117-3075
Telephone: 805-968-1911
800-368-6868
Fax: 805-685-9685
Website: http://www.abc-clio.com
> *Consumer Protection and the Law: A Dictionary* (L. Krohn)
> *Encyclopedia of Values and Ethics* (J.P. Hester)
> *Environmental Ethics: A Reference Handbook* (C. Palmer)
> *Heroes of Conscience: A Biographical Dictionary* (K. Gay, M.K. Gay)
> *Journalism Ethics: A Reference Handbook* (E.D. Cohen, D. Elliott)
> *Medical Ethics: A Reference Handbook* (L.H. Berlow)
> Book Series:
> *Contemporary Ethical Issues*
> *Contemporary Legal Issues*
> *Contemporary World Issues*

Academic Press
525 B Street, Suite 1900
San Diego, CA 92101-4495
Telephone: 619-231-6616
E-mail: ap@acad.com
app@acad.com
Website: http://www.apnet.com
> *Encyclopedia of Applied Ethics: A-Z* (R. Chadwick)
> *Encyclopedia of Violence, Peace and Conflict* (L.R. Kurtz)

918

Action Kit Publications
Horty, Springer & Mattern
The Fairfax
4614 Fifth Avenue
Pittsburgh, PA 15213
Telephone: 800-548-9346
Website: http://www.hortyspringer.com
   *Complete Conflict of Interest Package for Non-Profit Hospitals and Health
      Care Systems*
   Complete Corporate Compliance Policy and Procedure Manual

American Arbitration Association, NY
(see Ethics Standards section)
   A Handbook for Grievance Arbitration: Procedural and Ethical Issues

American Association for the Advancement of Science
Directorate for Science and Policy Programs, DC
(see Organizations: U.S.)
Website: http://www.aaas.org/spp/dspp/readroom.htm
   Directory of Human Rights Resources on the Internet (S. Hansen)
   Integrity in Scientific Research: Videos and Discussion and Resource Guide
   *Values and Ethics in Organization and Human Systems Development: An
      Annotated Bibliography* (M.S. Frankel)

American Bar Association
(see Ethics Standards section)
   *Advertising in the Legal Profession: A Descriptive Bibliography and
      Reference Guide*
   Compendium of Professional Responsibility Rules and Standards
   Directory of Lawyer Disciplinary Agencies
   Directory of Lawyers' Professional Liability Insurance Carriers
   Directory of State and Local Lawyer Assistant Programs
   Lawyer Specialization Bibliography
   Lawyer's Desk Guide to Legal Malpractice
   Legal Malpractice Claims in the 1990s
   National Legal Malpractice Data Center
      Website: http://www.abanet.org/legalserv/lpl.html

American College of Physicians
(see Ethics Standards section)
   Medical Ethics: An Annotated Bibliography

American Counseling Association
(see also Ethics Standards section)
P.O. Box 631396
Baltimore, MD 21263-1396

(American Counseling Association *cont'd*)
Telephone: 800-422-2648
Fax: 410-594-7570
   A Practitioner's Guide to Ethical Decision Making (H. Forester-Miller,
      T. Davis) (also online)
      Website: http://www.counseling.org/resources/pracguide.htm
   *The Professional Counselor: Competencies, Performance Guidelines, and
      Assessments* (D.W. Engels, J.D. Dameron)
   Professional Resource Bibliography: Ethical and Legal Issues
   Book Series:
   ACA Legal Series (T.P. Remley)

American Health Lawyers Association, DC
(see Organizations: U.S.)
   Peer Review Guidebook
   State Illegal-Remuneration and Self-Referral Laws (T.W. Mayo)

American Hospital Publishing, Inc.
American Hospital Association
P.O. Box 92683
Chicago, IL 60675-2683
Telephone: 800-242-2626
Fax: 312-422-4505
E-mail: orderservices@aha.org
Website: http://www.ahapress.com/press-home.html
(see also Ethics Standards section)
   *Ethics for Everyone: A Practical Guide to Interdisciplinary Biomedical
      Ethics Education* (L.C. Grafius)
   The Trustee Guide to Board Accountability in Health Care (J.E. Orlikoff ,
      M.K. Totten)
   U.S. Health Law & Policy 1999: A Guide to the Current Literature
      (D.H. Caldwell)

American Law Institute
4025 Chestnut Street
Philadelphia, PA 19104
Telephone: 215-243-1600
Fax: 215-243-1664
Website: http://www.ali.org/ali/LGL.htm
   Restatement of the Law Governing Lawyers (C.W. Wolfram, J. Leubsdorf,
      T.D. Morgan, L.S. Mullenix, et al.)

American Marketing Association Publications
250 South Wacker Drive, Suite 200
Chicago, IL 60606-5819
Telephone: 800-AMA-1150
Fax: 312-993-7542
Website: http://www.ama.org/pubs/index.html
   Marketing Ethics: A Selected, Annotated Bibliography of Articles (J.W. Bol,
      C.T. Crespy, S. Dunn, J.M. Stearns, J.R. Walton)

American Nurses Association
(see Ethics Standards section)
Annotated Bibliography for Ethical Guidelines

American Psychiatric Press, Inc.
American Psychiatric Association
(see Ethics Standards section)
A Comprehensive Guide to Malpractice Risk Management in Psychiatry
(F. Flach)
Assessing Competence to Consent to Treatment: A Guide to Physicians and Other Health Professionals (T. Grisson, P.S. Appelbaum)
Concise Guide to Psychiatry and Law for Clinicians (R.I. Simon)
The Mental Health Practitioner and the Law: A Comprehensive Handbook (L.E. Lifson, R.I. Simon)
Psychological Evalutions for the Courts: A Handbook for Mental Health Professionals and Lawyers (G.B. Melton, J. Petrila, N.G. Poythress, C. Slobogin)
Women's Health Research: A Medical and Policy Primer (F.P. Haseltine, B.G. Jacobson)

American Society of Association Executives, DC
(see Ethics Standards section)
Antitrust Guide for Association Members: An Outline of Procedures to Maintain Compliance with the Law (A.L. Herold)
Association Law Compendium (M. Baskin)
Ethics Survey (with Ethics Resource Center)
Book Series:
Background Kits
Nonprofit Governance

American Society of Civil Engineers
1801 Alexander Bell Drive
Reston, VA 20191-4400
Telephone: 800-548-2723
E-mail: marketing@asce.org
Website: http://www.pubs.asce.org/books.html
Quest for Quality: An Engineer's View on Responsibility and Liability: Proceedings of the 1990 Triennial Conference

Anderson Publishing Co.
2035 Reading Road
Cincinnati, OH 45202
Telephone: 800-582-7295
Fax: 513-562-8116
E-mail: andpubmail@aol.com
Website: http://www.legalpubs.com
Analytic Jurisprudence Anthology (A. D'Amato)
Corporate and White Collar Crime: An Anthology (L. Orland)
Professional Responsibility Anthology (T.B. Metzloff)

Jason Aronson Inc. Publishers
230 Livingston Street
Northvale, NJ 07647
Telephone: 800-782-0015
Fax: 201-767-4330
Website: http://www.aronson.com
  Jewish Encyclopedia of Moral and Ethical Issues (N. Amsel)

Aspen Publishers, Inc.
200 Orchard Ridge Drive
Gaithersburg, MD 20878
Telephone: 301-417-7500
800-638-8437
Fax: 301-417-7550
Website: http://www.aspenpub.com
  Directory of Federal Court Guidelines

Association for Investment Management and Research, VA
(see Ethics Standards section)
  Ethics in the Investment Profession: A Survey
  Ethics in the Investment Profession: An International Survey

Bioethics Consultation Group, CA
(see Organizations: U.S.)
  *Forming a Moral Community: A Resource for Healthcare Ethics
    Committees*

Bioethics Research Centre, University of Otago, New Zealand
(see Organizations: World)
  Euthanasia: Resourses for Community Discussion (B.R. Nicholas,
    S.E. Gordan)

Blackwell Publishers
108 Cowley Road
Oxford OX4 1JF
England
Telephone: 44 1865 791100
Fax: 44 1865 791347
U.S. Office: 350 Main Street
Malden, MA 02148
Telephone: 781-388-8200
Fax: 781-388-8210
Website: http://www.blackwellpublishers.co.uk
  Blackwell Encyclopedic Dictionary of Business Ethics (P. Werhane,
    R.E. Freeman)
  Ethical Issues in Behavioral Research: A Survey (A.J. Kimmel)
  Ethics in Practice: An Anthology (H. LaFollette)

BMJ Publishing Group
P.O. Box 299
London WC1H 9TD
England
Telephone: 44 171 383 6185/6245
Fax: 44 171 383 6662
E-mail: bmjsubs@dial.pipex.com
Website: http://www.bmjpg.com/data/jmesub.htm
New Dictionary of Medical Ethics (K.M. Boyd, R. Higgs, A. Pinching)

BNA Books
The Bureau of National Affairs, Inc.
1250 23rd Street, NW
Washington DC 20037
Telephone: 202-833-7470
800-960-1220
Fax: 202-833-7490
732-346-1624
E-mail: books@bna.com
Website: http://www.bna.com/bnabooks/index.html
Covenants Not to Compete: A State-by-State Survey (B.M. Malsberger,
A.H. Pedowitz, R.W. Sikkel)
Employee Duty of Loyalty: A State-by-State Survey (S.S. Manela,
A.H Pedowitz, B.M. Malsberger)

Bowne Publishing Division
345 Hudson Street
New York, NY 10014
Telephone: 212-924-5500
Website: http://pubs.bowne.com
The Best in D&O Duties and Liabilities

Business Ethics Foundation, MA
(see Organizations: U.S.)
Henderson's Ethictionary: A Practical Dictionary of Business Ethics Terms
(V.E. Henderson)

Butterworths Ltd.
Halsbury House
35 Chancery Lane
London WC2A 1EL
England
Telephone: 44 171 400 2500
Fax: 44 171 400 2842
Website: http://www.butterworths.co.uk
Canadian Office: 75 Clegg Road
Markham, Ontario L6G 1A1
Canada

(Butterworths Ltd. *cont'd*)
Telephone: 800-668-6481
905-479-2665
Fax: 905-479-2826
E-mail: info@butterworths.ca
Website: http://www.butterworths.ca
  Jurisprudence: Texts and Commentary (H. Davies, D. Holdcroft)
  Medical Negligence: A Practical Guide (C.J. Lewis)
  Medical Negligence Case Law (R. Nelson-Jones, F. Burton)
  Professional Negligence Cases (D. Pittaway, A. Hammerton)

Cambridge University Press
Edinburgh Bldg.
Cambridge CB2 2RU
England
Fax: 44 1223 325959
E-mail: customer_service@cup.org
U.S. Office: 110 Midland Avenue
Port Chester, NY 10573
Telephone: 800-872-7423
Fax: 914-937-4712
Website: http://www.cup.org
  A Bibliographic Guide to the Comparative Study of Ethics (J. Carman,
    M. Juergensmeyer)
  Bibliography of Comparative Religious Ethics (J. Carman,
    M. Juergensmeyer)
  Book Series:
  Cambridge Studies in Philosophy and Public Policy

Carswell Thomson Professional Publishing
1 Corporate Plaza, 11th Floor
2075 Kennedy Road
Scarborough, Ontario M1T 3V4
Canada
Telephone: 800-387-5164
416-609-3800
Fax: 416-298-5082
E-mail: orders@carswell.com
Website: http://www.carswell.com
  Professional Fiduciary Duties (M.V. Ellis)
  Professional Negligence (L.N. Klar)

Cassell plc
Wellington House
125 Strand
London WC2R 0BB
England
Telephone: 44 171 4205582
  Keyguide: Media Ethics (B. MacDonald)
  Professional Codes of Conduct in the United Kingdom: A Directory
    (N.G.E. Harris)

Center for Judicial Conduct Organizations, IL
(see Organizations: U.S.)
Digest of Judicial Ethics Advisory Opinions (D.L. Solomon)
Electing Justice: A Handbook of Judicial Election Reforms (S. Mathias)
*Judicial Disqualification: An Empirical Study of Judicial Practices and
Attitudes* (J.M. Shaman, J. Goldschmidt)
*Judicial Ethics and the Administration of Justice: A Videotaped Instructional
Program on Judicial Ethics*
*Justice at First Hand: A Videotape Curriculum on Ethics & Professionalism
for Nonjudicial Court Personnel*
Key Issues in Judicial Ethics Series (C. Gray)
Practices and Procedures of State Judicial Conduct Organizations
(J. Rosenbaum)

Center for the Study of Ethics in the Professions, IL
(see Organizations: U.S.)
Professional Ethics and Engineering: A Resource Guide

Centre de Recherche Interdisciplinaires en Bioethique
Universite Libre de Bruxelles, Belgium
(see Organizations: World)
Encyclopedia of Bioethics
Les Mots de Bioethique

Centre for Accounting Ethics, University of Waterloo, Canada
(see Organizations: World)
Annotated Bibliography

Centre for Research Ethics, Uppsala University and Swedish University of
Agricultural Sciences
(see Organizations: World)
Studies in Bioethics and Research Ethics

Chelsea House Publishers
1974 Sproul Road, Suite 400
Broomall, PA 19008
Telephone: 610-353-5166
800-848-2665
Fax: 610-359-1439
Website: http://www.chelseahouse.com
Encyclopedia of Health: Medical Ethics (J. Finn, E.L. Marshall,
D.C. Garrell)

Committee on Professional Ethics, Rights and Freedoms
American Political Science Assocation, DC
(see Organizations: U.S.)
A Guide to Professional Ethics in Political Science

Computer Ethics Institute, DC
(see Organizations: U.S.)
Ten Commandments of Computer Ethics

Congressional Quarterly
1414 22nd Street, NW
Washington, DC 20037
Telephone: 202-887-8621
800-432-2250
Website: http://www.cq.com
  Open Secrets: The Encyclopedia of Congressional Money and Politics
    (L. Makinson, J. Goldstein)
  Public Interest Profiles

Council on Licensure, Enforcement, and Regulation, KY
(see Organizations: U.S.)
  *Directory of Professional and Occupational Regulation in the United States
    and Canada* (L. Smith-Peters, B. Smith-Peters)

Crisp Publications
1200 Hamilton Court
Menlo Park, CA 94025
Telephone: 415-323-6100
800-442-7742
Fax: 415-323-5800
  *Ethics for Government Employees: Standards for Conduct for the Public
    Sector* (K. Keppler, C.P. Lickson)

Dartmouth Publishing Co.
Gower House
Croft Road
Aldershot, Hampshire GU11 3HR
England
Telephone: 44 1252 317707
Fax: 44 1252 317446
E-mail: gower@cityscape.co.uk
U.S. Office: Ashgate Publishing
Old Post Road
Brookfield, VT 05036-9704
Telephone: 800-535-9544
802-276-3162
Fax: 802-276-3837
E-mail: info@ashgate.com
Website: http://www.ashgate.com
  Book Series:
  Medico-Legal Series
  Onati International Series in Law and Society

DeAcklen-Terry Publishing Co.
1525 East 53rd Street, Suite 621
Chicago, IL 60615
Telephone/Fax: 312-791-9163
  *Dictionary of the Principles of Misconduct in the Workplace and a Glossary
    of Labor Terms* (C.C. Terry)

Division of Quality Assurance
U.S. Department of Health and Human Services
(see Organizations: Government)
Healthcare Integrity and Protection Data Bank
Website: http://www.hrsa.dhhs.gov/bhpr/dqa/hipmain.htm
Malpractice and Medical Discipline Research Information
Website: http://www.hrsa.dhhs.gov/bhpr/dqa/mmdr.htm
National Practitioner Data Bank
P.O. Box 10832
Chantilly, VA 20151
Telephone: 800-767-6732
Website: http://www.npdb.com

Duke University Press
Books Fulfillment
Box 90660
Durham, NC 27708-0660
Telephone: 919-688-5134
Fax: 919-688-2615
Website: http://www.duke.edu/web/dupress
Associate Degree Nursing Education: An Historical Annotated Bibliography
(P.T. Haase)
Constitutional Literacy: A Core Curriculum for a Multicultural Nation
(T.M. Massaro)
Social Medicine Reader (G.E. Henderson, N.M.P. King, R.P. Strauss,
S.E. Estroff, L.R. Churchill)

William B. Eerdmans Publishing Co.
255 Jefferson Avenue SE
Grand Rapids, MI 49503
Telephone: 616-459-4591
800-253-7521
Fax: 616-459-6540
Book Series:
Horizons in Bioethics Series
Institute of Religion Series on Religion and Health Care

Elsevier
P.O. Box 945
New York, NY 10159-0945
Telephone: 212-633-3730
888-4ES-INFO
Fax: 212-633-3680
E-mail: usinfo-f@elsevier.com
Website: http://www.elsevier.nl
Impact of Technology on Society: A Documentation of Current Research
(B. Schmeikal, H. Hogeweg-de Haart, W. Richter)
World Encyclopedia of Peace (E. Laszlo, J.Y. Yoo)
Book Series:
Foundations and Philosophy of Science and Technology
Technology, Innovation, Entrepreneurship and Competitive Strategy Series

Lawrence Erlbaum Associates, Inc.
10 Industrial Avenue
Mahwah, NJ 07430-2262
Telephone: 201-236-9500
800-9-BOOKS-9
Fax: 201-236-0072
Website: http://www.erlbaum.com
   Business and Environmental Accountability: An Overview and Guide to the
      Literature (L. Grayson, H. Woolston, J. Tanega)
   Ethics in Psychology: Professional Standards and Cases (P. Keith-Spiegel,
      G.P. Koocher)
   Handbook of Moral Behavior and Development (W.M. Kurtines, J. Gewirtz)
   Manager's Guide to Excellence in Public Relations and Communication
      Management (D.M. Dozier, L.A. Grunig, J.E. Grunig)
   Book Series:
   Applied Social Psychology
   Psychology and Its Allied Disciplines

EUR-OP: Office for Official Publications of the European Communities
2, rue Mercier
L-2985
Luxembourg
Telephone: 352 29 29-42053
Fax: 352 29 29-42025
Website: http://eur-op.eu.int
   Agriculture and Biotechnology (M. Chapuis)
   AIDS: Ethics, Justice and European Policy (C. Bardoux)
   Ethical Aspects of Cloning Techniques (Group of Advisers on the Ethical
      Aspects of Biotechnology)
   Ethical Implications of Biotechnology (Group of Advisers on the Ethical
      Aspects of Biotechnology)
   Ethical, Legal and Social Aspects of the R&D Programmes: Catalogue of
      Contracts (H. Pott)
   Individual Responsibility for Health: Moral Issues Regarding Life-Styles
      (C. Bardoux)

Fanlight Productions
47 Halifax Street
Boston, MA 02130
Telephone: 800-937-4113
Fax: 617-524-8838
E-mail: fanlight@fanlight.com
Website: http://www.fanlight.com
   Video Series:
   AIDS/HIV
   Death & Dying
   Ethics
   Genetics
   Nursing/Healthcare
   Psychiatry/Mental Health

Federal Reports, Inc.
1010 Vermont Avenue, NW, Suite 408
Washington, DC 20005
Telephone: 800-296-9611
202-393-3311
Website: http://www.attorneyjobs.com
  Career Opportunties in Ethics and Professional Responsibility

Fitzroy Dearborn Publishers
70 East Walton Street
Chicago, IL 60611
Telephone: 312-587-0131
800-850-8102
Fax: 312-587-1049
E-mail: FDPservice@aol.com
Website: http://www.fitzroydearborn.com
  *Encyclopedia of AIDS: A Social, Political, Cultural, and Scientific Record of
    the HIV Epidemic* (R.A. Smith)
  Encyclopedia of Animal Rights and Animal Welfare (M. Bekoff,
    C.A. Meaney)
  International Encyclopedia of Ethics (J.K. Roth)

Foundation Press
11 Penn Plaza, 10th Floor
New York, NY 10001
Telephone: 212-760-8700
877-888-1330
Fax: 212-760-8705
Website: http://www.fdpress.com
  Selected Standards on Professional Responsibility (T.D. Morgan,
    R.D. Rotunda)

Gale Research
27500 Drake Road
Farmington Hills, MI 48331-3535
Telephone: 800-877-GALE
248-699-GALE
Fax: 800-414-5043
Website: http://www.gale.com
  *Certification and Accreditation Programs Directory: A Descriptive Guide to
    National Voluntary Certification and Accreditation Programs for
    Professionals* (M.A. Pare)
  Job Seeker's Guide to Socially Responsible Companies
  National Directory of State Business Licensing and Regulation
  *Professional and Occupational Licensing Directory: A Descriptive Guide to
    State and Federal Licensing, Registration, and Certification Requirements*
    (D.P. Bianco, A. Moran)

Garland Publishing
19 Union Square West, 8th Floor
New York, NY 10003-3382
Telephone: 212-414-0650
Fax: 212-414-0659
E-mail: info@taylorandfrancis.com
Website: http://www.garlandpub.com
  Encyclopedia of Ethics (L.C. Becker)
  Mission Statements: A Guide to the Corporate and Nonprofit Sectors
    (J.W. Graham, W.C. Havlick)
  Book Series:
  Garland Studies in Applied Ethics

Georgetown University Press
P.O. Box 4866 Hampden Station
Baltimore, MD 21211-4866
Telephone: 410-516-6995
Fax: 410-516-6998
  Source Book in Bioethics: A Documentary History (A.R. Jonsen,
    R.M. Veatch, L. Walters)
  Book Series:
  Clinical Medical Ethics (H.T. Englehardt, K.W. Wildes)
  Hastings Center Studies in Ethics

Gold Standard Multimedia Inc.
3825 Henderson Blvd., Suite 200
Tampa, FL 33629-5002
Telephone: 813-287-1775
800-375-0943
Fax: 813-287-1810
E-mail: info@gsm.com
Website: http://www.ddonline.gsm.com
  Doctor's Dilemma: Essentials of Medical Ethics (online, CD)

Gordon and Breach Publishing Group
Knightsbridge House
8th Floor, North Wing
197 Knightsbridge
London SW7 1RB
England
Telephone: 44 171 584 7676
Fax: 44 171 823 7969
E-mail: info@gbhap.com
Website: http://www.gbhap.com
  Liability in Medical Practice: A Reference for Physicians (N.S. Blackman,
    C.P. Bailey)
  Medical Ethics and the Elderly: Practical Guide (G.S. Rai)
  Book Series:
  Advances in Medical Social Science
  Critical Voices in Art, Theory, and Culture
  Current Topics in Contemporary Thought
  Health, Society & Culture

Greenwood Publishing Group
88 Post Road West
P.O. Box 5007
Westport, CT 06881-5007
Telephone: 203-226-3571   800-225-5800
Fax: 203-222-1502
Website: http://www.greenwood.com
Criminal Justice Ethics: Annotated Bibliography and Guide to Sources
(F. Schmalleger, R. McKenrick)
Encyclopedia of U.S. Biomedical Policy (R.H. Blank, J.C. Merrick)
An Encyclopedia of War and Ethics (D.A. Wells)
Ethical Aspects of Health Care for the Elderly: An Annotated Bibliography
(M.B. Kapp)
*Malpractice Liability in the Business Professions: A Survey Guide for
Attorneys and Clients* (W. Freedman)
*Professional and Occupational Licensure in the United States: An Annotated
Bibliography and Professional Resource* (R.L. Hollings, C. Pike-Nase)
Professional Law Enforcement Codes: A Documentary Collection (J. Kleinig,
Y. Zhang)
Publication Peer Review: An Annotated Bibliography (B.W. Speck)
Sports Ethics in America: A Bibliography, 1970-1990 (D.G. Jones)

Walter de Gruyter GmbH & Co.
Genthiner Strasse 13
D-10785 Berlin
Germany
Telephone: 49 30 260 05-0
Fax: 49 30 260 05-222
U.S. Office: 200 Saw Mill River Road
Hawthorne, NY 10532
Telephone: 914-747-0110
Fax: 914-747-1326
E-mail: wdg-info@deGruyter.de
Website: http://www.deGruyter.de
Just Punishments: Federal Guidelines and Public Views Compared
(P.H. Rossi, R.A. Berk)
Social Movement Organizations: Guide to Research on Insurgent Realities
(J. Lofland)
Symmetries of Nature: A Handbook for Philosophy of Nature and Science
(K. Mainzer)
The Third Sector: Comparative Studies of Nonprofit Organizations
(H.K. Anheier, W. Seibel)
Book Series:
Communication and Social Order
Evolutionary Foundations of Human Behavior
Perspectives in Analytical Philosophy
Social Institutions and Social Change
Social Problems and Social Issues
Sociological Imagination and Structural Change
Sociology and Economics
Studies in Organization
Yahrbuch für Wissenschaft und Ethik

Harcourt Brace College Publishers
301 Commerce Street
Fort Worth, TX 76102
Telephone: 817-334-7500
Website: http://www.hbcollege.com
  A Handbook for Ethics (R.C. Solomon)
  Right and Wrong: Basic Readings in Ethics (C. Sommers)
  Thirteen Questions in Ethics and Social Philosophy (G.L. Bowie,
  K.M. Higgins, M.W. Michaels)

Harvard Business School Publishing
60 Harvard Way
Boston, MA 02163
Telephone: 617-496-1449
800-545-7685
Fax: 617-496-1029
Website: http://www.hbsp.harvard.edu
  *Can Ethics Be Taught? Perspectives, Challenges, and Approaches at
  Harvard Business School* (T.R. Piper, M. Gentile, S.D. Parks)
  Good Intentions Aside: A Manager's Guide to Resolving Ethical Problems
  (L.L. Nash)
  Managerial Decision Making and Ethical Values Course Module
  (K.E. Goodpaster, T.R. Piper)

Holden Meehan
Clifton Heights, 11th Floor
Triangle West
Clifton, Bristol BS8 1EJ
England
Website: http://www.arq.co.uk/holdenmeehan
  An Independent Guide to Ethical and Green Investment Funds

Hospital for Sick Children
Dept. of Bioethics
555 University Avenue
Toronto, Ontario M5G 1X8
Canada
Telephone: 416-813-5000
Fax: 416-813-4967
  *Codes of Ethics: Ethics Codes, Standards, and Guidelines for Professionals
  Working in a Health Care Setting in Canada* (F. Baylis, J. Downie)

Humana Press, Inc.
999 Riverview Drive
Totowa, NJ 07512
Telephone: 201-256-1699
Fax: 201-256-8341
E-mail: humana@mindspring.com
Website: http://www.humanapress.com:80/humana.html
  Book Series:
  Biomedical Ethics Reviews
  Contemporary Issues in Biomedicine, Ethics, & Society

Indiana University Press
601 North Morton Street
Bloomington, IN 47404-3797
Telephone: 800-842-6796
E-mail: iupress@indiana.edu
Website: http://www.indiana.edu/~iupress
  Guidelines on the Termination of Life-Sustaining Treatment and the Care of the Dying (Hastings Center)
  Book Series:
  Indiana Series in the Philosophy of Technology
  Medical Ethics

Institute for Social Inventions
20 Heber Road
London NW2 6AA
England
  The Book of Oaths: A Compendium of Ethical Codes for Scientists (P. Codling, N. Albery)

Institute of Management Accountants, NJ
(see Ethics Standards section)
  Corporate Codes of Conduct: An Examination and Implementation Guide (S. Landekich)

International Institute for the Sociology of Law, Spain
(see Organizations: World)
  List of Key Words in the Sociology of Law

InterVarsity Press
P.O. Box 1400
Downers Grove, IL 60515
Telephone: 800-843-9487
Fax: 630-734-4200
E-mail: order@ivpress.com
Website: http://www.gospelcom.net/ivpress
  New Dictionary of Christian Ethics & Pastoral Theology (D.J. Atkinson, D.F. Fields, A. Holmes, O. O'Donovan)

JAI Press
100 Prospect Street
P.O. Box 811
Stamford, CT 06904
Telephone: 203-323-9606
Fax: 203-357-8446
Website: http://www.jaipress.com
  Advances in Bioethics (R.B. Edwards, E.E. Bittar)
  Book Series:
  Empirical Studies of Business Ethics and Values

Johns Hopkins University Press
2715 North Charles Street
Baltimore, MD 21218-4363
Telephone: 410-516-6900
Fax: 410-516-6968
Website: http://www.press.jhu.edu/press/index.htm
　Book Series:
　Medical Ethics Series

Jones and Bartlett
40 Tall Pine Drive
Sudbury, MA 01776
Telephone: 978-443-5000
Fax: 978-443-8000
E-mail: info@jbpub.com
Website: http://www.jbpub.com
　Ethics Consultation: A Practical Guide (J. La Puma, D. Schiedermayer)

Jossey-Bass, Inc., Publisher
350 Sansome Street, Fifth Floor
San Francisco, CA 94104
Telephone: 800-956-7739
Fax: 800-605-2665
415-433-0499
Website: http://www.josseybass.com
　The Right Thing: Ten Years of Ethics Columns from the Healthcare Forum Journal (E. Friedman)

Kennedy Institute of Ethics, Washington, DC
(see Organizations: U.S.)
　Annual Bibliography of Bioethics
　Bioethics Thesaurus
　International Directory of Bioethics Organizations (A.L. Nolen, M.C. Coutts)
　Scope Note Series
　Syllabus Exchange Catalog

Kluwer Academic Publishers
P.O. Box 358
Accord Station
Hingham, MA 02018-0358
Telephone: 781-871-6600
Fax: 781-871-6528
E-mail: kluwer@wkap.com
Website: http://www.wkap.nl
　Bioethics Yearbook: Regional Developments in Bioethics (B.A. Lustig)
　Book Series:
　Clinical Medical Ethics
　Developments in Health Economics and Public Policy
　Environmental Ethics and Science Policy
　Issues in Business Ethics
　Law in a Social Context

(Kluwer Academic Publishers *cont'd*)
Philosophy and Medicine
Science and Philosophy
Theology and Medicine
Topics in Safety, Risk, Reliability and Quality

Krieger Publishing Co.
P.O. Box 9542
Melbourne, FL 32902-9542
Telephone: 407-724-9542
Fax: 407-951-3671
E-mail: info@krieger-pub.com
Website: http://www.web4u.com/krieger-publishing
  The Healthcare Ethics Committee Experience: Selected Readings from HEC Forum (S.F. Spicker)
  Medicine, Media and Morality: Pulitzer Prize-Winning Writings on Health-Related Topics (H.D. Fischer)

KTAV Publishing House
P.O. Box 6249
900 Jefferson Street
Hoboken, NJ 07030
Telephone: 201-963-9524
Fax: 201-963-0102
  Book Series:
  Library of Jewish Law and Ethics

LLP Limited
Sheepen Place
Colchester
Essex CO3 3LP
England
Telephone: 44 1206 772113
Fax: 44 1206 772771
E-mail: publications@llplimited.com
Website: http://www.llplimited.com
  Professional Liability: Law and Insurance (R. Hodgin)
  Professional Negligence in the Construction Industry: Practical Guide
  (J. Brown, I. Yule, M. Arrand)

Lockheed Martin
Ethics & Corporate Compliance Programs
310 North Westlake Blvd., Suite 200
Westlake Village, CA 91362
Telephone: 805-381-1492
Fax: 805-381-1482
Website: http://www.lmco.com/exeth
  Lockheed Martin Ethics Challenge Featuring DILBERT™ (board game)

Los Alamos National Laboratory
MS A187
Los Alamos, NM 87545
Fax: 505-665-4424
E-mail: msy@lanl.gov
   ELSI Bibliography: Ethical Legal & Social Implications of the Human Genome Project (M. Yesley, M. Roth, P. Ossorio)

LRP Publications
747 Dresher Road, Suite 500
P.O. Box 980
Horsham, PA 19044-0980
Telephone: 800-341-7874
Fax: 215-784-9639
E-mail: custserve@LRP.com
Website: http://www.lrp.com
   An Attorney's Guide to Protecting, Discovering and Producing Electronic Information (M.J. Patrick)
   An Overview of the Law: A Guide for Testifying and Consulting Experts
   Ethics in the American Workplace: Policies and Decisions
   Video Series:
   Medical Legal Video Library

Macmillan Press Ltd.
25 Eccleston Place
London SW1W 9NF
England
Telephone: 44 171 881 8000
Fax: 44 171 881 8001
Website: http://www.macmillan-press.co.uk:80
   Ethics and Nursing Practice: A Case Study Approach (R. Chadwick, W. Tadd)
   Nature, Risk and Responsibility: Discourses of Biotechnology (P. O'Mahony)

Macmillan Reference
Macmillan Publishing USA
Simon & Schuster
200 Old Tappan Road
Old Tappan, NJ 07675
Telephone: 800-257-5157
Fax: 800-445-6991
Website: http://www.mlr.com/macref/index.htm
   Bioethics Compendium: Sex, Genetics, and Human Reproduction (W.T. Reich)
   Encyclopedia of Bioethics (W.T. Reich)
   How Do We Know What's Right? (S.G. Post)

Management Assistance Program for Nonprofits
2233 University Avenue West, Suite 360
St. Paul, MN 55114
Telephone: 612-647-1216
E-mail: mcnam007@tc.umn.edu
Website: http://www.mapnp.org/library/ethics/ethxgde.htm
  Complete Guide to Ethics Management: An Ethics Toolkit for Managers
  (C. McNamara) (also online)

Matthew Bender & Co., Inc.
11 Penn Plaza
New York, NY 10001
Telephone: 212-967-7707
800-833-9844
Fax: 212-244-3188
Website: http://www.bender.com
  *Health Care Law Sourcebook: A Compendium of Federal Laws, Regulations
  and Documents Relating to Health Care*
  Shepard's Professional and Judicial Conduct Citations

McFarland & Co., Inc.
Box 611
Jefferson, NC 28640
Telephone: 336-246-4460
800-253-2187
Fax: 336-246-5018
Website: http://www.mcfarlandpub.com
  *Computer Law and Software Protection: A Bibliography of Crime, Liability,
  Abuse, and Security 1984 through 1992* (R.A. Best, D.C. Picquet)
  *Corporate Statements: The Official Missions, Goals, Principles and
  Philosophies of Over 900 Companies* (P.G. Haschak)
  *Human Rights: Sixty Major Global Instruments Introduced, Reprinted and
  Indexed* (W.E. Langley)
  Information Ethics for Librarians (M. Alfino, L. Pierce)
  *Mass Media Sex and Adolescent Values: An Annotated Bibliography and
  Directory of Organizations* (A.O. Alali)
  *Plagiarism, Copyright Violation, and Other Thefts of Intellectual Property:
  An Annotated Bibliography with a Lengthy Introduction* (J. Anderson)
  *Political Prisoners and Trials: A Worldwide Annotated Bibliography, 1900
  through 1993* (J.R. Bennett)
  *Sexual Harassment in the Workplace: A Guide to the Law and a Research
  Overview for Employers and Employees* (T. Aaron)
  Terrorism and the News Media: A Selected, Annotated Bibliography
  (A.O. Alali, G.W. Byrd)

McGraw Hill
11 West 19th Street, 4th Floor
New York, NY 10011

(McGraw Hill *cont'd*)
Telephone: 800-262-4729
Fax: 614-759-3641
E-mail: customer.service@mcgraw-hill.com
Website: http://www.pbg.mcgraw-hill.com
  Accountant's Guide to Legal Liability and Ethics: A Practice Guide
  (M.J. Epstein)
  Annual Editions: Business Ethics (J.E. Richardson)
  McGraw-Hill Pocket Guide to Managed Care: Business, Practice, Law,
  Ethics (J. LaPuma, D. Schiedermayer)

Medical and Public Health Law Site (online)
Public Health Law Project, University of Missouri at Kansas City School of
Law
(see Organizations: U.S.)
Website: http://plague.law.umkc.edu
  Law and the Physician: A Practical Guide (E.P. Richards, K.C. Rathbun)
  Medical Risk Management: Preventive Legal Strategies for Health Care
  Providers (E.P. Richards, K.C. Rathbun)

Medical Research Council
20 Park Crescent
London W1N 4AL
England
  Book Series:
  MRC Ethics Series

Meiklejohn Civil Liberties Institute, CA
(see Organizations: U.S.)
  Human Rights Organizations and Periodicals Directory

National Academy Press
2101 Constitution Avenue, NW
Lockbox 285
Washington, DC 20055
Telephone: 800-624-6242
202-334-3313
Fax: 202-334-2451
E-mail: amerchan@nas.edu
Website: http://www.nap.edu
  On Being a Scientist: Responsible Conduct in Research (Committee on
  Science, Engineering, and Public Policy, National Academy of Sciences,
  National Academy of Engineering, Institute of Medicine)

National Center for Clinical Ethics, VT
(see Organizations: Government)
  Annotated Bibliographies

National Center for State Courts
300 Newport Avenue
Williamsburg, VA 23185
Telephone: 757-253-2000
Fax: 757-220-0449
Website: http://www.ncsc.dni.us
  Access to Justice for Persons of Color: Selected Guides and Programs for Improving Court Performance (J. Richardson)
  Appellate Court Performance Standards (R.A. Hanson)
  Resolving Disputes Over Life-sustaining Treatment: A Health Care Provider's Guide (T.L. Hafemeister, P.L. Hannaford)

National Institute for Law, Ethics and Public Affairs, Griffith University, Australia
(see Organizations: World)
  Law, Ethics and Public Affairs Series

National Society of Professional Engineers
(see also Ethics Standards Section)
P.O. Box 1020
Sewickley, PA 15143-1020
Telephone: 800-417-0348
Fax: 412-741-0609
E-mail: nspeorders@abdintl.com
Website: http://www.nspe.org/ps-home.htm
  Engineering Licensure Laws: A State-by-State Summary and Analysis
  Ethics Resources Guide
  Gilbane Gold Ethics Video and Study Guide
  Quality, Risk, & Project Management: Guidelines for Engineers and Architects
  A State-by-State Summary of Liability Laws Affecting the Practice of Engineering
  Book Series:
  Guides to the Practice of Professional Engineering

Oceana Publications, Inc.
75 Main Street
Dobbs Ferry, NY 10522
Telephone: 914-693-8100
Fax: 914-693-0402
E-mail: info@oceanalaw.com
Website: http://www.oceanalaw.com
  Computer Crime Investigator's Handbook (A. Brill, F.N. Baldwin, R.J. Munro)
  Money Laundering, Asset Forfeiture and International Financial Crimes: Treaties, Statutes, and Cases (F.N. Baldwin, R.J. Munro)
  Book Series:
  Legal Almanac Series (M.C. Jasper)

Oryx Press
P.O. Box 33889
Phoenix, AZ 85067-3889
Telephone: 800-279-6799
Fax: 800-279-4663
Additional Office: 4041 North Central Avenue, Suite 700
Phoenix, AZ 85012-3397
Telephone: 602-265-2651
Fax: 602-265-6250
E-mail: info@oryxpress.com
Website: http://www.oryxpress.com
   Abortion & Reproductive Rights: A Comprehensive Guide to Medicine, Ethics, and the Law (J.D. Butler)

Oxford University Press
Great Clarendon Street
Oxford OX2 6DP
England
U.S. Office: 198 Madison Avenue
New York, NY 10016
Telephone: 212-726-6000
800-451-7556
Fax: 919-677-1303
Website: http://www.oup-usa.org
   Book Series:
   Environmental Ethics and Science Policy Series
   Issues in Biomedical Ethics
   Oxford Ethics Series
   Oxford Studies in Theological Ethics
   Practical and Professional Ethics
   Ruffin Series in Business Ethics
   Studies in Bioethics

Philosophy Documentation Center
Bowling Green State University
Bowling Green, OH 43403-0189
Telephone: 419-372-9902
800-444-2419
Fax: 419-372-6987
E-mail: pdc@mailserver.bgsu.edu.
Website: http://www.bgsu.edu/offices/phildoc/index.html
   Philosophy in Cyberspace: A Guide to Philosophy-Related Resources on the Internet (D. Alexander)

Pilgrim Press
700 Prospect Avenue East
Cleveland, OH 44115-1100

(Pilgrim Press *cont'd*)
Telephone: 216-736-3700
800-537-3394
Fax: 216-736-3703
  Book Series:
  Pilgrim Library of Ethics

Plenum Publishing Corp.
233 Spring Street
New York, NY 10013-1578
Telephone: 212-620-8000
800-221-9369
Fax: 212-463-0742
E-mail: info@plenum.com
Website: http://www.plenum.com
  Book Series:
  Critical Issues in Social Justice
  Hastings Center Series in Ethics

Practising Law Institute
810 Seventh Avenue
New York, NY 10019-5818
Telephone: 800-260-4PLI
212-824-5710
E-mail: info@pli.edu
Website: http://www.pli.edu/index-lo.html
  Accountants' Liability
  Antitrust Compliance Manual: A Guide for Counsel and Executives of
    Businesses and Professions
  Directors' and Officers' Liability
  Ethics in Litigation: From First Client Interview Through Trial (video)

Praxis Consulting Group
659 Edmands Road
Framingham, MA 01701
Telephone: 508-877-0591
Fax: 508-877-7935
E-mail: praxis@tiac.net
Website: http://www.tiac.net/users/praxis/EAIsample.html
  Ethical Awareness Inventory (training tool)

Prentice-Hall
1 Lake Street
Upper Saddle River, NJ 07458
Telephone: 800-643-5506
Fax: 800-835-5327
Website: http://www.prenhall.com
  A-Z Guide to Modern Social and Political Theorists (S. Sim, N. Parker)
  Business Ethics: A Philosophical Reader (T.I. White)
  Doing the Right Thing: A Real Estate Practitioner's Guide to Ethical
    Decision Making (D.H. Long)
  Ethical Manager: A New Method for Business Ethics (R.M. Green)

(Prentice-Hall *cont'd*)
Ethics in America Source Reader (L. Newton)
Medical Ethics: A Reader (A. Zucker)
Moral Competence: An Integrated Approach to the Study of Ethics
   (J. Liszka)

Princeton University Press
41 William Street
Princeton, NJ 08540-5237
Telephone: 609-258-4900
Fax: 609-258-6305
Website: http://pup.princeton.edu
   International Ethics: A Philosophy and Public Affairs Reader (C. Beitz,
      M. Cohen)
   Book Series:
   Ethikon Series in Comparative Ethics
   Princeton Studies in Culture, Power and History
   Studies in Moral, Political, and Legal Philosophy
   University Center for Human Values

Research Foundation of ICFA/Institute of Chartered Financial Analysts
P.O. Box 3668
Charlottesville, VA 22903
Telephone: 804-963-6826
Fax: 804-980-3634
   Ethics in the Investment Profession: A Survey (E.T. Veit)

Routledge
11 New Fetter Lane
London EC4P 4EE
England
Telephone: 44 171 583 9855
Fax: 44 171 842 2298
E-mail: info@routledge.com
Website: http://www.routledge.com
U.S. Office: 29 West 35th Street
New York, NY 10001
Telephone: 212-216-7800
Fax: 212-564-7854
   Dictionary of Ethics, Theology and Society (P.A.B. Clarke, A. Linzey)
   Book Series:
   Reflective Bioethics
   Social Ethics and Policy

Rowman & Littlefield Publishers, Inc.
4720 Boston Way
Lanham, MD 20706
Telephone: 301-459-3366
800-462-6420
Fax: 301-459-2118
Website: http://www.rowmanlittlefield.com

(Rowman & Littlefield Publishers, Inc. *cont'd*)
Book Series:
Issues in Academic Ethics
Social Ethics and Policy
Studies in Social, Political, and Legal Philosophy

Sage Publications
6 Bonhill Street
London, EC2A 4PU
England
Telephone: 44 171 374 0645
Fax: 44 171 374 8741
E-mail: market@sagepub.co.uk
Website: http://www.sagepub.co.uk/ltd_home.html
U.S. Office: 2455 Teller Road
Thousand Oaks, CA 91320
Telephone: 805-499-0721
Fax: 805-499-0871
E-mail: info@sagepub.com
Book Series:
Sage Series in Business Ethics

Salem Press
P.O. Box 1097
Englewood Cliffs, NJ 07632
Telephone: 201-871-3700
800-221-1592
Fax: 201-871-8668
E-mail: Salem@ix.netcom.com
Ethics: An Annotated Bibliography (J.K. Roth)
Magill's Ready Reference: Ethics (F.N. Magill)

W.B. Saunders Company
6277 Sea Harbor Drive
Orlando, FL 32887-4430
Telephone: 800-545-2522
E-mail: wbsbcs@harcourtbrace.com
Website: http://www.wbsaunders.com
Deciding Ethically: A Practical Approach to Nursing Challenges (V. Tschudin)

Scarecrow Press
4720 Boston Way
Lanham, MD 20706
Telephone: 301-459-3366
800-462-6420
Fax: 301-459-2118
Website: http://www.scarecrowpress.com/crow.html
Animal Rights Movement in the United States, 1975-1990: An Annotated Bibliography (B. Manzo)
Historical Dictionary of Human Rights and Humanitarian Organizations (R.F. Gorman, E.S. Mihalkanin)

Science Reference and Information Service
The British Library
Turpin Distribution Services Ltd.
Blackhorse Road
Letchworth, Herts SG6 1HN
England
   Scientific Deception: An Overview and Guide to the Literature of Misconduct and Fraud in Scientific Research (L. Grayson)

Sepher-Hermon Press
1265 46th Street
Brooklyn, NY 11219
Telephone/Fax: 718-972-9010
   The Essential Pele Yoetz: An Encyclopedia of Ethical Jewish Living (E. Papo)

Springer-Verlag
Tiergartenstrasse 17
D-69121 Heidelberg
Germany
Telephone: 49 6221 487 0
E-mail: Webmaster@springer.de
Website: http://www.springer.de
U.S. Office: 175 Fifth Avenue
New York, NY 10010
Telephone: 800-SPRINGER
212-460-1500
Fax: 212-473-6272
E-mail: custserv@springer-ny.com
Website: http://www.springer-ny.com
   AIDS Testing: A Comprehensive Guide to Technical, Medical, Social, Legal, and Management Issues (G. Schochetman, J.R. George)
   Key Words in Ethics, Law, and Aging: A Guide to Contemporary Usage (M.B. Kapp)
   Book Series:
   Springer Series on Ethics, Law, and Aging
   Studies in Economic Ethics and Philosophy

St. Martin's Press College Division
345 Park Avenue South
New York, NY 10010
Telephone: 800-470-4767
Website: http://www.smpcollege.com
   Cases in Bioethics: Selections from The Hastings Center Report (B.J. Crigger)
   Book Series:
   Contemporary Social Issues
   Ethics
   Professional Studies in Health Care

State University of New York Press
State University Plaza
Albany, NY 12246-0001
Telephone: 518-472-5000
E-mail: info@sunypress.edu
Website: http://www.sunypress.edu
  Book Series:
  Biopolitics
  Critical Issues in Criminal Justice
  Ethical Theory
  Health Care Politics and Policy
  Public Policy
  Science, Technology, and Society
  SUNY Case Studies in Applied Ethics, Technology, and Society

Technique & Documentation
11, Rue Lavoisier
F-75384 Paris Cedex 08
France
U.S. Office: 160 Implay Street
Brooklyn, NY 11231
  European Directory of Bioethics

Temple University Press
University Services 083-42
1601 North Broad Street
Philadelphia, PA 19122-6099
Telephone: 215-204-8787
Fax: 215-204-4719
E-mail: tempress@astro.ocis.temple.edu
Website: http://www.temple.edu/tempress
  Book Series:
  Animals, Culture, and Society
  Ethics and Action

Charles C. Thomas Publisher
2600 South 1st Street
Springfield, IL 62794-9265
Telephone: 217-789-8980
800-258-8980
Fax: 217-789-9130
  Life, Death, and the Law: A Sourcebook on Autonomy and Responsibility in Medical Ethics (W.N. Keyes)

University of California Press
2120 Berkeley Way
Berkeley, CA 94720

(University of California Press *cont'd*)
Telephone: 510-642-4247
Fax: 510-643-7127
E-mail: ucpress.comments@ucop.edu
Website: http://www.ucpress.edu
> *Choosing Justice: An Experimental Approach to Ethical Theory* (N. Frohlich,
>   J.A. Oppenheimer)
> *The Cigarette Papers* (S. Glantz, J. Slade, L. Bero, P. Hanauer, D.E. Barnes)
> *Earth's Insights: A Multicultural Survey of Ecological Ethics from the
>   Mediterranean Basin to the Australian Outback* (B. Callicott)
> *Lawyers in Society: An Overview* (R.L. Abel, P.S.C. Lewis)
> Book Series:
> *California Series on Social Choice and Political Economy*
> *Pittsburgh Series in Philosophy and History of Science*

University of Chicago Press
5801 South Ellis
Chicago, IL 60637
Telephone: 773-702-7700
Fax: 773-702-9756
E-mail: marketing@press.uchicago.edu
Website: http://www.press.uchicago.edu
> Book Series:
> *Language and Legal Discourse*
> *Morality and Society*
> *New Practices of Inquiry*
> *science.culture*
> *Studies in Business and Society*
> *Studies in Communication, Media, and Public Opinion*

University of Notre Dame Press
Notre Dame, IN 46556
Telephone: 219-631-6346
Fax: 219-631-8148
E-mail: nd.undpress.1@nd.edu
Website: http://www.nd.edu/~undpress
> *Eighty Exemplary Ethics Statements* (P.E. Murphy)
> Book Series:
> *Frank M. Covey Jr. Loyola Lectures in Political Analysis*
> *John W. Houck Notre Dame Series in Business Ethics*
> *Revisions: A Series of Books on Ethics*
> *Soundings: A Series of Books on Ethics, Economics, and Business*
> *Studies in Law and Contemporary Issues*
> *Studies in Science and the Humanities*
> *Theodore M. Hesburgh Lectures on Ethics and Public Policy*

University of Utah Press
1795 East South Campus Drive, Suite 101
Salt Lake City, UT 84112-9402

(University of Utah Press *cont'd*)
Telephone: 800-773-6672
801-581-6771
Fax: 801-581-3365
E-mail: info@upress.utah.edu
Website: http://www.media.utah.edu/upress
  Book Series:
  Ethics in a Changing World
  Tanner Lectures on Human Values

University Press of Florida
15 Northwest 15th Street
Gainesville, FL 32611-2079
Telephone: 800-226-3822
Fax: 352-392-7302
Website: http://nersp.nerdc.ufl.edu/~upf
  Judicial Misconduct: A Cross-National Comparison (M.L. Volcansek,
  M.E. De Franciscis, J.L. Lafon)

University Press of New England
23 South Main Street
Hanover, NH 03755
Telephone: 603-643-7100
Fax: 603-643-1540
E-mail: university.press@dartmouth.edu
Website: http://www.dartmouth.edu/acad-inst/upne/publish.html
  Ethics of Scientific Research: A Guidebook for Course Development
  (J.E. Stern, D. Elliott)
  Research Ethics: A Reader (D. Elliott, J.E. Stern)

University Publications of America
4520 East-West Highway
Bethesda, MD 20814-3389
Telephone: 301-657-3200
800-692-6300
Fax: 301-657-3203
E-mail: upainfo@lexis-nexis.com
Website: http://www.upapubs.com
  Book Series:
  Horatio R. Storer Series in Ethics, Law, and Medicine

U.S. Office of Government Ethics, DC
(see Organizations: Government)
  Ethics CD-ROM

West Group
(includes Clark Boardman Callaghan)
610 Opperman Drive
Eagan, MN 55123

(West Group *cont'd*)
Telephone: 612-687-7000
800-328-4880
Fax: 800-340-9378
Website: http://www.westgroup.com
  Black Letter on Professional Responsibility (R. Rotunda)
  Civil Rights Litigation and Attorney Fees Handbook (National Lawyers
    Guild, S. Saltzman, B.M. Volvovitz)
  Federal Sentencing Guidelines Handbook (R.W. Haines)
  Health Care Law and Ethics in a Nutshell (Hall, Ellman)
  Health Care Liability Deskbook (Kerns, Gerner)
  Hornbook on Modern Legal Ethics (C. Wolfram)
  Jurisprudence: Text and Readings on the Philosophy of Law (G.C. Christie,
    P.H. Martin)
  Law of Medical Liability in a Nutshell (Boumil, Elias)
  The Legal Audit: Corporate Internal Investigation (L.M. Brown, A.O.
    Kandel)
  Legal Handbook for Architects, Engineers & Contractors (A. Dib, A.H. Dib)
  Medical Malpractice: Checklists and Discovery
  A Practical Guide to Preventing Legal Malpractice
  Professional Responsibility in a Nutshell (Aronson, Weckstein)
  Professional Responsibility: Standards, Rules & Statutes
  Selected Standards on Professional Responsibility

Wilfrid Laurier University Press
75 University Avenue West
Waterloo, Ontario N2L 3C5
Canada
Telephone: 519-884-0710, ext. 6124
Fax: 519-725-1399
E-mail: press@mach1.wlu.ca
Website: http://info.wlu.ca/~wwwpress/home.html
  Book Series:
  Calgary Institute for the Humanities Series

3. Electronic Media

a. *Online Bibliographies*

This section lists bibliographies on topics in ethics, professionalism, and public policy, available online. They generally differ from the listings in the **Reference Works** section, above.

Website addresses change frequently. In addition to the URL address, the bibliography's title, author, and host or sponsor are provided, where available. This information will facilitate a search for the material, in the event that an address changes or a site is renamed.

A Select Bibliography (Partially Annotated) on Health Aspects of Human Rights (1984-1997) (S. Fluss)
Website: http://www.biol.tsukuba.ac.jp/~macer/HRBiblio.html
Author/Sponsor: Eubios Ethics Institute
(see Organizations: World)

Accounting Ethics Bibliography
Website: http://www.csu.edu.au/cgi-pub/anet/anetbib/htgrep?file=cgi-bin%2Fhtgrep%2Frefer_data&isindex=ethics&refer=plain&max=50
Host/Sponsor: A-Net International Accounting Network

Annotated Bibliography on Equity and Health Policy (R.K. Lie)
Website: http://www.hf.uib.no/i/Filosofisk/ethica/equity.html
Host/Sponsor: ETHICA - Ethics and Health: An International and Comparative Arena
(see Organizations: World)

Annotated Bibliography on Teaching Research Ethics (K.D. Pimple)
Website: http://www.indiana.edu/~poynter/tre-bib.html
Host/Sponsor: Poynter Center for the Study of Ethics and American Institutions
(see Organizations: U.S.)

Beginnings of a Partially Annotated Bibliography on Advance Directives
Website: http://ccme-mac4.bsd.uchicago.edu/CCMEDocs/AdvDir/Bib
Host/Sponsor: MacLean Center for Clinical Medical Ethics
(see Organizations: U.S.)

Bibliographies on Philosophy and Philosophers: Applied Ethics
Website: http://www.lib.ttu.edu/philosophy/PHIBIB.htm
Host/Sponsor: Texas Tech Library

Bibliography of Computing, Ethics, and Social Responsibility (H. Tavani)
Website: http://www.siu.edu/departments/coba/mgmt/iswnet/isethics/biblio/index.html
Host/Sponsor: Computer Professionals for Social Responsibility
(see Organizations: U.S.)

Bibliography of Professionalism & Ethics Topics
Website: http://www.txethics.org/frames37.htm
Host/Sponsor: Texas Center for Legal Ethics and Professionalism
(see Organizations: U.S.)

Bibliography of Scholarly Books on Buddhist Ethics and Ethics-Related Topics
Website: http://jbe.la.psu.edu/schoreso.html
Host/Sponsor: Journal of Buddhist Ethics
(see Information: Periodicals)

Bibliography of Useful Readings in Business Ethics (J.A. Baker)
Website: http://www.acs.ucalgary.ca/~baker/bus-biblio.html
Host/Sponsor: University of Calgary, Dept. of Philosophy

Bibliography on Law and Policy
Website: http://www.spatial.maine.edu/I-16/biblio2.html
Host/Sponsor: National Center for Geographic Information and Analysis

Bioethics Bibliographies
Website: http://www.bioethix.org/resources/biblio.html
Host/Sponsor: Center for Bioethics and Human Dignity
(see Organizations: U.S.)

Cloning Bibliography
Website: http://guweb.georgetown.edu/nrcbl/biblios/cloning.htm
Host/Sponsor: National Reference Center for Bioethics Literature
(see Organizations: Government)

Communitarian Bibliography
Website: http://www.gwu.edu/~ccps/biblio.html
Host/Sponsor: Communitarian Network
(see Organizations: U.S.)

Compilation of Federal Ethics Laws
Website: http://www.defenselink.mil/dodgc/defense_ethics/dod_oge/law.html
Host/Sponsor: U.S. Department of Defense, Standards of Conduct Office
(see Organizations: Government)

Directory of Lawyer Disciplinary Agencies
Website: http://www.abanet.org/cpr/disciplinary.html
Host/Sponsor: American Bar Association
(see Ethics Standards section)

Engineering Ethics References (W. P. Vann)
Website: http://www.niee.org/referenc.htm
Host/Sponsor: Murdough Center for Engineering Professionalism
(see Organizations: U.S.)

Freedom of the Press: An Annotated Bibliography (R.E. McCoy)
Website: http://www.lib.siu.edu/cni/homepage.html
Host/Sponsor: Southern Illinois University at Carbondale

Information Clearinghouse Index of Corporate Ethics Program Materials
Website: http://www.dii.org/clearindex.html
Host/Sponsor: Defense Industry Initiative on Business Ethics and Conduct
(see Organizations: U.S.)

Information Ethics: On the Philosophical Foundation of Computer Ethics
(L. Floridi)
Website: http://www.wolfson.ox.ac.uk/~floridi/ie.htm
Host/Sponsor: ETHICOMP98: Fourth International Conference on Ethical
Issues of Information Technology

ISEE Master Bibliography (H. Rolston, E. Katz)
Website: http://www.phil.unt.edu/bib
Host/Sponsor: International Society for Environmental Ethics
(see Organizations: U.S.)

JSCOPE Bibliography
Website: http://www.usafa.af.mil/jscope/articles.htm
Host/Sponsor: Joint Services Conference On Professional Ethics
(see Organizations: Government)

Media Ethics Bibliography (D. Shedden)
Website: http://www.poynter.org/research/biblio/bib_me.htm
Host/Sponsor: Poynter Institute for Media Studies
(see Organizations: U.S.)

National Center for Clinical Ethics Annotated Bibliographies
Website: http://wrjva1.hitchcock.org/Bib.html
Host/Sponsor: National Center for Clinical Ethics, U.S. Department of
Veterans Affairs
(see Organizations: Government)

National Patient Safety Foundation Web Bibliography
Website: http://www.ama-assn.org/med-sci/npsf/bibl1998.htm
Host/Sponsor: American Medical Association
(see Ethics Standards section)

Organizational Justice and Computers in the Workplace Bibliography
(N.D. Ainspan)
Website: http://shum.cc.huji.ac.il/jcmc/ainspanbib.html
Host/Sponsor: Journal of Computer-Mediated Communication
(see Information: Periodicals)

Philosophy of Action and Moral Psychology Bibliography
Philosophy of Psychiatry Bibliography: Ethical, Social, Political, Legal,
Historical and Philosophical Issues in Mental Health and Psychiatry
(C. Perring)
Website: http://www.uky.edu/~cperring
Host/Sponsor: University of Kentucky, Dept. of Philosophy

Resources for Science/Religion Discussion from A to Z
Website: http://www.iras.org/discussion/resources.html
Host/Sponsor: Institute on Religion in an Age of Science
(see Organizations: U.S.)

Science Ethics Bibliography (V. Hamner, B. Tissue)
Website: http://www.chem.vt.edu/ethics/vinny/ethxbibl.html
Host/Sponsor: Virginia Polytechnic Institute & State University, Dept. of
   Chemistry

South East Asian Health Ethics Network Bibliography
Website: http://www.hf.uib.no/i/Filosofisk/seahen/data.htm
Host/Sponsor: ETHICA - Ethics and Health: An International and Comparative
   Arena
(see Organizations: World)

Subject Bibliographies in Environmental Ethics (T.C. Weiskel)
Website: http://divweb.harvard.edu/csvpl/ee/bib
Host/Sponsor: Environmental Ethics and Public Research Policy Program,
   Center for the Study of Values in Public Life
(see Organizations: U.S.)

3. Electronic Media

b. *Selected Websites*

This section lists websites that are especially useful as meta-indexes, directories, and links to sources of further information on the topics of ethics, professionalism, and public policy. Most are not listed elsewhere in the **Resources** section.

Website addresses change frequently. In addition to the URL address, the website's title and author or sponsor are provided, where available. This information will facilitate a search for the material, in the event that an address changes or a site is renamed.

Please note that the website addresses and links *within* the websites listed here are themselves also subject to change.

A Call for Accountability, Competency, and Ethics in DOE
Website: http://www.mindspring.com/~jpcarson
Author/Sponsor: J.P. Carson

Advertising Law Internet Site
Website: http://www.advertisinglaw.com
Author/Sponsor: L. Rose, Arent Fox Kintner Plotkin & Kahn

American Legal Ethics Library
Website: http://www.law.cornell.edu/ethics
Author/Sponsor: Legal Information Institute, Cornell University

Applied Ethics in Professional Practice Case-of-the-Month Club
Website: http://www.engr.washington.edu/~uw-epp/Pepl/Ethics
Author/Sponsor: Professional Engineering Practice Liaison Program, University of Washington College of Engineering

Applied Ethics Resources on WWW
Website: http://www.ethics.ubc.ca/resources
Author/Sponsor: C. MacDonald, Centre for Applied Ethics, University of British Columbia
(see Organizations: World)

Astrolabe: Ethical Navigations through Virtual Technologies
Website: http://www.cgrg.ohio-state.edu/Astrolabe
Author/Sponsor: Advanced Computing Center for the Arts and Design, Ohio State University

Best Information on the Net: Ethics
Website: http://www.sau.edu/CWIS/Internet/Wild/Majors/Philos/Ethics/ethindex.htm
Author/Sponsor: O'Keefe Library, St. Ambrose University

Bioethics Information Website
Website: http://kenko.human.waseda.ac.jp/rihito/site.html
Author/Sponsor: Waseda University, Japan

953

Bioethics Online Service
Website: http://www.mcw.edu/bioethics/new98_99/bos.html
Author/Sponsor: Center for the Study of Bioethics, Medical College of
    Wisconsin
(see Organizations: U.S.)

Bioethics Resources
Website: http://www.smu.edu/~dcobb/pages/bioethics.html
Author/Sponsor: D.E. Cobb

BIOETHICSLINE
Website: http://guweb.georgetown.edu/nrcbl/nrcbl.htm#bioline
Author/Sponsor: National Reference Center for Bioethics Literature, National
    Library of Medicine
(see Organizations: Government)

Business Ethics Questionnaire
Website: http://trapeze.scs.unr.edu/~beekun/ethics
Author/Sponsor: University of Nevada at Reno, College of Business
    Administration

Business Ethics/Social Responsibility Links
Website: http://www.betterworld.com/Links/Get2?catid=18
Author/Sponsor: Better World Links

Canadian Ethical Investment Web Site
Website: http://www.web.apc.org/ethmoney
Author/Sponsor: E. Ellmen, Canadian Ethical Money Guide

Codes of Ethics Online
Website: http://csep.iit.edu/codes/codes.html
Author/Sponsor: Center for the Study of Ethics in the Professions
(see Organizations: U.S.)

Collection of Codes of Conduct/Practice/Ethics from Around the World
Website: http://ei.cs.vt.edu/~cs3604/lib/WorldCodes/WorldCodes.html
Author/Sponsor: J.A.N. Lee, Virginia Polytechnic Institute and State University

Computer Crime & Investigations Center
Website: http://www.ovnet.com/~dckinder/crime.htm
Author/Sponsor: D. Kinder

Computer Ethics
Website: http://homepage.seas.upenn.edu/~mengwong/comp.ethics.html
Author/Sponsor: M.W. Wong

*Corporate Governance NETwork: Enhancing the Return on Capital Through
    Increased Accountability*
Website: http://www.corpgov.net
Author/Sponsor: J. McRitchie

Corporate Power Information Center
Website: http://baobabcomputing.com/corporatepower
Author/Sponsor: Baobab Computing

Criminal Justice Resources on the Web
Website: http://www.nacj.com/links/mega.htm
Author/Sponsor: Nevada Attorneys for Criminal Justice, National Association
of Criminal Defense Lawyers

DeathNet: International Archive on All Aspects of Death and Dying
Website: http://www.islandnet.com/deathnet
Author/Sponsor: J. Hofsess, Right to Die Society of Canada, D. Humphry

DIANA International Human Rights Database
Website: http://www.law.uc.edu:81/Diana
Author/Sponsor: Center for Electronic Text in the Law, University of
Cincinnati College of Law

Ethical and Professional Issues in Computing
Website: http://www.rpi.edu/~johnsd/epic/epic.html
Author/Sponsor: D. Johnson, Rensselaer Polytechnic Institute, K. Miller,
University of Illinois at Springfield

Ethical Questions in Dentistry
Website: http://cpmcnet.columbia.edu/dept/dental/Dental_Educational_Software/
Dental-Ethics/ethics-welcome.html
Author/Sponsor: School of Dental and Oral Surgery, Columbia University

EthicNet: Databank for European Codes of Journalism Ethics
Website: http://www.uta.fi/ethicnet
Author/Sponsor: Dept. of Journalism and Mass Communication, University of
Tampere, Finland

Ethics and the Internet: Readings and Surfings
Website: http://www.duke.edu/~wgrobin/ethics/surfing.html
Author/Sponsor: W. Robinson, Duke University

Ethics at TI
Website: http://www.ti.com/corp/docs/ethics/home.htm
Author/Sponsor: Ethics Office, Texas Instruments Inc.

Ethics in Biomedicine
Website: http://www.mic.ki.se/Diseases/k1.316.html
Author/Sponsor: Karolinska Institutet Library, Stockholm, Sweden

Ethics in Science
Website: http://www.stat.wisc.edu/other/ethics
Author/Sponsor: B. Yandell, University of Wisconsin-Madison

Ethics in Science/Online Science Ethics Resources
Website: http://www.chem.vt.edu/ethics/ethics.html
Author/Sponsor: B. Tissue, Dept. of Chemistry, Virginia Polytechnic Institute
    and State University

Ethics Information Center
Website: http://www.gaiafriends.com/ethics
Author/Sponsor: R.E. Podolsky, G.R. Sulliger, Person to Person Promotions,
    Inc.

Ethics, Law and Computing Resource Center
Website: http://www.cs.ccsu.ctstateu.edu/~boconnel
Author/Sponsor: B.M. O'Connell, Central Connecticut State University, Dept.
    of Computer Science

Ethics on the Web
Website: http://www.gac.edu/Academics/philosophy/lethics.html
Author/Sponsor: Gustavus Adolphus College, Philosophy Dept.

Ethics on the World Wide Web
Website: http://commfaculty.fullerton.edu/lester/ethics/ethics_list.html
Author/Sponsor: P.M. Lester, California State University, Fullerton, School of
    Communications

*ETHICS OSCE: Standardized Patient Scenarios for Teaching and Evaluating
    Bioethics*
Website: http://wings.buffalo.edu/faculty/research/bioethics/osce.html
Author/Sponsor: Joint Centre for Bioethics, University of Toronto
(see Organizations: World)

Ethics Updates
Website: http://ethics.acusd.edu/index.html
Author/Sponsor: L.M. Hinman, University of San Diego, Dept. of Philosophy

ETHICSearch ABA Ethics Research Service
Website: http://www.abanet.org/cpr/ethicsearch/home.html
Author/Sponsor: American Bar Association
(see Ethics Standards section)

Euroethics: European Database on Medical Ethics
Website: http://www.spri.se/spriline/infome.htm
Author/Sponsor: SPRI Swedish Institute for Health Services Development

Federal Inspectors General Directory
Website: http://www.ignet.gov/ignet/internal/igdir.html
Author/Sponsor: IGNet: Internet for the Federal IG [Inspector General]
    Community

Genetics & Ethics
Website: http://www.ethics.ubc.ca/brynw
Author/Sponsor: B. Williams-Jones, Centre for Applied Ethics, University of
  British Columbia
(see Organizations: World)

GeoEthics
Website: http://www.geog.umn.edu/geoethics
Author/Sponsor: W.S. Lynn, University of Minnesota, Dept. of Geography

Harvard Law School Legal Ethics Web Site
Website: http://www.law.harvard.edu/groups/hlslews
Author/Sponsor: Harvard University

*Health Fraud Page: An Information Center on Legislation and Resources to
  Protect Those Who Encounter Unethical Counseling, Unscientific
  Evaluations, or Questionable Practices*
E-mail: dean@primenet.com.html
Author/Sponsor: D. Hughson

Healthcare Ethics Links
Website: http://members.tripod.com/~DianneBrownson/ethics.html
Author/Sponsor: BROWNson's Nursing Notes

Healthcare Integrity and Protection Data Bank
Website: http://www.hrsa.dhhs.gov/bhpr/dqa/hipmain.htm
Author/Sponsor: Division of Quality Assurance, U.S. Department of Health and
  Human Services
(see Organizations: Government)

Human Rights Library
Website: http://www.umn.edu/humanrts/index.html
Author/Sponsor: Human Rights Center, University of Minnesota
(see Organizations: U.S.)

Human Subjects/Participants and Research Ethics
Website: http://www.psych.bangor.ac.uk/deptpsych/Ethics/HumanResearch.html
Author/Sponsor: B.T. Maguire, University of Wales, Bangor, School of
  Psychology

*Interactive Computer Ethics Explorer: Online Ethical Scenarios with
  Interactive Surveys and Real-time Demographics*
Website: http://web.cs.bgsu.edu/maner/xxicee/html/welcome.htm
Author/Sponsor: W. Maner

International Calendar of Bioethics Events
Website: http://www2.umdnj.edu/ethicweb/upcome.htm
Author/Sponsor: Bioethics and Medical Humanities, University of Medicine
  and Dentistry of New Jersey-Robert Wood Johnson Medical School
(see Organizations: U.S.)

Issues in Christian Ethics
Website: http://honey.acu.edu.au/~yuri/ethics/index.html
Author/Sponsor: Y. Koszarycz, Australian Catholic University

ISWorld Net Information Systems Ethics: Computer Ethics - Cyberethics
Website: http://www.siu.edu/departments/coba/mgmt/iswnet/isethics/index.html
Author/Sponsor: D. Vance, A. Rai, Southern Illinois University, Dept. of
    Management

ISWorld Net Information Systems Ethics: Professional Ethics
Website: http://is.lse.ac.uk/iswnet/profact/ethics.htm
Author/Sponsor: F. Quek, Association for Information Systems

*JCMC Cite Site: Links to Bibliographies About Computer-Mediated
    Communication*
Website: http://jcmc.huji.ac.il/citesite.html
Author/Sponsor: Journal of Computer-Mediated Communication
(see Information: Periodicals)

Legal Ethics and Reform Home Page
Website: http://webusers.anet-stl.com/~hvmlr/hm_pgf.html
Author/Sponsor: H. Murray

Legalethics.com
Website: http://www.legalethics.com
Author/Sponsor: Practicing Attorney's Home Page, Internet Legal Services

Living Will and Values History Project
Website: http://www.netlink.co.uk/users/vess/lwvh.html
Author/Sponsor: C. Docker

Malpractice and Medical Discipline Research Information
Website: http://www.hrsa.dhhs.gov/bhpr/dqa/mmdr.htm
Author/Sponsor: Division of Quality Assurance, U.S. Department of Health and
    Human Services
(see Organizations: Government)

Mass Media Ethics
Website: http://www.interchange.ubc.ca/twthorne
Author/Sponsor: T.W. Thorne

Media Ethics
Website: http://www.usq.edu.au/faculty/arts/journ/medethic.htm
Author/Sponsor: University of Southern Queensland, Dept. of Mass
    Communication, Australia

Media Watchdog
Website: http://theory.lcs.mit.edu/~mernst/media
Author/Sponsor: M. Ernst

Medical Ethics: Where Do You Draw the Line?
Website: http://www.learner.org/exhibits/medicalethics
Author/Sponsor: Annenberg/CPB Project Exhibits Collection

MedWeb: Bioethics
Website: http://www.gen.emory.edu/medweb/medweb.bioethics.html
Author/Sponsor: Emory University Health Sciences Center Library

Metapsychology: Reviewing Books on Philosophical, Ethical, & Historical Issue in Mental Health
Website: http://www.cmhc.com/perspectives/metapsychology
Author/Sponsor: C. Perring, Perspectives: A Mental Health Magazine

Misconduct.com: A Resource Center for Investigating Attorney Misconduct
Website: http://www.misconduct.com
Author/Sponsor: A.M. Bond, Solstice Publishing Corp.

National Practitioner Data Bank
Website: http://www.npdb.com
Author/Sponsor: Division of Quality Assurance, U.S. Department of Health and Human Services
(see Organizations: Government)

Natural Philosophy Center
Website: http://www.baobabcomputing.com/naturalphilosophy
Author/Sponsor: Baobab Computing

Overview of Ethics in Government: Regulations and Statutes
Website: http://eos4.dcrt.nih.gov/dcrthr/ethics/overview.htm
Author/Sponsor: Division of Computer Research & Technology, Human Resource Management Section, National Institutes of Health

Photojournalism Ethics Page
Website: http://www.cris.com:80/~Mppa/ethics.html
Author/Sponsor: Michigan Press Photographers Association

PolicyFile: Public Policy Research and Analysis
Website: http://www.policyfile.com
Author/Sponsor: Chadwyck-Healey, Inc.

Public Radio Virtual Ethics and Style Guidebook
Website: http://www.npr.org/inside/styleguide/stylmain.htm
Author/Sponsor: National Public Radio Journalism Conference Project

Selected Sources. . . Civil Society; Ethics and Sustainable Development; Rights & Responsibilities
Website: http://iisd1.iisd.ca/ic/info/hottop.htm
Author/Sponsor: International Institute for Sustainable Development

Site on Scientific Misconduct
Website: http://www.nyx.net/~wstewart/main.ssi
Author/Sponsor: W.W. Stewart

Social Ethics and Moral Education Page
Website: http://re-xs.ucsm.ac.uk/ethics
Author/Sponsor: Religious Education Exchange Service, Electronic Media and
  Religion Project, University College of St. Martin, England

Social Issues Web Guide
Website: http://www.sirs.com/tree/social.htm
Author/Sponsor: Social Issues Resources Series, Inc.

Social, Political, and Ethical Dimensions of Business
Website: http://www.albany.edu/~pm157/teaching/ethics.html
Author/Sponsor: P. Miesing, State University of New York at Albany,
  Business School

Society, Religion and Technology Project
Website: http://webzone.ccacyber.com/www/srtproject/srtpage3.htm
Author/Sponsor: D. Bruce, Church of Scotland
(see Organizations: World)

Telemedicine & the Law
Website: http://www.arentfox.com/telemedicine.html
Author/Sponsor: R.J. Waters, Arent Fox Kintner Plotkin & Kahn

Theology Library: Morality
Website: http://www.mcgill.pvt.k12.al.us/jerryd/cm/moral.htm
Author/Sponsor: G. Darring, Catholic Mobile

Web Clearinghouse for Engineering and Computing Ethics
Website: http://www4.ncsu.edu/unity/users/j/jherkert/ethicind.html
Author/Sponsor: J.R. Herkert, North Carolina State University, Division of
  Multidisciplinary Studies

WWW Ethics Center for Engineering and Science
Website: http://ethics.cwru.edu
Author/Sponsor: National Science Foundation, C. Whitbeck, Case Western
  Reserve University

*WWW Virtual Library: Animal Health, Well-Being, and Rights; Human
  Computer Interaction; Law; Philosophy; Social Sciences; etc.*
Website: http://www.vlib.org/AlphaVL.html

3. Electronic Media

c. *Online Discussion Lists*

This section lists online discussion groups that address issues of ethics, professionalism, and public policy.

The list's name and title are provided, along with instructions (usually the contents and destination of an e-mail message) on how to subscribe or participate.

Online discussions, like those in person, often change locale or end altogether. The name and title information may facilitate a search for the list in the event that a host address changes or a discussion is renamed or terminated.

List name: 178TALK: Environmental Ethics
To subscribe, send the e-mail message:
   subscribe 178talk yourfirstname yourlastname
to: listserv@list.uvm.edu

List name: AAPAE-L: Australian Association for Professional and Applied Ethics
To subscribe, send the e-mail message: subscribe aapae-l emailaddress
to: majordomo@explode.unsw.edu.au

List name: Academic Dialogue on Applied Ethics
To participate and for more information, go to the website:
   http://www.lcl.cmu.edu/CAAE/Home/Forum/ethics.html

List name: ACCNET: Accounting Ethics Network
Part of CAERNETS (Canadian Applied Ethics Research Nets), Centre for Applied Ethics, University of British Columbia
To subscribe, send an e-mail request to the moderator:
   jgaa@gpu3.srv.ualberta.ca

List name: ADVERTISING-LAW: Advertising Law
To subscribe, send the e-mail message: subscribe
to: advertising-law-request@webcom.com

List name: AETHICS-L: Accounting Ethics
To subscribe, send an empty e-mail message with the subject line: subscribe
to: aethics-l-request@listserv.csu.edu.au

List name: ASLME-L : American Society for Law, Medicine, and Ethics
To subscribe, send the e-mail message:
   subscribe aslme-l yourfirstname yourlastname
to: listserv@lawlib.wuacc.edu

List name: BETS-L: Business Ethics Teaching Society
To subscribe, send the e-mail message:
   subscribe bets-l yourfirstname yourlastname
to: listserv@listserv.uic.edu

List name: BIOETH-LIST: University at Buffalo Bioethics Discussion List
To subscribe, send the e-mail message:
  subscribe bioeth-list yourfirstname yourlastname
to: listserv@listserv.acsu.buffalo.edu

List name: Bioethics Discussion Pages
To participate, send an e-mail message to: DoktorMo@aol.com
For more information, go to the website: http://www-hsc.usc.edu/~mbernste

List name: BIOETHICSLAW-L: Bioethics Law Scholars Forum
To subscribe, send the e-mail message:
  subscribe bioethicslaw-l yourfirstname yourlastname
to: listserv@lawlib.wuacc.edu

List name: BIOETHNET: Canadian Bioethics Network
Part of CAERNETS (Canadian Applied Ethics Research Nets), Centre for
  Applied Ethics, University of British Columbia
To subscribe, send an e-mail request to the moderator:
  mburgess@ethics.ubc.ca

List name: BIOMED-L: Biomedical Ethics
To subscribe, send the e-mail message:
  subscribe biomed-l yourfirstname yourlastname
to: listserv@listserv.nodak.edu

List name: BUSETH-L: Business Ethics Computer Network
To subscribe, send the e-mail message:
  subscribe buseth-l yourfirstname yourlastname
to: listserv@listserv.acsu.buffalo.edu

List name: BUSINESS-ETHICS: Business and Administrative Studies
To subscribe, send the e-mail message:
  join business-ethics yourfirstname yourlastname
to: mailbase@mailbase.ac.uk

List name: CBPENET: Canadian Business and Professional Ethics Network
Part of CAERNETS (Canadian Applied Ethics Research Nets), Centre for
  Applied Ethics, University of British Columbia
To subscribe, send an e-mail request to the moderator:
  boyd@sask.usask.ca

List name: CEI-L: Computer Ethics Institute
To subscribe, send the e-mail message:
  subscribe cei-l yourfirstname yourlastname
to: listserv@american.edu

List name: CHAETHIC: Policies, Ethics and Electronic Synchronous
  Communication
To subscribe, send the e-mail message: subscribe chaethic yourfirstname
  yourlastname
to: listserv@nic.surfnet.nl

List name: CIVIL-JUSTICE: Civil Justice
To subscribe, send the e-mail message:
    subscribe civil-justice yourfirstname yourlastname
to: listproc@essential.org

List name: CORP-WELFARE: Corporate Welfare
To subscribe, send the e-mail message:
    subscribe corp-welfare yourfirstname yourlastname
to: listserv@ursus.jun.alaska.edu

List name: CORPETHX-L: Corporate Social Responsibility
To subscribe, send the e-mail message:
    subscribe corpethx-l yourfirstname yourlastname
to: listserv@siu.edu

List name: CPAE: Center for Professional and Applied Ethics
To subscribe, send the e-mail message:
    subscribe cpae yourfirstname yourlastname
to: listserv@catfish.valdosta.peachnet.edu

List name: CPSR: Computer Professionals for Social Responsibility
To subscribe, send the e-mail message:
    subscribe cpsr-announce yourfirstname yourlastname
to: listserv@cpsr.org

List name: CYBERIA-L: Law and Policy of Computer Networks
To subscribe, send the e-mail message:
    subscribe cyberia-l yourfirstname yourlastname
to: listserv@listserv.cc.wm.edu

List name: CYBETH-L: Cyber-Ethics Discussion
To subscribe, send the e-mail message:
    subscribe cybeth-l yourfirstname yourlastname
to: listproc@sun.soci.niu.edu

List name: DEFININGDEATH-L: International Network for the Definition of
    Death/International Association of Bioethics
To subscribe, send the e-mail message:
    subscribe definingdeath-l yourfirstname yourlastname
to: listserv@uconnvm.uconn.edu

List name: E-ACTIVIST: Forest Service Employees for Environmental Ethics
To subscribe, send the e-mail message: subscribe afseee_activist
to: majordomo@efn.org.

List name: EBEN-L: European Business Ethics Network
To subscribe, send the e-mail message: subscribe eben-l
to: majordomo@nijenrode.nl

List name: EIT: Ethics and Interactive Technologies
To subscribe, send the e-mail message: subscribe eit
to: majordomo@cgrg.ohio-state.edu

List name: ENVIROETHICS: Environmental Ethics
To subscribe, send the e-mail message:
  join enviroethics yourfirstname yourlastname
to: mailbase@mailbase.ac.uk

List name: ETHCSE-L: Ethical Issues in Software Engineering/Social, Cultural
  and Political Aspects of Computing
To subscribe, send the e-mail message:
  subscribe ethcse-l yourfirstname yourlastname
to: listserv@utkvm1.utk.edu

List name: ETHEX: Exploratorium's Ethical Scenarios Forum/Diving Into the
  Gene Pool
To subscribe, send the e-mail message:
  subscribe ethex yourfirstname yourlastname
to: listproc@exploratorium.edu

List name: ETHICRND: Electronic Rountable Discussion on Ethics and
  Security
To subscribe, send the e-mail message:
  subscribe ethicrnd yourfirstname yourlastname
to: listserv@listserv.uic.edu

List name: Ethics & Genetics: A Global Conversation/Center for Bioethics,
  University of Pennsylvania
To participate and for more information, go to the website:
  http://www.med.upenn.edu/~bioethic/genetics.html

List name: ETHICS-DISCUSSION: Institute of Electrical and Electronics
  Engineers Ethics Committee
To subscribe, send the e-mail message:
  subscribe ethics-discussion
to: majordomo@majordomo.ieee.org

List name: ETHICS-ISRAEL-NET: Israeli Network for Social Responsibility
To subscribe, send the e-mail message:
  subscribe ethics-israel-net yourfirstname yourlastname
to: listserv@vm.tau.ac.il

List name: ETHICS-L: Discussion of Ethics in Computing
To subscribe, send the e-mail message:
  subscribe ethics-l yourfirstname yourlastname
to: listserv@vm.marist.edu

List name: ETHICS: Ethical Decision Making in the Psychiatric Treatment of the Elderly
To subscribe, send an empty e-mail message to:
  ethics-subscribe@makelist.com

List name: ETHICSFM: Ethics in Society of Teachers of Family Medicine
To subscribe, send the e-mail message:
  subscribe ethicsfm yourfirstname yourlastname
to: listserv@listserv.uic.edu

List name: ETHOS-L: Paleoanthropological & Biological Basis of Ethics & Aesthetics
To subscribe, send the e-mail message:
  subscribe ethos-l yourfirstname yourlastname
to: listserv@wvnvm.wvnet.edu

List name: ETHTALK-L: Public Administration Listserver
To subscribe, send the e-mail message:
  subscribe ethtalk-l yourfirstname yourlastname
to: listserv@nosferatu.cas.usf.edu

List name: EUROETH-L: European Data Base Network for Medical Ethics
To subscribe, send the e-mail message:
  subscribe euroeth-l yourfirstname yourlastname
to: listproc@gwdg.de

List name: FAB: Feminist Approaches to Bio-Ethics
To subscribe, send the e-mail message:
  subscribe fab yourfirstname yourlastname youremailaddress
to: fab-request@phil.ruu.nl

List name: FAIR-L: Fairness and Accuracy in Reporting
To subscribe, send the e-mail message:
  subscribe fair-l yourfirstname yourlastname
to: listserv@american.edu

List name: FORENSIC-PSYCH: Psychiatry, Medicine, Ethics, and the Law
To subscribe, send the e-mail message: subscribe
to: forensic-psych-request@world.std.com

List name: G-ETHIC: Global and Ecological Ethics
To subscribe, send the e-mail message:
  subscribe g-ethic yourfirstname yourlastname
to: listserv@vm.temple.edu

List name: GEN-ETHICS: The Human Genome Project:
  Ethical, Legal and Policy Issues/Association of Cancer Online Resources
To subscribe, send the e-mail message:
  subscribe gen-ethics yourfirstname yourlastname
to: listserv@acor.org

List name: GENETHICS: National Human Genome Research
    Institute
To participate, send an e-mail message to: webmaster@nhgri.nih.gov
For more information, go to the website:
    http://www.nhgri.nih.gov/About_NHGRI/Dir/Ethics/genethics.html

List name: HCELP: Health Care Ethics Leadership Program
To subscribe, send the e-mail message:
    subscribe hcelp yourfirstname yourlastname
to: listserv@listserv.iupui.edu

List name: HEALTHLAW-L: Health Law
To subscribe, send the e-mail message:
    subscribe healthlaw-l yourfirstname yourlastname
to: listserv@lawlib.wuacc.edu

List name: INT-CSR: AIESEC
    Global Corporate & Social Responsibility
To subscribe, send the e-mail message:
    subscribe int-csr yourfirstname yourlastname
to: listserv@lists.aiesec.org

List name: JBE-L: Journal of Buddhist Ethics
To subscribe, send the e-mail message: subscribe jbe-l yourfirstname
    yourlastname
to: listserv@lists.psu.edu

List name: JSCOPE: Joint Services Conference on Professional Ethics
To subscribe, send the e-mail message: subscribe jscope
to: majordomo@acpub.duke.edu

List name: JUPR: Journal of Universal Peer Review
To subscribe, send the e-mail message:
    subscribe jupr yourfirstname yourlastname
to: listserv@maelstrom.stjohns.edu

List name: LAWAND: Law and Society
To subscribe, send the e-mail message:
    subscribe lawand yourfirstname yourlastname
to: listproc@polecat.law.indiana.edu

List name: LEGALETHICS-L: Legal Ethics List
To subscribe, send the e-mail message:
    subscribe legalethics-l yourfirstname yourlastname
to: listserv@lawlib.wuacc.edu

List name: LEGALTEN: Topical Evaluation Network on Issues in Mental
    Health Care and Law
To subscribe, send the e-mail message: subscribe legalten
to: majordomo@world.std.com

List name: LEON: Law and Ethics on the Net
To subscribe, send the e-mail message:
  subscribe leon yourfirstname yourlastname
to: listserv@lawlib.wuacc.edu

List name: MCW-BIOETHICS: Medical College of Wisconsin Bioethics
  Discussion
To subscribe, send the e-mail message:
  subscribe mcw-bioethics yourfirstname yourlastname
to: listproc@its.mcw.edu

List name: MEDICAL-ETHICS: Medical Ethics Line
To subscribe, send the e-mail message:
  subscribe medical-ethics yourfirstname yourlastname
to: listserv@listserv.medec.com

List name: MEDMALPRACT: Medical Malpractice Law Forum
To subscribe, send the e-mail message:
  subscribe medmalpract yourfirstname yourlastname
to: listserv@groupserver.revnet.com

List name: NETFUTURE: Technology and Human Responsibility
To subscribe, send the e-mail message:
  subscribe netfuture yourfirstname yourlastname
to: listserv@infoserv.nlc-bnc.ca

List name: News Ethics Discussion Pages
To participate, send an e-mail message to: ethics@mediaone.net
For more information, go to the website:
  http://www.geocities.com/Athens/Parthenon/3285/index.html

List name: NURSING-ETHICS-L: Nursing Ethics
To subscribe, send the e-mail message:
  subscribe nursing-ethics-l yourfirstname yourlastname
to: listproc@lists.missouri.edu

List name: NYEN-L: New York Ethics Network
To subscribe, send the e-mail message:
  subscribe nyen-l yourfirstname yourlastname
to: listserv@health.nyam.org

List name: PEER TO PEER: Ethics: *Inc.* Magazine Online
To participate, send an e-mail message from the website:
  http://www.inc.com/bbs/list/20

List name: PRIVACY FORUM
To subscribe, send the e-mail message: subscribe privacy
to: privacy-request@vortex.com

List name: PSYLAW-L: Psychology and the Law
To subscribe, send the e-mail message:
  subscribe psylaw-l yourfirstname yourlastname
to: listserv@utepvm.ep.utexas.edu

List name: PUGWASH-L: Student Pugwash USA
To subscribe, send the e-mail message:
  subscribe pugwash-l yourfirstname yourlastname
to: listserv@cornell.edu

List name: SCIFRAUD: Discussion of Fraud in Science
To subscribe, send the e-mail message:
  subscribe scifraud yourfirstname yourlastname
to: listserv@cnsibm.albany.edu

List name: SOCETH-L: Social Ethics
To subscribe, send the e-mail message:
  subscribe soceth-l yourfirstname yourlastname
to: listserv@vm.usc.edu

List name: SPJ-ETHICS: Journalism Ethics/Society of Professional Journalists
To subscribe, send the e-mail message: subscribe spj-ethics
to: majordomo@dworkin.wustl.edu

List name: SPSR: Student Physicians for Social Responsibility
To subscribe, send the e-mail message:
  subscribe spsr yourfirstname yourlastname
to: listserv@itssrv1.ucsf.edu

List name: SRB: Socially Responsible Business Discussion Group
To subscribe, send the e-mail message: subscribe srb
to: listproc@bristlecone.together.net

List name: SR-SIS: Social Responsibility Special Interest Section/American
  Association of Law Libraries
To subscribe, send the e-mail message:
  subscribe sr-sis yourfirstname yourlastname
to: listserv@law.wuacc.edu:

List name: STS: Sci-Technology Studies/Society for Social Studies of Science
To subscribe, send the e-mail message:
  subscribe sts yourfirstname yourlastname
to: listcom@kant.ch.umkc.edu

List name: TEACHETHICS-L: Teaching Journalism Ethics
To subscribe, send the e-mail message:
  subscribe teachethics-l yourfirstname yourlastname
to: listproc@hawaii.edu

List name: TECH-SOCIETY: Technology and Society
To subscribe, send the e-mail message:
  subscribe tech-society youremailaddress
to: majordomo@majordomo.ieee.org

List name: TX-ETHICS: A Professional Ethics Public Forum
To subscribe, send the e-mail message:
  subscribe tx-ethics yourfirstname yourlastname
to: listserv@listserv.uh.edu

List name: WEB-ETHICS: Ethics of Using and Providing Information on the
  World Wide Web
To subscribe, send the e-mail message: subscribe web-ethics
to: majordomo@idyllmtn.com

List name: WEBETHICS: Lawyers' Web Ethics/Internet Use by Legal
  Professionals
To subscribe, send the e-mail message: subscribe webethics
to: majordomo@homecom.com

INDEXES

A. INDEX OF ISSUES

Page references are to texts of codes only, not to the introductory sections preceding each code. Cross-references are provided only for issues not listed below.

Issues are phrased generally, in order to apply to the full range of organizations and codes indexed, and to accommodate the perspectives of both professionals and clients, as well as third parties. For example, *refusing, declining, or withholding services or participation* would reference all of these code provisions: a journalist's turning down an assignment; a patient's reluctance to be part of a medical research program; and a lawyer's disqualification from taking on a certain client.

In a few instances, the code indexed is an excerpt, and so certain professions may not be listed under a particular issue (even though that issue is addressed elsewhere in that profession's code). Readers should contact the appropriate organization to obtain the complete text.

Please note that these organizations and codes are merely representative of a given profession. Federal, state, and local laws and regulations, and ethics standards of other public and private organizations, also may apply to the profession and/or to individual professionals.

List of Issues Indexed

access to or allocation of services
accountability, responsibility, obligations, or authority
advertising or promotional activities
advisory role or recommendations
advocacy role on behalf of client
alternative dispute resolution (arbitration, mediation, etc.)
antitrust or trade regulation
assistants, subordinates, paraprofessionals, or students
background, history, or development of code
bylaws, technical standards, or other codes or policies
candor, honesty, or accuracy
choosing or accepting client or professional or establishing professional-client relationship
clients or clients' interests
colleagues or intraprofessional relations
commissions, rebates, fee splitting, or financial incentives
communications with colleagues or other professionals, consultations, or referrals
communications with or information for client
communications with the public or news media
communications with third parties or ex parte proceedings
community, volunteer, or discount services
compassion, sensitivity, or respect
competence, ability, or qualifications
competition, competitors, or opposing professionals

973

computers, electronic data, or telecommunications
condoning or assisting misconduct of others
conferences, lectures, or continuing professional education
confidentiality, privacy, or professional-client privilege
conflicts of interests
consent of client
contingent or conditional fees or services
contracts, formal agreements, or contractual relations
credentials, degrees, or credentialing bodies
criminal or civilly liable conduct of client
criminal or civilly liable conduct of professional
criticism or disparagement
death or estate of client
death or estate of professional
delay, inaction, omissions, or negligence
delegation of responsibilities or activities
differentiation of personal opinion
diligence, due care, planning, or productivity
direction or request of client
disagreement between client and professional
disagreement between professionals
disclosure of information, interests, or status
discrimination, cultural diversity, or civil or human rights
education or training
emergencies, accidents, or imminent danger
employees of professional (professional as employer)
employer of professional (professional as employee)
endorsements or testimonials
enforcement of code, compliance, formal complaints, or disciplinary actions
ethical or moral standards generally
ethical or moral standards of individual
ethics committees
exceptions or limitations to code
experience or expertise
expert witnesses or testimony of professional
exploitation, abuse, coercion, or undue influence
family or personal contacts or relationships
fees, compensation, or costs
fiduciaries or trustees
financial, commercial, or property interests of client
financial, commercial, or property interests of professional
format of code, definitions, or terminology
fraud, deception, misrepresentation, or misleading information
gifts or favors
government, administrative agencies, or public officials
government employment
group practice, firms, partners, or associates
human reproduction or genetics
impaired professionals
impaired, vulnerable, or minor-age clients
impartiality or fairness

adverse effects (*see* risk, prevention, or protection from harm)

ADVERTISING OR PROMOTIONAL ACTIVITIES
accounting 17
advertising 29
arbitration 575
architecture 72
banking 83–84
chiropractic 276
counseling 427–29, 444
dentistry 289–92
direct marketing 36, 42–43, 45
dispute resolution 596–97
engineering 103–04, 106
executive search consulting 152–54
federal law practice 665, 725–26
financial planning 122, 135, 137
fund raising 224
health care management 261, 267, 269
insurance 174–76, 184
internal medicine 326
journalism 188, 200
judiciary 609
litigation 761
management education and consulting 211
mediation 557, 589–90
medicine 376–77, 382, 386, 404–05, 407
nursing 504
prosecution 777, 787, 811
psychology 475–76, 481–82, 484
public relations 60–62, 64
real estate 244–45, 247
sales 53–54
social work 525

advisory boards or committees
(*see* advisory role or recommendations; communications with colleagues or other professionals, consultations, or referrals; ethics committees; institutions, organizations, businesses, or investors; review of decisions or actions)

ADVISORY ROLE OR RECOMMENDATIONS
accounting 14, 16–18, 23–24
advertising 31
arbitration 568–69, 573, 577–84
architecture 70–71
banking 80
computing 96
counseling 420–21, 429, 431–32, 435–38, 441, 444–45
dentistry 285, 292
dispute resolution 595–96
engineering 103–04
executive search consulting 152–54
federal law practice 666–67, 671–73, 675, 677, 679–80, 682, 684–85, 690, 693–94, 696–97, 699–703, 705, 708–11, 715, 717–19, 721–22, 727, 730–33
financial planning 119–20, 124, 126, 129, 135–36
fund raising 224
health care management 260, 266, 268
human resource management 157
insurance 167, 169, 172, 182–83
internal medicine 314–22, 324–25, 327–29, 332
investment analysis 111–13
judiciary 606, 609–13
law practice 625–26, 629–32, 634, 636–40, 643–44, 646–48, 657–59
legal assistantship 746, 751–52, 754–55
litigation 761
lobbying 741
management education and consulting 207–08, 211
mediation 554–57, 586–87, 589
medicine 340, 342, 344, 347–50, 356–60, 371–74, 377–79, 381, 388, 391, 395, 404, 410–12
nursing 496, 499, 503–04
pharmacy 510
prosecution 774–75, 777, 788, 790, 792–93, 795, 799, 801–11
psychiatry 457–58
psychology 465–66, 469, 474–75, 487
public administration 147
public relations 62

e-mail communications
(*see* computers, electronic data, or telecommunications)

EDUCATION OR TRAINING
accounting 12–13, 19, 23
arbitration 575, 577
architecture 68–69, 71–72, 74
association management 218–19
chiropractic 277
computing 93, 95, 98
counseling 426–28, 430, 432, 435–37, 443, 446
dental hygiene 299–33, 302–03
dentistry 283–87, 289–95
direct marketing 45, 47
dispute resolution 594–96
engineering 102, 105
executive search consulting 150
federal law practice 667, 672, 715, 719, 721–22, 730, 732
financial planning 120–21, 124, 135
fund raising 223–24
health care management 266–67
insurance 162, 165–68, 172, 174, 177, 183
internal medicine 311, 315–16, 323, 326–30, 333
investment analysis 110–11, 113
law practice 625, 629–30
legal assistantship 746–50, 752–54
lobbying 218–19, 741–42
management education and consulting 206, 211
mediation 554, 556–58, 586, 588–90
medicine 340, 345, 352, 363, 373, 375–76, 394–95, 400, 403–08, 410–11, 413
nursing 500–02, 504
payroll management 142
prosecution 771, 779–85, 790, 792, 798, 800–01, 804–06, 810–11
psychiatry 454–55, 457
psychology 466–67, 469–70, 472, 476, 481–83, 485–86
public administration 146–47
public relations 58
sales 54
social work 517, 519–22, 525, 529–30, 532, 534, 536, 540–47

effectiveness (*see* diligence, due care, planning, or productivity; necessity or appropriateness of services; unconventional, unproven, or experimental services or methods)

effort (*see* advocacy role on behalf of client; diligence, due care, planning, or productivity)

elections or elected officials
(*see* government, administrative agencies, or public officials; legislative or social policies or reforms; political activities or lobbying)

electronic data (*see* computers, electronic data, or telecommunications)

embarrassment (*see* reputation, public image, or appearance of impropriety)

EMERGENCIES, ACCIDENTS, OR IMMINENT DANGER
chiropractic 275
counseling 424
dentistry 287, 289–90
federal law practice 675, 677, 713, 733
insurance 171
internal medicine 311–12, 314, 316
journalism 189
judiciary 611–12, 615
law practice 629, 634, 638–39
litigation 761
medicine 341, 344, 358, 370–73, 378, 380–81, 393, 395–97, 402–03, 406–07, 409
nursing 497–98, 503
psychiatry 456, 458
real estate 244
social work 524, 533, 535, 546–47

EMPLOYEES OF PROFESSIONAL (PROFESSIONAL AS EMPLOYER)
accounting 14
advertising 29–30

GIFTS OR FAVORS
accounting 23
arbitration 582
architecture 70
banking 81, 85–86
chiropractic 278
counseling 429, 444
direct marketing 40–41, 47
federal law practice 676, 684–85
fund raising 224
health care management 261
insurance 169
internal medicine 325–26
journalism 194, 200
law practice 646–48
management education and consulting
    207, 210
medicine 382, 393–95, 404–05
prosecution 774
public administration 147
public relations 59–60, 62
real estate 230
social work 522–23, 537, 540

Golden Rule (*see* ethical or moral
    standards generally)

good faith (*see* diligence, due care,
    planning, or productivity; judgment
    or decision of professional)

**GOVERNMENT,
    ADMINISTRATIVE AGENCIES,
    OR PUBLIC OFFICIALS**
accounting 9–10, 16–17
arbitration 574–82
architecture 70
association management 218
banking 82, 85
chiropractic 275–78
computing 97
counseling 428, 441
dental hygiene 303
dentistry 286–87, 289–90
direct marketing 36–37, 40, 44–45
engineering 102–03, 105
executive search consulting 150
federal law practice 665–70, 673–76,
    679–81, 683–86, 689–97, 700–02,
    704–05, 710–11, 713–17, 722–29,
    732

(GOVERNMENT,
    ADMINISTRATIVE AGENCIES,
    OR PUBLIC OFFICIALS *cont'd*)
financial planning 123, 125, 128–29,
    137–38
insurance 167, 169, 171–72
internal medicine 310, 316–17, 320,
    325–28, 330–31
investment analysis 110
journalism 194, 200
judiciary 605–06, 608–09, 614–15
law practice 625–28, 632–33, 637,
    643, 649, 652, 654–55, 658–59
legal assistantship 746–50, 752
litigation 761
lobbying 218, 741
management education and consulting
    211
mediation 587–88
medicine 343, 345, 348, 351, 357,
    362, 370, 372, 378–80, 383–84,
    388, 395, 400, 404, 406–08, 410
nursing 496, 504
payroll management 142
prosecution 766, 768, 770–71, 775,
    778–79, 781, 783–88, 790–92, 794,
    797–98, 801–02, 805–06, 809–12
psychiatry 454, 456, 458
psychology 465–66, 488
public administration 146–47
public relations 58–62
real estate 231, 238
social work 522, 531, 541

government contracts (*see* contracts,
    formal agreements, or contractual
    relations; government,
    administrative agencies, or public
    officials)

GOVERNMENT EMPLOYMENT
accounting 9, 12, 15
architecture 70
chiropractic 277
engineering 103–05
executive search consulting 150
federal law practice 665–67, 670–73,
    675–77, 680–81, 683–85, 687,
    689–96, 698, 700–02, 704–05, 713,
    716–18, 721–26, 728
financial planning 118

professionals, consultations, or referrals; communications with or information for client; communications with the public or news media; communications with third parties or ex parte proceedings; computers, electronic data, or telecommunications; conferences, lectures, or continuing professional education; disclosure of information, interests, or status; education or training; fraud, deception, misrepresentation, or misleading information; products, devices, methods, or treatments; publications, authorship, or plagiarism; records, documents, or data)

informed consent (*see* consent of client)

initiative (*see* advocacy role on behalf of client; diligence, due care, planning, or productivity)

inside information (*see* exploitation, abuse, coercion, or undue influence; financial, commercial, or property interests of client; financial, commercial, or property interests of professional; fraud, deception, misrepresentation, or misleading information; institutions, organizations, businesses, or investors)

institutional practice (*see* employer of professional; group practice, firms, partners, or associates; institutions, organizations, businesses, or investors)

institutional review boards (*see* ethics committees; institutions, organizations, businesses, or investors; review of decisions or actions)

INSTITUTIONS, ORGANIZATIONS, BUSINESSES, OR INVESTORS
accounting 9–12, 14–16, 19, 22–24
advertising 28–30
arbitration 564–67, 570, 573, 575–77, 583
architecture 75
association management 217–19
banking 80–87
chiropractic 276–78
computing 92–98
counseling 423, 425–27, 430–32, 434, 437–41, 444–45
dental hygiene 303–04
dentistry 286, 288–94
direct marketing 36, 41, 45–47
dispute resolution 594
engineering 102–03, 105–06
executive search consulting 150–53
federal law practice 669–70, 676, 680, 682, 684–85, 690, 692–96, 699, 712, 715–17, 719, 721–27, 729–30, 733
financial planning 118–19, 122–23, 125–28, 134–37
fund raising 224–25
health care management 259–61, 266–69
human resource management 157
insurance 165–67, 169–74, 183
internal medicine 309–12, 314–17, 319–27, 330–33
investment analysis 111
journalism 188
judiciary 606–07, 609–10
law librarianship 738
law practice 628, 631, 634, 640, 642–44, 652–53, 656–60
legal assistantship 747–50, 752, 755
litigation 761
lobbying 218–19, 741
management education and consulting 206–12
mediation 586–88, 590
medicine 339–41, 345–47, 351–54, 357–58, 363–64, 368–72, 374–78, 380–86, 388–90, 392–413
nursing 498–500, 502–05
payroll management 142

(INSTITUTIONS,
  ORGANIZATIONS,
  BUSINESSES, OR INVESTORS
  cont'd)
prosecution 766, 772, 774, 781,
  785–92, 794, 798–812
psychiatry 454–60
psychology 465–67, 469, 471–73,
  475–76, 479, 481–84, 486, 488
public administration 146–47
public relations 59, 63–64
real estate 242–43
sales 54
social work 517, 523–25, 529,
  531–32, 536, 538–39, 541–43,
  545–48

**INSURANCE, INSURERS, OR
  THIRD-PARTY PAYMENTS**
arbitration 570, 575
architecture 72
banking 82
counseling 429
dentistry 286, 288–89
federal law practice 676, 683–84,
  686, 698, 721
health care management 267
insurance 165–68, 170–75, 183–84
internal medicine 311–12, 315–16,
  323–25, 327
journalism 189
judiciary 607
law practice 631, 644–47
medicine 354, 358–59, 372, 376,
  382–88, 390–93, 397–401,
  409–10
nursing 498
psychiatry 456
psychology 473, 480
real estate 245
social work 517–19, 521–22, 525,
  531, 533, 536

insurance, malpractice
  (*see* malpractice liability, insurance,
  or indemnification)

INTEGRITY OR HONOR
accounting 10–13, 15
advertising 29

(INTEGRITY OR HONOR *cont'd*)
arbitration 565–66, 570–71, 574–75,
  580
architecture 68, 73
association management 217
chiropractic 277
computing 94–96
counseling 420, 439
dentistry 283, 288
direct marketing 39
dispute resolution 594–95
engineering 102, 104
executive search consulting 150–53
federal law practice 666–67, 712,
  716, 725–26, 731–33
financial planning 119–20, 122–23,
  128, 134, 137
fund raising 223
health care management 259
human resource management 157
insurance 171–73, 175, 177–78,
  184
internal medicine 309, 328, 331–32
investment analysis 110
journalism 194, 199–200
judiciary 605, 608, 610–11
legal assistantship 747, 752
litigation 761
management education and consulting
  206, 211
mediation 587–88
medicine 351, 368, 383, 402,
  412
nursing 496–97, 503–05
pharmacy 510
prosecution 775–76, 794, 798
psychiatry 454, 459–60
psychology 467, 475, 483, 485
public administration 147
public relations 58, 64
real estate 230, 238
social work 516–17, 521, 529, 531,
  545–46

**INTELLECTUAL PROPERTY
  RIGHTS (PATENTS,
  COPYRIGHTS, ETC.)**
architecture 70
computing 94
counseling 434, 440
dentistry 286, 289, 292

(JUDGMENT OR DECISION OF
  PROFESSIONAL *cont'd*)
dispute resolution 594–96
engineering 102–03, 105
executive search consulting 151
federal law practice 667, 669–70,
  672–79, 681–82, 684, 687, 689–94,
  697, 699–705, 707–12, 715–22,
  724–27, 731–34
financial planning 118–23, 129–30,
  135–36
health care management 259–61, 266,
  268
insurance 162, 164–66, 168–74, 178,
  182
internal medicine 309–19, 322,
  324–29, 331, 333
investment analysis 110–13
journalism 188, 195
judiciary 605, 607–12, 614–16
law librarianship 738
law practice 626–34, 637–46, 649,
  651, 654, 657–60
legal assistantship 747–49, 752–55
litigation 761
management education and consulting
  208, 211–12
mediation 555–57
medicine 342, 346–47, 349–50, 354,
  356, 362–64, 366, 368, 370–71,
  373–76, 378–79, 381, 384–86, 388,
  390–93, 395–98, 400–03, 408–09,
  411–13
nursing 495, 497–98, 500–02, 505
pharmacy 510
prosecution 769–70, 772–73, 775,
  778–81, 783–84, 787, 791–98, 800,
  802–03, 806–11
psychiatry 454–59
psychology 465–67, 469, 471–72,
  474–75, 484, 486–88
public administration 146
public relations 60
real estate 250
social work 516, 518–19, 521–23,
  530–31, 533–34, 536–37, 539, 541,
  543–45

judgments, procedural
  (*see* enforcement of code,
  compliance, formal complaints, or

disciplinary actions; legal process,
  litigation, courts, or rulings)

justice (*see* discrimination, cultural
  diversity, or civil or human rights;
  impartiality or fairness; laws,
  regulations, or legal requirements)

knowledge, professional
  (*see* competence, ability, or
  qualifications; education or training;
  experience or expertise; products,
  devices, methods, or treatments)

labor relations (*see* employees of
  professional; employer of
  professional; union activities or
  strikes)

law reform (*see* legislative or social
  policies or reforms)

**LAWS, REGULATIONS, OR
  LEGAL REQUIREMENTS**
accounting 10, 14, 16, 18–19, 23–24
advertising 31
arbitration 564–65, 568–71, 573,
  576–77, 579–84
architecture 68–73
association management 217–18
banking 82–85, 87
chiropractic 275–78
computing 92, 94–96
counseling 423–25, 432–35, 438–40,
  443
dental hygiene 299, 303–04
dentistry 283–86, 291–92
direct marketing 36–37, 40, 43–45
engineering 102, 105–06
executive search consulting 152, 154
federal law practice 665–70, 672–74,
  676–77, 680–81, 683–86, 690–91,
  695–702, 705–13, 715–19, 721–23,
  725, 727–28, 731–32
financial planning 118, 123–29,
  135–37
fund raising 223–25
health care management 259, 266,
  268
human resource management 157
insurance 163, 166, 168–69, 183–84

"letter and spirit" of code
  (*see* interpretations, guidance, or
  intent of code)

liability (*see* accountability,
  responsibility, obligations, or
  authority; criminal or civilly liable
  conduct of client; criminal or
  civilly liable conduct of
  professional; delay, inaction,
  omissions, or negligence; insurance,
  insurers, or third-party payments;
  malpractice liability, insurance, or
  indemnification)

libel (*see* criticism or disparagement;
  legal process, litigation, courts, or
  rulings; publications, authorship, or
  plagiarism)

**LICENSING, CERTIFICATION,
ACCREDITATION, OR
REGISTRATION**

**life-prolonging measures or life-
  support systems** (*see* death or
  estate of client; impaired,
  vulnerable, or minor-age clients;
  judgment or decision of
  professional; products, devices,
  methods, or treatments)

limitations (*see* competence, ability,
  or qualifications; exceptions or
  limitations to code; restrictions or
  limitations on practice or services)

literary rights (*see* intellectual
  property rights)

literature, professional
  (*see* publications, authorship, or
  plagiarism)

litigation or litigants (*see* clients or
  clients' interests; criminal or civilly
  liable conduct of client; criminal or

misconduct of others (*see* condoning or assisting misconduct of others; reporting misconduct or violations of law; third parties or third-party relationships)

MISCONDUCT OF PROFESSIONAL OR VIOLATIONS OF CODE
accounting 9, 14, 22–23
arbitration 564, 574–75, 577, 579, 582
architecture 70, 72–74
banking 81–83
chiropractic 277–78
computing 94, 96–98
counseling 422, 440–41, 447
dental hygiene 301, 303
dentistry 282, 285, 287–90, 292–93, 295
direct marketing 43
dispute resolution 595, 597
engineering 104–05
federal law practice 668, 670, 672–74, 677–79, 681–82, 685, 694, 699–700, 704, 706–12, 714–16, 718–20, 722–31, 733
financial planning 119–21, 127, 130, 134–35, 137
fund raising 224
health care management 259, 261, 267
insurance 162–64, 166, 168–70, 172, 174–77, 182, 184
internal medicine 309, 312–13, 316–18, 321, 325–32
investment analysis 110–11, 113–14
journalism 187, 194, 201
judiciary 605–06, 608–12, 614
law practice 627–32, 638–40, 643, 646, 649, 653
legal assistantship 746, 748–49, 751–54
litigation 761
management education and consulting 207, 209, 211
mediation 587, 589
medicine 341, 343–44, 349, 351–52, 357, 361, 363, 367, 369–70, 372–75, 382–88, 391–93, 395–97, 399–401, 403–06, 408–11, 413

(MISCONDUCT OF PROFESSIONAL OR VIOLATIONS OF CODE *cont'd*)
nursing 499, 501
prosecution 772–74, 791, 793–94, 796–98, 806, 809, 812
psychiatry 454–55, 457–58
psychology 465–68, 472, 478, 488–89
public administration 146–47
public relations 58–59
real estate 238, 240, 246, 251
sales 53–54
social work 516, 520, 522–23, 530–31, 533, 537–38, 541, 543

misleading information (*see* fraud, deception, misrepresentation, or misleading information)

misrepresentation (*see* fraud, deception, misrepresentation, or misleading information)

moonlighting (*see* outside activities or private conduct)

moral standards (*see* ethical or moral standards generally; ethical or moral standards of individual)

MULTIPLE CLIENTS
accounting 12
arbitration 564–72, 575–76, 578–84
architecture 72
association management 217
counseling 422, 425, 442–43, 446
dentistry 286
dispute resolution 595
engineering 103–04
executive search consulting 152–53
federal law practice 666, 675, 681–83, 685–91, 694–96, 701, 703–04, 709, 717, 720, 722, 728
financial planning 123
insurance 165, 183
internal medicine 322, 331
investment analysis 111
law practice 625, 627, 634, 642–55, 657–60
litigation 761

(MULTIPLE CLIENTS *cont'd*)
management education and consulting 211
mediation 554–55, 586–89
medicine 346, 362–64, 366, 387, 400
nursing 498
prosecution 778, 798–800
psychiatry 456
psychology 471–72, 478–79, 487
public relations 59, 62
real estate 239, 241, 243
social work 517, 519, 521, 523, 534–36

MULTIPLE PROFESSIONALS
arbitration 564–65, 567, 569–72, 579, 584
architecture 73–74
association management 218
chiropractic 276
counseling 421, 429, 435–36, 438, 440, 444, 446
dentistry 284
dispute resolution 596
engineering 105
federal law practice 684–90, 693–95, 700, 703–04, 716–17, 719–21
financial planning 124
health care management 268
insurance 182
internal medicine 322, 324, 329–30
law practice 627, 629, 635–39, 644, 646–53, 655, 659
legal assistantship 751–55
litigation 761
lobbying 218, 741
management education and consulting 208
mediation 558, 589–90
medicine 342, 346, 356, 363, 371–72, 385, 389–90, 399, 401–03
prosecution 790–91, 799–806, 810
psychiatry 456, 458–59
psychology 471–73, 478, 486
real estate 238, 241–42, 244, 246–51
social work 519, 521, 523

name of client (*see* disclosure of information, interests, or status; intellectual property rights)

NAME OR TITLE OF PRACTICE OR PROFESSIONAL
accounting 14, 18–19
arbitration 564, 573, 575
counseling 428
dental hygiene 304
dentistry 290, 292
engineering 102, 105
federal law practice 717
financial planning 124, 128–29, 137
insurance 175–76, 184
journalism 188
judiciary 609
legal assistantship 748
medicine 376–77, 396, 408
nursing 504–05
prosecution 777
public relations 64
sales 52, 54
social work 525

national security (*see* public safety, health, or environment)

NECESSITY OR APPROPRIATENESS OF SERVICES
arbitration 582, 584
chiropractic 276
counseling 423–24, 433–34, 438, 443, 445
dentistry 288–89
dispute resolution 596
federal law practice 702–04, 714–15, 731
financial planning 129
health care management 267–68
internal medicine 327
investment analysis 112
judiciary 614–15
law practice 629, 638, 640
legal assistantship 747–48
mediation 554, 556–57, 587
medicine 343, 346–47, 352–57, 360, 362–63, 366–67, 370–72, 375, 384–86, 388, 390, 392, 395, 398–400, 404, 413
nursing 498, 501–02
prosecution 769, 780, 783, 788, 809
psychiatry 456, 458–60
psychology 472, 474–75, 479, 483

(OUTSIDE ACTIVITIES OR
PRIVATE CONDUCT *cont'd*)
health care management 259, 261
insurance 167, 171, 183–84
internal medicine 310, 316
investment analysis 111
journalism 194, 200
judiciary 608–10, 613
law practice 644
legal assistantship 752
lobbying 741
management education and consulting
210, 212
mediation 555, 587
medicine 341, 349, 394, 404–05, 410,
412
nursing 505
payroll management 142
prosecution 769–70, 777–78, 788
psychiatry 458
psychology 465, 468, 471
public administration 146–47
social work 523, 543–45

paraprofessionals (*see* assistants,
subordinates, paraprofessionals, or
students)

parents (*see* family or personal
contacts or relationships; human
reproduction or genetics;
representative role or guardian)

**PART-TIME, TEMPORARY, OR
RETIRED PROFESSIONALS**
arbitration 564, 576
dentistry 292
engineering 105
judiciary 606–07
law practice 656
medicine 375, 387, 392
prosecution 769–70, 774–75, 778–80,
784–85
psychiatry 453
psychology 473
social work 536

**participation of client or
professional** (*see* choosing or
accepting client or professional or
establishing professional-client
relationship; communications with
or information for client; refusing,
declining, or withholding services
or participation)

parties or participants (*see* clients or
clients' interests; legal process,
litigation, courts, or rulings; third
parties or third-party relationships)

partisanship (*see* advocacy role on
behalf of client; impartiality or
fairness)

partnerships (*see* financial,
commercial, or property interests of
professional; group practice, firms,
partners, or associates)

patents (*see* intellectual property
rights)

patients (*see* clients or clients'
interests)

payments (*see* fees, compensation, or
costs; insurance, insurers, or third-
party payments)

PEER REVIEW
accounting 9, 16–17, 24
architecture 73
banking 81, 85, 87
computing 95
counseling 427, 430, 436, 440
dental hygiene 302–04
direct marketing 36
federal law practice 667–68
health care management 260, 267–68
internal medicine 324, 326, 330–33
law practice 626–27, 630
management education and consulting
208, 212
medicine 346, 351–54, 389, 400,
406–09, 411
nursing 496, 498–99, 501
prosecution 790
psychiatry 454–55, 460
psychology 480, 482, 486
social work 530–31, 533, 546

penalties (*see* enforcement of code, compliance, formal complaints, or disciplinary actions)

percentages (*see* commissions, rebates, fee splitting, or financial incentives; contingent or conditional fees or services)

performance (*see* diligence, due care, planning, or productivity; quality of services or excellence)

perjury (*see* candor, honesty, or accuracy; fraud, deception, misrepresentation, or misleading information; legal process, litigation, courts, or rulings)

personal contacts or relationships (*see* family or personal contacts or relationships)

personal matters (*see* confidentiality, privacy, or professional-client privilege; differentiation of personal opinion; direction or request of client; ethical or moral standards of individual; judgment or decision of professional; outside activities or private conduct)

picketing (*see* union activities or strikes)

plagiarism (*see* publications, authorship, or plagiarism)

plaintiffs (*see* clients or clients' interests; competition, competitors, or opposing professionals; criminal or civilly liable conduct of client; legal process, litigation, courts, or rulings; third parties or third-party relationships)

planning (*see* diligence, due care, planning, or productivity)

plea bargains (*see* contracts, formal agreements, or contractual relations)

policies (*see* bylaws, technical standards, or other codes or policies; legislative or social policies or reforms)

POLITICAL ACTIVITIES OR LOBBYING
architecture 68, 70
association management 218–19
banking 82, 85, 87
chiropractic 276
counseling 441
engineering 106
executive search consulting 151
federal law practice 672, 701, 726
health care management 261
insurance 170–71, 175
internal medicine 327
journalism 200
judiciary 605–09
law practice 625, 630
lobbying 218–19, 741–42
medicine 341, 344, 346, 353, 410
nursing 497, 503, 505
prosecution 768, 770–74, 776, 781, 784, 790, 792, 803–05, 808, 810
psychiatry 455, 458
psychology 468, 471
public administration 146
public relations 61–62
social work 519, 523, 529, 532, 534, 539, 544, 546–48

power (*see* accountability, responsibility, obligations, or authority; exploitation, abuse, coercion, or undue influence)

practice, professional (*see* group practice, firms, partners, or associates; name or title of practice or professional; profession or professional services generally; restrictions or limitations on practice or services; specialization or specialists)

PREAMBLES, INTRODUCTIONS, OR GENERAL CODE PROVISIONS
accounting 9–10, 13, 15–16, 22
advertising 28, 31
arbitration 564–66, 570, 573–74, 582
architecture 68–69, 73
association management 217–18
banking 80–81, 84–85
chiropractic 275
computing 92, 97
counseling 420, 441
dental hygiene 299–301
dentistry 282–83
direct marketing 36, 45
dispute resolution 594
engineering 102
executive search consulting 150–52
federal law practice 665–69, 729
financial planning 118–22, 134
fund raising 223
health care management 259, 266
insurance 162–64, 182
internal medicine 309–11
investment analysis 110
journalism 187, 194, 199
judiciary 605–06
law librarianship 738
law practice 625–26
legal assistantship 746, 748, 755
lobbying 218, 741
management education and consulting 206
mediation 554, 586
medicine 339–44
nursing 495–96
pharmacy 510
prosecution 766–68, 776, 778
psychiatry 453, 459
psychology 465–68, 474
public administration 146
public relations 58, 61
real estate 230, 232, 238–39
sales 52
social work 516–17, 529–33

prejudice (*see* discrimination, cultural diversity, or civil or human rights; impartiality or fairness)

preparation (*see* diligence, due care, planning, or productivity)

prescriptions (*see* products, devices, methods, or treatments)

press relations (*see* communications with the public or news media; interprofessional relations or other professionals; publications, authorship, or plagiarism; U.S. Constitution or First Amendment freedoms)

prevention of harm (*see* risk, prevention, or protection from harm)

printed materials (*see* advertising or promotional activities; contracts, formal agreements, or contractual relations; publications, authorship, or plagiarism; records, documents, or data)

prior consent (*see* consent of client)

priority of interests (*see* conflicts of interests; interpretations, guidance, or intent of code; loyalty, commitment, or dedication)

privacy of client or professional (*see* confidentiality, privacy, or professional-client privilege; outside activities or private conduct)

privilege, professional-client (*see* confidentiality, privacy, or professional-client privilege)

privileged communications (*see* communications with colleagues or other professionals, consultations, or referrals; communications with or information for client; communications with third parties or ex parte proceedings)

pro bono services (*see* community, volunteer, or discount services)

procedures (*see* bylaws, technical standards, or other codes or policies; products, devices, methods, or treatments)

procrastination (*see* diligence, due care, planning, or productivity)

productivity (*see* diligence, due care, planning, or productivity)

PRODUCTS, DEVICES, METHODS, OR TREATMENTS
accounting 17–18
advertising 28–29
arbitration 564, 566, 568, 570, 572, 574–75, 579–80, 582, 584
association management 218
chiropractic 275–78
computing 92, 97
counseling 420–21, 423–24, 428–36, 438–40, 446
dental hygiene 303–04
dentistry 283, 285–90, 293–94
direct marketing 36, 38, 40–47
dispute resolution 595–96
engineering 103–06
executive search consulting 150–53
federal law practice 666, 668, 671–73, 675, 677, 679, 682, 686, 689, 698–99, 702, 705–08, 710, 718, 720–21, 723, 725, 729–31, 733
financial planning 119, 127, 129, 135–36
fund raising 224–25
health care management 260–61, 266, 268–69
human resource management 157
insurance 166–67, 174
internal medicine 309–11, 313–28, 330, 332
investment analysis 111–12
journalism 187–89, 194–95, 199–200
judiciary 606, 609–11, 613, 616
law practice 630–32, 634–37, 640, 642, 645–47, 649, 654
legal assistantship 753, 755

(PRODUCTS, DEVICES, METHODS, OR TREATMENTS *cont'd*)
litigation 761
lobbying 218
management education and consulting 206–09, 211–12
mediation 554–55, 557, 586, 589–90
medicine 339, 342–54, 361–62, 364, 366–67, 369–73, 377–81, 383–84, 388–91, 393–97, 399–403, 407, 411, 413
nursing 495–98, 500–02, 504
payroll management 142
pharmacy 510
prosecution 66, 776, 782, 784–88, 790, 793, 797–805, 807, 809–11
psychiatry 455, 458–59
psychology 467, 469, 473–75, 477, 482–87
public administration 146–47
public relations 60
real estate 230, 233, 240, 243–47
sales 52–54
social work 516–21, 523–25, 530, 533, 541, 543, 546, 548

PROFESSION OR PROFESSIONAL SERVICES GENERALLY
accounting 9–19, 22–23
advertising 28–29, 31
arbitration 564–65, 573, 575, 580, 585
architecture 68–69, 71–74
association management 217–18
banking 80, 84–85
chiropractic 275–78
computing 92–97
counseling 420, 423, 429–30, 435–36, 440, 442, 444, 446
dental hygiene 299–304
dentistry 282–84, 286–89
direct marketing 36, 45
dispute resolution 594–97
engineering 102, 104, 106
executive search consulting 150–52, 154
federal law practice 665–67, 677, 680, 687–88, 692, 699, 701, 706, 715–16, 718, 720–23, 725–33

(RESEARCH WITH HUMANS OR
ANIMALS *cont'd*)
psychology 468, 482–85
social work 523–24, 546

residents, medical (*see* assistants,
subordinates, paraprofessionals, or
students; colleagues or
intraprofessional relations)

resolution of disputes (*see* alternative
dispute resolution; conflicts of
interests; disagreement between
client and professional;
disagreement between
professionals)

resource allocation (*see* access to or
allocation of services)

respect (*see* compassion, sensitivity,
or respect)

responsibility (*see* accountability,
responsibility, obligations, or
authority; judgment or decision of
professional; social responsibility,
the public interest, or public trust)

responsiveness (*see* candor, honesty,
or accuracy; communications with
or information for client; delay,
inaction, omissions, or negligence;
diligence, due care, planning, or
productivity)

**RESTRICTIONS OR
LIMITATIONS ON PRACTICE
OR SERVICES**
accounting 13–14, 19, 23
advertising 28
arbitration 569, 574, 578, 584–85
architecture 68
chiropractic 278
computing 94, 96
counseling 421, 423–26, 428–29,
431–39, 443–46
dental hygiene 302
dentistry 282, 284–86, 292–95
direct marketing 38, 41–42, 46–47
dispute resolution 595–96

(RESTRICTIONS OR
LIMITATIONS ON PRACTICE
OR SERVICES *cont'd*)
engineering 103–04
executive search consulting 152–54
federal law practice 668, 671–75,
678, 681–82, 684–92, 695,
697–700, 705, 707, 709, 712, 714,
716–18, 721–22, 724–25, 727,
731–33
financial planning 121, 124, 128–29,
135–36
fund raising 223
health care management 268
insurance 163, 168–69
internal medicine 310, 312, 315–18,
325, 327, 329
investment analysis 111
journalism 195
judiciary 605, 608–10, 612–13
law librarianship 738
law practice 629–33, 635–37,
639–40, 642–49, 653–57
legal assistantship 746–48, 751,
753–55
litigation 761
lobbying 741
management education and consulting
211
mediation 556, 587–88
medicine 344, 348–50, 355–56,
358–60, 363, 366, 369, 372,
376–77, 380–81, 387–90, 393,
398–400, 402, 405, 409–10,
412–13
nursing 496–97, 502
prosecution 769, 773, 777–79, 781,
783, 786–87, 789, 791–93, 805,
807–12
psychiatry 455–57, 459
psychology 467, 469, 471–75,
478–80, 482–84, 487
public relations 62
real estate 230, 232, 241, 246
sales 54
social work 516–17, 519–24, 533–36,
542–44, 547

**results of research, investigations,
or tests** (*see* research,
investigations, tests, or results)

results promised (*see* promised results or expectations of services)

retired professionals (*see* part-time, temporary, or retired professionals)

REVIEW OF DECISIONS OR ACTIONS
accounting 10, 13, 15–18, 24
advertising 30, 32
architecture 73
banking 81–82, 85–87
computing 93, 95
counseling 420, 424–25, 427, 431, 434, 436–37, 441, 446
dental hygiene 303–04
dentistry 285, 287, 291–92
engineering 102, 105
federal law practice 669–70, 685, 693–94, 700–01, 712, 718–20, 734
health care management 267–68
insurance 170, 176, 182
internal medicine 316–17, 324, 329–31
judiciary 615
law practice 647, 657–58
legal assistantship 749, 754–55
management education and consulting 208, 212
mediation 588
medicine 351–52, 354, 356–57, 363, 366, 368, 370–71, 384, 389–90, 396, 400, 402, 406–09, 411–12
nursing 496, 498–501, 503
prosecution 775, 785–86, 790, 793, 809
psychiatry 454, 457–60
psychology 468, 474, 478–80, 482, 484, 486, 488
public administration 146–47
public relations 61
real estate 246
sales 53–54
social work 517, 530, 533, 537–38, 546

revision of code (*see* promulgation, implementation, revision, or amendment of code)

"revolving door" (*see* conflicts of interests; employer of professional; government employment; refusing, declining, or withholding services or participation; termination, withdrawal, or removal from services)

"right to die" (*see* death or estate of client; direction or request of client; ethical or moral standards of individual; impaired, vulnerable, or minor-age clients; independence or autonomy)

RISK, PREVENTION, OR PROTECTION FROM HARM
accounting 11, 23
arbitration 566–67, 569, 577, 583–84
architecture 70–71, 73–74
association management 218
banking 80, 83–86
chiropractic 275–78
computing 93–98
counseling 421–30, 432–36, 438–39, 441–44, 447
dental hygiene 299–304
dentistry 282–86, 289–90
direct marketing 46–47
dispute resolution 595–96
engineering 102, 104
executive search consulting 151, 153
federal law practice 667, 669, 671, 673–79, 681–92, 694, 696–704, 706–07, 710–22, 724–32
financial planning 120–21, 126–27, 129, 135
fund raising 223
health care management 259–61, 268
human resource management 157
insurance 164, 168, 170–71, 174, 177–78, 182
internal medicine 310–19, 322–28, 330–32
investment analysis 111
journalism 189, 194, 200
judiciary 608, 611–14
law librarianship 738
law practice 629, 633–34, 636, 638–44, 646–49, 651–55, 657–59
legal assistantship 747, 752

(SOCIETY OR THE PUBLIC *cont'd*)
arbitration 564–65
architecture 68–71
association management 217–18
banking 80–81, 84, 86
chiropractic 275
computing 92–94, 97
counseling 420–22, 427–28, 441, 447
dental hygiene 299–300, 303
dentistry 282–86, 288, 290, 292–93
direct marketing 36
dispute resolution 594, 596
engineering 102–03
executive search consulting 150–52, 154
federal law practice 666, 668, 677–78, 695, 701, 712–13, 722, 728–29, 732
financial planning 119–20, 134, 136
fund raising 223
health care management 259–61, 266–67
human resource management 157
insurance 163, 165–66, 168, 170–75, 177, 182–84
internal medicine 310–12, 315, 317, 324, 326–28, 330, 333
investment analysis 110–11, 113–14
journalism 194–95, 199–201
judiciary 608, 610, 612
law librarianship 738
law practice 625–27, 639, 652–54
legal assistantship 747–50, 752
litigation 761
lobbying 218, 741–42
management education and consulting 206, 211–12
mediation 588, 590
medicine 339, 341–42, 345–47, 351–53, 355–56, 367, 369, 371, 376–78, 387–88, 395–96, 405–08, 411–13
nursing 495–96, 500–03, 505
pharmacy 510–11
prosecution 766, 769–70, 772–73, 779, 783–84, 787, 790, 792, 794–98, 804, 806, 808–12
psychiatry 457–59
psychology 466, 478, 489
public administration 146–47
public relations 58, 62–64

(SOCIETY OR THE PUBLIC *cont'd*)
real estate 238, 244–46
social work 516, 523, 525, 529–32, 545–48

SOLICITATION
accounting 17
arbitration 565, 575, 582
architecture 72
counseling 427, 444
dentistry 290, 292
direct marketing 37, 41, 44, 46
dispute resolution 596–97
engineering 103, 105–06
federal law practice 676, 728
financial planning 122
fund raising 224
insurance 176
internal medicine 330
judiciary 606, 616
law librarianship 738
litigation 761
mediation 589
psychology 477, 484
public relations 61
real estate 239, 247–48
sales 52–53
social work 522–23, 535, 538, 545

SPECIALIZATION OR SPECIALISTS
accounting 14
arbitration 564, 574–75
banking 80, 82–83
chiropractic 276
computing 98
counseling 426–28, 433, 446
dentistry 284–85, 291–95
dispute resolution 594–95
federal law practice 671, 695, 714–15
financial planning 118, 122, 124, 135, 137
insurance 166, 174, 177
internal medicine 315–16, 319, 332
journalism 199
judiciary 612
law librarianship 738
law practice 629, 637, 644, 649, 654
legal assistantship 747, 750
mediation 557

(SPECIALIZATION OR
SPECIALISTS *cont'd*)
medicine 345, 356, 363, 369, 373,
375, 379, 385, 393, 403–04, 407,
413
nursing 501
prosecution 771, 776, 778–83, 785,
790, 792, 805
psychiatry 457
psychology 482, 486–87
public relations 61–64
real estate 231, 244
social work 534, 540

"spirit and letter" of code
(*see* interpretations, guidance, or
intent of code)

split fees (*see* commissions, rebates,
fee splitting, or financial incentives)

sponsorship (*see* advertising or
promotional activities; conferences,
lectures, or continuing professional
education; endorsements or
testimonials; financial, commercial,
or property interests of
professional; independence or
autonomy; institutions,
organizations, businesses, or
investors; teaching, mentoring, or
supervising)

staff members (*see* assistants,
subordinates, paraprofessionals, or
students; colleagues or
intraprofessional relations;
employees of professional;
employer of professional; group
practice, firms, partners, or
associates; interprofessional
relations or other professionals)

state agencies or officials
(*see* government, administrative
agencies, or public officials)

statistics (*see* records, documents, or
data; research, investigations, tests,
or results)

statutes (*see* laws, regulations, or
legal requirements; legislative or
social policies or reforms)

strategies (*see* products, devices,
methods, or treatments)

strikes (*see* union activities or
strikes)

students (*see* assistants, subordinates,
paraprofessionals, or students;
clients or clients' interests;
teaching, mentoring, or supervising)

subordinates (*see* assistants,
subordinates, paraprofessionals, or
students; employees of
professional)

substitution of professional
(*see* choosing or accepting client or
professional or establishing
professional-client relationship;
consent of client; delegation of
responsibilities or activities;
direction or request of client; fraud,
deception, misrepresentation, or
misleading information; multiple
professionals; successor or
replacement professional)

**SUCCESSOR OR
REPLACEMENT
PROFESSIONAL**
accounting 18–19
arbitration 579
chiropractic 275
counseling 421, 439, 443
dentistry 283–85, 287, 292
dispute resolution 596
engineering 105
federal law practice 691, 696,
700–01, 714
financial planning 127
health care management 268
internal medicine 322, 329–30
judiciary 615
law practice 654
medicine 342, 347, 370–73, 386–87,
390–91, 397, 403

(UNAUTHORIZED PRACTICE
  cont'd)
law librarianship 738
law practice 645
legal assistantship 746, 748, 751,
  753–54
medicine 372–73, 396
nursing 501
psychiatry 455, 458
psychology 474–75, 482
real estate 233, 241, 246
social work 522, 546

UNCONVENTIONAL,
  UNPROVEN, OR
  EXPERIMENTAL SERVICES
  OR METHODS
counseling 434, 438
dental hygiene 303–04
dentistry 288, 292
engineering 105
federal law practice 706, 710, 720
internal medicine 317, 319, 324, 332
medicine 350–55, 366, 395–96,
  404–05, 410–11
nursing 499
prosecution 804
psychiatry 455
psychology 467, 469, 475, 482, 487
social work 534, 544

underage clients (*see* impaired,
  vulnerable, or minor-age clients)

undue influence (*see* exploitation,
  abuse, coercion, or undue influence)

unethical conduct (*see* misconduct of
  client; misconduct of professional
  or violations of code)

UNION ACTIVITIES OR
  STRIKES
arbitration 564, 573–76, 580, 583–84
dispute resolution 596
engineering 104
internal medicine 328
litigation 761
medicine 375
nursing 504
prosecution 790

(UNION ACTIVITIES OR STRIKES
  cont'd)
social work 544

unnecessary services (*see* necessity
  or appropriateness of services)

unorthodox treatments
  (*see* unconventional, unproven, or
  experimental services or methods)

unprofessional conduct
  (*see* misconduct of professional or
  violations of code; self-regulation
  or professionalism)

unproven services or methods
  (*see* unconventional, unproven, or
  experimental services or methods)

values (*see* ethical or moral standards
  generally; ethical or moral
  standards of individual)

victims of crimes (*see* clients or
  clients' interests; legal process,
  litigation, courts, or rulings; third
  parties or third-party relationships)

violations of code (*see* misconduct of
  professional or violations of code;
  reporting violations of code)

violations of law (*see* criminal or
  civilly liable conduct of client;
  criminal or civilly liable conduct of
  professional; reporting misconduct
  or violations of law)

voluntary acts (*see* consent of client)

volunteer services (*see* community,
  volunteer, or discount services)

vulnerable clients (*see* impaired,
  vulnerable, or minor-age clients)

waiver (*see* consent of client;
  direction or request of client)

B. INDEX OF PROFESSIONS

Page references are to texts of codes only, not to the introductory sections preceding each code. Cross-references are provided only for professions not listed below.

Issues are phrased generally, in order to apply to the full range of organizations and codes indexed, and to accommodate the perspectives of both professionals and clients, as well as third parties. For example, *refusing, declining, or withholding services or participation* would reference all of these code provisions: a journalist's turning down an assignment; a patient's reluctance to be part of a medical research program; and a lawyer's disqualification from taking on a certain client.

In a few instances, the code indexed is an excerpt, and so certain issues may not be listed under a particular profession (even though they are addressed elsewhere in that profession's code). Readers should contact the appropriate organization to obtain the complete text.

Please note that these organizations and codes are merely representative of a given profession. Federal, state, and local laws and regulations, and ethics standards of other public and private organizations, also may apply to the profession and/or to individual professionals.

List of Professions Indexed

accounting
advertising
arbitration
architecture
association management
banking
chiropractic
computing
counseling
dental hygiene
dentistry
direct marketing
dispute resolution
engineering
executive search consulting
federal law practice

financial planning
fund raising
health care management
human resource management
insurance
internal medicine
investment analysis
journalism
judiciary
law librarianship
law practice
legal assistantship
litigation
lobbying
management education and consulting
mediation

(List of Professions Indexed *cont'd*)

medicine
nursing
payroll management
pharmacy
prosecution
psychiatry

psychology
public administration
public relations
real estate
sales
social work

Key to Professions & Organizations

Accounting: American Institute of Certified Public Accountants; Institute of Management Accountants
Advertising: American Association of Advertising Agencies
Arbitration: American Arbitration Association
Architecture: American Institute of Architects
Association Management: American Society of Association Executives
Banking: American Bankers Association
Chiropractic: American Chiropractic Association
Computing: Association for Computing Machinery
Counseling: American Counseling Association
Dental Hygiene: American Dental Hygienists' Association
Dentistry: American Dental Association
Direct Marketing: Direct Marketing Association
Dispute Resolution: Society of Professionals in Dispute Resolution
Engineering: National Society of Professional Engineers
Executive Search Consulting: Association of Executive Search Consultants
Federal Law Practice: Federal Bar Association
Financial Planning: Certified Financial Planner Board of Standards; International Association for Financial Planning
Fund Raising: National Society of Fund Raising Executives
Health Care Management: American College of Healthcare Executives; American Hospital Association
Human Resource Management: International Personnel Management Association
Insurance: American Institute for Chartered Property Casualty Underwriters; Society of Financial Service Professionals (American Society of CLU & ChFC)
Internal Medicine: American College of Physicians - American Society of Internal Medicine
Investment Analysis: Association for Investment Analysis and Research
Journalism: American Society of Journalists and Authors; American Society of Newspaper Editors; Society of Professional Journalists
Judiciary: American Bar Association
Law Librarianship: American Association of Law Libraries
Law Practice: American Bar Association
Legal Assistantship: National Association of Legal Assistants
Litigation: Association of Trial Lawyers of America
Lobbying: American League of Lobbyists; American Society of Association Executives
Management Education and Consulting: Academy of Management
Mediation: Academy of Family Mediators; American Arbitration Association

Medicine: American Medical Association
Nursing: American Nurses Association
Payroll Management: American Payroll Association
Pharmacy: American Pharmaceutical Association
Prosecution: National District Attorneys Association
Psychiatry: American Psychiatric Association
Psychology: American Psychological Association
Public Administration: American Society for Public Administration
Public Relations: Public Relations Society of America
Real Estate: National Association of Exclusive Buyer Agents; National
    Association of REALTORS®
Sales: Direct Selling Association
Social Work: Clinical Social Work Federation; National Association of Social
    Workers

ACCOUNTING
**American Institute of Certified
Public Accountants 9–19**
Code of Professional Conduct **9–19**
**Institute of Management
Accountants 22–24**
*Standards of Ethical Conduct for
Practitioners of Management
Accounting and Financial
Management* **22–24**
accountability, responsibility,
obligations, or authority 9–14, 16,
19, 22–23
advertising or promotional activities
17
advisory role or recommendations 14,
16–18, 23–24
assistants, subordinates,
paraprofessionals, or students 12,
14, 23
background, history, or development
of code 9, 22
bylaws, technical standards, or other
codes or policies 9–16, 18–19,
22–24
candor, honesty, or accuracy 11–12
choosing or accepting client or
professional or establishing
professional-client relationship 13
clients or clients' interests 10–18
colleagues or intraprofessional
relations 9–10, 13–14, 16–17, 19,
24
commissions, rebates, fee splitting, or
financial incentives 17–18

(ACCOUNTING *cont'd*)
communications with colleagues or
other professionals, consultations,
or referrals 10, 12–13, 15–17,
23–24
communications with or information
for client 15–16, 23–24
communications with the public or
news media 9–10, 14–17, 19, 24
communications with third parties or
ex parte proceedings 12, 14, 16–18,
23–24
compassion, sensitivity, or respect
10–11
competence, ability, or qualifications
12–13, 15–16, 23
condoning or assisting misconduct of
others 14, 22–23
conferences, lectures, or continuing
professional education 12, 19, 23
confidentiality, privacy, or
professional-client privilege 11, 16,
23
conflicts of interests 11–13, 15–16,
23–24
consent of client 16, 23
contingent or conditional fees or
services 17
credentials, degrees, or credentialing
bodies 14–15, 19
delay, inaction, omissions, or
negligence 13
differentiation of personal opinion 23
diligence, due care, planning, or
productivity 11–13, 15, 23

(FEDERAL LAW PRACTICE
cont'd)

reputation, public image, or
appearance of impropriety 667–68,
674, 688, 703, 706, 709, 712, 718,
721, 724, 726, 729–32

research, investigations, tests, or
results 671, 691, 702, 704–06,
708–09, 712–13, 726–27, 731

restrictions or limitations on practice
or services 668, 671–75, 678,
681–82, 684–92, 695, 697–700,
705, 707, 709, 712, 714, 716–18,
721–22, 724–25, 727, 731–33

review of decisions or actions
669–70, 685, 693–94, 700–01, 712,
718–20, 734

risk or prevention of or protection
from harm 667, 669, 671, 673–79,
681–92, 694, 696–704, 706–07,
710–22, 724–32

scope or applicability of code
665–69, 671, 673–83, 685–92,
694–98, 701–05, 707–08, 710–30

self-regulation or professionalism
666–68, 709, 712, 727–30, 733

sexual contacts or relationships 728

social responsibility, the public
interest, or public trust 666–67,
692, 695, 713, 715, 722, 729

society or the public 666, 668,
677–78, 695, 701, 712–13, 722,
728–29, 732

solicitation 676, 728

specialization or specialists 671, 695,
714–15

successor or replacement professional
691, 696, 700–01, 714

teaching, mentoring, or supervising
670–71, 673–74, 678, 681, 683,
689–90, 694, 696, 700–01, 705,
711–12, 715, 718–22, 729

termination, withdrawal, or removal
from services 673–75, 678–81,
686–90, 692, 694, 696, 698–701,
703–04, 707–09, 715, 721, 728,
730

third parties or third-party
relationships 666–67, 670, 673–79,
681, 683–87, 690–91, 694, 697–99,
702–06, 710–18, 720–22, 724,
726–33

(FEDERAL LAW PRACTICE
cont'd)

U.S. Constitution or First Amendment
freedoms 680, 695

unauthorized practice 722

unconventional, unproven, or
experimental services or methods
706, 710, 720

FINANCIAL PLANNING
**Certified Financial Planner Board
of Standards 118–30**
*Code of Ethics and Professional
Responsibility* **118–30**
**International Association for
Financial Planning 134–38**
Code of Professional Ethics
134–38

accountability, responsibility,
obligations, or authority 118–20,
122–23, 125–26, 134, 136

advertising or promotional activities
122, 135, 137

advisory role or recommendations
119–20, 124, 126, 129, 135–36

alternative dispute resolution
(arbitration, mediation, etc.) 128

assistants, subordinates,
paraprofessionals, or students 118,
124, 130

background, history, or development
of code 118, 134

bylaws, technical standards, or other
codes or policies 118–19, 124, 128,
134, 136–37

candor, honesty, or accuracy 120–21,
123, 127, 135

choosing or accepting client or
professional or establishing
professional-client relationship 125,
129

clients or clients' interests 119–21,
123, 125–27, 129, 135–36

colleagues or intraprofessional
relations 118–24, 126–29, 136–38

commissions, rebates, fee splitting, or
financial incentives 119, 124–25

communications with colleagues or
other professionals, consultations,
or referrals 121, 124–29, 137

communications with or information
for client 121–29, 135–36

(FINANCIAL PLANNING *cont'd*)

institutions, organizations, businesses, or investors 118–19, 122–23, 125–28, 134–37

integrity or honor 119–20, 122–23, 128, 134, 137

interpretations, guidance, or intent of code 118, 120, 122, 126, 134

interprofessional relations or other professionals 118, 121, 124, 127–29, 136

judgment or decision of professional 118–23, 129–30, 135–36

laws, regulations, or legal requirements 118, 123–29, 135–37

legal process, litigation, courts, or rulings 121, 127–28

licensing, certification, accreditation, or registration 124, 126, 128–29, 138

loyalty, commitment, or dedication 123, 126–27, 135

memberships or professional societies 119, 122, 124, 127–29, 134–38

misconduct of professional or violations of code 119–21, 127, 130, 134–35, 137

multiple clients 123

multiple professionals 124

name or title of practice or professional 124, 128–29, 137

necessity or appropriateness of services 129

outside activities or private conduct 126, 129, 137

preambles, introductions, or general code provisions 118–22, 134

products, devices, methods, or treatments 119, 127, 129, 135–36

profession or professional services generally 118–23, 127, 129, 134–37

promised results or expectations of services 122, 135

promulgation, implementation, revision, or amendment of code 127

publications, authorship, or plagiarism 122, 137

quality of services or excellence 120, 122, 135

(FINANCIAL PLANNING *cont'd*)

records, documents, or data 119, 122–25, 127–29, 134, 136–38

reporting misconduct or violations of law (whistleblowing) 128–29, 138

reporting violations of code 127, 129, 137

representative role or guardian 119

reputation, public image, or appearance of impropriety 119, 121–22, 128–29, 136

research, investigations, tests, or results 136

restrictions or limitations on practice or services 121, 124, 128–29, 135–36

risk, prevention, or protection from harm 120–21, 126–27, 129, 135

scope or applicability of code 118–22, 125–27, 134–35

self-regulation or professionalism 118–19, 121, 127–29

social responsibility, the public interest, or public trust 120, 134, 136

society or the public 119–20, 134, 136

solicitation 122

specialization or specialists 118, 122, 124, 135, 137

successor or replacement professional 127

teaching, mentoring, or supervising 118, 122, 128, 130

termination, withdrawal, or removal from services 126–27

third parties or third-party relationships 119, 123–25, 135–37

unauthorized practice 129

FUND RAISING
National Society of Fund Raising Executives 223–25
Code of Ethical Principles and Standards of Professional Practice 223–25

accountability, responsibility, obligations, or authority 223

advertising or promotional activities 224

advisory role or recommendations 224

(INSURANCE *cont'd*)

improvement of the profession
164–67, 170–75, 177, 182–84

independence or autonomy 169, 173

institutions, organizations, businesses,
or investors 165–67, 169–74, 183

insurance, insurers, or third-party
payments 165–68, 170–75, 183–84

integrity or honor 171–73, 175,
177–78, 184

intellectual property rights (patents,
copyrights, etc.) 172, 176

interpretations, guidance, or intent of
code 162–66, 168–70, 172, 175,
177–78, 182–83

interprofessional relations or other
professionals 162–66, 168–69,
171–74, 182, 184

judgment or decision of professional
162, 164–66, 168–74, 178, 182

laws, regulations, or legal
requirements 163, 166, 168–69,
183–84

legal process, litigation, courts, or
rulings 170–71

legislative or social policies or
reforms 170–71, 174–75, 183

licensing, certification, accreditation,
or registration 167, 174

loyalty, commitment, or dedication
163, 168, 172, 182

memberships or professional societies
162–71, 175–78, 182, 184

misconduct of professional or
violations of code 162–64, 166,
168–70, 172, 174–77, 182, 184

multiple clients 165, 183

multiple professionals 182

name or title of practice or
professional 175–76, 184

outside activities or private conduct
167, 171, 183–84

political activities or lobbying
170–71, 175

preambles, introductions, or general
code provisions 162–64, 182

products, devices, methods, or
treatments 166–67, 174

profession or professional services
generally 163–65, 170–75, 177,
182, 184

(INSURANCE *cont'd*)

public safety, health, or environment
170–71, 174

publications, authorship, or plagiarism
167, 172, 176

quality of services or excellence 169,
171, 173, 175

records, documents, or data 162–64,
166, 168, 172, 175–76

refusing, declining, or withholding
services or participation 165, 169,
173, 178

reporting misconduct or violations of
law (whistleblowing) 172

reporting violations of code 172,
177–78

reputation, public image, or
appearance of impropriety 169–70,
173–74, 182–84

research, investigations, tests, or
results 167, 171–77

restrictions or limitations on practice
or services 163, 168–69

review of decisions or actions 170,
176, 182

risk, prevention, or protection from
harm 164, 168, 170–71, 174,
177–78, 182

scope or applicability of code
162–65, 169, 182, 184

self-regulation or professionalism 162,
164, 170, 184

social responsibility, the public
interest, or public trust 162–65,
170–72, 174, 177, 183

society or the public 163, 165–66,
168, 170–75, 177, 182–84

solicitation 176

specialization or specialists 166, 174,
177

teaching, mentoring, or supervising
166–67, 172–74

third parties or third-party
relationships 165–66, 168, 171–73

unauthorized practice 173–74, 177

INTERNAL MEDICINE
American College of Physicians-
American Society of Internal
Medicine 309–33
Ethics Manual **309–33**

(INVESTMENT ANALYSIS *cont'd*)

communications with third parties or ex parte proceedings 111–14

compassion, sensitivity, or respect 110, 112

competence, ability, or qualifications 110–13

condoning or assisting misconduct of others 110, 114

conferences, lectures, or continuing professional education 110

confidentiality, privacy, or professional-client privilege 113–14

conflicts of interests 111–13

consent of client 111

credentials, degrees, or credentialing bodies 110–13

criminal or civilly liable conduct of client 113

criminal or civilly liable conduct of professional 110–11, 113

differentiation of personal opinion 112

diligence, due care, planning, or productivity 110, 112, 114

disclosure of information, interests, or status 111–14

education or training 110–11, 113

employees of professional (professional as employer) 110

employer of professional (professional as employee) 110–11, 113

endorsements or testimonials 113

enforcement of code, compliance, formal complaints, or disciplinary actions 111

ethical or moral standards generally 110

exceptions or limitations to code 111, 113

experience or expertise 113

fees, compensation, or costs 111, 113

fiduciaries or trustees 112–13

financial, commercial, or property interests of client 112–14

financial, commercial, or property interests of professional 111, 113–14

format of code, definitions, or terminology 113

fraud, deception, misrepresentation, or misleading information 111–14

(INVESTMENT ANALYSIS *cont'd*)

government, administrative agencies, or public officials 110

group practice, firms, partners, or associates 113–14

impartiality or fairness 111–14

improvement of the profession 110

independence or autonomy 110, 112

institutions, organizations, businesses, or investors 111

integrity or honor 110

judgment or decision of professional 110–13

laws, regulations, or legal requirements 110–11

licensing, certification, accreditation, or registration 110

loyalty, commitment, or dedication 113

memberships or professional societies 110

misconduct of client 113

misconduct of professional or violations of code 110–11, 113–14

multiple clients 111

necessity or appropriateness of services 112

outside activities or private conduct 111

preambles, introductions, or general code provisions 110

products, devices, methods, or treatments 111–12

profession or professional services generally 110, 112

promised results or expectations of services 113–14

publications, authorship, or plagiarism 111

records, documents, or data 110–14

reporting misconduct or violations of law (whistleblowing) 113

reputation, public image, or appearance of impropriety 110–11

research, investigations, tests, or results 112

restrictions or limitations on practice or services 111

risk, prevention, or protection from harm 111

society or the public 110–11, 113–14

(JUDICIARY *cont'd*)
impartiality or fairness 605–06,
608–16
improvement of the profession 605,
608
independence or autonomy 605,
608–10, 612–16
institutions, organizations, businesses,
or investors 606–07, 609–10
insurance, insurers, or third-party
payments 607
integrity or honor 605, 608, 610–11
interpretations, guidance, or intent of
code 605–16
interprofessional relations or other
professionals 605–06, 609, 611–16
judgment or decision of professional
605, 607–12, 614–16
laws, regulations, or legal
requirements 605, 607–15
legal process, litigation, courts, or
rulings 605–15
legislative or social policies or
reforms 610
loyalty, commitment, or dedication
608, 613
memberships or professional societies
606, 609–10, 613
misconduct of professional or
violations of code 605–06, 608–12,
614
name or title of practice or
professional 609
necessity or appropriateness of
services 614–15
outside activities or private conduct
608–10, 613
part-time, temporary, or retired
professionals 606–07
political activities or lobbying 605–09
preambles, introductions, or general
code provisions 605–06
products, devices, methods, or
treatments 606, 609–11, 613, 616
profession or professional services
generally 605–06, 608–09, 611
promised results or expectations of
services 613
publications, authorship, or plagiarism
609
quality of services or excellence 614

(JUDICIARY *cont'd*)
records, documents, or data 606–07,
609, 612–13, 615–16
refusing, declining, or withholding
services or participation 610,
614–16
reporting violations of code 614
representative role or guardian 607,
611–16
reputation, public image, or
appearance of impropriety 605,
608–11, 613
research, investigations, tests, or
results 612
restrictions or limitations on practice
or services 605, 608–10, 612–13
review of decisions or actions 615
risk, prevention, or protection from
harm 608, 611–14
scope or applicability of code 605,
608, 610, 613–16
sexual contacts or relationships
609–11
social responsibility, the public
interest, or public trust 605, 612
society or the public 608, 610, 612
solicitation 606, 616
specialization or specialists 612
successor or replacement professional
615
teaching, mentoring, or supervising
612–13
third parties or third-party
relationships 606–16
U.S. Constitution or First Amendment
freedoms 605, 607, 610

labor-management arbitration
(*see* arbitration)

LAW LIBRARIANSHIP
American Association of Law
 Libraries 738
Code of Ethics **738**
access to or allocation of services 738
accountability, responsibility,
obligations, or authority 738
advocacy role on behalf of client 738
assistants, subordinates,
paraprofessionals, or students 738

(MEDICINE *cont'd*)
378–79, 381, 384–86, 388, 390–93,
395–98, 400–03, 408–09, 411–13
laws, regulations, or legal
requirements 341–45, 348–54,
356–57, 359–60, 362–64, 366–68,
371–74, 376–80, 385–88, 392–93,
396–97, 404, 406, 408–09, 411–12
legal process, litigation, courts, or
rulings 339, 341, 344, 349–50, 359,
365–66, 368, 378–80, 383, 387–88,
395, 397, 406, 408–10
legislative or social policies or
reforms 343, 346, 348–49, 353–54,
371, 399, 407, 410
licensing, certification, accreditation,
or registration 343, 372–73, 375,
388, 392, 398, 403–04, 406, 408
loyalty, commitment, or dedication
341, 344–45, 350–55, 363, 366–67,
370–71, 374–76, 383, 386, 388,
391, 399, 402
malpractice liability, insurance, or
indemnification 371, 383, 388, 395,
397
memberships or professional societies
339–41, 343–44, 348, 353, 361,
374, 378, 388, 394, 404–09,
411–12
misconduct of client 343, 345, 372,
379, 384
misconduct of professional or
violations of code 341, 343–44,
349, 351–52, 357, 361, 363, 367,
369–70, 372–75, 382–88, 391–93,
395–97, 399–401, 403–06, 408–11,
413
multiple clients 346, 362–64, 366,
387, 400
multiple professionals 342, 346, 356,
363, 371–72, 385, 389–90, 399,
401–03
name or title of practice or
professional 376–77, 396, 408
necessity or appropriateness of
services 343, 346–47, 352–57, 360,
362–63, 366–67, 370–72, 375,
384–86, 388, 390, 392, 395,
398–400, 404, 413
organ transplants or donors 343, 350,
353–54, 361–65, 380

(MEDICINE *cont'd*)
outside activities or private conduct
341, 349, 394, 404–05, 410, 412
part-time, temporary, or retired
professionals 375, 387, 392
peer review 346, 351–54, 389, 400,
406–09, 411
political activities or lobbying 341,
344, 346, 353, 410
preambles, introductions, or general
code provisions 339–44
products, devices, methods, or
treatments 339, 342–54, 361–62,
364, 366–67, 369–73, 377–81,
383–84, 388–91, 393–97, 399–403,
407, 411, 413
profession or professional services
generally 339, 341–43, 349,
351–52, 355, 357, 367, 369, 371,
373–74, 377–78, 385–86, 388–89,
391–95, 397–99, 402, 406–12
professional courtesy 386
promised results or expectations of
services 351–52, 372, 376–77, 383
promulgation, implementation,
revision, or amendment of code
339–41, 345
public safety, health, or environment
343, 353, 356–58, 367, 369, 372,
374, 380, 387–88, 406–07, 413
publications, authorship, or plagiarism
351, 376, 389, 394–95, 407–08,
411
quality of services or excellence 342,
346–47, 352–54, 361, 363, 366,
369, 371, 373–75, 377–78, 383–85,
389–90, 392, 396–97, 399–401,
403–04, 406–07, 409, 411–13
records, documents, or data 340,
342–43, 345, 348, 350–51, 354–60,
362, 364–65, 368, 370–71, 376–84,
386–89, 391–93, 395, 402–07,
409–10, 412
refusing, declining, or withholding
services or participation 342,
346–50, 356, 358–59, 362–63,
366–67, 369–74, 377, 385–87,
389–91, 393, 395, 397–401,
403–04, 406, 409–13
reporting misconduct or violations of
law (whistleblowing) 341, 343,

(PAYROLL MANAGEMENT
cont'd)
colleagues or intraprofessional
relations 142
communications with or information
for client 142
conferences, lectures, or continuing
professional education 142
confidentiality, privacy, or
professional-client privilege 142
conflicts of interests 142
diligence, due care, planning, or
productivity 142
disclosure of information, interests, or
status 142
education or training 142
employees of professional
(professional as employer) 142
employer of professional (professional
as employee) 142
enforcement of code, compliance,
formal complaints, or disciplinary
actions 142
experience or expertise 142
financial, commercial, or property
interests of client 142
financial, commercial, or property
interests of professional 142
government, administrative agencies,
or public officials 142
improvement of the profession 142
institutions, organizations, businesses,
or investors 142
interprofessional relations or other
professionals 142
laws, regulations, or legal
requirements 142
legislative or social policies or
reforms 142
loyalty, commitment, or dedication
142
memberships or professional societies
142
outside activities or private conduct
142
products, devices, methods, or
treatments 142
profession or professional services
generally 142
reputation, public image, or
appearance of impropriety 142

(PAYROLL MANAGEMENT
cont'd)
third parties or third-party
relationships 142

personnel management (*see* human
resource management)

PHARMACY
**American Pharmaceutical
Association 510–11**
*Code of Ethics for Pharmacists
510–11*
access to or allocation of services 511
accountability, responsibility,
obligations, or authority 510–11
advisory role or recommendations 510
advocacy role on behalf of client
510–11
background, history, or development
of code 510
bylaws, technical standards, or other
codes or policies 510
candor, honesty, or accuracy 510
clients or clients' interests 510–11
colleagues or intraprofessional
relations 510
commissions, rebates, fee splitting, or
financial incentives 510
communications with colleagues or
other professionals, consultations,
or referrals 510–11
communications with or information
for client 510
communications with the public or
news media 510
community, volunteer, or discount
services 511
compassion, sensitivity, or respect
511
competence, ability, or qualifications
510
condoning or assisting misconduct of
others 510
conferences, lectures, or continuing
professional education 510
confidentiality, privacy, or
professional-client privilege 510
contracts, formal agreements, or
contractual relations 510

(PROSECUTION *cont'd*)

communications with third parties or ex parte proceedings 776–79, 783–84, 786–88, 792–804, 807–11

community, volunteer, or discount services 801, 803–04, 810–11

compassion, sensitivity, or respect 766, 776–77, 780–81, 783, 788, 792–94, 797–98, 800, 808

competence, ability, or qualifications 771–75, 778–82, 785, 789–92, 794, 803, 806, 810

competition, competitors, or opposing professionals 766, 776–77, 783–84, 791, 793–98, 807, 809

computers, electronic data, or telecommunications 786–87

condoning or assisting misconduct of others 793–94, 797

conferences, lectures, or continuing professional education 771, 781–83, 785, 806, 810

confidentiality, privacy, or professional-client privilege 778, 784–85, 799–800

conflicts of interests 769–70, 772, 777–79, 793

consent of client 777–79, 796

contracts, formal agreements, or contractual relations 776, 795

credentials, degrees, or credentialing bodies 768, 776, 778

criminal or civilly liable conduct of client 771, 777, 795–97, 806

criminal or civilly liable conduct of professional 772–74, 793–94, 797–98, 811–12

criticism or disparagement 773, 776, 808

delay, inaction, omissions, or negligence 776, 786, 793, 803, 807

delegation of responsibilities or activities 771, 782, 784–85, 805, 810

differentiation of personal opinion 776, 793

diligence, due care, planning, or productivity 768, 772, 776–77, 779–89, 792–96, 799, 801, 803–04, 807, 812

direction or request of client 795–96

(PROSECUTION *cont'd*)

disagreement between professionals 770, 784, 791–92, 803, 805, 808–10

disclosure of information, interests, or status 777–79, 784–85, 794–807, 809, 811

discrimination, cultural diversity, or civil or human rights 773–74, 779, 781, 808

education or training 771, 779–85, 790, 792, 798, 800–01, 804–06, 810–11

employees of professional (professional as employer) 771–72, 778–86, 788, 805–06

employer of professional (professional as employee) 774, 788

enforcement of code, compliance, formal complaints, or disciplinary actions 767–68, 770, 772–73, 775–76, 780, 782, 789–91, 797, 809, 812

ethical or moral standards generally 766–67, 769, 773, 775–76, 778, 781, 783, 796–98, 805–08

ethical or moral standards of individual 773–74, 808

ethics committees 766

exceptions or limitations to code 766–68, 770, 773–74, 776–79, 795–96, 799, 807, 809

experience or expertise 774, 778–81, 783–85, 787, 790, 796, 805–06, 808, 811

exploitation, abuse, coercion, or undue influence 773, 776–78, 781, 783, 790, 793–95, 798–800, 802, 812

family or personal contacts or relationships 777–78, 783, 798, 800

fees, compensation, or costs 766, 772–75, 778–83, 786–88, 790, 796, 798–99, 809–12

financial, commercial, or property interests of client 778

financial, commercial, or property interests of professional 769, 774, 778, 809, 811–12

format of code, definitions, or terminology 767–68, 773, 776–79,

(PUBLIC RELATIONS *cont'd*)
advisory role or recommendations 62
advocacy role on behalf of client
61–62, 64
background, history, or development
of code 63
bylaws, technical standards, or other
codes or policies 59, 64
candor, honesty, or accuracy 58, 61–64
choosing or accepting client or
professional or establishing
professional-client relationship 61
clients or clients' interests 58–62, 64
colleagues or intraprofessional
relations 58–61
commissions, rebates, fee splitting, or
financial incentives 59, 62
communications with colleagues or
other professionals, consultations,
or referrals 58, 60–63
communications with or information
for client 58, 60–64
communications with the public or
news media 58–59, 62–64
communications with third parties or
ex parte proceedings 58, 60, 63
community, volunteer, or discount
services 58
compassion, sensitivity, or respect 58,
61–62
competence, ability, or qualifications
58–61
competition, competitors, or opposing
professionals 62
condoning or assisting misconduct of
others 62, 64
conferences, lectures, or continuing
professional education 58
confidentiality, privacy, or
professional-client privilege 59–60,
62–63
conflicts of interests 58–59, 62, 64
consent of client 59, 62
contingent or conditional fees or
services 60
contracts, formal agreements, or
contractual relations 60
credentials, degrees, or credentialing
bodies 61
criticism or disparagement 58–59,
61–62

(PUBLIC RELATIONS *cont'd*)
delay, inaction, omissions, or
negligence 63
differentiation of personal opinion 63
diligence, due care, planning, or
productivity 58, 62–64
disclosure of information, interests, or
status 59–60, 62–64
discrimination, cultural diversity, or
civil or human rights 58
education or training 58
employees of professional
(professional as employer) 58, 61
employer of professional (professional
as employee) 58–62, 64
endorsements or testimonials 64
enforcement of code, compliance,
formal complaints, or disciplinary
actions 59, 63
ethical or moral standards generally
58–59, 62
ethical or moral standards of
individual 61
ethics committees 59
exceptions or limitations to code
59–62, 64
expert witnesses or testimony of
professional 59
exploitation, abuse, coercion, or
undue influence 60, 62
family or personal contacts or
relationships 59
fees, compensation, or costs 59–60,
62, 64
financial, commercial, or property
interests of client 60, 62–64
financial, commercial, or property
interests of professional 62–64
format of code, definitions, or
terminology 58–63
fraud, deception, misrepresentation, or
misleading information 58–64
gifts or favors 59–60, 62
government, administrative agencies,
or public officials 58–62
impartiality or fairness 58–60
improvement of the profession 58
independence or autonomy 59–60
institutions, organizations, businesses,
or investors 59, 63–64
integrity or honor 58, 64

C. INDEX OF ORGANIZATIONS

Page references are to texts of codes only, not to the introductory sections preceding each code. Cross-references are to listings in **Index of Professions**. Organizations are also listed by key word.

In a few instances, the code indexed is an excerpt, and so certain organizations may not be listed (even though they are mentioned elsewhere in a profession's code). Readers should contact the appropriate organization to obtain the complete text.

Please note that these organizations and codes are merely representative of a given profession. Federal, state, and local laws and regulations, and ethics standards of other public and private organizations, also may apply to the profession and/or to individual professionals.